THE
ALL ENGLAND
LAW REPORTS

1990

Volume 3

Editor
PETER HUTCHESSON LL M
Barrister, New Zealand

Assistant Editor
BROOK WATSON
of Lincoln's Inn, Barrister
and of the New South Wales Bar

Consulting Editor
WENDY SHOCKETT
of Gray's Inn, Barrister

London
BUTTERWORTHS

UNITED KINGDOM Butterworth & Co (Publishers) Ltd,
88 Kingsway, **London** WC2B 6AB and
4 Hill Street, **Edinburgh** EH2 3JZ

AUSTRALIA Butterworths Pty Ltd, **Sydney, Melbourne,
Brisbane, Adelaide, Perth, Canberra**
and **Hobart**

CANADA Butterworths Canada Ltd, **Toronto** and **Vancouver**

IRELAND Butterworth (Ireland) Ltd, **Dublin**

MALAYSIA Malayan Law Journal Pte Ltd, **Kuala Lumpur**

NEW ZEALAND Butterworths of New Zealand Ltd, **Wellington** and **Auckland**

PUERTO RICO Equity de Puerto Rico Inc, **Hato Rey**

SINGAPORE Malayan Law Journal Pte Ltd, **Singapore**

USA Butterworth Legal Publishers,
Austin, Texas, **Boston**, Massachusetts,
Clearwater, Florida (D & S Publishers),
Orford, New Hampshire (Equity Publishing),
St Paul, Minnesota, **Seattle**, Washington

ISBN 0 406 85172 7

Butterworths

PART OF REED INTERNATIONAL PLC

House of Lords

The Lord High Chancellor: Lord Mackay of Clashfern

Lords of Appeal in Ordinary

Lord Keith of Kinkel
Lord Bridge of Harwich
Lord Brandon of Oakbrook
Lord Templeman
Lord Griffiths

Lord Ackner
Lord Oliver of Aylmerton
Lord Goff of Chieveley
Lord Jauncey of Tullichettle
Lord Lowry

Court of Appeal

The Lord High Chancellor

The Lord Chief Justice of England: Lord Lane
(President of the Criminal Division)

The Master of the Rolls: Lord Donaldson of Lymington
(President of the Civil Division)

The President of the Family Division: Sir Stephen Brown

The Vice-Chancellor: Sir Nicolas Christopher Henry Browne-Wilkinson

Lords Justices of Appeal

Sir Tasker Watkins VC
   (Deputy Chief Justice)
Sir Michael John Fox
Sir Christopher John Slade
Sir Francis Brooks Purchas
Sir George Brian Hugh Dillon
Sir Roger Jocelyn Parker
Sir Anthony John Leslie Lloyd
Sir Brian Thomas Neill
Sir Michael John Mustill
Sir Martin Charles Nourse
Sir Iain Derek Laing Glidewell
Sir Alfred John Balcombe
Sir Ralph Brian Gibson
Sir John Dexter Stocker

Sir Harry Kenneth Woolf
Sir Donald James Nicholls
Sir Thomas Henry Bingham
Sir Thomas Patrick Russell
Dame Ann Elizabeth Oldfield Butler-Sloss
Sir Peter Murray Taylor
Sir Murray Stuart-Smith
Sir Christopher Stephen Thomas Jonathan
   Thayer Staughton
Sir Michael Mann
Sir Donald Henry Farquharson
Sir Anthony James Denys McCowan
Sir Alexander Roy Asplan Beldam
Sir Andrew Peter Leggatt

Chancery Division

The Lord High Chancellor

The Vice-Chancellor

Sir John Evelyn Vinelott
Sir Jean-Pierre Frank Eugene Warner
Sir Peter Leslie Gibson
Sir David Herbert Mervyn Davies
Sir Jeremiah LeRoy Harman
Sir Richard Rashleigh Folliott Scott
(Vice-Chancellor of the County Palatine
of Lancaster)

Sir Leonard Hubert Hoffmann
Sir John Leonard Knox
Sir Peter Julian Millett
Sir Robert Andrew Morritt
Sir William Aldous
Sir John Frank Mummery
Sir Francis Mursell Ferris

Queen's Bench Division

The Lord Chief Justice of England

Sir William Lloyd Mars-Jones
(retired 4 September 1990)
Sir Leslie Kenneth Edward Boreham
Sir Alfred William Michael Davies
Sir Haydn Tudor Evans
Sir Kenneth Graham Jupp
(retired 5 November 1990)
Sir Walter Derek Thornley Hodgson
Sir Ronald Gough Waterhouse
Sir Frederick Maurice Drake
Sir Barry Cross Sheen
Sir Christopher James Saunders French
Sir Peter Edlin Webster
Sir Iain Charles Robert McCullough
Sir Hamilton John Leonard
Sir David Cozens-Hardy Hirst
Sir John Stewart Hobhouse
Sir Michael Patrick Nolan
Sir Oliver Bury Popplewell
Sir William Alan Macpherson
Sir Philip Howard Otton
Sir Paul Joseph Morrow Kennedy
Sir Michael Hutchison
Sir Simon Denis Brown
Sir Anthony Howell Meurig Evans
Sir Mark Oliver Saville
Sir Johan Steyn
Sir Christopher Dudley Roger Rose
Sir Richard Howard Tucker

Sir Robert Alexander Gatehouse
Sir Patrick Neville Garland
Sir John Ormond Roch
Sir Michael John Turner
Sir Harry Henry Ognall
Sir John Downes Alliott
Sir Konrad Hermann Theodor Schiemann
Sir John Arthur Dalziel Owen
Sir Denis Robert Maurice Henry
Sir Francis Humphrey Potts
Sir Richard George Rougier
Sir Ian Alexander Kennedy
Sir Nicholas Addison Phillips
Sir Robin Ernest Auld
Sir Malcolm Thomas Pill
Sir Stuart Neill McKinnon
Sir Mark Howard Potter
Sir Henry Brooke
Sir Igor Judge
Sir Edwin Frank Jowitt
Sir Michael Morland
Sir Mark Waller
Sir Roger John Buckley
Sir Anthony Brian Hidden
Sir John Desmond Augustine Fennell
Sir John Michael Wright
Sir Charles Barrie Knight Mantell
Sir John Christopher Calthorpe Blofeld
(appointed 9 November 1990)

Family Division

The President of the Family Division

Sir Alfred Kenneth Hollings
Sir John Kember Wood
Sir Thomas Michael Eastham
Dame Margaret Myfanwy Wood Booth
Sir Anthony Leslie Julian Lincoln
Sir Anthony Bruce Ewbank
Sir John Douglas Waite
Sir Anthony Barnard Hollis
Sir Swinton Barclay Thomas

Sir Mathew Alexander Thorpe
Sir Edward Stephen Cazalet
Sir Alan Hylton Ward
Sir Thomas Scott Gillespie Baker
Sir Robert Lionel Johnson
Sir Douglas Dunlop Brown
Sir Donald Keith Rattee
Dame Joyanne Winifred Bracewell
(appointed 2 October 1990)

CITATION

These reports are cited thus:

[1990] 3 All ER

REFERENCES

These reports contain references to the following major works of legal reference described in the manner indicated below.

Halsbury's Laws of England

The reference 26 Halsbury's Laws (4th edn) para 577 refers to paragraph 577 on page 296 of volume 26 of the fourth edition of Halsbury's Laws of England.

The reference 7(1) Halsbury's Laws (4th edn reissue) para 267 refers to paragraph 267 on page 177 of reissue volume 7(1) of the fourth edition of Halsbury's Laws of England.

Halsbury's Statutes of England and Wales

The reference 27 Halsbury's Statutes (4th edn) 208 refers to page 208 of volume 27 of the fourth edition of Halsbury's Statutes of England and Wales.

The reference 19 Halsbury's Statutes (4th edn) (1990 reissue) 499 refers to page 499 of the 1990 reissue of volume 19 of the fourth edition of Halsbury's Statutes of England and Wales.

The reference 45 Halsbury's Statutes (3rd edn) 1196 refers to page 1196 of volume 45 of the third edition of Halsbury's Statutes of England.

The Digest

References are to the green band reissue volumes of The Digest (formerly the English and Empire Digest).

The reference 37(2) Digest (Reissue) 424, 2594 refers to case number 2594 on page 424 of Digest Green Band Reissue Volume 37(2).

The reference 27(1) Digest (2nd reissue) 330, 2849 refers to case number 2849 on page 330 of Digest Green Band Second Reissue Volume 27(1).

Halsbury's Statutory Instruments

The reference 1 Halsbury's Statutory Instruments (Grey Volume) 278 refers to page 278 of Grey Volume 1 of Halsbury's Statutory Instruments.

The reference 17 Halsbury's Statutory Instruments (4th reissue) 256 refers to page 256 of the fourth reissue of volume 17 of Halsbury's Statutory Instruments.

Cases reported in volume 3

Digest of cases reported in volume 3

House of Lords petitions

This list, which covers the period 4 August 1990 to 14 December 1990, sets out all cases which have formed the subject of a report in the All England Law Reports in which an Appeal Committee of the House of Lords has, subsequent to the publication of that report, refused leave to appeal. Where the result of a petition for leave to appeal was known prior to the publication of the relevant report a note of that result appears at the end of the report.

W v Egdell [1990] 1 All ER 835, CA. Leave to appeal refused 27 November 1990 (Lord Bridge, Lord Brandon and Lord Templeman)

CORRIGENDUM

[1990] 3 All ER
p 9. **The Iran Nabuvat.** Line *c* 1, should read: 'reconsideration inter partes . . .'

Re White (deceased)
Barker v Gribble and another

CHANCERY DIVISION
ANDREW PARK QC SITTING AS A DEPUTY JUDGE OF THE HIGH COURT
27, 28 NOVEMBER 1989, 15 JANUARY 1990

Will – Alteration – Alteration after execution – Alterations made by hand on original at testator's direction – Alterations witnessed but not signed by testator – Whether will in amended form could be admitted to probate as an altered will – Whether will in amended form could be admitted to probate as an original will – Wills Act 1837, ss 9, 21.

In 1981 the testator made a valid will appointing the first defendant to be his executor and trustee. In 1984 the testator decided to alter his will and dictated certain alterations to the second defendant, who copied them by hand onto the will. The testator checked the alterations, then wrote 'Alterations to Will dated 14–12–84' and asked two witnesses to sign it. The testator did not sign the will again although the will still bore his signature from the original execution in 1981. Following the testator's death the question arose whether the will in its original or amended form should be admitted to probate. The plaintiff, a residuary beneficiary under the will in its original form, contended that the alterations did not comply with s 21[a] of the Wills Act 1837, which provided that 'no . . . alteration made in any will after the execution thereof shall be valid or have any effect . . . unless such alteration shall be executed in like manner as . . . is required for the execution of the will', because the alterations were not signed by the testator, nor could the will in its amended form be treated as an original will because it did not comply with s 9[b] of the 1837 Act, which required a valid will to be in writing and signed by the testator and further provided that a will was not valid unless it appeared that the testator intended by his signature to give effect to the will and each witness attested and signed the will in the presence of the testator.

Held – (1) The will in its amended form could not be admitted to probate as an altered will because the alterations did not comply with s 21 of the 1837 Act, because the alterations had to meet all the formal requirements under s 9 for the execution of a will and had not been signed by the testator or any other person in his presence and by his direction as required by s 9 (see p 5 e, post); dictum of Buckley J in *Re Hay, Kerr v Stinnear* [1904] 1 Ch 317 at 321 applied.

(2) The will in its amended form could not be admitted to probate as an original will because it had not been signed by the testator as required by s 9(a) of the 1837 Act, since the testator's signature to the original will in 1981 did not suffice to make the amended will made in 1984 a will 'signed by the testator' because the testator's signature in 1981 was not part of the process of making an entirely new will in 1984. Furthermore, that signature could not be said to have been intended by the testator 'to give effect' to the will made in 1984, as required by s 9(b), and the witnesses to the alterations had not attested a new will in 1984 but merely the alterations to the original will made in 1981 and therefore the requirement of s 9(d) that each witness 'attests . . . the will' was not

---

a   Section 21 is set out at p 4 *j* to p 5 *a*, post
b   Section 9 is set out at p 4 *h* post

satisfied. It followed that since the will in its amended form could not be admitted to probate the original will made in 1981 would be admitted to probate (see p 5 *h*, p 6 *b d g* *a* to *j*, p 7 *b e f* and p 8 *c d*, post); *Re Martin's goods* (1849) 1 Rob Eccl 712 and *Re Shearn's goods* (1880) 50 LJP 15 applied.

Notes

For attestation and alteration of wills, see 50 Halsbury's Laws (4th edn) paras 261, 273, *b* and for cases on the subjects, see 50 Digest (Reissue) 151–156, 179–186, *1369–1435*, *1700–1766*.

Cases referred to in judgment

Daintree v Butcher (1888) 13 PD 102, CA.
Dewell's goods, Re (1853) 1 Ecc & Ad 103, 164 ER 60.   *c*
Hay, Re, Kerr v Stinnear [1904] 1 Ch 317.
Martin's goods, Re (1849) 1 Rob Eccl 712, 163 ER 1188.
Shearn's goods, Re (1880) 50 LJP 15.

Cases also cited

Cunningham's goods, Re (1860) 4 Sw & Tr 194, 164 ER 1491.   *d*
Locke v James (1843) 11 M & W 901, 152 ER 1071.
Robinson, Re, Lamb v Robinson [1930] 2 Ch 332, [1930] All ER Rep 658.
Treeby's goods, Re (1875) LR 3 P & D 242.
Trotter, Re, Trotter v Trotter [1899] 1 Ch 764.
Wilson's goods, Re (1866) LR 1 P & D 269.
Wright v Sanderson (1884) 9 PD 149, CA.   *e*

Action and counterclaim

The plaintiff, Frederick John Barker, who was entitled under a partial intestacy arising if a will made by the testator, John Graham White deceased, on 2 January 1981 and amended on 14 December 1984 was admitted to probate in its amended form, brought an action, by a writ dated 18 February 1988, claiming that the court pronounce for the *f* force and validity of the amended will in solemn form of law. The defendants to the action were Michael Sinclair Gribble, the executor named in the will, and Guy Williams, who was a witness to the will in its amended form and was therefore unable to take a legacy bequeathed to him under the will in its amended form. By counterclaims dated 13 April 1988 and 3 August 1988 the defendants counterclaimed, inter alia, that the court pronounce for the will with the omission of the alterations made on 14 December *g* 1984. The facts are set out in the judgment.

Vivian Chapman for the plaintiff.
Christopher Semken for the first defendant.
David Stockill for the second defendant.   *h*

Cur adv vult

15 January 1990. The following judgment was delivered.

ANDREW PARK QC. Mr John Graham White, the testator, died on 26 February *j* 1985. In 1981 he made a will (the original will). In 1984 he caused it to be amended. The principal question I have to decide is whether what should be admitted to probate is the original will or the amended will. In my judgment the answer is: the original will. It follows that a secondary question which would have arisen if the amended will had been admitted to probate does not arise.

I now set out the facts more fully and describe the reasons for my conclusion.

a

The facts
The original will was executed on 2 January 1981. By cl 1 the testator appointed Mr Gribble, the first defendant in this case, as executor and trustee of the will. Clause 2 is a common form provision for the trustee to collect in the estate, and includes a trust for sale with power to postpone sale. Clause 3 is another common form provision for the

b   payment of funeral and testamentary expenses and debts.
Clause 4 is the provision which matters:

'MY TRUSTEE shall stand possessed of the residue of the said monies and the investments for the time being representing the same and of such part of my estate as shall for the time being remain unsold and unconverted upon the following

c   trusts: (a) as to 47% thereof for the said MICHAEL ST. CLAIR GRIBBLE . . .'

There follows a list of residuary bequests, 18 in all (ie paras (a) to (r)), the highest percentage being the 47% in favour of the first defendant and the lowest being a 0·6% share to a Mr Leslie Lancaster. Paragraph (b) gave 12% to Mr Guy Williams, the second defendant, and paragraph (c) gave 4·6% to Mr Frederick Barker, the plaintiff. Thirteen of

d   the beneficiaries were named individuals. Four were charities, and the other was the Conservative Party. The original will was duly witnessed by persons having no interest under the will. There is no doubt that the original will was in every respect a valid and effective will.

However, in December 1984 the testator decided that he wished to alter the will. The problems in this case arise from the way in which he went about doing so. The second

e   defendant was with him at his house at 66 Brunswick Road, Ealing, London W5. The second defendant had the original will and the testator had a copy of it. The testator made the alterations he desired in manuscript on his copy of the will. He read them out to the second defendant, and he at the testator's dictation, wrote them in manuscript on the original will. I describe the contents of the alterations in the next paragraph. The second defendant then handed the original will, with his manuscript alterations written

f   on it, to the testator. The testator checked it, and then wrote in his own handwriting in a blank space at the foot of the last page of the will:

'Alterations to Will dated 14–12–84
Witnesses . . .'

The testator had already by telephone asked Mr Lancaster (the beneficiary of a 0·6% share)

g   to come to the house. When Mr Lancaster arrived he was asked to sign as a witness. He did so in the space after the word 'witnesses', which the testator had written on the original will as I described above. The second defendant also added his signature at that point. Thus the last page of the will bears the testator's signature as written by him at the execution of the original will on 2 January 1981, that signature being duly attested by the two witnesses to the original will. In the space to the right of their signatures appear

h   the words:

'Alterations to Will dated 14–12–84
Witnesses   L. L. Lancaster
               G. Williams.'

The testator, who had signed the will in 1981, did not sign it again in 1984.

j   The manuscript amendments made to the will were six in number. Four of them were deletions of the residuary bequests to four beneficiaries. The second defendant ruled a line through the deleted bequests and wrote after each one 'Cancelled 14/12/84'. One of the deleted shares was the 4·6% share in favour of the plaintiff. The other two alterations were changes to the shares of two beneficiaries. The first defendant's share was reduced from 47% to 20%, and the second defendant's share was increased from 12% to

15%. This was done (or was sought to be done) by the second defendant crossing out the two figures of 47% and 12%; above the line in each case he write 'Cancelled' and below *a* the line he wrote in the one case '20% only' and in the other case '15% only'. I should mention, since a point was taken on it though not one to which I myself attach any significance, that he did not add a date to those individual alterations, whereas, as I have described, he did do so in relation to the four other alterations. There are no signatures or initials in the margins against any of the alterations.

b

The issues

The testator having died in 1985 the main issue which is in dispute is whether the manuscript alterations to the will take effect in law. The plaintiff contends that they do and that the will should be admitted to probate as amended in 1984. At first sight this is suprising, because one of the 1984 alterations deleted his 4·6% share under the original will. The explanation, however, is that if the amendments are valid only 67·5% of the *c* residury estate is disposed of by the will, whereas the original will disposed of 100% of the residuary estate. Therefore the amended will, if valid, leaves an intestacy, and the plaintiff would be entitled to a substantial share of the undisposed of estate to which the rules of intestacy would apply. There are other intestacy beneficiaries who would also benefit if the plaintiff was successful in this case.

Mr Gribble is a defendant in two capacities. First he is the executor. Second his 47% *d* share under the original will is reduced to 20% if the amendments are valid. He contends that the amendments are ineffective, and that the original will should be admitted to probate in its unamended form. The second defendant also contends that the original will should be admitted to probate. This also is surprising at first sight, since the amendments purported to increase his share from 12% to 15%. However, the second defendant was a witness on the occasion of the making of the amendments in 1984, and *e* by virtue of the rule that no attesting witness to a will may take a beneficial interest thereunder (see the Wills Act 1837, s 15) there is no basis on which he could claim a 15% share. If the original will is admitted to probate without the amendments, the second defendant was not a witness to the original will and there is no problem over him taking his 12% share. In the alternative, if the amended will is admitted to probate, while accepting that he cannot take his 15% share, he contends that he is still entitled to the *f* original 12%. Whether he is right in that alternative contention is the issue, to which I referred at the beginning of this judgment, which does not arise given my conclusion that it is the original will which is valid.

The relevant provisions

There are two sections of the Wills Act 1837 which I should set out. Section 9, as *g* substituted by s 17 of the Administration of Justice Act 1982, reads as follows:

> '*Signing and attestation of wills.*—No will shall be valid unless—(a) it is in writing, and signed by the testator, or by some other person in his presence and by his direction; and (b) it appears that the testator intended by his signature to give effect to the will; and (c) the signature is made or acknowledged by the testator in the *h* presence of two or more witnesses present at the same time; and (d) each witness either—(i) attests and signs the will; or (ii) acknowledges his signature, in the presence of the testator (but not necessarily in the presence of any other witness), but no form of attestation shall be necessary.'

Section 21, which is still in the original 1837 form, reads as follows: *j*

> '*No alteration in a will shall have any effect unless executed as a will.*—No obliteration, interlineation, or other alteration made in any will after the execution thereof shall be valid or have any effect, except so far as the words or effect of the will before such alteration shall not be apparent, unless such alteration shall be executed in like

a
manner as herein-before is required for the execution of the will; but the will, with such alteration as part thereof, shall be deemed to be duly executed if the signature of the testator and the subscription of the witnesses be made in the margin or on some other part of the will opposite or near to such alteration, or at the foot or end of or opposite to a memorandum referring to such alteration, and written at the end or some other part of the will.'

b
Discussion and conclusions

When amendments are made on the document which constitutes a will there are two ways in which the alterations might be effective. First, if they comply with s 21 of the 1837 Act, they are valid as alterations. Second, the process by which the amendments are made might amount to the making of an entirely new and valid will, complying with s 9.

c
I comment first on s 21. Counsel for the plaintiff relied on s 21 to give validity to the amendments, but I think only faintly. The problem is that if an alteration to a will is to be valid under s 21, then the alteration itself has to be 'executed in like manner as herein-before is required for the execution of the will'. That means that the alteration must meet all the formal requirements of s 9. In *Re Hay, Kerr v Stinnear* [1904] 1 Ch 317 at 321 Buckley J said:

d
'. . . it is quite plain that an alteration in a duly executed will made after the execution thereof is not effective unless the alteration is executed in the manner required by the statute for the execution of the will.'

One of the requirements of s 9 is that the will (and thus, in a s 21 case, the alteration) must be 'signed by the testator, or by some other person in his presence and by his direction'. In this case the alterations to the will were not signed by the testator nor were they signed by any other person in his presence and by his direction. When Mr Lancaster and the second defendant wrote their names against the word 'witnesses' they were not purporting to sign the alterations.

e

It follows that the alterations cannot be valid by virtue of s 21.

I turn to the argument under s 9, around which most of the hearing revolved. Did what happened on 14 December 1984 amount to the creation of a will, complying with all the formal requirements of s 9? Section 9 sets out the requirements in four paragraphs, paras (a) to (d). They are cumulative, and all must be satisfied. I shall now consider each paragraph in turn.

f

Paragraph (a) of s 9

g
So far as relevant in this case, s 9(a) requires that the will must be in writing and must be signed by the testator. It is important to remember that this test must be applied, not to the original 1981 will, but to what I might call 'the 1984 will', that is a will regarded conceptually as an entirely new will expressed in the terms of the 1981 will as amended in 1984.

The 1984 will is plainly in writing, and prima facie it is signed by the testator. Certainly his signature appears at the end of it. Nevertheless, counsel for the second defendant submits that the statutory condition is not satisfied, and after considerable deliberation I have decided that I agree with him.

h

Let me illustrate my reasoning by an example somewhat in the nature of a reductio ad absurdum. Suppose that a man finds a sheet of paper on which he wrote his signature months ago. It might, for example, be a letter which he wrote. He crosses out everything except his signature and writes on a blank space above where his signature appears: 'This is my last will and testament. I leave all my estate to my wife.' He then gets two witnesses to attest his signature. In my judgment that is not an instance of a will which is signed by the testator. What was signed by the testator was a different document altogether, and the will itself is not signed by him. Moving the example a little closer to the actual facts,

j

suppose that the document which he had signed months ago was not a letter or something similar, but an earlier will which he does not like any more. So, leaving his original *a* signature on the document, he crosses out everything else, writes in his new will and gets his original signature witnessed a second time. In principle that case appears to me to be the same as the previous one, and it is not a case of a will which is signed by the testator.

The present case appears to me in principle to be exactly the same. What I have called 'the 1984 will' is conceptually a different will, and the signature which almost four years before the testator had written on the 1981 will does not in my judgment suffice to meet *b* the requirement that the 1984 will must be a will signed by the testator.

Having regard to some of the argument on this issue I should make one point. I would have no difficulty over accepting as valid a will created in the following way. First, the testator takes a blank piece of paper and signs it at the bottom. Second, as part of the same continuing process, he writes above his signature: 'This is my last will and testament. I leave everything to my wife.' Third, he gets his signature attested by two *c* witnesses. In that case it is all one operation, and it could not matter that he wrote his signature on the document before the dispositive wording of the will. The case I have to decide, however, is altogether different. The writing by the testator of his signature on the document in 1981 was in no sense part of the process of the creation of the 1984 will on 14 December 1984.

I ought to acknowledge that my conclusion on this point is probably inconsistent with *d* the decision of Sir John Dodson in the Prerogative Court in the old case of *Re Dewell's goods* (1853) 1 Ecc & Ad 103 at 104, 164 ER 60. In that case the testator had made a will in 1847 and in 1848 he made a number of manuscript alterations to it ('interlineations'). At the end of the will he wrote: 'Republished and declared by the testator, with [the interlineations] in the presence of [two witnesses].' The witnesses added their signatures, but the testator did not. This will as amended was admitted to probate, and Sir John *e* Dodson is reported as saying:

> 'The proper course, perhaps, would have been for the testator to have re-signed his name, as the witnesses did; but I don't know that the omission is fatal to the validity of these interlineations.'

f

It is not clear from the report whether the case was argued on the basis of ss 21 or 9 (in its original form) or both, but, however it was presented, I respectfully disagree with the result.

Paragraph (b) of s 9

The requirement is: 'No will shall be valid unless . . . it appears that the testator, *g* intended by his signature to give effect to the will . . .' In my judgment this condition is not satisfied either. Counsel for the plaintiff said that, when the testator presented the amended will to Mr Lancaster and the second defendant for them to witness in 1984, he intended to give effect to it. I am sure that he did, but the statute requires that it must have been by the testator's signature (not, for example, by the testator's presentation of the will to the witnesses) that he intended to give effect to the will. The reference in the *h* statute to 'his signature' might be read in two ways. It might refer to the act of signing the will. Alternatively, it might refer to the presence on the document of the testator's signature. The former seems to me the more natural reading, and if it is correct there is no doubt that this statutory condition is not satisfied. The act of signing happened in 1981, and there is no conceivable basis on which, by signing the will in 1981 the testator intended to give effect to the amended 1984 will. Even if 'his signature' merely refers to *j* the presence on the document of the signature, I can still see no basis on which it can be said to appear that it was by the presence of that signature that the testator intended in December 1984 to give effect to the will.

I should mention that the condition which is set out in the present para (b) of s 9 was not to be found in the section as originally enacted in 1837. Something similar was

provided for in s 1 of the Wills Act Amendment Act 1852, but as far as I am aware there
a is no authority on the meaning of that particular requirement. In *Re Dewell's goods* Sir
John Dodson appears not to have considered the 1852 Act at all, possibly rightly because,
although the testator in that case died after the Act, the will and the interlineations were
made before it. I do not believe that there is any authority which need inhibit me from
concluding that, although the signature which the testator in this case had written in
1981 appears on the document, it does not appear that it was by that signature that he
b intended to give effect to the 1984 will.

Paragraph (c) of s 9
The effect of this requirement is that the testator's signature must have been either
made or acknowledged by him in the presence of the two 1984 witnesses, that is Mr
c Lancaster and the second defendant. It was certainly not made in their presence, but it
may be that it was acknowledged in their presence. In *Daintree v Butcher* (1888) 13 PD
102 at 103 Cotton LJ said:

> '... it is not necessary for the testator to say "this is my signature", but if it is
> placed so that the witnesses can see it, and what takes place involves an
d > acknowledgment by the testator that the signature is his, that is enough.'

Although my general conclusion is that the conditions of s 9 are not satisfied, I would be
disposed to accept that this particular condition (c) was satisfied.

Paragraph (d) of s 9
The relevant wording of this requirement is as follows: 'No will shall be valid unless
e ... each witness ... attests and signs the will ... in the presence of the testator ...' This
wording effectively reproduces a requirement of the original wording from 1837.
The principal submission of counsel for the first defendant, concurred in by counsel
for the second defendant, was that this condition is not satisfied. I agree. It is of course
true that both Mr Lancaster and the second defendant placed their signatures on the
f document in the presence of the testator. It is, however, necessary that, by doing so, they
should have attested *the will*, that is what I have called the 1984 will. If all that they were
attesting were the alterations to the 1981 will, that does not satisfy s 9.
The principle of law is clearly established by authority. First I refer to *Re Martin's goods*
(1849) 1 Rob Eccl 712 at 714, 163 ER 1188. The testatrix caused certain manuscript
alterations to be made to her will and thereafter it is at least possible that she re-signed
g the will herself. The witnesses, however, merely initialled against the manuscript
amendments. It was held that the amended will could not be admitted to probate,
because the witnesses had not attested the altered will as a whole 'as the instrument
appears on the face of it they attested the *alterations* only' (my emphasis). Second I refer
to *Re Shearn's goods* (1880) 50 LJP 15. This was another case in which manuscript
alterations were made to a will, and the witnesses merely initialled in the margin against
h the alterations. It was alleged that the testatrix, after the alterations, acknowledged her
earlier signature, and that that was sufficient to meet the requirement of signature. Even
if it was (and in my judgment it would not have been) the amended will was not valid
because what the witnesses attested were merely the alterations, not the amended will as
a whole. Hannen P said (at 16):

> 'My decision proceeds on this ground, that when a second execution is alleged to
j > have taken place that second execution must have been attested by the witnesses. In
> this case there has been no attestation by the witnesses.'

Counsel for the plaintiff does not dispute the proposition that, if all that Mr Lancaster
and the second defendant attested were the amendments to the will, the amended will
would not be valid. He says, however, that they attested the amended will as a whole. I

am afraid that I cannot agree. Their evidence (in affidavit form from Mr Lancaster, who
has since died, and in both affidavit and oral form from the second defendant) is entirely
inconclusive as to what they were attesting. Counsel for the plaintiff says that they
thought there was no difference between attesting the will and merely attesting the
alterations. I think that is probably right, but there is a difference, and, if their evidence
does not resolve the question of what they were attesting, then it must be determined by
the document. As I have said, the words are:

> 'Alterations to Will dated 14–12–84
> *Witnesses*   L. L. Lancaster
>   G. Williams.'

What the testator wrote was 'Alterations to Will', not, for example, 'Altered Will'. In the
circumstances I can only conclude that what the two witnesses attested were merely the
alterations to the will, not the will as a whole. I take the point, forcefully made by counsel
for the plaintiff that the words are written at the end of the will and underneath the
testator's signature, but the force of the point is substantially removed by the circumstance
that the words appear on the only convenient blank space on either of the two pages to
which the alterations had been made.

My conclusion, therefore, is that the amended will fails to satisfy three of the four
conditions which it has to satisfy if it is to take effect under s 9 as a valid will newly made
in 1984. The result on the whole matter is that the original will in its unamended form
continued to be valid and in my judgment falls to be admitted to probate. As I indicated
earlier, it follows that the question of whether, had the position been otherwise, the
second defendant would have lost his entire interest or would have been entitled to keep
12% does not arise, and I propose to say nothing about it.

Order accordingly.

Solicitors: *Male & Wagland*, Potters Bar (for the plaintiff); *Rumbolds* (for the first
defendant); *Longueville Gittins*, Oswestry (for the second defendant).

Hazel Hartman   Barrister.

a

The Iran Nabuvat

COURT OF APPEAL, CIVIL DIVISION
LORD DONALDSON OF LYMINGTON MR, BUTLER-SLOSS AND TAYLOR LJJ
12 JUNE 1990

b *Court of Appeal – Practice – Leave to appeal – Application for leave to appeal – Reconsideration inter partes in open court of leave to appeal granted ex parte – Test to be applied by court in deciding whether to grant leave – RSC Ord 59, r 14(2B).*

The purpose of requiring leave to appeal is to screen out appeals which will inevitably fail. Accordingly, where a party applies pursuant to RSC Ord 59, r 14(2B)[a] for the
c reconsideration inter partes in open court of leave to appeal which was granted ex parte the test to be applied by the court in deciding whether leave should be granted is whether there is an arguable case by way of appeal and not whether there is a probability or reasonable likelihood of the appeal succeeding, since the bias must always be towards allowing the Full Court to consider the complaint of the dissatisfied litigant (see p 10 *f* to *h*, p 11 *b* and p 12 *d*, post).

d
Notes
For applications to the Court of Appeal, a single judge or the registrar for leave to appeal, see 37 Halsbury's Laws (4th edn) paras 683, 695.

Case cited
e *Carter (R G) Ltd v Clarke* [1990] 2 All ER 209, [1990] 1 WLR 578, CA.

Application for leave to appeal
The defendants, the owners of the vessel Iran Nabuvat, applied for an inter partes review, under RSC Ord 59, r 14(2), of the order made ex parte by Bingham LJ granting the plaintiffs, Credit Commercial de France, a body corporate according to the laws of France
f leave to appeal against the order of Sheen J dated 8 May 1989 whereby he set aside the judgment of Hobhouse J dated 12 June 1987 giving judgment for the plaintiffs in the sum of $US405,015 in default of acknowledgment of service and substituted judgment for the sum of $US259,488·65. The facts are set out in the judgment of Lord Donaldson MR.

g *Angus Glennie* for the defendants.
Nigel Meeson for the plaintiffs was not called on.

LORD DONALDSON OF LYMINGTON MR. On 1 October 1989 RSC Ord 59, r 14(2) was amended by RSC (Amendment No 3) 1989, SI 1989/1307, to read as follows:

h   '(2) An application to the Court of Appeal for leave to appeal shall—(a) include, where necessary, any application to extend time for appealing, and (b) be made ex parte in writing setting out the reasons why leave should be granted and, if the time for appealing has expired, the reasons why the application was not made within that time; and the Court may grant or refuse the application or direct that the application be renewed in open court either ex parte or inter partes.

j   (2A) If an application under paragraph (2) is refused otherwise than after a hearing in open court, the applicant shall be entitled, within 7 days after he has been given notice of the refusal, to renew his application; and such renewed application shall be heard ex parte in open court.

---

a   Rule 14(2B) is set out at p 10 *a*, post

(2B) If an application under paragraph (2) is granted otherwise than after a
hearing inter partes, notice of the order is to be served on the party or parties affected *a*
by the appeal and any such party shall be entitled, within 7 days after service of the
notice, to apply to have the grant of leave reconsidered inter partes in open court.'

It is the power to ask for a reconsideration inter partes in open court which has been
exercised by the defendants in this case. They seek a reconsideration of the leave to appeal
which was granted by Bingham LJ on a consideration of the written application of the *b*
plaintiffs for leave to appeal, and in the light of the documents which accompanied that
written application.

In para 7 of the note which the sixth cumulative supplement to *The Supreme Court
Practice 1988* adds to para 59/14/7 of the main work the following words appear:

'. . . Since the single Lord Justice will (prior to granting leave to appeal) have seen
and considered the draft grounds of appeal, a transcript or note of judgment *c*
appealed against, and (where the application was made out of time) the reasons for
the delay, it is envisaged that respondents will not apply for the grant of leave to be
set aside unless there are cogent grounds for believing that there is some point
which was not before the single Lord Justice and which renders the appeal so weak
as to justify rescinding the grant of leave to appeal.'
                                                                                    d

Before I come to the facts, let me say at once that counsel for the defendants does not
accept that note as being a proper approach by this court. He submits that arguability
should not be the test. The true test, as he submits, should be that leave to appeal should
only be granted where there is a probability or a reasonable likelihood of the judge
having gone wrong. He says, particularly in the context of discretionary decisions, that
there should be a strong bias against granting leave and, if leave is granted, there should *e*
be a favourable wind given to any application to reconsider.

I am bound to say that, for my part, I do not accept that proposition at all. The grant
or refusal of leave to come to the Court of Appeal is a very sensitive power which has to
be exercised by the court. The bias must always be towards allowing the Full Court to
consider the complaints of the dissatisfied litigant, and the justification for leave to appeal *f*
in its present form or (if as I hope will come to pass) in an extended form must be that it
is unfair to the respondent that he should be required to defend the decision below,
unfair to other litigants because the time of the Court of Appeal is being spent listening
to an appeal which should not be before it and thereby causing delay to other litigants,
and unfair to the appellant himself who needs to be saved from his own folly in seeking
to appeal the unappealable.
                                                                                    g

The test of counsel for the defendants would really involve the single Lord Justice or,
as is likely to be the case when there are changes in legislation, two Lords Justices hearing
the application and deciding, if not whether the appeal should succeed, at least, as counsel
would have us say, whether there was a probability and a reasonable likelihood of the
appeal succeeding. This comes very near to actually hearing the appeal.

For my part, I have no doubt at all that no one should be turned away from the Court *h*
of Appeal if he has an arguable case by way of appeal.

That leads one on to the question of whether there is an arguable case in these
particular circumstances. Again, for my part, if a Lord Justice of Appeal, having studied
the matter on paper, is satisfied that there is an arguable case and grants leave, I think it
would require some very cogent reasons for disagreeing with his decision, and it certainly
would not be a reason that the court which was asked to reconsider his decision did not *j*
itself think that the matter was arguable.

It is certainly within my experience, and I do not doubt within the experience of every
member of the Court of Appeal, that, having preread an appeal, one member of the court
will say, 'I really think this is unarguable,' and other members of the court will say, 'I do
not know, I really think there is a point here which needs looking at seriously.' In the

end, you may get a dissenting judgment or it may be that they will all come to the
a conclusion that the appeal is arguable or even that it should succeed.

But the point that I am making is that, if one Lord Justice thinks that an appeal is
arguable, it is really necessary, in my view, for anybody seeking a reconsideration of that
to be able to point fairly unerringly to a factor which was not drawn to the Lord Justice's
attention, because, perhaps, it did not feature in the documents which had been studied,
or to the fact that he has overlooked some statutory provision which is decisive, or some
b authority which is decisive, in the sense that the appeal will inevitably fail. That is really
what leave to appeal is directed at, screening out appeals which will inevitably fail.

Having rejected the approach of counsel for the defendants, may I deal briefly with
the facts of this particular application. The action itself was begun in November 1985,
when the plaintiffs, Credit Commercial de France, issued a writ in rem against the
defendants' ship the Iran Nabuvat, claiming demurrage due from the defendants under
c the terms of a charterparty between Sunflower Maritime Co SA, the owners of the ship
concerned, the motor vessel IO, and the Islamic Republic of Iran Shipping Lines, who
were charterers.

It matters not, but I gather that the right to receive the unpaid demurrage was assigned
to the plaintiffs and hence their appearance on the scene. What matters is that no
acknowledgment of service was received from the defendants and, accordingly, on
d 12 June 1987 Hobhouse J entered a default judgment for the not insignificant sum of
$US405,105, with interest to run from 1 January 1985.

The parties then entered into negotiations, the details of which do not matter, save
that the result was that no steps were taken by the plaintiffs to enforce that judgment for
a considerable period. When the negotiations failed to reach a happy, or indeed any,
conclusion, the defendants applied to Sheen J in or about May 1989 to have the judgment
e set aside. This, it will be appreciated, was some 21 months later. On that hearing the
defendants admitted that they owed the plaintiffs at least $245,700. They claimed to
have an arguable defence to the balance in excess of that sum. The plaintiffs, on the other
hand, admitted that there was an arguable defence to part of the larger sum of $405,000,
but they put the cut-off line between the arguable and the unarguable at $259,488.

f On 8 May Sheen J set aside the whole of the default judgment and gave judgment for
the plaintiffs in the sum of $259,488 with interest. He stayed that part of the judgment
which exceeded $245,700, ie the interface between the two parties' contentions, pending
an appeal to the House of Lords in another case[1] which was thought to have some bearing
on the matter, and he ordered that interest on the sum due was to be awarded at the rate
of 11% up to the date of his judgment. That, of course, includes the 21 months between
g the date when Hobhouse J had given judgment, the judgment which Sheen J had set
aside, and the date of Sheen J's judgment. The order for interest was made under the Law
Reform (Miscellaneous Provisions) Act 1934 and 11% was specified as being the
appropriate commercial rate for dollar currency. Thereafter, of course, his judgment
would bear interest at the current rate under the Judgments Act 1838, which was 15%.

The commercial basis of the dispute which has arisen is that, in substituting a new
h judgment for that which he had set aside and awarding interest at 11%, Sheen J effectively
deprived the plaintiffs of 4% (the difference between 15% under the 1838 Act and 11%
under the 1934 Act) for a period of 21 months on the sum of $245,700, which was
admittedly due at the time when Hobhouse J gave his judgment.

Counsel for the defendants says that that is right and proper because it is wholly wrong
that a sterling rate of interest should be applied to a dollar debt. Well, that is as may be.
j That is one of the points which will fall to be argued on this appeal. Bingham LJ said that
it was highly arguable, and certainly that would appear to be a point of principle.
Bingham LJ also said that it was a novel point, and counsel for the defendants accepts

1   *President of India v Jebsens (UK) Ltd, The General Capinpin* (not yet decided); on appeal from [1989] 1
    Lloyd's Rep 232, CA.

that it is a novel point, at any rate arising in this form. That is likely to be right because it really only achieves commercial significance if you have a delay, such as occurred here, *a* of 21 months between the original judgment and the date when there was a new judgment. It is, of course, contended, and it is right, that Sheen J could have simply amended Hobhouse J's judgment as to amount and left the interest position undisturbed. Counsel for the defendants says that this is essentially a discretionary decision by Sheen J, and on that ground alone is unappealable.

I am bound to say that, while it is difficult to dislodge discretionary decisions by judges *b* where they are truly discretionary, it is surprising in some fields, and particularly in the field of commercial law, how often a point of principle emerges from the woodwork when the discretion of the judge is being analysed.

However, I would dismiss this application with a good deal of emphasis, if one can dismiss with emphasis, because here was a Lord Justice saying not only that this appeal was arguable but that it was highly arguable, and that it was a novel point, and in those *c* circumstances it seems to me that any attempt to achieve a reversal of that decision was and is doomed to failure. I would dismiss the application.

BUTLER-SLOSS LJ. I agree.

TAYLOR LJ. I also agree.   *d*

Application dismissed.

Solicitors: *Lovell White Durrant* (for the defendants); *Clifford Chance* (for the plaintiffs).

Mary Rose Plummer   Barrister.   *e*

R v Harrow London Borough Council, ex parte D   *f*

COURT OF APPEAL, CIVIL DIVISION
FOX, WOOLF AND BUTLER-SLOSS LJJ
14, 28 JULY 1989

Child – Child abuse – Child abuse register – Register maintained by local authority – Registration *g* *of alleged abuser – Child making allegations of abuse against applicant – Local authority convening case conference to consider allegations – Applicant given opportunity to make written submissions but not allowed to attend case conference – Case conference deciding to place applicant's name on register – Whether case conference acting unfairly and contrary to natural justice.*

Judicial review – Availability of remedy – Child abuse register – Register maintained by local *h* *authority – Registration of alleged abuser – Child making allegations of abuse against applicant – Local authority convening case conference to consider allegations – Applicant given opportunity to make written submissions but not allowed to attend case conference – Case conference deciding to place applicant's name on register – Whether case conference's decision part of authority's internal administrative procedures – Whether case conference's decision subject to judicial review.*   *j*

The applicant was the mother of three children. She was divorced from the children's father and relations between the applicant and the father were acrimonious. The applicant had custody of the children, while the father had access. Following a visit by the two older children the father complained to a social worker that the applicant was hitting the children. The eldest child was independently examined by two paediatricians, who both found serious bruising and formed the view that the injuries were non-

accidental. The local authority called a case conference to determine what action, if any,
a should be taken with regard to the children. The applicant asked to be permitted to
attend the case conference but the local authority refused that request although it
informed her that she could make written submissions, which she did. Following the
case conference the local authority decided to place the children on its child abuse register
with the applicant being named as the abuser. The applicant applied for judicial review
of the local authority's decision on the grounds that it was unfair, unreasonable and
b contrary to natural justice because although the applicant had been given the opportunity
of making written submissions to the case conference she had not been given an
indication of the allegations against her to enable her to rebut them. The judge refused
the application and the applicant appealed.

Held – Since the applicant had been given an opportunity to give her account of how
c the injuries to the children had occurred and had done so, the local authority's decision
to place the children and the applicant on its child abuse register was not unfair,
unreasonable or contrary to natural justice because what was critical was whether the
applicant was responsible for the oldest child's injuries and the local authority was
justified in reaching its decision in the light of the findings and conclusions of the
paediatricians. The appeal would therefore be dismissed (see p 16 *a* to *f* and p 17 *g h*,
d post).
    Per curiam. Although the decision of a local authority to place a child's name on its
child abuse register will be subject to judicial review if it can be shown to be utterly
unreasonable, recourse to judicial review of such decisions should be very rare because
the welfare of the child is paramount and the interest of an adult accused of abuse may
have to be subordinated to the child's interest, the local authority is not carrying out a
e judicial process when making its decision, an entry in the register as an abuser is neither
a finding of fact nor a finding of guilt, and unbridled resort to judicial review could
frustrate efforts to protect the victims of child abuse. Accordingly, criticism of some
individual aspect of the procedure carried out by the local authority which does not raise
a point of principle should not normally be a ground for judicial review (see p 16 *h* to
p 17 *d*, post); *R v Norfolk CC, ex p* M [1989] 2 All ER 359 approved.

f **Notes**
For care and welfare of children by local authorities, see 24 Halsbury's Laws (4th edn)
para 786.
    For judicial control of administrative action, see 1(1) Halsbury's Laws (4th edn reissue)
paras 51–65.
g   For natural justice and fairness, see ibid paras 84–85.

Cases referred to in judgments
Associated Provincial Picture Houses Ltd v Wednesbury Corp [1947] 2 All ER 680, [1948] 1
    KB 223, CA.
R v Norfolk CC, ex p M [1989] 2 All ER 359, [1989] QB 619, [1989] 3 WLR 502.

h **Appeal**
The applicant, D (the mother), appealed against the order of Anthony Lincoln J sitting as
an additional judge of the Queen's Bench Division on 25 November 1988 whereby he
dismissed her motion for orders of judicial review of decisions made by the respondents,
Harrow London Borough Council, on or about 4 June 1986 (1) that the mother's three
children should be placed on the child abuse register kept by the council and (2) that the
j mother should sign a form of agreement as to the future supervision of her children
before they were returned to her care and custody. The facts are set out in the judgment
of Butler-Sloss LJ.

Anthony Scrivener QC and *Nigel Ley* for the mother.
Roger McCarthy for the council.

                                                                    Cur adv vult

28 July. The following judgments were delivered.

a

BUTLER-SLOSS LJ (giving the first judgment at the invitation of Fox LJ). This appeal is from the refusal by Anthony Lincoln J of an application for judicial review of the decision of the Harrow London Borough Council of 4 June 1986 that the names of three children be placed on the child abuse register. The applicant is the mother of the children, and the council is responsible for the register.

The applicant has been divorced from the father of the children. She was granted a *b* custody order in 1983, with fortnightly access to the father and a supervision order to the local authority. The divorce and subsequent proceedings have clearly been acrimonious, including a dispute over the paternity of the youngest child. Access to the two elder children by the father has been a cause of continuing litigation between the parents.

On 31 May 1986 the father took out the two elder children on an access visit. He got in touch with a social worker from the respondent council, and alleged that the mother *c* was hitting them. He was advised to take them to the local hospital. The eldest child, J, was examined by a paediatrician, who found serious bruising and formed the view that these injuries were non-accidental. The social worker, having heard an account from the child accusing the mother of inflicting them, applied to a magistrate under s 28 of the Children and Young Persons Act 1969 for a place of safety order, which was granted. The children remained in hospital overnight. On the following day, 1 June, a consultant *d* paediatrician, Dr Valman, examined both children. I take the description from the judgment:

'He found a large bruise surrounding the right eye in J's case and involving the whole orbital cavity. He also found four bruises on the left chest posteriorly and one bruise on the right chest posteriorly. The bruise surrounding the orbit, he stated, was compatible with an injury caused by a punch and the bruises on the back could *e* have been caused by being struck with a fist. He added: "I would say that all of these bruises were probably inflicted in a non-accidental manner." He was uncertain about the injuries to D. The applicant mother also was present on this occasion. She told Dr Valman that all the bruises were due to the children fighting with each other. He was unable to accept the mother's explanation, the injuries being *f* incompatible with her account of what had happened.'

The mother also says that the boy is prone to fantasise.

A case conference was arranged for 4 June. The two paediatricians and the headmistress of the children's school were among those who attended. The mother, through her solicitor, asked to attend. That request was refused, but she was told that she could make written submissions, which she did. A close friend of the mother also made written *g* submissions, which were placed before the case conference.

As a result of the case conference, the children's names, including the youngest, R, were placed on the child abuse register. At the same time the two elder children were returned to their mother. The youngest child was never removed from home. The names of all three children were thereafter removed from the register, J and D on 9 October 1987 and R on 20 March 1988. *h*

Before turning to the issues raised by this appeal, I shall look briefly at the procedures the subject of the appeal. Social services departments of local authorities since the early 1970s have been charged with the duty of keeping child abuse or child protection registers. They are given guidance in this task by successive circulars and guides issued by the former Department of Health and Social Security: see DHSS handbook *Child Abuse—Working Together* (1988): *j*

'Child protection registers.

5.30. In each area covered by a social services department a central register must be maintained which lists all the children in the area who have been abused or who are considered to be at risk of abuse and who therefore are currently the subject of an inter-agency plan to protect them . . .

a   5.32. The entry of a child's name on the register should normally only occur following discussion at a case conference when abuse or potential abuse is confirmed and an inter-agency agreement is made to work co-operatively to protect the child . . . A child's name will normally only be removed from the register when it is agreed in a case conference that formal inter-agency working is no longer necessary to protect the child.'

b   It is normally a prerequisite of entry on the register that a case conference has been called, but the case conference is not a decision-making body. However, its recommendation will in practice be followed by the local authority (or the National Society for the Prevention of Cruelty to Children), which is the decision-making body and has the responsibility for keeping the register. The guides and circulars are advisory in tone, but expected in practice to be followed.

c   The Harrow guidelines are similar, but not identical, to other local authority guidelines, and set out the people to be invited to attend case conferences. There is no statutory basis for the case conference or the register, but both are considered by the DHSS to be good social work practice and necessary elements for, inter alia, protection of children at risk. The Harrow guidelines set out the list of those with a right of access to the information on the register, which is otherwise confidential. It is a carefully defined section of the community, not restricted to social workers, and very broadly consists of those invited to case conferences or agencies in other areas to which the family may have moved.

d   Three issues were raised on the initial application for judicial review. One only remains for consideration on this appeal, that the conclusions of the case conference on 4 June, and the subsequent placing of the children's names, together with the name of the mother as the abuser on the child abuse register, were unfair and unreasonable and contrary to natural justice. A declaration is sought that the mother's name should never have been entered on the register.

e   Before the judge it was argued that the mother should have been permitted to attend the case conference and to have been heard. That suggestion is not pursued before this court. Rather, it is urged on us that the lowest degree of fairness to the mother, the opportunity to know about and to be allowed to meet the material allegations made against her, was not afforded to her. It is said that the decision was unfair, and the decision-making process was defective on Wednesbury principles (see Associated Provincial Picture Houses Ltd v Wednesbury Corp [1947] 2 All ER 680, [1948] 1 KB 223).

f   Counsel for the mother made a number of points. The effect of entry on the register, even if the names of the children are subsequently removed, is to leave a stigma on the character of the mother. He asserts that the inclusion of the name of the mother in the register was the equivalent of a 'finding of guilt' that she had physically abused J. The record for J reads:

g
        'Nature of injury and by whom inflicted, whether child abuse has been substantiated: bruise on back and forehead, graze on side of nose, near eye (black eye), inflicted by mother. Child abuse substantiated.'

h   That finding had to be on the basis of suitable evidence which she was entitled to know about and to have an opportunity to answer. He accepts that not all the minutiae require to be disclosed, but asserts that relevant and important matters were taken into account without prior disclosure.

       The case conference was given background information about the family, which included the information that the child J had previously been on the register shortly after birth in 1979 for about two years. The mother says that she was unaware of that fact, and the accuracy of that statement was not explored. There were other matters relating to why J did not attend swimming lessons, why the children did not drink milk at school, the failure of the mother to take the youngest for medical check-ups, the explanation for an earlier accident to D and the failure of the social workers to ask the mother for an explanation of the injuries to J.

In the context of these facts, the earlier registration was of peripheral relevance. With
the exception of the last point, all the other matters relate to history and do not disclose, *a*
as was suggested, a pattern of behaviour. They are most unlikely to have had any decisive
influence on the recommendation to place on the register.

What was critical was whether the mother was responsible for J's injuries. What the
mother required was an opportunity of giving her account how these injuries could have
occurred, and this was given to her by the consultant paediatrician. She took advantage
of the opportunity to give her account, both orally and in written representations.   *b*

The child J was clearly on the register as a result of the findings and conclusions of the
consultant paediatrician, together with the allegations of the child J and the unsatisfactory
explanations of the mother. The failure of a social worker to elicit an explanation from
the mother was not only understandable but, in my view, probably wise. In allegations
of physical injury, the most appropriate person to be given the account of the parent is
likely to be the paediatrician, who is often specially qualified to assess its probability in *c*
the light of the type, place, severity and other aspects of the injuries which have occurred.

Although the mother's request to attend, be represented and speak at the case
conference was refused, counsel for the mother does not submit that the case conference
erred in that respect. She was permitted to make written representations, both from
herself and a friend. The representations were placed before the case conference. The
decision to place the name of J on the register cannot, in my view, be faulted. Counsel *d*
for the mother accepts that, if J's name was properly there, the inclusion of the other
children was reasonable since they would be at risk. It is said that the mother was found
as a fact to be an abuser. This I do not consider to be the case, and I shall refer to it further
below.

The facts and circumstances must be looked at as a whole, and it becomes clear that
the level of fairness contended for by counsel for the mother in respect of all material *e*
matters was amply met by the procedure in fact followed.

I am satisfied that the procedure and the result did not in any way offend the
Wednesbury principles. The conclusion of the judge was that the mother failed 'to show
that the decision was in any way unfair, unreasonable or contrary to natural justice'. I
agree with him.

That would be sufficient to dispose of this matter, but it has been contended by the *f*
council that judicial review does not lie in respect of a decision to place a name on the
child abuse register. Counsel for the council also submits that the decision of Waite J to
grant judicial review of such a decision in *R v Norfolk CC, ex p M* [1989] 2 All ER 359,
[1989] QB 619 was wrong. The facts in the *Norfolk* case were: a plumber was working in
a house where a teenage girl made allegations that whe was sexually abused by him. She
had twice previously been the victim of sexual abuse, and a few days later made similar *g*
allegations against another man. The plumber's name was entered in the child abuse
register as an abuser, after a case conference. His employers were informed and they
suspended him, pending an internal inquiry. The first knowledge that the plumber had
of the allegations was the letter informing him of the decision to place his name on the
register. He was not told that his employers had been informed.   *h*

Although the contents of the register are confidential, a significant number of people
inevitably have to be aware of the information contained in it. As the *Norfolk* case
demonstrates, the effect on outsiders may be dramatic. If the decision to register can be
shown to be utterly unreasonable, in principle I cannot see why an application to review
the decision cannot lie. In coming to its decision, the local authority is exercising a most
important public function, which can have serious consequences for the child and the *j*
alleged abuser. I respectfully agree with the decision of Waite J.

It would also seem that recourse to judicial review is likely to be, and undoubtedly
ought to be, rare. Local authorities have laid on them by Parliament the specific duty of
protection of children in their area. The case conference has a duty to make an assessment
as to abuse and the abuser, if sufficient information is available. Of its nature, the

a mechanism of the case conference leading to the decision to place names on the register, and the decision-making process, is unstructured and informal.

It is accepted by counsel for the mother that it is not a judicial process. It is part of a protection package for a child believed to have been the victim of abuse. Unlike other areas of judicial review, the considerations are not limited to the individual who may have been prejudiced and the tribunal or organisation being criticised. In this field, unusually, there is a third component of enormous importance, namely the welfare of b the child which is the purpose of the entry in the register. In proceedings in which the child is the subject, his or her welfare is paramount.

In balancing adequate protection for the child and fairness to an adult, the interest of an adult may have to be placed second to the needs of the child. All concerned in this difficult and delicate area should be allowed to perform their task without looking over their shoulder all the time for the possible intervention of the court. The important c power of the court to intervene should be kept very much in reserve, perhaps confined to the exceptional case which involves a point of principle which needs to be resolved, not only for the individual case but in general, so as to establish that registration is not being conducted in an unsatisfactory manner. In the normal case where criticism is made of some individual aspect of the procedure which does not raise any point of principle leave should be refused. The decision of Waite J, right though it was in that case, should d not be the excuse for over-formalising the procedure, which is not intended to be confined within a rigid legal structure. In this area unbridled resort to judicial review could frustrate the ability of those involved in their effort to protect the victims of child abuse.

A record, not only that the child is at risk, but also recording who is the most likely abuser, may be an important element of protection in returning the child home. It is e important to remember that the children here were returned after 24 hours to their mother. The purpose of the entries and the letter the mother was asked to sign, about which she complained in the court below, was to provide a protection package for the children on their return to their mother. The purpose of the inclusion of the name of the adult needs to be clearly understood by those with knowledge of the entry. To pass that information to the employers was, as Waite J held, unreasonable and unfair. To have f the name on the register is not. The nature of the information recorded, the machinery by which it has been inserted and the limited purpose for which it is included must be recognised. Having said that, I do not consider that such an entry is in any way a finding of fact, even less a finding of guilt, nor should it be seen as such.

Unless there are exceptional features leading to a conclusion such as there were in the *Norfolk* case, I for myself would hesitate long before encouraging a review of the way in g which a particular case conference arrived at the recommendation required before the register entry is made.

I agree with the conclusion of the judge that the process and the decision of the council was neither unfair nor unreasonable, and would dismiss this appeal.

h **WOOLF LJ.** I agree.

FOX LJ. I also agree.

Appeal dismissed. Leave to appeal to the House of Lords refused.

j Solicitors: *Cheek Lesson & Co*, Harrow (for the mother); *Keith Gowling*, Harrow (for the council).

Sophie Craven   Barrister.

Legal Aid Board v Russell

COURT OF APPEAL, CIVIL DIVISION
LORD DONALDSON OF LYMINGTON MR, BUTLER-SLOSS AND TAYLOR LJJ
12, 13, 28 JUNE 1990

Costs – Interest on costs – Payment into court by defendant – Plaintiff accepting money paid into court in satisfaction of claim – Whether plaintiff entitled to payment of interest on his costs of action – Judgments Act 1838, s 17 – RSC Ord 22, r 3.

The court has no power to award interest on costs under s 17[a] of the Judgments Act 1838 except under a judgment or order, either formal or informal. Accordingly, where under RSC Ord 22, r 3 a plaintiff accepts money paid into court by the defendant in full settlement of his claim the court has no jurisdiction to make an order for payment of interest on his costs, because his entitlement to costs arises under the Rules of the Supreme Court and not by virtue of any judgment or order of the court. If the defendant fails to pay the plaintiff's taxed costs and the plaintiff applies for judgment for those costs under Ord 45, r 15 interest will only accrue from the date of that judgment (see p 19 hj, p 22 c to e and p 23 b, post).

Notes

For interest on costs, see 37 Halsbury's Laws (4th edn) para 753, and for cases on the subject, see 30 Digest (Reissue) 248–250, 540–564.

For the Judgments Act 1838, s 17, see 22 Halsbury's Statutes (4th edn) 263.

Cases referred to in judgments

Fishing v Dudding (1841) 9 Dowl 872.
Hunt v R M Douglas (Roofing) Ltd [1988] 3 All ER 823, [1990] AC 398, [1988] 3 WLR 975, HL.

Cases also cited

Coote v Ford [1899] 2 Ch 93; *affd* [1899] 2 Ch 93, [1895–9] All ER Rep 673, CA.
Debtor (no 5883 of 1979), Re a (1981) Times, 20 February.
Frankland, Re (1872) LR 8 QB 18.
French (A Martin) (a firm) v Kingswood Hill Ltd [1960] 2 All ER 251, [1961] 1 QB 96, CA.
Hill v Brown (1847) 16 M & W 796, 153 ER 1412.
Jones v Williams (1841) 8 M & W 349, 151 ER 1073.
Parsons v Mather & Platt Ltd [1977] 2 All ER 715, [1977] 1 WLR 855.
R v Essex County Court Judge and Clarke (1887) 18 QBD 704, CA.
Shaw v Neale (1858) 6 HL Cas 580, 10 ER 1422.
Waite v Redpath Dorman Long Ltd [1971] 1 All ER 513, [1971] 1 QB 294.

Interlocutory apppeal

The defendant, Dennis Russell, appealed with leave of the judge against the order of his Honour Judge Dobry QC sitting as a judge of the High Court in the Queen's Bench Division on 21 March 1989 whereby he dismissed the defendant's appeal against the decision of Mr District Registrar Donaldson dated 20 January 1989 in the Oxford District Registry holding that the plaintiff, John Edward Woodley, was entitled to interest on taxed costs in his action against the defendant for damages for personal injuries arising out of a traffic accident in which the plaintiff had accepted the amount paid into court by the defendant in full satisfaction of his claim. By order made by Mr Registrar Adams

---

a Section 17, so far as material, is set out at p 21 c to e, post

in chambers on 7 June 1989 the Legal Aid Board was substituted as the plaintiff for the
a purposes of the appeal. The facts are set out in the judgment of Lord Donaldson MR.

Dermod O'Brien QC and *Lord Meston* for the defendant.
Duncan Matheson QC and *Christopher Frazer* for the board.

Cur adv vult

b
28 June. The following judgments were delivered.

LORD DONALDSON OF LYMINGTON MR. It is a well-known fact that only a
very small proportion of the writs issued out of the High Court ever result in a trial. In
most cases the parties reach a settlement at an earlier stage and it is wholly in the public
c interest that this should be the case. Many such settlements result from defendants
making a payment into court under RSC Ord 22. The plaintiff then has a short time,
usually 21 days, in which he has to decide whether or not to accept the money in
satisfaction of his claim or whether he will continue with the action. It can be a decision
of crucial importance because, if the plaintiff fails to accept the payment in and eventually
recovers less than that amount, he will usually be ordered to pay the defendant's costs
d incurred after the money was paid into court. If, however, he accepts the money in full
satisfaction of his claim, he will be entitled to his costs of the action.
      So many actions settle in this way that the rules provide an automatic 'drill'. The
defendant pays the money into court and gives notice of the payment in to the plaintiff,
using Form 23 in RSC, App A. The plaintiff, if he decides to accept the money in
settlement of his claim, gives notice to the defendant using Form 24. The effect of this
e acceptance is to stay all further proceedings in relation to the cause of action (Ord 22,
r 3(4) or (5)), to authorise the Accountant General to pay the money to the plaintiff
(Ord 22, r 3(6)), to entitle the plaintiff to payment of his taxed costs of the action up to
the date of payment in and to authorise the taxation of those costs without any specific
order of such taxation and payment (Ord 62, r 5(1) and (4)). The only circumstances in
which the plaintiff needs to, or can, do more than give notice of acceptance is if the
f defendant fails to pay the taxed costs within four days after taxation. The plaintiff may
then, if he wishes, sign judgment for the amount of the costs pursuant to Ord 45, r 15.
      In every case in which a specific order for costs is made, the beneficiary under the order
is entitled to interest on the amount of those costs from 'the time of entering up the
judgment . . . until the same shall be satisfied'. This entitlement arises under s 17 of the
Judgments Act 1838. Recently, the House of Lords has ruled in *Hunt v R M Douglas*
g *(Roofing) Ltd* [1988] 3 All ER 823, [1990] AC 398 that the 'time of entering up the
judgment' is when the order for costs is made (the *incipitur* rule) and not, as had for
some years been thought to be the case, from the date on which the taxation of costs was
completed (the *allocatur* rule). What is suggested in this appeal is that the streamlined
procedure which relieves the plaintiff of any need to apply to the court for an order for
costs and a taxation of those costs where he is simply accepting money paid into court in
h satisfaction of his claim has, incidentally and I doubt not accidentally, deprived him of
any right to interest on those costs, unless and until he becomes entitled to apply for a
judgment for those costs under Ord 45, r 15. Even then, interest will only accrue from
the date of that judgment.
      It is with the greatest regret, and after a struggle to find a way in which such an
j anomalous result could be avoided, that I have come to the conclusion that there is no
escape. Let me explain how this point has arisen and why I have reached this conclusion.
      Before the decision in *Hunt's* case I doubt whether anyone gave any very serious or
prolonged consideration to whether there was any difference between the entitlement to
interest on costs of a plaintiff who accepted money paid into court in settlement of his
claim and one who succeeded at the trial of the action and obtained a specific order for

costs. Neither was thought to be entitled to interest before the issue of the allocatur by
the taxing master and the plaintiff who had accepted money paid into court could start   *a*
the interest clock ticking four days later by applying for judgment under Ord 45, r 15.
The decision in *Hunt's* case opened up the possibility that there was a very significant
difference between the position of the two categories of plaintiff.

The present action arose out of a road traffic accident on 18 September 1984 in which
the plaintiff, Mr John Woodley, was injured. In due course he claimed damages from the
defendant, Mr Dennis Russell, and later gave notice of his acceptance of sums which had   *b*
been paid into court and amounted to £35,500. The plaintiff had the benefit of legal aid
but was, of course, concerned to obtain interest on the costs incurred in prosecuting his
claim, since this would reduce the amount for which the Legal Aid Board will have a
charge on the damages which he has received from the defendant or, more accurately,
the defendant's insurers.

The taxation of costs by Mr Registrar Donaldson of the Oxford district registry was   *c*
completed in January 1989 and both parties then asked him to rule on whether, as the
plaintiff contended, interest on the amount of the costs began to accrue as from the date
of the acceptance of the money in court (August 1988) or, as the defendant contended,
from at the earliest January 1989, a difference of five months. As the appropriate rate of
interest was 15% and the costs were taxed at £10,200, the sum immediately in issue was
of the order of £630. This was no doubt of some significance to Mr Woodley, but the   *d*
principle involved was of vastly greater significance to the legal aid fund and to motor
and other liability insurers in view of the number of such claims with which each is
concerned.

Mr Registrar Donaldson did not have a full report of *Hunt's* case, but found for the
plaintiff on the footing that it would be wholly illogical to disqualify a successful litigant
from interest on costs simply because his entitlement arose from a rule rather than from   *e*
a specific order for costs. He pointed out that Ord 62, r 5(1) stated: 'No order for costs *is
required* in the circumstances mentioned in this rule.' From this he deduced that a
plaintiff could seek a specific order for costs, notwithstanding that the rules did not
require him to do so, and that no court would deny him such an order. However, the
adoption of this course would only result in increasing the costs incurred by the plaintiff
for which the defendant would ultimately be liable.   *f*

I have every sympathy with the registrar's approach, but I fear that he was in error in
thinking that a court could make a specific order for costs in a case such as this. It has to
be remembered that the court has no power to order the payment of interest on costs.
Where that entitlement exists, it is based on the happening of the event predicated by
s 17 of the Judgments Act 1838, namely the existence of a judgment debt for costs *and* a
'time of entering up the judgment'. The true interpretation of this section and of s 18   *g*
lies at the heart of this appeal and I will return to them hereafter. In the context of the
registrar's decision, I would only say that I do not think it would be a proper exercise of
discretion to make a specific order for costs in favour of a litigant who was already
entitled to those costs pursuant to Ord 62, r 5(4) with the extraneous objective of
indirectly granting him an entitlement to interest.

The defendant appealed to his Honour Judge Dobry QC, sitting as a Judge of the High   *h*
Court, who had the benefit of a full report of *Hunt's* case and was able to, and did, go into
the matter in much greater depth. He concluded that the legislative intention was clear,
namely to allow interest where the principal sum arose under a judgment or order of the
court which had the effect of a judgment and that, on the authorities, an informal record,
such as an entry in the master's book, was sufficient even if a formal judgment had   *j*
subsequently to be entered if execution was to be levied. There was no logical distinction
between *Hunt's* case, where there was a settlement and a stay of proceedings on agreed
terms, and a case in which there was an acceptance of money paid into court. If anything,
the automatic liability for costs after the date of notice of acceptance provides an even

clearer reason for interest to run from that date and with the effect of creating a judgment
a debt.

The defendant (or his insurers) were vastly dissatisfied with this decision and gave
notice of appeal to this court. Mr Woodley, who clearly has a sense of proportion, lost his
enthusiasm for creating a leading case and it was agreed that the Legal Aid Board, which
had far more at stake and some interest in the appeal, should be substituted for Mr
Woodley. It was in any event very much in the public interest that both sides of the
b argument should be fully deployed and we are most grateful to counsel for the assistance
which they have given us.

The Judgments Act 1838

Sections 17 and 18 have been amended only in relation to the rate of interest and, as
originally enacted, read as follows:

c   'XVII ... every Judgment Debt shall carry Interest at the Rate of Four pounds *per
centum per Annum* [the statutory rate of interest has been increased from time to
time] from the Time of entering up the Judgment ... until the same shall be
satisfied, and such interest may be levied under a Writ of Execution on such
Judgment.

        XVIII ... all Decrees and Orders of Courts of Equity, and all Rules of Courts of
d   Common law ... whereby any Sum of Money, or any Costs, Charges, or Expences,
shall be payable to any Person, shall have the Effect of Judgments in the Superior
Courts of Common Law, and the Persons to whom any such Monies, or Costs,
Charges, or Expences, shall be payable, shall be deemed Judgment Creditors within
the Meaning of this Act; and all Powers hereby given to the Judges of the Superior
Courts of Common Law with respect to Matters depending in the same Courts shall
e   and may be exercised by Courts of Equity with respect to Matters therein depending
... and all Remedies hereby given to Judgment Creditors are in like Manner given
to Persons to whom any Monies, or Costs, Charges, or Expences, are, by such Orders
or Rules respectively directed to be paid.'

Hunt's case

f   In *Hunt's* case there was a settlement and there was money in court, but the action was
not settled by an acceptance of that money under Ord 22, r 3. Instead, the parties by
agreement came to the court to obtain an order, and did obtain an order, that 'all further
proceedings in this action be stayed (except for the purpose of carrying into effect the
terms hereof) upon the following terms', which included a term that the money in court
be paid out in part satisfaction of the claim, that the balance be paid within seven days
g and that the defendants should pay the costs of the plaintiff. It was common ground
between the parties, and was accepted by the House of Lords, that this order was a
judgment or order which carried interest as if it were a judgment (see [1988] 3 All ER
823 at 824, [1990] AC 398 at 404). Here this is precisely what is in issue.

Hunt's case is not without interest because it, and *Fisher v Dudding* (1841) 9 Dowl 872,
which is cited extensively (see [1988] 3 All ER 823 at 825–826, [1990] AC 398 at 405–
h 40), shows that it is not necessary to have a formal judgment or order to attract the
operation of the 1838 Act. The pronouncement of a decision that the costs shall be paid
by one party to another is sufficient, at least if a note is made in the cause book or other
official record. As Maule J put it, the fact that the record is not generally filled up, but
only when special circumstances require it—

        'affords a clue to the intentions of the legislature, and shews that the statute was
j   not meant to refer to the entering up of the judgment on the roll, which would
often produce more expense than the interest would amount to, but to the general
entering up of judgment in the Master's book in the form of an incipitur.'

(See 9 Dowl 872 at 876.)

The insuperable difficulty which confronts the plaintiff and the Legal Aid Board in this case lies in the fact that, as we have confirmed by inquiry, there is no record, formal *a* or informal, of a decision that the plaintiff should be entitled to his costs, and indeed there is not such specific decision. There is a record of the notice of acceptance of the money in court and of the payment out, but the first is merely an authority to the Accountant General to pay out and the second is merely his record that he did so.

This led counsel for the board to advance two arguments and they are the only two which could be advanced. The first is that the combined effect of Ord 22, r 3 and of *b* Ord 62, r 5(4) is that, in every case in which the plaintiff accepts money in court, the court notionally awards the plaintiff his costs, refraining from doing so on an individual and specific basis in the interests of efficiency and economy and instead doing so by standing order. The second is that s 18 is drawn sufficiently widely to cover an entitlement arising under the Rules of the Supreme Court, since it refers to 'all Rules of Courts of Common Law' which 'shall have the Effect of Judgments'. *c*

It is, I think, quite impossible to contend that the plaintiff's entitlement to costs in this case, or in other cases in which money is taken out of court in satisfaction of a claim, arises out of any judicial decision, either generally or specifically. It arises because the Rules of the Supreme Court so provide and those rules are legislative and not judicial in character. The authority to make the rules is derived from s 84 of the Supreme Court Act 1981, and they are made by statutory instrument which is subject to the negative *d* resolution procedure (see sub-s (8)). The fact that the majority of the members of the Supreme Court Rule Committee, which is constituted by s 85, happen to be judges does not alter the character of their activity, which is a subordinate legislative activity. The plaintiff becomes entitled to his costs, not because the judges so decide, but because the law gives him that entitlement.

This is not a novel situation. The first such rule-making body was constituted in 1833 *e* by s 1 of the Civil Procedure Act 1833 and again the rules, orders and regulations which the judges were empowered to make had to be laid before Parliament. In other words, it was even then a legislative activity. The rules and regulations which the judges made in 1834 are set out in Crompton & Meeson's Reports (see 2 Cr & M 10–30, 149 ER 655–663). Rule 19 provided (2 Cr & M 11 at 19, 149 ER 655 at 658): *f*

> 'The plaintiff, after the delivery of a plea of payment of money into Court, shall be at liberty to reply to the same, by accepting the sum so paid into Court in full satisfaction and discharge of the cause of action in respect of which it has been paid in; and, he shall be at liberty in that case to tax his costs of suit, and in case of non-payment thereof within forty-eight hours, to sign judgment for his costs of suit so taxed...' *g*

The second argument fares no better. The 1838 Act has to be construed in the light of the meaning which the words used had at the time of its enactment. At that time 'rules' was a term denoting decisions of rulings by the judiciary on a case by case basis, as is clear from contemporary law reports, which constantly conclude with such expressions as 'rule nisi', 'rule absolute' or 'rule discharged' and it is clearly in this sense that s 18 refers *h* to 'Rules of Courts of Common Law'.

Under Ord 62, r 3(2) the general rule is that no party is entitled to recover any of the costs of the proceedings from any other party except under an order of the court and r 3(3) gives the court a discretion whether to make such an order. If it does so, the entitlement to interest arises under the Judgments Act 1838. The only cases which provide exceptions to the general rule in that no order is required, no order is ever made *j* and a party becomes entitled to costs nevertheless, are set out in Ord 62, r 5. Of these cases far the largest category is that with which we have been concerned and the slightly more complex version which involves a counterclaim and is the subject of r 5(6).

Earlier in this judgment I expressed my belief that this situation was unintended. It is certainly wholly illogical, as Mr Registrar Donaldson pointed out. It needs to be remedied a at the earliest possible moment. This could be achieved by revoking Ord 62, r 5, but this would involve litigants and the courts in the wholly unnecessary labour of applying for and making specific orders for costs in all these cases. Alternatively, and this must be the preferred course, a short and relatively simple amendment could be made to the Judgments Act 1838 when parliamentary time allows.

Meanwhile, in my judgment, we have no option but to allow the appeal.

b **BUTLER-SLOSS LJ.** I agree.

   TAYLOR LJ. I also agree.

Appeal allowed. Leave to appeal to the House of Lords granted.

c Solicitors: *Vizards* (for the defendant); *Cole & Cole*, Reading (for the plaintiff).

Mary Rose Plummer   Barrister.

d

Note

Sekhon v British Airways plc

e QUEEN'S BENCH DIVISION
EVANS J SITTING WITH CHIEF MASTER BERKELEY AND MR HARVEY CRUSH AS ASSESSORS
27 JULY 1989

Costs – Taxation – Misconduct, neglect etc – Notice of intention to make application – Allegation that costs have been unreasonably or improperly incurred – Respondent entitled to be present at f taxation and to be given time to prepare response – RSC Ord 62, r 28.

EVANS J, having determined an appeal against the taxing off by the master under RSC Ord 62, r 28 of a sum to reflect the plaintiff's misconduct, said: There is one more matter, that is the question of an application under RSC Ord 62, r 28 being made without prior notice to the plaintiff. In the nature of things, notice is not given on points likely to g be raised at a taxation. However, it does seem to be clearly desirable that advance notice should be given if an Ord 62, r 28 application is going to be made. This is for two reasons. (1) The plaintiff should be entitled to be present in person; if he is not, then clearly there are risks of adjournment and delay. (2) An allegation of misconduct can have substantial repercussions in terms of costs, and the plaintiff and his advisers should be given sufficient time to prepare a response. If there is no time then there is a risk of an adjournment as h the solicitor/partner will not be present or even if present he may need time to prepare his response.

It seems to me that in fairness the party concerned should give notice of his intention to make such an application.

K Mydeen Esq   Barrister.

Practice Direction

SUPREME COURT TAXING OFFICE

Costs – Taxation – Misconduct, neglect etc – Notice of intention to make application – Allegation that costs have been unreasonably or improperly incurred – Form of notice – Length of notice – Notice to indicate whether applicant relying on misconduct or neglect, on personal liability of solicitor or on failure or delay in taxation – Notice to give brief particulars of facts relied on and relief sought – RSC Ord 62, rr 10(1), 11(1)(a), 28(1)(2)(4).

Consequent on the decision on 27 July 1989 of Evans J sitting with assessors in *Sekhon v British Airways plc* [1990] 3 All ER 23, [1990] 1 WLR 577 the following practice will be introduced.

1. Any party wishing to make any application under RSC Ord 62, r 28 should give not less than 14 days' written notice to the other parties and to the Taxing Office. The notice may be given any time after a reference to tax is taken. Leave to give short notice will be granted only in exceptional circumstances.

2. The notice should be so drawn as to give the other parties adequate notice of the case to be met and thus to minimise the risk of application for adjournments.

3. The notice should indicate whether the party intends to rely on (a) rr 28(1) and 10(1) (misconduct or neglect in the conduct of any proceedings), (b) on rr 28(2) and 11(1)(a) (personal liability of solicitor for costs) or (c) on r 28(4) (failure and delay in taxation).

4. A notice under r 28(1) or r 28(2) should give brief particulars of the facts complained of and the relief sought.

5. A notice under r 28(4) should identify any failure or delay relied on, the facts complained of and the relief sought.

6. This direction amends para 4 of the Practice Direction of 27 June 1986 ([1986] 3 All ER 724, [1986] 1 WLR 1054).

F G BERKELEY
Chief Taxing Master.

26 June 1990

Blackpool and Fylde Aero Club Ltd v Blackpool Borough Council

COURT OF APPEAL, CIVIL DIVISION
STOCKER, BINGHAM AND FARQUHARSON LJJ
24, 25 APRIL, 25 MAY 1990

Contract – Invitation to tender – Contractual obligations arising out of invitation – Tenders solicited from selected parties known to invitor – Prescribed common form of tender – Envelope provided to preserve anonymity of tenderer – Tenders required to be submitted by deadline – Invitee submitting tender by due time but tender not considered – Whether implied contractual obligation on invitor to consider tender if conforming with conditions of tender.

The council owned and managed an airport and raised revenue by granting a concession to an air operator to operate pleasure flights from the airport. The plaintiff club was granted the concession in 1975, 1978 and 1980. Shortly before the last concession was due to expire in 1983 the council sent invitations to tender to the club and six other parties, all of whom were connected with the airport. The invitations to tender stated that tenders were to be submitted in the envelope provided and were not to bear any name or mark which would identify the sender, and that tenders received after the date and time specified, namely 12 noon on 17 March 1983 would not be considered. Only the club and two other tenderers responded to the council's invitation. The club's tender was put in the Town Hall letter box at 11 am on 17 March but the letter box was not cleared by council staff at noon that day as it was supposed to be. The club's tender was recorded as being received late and was not considered. The club brought an action against the council claiming damages for breach of contract, contending that the council had warranted that if a tender was received by the deadline it would be considered and that the council had acted in breach of that warranty. The judge held that the council was liable in damages to the club for breach of contract and negligence. The council appealed.

Held – In certain circumstances an invitation to tender could give rise to binding contractual obligations on the part of the invitor to consider tenders which conformed with the conditions of tender. Since tenders had been solicited by the council from selected parties, all of whom were known to the council as invitor, and since the council's invitation to tender prescribed a clear, orderly and familiar procedure, which included draft contract conditions available for inspection but not open to negotiation, a prescribed common form of tender, the supply of envelopes designed to preserve the absolute anonymity of tenderers and an absolute deadline, it was to be implied that if an invitee submitted a conforming tender before the deadline he would be entitled as a matter of contractual right to have his tender opened and considered along with any other tenders that were considered. It followed that the appeal would be dismissed (see p 30 *h* to p 31 *a e f* and p 32 *a b f* to *h*, post).

Notes

For invitations to tender, see 9 Halsbury's Laws (4th edn) para 230, and for cases on the subject, see 12 Digest (Reissue) 69–70, 351–356.

Cases referred to in judgments

American Express International Banking Corp v Hurley [1985] 3 All ER 564, DC.
Caparo Industries plc v Dickman [1990] 1 All ER 568, [1990] 2 WLR 358, HL.
Carlill v Carbolic Smoke Ball Co [1893] 1 QB 256, [1891–4] All ER Rep 127, CA.
CBS Songs Ltd v Amstrad Consumer Electronics plc [1988] 2 All ER 484, [1988] AC 1013, [1988] 2 WLR 1191, HL.

Harris v Nickerson (1873) LR 8 QB 286.
Heilbut Symons & Co v Buckleton [1913] AC 30, [1911–13] All ER Rep 83, HL.   *a*
Hispanica de Petroleos SA v Vencedora Oceanica Navegacion SA, The Kapetan Markos NL
      [1987] 2 Lloyd's Rep 321, CA.
Lavarack v Woods of Colchester Ltd [1966] 3 All ER 683, [1967] 1 QB 278, [1966] 3 WLR
      706, CA.
Liverpool City Council v Irwin [1976] 2 All ER 39, [1977] AC 239, [1976] 2 WLR 562, HL.
Ministry of Housing and Local Government v Sharp [1970] 1 All ER 1009, [1970] 2 QB 223, *b*
      [1970] 2 WLR 802, CA.
Ross v Caunters (a firm) [1979] 3 All ER 580, [1970] Ch 297, [1970] 3 WLR 605.
Spencer v Harding (1870) LR 5 CP 561.
Tai Hing Cotton Mill Ltd v Liu Chong Hing Bank Ltd [1985] 2 All ER 947, [1986] AC 80,
      [1985] 3 WLR 317, PC.
White & Carter (Councils) Ltd v McGregor [1961] 3 All ER 1178, [1962] AC 413, [1962] 2 *c*
      WLR 17, HL.

Cases also cited
Bank of Nova Scotia v Hellenic Mutual War Risks Association (Bermuda) Ltd, The Good Luck
      [1989] 3 All ER 628, [1990] 2 WLR 547, CA.   *d*
Banque Financière de la Cité SA v Westgate Insurance Co Ltd [1989] 2 All ER 952, sub nom
      Banque Keyser Ullman SA v Skandia (UK) Insurance Co Ltd [1989] 3 WLR 25, CA.
China and South Sea Bank Ltd v Tan [1989] 3 All ER 839, [1990] AC 536, PC.
Reid v Rush & Tompkins Group plc [1989] 3 All ER 228, [1990] 1 WLR 212, CA.

Appeal   *e*
The defendant, Blackpool Borough Council, appealed against the judgment of his Honour
Judge Jolly sitting as a judge of the High Court on 17 April 1989 whereby it was ordered
that judgment be entered for the plaintiff, Blackpool and Fylde Aero Club Ltd (the club),
for damages to be assessed in respect of the council's failure to consider a tender received
in accordance with its standing orders. The facts are set out in the judgment of Bingham
LJ.   *f*

Roger Toulson QC and *Hugh Davies* for the council.
Michael Shorrock QC and *M P Sylvester* for the club.

Cur adv vult
                                                                                        g

25 May. The following judgments were delivered.

BINGHAM LJ (giving the first judgment at the invitation of Stocker LJ). In this action
the plaintiff (the club) sued the defendant (the council) for damages for breach of contract
and common law negligence. It was in issue between the parties whether there was any *h*
contract between them and whether the council owed the club any duty of care in tort.
These issues of liability came before his Honour Judge Jolly sitting as a judge of the High
Court in the Queen's Bench Division and he decided them both in favour of the club (all
questions of quantum being deferred). The council appeals, contending that the judge
was wrong on each point.
      The council owns and manages Blackpool airport. For purposes of raising revenue the *j*
council has made it a practice to grant a concession to an air operator to operate pleasure
flights from the airport, no doubt largely for the entertainment of holidaymakers. The
club (one of whose directors was and is a Mr Bateson) tendered for and was granted this
concession in 1975 and again in 1978 and again in 1980.
      In 1983 the most recently granted concession was due to expire. The council
accordingly prepared an invitation to tender. This was sent to the club and to six other

parties, all of them in one way or another connected with the airport. This documen
a was headed and began as follows:

'BLACKPOOL BOROUGH COUNCIL

BLACKPOOL AIRPORT

PLEASURE FLYING CONCESSION

INSTRUCTIONS TO TENDERERS
b
The Council do not bind themselves to accept all or any part of any tender. N
tender which is received after the last date and time specified shall be admitted fo
consideration.

The concession will be for a period of three years commencing on the 1st day of
April 1983. Tenderers should note that the concession is *NOT* to be a sole concession
c and the Council may accept all or any of the tenders submitted in respect of each
class of aircraft.

Tenderers may tender for both classes of aircraft or one only.

Successful tenderers will be required to execute an Agreement prepared by the
Town Clerk for the time being of the Council. A specimen form of agreement may
be examined on application to the Airport Director and it will be assumed that
d tenderers are aware of the covenants and conditions contained therein.

FORM OF TENDER

I/We the undersigned hereby take the following offers for the privilege of
operating pleasure flights from Blackpool Airport for a period of three years from
the 1st day of April 1983.'
e
There then followed provision, with blank spaces to be filled in by the tenderer, for
alternative offers for different sizes of aircraft and for the naming of willing sureties. The
invitation then continued:

'This form of tender, fully completed and enclosed in the envelope provided
endorsed "TENDER FOR PLEASURE FLYING CONCESSION" and not bearing any name or
f mark indicating the identity of the sender, is to be received by:—

THE TOWN CLERK

P.O. BOX 11,

TOWN HALL

BLACKPOOL
g
FY1 1NB.

not later than 12 o'clock noon on Thursday 17th March 1983.

PLEASE NOTE THE ATTACHED NOTICE PRINTED IN RED'

'The attached notice in red' was an extract from the Council's Standing Orders in these
h terms:

'IMPORTANT NOTE

The Council's Standing Orders with respect to Contracts include the following
provisions:—

1.—Tenders shall be submitted in a plain, sealed envelope bearing the words
j "Tender . . . (followed by the subject to which it relates) . . ." and shall not bear any
name or mark indicating the identity of the sender, and

2.—No tender which is received after the last date and time specified shall be
admitted for consideration.

STRICT COMPLIANCE WITH THESE STANDING ORDERS IS REQUESTED.

[Signature]
Town Clerk.'

The envelope provided to the selected tenderers was printed and addressed to the town
clerk at the post office box number given in the invitation. The envelopes also bore the   a
printed words 'Tender for' and 'Due in' to which the council's employees had added in
manuscript 'Pleasure Flying Concession' and '12 noon Thursday 17th March 1983'.
Only three of the selected tenderers responded to the council's invitation. One put in
a low bid for the lighter size of aircraft only. The second, Red Rose Helicopters Ltd,
submitted a larger bid, also for the lighter size of aircraft.

Mr Bateson for the club filled in the form of tender, submitting a bid substantially   b
larger (on its face) than that of the others for the lighter size of aircraft, and also
submitting a bid for the heavier size. He put it in the envelope provided by the council,
took it to the town hall and posted it in the town hall letter box at about 11.00 am on
Thursday, 17 March. This was about an hour before the advertised deadline expired. The
town clerk's staff were supposed to empty the letter box each day at 12 o'clock. They
failed to do so. The club's tender accordingly remained in the letter box until the next   c
morning, 18 March, when the letter box was next opened. The envelope was then taken
out and date-stamped 18 March 1983 by the town clerk's department. At some time
thereafter the word 'LATE' was written on the envelope, because that is what the club's
tender was mistakenly thought to be.

On 29 March 1983 the chairman of the council's relevant committee considered which
tender to accept. The club's tender had been recorded as being late, and was in accordance   d
with the council's standing orders excluded from consideration when the chairman made
his decision. He accordingly made his choice between the two tenders believed to be in
time, recommending acceptance of Red Rose Helicopters' tender, no doubt because it
was bigger.

An indication that its tender was accepted was given to Red Rose Helicopters. The
town clerk wrote to the club to say that its tender was not received until 18 March and   e
was therefore received too late for consideration. Mr Bateson replied that the club's
tender had been delivered to the town hall before the deadline. He wrote:

'You will appreciate that this matter is of some considerable importance to our
company.'

The council evidently made inquiries and established that the club's tender had been   f
received in time.

On 30 March the airport director accordingly wrote to Mr Bateson saying:

'Due to an error in the administration of the terms of tender for the above
Concession I regret to inform you that the tenders recently received have been
declared invalid.'
                                                                                            g
Amended tender documents were accordingly sent for a rescheduled tendering procedure.
In a letter of 31 March the town clerk wrote to the club (and, I infer, other potential
tenderers) outlining the facts summarised above and concluding:

'. . . I trust that you will appreciate that the only course of action open to us is to
go through the formalities of seeking tenders for a second time.'   h

It seems that as a result of this second invitation further tenders were submitted. At this
stage, however, Red Rose Helicopters, having taken legal advice, contended that its
earlier tender had been accepted and that the council was contractually bound to proceed
on that basis. Proceedings were threatened. The council then decided to disregard the
tenders received in response to its second invitation and to honour the contract made
with Red Rose Helicopters.   j

The contractual argument hinges on para 4 of the club's amended statement of claim
in which it was alleged that the council:

'. . . warranted that if a tender was returned to the Town Hall, Blackpool before
noon on Thursday the 17th March 1983 the same would be considered along with
other tenders duly returned when the decision to grant the concession was made.'

Council for the club declined to put the contractual term contended for in any other
a way, save that he accepted that 'when' might with advantage be read as 'when or if'. It
was for breach of this warranty that damages in contract were claimed.

Mr Bateson was the only witness called. His examination in chief included this passage:

'Q . . . when you submitted your tender before noon on 17 March, did you believe
or not that that tender would be considered along with others that had been
submitted? A. We were under no doubt that it would be considered as other tenders
b had been considered in previous years.

Q. If you had known or thought that a tender submitted by you would not have
been considered, would you have bothered to tender in the first place? A. It would
have been very questionable whether to bother to tender, but we would have,
probably pursued the matter beforehand.'

c Mr Bateson was not cross-examined.

The judge resolved the contractual issue in favour of the club, holding that an express
request for a tender might in appropriate circumstances give rise to an implied obligation
to perform the service of considering that tender. Here, the council's stipulation that
tenders received after the deadline would not be admitted for consideration gave rise to a
contractual obligation (on acceptance by submission of a timely tender) that such tenders
d would be admitted for consideration.

In attacking the judge's conclusion on this issue, four main submissions were made on
behalf of the council. Firstly, it was submitted that an invitation to tender in this form
was well established to be no more than a proclamation of willingness to receive offers.
Even without the first sentence of the council's invitation to tender in this case, the
council would not have been bound to accept the highest or any tender. An invitation to
e tender in this form was an invitation to treat, and no contract of any kind would come
into existence unless or until, if ever, the council chose to accept any tender or other
offer. For these propositions reliance was placed on *Spencer v Harding* (1870) LR 5 CP 561
and *Harris v Nickerson* (1873) LR 8 QB 286.

Secondly, counsel submitted that on a reasonable reading of this invitation to tender
the council could not be understood to be undertaking to consider all timely tenders
f submitted. The statement that late tenders would not be considered did not mean that
timely tenders would. If the council had meant that it could have said it. There was,
although counsel did not put it in these words, no maxim exclusio unius, expressio
alterius.

Thirdly, the court should be no less rigorous when asked to imply a contract than
when asked to imply a term in an existing contract or to find a collateral contract. A term
g would not be implied simply because it was reasonable to do so: *Liverpool City Council v
Irwin* [1976] 2 All ER 39 at 43, [1977] AC 239 at 253. In order to establish collateral
contracts, Not only the terms of such contracts but the existence of an animus contrahendi
on the part of all the parties to them must be clearly shewn': see *Heilbut Symons & Co v
Buckleton* [1913] AC 30 at 47, [1911–13] All ER Rep 83 at 91. No lower standard was
h applicable here and the standard was not satisfied.

Fourthly, counsel submitted that the warranty contended for by the club was simply a
proposition' tailor-made to produce the desired result' (to quote Lord Templeman in *CBS
Songs Ltd v Amstrad Consumer Electronics plc* [1988] 2 All ER 484 at 497, [1988] AC 1013
at 1059) on the facts of this particular case. There was a vital distinction between
expectations, however reasonable, and contractual obligations: see *Lavarack v Woods of
j Colchester Ltd* [1966] 3 All ER 683 at 690, [1967] 1 QB 278 at 294 per Diplock LJ. The
club here expected its tender to be considered. The council fully intended that it should
be. It was in both parties' interests that the club's tender should be considered. There was
thus no need for them to contract. The court should not subvert well-understood
contractual principles by adopting a woolly pragmatic solution designed to remedy a
perceived injustice on the unique facts of this particular case.

In defending the judge's decision counsel for the club accepted that an invitation to tender was normally no more than an offer to receive tenders. But it could, he submitted, in certain circumstances give rise to binding contractual obligations on the part of the *a* invitor, either from the express words of the tender or from the circumstances surrounding the sending out of the invitation to tender or (as here) from both. The circumstances relied on here were that the council approached the club and the other invitees, all of them connected with the airport, that the club had held the concession for eight years, having successfully tendered on three previous occasions, that the council as a local authority was obliged to comply with its standing orders and owed a fiduciary *b* duty to ratepayers to act with reasonable prudence in managing its financial affairs and that there was a clear intention on the part of both parties that all timely tenders would be considered. If in these circumstances one asked of this invitation to tender the question posed by Bowen LJ in *Carlill v Carbolic Smoke Ball Co* [1893] 1 QB 256 at 266 [1891–4] All ER Rep 127 at 132, 'How would an ordinary person reading this document construe it?', the answer in the submission of counsel for the club was clear: the council might or *c* might not accept any particular tender; it might accept no tender; it might decide not to award the concession at all; it would not consider any tender received after the advertised deadline; but if it did consider any tender received before the deadline and conforming with the advertised conditions it would consider all such tenders.

I found great force in the submissions made on behalf of the council and agree with much of what was said. Indeed, for much of the hearing I was of opinion that the judge's *d* decision, although fully in accord with the merits as I see them, could not be sustained in principle. But I am in the end persuaded that the argument proves too much. During the hearing the following questions were raised: what if, in a situation such as the present, the council had opened and thereupon accepted the first tender received, even though the deadline had not expired and other invitees had not yet responded? or if the council had considered and accepted a tender admittedly received well after the deadline? *e* Counsel answered that although by so acting the council might breach its own standing orders, and might fairly be accused of discreditable conduct, it would not be in breach of any legal obligation because at that stage there would be none to breach. This is a conclusion I cannot accept, and if it were accepted there would in my view be an unacceptable discrepancy between the law of contract and the confident assumptions of *f* commercial parties, both tenderers (as reflected in the evidence of Mr Bateson) and invitors (as reflected in the immediate reaction of the council when the mishap came to light).

A tendering procedure of this kind is, in many respects, heavily weighted in favour of the invitor. He can invite tenders from as many or as few parties as he chooses. He need not tell any of them who else, or how many others, he has invited. The invitee may *g* often, although not here, be put to considerable labour and expense in preparing a tender, ordinarily without recompense if he is unsuccessful. The invitation to tender may itself, in a complex case, although again not here, involve time and expense to prepare, but the invitor does not commit himself to proceed with the project, whatever it is; he need not accept the highest tender; he need not accept any tender; he need not give reasons to justify his acceptance or rejection of any tender received. The risk to which the tenderer *h* is exposed does not end with the risk that his tender may not be the highest (or, as the case may be, lowest). But where, as here, tenders are solicited from selected parties all of them known to the invitor, and where a local authority's invitation prescribes a clear, orderly and familiar procedure (draft contract conditions available for inspection and plainly not open to negotiation, a prescribed common form of tender, the supply of envelopes designed to preserve the absolute anonymity of tenderers and clearly to *j* identify the tender in question and an absolute deadline) the invitee is in my judgment protected at least to this extent: if he submits a conforming tender before the deadline he is entitled, not as a matter of mere expectation but of contractual right, to be sure that his tender will after the deadline be opened and considered in conjunction with all other conforming tenders or at least that his tender will be considered if others are. Had the

club, before tendering, inquired of the council whether it could rely on any timely and
a conforming tender being considered along with others, I feel quite sure that the answer
would have been 'of course'. The law would, I think, be defective if it did not give effect
to that.

It is of course true that the invitation to tender does not explicitly state that the council
will consider timely and conforming tenders. That is why one is concerned with
implication. But the council does not either say that it does not bind itself to do so, and
b in the context a reasonable invitee would understand the invitation to be saying, quite
clearly, that if he submitted a timely and conforming tender it would be considered, at
least if any other such tender were considered.

I readily accept that contracts are not to be lightly implied. Having examined what
the parties said and did, the court must be able to conclude with confidence both that the
parties intended to create contractual relations and that the agreement was to the effect
c contended for. It must also, in most cases, be able to answer the question posed by Mustill
LJ in *Hispanica de Petroleos SA v Vencedora Oceanica Navegacion SA, The Kapetan Markos NL
(No 2)* [1987] 2 Lloyd's Rep 321 at 331: 'What was the mechanism for offer and
acceptance?' In all the circumstances of this case (and I say nothing about any other) I
have no doubt that the parties did intend to create contractual relations to the limited
extent contended for. Since it has never been the law that a person is only entitled to
d enforce his contractual rights in a reasonable way (*White & Carter (Councils) Ltd v
McGregor* [1961] 3 All ER 1178 at 1182, [1962] AC 413 at 430 per Lord Reid), counsel
for the club was in my view right to contend for no more than a contractual duty to
consider. I think it plain that the council's invitation to tender was, to this limited extent,
an offer, and the club's submission of a timely and conforming tender an acceptance.

Counsel's fourth submission on behalf of the council is a salutary warning, but it is not
e a free-standing argument: if, as I hold, his first three submissions are to be rejected, no
subversion of principle is involved. I am, however, pleased that what seems to me the
right legal answer also accords with the merits as I see them.

I accordingly agree with the judge's conclusion on the contractual issue, essentially for
the reasons which he more briefly gave.

f This conclusion makes it unnecessary to consider at length the club's alternative
argument, which the judge also accepted, that if there was no contract at all between the
parties the council none the less owed the club a duty to take reasonable care to see to it
that if the club submitted a tender by the deadline it would be considered along with
other tenders duly returned when the decision to grant the concession was made.

Counsel for the club sought to sustain this argument in particular by reliance on
g *Ministry of Housing and Local Government v Sharp* [1970] 1 All ER 1009, [1970] 2 QB 223,
Ross v Caunters (a firm) [1979] 3 All ER 580, [1980] Ch 297 and *American Express
International Banking Corp v Hurley* [1985] 3 All ER 564, none of which, he submitted,
was inconsistent with the principles laid down in the recent decision of the House of
Lords in *Caparo Industries plc v Dickman* [1990] 1 All ER 568, [1990] 2 WLR 358.

On behalf of the council it was urged that the court should not introduce a common
h law duty of care into an area of pre-contractual negotiations where the parties could, if
they wished, have introduced such a duty by agreement but had not done so: see *Tai
Hing Cotton Mill Ltd v Liu Chong Hing Bank Ltd* [1985] 2 All ER 947, [1986] AC 80.
Although a duty to take reasonable care not to cause pure economic loss could be held to
exist, such cases were rare and confined to limited classes of case which did not include
the present case and with which the present case had no analogy. The plaintiff's task was
j even harder where, as counsel argued was the case here, his complaint was of a mere
omission. Counsel argued, if it was necessary to do so, that *Ross v Caunters* was wrongly
decided.

I am reluctant to venture into this somewhat unvirginal territory when it is
unnecessary to do so for the purpose of deciding this case. Having heard the argument, I
am tentatively of opinion that the objections on behalf of the council are correct and that

the club cannot succeed on this point if they fail on the other. But I do not think it necessary or desirable to express a final conclusion.

I would accordingly dismiss the appeal. The practical consequences of deciding the contractual issue on liability in the club's favour must, if necessary, be decided hereafter.

STOCKER LJ. I agree. I have had the advantage of reading in draft the judgment of Bingham LJ and add short observations of my own solely in deference to the lucid and interesting arguments of counsel put before the court.

The format of the invitation to tender document itself suggests, in my view, that a legal obligation to consider to tender submitted before any award of a concession was made to any other operator was to be implied in the case of any operator of aircraft to whom the invitation was directed who complied with its terms and conditions. The fact that the invitation to tender was limited to a very small class of operators is itself of significance. The circumstances surrounding the issue of the invitation to tender and the formal requirements imposed by it support the conclusion. Of particular significance, in my view, was the requirement that tenders be submitted in the official envelope supplied and indorsed, as described by Bingham LJ, by the council. The purpose of this requirement must surely have been to preserve the anonymity of the tenderer and, in conjunction with the council's standing orders, to prevent any premature leak of the nature and amount of such tender to other interested or potentially interested parties. Such a requirement, as a condition of the validity of the tender submitted, seems pointless unless all tenders submitted in time and in accordance with the requirements are to be considered before any award of the concession is made. There can be no doubt that this was the intention of both parties, as exemplified by the council's actions when its error with regard to the time of receipt of the club's tender was appreciated. Such a common intention can, of course, exist without giving rise to any contractual obligations, but the circumstances of this case indicate to me that this is one of the fairly rare exceptions to the general rule expounded in the leading cases of *Spencer v Harding* (1870) LR 5 CP 561 and *Harris v Nickerson* (1873) LR 8 QB 286. I therefore agree that in all the circumstances of this case there was an intention to create binding legal obligations if and when a tender was submitted in accordance with the terms of the invitation to tender, and that a binding contractual obligation arose that the club's tender would be before the officer or committee by whom the decision was to be taken for consideration before a decision was made or any tender accepted. This would not preclude or inhibit the council from deciding not to accept any tender or to award the concession, provided the decision was bona fide and honest, to any tenderer. The obligation was that the club's tender would be before the deciding body for consideration before any award was made. Accordingly, in my view, the conclusion of the judge and his reasons were correct.

I agree that in the light of this conclusion no useful purpose can be served by consideration of the difficult questions which arise on the claim formulated in tort.

Accordingly I agree with the conclusions reached by Bingham LJ, and with the detailed reasoning contained in his judgment and agree that this appeal should be dismissed.

FARQUHARSON LJ. I agree.

Appeal dismissed. Leave to appeal to the House of Lords refused.

Solicitors: *Sharpe Pritchard*, agents for *John B Turner*, Blackpool (for the council); *Berg & Co*, Manchester (for the club).

Raina Levy   Barrister.

Hazell v Hammersmith and Fulham London Borough Council and others

QUEEN'S BENCH DIVISION
WOOLF LJ AND FRENCH J
2, 4, 5, 6, 10, 11, 12, 13, 16, 17, 18 OCTOBER, 1 NOVEMBER 1989

COURT OF APPEAL, CIVIL DIVISION
SIR STEPHEN BROWN P, NICHOLLS AND BINGHAM LJJ
16–19, 22–25, 29–31 JANUARY, 1, 5–8, 22, 28 FEBRUARY 1990

Local authority – Statutory powers – Implied power – Implied power used for improper purpose – Interest rate swap transactions – Local authority incorporated by charter entering into financial transactions involving speculation on interest rate movements – Auditor claiming that local authority having no power to enter into transactions – Auditor seeking declaration that local authority's capital market activity ultra vires – Whether local authority having capacity to enter into swap transactions – Whether capacity conferred by statute – Whether local authority having capacity to enter into swap transactions for limited purpose of interest rate risk management – Whether swap transactions tainted with improper purpose of speculative trading – London Government Act 1963, s 1(2) – Local Government Act 1972, ss 101(6)(12), 111(1) – Local Government Finance Act 1982, s 19.

In 1983 a local authority, which was a London borough which was incorporated by royal charter pursuant to s 1(2)[a] of the London Government Act 1963, established a capital market fund for the purpose of conducting transactions involving speculation on interest rate movements. Between 1987 and 1988 the local authority's activity in the capital markets increased dramatically in both the volume and the range of transactions, which by then included interest rate swaps, swap options, interest rate caps, floors and collars, forward rate agreements and gilt and cash options. In the majority of transactions the local authority would benefit if interest rates fell, but would incur substantial losses if interest rates rose. In July 1988 the auditor appointed by the Audit Commission examined the local authority's accounts and determined from the emerging pattern of its capital market activities that the interest rate swap transactions amounted to speculative trading for profit, since the authority had made no attempt to match its actual debts and investments with any of the transactions, all of which had been entered into without any detailed analysis of the interest that was due to be paid or received, or of the interest rate risks involved or the steps which could be taken to mitigate or secure protection against losses. The auditor challenged the legality of the local authority's capital market activities and thereafter the local authority ended all further participation in swap transactions and pursued an interim strategy of containment designed to limit the extent of its exposure to losses which had resulted from a rise in interest rates, while gradually extricating itself from the market. In February 1989 the local authority terminated its capital market activities, apart from seven transactions which were consequent on other parties exercising options, on advice from counsel that the scale of those activities was unlawful. The auditor later applied pursuant to s 19[b] of the Local Government Finance Act 1982 for a declaration that the items appearing in the local authority's capital market fund account for the financial years 1987 and 1988 were contrary to law and for an order for rectification of the accounts. A number of banks involved in the local authority's capital market activities applied for and were granted leave to be joined as respondents to the auditor's application in order to protect their

---

a   Section 1(2) is set out p 76 *f g*, post
b   Section 19, so far as material, is set out at p 70 *j* to p 71 *c*, post

commercial interests. The Divisional Court granted the declaration sought by the auditor
and ordered the 1987 and 1988 accounts to be rectified, holding (i) that the local authority *a*
could not rely on its status as an incorporated municipal corporation to give it the
capacity of a natural person to enter into contracts and that its capacity to contract was
therefore limited to the powers conferred on it by statute and (ii) that, although a local
authority had an implied power under s 111(1)ᶜ of the Local Government Act 1972 to do
anything which facilitated the discharge of any of its functions, the swap transactions
entered into by the local authority did not fall within the ambit of s 111(1) because there *b*
was insufficient connection between the permitted discharge of the local authority's
function to raise and invest money, which was strictly circumscribed by the provisions
of Pt I of Sch 13 to the 1972 Act, and the transactions, which at best merely alleviated the
consequences of borrowing, ie the payment of interest, by speculating on interest rate
movements rather than facilitating the discharge of the borrowing itself, and because the
capacity to enter into swap transactions was not within the scope of the relevant statutory *c*
provisions. The banks appealed.

Held – The appeal would be allowed in part for the following reasons—

(1) Although a local authority which had been incorporated by royal charter was a
legal entity with all the powers of a natural person, it did not have the capacity to enter
into contracts and use its funds to defray obligations under those contracts, since the *d*
functions vested in local authorities by the 1972 Act were vested in them as
unincorporated councils created by statute rather than incorporated municipal
corporations and therefore an authority's ability to use its funds to defray obligations
under interest rate swap transactions depended on the existence of an express or implied
statutory power which empowered it to enter into such transactions (see p 77 *b c g* and
p 78 *d e j* to p 79 *a*, post); dicta of Farwell J in *A-G v Manchester Corp* [1906] 1 Ch 643 at *e*
651 and of Lord Hanworth MR in *A-G v Smethwick Corp* [1932] All ER Rep 304 at 306
applied; *A-G (ex rel Birmingham and Midland Motor Omnibus Co Ltd) v Leicester Corp* [1943]
1 All ER 146 considered.

(2) A local authority had implied power under s 111(1) of the 1972 Act to enter into
interest rate swap transactions provided that such transactions were entered into for the
limited purpose of interest rate risk management and not for speculative trading *f*
purposes, which meant that the authority could only enter into a swap transaction with
reference to a specific debt in order to regulate to the best advantage the rate payable on
its indebtedness. Since that power was ancillary to the local authority's duty to take
reasonable care to manage its borrowings and investments prudently, it was subject to
the provisions of Pt I of Sch 13 to the 1972 Act, which provided a detailed code for the
proper discharge of an authority's functions to raise and invest money. Where a local *g*
authority had unwittingly and in good faith exceeded its powers but was with good
reason uncertain whether it had done so, it had implied power for such period as it
reasonably took to resolve that uncertainty to take such steps as it reasonably and
prudently could to limit and reduce the loss which its earlier conduct might cause to its
ratepayers. Accordingly, all the categories of swap transactions identified by the auditor *h*
in the local authority's capital market fund account were capable of being lawfully
entered into by a local authority in the exercise of its powers under the 1972 Act, in the
sense that there might be circumstances in which they could be lawfully undertaken by
the authority. However, on the facts, all the transactions up to July 1988 were tainted
with the improper purpose of speculative trading, since prior to that time the local
authority had not made any attempt to match those transactions with its actual debts and *j*
investments and neither had it made any detailed analysis of the risk involved. On the
other hand, during the interim strategy period from July 1988 to February 1989 the
local authority had entered into swap transactions for the purpose of mitigating or

c Section 111(1) is set out at p 83 h j, post

averting any potential loss to its ratepayers which might result from the earlier
a transactions and consequently those transactions had been carried out for a lawful
purpose. The auditor was consequently entitled to a declaration that the swap transactions
entered into by the local authority prior to July 1988 were ultra vires, but was not entitled
to such a declaration in respect of the transactions entered into during the interim
strategy period, which, in any event, had been entered into in good faith and with the
auditor's knowledge and, albeit qualified, acquiescence. No order for rectification of the
b accounts would be made (see p 79 *h j*, p 80 *a b d e g* to p 81 *b f h j*, p 82 *c d*, p 83 *a b*, p 86 *b*
to *f*, p 88 *b* to *e*, p 89 *b*, p 90 *h* to p 91 *c* and p 96 *c* to *g*, post); *A-G v Great Eastern Rly Co*
(1880) 5 App Cas 473 applied.

Per curiam. On its true construction, s 101(12)[d] of the 1972 Act makes it plain that the
general power of delegation contained in s 101(1), whereby a local authority may arrange
for its its functions to be discharged by another administrative body, applies as much to
c the authority's exercise of subsidiary powers under s 111(1) of the Act as to the discharge
of its functions and, therefore, the ban on delegation in s 101(6) in respect of the levying
or issuing of a precept for a rate or the borrowing of money does not encompass the
exercise of a subsidiary power to do all things incidental to that function, with the result
that the day-to-day discharge of the authority's power to enter into interest rate swap
transactions, which is incidental to its borrowing and investment function, may be
d properly delegated (see p 84 *e f* and p 85 *b c e f*, post); dicta of Lord Widgery CJ in *Bar Hill
Developments Ltd v South Cambridgeshire DC* (1979) 252 EG 915 at 918 and of Lord Roskill
in *Provident Mutual Life Assurance Association v Derby City Council* [1981] 1 WLR 173 at
180 applied.

Notes
e For a local authority's power to incur expenditure in general, see 28 Halsbury's Laws (4th
edn) paras 1245, 1247, and for cases on the subject, see 33 Digest (Reissue) 31–34, 96–
104.

For the London Government Act 1963, s 1, see 26 Halsbury's Statutes (4th edn) 414.

For the Local Government Act 1972, ss 101, 111, Sch 13, see 25 Halsbury's Statutes
f (4th edn) (1990 reissue) 263, 272, 445.

For the Local Government Finance Act 1982, s 19, see ibid 697.

As from 1 April 1990 Pt I of Sch 13 to the 1972 Act was repealed by s 194(2) of and
Pt I of Sch 12 to the Local Government and Housing Act 1989, which Act makes further
provision about the finances of local authorities.

Cases referred to in judgments
g *A-G v Great Eastern Rly Co* (1880) 5 App Cas 473, HL.
A-G v Great Northern Rly Co (1860) 29 LJ Ch 794.
A-G v Leeds Corp [1929] 2 Ch 291.
A-G v London CC [1901] 1 Ch 781, CA; *affd* [1902] AC 165, HL.
A-G v Manchester Corp [1906] 1 Ch 643.
A-G v Newcastle-upon-Tyne Corp (1889) 23 QBD 492, CA; *affd* [1892] AC 568, HL.
h *A-G v Smethwick Corp* [1932] 1 Ch 562, [1932] All ER Rep 304, CA.
A-G (ex rel Birmingham and Midland Motor Omnibus Co Ltd) v Leicester Corp [1943] 1 All ER
146, [1943] Ch 86.
Amalgamated Society of Railway Servants v Osbourne [1910] AC 87, HL.
Ashbury Railway Carriage and Iron Co Ltd v Riche (1875) LR 7 HL 653; *rvsg* (1874) LR 9
Exch 224, Ex Ch.
j *Associated Provincial Picture Houses Ltd v Wednesbury Corp* [1947] 2 All ER 680, [1948] 1
KB 223, CA.
Bar Hill Developments Ltd v South Cambridgeshire DC (1979) 252 EG 915, DC.
Beauforte (Jon) (London) Ltd, Re [1953] 1 All ER 634, [1953] Ch 131, [1953] 2 WLR 465.

---

d   Section 101, so far as material, is set out at p 84 *b* to *d*, post

Beecham v Metropolitan District Auditor (1976) 75 LGR 79, DC.
Belvoir Finance Co Ltd v Stapleton [1970] 3 All ER 664, [1971] 1 QB 210, [1970] 3 WLR *a*
530, CA.
Binder v Alachouzos [1972] 2 All ER 189, [1972] 2 QB 151, [1972] 2 WLR 947, CA.
Bonanza Creek Gold Mining Co Ltd v R [1916] 1 AC 566, [1916–17] All ER Rep 999, PC.
Bromley London BC v Greater London Council [1982] 1 All ER 129, [1983] 1 AC 768, [1982]
2 WLR 62, CA and HL.
Charterbridge Corp Ltd v Lloyds Bank Ltd [1969] 2 All ER 1185, [1970] Ch 62, [1969] 3 *b*
WLR 122.
Council of Civil Service Unions v Minister for the Civil Service [1984] 3 All ER 935, [1985] AC
374, [1984] 3 WLR 1174, HL.
Evans v Bartlam [1937] 2 All ER 646, [1937] AC 473, HL.
Feret v Hill (1854) 15 CB 207, [1843–60] All ER Rep 924, 139 ER 400.
Great North-West Central Rly Co v Charlebois [1899] AC 114, PC.   *c*
Holsworthy UDC v Holsworthy RDC [1907] 2 Ch 62.
Hurle-Hobbs, Re [1944] 2 All ER 261, CA.
Institution of Mechanical Engineers v Cane [1960] 3 All ER 715, [1961] AC 696, [1960] 3
WLR 978, HL.
Introductions Ltd v National Provincial Bank Ltd [1969] 1 All ER 887, [1970] Ch 199, [1969]
2 WLR 791, CA.   *d*
Jenkin v Pharmaceutical Society of GB [1921] 1 Ch 392.
Norwich Provident Insurance Society, Re, Bath's Case (1878) 8 Ch D 334, CA.
Prescott v Birmingham Corp [1954] 3 All ER 698, [1955] Ch 210, [1954] 3 WLR 990, CA.
Provident Mutual Life Assurance Association v Derby City Council [1981] 1 WLR 173, HL.
R v Eastern Archipelago Co (1853) 2 E & B 856, 118 ER 988, Ex Ch.
R v Eden DC, ex p Moffat (1988) Independent, 16 December, [1988] CA Transcript 919.   *e*
R v Greater London Council, ex p Westminster City Council (1984) Times, 27 December.
R v Roberts [1908] 1 KB 407, CA.
R (Duckett) v Calvert [1898] 2 IR 511, Ir QB.
Roberts v Hopwood [1925] AC 578, [1925] All ER Rep 24, HL.
Rolled Steel Products (Holdings) Ltd v British Steel Corp [1985] 3 All ER 52, [1986] Ch 246,
[1985] 2 WLR 908, CA.   *f*
Rutter v Chapman (1841) 8 M & W 1, 151 ER 925, Ex Ch.
Singh v Ali [1960] 1 All ER 269, [1960] AC 167, [1960] 2 WLR 180, PC.
Sutton's Hospital Case (1612) 10 Co Rep 1a, [1558–1774] All ER Rep 11, 77 ER 937, Ex
Ch.
Thomas v Devonport Corp [1900] 1 QB 16, CA.
Webb v Herne Bay Comrs (1870) LR 5 QB 642.   *g*
Wenlock (Baroness) v River Dee Co (1883) 36 Ch D 675, CA; *affd* (1885) 10 App Cas 354,
HL.

Cases also cited

A-G v Aspinall (1837) 2 My & Cr 613, [1835–42] All ER Rep 525, 40 ER 793.
A-G v Crayford UDC [1961] 3 All ER 1002, [1962] Ch 246; *affd* [1962] 2 All ER 147,   *h*
[1962] Ch 575, CA.
A-G v De Winton [1906] 2 Ch 106.
A-G v Fulham Corp [1921] 1 Ch 440.
A-G v Guardians of the Poor Law Union of Tynemouth [1930] 1 Ch 616.
A-G v Mersey Rly Co [1907] AC 415, HL.
A-G v West Ham Corp [1910] 2 Ch 560.   *j*
A-G v Wilson (1840) Cr & Ph 1, 41 ER 389, LC.
Allchin v Coulthard [1943] 2 All ER 352, [1943] AC 607, HL; *affg* [1942] 2 All ER 39,
[1942] 2 KB 228, CA.
Anisminic Ltd v Foreign Compensation Commission [1969] 1 All ER 208, [1969] 2 AC 147,
HL.

Baccus SRL v Servicio Nacional del Trigo [1956] 3 All ER 715, [1957] 1 QB 438, CA.

a *Barrs v Bethell* [1982] 1 All ER 106, [1982] Ch 294.

Blackburn Building Society v Cunliffe Brooks & Co (1882) 22 Ch D 61, CA; *affd* (1884) 9 App Cas 857, HL.

Blackburn v Flavelle (1881) 6 App Cas 628, PC.

Bradford Metropolitan DC v Secretary of State for the Environment (1977) 76 LGR 454.

British South Africa Co v De Beers Consolidated Wines Ltd [1910] 1 Ch 354; *affd* [1910] 2 Ch
b   502, CA; *rvsd* [1912] AC 52, [1911–13] All ER Rep 882, HL.

Cannock Chase DC v Kelly [1978] 1 All ER 152, [1978] 1 WLR 1, CA.

Chief Constable of North Wales Police v Evans [1982] 3 All ER 141, [1982] 1 WLR 1155, HL.

Cocks v Thanet DC [1982] 3 All ER 1135, [1983] 2 AC 286, HL.

Commission for Local Authority Accounts in Scotland v Stirling DC 1984 SLT 442, Ct of Sess.

Crown Estate Comrs v Dorset CC [1990] 1 All ER 19, [1990] 2 WLR 89.

c *Cudgen Rutile (No 2) Pty Ltd v Chalk* [1975] AC 520, [1975] 2 WLR 1, PC.

Deuchar v Gas Light and Coke Co [1925] AC 691, [1925] All ER Rep 720, HL.

Dundee Harbour Trustees v D & J Nicol [1915] AC 550, HL.

Elve v Boyton [1891] 1 Ch 501, CA.

Equal Opportunities Commission v Birmingham City Council [1989] 1 All ER 769, [1989] AC
     1155; *affg* [1989] AC 1155, CA.

d *Findlay v Secretary of State for the Home Dept* [1984] 3 All ER 801, [1985] AC 318, HL.

Maclaine Watson & Co Ltd v Dept of Trade and Industry [1988] 3 All ER 257, [1987] Ch
     419, CA; *affd* [1989] 3 All ER 523, [1989] 3 WLR 969, HL.

Magrath (H W), Re a decision of [1934] 2 KB 415, CA.

Manchester City Council v Greater Manchester Metropolitan CC (1979) 78 LGR 71, CA; *affd*
     (1980) 79 LGR 560, HL.

e *Mixnam's Properties Ltd v Chertsey UDC* [1963] 2 All ER 787, [1964] 1 QB 214, CA.

Municipal Mutual Insurance Ltd v Pontefract Corp (1917) 116 LT 671, [1916–17] All ER
     Rep 543.

O'Reilly v Mackman [1982] 3 All ER 680, [1983] 2 AC 237, CA.

Pallister v Gravesend Corp (1856) 25 LJ Ch 776.

Parr v A-G (1842) 8 Cl & Fin 409, 8 ER 159, HL.
f *Pickering v Stephenson* (1872) LR 14 Eq 322.

Pickwell v Camden London BC [1983] 3 All ER 602, [1983] QB 962, DC.

Poppetts (Caterers) Ltd v Maidenhead BC [1970] 3 All ER 289, [1971] 1 WLR 69, CA.

Prest v Secretary of State for Wales (1983) 81 LGR 193, CA.

R v Criminal Injuries Compensation Board, ex p Lain [1967] 2 All ER 770, [1967] 2 QB 864,
     DC.

g *R v East Berkshire Health Authority, ex p Walsh* [1984] 3 All ER 425, [1985] QB 152, CA.

R v Educational Services Committee of Bradford Council, ex p Professional Association of Teachers
     (1986) Independent, 16 December.

R v Greater London Council, ex p Burgess [1978] ICR 991, DC.

R v Greater London Council, ex p Westminster City Council (1985) Times, 22 January.

h *R v Monopolies and Mergers Commission, ex p Argyll Group plc* [1986] 2 All ER 257, [1986]
     1 WLR 763, CA.

R v National Coal Board, ex p National Union of Mine Workers [1986] ICR 791.

R v Panel on Take-overs and Mergers, ex p Datafin plc (Norton Opax plc intervening) [1987] 1
     All ER 564, [1987] QB 815, CA.

R v Reed (1880) 5 QBD 483, CA.

j *R v Richmond upon Thames London BC, ex p McCarthy & Stone (Developments) Ltd* [1990] 2
     All ER 852, [1990] 2 WLR 1294, CA.

R v Secretary of State for Foreign and Commonwealth Affairs, ex p Everett [1989] 1 All ER
     655, [1989] AC 1014, CA.

R v Secretary of State for Social Services, ex p Association of Metropolitan Authorities [1986] 1
     All ER 164, [1986] 1 WLR 1.

R v Secretary of State for the Environment, ex p Hillingdon London BC [1986] 1 All ER 810,
    [1986] 1 WLR 192, DC; *affd* [1986] 2 All ER 273, [1986] 1 WLR 807, CA.
R v Sheffield Corp (1871) LR 6 QB 652.
R v Stafford Justices, ex p Stafford Corp [1940] 2 KB 33, CA.
R v Wirral Metropolitan BC, ex p Milstead (1989) Independent, 28 March, DC.
Riches v Westminster Bank Ltd [1947] 1 All ER 469, [1947] AC 390, HL.
Ridge v Baldwin [1963] 2 All ER 66, [1964] AC 40, HL.
Roberts v Cunningham (1925) 24 LGR 61, HL.
Smith v Southampton Corp [1902] 2 KB 244.
Stockdale v Haringey London BC (1989) Independent, 28 April, [1989] CA Transcript 392.
Swain v Law Society [1982] 2 All ER 827, [1983] 1 AC 598, HL.
Taylor v Munrow [1960] 1 All ER 455, [1960] 1 WLR 151, DC.
Tower Hamlets London BC v Chetnick Developments Ltd [1988] 1 All ER 961, [1988] AC 858,
    HL.
Town Investments Ltd v Dept of the Environment [1977] 1 All ER 813, [1978] AC 359, HL.
Tynemouth v A-G [1898] 1 QB 604, CA; *affd* [1899] AC 293, HL.
Wandsworth London BC v Winder [1984] 3 All ER 976, [1985] AC 461, HL.
Westminster City Council, Re [1986] 2 All ER 278, [1986] AC 668, HL.
Wheeler v Leicester City Council [1985] 2 All ER 1106, [1985] AC 1054, HL.

Motion
By motion dated 30 May 1989 Anthony John Hazell, the district auditor responsible for
the audit of the accounts of the first respondent, the Hammersmith and Fulham London
Borough Council, applied for a declaration that items appearing in the capital market
fund account of the council for the financial years beginning 1 April 1987 and 1 April
1988 were contrary to law on the ground, inter alia, that the itemised interest rate swap
transactions constituted purely speculative trading and, as such, did not fall within the
scope of a local authority's subsidiary powers under s 111(1) of the Local Government
Act 1972, and for an order for rectification of the accounts for those years. The second,
third, fourth and sixth respondents, Midland Bank plc, Security Pacific National Bank
NA, Chemical Bank and Mitsubishi International Finance plc (the banks), and the fifth
respondent, Barclays Bank plc (Barclays), through whom the transactions had been
carried out, applied for leave under RSC Ord 15, r 6 or the court's inherent jurisdiction
to joined as parties to the proceedings and by orders made by Otton J on 19 July and 21
September 1989 they were ordered to be joined as respondents. By a second order on 21
September 1989 Otton J ordered that the hearing of the application be confined to the
consideration of certain issues (set out at p 44 *e* to *h*, post). The facts are set out in the
judgment of the court.

John Howell for the auditor.
Anthony Scrivener QC and *Catherine Newman* for the council.
J M Chadwick QC, Rhodri Davies and *Alan Griffiths* for the banks.
Nicholas Chambers QC and *Catharine Otton-Goulder* for Barclays.

Cur adv vult

1 November. The following judgment of the court was delivered.

WOOLF LJ. This is a judgment of the court to which both members have contributed.
It relates to an application by Anthony John Hazell (the auditor), a partner in a well-
known firm of chartered accountants, who was appointed by the Audit Commission for
Local Authorities in England and Wales to audit the accounts of Hammersmith and
Fulham London Borough Council from 1 April 1983. The application is made under
s 19 of the Local Government Finance Act 1982 and RSC Ord 98. Section 19 of the 1982
Act, so far as relevant, provides:

a
'(1) Where it appears to the auditor carrying out the audit of any account under this Part of this Act that any item of account is contrary to law he may apply to the court for a declaration that the item is contrary to law except where it is sanctioned by the Secretary of State.

(2) On an application under this section the court may make or refuse to make the declaration asked for, and where the court makes that declaration, then, subject to subsection (3) below, it may also . . . (c) order rectification of the accounts . . .'

b
The events leading up to the application

The application of the auditor has been made necessary because during the financial years 1987 to 1989 very substantial financial transactions (the transactions) of a sophisticated nature have been conducted in the name of the council. The transactions are known by exotic names, namely interest rate swaps (swaps), interest rate swap options

c (swap options), interest rate caps (caps), interest rate floors (floors), interest rate collars (collars), forward rate agreements (FRA) and gilt and cash options.

In his evidence the auditor distinguishes between three types of financial transactions, namely (i) debt restructuring (an arrangement whereby a party borrows money for the purpose of repaying a loan during the period in which that loan is to be repaid and thus replaces one loan with another, which may have implications as to the amount of interest

d payable), (ii) an exchange of obligations to pay interest (an arrangement where a party undertakes to discharge an obligation to pay interest on another's debts in return for that other person's undertaking to discharge the first party's obligation to pay interest on his own debts of an equivalent amount; again the transaction can have interest implications), and (iii) an income generating scheme (which leaves untouched any existing rights or obligations and is designed to produce a profit). The auditor regards the transactions with

e which this application is concerned as falling within the last mentioned category.

It was intended that as a result of entering into the transactions that the council would benefit financially and so far there have been no immediate adverse consequences if regard be had only to money actually paid and received as at the date the council ceased payment, ie 23 February 1989. However, if the transactions are enforceable they will result in a loss to the council well in excess of £100m.

f
Whether the transactions produced a profit or loss depends on whether the movement of interest rates has been correctly anticipated by the council. With isolated exceptions the transactions entered into by the council were ones in which the council would benefit if interest rates fell. In fact, interest rates have risen substantially since August 1988 and this is why the council could now incur substantial losses. What has happened demonstrates the highly speculative nature of the council's activities.

g
The council now accepts and contends that the transactions which were entered into in its name during the financial years 1987 to 1989 were not undertaken for a lawful purpose and thus are ultra vires. It has stopped making payments which are due, according to the terms of the transactions, to the institutions which were the other parties. The institutions or some of them not unnaturally fear that if this application is successful it could have serious adverse financial consequences for them. The second to

h sixth respondents (the banks) have intervened in the proceedings as parties to protect their position and have contested the application.

The nature of the different transactions is summarised in Appendix A to this judgment. The activities of the council in transactions over the two financial years were very extensive and the following features should be observed.

j
(1) On 31 March 1989 the council was involved in 72 open swaps with a total notional principal sum of £707m. With one exception (a swap with Brent London Borough Council) they all involve the council being the variable interest payer and taking an interest rate risk, that is a risk that the interest rates will move adversely to the council. Even in the case involving Brent counsel for the auditor submits that the council was taking a risk, the risk being that the council will lose the benefit of lower interest rates if

interest rates fall below the fixed rate. However, we regard it as more realistic to treat
such a transaction as one in which the council buys off the risk of interest rates rising at
the cost of losing the benefit if the interest rate falls. There is also a credit risk, that is that
the other party is unwilling or unable to meet the obligations under the agreement
should the transaction prove favourable to the council. It is suggested that in addition
there are risks which arise because of the informal nature of transactions on the capital
market and the need for fast dealing decisions, retrospective formalisation of contracts
and the complex system required to record transactions.

(2) The total number of transactions involved in the two financial years was 592
involving a notional principal sum of £6,002m. At 31 March 1989 297 of these
transactions were still extant and they involved a notional sum of £2,996m. These
figures are put into context by comparing them with the council's total expenditure
during the year 1988/89 in discharging its functions other than those in dispute, which
amounted to £85·7m.

(3) The council's activities in relation to the transactions were initiated and substantially
expanded without any report to the members of the council describing what was
happening or the members considering the advantages and disadvantages or legality of
the transactions and without any authorisation from the council, its committees or sub-
committees.

(4) If the result of a transaction is that the council is to be liable to pay interest on a
notional sum at variable rate, then while the council will benefit if interest rates fall, the
council is exposed to the danger that interest rates may rise and if this happens the
council could, particularly having regard to the size of the notional principal sums
involved, suffer substantial losses.

(5) The majority of the transactions involved the council being obliged to make
payments calculated on the basis that the council was to pay interest at a variable rate.
This was in contrast with the practice of the council in relation to its exercise of its
ordinary statutory borrowing powers where at the material times 98% of the loans were
at fixed rates.

(6) There is a significant difference between option transactions where the council
purchased the option from those where the option was sold. If the option was sold, the
council would receive a premium but the council would have no control over whether
the purchasing institution would exercise its option. In practice, however, the council
could expect the option to be exercised against it if at the time the right to exercise the
option arose it would be in the interest of the holder to exercise the option. The effect of
interest rates on such an option would depend on whether it was a cash or gilt option
which was sold. If, for example, interest rates go up the value of the gilts which are the
subject of the upturn will go down and so the option will be less valuable to the buyer.
In the case of the cash option the attractiveness of the underlying loan will increase,
making the option more valuable to the buyer if interest rates rise.

The history of the council's activity can be conveniently considered in four phases.
The dates of the phases are as follows: (1) December 1983 to March 1987; (2) April 1987
to July 1988; (3) August 1988 to 23 February 1989. (4) 23 February 1989 onwards.

(1) December 1983 to March 1987

The first phase precedes the two financial years (April 1987–88, April 1988–89) the
accounts of which are the subject of the auditor's application. However, because
transactions entered into in this period could result in the council having to make or
receive payments during the relevant financial years, transactions entered into during
this period are relevant. However, in fact very few transactions were made during this
period and those which were entered into were swaps. December 1983 is taken as the
commencement of the phase because it was in that month that the first swap was entered
into. In each of the first and second financial years in this phase two transactions were
carried out, in the third year three and in the last year 17 transactions were entered into
involving a notional principal of £112m.

(2) *April 1987 to July 1988*

a   The beginning of this period marked an increase in the scale and range of the council's activities in transactions. Combining all the instruments involved in the transactions the notional premium of current transactions during the period increased from £135m to £3,727·5m on 31 July 1988. August 1988 marks the end of the phase because on 15 July 1988 the auditor received copies of three opinions obtained by the Audit Commission relating to the legality of the transactions. The first of the opinions was a joint opinion

b by leading and junior counsel and the remaining opinions were by leading and junior counsel respectively. The reason for the three opinions was that leading and junior counsel were agreed that the majority of the transactions were unlawful but differed as to whether a swap which related to a parallel contract under which the council had an actual borrowing was unlawful. Leading counsel took the view that it was not, junior counsel took the view that it was.

c   After the opinions had been received a meeting took place on 25 July 1988 between a representative of the audit team and the council's head of loans and investments (Mr Terry Price) who supplied details of the council's activities and indicated that no legal advice had been obtained from within or on behalf of the council about the legality of the transactions. This meeting was followed by a letter from the auditor dated 27 July

d 1988 in which the auditor stated his view that a large number of the transactions would appear to be ultra vires and sought confirmation from the council that it would not enter into any swap agreements which did not fall within the category defined by leading counsel as intra vires. On 1 August 1988 the council's director of finance replied to that letter and indicated that he was temporarily suspending all swaps and swap option transactions as was required but he would continue to manage existing swap and swap option positions and other instruments as failure to do so could result in actual losses to

e the council in relation to its existing portfolio. He added:

> 'I thus propose to close existing "open" swap positions at suitable times as well as use for example forward rate agreements and gilt options to hedge existing "open" swaps, depending on the future movement in interest rates, swap prices and gilt prices. I believe this is the most prudent response to the present uncertain

f > position . . .'

This exchange of correspondence was followed by further correspondence and a meeting on 9 August 1988. The attitude of the auditor at this stage was, according to his first affidavit sworn in support of the application, as follows:

> 'The position I took was that I should let the council seek its own advice from

g > counsel and make representations to me before I considered whether or not to exercise my powers to apply to the court and that the interim strategy which was intended to close the existing deals was acceptable in that context given that the council did not accept it was acting unlawfully.'

During this period the activity in transactions by the council was conducted through

h what was called a capital market fund (CMF) with income credited and expenditure debited to the CMF. The CMF was established without any specific resolution of the council and the council's director of legal services acknowledged, in a letter dated 21 April 1988, 'that there are no internal documents establishing the [CMF] although there are references in internal memos to exploring the possibility of establishing the [CMF] and, later, that work on setting up the fund had commenced'. From the second of these

j 'memos', which is dated 14 March 1988, it appears that it was shortly before that date that the CMF was established, in the sense that an account was kept in which transactions were recorded, that account being called the CMF account. The memo, however, also says that the council never, so far as the director is aware, established or maintained an actual separate fund for these activities.

As already indicated, the initiation and the main extension in transactions was carried out without any report to the members describing it or considering its advantages, disadvantages or legality and without any authorisation from the council, its committees and sub-committees themselves. An annual borrowing report dated 4 January 1988 was, *a* however, submitted to the finance administration sub-committee on 17 February 1988, by which date the scale of the dealings in swaps, swap options, caps, floors and FRA's involved a notional principal sum exceeding £1·7bn. The report, in Part 2, entitled 'Borrowing 1986/78', noted:

> 'The Director of Finance has also continued to arrange where applicable, *b* transactions in the London Money/Capital Markets in order to maximise gains on favourable interest rate movements.'

The committee were asked to recommend the council to authorise the director of finance to 'arrange transactions in the London Money/Capital Markets in order to take advantage of favourable interest rate movements on such terms and conditions as are agreed by the Director of Finance', and the recommendation which the sub-committee *c* made was the one which was agreed by the council on 24 February 1988. The council was given no further information as to the type and scale of the transactions or the risks they involved.

(3) *August 1988 to 23 February 1989 (the interim strategy)*
During this phase the council continued to carry out transactions but as part of an *d* interim strategy designed to reduce the extent of the council's exposure to loss which would result from a rise in interest rates. Although the auditor makes criticisms of the diligence shown by the council during this phase which are not without justification, in general the transactions which were carried out during this phase were carried out in accord with the policy which had been agreed with the auditor. However, the auditor did, in a letter dated 22 August 1988, indicate that 'our acceptance of the strategy does *e* not prejudice the rights of the Borough's electors'. The council was urged to obtain its own legal advice but instructions were not in fact given until 27 October 1988, and those instructions resulted in an opinion which was obtained from leading counsel in December 1988. Leading counsel advised:

> 'If the rate swap is undertaken as part of the proper management of the Council's *f* funds then as long as all relevant market factors are taken into account the swap will be intra vires. If the Council are carrying on a business of interest rate swaps, then to exercise a discretion in favour of such transactions would be ultra vires . . . Since swap transactions are lawful within s. 111 as being ancillary to good management of debts it would obviously not be lawful to enter into such transactions above the level of the current debt. A sufficient leeway should always be allowed between the *g* level of the rate swaps and the level of the total indebtedness so as to ensure that any decision made with respect to each individual rate swap transaction will be made on the merits of the particular transaction and not just because of the need to keep below the ceiling . . . The Council is entitled to enter into swap transactions because it is a means of securing good debt management. It should reduce the overall cost *h* of borrowing; it assists in making the debt portfolio more manageable. It is to the benefit of the ratepayers.'

That opinion did not, however, advise the council on what action the council should take having regard to the advice which is given as to the law. This further advice was not immediately forthcoming and the auditor became concerned about the continuation of the interim strategy. On 14 February 1989 he wrote to the chief executive of the council *j* stating, inter alia:

> 'In view of the legal position, you need to seriously consider whether further transactions should be entered [into] pending the outcome of the legal opinion.'

a
A meeting took place between the auditor and the director of finance on 22 February 1989, at which the auditor indicated that the council must desist from any further activity (including making any payments on existing contracts) unless supported by legal opinion and that he would consider a prohibition order if it did not do so, that he would make an application to the court to determine the legality of the council's activity and that he would issue a report under s 15 of the 1982 Act. However, on the same day the further written advice was given to the council by leading counsel in which he said:

b
'I can say that in my opinion the council have been engaged in various types of interest swap transactions which as a whole are on a scale outside the parameters I explained in (my earlier) written opinion and that therefore looking at the totality of the transactions it is not possible to say that these transactions were part and parcel of debt management so as to be lawful.'

c
The auditor was informed the same day that the council had decided not to make any further payments under its 'capital market agreements unless sanctioned by the Secretary of State for the Environment, or unless the courts declare it lawful to do so'.

The Secretary of State is given powers to sanction payments which would otherwise be unlawful under s 19 of the 1982 Act. However, on 28 February 1989 he refused to grant his sanction.

d
In February 1989 there was also the only other report to members before the council decided to cease making payments. This was the annual borrowing report submitted to the finance administration committee on 8 February 1989, by which time the notional principal involved in all the deals exceeded £5·9bn. The report and the recommendation it contained were very much in the same terms as in the previous year and the council accepted that recommendation on 15 February 1989. The auditor in his affidavit

e
contends, with obvious justification, that—

'the information as supplied to the council, its committees and sub-committees in the reports in 1988 and 1989 was in my view inadequate to enable members of them to consider properly the legality, reasonableness and prudence of the activities in the London Money/Capital Market.'

f
(4) *After 23 February 1989*

On 23 February 1989 the auditor delivered a report under s 15(3) of the 1982 Act, which provides:

'The auditor shall consider whether, in the public interest, he should make a report on any matter coming to his notice in the course of the audit in order that it

g
may be considered by the body concerned or brought to the attention of the public, and shall consider whether the public interest requires any such matter to be made the subject of an immediate report rather than of a report to be made at the conclusion of the audit.'

h
This was followed by the auditor on 28 February 1989 requesting the council to produce various items of information to him under s 16 of the 1982 Act. The auditor acknowledges that the council has helpfully co-operated in providing him with the necessary information.

Since 23 February 1989 the council has been involved in only seven transactions. These are seven swaps consequent on other parties exercising earlier swap options. In additon, the council exercised a gilt option which resulted in it receiving £250,000 from

j
a bank.

The scale of the council's activities during the financial years 1987 to 1989

In considering the issues it is necessary to bear in mind the extent to which the council was involved in the transactions over the relevant financial years. A summary of the

relevant information is contained in Appendix B to this judgment. The references we
have made in this judgment and in the Appendices to the notional principal sum can be   *a*
misleading unless it is remembered that at any one time the actual total of the notional
principal sums will be less because transactions will have lapsed, been cash settled,
assigned, cancelled and, in the case of options, exercised or have been offset by 'hedging'
transactions.

The auditor's application   *b*
   The auditor made his application to the court by notice of motion dated 30 May 1989.
The auditor sought two orders: (1) a declaration that the items of account appearing in
the CMF account for financial years beginning 1 April 1987 and 1988 are contrary to
law; and (2) an order for rectification of the accounts. The grounds of the application are
that (1) there was no authority in law for the said items of account; (2) the rectification of
accounts is required for them to comply with the law.   *c*
   As the council is not proposing to dispute the application the other respondents, the
banks, sought to be joined in the proceedings. The banks are by no means all the banks
which are involved in these transactions but they have been selected because they have
between them been involved in a cross-section of the transactions. They do not, however,
represent the other banks who have not been joined.
   The notice of motion was not served on any of the banks because this is not required   *d*
by RSC Ord 98, r 2(2), which requires the notice of motion to be served 'on the body to
whose accounts the application relates and on any person against whom an order is
sought' under the 1982 Act.
   In order to avoid the courts having to examine each transaction, and to simplify the
proceedings, on 21 September 1989 Otton J made a number of orders, including two
which affected the scope of the proceedings. These were in the following terms: *e*

   '2. The scope of the hearing fixed to commence on 2nd October 1989 shall be to
   consider the following issues, namely: (1A) Whether transactions within the eight
   categories referred to in paragraph 4 of the affidavit sworn by the Applicant herein
   on 30th May 1989 are capable of being within the powers conferred on local
   authorities by Parliament; (1B) If so, whether transactions within all or any of those   *f*
   categories were in fact entered into by the First Respondent in a proper exercise of
   those powers; (2) Whether the transactions were not such that a reasonable authority
   could have engaged in organised as the First Respondent was; (3) Whether the
   transactions were authorised properly or at all by the First Respondent; (4) Whether
   the Capital Markets Fund was validly established or maintained by the First
   Respondent.   *g*
   3. The hearing of the following issues, namely: (5) Whether, if the Applicant's
   contentions with regard to issue (1A) is wrong but his contentions with regard to
   one or more of issues (1B) to (4) are correct, the transactions between the Second to
   Sixth Respondents and the first Respondent can nevertheless be enforced in
   circumstances where those Respondents had no notice of any improper exercise of
   powers, lack of authority or other defect, and (6) Whether, if any of the Applicant's   *h*
   contentions are correct, payments already made by the First Respondent to any of
   the Second to Sixth Respondents, and vice versa, should be restored to the payer: be
   adjourned for further directions to be given upon the determination of the above
   issues.'

   The eight categories of transactions are the categories which have been identified   *j*
earlier in this judgment.
   There is no dispute between the parties that if the transactions fall within para (1A)
then the transactions are unlawful and not capable of being enforced by the parties to the
transactions. If, however, the transactions or any of them fall within para (1B) there is a
dispute as to the extent to which they would be enforceable.

a   The outcome of these proceedings is of great importance not only to the council and the banks who are parties to the proceedings but many other banks and approximately 70 other local authorities who have also entered into transactions of this nature, but not on the same scale as the council.

Applications were made for oral evidence and cross-examination. However, prior to the hearing this court adjourned those applications allowing the parties to renew them if necessary, in the hope that it would not in the end prove necessary for the witnesses to be b   called. This has in fact proved to be the position and no witnesses have in fact given oral evidence.

The case raises a number of difficult issues and, before considering those issues, we would like to acknowledge the very great assistance that we have had from all the lawyers involved in presenting the case before us. A large number of documents have been involved and they have been put before us in a form which makes them as simple to c   refer to as is possible in the circumstances. Excellent outline (the word 'skeleton' is not used) written arguments have been presented to us, and they have been amplified by oral argument of the highest order. However, even with this assistance, the issues which the case raises are by no means easy to resolve. In particular, the case raises in an acute form the effect of a public body such as a council failing to exercise its powers properly on the private rights which the banks have under the contracts entered into with the d   Hammersmith council.

Municipal corporation

An argument was advanced by counsel for the banks which, if it is correct, has surprising consequences. The argument is based on the fact that the London Borough of Hammersmith and Fulham embraces not only the council but also a separate corporate e   body created by royal charter and originally known by the name 'The Mayor, Aldermen and Burgesses of the London Borough of Hammersmith' and now known (as a result of a resolution of 1 April 1979) as 'The Mayor and Burgesses of the London Borough of Hammersmith and Fulham' (the borough). Counsel for the banks submits that the borough as a chartered corporation has at common law the full capacity of a natural f   person. This includes the power to enter into contracts without restriction as to purpose and therefore the doctrine of ultra vires which is applicable to statutory corporations has no application to the borough as a chartered corporation. That in relation to ultra vires there is a distinction between the approach which must be adopted in relation to corporations created by charter under the royal prerogative and the approach which must be adopted in relation to statutory corporations is confirmed by a judgment of Bowen LJ g   in *Baroness Wenlock v River Dee Co* (1883) 36 Ch D 675 at 685, which is reported as a note to a case concerning the same parties. The relevant passage of the judgment is in the following terms:

'At common law a corporation created by the King's charter has, *primâ facie*, and has been known to have ever since *Sutton's Hospital Case* ((1612) 10 Co Rep 1a, h   [1558–1774] All ER Rep 11), the power to do with its property all such acts as an ordinary person can do, and to bind itself to such contracts as an ordinary person can bind himself to; and even if by the charter creating the corporation the King imposes some direction which would have the effect of limiting the natural capacity of the body of which he is speaking, the common law has always held that the direction of the King might be enforced through the Attorney-General; but although j   it might contain an essential part of the so-called bargain between the Crown and the corporation, that did not at law destroy the legal power of the body which the King had created. When you come to corporations created by statute, the question seems to me entirely different, and I do not think it is quite satisfactory to say that you must take the statute as if it had created a corporation at common law, and then see whether it took away any of the incidents of a corporation at common law, because that begs the question, and it not only begs the question, but it states what is an untruth, namely, that the statute does create a corporation at common law. It *a* does nothing of the sort. It creates a statutory corporation, which may or may not be meant to possess all or more or less of the qualities with which a corporation at common law is endowed. Therefore, to say that you must assume that it has got everything which it would have at common law unless the statute takes it away is, I think, to travel on a wrong line of thought. What you have to do is find out what this statutory creature is and what it is meant to do; and to find out what this *b* statutory creature is you must look at the statute only, because there, and there alone, is found the definition of this new creature. It is no use to consider the question of whether you are going to classify it under the head of common law corporations. Looking at this statutory creature one has to find out what are its powers, what is its vitality, what it can do.'

That for every London borough there is in addition to the council a municipal *c* corporation is not in dispute. Paragraph 1(2) of Sch 2 to the Local Government Act 1972 provides:

'For every London borough there shall be a council consisting of the mayor and councillors and the council shall exercise all such functions as are vested in the municipal corporation of the borough or in the council of the borough by this Act *d* or otherwise.'

The London Government Act 1963, s 1, established new administrative areas to be known as 'London boroughs'. That section provided:

'(1) There shall be established new administrative areas, to be known as London boroughs, which shall comprise the areas respectively described (by reference to *e* existing administrative areas) in column 2 of Part I of Schedule 1 to this Act; and in this and any other . . . Act—(a) any reference to an inner London borough shall be construed as a reference to one of the London boroughs numbered from 1 to 12 in the said Part I; (b) any reference to an outer London borough shall be construed as a reference to one of the London boroughs numbered from 13 to 32 in the said Part I. *f*
(2) If in the case of any London borough, on representations in that behalf made to the Privy Council by the Minister, Her Majesty by the advice of Her Privy Council thinks fit to grant a charter of incorporation of the inhabitants of that borough, Her Majesty may by that charter—(a) make provision with respect to the name of the borough; and (b) subject to the provisions of this Act, make any provision such as may be made by virtue of section 131 of the Local Government Act 1933 by a *g* charter granted under Part VI of that Act; and any charter which purports to be granted in pursuance of the Royal prerogative and this subsection shall be deemed to be valid and within the powers of this Act and Her Majesty's prerogative and the validity thereof shall not be questioned in any legal proceeding whatever.
(3) In the case of any London borough whose inhabitants are not incorporated by such a charter as is referred to in the last foregoing subsection, provision for their *h* incorporation shall be made by the Minister by order (hereafter in this Act referred to as an "incorporation order") which may include any such provision as is mentioned in paragraph (a) or (b) of that subsection . . .
(6) The Municipal Corporations Act 1882 shall apply to every London borough . . . the expression "borough" when used in relation to local government in any enactment whether passed before or after this Act . . . shall except where the context *j* otherwise requires (and except in particular in the expressions "county borough" and "non-county borough") include a London borough . . .'

As envisaged by s 1(2) a charter of incorporation was granted by Her Majesty in respect of the areas of the existing metropolitan boroughs of Fulham and Hammersmith to be

named the 'The London Borough of Hammersmith'. That charter provided that the
a borough should be named the London Borough of Hammersmith. The charter records
that it is granted, ordered and declared 'by virtue of Our Prerogative Royal and in
pursuance of the London Government Act 1963' and goes on to state:

> '3. The said corporation shall have the powers, authorities, immunities and
> privileges usually vested by law in the Mayor, Aldermen and Burgesses of a
> *b* municipal borough.'

Counsel for the auditor and counsel for the council do not dispute that there would be
considerable force in the submission of counsel for the banks if the incorporation of the
borough was under the royal prerogative alone as, for example, in the case of an ordinary
chartered corporation. However, they submit that in the case of a London borough the
incorporation is not under the royal prerogative alone but in the exercise of the royal
c prerogative under statutory powers conferred for particular purposes. Section 1 of the
1973 Act is an enabling provision which provides an additional power of incorporation
exercisable by Her Majesty by virtue of the royal prerogative. This provision is supported
by the terms of s 93(5) of the 1963 Act, which states:

> 'Any enabling provision contained in this Act shall be deemed to be in addition
> *d* to, and not in derogation of, any powers exercisable by Her Majesty by virtue of Her
> Royal prerogative.'

On that basis counsel for the auditor goes on to make a precise submission that where
a statute provides for incorporation as a result of the exercise of the royal prerogative, it
is a question of the construction of the Act whether Parliament intended that a
corporation so created is to have such general capacity as the common law may attach to
e the corporation created by charter. He distinguishes the decision of the Privy Council in
Bonanza Creek Gold Mining Co Ltd v R [1916] 1 AC 566, [1916–17] All ER Rep 999 relied
on by counsel for the banks because in that case the statute did not restrict the general
capacity of a corporation created by a charter but restricted the situations in which it was
open to the Lieutenant-Governor on behalf of the Crown to create a corporation by
f charter. The judgment of the Privy Council was given by Viscount Haldane who said
([1916] 1 AC 566 at 578, [1916–17] All ER Rep 999 at 1004):

> 'Or the statute may be in such a form that a new power to incorporate by charter
> has been created, directed to be exercised with a view to the attainment of, for
> example, merely territorial objects, but not directed in terms which confine the
> legal personality which the charter creates to existence for the purpose of these
> *g* objects and within territorial limits. The language may be such as to show an
> intention to confer on the corporation the general capacity which the common law
> ordinarily attaches to corporations created by charter.'

Then, having summarised the situation in relation to the statute which was being
considered in that case, Viscount Haldane added ([1916] 1 AC 566 at 563–584,
h [1916–17] All ER Rep 999 at 1007):

> 'In the case of a company created by charter the doctrine of ultra vires has no real
> application in the absence of statutory restriction added to what is written in the
> charter.'

In our judgment, as was accepted by counsel for the banks in his final submissions in
j reply, counsel for the auditor is correct in stating that the extent of the powers of a
London borough have to be determined by a construction of the 1963 Act. There is
nothing inconsistent with this approach in the other cases to which we were referred on
this subject, including, in particular, *A-G v Newcastle-upon-Tyne Corp* [1892] AC 568 and
A-G v Manchester Corp [1906] 1 Ch 643.

When it comes to construing s 1 of the 1963 Act we accept that it does place a limit on
the extent of the powers that Her Majesty is entitled to grant by the charter. Those *a*
powers are limited to making provision in respect of the name of the borough and
dealing with the specific matters referred to in s 131 of the Local Government Act 1933
which include, inter alia, fixing the number of councillors and the other matters relating
to the constitution of the borough. We regard the alternative power given to the minister
under s 1(3) as confirming this approach. His powers of incorporation, which are clearly
wholly dependant on the section, are specifically confined to those matters referred to in *b*
sub-s (2) and if that is the position in relation to the minister so also should it be the
position with regard to a charter granted by Her Majesty.

We also find confirmation in sub-s (6) which applies the Municipal Corporation Act
1882 to the borough. If the borough was intended to have all the powers of a municipal
corporation, then it would not in our view have been necessary to apply the whole of
that Act, in so far as it had not already been repealed, to London boroughs. The remaining *c*
language of sub-s (6) is also inconsistent with the proposition that the borough should
have all the powers of a common law corporation. Outside London, boroughs certainly
did not have those powers and the effect of sub-s (6) in applying the expression 'borough',
which when used in relation to local government in any enactment whether passed
before or after this Act is to include a London borough, indicates an intention that the
position of London boroughs should in general be assimilated with that of non-London *d*
boroughs.

Our view furthermore appears to be in accord with the views of the editors of two
leading textbooks on this subject, namely *Hart's Local Government and Administration* (9th
edn, 1973) p 309 and the *Encyclopedia of Local Government Law* (1980) para 1–07.

In coming to our conclusion, however, we do not rely on the terms of the charter
itself, although they are consistent with our conclusion. The reason for this is: *e*

> 'If there are limitations upon its actions expressed in the charter creating it,
> nevertheless these do not prevent the corporation from validly doing the acts in
> question, though, if it thus infringes its charter, a *scire facias* will lie against it at the
> suit of the Crown to forfeit or revoke the charter.'

(See *Hart* p 306 and the passage from the judgment of Bowen LJ already cited.) *f*

Counsel for the auditor also argued that purely on a factual basis it was not possible for
counsel for the banks to rely on this argument to sidestep the issues as to ultra vires.
Having regard to our conclusions on the interpretation point, it is not necessary for us to
go into the factual issues which are involved in the submission of counsel for the auditor
and it will suffice if we indicate that we are far from satisfied that if the submission of
counsel for the banks was right in law it would fail on the facts. *g*

We therefore proceed to consider the other issues raised before us on the basis that the
council's functions are confined, so far as is relevant for present purposes, to those
expressly or implicitly conferred on it by statute and therefore for those purposes do not
differ from those of a borough situated outside London.

h

Issue (1A): was the transaction capable of being within the powers of the council?

On the question whether the council was ever capable of entering into any of these
transactions three different opinions had been expressed by counsel prior to the
commencement of these proceedings in written opinions which were before the court.
The conclusion of counsel for the auditor, which is that which is now contended for by
the auditor, is that a local authority is never capable of lawfully entering into swap *j*
transactions. Leading counsel who previously jointly advised with counsel for the auditor
was of the opinion that the council was only capable of lawfully entering into a swap
which was a parallel contract. That is a swap which is—

> 'arranged in parallel to an existing debt of a local authority which it has lawfully

a   incurred by borrowing where the notional principal involved in the swap is equal to the debt outstanding or part of it and where the profit which it is hoped or sometimes known, subject to continued solvency, that the swap will yield is to be used in order to reduce the burden or eliminate interest rate variation risks imposed on that authority by its previous borrowing.'

The third view was that expressed by counsel for the council and is the basis for his
b   submissions. It only applies to certain of these transactions, and depends on the council at the time being engaged in what has become known for convenience during the hearing, as a result of the submissions of counsel for the banks, as 'interest rate risk management' and which counsel for the council described as debt management. On this view transactions could be used for the purposes of enabling the council to manage the burden of interest rates which it had to pay on its lawful borrowing and the interest
c   which it received on its lawful investments so as to achieve the most satisfactory financial result for the council. On this approach the transactions were capable of being lawful if the object which the council was seeking to achieve was debt or interest risk management. They would not be lawful if they were not in fact used for the purpose or were not capable of being used for this purpose.

A category of transactions which would manifestly not be capable of being used for
d   this purpose would be swap transactions in which the council was acting as an intermediary for a 'turn', that is a profit. Counsel for the council, however, in a later opinion dated 23 February 1989 accepted that all the transactions entered into during the two financial years which are the subject of the auditor's application are unlawful because when the totality of the transactions are examined it is clear that the transactions were not part and parcel of management but involved trading which is ultra vires.

e   At the hearing, the approach of counsel for the banks and counsel for Barclays differed from that of counsel for the council. They differed as to whether the transactions were outside the parameters of management and as to the consequences of a decision of the court that the transactions, or some of them, were capable of being intra vires if they were being used for management purposes. Counsel for the banks and counsel for Barclays argued that once it was accepted that the transactions were capable of being intra
f   vires, then the contracts which the council entered into with third parties in connection with the transactions were enforceable by and against those parties (here the banks).

If the transactions were ones which the council was incapable of entering into lawfully, then it was not really in dispute that the auditor is entitled to the declaration which he seeks. This issue is therefore of the greatest importance in these proceedings.

On the assumption that the extent of the authority of the council was not materially
g   affected by para 1(2) of Sch 2 to the 1972 Act then it is accepted that there is no express specific statutory power which entitles the council to enter into the transactions. If authority to do so exists it is derived from the provisions of s 111(1) of the 1972 Act. The sidenote to s 111 reads 'Subsidiary powers of local authorities', and s 111(1) provides:

'Without prejudice to any powers exercisable apart from this section but subject
h   to provisions of this Act and any other enactment passed before or after this Act, a local authority shall have power to do anything (whether or not involving the expenditure, borrowing or lending of money or the acquisition or disposal of any property or rights) which is calculated to facilitate, or is conducive or incidental to, the discharge of any of their functions.'

This sub-section puts in a statutory form the long-established principle that local
j   authorities have implied power to do anything which is ancillary to the discharge of any of their functions.

The fact that s 111(1) is expressly made subject to 'the provisions of this Act' makes it clear that it is important to construe s 111(1) in its context. The references to expenditure, borrowing or lending etc within the brackets in the sub-section do not themselves confer any power to expend, borrow or lend money etc, but only make it clear that the fact that those activities are involved does not prevent the activities being within the power of the *a* authority which is authorised by this subsection.

The critical part of the subsection is the words 'calculated to facilitate, or is conducive or incidental to, the discharge of any of their functions'. Before the subsection can authorise an activity which is not otherwise authorised there must be some other underlying function which is authorised, to the discharge of which the activity will facilitate or be conducive or incidental. *b*

What is a 'function' for the purposes of the subsection is not expressly defined but in our view there can be little doubt that in this context 'function' refers to the multiplicity of specific statutory activities the council is expressly or impliedly under a duty to perform or has power to perform under the other provisions of the 1972 Act or other relevant legislation. The subsection does not of itself, independently of any other provision, authorise the performance of any activity. It only confers, as the sidenote to *c* the section indicates, a subsidiary power, a subsidiary power which authorises an activity where some other statutory provision has vested a specific function or functions in the council and the performance of the activity will assist in some way in the discharge of that function or those functions.

For example, s 172 of the 1972 Act provides that Pt I of Sch 13 to the Act is to have effect as to the powers of local authorities to borrow and lend money with respect to their *d* funds. Paragraph 2(1) specifies the methods by which the council can borrow money and they include by mortgage, issue of stock, debentures, bonds, bills, agreements entered into with the Public Work Loan Commissioners and other means approved by the Secretary of State with the consent of the Treasury, and para 2(2) goes on to provide that the powers conferred by that paragraph shall be exercisable 'subject to and in accordance with the following provisions of this part of the Schedule'. The following provisions then *e* contain extremely detailed provisions dealing with the powers of the local authority to borrow money, including the power of the Secretary of State to make regulations as to the exercise of the power.

None of the transactions with which we are concerned fall within the provisions of Sch 13, nor do they in fact themselves involve borrowing money. Apart from cash *f* options the transactions do not lead to actual or future borrowing. In the case of cash options there can be a borrowing in the future but a borrowing which may not be authorised by the specific provisions of Sch 13.

Are the transactions then capable of helping the authority to discharge the function of borrowing which it is given by the 1972 Act? Our view is No. The performance of the transactions will not in any way assist the council to borrow. What some of the transactions are capable of doing is assist the council to alleviate the consequence of *g* borrowing, ie assist the council to pay interest. But so also would any profit-making activity. Indirectly, but not directly, they can have the effect of converting what is an obligation to pay a fixed rate of interest into a variable rate and vice versa. It is for this reason that counsel for the council in his submissions identifies debt management as the function and counsel for the banks identifies interest risk management as the function *h* which the transactions are said to be capable of facilitating.

This way of approaching the issue involves asking the question whether s 111(1) can authorise the performing of some activity if it facilitates the management not of a function itself but the consequence of a function or functions, a function in the case of debt management or functions in the case of interest risk management (since interest risk management can be necessary either as a result of borrowing or investing or a *j* combination of both). In our judgment there must be a sufficient nexus between the activity and the function or functions if the activity is to be authorised by the subsection. Whether or not there is such a nexus can involve problems of degree. The necessary nexus can be broken if the acitivity is not subsidiary to the discharge of the function of the council or if it involves setting up a separate business or undertaking.

In *A-G v London CC* [1901] 1 Ch 781 the London Council Council acted ultra vires,
a although it had statutory powers to own and work tramways, when it set up a bus
business, even though the buses were being used as feeders to the trams. The running of
the buses in that case was a separate undertaking. The nexus was not sufficient because
of the scale of the bus business.

The necessary link may also not exist because the activity is not sufficiently closely
related to the function to which it is said to be subsidiary. Here assistance is provided by
b the rather similar case of *A-G v Manchester Corp* [1906] 1 Ch 643. In that case the
corporation was also authorised to run a tramway but it commenced a general parcel
delivery business within and beyond the area covered by its tramways which was not
confined to parcels and goods carried on the tramways. Farwell J concluded that the
delivery activities had to be confined to parcels or goods carried on the tramways. He
said (at 656):
c

'The question, as is pointed out in *Attorney-General v. London County Council* ([1901]
1 Ch 781), is not whether the business can be conveniently or advantageously
conducted with the tramway business, but whether it is by necessary implication
incidental or accessory to it, and I think that it is not. To collect and deliver parcels
for the tramway is fairly incidental; to collect and deliver parcels outside the radius
d of the tramway, and without any connection with the tramway, is not incidental to
the tramway business, but distinct from it. At the best it could be said to be
incidental to the incidental, and such reasoning would authorize a railway company
to carry on a coal merchant's business, because they must buy coal; but this was
restrained in *Attorney-General v. Great Northern Ry. Co.* ((1860) 29 LJ Ch 794). For the
same reasons I hold that the corporation cannot act as general agents for the railway
e companies, but only in respect of tram-borne goods.'

Seeking to apply Farwell J's reasoning to this case, we would, both in respect of the
council's functions of borrowing and investing, regard the transactions as only capable of
being 'incidental to the incidental'. It is an incident of borrowing that you pay interest
and of investing that you receive interest, it is also an incident of the transactions that
f you pay or receive interest or a sum of money that represents interest, but the transactions
do not involve borrowing or investing though they can involve borrowing or investing
in the future in the case of options and FRAs.

There is, however, in our view, another and more fundamental difficulty in the way
of regarding the transactions as capable of falling within s 111. The powers of an
authority such as a council to raise and invest money are strictly prescribed by a statutory
g framework. Reference has already been made to Sch 13. One of the specific powers
contained in Sch 13 is para 8, which provides:

'A local authority who borrows money under paragraph 1(b) above may during
the fixed period borrow further sums, without the approval of the Secretary of State
under that sub-paragraph, for the purpose of repaying the money so borrowed.'

h This paragraph expressly authorises debt restructuring (the first of the auditor's three
types of financial transactions). The paragraph is a statutory provision which enables a
local authority to engage in a form of debt or interest rate management but which is very
narrowly confined. When that paragraph is considered together with the specific nature
of the provisions which govern investing money, raising money and establishing funds
it appears to us that it would be inconsistent with the structure of the 1972 Act as a
j whole, to which the provisions of s 111(1) are expressly made subject, to regard the
transactions (which fall within the third of the auditor's three categories) as falling within
that subsection. The same can be said with regard to other statutory powers to which the
subsection could be regarded as being subsidiary, such as the Local Loans Act 1875.

The fact that the activities involving the transactions are inconsistent with the structure
of the Act is demonstrated by the manner in which the activities were dealt with by the

council after the initial period. They were treated as falling within a so-called capital market activities fund (the CMA fund). Schedules 13 to 19 of the 1972 Act deal with the establishment of funds by a local authority but the so-called CMA fund would not fall within these paragraphs.

We therefore come to the conclusion that none of the transactions are capable of being lawfully entered into by the council. In coming to this conclusion we are not indicating that the transactions were not capable of being advantageously used by the council in connection with its interest obligations. On the contrary, we can see that properly controlled activities of this nature could provide a useful tool which, if it were available to the council, would enable it to minimise its expenditure on interest and increase its income from investments. However, as was pointed out in argument, it is not for the court to confer powers on the council which the language of s 111 does not confer.

Before leaving this issue, we should make it clear that we have not forgotten the cases of *R v Greater London Council, ex p Westminster City Council* (1984) Times, 27 December and *R v Eden DC, ex p Moffat* (1988) Independent, 16 December. In the former case a function, namely the maintenance of a good and harmonious relationship between a local authority and staff, was recognised as falling within s 111 and in *Moffat's* case the function of improving the council's structure and efficiency was also recognised. Counsel for the banks submitted that these were functions of the local authority implied from their express powers and duties. We would not question that functions can arise from implied powers and duties in the same way as they can arise from express powers and duties. However, the functions identified in these cases were not connected with the financial activities of a council. As we have sought to indicate, the financial activities are statutorily constrained in a way which makes it impossible, in our view, to imply functions of debt management or interest risk management which are not expressly referred to in the legislation. It is for this reason that we did not receive the assistance which we would otherwise have done from these cases.

Having come to the conclusion that the transactions as a whole are not capable of being within the powers conferred on the local authority, we have disposed of the first issue which Otton J in his order of 27 July 1989 ordered to be determined. Strictly speaking therefore it is not necessary for us to go on to express our views on the remaining issues which are before the court. However, extensive argument has been advanced before us on the remaining issues and we feel we should deal with those issues as briefly as we can commensurate with assisting the parties and superior courts if this case goes to appeal. Our views are as follows.

If there was power to embark on capital market activities, were the officials in a position lawfully to do so?

It was submitted by the auditor and by the council that there was no, or no proper, delegation by the council to any officer of any power the council might have to enter into capital market activity nor was any CMA fund validly established; further, that in any event the decision of the council, if such there was, to undertake dealings on the capital market was a decision so unreasonable that no reasonable local authority could ever have come to it and equally that the council's capital market activity was such that no reasonable authority could have undertaken it organised as the council was (see *Associated Provincial Picture Houses Ltd v Wednesbury Corp* [1947] 2 All ER 680, [1948] 1 KB 223).

These three submissions are inter-related in that the absence of delegation or of the establishment of such a fund or at least the lack of formality leading to any delegation or any establishment of such a fund are themselves part of the evidence to show that the council's decision to deal and its dealing on the capital market was unreasonable within *Wednesbury* principles.

Delegation of any power

a   The council's 'General scheme of delegation' records that the 'Council has delegated under Section 101 of the Local Government Act 1972, in so far as it lawfully may, all its powers, duties and functions to the several Committees appointed under the standing orders'. Paragraph 4(a) provides:

b   'No Committee, Sub-Committee, or officer to whom powers are delegated shall exercise those powers where revenue expenditure will be incurred, or new sources of revenue secured, which are not included in appropriate approved revenue estimates, without reference to the appropriate Committee if the amount exceeds that stipulated in the Financial Regulations.'

In their standing orders concerning 'General delegation to officers', para 3 of Section A provides:

c   'The Director of Finance . . . shall be the Officer responsible for the administration of the Authority's financial affairs (Section 151 Local Government Act 1972) but subject in all respect to the principles of corporate management established in the Authority.'

d   Paragraph 3.1 of Section A appoints the director of finance as the proper officer in relation to certain immaterial matters and Section B delegates certain functions to all chief officers, of whom the director of finance is one. The terms of Section B and Section C (which it would be burdensome to quote) serve to indicate how narrowly the terms of para 3 of Section A are properly to be construed. The auditor submits that undertaking the transactions is well outside any delegated authority granted by the standing orders.

e   In response to the auditor's request for copies of all the reports to the council, its committees, sub-committees or members which provide information as to the council's 'capital market activity', the council supplied the auditor with copies of certain 'Annual Borrowing Reports'. Before the report dated 17 February 1988 there was nothing in any report which would have led a member reading them to understand that the council had been using any of the financial instruments with which the court is concerned or that the council had been engaged in 'capital market activity'. It appears, therefore, that the

f   initiation and main expansion of such activity was carried out without any report to members and, in consequence, without any express delegation of authority, if such there could be, by the finance and administration committee. The report dated 17 February 1988 includes the following item:

g   'The Director of Finance has also continued to arrange where applicable, transactions in the London money/capital markets in order to maximise gains on favourable interest rate movements.'

The report ends by recommending the committee to authorise the director of finance, inter alia, to—

h   'arrange transactions in the London money/capital markets in order to take advantage of favourable interest rate movements on such terms and conditions as are agreed by the Director of Finance.'

The finance and administration committee duly resolved that the council be recommended accordingly. On 24 February 1988 the council duly accepted the committee's recommendation. On 8 February 1989 the committee received a similar

j   recommendation from the director of finance in the annual borrowing report and recommended the council to resolve accordingly, as no doubt it did. Neither of the reports referred to gave any indication of the number of transactions arranged or to be arranged or as to any income or expenditure past or future or any information as to the type of risks involved or the scale of any potential gains or exposure to loss.

In any event, the auditor submits, the delegation to the director of finance, if such there was, contravened the financial regulations of the council. These regulations provide *a* for the preparation of estimates and for budgetary control. They require the preparation and approval of estimates and, at para 2.7 read:

'Committees shall have the authority to incur expenditure up to the amount of the approved estimate. When, in the opinion of the Director of Finance, actual or proposed expenditure has resulted or is likely to result in overspending of the appropriate annual estimate provision, the chief officer concerned shall, wherever *b* possible, see virement of estimates so as to avoid a supplementary estimate.'

Paragraph 2.10 reads:

'The Director of Finance shall report to the relevant committees on the financial implications of any proposed new scheme or development, except where in his/her opinion it would be inappropriate to do so.' *c*

No provision was made in the approved estimates for any expenditure to be incurred under any of the financial instruments with which this court is concerned nor was any specific authority given for such expenditure. Our conclusion is that there was no proper delegation.

d

Capital markets fund
There was, as the council accepts, no specific resolution establishing such a fund. It claims, however, that such a fund was established under para 16 of Sch 13 to the 1972 Act, as substituted by the Local Government (Miscellaneous Provisions) Act 1976, s 28(1) and (2). Paragraph 16(1) empowers a local authority to establish such funds as they consider appropriate for the purpose of meeting any expenditure they incur in connection *e* with their functions. Paragraph 16(3) provides:

'Any fund maintained by a local authority for the purposes for which the authority have power by virtue of this paragraph to establish a fund shall be deemed to be established by the authority under this paragraph and may be dealt with accordingly; and it is hereby declared that references in any enactment to a fund *f* established under this paragraph or to an authority by whom a fund is established include references to a fund which is deemed to be so established . . .'

The evidence relevant to the issue as to whether or not a CMA fund was established is as follows. In response to a request by the auditor's solicitor the council's director of legal services replied by letter dated 21 April 1989 stating:
g
'I am advised that there are no internal documents establishing the Capital Markets Fund although there are references in internal memo's to exploring the possibility of establishing the fund and, later, that work on setting up the fund had commenced.'

The first memorandum referred to is from the head of loans and investments to the *h* director of finance and is dated 8 December 1987. It states:

'I am currently exploring the possibility of setting up a Capital Markets Fund or similar into which all credits/debits related to notional borrowing and lending could be posted. Hopefully we could then carry forward a balance each year which to some extent ought to be prudent in case, for example, any of the swap options are exercised.' *j*

The second memorandum, also from the head of loans and investments to the director of finance is dated 14 March 1988 and states:

'Work on setting up the Capital Markets Fund has commenced. All premiums

a
and swap payments since 1/4/87 to be credited and brokerage debited. Virtually all
the balance will be carried forward on 31/3/88. In future credit direct to GRF
[general rate fund] (not CLF [consolidated loans fund]) in line with the risk period
i.e. up to five years. I now propose to also include the small number of reverse swaps
prior to 1/4/87 in the CM fund and not CLF as last year—only five reversed swaps
(£15m notional) actually had payments and receipts in 1986/87—net £120K. Could
be argued that this is not a change of accounting practice on basis of very small

b
volumes in previous years.'

It is to be noted (a) that 'work on setting up the CMF' is said to have started but there
is no reference to completion of that work, (b) that the 'fund' contemplated was not a
'fund' for the purpose of meeting any expenditure that the council incurred in connection
with their functions (see para 16 of Sch 13 to the 1972 Act) nor was there evidence that
the council maintained for this purpose any fund, in the sense of a 'portion of revenue
c
set apart as security for specified payments'. Accounts were no doubt kept but this is not
equivalent to maintaining a fund. In the first place, credits were to be directed to the
general rate fund and secondly, the council having no function of dealing on the capital
market, para 16 of Sch 13 conferred no power to set up such a fund, (c) there being, as
we conclude, no delegation by the council at best until the resolution of 24 February
d
1988 of authority to deal on the London money/capital markets no CMF could in any
event have been established before that date.

We therefore conclude that no CMF was ever validly established.

Wednesbury unreasonableness

It was contended on behalf of the auditor that no reasonable authority, organised as
e
the council was, could have engaged in the council's scale of capital market activity.
During the first phase down to March 1987 the scale of such activity was relatively small
and the evidence did not satisfy us that it was conducted in a manner which was
unreasonable within *Wednesbury* principles. Although a greater increase occurred in the
early months of 1988 we regard the initiation of serious dealing by the council in the
transactions to have taken place during the second phase from April 1987.

f
In broad outline the auditor draws attention to the following. First, no legal advice
was obtained within or on behalf of the council before it undertook its capital market
activity. Secondly, the local government officers engaged in the activity were not
equipped by training or experience to operate within a highly technical, sophisticated
and competitive market. The 'post holders' who actually entered into deals were identified
by the council's legal services in their letter dated 25 April 1989 as having been the loans
g
accountant between 1983 and 9 November 1987 and the head of loans and investments
between 10 November 1987 and 26 September 1988 (with a few exceptions) and we
were by no means satisfied that these 'post holders' had the necessary expertise or
guidance. Thirdly, the council's lack of appropriate expertise and resources is exemplified
by (a) its inability as late as February 1989 to produce an assessment of its total exposure
to risk despite the auditor's urgent request for such estimates as far back as 27 July 1988,
h
and (b) by the fact that certain steps taken by the council for the purpose of reducing risk
in fact had the opposite effect. Fourthly, the lack of information in the reports to the
finance and administration committee and to the council (the content of the reports is
referred to above). In the result, we consider that the entire conduct of the capital market
dealings from April 1987 until August 1988 was unreasonable within *Wednesbury*
principles.

j
Different considerations in our judgment apply to the third phase, the interim strategy
period, that is to say, from about the end of August 1988 until dealing virtually ceased in
February 1989. We have already set out in brief the history of the interim strategy.

The question which arises as to the interim strategy is: was the conduct of the interim
strategy by the council unlawful either in the sense that no reasonable council could have

decided to undertake it or in the sense that no reasonable council could have implemented
the interim strategy in the way the council did (disregarding for this purpose the absence   *a*
of any proper delegation and the ignorance of the members of the council as to what was
happening which prevented them considering the reasonableness of the council's
activities)?

We see no reason to doubt the bona fides of the council officers' intention during this
period to limit potential losses to ratepayers and/or to the council or the genuineness of
their belief that some, at least, of the transactions in question, including those which they   *b*
proposed in future to undertake, were capable in law of being intra vires the council. In
this regard the solicitor to the Audit Commission had, on 28 July 1987, expressed the
following view:

> '2. Interest rate swaps *as part of the normal process of debt management* are within
> the powers conferred on Local Authorities by section 111 of the Local Government   *c*
> Act 1972.
> 3. The taking of a premium (front loading) is also permissible, subject to normal
> principles of financial prudence.' (Our emphasis.)

The council was aware that this view had been expressed and there was evidence to
satisfy us that a number of local authorities had entered into such transactions as part of
what they conceived to be the normal process of debt management, nor do we doubt   *d*
that the council implemented the measures referred into in its letter to the auditor dated
5 October 1988 (these included measures to increase staff and to employ, temporarily, a
capital markets dealer and to install a more sophisticated computer) with a view to
improvements in risk calculation and control generally. While recognising that delay
occurred in instructing counsel, this may well have been due, at least in part, to
insufficiency and inefficiency of past recording procedures and to difficulty in preparing   *e*
instructions having regard to the complication of the matter. Inefficiency is not the same
thing as *Wednesbury* unreasonableness and we are not satisfied, therefore, that either in
deciding to implement or in implementing the interim strategy the council was acting
in a way that no reasonable council could. We will set out our views on the consequences
of the activities during the second phase being *Wednesbury* unreasonable on the interim
strategy when considering the question whether the council was in fact engaged in   *f*
interest risk management.

Was the council engaged in interest risk management?

If the council is authorised to engage in interest risk management, the question arises
as to whether it did in fact do so. The history of the council's dealing has already been set
out and, as indicated, the history falls within three periods. During the first period   *g*
(December 1983 to March 1987) the limited nature of the council's activities does not
enable us to hold that it was not engaged in interest risk management. In the second
period (from April 1987 to August 1988) the position is, however, wholly different. The
scale and range of transactions makes it clear that the council was not engaged in interest
risk management but engaged in a trade designed to exploit the market in these   *h*
transactions with a view to profit. It is not possible to identify precisely the date on which
that trade commenced; all that can be said is that it started towards the beginning of this
period. If in subsequent proceedings it is necessary to identify the precise date on which
the trade commenced then that would require more detailed examination than is possible
in these proceedings. As counsel for the banks pointed out, the transactions can be put
into effect long after they are entered into (e g when an option is exercised) and continue   *j*
to have effect for a long period thereafter (ie during the currency of the agreement to
which an option relates). It is the date of the transaction which is critical in considering
the validity of the transactions. However, once the trade began this would be fatal to the
argument advanced by counsel for the banks that the transactions entered into during
this period were capable of being within the powers of the authority because they were

entered into for the purposes of interest risk management and therefore fell within s 111
a of the 1972 Act.

The third or interim strategy period (from August 1988 to 23 February 1989) raises
different questions. In this period the evidence referred to earlier in this judgment
indicates that the council was seeking to reduce its exposure as a result of its earlier
activities which it by that time appreciated were arguably beyond its powers. If
transactions which were undertaken as part of interest risk management were capable of
b being within the powers of the Act, then in our view so must activities which the council
undertook with a view to minimising the risks to which the council was exposed by
earlier transactions.

The argument against this being within the powers of the council, which was advanced
by both counsel for the council and for the auditor, was that if the council had engaged
in activities outside the activities permitted by the statute or which were otherwise
c unlawful for offending *Wednesbury* principles it could not be within the council's
statutory power to enter into transactions of the same nature in order to reduce the risks
created by the unlawful earlier transactions. We do not accept this argument if the
activities are capable of being permitted by the statute.

There is no presumption that the council knew what the law was on the point, or in
more realistic terms, what it would turn out to be (see *Evans v Bartlam* [1937] 2 All ER
d 646 at 649, [1937] AC 473 at 479 per Lord Atkin). The council had reason to suppose,
albeit wrongly as we find, that in some circumstances the transactions it proposed to
carry out during the interim strategy period were capable of being intra vires. During
the period of the interim strategy the legality of the earlier transactions was in dispute. If
those transactions were lawful then the council was exposed to a very considerable risk
indeed. While it is true that if the transactions were unlawful the council would probably
e be under no risk, this does not mean that prudent management did not require that the
risk should be reduced in case the transactions should prove to be enforceable. The
transactions existed, the council was not then in a position to repudiate its liability under
the transactions and if further transactions, which for this purpose must be assumed to
be capable of being within the powers of the council, were taken to reduce that risk, that
would be sensible management on the part of the council. A local authority owes, we
f consider, a duty to its ratepayers to preserve their funds from erosion due to anticipated
financial claims even if such claims result from imprudent or ultra vires actions on the
part of the authority itself and even if its anticipation of such claims proves groundless.
For this council simply to have ceased its capital market activities in August 1988 and
done nothing further would, in our judgment, have been irresponsible. In the absence
of any authority compelling the contrary conclusion, we cannot accept that the council,
g pending the clarification of the enforceability of the earlier transactions, was compelled
to stand by and take no action. We therefore conclude that if the transactions during this
period were capable of being lawful they were in fact lawful.

Transactions which are incapable of being used for interest risk management even if the
h *use of the transactions for interest risk management is authorised by the 1972 Act*
Where the council was acting as an intermediary and merely entering into swaps with
a view to obtaining a 'turn', for example to assist another council which was rate-capped
or whose credit standing was not as high as that of the council, then in our view the
transactions are self-evidently nothing to do with interest risk management.

We would take the same view of any transactions in which the council sold options or
j otherwise received premiums for entering into any of the transactions. The fact that in
this group of transactions the underlying contract would only be implemented in the
case of options if the interest rates moved against the council and if they did not the
council would make a profit indicates that the nature of the transactions is not such that
they can be regarded as falling within s 111 for the purposes of interest risk management.
It is true that Mr Eastment (the head of investment banking credit and risk at Midland

Bank plc) has managed to envisage circumstances where this group of transactions can be linked with interest risk management; however, we do not regard the link as being *a* sufficiently close. Into this group we would place selling of swap options, gilt option, cash option and caps, floors and collars.

Counsel for the auditor identified other groups, swaps, FRAs, the *purchase* of caps and floors and the purchase of swap options. We regard this category as being capable of being used for interest risk management. However, we would accept that whether they were to be so regarded would depend on the facts and whether, in the sense these terms *b* were used by counsel for the auditor, the transactions were open and current. Counsel for the auditor identified four criteria which he suggested would be relevant. Without lengthening this judgment even further by going into the criteria, we do agree that factors such as counsel identified would be relevant in determining the issues of fact.

The jurisdiction of the court under s 19 of the 1982 Act   *c*
The issues raised in these proceedings make it important to identify the court's role under s 19 of the 1982 Act. In many applications under s 19 there will be no possibility of the decision of the court affecting the rights of third parties under contracts with the local authority. However, in this case the banks are deeply concerned that their rights in relation to the transactions could be prejudiced by the decision of the court. It was this *d* concern which caused them to seek to be joined as parties to the proceedings.

If the banks had not been joined as parties to the proceedings, then the decision of the court would not have had any direct effect on them. Any declaration which the court made would resolve any issue which existed between the council and the auditor. However, the declaration would not affect third parties. It is for this reason that the auditor was not required by RSC Ord 98, rr 2 and 4 to serve the notice of motion on third parties such as the banks. Thus in *Re Hurle-Hobbs* [1944] 2 All ER 261 the Court of *e* Appeal held that a contractor was not entitled to be represented on an appeal against the disallowance of expenditure on sums paid to him because his legal rights were not affected by the disallowance, with the result that he was not a 'person aggrieved'.

However, this does not mean that it was not right for the banks to be represented and be parties to the present proceedings. These proceedings are unusual in that the council is conceding that it was acting ultra vires in entering into the transactions and it is *f* important that the banks who do not accept that this is the situation should have an opportunity of putting forward their arguments for taking a different view from that of the auditor and the council. While a declaration would not have affected them if they were not parties, it is clearly undesirable that a situation should arise where different courts could take a different view as to the legality of the activities of the council. If this court had not had the benefit of the arguments of the banks this would increase the *g* possibility of a conflict between the decision of the court in these proceedings and the decision of the court in proceedings between the council and the banks.

The intervention of the banks cannot, however, change the nature of the present proceedings, the jurisdiction of which is dependent on the terms of s 19 of the 1982 Act. Under that section what the court is concerned with is the correct auditing of the accounts of the council. The audit process is designed to protect the interests of the ratepayers, *h* who may have considerable difficulty in obtaining redress against the council in respect of wrongdoing except under the audit process and ss 19 and 20 of the 1982 Act.

While in theory judicial review may also be available in relation to performance by the auditor of his statutory role and in relation to the activities of the council, in practice, having regard to the remedies given to a local government elector under s 17(3) to make objection and the right of an objector to appeal to the court under ss 19 and 20, in the *j* ordinary case it may be difficult to persuade the court to grant leave on an application for judicial review.

'Contrary to law'
The fact that the auditor in performing his role is protecting the interests of the

ratepayers and that the local government electors in the area are also able to bring
a disputed items of account before the court indicates, in our view, that an item of account
'is contrary to law' when its treatment in the accounts, when considered from the point
of view of the ratepayers and the electors, is not in accordance with the law. We consider
that assistance as to the approach to the meaning of 'contrary to law' is to be derived from
the judgment of Boreham J in *Beecham v Metropolitan District Auditor* (1976) 75 LGR 79
at 83 where he said, in relation to the earlier provisions contained in the Local
b Government Act 1933:

> '. . . it is the item of account which must be contrary to law if it is to be disallowed,
> and I take that to mean, if I may enlist a paraphrase, that it must be an item which
> by law ought not to have appeared in the accounts; in other words, an item of
> expenditure which the council had no power to incur or which was incurred
> without authority, expenditure, in other words which was ultra vires. In my view
> c the accounts must contain every item of expenditure which was intra vires. They
> should not contain any item which was ultra vires or which was incurred without
> express authority.'

In adopting this approach, we would give a generous interpretation to what is an item
of account and what is to be said to be 'contrary to law'. We would also point out that the
d description of an item in an account or the omission of a provision may make an item
unlawful. However, for the purpose of these proceedings, it is not necessary to define
closely the parameters of what is contrary to law. However, what is important for the
purpose of these proceedings is the fact that in deciding whether or not an item is
contrary to law the auditor and, if proceedings are commenced, the court are not
normally required to determine whether or not a contract which is entered into by the
e council is enforceable by or against third parties because the item is associated with that
contract.

Where, however, the court is asked to make an order that the person responsible for
incurring or authorising any expenditure declared unlawful shall repay it in whole or in
part, it appears that a court must be concerned with the rights of third parties although
its decision would not normally be binding on them. This is because whether or not the
f council can recover the expenditure could be critical as to whether an order should be
made for repayment. On rectification of the accounts the court will be concerned
primarily to ensure they are in accordance with the law in the sense already indicated.

Discretion of the court
g   Furthermore, it is accepted by all parties in the proceedings, in our view rightly, that
the court has a discretion whether or not to make a declaration. The question therefore
arises as to whether the interests of third parties are a relevant matter to be taken into
account in deciding whether a declaration should be made. As to this, as we have come
to the conclusion that the declaration is not concerned with the enforceability of the
h rights of the council by or against third parties it is only logical to regard those rights as
not being relevant to the exercise of discretion.

This was a matter of importance to the banks because they were concerned that the
effect of granting a declaration could have a similar effect to a court declaring a transaction
void on an application for judicial review. The banks were concerned to argue that if the
position was the same as on an application for judicial review the court should not in any
j event grant a declaration as a matter of discretion, since it might be to their advantage to
be able to contend that even if those transactions with the council were void they were
perfectly valid until this had been declared. In our view, this concern is misplaced not
only because the declaration would not normally bind third parties but also because the
declaration relates to the items of account and not to any transactions to which the items
of account may relate.

However, if the lawfulness of a transaction to which an item relates has already been established, then that may be decisive as to the treatment of an item in the accounts. This is the explanation of the decision in R (Duckett) v Calvert [1898] 2 IR 511 which was strongly relied on by counsel for Barclays. If a court of competent jurisdiction had already decided the validity of a transaction between the council and the banks then the court on an application under s 19 would take that decision into account in deciding how the item should be dealt with in the accounts (see also Lord Sumner's speech in Roberts v Hopwood [1925] AC 578 at 603, [1925] All ER Rep 24 at 37).

The Rolled Steel point

It is now convenient to deal with what we will call 'the Rolled Steel point' (see Rolled Steel Products (Holdings) Ltd v British Steel Corp [1985] 3 All ER 52, [1986] Ch 246). The issue arises because of an argument which counsel for the banks advanced with considerable skill. He submits that there are three different situations which can make an item contrary to law for the purposes of s 19 of the 1982 Act.

(1) Where the contract under which a payment was made or was payable was void in the sense that it gave rise to no private law rights in either party. Counsel for the banks described this category as 'the void contract category'.

(2) Where the contract under which the payment is made or is payable is enforceable in the sense that the contract gives rise to private law rights and obligations but the contract is one into which a public body ought not as a matter of public law to have entered. This category he labels as 'the improper contract category'.

(3) Where the contract under which the payment was made or was payable was enforceable and was one in which it was proper for the public body to enter but the payment is made from a fund or source which ought not to be used for that purpose. This category he labels 'the improper payment category'.

Counsel for the banks submits that there is no problem with regard to the first category. In the case of contracts which fall within this category, which corresponds with the category identified in issue (1A) of Otton J's order, both from a public law point of view and a private law point of view the contract would not only be contrary to law but absolutely void; that is to say void for all purposes and properly described as ultra vires. No private rights could be obtained or given under such a contract. However, with regard to the second and third categories counsel submits there is a divergence between the situation viewed from a public law point of view and the situation viewed from a private law point of view. Judged under public law, payments made under such contracts could properly be described as being contrary to law but under private law they would not be void and could give rise to rights enforceable by third parties as long as third parties did not know and ought not to have known that the contract was improper or a payment was improper.

Counsel for the banks submits that this distinction between the first category and the other two categories could be critically important in this case to the banks. If he is right in his contention, then if the transactions which were entered into by the council were capable of being lawful but were only unlawful because of the purpose for which they were entered into or because they were Wednesbury unlawful or because the payments were made out of the wrong fund, the contracts would not be void and would be enforceable in private law against the council by the banks as long as the banks neither knew or ought to have known of the facts which would make them contrary to law.

Counsel for the banks accepts that there is no binding authority which indicates so far as public bodies are concerned that the difference between the categories which he would draw is right. However, he submits Roberts v Hopwood [1925] AC 578, [1925] All ER Rep 24 is an example of the second category and the views expressed by Lord Sumner ([1925] AC 578 at 603, [1925] All ER Rep 24 at 37) are consistent with his submissions. Similarly, in relation to the third category he relies on A-G v Newcastle-upon-Tyne Corp (1889) 23 QBD 492 and the passage in the speech of Lindley LJ (particularly at 500) when he *a* indicates that the contract 'in question is not illegal and void' and 'no injunction, therefore ought to be granted at present, but the Court ought to declare what can and cannot be done, and the plaintiffs ought to have liberty to apply for an injunction hereafter if the corporation should manifest an intention to misapply their funds'.

Counsel for the banks then submits that while the positon may not be clear with regard to the activities of public bodies, the position is now clear in relation to companies and the decisions which relate to companies should be applied by analogy to statutory *b* bodies so that the statute under which they are created is treated as being the equivalent of the memorandum of the company which sets out its objects.

That there is the clear distinction to which we will draw attention under company law we accept. We were referred to *Charterbridge Corp Ltd v Lloyds Bank Ltd* [1969] 2 All ER 1185 at 1189, [1970] Ch 62 at 69 and *Introductions Ltd v National Provincial Bank Ltd* [1969] 1 All ER 887, [1970] Ch 199, and in particular the decision of the Court of Appeal in *c* *Rolled Steel Products (Holdings) Ltd v British Steel Corp* [1985] 3 All ER 52, [1986] Ch 246. Those cases do establish that in company law the term 'ultra vires' should strictly be confined to describe the acts which are beyond the corporate capacity of a company, that is to say, outside its objects altogether, and not applied to situations where 'a transaction falls within the objects of the company (and is therefore within its capacity)'. Then, 'it is effective to vest rights in a third party even if the transaction was carried out in excess or *d* abuse of the powers of the company' (see [1985] 3 All ER 52 at 91, [1986] Ch 246 at 303 per Browne-Wilkinson LJ).

We recognise that the law in relation to ultra vires both in respect of public bodies and companies has a common source in the decision of the House of Lords in *Ashbury Railway Carriage and Iron Co Ltd v Riche* (1875) LR 7 HL 653 and the argument advanced by counsel for the banks could provide a satisfactory foundation for reconciling the interests *e* of third parties who have private rights against a public body and the duties which the public body, if this is a public authority, owes to its ratepayers. We also, however, appreciate, as was strongly argued on behalf of the council and the auditor, that there are difficulties in applying the *Rolled Steel* principle to public bodies which have a very different constitution to that of a company. We are also mindful that the argument of counsel for the banks makes statutory provisions which are designed to protect third *f* parties, such as para 20 of Sch 13 to the Local Government Act 1972 (which protect persons lending money from being bound to inquire whether the borrowing of the money is legal or regular) superfluous.

A decision on this subject would be of great significance. We have come to the conclusion that it would be wrong for us to do more than recognise the force of the argument of counsel for the banks without expressing any conclusion upon it. Our *g* reasons for this conclusion are as follows: having regard to our decision that the transactions fall within issue (1A) the point does not even indirectly arise. Even if we had come to a different decision and regarded the transactions as falling within issue (1B) the point would still not directly arise and would only need to be considered if our earlier view as to discretion was wrong in so far as it could possibly influence us in our view as *h* to whether or not it was appropriate to grant a declaration. Counsel for the banks accepts that his argument does not affect whether an item is contrary to law, it merely affects the consequences of an item being contrary to law in cases where the transactions are capable of being lawful. Our conclusions on this subject would therefore certainly be obiter and the parties might be in difficulties in challenging them on appeal in these proceedings. If the issue is to be ventilated, it is preferable for it to be finally determined in proceedings *j* between the banks and the council in which the issue directly arises.

Public rights and private rights

Counsel for Barclays advanced a separate argument from that advanced by counsel for the banks based on the *Rolled Steel* case. He submits that it is now well established by a series of authorities that the English legal system has a separate procedure and separate remedies for enforcing public duties from those which exist for establishing private rights, that an inevitable consequence of those separate procedures and remedies is that it is now necessary to draw a distinction between the consequences on its position in public law of a public authority being in breach of its public duty from the consequences on its position and duties in private law under a contract.

Again we appreciate the force of the argument which is being advanced by counsel for Barclays. The extent of the supervision of the court over the performance by public bodies of their functions has undoubtedly been extended over the years but so far what flows from a decision being quashed by the courts or, equally important, from a decision being liable to be quashed by the courts because a power or duty entrusted to a public body has not been properly exercised according to public law, has not been laid down by the courts. Unlike the majority of Continental legal systems, in English law contracts entered into by public bodies are subject to the ordinary procedures of and are governed by private law. Counsel for Barclays submits that a line has to be drawn limiting the consequences to third parties of a public body being in breach of its public law obligations. He accepts that if a public body is incapable of lawfully doing what it has done (an issue (1A) situation) then that has the same consequences in public or private law. However, he submits that if the public body is perfectly capable of entering into a private obligation but has gone outside its powers because of the reasons for which or the manner in which it has entered into that obligation then this should not adversely affect a third party at least if that third party did not know and ought not to have known that there was anything wrong with the transaction.

We are aware that there are authorities, particularly in the field of local authorities acting as landlord, which can be said to be inconsistent with the submission of counsel for Barclays. However, the argument which counsel is advancing was not raised in those decisions and there are dangers in reading too much into a decision where the only issue which was involved was whether a party was abusing the process of the court. It is possible, for example, that the position will be different where the person seeking to rely on the improper exercise of its powers by a public body is a person to whom both public law and private law obligations are owed as in the case of a tenant. There is also the problem, which has not yet been tackled by the courts, of integrating into private law proceedings in which private rights are involved the discretions which are built into judicial review and which can deprive a litigant in judicial review of a remedy to which he would otherwise be entitled.

However, again the implications involved in this issue, which we have stated not in precisely the same terms as counsel, are extremely far-reaching and for the same reasons which we have indicated in the case of the argument of counsel for the banks we again do not feel that it is right to express any firm view.

What we have said, however, in relation to both arguments may achieve the object which the banks sought to achieve. This is that we accept that if as a consequence of this judgment we grant any declaration under s 19 of the 1982 Act, that declaration does not prevent the banks from contending that if the transactions were capable of being entered into lawfully, they do not inevitably adversely affect the banks' rights.

The exercise of discretion

This is the final matter with which we should deal. If as a result of our judgment we are required by the auditor to consider granting him a declaration, then while we accept that we have a discretion to refuse to grant a declaration, we can see no reason why we should exercise that discretion adversely to the auditor. The only matter which caused us to question whether it was appropriate to exercise our discretion against the auditor was the fact that during the interim strategy the further transactions were entered into with his knowledge. However, while his acquiescence pending the receipt of counsel's advice might be significant if the transactions were capable of being lawful, as in our view they a were not, having regard to our conclusions on issue (1A) we can see no reason why we should not exercise our discretion to grant a declaration, subject to any further arguments of the parties.

Appendix A

Swaps

b A swap is an agreement between two parties by which each agrees to pay the other on a specified date or dates an amount calculated by reference to the interest which would have accrued over a given period on the same notional principal sum assuming different rates of interest are payable in each case. For example, one rate may be fixed at 10% and the other rate may be equivalent to the six-month London Inter-Bank Offered Rate (LIBOR). If the LIBOR rate over the period of the swap is higher than 10% then the party

c agreeing to receive 'interest' in accordance with LIBOR will receive more than the party entitled to receive the 10%. Normally neither party will in fact pay the sums which it has agreed to pay over the period of the swap but instead will make a settlement on a 'net payment basis' under which the party owing the greater amount on any day simply pays the difference between the two amounts due to the other.

There are a considerable number of variations of detail possible in a swap transaction

d but the council only engaged in swaps of fixed and variable rates in a single currency, namely sterling.

Reverse swaps

The council also entered into reverse swaps. A reverse swap is a swap in which a party to a previous swap agrees to make payments calculated by reference to the type of interest

e which he is to receive under the earlier swap and to receive payments calculated by reference to the type of interest on which he is to make payments under the first swap. So if he is paying a variable rate under the first swap under the second swap he will be paying a fixed rate. If the variable rate in each swap is calculated in the same way, the party's net position on the two swaps will depend on the margin between the two fixed rates. A reverse swap may therefore, subject to the other risks involved, limit the loss or

f secure the profits which a party would receive without exposing him to the consequences of further interest rate movements.

Swap options

A swap option is an agreement by which one party (the seller) agrees in return for a premium that the other party (the purchaser) shall have the right to require the seller to

g enter into a swap on agreed terms at a later date. The option may be European or American. The former can only be exercised on a specified future date while the latter can be exercised over a specified period. The agreement may provide for cash settlement under which the purchaser receives if he exercises his option the sum equivalent to the profit he might expect to receive under the swap discounted to reflect its accelerated

h receipt.

Caps, floors and collars

A cap is a transaction in which the seller of the cap will make a payment or payments to the buyer if interest rates rise above a rate specified in the agreement (the cap rate). The payment to be made will be calculated by reference to the amount by which the

j current variable rate exceeds the cap rate applied to a notional principal sum specified in the agreement for an agreed period of time. In return the purchaser pays the seller a premium fee for entering into the cap. The transaction thus enables the purchaser in return for a premium to insure against the consequences of interest rates rising above a predetermined level. An interest rate floor is the reverse of a cap. There is a dispute between Mr Eastment and the auditor as to what technically constitutes a collar.

However, as the council only entered into a collar of the 'auditor's variety' for the purposes of this case, we can use the auditor's definition, which is an agreement in which both a cap and a floor are sold in the same transaction. The council in fact sold three collars of this type with a notional principal of £30m. In these transactions, if the rate fell below the lowest specified fixed rate of interest or rose above the highest specified fixed rate of interest during the lifetime of the transaction, the council, the seller, was obliged to make payments to the buyer. By the transaction the buyer insures that if the rates of interest move outside an agreed range he will receive payment from the seller, here the council.

Forward rate agreements

An FRA is an agreement under which one party undertakes to make to the other party payments calculated by reference to a specified rate on a notional principal sum in respect of a period in the future and the other party agrees to make a payment calculated by reference to a variable rate on the same notional principal over the same future period.

Gilt or cash options

It is not necessary to give an explanation of gilt and cash options, which are more well-known transactions. A feature to be noted about the options entered into by the council is that frequently settlement, if the option is exercised (because in the case of call options of gilts the price of gilts has risen above the option price or in the case of cash options rates of interest have risen above the agreed rate), does not necessarily involve physical delivery of the gilts or the entering into the cash agreement. Usually settlement is made by the seller making a cash payment to the purchaser.

Appendix B

The auditor summarised the extent of the council's dealings as follows:

Instrument	No of deals	Notional principal sum
Interest rate swaps (including reversed swaps)	183	£1,563m
Interest rate swap options	218	£2,570m
Interest rate caps	26	£ 290m
Interest rate floors	14	£ 155m
Interest rate collars	3	£ 30m
Gilt options	107	£1,135m
Forward rate agreements	26	£ 240m
Cash options	15	£ 69·5m
	592	£6,052·5m

The figure of over £6 bn is of course not an amount which in any event would be payable but indicates the figures by reference to which interest and other payments are to be calculated.

At 31 March 1989 the auditor indicated that the council's portfolio may be summarised as follows:

Instrument	No of deals	Notional principal sum
Interest rate swaps (including reversed swaps)	114	£1,009m
Interest rate swap options	110	£1,255m
Interest rate caps	26	£ 290m
Interest rate floors	14	£ oxf,155m

Interest rate collars	3	£ 30m
Gilt options	16	£ 190m
Forward rate agreements	nil	nil
Cash options	14	£ 67m
	297	£2,996m

b   This portfolio can usefully be contrasted with the council's estimated total expenditure for the year 1988–89 of £85·7m, its capital budget of £44·6m and its total debt (representing outstanding borrowing incurred to undertake capital projects over many years) of £390m at 31 March 1989.

c *The swaps*
    Of the 114 interest rate swaps referred to in the above table 42 comprised 21 open interest swaps, which were matched by a further 21 reverse swaps. The remaining 72 swaps were, with one exception, swaps in which the council is the variable interest rate payer and receives payments calculated by reference to a fixed rate of interest, thus exposing the council to the risk of adverse movements in interest rates.
d   In the case of the 21 swaps which were matched by a further 21 reverse swaps, in most of the reverse swaps the council contracted to receive payment by reference to a higher fixed rate than the fixed rate by reference to which it had contracted to pay matched deals so on these the transactions the council had an estimated secure profit of £1·5m over the life of the transactions. In seven of the reverse interest swaps the council was acting as an interemediary receiving a marginal profit for assuming the credit risk which
e one party would incur if they contracted directly with the other. An example cited by the auditor is the reverse swap entered into by the council with Chemical Bank on the one hand and Haringey London Borough Council (Haringey) on the other. Haringey at the material time was rate-capped and according to Haringey's district auditor wished to raise money to assist in maintaining a level of expenditure above the cap with the income
f from rates, block grants, rents and other charges.

Swap options
    All but one of the 218 interest rate swap options which were entered into by the council were sold rather than purchased. The only purchase was from another local borough council. If the options are exercised the council will be required to make
g payment by reference to six months LIBOR and in present circumstances will receive what will be a much lower rate of interest, which means that the council will suffer a significant loss unless there is a material decline in interest rates. A number of these swap options had a feature which is known as a 'mandatory cash exercise strangle option'. This means that if the option is exercised, the seller of the option (here the council) is required
h to make a cash settlement calculated by reference to the profit which the counter-party would expect to achieve over the life of the notional swap, discounted to reflect accelerated receipt. This enables the counter-party to realise a gain without the risk that interest rates might subsequently move against him during the life of the swap. In 27 such transactions the counter-party has exercised the option and in accord with the strangle provision acquired a once and for all cash payment resulting in the respective banks earning a profit of approximately £10m at the expense of the council.
j   Approximately 60% of the options sold by the council were 'straddle' or 'double' options. In these transactions the council sold two options under which, unless option rates remained within a limited band, the option would be exercised at the expense of the council, who would be required to make a cash payment in accordance with the strangle option.

Caps and floors

Of the caps which the council entered into 18 were sold by the council and 8 were *a* purchased. Of the floors, 11 were sold and 3 were purchased. The council has so far profited from the selling of floors. The 3 floors were all sold so the council was in effect betting on interest rates remaining within the band set by the cap and floor.

Gilt options and cash options

Up to 8 November 1988 the council had not purchased any gilt options but had sold *b* 84 gilt options. They later sold a further four. The council was apparently continuing to sell gilt options during the period of the interim strategy until the auditor pointed out that the correct action to take in order to reduce interest risks was to purchase options rather than sell options. Each of the cash options was sold by the council. Only one of these options has been exercised and then only exercised in part and cancelled in part. Because of the current interest rate the remaining options are unlikely to be exercised. *c* The council's loss in respect of the gilt options will be small and in the case of the cash options it appears likely that they will make a profit of over £300,000.

Forward rate agreements

By 31 March 1989 none of the 26 FRAs in which the council was involved was current. Fourteen had been sold and 12 purchased, all on a mandatory cash settlement basis. The *d* council's loss on the transactions is modest in relation to the position as a whole, amounting to £218,000 including brokerage.

The overall picture is, however, a grave one for the council unless because the transactions are unlawful they cannot be enforced against the council by the banks and the other parties who have entered into them. In February 1989 Deloittes were asked to form an assessment of the risk with which the council is faced if it is obliged to honour *e* its obligations under the transactions. The conclusion, which is not a precise one, which Deloittes came to is that at the date of valuation, which was February 1989, the council would have to pay something like £69·1m to someone to acquire its portfolio. This figure would be substantially in excess of that figure now because of the rise in interest rates actually received, down to the date it ceased payment. Although the council has so far a surplus in relation to the transactions the results of its activities has exposed its *f* ratepayers to very substantial losses if the transactions are enforceable.

Application granted.

Dilys Tausz Barrister.

g

Appeal

The banks and Barclays appealed.

h

Gordon Pollock QC, Rhodri Davies and *Alan Griffiths* for the banks.
Nicholas Chambers QC and *Catharine Otton-Goulder* for Barclays.
Anthony Scrivener QC and *Catherine Newman* for the council.
John Howell for the auditor.

Cur adv vult *j*

28 February. The following judgment of the court was delivered.

SIR STEPHEN BROWN P. This is the judgment of the court. It is given on an appeal against a decision of the Queen's Bench Divisional Court (Woolf LJ and French J) given

on 1 November 1989. On the application of Mr Hazell (the auditor) under s 19(1) of the
Local Government Finance Act 1982 the Divisional Court made a declaration 'that the
items of account appearing within the Capital Markets Fund Account of the Council of
the London Borough of Hammersmith and Fulham for the financial years beginning on
1st April 1987 and 1st April 1988 [are] contrary to law' and ordered that the accounts of
that council for those years be rectified. That order is not challenged on appeal, and was
not opposed below, by the council, which was, as RSC Ord 98, r 2(2) requires, the
respondent to the auditor's notice of originating motion. The resistance of the auditor's
application, below and on appeal, has been mounted by the other respondents, all of
them banks which (among others) entered into transactions with the council (or, it may
be, the corporation of the London Borough of Hammersmith and Fulham). Before this
court Barclays Bank plc (Barclays) and the other appellant banks (the banks) have been
represented by separate counsel. Save on one point the banks and Barclays have
substantially made common cause.

The joinder of the banks and Barclays as respondents to the auditor's application
against the council was on their own application. They feared that, if the items in the
accounts of the council to which the auditor objected were declared to be contrary to law,
this would or might prejudice their right to enforce a number of outstanding contracts.
They accordingly applied to be joined in order to defend their commercial interests, and
the application was granted.

Before the hearing of the auditor's application by the Divisional Court an interlocutory
order was made on 21 September 1989 that certain issues only be heard in the first
instance and that the remaining issues be deferred. The issues ordered to be heard were:

'(1A) Whether transactions within the eight categories referred to in paragraph 4
of the affidavit sworn by the [auditor] herein on 30th May 1989 are capable of being
within the powers conferred on local authorities by Parliament;
(1B) If so, whether transactions within all or any of those categories were in fact
entered into by the [council] in a proper exercise of those powers;
(2) Whether the transactions were not such that a reasonable authority could
have engaged in organised as the [council] was;
(3) Whether the transactions were authorised properly or at all by the [council];
(4) Whether the Capital Markets Fund was validly established or maintained by
the [council].'

The issues ordered to be deferred related (a) to the enforceability of contracts by the banks
or Barclays if the auditor was wrong on issue (1A) but right on any other issue, and (b) if
the auditor was right on any issue, to the restitutionary rights of the respective contracting
parties.

The Divisional Court answered issue (1A) in the auditor's favour. All parties before us
accepted that this answer, if correct, renders unenforceable any outstanding claim by the
banks and Barclays against the council and must, since issue (1A) raises an issue of pure
principle, preclude successful claims on similar facts by any other bank against the
council or by any bank against any other local authority. It seems clear on the evidence
before us that this result would cause the banks losses running into many millions of
pounds.

Having decided issue (1A) in the auditor's favour, it was strictly unnecessary for the
Divisional Court to decide the other issues, but it helpfully expressed its views on these
issues in case it was wrong on issue (1A). Making the assumption (contrary to their
decision) that transactions of the kind in question might in principle be lawfully entered
into by a local authority, the Divisional Court was broadly of opinion that issues (1B) to
(4) inclusive should also be decided in the auditor's favour, although they qualified that
opinion in respect of the period up to March 1987 and after August 1988. Even on the
assumption stated the Divisional Court was of opinion that the council's capital market
activities between those dates could not be justified.

The items of account which the auditor challenges relate to what have for convenience been generically described as interest rate swaps, but the genus comprises financial transactions more specifically called interest rate swaps, interest rate swap options, interest rate caps, interest rate floors, interest rate collars, forward rate agreements, gilt options and cash options. In Appendix A to its judgment the Divisional Court has given a clear and succinct explanation of these transactions which has not been criticised and which therefore we gratefully adopt and need not repeat (see pp 63–64, ante). But it is important to see these transactions in context.

The contract for the loan of money is one of the oldest known to the law and it is in essence very simple. A makes money available to B for a period in consideration of B's covenant to repay the money during or at the end of the period and to pay interest on the sum outstanding until repayment. Like all commercial transactions this is not free of risk, the most obvious being that B will be unwilling or unable to repay. But even if B's financial integrity and credit are unimpeachable, risk of a less obvious kind remains. If the rate of interest is fixed and market rates rise over the period of the loan, the contract, although advantageous to B, leaves A out of his money and earning a reward less than it would command in the market. Conversely, if rates fall the contract benefits A, but results in B paying more for the use of A's money than he would if he contracted afresh. If the contractual rate of interest is expressed to be variable it may be assumed that the rate payable will follow the market, perhaps subject to some time lag, but risk is not thereby eliminated. If interest rates fall over the period of the loan A will earn less than he expected and may have relied on. If interest rates rise B may find the burden of repayment greater than he expected or budgeted for, and may in an extreme case find that the project for which he borrowed the money is turned from profit into loss by the increased cost of borrowing. In a genuinely commercial context, where the lessening of risk and uncertainty will almost always be desirable, it is understandable that both A and B will seek for their own differing reasons to protect themselves against changes in the market rate of interest which might prove prejudicial to their respective interests.

If B has borrowed at a fixed rate for a term and market rates have fallen below that fixed rate, his most obvious remedy is of course to borrow at the lower market rate and use the proceeds of the loan to repay A. But the fall in the market which makes it advantageous for B to repay A makes it correspondingly disadvantageous for A at that time to receive premature repayment. So, subject always to the terms of the contract, A will attempt to ensure that the price payable by B on premature redemption so far as possible compensates A for the loss he will necessarily suffer on re-lending in the market at a less favourable rate. Once the fall has occurred, therefore, it may not be open to B simply to replace his existing borrowing with a new loan at a lower rate of interest without significant expense. The desirability from B's point of view of protecting himself in advance is obvious.

To meet the legitimate concerns of parties such as A and B a new market has grown up over the last decade, trading in interest rate swaps and the other related transactions we have mentioned. The volume of trade has been enormous and the range of institutions participating in the market diverse. We do not think it useful or necessary to retail examples of situations in which these transactions may for legitimate commercial reasons be entered into, although many notional examples have been elaborated for our consideration. It suffices to say, without at this stage differentiating between the different types of transaction or different classes of participant, that these are transactions into which a prudent institution may bona fide enter for the purpose of lessening risk and reducing uncertainty, whether by seeking to maximise the return to A or to minimise the effective (or net) rate of interest which B may be obliged to pay. So used they provide (in effect, but not of course in law) a form of insurance.

This conclusion does not have as its corollary that this market may not, like others, be used for purposes of pure speculation. It undoubtedly may. Futures markets are notoriously attractive to wealthy gamblers, but a chocolate manufacturer who enters the

market in cocoa futures to protect himself against loss on a future purchase of physical
a cocoa is not a gambler. If A and B, independently of any other transaction, agree to make
payment one to the other depending on the market value of one currency in relation to
another on a specified date in the future, they are wagering. But if a banker who has
agreed to sell foreign currency to a customer at a future date at its then market value
makes a back-to-back purchase contract, he is simply ensuring that he cannot lose. In the
interest rate swap market, as in these others, the true commercial character of a
b transaction will become apparent only when the full circumstances of it are examined. If
a transaction of this kind is not to be regarded as speculative trading, however, it must be
made, by one party at least, with clear reference to an underlying obligation or asset.

Hammersmith council entered into its first relevant deal, an interest rate swap in the
strict sense, in December 1983. Between that date and March 1987 it entered into some,
but very few, transactions and those into which it did enter were swaps. The items of
c account which the auditor challenges relate to the two financial years of the council's
accounts which follow this period, but the period is relevant because transactions entered
into then could have financial consequences during the financial years under review. But
the Divisional Court held (see p 56, ante):

> 'During the first period (December 1983 to March 1987) the limited nature of
d the council's activities does not enable us to hold that it was not engaged in interest
risk management.'

By 'interest risk management' the Divisional Court meant use of these transactions for
legitimate as opposed to speculative profit-making purposes.

Between April 1987 and July 1988 the council's participation in this market increased
very markedly, both in volume and in the range of transactions entered into. The
e Divisional Court has given figures (see pp 41, 64–65, ante). These figures are, as the
Divisional Court emphasised, to be treated with caution, since in a more complicated
transaction the principal of the original transaction may be duplicated several times over.
In respect of this period the Divisional Court was of opinion that (see p 56, ante):

> 'The scale and range of transactions makes it clear that the council was not
f engaged in interest risk management but engaged in a trade designed to exploit the
market in these transactions with a view to profit.'

But the Divisional Court also observed (see p 56, ante):

> 'It is not possible to identify precisely the date on which that trade commenced;
all that can be said is that it started towards the beginning of this period. If in
subsequent proceedings it is necessary to identify the precise date on which the trade
g commenced then that would require more detailed examination than is possible in
these proceedings.'

In July 1988 the auditor received from the Audit Commission written opinions of
counsel on the legality of transactions of the type into which the council had entered.
These opinions showed some divergence of view between leading and junior counsel but
h both counsel agreed that most transactions of this type, if entered into by a local authority,
would be unlawful. On receipt of these opinions the auditor investigated the situation of
the council and discovered the nature and range of its activities in this field. The opinions
were drawn to the attention of the council, which naturally wished to seek its own
advice. This took some months, during which an interim strategy of containment and
gradual extrication from the market was followed. The Divisional Court's conclusion on
j this period is (see p 57, ante):

> 'If transactions which were undertaken as part of interest risk management were
capable of being within the powers of the Act, then in our view so must activities
which the council undertook with a view to minimising the risks to which the
council was exposed by earlier transactions.'

The view that no transaction of this kind may lawfully be entered into by a local authority, however prudent and however closely related to the local authority's *a* management of its assets and debts, is one which junior counsel for the auditor first expressed in July 1988 and has argued on behalf of the auditor in the Divisional Court and before us. It is a view which runs counter to what appears to have been the trend of orthodox opinion before July 1988. In an article entitled 'Recent developments in the swap market' the Bank of England Quarterly Bulletin (1987) vol 27, p 66 suggested:

> 'Swaps provide a mechanism for exploiting market imperfections and are also a *b* valuable technique for managing financial flows—on both the liability and asset side. As such they are widely used by all kinds of institution in the financial, corporate and government sectors.'

In its annual report for 1986–87 the Audit Commission, having referred to 'front end premiums on interest swaps' and 'so called parallel loans', accepted that it was 'right that *c* local authorities should take advantage of the opportunities to reduce borrowing costs offered by new types of financial instrument', although the commission warned of possible dangers. In July 1987 the (unpublished) opinion of the solicitor to the commission was that interest rate swaps as part of the normal process of debt management were within the powers of local authorities. In August 1987 the controller of the commission, addressing a conference of local government auditors, described interest *d* rate swaps as 'a legitimate tool of debt management', a description publicised in a contemporaneous news release of the commission. If, until the auditor's intervention, the council and the banks dealing with it believed transactions of this kind to be lawful if genuinely used for purposes of debt or asset management, they were not alone. The evidence shows that many local authorities entered into this market, but none entered into as many or as varied transactions as the council. *e*

The auditor is a chartered accountant in private practice appointed by the Audit Commission under s 13 of the Local Government Finance Act 1982 to audit the accounts of the council. His general duties are prescribed by s 15(1) and (2) of that Act:

> '(1) In auditing any accounts required to be audited in accordance with this Part of this Act, an auditor shall by examination of the accounts and otherwise satisfy *f* himself—(a) that the accounts are prepared in accordance with regulations made under section 23 below and comply with the requirements of all other statutory provisions applicable to the accounts; (b) that proper practices have been observed in the compilation of the accounts; and (c) that the body whose accounts are being audited has made proper arrangements for securing economy, efficiency and effectiveness in its use of resources. *g*
> (2) The auditor shall comply with the code of audit practice as for the time being in force.'

The code referred to, that is the code provided for by s 14, makes plain that an auditor's function is to check not only the regularity of a local authority's accounts, but also the efficiency of its financial and commercial management, while not questioning the policy *h* of the authority.

Section 19 of the Act, on which the auditor's present application is founded, provides in sub-ss (1) and (2):

> '(1) Where it appears to the auditor carrying out the audit of any accounts under this Part of this Act that any item of account is contrary to law he may apply to the *j* court for a declaration that the item is contrary to law except where it is sanctioned by the Secretary of State.
> (2) On an application under this section the court may make or refuse to make the declaration asked for, and where the court makes that declaration, then, subject to subsection (3) below, it may also—(a) order that any person responsible for

a incurring or authorising any expenditure declared unlawful shall repay it in whole or in part to the body in question and, where two or more persons are found to be responsible, that they shall be jointly and severally liable to repay it as aforesaid; (b) if any such expenditure exceeds £2,000 and the person responsible for incurring or authorising it is, or was at the time of his conduct in question, a member of a local authority, order him to be disqualified for being a member of a local authority for a specified period; and (c) order rectification of the accounts.'

b The Secretary of State was asked by the council to sanction the items of account which the auditor challenges, but declined to do so. No order has been sought against any person responsible for incurring or authorising any expenditure.

Section 19(1) of the 1982 Act re-enacts s 161(1) of the Local Government Act 1972. That section differed in its effect from its predecessor section (s 228(1) of the Local Government Act 1933), but the expression 'contrary to law' may be traced back at least c to s 247(7) of the Public Health Act 1875. The decided cases since that date have clearly illustrated the grounds on which items of account may be held to be contrary to law. Such a conclusion may be reached where the items of account relate to payments which were not authorised by the duty of the authority, or were contrary to the duty of the authority, or were beyond the powers of the authority, or were made in the exercise of a d discretion vitiated by misdirection, consideration of irrelevant matters, failure to consider relevant matters or gross unreasonableness: see *Thomas v Devonport Corp* [1900] 1 QB 16, *R v Roberts* [1908] 1 KB 407 and *Roberts v Hopwood* [1925] AC 578, [1925] All ER Rep 24. Breach of the fiduciary duty owed by a local authority to its ratepayers would found a s 19 application: see *Roberts v Hopwood* [1925] AC 578, [1925] All ER Rep 24 *Prescott v Birmingham Corp* [1954] 3 All ER 698, [1955] Ch 210 and *Bromley London BC v Greater* e *London Council* [1982] 1 All ER 129, [1983] 1 AC 768. In short, the auditor is entitled to seek relief if he can show that an item of account is for any reason unlawful or improper.

We do not understand the foregoing summary to be controversial. We would, however, emphasise two points: (1) as Lord Sumner pointed out in *Roberts v Hopwood* [1925] AC 578 at 604, [1925] All ER Rep 24 at 37, the purpose of the audit is to ensure wise and prudent administration and to protect the ratepayers' pockets; and (2) while an f auditor may obtain a declaration that an item of account is contrary to law on a very wide variety of grounds, any one of which may entitle the court to surcharge any person responsible, the ground of unlawfulness established may have a crucial bearing on the rights of a third party to enforce an outstanding claim against a local authority.

Suppose, for example, that a local authority paid the first instalment under a contract into which the authority was statutorily prohibited from entering. The auditor would, g in the absence of extraordinary circumstances, obtain a declaration under s 19 that the relevant item of account was contrary to law. The other contracting party, if a party to the application, would plainly be estopped from seeking to enforce payment of any subsequent instalment. If not a party to the application, he would not be estopped, but could succeed only if he could persuade a court called on to enforce a claim for any subsequent instalment that the earlier decision had been wrong and should not be h followed. This result is to be contrasted (for instance) with a case falling within para 20 of Sch 13 to the 1972 Act, which provides:

'A person lending money to a local authority shall not be bound to inquire whether the borrowing of the money is legal or regular or whether the money raised was properly applied and shall not be prejudiced by any illegality or j irregularity, or by the misapplication or non-application of any of that money.'

If the local authority has borrowed money illegally or irregularly or has misapplied or failed to apply it, an auditor may no doubt be entitled to his declaration under s 19, but it seems plain that the rights of the other contracting party are not thereby prejudiced. The same is so in a case governed by s 135(4) of the 1972 Act, which provides:

'A person entering into a contract with a local authority shall not be bound to inquire whether the standing orders of the authority which apply to the contract have been complied with, and non-compliance with such orders shall not invalidate any contract entered into by or on behalf of the authority.'

The same may be so where the declaration under s 19 is made on some at least of the grounds familiar in the field of judicial review. In *Roberts v Hopwood* [1925] AC 578 at 602–603, [1925] All ER Rep 24 at 36–37 Lord Sumner did not doubt the validity of the contract to pay wages at the specified rate as between the council and its employees, but upheld the auditor's decision to disallow a proportion of such wages as contrary to law because they were unreasonable in amount and paid in the improper exercise of a discretion. The making of a declaration under s 19 does not, of itself and without more, preclude a party who has made an apparently valid contract with a local authority from enforcing the contract.

The legal capacity of the corporation as a body incorporated by charter
Of the various issues raised on the appeals, it is convenient to consider first a submission made by the banks, but not by Barclays. This raised a somewhat arcane point, founded on the distinction, which in law undoubtedly exists, between the municipal corporation of a borough and the council of a borough. In the present case the municipal corporation, to which we shall refer as 'the corporation', is a body incorporated by a royal charter granted on 10 March 1964 by virtue of the royal prerogative and in pursuance of the London Government Act 1963. By the charter the inhabitants of the area comprising the newly-created 'London Borough of Hammersmith', as it was then known, were incorporated by the name of 'The Mayor, Aldermen and Burgesses of the London Borough of Hammersmith'. In contrast, Hammersmith council is not a corporate body. Paragraph 1(2) of Pt I of Sch 2 to the 1972 Act provided that for every London borough there should be a council consisting of the mayor and councillors. This superseded a provision in the 1963 Act (s 1(6)) which had the same effect, save that the 1972 Act omitted reference to aldermen. The council was to exercise 'all such functions as are vested in the municipal corporation of the borough or in the council of the borough by this Act or otherwise'. Shortly stated, the banks' argument was that the swap transactions under challenge were entered into by the banks with the corporation, which is a legal entity, and not with Hammersmith council, which does not in law exist as a legal entity, and that the corporation, as a body incorporated by charter, has all the powers of a natural person. Hence there can be no question of the swap transactions being ultra vires.

Several points arise on this submission. First, as to the legal capacity of a chartered corporation. Viewing it through the eyes of twentieth century lawyers, one might have expected to look to the charter itself to see what the activities of the body were intended to be and, hence, to see what were to be the limits to its legal capacity, in the same way as one looks at the objects clause in the memorandum of association of a company formed under the Companies Acts. In the present case the charter provided that the corporation should have the powers, authorities, immunities and privileges usually vested by law in the mayor, aldermen and burgesses of a municipal corporation. But for a long time now it has been generally accepted that *Sutton's Hospital Case* (1612) 10 Co Rep 1a, [1558–1774] All ER Rep 11 decided that a corporation created by charter, as distinct from a corporation created by or under a statute, has the same power to contract as a natural person and that this is so regardless of the terms of the charter of incorporation. On this it is sufficient to refer to dicta in two cases. In *Riche v Ashbury Railway Carriage and Iron Co Ltd* (1874) LR 9 Exch 224 at 263–264 Blackburn J said, with regard to the *Sutton's Hospital* case:

'This seems to me an express authority that at common law it is an incident to a corporation to use its common seal for the purpose of binding itself to anything to

a
which a natural person could bind himself, and to deal with its property as a natural person might deal with his own. And further, that an attempt to forbid this on the part of the King, even by express negative words, does not bind at law. Nor am I aware of any authority in conflict with this case. If there are conditions contained in the charter that the corporation shall not do particular things, and these things are nevertheless done, it gives ground for a proceedings by sci. fa. in the name of the Crown to repeal the letters patent creating the corporation: see *Reg. v. Eastern*

b
Archipelago Company ((1853) 2 E & B 856, 118 ER 988). But if the Crown take no such steps, it does not, as I conceive, lie in the mouth either of the corporation, or of the person who has contracted with it, to say that the contract into which they have entered was void as beyond the capacity of the corporation. I am aware of no decision by which a corporation at common law has been permitted to do so. I take it that the true rule of law is, that a corporation at common law has, as an incident

c
given by law, the same power to contract, and subject to the same restrictions, that a natural person has.'

Next, the very well known passage in the judgment of Bowen LJ in *Baroness Wenlock v River Dee Co* (1883) 36 Ch D 675 at 685:

d
'At common law a corporation created by the King's charter has, *primâ facie*, and has been known to have ever since *Sutton's Hospital Case* ((1612) 10 Co Rep 1a, [1558–1774] All ER Rep 11), the power to do with its property all such acts as an ordinary person can do, and to bind itself to such contracts as an ordinary person can bind himself to; and even if by the charter creating the corporation the King imposes some direction which would have the effect of limiting the natural capacity

e
of the body of which he is speaking, the common law has always held that the direction of the King might be enforced through the Attorney-General; but although it might contain an essential part of the so-called bargain between the Crown and the corporation, that did not at law destroy the legal power of the body which the King had created.'

f
More recent affirmations of these principles can be found in the judgment of Viscount Haldane in *Bonanza Creek Gold Mining Co Ltd v R* [1916] 1 AC 566 at 583–584, [1916–17] All ER Rep 999 at 1007–1008 and in the speech of Lord Denning in *Institution of Mechanical Engineers v Cane* [1960] 3 All ER 715 at 728–729, [1961] AC 696 at 724–725.

Arising from these two passages a further important point is to be noted. It is that care must be taken when using terms such as 'capacity' and 'powers' in this context. In the context now under consideration, the issue being addressed is the legal capacity of a

g
corporation. At common law a chartered corporation has the 'capacity', as a legal entity, to do acts even though these may be unauthorised as outside conditions or directions contained in the charter. The corporation has no 'power' lawfully to carry out such unauthorised acts, and the doing of them may be restrained by injunction (see *Jenkin v Pharmaceutical Society of GB* [1921] 1 Ch 392). Today, in appropriate cases, relief would be available by way of judicial review. And steps can be taken to repeal the charter. But, if

h
not restrained, such acts are none the less valid in law in the sense that they are not, as between the corporation and those contracting with it, void for being beyond the capacity of the corporation.

In the present case, as already noted, the corporation's charter was not granted by virtue of the royal prerogative alone. It was granted by virtue of the royal prerogative

j
and in pursuance of the 1963 Act. On this a question of statutory construction arises. But before identifying or addressing this question of contruction, we must sketch in barest outline some of the complicated legislative history, so that the relevant provision in the 1963 Act, which has a lengthy ancestry, can be seen in its context. We can start with the Municipal Corporations Act 1835. Before 1835 there was considerable diversity in the contents of the charters granted to municipal corporations. The 1835 Act represented an

attempt to establish a common form for local government administration for the future, and to place borough funds under the control of an elected council. By s 1 so much of all charters then in force relating to the boroughs named in the Act as was inconsistent with or contrary to the provisions of the Act was annulled. Section 6 provided that in future each body corporate relating to the respective boroughs should have a common form name, that is the mayor, aldermen and burgesses of the borough in question. By that name the corporation body should be capable in law, by the council created by the Act, to do everything which it could then lawfully do. Section 25 provided for each borough to have a council consisting of a mayor, aldermen and councillors. Section 141 provided that, for the future, if the inhabitant householders of a town or borough should petition for the grant to them of a charter of incorporation, it should be lawful for the King, if he should think fit to grant the same, to extend to the inhabitants the powers and provisions contained in the Act. In 1841 Patteson J in *Rutter v Chapman* M & W 1 at 74, 151 ER 925 at 955 said concerning a corresponding section, s 49, of the Municipal Corporations (General) Act 1837:

> '. . . s. 49, enacts that if the *inhabitant householders* of any town or borough shall petition for a charter, it shall be lawful for her Majesty (if she should think fit, by the advice of her Privy Council, to grant the same,) to extend to the inhabitants of any such town or borough, within the district to be set forth in such charter, all the *powers and* provisions of the Municipal Corporations Act [1835]. This is not in derogation or abridgment of the power of the Crown to grant charters of incorporation at common law, which it may still do without any petition; but it is to enable the Crown, in case of any such petition, to extend to any new corporation, when created, the powers of the Municipal Corporations Act, some of which, as for instance the taxing the inhabitants by a borough rate, may not have been grantable by the Crown at common law. The act does not profess to enable the Crown to grant charters, but only, if it shall think fit to grant them upon petition, to extend to the grantees, by those charters, certain powers and provisions.' (Patteson J's emphasis.)

In 1882 the Municipal Corporations Act of that year consolidated, with some amendments, the existing enactments relating to municipal corporations in England and Wales. The Act applied to every city and town to which the 1835 Act applied, and to any town, district or place the inhabitants whereof were incorporated after the commencement of the 1882 Act and to which the provisions of the Municipal Corporations Acts were under the 1882 Act extended by charter. The 1882 Act contained similar provisions to those of the 1835 Act concerning the name of the municipal corporation of a borough, that is the corporate body constituted by the incorporation of the inhabitants. Likewise with the provisions regarding the municipal corporation being capable of acting by the council of the borough, which should exercise all powers vested in the corporation by the 1882 Act or otherwise. Section 210, concerning the grant of charters, was in terms not materially different from s 141 of the 1835 Act. Section 212 provided that by a charter the Queen might make provision for the number of councillors, the number and boundaries of the wards, and other electoral matters.

The Local Government Act 1888 established county councils, to which were entrusted the management of the administrative and financial business of administrative counties (including county boroughs). The council of each county was a body corporate. The metropolis of London became an administrative county, having as its council the London county council.

London government was further reorganised in 1889. The London Government Act of that year provided for the administrative county of London to be divided into 28 metropolitan boroughs, and for a council for each metropolitan borough to be incorporated by Order in Council.

In the 1930s there were two Acts which essentially consolidated the existing legislation. The Local Government Act 1933 consolidated, with some amendments, the previous

legislation relating to local government outside London. The position continued to be
a that the country was divided into administrative counties and county boroughs.
Administrative counties were divided into county districts, and those districts were either
non-county boroughs, urban districts or rural districts (s 1). For each administrative
county there was to be a county council, which was to be a body corporate by the name
of the county council (s 2). For boroughs, the existing structure of an incorporated
municipal corporation acting through an unincorporated council remained intact (s 3).
b Section 129 contained a provision concerning the grant of charters to urban or rural
district councils, in terms not materially different from those already noted in the earlier
legislation. In that regard, s 131 contained provisions corresponding to s 212 of the 1882
Act. As to London, the London Government Act 1939 consolidated, with amendments
immaterial for present purposes, the legislation relating to local government in London.
   That, in short, was the relevant legislative position when the 1963 Act reformed local
c government in London. In particular, it is to be noted that outside London at that time
were numerous boroughs incorporated by charter: many of the charters were ancient,
but others had been granted after the 1835 Act introduced on to the statute book the
provision regarding charters which started as s 91 of the 1835 Act and carried through to
s 129 of the 1933 Act.
   It is also to be noted that, on several occasions between 1835 and 1963, disputes came
d before the court in which questions arose concerning the capacity of municipal
corporations, incorporated by charter, to enter into particular activities to which
ratepayers, carrying on similar activities themselves, objected, and to charge the expenses
of such activities against local authority funds. Tramways were a notable example of this.
Through all these cases runs the thread that it was accepted as established law by the
judges who decided them, and usually it was not disputed by counsel, that the capacity
e of a municipal corporation created by charter was as enunciated in *Sutton's Hospital Case*
(1612) 10 Co Rep 1a, [1558–1774] All ER Rep 11, and that the Municipal Corporation
Acts had not taken away that capacity although the Acts had restricted the applications
which could be made of corporate funds. No suggestion was put forward that s 1 of the
1835 Act, repealing so much of the existing charters as was inconsistent with the
f provisions of the Act, had operated to curtail the existing legal capacity of corporations
which the common law regarded as an incident flowing from incorporation regardless
of the terms of the charter. Nor was any suggestion advanced that, in this regard,
corporations created by charter after 1835 were in a different position from those created
by charter before 1835.
   The cases in question are *A-G v Newcastle-upon-Tyne Corp* (1889) 23 QBD 492; *affd*
g [1892] AC 568, *A-G v London CC* [1901] 1 Ch 781; *affd* [1902] AC 165, *A-G v Manchester
Corp* [1906] 1 Ch 643, *A-G v Leeds Corp* [1929] 2 Ch 291 and *A-G (ex rel Birmingham and
Midland Motor Omnibus Co Ltd) v Leicester Corp* [1943] 1 All ER 146, [1943] Ch 86. Of
these it is unnecessary to do more than cite a passage from the judgment of Farwell J in
the *Manchester Corp* case [1906] 1 Ch 643 at 651, noting that Manchester corporation was
incorporated by a charter granted in 1839:
h
   'Now the difference between a statutory corporation and a corporation
   incorporated by Royal Charter is well settled; the former can do such acts only as are
   authorized directly or indirectly by the statute creating it; the latter (speaking
   generally) can do everything that an ordinary individual can do. If, however, the
   corporation by charter be (as are the defendants) a municipal corporation, then they
j   are subject to the restrictions imposed by the Municipal Corporations Act, 1882,
   and will be restrained from applying their borough funds to purposes not authorized
   by that Act: *Attorney-General v Newcastle-upon-Tyne Corporation*. If the defendants in
   this case had no statutory powers, it is plain that they could not apply their borough
   fund either for the purposes of the tramways or of the business of general delivery
   agents or common carriers. Granting that theoretically a corporation by charter

could lawfully run tramways or carry on such a business, they could not do so in practice without the expenditure of money.'

We do not consider that Lord Hanworth MR or Romer LJ, in their observations in A-G v Smethwick Corp [1932] 1 Ch 562, [1932] All ER Rep 304, were speaking with a different voice on this point. In particular, Lord Hanworth MR's observation that 'The powers of this corporation, although incorporated by charter, are stated by the terms of the Act of 1882, which none the less bind them', was directed at the corporation's powers with regard to the expenditure of money out of the general rate fund (see [1932] 1 Ch 562 at 575, [1932] All ER Rep 304 at 306). The primary relief sought in that action was a declaration that it was unlawful and ultra vires the 1882 Act for Smethwick corporation to expend any part of the general rate fund in carrying on a printing works.

Against this background we turn to consider the 1963 Act. Section 1(1) provides that in London there should be new administrative areas, to be known as London boroughs. The old metropolitan boroughs and their councils ceased to exist (s 3). For the local governance of the new boroughs Parliament did not adopt a structure comparable to that which had existed in London ever since 1899 regarding the metropolitan boroughs, namely an incorporated council. Instead, the new London boroughs were to have a legal framework similar to that existing at the time outside London in the case of boroughs: an incorporated municipal corporation and an unincorporated council. The key statutory provision on this point is s 1(2), which provided:

'If in the case of any London borough, on representations in that behalf made to the Privy Council by the Minister, Her Majesty by the advice of her Privy Council thinks fit to grant a charter of incorporation of the inhabitants of that borough, Her Majesty may by that charter—(a) make provision with respect to the name of the borough; and (b) subject to the provisions of this Act, make any provision such as may be made by virtue of section 131 of the Local Government Act 1933 by a charter granted under Part VI of that Act; and any charter which purports to be granted in pursuance of the Royal prerogative and this subsection shall be deemed to be valid and within the powers of this Act and Her Majesty's prerogative and the validity thereof shall not be questioned in any legal proceeding whatever.'

In our view s 1(2) did not confer on Her Majesty a power to grant a charter of incorporation of the inhabitants of the borough in question. The subsection followed a well-established legislative pattern in this field. It proceeded on the assumption, as was the case, that the Crown already had power under the royal prerogative to grant such a charter. What the subsection did was to authorise the Crown, if the charter-granting power were exercised, to make provision in the charter on two subjects which were not or might not be within the scope of the matters which, under the prerogative, could be provided for in a charter: 'if ... Her Majesty ... thinks fit to grant a charter of incorporation ... Her Majesty may by that charter—(a) ... and (b) ...'

Of course, when granting a charter the Sovereign can name the corporate body being created. But para (a) is not directed at the name of the corporate body. Paragraph (a) is directed at the name of the borough, that is the geographical area in question. By virtue of para (a), the charter may make provision for a name for the new administrative area in question. That was done in the instant case. Article 1 of the charter provided that the London borough consisting of the areas of the then-existing metropolitan boroughs of Fulham and Hammersmith should be named the 'London Borough of Hammersmith' (since changed to the 'London Borough of Hammersmith and Fulham'). Paragraph (b) enabled the Crown to include in the charter provision on the electoral matters mentioned in the corresponding section in the 1933 Act. That power was also exercised in the instant case, in arts 4 to 9 of the charter: the borough was to be divided into 21 wards, with specified boundaries, there were to be 60 councillors, and so forth.

In our view, a charter granted by the Crown as envisaged in s 1(2) is, save as to the

matters included therein by virtue of paras (a) and (b), a charter granted in pursuance of
a the royal prerogative. The incorporation thereby achieved is pursuant to the prerogative
and not pursuant to a statutory power. Thus unless a contrary intention can be found in
the statutory language, the body thereby incorporated will have the attributes which a
body so incorporated, viz under the royal prerogative, normally has; in particular, it will
have the same capacity to enter into contracts as a natural person.

No contrary intention is expressed, but is a contrary intention implicit in s 1(2)? In
b our view it is not. It is not possible, from the provision enabling para (a) and (b) matters
to be included in the charter, to spell out an intention by Parliament that the legal
consequences of incorporation pursuant to the charter should be different from what
otherwise they would be. This is supported by s 93(5), which provides that any enabling
provision in the Act should be deemed to be in addition to, and not in derogation of, any
powers exercisable by Her Majesty by virtue of the royal prerogative. Nor do we think
c that the existence, cheek by jowl with s 1(2), of a power for the minister to make an
incorporation order under s 1(3) assists: a power, incidentally, which has never been
exercised. The section contemplates two alternative modes of incorporation, and there is
a long-established distinction between the two, so far as the application of ultra vires
principles is concerned. We accept that, civic dignity apart, Parliament presumably did
not intend that there should be any difference in the practical consequences ensuing
d from incorporation by one route rather than the other. But in our view that result is
achieved by a different means, namely by the permitted use of council funds not being
affected by the extent of the theoretical, legal capacity of the corporation.

Corporations and council funds
e   To that point we now turn. Thus far we have accepted the banks' submission. But this
case concerns money: the use or misuse of the council's funds. The auditor is claiming
that these funds cannot properly, that is lawfully, be used by the council to finance swap
transactions. The banks and Barclays dispute this. So the next step in the banks'
submission, based on the vires of the corporation as a chartered body, is to consider
whether council funds can be used to finance activities carried on by the corporation as
f distinct from the council. By way of general introduction we observe that, although not
an incorporated body, it is the council which is the 'local authority' and a 'principal
council' for the purposes of the 1972 Act: see the definitions in s 270. Thus the functions
vested by the Act in a local authority are vested in the council, not the corporation.

Again, as an aid to understanding the position under the present legislation, it is
helpful to note first the earlier legislation, some of which is still in force. On this, we
g have already noted that one of the objects of the 1835 Act was to place borough funds
under the control of an elected council. For present purposes it is sufficient to start in
1882. Under the 1882 Act, all rents and interest payable to a municipal corporation were
to go to the borough fund (s 139). Likewise, under s 149, in respect of all sums levied in
pursuance of the borough rate. Section 140 made provision for the application of the
h borough fund. The fund was to be applicable to 15 heads of expenditure specified in
Sch 5 (s 140(1)). Section 140 (3) provided that, with stated exceptions, no other payments
were to be made out of the borough fund. The 1933 Act repealed, amongst other
provisions, s 140(3) of the 1882 Act. The 1933 Act, and other legislation, also amended
Sch 5 by excluding all the items there listed save for part of item 3: 'the expenses of
providing, furnishing, maintaining or improving the corporate buildings.' Section 185(1)
j provided that all receipts of the council of a borough should be carried to the general rate
fund of the borough and that 'all liabilities falling to be discharged by the council should
be discharged out of that fund'. Section 185(3) provided that, if the general rate fund was
more than sufficient 'for the purposes to which it is applicable', the surplus might be
applied under the direction of the council for the public benefit of the inhabitants and
improvement of the borough.

The position under the current legislation can be summarised as follows. The effect of
s 148 of the 1972 Act, so far as material for present purposes, is that all receipts of the   *a*
council of a London borough are to be carried to the general rate fund which is to be
kept by the council, and that 'all liabilities falling to be discharged by . . . such council
shall be discharged out of the [general rate] fund'. Section 137 provided that 'a local
authority' might incur expenditure which in its opinion was in the interests of its area or
any part of it or all or some of the inhabitants. However, the section set strict bounds on
the amount of such expenditure. Basically the limit was the product of a rate of 2p in the   *b*
pound (see sub-s (8)). That section has now been amended, but the amendments do not
affect the point on which the section is relevant for present purposes: namely that the
statute contains express, but limited, authority for expenditure on matters not otherwise
provided for in the legislation.

In our view the scheme of the legislation makes plain that the general rate fund to be
kept by a council under s 148 is applicable only for the purpose of meeting liabilities   *c*
which, under the 1972 Act or other legislation, fall to be discharged by the council. The
council is a statutory creation, and it is to the statutes that one must look to discover the
liabilities falling to be discharged by the council. Those are the liabilities which may be
discharged out of the general rate fund.

We add that we do not think that para 1(2) of Pt I of Sch 2 to the 1972 Act assists in
determining what are the expenses which may be paid out of a general rate fund. Under   *d*
this paragraph there continued to be a council for each London borough, clothed with
authority, amongst other matters, to act on behalf of the municipal corporation of the
borough. But, even so, before the general rate fund can be resorted to by the council, it is
necessary to find the power which authorised the council to incur the particular liability
which it is seeking to discharge out of the fund.

Reliance was placed on some observations in *A-G* (*ex rel Birmingham and Midland Motor*   *e*
Omnibus Co Ltd) v *Leicester Corp* [1943] 1 All ER 146, [1943] Ch 86. The issue there was
whether the corporation was entitled to use a reserve fund to pay for the purchase of a
business which operated certain bus services. Bennett J decided that it could not, but in
the course of his judgment he considered what the position would be if, as was not the
case, the corporation had sought to use the general rate fund for this purpose. He stated
that since the 1933 Act repealed s 140(2), (3) and (4) of the 1882 Act, the only ban against   *f*
making such a payment had been removed, that the corporation, being a chartered body,
was no longer prohibited by any legislation from making such a payment, and that
s 185(1) of the 1933 Act gave the corporation power to make the payment out of the
general rate fund. We are unable to accept this. The wide power given to a council by
s 185(3) of the 1933 Act, in respect only of any surplus in the general rate fund, is
inconsistent with the council having the like wide power in respect of the entire fund.   *g*
That this is so is confirmed by the terms of s 7 of the Local Authorities (Land) Act 1963.
This section provided that the liabilities falling to be discharged by the council of a
borough that might be discharged out of the general rate fund under s 185 of the 1933
Act should include liabilities incurred by them in the exercise of any power exercisable
by virtue of the charter of the municipal corporation of the borough for, in short, the   *h*
acquisition of land and the construction and repair of buildings or works on corporate
land. There would have been no need for such a provision if a council in any event could
discharge out of the general rate fund liabilities incurred by them in the exercise of any
powers exercisable by virtue of the charter of a municipal corporation.

Thus we do not think that the vires of the corporation as a chartered body leads to a
conclusion which assists the banks. Hammersmith council's ability to use its funds to   *j*
defray obligations under the instruments under challenge depends on there being a
statutory power, express or implied, authorising the council to enter into these
instruments.

To that issue we shall turn in a moment, but before doing so one further point is to be
noted. Before the Divisional Court and before us there was no evidence directed at

identifying precisely the party with whom the banks had contracted. We were informed
a   by counsel that in the documents most contracts were expressed to be made with the
'London Borough of Hammersmith and Fulham', and some with Hammersmith council,
but in no instance did the full name of the corporation appear. Having regard to the
view we have expressed regarding the use which may be made of the council's funds, it
is not necessary to consider this question further.

b   *The council's powers under the 1972 Act*
The 1972 Act contains no express power enabling local authorities to enter into all or
any of the various types of transactions under challenge. Nor does it contain an express
prohibition against such transactions. The absence of express provision is not surprising,
since these transactions are such a recent development. Thus the question which arises
c   for determination is whether, despite the absence of express authorisation, local
authorities are impliedly authorised by the Act to enter into such transactions.
Two preliminary points can be noted. First, the general approach to this question is
well established. In *A-G v Great Eastern Rly Co* (1880) 5 App Cas 473 at 478 Lord
Selborne LC said:

d   '... whatever may fairly be regarded as incidental to, or consequential upon,
those things which the Legislature has authorised, ought not (unless expressly
prohibited) to be held, by judicial construction, to be *ultra vires*.'

In different language, but to the like effect, Lord Watson said in *Baroness Wenlock v River
Dee Co* (1885) 10 App Cas 354 at 362–363:

e   'Whenever a corporation is created by Act of Parliament, with reference to the
purposes of the Act, and solely with a view to carrying these purposes into execution,
I am of opinion not only that the objects which the corporation may legitimately
pursue must be ascertained from the Act itself, but that the powers which the
corporation may lawfully use in furtherance of these objects must either be expressly
conferred or derived by reasonable implication from its provisions.'

f   The same approach is applicable to an unincorporated body owing its constitution to a
statute which defines its objects and powers (see *Amalgamated Society of Railway Servants v
Osborne* [1910] AC 87 at 94).
Secondly, it was accepted by the banks and Barclays, and in our view rightly so, that
local authorities are not empowered to carry on a trade or business of entering into
interest rate swaps and related transactions, even if the object is to apply the profits which
g   they hope to earn in reducing their cost of borrowing. Such a trade or business would
stand on no different footing from any other trade or business in which a local authority
might seek to engage, in the hope of profit. But, in general, local authorities have no
implied power to engage in a trade or business for profit. And an intention to apply the
profits in reducing the local authority's costs or expenses in a particular way would not
h   render intra vires an activity which would otherwise be ultra vires.
What, then, is the basis on which the banks and Barclays contend that, in certain
circumstances, interest rate swaps and related transactions are within the powers of local
authorities? Reduced to the simplest terms, it is this. Local authorities borrow large sums
of money to finance certain types of expenditure, often for long periods. They borrow
mostly from the Public Works Loan Commissioners, but also through the money
j   markets. Local authorities are, of course, concerned to borrow as cheaply as possible
consistent with the orderly and prudent conduct of their financial affairs. Nowadays
interest rates are highly volatile. Thus local authorities are concerned to protect
themselves against unfavourable movements in interest rates, and to take advantage of
favourable movements. To this end it would be open to, and proper for, a local authority,
in appropriate circumstances, to repay an existing loan and substitute for it a replacement

loan on different interest terms as the authority's perception of interest rate trends might
dictate. For instance, an existing loan at a floating rate of interest might be replaced by a   *a*
loan having a fixed rate of interest. Or an initial loan at a fixed rate of interest might be
replaced by a loan with a fluctuating rate of interest such as a 6-month London Interbank
Offered Rate (LIBOR), or 6-month LIBOR with a specified maximum, or minimum, or
between a specified maximum and minimum. Likewise, a local authority might agree
with a lender to vary the rate of interest payable on an existing loan, for the residue of
the period of the loan or for a lesser period. Entering into interest rate swaps, and   *b*
purchasing swap options and interest rate caps and floors and collars, to mention some of
the ranges of instruments in use, can achieve the same commercial result as in these
examples, but more cheaply and simply. The expenses attendant on swap transactions
are often appreciably less than the expenses involved in the early redemption of an
existing long-term loan and taking up a fresh loan, and swap transactions can be entered
into speedily and easily.   *c*

   Expressed in these simple terms, a swap transaction which is entered into by a local
authority with reference to a particular debt or debts of the authority, and for the purpose
of (in effect) varying the rate of interest which the local authority has to pay in respect of
that debt or debts, can be seen for what it is: an economical and convenient method of
achieving the same financial result as could have been achieved by repayment and
replacement borrowing or by agreement with a lender without repayment of the loan.   *d*
So expressed, swap transactions, entered into for such a purpose, are a novel method of
achieving an unexceptional end: regulating to best advantage the rate of interest payable
on an authority's indebtedness.

   Of course, entering into a swap transaction with reference to a particular debt does not
have the effect in law of altering the rate of interest payable by the local authority as
borrower to the lender. But, commercially, the combined effect of the original loan and   *e*
the swap transaction is the same as if the interest rate in the actual loan had been varied.
In theory there is a risk that the party to the swap transaction might become insolvent or
default for some other reason; but with parties of the standing of the banks and others
involved in the swap transactions under challenge, that credit risk is more theoretical
than real.

   So far we have referred to the use of a simple swap transaction entered into with   *f*
reference to a particular debt or debts. But what is said above would be equally applicable
to entering into swap transactions, such as the purchase of an interest rate swap option or
a cash option, with reference to a particular borrowing which the local authority is about
to undertake or envisages undertaking in the near future. Again, the same reasoning
would be applicable to successive swap transactions entered into with reference to a
particular debt. This would include reverse swaps. Yet further, the like reasoning would   *g*
be applicable to the converse case of entering into a swap transaction with reference to
the interest payable to a local authority in respect of a loan or loans made by it. For
convenience we shall refer to entering into swap transactions in the circumstances and
for the limited purpose we have so far described as 'interest rate risk management'.

   In principle, we have no difficulty in concluding that interest rate risk management,   *h*
as described above, is fairly to be regarded as incidental to or consequential on a local
authority's powers of borrowing and investment and the attendant duty resting on it to
take reasonable care to manage its borrowings and investments prudently in the best
interests of the ratepayers and those for whom the authority provides services. In
discharging this duty a local authority is entrusted with an area within which to exercise
its own judgment and discretion. We can see no compelling reason why a local authority   *j*
cannot, in appropriate circumstances and exercising due caution, make use of a newly-
fashioned tool which achieves, more economically and expeditiously, substantially the
same commercial result as could lawfully be achieved in the discharge of the duty by
more traditional means. Indeed, this is a case in which, to adopt the language of Lord
Hanworth MR in *A-G v Smethwick Corp* [1932] 1 Ch 562 at 578, [1932] All ER Rep 304 at

308, it seems impossible to hold that a local authority is not authorised to take a step
a 'which prudence dictates and modern mechanism renders possible'.

In passing, we notice that in line with this approach, and as already observed, one of
the general duties of an auditor under s 15(1) of the Local Government Finance Act 1982
is to satisfy himself that the local authority has made proper arrangements 'for securing
economy, efficiency and effectiveness in the use of its resources'. And under s 26 the
Audit Commission is required to undertake or promote studies designed to enable it to
b make recommendations for improving, amongst other matters, the financial or other
management of local authorities.

However, this initial, preliminary view based on a simple appraisal of the financial
purposes sought to be achieved by interest rate risk management, has to be considered
and tested against the framework of the legislation. For on these appeals, as in the
Divisional Court, the auditor's case was that, whatever the circumstances, and whatever
c the object, and however careful and prudent they may be, local authorities have no
power ever to enter into any swap transactions of any sort. Swap transactions are never
an option available to a local authority, in any circumstances. The gist of the argument
of counsel for the auditor was that dealings with the funds of a local authority are
regulated by a set of statutory powers and duties, and that a power to use swap
instruments would be incompatible with these powers and duties. He placed particular
d reliance on the detailed code respecting the powers of local authorities to borrow and
lend money, and respecting their funds, set out in Pt I of Sch 13 to the 1972 Act. He
submitted that it would be inconsistent for Parliament to have legislated in such close
detail but to have left local authorities free to expose ratepayers to the financial risks
which can arise from swap transactions.

There is some force in this argument. We cannot help but feel that if the swaps market
e had existed in 1972 Parliament would be likely to have made some provision regarding
local authorities' participation in it, in the same way as Parliament has now regulated
building societies' participation in this market, by s 23 of the Building Societies Act 1986
and the Building Societies (Prescribed Contracts) Order 1988, SI 1988/1344. But we do
not think that this consideration leads inexorably to the extreme conclusions for which
the auditor contended. It is to be noted that, while Sch 13 makes comprehensive
f provision on matters such as the purposes for which, and the means by which, local
authorities may borrow, Parliament has not sought to regulate the rate of interest payable
by local authorities to lenders. That, as one would expect, is a matter left to the discretion
of local authorities, to be exercised by them from time to time in the light of their own
needs and current market conditions. And it is with this field of interest rates that
interest rate risk management is concerned.
g   Counsel for the auditor relied on para 8 of Sch 13. He submitted that this paragraph
expressly authorised a limited form of debt restructuring and, hence, that this impliedly
negatived the existence of any wider power. We do not think that the paragraph is to be
so understood. The paragraph obviates the need for a local authority to seek approval for
replacement borrowings. But that is not inconsistent with a local authority being at
h liberty to take steps to restructure its interest rate exposure other than by replacement
borrowing, e g by agreeing a changed interest rate with a lender.

Nor are we persuaded that interest rate risk management cannot be accommodated
within the due operation of a loans fund in accordance with para 15. The loans fund
scheme made by the council under this paragraph in 1982 seems to offer adequate scope
for making payments and accepting receipts from swap transactions through the revenue
j account of the loans fund. On this we are comforted by noting that the Audit
Commission, with its unrivalled knowledge and understanding of local authority
accounts, seems not to have perceived herein any obstacle to interest rate risk
management.

The third paragraph in Sch 13 on which counsel for the auditor placed particular
reliance was para 7. He submitted that the obligation to debit a borrowing account

annually with an amount which includes a calculation made by reference to the 'interest at the due rate' on the outstanding principal would preclude bringing into account the effect of a related interest swap, because the latter does not alter the actual rate of interest payable on the loan. In practice, however, and quite apart from interest rate risk management, this paragraph is given a sensibly liberal interpretation. Local authorities operate loans funds on a pooled basis. In general they do not earmark particular loans to particular items of expenditure. Accordingly, they debit borrowing accounts with the average rate of interest payable by them on their overall borrowings. It seems that, in calculating this average, any interest received on loans made by the loans fund is also taken into account. We think that an acceptably liberal interpretation can also accommodate the net effect of swap transactions when making the interest calculation required by para 7.

Counsel for the auditor emphasised that an interest rate swap is a transaction unconnected, in law, with any existing debt of the local authority: the lender is still entitled to be paid the agreed rate of interest. By a swap the local authority purchases a stream of income, which will enable it to reduce the net cost of its borrowing. This analysis is undoubtedly correct. But what is in issue is the conclusion which flows from this. The absence of legal connection is equally a feature of insurance policies. The justification for a local authority taking out a policy of insurance has to be found elsewhere than in the terms of the policy. So it is with interest rate risk management. In the case of swap transactions entered into as part of interest rate risk management, their justification lies in the existence of the particular debt or debts with reference to which they were entered into.

Nor do we think that entering into swap transactions by way of interest rate risk management should cause difficulties with local authorities' annual budgeting arrangements. Local authorities are able to cope with loans at fluctuating rates of interest. They have to make the best assessments they can concerning the likely cost of their borrowings over the year, including future borrowings. There is no evidence before us that the adjustment of their cash flow by swap transactions does, or will, create insuperable budgeting difficulties.

That swap transactions can give rise to enormous losses (or profits) is obvious. The prognosis, as matters now stand, of the council's dealings speaks for itself in this regard. But that unhappy history must be kept in perspective. In so far as council's swap activities were not by way of interest rate risk management but were by way of conducting a trade or business in swap transactions, which is a question we shall deal with later, those activities should not be allowed to colour an appraisal of the use by local authorities of swap transactions by way of interest rate risk management.

For it must be kept in mind that the decision made in these proceedings on issue (1A) will apply to all local authorities. The evidence showed that 77 local authorities, other than the Hammersmith council, have entered into interest rate swaps. Of these, 59 have entered into five deals or fewer. Only ten local authorities have entered into more than ten interest rate swaps. The evidence of Mr D J Hopkins, the treasurer of the City of Westminster, was that Westminster council has entered into some 12 swap contracts, and that each one was related to a specific loan in the council's portfolio. The tenor of his evidence was that he made these contracts in the course of handling Westminster council's finances in a prudent and conservative manner, that it would be detrimental to the interests of local authorities and ratepayers if the use of swap transactions were to be denied to local authorities, and that this view is shared by many other local authority treasurers.

Our conclusion is that the detailed code in Sch 13, and the other statutory provisions regarding borrowing and lending to which our attention was drawn, are not inconsistent with local authorities being able, in appropriate circumstances, to enter into swap transactions as part of interest rate risk management in the limited terms we have described above. We are unable to accept the sweeping submission of counsel for the

auditor that in no circumstances at all can a local authority ever enter into any swap
a transaction. We respectfully differ from the narrower interpretation of the powers of
local authorities accepted by the Divisional Court.

We should add that we were referred by counsel to many reported cases in which
courts have been concerned to decide whether this or that activity was or was not
impliedly within the powers of local authorities. These cases are no more than illustrations
of the application, in particular instances, of the general principle outlined at the
b beginning of this section of our judgment. We do not think that to undertake an analysis
of these authorities would assist in resolving the questions we have to decide.

That leaves open the question of where precisely the boundary line is drawn between
interest rate risk management, which is permissible, and trading, which is not. The
feature to which we attach importance is the clear linkage between a swap transaction
and a particular debt or debts (or investment or investments). The purpose and
c commercial effect of the swap transactions in the case of such 'parallel contracts' are to
substitute for a cash flow in respect of a debt or investment a different cash flow.
However, a suggestion has been advanced that interest rate risk management is not
confined so narrowly as this, but that it includes altering the 'profile' of a local authority's
'loan portfolio' by, for example, entering into swaps from fixed to fluctuating rates of
interest although the swaps are not related to any particular debt or debts.
d   We express no view on this suggested extension of interest rate risk management, for
two reasons. First, the point does not arise for decision in these proceedings. The issue to
which we are directing our attention is issue (1A), namely whether swap transactions are
ever capable of being within the powers conferred on local authorities by Parliament.
Second, we do not have before us the evidential material with which to consider this
point properly. The arguments each way on the point could be weighed more
e satisfactorily in a case where there is evidence of how such a 'reprofiling' works in
practice.

Sections 101 and 111 of the 1972 Act
We must turn now to a point which loomed large in the argument. Thus far we have
f considered whether, having regard to the statutory framework within which they
operate, local authorities are impliedly authorised to undertake interest rate risk
management. In so doing we have applied the principle enunciated in *A-G v Great Eastern
Rly Co* (1880) 5 App Cas 473 and other cases. In the 1972 Act Parliament codified this
principle so far as local authorities are concerned. Section 111(1), headed 'Subsidiary
powers of local authorities', provides:

g   'Without prejudice to any powers exercisable apart from this section but subject
to the provisions of this Act and any other enactment passed before or after this Act,
a local authority shall have power to do any thing (whether or not involving the
expenditure, borrowing or lending of money or the acquisition or disposal of any
property or rights) which is calculated to facilitate, or is conducive or incidental to,
the discharge of any of their functions.'
h
Standing by itself, this subsection would not seem to give rise to any particular
difficulty. We agree with the Divisional Court that in this subsection the word 'functions',
which is accompanied by no statutory definition, is used in a broad sense, and is apt to
embrace all the duties and powers of a local authority: the sum total of the activities
Parliament has entrusted to it. Those activities are its functions. Section 111(1) confirms
j that, subject always to any contrary statutory provision, a local authority has power to do
all the ancillary things requisite for carrying out those activities properly. This
construction accords with the codifying purpose for which the subsection was enacted.
It also accords with the views expressed by Glidewell J in *R v Greater London Council, ex p
Westminster City Council* (1984) Times, 27 December, and by Nourse LJ and Sir Denys
Buckley in *R v Eden DC, ex p Moffat* (1988) Independent, 16 December.

Difficulty arises from the combined operation of sub-ss (6) and (12) in s 101. The material provisions in s 101 read:

'(1) Subject to any express provision contained in this Act or any Act passed after this Act, a local authority may arrange for the discharge of any of their functions— (a) by a committee, a sub-committee or an officer of the authority; or (b) by any other local authority . . .
(6) A local authority's functions with respect to levying, or issuing a precept for, a rate or borrowing money shall be discharged only by the authority . . .
(12) References in this section and section 102 below to the discharge of any of the functions of a local authority include references to the doing of anything which is calculated to facilitate, or is conducive or incidental to, the discharge of any of those functions . . .'

Subsection (12) echoes the language of s 111(1). Thus, if entering into swap transactions by way of interest rate risk management falls within s 111(1) as the doing of something conducive or incidental to the discharge of one of the local authority's functions, viz borrowing and investment and the attendant duty to which we have referred, there might seem, at first sight, to be no escape from the conclusion that, by virtue of ss 101(6) and (12), entering into such swap transactions is an activity which can be discharged only by the authority itself. It is an activity which, by virtue of those two subsections, is excepted from the general power of delegation contained in s 101(1).

This proposition has only to be stated for it to be obvious that Parliament cannot have intended such a result. By including sub-s (12) in s 101, so as to make it plain that the power of delegation applied as much to the exercise of subsidiary powers as to the discharge of functions themselves, Parliament cannot have intended that the ban on delegation in sub-s (6) should also embrace the exercise of the power to do all the subsidiary things, however trivial, which are incidental to levying, or issuing a precept for, a rate or borrowing money. In consequence, all counsel exercised much ingenuity in seeking to find a way in which to escape, Houdini-like, from the chains which these two subsections apparently impose.

This question has been before the court on at least two previous occasions. In 1979, in *Bar Hill Development Ltd v South Cambridgeshire DC* (1979) 252 EG 915 one of the issues was whether a completion notice under para 8(1) of Sch 1 to the General Rate Act 1967, sent by an officer of the local authority, to the effect that certain properties would be rated as unoccupied property from a stated date, was caught by s 101(6) and, hence, required specific authorisation by a resolution of the council. Eveleigh LJ, with whose judgment Lord Widgery CJ and Woolf J agreed, declined to construe s 101(6) as having such a wide operation. The subsection could not refer to every single aspect of a local authority's actions which might have some effect on the rate. He then rejected the argument based on sub-s (12):

'I regard subsection (12) as relating back to subsection (1) and applying to cases where the council can delegate, not to subsection (6) which states when a council may not delegate. Subsection (1) of section 101 permits the council to delegate its function in a broad way and subsection (12) is making it clear that it is not merely the function that may be delegated but all incidental matters necessary for that function to be performed.'

(See 252 EG 915 at 918.)

The same point came before the House of Lords in *Provident Mutual Life Assurance Association v Derby City Council* [1981] 1 WLR 173. Lord Roskill declined to treat the giving of a para 8 completion notice as making or levying a rate and thus to require a formal resolution of the council (at 180). He referred to the decision in the *Bar Hill* case with apparent approval.

a   Likewise, in the present case: in our view the local authority's duty to take reasonable care to manage its borrowings and investments prudently, to which duty entering into swap transactions by way of interest rate risk management is an ancillary power, is not a function falling within the ambit of sub-s (6) as one of a local authority's 'functions with respect to . . . borrowing money'. It is a duty which arises out of, and in connection with, its borrowing (and investment) functions. But the discharge of that duty, day by day, cannot be regarded as the discharge of a function in respect of borrowing within the

b   meaning of the section, so as to require every step taken to be considered and approved by resolution of the council itself.

On this we note that Parliament has now intervened and provided for a like result in the course of imposing further obligations on local authorities in this field. Section 45 of the Local Government and Housing Act 1989 imposes on every local authority an obligation to determine each year an overall borrowing limit, a short-term borrowing

c   limit, and a limit on the proportion of the total amount of interest payable by the authority which is at a fluctuating rate. That duty, and the power to vary limits decided on, are excepted from the power of delegation contained in s 101 of the 1972 Act. Section 45(5) then provides that henceforth the words 'or borrowing money' shall be omitted from s 101(6). So for the future any difficulty under s 101(6) is altogether disposed of, so far as borrowing is concerned.

d   We think, further, that the same result is to be arrived at by a different route. Should we be wrong in our narrow interpretation of 'functions with respect to . . . borrowing money' in s 101(6), in our view the same result is to be achieved by construing s 101(12) in the manner described by Eveleigh LJ in the Bar Hill case. As already noted, sub-s (12) cannot have been intended to put within the scope of sub-s (6) everything done by a local authority in connection with its borrowing functions. The draftsman, for once, nodded.

e   He failed to observe the impact of sub-s (6) when introducing sub-s (12) into this non-delegation section. Parliament must have intended that sub-s (12) should not apply to sub-s (6). Subsection (12) is to be construed accordingly.

We must refer to one final point on s 111. Counsel for the auditor submitted that, since an interest rate swap is the purchase of an income, it will always constitute an unauthorised means of raising money. Section 111, it was submitted, does not of itself

f   empower a local authority to raise money: see s 111(3). That subsection, it was contended, applies to all raising of money: rates, precepts and borrowing are not intended to be an exhaustive list. The ambit of s 111(3) is not a matter we need to pursue in these proceedings, because we cannot accept counsel's characterisation of an interest rate swap, which is the starting point of his submission. When an interest rate swap is entered into by way of interest rate risk management, the commercial substance of the transaction is

g   no more a means of 'raising money' than would be taking out an insurance policy, or varying the rate of interest payable on a loan by agreement with the lender. (This is not to say that some swap transactions do not lend themselves to being used, improperly, for money raising purposes; 'deep discounted' swaps, where the interest rate is reduced in order to generate a large front-end premium, are an example.)

h   *Whether particular types of swap transactions are incapable of being used by way of interest rate risk management*

The Divisional Court identified two types of swap transactions as incapable of being used for interest rate risk management even if the use in general of swap transactions for interest rate risk management by local authorities is authorised by the 1972 Act. First,

j   'intermediation'; that is where Hammersmith council acted as an intermediary and entered into swaps with a view merely to obtaining a 'turn', for example, to assist another council which was rate-capped or whose credit standing was not so high as that of Hammersmith council. Before us it was accepted that swap transactions entered into for such a purpose were not entered into by way of interest rate risk management and that, as such, they were outside the powers of the council. But in our view the banks and

Barclays were correct in submitting that 'intermediation' is a type of purpose, not a type of swap transaction (such as an interest rate swap, or a cash option and so forth). The purpose for which a local authority enters into a swap transaction goes to whether the local authority was empowered to enter into that particular transaction: if it was by way of interest rate risk management, it was so empowered; if it was not by way of interest rate risk management but was by way of trading, the authority was not so empowered. In this context 'intermediation' is a form of trading.

The Divisional Court identified, as its second prohibited group, transactions in which the council sold options or otherwise received premiums for entering into any of the transactions. This group comprised the sale by the council of swap options, gilt options, cash options and caps and floors and collars. Once again it is essential to keep clearly in mind that the question being considered is whether transactions of this type are ever capable of being used by a local authority by way of interest rate risk management. At this stage the question is not whether the council did use this type of transaction for interest rate risk management. With this in mind, in our view the answer is clear. There may be circumstances in which a local authority is entitled, by way of interest rate risk management, to *buy* a swap option, or a gilt option, or a cash option or interest rate caps and floors and collars. If that is so, it must follow there may be circumstances in which a local authority is entitled to *sell* such options, if only by way of sale of a 'mirror' transaction should an option which has been bought be found later to be unwanted.

Overall conclusion on issue (1A)

Our overall conclusion on issue (1A) is that all the categories of swap transactions which have featured in these proceedings are *capable* of being lawfully entered by a local authority in the exercise of its powers under the 1972 Act, in the sense that there *may* be circumstances in which they can lawfully be undertaken by a local authority.

We must explain briefly what is the significance of this question. Although the issues concerning the enforceability of the transactions by the banks and others against the council do not as such arise in the present proceedings, the banks and Barclays are greatly concerned that the answers given to the issues which do arise shall not prejudice their claims that, whatever unlawfulness may have tainted the transactions so far as the council is concerned, the transactions remain enforceable by the banks and Barclays. Issue (1A) was, we apprehend, formulated by the banks having very much in mind an argument that a principle analogous to that applied in the field of company law as enunciated in *Rolled Steel Products (Holdings) Ltd v British Steel Corp* [1985] 3 All ER 52, [1986] Ch 246 applies to persons dealing with local authorities. In this regard, Slade LJ and Browne-Wilkinson LJ referred to the particular exercise of powers being 'capable of' falling within the objects of the relevant company (see [1985] 3 All ER 52 at 85, 93–94, [1986] Ch 246 at 295, 306). So it is that in the present proceedings, the conduct of which was shaped by the order made on 21 September 1989, it has become necessary to address the general issues to which thus far we have directed our consideration, unrelated to the circumstances in which any actual swap transaction was entered into by the council. We now turn to address issue (1B) and consider the evidence.

The transactions entered into by the council up to July 1988

In his submissions for the banks (which counsel for Barclays adopted on this aspect) counsel came close to accepting that many, if not most or even all, of the transactions entered into by the council during the halcyon period of April 1987 to July 1988 might on close examination turn out to have been entered into for the improper purpose of trading. But he argued that such a conclusion could not be reached without close investigation of each relevant transaction, which the Divisional Court had not attempted to carry out and had lacked the evidence to carry out. Accordingly, the case should be remitted to the Divisional Court for that investigation to be carried out. In making this submission counsel urged (1) that the Divisional Court had not been satisfied of any

improper purpose on the part of the council during the first period, up to April 1987 (see
a p 56 g, ante), (2) that the Divisional Court erred in treating the scale and range of
transactions entered into during the second period as conclusive evidence of improper
purpose (see p 56 h, ante), since these features only appeared as time went on and
transactions multiplied and so could not vitiate the first transactions in the series, (3) that,
since the Divisional Court could not identify the date when the objectionable transactions
began (see p 56 h, ante), a blanket condemnation of all transactions after an initial,
b arbitrarily chosen, date could not be upheld, and (4) that the Divisional Court could not
safely draw an inference of improper purpose in the absence of any evidence at all from
Mr Robb and Mr Price, the officers of the council who for most of the relevant time had
held the appointments of financial controller and head of loans and investments and had
thus exercised the responsibility of deciding whether to enter into these transactions: if
their motives were in issue, their evidence was needed.

c   Counsel for the banks was, of course, correct in suggesting that there was no evidence
from Messrs Robb and Price before the Divisional Court, orally or on affidavit. This is
not surprising. The auditor, as was right, proceeded against the council alone. The
council did not contest this entitlement to the relief he sought. In accepting that all the
transactions in issue were unlawful, the council acted in accordance with clear advice
tendered by counsel and cannot fairly be accused of opportunism. But it is the case that,
d as matters appeared to stand, it was or might prove to be very much in the financial
interest of the council that these transactions should be declared unlawful. It is also the
case that, faced with an admission by the council, the auditor was (subject always to the
discretion of the court) in a position to claim a declaration in his favour without adducing
direct evidence from Messrs Robb and Price, provided always that the council's
contemporary documents and records supported his contention and the council's
e admission that the transactions had been entered into for the improper purpose of
trading. It was the banks and Barclays who had the strongest incentive to rebut or throw
doubt on that conclusion. This they could reasonably hope to do only in reliance on the
contemporary documents and records themselves or by adducing oral evidence, perhaps
from Messrs Robb and Price. It was partly in order to do this, as we understand, that they
sought to be joined to the application, which could otherwise have given rise to no issue
f estoppel against them.

We were told, and it was not challenged, that the council gave the banks and Barclays
full discovery of all documents relating to the genesis and execution of these transactions
by itself and its officers. So no further relevant documentation would be before the court
if the facts were to be further investigated on a later occasion. We were also told, and
again it was not challenged, that for several days during the Divisional Court hearing the
g council held Mr Robb and Mr Price available in court for questioning by the banks and
Barclays if they wished, such attendance coming to an end only when it was indicated
that the banks did not wish to avail themselves of this opportunity. While we fully
appreciate the banks' dilemma, it was none the less for them to choose between the risk
of asking Messrs Robb and Price questions which might elicit unhelpful answers and the
h risk of proceeding without any evidence from them at all. They adopted the latter course.
This obliged the Divisional Court to draw such inferences from the documents, read in
the light of such affidavit evidence as there was, as seemed proper. We are in the same
position save only that we sit as a court of review.

Since, as pointed out by counsel for the banks in his point (1), the Divisional Court did
decline to make a finding of improper purpose in respect of the first period up to April
j 1987, we could not (if the matter rested there) resist the logic of his points (2) and (3).
There would be no alternative but to direct an investigation, which we could not
ourselves undertake, of when exactly a purpose not shown to be improper was superseded
by the improper purpose of trading. However, having carefully considered all the
submissions of counsel and all the material drawn to our attention, we are satisfied that
all the transactions to which the challenged items of account relate during the first two

periods are shown by the auditor to have been tainted with the improper purpose of trading.

We base this conclusion primarily on one clinching fact, fatal to the inference that any of these transactions was entered into for a purpose which could have been proper: neither before the transactions began, nor at any time before July 1988, did the council or its officers make any careful and detailed analysis of the interest which was due to be paid or received at any time in the future, or of the losses which the council might (on varying assumptions) suffer, or of the risk that those losses might eventuate, or of the steps which it was desirable to take to mitigate or secure protection against those losses. There was, in short, no attempt to match the council's actual debts and investments, either singly or in aggregate, with any of these transactions. Such an attempt, if made, would involve much sophisticated and time-consuming work and we cannot believe that no documentary record of this work would remain if it had ever been done. There is no suggestion that it ever was done. As time went on and the pattern of the council's activity became established, the inference that it was engaged in trade (or speculation) becomes even clearer, as the Divisional Court rightly held. Counsel were not able to suggest any proper purpose which could have led the officers to sell 18 caps while buying only 8, or to sell 217 swap options while buying only one. But in our judgment the absence of any proper purpose is manifest from the beginning and one does not have to wait until the pattern of the activity was fully established.

In resisting this conclusion, counsel for the banks directed out attention to a number of references in the documents which taken alone suggested or were at least consistent with a proper purpose on the part of the officers entering into these transactions. For example: (1) the Annual Loans and Investments Report 1986, apparently prepared early in that year, spoke of administering and servicing the council's debt so as to minimise its interest and debt-servicing costs; the key element of the council's borrowing strategy was described as 'the management of the sensitivity of the council's debt to interest rates' by means which included interest rate swaps, caps and floors; (2) the annual report, it would seem for 1986–87, referred to the use of interest rate swaps 'to maximise gains on favourable interest rate movements, and in turn, reduce the average rate of the Council's borrowings'; and (3) the paper relating to two projects, which did not in the event proceed (the acquisition of a freehold in King Street and of System Text House), referred in early 1987 and December 1987 to interest rate swaps as a means of minimising risk and uncertainty and minimising the interest rate risk.

These references deserve to be given their full weight, but on the other side we note (1) that as early as August 1987 Mr Price was reporting a '£950K surplus to date 1987/88', (2) that in a borrowing update of December 1987 Mr Price, while referring to 'locking in our "profit"', made no analysis of the council's debt, (3) that as time went on references increased to 'reversing at a profit', to generating surpluses and to generating income, (4) that in a formal report by the chief executive of the council on 15 March 1989 it was stated 'The original intention was that accumulated surplus from the [capital markets] fund would have been released to support revenue expenditure in future years once the capital markets fund had met all its major liabilities', and (5) that, save arguably in the two cases which did not proceed, there was, as we have said, no attempt at any time to match the council's actual debts and investments with any of these transactions.

Further, the auditor's account of these transactions, given in some detail in his affidavits, has not been effectively challenged.

In the absence of any evidence of lawful purpose from those primarily involved, in the face of the council's admission and on consideration of the evidence as a whole, we cannot accept the references (some of which are not free of ambiguity) of counsel for the banks as displacing the clear impression that these transactions, although no doubt entered into by the officers with an honourable and disinterested intention to benefit the council, were entered into for a purpose which the law cannot accept as proper for a local

authority, namely trading. This conclusion is, in our judgment, as true of the first period
a as of the second. In respect of these periods the declaration was rightly made.

Transactions entered into from July 1988 to February 1989: the interim strategy period
The Divisional Court's conclusion on the interim strategy period from July 1988 to
February 1989 has been quoted above: if there was power to enter into transactions such
as these at all, then there was power to take steps to mitigate the potential losses which
b might flow from earlier transactions even if they had been entered into unlawfully. The
auditor challenged this conclusion: it could not, he argued, be a lawful purpose to undo
damage caused in the course of effecting an unlawful purpose. The banks and Barclays
broadly supported the Divisional Court's view. The council, perhaps surprisingly, aligned
itself with the auditor.
For the purposes of considering this question we make the following assumptions of
c fact, all of them in our judgment justified by the evidence which has been filed.
(1) Until July 1988 the council and its officers believed that the swaps transactions
into which they were entering were lawful.
(2) On being confronted with the opinions obtained by the Audit Commission in July
1988 the council and its officers were genuinely doubtful, pending the receipt of legal
advice, whether the transactions had been lawful or not.
d (3) The council, its officers, the auditor and the Audit Commission recognised that, if
the council's capital market swaps activity ceased altogether pending receipt of legal
advice, it stood to suffer losses which could be averted or mitigated by taking appropriate
defensive action in the market.
(4) While the auditor expressly acted without prejudice to the rights of the borough's
electors, an interim strategy was agreed between the council, its officers and the auditor
e (apparently with the blessing of the Audit Commission and with help from the auditor's
associated consultancy firm) for handling the council's portfolio of swap transactions
until the council's legal position was clarified.
(5) The agreed interim strategy was thereafter followed.
(6) No indication was given to those dealing with the council during the interim
strategy period that the legality or enforceability of those deals might be in doubt.
f
(7) The council did not receive definitive advice on the legality of its previous
transactions until about 23 February 1989, the auditor having pressed for such advice to
be obtained since September.
(8) On about 22 February 1989 all dealing by the council in the swaps market ceased.
(9) It is still uncertain whether all or any of the council's swap transactions can be
enforced against it, and this uncertainty will remain even after the present litigation is
g finally determined.
(10) The council remains exposed to possible losses which prudent and expert dealing
in the market might avert or mitigate.
(11) Any losses which the council suffers in these transactions are likely to fall
ultimately on the ratepayers and community charge payers of the borough, at least in
h large measure.
If, as the auditor and the council submitted, the auditor is entitled to a declaration that
items of account arising from transactions entered into during the interim strategy
period are contrary to law because the transactions were entered into for an improper
purpose and in that sense are ultra vires, the implications are striking. Such a declaration
would be made in respect of transactions entered into with the knowledge and qualified
j acquiescence of the auditor and the Audit Commission and pursuant to arrangements
devised by the auditor's associated consultancy firm, retained at his suggestion. Doubts
would be raised (which cannot now be resolved) concerning the enforceability of
contracts made by the council in an attempt to protect the interests of those to whom it
owed a fiduciary duty while the legal position remained unclear and made by

counterparties in the ordinary course of business (without, it may be, knowledge of the legal issue which engaged the council). Such a decision would leave the council powerless to make any contract of this kind after February 1989 to avert or mitigate losses which might flow from earlier transactions; the council would have to stand and watch the flood-waters rise, impotent to raise a sandbag. These conclusions may be inescapable, but they do not seem to reflect that fundamental fairness and pragmatic good sense which are boasted to infuse the common law.

The researches of counsel failed to unearth authority bearing at all closely on this problem, and our own researches since the hearing ended have proved scarcely more fruitful. We were, however, referred to authority which appears to establish that, where the vires of a corporation to do an act are in doubt, the corporation may (if acting bona fide) make a binding agreement to compromise any questing arise out of that act (see *Re Norwich Provident Insurance Society, Bath's Case* (1878) 8 Ch D 334). The better view probably is, however, that the issue of vires must have been raised before a compromise can bind: see *Great North-West Central Rly Co v Charlebois* [1899] AC 114, *Re Jon Beauforte (London) Ltd* [1953] 1 All ER 634, [1953] Ch 131, cf *Holsworthy UDC v Holsworthy RDC* [1907] 2 Ch 62 (in which the *Charlebois* case was not cited). Further, in the field of company law, as pointed out in *Rolled Steel Products (Holdings) Ltd v British Steel Corp* [1985] 3 All ER 52 at 85, 93–94, [1986] Ch 246 at 295, 306, ultra vires principles have not been applied at every stage with ruthless logic. It also appears that, even where a corporation had no power to issue a security, it may be estopped from asserting the invalidity of the security against a third party holding it without notice of the corporation's lack of vires (see *Webb v Herne Bay Comrs* (1870) LR 5 QB 642 and *Spencer Bower and Turner* on *Estoppel by Representation* (3rd edn, 1974) p 236). The authorities also show that a dispute on whether a contract is an unlawful moneylending transaction may be the subject of a bona fide compromise (*Binder v Alachouzos* [1972] 2 All ER 189, [1972] 2 QB 151); and even an illegal contract may be effective to transfer the property in goods or an interest under a lease (*Singh v Ali* [1960] 1 All ER 269, [1960] AC 167, *Belvoir Finance Co Ltd v Stapleton* [1970] 3 All ER 664, [1971] 1 QB 210, *Feret v Hill* (1854) 15 CB 207, [1843–60] All ER Rep 924). The law has thus eschewed a rigid, doctrinaire principle that all transactions tainted by lack of vires or illegality are necessarily and for all purposes void. The policy of the law must of course be to discountenance excesses of power by statutory bodies; if that were not so the boundaries which Parliament has set would be quickly eroded. On the other hand, it is sometimes necessary to accept that 'what's done is done' and, even if it should not have been done, the law should lean in favour of such solution as enables the situation to be so far as possible rectified with minimum loss and inconvenience to all involved.

The purpose of the council in its transactions entered into after July 1988 was, as it seems to us, radically different from what it had been before. The vice of the council's transactions up to then had been its purpose of trading in the market in order to make a profit with which to fund the council's activities. After that date the council was not trading. It was seeking, in the interests of its ratepayers, to limit the damage which might flow from what might turn out to be unlawful excesses of power. It was not seeking to do this by making a profit on the market but by defensive steps designed to protect its, and its ratepayers', financial interests. We think it possible to date this change of purpose with sufficient accuracy as taking place on 25 July. The correct principle in our view is that if a local authority has unwittingly and in good faith exceeded its powers, but is with good reason uncertain whether or not it has done so, it has implied power for such period as it reasonably takes to resolve that uncertainty to take such steps as it reasonably and prudently can to limit and reduce the loss which its earlier conduct may cause to its ratepayers or community charge payers. In the present case the time taken to obtain legal advice could well be thought unreasonably long, but that is not a view which has been urged on us and the facts have not been sufficiently explored to permit a fair adjudication. Our conclusion accordingly is that the auditor is not entitled to a declaration

that the items of account are contrary to law as having been entered into for an improper
purpose in so far as they relate to transactions entered into during the interim strategy
period. If, however, that conclusion of law is wrong, then in all the circumstances we
would exercise our discretion against making a declaration on grounds of improper
purpose in respect of transactions entered into during that period: it would not seem fair
to condemn as unlawful on the auditor's application steps taken in good faith and with
his knowledge and (albeit qualified) acquiescence.

To say more would be to stray beyond the issue raised for the court's decision, which
would probably be unwise. We can see powerful grounds for contending that the council
should have been entitled to continue to take defensive steps to protect the interests of
ratepayers and community charge payers even after February 1989, since the
enforceability of previous transactions against the council then remained, as it still
remains, undecided. But we have not been asked to consider this and, as counsel aptly
observed, it might now be hard to find counterparties willing to deal in this market with
the council or, perhaps, any other local authority.

'Wednesbury' unreasonableness

In answering issue (2), the Divisional Court was of opinion that a reasonable local
authority, organised as the council was, could not (or would not) have engaged in the
transactions which the council did during the second period (April 1987 to July 1988)
but was not so satisfied in respect of the earlier period up to April 1987 or the interim
strategy period from July 1988 to February 1989. The Divisional Court's opinion adverse
to the council for the second period was based on the council's lack of legal advice, its
officers' lack of competence in this market, its lack of expertise and resources and the lack
of information given to council members.

The auditor argued that the Divisional Court should have formed the same opinion of
the first and interim strategy periods as of the second. The banks and Barclays argued
that these transactions were entered into by Hammersmith council in exercise of a
managerial discretion which is governed by principles of private law and to which
Wednesbury principles (see *Associated Provincial Picture Houses Ltd v Wednesbury Corp*
[1947] 2 All ER 680, [1948] 1 KB 223), being part of public law, have no application.
This issue gave rise to prolonged argument and the citation of much authority.

Most of this argument was in our judgment misdirected. The auditor is not applying
for judicial review under RSC Ord 53. He is not therefore obliged to identify the
'judgment, order, decision or other proceeding in respect of which relief is sought' as
Form 86A requires. Nor, of course, does he require leave to move. The public law
principles developed by the courts in ruling on the old prerogative writs and now applied,
with modifications, in applications for judicial review are accordingly not directly
applicable to an auditor seeking a declaration under s 19 that an item of account is
contrary to law. But it does not follow from that conclusion that none of the grounds
which invalidate a decision of a body in public law may be relied on by analogy by an
auditor seeking to show that an item of account is contrary to law. Such a proposition
would be plainly false. A local authority which acts outside its statutory powers is clearly
susceptible to certiorari or prohibition on an application for judicial review. Any item of
account to which such action gives rise is, equally clearly, contrary to law and liable to be
declared so under s 19.

So, too, with *Wednesbury* unreasonableness. It is certainly not an auditor's function to
monitor the wisdom, still less the political judgment, of any local authority. He is an
accountant appointed to audit the local authority's accounts, not a commissar appointed
to ensure its political rectitude. On any question of fact or judgment which might lead
reasonable local authority members or officers, viewing the question objectively, to take
differing views he has no place to intervene. If, however, he can identify to the court an
item of account reflecting a decision or course of conduct by a local authority, which is,
in Lord Diplock's famous phrase in *Council of Civil Service Unions v Minister for the Civil*

Service [1984] 3 All ER 935 at 951, [1985] AC 374 at 410, 'so outrageous in its defiance of logic or of accepted moral standards that no sensible person who had applied his mind to the question' could have so decided or acted, we have no doubt that the auditor may seek, and the court make a declaration that such item is contrary to law. That is in effect what the House of Lords did in *Roberts v Hopwood* [1925] AC 578, [1925] All ER Rep 24.

We do not consider that this issue calls for detailed discussion in this judgment. The auditor's real complaint under this head is, we think, that, even if (contrary to his contention) swap transactions are within the powers of a local authority, and even if (again contrary to his contention) these transactions or any of them were entered into for a proper purpose, it was none the less unreasonable in the *Wednesbury* sense for the council and its officers to plunge into the market on the extravagant scale they did. This is a very weighty complaint. But if, as we have concluded, all the transactions entered into by the council up to July 1988 were entered into for an improper purpose, the auditor is entitled to an appropriate declaration and it can make no difference, either to the grant of the declaration or at any later stage when questions of enforceability are resolved, whether the relevant items of account are contrary to law also on the ground that the transactions giving rise to them were irrational on the part of a local authority organised as the council was. As to transactions entered into after July 1988, we did not understand that the auditor directed this ground of complaint at these transactions entered into during the interim strategy period. If he did, the criticism in respect of this period would be misdirected.

In these circumstances we think it unnecessary and undesirable to pursue this issue further, beyond making one general observation. If, contrary to our view, the swap transactions entered into up to July 1988 were entered into for a proper purpose, the council's lack of the equipment and expertise reasonably necessary for engaging in this activity on the scale involved would not of itself lead to the conclusion that the resulting items of account were contrary to law. An auditor would, no doubt, be justified in warning a local authority strongly of the dangers inherent in such a situation. But whether all or any of the transactions entered into were contrary to law, even though entered into for a proper purpose, would depend on whether the terms of each transaction, considered separately but in the context of the transactions already undertaken by the authority, were such that no reasonable authority, applying its mind aright, would have entered into that transaction. The court might readily reach that conclusion where outside advice was not sought and the necessary skills and expertise were lacking within the authority itself. But those facts would be evidence, and would not in themselves found a conclusion in law.

Authorisation

The Divisional Court was of opinion that the council's capital market transactions were never authorised properly or at all by the council because there was no proper delegation of authority (see p 54, ante). The steps leading to that conclusion were: (1) the council's general scheme of delegation and standing orders did not of themselves confer authority to enter into these transactions; (2) there was no specific delegation of authority before February 1988; (3) recommendations made by the finance and administration committee and accepted by the council in February 1988 and February 1989, although purporting to confer express authority on the director of finance, were based on inadequate information as to the scale and risk of the transactions; and (4) any delegation to the director of finance was in any event in breach of the financial regulations of the council.

The Divisional Court's reasoning and conclusion were attacked by the banks and Barclays, reinforced by counsel for the council, but were supported by the auditor.

In considering this issue, we start from s 151 of the 1972 Act, which provides:

'Without prejudice to section 111 above, every local authority shall make arrangements for the proper administration of their financial affairs and shall secure that one of their officers has responsibility for the administration of these affairs.'

The reference to s 111, and the absence of any reference to s 101, are perhaps a little puzzling, but plainly the section imposes two distinct administrative duties on local authorities. The House of Lords had occasion to consider s 151 in *Provident Mutual Life Assurance Association v Derby City Council* [1981] 1 WLR 173. As already noted, that case concerned rating, and the facts were remote from the present. From the speech of Lord Roskill, adopted by the majority, it appears that for practical administrative reasons an appointment under s 151 is to be given a reasonably generous interpretation and that some reasonable freedom to sub-delegate must be accorded to a responsible officer so appointed.

By para 3 of section A of the council's 'General Delegation to Officers' it was provided:

'The Director of Finance or if he/she is unable to act for any reason, the Financial Controller, shall be the Officer responsible for the administration of the Authority's financial affairs (Section 151 Local Government Act 1972) but subject in all respects to the principles of corporate management established in the Authority.'

This was, we have no doubt, an effective discharge of the council's duty under s 151, and the director of finance (or the financial controller) became the responsible officer for all statutory purposes and for purposes of the Accounts and Audit (Transitional Provisions) Regulations 1983, SI 1983/249. The director of finance was also, no doubt, authorised to conduct all routine tasks of financial administration. But this provision did not stand alone. The council's general scheme of delegation also provided, in para 1:

'For the better and speedier conduct of the Council's lawful business the Council has delegated under section 101 of the Local Government Act 1972, in so far as it lawfully may, all its powers, duties and functions to the several Committees appointed under Standing Order 37 subject to this General Scheme of Delegation . . .'

Paragraph 4(a), (b) and (c) provided:

'(a) No Committee, Sub-Committee, or officer to whom powers are delegated shall exercise those powers where revenue expenditure will be incurred, or new sources of revenue secured, which are not included in appropriate approved revenue estimates, without reference to the appropriate Committee if the amount exceeds that stipulated in the Financial Regulations.
(b) Each Committee, Sub-Committee or officer to whom powers are delegated shall not exercise those powers where any capital expenditure will be incurred except in accordance with Financial Regulations . . .
(c) Each Committee, Sub-Committee or officer shall exercise all delegated powers subject to the Standing Orders, Delegation Schemes and Financial Regulations.'

The financial regulations referred to are, as one would expect, detailed. They give the director of finance responsibility for organisation and supervision of the council's financial arrangements, including a number of specified matters which do not include interest rate risk management. They provide for the preparation and approval of budgets and estimates. Committees have authority to incur expenditure up to the amount of an approved estimate. If expenditure above the estimate occurs or is likely to occur, money should if possible be moved from an estimate where the estimated sum has not been and is no longer expected to be spent, but the approval of the finance and administration committee has to be sought if more than £25,000 (or in some cases £50,000) is involved. Where such a move is not possible the approval of the finance and administration committee to a supplementary estimate must be sought. The director of finance is required to report to the relevant committee on the financial implications of any proposed new scheme or development, except where he considers it would be inappropriate to do so.

For the year 1983–84 the finance and general purposes policy committee recommended, and the council resolved, to borrow—

'up to the maximum allowed by government regulation in the form of negotiable
bonds on such terms and conditions as the director of finance thinks fit, bearing in
mind the alternative sources of borrowing.'

For the year 1984–85 the same procedure was followed but the wording was somewhat
different and the director of finance was 'authorised to administer the statutory provisions
and regulations relating to the borrowing of such monies, subject also to the Council's
financial regulations'. The same procedure and language were used for the year 1985–
86. There was another change of language but no change of substance for the year 1986–
87. Although express reference was made to interest rate swaps in the annual loans and
investments report for 1986 and the annual report for 1986–87, no detail was given.

The financial year 1987–88 is the first of those to which the auditor's application
directly relates. Up to this time the council had confined its activity to some 24
transactions, all of them interest rate swaps. No written report on these, or any
contemplated activity in future, was (so far as we know) made to the council or any
committee before the 1987–88 financial year began, other than in the most general
terms. There had been no written authority to the director of finance or any other officer
beyond those we have quoted. We have no evidence of any oral report or authority. For
the year 1987–88 the financial and administration committee recommended and the
council resolved in the terms:

'That the Council borrows to meet its revenue and capital payments during the
year ending 31 March 1988 and authorises the Director of Finance to arrange and
administer the Council's borrowing on its behalf. That the Council authorises the
Director of Finance, on its behalf, to borrow in the year ending 31 march 1988 up
to £10 million in the form of negotiable bonds on terms and conditions to be agreed
by the Director of Finance.'

This very bland and general resolution could not reasonably be understood, in our
opinion, as authorising the director of finance or any other officer to enter into interest
rate swap and related transactions which, however prudently judged, were liable to
involve a degree of risk. This appears to have been the view of Mr Price also, since in a
message to Mr Robb of 12 January 1988 he drew attention to the need to establish the
extent of the powers delegated to the officers. During this financial year (1987–88) some
200 transactions were entered into.

On 17 February 1988 it was reported to the finance and administration committee:

'The Director of Finance has also continued to arrange, where applicable,
transactions in the London money/capital markets in order to maximise gains on
favourable interest rate movements.'

No detail of any kind was given, at least in writing. In addition to the standard authority
to arrange and administer the council's borrowing on its behalf, and perhaps as a result
of Mr Price's memo, the director of finance was on this occasion (24 February 1988)
authorised by the council—

'to arrange transactions in the London money/capital markets in order to take
advantage of favourable interest rate movements on such terms and conditions as
are agreed by the Director of Finance.'

A similar procedure was followed in February 1989 for the then forthcoming year,
but the auditor's intervention and the receipt of counsel's final opinion prevented action
being taken on the council resolution.

On these materials, and in the absence of evidence from the officers involved, we feel
bound to conclude that until February 1988 neither the council nor any committee
authorised the director of finance or any of his subordinates to enter into these capital
market transactions. Section 151, the council's schemes of delegation and the minutes

and resolutions relied on do not purport to give such authority. The resolution of February 1988 cannot in our judgment be relied on as ratification of what had gone before (a) because ratification requires knowledge, and we are not persuaded that council members appreciated what had happened, and (b) because the resolution was not expressed to relate to the past.

Was the council resolution of February 1988 authority to the director of finance to enter into transactions of this type during the financial year 1988–89? Assuming, without deciding (for the contrary was not argued), that the resolution was in terms wide enough to authorise what followed, in our judgment the auditor is justified in submitting that it was unreasonable to the point of gross irrationality for any local authority on the exiguous material apparently put before the finance and administration committee and the council, to authorise the director of finance to enter into swap transactions without any limit as to type, amount, terms or period. Accordingly, in our judgment the council's decision to accord such authority was vitiated by irrationality.

When the auditor intervened in July 1988 the council did not, it appears, adopt any further resolution to authorise the steps thereafter taken during the interim strategy period. In our judgment a council meeting should then have been called to receive a report on the transactions entered into in the past and to give such authority as the council thought fit for the immediate future. We do not, however, consider it appropriate to grant a declaration in respect of items of account arising from transactions entered into during the interim strategy period. Had a meeting been called and a full report made, with an explanation of the procedure and safeguards suggested by the auditor to protect the council's position pending receipt of legal advice, we think it probable that the council would (and we think it could quite rationally) have authorised substantially the steps which were in fact taken. We do not think these steps, taken in the circumstances and for the purpose they were, should be stigmatised as unlawful. We feel sure that the Divisional Court would have been influenced by these considerations had it been drawn to its attention.

The establishment of the capital market fund

The Divisional Court was of opinion that no capital market fund was ever validly established (see p 55, ante). Having set out the salient facts (see p 54, ante), which we need not repeat, they based this opinion on the grounds (1) that although the documents referred to the beginning of work to set up the fund they contained no reference to completion of the work, (2) that the intended fund was not a fund for meeting the council's expenditure in connection with its functions within the meaning of para 16(1)(b) of Sch 13 to the 1972 Act, (3) that there was no evidence that the council maintained any fund in the sense of a 'portion of revenue set apart as security for specified payments', (4) that the council had no function of dealing in the capital markets and therefore no power to set up such a fund and (5) that no authority to deal on the capital markets was delegated until at earliest 24 February 1988 and no fund could therefore have been established before that date.

We do not think this topic merits protracted discussion, since there is in our judgment no answer to the points that the council never resolved to establish such a fund and never in fact did so. Whether, in any event, it is appropriate for an authority entering into swap transactions for the purposes of interest rate risk management to establish a separate fund for the purpose of meeting expenditure arising from these transactions seems doubtful, but we need not and do not express any concluded view on this. The question of the capital market fund in the present proceedings is, in truth, a peripheral question since, if the only issue between the auditor and the council had been whether transactions properly entered into had been properly accounted for, we cannot think that an application under s 19 would have been necessary to resolve it. Understandably, the banks addressed no argument on this issue.

Conclusions

It may be of assistance if we briefly summarise our conclusions. We conclude that *a* interest rate swap transactions within the eight categories identified by the auditor are capable of being within the powers conferred on local authorities by Parliament. Such transactions, however, must be entered into for purposes of interest rate risk management and not for trading purposes. The transactions entered into by the council up to 25 July 1988 were without exception entered into for the purpose of trading and not for purposes of interest rate risk management. They were accordingly entered into for an improper *b* purpose and were in that sense outside the powers of the council. The items of account relating to those transactions are accordingly contrary to law within the meaning of s 19 of the 1972 Act and the auditor is entitled to a declaration to that effect. The transactions entered into by the council from 25 July 1988 to February 1989 were entered into for the purpose of mitigating or averting potential loss to the ratepayers and community charge payers of the borough, which was a lawful and proper purpose. The auditor is not *c* entitled to a declaration that items of account relating to those transactions are contrary to law as entered into for an improper purpose. Nor, in the exercise of our discretion, do we grant such a declaration on the grounds that those transactions were not properly authorised. No capital markets fund was validly established by the council. The question whether any outstanding contract is enforceable as between the council and any other party is not before us and we express no opinion on it. *d*

We shall make a declaration accordingly. We shall not make an order for rectification of the accounts unless persuaded that there is some point in doing so and that it is appropriate to do so at this stage.

The appeals are therefore allowed in part to the extent that I have indicated in the summary of our conclusions.

e

Declaration of Divisional Court affirmed save in so far as it related to transactions entered into after 25 July 1988. No order for rectification of accounts. Leave to appeal to the House of Lords granted.

Solicitors: *Clifford Chance* (for the banks); *Linklaters & Paines* (for Barclays); *Herbert Smith* (for the council); *A A Child* (for the auditor).

Bebe Chua   Barrister.

a   # Re F (minor: abduction: jurisdiction)

COURT OF APPEAL, CIVIL DIVISION
LORD DONALDSON OF LYMINGTON MR, NEILL AND BALCOMBE LJJ
30 JULY 1990

b   *Minor – Custody – Rights of custody – Foreign custody rights – Jurisdiction – Wrongful removal
or retention – Removal from non-convention country – Father removing child from Israel to
England in breach of mother's rights of custody – Mother obtaining interim custody order from
Israeli court – Father subsequently obtaining similar order from English court – Principles
applicable in deciding appropriate forum to determine child's welfare – Whether English court
should order child to be returned to Israel – Child Abduction and Custody Act 1985, Sch 1,*
c   *art 13.*

The father, who had both English and Israeli nationality, married the mother, an Israeli
national, in Israel in 1979. They had two boys, one born in 1980 and another born in
1986. The parties resided in Israel except for a period between 1982 and 1985 when they
lived in England. The marriage was not happy and throughout there were difficulties,
d   separations and reconciliations. In 1989 they finally separated. Under Israeli law they
were joint guardians of the children. On 4 April 1990 the father came to England with
the youngest child, B, and, in breach of the mother's rights of custody under Israeli law,
refused to return the child to the mother. On 15 April the mother applied to an Israeli
court for interim custody of both children. Three weeks later the father made a similar
application to a county court in England. The Israeli court found in favour of the mother
e   and ordered the father to return the child to Israel. The mother then applied to the
county court for an order requiring the father to return the child to Israel but the judge
gave interim care and control of the child to the father pending further inquiries by the
court welfare officer and ordered the case to be transferred to the High Court and also
forbade the mother to remove the child out of the jurisdiction. The mother appealed
against those orders. Since Israel was not a party to the Convention on the Civil Aspects
f   of International Child Abduction as set out in Sch 1 to the Child Abduction and Custody
Act 1985 the question arose as to the extent to which convention principles were
applicable.

Held – Where a child was wrongfully removed from a foreign jurisdiction to the United
Kingdom an English court should not retain jurisdiction merely on the basis that a
g   possible outcome of custody proceedings, whether in the United Kingdom or the foreign
jurisdiction, was that the child may be ordered to remain in the United Kingdom.
Instead, applying the principle that the welfare of the child was paramount, it was
normally in the interests of a child that it should not be abducted and any decision
relating to the custody of the child was normally best decided by the court in the state
where the child was habitually resident. Accordingly, the English court should order the
h   return of an abducted child to the jurisdiction of the court in the state where the child
was habitually resident if that court would apply principles which were acceptable to
English courts, there were no contraindications such as those referred to in art 13[a] of the

---

a   Article 13, so far as material, provides: '. . . the judicial or administrative authority of the requested
State is not bound to order the return of the child if the person, institution or other body which
j   opposes its return establishes that—(a) the person, institution or other body having the care of the
person of the child was not actually exercising the custody rights at the time of removal or
retention, or had consented to or subsequently acquiesced in the removal or retention; or (b) there
is a grave risk that his or her return would expose the child to physical or psychological harm or
otherwise place the child in an intolerable situation. The judicial or administrative authority may
also refuse to order the return of the child if it finds that the child objects to being returned and
has attained the age and degree of maturity at which it is appropriate to take account of its views.'

convention and there was no risk of persecution or discrimination. Where the removal
of a child was in breach of rights of custody, the existence of prior orders by a foreign
court did no more than affirm or reinforce those rights and, furthermore, the fact that
there were ties with England was merely one of the matters to be considered by the court
charged with resolving the dispute between the parents and did not point to the English
court as being the appropriate court for that purpose. Moreover, possible outcomes of
any proceedings had no bearing on which court should decide the issue of custody.
Applying the normal rule that abducted children should be returned to their country of
habitual residence the father would be ordered to arrange for the immediate return of
the child to Israel. The mother's appeal would accordingly be allowed (see p 100 b to g j
to p 101 d, post).

Notes

For the return of abducted children, see Supplement to 8 Halsbury's Laws (4th edn) para
525A.

Cases referred to in judgments

Barrios and Sanchez [1989] FLC 92-054, Aust Fam Ct.
G (a minor) (wardship: jurisdiction), Re [1984] FLR 268, CA.
Giraudo v Giraudo [1989] CA Transcript 527.
H (infants), Re [1966] 1 All ER 886, [1966] 1 WLR 381, CA.
H and H [1985] FLC 91-640, Aust Fam Ct.
Khamis and Khamis [1978] FLC 90-486, Aust Fam Ct.

Case also cited

L (minors) (wardship: jurisdiction) [1974] 1 All ER 913, [1974] 1 WLR 250, CA.

Appeal

The mother of a minor appealed against the order of her Honour Judge Viner QC sitting
in the Hastings County Court on 2 July 1990 granting interim custody, care and control
of the child Ben to the father until final disposal of the matter, refusing the mother's
application for the return of the child to Israel, ordering the parties' claims for custody of
the child to be heard by the Family Division of the High Court and restraining the
mother from removing the child from the father's care or from the jurisdiction of the
court. The facts are set out in the judgment of Lord Donaldson MR.

Adrian Salter for the mother.
Judith Rowe for the father.

LORD DONALDSON OF LYMINGTON MR. This is an international child
abduction case. It is not, however, one to which the Child Abduction and Custody Act
1985 applies because Israel has not yet been named in an Order in Council made under
s 2, and may indeed not be a party to the Convention on the Civil Aspects of International
Child Abduction (The Hague, 25 October 1980; TS 66 (1986); Cm 33) to which that Act
gives effect. Nevertheless, like all international child abduction cases, it is in a special
category.
    The facts are these. The father is English by birth, but has acquired additional Israeli
nationality. The mother is Israeli by birth. They met at Kibbutz Yif'at in Israel in 1975
and in 1977 the father was converted to Judaism. He returned to England and in January
1979 sent the mother a telegram announcing that he was coming to Israel and proposing
marriage. His proposal was accepted and he went to Israel. However, in May 1979 he
had second thoughts and broke off the engagement. In the following month the couple
were in fact married, when the mother told him that she was pregnant, and the child,
Ron, was born in January 1980. Ron is therefore ten and a half years old. Ben, the child

with which these proceedings are primarily concerned, was born in September 1986, and
a   is therefore just under four years old.

The marriage has not been a happy one and in May 1989 the parties were considering
a divorce. Nothing came of this, but in September 1989 they executed an informal
separation agreement and were rehoused in separate accommodation in the kibbutz.
Under the agreement both parents had 'control', to use the word used in the agreement,
of the children and it provided for divided care. Whatever the status of that agreement,
b   it is clear that under ss 14 and 15 of the Israeli Capacity and Guardianship Law 1962 the
parents are joint guardians of their minor children, and have joint custody and the joint
right to determine their place of residence.

The basic disagreement between the parents is clearly concerned with where they shall
live, although there are no doubt other problems. The father wants to live in England.
Indeed, he left the mother and Ron, the elder child, in Israel in October 1980, and it was
c   not until September 1982 that he and the mother were reconciled. That reconciliation
was achieved when the mother and Ron joined him in England. The mother was
unhappy in England, but stayed here until 1985 when the family moved back to Israel.
Since then, both parties have lived in Israel, although the father paid a short visit to
England last Christmas, accompanied by the younger son, Ben. Before the mother would
agree to that visit, she required the father to give security for the prompt return of Ben.
d   On or about 4 April of this year the father came to England, taking Ben with him.
They are now living with the paternal grandparents. He neither obtained nor even
sought the consent of the mother, and left her a letter falsely promising to return Ben on
18 April. On 15 April the mother applied to the District Court of Nazareth for interim
custody of both children, and on 26 April the father made a similar application to the
Hastings County Court in relation to Ben. The Nazareth court made an order in favour
e   of the mother and ordered the father to return Ben. The mother applied to the Hastings
court for an order requiring the return of Ben to Israel, but this was refused pending
further inquiries in the form of a court welfare officer's report which was to include the
result of inquiries in Israel. Meanwhile, the father was given interim custody and care
and control, the case was transferred to the Family Division of the High Court and the
mother was forbidden to remove Ben from the jurisdiction.
f   The Hastings County Court orders were made by her Honour Judge Viner QC, and it
is from those orders that the mother now appeals.

No one could or would criticise the judge's decision to order further inquiries and to
give interim care, custody and control to the father, who is, after all, the only parent
present in England, provided always that it was appropriate that the English rather than
the Israeli courts should decide what the welfare of Ben required. If it was more
g   appropriate that this should be decided by the Israeli courts, as I have no doubt that it
was, she should have ordered the return of Ben to Israel at the earliest possible moment.

If this had been a convention case, there would have been no argument. The father's
action in bringing Ben to England was a 'wrongful removal' within the meaning of the
convention, having been undertaken in breach of the mother's rights of custody under
h   the law of Ben's habitual place of residence immediately before the removal. There are
no contraindications, such as those contemplated by art 13. But this is not a convention
case and the question inevitably arises of the extent to which convention principles are
applicable.

I agree with Balcombe LJ's view expressed in *Giraudo v Giraudo* [1989] CA Transcript
527 that, in enacting the 1985 Act, Parliament was not departing from the fundamental
j   principle that the welfare of the child is paramount. Rather it was giving effect to a
belief—

'that in normal circumstances it is in the interests of children that parents or
others shall not abduct them from one jurisdiction to another, but that any decision
relating to the custody of the children is best decided in the jurisdiction in which
they have hitherto been normally resident.'

This decision was not drawn to the judge's attention, although she was referred to two earlier cases, *Re H (infants)* [1966] 1 All ER 886, [1966] 1 WLR 381 and *Re G (a minor)* *a* *(wardship: jurisdiction)* [1984] FLR 268, in which children were ordered to be returned. She distinguished those cases on the grounds that in each case there had been orders by foreign courts relating to the children prior to their removal and that in *Re G* the family had no fixed ties with England, although the mother was of English nationality. In the instant case, by contrast, she held that the father had important ties with England and that not all Ben's ties were with Israel.

For my part, I consider that the existence of prior orders by a foreign court is of little, if any, significance so long as the removal was in breach of rights of custody. The existence of a prior order would do no more than affirm and reinforce those rights. So far as ties with England are concerned, this is one of the matters which falls to be considered by the court charged with resolving the dispute between the parents. It does not point to the English courts as the courts appropriate for that purpose.

Similarly, I reject the judge's reliance on her view of Ben's future. As she put it: '. . . this is not a case where his future is inevitably tied up with Israel. It might be so, but that is not an inevitable certainty.' That is something which has to be taken into account by the appropriate court, be it English or Israeli, but does not point to one rather than the other.

Finally, the judge expressed doubts as to the extent to which the father is free to return to Israel without adverse consequences as a result of his abduction of Ben. If, for example, he were imprisoned, this would deprive Ben of his father's care and attention for a period. Quite apart from the fact that this involves the father being allowed to rely on his own wrong, it ignores the fact that, so long as Ben remains in England, he is cut off from his mother and younger brother. In fact, the criminal charges were instituted in Israel by the mother when she discovered that Ben had been abducted, and we are told that she does not intend to press those charges. Of course, it will be for the Israeli authorities to decide what difference that makes.

There is no evidence that the Israeli courts would adopt an approach to the problem of Ben's future which differs significantly from that of the English courts. It is not a case in which Ben or his father are escaping any form of persecution or ethnic, sex or other discrimination. In a word, there is nothing to take it out of the normal rule that abducted children should be returned to their country of habitual residence.

The welfare of the child is indeed the paramount consideration, but it has to be considered in two different contexts. The first is the context of which court shall decide what the child's best interests require. The second context, which only arises if it has first been decided that the welfare of the child requires that the English rather than a foreign court shall decide what are the requirements of the child, is what orders as to custody, care and control and so on should be made.

In my judgment, the judge mixed the two questions. Thus, in her judgment, having distinguished *Re G (a minor) (wardship: jurisdiction)* [1984] FLR 268, on the basis that the parents were of different nationalities, but the mother, though English, had no fixed ties with Britain, she continued in this way:

> 'In this case the applicant clearly has important ties with this country notwithstanding his conversion and acceptance of dual nationality. It could not be said that on common sense all Ben's ties are with Israel. As regards the future and Ben, this is not a case where his future is inevitably tied up with Israel. It might be so, but that is not an inevitable certainty.'

In other words, she was saying that, if one possible outcome of any proceedings, whether in Israel or England, would be that Ben might remain in England, the English courts should retain jurisdiction.

This is an error in principle. Possible outcomes have no bearing on which court should decide. Which court should decide depends, as I have said, on whether the court will

apply principles which are acceptable to the English courts as being appropriate, subject
a always to any contraindication such as those mentioned in art 13 of the convention, or a
risk of persecution or discrimination, but prima facie the court to decide is that of the
state where the child was habitually resident immediately before its removal.

I would allow the appeal accordingly and order the immediate return of Ben to Israel.

NEILL LJ. I agree. The general principle is that, in the ordinary way, any decision
b relating to the custody of children is best decided in the jurisdiction in which they have
normally been resident. This general principle is an application of the wider and basic
principle that the child's welfare is the first and paramount consideration. This principle
is subject to exceptions and these exceptions will no doubt be worked out in future cases.
In the present case, however, I can see no reason whatever why the general principle
should not be applied. I too consider that the judge erred in this case and applied the
c wrong principle. Accordingly, this court is entitled to, and should, interfere. I too, for
the reasons explained by Lord Donaldson MR, would allow this appeal.

BALCOMBE LJ. I agree that this appeal should be allowed for the reasons given by
Lord Donaldson MR and Neill LJ and following the decision of this court in *Giraudo v
Giraudo* [1989] CA Transcript 527.
d   I add that the effect we are giving to the Child Protection and Custody Act 1985 in
relation to non-convention countries is consistent with the practice which the Australian
courts have adopted.

By 1976 Australia had entered into bilateral treaties with New Zealand and Papua New
Guinea with respect to children removed from those jurisdictions, and those treaties
were enshrined in the provisions of s 68 of the Australian Family Law Act. That
e enactment helped then to shape the common law. In *Khamis and Khamis* [1978] FLC 90-
486, when dealing with a child who had been removed from California, the Full Court
of the Family Court of Australia indicated that, in determining an appropriate forum,
the court should endeavour to apply principles identical to those outlined in s 68 of the
Family Law Act, notwithstanding that California was not a signatory to any bilateral
treaty, nor did the legislation particularly apply to it.
f   Australia, but not Chile, is a party to the Convention on the Civil Aspects of
International Child Abduction (The Hague, 25 October 1980; TS66 (1986); Cm 33), and
in *Barrios and Sanchez* [1989] FLC 92-054 the Full Court of the Family Court of Australia
was concerned with children who had been removed from Chile to Australia. In its
judgment the court said (at 77, 609):

g   '. . . the clear policy of the Convention is that save in exceptional circumstances,
        children who have been removed from their lawful custodial parent in another
        country without the authority of a court should be returned to that parent. In the
        present case we think it is appropriate to take this into account as an element to be
        considered . . .'

h   I also agree with what the Full Court of the Family Court of Australia said in *H and H*
[1985] FLC 91-640 that, as a general principle, courts should act in comity to discourage
the abduction of children across national borders. The forum which has the pre-eminent
claim to jurisdiction is the place where the child habitually resided immediately prior to
the time when it was removed or retained without the consent of the other parent.

In my judgment, a rapid accession to the Hague Convention by all nations would be a
j welcome advance towards the recognition of the rule of law by all nations.

Appeal allowed.

Solicitors: *Cartier & Co* (for the mother); *Morgan & Lamplugh*, Hastings (for the father).

                                        Mary Rose Plummer   Barrister.

Re G (a minor) (ward: criminal injuries compensation)

COURT OF APPEAL, CIVIL DIVISION

LORD DONALDSON OF LYMINGTON MR, BUTLER-SLOSS AND TAYLOR LJJ

14 JUNE 1990

Ward of court – Practice – Criminal injuries compensation claim – Application for leave to claim compensation – Application made by Official Solicitor acting as guardian ad litem of ward – Ward a victim of sexual abuse by father – Test to be applied by judge in deciding whether to allow application to proceed.

In 1983 the mother and father were married and had a child. In 1985 the parents separated and the father was granted custody of the child and the mother was granted access. The mother presented a divorce petition and in 1987 retained the child following an access visit. Subsequently, matters came to light indicating that the child had been the victim of sexual abuse for which the father was later found to be responsible. A place of safety order was obtained by the police and the child was placed with the local authority, which issued wardship proceedings. The child remained in the care of the local authority but was currently living with her mother and grandparents. The father's access to the child was terminated in October 1989. After the order terminating access was made, the Official Solicitor, as guardian ad litem, applied for leave to make an application on behalf of the child to the Criminal Injuries Compensation Board. The judge refused the application on the grounds that there was no reasonable prospect of such an application succeeding, that there had been no violent sexual abuse and that it would be against the interests of the child for the application to be made. The Official Solicitor appealed.

Held – Applications for leave to make a claim on behalf of a ward of court to the Criminal Injuries Compensation Board should be filtered in a manner analogous to applications for leave to apply for judicial review. Accordingly, a judge hearing such an application should consider whether it was arguable or hopeless rather than whether it would succeed before the board. If it was arguable then it was for the board and not for the judge to decide whether it came within their criteria and whether an ex gratia payment should be made. Where an application was made on behalf of a child and the judge decided it was not a hopeless application the judge should go on to consider whether, having regard to the paramount interest of the welfare of the child, it was in the interests of the child that the application should go forward to the board. Where the application was made by the Official Solicitor it would only be in rare circumstances that the court would find it necessary to hold that it was not appropriate to make an application, since not only did the Official Solicitor have great experience in dealing with wards of court but he was an officer of the court charged to act as guardian ad litem for children in High Court proceedings and accordingly his position was different from a member of the family who might wish to make a speculative claim in respect of a ward of court and whose claim ought accordingly to be more carefully filtered. Since the application was arguable and on balance would be in the child's interests the Official Solicitor should be permitted to act on the child's behalf in making the application to the board. Accordingly, the appeal would be allowed (see p 105 *b c e* to *g* and p 106 *c* to *g*, post).

Notes

For compensation for victims of crimes of violence, see 11(2) Halsbury's Laws (4th edn reissue) paras 1505–510, and for cases on the subject, see 14(2) Digest (Reissue) 865–867, 7493–7499.

For the duties of the Official Solicitor, see 10 Halsbury's Laws (4th edn) para 950.

Case referred to in judgments
a G (a minor) (child abuse: standard of proof), Re [1987] 1 WLR 1461.

Case also cited
R v Criminal Injuries Compensation Board, ex p Warner [1986] 2 All ER 478, sub nom R v Criminal Injuries Compensation Board, ex p Webb [1987] QB 74, CA.

b **Interlocutory appeal**
The minor, a ward of court in the care of a local authority but living with her mother and her maternal grandparents, suing by the Official Solicitor as her guardian ad litem, applied for an extension of time in which to appeal, and also appealed, against the order of Rattee J sitting in chambers at Bristol on 19 October 1989 refusing an application by the Official Solicitor on behalf of the ward for leave to make an application to the Criminal Injuries Compensation Board. The father of the ward opposed the application and was the respondent to the appeal. The facts are set out in the judgment of Butler-Sloss LJ.

Allan Levy QC and Richard Bond for the ward.
d Andrew Kirkwood QC and Suzan Matthews for the father.
The local authority was not represented.
The mother and the grandparents did not appear.

BUTLER-SLOSS LJ (delivering the first judgment at the invitation of Lord Donaldson MR). This is an application for leave to appeal out of time, which is not opposed, and, e therefore, leave has been granted. It is also an appeal by the Official Solicitor on behalf of the ward, in respect of whom he acts as guardian ad litem, from the decision of Rattee J given on 19 October 1989. On that occasion the judge refused an application for leave by the Official Solicitor to make an application on behalf of the ward to the Criminal Injuries Compensation Board.

This case has a very complicated history. But it is only necessary to provide a few facts f for the purpose of this particular application.

The parents were married on 2 September 1983 and the little girl was born a month or so after the marriage of the parents, on 22 October 1983. The parents separated in 1985 and the little girl remained with her father. There was a magistrates' court custody order to the father with access to the mother. The mother issued a divorce petition and, after an access visit to the mother on 30 January 1987, the mother retained the child.

g Thereafter, the matters came to light which have come before the courts over a number of years. As a result of allegations by the grandmother which were not sustainable, a place of safety order was obtained by the police and the child was placed with the local authority, who issued wardship proceedings on 5 February 1987 and the child remains to this day in the care of the local authority, although currently she is living with her mother and her grandparents.

h There have been numerous hearings. The main hearing before Sheldon J took some ten days in May and June of 1987 and the judge made various findings, including one which is highly relevant to today's appeal, that is to say that the child had been the victim of sexual abuse: see Re G (a minor) (child abuse: standard of proof) [1987] 1 WLR 1461. In his judgment Sheldon J said (at 1469):

i 'In all the circumstances, however, even applying a more stringent test than a mere "balance of probabilities" I have been driven to the conclusion, without considering it necessary to spell it out in greater detail, that [the father] has been guilty of an over-familiar and sexually inappropriate relationship with her, amounting in the present context to sexual abuse, which could bode ill for the future and which has created the "particularly vulnerable" little girl described by Dr Gaye. Nor, in my judgment, is there any evidence to justify the conclusion that anyone but [the father] could be held responsible for that state of affairs.'

The judge confirmed the wardship, confirmed that the child remain in the care and control of the local authority with a view to the child going to live with her mother in *a* due course, as she did, but he also made an order that there should be continued access to the father on evidence that such access would be beneficial to the little girl.

The access to the father was limited and supervised, and there were a considerable number of hearings after the main judgment of Sheldon J in relation to access. The access was unsuccessful and it became the view of the medical experts who had earlier supported access before Sheldon J that by 1989 it was disadvantageous to the child and should be *b* brought to an end. The application before Rattee J which was concluded on 19 October 1989 was that the access to the father should be terminated.

The judge heard evidence over three days and he made the order that access should be terminated. He said:

> 'In my judgment it is clearly in [the child's] interests to terminate access by her father . . . I am, nevertheless, convinced that the potential harm to [the child] of *c* again subjecting her to the distress suffered by her both before and after access in the circumstances of this case outweighs the advantage of access to her. In my judgment there should be no more access by the father to [the child] during her minority, or until further order.'

He also said that he hoped that the mother and the grandparents— *d*

> 'should do their best not impose their opinion on [the child]. To express to the child antagonism against the father can only be harmful to [the child], whatever the truth of the circumstances giving rise to that antagonism . . . For her future well-being she must be allowed, in my judgment, in time, and freely, to form her own views of him, and must not be made to inherit the views of her mother and her *e* grandparents, however justified those views may be.'

Immediately after the decision on termination of access, the judge made the decision which is appealed to this court on two grounds: that there was no reasonable prospect of success of an application to the Criminal Injuries Compensation Board and that it would be against the interests of the child to make that application.

The judge referred to the high degree of animosity and hostility between the mother *f* and her parents on the one side and the father on the other, and was very concerned about the adverse effect of such hostility on the child and made the comments which I have just read out. That clearly had a very marked effect on his approach to this application to the Criminal Injuries Compensation Board. He saw the need to reduce tension and he saw in the application a risk of perpetuating the concentration on the sexual abuse caused to the child by making such an application. *g*

This is an application by the Official Solicitor, who appeals to this court. He is very experienced in making these applications and has made many in the past on behalf of wards. It is the normal practice for such an application to be made ex parte. There is a Practice Direction which requires: 'Where a ward of court has a right to make a claim for compensation to the Criminal Injuries Compensation Board application must be made *h* by the guardian ad litem of the child for leave to apply and' to disclose the confidential documents in wardship which otherwise would not be disclosed to the board (see [1988] 1 All ER 182, [1988] 1 WLR 33). Such an application may be made ex parte to a registrar if leave has not been given by the judge at the wardship hearing.

Therefore, the standing of the father, who opposed the application before the judge and is the respondent to this appeal, is somewhat tenuous. Technically, he is a party to *j* the proceedings. He has a right, obviously, to be heard on the welfare of the child. He would not, in the normal course of events, be served with notice of the application, which can, according to the Practice Direction, be made ex parte, and he would not necessarily have any knowledge that such an application has been made. In this case he

has that knowledge and he has strenuously opposed the application being made to the
a board. He opposed it before the judge and before this court on the grounds that there
was no crime of violence and there was no reasonable prospect of success, and also that it
is not in the interests of the child.

The judge found that there was no violent sexual abuse and he also found that it was
against the interests of the child that this application should be made.

Both of those, of course, are matters for the board. The board has to consider whether
b it is against the interests of the child to make such an application, when the child has
lived in the household of the person in respect of whom the application has been made:
see para 8(*d*) of the Criminal Injuries Compensation Scheme 1979 (now para 8(*c*) of the
1990 scheme). This child has, according to the Official Solicitor acting as guardian ad
litem, a claim. It is one which may or may not succeed before the board. There are facts
found by Sheldon J which show sexual abuse. It is, in my judgment, a matter for them
c whether those facts amount to sufficient for them to make an order for compensation
which is ex gratia, this being a non-statutory scheme.

It is an application which is made in writing and the consideration is on the papers. It
is, I would have thought, in this case unlikely that the Official Solicitor would go forward
to an oral hearing before the board. If he did so, it would not in this case involve the
child, and could not involve the child's mother and grandparents because they would
d have no information which they would be able to give to the board.

The first question on which the judge refused this application was that there was no
crime of violence. Counsel for the father accepts that, if it is a crime at all, it is a violent
crime or is capable of being a violent crime in the circumstances of the evidence found
by Sheldon J.

In my view, it is not for the judge, on the making of such an application for leave to
e go to the Criminal Injuries Compensation Board, to try the very issue which is specifically
within the remit of the board. The position is, in my view, that the court should act as a
filter somewhat analogous to an application for leave to apply for judicial review. Is this
a hopeless application; alternatively, is it arguable, rather than will it succeed? If the
application is hopeless or is not arguable, then it is right for the court to say that it is not
a proper case to make an application. If it is arguable, then it is a matter for the board to
f decide whether it comes within their criteria and whether they should make their ex
gratia payment.

There are two stages to this. First, whether it is a hopeless application. If it is not a
hopeless application, then the judge will go on to consider whether it is in the interests
of the child, since the welfare of the child is paramount, that the application should go
forward to the board. The interests of the child here will not, in my judgment, be
g adversely affected, or so adversely affected that this claim should not be made. The
prospects of access to the father are very, very unlikely for the foreseeable future. The
judge himself has terminated access. Although the judge asked the mother and the
grandparents not to impose their views on the child, she is now six, she is aware that she
has had access to her father and that that has not been successful, and the degree of
h distress which has been exhibited by this child is unlikely, in my view, to go away
quickly. In so far as she may ask about her father, however much the mother and the
grandparents try to be protective, human nature being what it is, they are not likely to
speak positively of the father. One of these days this child may come back to seeing her
father. She may come back to having a relationship with him, but that is not for the
foreseeable future and was not believed to be so by the judge.

j In those circumstances, an application made by the Official Solicitor and not by the
family is one which is not likely to heighten the tension to any great extent or exacerbate
unduly the existing situation of the child and the family with whom she lives. If the
application succeeds, the child will receive a sum of money which, to a child who one
would assume has no money of her own, is bound to be substantial and will be of value

to her. The fact that in due course she may learn the source of such money is not likely dramatically to increase the adverse effect on a child who will know, if she asks, why it is *a* that she has ceased to see her father and is bound, sooner or later, to know what has been alleged. These are not matters that can be kept from children for ever, and I do not, in the context of this case, see that this child will be much more affected by this application and by a finding that the Criminal Injuries Compensation Board have awarded her money because she was sexually abused than by the facts which gave rise to the application. *b*

The other aspect which was raised by counsel for the father, interestingly enough, at the end of his submissions is that this is a claim that may not succeed. If it does not succeed, it could, indeed, be a matter which would help the father and might, I suppose, consequently help the child if or when it is right that the child should recommence in the future a relationship with the father.

I do not agree with the judge that this is a case with no reasonable prospect of success. *c* It is, at its lowest, arguable and, therefore, the second stage arises: is it in the interests of the child that the application should go ahead? In my judgment, the judge misdirected himself, first, in finding that this was an application which should not be made and, second, in over-stressing one aspect of the case, that is to say the adverse effect on the child of making the application, without putting into the balancing exercise all the other matters to which I have just referred. *d*

I would only just add this. I do, speaking entirely for myself, consider that the Official Solicitor is in a special position, not only because he has great experience in dealing with wards of court, but he is an officer of the court charged to act as a guardian ad litem for children in High Court proceedings and, if he makes an application that a child should be permitted to apply to the Criminal Injuries Compensation Board, it can only in rare circumstances be necessary for the court to find that it is not an appropriate application *e* to make. If he were to make frivolous applications, the consequences would rebound on him, and I am sure he will deal with this particular application with moderation and sensitivity so that it will minimise any adverse effect upon the child. The position of the Official Solicitor is somewhat different from a member of the family who might wish to make a speculative claim in respect of a ward of court that ought to be more carefully *f* filtered through in the way to which I have already referred.

For those reasons I take the view that this appeal should be allowed and the Official Solicitor should be permitted to act on behalf of the child in making an application to the Criminal Injuries Compensation Board.

TAYLOR LJ. I agree. *g*

LORD DONALDSON OF LYMINGTON MR. I also agree and, in particular, with the remarks that Butler-Sloss LJ has made about the special position of the Official Solicitor.

Appeal allowed. No order for costs. *h*

Solicitors: *Official Solicitor*; *Thomas Eggar Verrall Bowles*, Horsham (for the father).

Mary Rose Plummer   Barrister.

a Hastingwood Property Ltd v Saunders Bearman Anselm (a firm)

CHANCERY DIVISION

EDWARD NUGEE QC SITTING AS A DEPUTY JUDGE OF THE HIGH COURT

b 4, 11 APRIL 1990

Solicitor – Stakeholder – Deposit paid to solicitor as stakeholder – Solicitor paying out deposit to one party on happening of specified event – Other party objecting to payment out – Whether stakeholder required to retain deposit pending arbitration of dispute between parties – Whether stakeholder's position affected by his position as solicitor for one of the parties.

c *Solicitor – Undertaking by solicitor – Summary jurisdiction – Extent of jurisdiction – Whether court's summary jurisdiction over solicitors exercisable whenever solicitor has accepted obligation in capacity as solicitor.*

The plaintiff company entered into a joint venture with a company which was set up by *d* the two partners in the defendant firm of solicitors, for the purchase, development and sale of a property. In accordance with the terms of the joint venture agreement the plaintiff company paid £80,000 to the defendant solicitors to be held by them as stakeholders and deposited in a designated deposit account until either 1 June 1989 or the obtaining of vacant possession and planning permission by 1 December 1989, whichever was the later. In the event of the venture not proceeding the deposit of *e* £80,000 plus interest but less half the professional fees and expenses incurred in the project was to be returned to the plaintiff company. In the event planning permission was not obtained by 1 December 1989 and the defendant solicitors, acting on behalf of their company, gave notice to determine the agreement, enclosed a schedule of expenses amounting to £205,405 and claimed that accordingly nothing was repayable to the plaintiff company, which disputed that any expenses were deductible or that the *f* defendant solicitors were entitled to close the designated deposit account and issued a motion seeking an order that the defendant solicitors reopen the account and also seeking damages for breach of the defendants' obligations as stakeholders.

Held – A stakeholder, whether a solicitor for one of the parties or not, was a principal rather than an agent for both parties and accordingly if the event happened on which the *g* stake was payable and the stakeholder took the view that he knew to which of the two parties the stake should be paid he was not bound to retain the stake but could pay it out to that party, subject to the risk that if his view was wrong he might be personally liable to pay the amount of the stake to the other party. Furthermore, it made no difference that the stakeholder was a solicitor since the court would not impose on a solicitor stakeholder obligations which would not be imposed on a non-solicitor stakeholder. It *h* followed that the defendant solicitors were under no obligation to retain the deposit in the designated deposit account. The plaintiff company's motion would accordingly be dismissed (see p 111 *j* to p 112 *a c*, p 113 *d* to *f h j* and p 115 *c* to *f h*, post).

Potters (a firm) v Loppert [1973] 1 All ER 658 followed.

John Fox (a firm) v Bannister King & Rigbeys (a firm) [1987] 1 All ER 737 and *Udall v Capri Lighting Ltd* [1987] 3 All ER 262 considered.

j Per curiam. The court's summary jurisdiction over solicitors is not restricted to a solicitor's liability in respect of contempt of court, enforcement of undertakings, misconduct or acting without authority, loss in the course of proceedings and dealing with or retention of clients' money or papers, but is exercisable whenever a solicitor has accepted an obligation in his capacity as a solicitor, subject to the safeguard that it will only be used in a clear case (see p 114 *j* to p 115 *c*, post); *Re a solicitor, ex p Hales* [1904–7]

All ER Rep 1050, *Geoffrey Silver & Drake v Baines* [1971] 1 All ER 473 and *John Fox (a firm) v Bannister King & Rigbeys (a firm)* [1987] 1 All ER 737 applied.   a

Notes

For money received as deposit by stakeholder, see 9 Halsbury's Laws (4th edn) para 681, and for cases on the subject, see 12 Digest (Reissue) 700, 5054–5058.

For liability on undertakings given as a solicitor, see 44 Halsbury's Laws (4th edn) paras 255–258, and for cases on the subject, see 44 Digest (Reissue) 410–420, 4470–4572.   b

Cases referred to in judgment

Collins v Stimson (1883) 11 QBD 142, [1881–5] All ER Rep 382.
Fox (John) (a firm) v Bannister King & Rigbeys (a firm) [1987] 1 All ER 737, [1988] QB 925, [1987] 3 WLR 480, CA.
Harington v Hoggart (1830) 1 B & Ad 577, [1824–34] All ER Rep 471, 109 ER 902.   c
Myers v Elman [1939] 4 All ER 484, [1940] AC 282, HL.
Potters (a firm) v Loppert [1973] 1 All ER 658, [1973] Ch 399, [1973] 2 WLR 469.
Silver (Geoffrey) & Drake v Baines [1971] 1 All ER 473, [1971] 1 QB 396, [1971] 2 WLR 187, CA.
Solicitor, Re a [1966] 3 All ER 52, [1966] 1 WLR 1604.
Solicitor, Re a, ex p Hales [1907] 2 KB 539, [1904–7] All ER Rep 1050, DC.   c
Udall v Capri Lighting Ltd [1987] 3 All ER 262, [1988] QB 907, [1987] 3 WLR 465, CA.
United Mining and Finance Corp Ltd v Becher [1910] 2 KB 296, [1908–10] All ER Rep 876; *on appeal* [1911] 1 KB 840, CA.
Wiggins v Lord (1841) 4 Beav 30, 49 ER 248.

Cases also cited   e

Evans v Duncombe (1831) 1 Cr & J 372, 148 ER 1465.
Greaves, Re (1827) 1 Cr & J 374, 148 ER 1466.
Grey, Re [1892] 2 QB 440, CA.

Motion

The plaintiff, Hastingwood Property Ltd (Hastingwood), by a motion dated 19 March   f
1990, sought an order that within seven days the defendants, Saunders Bearman Anslem (Saunders Bearman), a firm of solicitors, open a bank account in their own name with a credit of £92,412·78 plus £35·44 per day for the number of days between 19 March 1990 and the date of the deposit and maintain such account without making any withdrawal therefrom unless and until directed how to dispose thereof either by Hastingwood and Wimpole Street Securities Ltd jointly or by the arbitrator appointed   g
under an agreement dated 17 February 1989 setting out the terms of a joint venture entered into by the two companies. The facts are set out in the judgment.

Dirik Jackson for Hastingwood.
Jonathan Tecks for Saunders Bearman.

Cur adv vult

11 April. The following judgment was delivered.

EDWARD NUGEE QC. The matter before me is a motion by which the plaintiff,   j
Hastingwood Property Ltd (Hastingwood), seeks an order under the court's summary jurisdiction over solicitors to compel the defendants, Saunders Bearman Anslem (Saunders Bearman), to pay a sum in excess of £90,000 into a bank deposit account to await the outcome of a dispute between Hastingwood and another company, Wimpole Street Securities Ltd (Wimpole), which is a company of which Mr Saunders and Mr Bearman,

the only two partners in Saunders Bearman, are directors. By an agreement dated 17

a February 1989 made between Wimpole and Hastingwood it was recited that Wimpole
had acquired a property known as 280 and 280A St Paul's Road, Islington, and that
Wimpole and Hastingwood had agreed to enter into a joint venture with a view to the
development and onward sale of the property. The agreement provided for the carrying
out by 'the joint venture', which was defined to mean Wimpole and Hastingwood, of a
31,000 sq ft development on the property in accordance with a planning permission to

b be granted pursuant to an application which had been made by a firm of architects who
were designated the project consultants. The project was to be financed by bank
borrowing and, so far as necessary, additional sums contributed by Wimpole and
Hastingwood equally. The parties declared that it was their intention that the
development should be completed as soon as possible and that the developed land should
be sold either in whole or in parts or leased at a rack rent or at a premium and a ground

c rent. The ultimate proceeds of the sale were to be divided between Wimpole and
Hastingwood in the manner set out in the agreement. Clause 20 contained provisions
for disputes between the parties to be referred to arbitration.

Clause 2 provided as follows (with appropriate alterations to the names of the parties):

'(a) On the execution hereof Hastingwood shall pay to Saunders Bearman of 73

d Wimpole Street, London, w1m 7dd Solicitors for Wimpole by way of a preliminary
deposit the sum of EIGHTY THOUSAND POUNDS (£80,000·00) which said sum shall be
deposited by the Solicitors in an special designated deposit account to be held by the
said Solicitors as Stakeholders until either (whichever event shall be the later in
time):—(i) the 1st of June 1989; or (ii) vacant possession being obtained of the
Property and the granting of the Planning Permission PROVIDED THAT both vacant

e possession and the said Planning Permission is obtained by not later thatn the 1st of
December 1989 (iii) at any time by a twenty-one working day notice given by
Hastingwood to Wimpole indicating the willingness of Hastingwood to proceed
notwithstanding the contingencies set forth in the preceding sub-clauses (i) and (ii)
have not arisen . . .'

f There then followed provisions which were to take effect in the event of conditions (ii)
or (iii) being satisfied. Clause 2 continues:

'(b) In the event of none of the contingencies (that is to say (i), (ii) or (iii) set forth
in the previous sub-clause) occuring by the 1st of December 1989 on service of a five
working day notice by either party on the other this Agreement shall determine
and the deposit of EIGHTY THOUSAND POUNDS (£80,000) repaid to Hastingwood

g together with the actual interest earned thereon less one half of all professional fees
and expenses incurred by the Joint Venture in relation to the Project since the date
hereof.'

Hastingwood duly paid the preliminary deposit of £80,000, and on the same day, 17
February 1989, Mr Saunders wrote to Mr Roberts of Hastingwood saying, inter alia:

h 'I am today setting up at Barclays Bank plc, 27 Regent Street, London W1 a
separate designated deposit account in the name of Wimpole Street Securities
Limited/Hastingwood Property Limited into which the £80,000 deposit will be
paid. I sincerely hope that we all make a great deal of money out of our joint
venture.'

j It is common ground that the planning permission referred to in the agreement was
not obtained by 1 December 1989, and on that day Wimpole, acting by Mr Saunders,
wrote to Hastingwood giving a five working day notice to determine the agreement.
The notice expired at close of business on 8 December, and on the same day Mr Saunders
wrote to Hastingwood enclosing a schedule of the expenses which he claimed had been
incurred since the date of the agreement, which amounted to £205,405·60. Since half of

this exceeded the deposit plus accrued interest, Mr Saunders claimed that nothing was
repayable to Hastingwood under cl 2(b) of the agreement, and stated that he had   a
instructed the bank to close the special designated account. Hastingwood's solicitors
replied on 11 December denying that any of the expenses shown on Mr Saunders'
schedule were deductible, pointing out that the deposit was to be held by Saunders
Bearman in a stakeholder client account with all the extra protection which that entailed,
and requesting confirmation that on the closing of the designated deposit account he
would remit the £80,000 plus all accrued interest to Hastingwood. Mr Saunders replied   b
accepting that the funds were held by his firm as stakeholders but stating that he had
been advised by counsel as to the amount deductible from them.

On 7 February 1990 Hastingwood's solicitors wrote making a further demand for
repayment of the entire deposit plus interest until payment, and also asking for
confirmation that the funds were still held on deposit either in the name of Saunders
Bearman or in the joint names of the parties and would remain so deposited until the   c
dispute was resolved.

On 21 February Hastingwood's solicitors wrote to the President of the Law Society
requesting him to appoint an arbitrator under cl 20 to determine the construction of
cl 2(b) and the amount, if any, of the professional fees and expenses which were
deductible under that subclause. On 22 February they wrote again to Saunders Bearman
requiring confirmation as to the present whereabouts of the funds deposited and as to   d
the amount of the fund at 8 December 1989 by means of a bank statement showing the
balance with accrued interest at that date. Saunders Bearman replied on 23 February
stating that they had been advised by counsel that Wimpole were entitled to retain the
full amount of the deposit and interest and that they (Saunders Bearman) had not in any
way acted improperly with regard to the deposit, and they sent a copy of the bank
statement showing the balance with accrued interest as at 8 December, but added that   e
the funds were no longer in the designated account. Hastingwood's solicitors wrote on
27 February stating that the deposit should not have been released from the stakeholder
account. On 19 March Hastingwood issued proceedings against Saunders Bearman
seeking the following relief:

> 'An order that the Defendants do within such time as may be specified open a   f
> bank deposit account in their own name designated "Wimpole/Hastingwood" with
> a credit in the sum of £92,412·78+(£35·44 × n) where n is the number of days
> between 19th March 1990 and the date of the deposit (including in such number
> the first and last days of the period mentioned) and do maintain such account
> without making any withdrawal therefrom unless and until directed how to dispose
> thereof either by the Plaintiff and Wimpole Street Securities Limited jointly or by   g
> the arbitrator appointed under the agreement dated 17th February 1989 . . .'

There was a second claim for damages for breach of the defendant's obligations as
stakeholders under the said agreement. Notice of motion was given the same day seeking
an order in the terms of para 1.

It has been agreed between the parties that the amount of the deposit plus interest   h
accrued to 3 April is £91,822·40, and the daily rate of interest has also been agreed. The
facts are not now in dispute in any respect.

Two issues have been argued before me. First, where a sum of money has been paid to
a person as stakeholder on terms that he will pay it to one of two contracting parties in
one event and to the other in another event, is he under a duty if a dispute arises between
the parties to retain the money under his own control until the dispute has been   j
determined, either by agreement between the parties or by the decision of a tribunal
having jurisdiction to determine it? Secondly, if the stakeholder is a solicitor, and he has
paid the money to one or other of the parties while the dispute is still unresolved, should
the court exercise its inherent supervisory jurisdiction over solicitors by ordering him to
replace the money pending the determination of the dispute?

Counsel for Hastingwood submitted that in the absence of an express agreement a
a person who accepts the position of stakeholder comes under an obligation, on his receipt
of the stake, to hold the stake as the agent of both parties to the contract and cannot part
with it until directed by the parties jointly how to dispose of it or so directed by a tribunal
having jurisdiction to decide the issue. In support of this proposition he relied on *Collins
v Stimson* (1883) 11 QBD 142 at 144, cf [1881–5] All ER Rep 382 at 383, where Pollock CB
said:

b
'In the present case the deposit was paid not to the vendor but to an auctioneer,
and the law, as is well known, is that an auctioneer to whom a deposit is paid under
such circumstances receives it as the agent of both parties, and cannot part with it
without the sanction of both of them.'

He also relied on certain passages in the judgments in *Harington v Hoggart* (1830) 1 B
c & Ad 577, [1824–34] All ER Rep 471. In that case Lord Tenterden CJ said (1 B & Ad 577
at 586, [1824–34] All ER Rep 471 at 472):

'A stakeholder does not receive the money for either party, he receives it for both;
and until the event is known, it is his duty to keep it in his own hands.'

d Parke J said (1 B & Ad 577 at 588–589, [1824–34] All ER Rep 471 at 473):

'It appears to me that the situation of an auctioneer is this: He receives a sum of
money, which is to be paid in one event to the vendor, that is, provided the purchase
is completed; and in the other, if it is not completed, to the vendee: he holds the
money, in the mean time, as stakeholder; and he is bound to keep it, and pay it
over, upon either of those events, immediately.'

e
Counsel for Hastingwood also referred to me to *Wiggins v Lord* (1841) 4 Beav 30, 49
ER 248. In that case, on a contract for the purchase of land, a part of the purchase money
was paid as a deposit to the vendor's solicitor who, without the concurrence of the
purchaser, paid it away according to the order of the vendor. This created a difficulty in
completing the purchase, because the vendor's mortgagees required the whole of the
f purchase money to be paid to them. The purchaser sought an order that the solicitor
should repay the deposit. Lord Langdale MR said (4 Beav 30 at 32, 49 ER 248 at 249):

'The Defendants. . . had clearly a duty to perform, which was, to keep the money
in their hands as a deposit for the person ultimately entitled. Instead of doing that,
they paid it away, according to the direction of the vendor, without regarding their
duty to the Plaintiff. It is argued they are not in any way liable for what they have
g done, because at present it is unknown whether the contract can be completed. But
is the purchase money to remain in the meanwhile in its present situation? The case
is put thus: if the contract is to be performed, the deposit will belong to the vendor,
and if not performed, then that they must either pay voluntarily, or an action at law
must be brought against them for its recovery. I think they and the estate of the
vendor [the word 'vendee' in the report is a misprint, although it appears in both
h the original and the English Reports] are liable to pay this sum, and it must be
brought into court.'

Counsel for Hastingwood relied on *Wiggins v Lord* as an example of a case in which the
court had ordered a solicitor-stakeholder to reconstitute the fund in circumstances in
which he had paid it away before the outcome of the event was known.
j Counsel for Saunders Bearman submitted in the first instance that a stakeholder is not
permitted to continue to hold the stake once the event has happened on which it is
payable to one or other of the contracting parties. If he is in doubt, his only course is to
interplead. In the alternative, he submitted that if the stakeholder takes the view that he
knows to which of the two parties the stake should be paid, there is nothing to prevent
him from acting accordingly, subject, of course, to the risk that if the view which he has

formed turns out to be wrong he may be liable to pay the amount of the stake over to the other party out of his own resources.

The two submissions may be summarised as being that if the event has happened on which the stake is payable (i) he is not entitled to retain the stake or (ii) he is not bound to retain the stake. The submission of counsel for Hastingwood may be summarised as being that in that situation the stakeholder is bound to retain the stake until the dispute is resolved and he is not entitled to part with it, however clearly he considers that one of the two parties has a right to it; the parties have agreed that if there is a dispute between them the dispute should be referred to arbitration, and it is not open to the stakeholder to anticipate the decision of the arbitrator.

In my judgment, the second submission of counsel for Saunders Bearman represents the true position. The judgments on which counsel for Hastingwood relies have to be read in the context of the cases in which they were delivered. In *Collins v Stimson* (1883) 11 QBD 142, [1881–5] All ER Rep 382 the money was paid to the auctioneer as a deposit on a contract for the purchase of land. The contract went off when the purchaser went bankrupt and the deposit was forfeited to the vendor. The purchaser's trustee in bankruptcy sued to recover the deposit from the auctioneer, who had not yet paid it over to the vendor. The decision of the court was that the vendor was in the same position as an ordinary tradesman who receives money in part payment of his debt, and that the trustee could not follow and recover the deposit. The passage from the judgment of Pollock CB which I have quoted must, in my judgment, be read as stating the position of the auctioneer at a time when it is not known whether the contract will be completed or not. At that time it is correct to say that the auctioneer cannot part with a deposit without the sanction of both vendor and purchaser. Once it is known that the contract has gone off, however, and the deposit is forfeited to the vendor, the auctioneer is at liberty to pay it over to the vendor; and I can see nothing in Pollock CB's judgment which lends support to the view that the auctioneer has to obtain the further sanction of the purchaser in that situation before he can make the payment. In so far as the sanction of the purchaser is required at all in that situation, it is given when the purchaser pays the deposit to the auctioneer on the express or implied condition that it will be paid to the vendor if the purchaser, through no fault of the vendor, is unable to complete the purchase. In *Harington v Hoggart* (1830) 1 B & Ad 577, [1824–34] All ER Rep 471 the issue was whether the stakeholder was bound to account for interest which he had earned by investing the deposit pending the completion of the purchase. The observations of Lord Tenterden CJ and Parke J were directed to the position of the stakeholder during the period before it was known whether the contract would be completed or not. They were not considering what the position of the stakeholder would be in a case like the present, where it is clear that the event has happened on which the stakeholder is bound to pay over the deposit but there is a dispute between the parties as to which of them is entitled to receive payment. In *Wiggins v Lord* (1841) 4 Beav 30, 49 ER 248 the issue was whether the stakeholder should reconstitute the fund at a time when it was uncertain whether the contract would be completed, and again the case is of no assistance in relation to a time after the event has happened on which the stakeholder is to pay over the stake.

More relevant, in my judgment, is the decision of Pennycuick V-C in *Potters (a firm) v Loppert* [1973] 1 All ER 658, [1973] Ch 399. The case related to a pre-contract deposit paid to an estate agent as stakeholder, but in the course of considering whether the estate agent was entitled to retain for his own benefit the interest earned on the deposit during the period before the prospective purchaser asked for its repayment, Pennycuick V-C sought guidance from the cases on contract deposits. In relation to such deposits he said ([1973] 1 All ER 658 at 661–662, [1973] Ch 399 at 405–406):

'Looking at the position apart from authority, one might perhaps at first sight rather expect that where any property is placed in medio in the hands of a third party to await an event as between two other parties the third party receives that a property as trustee, and that the property and the investments for the time being representing it represent the trust estate. Where the property is something other than money—for example, an investment—that must in the nature of things almost certainly be the position. But where the property is money—that is, cash or a cheque resulting in a bank credit—this is by no means necessarily so. Certainly the money may be paid to the third party as trustee, but equally it may be paid to him as principal on a contractual or quasi-contractual obligation to pay the like sum to one

b or other of the parties according to the event. It must depend on the intention of the parties, to be derived from all the circumstances, including any written documents, in which capacity the third party receives the money . . . Turning now to authority, it is to my mind conclusive that, apart from agreement to the contrary, a contract deposit paid to a stakeholder is not paid to him as trustee, but on a contractual or quasi-contractual liability with the consequence that the stakeholder

c is not accountable for profit on it. The decisive case on this point is *Harington v Hoggart* . . .'

It follows from this that neither party to the contract of sale has any proprietary interest in the deposit. Each has merely a contractual or quasi-contractual personal right of action to recover it from the stakeholder which is dependent on whether the contract

d proceeds to completion or not. In my judgment Pennycuick V-C's description of the stakeholder as principal is more accurate than Pollock CB's description of him as agent for both parties and emphasises the fact that he is not accountable to either party for his use of the deposit during the period while it is uncertain which of the parties will become entitled to it. It seems to me clear that in the common case of a deposit paid to a stakeholder on the signing of a contract for the sale of land, if the stakeholder repays the

e deposit to the purchaser in the belief that the contract is at an end the remedy of the vendor who claims to be entitled to forfeit the deposit is, so far as the stakeholder is concerned, limited to an action to recover the amount of the deposit, which will be an action in contract or, more usually, an action for money had and received. It may be that in special circumstances the vendor could obtain a Mareva injunction to protect his position pending the outcome of his action against the stakeholder; but I do not consider

f that the vendor would be entitled to an interlocutory order requiring the stakeholder to replace the amount of the deposit in a designated account or to pay it into court. The fact that the vendor did not consent to the stakeholder repaying the deposit to the purchaser would not affect this conclusion.

The present case is not quite as simple as the common case of a deposit paid on a contract for the sale of land, since cl 2(b) envisages that the amount to be repaid to

g Hastingwood on the determination of the agreement may be reduced by one half of the professional fees and expenses incurred by the joint venture, and there may clearly be scope for argument as to the amount of the professional fees and expenses which fall to be deducted. Moreover, the interest earned on the deposit is to be added to it and is not to be retained by the stakeholders for their own benefit. However, disregarding for the moment the fact that the stakeholders, Saunders Bearman, are at the same time the

h solicitors for Wimpole, one of the parties to the agreement, I do not consider that the additional complexity of the provisions relating to the deposit places the stakeholder in a different position from that of a stakeholder in the more common case. He might well be more reluctant to part with the deposit to either Hastingwood or Wimpole so long as they were in dispute about the amount to be deducted, but if he chose to pay it to one of them, I do not consider that the other would be entitled to an order that he replace the

j amount in the designated account or would have any other remedy against him except an action in contract or for money had and received.

Does it make any difference that the stakeholders in the present case were the solicitors for one of the parties, and indeed were directors of that party? Counsel for Hastingwood submits that it does and that it is not satisfactory that a solicitor who accepts a deposit as stakeholder should be able to take it on himself to pay the deposit to his own client when the entitlement of his client to the deposit is disputed by the other party to the agreement. *a* Counsel submitted that Saunders Bearman had undertaken to act as stakeholders and that they were under an implied obligation to act fairly as between the parties. It was unfair, he said, that where money had been paid into a special designated account to be kept from both parties, Saunders Bearman should favour their own client. He suggested that if they were going to make any payment in respect of the deposit, they ought to have paid £40,000 to each party and left them to resolve the dispute about their rights under *b* cl 2(b) by arbitration. His primary submission, however, was that they should be ordered to replace the deposit in the special designated account with the interest which accrued up to the time the account was closed and a further sum in respect of the interest which would have accrued had the money remained in the account, and keep it there until the outcome of the arbitration. This, he said, is what they had undertaken to do when they accepted the position as stakeholders; and the court should order them to perform their *c* undertaking, for this was the very purpose of paying the deposit to solicitors. In support of his submission counsel for Hastingwood relied on two recent cases in which the court exercised its summary jurisdiction over solicitors. In *John Fox (a firm) v Bannister King & Rigbeys (a firm)* [1987] 1 All ER 737 at 743, [1988] QB 925 at 931 Sir John Donaldson MR said:

d
'The jurisdiction is indeed "extraordinary", being based on the right of the court to see that a high standard of conduct is maintained by its officers acting as such . . . It is, in a sense, a domestic jurisdiction to which solicitors are only amenable because of their special relationship with the court and it is designed to impose higher standards than the law applies generally. Thus, for example, it is no answer to a complaint that a solicitor acted in breach of an undertaking given by him that there *e* was no consideration for it (*United Mining and Finance Corp Ltd v Becher* [1910] 2 KB 296 at 303, [1908–10] All ER Rep 876 at 880).'

That case was applied in *Udall v Capri Lighting Ltd* [1987] 3 All ER 262 at 269, [1988] QB 907 at 917–918, where Balcombe LJ summarised the position in seven numbered paragraphs. Paragraph (6) was as follows:
f
'The summary jurisdiction involves a discretion as to the relief to be granted: see *Myers v Elman* [1939] 4 All ER 484 at 508, [1940] AC 282 at 318 per Lord Wright. In the case of an undertaking, where there is no evidence that it is impossible to perform, the order will usually be to require the solicitor to do that which he has undertaken to do: see *Re a solicitor* [1966] 3 All ER 52, [1966] 1 WLR 1604.'

So here, said counsel for Hastingwood, Saunders Bearman had undertaken to hold the *g* deposit as stakeholders, and they should be ordered to perform that undertaking.

There is a preliminary question, namely whether Saunders Bearman ever gave an undertaking of the kind which will be enforced by the court in the exercise of the summary jurisdiction. They were not parties to the agreement of 17 February 1989 and all that they did was to receive the deposit and pay it into the designated deposit account. *h* Counsel for Saunders Bearman submitted that there was nothing in Mr Saunders's letter of 17 February 1989 or elsewhere which amounted to an undertaking. He was constrained to admit that if, after the dispute between the parties had been resolved by arbitration, Saunders Bearman refused to pay over the deposit and accrued interest in accordance with the rights of the parties as determined by the arbitrator, they might be compelled to do so under the summary jurisdiction; but he said that this would be *j* regarded as analogous to the enforcement of a solicitor's duty to pay over clients' money, which is a distinct head under which the summary jurisdiction is exercisable, rather than the enforcement of an undertaking.

In my judgment, the exercise of the summary jurisdiction is not dependent on bringing the case under one of the five heads under which a solicitor's liability is classified

in the textbooks, namely contempt of court, enforcement of undertakings, misconduct
a or acting without authority, loss in the course of proceedings and dealing with or
retention of client's money or papers: see *Cordery on Solicitors* (8th edn, 1988) pp 105–122
and 44 Halsbury's Laws (4th edn) paras 252–273. The use of the word 'undertaking' is
not essential in order that a solicitor's obligation shall be enforceable summarily: in *John
Fox (a firm) v Bannister King & Rigbeys (a firm)* the solicitor did not in terms give an
undertaking, nor did he in *Re a Solicitor, ex p Hales* [1907] 2 KB 539, [1904–7] All ER Rep
b 1050, but in both cases the court enforced the obligations of the solicitor as if he had
done so.

In my judgment, the summary jurisdiction is exercisable whenever a solicitor has
accepted an obligation in his capacity as solicitor, but this is subject to the safeguard that
it will only be exercised in a clear case (see *Geoffrey Silver & Drake v Baines* [1971] 1 All ER
473, [1971] 1 QB 396). Accordingly, the mere fact that Mr Saunders did not use the word
c 'undertaking' or an equivalent word in his letter of 17 February 1989 will not in my
judgment prevent me from ordering him to perform the obligations which he had
accepted by accepting the deposit and dealing with it in accordance with cl 2 of the
agreement. However, the obligation accepted by Mr Saunders was an obligation to act as
stakeholder until the later in time of the events specified in cl 2(a); and I agree with
counsel for Saunders Bearman that the fact that a stakeholder is a solicitor does not alter
d the nature of the stakeholder's obligations. It is true that the court in certain respects
imposes higher standards on a solicitor than the law applies generally, but so far as is
material to the present case this appears to be limited to preventing the solicitor from
relying on defences such as absence of consideration or the Statute of Frauds (1677) or
delay short of the statutory period. The summary jurisdiction enables the court to compel
solicitors to perform their obligations. It does not, except in relation to these defences,
e which are sometimes regarded as unmeritorious, enable the court to impose more
extensive obligations than those to which they are already subject. I do not consider that
the court can impose on Saunders Bearman obligations as stakeholders which would not
be imposed on stakeholders who were not solicitors. Of course they take a risk if they
part with the deposit before Hastingwood and Wimpole have resolved their dispute; but
the close association between the firm and Wimpole no doubt makes that risk acceptable
f to them, and I do not know what arrangements have been made between them to meet
the possibility that Hastingwood will obtain a decision in the arbitration which entitles
them to be repaid part or all of their deposit.

Saunders Bearman have since these proceedings began offered Hastingwood an
undertaking in the following terms:

g   'We hereby undertake to make payment to you or to whomever you may direct
of any award which the arbitrator might make (if any) against our clients Wimpole
Street Securities Limited including interest within seven days of the award being
made.'

I doubt whether an undertaking in this form adds significantly to the obligations to
h which Saunders Bearman are already subject by virtue of their having accepted the
deposit on the terms of the agreement, but it removes any doubt there may be, and I am
informed that the offer of such an undertaking is still open. Be that as it may, I decline
to make the order sought by the notice of motion, and it follows that the motion will be
dismissed.

j *Motion dismissed.*

Solicitors: *Stilgoes* (for Hastingwood); *Saunders Bearman Anselm.*

Hazel Hartman   Barrister.

R v Kemble

COURT OF APPEAL, CRIMINAL DIVISION
LORD LANE CJ, OWEN AND AULD JJ
8 JUNE 1990

Evidence – Oath – Person who is neither Christian nor Jewish – Oath required to be administered 'in a lawful manner' – Oath must appear to be binding on person's conscience and he himself must consider it to be binding on his conscience – Oaths Act 1978, s 1(3).

Whether an oath is administered 'in a lawful manner' within s 1(3)[a] of the Oaths Act 1978 to a person at a trial who is neither a Christian nor a Jew does not depend on the intricacies of the particular religion adhered to by that person but on whether the oath appears to the court to be binding on his conscience and whether it is an oath which that person himself considers to be binding on his conscience (see p 117 j, post).

R v Chapman [1980] Crim LR 42 applied.

Notes

For evidence on oath, see 17 Halsbury's Laws (4th edn) para 264, and for cases on the subject, see 22(2) Digest (2nd reissue) 224–226, 8390–8430.

For the Oaths Act 1978, s 1, see 17 Halsbury's Statutes (4th edn) 200.

Case referred to in judgment

R v Chapman [1980] Crim LR 42, CA.

Application for leave to appeal against conviction

Peter Kemble applied for leave to appeal against his conviction on 19 January 1989 in the Central Criminal Court before his Honour Judge Machin QC and a jury of having a firearm with intent to commit an indictable offence, namely blackmail, for which he was sentenced to two and a half years' imprisonment. On 16 January 1989 he had pleaded guilty to two offences of possessing a firearm without a certificate, for which he was sentenced to 12 months' imprisonment to run concurrently with the sentence for the offence of which he was convicted. The ground of the application was that the main prosecution witness, Tareq Hijab, who was a Muslim, took the oath using the New Testament before he gave evidence. The facts are set out in the judgment of the court.

Robert J Banks for the applicant
Samuel Wiggs for the Crown.

LORD LANE CJ delivered the following judgment of the court. On 16 January 1989 in the Central Criminal Court before his Honour Judge Machin QC the applicant pleaded guilty to two counts of possessing a firearm without a firearms certificate (counts three and four). On 19 January before the same court he was convicted by verdict of a jury of having a firearm with intent to commit an indictable offence (count two), the indictable offence being blackmail. He was sentenced to 12 months' imprisonment to run concurrently on counts three and four to which he had pleaded guilty, and he was sentenced to two and a half years' imprisonment on count two, the count to which he had pleaded not guilty but of which he was found guilty, namely having a firearm with intent to commit an indictable offence. All those sentences were to run concurrently.

This application for leave to appeal against conviction has been referred to the full court by the registrar, and the sole ground of the application is that the main, if not the

---

a Section 1, so far as material, is set out at p 117 b to d, post

only relevant, prosecution witness, namely a man called Tareq Hijab, who is a Muslim
a by religious conviction, took the oath using the New Testament before he gave evidence.
Those are the basic facts of the case.

Counsel who has argued the case on behalf of the applicant argues that s 1 of the Oaths
Act 1978 has not been complied with, that the chief witness for the prosecution was not
properly sworn, that therefore there was a material irregularity and that the conviction
accordingly was in any event unsafe and unsatisfactory.

b The relevant section, s 1 of the 1978 Act, provides:

'(1) Any oath may be administered and taken in England, Wales or Northern
Ireland in the following form and the manner—The person taking the oath shall
hold the New Testament, or, in the case of a Jew, the Old Testament, in his uplifted
hand, and shall say or repeat after the officer administering the oath the words "I
swear by Almight God that . . .", followed by the words of the oath prescribed by
c law.

(2) The officer shall (unless the person about to take the oath voluntarily objects
thereto, or is physically incapable of so taking the oath) administer the oath in the
form and manner aforesaid without question.

(3) In the case of a person who is neither a Christian nor a Jew, the oath shall be
administered in any lawful manner . . .'
d

The argument of counsel for the applicant goes as follows. The witness, he says rightly,
is a Muslim by faith. Secondly he says, according to the strict tenets of the Muslim faith
(which we have had explained to us carefully and in detail by an expert in the matter in
the shape of Professor Yagub-Zaki, evidence which we of course accept unreservedly), no
oath taken by a Muslim is valid unless it is taken on the Koran, and moreover taken on a
e copy of the Koran in Arabic. A translation into English or into any other language will
invalidate, so to speak, the book so far as the oath is concerned under these strict religious
tenets.

There are also many sub-rules which govern the taking of oaths by persons of the
Muslim faith, according to the professor. For instance, a woman who is menstruating,
and therefore considered to be unclean, cannot take a valid oath on the Koran.
f What we have to consider however is something else. Whilst respecting, as of course
we do, the religious tenets of other faiths, be it Muslim or Jewish or anything else, it is
the 1978 Act which must govern our decision.

Assuming that one cannot simply stop after sub-s (2) of s 1, which appears to be the
case, we have to ask ourselves this: in the case of a person who is neither a Christian nor a
Jew, that is to say this particular witness, 'the oath shall be administered in any lawful
g manner'. Accordingly, was the oath in the present case administered in a lawful manner?

We had our attention drawn by counsel for the applicant, helpfully if we may say so,
to the decision in *R v Chapman* [1980] Crim LR 42. The only passage I need read is a short
passage in the part of the report which deals with the decision of the court. The court
consisted of Roskill, Ormrod LJJ and Bristow J. The passage runs as follows:

h 'The efficacy of an oath must depend on it being taken in a way binding, and
intended to be binding, upon the conscience of the intended witness.'

The case was on cognate facts, although the facts were not by any means precisely the
same.

We take the view that the question of whether the administration of an oath is lawful
j does not depend on what may be the considerable intricacies of the particular religion
which is adhered to by the witness. It concerns two matters and two matters only in our
judgment. First of all, is the oath an oath which appears to the court to be binding on the
conscience of the witness? And if so, secondly, and most importantly, is it an oath which
the witness himself considers to be binding on his conscience?

So far as the present case is concerned, quite plainly the first of those matters is satisfied.

The court did obviously consider the oath to be one which was binding on the witness.
It was the second matter which was the subject so to speak of dispute before this court. *a*
Not only did we have the evidence of the professor, the expert in the Muslim theology,
but we also had the evidence of the witness himself. He having on this occasion been
sworn on a copy of the Koran in Arabic gave evidence before us that he did consider
himself to be bound as to his conscience by the way in which he took the oath at the trial.
Indeed he went further. He said,

> 'Whether I had taken the oath on the Koran or on the Bible or on the Torah, I *b*
> would have considered that to be binding on my conscience.'

He was cross-examined by counsel for the applicant in an endeavour to show that that
was not the truth, but we have no doubt, having heard him give his evidence and seen
him give his evidence, that that was the truth, and that he did consider all of those to be
holy books, and that he did consider that his conscience was bound by the form of oath *c*
he took and the way in which he took it. In other words we accept his evidence.

Consequently, applying what we believe to be the principles which we have
endeavoured to set out to those facts, we conclude that the witness was properly sworn.
We conclude accordingly that there was no irregularity, material or otherwise. There
was nothing unsafe or unsatisfactory about the conviction. Accordingly this application
is refused. *d*

Application refused.

Solicitors: *Saunders & Co* (for the applicant); *Crown Prosecution Service.*

N P Metcalfe Esq　　Barrister. *e*

Douihech v Findlay and another

QUEEN'S BENCH DIVISION
HIS HONOUR JUDGE DOBRY QC SITTING AS A JUDGE OF THE HIGH COURT　　　*f*
23 MAY, 13 JUNE 1989

*Practice – Parties – Joinder of parties – Inspection of property – Joinder of defendant to enable
property to be inspected – No rights to be adjusted between person joined and any other party to
action – Whether jurisdiction to join person as party to action solely for purpose of obtaining
order for inspection of his property – RSC Ord 29, r 2.*
　　　　　　　　　　　　　　　　　　　　　　　　　　　　　　　　　　　　　　g

The plaintiff bought what was reputed to be a sixteenth century Italian cello for £50
from the first defendant, who was an antique dealer. The cello had been stolen from the
second defendant and was returned to her when the theft was discovered. The plaintiff
issued a writ against the first defendant claiming damages for breach of an implied *h*
condition that the first defendant had title to the cello. The first defendant admitted
liability but disputed the amount of damages payable. The plaintiff contended that the
correct measure of damages was the difference between the purchase price of £50 and
the market price and sought to join the second defendant as a party to the action so that
he could obtain an order under RSC Ord 29, r 2[a] for the cello to be inspected and valued
by experts to ascertain the market price. The master made an order joining the second *j*
defendant as a party. The second defendant appealed against the order.

Held – A person whose property was the subject matter of an action but who was not in
dispute with any of the parties to the action could not be joined as a party to the action

a　Rule 2, so far as material, is set out at p 120 *d e f*, post

a solely for the purpose of obtaining an order under RSC Ord 29, r 2 for the inspection of his property, since in such a case there were no rights to be adjusted between him and any of the parties to the action. Since the only reason for the second defendant being joined as a party to the action was to enable the cello to be inspected the court had no jurisdiction to make an order joining her. The appeal would therefore be allowed (see p 122 c d and p 123 b c g, post).

Shaw v Smith (1886) 18 QBD 193 followed.

b Coomes & Son v Hayward [1913] 1 KB 150 and Penfold v Pearlberg [1955] 3 All ER 120 not followed.

Notes

For joinder of parties, see 37 Halsbury's Laws (4th edn) para 218, and for cases on the subject, see 37(2) Digest (Reissue) 343–351, 2139–2189.

c

Cases referred to in judgment

Coomes & Son v Hayward [1913] 1 KB 150, DC.
Harrington v North London Polytechnic [1984] 3 All ER 666, [1984] 1 WLR 1293, CA.
Hetherington (decd), Re, Gibbs v McDonnell [1989] 2 All ER 129, [1990] Ch 1, [1989] 2 WLR
d   1094.
Norwich Pharmacal Co v Customs and Excise Comrs [1973] 2 All ER 943, [1974] AC 133, [1973] 3 WLR 164, HL.
Penfold v Pearlberg [1955] 3 All ER 120, [1955] 1 WLR 1068.
Shaw v Smith (1886) 18 QBD 193, CA.

e **Appeal**

The second defendant, Vivian Mackie, the owner of a cello which was the subject of an action brought by the plaintiff, Kamel Douihech, against the first defendant, Dennis Findlay, claiming damages for breach of an implied condition as to title in the contract of sale of the cello and who had been joined as a defendant in the action, appealed against the order of Master Creightmore made on 10 May 1989 ordering the inspection of the
f cello, and also applied to strike out paras 6 and 7 of the statement of claim in which the plaintiff claimed to be entitled to inspect and photograph the cello for the purpose of compiling an expert's report so as to give full particulars of loss and damage suffered as the result of the first defendant's breach of contract. The appeal was heard in chambers but judgment was given by his Honour Judge Dobry QC in open court. The facts are set out in the judgment.

g

Stephen de B Bate for the plaintiff.
Mr Simon Davies, solicitor, for the second defendant.
The first defendant did not appear.

Cur adv vult

h

13 June. The following judgment was delivered.

HIS HONOUR JUDGE DOBRY QC. The issue in this appeal is whether a person can be joined as a defendant solely to obtain an order for inspection and photography of a cello under RSC Ord 29, r 2(1).
j   The claim is for damages for breach of contract against Mr Dennis Findlay, the first defendant. He is an antique dealer and sold the cello to the plaintiff in March 1983 for £50. It then transpired that the cello had been stolen from a Mrs Vivian Mackie, who is now the second defendant. The cello was returned to her on 16 March 1983 a few days after the theft. It is reputed to have been made by Gasparo Da Salo, a sixteenth century Italian instrument maker. It is worth a great deal of money, considerably more than

£50. The writ was issued in December 1984 and later amended joining Mrs Mackie as a
defendant.

The claim against the first defendant is for breach of an implied condition that the first
defendant had title to the cello and of a warranty of quiet possession. In the amended
defence these breaches are admitted by the first defendant but the proper measure of
damages is in issue. The plaintiff contends that it is the difference between the purchase
price and the market price of the cello and wishes to have an inspection by his experts.

The plaintiff made an application under Ord 29, r 2(1) and on 10 May 1989 Master
Creightmore made the order applied for and the second defendant has appealed to this
court.

Further, on 18 May the master transferred another application to a judge in chambers,
under Ord 32, r 12. That other application was for a striking-out of paras 6 and 7 of the
rereamended statement of claim. In these there is a claim that the plaintiff is entitled to
inspection which has been refused.

Order 29, r 2 provides:

'(1) On the application of any party to a cause or matter the Court may make an
order for the detention, custody or preservation of any property which is the subject-
matter of the cause or matter, or as to which any question may arise therein, or for
the inspection of any such property in the possession of a party to the cause or
matter.

(2) For the purpose of enabling any order under paragraph (1) to be carried out
the Court may by the order authorise any person to enter upon any land or building
in the possession of any party to the cause or matter . . .

(4) An order under this rule may be made on such terms, if any, as the Court
thinks just.

(5) An application for an order under this rule must be made by summons or by
notice under Order 25, rule 7 . . .'

I shall consider the effect of r 2, para (1) later but must observe that under para (4) an
order for inspection may be made subject to terms. Paragraph (6) is also of some
significance and reads:

'Unless the Court otherwise directs, an application by a defendant for such an
order may not be made before he acknowledges service of the writ or originating
summons by which the cause or matter was begun.'

Rule 29(2) was taken from RSC 1883, Ord 50, r 3. It was in identical terms.

It is appropriate to refer to two notes in The Supreme Court Practice 1988, vol 1. The
first deals with the opening words of the rule, 'On the application of any party', and,
under the heading 'Any party', reads as follows (para 29/2–3/2):

'One defendant cannot obtain an order against another defendant for inspection,
when there is no right to be adjusted between them in the action (Shaw v. Smith
((1886) 18 QBD 193)) . . .'

The second relevant note, under the heading 'Possession of party necessary', reads as
follows (para 29/2–3/4):

'. . . In Penfold v. Pearlberg ([1955] 3 All ER 120, [1955] 1 WLR 1068) an order
was made against a party not in possession, subject to the consent of a requisitioning
local authority. If they had refused they would have had to have been made by
parties solely for the purpose of having the inspection authorised . . .'

This note suggests that, as between a plaintiff and a defendant, an inspection order can be
made although there is no other 'right' to be adjusted.

The crux of the case is whether an action can be brought for inspection alone. Master

Creightmore felt bound by *Penfold v Pearlberg* and made the order asked for but stayed
a execution so that there could be full argument before a judge.

The case law

In *Penfold v Pearlberg* the defendant contracted to buy a house, at an auction, described
in the particulars as 'Practically rebuilt under War Damage Act' and 'Requisitioned by
the local authority . . .' In an action by the vendor for specific performance an application
b was made by her under the 1883 Ord 50, r 3 for inspection before delivery of defence.
Roxburgh J held that the general power under Ord 50, r 3 to make an order for inspection
of property is not limited by the provision in the rule authorising persons to enter land
in the *possession* of a party. He made an order for inspection subject to the consent of the
requisitioning local authority and indicated that in the event of their refusal they could
be added as parties to the action solely for the purpose of having the inspection authorised.
c The judge explained his approach thus ([1955] 3 All ER 120 at 121, [1955] 1 WLR 1068
at 1070):

> 'It is said that I cannot do anything, notwithstanding the positive refusal of the
> plaintiff to give inspection now, unless I, by the pressure of my decision, compel the
> defendant to add the local authority as a party to the action, solely for the purposes
d > of the inspection.'

He referred to *Coomes & Son v Hayward* [1913] 1 KB 150 as indicating that the proper
course could be to add the local authority as defendants if they refused. There was no
cause of action against them but the judge assumed that they could do this. But *Shaw v
Smith* (1886) 18 QBD 193 was not cited.

The effect of the judgment of Roxburgh J is (1) that a conditional order for inspection
e can be made although the defendant is not in actual possession, and (2) (obiter) that, if
the third party (the local authority in that case) is in actual possession and does not
consent to inspection, it could be added as a defendant.

The second point was obiter and thus the master was not bound by *Penfold*'s case, as
the question whether it is possible to sue solely for an inspection order was commented
on but not decided.

f In *Coomes & Son v Hayward* the plaintiffs, a firm of builders, brought proceedings
against the defendant for payments due for work done and materials supplied in respect
of certain houses. The defendant was one of three tenants in common of the houses and
the co-tenants were not parties to the action. The county court made an order for
inspection (under CCR 1903 Ord 12, r 3, which was similar to RSC 1883 Ord 50, r 3).
This was held to be wrong in relation to the tenants in common who were not parties to
g the action, although the county court judge held that the defendant was an agent for the
two other tenants in common. Both Ridley and Scrutton JJ observed that the other
tenants in common, who had a proprietary interest in the houses, ought to have been
made parties to the action. Their remarks were also obiter as was acknowledged by
Roxburgh J in *Penfold v Pearlberg*. In any event this decision is distinguishable from the
h present case as it appears that in *Coomes & Son v Hayward* there was a cause of action
against the other tenants in common other than the claim to inspect. This decision is of
no direct assistance in the present case: it contains an obiter dictum based on a supposition
that there is a right to sue for inspection.

Shaw v Smith (1886) 18 QBD 193 is a decision of the Court of Appeal in which the 1883
Ord 50, r 3 was considered. The plaintiff was suing Smith for breach of covenant of quiet
j enjoyment and the other defendant for letting down his surface by working their mines.
Smith had applied for an order for inspection of the mines of the other defendant under
Ord 50, r 3. The court held that on a proper construction of Ord 50, r 3 the court had no
jurisdiction to make an order for inspection by one defendant against another defendant.
Lord Esher MR compared the words of Ord 50, r 3 with the words of the 1883 Ord 31,
r 12 (which dealt with discovery), and concluded that an order for inspection or discovery

is not limited to 'opposite parties' as it may often be necessary to adjust rights between
two plaintiffs or two defendants. Lord Esher MR said that there may be an inspection, *a*
not only between plaintiff and defendant but as between two defendants, if there are
rights which have to be adjusted between them in the action and to which such
inspection is material. Lindley LJ agreed that the opening words of r 3, '. . . upon the
application of *any party*', are wide enough to cover an order between two defendants. He
said (at 200):

'. . . the right to discovery or inspection must have some foundation and must *b*
depend on some other right . . . The mere fact that persons are co-defendants does
not give the right, as it appears to me, in the absence of any community of interest
or right to be adjusted between them.'

Submissions
Counsel for the second defendant submits that Roxburgh J's observations in *Penfold v* *c*
Pearlberg cannot stand with *Shaw v Smith* and that a person cannot be made a party to an
action, unless expressly authorised by statute, where there is no substantive right required
to be adjusted between the parties. In the present case the only relief sought against the
second defendant is an order for inspection under Ord 29 and the Rules of the Supreme
Court do not, in the absence of specific statutory authority, found a cause of action. *d*
Counsel for the plaintiff points out that in *Shaw v Smith* it was assumed that a right to
inspection or discovery would not lie in the absence of a substantive right but the precise
point which arises in the present case was not argued. The submission of counsel for the
successful appellant was that the rule, on its proper construction, did not enable one
defendant to get inspection from another defendant merely for the purpose of obtaining
evidence. Therefore, he submits, *Shaw v Smith* is not binding on this court. He points out *e*
that the assumption was contrary to the views expressed subsequently in *Penfold v*
Pearlberg.
Counsel for the plaintiff relies on *Re Hetherington (decd)* [1989] 2 All ER 129 at 133,
[1990] Ch 1 at 10, in which Sir Nicolas Browne-Wilkinson V-C said:

'In my judgment the authorities therefore clearly establish that even where a *f*
decision of a point of law in a particular sense was essential to an earlier decision of a
superior court, but that superior court merely assumed the correctness of the law on
a particular issue, a judge in a later case is not bound to hold that the law is decided
in that sense.'

I accept counsel's submission that *Shaw v Smith* is distinguishable and that the Court of
Appeal has assumed, rather than decided, the main point in the present case. But, for all *g*
that, the decision in *Shaw v Smith* is of much greater weight and provides clearer guidance
than the other decided cases.
The ratio in *Shaw v Smith* treated the right to a claim for inspection and discovery alike:
see per Lindley LJ (at 200). Counsel for the plaintiff referred me to *Norwich Pharmacal Co*
v Customs and Excise Comrs [1973] 2 All ER 943, [1974] AC 133, in which the House of *h*
Lords held that in the special circumstances of that case an action for discovery alone can
exist. But the effect of the *Norwich Pharmacal* case is explained in *The Supreme Court*
Practice 1988 vol 1, para 24/1/4 as follows:

'An action for discovery alone does not lie against a defendant who is not himself
a wrongdoer and has no connection with the wrong-doing. But where a defendant *j*
through no fault of his own (and whether voluntarily or not) "has got mixed up in
the tortious acts of others so as to facilitate their wrong-doing he may incur no
personal liability but he comes under a duty to assist the person who had been
wronged by giving him full information and disclosing the identity of the
wrongdoers" (*per* Lord Reid in *Norwich Pharmacal Co. v. Commrs. of Customs and*

Excise ([1973] 2 All ER 943, [1974] AC 133). See also *Harrington v North London Polytechnic* ([1984] 3 All ER 666, [1984] 1 WLR 1293).'

I should add that other speeches of their Lordships, in particular the speech of Lord Kilbrandon, make the effect of the ratio decidendi in the *Norwich Pharmacal* case equally clear.

The *Norwich Pharmacal* case is probably the most exhaustive and profound authority on discovery. Counsel for the plaintiff asks me to infer from it that an action for *b* inspection alone is within the court's jurisdiction in the present case. I cannot do so because the second defendant did not facilitate the theft.

Conclusion

My conclusion is that in the absence of an express statutory authority to bring an action for inspection simpliciter, the plaintiff's application must fail. I adopt the *c* reasoning in *Shaw v Smith* which I have already fully explained and must hold that the obiter dicta in *Coomes & Son v Hayward* [1913] 1 KB 150 and *Penfold v Pearlberg* [1955] 3 All ER 120, [1955] 1 WLR 1068 are not to be followed.

For the sake of completeness I must refer to Ord 29, r 7A(2), which provides:

d 'An application after the commencement of proceedings for an order under section 34(3) of the Act in respect of property which is not the property of or in the possession of any party to the proceedings shall be made by summons, which must be served on the person against whom the order is sought and on every party to the proceedings other than the applicant.'

Rule 7A is derived from s 34(3) of the Supreme Court Act 1981, which, inter alia, *e* makes provision for inspection against a new party in a personal injury action or one arising out of death, but the provisions are without prejudice to other powers of the High Court to order discovery or inspection apart from these sections: s 34(4). Rule 7A sets out the machinery for s 34.

I have referred to Ord 29, r 7A for two reasons: first, because the plaintiff cannot claim inspection under r 7A and, second, Ord 29 thus leaves the plaintiff without a remedy. He *f* cannot quantify his claim without inspection of the cello. This is unjust. Counsel for the second defendant says that the second defendant is entitled to refuse inspection by reason of what he has described as right of privacy. I accept that the second defendant may have good reasons but I must observe that an extension of the principle in the *Norwich Pharmacal* case by a higher court, or an amendment of the rules, might provide machinery whereby the merits of the plaintiff's claim to inspection could be justly determined.

g As it is, the appeal must be allowed. I consequently also make an order holding that the court has no jurisdiction, and accede to the application of counsel for the second defendant to strike out paras 6 and 7 of the statement of claim.

Costs

I do not think that the fact that the plaintiff took a proper course in making the *h* application is the overriding consideration as to costs. The difficulty is that my decision was not in fact covered by any authority. I have held that none of the three cases cited in *The Supreme Court Practice 1988* applies. In those circumstances, in my judgment, the proper order is no order as to costs.

i *Appeal allowed. Paragraphs 6 and 7 of statement of claim struck out. No order as to costs. Leave to appeal granted.*

Solicitors: *Bruce Weir & Co* (for the plaintiff); *Booth v Blackwell* (for the second defendant).

K Mydeen Esq   Barrister.

Bell v Peter Browne & Co (a firm)   *a*

COURT OF APPEAL, CIVIL DIVISION
MUSTILL, NICHOLLS AND BELDAM LJJ
21 FEBRUARY, 11 APRIL 1990

Solicitor – Negligence – Cause of action – Parallel claims in tort and contract – Limitation of *b*
action – Accrual of cause of action – Divorce – Matrimonial home in joint names of husband and
wife – Property transferred into sole name of wife under agreement entitling husband to share of
proceeds on sale – Solicitors failing to prepare declaration of trust or mortgage or register caution
to protect husband's interest – Wife selling property eight years later and spending proceeds –
Husband losing share in proceeds of sale and suing solicitors – When cause of action against
solicitors accruing in contract and tort – Whether husband's cause of action time-barred.   *c*

The plaintiff employed the defendant solicitors to act on his behalf in divorce proceedings
when his marriage broke down. The plaintiff and his wife agreed that the matrimonial
home, which was in their joint names, be transferred into the sole name of the wife, who
was to be entitled to live in it for the time being, and that the plaintiff's interest in it,
which was agreed to be one-sixth of the proceeds of sale, be protected by a trust deed or   *d*
mortgage. The house was duly transferred to the wife but the defendants neglected to
take any steps to protect the plaintiff's interest either by arranging for a declaration of
trust or a mortgage to be prepared or by registering a caution in the Land Registry. Eight
years later the wife sold the property and spent the proceeds. The plaintiff brought an
action against the defendants claiming damages for breach of contract and negligence.
The defendants applied to have the action struck out on the ground that it was time-   *e*
barred. The registrar granted the application and his decision was upheld by the judge
on appeal. The plaintiff appealed.

Held – Where a solicitor negligently failed to take precautions, such as the registration
of a caution or a charge, to protect his client's equitable interest in the proceeds of sale of   *f*
a property in the sole name of another party who had agreed that the proceeds would be
shared, the client's cause of action against the solicitor arose in contract when the breach
of duty occurred and in tort when the client parted with his legal interest in return for
an equitable interest or at the latest when a careful solicitor would have registered a
caution or charge because that was when the client suffered damage. The defendants
were in breach of contract when, at the time of the transfer to the wife or as soon as   *g*
practicable thereafter, they failed to take the necessary steps to protect the plaintiff's
interest but since that breach had occurred more than six years before the issue of the
writ, the plaintiff's action in contract was time-barred. Furthermore, the plaintiff had
suffered damage in tort both at the time when the defendants failed to prepare a
declaration of trust, because he had suffered prejudice in entering into the transfer
without the benefit of the protection of a declaration of trust, and at the time when they   *h*
failed to register a caution in the Land Registry, because although that breach was
remediable by the plaintiff up until the wife's sale of the house remedying it depended
on the plaintiff being aware of the breach, which he was not, but since that damage had
also occurred more than six years before the issue of the writ the plaintiff's action in tort
was time-barred. The appeal would therefore be dismissed (see p 126 *f g*, p 127 *j* to p 128
b e to *j*, p 129 *b*, p 132 *j* to p 133 *e*, p 134 *b c g j* and p 136 *b c e*, post).   *j*

Baker v Ollard & Bentley (a firm) (1982) 126 SJ 593 and D W Moore & Co Ltd v Ferrier
[1988] 1 All ER 400 applied.

Midland Bank Trust Co Ltd v Hett Stubbs & Kemp (a firm) [1978] 3 All ER 571 not
followed.

Notes

a For the limitation period for actions in contract and tort, see 28 Halsbury's Laws (4th edn) para 657, for when time begins to run where damage is the gist of the action, see ibid paras 685, 690, and for cases on the subject, see 32 Digest (Reissue) 503–511, 3842–3888.

Cases referred to in judgments

b *Baker v Ollard & Bentley (a firm)* (1982) 126 SJ 593, CA.
Bean v Wade (1885) 2 TLR 157, CA.
Birkett v James [1977] 2 All ER 801, [1978] AC 297, [1977] 3 WLR 38, HL.
Forster v Outred & Co (a firm) [1982] 2 All ER 753, [1982] 1 WLR 86, CA.
Harmer v Cornelius (1858) 5 CBNS 236, [1843–60] All ER Rep 624, 141 ER 94.
Iron Trade Mutual Insurance Co Ltd v J K Buckenham Ltd [1990] 1 All ER 808.
c *Kitchen v Royal Air Forces Association* [1958] 2 All ER 241, [1958] 1 WLR 563, CA.
Mersey Steel and Iron Co Ltd v Naylor Benzon & Co (1884) 9 App Cas 434, [1881–5] All ER Rep 365, HL.
Midland Bank Trust Co Ltd v Hett Stubbs & Kemp (a firm) [1978] 3 All ER 571, [1979] Ch 384, [1978] 3 WLR 167.
Moore (D W) & Co Ltd v Ferrier [1988] 1 All ER 400, [1988] 1 WLR 267, CA.
d *Ronex Properties Ltd v John Laing Construction Ltd (Clarke Nicholls & Marcel (a firm), third parties)* [1982] 3 All ER 961, [1983] QB 398, [1982] 3 WLR 875, CA.
Spoor v Green (1874) LR 9 Exch 99.

Appeal

e The plaintiff, Barry Bell, appealed against the order of Auld J on 22 May 1989 dismissing his appeal against the order of the deputy district registrar in chambers on 14 October 1988 striking out his statement of claim for damages against the defendants, Peter Browne & Co, a firm of solicitors, for negligence and/or breach of contract on the ground that it was frivolous and/or vexatious and an abuse of the process of the court, since the action was time-barred by virtue of ss 2 and 5 of the Limitation Act 1980 having been commenced more than six years after the date on which the cause of action accrued. The

f facts are set out in the judgment of Nicholls LJ.

Peter W Smith for Mr Bell.
Paul Rees for the solicitors.

Cur adv vult

g

11 April. The following judgments were delivered.

NICHOLLS LJ (giving the first judgment at the invitation of Mustill LJ). This appeal raises some short points concerning the date of accrual of the plaintiff's causes of action,

h for breach of contract and in tort, arising out of his solicitors' alleged negligence. The facts as pleaded lie in a very small compass. In October 1977 Mr Barry Bell consulted the defendant firm regarding the breakdown of his marriage. One of the points he discussed with his solicitors concerned what was to happen to the matrimonial home, 60 Lower High Street, Shirehampton, Bristol. The house was registered in the joint names of himself and his wife Sandra. It was worth about £12,000 and subject to a mortgage for

j about £8,000. So if the house had then been sold, Mr Bell would have received about £2,000, that is about one-sixth of the gross proceeds. Mr Bell was agreeable to the house not being sold for the time being, but he was to receive one-sixth of whatever might be the gross proceeds when a sale took place. Meanwhile the house would be transferred into the sole name of his wife. This would help Mr Bell to obtain a mortgage to buy

other accommodation for himself. His continuing interest in 60 Lower High Street
would be protected by a trust deed or a mortgage.   *a*

These arrangements were agreed between Mr and Mrs Bell and their respective
solicitors. On 1 September 1978 Mr Bell executed a transfer of the house into his wife's
sole name. But no steps were taken by Mr Bell's solicitors to protect his one-sixth share in
the proceeds of sale. No declaration of trust or mortgage was prepared or executed. No
caution was registered at the Land Registry. The parties were divorced in the following
year.   *b*

In December 1986 Mr Bell learnt from his former wife that she had sold the property
in July 1986 for £33,000. That is almost eight years after the property had been
transferred into her sole name. She had spent all the proceeds. Thus Mr Bell had lost his
one-sixth interest in the proceeds of sale.

So Mr Bell brought this action against his former solicitors for damages for professional
negligence. The writ was issued on 20 August 1987. The sole question arising on this   *c*
appeal is whether the action is bound to fail because it is statute-barred.

The claim for breach of contract

It was common ground before us that, on the pleaded facts, Mr Bell has or had claims
against his former solicitors in contract and also in tort. I shall consider the two claims in
that order. The basic limitation provision regarding claims founded on contract appears   *d*
now in s 5 of the Limitation Act 1980. That section precludes the bringing of an action
founded on simple contract after the expiration of six years from the date on which the
cause of action accrued. Ascertaining that date involves identifying the relevant terms of
the contract and also the date on which the breach relied on occurred. In the present case
there is no difficulty under either head. Mr Bell's solicitor was retained to take all those
steps which a reasonably careful solicitor would take in respect of the agreed arrangements   *e*
for the transfer of the house to Mr Bell and the retention by him of a beneficial interest
in a one-sixth share. He was to see to the preparation and execution of a formal declaration
of trust or other suitable instrument. He was also to see that Mr Bell's interest would be
protected when Mrs Bell came to sell the house. Under the agreed arrangements she was
to become the sole registered proprietor. By causing appropriate entries to be made on
the land register, such as a caution against dealings, Mr Bell's solicitor was to ensure that   *f*
on a sale of the house Mr Bell would receive his share of the proceeds.

Clearly, all those steps needed to be taken at the time of the transfer or, in the case of
lodging a caution, as soon as reasonably practicable thereafter. When the solicitor failed
to take those steps in 1978 he was, thereupon, in breach of contract. This was so even
though the breach, so far as it related to lodging a caution, remained remediable for
many years. Indeed, it remained remediable until Mr Bell's former wife sold the house.   *g*
Thus the six-year limitation period began to run from the date of the breach, in
September 1978, and it expired long before the writ was issued nearly nine years later, in
August 1987. Accordingly, in my view, Auld J was correct in holding that the claim
based on breach of contract is statute-barred.

It is, of course, true that the solicitor's breach of contract in 1978 did not *discharge* his
obligations. Had Mr Bell learnt, a year or two later, of what had happened, he would still   *h*
have been entitled to go back to his former solicitor and require him to carry out,
belatedly, his contractual obligations so far as they could still be performed. For example,
lodging a caution. Despite this, it was in 1978 that the breach occurred. Failure thereafter
to make good the omission did not constitute a further breach. The position after 1978
was simply that, in breach of contract, the solicitor had failed to do what he ought to
have done in 1978 and, year after year, that breach remained unremedied. Nor would   *j*
the position have been different if in, say, 1980 Mr Bell's solicitor had been asked to
remedy his breach of contract and he had failed to do so. His failure to make good his
existing breach of contract on request would not have constituted a further breach of
contract: it would not have set a new six-year limitation period running. Once again, the

position would have been simply that the solicitor remained in breach. Nor, finally, is
a the position any different because, in respect of lodging a caution, the breach remained
remediable until 1986 when the house was sold. A remediable breach is just as much a
breach of contract when it occurs as an irremediable breach, although the practical
consequences are likely to be less serious if the breach comes to light in time to take
remedial action. Were the law otherwise, in any of these instances, the effect would be to
frustrate the purpose of the statutes of limitation, for it would mean that breaches of
b contract would never become statute-barred unless the innocent party chose to accept the
defaulting party's conduct as a repudiation or, perhaps, performance ceased to be possible.

For completeness I add that the above observations are directed at the normal case
where a contract provides for something to be done, and the defaulting party fails to
fulfil his contractual obligation in that regard at the time when performance is due under
the contract. In such a case there is a single breach of contract. By way of contrast are the
c exceptional cases where, on the true construction of the contract, the defaulting party's
obligation is a continuing contractual obligation. In such cases the obligation is not
breached once and for all, but it is a contractual obligation which arises anew for
performance day after day, so that on each successive day there is a fresh breach. A
familiar example of this is the usual form of repairing clause in a tenancy agreement.
Non-repair for six years does not result in the repairing obligation becoming statute-
d barred while the tenancy still subsists. The obligation of the tenant or the landlord to
keep the property in repair is broken afresh every day the property is out of repair, as
Bramwell B observed in *Spoor v Green* (1874) LR 9 Exch 99 at 111.

We were much pressed with the decision of Oliver J in *Midland Bank Trust Co Ltd v
Hett Stubbs & Kemp (a firm)* [1978] 3 All ER 571, [1979] Ch 384. That case may be
distinguishable on its facts. There the defendant firm of solicitors never treated
e themselves as functi officio in relation to the option. They continued to have dealings
with their client in respect of the unregistered option (see [1978] 3 All ER 571 at 614,
[1979] Ch 384 at 438). The instant case stands in marked contrast. There is no suggestion
that the solicitors had any further contact with Mr Bell or his affairs after the conclusion
of the divorce proceedings. That was more than six years before the writ was issued. The
amended statement of claim, indeed, alleges that the solicitors owed a 'continuing duty'
f to protect Mr Bell's one-sixth beneficial interest until that duty could no longer be
fulfilled or Mr Bell accepted the solicitors' breach as repudiation. But this alleged
continuing duty is not founded on any facts other than the initial retainer I have
mentioned. This allegation takes Mr Bell's case no further.

The claim in tort
g One might have expected that parallel professional negligence claims based on contract
and the tort of negligence would have a common starting date for the running of the six-
year limitation periods applicable in most cases under the 1980 Act. But this is not so,
because a cause of action based on negligence does not accrue until damage is suffered. It
is from that date, not the date on which the negligent act or omission occurred, that the
six-year limitation period prescribed by s 2 of the Limitation Act 1980 runs.
h The question of damage and the limitation period in negligence claims has been a
troublesome one for some years. Most recently this matter was, in 1984, the subject of
recommendations in the Law Reform Committee's 24th Report *Latent Damage* (Cmnd
9390 (1984)). This report led to the Latent Damage Act 1986. The 1986 Act made
amendments to the 1980 Act, which it is hoped will provide a sounder and fairer legal
j framework for the future. In future, in cases comparable to the present one, the new
ss 14A and 14B of the 1980 Act, and not s 2, will apply. But the 1986 Act is of no assistance
to Mr Bell. The changes to the 1980 Act made by the 1986 Act do not enable any action
to be brought which had already been barred by the 1980 Act (see s 4 of the 1986 Act).

So when did Mr Bell first sustain damage by reason of his solicitor's negligence? On
this it is necessary to distinguish between (a) the solicitor's failure to see that the parties'

agreement was recorded formally in a suitable declaration of trust or other instrument
and (b) their failure to protect Mr Bell's interest in the house or the proceeds of sale by   a
lodging a caution. As to failure (a), clearly the damage, such as it may have been, was
sustained when the transfer was executed and handed over. At that point Mr Bell parted
with title to the house, and he became subject to the practical inconveniences which
might flow from his not having Mrs Bell's signature on a formal document. If Mrs Bell
thereafter chose to deny his entitlement to one-sixth of the proceeds of sale, Mr Bell
would have to rely on the correspondence between the solicitors coupled with part   b
performance. To the extent that this was less satisfactory than a formal document
recording the deal, Mr Bell suffered prejudice. He suffered that prejudice when the
transaction was implemented without his having the protection of a formal document.
    The extent of that prejudice depended on the attitude adopted thereafter by his former
wife. All we know is that, according to the pleadings and Mr Bell's affidavit evidence,
when she sold the house she disposed of all the proceeds and did not account to her   c
former husband for his agreed one-sixth share. But the uncertainty surrounding her
future intentions goes only to the quantum of the loss Mr Bell sustained when the
transfer was executed without him having the same degree of protection as would be
provided by a formal document. Likewise in the decision of the Court of Appeal in *Baker
v Ollard & Bentley (a firm)* (1982) 126 SJ 593 cited in *D W Moore & Co Ltd v Ferrier* [1988]   d
1 All ER 400 at 407–408, [1988] 1 WLR 267 at 275–276. There the plaintiff acquired a
share in a property, rather than, as she ought to have received, the security of a long lease
of one floor of the property. The amount of her loss depended on the attitude of her co-
owners. But, even so, the damage was held to be suffered by the plaintiff at the time of
the conveyance, when she received her precarious interest.
    Failure (b) comprised the solicitors' omission to protect Mr Bell's interest by making
an appropriate entry in the land register. This failure stands on a different footing from   e
failure (a) in that it was within Mr Bell's own power to remedy failure (b) so long as the
house continued to belong to his former wife. So long as she did not sell or mortgage the
property, he could protect his interest by taking the simple step of lodging a caution. To
do so he did not need her consent or co-operation.
    Is this difference material? On the one hand Mr Bell, in the case of failure (b) as much
as in the case of failure (a), did not receive the protection he ought to have received when   f
he executed the transfer and parted with his title to the house. He was at risk from the
outset. His interest was vulnerable. On the other hand, so long as Mr Bell's wife did not
deal with the property, failure (b) could easily be put right and at little expense and, had
it been remedied, the failure to lodge a caution promptly in 1978 would have caused no
financial loss to Mr Bell.
    I am unable to accept that remediability puts failure (b) on the other side of the line   g
from failure (a). The solicitors' breach of duty in 1978 was remediable by Mr Bell, but
that was only possible after he became aware that there had been a breach of duty. Apart
from any other consideration, to treat Mr Bell's ability to remedy the breach himself
without the concurrence of his former wife as a ground of distinction between this case
and cases such as *Baker v Ollard & Bentley* would be to disregard the unlikelihood in   h
practice of Mr Bell ever being in a position to remedy the breach. Once the solicitors
closed their file, it was unlikely that failure (b) would come to the notice of Mr Bell, or
the solicitors, until the house was sold and it was too late. That, on the pleaded facts, is
exactly what happened. The first Mr Bell knew that his one-sixth share was not properly
protected was after it had gone beyond recall. So his ability to remedy the breach before
the house was sold was a matter of more theoretical interest than practical importance.   j
    In considering whether damage was suffered in 1978 one can test the matter by
considering what would have happened if in, say, 1980 Mr Bell had learnt of his solicitors'
default and brought an action for damages. Of course, he would have taken steps to
remedy the default. But he would have been entitled at least to recover from the solicitors
the cost incurred in going to other solicitors for advice on what should be done and for

their assistance in lodging the appropriate caution. The cost would have been modest,
a but not negligible.

I am very conscious that in *Midland Bank Trust Co Ltd v Hett Stubbs & Kemp* [1978] 3 All
ER 571, [1979] Ch 384 Oliver J treated it as axiomatic that the client suffered no loss
from non-registration of the option until the farm was sold. But I can see no sound
distinction between the present case and binding decisions of this court, such as *Baker v
Ollard & Bentley* and *D W Moore & Co Ltd v Ferrier*, which were decided subsequent to
b the *Midland Bank* case.

I reach the conclusion that Mr Bell's claim in tort, as well as his claim in contract, is
statute-barred, with reluctance. It will be cold comfort to Mr Bell to be told of the Latent
Damage Act 1986 and that cases such as his will be subject to different rules in future.
But I do not think that shortcomings in the applicable Limitation Act are to be cured by
drawing unsound distinctions between one case and the next. I would dismiss this appeal.
c

BELDAM LJ. This appeal raises again the question: when does a cause of action arise
for failure by a solicitor to exercise reasonable care and skill in handling the property
affairs of his client? If due to such a breach the client does not get the security for which
it is the elementary duty of the solicitor to provide, does he suffer loss at the moment of
that failure or only when the contingency against which it is intended to guard occurs
d some years later?

The question arises in these circumstances. The plaintiff, Mr Barry Bell, consulted the
defendant solicitors, Messrs Peter Browne & Co, about his matrimonial affairs in October
1977. The defendants practice as solicitors in Shirehampton, Bristol. Mr Bell and his
former wife had their matrimonial home at 60 Lower High Street, Shirehampton,
Bristol. Subject to a mortgage, they owned the property as joint tenants on trust for sale
e equally entitled to the balance of any proceeds after discharge of sums outstanding on
the mortgage. As is so often the case, it was their only substantial asset. There was one
child of the marriage, who at that time was 14 years old. Mr Bell's marriage had
irretrievably broken down although at that time he continued to live separately in the
matrimonial home. He and his wife reached an amicable agreement, no doubt as part of
f the overall settlement of their affairs, that if he would relinquish his half-share in the
proceeds of sale she alone would become responsible for the mortgage repayments and
would undertake, when she disposed of the property, to pay Mr Bell one-sixth of the
gross sale price realised.

It is clear from a letter written by the solicitors to Mr Bell on 11 October 1977 that as
part of their instructions to act for him they were retained to implement the agreement
between Mr Bell and his former wife. The letter was written very shortly after Mr Bell
g had instructed them and included the sentence: 'Your interest could be legally protected
either by Declaration of Trust or by mortgage and this is something we would have to
discuss with your wife's solicitors.'

On 1 September 1978 Mr Bell executed a transfer of his interest in the matrimonial
home to his former wife but for the purposes of this appeal it has to be assumed that the
h solicitors took no steps to protect Mr Bell's interest in the future proceeds of sale either
by requiring a deed of trust to be executed by his former wife, by securing a charge on
the property or by registering a caution. Nor did they tell Mr Bell that they had failed to
do so. He was unaware that he had surrendered his interest in the property for an interest
in the proceeds of sale which depended entirely on the ability and willingness of his
former wife to fulfil her side of the bargain when the house was sold.

j Mr Bell's marriage ended in 1979 and in 1982 he remarried. On 4 July 1986 60 Lower
High Street was sold by his former wife for the sum of £33,000. According to an affidavit
of Mr Bell he first heard of the sale from his former wife in a telephone conversation on
12 December 1986. On the same occasion she informed him that she had already spent
the proceeds of sale and could not pay him his one-sixth share.

On 20 August 1987 Mr Bell commenced these proceedings claiming breach of duty by the solicitors. His original statement of claim condescended to few particulars though it set out the material facts as I have outlined them. By their defence the solicitors contended that any claim by Mr Bell was barred by limitation since his cause of action arose more than six years prior to the issue of the writ.

Relying on observations of this court in *Ronex Properties Ltd v John Laing Construction Ltd (Clarke Nicholls & Marcel (a firm), third parties)* [1982] 3 All ER 961, [1983] QB 398, the solicitors took out a summons to strike out the statement of claim as frivolous and vexatious and an abuse of the process of the court, contending that this was the appropriate course because on the face of the pleadings they disclosed no cause of action which was not barred by statute.

The registrar upheld the solicitors' claim and struck out the action. Mr Bell appealed to Auld J who on 22 May 1989 dismissed the appeal. In the course of the hearing he allowed amendments to the statement of claim. The significance of the amendments is to be found in the particulars set out in para 7 of the amended statement of claim. In para 7(ii) Mr Bell contended that the duty owed by the solicitors was a duty to protect his interest which continued until the solicitors repudiated it or until it became incapable of fulfilment. By para 8 it was averred that the duty only became incapable of being fulfilled when the property was sold on 4 July 1986.

The purpose of these amendments was to reflect an argument which had been addressed to the judge based on the decision of Oliver J in *Midland Bank Trust Co Ltd v Hett Stubbs & Kemp (a firm)* [1978] 3 All ER 571, [1979] Ch 384.

Auld J rejected the argument based on that decision, holding that there was no continuing contractual obligation on the present defendant solicitors, and relying on a decision in this court, *Forster v Outred & Co (a firm)* [1982] 2 All ER 753, [1982] 1 WLR 86, he held that Mr Bell's claim was clearly statute-barred.

Although in the final analysis it did not affect the result of this appeal, in the course of argument the parties canvassed the question of the nature and extent of the solicitors' retainer. From the discussion it was clear that an issue of fact might have arisen over the terms of the retainer which would have made the application to strike out the proceedings inappropriate. This is not the first case in which such a state of affairs has arisen. It is, I feel, necessary to emphasise that as Donaldson LJ in his judgment in the *Ronex Properties* case [1982] 3 All ER 961 at 966, [1983] QB 398 at 405 made clear, such a procedure is only appropriate in 'a very clear case'. If, from the issues raised in the pleadings, arguable questions of fact could arise, the procedure will not be appropriate. Similarly if the pleadings are in such a form that the full extent of the issues have not been defined, the procedure will not be appropriate until they have been. This may perhaps seem obvious, but it can only add to the cost and delay of proceedings if such applications are made other than in cases in which on the face of the pleadings it is beyond argument that the cause of action is statute-barred.

The argument for Mr Bell may be summarised in this way. A plaintiff who alleges that he has suffered loss by reason of breach of duty of his solicitor may found his cause of action either in contract or in tort. Although in the ordinary case his cause of action in contract will arise when the breach of duty occurs, in cases where the solicitor's duty includes a duty to protect the plaintiff's interest by taking some positive action, such as registering an interest in or charge over property, the duty is to be regarded as a continuing duty. If the solicitor fails to take the appropriate steps, there may come a time when it could be said that he has repudiated that duty. It is, however, trite law that his repudiation does not put an end to his duty unless it is accepted by the other party to the agreement. Thus it is argued that until the duty becomes incapable of performance or until a repudiation of the duty is accepted, the breach is a continuing one capable of giving rise to a cause of action. Alternatively Mr Bell bases his claim in tort, contending that his cause of action did not arise until he suffered damage. On the facts of the present case, since Mr Bell's ex-wife's obligation to pay over to him the agreed portion of the net proceeds of sale only arose on sale of the property, Mr Bell suffered no loss until she failed

to comply with her obligation. Thus his cause of action only arose in the present case
a after the sale of the property in July 1986 and was therefore not barred by statute.

Mr Bell's claim in contract is, as I have said, founded firmly on the judgment of
Oliver J in the *Midland Bank Trust Co* case. Auld J considered that that case could be
distinguished on its facts. In that case the plaintiffs were the executors of a client of the
defendant firm. In March 1961 the defendants' senior partner had been instructed to
draw up an option agreement for the purchase by the client of his father's farm at a
b favourable price. The option was to remain effective for ten years. The client paid a
nominal consideration for the option, which the defendants failed to register as an estate
contract under the Land Charges Act 1925. On a number of occasions subsequently the
client consulted the defendants and sought their advice whether he should exercise the
option. In due course in August 1967 the client's father, wishing to resile from the option
he had granted his son, discovered through other solicitors that the option had not been
c registered and conveyed the farm to his wife for the sum of £500 within the ten-year
period. In October 1967 the client sought without success to exercise the option. In July
1972 he issued proceedings against the defendants, claiming damages for negligence and
breach of duty.

Oliver J held that there was no general or continuing duty arising out of the client's
retainer to consider the enforceability of the option on every occasion on which they
d were consulted as to a possible exercise of it. He held that the defendants were liable in
tort for breach of duty because the damage suffered by their client did not arise until his
father conveyed the farm to his wife, thereby defeating the option. The client's cause of
action therefore arose within the period of limitation.

Finally he held that the defendants' breach of their contractual duty amounted to non-
feasance of the duty to register the option, and that that duty continued to bind them
e until it ceased to be effectively capable of performance when the father conveyed the
farm to his wife. Thus an action based in contract against the defendants was not statute-
barred.

The principal question considered in the judgment was whether the relationship of
solicitor and client gives rise to a duty of care in tort as well as to a duty in contract. After
concluding that there were concurrent duties, the judge turned to the question whether
f the defendants were liable in contract. After noting that a contract gives rise to a complex
of rights and duties of which the duty to exercise reasonable care and skill is but one,
Oliver J illustrated by analogy from a contract to supply goods and services the differing
consequences which may flow from the different types of obligation undertaken.

It was important in that case to note that it was not a case of the giving of wrong and
negligent advice, where the breach of contract necessarily occurred at a fixed point of
g time, but of simple non-feasance. So far as the client was concerned, it was a matter of
total indifference to him at what date the solicitor chose to fulfil his contractual
obligations to effect registration so long as it is effectively fulfilled. No doubt a normal
careful practitioner would fulfil that obligation as soon as was reasonably practicable. In
an appropriate case he might give a priority notice. But if he failed to do so and an
h effective registration could still be and was effected, his client can have no complaint
except the purely technical one that he had been a bit careless and might have done it
sooner. He had, no doubt, exhibited a failure to show the normal competence and care
for his client's affairs by carelessly allowing a period to elapse during which a third party
might have, but had not in fact, acquired an interest. But such a failure could not affect,
much less discharge, the primary obligation to effect registration timeously, which
j continued until it was performed or became impossible of performance or until the
client elected to treat the continued non-performance as a repudiation of the contract.

He next considered the decision of the Court of Appeal in *Bean v Wade* (1885) 2 TLR
157. A husband, who had an interest in trust funds, assigned that interest to the trustee
of his marriage settlement. No notice of the assignment was given to the trustees of the
fund. Subsequently proceedings were brought by his wife for the removal of the trustees

of the marriage settlement and the appointment of fresh trustees. The defendants acted as solicitors for the wife in those proceedings. In due course the plaintiffs were appointed *a* as trustees of the marriage settlement and a deed of assignment from the former trustees to them was executed in 1875 but the defendant solicitors, assuming that notice of the marriage settlement had already been given to trustees of the head settlement, omitted to give any notice to them of the assignment to the plaintiffs. Subsequently the husband executed a mortgage of his interest under the head settlement to a mortgagee who took without notice of the prior assignment to the plaintiffs. In April 1879 the mortgagee *b* gave notice of his interest to the trustees of the head settlement, thus gaining priority. In due course the plaintiffs were called on to make good a deficiency of interest and capital to the wife and they sought to claim this loss from the defendant solicitors. At first instance Cave J found for the plaintiffs but on appeal his decision was reversed on the ground that more than six years had elapsed between the time when notice should have been given and the commencement of the action. Accordingly it was statute-barred. The *c* basis of the decision was that the solicitors' obligation under their retainer was an obligation to give notice within a reasonable time. There was no separate or co-existing continuing duty on which the action could be founded.

Oliver J acknowledged the striking resemblance to the case before him. In distinguishing it he emphasised the fact that in that case the solicitors had failed to give notice within a reasonable time of their appointment as trustees; there was no allegation *d* of a continuing breach of duty as there was in the case before him. Finally, he said ([1978] 3 All ER 571 at 614, [1979] Ch 384 at 438):

> 'The defendants here never treated themselves as functi officio in relation to the option. They kept the document on Geoffrey's behalf in their strongroom. They opened a file relating to the matter. They were consulted about it at intervals over *e* the next 6½ years. In my judgment the obligation to register which they assumed when they were first consulted continued to bind them. It was an obligation to protect the interest from third parties by registration and without their client's knowledge they failed to perform it until it ceased to be effectively capable of performance on 17th August 1967. It seems to me that it was *then* that the contract was broken once and for all.' (My emphasis.) *f*

Later he said:

> 'In my judgment the breach of contract on which this action is based occurred on 17th August 1967 and the defence of limitation fails under this head also.'

Naturally before us the solicitors relied strongly on this paragraph as showing that *g* there was an essential difference between that case and the present. Here they said the solicitors were never consulted again after they had effected the conveyance of Mr Bell's interest in the property to the wife. They rendered Mr Bell a bill and from that moment on they were functi officio. For my part, however, I do not think that the liability of a solicitor for breach of contract should depend on such a distinction. Moreover, although it is with the greatest diffidence that I would express any view contrary to that of Oliver J, *h* I am not persuaded that that case was distinguishable on its facts from *Bean v Wade*, nor from the facts in the present case.

The obligation of a solicitor in carrying out his retainer is to exercise the care and skill of a competent solicitor. His duty to act with that degree of care and skill arises originally from the fact that a professional man warranted that he possessed and would exercise in the execution of the task he undertook the care and skill expected of a person practising *j* that profession (see *Harmer v Cornelius* (1858) 5 CBNS 236, [1843–60] All ER Rep 624). It is now established that an action may be brought for breach of the duty either founded in contract or in tort.

Whether in any particular case there has been a failure by a solicitor to exercise that degree of care and skill depends on the circumstances of each case and on the finding of

the court as to how the competent solicitor would discharge his duty in those
a circumstances. Where, as in the present case and in the *Midland Bank Trust Co Ltd* case
and *Bean v Wade*, the duty is to protect the interests of the client by giving notice or by
registration of a charge or caution, I cannot believe that a competent solicitor would
regard it as a satisfactory discharge of that duty to postpone action for months or years.
Indeed, there would be many cases when even postponement for a day would be regarded
as negligent and a breach of duty. Further, in a case in which it is necessary to take
b precautions to preserve a client's interest against the failure by another to fulfil an
obligation whether by requiring the execution of a charge or a deed of trust, it seems to
me clear that the exercise of reasonable care requires the transactions to be
contemporaneous. I do not believe, therefore, that it is correct to say that in a case such
as the present the obligation of the solicitor in contract was one which was capable of
performance at any time up until the property was sold. If by chance he realised his
c mistake in time, he could take steps to prevent the consequences of breach of the
obligation and to that extent repair the damage caused. I believe that the solicitors were
in breach of their duty when they permitted Mr Bell to execute a conveyance of his
interest in the freehold property without securing by deed of trust or charge an interest
in the proceeds of sale. They ought to have appreciated that Mr Bell had only executed at
that stage in escrow and should have insisted on the performance by his wife of the
d condition to which she had agreed. Whilst it may not have been a breach of duty to fail
to register Mr Bell's interest immediately or within a day or two on the facts of this
particular case, nevertheless experience shows that such a duty should be discharged as
soon as is practicable. Consequently, although Mr Bell only suffered nominal damage
until the property was sold in July 1986, his cause of action arose when he conveyed his
interest in the property to his former wife without proper precautions being taken to
e protect his future interest in the proceeds of sale. Accordingly, I would hold that his
cause of action in contract was barred by statute. I now turn to consider his claim in tort.

In the tort of negligence, damage is the gist of the action. So until actual loss is suffered,
no cause of action can arise. Thus Mr Bell argued that until the sale of the house he had
no right to receive any part of the proceeds from the sale of the property. Until his
former wife failed to fulfil her side of the bargain, he had in fact suffered no loss.
f Consequently no cause of action arose until she failed to fulfil her promise to pay over a
part of the proceeds of sale.

The solicitors, however, contended that the case was indistinguishable from *Forster v
Outred & Co (a firm)* [1982] 2 All ER 753, [1982] 1 WLR 86. In that case the plaintiff had
executed a mortgage of her property in the presence of her solicitors to secure a loan
made to her son, who subsequently went bankrupt. Some time later she was called on to
g repay the loan, which she did. About two years later she claimed damages for negligence
and breach of contract of her solicitors, who were the defendants. The plaintiff and her
new advisers were guilty of inordinate and inexcusable delay in proceeding with the
action and the defendants applied to dismiss it for want of prosecution. The plaintiff's
solicitors thereupon issued another writ claiming damages against the defendants for
h negligence in connection with the execution of the mortgage. This writ was issued more
than six years after she had executed the mortgage but was within six years of the date
when she repaid the loan. It was contended on behalf of the plaintiff that the court
should not dismiss her action for want of prosecution because, in accordance with the
decision in *Birkett v James* [1977] 2 All ER 801, [1978] AC 297, the plaintiff could still
proceed with her alternative action started by the issue of the fresh writ. The defendants
j contended that the claim in the second writ was statute-barred and that consequently the
decision in *Birkett v James* was no bar to dismissal of the first action. Thus the question in
issue before the court was whether the plaintiff has suffered damage at the time when
she executed the original mortgage or only when she discharged the loan, being called
on to pay it.

The court held that the plaintiff in that case had suffered actual damage through the negligence of her solicitors by entering into the mortgage deed which had the effect of encumbering her interest in the freehold estate by a legal charge which could, in the *a* future, mature into an actual loss. The fact that it only did so subsequently did not alter the fact that she had suffered loss at the moment she had executed the deed.

I can see no ground for distinguishing the present case. Due to the solicitors' negligence, Mr Bell parted with his legal estate in the property conveyed to his wife in exchange for an equitable interest in the proceeds of sale. That equitable interest until secured by a charge or acknowledged by a deed of trust was clearly less valuable to Mr Bell. *b* Unprotected against the interests of third parties by registration of a charge or of a caution, it was less valuable still. I consider therefore that Mr Bell's cause of action arose when he parted with his property or at the latest at the time when the careful solicitor would have effected registration either of a charge or of a caution. For those reasons I would dismiss this appeal. I desire, however, to add that it is a conclusion at which I arrive with no enthusiasm. As Lord Evershed MR said in *Kitchen v Royal Air Forces* *c* *Association* [1958] 2 All ER 241 at 245, [1958] 1 WLR 563 at 567–568:

> 'An action against a firm of solicitors for alleged negligence by one who says that she was their client is always a matter of special anxiety to the court; for to some extent, inevitably, our system and profession of the law is impugned and its adequacy and competency challenged. Especially is this so in the present case.' *d*

Although such claims are now much more frequent, I hope that these words have lost none of their force. Indeed on the assumed facts of the present case it would be difficult to imagine a case of greater neglect of a client's interest. When it is conceded that Mr Bell, who had relied on the defendants' competence as solicitors had no means of knowing that they had by their negligence left him unprotected, it seems to me an added indictment of our system and profession of the law that they should escape liability by *e* reliance on the rule designed to secure efficiency. The judge regarded the outcome as 'unfortunate' for the plaintiff in this instance though in the future he thought such an injustice should in most cases be avoided by the operation of the Latent Damage Act 1986.

How effective the operation of that Act will prove to be in the future to enable persons who have suffered damage in circumstances similar to Mr Bell to recover their loss *f* remains to be seen; it will not avail those who from the negligent performance of duty before July 1980 suffer damage in the future. Nor will it avail those who may become aware of their loss after a period of 15 years. For my part I would have hoped that consideration could be given to a more comprehensive assurance against similar loss in the future.

g

MUSTILL LJ. I agree, but with the same regret as Nicholls and Beldam LJJ have already expressed. The hardship to a person in the position of Mr Bell, whose justifiable reliance on the professional skills of his advisers was precisely the reason that he had no cause to suspect that there had been a failure to exercise those skills, will be greatly mitigated for the future by the Latent Damage Act 1986. This will be cold comfort to Mr Bell, who *h* could have hoped for better from the legal system and its practitioners. On the more general plane, I think it a pity that English law has elected to recognise concurrent rights of action in contract and tort. Other legal systems seem to manage quite well by limiting attention to the contractual obligations which are, after all, the foundation of the relationship between the professional man and his client: as for example, in the case of French law, via the doctrine of non cumul. That precisely the same breach of precisely *j* the same organisation should be capable of generating causes of action which arise at different times is in my judgment an anomaly which our law could well do without. Nevertheless the law is clear and we must apply it.

As regards the breach of contract, I entirely agree with Nicholls and Beldam LJJ and would add only a few brief observations on one aspect of *Midland Bank Trust Co Ltd v Hett*

Stubbs & Kemp (a firm) [1978] 3 All ER 571 at 611, [1979] Ch 384 at 434–435, namely the
a proposition that in cases where there is a breach of contract, not accepted by the promisee
as a repudiation, the promisee has no cause of action. In this respect I believe that a
distinction must be drawn between two situations.

In the first, the promisor makes it plain by words or conduct, before the time fixed for
performance, that when the time arrives he cannot or will not perform. This is the case
of anticipatory breach of contract, where under English law the promisee has an option
b whether or not to continue with the contract. If he elects to 'accept' the promisor's
conduct as a wrongful repudiation the obligations for the future of both parties are
discharged, and the promisee may sue at once to recover damages for loss of the bargain.
If, however, he elects not to treat the contract as repudiated the obligations of both sides
continue in existence and the promisor's renunciation has no effect as a breach of contract
and gives no immediate cause of action for damages, although it may create certain rights
c in equity.

The second situation exists where there is no renunciation in advance, but where when
the day for performance (if the obligation is to do a once-for-all act) or the first day for
performance (if the contract requires acts to be done continually or intermittently over a
period of time) arrives the promisor either performs badly or does not perform at all.
Here the fate of the bilateral obligation will depend on a number of factors. First, on the
d nature of the obligation and magnitude of the breach. If the obligation is a condition of
the contract, or if the breach is serious enough to go to the root of the contract, the
promisee will have the option to treat himself as discharged from his present and future
obligations. Second, on whether the breach, even if insufficient in itself to justify a
termination, nevertheless demonstrates when placed in the context of other relevant
facts, an unwillingness or inability on the part of the promisor to go ahead and perform
e his obligations in the future. If it does, the promisee may elect to treat himself as
discharged by anticipatory breach of those future obligations: see *Mersey Steel and Iron Co
Ltd v Naylor Benzon & Co* (1884) 9 App Cas 434, [1881–5] All ER Rep 365. Third, on the
conduct of the promisee himself. This may be such as to be a waiver of the right to treat
a breach of condition, or a serious breach of an 'innominate' term, as a ground to
terminate the contract. Or it may show an election not to treat the future obligations as
f having been the subject of an anticipatory breach. In such cases the contract remains
alive for the future. The point, however, for present purposes is that even if the promisee
does not 'accept' the promisor's breach as a repudiation, it retains its character as a breach
and is actionable at once, even though the continuing obligation to perform in the future
will also be capable of founding new causes of action when the time becomes ripe. Thus
I would not for my part accept that there is no right of suit, and hence no commencement
g of the limitation period, until the promisee finally loses patience and elects to bring the
contract to an end.

In fact, however, I doubt whether this theoretical question is material to the present
case. Certainly, a solicitor may have a continuing retainer from his client, and no doubt
there are retainers which require the solicitor to be constantly on watch for new sources
h of potential danger, and to take immediate steps to nip them in the bud. I confess,
however, that I cannot see the relationship between the present parties in any such light.
The proposition entails that the solicitor had two duties, one express and the other
implied. The express duty would be to perform the task for which he was retained and
paid, namely to put into effect in a legally appropriate manner the informal arrangement
between his client and his wife. The second duty, implied and presumably gratuitous,
j and commencing immediately after the last moment when a careful solicitor would
have taken the necessary steps to formalise and protect his client's interest in the future
proceeds of sale, would be to exercise continuing vigilance to discover any mistake which
he might have made, and then to busy himself in putting it right. Evidently, this
obligation would continue up to, but not beyond, the time when the mistake became
irretrievable. I find it impossible to imply such a strange obligation from the mundane

facts of the present case, and equally improbable to suppose that if it did exist the
obligation would be broken at any time other than the time when the mistake should   *a*
have been discovered and put right, namely straight away. To my mind the solicitor was
employed to complete the transaction, and to complete it within the appropriate time.
No more than that. Any further steps taken or not taken would relate to mitigating the
consequences of a breach which had already occurred.

As to the claim in tort, I have little to add. The transaction caused Mr Bell to exchange
his valid legal estate for an equitable interest in the proceeds of sale which was dependent   *b*
on the goodwill and solvency of the wife unless and until protected by a formal
declaration of trust and the lodging of a caution. The failure to see that these steps were
taken promptly meant that Mr Bell was actually, and not just potentially, worse off than
if the solicitor had performed his task competently. The sale in 1986 simply meant that
the breach and its consequences were irremediable. As Nicholls LJ has pointed out, the
solicitors' negligence had two different aspects: the failure to obtain the wife's participation   *c*
in a formal instrument and the failure to protect the interests by a caution, but I
respectfully agree with his view that this characteristic forms no ground for distinguishing
Baker v Ollard & Bentley (a firm) (1982) 126 SJ 593 and *D W Moore & Co Ltd v Ferrier*
[1988] 1 All ER 400, [1988] 1 WLR 267, which are binding on this court.

I would add that since the conclusion of argument a report has appeared of the decision
of Kenneth Rokison QC in *Iron Trade Mutual Insurance Co Ltd v J K Buckenham Ltd* [1990]   *d*
1 All ER 808, where a similar point to the present arose in the context of clauses against
insurance brokers. After an extensive discussion of the cases to which Nicholls and
Beldam LJJ have referred, the deputy judge arrived at a conclusion identical to our own.

With regret, therefore, I must concur in the opinion that the appeal should be
dismissed.

e

Appeal dismissed.

Solicitors: *Hyde Mahon Bridges*, agents for *Croftons*, Manchester (for Mr Bell); *Willey
Hargrave*, agents for *Wansbroughs*, Bristol (for the solicitors).

Raina Levy   Barrister.

a # R v General Council of the Bar, ex parte Percival

QUEEN'S BENCH DIVISION

WATKINS LJ AND GARLAND J

6, 7, 8, 9 NOVEMBER, 20 DECEMBER 1989
b

Judicial review – Availability of remedy – Disciplinary proceedings – Professional Conduct Committee of Bar Council – Decision of committee to bring charges against barrister – Head of chambers lodging complaint that member of chambers guilty of professional misconduct – Committee deciding to prefer lesser charge of breach of proper professional standards against barrister – Head of chambers applying for judicial review of committee's decision – Whether head
c *of chambers having locus standi to apply for judicial review of committee's decision – Whether court having jurisdiction to hear and determine application – Whether prosecuting authority's decision to prosecute reviewable – Whether public policy preventing court considering application – Whether committee's decision unreasonable or tainted by procedural irregularity – Code of Conduct for the Bar of England and Wales (3rd edn), paras 6, 7, 8.*

d The applicant, who was the head of a set of barristers' chambers, accused another member, who was the financial and general administrator of the chambers, of mishandling chambers money and reported him to the Bar Council as being in breach of para 6 of the Code of Conduct for the Bar of England and Wales (3rd edn), which provided that a barrister should not engage in conduct which was, inter alia, dishonest or which would bring the profession into disrepute. A serious breach of para 6 amounting
e to professional misconduct could result in disbarment under para 7, while the lesser offence of breach of proper professional standards could render the barrister liable under para 8 to an admonishment. The applicant's complaint was referred to the Professional Conduct Committee of the Bar Council, to which, pursuant to r 2 of its rules, was delegated the power 'to investigate and sift complaints . . . to prefer charges . . . and be responsible for prosecuting any such charges' before a disciplinary tribunal. The
f committee decided that the barrister should be charged with a breach of proper professional standards under para 8. The applicant, who considered that the barrister should have been charged with the more serious charge of professional misconduct under para 7, applied for judicial review of the committee's decision, seeking (i) a declaration that the committee was required by r 3(e)(viii) of its rules to prefer a charge of professional misconduct against the barrister because a prima facie case of professional misconduct
g had been disclosed by the complaint and (ii) an order that the committee prefer a charge of professional misconduct against the barrister rather than a charge of breach of proper professional standards. The questions arose (i) whether the applicant had locus standi to make the application, (ii) whether the Divisional Court had jurisdiction to hear and determine the application or whether the application fell within the exclusive jurisdiction
h of the judges, as visitors of the Inns of Court, to discipline members of the Bar, (iii) whether a prosecuting authority's decision to prosecute or not was reviewable at all, (iv) whether public policy prevented the court considering the application and (v) whether the committee's decision was unreasonable or tainted by procedural irregularity.

Held – (1) The applicant had sufficient interest in the Professional Conduct Committee's
j decision by reason of the fact that as the head of chambers of the barrister against whom the complaint had been made he had a responsibility to ensure that any lapse from proper professional conduct or the observance of proper professional standards by a member of his chambers was properly investigated and if necessary referred to a disciplinary tribunal. Moreover, as the complainant, he was the only person in a position to challenge a decision by the committee not to investigate a complaint or not to initiate

a prosecution of a complaint (see p 149 *f g*, post); *O'Reilly v Mackman* [1982] 3 All ER
1124, *R v Metropolitan Police Comr, ex p Blackburn* [1968] 1 All ER 763 and *Public Disclosure* **a**
Commission v Isaacs [1989] 1 All ER 137 considered.

(2) The acts and omissions of the Professional Conduct Committee were susceptible to
judicial review because, as the body to whom the Bar Council's prosecuting functions of
sifting and assessing complaints and prosecuting complaints before the disciplinary
tribunal had been delegated, the committee was required to carry out those functions in
accordance with its own rules and was subject to judicial review if it did not. Furthermore, **b**
there were no public policy reasons which prevented the court considering the application.
However, since the committee had acted within the limits of its discretion and had not
acted unreasonably, perversely or with any procedural irregularity the application would
be dismissed (see p 147 *h j*, p 153 *a b e*, p 156 *e to j* and p 157 *b*, post); *R v Benchers of Gray's
Inn* (1780) 1 Doug 353 and *Lincoln v Daniels* [1961] 3 All ER 740 considered.

Per curiam. A prosecuting authority's discretion whether to prosecute or not is plainly **c**
reviewable but given the fact that there is potentially an almost infinite variety of
circumstances in which that discretion may be exercised it would not be right to set
strictly defined limits to the judicial review of a prosecuting authority. Each case is to be
considered with due regard to the powers, functions and procedures of the authority and
the manner in which it has dealt with the particular complaint (see p 152 *b c*, post); *R v
Metropolitan Police Comr, ex p Blackburn* [1968] 1 All ER 763, *Selvarajan v Race Relations* **d**
Board [1976] 1 All ER 12 and *R v Police Complaints Board, ex p Madden* [1983] 2 All ER
353 considered.

Notes

For the Bar Council and for disciplinary proceedings in relation to barristers, see 3(1) **e**
Halsbury's Laws (4th edn reissue) paras 367, 493–498.

For judicial review of non-statutory tribunals, see 1(1) ibid paras 52, 112.

Cases referred to in judgment

Associated Provincial Picture Houses Ltd v Wednesbury Corp [1947] 2 All ER 680, [1948] 1
   KB 223, CA. **f**
Bhattacharya v General Medical Council [1967] 2 AC 259, [1967] 3 WLR 498, PC.
Booreman's Case (1641) March 177 pl 235, 82 ER 464.
Council of Civil Service Unions v Minister for the Civil Service [1984] 3 All ER 935, [1985] AC
   374, [1984] 1 WLR 1174, HL.
General Medical Council v Spackman [1943] 2 All ER 337, [1943] AC 627, HL.
Lincoln v Daniels [1961] 3 All ER 740, [1962] 1 QB 237, [1961] 3 WLR 866, CA. **g**
Nottingham CC v Secretary of State for the Environment [1986] 1 All ER 119, [1986] AC 240,
   [1986] 2 WLR 1, HL.
Oakes v Sidney Sussex College, Cambridge [1988] 1 All ER 1004, [1988] 1 WLR 431.
O'Reilly v Mackman [1982] 3 All ER 1124, [1983] 2 AC 237, [1982] 3 WLR 1096, HL.
Public Disclosure Commission v Isaacs [1989] 1 All ER 137, [1988] 1 WLR 1043, PC.
R v Benchers of Gray's Inn (1780) 1 Doug 353, 99 ER 227. **h**
R v General Council of Medical Education and Registration of the UK [1930] 1 KB 562.
R v Metropolitan Police Comr, ex p Blackburn [1968] 1 All ER 763, [1968] 2 QB 118, [1968]
   2 WLR 893, CA.
R v Police Complaints Board, ex p Madden [1983] 2 All ER 353, [1983] 1 WLR 447.
Rajasooria v Discipline Committee [1955] 1 WLR 405, PC.
S (a barrister), Re [1981] 2 All ER 952, [1981] QB 683, [1981] 3 WLR 129. **j**
Selvarajan v Race Relations Board [1976] 1 All ER 12, [1975] 1 WLR 1686, CA.

Cases also cited

Adams v Comr of Police of the Metropolis [1980] RTR 289, DC.

Breen v Amalgamated Engineering Union [1971] 1 All ER 1148, [1971] 2 QB 175, CA.

a *Calvin v Carr* [1979] 2 All ER 440, PC.

Currie v Barton [1988], CA Transcript 430.

Finnigan v New Zealand Rugby Football Union Inc [1985] 2 NZLR 159, NZ CA.

McInnes v Onslow-Fare [1978] 3 All ER 211, [1978] 1 WLR 1520.

R v BBC, ex p Lavelle [1983] 1 All ER 241, [1983] 1 WLR 23.

R v Committee of Lloyd's, ex p Posgate (1983) Times, 12 January, DC.

b *R v Criminal Injuries Compensation Board, ex p Lain* [1967] 2 All ER 770, [1967] 2 QB 864, DC.

R v East Berkshire Health Authority, ex p Walsh [1984] 3 All ER 425, [1985] QB 152, CA.

R v General Medical Council, ex p Gee [1987] 2 All ER 193, [1987] 1 WLR 565, HL.

R v Justice of the Central Criminal Court, ex p London CC [1925] 2 KB 43, [1925] All ER Rep 429, DC.

c *R v Metropolitan Police Comr, ex p Blackburn (No 3)* [1973] 1 All ER 324, [1973] QB 241, CA.

R v National Coal Board, ex p National Union of Mine Workers [1986] ICR 791.

R v Panel on Take-overs and Mergers, ex p Datafin plc (Norton Opax plc intervening) [1987] 1 All ER 564, [1987] QB 815, CA.

R v Panel on Take-overs and Mergers, ex p Guinness plc [1989] 1 All ER 509, [1990] QB 146, d CA.

R v Pharmaceutical Society of GB, ex p Sokah (1986) Times, 4 December.

S (a barrister), Re [1969] 1 All ER 949, [1970] 1 QB 160, [1969] 2 WLR 708.

Stoke-on-Trent City Council v B & Q (Retail) Ltd [1984] 2 All ER 332, [1984] AC 45, HL.

Thomas v University of Bradford [1987] 1 All ER 834, [1987] AC 795, HL.

e **Application for judicial review**
The Rt Hon Sir Walter Ian Percival QC, the complainant in proceedings before the Professional Conduct Committee of the Bar Council concerning a member of his chambers, John Samuels QC, applied with the leave of McCowan J given on 5 May 1989 for judicial review of a decision of the committee contained in a letter dated 16 January 1989 not to prefer charges of professional misconduct against Mr Samuels. The relief f sought was (1) a declaration that the committee was obliged pursuant to r 3(e)(viii) of its rules to prefer charges of professional misconduct against Mr Samuels arising out of the applicant's complaint alleging serious breaches by Mr Samuels of his duties under para 6 of the Code of Conduct for the Bar and (2) an order that the committee should forthwith prefer such charges. The facts are set out in the judgment of the court.

g Michael Beloff QC and Nicholas Underhill for the applicant.
Sydney Kentridge QC and Paul J Walker for the Bar Council.

Cur adv vult

h 20 December. The following judgment of the court was delivered.

WATKINS LJ. The Bar takes justifiable pride in a reputation for the maintenance of high professional standards. That is a reputation which it jealously guards by, among other ways, expected conformity with a code which is entitled the 'Code of Conduct for the Bar of England and Wales'.
j   In this unique case, said by leading counsel for the applicant to be of major importance, the applicant, a former Solicitor General and a Queen's Counsel in active practice from chambers in Paper Buildings in the Temple, accuses another Queen's Counsel in active practice, Mr John Samuels, of acting dishonestly and of being engaged in conduct which otherwise might have brought the profession of barrister into disrepute in failing time and again to observe the ethics and etiquette of the profession.

At the time they both belonged to chambers in Hare Court. The applicant was the head of them and Mr Samuels their financial and general administrator.   *a*

Practising from a set of chambers is traditional for barristers. It has been going on for centuries. It is a most convenient, economic and usually efficient manner of practising in a profession which otherwise knows no kind of partnership, every member being independent of one another.

Members of chambers share a clerk and expenses. To be head of chambers is quite prestigious. A conscientious head (very few are not) is infinitely valuable, in among other   *b* things exercising discreet control over men and women of different ages and characters as well as being an adviser and friend to them and overseeing chambers' finances. In that task he needs assistance from another senior member, with whom he should (they usually do) get on well.

The applicant and Mr Samuels are experienced lawyers of widely different dispositions. They did not get on at all well almost from the time they shared responsibility for the   *c* manifold affairs of their chambers, and as time went by the applicant began to distrust Mr Samuels, who does not seem to have gone out of his way to sweeten their sour relationship.

Distrust turned to a suspicion that Mr Samuels was mishandling chambers money. It was and is not said by the applicant that Mr Samuels was putting some of the money into his own pocket. What is said is that he was devious and secretive in the management of   *d* it when not only was complete frankness obviously called for in any event but especially when the levels of contributions by members of chambers to expenses were under discussion, as they quite frequently in all chambers are and need to be.

In a worsening atmosphere the applicant levelled the charge of dishonesty and other disreputable conduct at Mr Samuels and, giving chapter and verse for it in a volume of documents and otherwise, he on 30 December 1987 reported him to the General Council   *e* of the Bar (usually referred to as the Bar Council) as being in breach of para 6 of the code. He gave notice to Mr Samuels of what he had done. Chambers was split asunder, some members going out of it with Mr Samuels, and others remaining with the applicant.

It goes without saying that so to accuse a fellow barrister is a very serious matter indeed. If such a charge is substantiated before a disciplinary tribunal the charge of   *f* dishonesty or other serious misconduct could have dire consequences as the following leading paragraphs of the *Code of Conduct for the Bar of England and Wales* (3rd edn, 1985) show:

'4. Every barrister, whether in practice or not, should uphold at all times the standard set out in this Code, the dignity and high standing of the profession of barrister and his own standing as a member of it . . .   *g*

6. It is the duty of every barrister: (a) to comply with the provisions of this Code and with the Declaration which he made on his call to the Bar; (b) not to engage in conduct (whether in pursuit of his profession or otherwise) which is dishonest or which may otherwise bring the profession of barrister into disrepute, or which is prejudicial to the administration of justice; (c) to observe the ethics and etiquette of his profession . . .   *h*

7. Serious failure to comply with the duties set out in paragraph 6 shall be professional misconduct and, if proved before a Disciplinary Tribunal, shall render the barrister liable to be disbarred, to be suspended (either unconditionally or subject to conditions), to be ordered to repay or forgo fees, or to be reprimanded . . .

8. Any failure to comply with the duties set out in paragraph 6, which does not amount to a serious failure under the terms of paragraph 7, shall be a breach of   *j* proper professional standards and: (a) if proved or admitted before a Disciplinary Tribunal, shall render the barrister liable to be admonished or to be given advice as to his future conduct; or (b) if proved or admitted before the Professional Conduct Committee, shall render the barrister liable to be ordered to attend upon the

a Chairman or some other person nominated by the Committee to be admonished or to be given advice as to his future conduct.'

(The code in the fourth edition, 1 February 1989, has been substantially revised and is in the process of further revision.)

It is plain from those provisions, which were relevant at all material times, that professional misconduct carries far greater penalties (to disbar is to put an end to a career, b an awful fate) than does a breach of proper professional standards.

The applicant maintained and still does that Mr Samuels should have been charged before the disciplinary tribunal with professional misconduct. The Professional Conduct Committee (the PCC) of the Bar Council who are responsible for such a matter have charged Mr Samuels with a breach of proper professional standards (para 8) only. The applicant maintains that not to charge him with professional misconduct (para 6) is a c wrong decision to have been made by the PCC. He was informed of that decision by letter of 16 January 1989.

He comes before us with leave seeking a declaration that the PCC are obliged pursuant to their rules to prefer a charge, or charges, of professional misconduct against Mr Samuels and an order that the PCC prefer such a charge or charges.

He also sought relief from a refusal by the PCC to inform him of the nature of the d charges made under para 8. This is not now pursued. He has that information. Those charges have not been adjudicated on by the disciplinary tribunal, which awaits the decision of this court.

The grounds relied on for relief are that the applicant's complaint disclosed prima facie breaches of para 6. Thus the PCC were obliged, pursuant to r 3(e)(viii) of their rules, to prefer charges of professional misconduct against Mr Samuels before a disciplinary e tribunal.

That rule, inter alia, provides:

'As soon as practicable following the receipt of the response (if any) of the barrister concerned to the letter referred to at Paragraph (d) above, the Committee shall consider the complaint in the light of all the material then available and may ... f (viii) If a prima facie case of professional misconduct as defined in Paragraph 7 of the Code be disclosed by the complaint, direct that the complaint shall form the subject matter of a charge or charges before a Disciplinary Tribunal ...'

It is also contended that the PCC's decision was contrary to the obligation in that rule and, in so far as it involved any exercise of discretion or judgment, it was a decision which no PCC property directing themselves as to the nature of the complaint and the g terms of r 3 could have come.

The structure of the disciplinary procedures affecting barristers is founded on the PCC. In addition to r 3(e)(viii) the following other parts of the rules of the PCC, who are, of course, a committee of the Bar Council, are of significance:

'2. *Powers and Functions.* The powers and functions of the Committee shall be as h follows: (a) to investigate and sift complaints ... (b) to prefer charges of professional misconduct and or breach of proper professional standards before Disciplinary Tribunals (as provided by the Regulations appended by way of Schedule, as amended from time to time, to the Constitution of the Council of the Inns of Court) and be responsible for prosecuting any such charges before such tribunals ...

3. *Procedures for Dealing with Complaints.* (a) Any complaint received by the Bar Council alleging misconduct by a barrister shall be referred to the Committee, which shall investigate the complaint in accordance with the provisions of these Rules. (b) Upon receipt of the complaint, the Secretary shall make such further investigations or inquiries (if any) as appear to him to be necessary at that stage for the purpose of enabling the Committee to deal with it. (c) It if appears to the

Secretary that the complaint is trivial or obviously lacking in validity, or that it is
for any other reason expedient that it should be considered by the Committee before a
the steps referred to in paragraph (d) below are taken, he shall place it before the
Committee, which may thereupon dismiss it summarily, or determine that no
action be taken upon it. (d) In any other case, the Secretary shall write to the barrister
concerned, in such terms as the Committee may from time to time specify inviting
him to comment in writing or in person on the complaint . . . (e) . . . (vi) if a prima
facie case of a breach of proper professional standards as defined in Paragraph 8 of b
the Code of Conduct, is disclosed by the complaint, and if it appears to the
Committee that there is a relevant and significant dispute of fact requiring to be
resolved by oral or other evidence, direct that the complaint shall form the subject
matter of a charge or charges before a Disciplinary Tribunal. (vii) If a prima facie
case of a breach of proper professional standards as defined in Paragraph 8 of the
Code of Conduct is disclosed by the complaint, and if it appears to the Committee c
that there is no such dispute of fact as aforesaid, deal with the matter summarily in
accordance with the procedure prescribed in Paragraph 5 below . . .
    8. *Disciplinary Charges.* (a) If the Committee decides that a complaint shall form
the subject matter of a charge or charges before a Disciplinary Tribunal it shall
nominate one of its members (the "PCC Representative") to take charge of the
proceedings on its behalf . . . (b) The Secretary after consultation with the PCC d
Representative shall arrange for the appointment of Counsel to formulate the charge
or charges and to present the case before the Disciplinary Tribunal, and may arrange
for the appointment of a solicitor or such other person as may be necessary to assist
Counsel and prepare the case. (c) The Counsel appointed as aforesaid shall formulate
such charges as he considers appropriate, provided such charges are founded upon
the same facts or evidence from which the complaint arose . . .'   e

    The PCC consist of practising barristers and a small number of lay persons. At the
time the chairman was Mr Gareth Williams QC, and Mr Scott Baker QC (now Scott Baker
J) became, for the purpose of the applicant's complaint, sponsor and afterwards the
professional representative. The counsel appointed to formulate the charge or charges
was Mr Lionel Read QC. He not only formulated the charges now before the disciplinary f
tribunal but advised the PCC what they should be. His advice was, as will be seen,
accepted.
    A disciplinary tribunal consists at any one time of a judge as chairman, a lay person
and three practising members of the Bar. An appeal lies from a disciplinary tribunal to
the Visitors of the Inns of Court and is normally comprised of three High Court judges.
    Why should the applicant go to the lengths he now does to challenge the decision of g
the PCC to forward to the disciplinary tribunal the less serious charges of breaches of
proper professional standards? Is it a high-minded desire to ensure that what might be
called proper proceedings are set afoot or vindictiveness, which was more than faintly
suggested during the course of the hearing before us?
    The applicant in his affidavit says, and we accept, that both for his own sake and that h
of the Bar he would rather that his complaint could have been left in the hands of the
PCC and the disciplinary tribunal. He believes, he says, that the way in which his
complaint has been treated raises a very serious question about the standards of conduct
expected of members of the Bar. If conduct of the kind of which he has complained,
involving as it does misrepresentation and deliberate concealment of matters of
importance between fellow members of chambers, is to be regarded by the PCC, in j
advance of being examined by a tribunal, as no more than a misdemeanour, meriting at
most a private admonishment, he would regard that as marking a serious decline in the
standards of the profession. So he asks us to confirm his belief that on a proper
construction of the code a complaint of behaviour of the kind he alleges must be regarded
as a complaint of dishonesty, or, by any standards, a serious breach of professional ethics

and accordingly should necessarily be dealt with before the disciplinary tribunal as a
complaint of professional misconduct.

a   Bearing in mind that a disciplinary tribunal will, so it seems inevitable, hear the
applicant's complaint against Mr Samuels on some charge or charges it would be
inappropriate in this judgment to cast any reflection on either the applicant's or Mr
Samuels's conduct and especially on the evidence as to it that the disciplinary tribunal is
likely to hear. But, a brief recital of what the applicant says as to the relevant facts and
b   the way in which this complaint was dealt with the PCC is unavoidably necessary in
order to deal sensibly with the issues which were so outstandingly well argued by counsel
for the applicant and counsel for the Bar Council.

It was in 1960 that the applicant first became head of chambers. Between 1979 and
1983 he was Solicitor General. In 1983 he returned to practice and resumed his position
as head of chambers as well as appointing Mr Samuels to be in charge of administration,
c   which included the chambers' finances.

This involved Mr Samuels in making recommendations to meetings of chambers on
the level of rent and levy on income to be charged to members each year. The policy was
that the amount payable should, generally speaking, match the budgeting expenses of
chambers, including rent, for the year. The creation of a modest surplus was contemplated
to cater for any future major expenditure. In this connection it had to be borne in mind
d   that that could be achieved only out of payments made by members of chambers, many
of whom could ill afford to pay any more than was necessary to cover ordinary expenses.
The size of the surplus was of obvious interest and importance, therefore, to members of
chambers. It was complicated to some extent by the incidence of taxation of surplus
moneys, the surplus being regarded as having been created out of untaxed income.

In August 1985 Mr Samuels and the clerk to chambers opened an account with the
e   Bristol and West Building Society in the name of the trustees of 'Sir I Percival Chambers
Account' and paid into it the sum of £15,000 from the chambers' current account. No
one else in chambers was told of that.

In November 1985 a chambers' meeting was held to discuss the budget for the
following year. The surplus was part of the discussion, as was the best way of earning
interest on it. Mr Samuels made no mention of the opening of an account in the building
f   society.

In January 1986 Mr Samuels paid a further £5,000 from the chambers' current account
into the building society account. No one else in chambers was told of that. In February
Mr Samuels circulated a paper about banking arrangements without mentioning the
£20,000 in the building society account.

On 18 March 1986 Mr Samuels paid a further £5,000 into the building society account
g   out of the chambers' current account. No one else was told of that. Two days later there
was a further chambers' meeting to discuss banking arrangements. Surplus moneys were
spoken of but nothing was said by Mr Samuels of the sum of £25,000 in the building
society account. The impression other members of chambers had about the surplus was
that it was in a current account and amounted to something in the region of £10,000.

Shortly after that the applicant discovered from bank accounts two debit items each of
h   £5,000. Later on he spoke to Mr Samuels about that and for the first time was told of the
building society account but was left with the impression that there was only £10,000 in
it.

Mr Samuels said that he would return £10,000 to the chambers' current account
forthwith and he did. But, again without informing anyone else in chambers, he
transferred the remaining £15,000 into a new account in the same building society and
j   then proceeded over the following two months to run down that account by returning
that sum in dribs and drabs to the chambers' current account.

The applicant clearly thought that Mr Samuels was generally handling chambers'
financial affairs in a high-handed and secretive way. His discontent over that simmered
over a number of months in 1987. The atmosphere in chambers was bad. Mr Samuels

was removed in February from being in charge of the administration and reinstated a short time later, but in June of that year the applicant heard for the first time that the *a* building society account had held not £10,000 but £25,000. This obviously had been levied from members of chambers over and above ordinary expenses and was thought to be an extravagant and unnecessary imposition on them. The applicant then asked Mr Samuels to leave the chambers.

This account of relevant matters is, of course, shorn of a vast amount of detail and may not be altogether agreed to by Mr Samuels. With that reservation it probably suffices for *b* present purposes to sufficiently indicate a very unsatisfactory state of affairs on any view of it.

Once the PCC were seised of the applicant's complaint, procedures according to the rules were followed, it rightly being considered by the chairman that a conciliation process going on on issues arising out of the division of chambers was an entirely independent matter. There was a good deal of correspondence between Mr Samuels and *c* the secretary to the Professional Standards Committee and between him and the secretary to the PCC. Mr Samuels attempted unsuccessfully to persuade Mr Williams and the other members of the PCC to consider dismissing the applicant's complaint without further investigation.

In the middle of February 1988 the secretary to the PCC informed Mr Samuels that the matter was being referred to the PCC for consideration. On 30 March the matter was *d* first considered by the PCC; after that Mr Samuels was asked to reply in detail to the applicant's allegations. He did so. On 27 April the PCC decided to refer the matter to a disciplinary tribunal. They had before them a report from Mr Scott Baker in which he expressed doubts about whether Mr Samuels was guilty of serious misconduct but thought that the allegations were undoubtedly serious and that he saw no alternative to a referral to the disciplinary tribunal. The PCC accepted his advice, deciding that if the *e* facts and the interpretation placed on them by the applicant were proved there could be a case of professional misconduct. They did not, Mr Williams says in his affidavit, determine that 'there would be a prima facie case of professional misconduct'.

Mr Lionel Read was then appointed to formulate the charges.

On 11 May the PCC met again. A letter from Mr Samuels was before them. Despite its contents it was decided that referral to the disciplinary tribunal should stand. This *f* decision was conveyed to Mr Samuels in a letter of 16 May from the secretary, which stated:

> 'The committee's view was that 1. the complaint if proved could amount to professional misconduct and 2. there are significant disputes of fact which require to be resolved before the complaint can be brought to a conclusion, thus they feel *g* reference to a tribunal inevitable.'

Mr Read was actually instructed on 8 August. He wrote a long and careful advice in which he stated that in his opinion the papers did not disclose a prima facie case of professional misconduct. He advised that only charges of breach of professional standards would be appropriate. But he left it to the PCC to consider whether more serious charges *h* should be made.

On 14 September, the chairman being present, the view of the PCC was, Mr Williams states, that they would have been prepared to forward to the disciplinary tribunal charges of professional misconduct if Mr Read had advised such charges had a reasonable prospect of success. Seeing that he advised to the contrary it was decided that the less serious charges should go to the disciplinary tribunal.

This decision was conveyed to the applicant in a letter from the secretary in the *j* following terms:

> 'At their meeting on 14 September 1988, the Professional Conduct Committee re-considered your complaint in the light of detailed advice from Lionel Read QC. The committee concluded that the complaint should proceed to a tribunal on two

charges of breaches of proper professional standards but not on any charge of
professional misconduct. Their revised view, in the light of leading counsel's advice,
was that while there is a prima facie case on the former, there is not on the latter.'

The applicant protested. He asked the PCC to reconsider their decision in the light of
a letter from Mr Thomas Morison QC which he sent to them. Mr Samuels's solicitors
wrote to the PCC alleging that they had not complied with their rules and that there was
no justification for dealing with the matter other than summarily. On 19 October 1988
the PCC again met and, replacing Mr Scott Baker (by then elevated to the High Court
bench) with Mr Ronald Walker QC, confirmed the decision already made. On
16 November there was again a meeting of the PCC at which Mr Walker's advice was
considered. He advised that further material be obtained from Mr Samuels. It was
obtained.

On 11 January 1989 the PCC, having considered Mr Walker's advice, finally confirmed
their decision to charge Mr Samuels only with breaches of proper professional standards.
On 16 January the secretary wrote the letter already referred to, which stated:

'In confirmation of our telephone conversation of Friday, 13 January 1989, the
above-mentioned complaint was re-considered by the Professional Conduct
Committee at their meeting on 11 January in the light of the additional material
which you submitted and of all other material received to date. The committee
agreed that they should adhere to their previous decision that the matter should be
referred to a disciplinary tribunal on the basis recommended by counsel to the
Committee, i.e. on charges of breaches of proper professional standards. The
committee further agreed that, while remaining within these parameters, counsel
should be asked to consider the desirability or otherwise of certain slight changes to
the detailed wording of the charge as already notified to you. Subject to any changes
which may result, a formal charge sheet will be prepared in due course and served
on Mr. Samuels in the usual way.'

Thus, it took the PCC twelve months from the time they first considered whether
charges should go to the disciplinary tribunal to finally confirming their decision that
they should go there. One of the complaints which the applicant makes of the PCC is of
protracted delay in coming to a conclusion. We feel bound to say that whilst appreciating,
fully we hope, the difficulties involved it should have been possible for a much swifter
resolution to have been achieved.

The issues as we perceive them are as follows.

(1) Is the jurisdiction of the Divisional Court excluded because the judges as visitors
are the only source of power to discipline the Bar and their jurisdiction is exclusive, albeit
delegated so far as disciplinary tribunals are concerned at present to the Council of the
Inns of Court?

(2) Has the applicant locus standi to make the application, or is he only entitled to
have his complaint fairly considered consistently with the rules and no more?

(3) Is a prosecuting authority's decision whether or not to prosecute reviewable at all?
If so, is review limited to the extreme cases of failure to consider a complaint at all, the
adoption of an impermissible policy to exclude certain types of complaint or illegality?

(4) Do any principles of public policy require the Divisional Court to decline to review
the PCC decision to prefer the lesser charges because, inter alia: (a) it should not interfere
with the particularly wide discretion of the PCC to be inferred from the rules; (b) a
committee of professional men required to consider the standards of their own profession
are better judges of these than the court; (c) the publicity resulting from judicial review
wholly breaches the confidentiality attaching to Bar disciplinary proceedings until an
adverse finding by the disciplinary tribunal; (d) judicial review of a PCC's decision not to
prosecute or to prosecute at a particular level may result in the Divisional Court
substituting its own view of the conduct of a barrister against whom the complaint is
made. This is undesirable and may in some cases pre-empt the function of the disciplinary

tribunal; (e) to allow judicial review in the instant case makes the PCC vulnerable to many similar applications (the floodgates argument) and these would cause undesirable *a* delay.

(5) Was the PCC decision *Wednesbury* unreasonable (see *Associated Provincial Picture Houses Ltd v Wednesbury Corp* [1947] 2 All ER 680, [1948] 1 KB 223) because of, or alternatively was there, (6) a fundamental procedural irregularity when the PCC having originally decided that there could be a prima facie case of professional misconduct attempted, following the advice of Mr Read, to resolve disputed issues of fact about *b* motive in a manner not contemplated by the rules, which expressly required disputes of fact to be referred to the disciplinary tribunal.

We now consider these issues.

The jurisdiction of the Divisional Court
The history of the organisation of the practising Bar and of the exercise of disciplinary *c* powers over its members is set out in 3 Halsbury's Laws (4th edn reissue) paras 352–372, 493–514. The Court of Appeal in *Lincoln v Daniels* [1961] 3 All ER 740, [1962] 1 QB 237 and Vinelott J in *Re S (a barrister)* [1981] 2 All ER 952, [1981] QB 683 considered the origin of those disciplinary powers and the manner of their exercise.

From as early as the late thirteenth century the judges, deriving their authority from the Crown, had both the duty and the right to provide and regulate lawyers to conduct *d* the business of the royal courts. Lawyers then began their careers as apprentices-at-law residing at a fairly large number of inns. By the middle of the fourteenth century the Inns of Court, as they became, ceased to be purely residential and began to assume an educational role including the call of successful students to the utter Bar. This did not mean that the utter barrister necessarily had a right to appear in the superior courts: the exact extent of education and seniority required of such an advocate was variously a *e* matter for royal proclamation, orders of the Privy Council and above all of the judges' orders.

From the mid-sixteenth century to the mid-seventeenth century, call to the Bar and rights of audience became increasingly closely connected: the judges issued numerous directives to the Inns concerning conduct, etiquette and discipline. In the later seventeenth century, although the educational role of the Inns declined, they still controlled matters *f* of professional conduct and discipline, those functions having been left to them by the judges, who nevertheless retained an appellate jurisdiction and also the power to punish a barrister for contempt of court.

In *R v Benchers of Gray's Inn* (1780) 1 Doug 353, 99 ER 227 Lord Mansfield CJ said that the original institution of the Inns of Court nowhere precisely appears, but all the power they have concerning the admission to the Bar is delegated to them from the judges and *g* in every instance their conduct is subject to their control as visitors. He referred to *Booreman's Case* (1641) March 177 pl 235, 82 ER 464, in which the Inns of Court were described as voluntary societies 'submitting to government; and the ancient and usual way of redress for any grievance in the Inns of Court, was by appealing to the Judges' (see 1 Doug 353 at 355, 99 ER 227 at 228).

In *Lincoln v Daniels* [1961] 3 All ER 740 at 745, [1962] 1 QB 237 at 250 Sellers LJ said: *h*

'I would regard the Inns of Court in their disciplinary power in relation to the practising member of the Bar as equivalently established over the centuries by its practice and acceptance as if the power had been derived from statute and as unassailable. If the Inns of Court had not controlled the professional conduct of the *j* Bar the judges themselves would have had to do so. The judges themselves, deriving their authority from the Crown, were minded in the distant past to delegate, and the undisputed view in LORD MANSFIELD's time was that the judges had delegated, their disciplinary power over the Bar to the Inns of Court.'

In 1967 the Inns delegated that disciplinary authority to the Senate of the Four Inns of
a Court and then in 1974 to the Senate of the Inns of Court and the Bar. In 1987 that
delegated power was transferred to the Council of the Inns of Court by resolution of the
judges of Her Majesty's High Court of Justice.

The present system for investigating and determining breaches of discipline by
members of the Bar requires brief consideration of the role of the Bar Council. Until the
latter part of the last century there was no organisation representing the English Bar as a
b whole, although by that time each circuit had assumed responsibility for the conduct,
etiquette and observance of circuit rules by those barristers practising on the circuit. It
was not until 1883 that a 'Bar Committee' was formed to represent the Bar as a whole. In
1894 it was replaced by the Bar Council constituted by regulations approved by the Bar
in general meeting.

One of the functions of the Bar Council was the publishing of rules of conduct and
c etiquette for the guidance of members of the Bar. In 1966 the four Inns established a
single body, the Senate, to act on behalf of the Inns collectively in matters of common
interest. This was the body that until 1974 exercised the disciplinary powers orginally
delegated by the judges to the Inns. In 1974 the Senate of the Four Inns of Court was
replaced by a body called the Senate of the Inns of Court and the Bar combining the
existing Senate and the Bar Council. However, the latter, reconstituted as the Bar Council,
d remained autonomous within the combined body. The delegated disciplinary powers of
the old Senate were vested in the new combined body, which, with effect from 1 January
1987, was dissolved and split into two separate bodies, the Council of the Inns of Court
representing and acting for the four Inns, and the Bar Council being restored to a
completely separate as well as autonomous position.

The Bar Council is responsible, amongst other things, for promulgating the Code of
e Conduct, and it is the duty of every barrister to comply with the provisions of that code:
non-compliance gives rise to the disciplinary offences which lie at the heart of these
proceedings. The PCC of the Bar Council are, as we have already indicated, by their own
rules charged with the investigation and sifting of complaints against barristers and the
task of preferring charges of professional misconduct in accordance with its rules.

f Counsel for the Bar Council argued that all disciplinary powers derive from the judges,
so that any complaint about the incorrect or improper exercise or failure to exercise those
powers must go to the judges and not to the Divisional Court. He did not deal in detail
with the summary powers of the Bar Council delegated to the PCC. This we assume is a
sub-delegation acquiesced in by the judges.

Despite this summary jurisdiction the role of the PCC is, it was said, essentially that of
g prosecutor. In so acting, it is not an adjudicating body but a body charged with deciding
whether or not to prosecute and, if so, what charges should be preferred. This whole
disciplinary process is derived from the visitatorial jurisdiction of the judges and that
jurisdiction must be exclusive: see *Oakes v Sidney Sussex College, Cambridge* [1988] 1 All
ER 1004, [1988] 1 WLR 431.

We do not agree. The Bar Council, which is an autonomous and wholly separate
h organisation from the Council of the Inns of Court, is fulfilling the role of a prosecutor
exercising discretion in the sifting and assessment of complaints and empowered by its
rules when certain conditions are fulfilled to prosecute that complaint before the
disciplinary tribunal as an adjudicating body exercising powers delegated by the judges.
The PCC to whom those functions are delegated must carry them out in accordance with
their own rules. Consequently, its acts and omissions can, in our view, be challenged by
j way of judicial review.

Locus standi
The rival contentions can be very briefly stated. Counsel for the Bar Council maintained
that once a complaint has been accepted for consideration the complainant's legal rights

are exhausted. In order to bring an application for judicial review the applicant must show that he has suffered damage in law or is likely to suffer damage by reason of the *a* exercise of a discretion by the body being reviewed. *O'Reilly v Mackman* [1982] 3 All ER 1124, [1983] 2 AC 237 is, he said, an authority for the proposition that an applicant must have a legal interest in the result or outcome of the decision-making. The more modern approach is to ask whether he has a sufficient interest rather than a legal right to protect.

Reference was made to a number of other authorities. In *R v Metropolitan Police Comr, ex p Blackburn* [1968] 1 All ER 763, [1968] 2 QB 118 locus standi was not in issue and was *b* assumed. Lord Denning MR thought it an open question whether Mr Blackburn had a sufficient interest to be protected, having said ([1968] 1 All ER 763 at 770, [1968] 2 QB 118 at 137):

> 'No doubt the party who applies for mandamus must show that he has sufficient interest to be protected and that there is no other equally convenient remedy . . .'   *c*

Salmon LJ said ([1968] 1 All ER 763 at 771, [1968] 2 QB 118 at 139):

> 'For example, if, as is quite unthinkable, the chief police officer in any district were to issue an instruction that as a matter of policy the police would take no steps to prosecute any housebreaker, I have little doubt but that any householder in that district would be able to obtain an order of mandamus for the instruction to be *d* withdrawn.'

Edmund Davies LJ said ([1968] 1 All ER 763 at 777, [1968] 2 QB 118 at 148–149):

> '. . . I agree with them in holding that the law enforcement officers of this country certainly owe a legal duty to the public to perform those functions which are the raison d'être of their existence. How and by whom that duty can be enforced is *e* another matter, and it may be that a private citizen, such as the applicant, having no special or peculiar interest in the due discharge of the duty under consideration, has himself no legal right to enforce it. That is widely different, however, from holding that no duty exists, enforceable either by a relator action or in some other manner which may hereafter have to be determined.'

In *Selvarajan v Race Relations Board* [1976] 1 All ER 12, [1975] 1 WLR 1686 Lawton LJ *f* contemplated the challenge of a decision of a prosecuting authority by judicial review: counsel for the applicant submitted that the obvious challenger would be the victim of the alleged crime. The court did not deal with this broader issue and had no need to. Lord Denning MR in the passage quoted earlier confined his observations to those persons against whom allegations or adverse reports were made.

Counsel for the Bar Council referred to *O'Reilly v Mackman* [1982] 3 All ER 1124 at *g* 1134, [1983] 2 AC 237 at 285 where Lord Diplock said:

> 'Now that those disadvantages to applicants have been removed and all remedies for infringements of rights protected by public law can be obtained on an application for judicial review, as can also remedies for infringements of rights under private law if such infringements should also be involved, it would in my view as a general *h* rule be contrary to public policy, and as such an abuse of the process of the court, to permit a person seeking to establish that a decision of a public authority infringed rights to which he was entitled to protection under public law to proceed by way of an ordinary action and by this means to evade the provisions of [RSC] Ord 53 for the protection of such authorities.'

Counsel for the Bar Council also referred to *Public Disclosure Commission v Isaacs* [1989] *j* 1 All ER 137, [1988] 1 WLR 1043 as authority for the proposition that once an applicant's complaint had been received and considered he had no further rights requiring protection. The reply of counsel for the applicant to that was that that applicant failed, not for want of standing but because of the substantive provisions of the Public Disclosure Act 1976 of the Commonwealth of the Bahamas. The complainant had submitted a

written complaint supported by factual material to the Public Disclosure Commission
a alleging that the prime minister had not made a sufficient statutory declaration of his
assets, income and liabilities in the prescribed form. The commission were of the opinion
that the complaint should be investigated; the prime minister clarified and explained
particular aspects of his declarations but the complainant was not given an opportunity
further to substantiate his complaint or to rebut the prime minister's answer to it. After
conducting their investigation the commission decided that the complaint had not been
b substantiated. The complainant challenged this decision. The Privy Council held that
under the provisions of the 1976 Act the commission had to follow inquisitorial and not
adversarial procedure, that the commission had to carry out their investigation in private,
making such further inquiry with regard to the material supplied by the complainant
and requesting information and explanations from the prime minister as considered
necessary, and finally reaching a decision, but that although the commission were under
c a duty to act fairly, since publication that the complaint had not been substantiated
would have no adverse effect on the complainant, the commission were not required to
tell him the prime minister's response to the complaint or to give the complainant an
opportunity to answer it. The commission had followed the proper procedure and were
entitled to conclude that the complaint had not been substantiated.

In our view the submission of counsel for the applicant is correct: the complainant did
d not fail for want of standing. The Privy Council did express the view that if the
commission were provisionally minded to find a complaint frivolous, vexatious or
groundless, exposing the complainant to the risk of prosecution for an offence, they
would have to indicate to a complainant the reasons for their provisional view and give
him a fair opportunity to demonstrate that the provisional view was unfounded and that
he had at least good grounds for making the complaint. On our reading their Lordships
e were saying that in certain circumstances the complainant would undoubtedly have had
locus standi but on the facts it was not necessary to decide whether he had locus standi or
not, because the proceedings of the commission were unimpeachable.

The concluding argument of counsel for the applicant was to this effect: granted that
there are circumstances where a decision not to proceed with the investigation of a
complaint or the initiation of a prosecution should be challengeable, who is to mount the
f challenge? He submitted that the obvious person was the victim. Again, in our view this
submission is correct. Unless the disappointed complainant is regarded as having
sufficient locus standi to challenge the decision it is difficult to see who else could be
expected to do it. We are fortified in our view by the fact that the applicant here was
head of chambers, his interest being the greater in order to ensure that any lapse from
proper professional conduct or the observance of proper professional standards by a
g member of his chambers for whom he was responsible should be properly investigated
and referred to a disciplinary tribunal if necessary. If that does not amount to a sufficient
interest for present purposes we should find it difficult to envisage what circumstances
possibly could.

We conclude that the applicant had and retains locus standi.

h

Is a prosecuting authority's decision whether or not to prosecute reviewable at all?
The Bar Council accepted that the PCC are a body the decision of which could be
subject to judicial review, but submitted that the scope of any review must be confined
to (1) a refusal to perform their functions at all or (ii) a refusal to entertain particular
j types of complaint, for example where the complainant and the respondent are both
members of the same set of chambers. It was submitted that the PCC should not be
regarded in any different way from any other prosecuting authority. Only in the most
exceptional cases, such as failure to act on a complaint or a refusal to receive a complaint
because of the application of a prior policy that has no legitimate or reasonable
justification, can there be a review of a body charged with the prosecution of offences,
granted that there is someone with locus standi to make the application.

Counsel for the Bar Council in this context relied on the following passages in *R v Metropolitan Police Comr, ex p Blackburn* [1968] 1 All ER 763 at 769, [1968] 2 QB 118 at 136, where Lord Denning MR said:

> 'Although the chief officers of police are answerable to the law, there are many fields in which they have a discretion with which the law will not interfere. For instance, it is for the Commissioner of Police, or the chief constable, as the case may be, to decide in any particular case whether enquiries should be pursued, or whether an arrest should be made, or a prosecution brought. It must be for him to decide on the disposition of his force and the concentration of his resources on any particular crime or area. No court can or should give him direction on such a matter. He can also make policy decisions and give effect to them, as, for instance, was often done when prosecutions were not brought for attempted suicide; but there are some policy decisions with which, I think, the courts in a case can, if necessary, interfere. Suppose a chief constable were to issue a directive to his men that no person should be prosecuted for stealing any goods less than £100 in value. I should have thought that the court could countermand it. He would be failing in his duty to enforce the law.'

Salmon LJ said ([1968] 1 All ER 763 at 771, [1968] 2 QB 118 at 138–139):

> 'In my judgment the police owe the public a clear legal duty to enforce the law— a duty which I have no doubt they recognise and which generally they perform most conscientiously and efficiently. In the extremely unlikely event, however, of the police failing or refusing to carry out their duty, the court would not be powerless to intervene. For example, if, as is quite unthinkable, the chief police officer in any district were to issue an instruction that as a matter of policy the police would take no steps to prosecute any housebreaker, I have little doubt but that any householder in that district would be able to obtain an order of mandamus for the instruction to be withdrawn. Of course, the police have a wide discretion whether or not they will prosecute in any particular case. In my judgment, however, the action which I have postulated would be a clear breach of duty. It would be so improper that it could not amount to an exercise of discretion.'

Salmon LJ then went on to reject an argument which had been advanced that the discretion whether or not to prosecute is absolute and unchallengeable in the courts.

Reliance was also placed on *Selvarajan v Race Relations Board* [1976] 1 All ER 12, [1975] 1 WLR 1686. There the applicant had complained to the Race Relations Board that his employers had unlawfully discriminated against him. A conciliation committee found that unlawful discrimination had occurred but the employment committee of the board decided to reinvestigate the matter and formed the opinion that no unlawful discrimination had occurred. At that time the complainant could not himself have brought proceedings in respect of any alleged discrimination so that rejection of his complaint by the board exhausted his remedies. The Court of Appeal held that the board though not a judicial body was as an administrative or investigating body under an obligation to act fairly, but that subject to that obligation and its enforcement by the courts the board was master of its own procedure and that on the facts no unfairness had occurred. Counsel for the Bar Council drew attention to the emphasis laid on the width of the discretion of a body which was master of its own procedures. Lord Denning MR said ([1976] 1 All ER 12 at 20, [1975] 1 WLR 1686 at 1695):

> 'The most troublesome point is that several members of the board did not have all the papers. Four of them had only the summary of a "clearly predictable case" of 1½ pages and a recommendation that the committee should form the opinion of no unlawful discrimination ... If this had been a judicial body, I do not think this

a would be right. Every member of a judicial body must have access to all the evidence and papers in the case, he must have heard all the arguments, and he must come to his own conclusion ... But it is different with a body which is exercising administrative functions or which is making an investigation or conducting preliminary enquiries, especially when it is a numerous body.'

b Lawton LJ drew an analogy between the functions of the board and the powers of the Director of Public Prosecutions. He said ([1976] 1 All ER 12 at 21, [1975] 1 WLR 1686 at 1696):

'Forming an opinion that there has been no discrimination, as the board did in this case, is not a definitive determination of an issue: it is a preliminary to a decision whether proceedings should be initiated. In some respects its powers are like those of the Director of Public Prosecutions. He receives complaints from public bodies c and members of the public; he can start investigations; and if he is of the opinion that there is sufficient evidence to justify a prosecution, he can initiate one; but he does not decide guilt or innocence. As far as I know, the courts have never interfered with the exercise of the director's discretion; but it does not follow that they could not do so if he refused or failed to perform his public duties or acted corruptly or unfairly.'

d Counsel for the Bar Council submitted that the ratio of the decision in R v Police Complaints Board, ex p Madden [1983] 2 All ER 353, [1983] 1 WLR 447 was that the board had rejected the complaint on a wholly mistaken basis and not after due consideration of the merits. The applicant had made a formal complaint alleging mistreatment by police officers but the Director of Public Prosecutions concluded that there was insufficient e evidence to charge them with any criminal offence. The matter was then referred to the Police Complaints Board, which considers the institution of disciplinary charges. The board was required as a matter of law to 'have regard to any guidance' given by the Secretary of State. This took the form of 'Guidance by the Secretary of State on the Preferring and Withdrawing of Disciplinary Charges'. The board misread the paragraphs which required a police officer to be protected from disciplinary proceedings that were f in substance the same as criminal charges for which he had been tried, and concluded that it could not prefer disciplinary charges against an officer in circumstances where the Director of Public Prosecutions had decided not to prefer criminal charges on substantially the same evidence. McNeill J said ([1983] 2 All ER 353 at 371, [1983] 1 WLR 447 at 468):

g '... the concept of "fairness", even a policy of "fairness" (and it is quite plain from Sir George Ogden's affidavit that the board regarded itself as motivated by "fairness", although confusing that with the double jeopardy principle), cannot limit the board's statutory obligation to consider complaints. It goes without saying that the board should and would be "fair" in considering complaints but, in my view, it could not treat fairness as a justification for declining to consider complaints further h when the Director of Public Prosecutions has advised against criminal proceedings, save in the exceptional paras 5.11 and 5.12 [of the Guidance] situations.'

Those authorities, counsel for the Bar Council said, indicate that only in the most exceptional cases can an applicant seek a review of a body whose function it is to investigate, consider if there is prima facie evidence and decide whether or not to prefer charges or prosecute offences.

j The following submissions were made by counsel for the applicant. (i) As to the decision in Blackburn's case, Lord Denning MR was saying that it was not for the court to interfere when there was a wide discretion save in the exceptional case, but the court did not accept that the discretion was absolute and clearly regarded it as reviewable in some circumstances. (ii) As to Selvarajan's case it was accepted that the decisions of both the

conciliation committee and the board could be challenged. (iii) As to *Madden's* case it
was clearly the view of the trial judge that a decision of the Police Complaints Board   *a*
could be challenged. Reference was also made by counsel for the applicant to a passage in
de Smith's Judicial Review of Administrative Action (4th edn, 1980) pp 549–550, to the effect
that the discretion of a prosecuting authority though broad is not unreviewable.

In our view such discretion is plainly reviewable but the question is whether the limits
of review should be as strict as those contended for by the Bar Council. Much will
depend, we think, on the powers of the body subject to review, the procedures which it   *b*
is required to follow and on the way in which a particular proceeding has been conducted;
there is potentially an almost infinite variety of circumstances. We do not think it right
that strictly defined limits should be set to the judicial review of a body which can
broadly be described as a prosecuting authority. Each case must be considered with due
regard to the powers, functions and procedures of the body concerned and the manner
in which it has dealt (or not dealt) with the particular complaint or application. This   *c*
complaint should not, we think, fail because the applicant is unable to demonstrate that
it was not dealt with at all or excluded by the adoption of an illegitimate prior policy. It
falls to be decided, in our view, on the substantive issues of irrationality and/or procedural
irregularity, with due regard to the nature of the discretion involved.

Public policy   *d*
    This court could and should, it was submitted by counsel for the Bar Council, so
exercise its discretion as to decline to review the decision of the PCC.
    We should not, he said, first, interfere with the particularly wide discretion of the PCC
which is to be inferred from their own rules. A decision whether or not to prefer a
particular charge or charges involves a wide element of discretion, and the PCC are
charged with the exercise of that discretion. It is very undesirable for the courts to   *e*
intervene in the functions of such a body in order to determine whether it acted
reasonably or not, or whether it had misdirected itself or committed a procedural error.
    Counsel for the applicant contended that merely because a discretion exists, however
broad or narrow it be, is no ground for excluding judicial review if the discretion has
been exercised unreasonably or is based on a procedural irregularity. The court should
grapple with the substantive issues rather than decline to entertain them as a matter of   *f*
discretion.
    Second, counsel for the Bar Council urged that the applicant's complaints should be
viewed in the light of the approach to be adopted by the court when judicial review is
sought of a professional body, the decisions of which as to what does or does not constitute
professional misconduct involving questions of opinion and degree which are supremely
a matter for the professional body concerned. As such these are matters best dealt with   *g*
through the profession's own committees and tribunals, and the court should be reluctant
to interfere with the decisions of such bodies since they are in the best position to
determine what constitutes misconduct and to examine the degrees of misconduct.
    He referred to *R v General Council of Medical Education and Registration of the UK* [1930]
1 KB 562 at 569, where Scrutton LJ said: *h*

> 'As in the case of the Bar so in the medical profession advertising is serious
> misconduct in a professional respect and that is all that is meant by the phrase
> "infamous conduct"; it means no more than serious misconduct judged according
> to the rules written or unwritten governing the profession.'

    He referred also to *General Medical Council v Spackman* [1943] 2 All ER 337 esp at 342,   *j*
[1943] AC 627 esp at 639–640 per Lord Wright (this case may properly be described as
the high-water mark of non-interference with a disciplinary tribunal having a wide
discretion) and to *Rajasooria v Disciplinary Committee* [1955] 1 WLR 405 and *Bhattacharya
v General Medical Council* [1967] 2 AC 259.

These authorities were, of course, concerned with the decisions of disciplinary tribunals
a whether or not in particular instances the rules or standards of professional conduct had
been transgressed. We are concerned with the decision of a body charged with
investigating and securing the prosecution of an alleged transgression of the code. The
mere fact that professional standards thereby are called in question does not, in our view,
mean that we should exercise our discretion not to interfere.

Third, it was suggested that the publicity resulting from judicial review breaches the
b confidentiality attaching to disciplinary proceedings up to the moment of an adverse
finding by the disciplinary tribunal. In our view the unavoidable publicity attendant on
an application for judicial review cannot justify, save possibly in the most exceptional
circumstances, declining to review that which is otherwise reviewable.

Fourth, it was submitted that judicial review of a decision of the PCC not to prosecute
or to prosecute at a particular level could result in this court substituting its own view of
c the conduct of the barrister against whom the complaint is made. Such a substitution
would be very undesirable and could pre-empt the function of the disciplinary tribunal.
We do not accept that the applicant is contending that Mr Samuels should be charged
with a particular offence: the outcome is a matter for the disciplinary tribunal alone after
it has heard all the evidence.

Fifth, there was the floodgates argument: to allow judicial review in the instant case
d would, it was said, make the PCC vulnerable to many similar applications which would
cause undesirable delay and an application for judicial review might well become a
delaying tactic.

Counsel for the applicant submitted that excessive applications, whether tactical or
merely optimistic, could properly be contained by the filtering process of obtaining leave
and by the penalty of costs for the unsuccessful. We find this argument convincing.
e There is accordingly, in our view, no ground of public policy which should inhibit
this court from reviewing a decision of the PCC.

The decisions

At the heart of the applicant's complaint is, counsel for the applicant told us, the
deliberate concealment by Mr Samuels of the state of chambers finances, in particular the
f full amount and whereabouts of moneys held in reserve, ie the surplus. In the whole of
the circumstances known to the PCC the decision to find as to them that a prima facie
case of a breach of proper professional standards and no more was, he submitted, badly
flawed. It was irrational, unreasonable, no matter how regarded and arrived at after
much changing of minds via the route of procedural irregularity. No reasonable
committee interpreting its own rules properly and acting accordingly could, he said,
g possibly have made it.

He maintained, and in so doing we think he was justified, that a change of mind
appears to have occurred following the PCC's contemplation of the opinion of Mr Read.
That, counsel for the applicant contended, was an unsought opinion from counsel whose
only role according to the rules was to advise on evidence and to draft charges the level
h of which was for the sole determination of the PCC. Mr Read, counsel for the applicant
said, exceeded his brief.

In his opinion Mr Read, having referred to the secretary's letter to Mr Samuels of
18 May 1988, stated, inter alia:

'There was no need for the committee to form the view that there were significant
j disputes of fact requiring to be resolved before the complaint could be brought to a
conclusion if they had concluded that there was a prima facie case of professional
misconduct. I am accordingly left in some doubt as to whether the committee
intended to find a prima facie case of breach of proper professional standards, and if
so whether to the exclusion of a case of professional misconduct, or alternatively or

additionally to such a case—and, if additionally, on which separate aspects of the complaint.'

a

He went on:

'I raise the points made in the last two paragraphs for two principal reasons. First
... there would be substantial advantage in the committee reviewing their decision
and expressing themselves unequivocally for the purposes of the record if the
complaint is referred to the tribunal on a charge of professional misconduct. Second, *b*
if the committee has formed the view that there is a prima facie case of professional
misconduct, they will note from the views I express hereafter that I cannot see that
the papers disclose such a case and I do not believe that any prima facie sustainable
point or points of complaint qualify for such a serious charge.'

Later, he went on:

c

'Dishonesty by a member of the Bar, let alone of the kind alleged, is plainly prima
facie professional misconduct. In my view, however, neither the documentary
material before me—which largely takes the form of letters and documents
contemporaneously written by the principal parties and minutes of chambers
meeting—nor any of the specific instances of conduct particularised in paragraph
10 of the complaint begins to support these very serious allegations of dishonesty. *d*
There is no doubt that Samuels deliberately did not tell Percival about the payments
into the building society account. I find nothing, however, prima facie dishonest in
this "concealment" either in any motive alleged or in the circumstances alleged. The
highest one could reasonably put the last sentence of the much quoted paragraph
5.2 of Samuels' note of 5 February 1987 is that it was less than frank. In my opinion,
therefore, a charge could not properly be preferred alleging dishonest conduct or *e*
accordingly professional misconduct on that basis. There can, in my view, be no
half-way house on this point. If there is no prima facie case of dishonest conduct,
there is no room for alleging dishonest conduct as a failure, but less than a serious
failure, to comply with the duties imposed by paragraph 6 of the Code to support a
charge of breach of proper professional standards. It is all or nothing, and in my *f*
view it is nothing.'

That was strong stuff. It was supported, in effect, later on by Mr Walker and was
almost certainly the decisive viewpoint which swayed the PCC into deciding that only
the lesser charges should be referred to the disciplinary tribunal. Counsel for the applicant
fired a heavy broadside at it in this court, maintaining that not only was that view wrong
but that providing it was an unwarranted intrusion into the PCC's exclusive decision- *g*
making domain. It was wrong, he said, because it was based on an erroneous appreciation
of the relevant facts, not all of which were available to him, and it was based on wholly
insupportable inferences. If all that be right, it must be pointed out that the PCC were
able for themselves to see from the whole comprehensive opinion how mistaken Mr
Read was or might have been.

Whatever room there may be for criticism of Mr Read it cannot be denied that he *h*
clearly exposed the ambiguity, as he saw it, of the words used in the letter of 16 May.
Counsel for the applicant, of course, asserts there was no ambiguity: the PCC had at that
time made up their minds to refer the more serious charges to the disciplinary committee,
albeit that they also referred in the letter to unresolved issues of fact when it was
inappropriate to do so. Anyway, he said, they had all the material they needed then to *j*
reach a final resolution and if they did not, contrary to what the applicant says, they
failed in their duty to do so. It was wholly unreasonable and perverse of them to go back
on a proper decision to refer.

The PCC, it is submitted, should be regarded as having in reality found at that time
that there was a prima facie case of professional misconduct and were, therefore, bound
to refer such a charge to the tribunal: see r 3(e)(viii).

It is further submitted that the PCC misdirected themselves as to dishonesty as that

word appears in r 3. It does not, as the Bar Council or those advising seem to have
a thought, necessarily mean dishonesty in the criminal sense. They should have acted, and
they did not, as a prosecuting authority determining whether or not to begin a
prosecution. If they had conformed to their own rules that is precisely what they would
have done. Instead, they took their eyes off the only test they had to apply, namely: 'is
there on the available evidence a prima facie case of professional misconduct? A short
straightforward answer to that question was plainly available. Instead, they allowed
b themselves to be influenced by an opinion of dubious value. Such conduct as that was
unreasonable in the *Wednesbury* sense and should be condemned as such. Those
submissions, which were developed in considerable depth, we have encapsulated in
summary form without, we hope, diminishing either the breadth or the force of them.

Counsel for the Bar Council responded to them by submitting that the applicant's
complaint should be viewed in the light of the approach to be adopted by the court
c where judicial review is sought of a professional body: the decisions of a professional
body as to what does or does not constitute professional misconduct must involve
questions of opinion and degree which are supremely a matter for the professional body
concerned.

In this context he referred to *Rajasooria v Disciplinary Committee* [1955] 1 WLR 405 at
415–416:
d
'Their Lordships . . . would add that had they felt any hesitation in the matter
they would require a very strong case before they substituted their own opinion of
what is professional misconduct . . . for the conclusion reached by the disciplinary
committee and the Supreme Court. As Darling J. said in relation to England in *In re
A Solicitor, Ex Parte Law Society* ([1912] 1 KB 302 at 312): "The Law Society are very
e good judges of what is professional misconduct as a solicitor, just as the General
Medical Council are very good judges of what is misconduct as a medical man."'

He also referred to what Lord Hodson said in *Bhattacharya v General Medical Council*
[1967] 2 AC 259 at 265:

'In their Lordships' view that jurisdiction on appeal is not confined to considering
f whether the alleged facts, if proved, are capable of amounting to infamous conduct
in a professional respect, but extends to the consideration whether in the particular
circumstances of the case these facts justify a finding of infamous conduct in a
professional respect; but in the latter case their Lordships' board would naturally be
very slow to differ from the conclusion of the General Medical Council, to whom is
entrusted the decision of those matters as representing the responsible body of
g opinion in the medical profession upon professional matters.'

Counsel for the Bar Council disputed that r 3(e)(viii) imposes any kind of obligation
on the PCC. The operative word in the leading words of the rule is 'may', not 'must', be
pointed out. Therefore, the PCC, no matter what their findings, are not bound to prefer
a charge to the disciplinary tribunal. They have a discretion whether to do so or not.
h Thus, it cannot be said that the PCC at any time following receipt of the complaint from
the applicant acted in breach of rule, that is to say unlawfully.

He further submitted that it could not possibly be argued that the PCC did not take
account of professional ethics and etiquette. Such matters were referred to with some
emphasis in Mr Read's opinion and cannot possibly have been left out of account by a
committee composed of experienced barristers, one reason for the presence of whom on
j that committee was care for professional ethics and etiquette.

He contested the alleged misdirection as to dishonesty. There is nothing to show, he
said, that the PCC regarded dishonesty as requiring proof of intended gain. This ground
of complaint, he maintained, is wholly without foundation.

The charge made on behalf of the applicant that the PCC did not take account of all of
the conduct of Mr Samuels of which the applicant complains is, he said, without
substance. One has only to look at the charges which are now before the disciplinary
tribunal to find that they specifically address especially the question of concealment.

As for unreasonableness or perversity this, he submitted, entails showing that the decision of the PCC is 'so outrageous in its defiance of logic or of accepted moral standards that no sensible person who had applied his mind to the question to be decided could have arrived at it' (see Lord Diplock in *Council of Civil Service Unions v Minister for Civil Service* [1984] 3 All ER 935 at 951, [1985] AC 375 at 410) or that it is 'A perversely unreasonable exercise of power' (see Lord Scarman in *Nottinghamshire CC v Secretary of State for the Environment* [1986] 1 All ER 199 at 201, [1986] AC 240 at 246).

He contended that in meeting after meeting the PCC showed an anxiety to be fair to both parties in what was a very anxious inquiry into a most regrettable piece of chambers history. The criticisms of Mr Read were, he maintained, baseless. That learned counsel was under the impression that his advice was called for and he gave it in a finely balanced opinion in a most meticulous manner. It was entirely right for the PCC to study that opinion and to give regard to it as they thought fit. In one passage in his skeleton argument counsel for the Bar Council wrote:

'The question for the committee was what interpretation should be put on the facts alleged. If the applicant's interpretation was accepted, then a case of professional misconduct could be made out. That was the position adopted in April 1988 by the P.C.C. ... It must be a matter of opinion and degree for the committee as to whether it would be right on the basis of the facts alleged to make an allegation of dishonest intent. In the circumstances where both Mr. Read and Mr. Walker had concluded that the applicant's interpretation could not be supported and the P.C.C. considered and agreed with these views, the P.C.C.'s decision was not perverse or irrational.'

We have come to the conclusion, following careful consideration of all those submissions directed to unreasonableness, perversity and procedural irregularity, that those of counsel for the Bar Council must be preferred. We cannot find anything irregular or out of conformity with the rules in the conduct of the PCC. They were not bound to refer the applicant's complaint to the disciplinary tribunal. Nevertheless, they plainly resolved to do that at a fairly early stage of the deliberations and never afterwards resiled from that position. They may very well have changed their minds or have been taken back from the brink of referring the matter to the disciplinary tribunal on the basis of the more serious charges by the opinions of Mr Read and Mr Walker.

However that may be, we regard them as acting well within their discretion in receiving those opinions and allowing them to influence their judgment. But that they allowed a final resolution of their unenviable task to drag on for much too long cannot, we think, be gainsaid, even accounting for the fact that difficulties are encountered in bringing together busy professional men at short notice. Moreover, they did not with sufficient clarity give expression to their original determination, thus allowing an impression to be gained by the applicant, if no one else, that Mr Read really did change their minds.

The test we have had to apply in deciding whether or not the decision of the PCC is flawed is obviously not whether were we in their position we would have come to the same decision as they did. There may very well be room on the special facts for divergent views as to the proper charge that Mr Samuels should face before the disciplinary tribunal. What we believe cannot be controverted is that the PCC acted within a broad discretion, which undoubtedly they had, on correct principles and with impartiality and fairness. Even if they did in fact change their minds following the receipt of Mr Read's opinion we would not regard them in the particular circumstances as having acted unreasonably or perversely or otherwise wrongly in the exercise of their discretion in that respect. Moreover, we are confident that the PCC relied on the proper test of 'prima facie case' although Mr Williams, inadvertently we suppose, mistakenly referred to the test as 'unreasonable prospect of success' in his affidavit. This caused counsel for the applicant to suggest with some force that the PCC had thus directed themselves.

In conclusion, observing what we trust is a proper regard for the need to avoid a embarrassing the disciplinary tribunal, which has, of course, to dispose finally of this matter, we think it right to say that we have not detected the presence of any improper motive in the applicant in pursuing this application. What the rights and wrongs are about his complaints against Mr Samuels can, we have no doubt, be fully and properly ventilated within the ambit of the charges which the PCC have preferred. The sooner these charges are dealt with the better it will be in the interests of all concerned.

For the reasons which we have explained we are obliged to deny the applicant the
b relief which he seeks.

Application dimissed. No order as to costs.

Solicitors: *Farrer & Co* (for the applicant); *Allison & Humphreys* (for the Bar Council).

c
Sophie Craven   Barrister.

Ventouris v Mountain and another
The Italia Express

d
QUEEN'S BENCH DIVISION (COMMERCIAL COURT)
SAVILLE J
2, 23 FEBRUARY 1990

e *Discovery – Production of documents – Representative action – Documents in possession, custody or power of represented persons – Whether court having power to order representative party or represented person to make discovery of documents in possession, custody or power of represented persons – Whether represented person party to representative proceedings – RSC Ord 15, r 12(3), Ord 24, r 3.*

f *Discovery – Legal professional privilege – Document obtained for purpose of actual or contemplated litigation – Document not coming into existence for purpose of litigation – Whether privilege attaching to document.*

The plaintiff brought an action against the first defendant, who was sued as representing himself and all other underwriters who subscribed to the marine war risks policy on which the plaintiff claimed. In the course of the proceedings the plaintiff issued a
g summons under RSC Ord 24, r 3[a] seeking an order that the first defendant, within seven days, make and serve on the plaintiff a further and better list of documents stating what documents were or had at any time been in his possession, custody or power and/or the possession, custody or power of the underwriters whom he represented. The first defendant contended that as regards the represented underwriters he was not in a position to provide such a list and that the court had no jurisdiction to make such an order. The
h first defendant also claimed privilege in respect of documents which, although not prepared for the proceedings, had been obtained by his solicitors from third parties for the purpose of the proceedings.

Held – (1) The court had no power under RSC Ord 24, r 3 to order either the
j representative party or the represented persons in representative proceedings to make discovery of documents in the possession, custody or power of the represented persons since the power under that rule to order discovery of documents only applied to parties to proceedings and, as Ord 15, r 12(3)[b] made clear, represented persons in representative

---

a   Rule 3, so far as material, is set out at p 159 c, post
b   Rule 12(3) is set out at p 159 e, post

proceedings were not party to the proceedings. Accordingly, the court would not order
the first defendant to provide a list of documents in the possession, custody or power of
the represented underwriters (see p 159 f, post).

(2) Legal professional privilege attached to documents which had not previously been
in the possession, custody or power of a party to actual or contemplated litigation and
which had not come into existence for the purpose of that litigation but which had been
obtained by the solicitors of that party for that purpose. Accordingly, the first defendant's
claim for privilege in respect of documents which had been obtained by his solicitors
from third parties for the purpose of the proceedings succeeded (see p 160 b to e, post).

Notes

For representative proceedings, see 37 Halsbury's Laws (4th edn) paras 232–234, and for
cases on the subject, see 37(2) Digest (Reissue) 382–391, 2369–2418.

For legal professional privilege generally, see 13 Halsbury's Laws (4th edn) paras 71–
75, and for cases on the subject, see 18 Digest (2nd reissue) 154–169, 1379–1482.

Cases referred to in judgment

Anderson v Bank of British Columbia (1876) 2 Ch D 644; *affd* 2 Ch D 644, [1874–80] All ER
    Rep 396, CA.
Balabel v Air-India [1988] 2 All ER 246, [1988] Ch 317, [1988] 2 WLR 1036, CA.
Palermo, The (1883) 9 PD 6, CA.
Taylor v Batten (1878) 4 QBD 85, CA.
Watson v Cammell Laird & Co (Shipbuilders and Engineers) Ltd [1959] 2 All ER 757, [1959]
    1 WLR 702, CA.

Application

The plaintiff, Apostolos Konstantinos Ventouris, the owner of the vessel Italia Express,
brought an action by writ issued on 11 April 1989 claiming damages and an indemnity
against the defendant, Trevor Rex Mountain, sued on his own behalf and on behalf of all
other insurers and/or underwriters subscribing to a marine war risks policy under which
the plaintiff was the assured. Pursuant to an order of Saville J dated 17 November 1989
Nicholas Colwyn Sturge was added as second defendant, sued on his own behalf and on
behalf of all other insurers and/or underwriters subscribing to a marine port risks policy
under which the plaintiff was the assured. By consent the action against the second
defendant was discontinued on 20 February 1990. By a summons issued on 1 December
1989 the plaintiff applied to the judge in chambers for an order that the first defendant,
within seven days of the order, make and serve on the plaintiff a further and better list of
documents stating what documents were or had been in his possession, custody or power
and/or in the possession, custody or power of the underwriters whom he represented
relating to the matters in question in the action and within like period file an affidavit
verifying such list. The summons was heard in chambers but at the request of the parties
judgment was given by Saville J in open court. The facts are set out in the judgment.

Stephen Hofmeyr for the plaintiff.
Andrew Popplewell for the first defendant.

Cur adv vult

23 February. The following judgment was delivered.

SAVILLE J. In this application under RSC Ord 24, r 3 the plaintiff seeks an order that
the first defendant make and serve a better list of documents. During the course of the
submissions on this application it became apparent that two points of general importance
arose for decision and both parties requested that I should give my ruling on these points
in open court.

The first point arises from the fact that the first defendant is sued in representative
proceedings, as representing himself and all other underwriters subscribing to the marine

war risks policy on which the plaintiff is claiming. The question is raised whether the
a court has power to order either the representative underwriter, or the represented
underwriters, to make discovery of documents which are or have been in the possession,
custody or power of the latter, but not the former.

The plaintiff's summons seeks an order that:

> 'The First Defendant do, within seven days of this Order, make and serve on the
> Plaintiff a further and better list of documents stating what documents are or have
b
> been at any time in his possession, custody or power and/or in the possession,
> custody or power of the underwriters whom he represents relating to the matters in
> question in the action and do within the like period file an affidavit verifying such
> list . . .'

Order 24, r 3(1) provides:
c
> '. . . the Court may order any party to a cause or matter . . . to make and serve on
> any other party a list of the documents which are or have been in his possession,
> custody or power relating to any matter in question in the cause or matter . . .'

It is clear from this rule that the court only has power to order a party to proceedings
to make discovery of documents that are or have been in the possession, custody or power
d of that party. So far as representative proceedings are concerned, it is to my mind clear
from Ord 15, r 12(3) that represented persons are not party to the proceedings, for this
rule provides:

> 'A judgment or order given in proceedings under this Rule shall be binding on
> all the persons as representing whom the plaintiffs sue or, as the case may be, the
e
> defendants are sued, but shall not be enforced against any person not a party to the
> proceedings except with the leave of the Court.'

To my mind it must follow from the foregoing that (however the summons is worded)
I cannot make any order under Ord 24, r 3 against the represented underwriters, since
they are not party to the proceedings, nor can I make any order against the first defendant
f in respect of any documents that are not or have not been in this possession, custody or
power, since such documents also fall outside the ambit of the rule.

I should add that in the present case I would not be minded to make the order sought
in relation to documents of the represented underwriters even if I was persuaded that I
had power to do so. The basis for seeking such an order is an alleged admission in a draft
affidavit prepared by Mr Deering, the solicitor acting for the first defendant. This draft
can indeed reasonably be read as expressing Mr Deering's view that the represented
g
underwriters may have relevant documents in their possession, custody or power.
However, the draft was prepared in a hurry (through no fault of Mr Deering or his
clients) and I accept without qualification (as does counsel for the plaintiff) Mr Deering's
assurance, given to me through the first defendants' counsel, that his true intent (which
will appear in the affidavit in its final sworn form) was to say that he simply does not
h know whether the represented underwriters have or have had any such documents in
their possession, custody or power. In such circumstances on the material before me I
can see no good reason for seeking an order against those underwriters.

The second question is whether legal professional privilege can be claimed for
documents which were not previously in the possession, custody or power of a party to
actual or contemplated litigation, which have not come into existence for the purposes
j of that litigation, but which have been obtained by the solicitors of that party for that
purpose.

It is settled law that the privilege attaches to information obtained by a solicitor from
a third party for the purpose of actual or contemplated litigation: see, for example, per
Jessell MR in *Anderson v Bank of British Columbia* (1876) 2 Ch D 644 at 649–650. It is also
settled law that the privilege attaches to copies taken by solicitors of documents held by
third parties, where the copying is done for the purpose of actual or contemplated
litigation: see *The Palermo* (1883) 9 PD 6 and *Watson v Cammell Laird & Co (Shipbuilders*

and Engineers) Ltd [1959] 2 All ER 757, [1959] 1 WLR 702. The reason why privilege attaches in such cases is that to require disclosure of the documents in question would be   *a* to undermine the very reason for the existence of the privilege at all, the basic principle of which is that the public interest requires full and frank exchange of confidence between solicitor and client to enable the latter to receive necessary legal advice and assistance: see *Anderson v Bank of British Columbia* and *Balabel v Air-India* [1988] 2 All ER 246 at 249, [1988] Ch 317 at 324 per Taylor LJ.

To my mind this basic principle applies equally to the documents in question. If a   *b* party to actual or contemplated litigation had to disclose such documents, then in the nature of things such disclosure would be calculated to diminish or destroy the confidential relationship between solicitor and client, and gravely hamper proper and effective preparations for trial by the solicitors. Indeed, just as Jessell MR pointed out in *Anderson v Bank of British Columbia* (at 649), it might otherwise be dangerous, if not impossible, to employ a solicitor at all.   *c*

It is suggested that unless the documents have come into existence for the purpose of actual or contemplated litigation (as would be the case where a solicitor copies a document) legal professional privilege cannot attach to them. I disagree. The privilege is an exception to the general rule that a party to litigation must disclose all documents that are or have been in his possession, custody or power. If the reason why documents fall within the general rule is because they have been obtained by solicitors for the purposes   *d* of the litigation, i e by that means are brought within the possession, custody or power of the party, and if (as I consider to be the case) the disclosure of such documents would be likely to undermine the public interest in preserving the confidence between solicitor and client, I can see no good reason for distinguishing in this context between documents that have and those that have not been brought into existence for the purpose of the litigation.   *e*

It might be suggested that, if the privilege extends to original documents (as opposed to copies) obtained by solicitors for the purposes of actual or contemplated litigation, a ready means presents itself for obtaining and then suppressing material adverse evidence. This is not so. Solicitors who obtained documents for the purposes of suppressing them would not be acting in the course of giving necessary legal advice and assistance, but in breach of their duties as officers of the court. Thus no privilege would attach to such   *f* documents. Quite apart from this, the source or maker of the document is likely to remain available; and, even if the original owner of the document has given up to the party in question all rights to it, there would be, as I see it, nothing to prevent that person from revealing its contents or indeed what he had done with the document.

It remains to say that in my view the correct way to list documents of the kind under discussion in part II of schedule 1 of the list is to use some such phrase as the following: *g*

> 'Original documents not previously in the possession, custody or power of (the party (*naming the party concerned*)) but obtained by (the party's) solicitors from third parties for the purposes of these proceedings.'

The purpose of such wording is to identify the documents in respect of which privilege   *h* is claimed so that, assuming the identification to be true, it can be seen whether or not the claimed privilege attaches to such documents. It is not necessary to provide a description that enables the asserted identity to be tested or which reveals the contents, maker or particular provenance of the documents: see RSC Ord 24, r 5(2) and *Taylor v Batten* (1878) 4 QBD 85 at 87–88.

It will be noted that in this judgment I have referred to documents obtained by   *j* solicitors for the purpose of actual or contemplated litigation. Whether the privilege attaches in other circumstances is not relevant to the present proceedings and accordingly I express no view on what the position would be in such cases.

Application dismissed.

Solicitors: *Hill Taylor Dickinson* (for the plaintiff); *Ince & Co* (for the first defendant).

K Mydeen Esq   Barrister.

Derby & Co Ltd and others v Weldon and others (No 7)

CHANCERY DIVISION

VINELOTT J

2, 5, 6, 12 MARCH 1990

Discovery – Legal professional privilege – Legal advice obtained in furtherance of crime or fraud – Loss of privilege – Communications passing between solicitors and defendants regarding creation of trusts and transfer of assets to them – Plaintiffs asserting proprietary claim over transferred assets – Plaintiffs seeking disclosure of communications regarding creation of trusts and transfer of assets to them on basis that they were made in furtherance of fraudulent design – Defendants asserting privilege as ground for refusing to disclose communications to plaintiffs – Whether privilege lost – Factors to be considered in deciding whether to deprive a party of the protection of privilege.

Discovery – Legal professional privilege – Affidavit and list of documents in support of claim – Need for list to be specific – Circumstances giving rise to claim for privilege required to be stated clearly – Privilege claimed for professional communications of confidential character obtained for purpose of getting legal advice – Party seeking disclosure requesting list and full particulars of professional communications – Whether party seeking disclosure entitled to further particularisation – Whether claim for privilege sufficient description of communications.

The plaintiffs were seven associated companies which were all part of a United States banking group. In 1981 the plaintiff group purchased a London commodity dealer, CML, from the first and second defendants, who were the directors and effective owners of CML. The sale of CML was made through the third and fourth defendants, a Panamanian company and a Luxembourg company, both of which were controlled by the first and second defendants. After the sale CML continued to be managed by the first and second defendants and while under their management CML offered very extensive credit to a Far Eastern commodity dealer which in 1984 became insolvent owing over £35m to CML. The plaintiff group recovered less than £1·5m in the insolvency and brought an action against the defendants alleging deceit, conspiracy to defraud and fraudulent breach of fiduciary duty and seeking delivery up of secret profits. The plaintiffs were granted a worldwide Mareva injunction against the first and second defendants and later obtained similar relief against the third and fourth defendants and also receivership and disclosure orders in respect of their assets. The plaintiffs subsequently sought and obtained leave to join as defendants another seven individuals and companies, including a Liechtenstein stiftung (which owned, among other companies, the parent company of the fourth defendant and a Liberian company, CMFE, in which the first and second defendants had undisclosed interests), the trustees of two other Liechtenstein trusts (which the plaintiffs discovered had been created to hold the assets of companies previously under the direct or indirect ownership of the stiftung), two Panamanian companies owned by the two trusts, and the Swiss lawyer who acted for the stiftung and the fourth defendant. The basis of the claim against the added defendants was that they had been parties to the conspiracy or had assisted in the commission of unlawful acts by the first four defendants or had received assets for which they were accountable. The plaintiffs also obtained the appointment of a receiver of the assets of the added corporate defendants and the two Liechtenstein trusts. Under their claim for secret profits the plaintiffs then sought (i) discovery by the defendants of confidential documents from their legal advisers relating to the creation of the two Liechtenstein trusts and the transfer of assets to them, on the ground that the documents had been obtained in furtherance of a fraudulent design to conceal and render irrecoverable profits of more than $US8·5m

made by CMFE from fraudulent foreign exchange dealings with CML and the first
plaintiff, for which the first two defendants were accountable to the plaintiffs and which
were therefore outside the protection of legal professional privilege claimed by the
defendants, and (ii) further lists of the confidential documents identifying 'with full
particularity' the circumstances alleged to give rise to the claim for privilege. The
defendants contended (i) that the plaintiffs' allegation of fraud did not defeat their claim
to privilege, since it amounted to nothing more than a mere allegation in view of the fact
that the creation and transfer of assets to the two trusts were not steps taken in furtherance
of the alleged fraud, but were rather steps taken to protect the assets of the stiftung and
to enable them to be used for the purpose of the stiftung free from interference from any
Mareva injunction which the plaintiffs might obtain in the course of prosecuting the
claims, which the first two defendants regarded as ill-founded, and (ii) that the plaintiffs
were not entitled to further particulars of the confidential documents, since the claim for
privilege in respect of those documents, which was expressed in standard form and
referred to the documents as 'confidential correspondence... for the purpose of obtaining
legal advice', constituted a sufficient description of the documents.

Held – (1) Where communications which would otherwise be within the protection of
legal professional privilege had been made in furtherance of a fraudulent design, a person
was not entitled to assert legal professional privilege as a ground for refusing to disclose
those communications in circumstances where the party seeking disclosure was able to
establish a strong prima facie case of fraud. However, the court would be very slow to
deprive a party of the important protection of legal privilege on an interlocutory
application and would judge each case on the facts, striking a balance between the
important considerations on which legal privilege was founded and the gravity of the
charge of fraud that was made. Nevertheless, since the creation of the trusts and the
transfer of assets to them were steps taken in furtherance of the initial fraud alleged, in
the sense that they were taken to conceal or render irrecoverable profits made by CMFE
to which the plaintiffs had asserted a proprietary claim, the plaintiffs were able to
establish a strong prima facie case of fraud and as a result were entitled to the disclosure
sought. An order for disclosure of the requested documents would therefore be made,
reserving liberty to the defendants to apply to exclude any documents that were obtained
or created for the dominant purpose of being used in pending or contemplated
proceedings (see p 176 h to p 177 b and p 178 a to g, post); dicta of Lord Wrenbury in
O'Rourke v Darbishire [1920] All ER Rep 1 at 19–20 and of Lord Denning MR and of
Donaldson LJ in Buttes Gas and Oil Co v Hammer (No 3) [1980] 3 All ER 475 at 486, 490
applied.
   (2) Where privilege was claimed for professional communications of a confidential
character obtained for the purpose of getting legal advice, the claim for privilege was to
be treated as itself a sufficient description of the communications, irrespective of the scale
of discovery and the complexity of the issues involved, and consequently the party
seeking disclosure was not entitled to satisfy himself by means of a fuller description of
the communications for which privilege was claimed that it was not claimed for
documents outside its proper scope. Moreover, the court would not order the party
claiming privilege to disclose all communications with his legal advisers or to provide
fuller particulars of those communications even where it had been shown in relation to
one transaction that the advice was sought in furtherance of a fraudulent design, since to
order such disclosure would be contrary to the public policy on which legal privilege was
founded. Accordingly, the plaintiffs were not entitled to require the defendants to file
further lists identifying in the case of documents for which privilege was claimed the
circumstances allegedly giving rise to such a claim. The leave sought in the second part
of the plaintiffs' application would therefore be refused (see p 182 a b h to p 183 a, post);
dictum of Eveleigh J in Alfred Crompton Amusement Machines Ltd v Customs and Excise
Comrs [1971] 2 All ER 843 at 847–848 explained; dicta of Cotton LJ in Taylor v Batten

(1878) 4 QBD 85 at 87 and of Cotton LJ in *Gardner v Irvin* (1878) 4 Ex D 49 at 53
a considered.

Notes
For legal professional privilege generally, see 13 Halsbury's Laws (4th edn) paras 71–75,
and for cases on the subject, see 18 Digest (2nd reissue) 154–169, *1379–1482*.
   For confidentiality of communications between solicitor and client, see 44 Halsbury's
b Laws (4th edn) para 74, and for cases on the subject, see 44 Digest (Reissue) 38–40, *359–
367*.

Cases referred to in judgment
A v C [1980] 2 All ER 347, [1981] QB 956, [1981] 2 WLR 629.
Anderson v Bank of British Columbia (1876) 2 Ch D 644, [1874–80] All ER Rep 396, CA.
c *Bankers Trust Co v Shapira* [1980] 3 All ER 353, [1980] 1 WLR 1274, CA.
Birmingham and Midland Motor Omnibus Co Ltd v London and North Western Rly Co [1913]
   3 KB 850, CA.
Bullivant v A-G for Victoria [1901] AC 196, [1900–3] All ER Rep 812, HL.
Buttes Gas and Oil Co v Hammer (No 3) [1980] 3 All ER 475, [1981] QB 223, [1980] 3 WLR
   668, CA; stayed [1981] 3 All ER 616, [1982] AC 888, [1981] 3 WLR 787, HL.
d *Crescent Farm (Sidcup) Sports Ltd v Sterling Offices Ltd* [1971] 3 All ER 1192, [1972] Ch 553,
   [1972] 2 WLR 91.
Crompton (Alfred) Amusement Machines Ltd v Customs and Excise Comrs [1971] 2 All ER
   843.
Derby & Co Ltd v Weldon (No 1) [1989] 1 All ER 469, [1990] Ch 48, [1989] 2 WLR 276,
   CA.
e *Derby & Co Ltd v Weldon (No 2)* [1989] 1 All ER 1002, sub nom *Derby & Co Ltd v Weldon
   (Nos 3 and 4)* [1990] Ch 65, [1989] 2 WLR 412, CA.
Films Rover International Ltd v Cannon Film Sales Ltd [1986] 3 All ER 772, [1987] 1 WLR
   670.
Gamlen Chemical Co (UK) Ltd v Rochem Ltd (No 2) (1979) 124 SJ 276, CA.
f *Gardner v Irvin* (1878) 4 Ex D 49, CA.
Kain v Farrer (1877) 37 LT 469, DC.
O'Rourke v Darbishire [1920] AC 581, [1920] All ER Rep 1, HL; affg [1919] 1 Ch 320, CA.
R v Cox and Railton (1884) 14 QBD 153, [1881–5] All ER Rep 68, CCR.
Taylor v Batten (1878) 4 QBD 85, CA.
Taylor v Oliver (1876) 34 LT 902.
Williams v Quebrada Railway Land and Copper Co [1895] 2 Ch 751.
g *Willmott v London Celluloid Co* (1886) 34 Ch D 147, CA.

Cases also cited
A-G v Guardian Newspapers Ltd (No 2) [1988] 3 All ER 545, [1990] 1 AC 109, CA and HL.
Banque Keyser Ullmann SA v Skandia (UK) Insurance Co Ltd [1986] 1 Lloyd's Rep 336, CA.
h *Bewicke v Graham* (1881) 7 QBD 400, CA.
Budden v Wilkinson [1893] 2 QB 432, CA.
Butler v Board of Trade [1970] 3 All ER 593, [1971] Ch 680.
Crompton (Alfred) Amusement Machines Ltd v Customs and Excise Comrs (No 2) [1972] 2 All
   ER 353, [1972] 2 QB 102, CA; affd on other grounds [1973] 2 All ER 1169, [1974] AC
   405, HL.
j *Dependable Upholstery Ltd, Re* [1936] 3 All ER 741.
Doland (George) Ltd v Blackburn Robson Coates & Co (a firm) [1972] 3 All ER 959, [1972] 1
   WLR 1338.
Gamlen Chemical Co (UK) Ltd v Rochem Ltd [1983] RPC 1.
O'Shea v Wood [1891] P 286, CA.
Thompson's Settlement, Re [1985] 2 All ER 720, [1986] Ch 99.

Motion

The plaintiffs, Derby & Co Ltd, Cocoa Merchants Ltd (CML), Phibro-Salomon Finance *a* AG, Phibro-Salomon Ltd, Philipp Bros Inc, Philipp Bros Ltd and Salomon Inc (the holding company of the other plaintiff companies), by a writ issued on 25 June 1987 brought an action against (1) Anthony Henry David Weldon, (2) Ian Jay, (3) Milco Corp, a Panamanian company, and (4) CML Holding SA of Luxembourg, claiming damages for breach of contract, misrepresentation, negligence, deceit, conspiracy to defraud and fraudulent breach of fiduciary duty arising out of the trading activities of CML between *b* June 1981 and February 1984 while under the management of the first and second defendants as executive directors of CML after it had been purchased by Salomon Inc from the liquidator of a subsidiary of the third defendant, which was itself a subsidiary · of the fourth defendant. The statement of claim in the action was served on the four defendants on 4 December 1987 and on the same day Sir Nicolas Browne-Wilkinson V-C granted ex parte Mareva injunctions against the first and second defendants restraining *c* them from removing their assets out of the United Kingdom or those countries which were parties to the Convention on Jurisdiction and the Enforcement of Civil and Commercial Judgments 1968 (Brussels, 27 September 1968; EC 46 (1978); Cmd 7395; and set out as amended in the Civil Jurisdiction and Judgments Act 1982, Sch 1) or from dealing in any way with those assets except to the extent that they exceeded £25m and requiring the first and second defendants to file an affidavit disclosing the full value of *d* their assets. On 20 June 1988 Mervyn Davies J granted, inter alia, a Mareva injunction restricted to the first and second defendants' assets in the United Kingdom but on appeal by the plaintiffs the Court of Appeal (May, Parker and Nicholls LJJ) ([1989] 1 All ER 469, [1990] Ch 48) granted a worldwide Mareva injunction against the first and second defendants. By notices of motion dated 16 August and 4 November 1988 the plaintiffs sought worldwide Mareva injunctions and receivership and disclosure orders against the *e* third and fourth defendants which were granted by Sir Nicolas Browne-Wilkinson V-C on 4 November 1988 and upheld with variations by the Court of Appeal (Lord Donaldson MR, Neill and Butler-Sloss LJJ) ([1990] 1 All ER 1002, [1990] Ch 65). On 8 March 1989 Vinelott J gave leave to join as defendants (5) Wollstein Stiftung, a Liechtenstein stiftung which was the ultimate owner of a Liberian company, Cocoa Merchants (Far East) Ltd *f* (CMFE), and therefore holder of profits made from foreign exchange dealings with CML and Derby & Co Ltd, (6) Tim Schneider, (7) Ernst Aeschbacher and (8) Peter Ritter, the trustees of two other Liechtenstein trusts (the Lagor trust and the Ralgo trust) and (9) Steelburg Management Inc and (10) Pilgrim Enterprises Inc, two companies owned by the two trusts, on the basis that they had been parties to the conspiracy or had assisted in the commission of unlawful acts by the first four defendants or had received funds for *g* which they were accountable, and also granted an ex parte worldwide Mareva injunction against the fifth defendant and receivership orders in respect of the assets of the added corporate defendants and the two trusts. On 21 December 1989 Vinelott J gave leave to the plaintiffs to join as defendant (11) Dr Louis Rohner, the Swiss lawyer for the fourth and fifth defendants. By a notice of motion dated 19 January 1990 the plaintiffs applied for (i) an order for disclosure by the defendants of confidential documents relating to the *h* creation of the Lagor trust and the Ralgo trust and the transfer of assets to the trusts or companies owned by them on the ground that the advice was sought from legal advisers in furtherance of a fraudulent design and was therefore within the exclusion from legal professional privilege and (ii) an order that the third to fifth defendants provide the defendants with a further list of the documents for which legal privilege had been claimed identifying with full particularity the circumstances alleged to give rise to the *j* claim.

Michael Lyndon-Stanford QC and *J Stephen Smith* for the plaintiffs.
Nicholas Chambers QC and *Mark Hapgood* for the first and second defendants.
David Hunt QC and *Terence Mowschenson* for the third to eleventh defendants.

Cur adv vult

12 March. The following judgment was delivered.

VINELOTT J.

The first issue

In these applications the plaintiffs seek discovery by the defendants of documents for which the protection of legal professional privilege is claimed. The interlocutory judgments that have been given and the orders that have so far been made in this action occupy four large ring binders. At least three of the judgments have been reported. I am reluctant to add another lengthy judgment to their bulk. However, the public policy which requires that confidential communications between a client and his solicitor made in the course of obtaining legal advice are not to be subject to production is of fundamental and constitutional importance. It is only in very exceptional circumstances that the privilege can be displaced. I must, therefore, set out in some detail the grounds on which the plaintiffs seek to displace or breach that privilege.

The action was started by writ issued on 25 June 1987. The plaintiffs are all members of a banking group headed by the seventh plaintiff, Salomon Inc (Salomon). The litigation concerns the acquisition by the Salomon Group of the shares of the second plaintiff, Cocoa Merchants Ltd (CML). When the writ was issued, the first two defendants, Mr Weldon and Mr Jay, and the third defendant, Milco Corp, a Panamanian company, were the only defendants. On 4 December 1987 Sir Nicolas Browne-Wilkinson V-C, on the application of the plaintiffs ex parte, granted a Mareva injunction in usual form until the hearing of the plaintiffs' application inter partes, restraining the individual defendants from disposing of assets in the United Kingdom or in countries within the European Economic Community except to the extent that they exceed £25m in the case of each defendant. The writ was amended shortly afterwards by adding the fourth defendant, CML Holding SA Luxembourg (which is referred to in the pleadings as 'CMI') and was reissued on 8 December 1987.

The statement of claim was served on 15 January 1988. In the course of the action the statement of claim has undergone many alterations and additions. Even in its original form it is a very lengthy document. Fortunately it is unnecessary to explain all the claims made by the plaintiffs. It will be sufficient at this stage to outline the general background to the claims and the substance of one of them.

The background

The allegations are as follows.

(a) In June 1981 Mr Weldon and Mr Jay were directors of CML, which traded as principal or as broker in commodities and as foreign exchange dealer.

(b) By an agreement of 26 June 1981 made between the fourth plaintiff, Phibro-Salomon Ltd (PSL) and Cocoa Merchants Group Ltd (CMGL) (the sale agreement) PSL agreed to buy the shares of CML for a very considerable sum.

(c) The shares of CMGL were owned beneficially by CMI and the liquidator of CMGL assigned the benefit of the sale agreement to Milco Corp, the shares of which were in turn owned by CMI.

(d) After the takeover Mr Weldon and Mr Jay remained managing directors of CML. In addition, Mr Weldon became a director of the first plaintiff, Derby & Co Ltd (Derby), and of PSL and was employed as an executive of the fifth plaintiff, Philipp Bros Inc (PBI). He spent most of his time dealing with the affairs of CML. Mr Jay also became a director of Derby and of PSL.

(e) In 1983 CML suffered very severe losses as a result of the insolvency of a major customer known as the Allied Group. Following an investigation into the causes of the collapse, an agreement was entered into on 11 May 1984 (the May agreement) between Milco, PSL, Salomon, CMGL, Mr Weldon and Mr Jay under which, so far as is material, Salomon, on behalf of its subsidiaries, released Milco, CMGL, Mr Weldon and Mr Jay from all claims in respect of, amongst other things, the purchase of CML and any transactions between CML and any other party, and any advice given by Milco, CMGL,

Mr Weldon or Mr Jay to Salomon or its subsidiaries, and Milco agreed to repay part of
the purchase price paid for CML.   a
(f) In the action it is sought to set aside the May agreement on the ground that
Salomon and PSL were induced to enter into it by means of misrepresentations.

The related party dealings
The claims in the action include a claim that, shortly stated, Mr Weldon and Mr Jay,
in breach of fiduciary duties owed to CML and others of the plaintiffs of which they were   b
directors and (where employed under a contract of service) of the terms of the contract,
caused CML to enter into transactions with companies or other entities in which they
had an interest, as a result of which profits were made at the expense of or improperly
diverted from CML and other companies in the Salomon group. The allegations are spelt
out in great detail in the amended statement of claim. It is only necessary to refer to one
group of transactions, namely the foreign exchange dealings. One of the allegations   c
made is that profits were made by a Liberian company, called Cocoa Merchants (Far East)
Ltd (CMFE), whereby CML or Derby sold to or purchased from CMFE foreign exchange
for immediate or forward delivery (forex deals) and that, unknown to the plaintiff, Mr
Weldon and Mr Jay had an interest in CMFE. Again, those allegations are set out in great
detail in the statement of claim. For instance, it is said that in the case of three forex deals
all entered into on 29 October 1981 a profit was made by CMFE by purchasing   d
Deutschmarks at one price and selling Deutschmarks back to CML at a higher price. The
claim is that these profits are the property of the plaintiffs, or one of them, traceable in
equity and that, if they have been mixed with other moneys, the plaintiffs are entitled to
a charge on those moneys, whether they are in the hands of CMFE (which has in fact
ceased to exist) or in the hands of volunteers or anybody else taking with notice of the
claim.   e
The sums claimed under the general heading of related dealings are very large. In the
case of forex deals routed through CMFE alone, the plaintiffs in the amended statement
of claim specify forex deals which, it is said, yielded a profit of over $US8·5m.
Defences were not served until February 1989. I will have to say something about the
defences raised later.
Returning to the history of the action, the application for Mareva injunctions against   f
Mr Weldon and Mr Jay came on for hearing before Mervyn Davies J in June 1988. He
gave judgment on 20 June. He continued the Mareva injunctions but limited them to
the defendants' United Kingdom assets. He also found that there were ample grounds
for supposing that Mr Weldon and Mr Jay had interests in CMI and Milco and so
indirectly in CMFE, and he made an order requiring Mr Weldon and Mr Jay to disclose
what had happened to the profit made by CMFE on Forex deals and to disclose any   g
documents relating to dealings with such moneys.
Both parties appealed against this decision. The appeals were heard by the Court of
Appeal in July and on 29 July 1988 the Court of Appeal gave judgment: see *Derby & Co
Ltd v Weldon (No 1)* [1989] 1 All ER 469, [1990] Ch 48. The plaintiffs' appeal was allowed.
The Mareva injunctions were extended to Mr Weldon and Mr Jay's assets worldwide,   h
subject to a proviso designed to protect third parties dealing with assets outside the
jurisdiction of the United Kingdom courts. The Court of Appeal dismissed the defendants'
appeal against that part of the order of Mervyn Davies J which had required disclosure of
dealings with Forex profits made by CMFE. I should at this stage cite a short passage in
the judgment of Nicholls LJ where he said ([1989] 1 All ER 469 at 480, [1990] Ch 48 at
64):   j

'If the plaintiffs have a seriously arguable case that they had a proprietary interest,
under a constructive trust, in certain sums of money paid to CMFE, then in my
view the court has jurisdiction, under the principles set out in *A v C* [1980] 2 All ER
347, [1981] QB 956 and *Bankers Trust Co v Shapira* [1980] 3 All ER 353, [1980] 1
WLR 1274, to require the defendants to provide information about what has

a happened to those sums. In the exercise of his discretion Mervyn Davies J considered that an order to that effect should be made in this case. I can see no ground entitling or requiring this court to interfere with that exercise of his discretion.'

Next the plaintiffs applied for worldwide Mareva injunctions against the third and fourth defendants, Milco and CMI. That came before Mervyn Davies J ex parte on 11 August 1988. He granted the injunction sought until the effective hearing of the motion.
b As regards these defendants, the limit in the Mareva injunctions was again fixed at £25m each. The application was adjourned from time to time until 4 November. In the meantime, on 2 November Sir Nicolas Browne-Wilkinson V-C had made an order requiring Mr Weldon and Mr Jay to serve further affidavits disclosing the amounts and the whereabouts of their assets and requiring them to attend for cross-examination. The main reason given by Sir Nicolas Browne-Wilkinson V-C was that there was considerable
c uncertainty in the evidence then filed as to the interest in and degree of control exercised by these defendants over CMI and Milco and as to their knowledge of forex dealings between CML and CMFE.

Then on 4 November Sir Nicolas Browne-Wilkinson V-C confirmed the Mareva injunction granted by Mervyn Davies J against CMI. He also appointed a receiver of the assets of CMI. He declined to continue the Mareva injunctions over or to appoint a
d receiver of the assets of Milco.

At this stage there was a very important departure. The cross-examination of the first and second defendants had been fixed for 10 November. Shortly before it commenced, the solicitors acting for Mr Weldon and Mr Jay, Messrs Hopkins & Wood, disclosed to the plaintiffs' solicitors a letter written by them to the solicitors then acting for Milco and CMI, Messrs Theodore Goddard, dated 9 November. I should read this letter in full:

e
'We should like to make plain the views of our client, Mr. Weldon, who is a discretionary beneficiary of the Stiftung which is the ultimate beneficial owner of CMI. Although it is not within Mr. Weldon's power to require your clients to do so, please will you convey to your clients Mr. Weldon's wishes that full disclosure of the assets of CMI, Milco and all of their subsidiary companies and of any other companies
f which may underlie the Stiftung, be disclosed to the Plaintiffs and to the court forthwith. Mr. Jay concurs with these sentiments, although he is of course not even a beneficiary. Neither Mr. Jay nor Mr. Weldon are in a position to procure the compliance by your clients with the Order of the Vice-Chancellor dated 7th November, but we should like to repeat that, regardless of any appeal which you may be making as to the Order appointing the Receiver, full disclosure of assets
g should be made forthwith in our clients' view.'

This was the first the plaintiffs had known of what is now known to be the fifth defendant, the Wollstein Stiftung. In the course of the cross-examination it was revealed that the stiftung owned CMI and, through CMI, CMFE while it was in existence, and that Mr Weldon was a beneficiary, if not the primary beneficiary, under the discretionary
h trust constituted by the stiftung. Mr Jay estimated that the assets controlled by the stiftung were worth £30m to £40m. Mr Weldon agreed and, asked whether he knew of other trusts in which he had any hope or expectation of benefit, said: 'Not that I know of.'

The plaintiffs appealed against the decision of Sir Nicolas Browne-Wilkinson V-C not to grant a Mareva injunction over or to appoint a receiver of assets of Milco, and CMI
j appealed against the grant of a Mareva injunction over and the appointment of a receiver of its assets. The appeal was heard in December and the Court of Appeal gave judgment on 16 December: see Derby & Co Ltd v Weldon (No 2) [1989] 1 All ER 1002, sub nom Derby & Co Ltd v Weldon (Nos 3 and 4) [1990] Ch 65. The Court of Appeal affirmed the orders made as regards CMI but reversed the decision of Sir Nicolas Browne-Wilkinson V-C not to make similar orders in the case of Milco.

That takes the history to the end of 1988. Early in 1989 Sir Nicolas Browne-Wilkinson V-C decided that he could not properly hear applications by the receiver and interlocutory *a* applications in the action, and since February 1989 I have heard all interlocutory applications in the action.

Early in March there was a further unexpected development. In January Messrs Allen & Overy had replaced Theodore Goddard as solicitors for Milco and CMI. On 2 March 1989 Allen & Overy wrote to the plaintiffs' solicitors, Messrs Lovell White Durrant, in the following terms: *b*

'The Lagor Trust, of which you were informed in the Affirmation served in draft upon you recently is the sister trust of the Ralgo Trust. Lagor is an obvious anagram of Ralgo, and vice versa. Both trusts were created under deeds dated 9th August 1988 on identical terms and the range of beneficiaries of both trusts is identical to those under the Wollstein Stiftung of which you are already aware. The Trust Deeds are dated 9th August 1988 and originally the trustees of the trust were "Protec Trust *c* Management Establishment" of Liechtenstein. However by two Deeds of Appointment dated 15th February 1989 they were replaced by Mr. Aeschbacher, Mr. Schneider and Dr. Ritter in the case of each trust. The trusts were designed and intended to hold assets of companies previously in the direct or indirect ownership of the Wollstein Stiftung Group. Lagor owns Steelburg Company ("Steelburg") a *d* Panamanian company. As at 6th February 1989 Steelburg had assets exceeding £8·5 million. All these sums are in the control of the receiver. Steelburg had received its monies from Lock Investment Limited ("Lock") and Woodroffe Investment Limited ("Woodroffe"), both incorporated under the laws of Liberia. Following the transfer Lock was left with no assets of any nature and was dissolved, as you are aware. Woodroffe retained and continued to retain some assets and this *e* company is still in existence. Its assets are, of course, in control of the receiver. Two other service companies, Pollux Business S.A. ("Pollux"), and Cat Spring Management Inc. ("Cat") already known to you held the monies which were being transferred from Lock and Woodroffe prior to them being paid to Steelburg. We are instructed, however, that all sums received from Lock and Woodroffe by these companies were paid to Steelburg. The sole asset of the Ralgo Trust is its shares in a company called *f* Pilgrim Enterprises Inc. ("Pilgrim"), also incorporated under the laws of Panama. These were acquired indirectly from Dumaine Investment Corporation, having been transferred to a private individual, who transferred them to Pilgrim. We are instructed that Pilgrim acquired its assets from Milco, although this is a matter which our clients are still checking.'

The plaintiffs applied immediately to join the stiftung, the trustees of these two trusts, *g* the sixth, seventh and eighth defendants, and Steelburg and Pilgrim as defendants. On 8 March I made an order in those terms. I also granted Mareva injunctions over the assets of the stiftung and appointed the receiver of the assets of Milco and CMI to be receiver of the assets of the stiftung, Steelburg and Pilgrim and of the assets of the trusts.

In the course of the summer orders for discovery of documents were made. Then in July the receiver, at the direction of Sir Nicolas Browne-Wilkinson V-C, prepared a *h* memorandum of contradictions between the evidence of the defendants and the information obtained by the receiver. One contradiction was between the statements by Mr Weldon and Mr Jay that assets under the control of the stiftung were between £30m and £40m, and the fact revealed by the receiver's researches that the assets of the stiftung at the commencement of the proceedings were in excess of £60m. Mr Weldon and Mr *j* Jay were then ordered to depose to a further affidavit explaining these contradictions. The explanation of the discrepancy between the figure of £30m and £40m given in their earlier cross-examination and the figure of £60m given by the receiver as the value of the assets of the stiftung at the commencement of the proceedings was that, in order,

to use Mr Weldon's words, to 'protect the assets of the stiftung' and in the expectation
a that injunctions similar to those granted by the Court of Appeal against him and Mr Jay
would be granted against Milco and CMI, it was agreed to put some of the assets of the
CMI Group into two new trusts, the beneficiaries of which would be identical to those
interested under the stiftung. One would hold assets derived from Far Eastern companies
and the other assets derived from other companies. The Lagor trust was chosen for the
assets from the Far Eastern companies, including profits made by CMFE, which were put
b into Steelburg. The other trust, Ralgo, took over the shares of Pilgrim, into which assets
from other companies had been put. Mr Weldon describes the way in which the shares
of Pilgrim were acquired by Ralgo in a passage I should cite in full:

> 'Between, I believe, 2nd and 5th August I had meetings in Switzerland with Dr.
> Rohner [who has now been added as the eleventh defendant], Dr. Bar and Dr.
> Wettenschwiler, both individually and together. At a meeting on, I believe, 5th
c August Dr. Bar rejected all the ideas which had previously been discussed and said
> that Dr. Wettenschwiler had come up with a "brilliant idea" of selling Pilgrim for
> its paid up share capital, i.e. $5,000, rather than its net asset value. Dr. Bar there and
> then approved the transfer of ownership of Pilgrim and Lock. This proposal had
> my full support, and indeed I believe it was I who suggested that the existing
> division between the Far East and non-Far East interests should be maintained via
d the creation of the two trusts.'

The shares of Pilgrim were sold to a nominee, a Mr Ilsley, who then transferred them to
the trustees of the Ralgo trust. The assets of Pilgrim were then worth some £20m. The
transfers of the shares of Steelburg were made for no consideration.
All these matters came to the knowledge of the plaintiffs following a direction of Sir
e Nicolas Browne-Wilkinson V-C that a report by the receiver and the joint affidavit should
be disclosed to them.
Returning to the course of the main proceedings, lists of documents were exchanged
on 21 August 1988. The lists of Milco and CMI contained in schedule 2 the following
reference:

f 'The documents numbered (1) and (2) in Schedule 2 hereto were last in the
> possession or power of the Third and/or Fourth and/or Fifth Defendants on the
> respective dates thereof when they were posted to the person firm or company to
> whom they were addressed. The file numbered (3) was last in the Third to Fifth
> Defendants' possession when it was posted to Mr. H Schwartz, Casa Atrium, Via
> Borenco 22, 6648 Minusio, Switzerland, on 30th August 1988. The documents
> numbered (4) were last in the Third and/or Fourth and/or Fifth Defendants'
g possession when they were left in the offices of Kara (HK) Ltd. in or around October–
> December of 1985.'

When they had studied these lists, the plaintiffs sought further information about the
'Pilar' file. It transpired later that there had been a mistake in the list. The reference
should have been to a Pilgrim file. The plaintiffs of course were equally concerned to
h know what had happened to documents in the Pilgrim file, which might throw light on
the origins of moneys that had been effectively transferred to the Ralgo trust. That
information would be important in the context of their proprietary claim.
On 15 January 1990, on an application of the plaintiffs, I made an order giving the
plaintiffs leave to serve interrogatories, calling on the defendants to say, amongst other
things, if the file had been sent to a third person, when it was sent, why it was sent, how
j it was sent, which individual sent it, on which individual's ultimate instructions it was
sent, whether receipt was acknowledged and, if so, when and how and by whom, and
what the file contained when it was sent.
The affidavit in answer revealed that the Pilgrim file was sent to Mr Hugo Schwartz

between 5 August and mid-September 1988. Mr Weldon says the disposal of the shares of Pilgrim was agreed at meetings attended by Dr Rohner, now the eleventh defendant, Dr Bar, and his partner, Dr Wettenschwiler. Dr Wettenschwiler advised that there was no requirement for any financial records to be retained since most of the companies were Panamanian and Panamanian law does not require Panamanian companies to keep any records or file accounts. She suggested that steps should be taken to dispose of all files relating to stiftung companies which were not, in her words, 'legal files'. She put forward what Dr Bar described as the brilliant idea of selling shares to Pilgrim for a sum equal to the paid-up capital. That, of course, together with the destruction of files, banking documents and other financial records, would conceal, at least on superficial inquiry, the transfer of assets of £20m to the trust.

The file was sent to Mr Schwartz by post. He had previously agreed with Dr Bar to destroy all papers in his possession concerning the stiftung and its underlying companies' affairs. Later, in September or October, he confirmed that he had destroyed the file.

An affidavit of a solicitor with Allen & Overy recording a conversation she had had with Dr Wettenschwiler confirms this account, save in one particular. Mr Weldon in his affidavit asserted that the individual on whose ultimate instructions the file was sent to Mr Schwartz was Dr Bar, though he, Mr Weldon, made it clear that he was in favour of this course. Dr Wettenschwiler is said to have made the following statement to the solicitor with Allen & Overy who has deposed to an affidavit:

'Dr. Wettenschwiler says that Mr. Weldon told her to send the File. In a telephone conversation in February 1989 with myself and Robert Hunter of this firm she said that she was aware of the fact that this was to dispose of the evidence that the Pilgrim shares were worth more than £5,000 allegedly paid by Mr. Ilsley on the sale to him of Pilgrim. However, more recently Dr. Wettenschwiler has told Markus Dorig that she was not aware of the purpose of sending the File and that she would not know what Mr. Schwartz did with the File . . . Dr. Wettenschwiler and Dr. Bar have said that Mr. Weldon gave instructions to send the File.'

That is all I need say about the evidence and the historical background at this stage. In this application the plaintiffs seek an order for the discovery of all documents relating to the creation of the two trusts and the transfer of assets to the trusts or to Steelburg or to Pilgrim, notwithstanding that a claim for privilege may have been made in respect of any of these documents.

Counsel's two main submissions on behalf of Milco, CMI and the stiftung were as follows. He submitted, first, that to bring a case within the exclusion from legal professional privilege the plaintiffs must satisfy the court that advice was sought from the legal advisers in furtherance of a fraudulent design. A mere allegation of fraud in a pleading can never suffice. The plaintiffs must be able to show on the material before the court that the defendant was probably guilty of the fraud alleged or at least that the plaintiffs' case is an exceptionally strong one. Second, the plaintiffs must show that the advice was sought in furtherance of that fraudulent design.

Counsel, while conceding that the allegations in the statement of claim that Mr Weldon and Mr Jay improperly made or diverted profits from forex deals for which they were accountable to the plaintiffs are allegations of fraud in the relevant sense, submitted that the creation of and transfer of assets to the Ralgo and Lagor trusts were not steps taken in furtherance of that initial fraud. And he submitted that taken in isolation from the initial fraud these steps were not in themselves dishonest. They were steps taken to protect the assets of the stiftung and to enable them to be used for the purposes of the stiftung free from interference in the form of a Mareva injunction which the plaintiffs might obtain in the course of prosecuting claims which his clients, Mr Weldon and Mr Jay, regarded as ill-founded.

Counsel for the third to eleventh defendants referred me to a large number of
a authorities in support of these submissions. A convenient starting point is the decision
of the full Court of Queen's Bench in *R v Cox and Railton* (1884) 14 QBD 153, [1881–5]
All ER Rep 68. That was an appeal against a conviction of the two defendants for a
conspiracy with intent to defraud. The question was whether at the trial the evidence of
a solicitor who had been consulted by the defendants had been properly admitted. The
solicitor's evidence was that the defendants consulted him after the plaintiff in an action
b against a firm, Railton & Co, in which the defendants were partners had recovered
judgment, as to how they could defeat the judgment. The case for the Crown at the
prosecution was that a memorandum indorsed on a deed of partnership between Cox
and Railton purporting to record the dissolution of the partnership at a date antecedent
to the action had been falsely antedated. The object was to conceal the existence of the
partnership so that a bill of sale of Railton's business assets to Cox would not be open to
c attack on the ground that it was a transaction between partners.

Stephen J gave the judgment of the court. Having explained the scope of the rule that
a legal adviser is not only justified but bound to withhold disclosure of a communication
received in his professional capacity and having held that the rule cannot include the case
of communications criminal in themselves or intended to further any criminal purpose,
he concluded with a passage which is often cited, which I will read again (14 QBD 153 at
d 175–176, [1881–5] All ER Rep 68 at 76):

> 'We were greatly pressed with the argument that, speaking practically, the
> admission of any such exception to the privilege of legal advisers as that it is not to
> extend to communications made in furtherance of any criminal or fraudulent
> purpose would greatly diminish the value of that privilege. That privilege, must, it
e > was argued, be violated in order to ascertain whether it exists. The secret must be
> told in order to see whether it ought to be kept. We were earnestly pressed to lay
> down some rule as to the manner in which this consequence should be avoided. The
> only thing which we feel authorized to say upon this matter is, that in each particular
> case the Court must determine upon the facts actually given in evidence or proposed
> to be given in evidence, whether it seems probable that the accused person may
f > have consulted his legal adviser, not after the commission of the crime for the
> legitimate purpose of being defended, but before the commission of the crime for
> the purpose of being guided or helped in committing it. We are far from saying
> that the question whether the advice was taken before or after the offence will
> always be decisive as to the admissibility of such evidence. Courts must in every
> instance judge for themselves on the special facts of each particular case . . .'

g   The scope of the exclusion from legal professional privilege in civil litigation (what is
meant in this context by 'fraud') was very widely defined by Kekewich J in *Williams v
Quebrada Railway Land and Copper Co* [1895] 2 Ch 751. The plaintiff held debentures and
debenture stock in the company. The debenture stock had been issued in 1883 and in
1885 and the debentures in 1886. Both created a floating charge on the company's assets.
h The company had defaulted in payment of interest and the action was commenced on
1 September 1894. In his statement of claim the plaintiff alleged that on 22 February
1894 the company, without disclosing the prior charges, entered into an agreement
purporting to charge its assets with another company, which was its sole agent, to secure
moneys due to it and that that agreement had been entered into when the defendant
company was insolvent and when its stoppage was imminent and not in the ordinary
j course of its business. It had been entered into solely to defeat or delay the debenture
holders. The plaintiff could not rely on the fraudulent preference provisions then
contained in s 164 of the Companies Act 1862 as enlarged by the Bankruptcy Act 1869,
first because the action was started before the winding up of the company commenced
in October or November 1894 and, also, because a transaction could not be impeached

under that section for the benefit of a single class of creditors: see *Willmott v London Celluloid Co* (1886) 34 Ch D 147. But the claim was analogous to a claim to set aside a transaction for fraudulent preference. The claim was that the charge had been created when the cesser of business by the company was inevitable and to remove the assets from the scope of the floating charge before it crystallised. The case for the company was that the fraud was 'of a very mild character' and fell short of the cases in which it had been held that a charge of fraud prevents privilege. Kekewich J rejected that argument. He said ([1895] 2 Ch 751 at 755):

> '... where there is anything of an underhand nature or approaching to fraud, especially in commercial matters, where there should be the veriest good faith, the whole transaction should be ripped up and disclosed in all its nakedness to the light of the Court ... Then it is alleged that the company was insolvent, and that they found it useless for them to continue to carry on business and they had to stop, but that in order to prevent for a time this inevitable result they gave a charge in favour of their agents, and, as the plaintiff alleges, they did it in such a way as to defeat the holders of first debentures. That is what I understand the plaintiff's case to be, and it is said that is not a charge of fraud. It is difficult to say it is not commercial dishonesty. It is, in my opinion, commercial dishonesty of the very worst type; and that is fraud.'

The question whether a communication between a legal adviser and his client could be displaced or breached on this ground was first considered by the House of Lords in *Bullivant v A-G for Victoria* [1901] AC 196, [1900–3] All ER Rep 812. The case arose on an application to examine witnesses in England. The Attorney General for Victoria claimed that voluntary conveyances had been executed by a testator to evade the payment of the colonial equivalent of estate duty, and sought from the solicitor who had prepared the conveyances notes and records of his instructions. Under the colonial Act (the Administration and Probate Act 1890) it was provided that, if property had been conveyed with intent to evade the payment of duty, the property conveyed should be treated as part of the estate of the disponor on his death. The decision of the House of Lords was that it could not be said that an outright conveyance executed in order to ensure that the property conveyed was outside the scope of the charge to duty had been executed with intent to evade the payment of duty, a proposition which, to the modern reader, occasions no surprise.

However, the Earl of Halsbury LC made some important observations as to the circumstances in which the court is entitled to require production of communications passing between client and his legal adviser. He said ([1901] AC 196 at 201, [1900–3] All ER Rep 812 at 814):

> '... if it is sufficient for the party demanding the production to say, as a mere surmise or conjecture, that the thing which he is so endeavouring to inquire into may have been illegal or not, the privilege in all cases disappears at once. The line which the Courts have hitherto taken, and I hope will preserve, is this—that in order to displace the primâ facie right of silence by a witness who has been put in the relation of professional confidence with his client, before that confidence can be broken you must have some definite charge either by way of allegation or affidavit or what not. I do not at present go into the modes by which that can be made out, but there must be some definite charge of something which displaces the privilege.'

The question came before the House of Lords again in *O'Rourke v Darbishire* [1920] AC 581, [1920] All ER Rep 1. The plaintiff claimed as heiress-at-law of one of the next of kin of a testator. The claim was that the residuary estate which had been given to his executors subject to precatory provisions was not disposed of by the testator's will either because it had been the subject of a secret trust which was void for uncertainty or as contravening the Mortmain Acts or, alternatively, that the disposition in favour of the

executors had been procured by fraud. In the Court of Appeal Bankes LJ said of this last
claim ([1919] 1 Ch 320 at 336):

> 'The statement of claim in the present case does not allege any definite charge of
> fraud. It is manifest, in my view, that the pleader had no materials before him
> which would enable him to state definitely what was the fraud complained of.'

Scrutton LJ described the pleading in that case in even more damning terms (at 346–
347):

> 'It is a pleading obviously framed to take the benefit of anything that may turn
> up, without any clear idea of the case which the plaintiff is alleging. The pleader
> charges either that there was a secret trust which was never defined, or that there
> was a secret trust which was defined, or that there was no secret trust at all; and
> whichever it was it was a fraudulent device for appropriating to the use of the
> executors a large portion of the estate . . .'

It is important to bear in mind the flimsy nature of the claim when considering the
observations in the Court of Appeal and in the House of Lords relied on by counsel for
the third to eleventh defendants. Bankes LJ rejected a submission that a mere allegation
of fraud in a statement of claim is sufficient to induce the court to refuse to recognise a
claim for privilege and added (at 336):

> 'I do not think that there can be any general rule on this matter. Each case must
> depend upon its own circumstances. There may be cases in which the mere
> allegation in the statement of claim is sufficient. On the other hand there may be
> cases in which the statement of claim or other document relied upon, when looked
> at, will indicate that the case made is a mere fishing case, what I may call a bow
> drawn at a venture; that it is a mere pleader's statement put forward in the hope
> that it may result in permission being given to inspect all documents in the
> possession of the other side and that some materials may be discovered on which to
> found a case.'

Scrutton LJ said (at 347):

> 'Therefore, while it is, in my view, impossible to lay down any fixed rule as to
> when the Court should, or when it should not, order disclosure, this I think is clear,
> that the mere fact that there is an allegation of fraud in the pleadings should not of
> itself render it a matter of course to order disclosure of documents which may be
> material to the allegation. I hesitate to state in any way the exact amount of evidence
> which the Court should require, but I think that the Court should be satisfied in
> cases which involve any extensive disclosure that the plaintiff has some prima facie
> case, or some substantial reason for thinking that, though he has not in his possession
> evidence, there is in the possession of the defendant evidence which supports his
> case, and that in cases where the Court is not satisfied that the plaintiff is in that
> position it should not order discovery until the plaintiff satisfies the Court that he is
> in that position.'

In the House of Lords, Lord Finlay said ([1920] AC 581 at 604, [1920] All ER Rep 1 at 6):

> 'The statement must be made in clear and definite terms, and there must further
> be some prima facie evidence that it has some foundation in fact.'

Lord Sumner, on whose speech counsel for the third to eleventh defendants places
particular reliance, said ([1920] AC 581 at 613–614, [1920] All ER Rep 1 at 10–11):

> 'No one doubts again that you can neither try out the issue in the action on a mere
> interlocutory proceeding, nor require the claimant to carry the issue raised to a
> successful trial before he can obtain production of documents which are only

relevant to that issue and only sought for the purpose of proving it. I am, however, sure that it is equally clear in principle that no mere allegation of fraud, even though *a* made in the most approved form of pleading, will suffice in itself to overcome a claim of professional privilege, properly formulated . . . The imperfections of his pleadings or the dubious character of his procedure in the action may militate against the claimant's case. The fact that a motion to strike out his pleading has been made and has failed, does not establish that he has a sufficient prima facie case for this purpose. The stage in the action is only an interlocutory one, and the materials *b* must be weighed, such as they are, without the apparatus of a formal trial of an issue. On such materials the Court must judge whether the claim of privilege is displaced or not.'

Lord Parmoor posed the question whether such a prima facie case of a definite character has in some way been brought to the notice of court so as to justify the court in holding that the appellant has the ordinary right of production of documents relating to *c* his case. He said ([1920] AC 581 at 623, [1920] All ER Rep 1 at 15):

'Whether the circumstances brought to the notice of the Court in a particular case are sufficiently explicit to establish a prima facie case of definite fraud, either by allegation, affidavit, or in some other way, will depend on the special facts in each case: *Reg. v. Cox* ((1884) 14 QBD 153, [1881–5] All ER Rep 68). But something *d* more is required than mere pleading, or than mere surmise and conjecture. If in the present appeal there is disclosed a real prima facie case of definite fraud, this must be found in the allegations contained in the pleadings and particulars, seeing that there had been no affidavit, and no information from any other source.'

Lord Wrenbury expressed this test in the following terms ([1920] AC 581 at 632, *e* [1920] All ER Rep 1 at 19):

'. . . the plaintiff must . . . go at any rate so far as to satisfy the Court that his allegations of fraud are not merely the bold assertions of a reckless pleader, but are such as to be regarded seriously as constituting prima facie a case of fraud resting on solid grounds.'

He elaborated this test later in a passage I should read in full. After citing this passage in *f* the speech of Lord Halsbury LC in *Bullivant's* case that I have cited, he said ([1920] AC 581 at 633, [1920] All ER Rep 1 at 20):

'If I may venture to express this in my own words I should say that to obtain discovery on the ground of fraud the plaintiff must show to the satisfaction of the Court good ground for saying that prima facie a state of things exists which, if not *g* displaced at the trial, will support a charge of fraud. This may be done in various ways—admissions on the pleadings of facts which go to show fraud—affidavits in some interlocutory proceedings which go to show fraud—possibly even without admission or affidavit allegations of facts which, if not disputed or met by other facts, would lead a reasonable person to see, at any rate, a strong probability that *h* there was fraud, may be taken by the Court to be sufficient. Every case must be decided on its merits.'

It is, I think, only necessary to refer to three of the many subsequent authorities on this point. In *Crescent Farm (Sidcup) Sports Ltd v Sterling Offices Ltd* [1971] 3 All ER 1192, [1972] Ch 553 the plaintiff sought to extend the principle on which the courts have held that privilege does not attach to communications between a party and his solicitor for *j* the purpose of obtaining advice in furtherance of a fraud to cover an alleged conspiracy to induce a breach of contract. Goff J said ([1971] 3 All ER 1192 at 1200, [1972] Ch 553 at 565):

'. . . I think the wide submission of the plaintiffs would endanger the whole basis

of legal professional privilege. It is clear that parties must be at liberty to take advice
as to the ambit of their contractual obligations and liabilities in tort and what
liability they will incur whether in contract or tort by a proposed course of action
without thereby in every case losing professional privilege. I agree that fraud in this
connection is not limited to the tort of deceit and includes all forms of fraud and
dishonesty such as fraudulent breach of trust, fraudulent conspiracy, trickery and
sham contrivances, but I cannot feel that the tort of inducing a breach of contract or
the narrow form of conspiracy pleaded in this case come within that ambit.'

The scope of the exception from legal professional privilege was also considered in a
decision of the Court of Appeal in an interlocutory application in the well-known *Rochem*
litigation, *Gamlen Chemical Co (UK) Ltd v Rochem Ltd (No 2)* (1979) 124 SJ 276, a transcript
of the judgments in which are before me. In that case it was admitted that in the case of
one transaction the plaintiffs had sufficiently established on the pleadings and on the
plaintiffs' unanswered affidavit evidence that the defendant had been guilty of fraud.
The Court of Appeal also held more generally that the plaintiffs had sufficiently
established that the defendants were senior employees who had used their employer's
time and money to prosecute their own interests and to organise a competing business.
Having referred to the passage in the judgment of Kekewich J in *Williams v Quebrada
Railway Land and Copper Co* [1895] 2 Ch 751 at 755 and to his own judgment in the
Crescent Farm Sports case, which I have cited, and having held that what had taken place
fell well within the word 'trickery', Goff LJ cited and approved a passage in the judgment
of Goulding J in the court below, where Goulding J said:

'For servants during their employment and in breach of their contractual duty of
fidelity to their master to engage in a scheme, secretly using the master's time and
money, to take the master's customers and employees and make profit from them
in a competing business built up to receive themselves on leaving the master's
service, I would have thought that commercial men and lawyers alike would say
that that is fraud.'

Goff LJ added:

'Where you draw the line in the infinite gradation of good and evil between
Williams's case (Kekewich J) and the *Crescent Farm Sports* case . . . I do not attempt to
say, but I have no doubt the present case is on the same side as *Williams*'s case and
that discovery ought to be given . . . I wish only to add two further observations.
First the court must in every case, of course, be satisfied that what is prima facie
proved really is dishonest, and not merely disreputable or a failure to maintain good
ethical standards and must bear in mind that legal professional privilege is a very
necessary thing and is not lightly to be overthrown, but on the other hand the
interests of victims of fraud must not be overlooked. Each case depends on its own
facts.'

Templeman LJ stated the test in the following way:

'In the light of the existing evidence, and without knowing if, at the trial, that
evidence will be disproved, we must, adopting the words of Stephen J, determine
whether it seems probable that the defendants may have consulted their legal
advisers before the commission of fraud and for the purpose of being guided and
helped wittingly or unwittingly in committing the fraud. A fortiori, if the
defendants embarked on a fraudulent activity, communications between the
defendants and the solicitors made in the course of that activity cannot be entitled
to privilege and must be disclosed so that, in the words of Kekewich J, quoted by
Goff LJ, "the whole transaction shall be ripped up and disclosed in all its nakedness
to the light of the Court".'

Lastly, in one of the interlocutory applications in the very complex case of *Buttes Gas and Oil Co v Hammer (No 3)* [1980] 3 All ER 475, [1981] QB 223 a claim was made to a displace legal professional privilege. Lord Denning MR, having described the scope of the professional privilege and before turning to examine the categories of documents in which privilege had been claimed, said ([1980] 3 All ER 475 at 486, [1981] QB 223 at 246):

> 'No privilege can be invoked so as to cover up fraud or iniquity. But this principle b must not be carried too far. No person faced with an allegation of fraud could safely ask for legal advice. To do away with the privilege at the discovery stage there must be strong evidence of fraud such that the court can say: "This is such an obvious fraud that he should not be allowed to shelter behind the cloak of privilege."'

Donaldson LJ cited a passage of McNeill J in the court below where he described the allegations of fraud as— c

> 'no more than the key to an intended fishing operation, to be carried out in the hope that discovery of otherwise privileged documents will produce some peg on which the defendants could seek to justify and to sustain the counterclaim.'

He added ([1980] 3 All ER 475 at 490, [1981] QB 223 at 252): d

> 'I respectfully agree and find it unnecessary to express any view on how strong a prima facie case of fraud is necessary to defeat a claim for disclosure based on legal professional privilege, but something exceptional is called for.'

Counsel for the third to eleventh defendants also referred me to the decision of the Court of Appeal in *Bankers Trust Co v Shapira* [1980] 3 All ER 353, [1980] 1 WLR 1274, where the plaintiffs sought disclosure of confidential banker/customer information on e an interlocutory application. He relied in particular on the observation of Waller LJ where he said ([1980] 3 All ER 353 at 358, [1980] 1 WLR 1274 at 1283):

> 'Clearly it is undesirable that an order such as this should be lightly made. But the answer to this part of [the submission of counsel for the bank against which the discovery was sought], in my judgment, is that here there is very strong evidence f indeed of fraud on the part of the other two defendants . . .'

The first two defendants had not entered an appearance and were charged in the proceedings with having perpetrated a plain fraud on the plaintiff bank. Counsel submitted that the test to be applied where a plaintiff attacks a claim for legal professional privilege on the ground of fraud must be at least as stringent. However, Nicholls LJ in *Derby & Co Ltd v Weldon (No 1)* [1989] 1 All ER 469 at 480, [1990] Ch 48 at 64 had the g *Bankers Trust* case in mind when he declined to interfere with the tracing order made by Mervyn Davies J and must, I think, have taken the view that the plaintiffs' case met the test stated by Waller LJ. The pleadings and other materials that have come into existence and have come to light since then have certainly not weakened the plaintiffs' case.

As I have said, counsel's primary submission was that the authorities (and, in deference to his argument, I have referred to all the authorities he relied on on this point) showed h that unless the relevant facts are admitted or beyond dispute, as they were in *Williams v Quebrada Railway Land and Copper Co* [1895] 2 Ch 751, there must be positive evidence sufficient to satisfy the court on the balance of probabilities that an allegation of fraud will probably succeed. I think this puts the test too high. In all the cases I have cited what is stressed is that every case must be judged on its own facts. In any given case, the court j must weigh, on the one hand, the important considerations of public policy on which legal professional privilege is founded (the necessity that the citizen should be able to make a clean breast to his legal adviser: see *Anderson v Bank of British Columbia* (1876) 2 Ch D 644 at 649 per Jessel MR) and, on the other, the gravity of the charge of fraud or dishonesty that is made. There are many contexts in which the court similarly has to a strike a balance between the need to do justice to the plaintiff, on the one hand, and, on the other, the extent to which interlocutory relief may result in an unjustified interference with the defendant's property and his right to privacy. The point at which the balance is struck must depend on the extent to which the relief sought may unjustifiably invade the defendant's rights. So, if a plaintiff can show that he has a fairly arguable case and if the defendant can be fully protected by a cross-undertaking in damages, the court in granting or refusing a purely negative injunction will be primarily concerned with a

b balance of convenience. More is required (in ascending order of importance) if the plaintiff seeks a mandatory injunction or a negative injunction which, in the words of Hoffmann J, may have 'intrusive' effect (see *Films Rover International Ltd v Cannon Film Sales Ltd* [1986] 3 All ER 772 at 781, [1987] 1 WLR 670 at 681), or if the plaintiff seeks Mareva relief or an Anton Piller order or the disclosure of confidential banking documents.

c There is a continuous spectrum and it is impossible to, as it were, calibrate or express in any simple formula the strength of the case that the plaintiff must show in each of these categories. An order to disclose documents for which legal professional privilege is claimed lies at the extreme end of the spectrum. Such an order will only be made in very exceptional circumstances but it is, I think, too restrictive to say that the plaintiff's case must always be founded on an admission or supported by affidavit evidence or that the

d court must carry out the preliminary exercise of deciding on the material before it whether the plaintiff's case will probably succeed, a task which may well present insurmountable difficulties in a case where fraud is alleged and the court has no more than affidavit evidence.

Both Lord Parmoor and Lord Wrenbury in *O'Rourke v Darbishire* [1920] AC 581 at 623, 632–635, [1920] All ER Rep 1 at 15, 19–20 contemplated that allegations in a

e statement of claim, apart from any other source of information, might in themselves be sufficiently explicit to negative the claim for professional privilege. That might, as I see it, be the case if the statement of claim set out allegations of misconduct with very great particularity and if the defence was couched in very general terms and was unsupported by affidavit or other admissible evidence. But no clear line can be drawn. All that can be said is that all the circumstances must be taken into account and that the court will be

f very slow to deprive a defendant of the important protection of legal professional privilege on an interlocutory application.

Turning to the material before the court in the instant case, the claim that Mr Weldon and Mr Jay and, through them, CMI, became constructive trustees of, in particular, the profits made by CMFE on forex deals with one or more of the plaintiffs is, prima facie, a strong one. It is not in dispute that CMFE made large profits on forex deals with one or

g other of the plaintiffs. It is not in dispute that Mr Weldon and Mr Jay were directors and, in some instances, employees of the plaintiff companies concerned. It is not in dispute that, if Mr Weldon and Mr Jay had interests in CMFE which required to be disclosed, those interests were not in fact disclosed.

Three defences are relied on. The first is that Mr Weldon and Mr Jay had no interest

h in CMFE which required to be disclosed. As to that, it is not now in dispute that the ultimate owner of CMFE was the stiftung and that Mr Weldon was a beneficiary, if not the primary beneficiary, of the trust on which the assets of the stiftung were held. Mervyn Davies J and Sir Nicolas Browne-Wilkinson V-C have also expressed disquiet at different times at the extent to which Mr Weldon appears to be able to influence, if not control, the acts of CMI and the stiftung. The evidence as to the role of Mr Weldon in

j the creation of the new trusts and the transfer of assets to them reinforces the inference that he was able to control the acts of the stiftung.

The second defence is that the defendants had some general authority to deal with the plaintiffs through companies in which they were interested and were not bound to disclose any indirect interest through the stiftung.

The third defence is that the profits on the forex deals were made at the expense of

banks through which the deals were backed. It may be that these defences will succeed
at the trial but the burden will be on the defendants to establish them. On the material   *a*
before the court the plaintiffs have, in my judgment, established a strong prima facie
case of fraud in relation to the profits made by CMFE.

Counsel for the third to eleventh defendants submitted that there is no foundation for
the claim that the creation of the new trusts and the transfer of assets to them were steps
taken in furtherance of the initial fraud. The ground of this submission, as I understand
it, is that these steps were not in contemplation when the initial fraud was committed.   *b*
In my judgment, that involves reading the words 'in furtherance of' too narrowly. These
steps were taken in furtherance of the initial fraud in that they were taken to conceal and
render irrecoverable profits to which the plaintiffs asserted a proprietary claim. Moreover,
these steps, even if taken in isolation from the initial fraud, were, in my judgment,
themselves so dishonest as to negate the claim for professional legal privilege. They
involved, in the words of Goff J in the *Crescent Farm Sports* case, 'trickery and sham   *c*
contrivances'. The sale of the shares of Pilgrim at a price equal to the nominal amount of
the subscribed capital, and the destruction of files that would have revealed the true
nature of the assets of that company, and the later assertions by Mr Weldon that he had
no interest under any trusts except the stiftung and that the assets of the stiftung
amounted to £30m or £40m, in my judgment, themselves amount to trickery and sham
contrivance within this rule. These steps were taken to defeat or delay a proprietary claim   *d*
asserted by the plaintiffs. In my judgment, these facts alone would justify the conclusion
that legal advice sought in furtherance of a scheme to conceal these assets is not entitled
to the protection of legal professional privilege.

Finally, counsel submitted that a distinction must be drawn between the initial
constitution of the trusts and the transfer of assets to them. That distinction seems to me
entirely unreal. The trusts simply reproduce the trust affecting the assets of the stiftung.   *e*
They were created for the sole purpose of receiving and concealing assets of the stiftung.

I do not underestimate the importance of the privilege attaching to documents which
came into existence in the course of obtaining legal advice. However, in my judgment,
the plaintiffs have established clear grounds for the disclosure which they seek. There is
one qualification. The plaintiffs are not entitled to disclosure of any documents which
fall under a different head of privilege: legal advice obtained and documents coming into   *f*
existence for the dominant purpose of being used in pending or contemplated
proceedings. The order sought must be amended to exclude this category of documents.
Counsel submitted that the disclosure should be limited to the steps actually taken in the
preparation of or in the course of transferring assets to the trustees of the new trusts. I
think that might be too restrictive. I think the right course is to make the order sought,
with the qualification I have explained, and to give the defendants liberty to apply to   *g*
exclude any document or class of documents which may fall within the terms of the
order of disclosure but which they consider to fall outside the scope of the principles I
have explained.

The second issue   *h*
In these applications the plaintiffs make a further claim. It is that the first five
defendants should file further lists identifying in the case of documents for which
professional privilege is claimed 'with full particularity the circumstances alleged to give
rise to such a claim'. The claim for privilege made in Mr Weldon's and Mr Jay's list is in
usual form and refers to:

j
> '. . . confidential correspondence, both original and copies, memoranda of
> instructions, opinions and other documents and notes of meetings and telephone
> conversations between the First and Second Defendants, their solicitors and Counsel
> and other legal advisers, or any of them, and drafts of the same for the purpose of
> obtaining legal advice.'

The claim for privilege in the list of the third to fifth defendants is in similar terms,
a except that it refers to 'correspondence for the purpose of obtaining legal advice' but does
not add the qualification that the documents must be confidential.

Counsel for the plaintiffs referred me to the decision of Eveleigh J in *Alfred Crompton
Amusement Machines Ltd v Customs and Excise Comrs* [1971] 2 All ER 843 esp at 847–848.
Eveleigh J cited a passage in the decision of Cotton LJ in *Gardner v Irvin* (1878) 4 Ex D 49
at 53, where Cotton LJ said:

b   'An affidavit in answer to an application for discovery must be construed strictly,
because the other side cannot adduce evidence to contradict it. The person seeking
discovery is bound by the affidavit made by his opponent, and therefore it ought to
be full. It is not sufficient for the affidavits to say that the letters are a correspondence
between a client and his solicitor, the letters must be professional communications
of a confidential character for the purpose of getting legal advice. I think that the
c   plaintiffs are not entitled to have the dates of the letters and such other particulars
of the correspondence as may enable them to discover indirectly the contents of the
letters, and thus to cause the defendants to furnish evidence against themselves in
this action.'

Eveleigh J commented:
d
        'However, the opening two sentences demonstrate the need for the affidavit to be
specific, particularly so that the nature of the privilege claimed can be ascertained.
There are a variety of situations which can give rise to a claim for privilege. Which
situation is relied on must be clearly stated in relation to the particular document,
or to the type or class of documents alleged to be protected.'

e   Counsel for the plaintiffs submitted that the claims for professional privilege which I
have cited, though they may be sufficient in a straightforward case, do not in the context
of this case sufficiently identify the categories of document for which privilege is claimed
or the circumstances relied on as giving rise to that claim. He accepted that the plaintiffs
are not entitled to any information which might lead by a process of inference to a
conclusion as to the probable nature or content of the advice sought. But he submitted
f that the plaintifffs are entitled to know at least the identity of the persons or firms from
whom advice was sought, the time when it was sought and, subject to the qualification I
have explained, the category of advice sought.

It is important that the observations of Eveleigh J should be read in the context of the
very special facts of that case. Discovery was sought in the course of an arbitration under
s 36 of the Purchase Tax Act 1963. Privilege was claimed in part 2 of schedule 1 to the
g commissioners' list in respect of two distinct categories of documents. The first, sub-para
(a), comprised correspondence between the commissioners and their solicitors in their
professional capacity. I will call that 'the first head'. The second, sub-para (b), comprised
documents prepared or obtained by the commissioners' solicitors for the purpose of
providing information or evidence for use in the arbitration or to uncover sources of
h evidence or for use in deciding whether to prosecute the arbitration and to advise the
commissioners in relation to it. I will call that 'the second head'. The commissioner also
claimed in part 3 of schedule 1 the protection of Crown or public interest privilege.

The claim for privilege under the first head was not challenged before Eveleigh J. The
relevant part of his judgment is concerned with the claim under the second head. It is in
the context of that claim that Eveleigh J made the observation I have cited. He came to
j the conclusion that, for reasons which it is unnecessary to detail, the manner in which
the claim for privilege had been made, in the wording of the list and the affidavit, was
unsatisfactory and equivocal. Again I stress that the reference to legal privilege is to the
privilege claimed under the second head.

The commissioners prepared a further affidavit of documents, again in part 2 of
schedule 1. The claim was made under these two heads. Paragraph (a) repeated para (a)

of the earlier list. It may have been slightly elaborated but there is no distinction in principle. Paragraph (b) was framed in a less confusing way to meet the criticism made *a* by Eveleigh J. The claim for Crown or public interest privilege was again set out in part 3 of schedule 1. These claims for privilege were challenged in a summons taken out by the plaintiff and the summons came on before Forbes J, Eveleigh J being on circuit.

Matters then took an unexpected turn. Forbes J took the view that the commissioners were not entitled to claim legal professional privilege under the first head for communications between the commissioners and their own internal legal advisers. *b* Privilege could be claimed for such communications only under the second head, if and in so far as applicable. It is not clear to me that the plaintiffs in fact challenged or could have challenged the claim for privilege under the first head. This claim had been conceded before Eveleigh J and the further affidavit and lists were designed to meet his criticism of the claim under the second head. But, be that as it may, the Court of Appeal allowed an appeal against the decision of Forbes J.   *c*

In my judgment, on analysis, the *Crompton Amusement Machines* case does not assist the plaintiffs.

Nor, I think, is the plaintiffs' case assisted by the decision of the Court of Appeal in *Gardner v Irvin* (1878) 4 Ex D 49. In that case the defendants made an affidavit in which they stated boldly that they objected to the production of documents set out in the second part of their schedule of documents and that one reason for objecting was that the same *d* were privileged. The documents in the second part of the schedule were a mixed bag and included in addition to correspondence between 'ourselves and our solicitors', 'cash books, ledgers and accounts'. The affidavit was plainly insufficient since it did not segregate the different categories of documents or set out the ground on which privilege was claimed. Cotton LJ, immediately before the passage cited by Eveleigh J in the *Crompton Amusement Machines* case [1971] 2 All ER 843 at 847–848, said (4 Ex D 49 at 53):   *e*

> 'How can it be said that this affidavit is sufficient; in the body of the affidavit the defendants simply say "that the same are privileged," and in the schedule they set out the documents, some of which clearly are not privileged. They ought to say not only that the documents are privileged, which is a statement of law, but they ought to set out the facts from which we can see that the defendants' view of the law is *f* right. Cash-books and ledgers primâ facie are not privileged.'

It is also significant that Cotton LJ in the passage which Eveleigh J does cite refers to the correspondence in respect of which professional privilege could have been claimed in these terms (4 Ex D 49 at 53):

> '. . . the letters must be professional communications of a confidential character *g* for the purpose of getting legal advice.'

That formula is, of course, the one that was used in para (a) of the second part of the schedule in the *Crompton Amusement Machines* case and the formula used in the lists of Mr Weldon and Mr Jay. It is the formula by which legal professional privilege is normally claimed. It is also significant that in *Gardner v Irvin* 4 Ex D 49 at 51 counsel for the *h* plaintiffs had claimed that:

> '. . . the plaintiffs are entitled to have the dates and addresses of the letters, in order to judge whether they were confidential communications between the defendants and their solicitors in their character of solicitors, and whether it was with reference to this litigation.'

j

That argument was clearly rejected by Cotton LJ in the passage cited by Eveleigh J.

It is also clear from an earlier decision of the Court of Appeal that a party claiming legal professional privilege under either head cannot be required to give the dates and addresses of letters so that the other party can judge whether privilege is properly

claimed. That is the decision of the Court of Appeal in *Taylor v Batten* (1878) 4 QBD 85,
a which was decided a few weeks before *Gardner v Irvin* (1878) 4 Ex D 49, and in which
Cotton LJ gave the judgment of the court. The facts are set out in a passage in the
judgment of Cotton LJ which I will read in full (4 QBD 85 at 87):

> 'The plaintiff in this action called on the defendant to make an affidavit of
> documents in his possession. The first affidavit made by the defendant was clearly
> insufficient; the plaintiff applied for and obtained a further affidavit, and the
b > question is whether that second affidavit was sufficient. The question arises as to
> documents, for which privilege was claimed on the ground that they consist of
> correspondence with the defendant's legal advisers, cases for the opinion of counsel
> and counsel's opinion. There is no question as to the first affidavit, it was clearly
> insufficient; it ran thus: "I have also in my possession or power certain documents,
> letters, and correspondence, which have passed between my legal advisers and
c > myself in relation to the matters in queston in this case, and with a view to my
> defence to the plaintiff's claim, and certain instructions to and opinions of counsel
> in relation to the same matters, all of which I claim to be privileged from
> production." This is clearly insufficient, as it only describes the documents as
> "certain documents, letters," &c., without any further identification. In the further
d > affidavit, the second paragraph is as follows: "The documents referred to in paragraph
> 2 of my former affidavit are numbered 50 to 76 inclusive, and are tied up in a
> bundle marked with the letter A and initialed by me."'

The requirement that the documents should be tied up in a numbered bundle is
surprising to modern eyes. The explanation is that it was the practice of the Court of
Equity when exercising its auxiliary jurisdiction to assist parties in litigation in the
e common law courts by making orders for discovery to require them to be identified so
that the court could order production of any which the other party wished to see. That
was done by tying them up in bundles and numbering the bundles. The practice is fully
explained in *Bray on Discovery* (1885) p 485 and in *Daniell's Chancery Practice* (8th edn,
1914) vol 1, p 591. Moreover, at that time the grounds on which privilege could be
claimed were more extensive than now. In particular a party did not have to disclose
f documents which supported his own but did not assist the other party's case. The extent
of the documents for which privilege was claimed might not in all cases be sufficiently
clear from the grounds on which the privilege was claimed to enable the court to order
disclosure.

That historical background must be borne in mind when considering the principle
laid down by Cotton LJ where he said (4 QBD 85 at 88):
g
> 'But it is said that the plaintiffs are entitled to be put in such a position as to test
> the truth of the affidavit by the description of the documents. That, however, is, in
> our opinion, erroneous. The only object of the affidavit is to enable the Court to
> order the documents to be produced, if it thinks fit to make an order to that effect;
> and if words are used which, if true, protect the documents, no further particularity
h > is necessary than in the case of documents for which protection is not claimed. If an
> affidavit claiming protection for documents some of which are, while others are
> not, privileged did not sufficiently shew which were entitled to protection, the
> Court would either order production of all or, as under ordinary circumstances
> would be the proper course, allow the party an opportunity of making a further
> affidavit to identify the documents entitled to protection.'

j The purpose of bundling or numbering documents for which privilege was claimed
was to enable the court to make an order for production if it was later held that the party
claiming privilege had erroneously represented or misconceived the claim. He was not
required to give the date or heading or any description of each document or, in the case

of a letter, the addressee. That was made clear in two cases decided shortly before *Taylor v Batten*, namely *Taylor v Oliver* (1876) 34 LT 902 and *Kain v Farrer* (1877) 37 LT 469. If *a* a document is privileged, the whole of it is privileged.

Where privilege is claimed for professional communications of a confidential character obtained for the purpose of getting legal advice, it has not in modern times been the practice to require the party claiming privilege to bundle and number them. The claim for privilege is treated as itself a sufficient description of them.

Counsel for the plaintiffs submitted that this general rule should be departed from in *b* the instant case on three grounds. The first is that the case is one of exceptional complexity in which wide ranging issues are raised and which has called for discovery on an unprecedented scale. I cannot, for my part, see that the complexity of the issues and the scale of discovery have any relevance.

The second is that the evidence shows that the lawyers, in particular foreign lawyers, have been employed to do work which is not strictly within the scope of legal professional *c* privilege. The plaintiffs are entitled to satisfy themselves, by means of a fuller description of the documents for which the privilege is claimed, that it is not claimed for documents outside its proper scope. The answer to that submission is to be found in the correspondence. In a letter of 20 December 1989 Lovell White Durrant, writing to Allen & Overy, say:

> 'In view of the extensive use of lawyers by the First and Second Defendants as *d* business intermediaries and nominees, the question of identifying the precise scope of what is and what is not privileged is more complex than in a straightforward case.'

And then, having referred to what is said at an earlier stage, they continue:

> '. . . you agreed that as far as you were able you would specifically describe the *e* papers of your clients which were in the files of Johnson Stokes & Master in a separate part of the List specifically designated for that purpose; unfortunately, you appear not to have done so. The claim for privilege which is made in your clients' List of Documents is very general and, therefore, too vague in the circumstances of the dealings by the Defendants.'   *f*

Allen & Overy, replying on 29 December, confirmed that the expression 'legal advice' is not used in their list of documents to 'embrace administrative functions regarding the running of the various companies and trusts', and that all documents for which legal professional privilege is claimed under either head 'were carefully considered by this firm and counsel before a claim to privilege was made'.

A similar letter was sent to Hopkins & Wood on 27 December. In their reply they say: *g*

> 'We and our Counsel have been through the documents in respect of which privilege has been claimed and are satisfied that in each case there is a valid claim to privilege.'

The plaintiffs, in my opinion, are clearly not entitled to go behind these assurances. It *h* is important, as Hamilton LJ observed in *Birmingham and Midland Motor Omnibus Co Ltd v London and North Western Rly Co* [1913] 3 KB 850 at 860 (in a passage also cited by Eveleigh J in the *Crompton Amusement Machines* case) that a claim for privilege should not be treated as if it were 'pronouncing a spell, which, once uttered, makes all the documents taboo'. It is, I think, for that reason, better that the claim should state that the documents for which privilege is claimed are described as confidential communications passing *j* between the client and his legal advisers for the purposes of obtaining legal advice, even though that formula may appear to be pleonastic and was treated as such by Allen & Overy when they omitted the word 'confidential'. But in this case the formula was not treated as a mere incantation.

Counsel's third ground was that it has been shown that privilege was not properly

claimed in respect of the documents the disclosure of which I have directed in the earlier
a part of this judgment. But, in my judgment, it would be contrary to the public policy
on which the privilege is founded to compel disclosure of all documents passing between
a party and his legal advisers once it has been shown that in relation to one transaction
the advice was sought in furtherance of a fraud. In my judgment, therefore, the plaintiffs
are not entitled to the leave sought on this part of their application.

b *Order for disclosure granted. Further particularisation of claim to privilege refused.*

Solicitors: *Lovell White Durrant* (for the plaintiffs); *Hopkins & Wood* (for the first and
second defendants); *Allen & Overy* (for the third to eleventh defendants).

Jacqueline Metcalfe   Barrister.

c

R v Hancock

d COURT OF APPEAL, CRIMINAL DIVISION
WATKINS LJ, TUDOR EVANS AND AULD JJ
19 JUNE, 24 JULY 1989

*Criminal law – Theft – Treasure trove – Theft of treasure trove – Whether for jury to decide if
property is treasure trove – Whether coroner's inquest necessary – Burden and standard of proof.*

e
On a charge of theft of treasure trove it is for the jury to determine as part of the issue of
the defendant's guilt or innocence whether the property in question was in fact deposited
by someone who intended to retrieve it and is thus treasure trove which is the property
of the Crown. In determining that issue the jury are required to apply the ordinary
criminal burden and standard of proof and may only convict if they are sure that the
f property is treasure trove and not if there is merely a real possibility that it might be, and
they should be directed accordingly (see p 188 e f and p 189 d to f, post).
    Since it is not necessary for the offence of theft that the property alleged to have been
stolen was in the actual or constructive possession of the owner at the time of the
appropriation, a coroner's inquest to establish that the property is treasure trove is no
longer a prerequisite for bringing a charge of theft of treasure trove (see p 188 j, post); *R
g v Toole* (1867) 16 WR 439 considered.

Notes
For inquests on treasure trove, see 9 Halsbury's Laws (4th edn) paras 1177–1178, and for
cases on the subject, see 11 Digest (Reissue) 784, 943–944.

h **Cases referred to in judgment**
A-G v Moore [1893] 1 Ch 676, [1891–4] All ER Rep 880.
A-G v Trustees of the British Museum [1903] 2 Ch 598.
A-G of the Duchy of Lancaster v G E Overton (Farms) Ltd [1982] 1 All ER 524, [1982] Ch 277,
    [1982] 2 WLR 397, CA.
j *King's Prerogative in Saltpetre* (1606) 12 Co Rep 12, 77 ER 1294.
R v Church (1845) 5 LTOS 314.
R v Ghosh [1982] 2 All ER 689, [1982] QB 1053, [1982] 3 WLR 110, CA.
R v Roberts (1985) 84 Cr App R 117, CA.
R v Thomas (1863) Le & Ca 313, 169 ER 1409, CCR.
R v Toole (1867) 16 WR 439, Ir CCR.

Appeal against conviction

Stephen Frederick Hancock appealed with the leave of the single judge against his conviction on 11 October 1988 in the Crown Court at Guildford before his Honour Judge Main QC and a jury of theft of treasure trove for which he was placed on probation for 12 months. The facts are set out in the judgment of the court.

Patrick Mullen (assigned by the Registrar of Criminal Appeals) for the appellant.
Jeremy Benson for the Crown.

Cur adv vult

24 July. The following judgment of the court was delivered.

AULD J. On 11 October 1988, before his Honour Judge Main QC in the Crown Court at Guildford, the appellant was convicted of theft, and on 8 November 1988 was placed on probation for 12 months. He appeals against conviction by leave of the single judge.

The case concerns the alleged theft of treasure trove, that is to say coin or other articles of gold or silver hidden at some time in the past by someone who intended to recover them and who, or whose successors, are unknown. Treasure trove belongs to the Crown.

The prosecution came about in the following circumstances. On 18 February 1988 the appellant, when being interviewed by the police about another matter, told them that he had found some ancient coins at a site in Wanborough, near Guildford. The coins, as the police later discovered, were Celtic silver coins which had been minted some time between 50 BC and AD 30. They are unique. No such coins have been found on any other site in this country. They are now in the British Museum. The Wanborough site appears to have been the site of a Romano-Celtic temple.

The appellant told the police that he had found the coins with the help of a metal detector and had dug them up. He claimed that when he had found them they were not altogether in one place, but scattered about. The significance of that for the purpose of the prosecution is that, if they had all been found together in one place, there was at least an inference that they had been deposited or hidden there at some distant time in the past by someone who intended to return and recover them. Where, as here, the coins were scattered about, it may suggest that the coins were dropped there at different times and by different people as sacrifices or votive offerings. In that event, they would be unlikely to be treasure trove. However, as the appellant acknowledged when being questioned by the police officers, the coins could have been deposited in one hoard and then scattered by ploughing over the centuries.

The appellant told the police that he had had earlier dealings with the Wanborough site and knew that the police had retained some coins recovered from it previously.

The police saw the appellant again about the matter on 18 March 1988. He told them this time exactly where on the site he had found the coins. He said that he had found them on the side of a footpath, known as Green Lane path, and by a hedge. He volunteered the view that because they came from the path that made his finding and keeping of them lawful. The police then asked him a number of questions about his story, but he refused to tell them any more.

After that interview the police and those now responsible for the prosecution obtained advice from the British Museum about the likely history and status of the coins. As a result they took the view that the coins when found by the appellant were treasure trove and, therefore, belonged to the Crown. They charged him with the theft of the coins from the Crown.

The evidence for the prosecution consisted of the police account of their two interviews with the appellant, the production of the coins, and evidence from Mr Kent, an expert from the British Museum. He expressed the opinion that a large number of the coins

had been deposited at one time because the older ones were much worn and the newer
ones were not. He said that if the coins had been deposited over a period of time he
would have expected all of them to have an average degree of wear. His view was that it
was at least possible that the coins had been deposited there by somebody who had
intended to retrieve them. He put it no higher than that.

The appellant gave evidence. Contrary to the account that he had given to the police,
he said that his father had given him the coins. He said that he had told the police that
he, the appellant, had dug them up because he had wanted to protect his father. His
father had apparently had some difficulties of his own over some coins that he had found
at the Wanborough site. The appellant said that after his first interview with the police,
on 18 February 1988, his father had told him to go back to the police and tell them the
truth, but that he had not done so. The appellant acknowledged that if he, the appellant,
had found the coins at the Wanborough site, he would have known from his experience
of treasure hunting and from his previous dealings with the site that he had a duty to
hand them in.

The appellant's father gave evidence, saying that he had obtained the coins from a man
in Charing Cross and had given them to his son. He said that he had told the appellant to
return to the police and tell them the truth. However, he said that that was after the
appellant's second interview with the police, the one on 18 March 1988, not the one on
18 February 1988.

Finally, Professor Collis of Sheffield University gave evidence for the defence. He said
that the Wanborough site appears to have been a religious site and that on such sites coins
and precious articles were often found, having been left there as sacrifices or votive
offerings by people who had no intention of returning to retrieve them.

The jury by their verdict of guilty clearly found that the appellant was lying in his
evidence to them that his father had given him the coins. As will appear, however, it
does not follow from their verdict that they were satisfied so as to be sure that the coins
were treasure trove and, on that basis, the property of the Crown.

The first ground of appeal is that the judge erred in directing the jury that they should
regard the coins as property belonging to the Crown if they were satisfied merely that
there was a real possibility that they might be found to be treasure trove.

The judge's direction to the jury on the law was as follows:

'I direct you as a matter of law that the Crown has a proprietary right or interest
in coins in the ground which may be treasure trove, which means that a person who
finds them and does not hand them in may well be guilty of theft, if the other
elements in the definition are satisfied. It follows that in this case it is not necessary
for the prosecution to prove that the coins which you are concerned with were
found to be treasure trove, or that they were bound to be found to be treasure trove
when the question was looked into. It is sufficient for the prosecution to prove that
the coins with which you are concerned, the property appropriated, was capable of
being found as treasure trove, because the Crown has an interest in the ascertainment
of the question whether such coins are treasure trove or not. The subsequent finding
of the coroner's jury . . . that these coins were in fact treasure trove is really neither
here nor there as far as you are concerned. It is a piece of knowledge which . . . does
not really decide the question which is whether the Crown was entitled to have
these coins in proper custody when they were found, until the coroner could
pronounce. The key to that is whether the circumstances were such that there was a
real possibility that the coins might be found to be treasure trove.'

Counsel for the appellant argued before us that the judge should have directed the
jury that, before they could convict, they had to be sure on the evidence before them that
the coins were treasure trove. On this argument the outcome of a coroner's inquest, if
any, into the matter is irrelevant, and it fell to the jury in the criminal proceedings to

determine whether they were sure that the coins were treasure trove at the time when
the appellant found them.

Counsel for the Crown submitted that, regardless of any final ruling on the status of
the coins, the Crown had a properietary right or interest in them when they were found
by the appellant, namely to have their status determined by a coroner's jury. He argued
that, unless such an intermediate right or interest is recognised by law, the Theft Act
1968 would give no protection to the Crown against the dishonest finder of treasure,
who appropriates it before its legal status has been determined. In so arguing counsel
placed much emphasis on the protection formerly given to the Crown by the old
common law offence of concealment of treasure trove, which was abolished by s 32(1)(a)
of the 1968 Act.

As we have already indicated, the Crown has a prerogative right to all treasure trove,
that is objects of gold or silver, or substantially of gold or silver, which were hidden by
their owner at some time with a view to later recovery, and where the owner or his
present heirs or successors are unknown: see *Jervis on Coroners* (10th edn, 1986) pp 231,
232, citing 3 Co Inst 132 and Chitty *Law of the Prerogatives of the Crown* p 152; see also *A-
G v Trustees of the British Museum* [1903] 2 Ch 598 at 608 per Farwell J, citing *Chitty* with
approval and *A-G of the Duchy of Lancaster v G E Overton (Farms) Ltd* [1982] 1 All ER 524,
[1982] Ch 277.

Thus, property is only capable of being treasure trove if its last owner left it, intending
to recover it. If he deliberately abandoned it or accidentally lost it, it is not treasure trove
(see *Jervis* p 232, citing *Chitty* p 152). If, as was the defence case here, silver coins were
buried at a religious site or burial ground as sacrifices or votive offerings, they are unlikely
to be treasure trove. We put it in that way because that is the view of twentieth century
commentators on the point: see *Jervis* p 232, footnote 12, the Law Commission's
publication *Treasure Trove: Law Reform Issues* (September 1987) p 3 and also because, in
the only authority drawn to our attention when the point was considered *A-G v Trustees
of the British Museum* [1903] 2 Ch 598 at 611, Farwell J expressly declined to rule whether
votive offerings could be treasure trove.

Certainly the trial appears to have been conducted by both parties on the basis that the
coins in question could not be treasure trove if they had been left at the Wanborough site
as sacrifices or votive offerings. This was the sole or main issue of fact canvassed in
evidence before the jury on the important point of the status and ownership of the coins.
As we have mentioned, expert opinion evidence for the prosecution was that it was
possible that the coins had been deposited at one time by someone who had intended to
retrieve them, and contrary expert opinion evidence for the defence was that Wanborough
appeared to have been a religious site and that coins and other precious things had often
been left on such sites as sacrifices.

However eminent and well informed the two experts were, their evidence on this
crucial point lacked sureness. In particular, the view of the prosecution expert, Mr Kent,
that it was at least possible that the coins had been deposited there by somebody who had
intended to retrieve them was hardly a basis on which the jury could have been sure that
they were treasure trove. It is likely, therefore, that the jury's finding of guilt depended
on their application of the judge's direction that they should regard the coins as the
Crown's property if they were satisfied merely that there was a real possibility that they
might be found to be treasure trove.

We start our examination of the issue by going back to the Theft Act 1968. Section
1(1) provides, so far as material:

'A person is guilty of theft if he dishonestly appropriates property belonging to
another with the intention of permanently depriving the other of it . . .'

No question turns on the meaning of property as defined in s 4(1) of the Act; the coins
are the property alleged in the indictment as having been stolen. It is the meaning of the

expression 'belonging to any person', which is dealt with in s 5(1) of the Act, that is in
a question. That provision reads, so far as material:

> 'Property shall be regarded as belonging to any person having possession or
> control of it, or having in it any proprietary right or interest . . .'

On the argument of counsel for the appellant the proprietary right or interest of the
Crown in the coins that the prosecution had to establish was a right to ownership of them
b as treasure trove at the time when the appellant found them. On the argument of counsel
for the Crown the proprietary right or interest that the prosecution had to prove was no
more than a right to have the question of the status and ownership of the coins
determined. It is implicit in counsel's argument that the Crown's entitlement to the
property itself depends on and does not take effect until there has been a determination
c of these issues by a coroner's jury or by some other tribunal.

The judge appears to have adopted counsel's approach in reliance on *R v Toole* (1867)
16 WR 439, a decision of the Irish Court for Crown Cases Reserved. To put that case in
context, we should say that before it the practice appears to have been to commit for trial
persons charged with concealment of treasure trove by both a grand jury's indictment
and a coroner's inquisition: see e g *R v Thomas* (1863) Le & Ca 313, 169 ER 1409 and *R v*
d *Toole* (1867) 16 WR 439 at 441 per Pigot CB, giving the judgment of the court. In *R v*
Toole the accused was committed for trial for that offence, but on indictment only, and
without evidence of any finding by coroner's inquisition as to the Crown's entitlement
to the treasure in question. There does not appear to have been any real dispute that the
property was in fact treasure trove. There was a conviction, and the trial judge referred
for the decision of the Court for Crown Cases Reserved the effect on the trial of there
e having been no coroner's inquisition. The court, after a careful review of the authorities,
held that a coroner's inquisition was not a necessary prerequisite of a successful
prosecution for concealment of treasure trove.

Pigot CB, in his judgment, made a number of observations, derived from authorities
in other contexts, which point clearly to the Crown's right to treasure trove arising
before, and independently of, any finding by a coroner's jury. He referred to the *King's*
f *Prerogative in Saltpetre* (1606) 12 Co Rep 12 at 13, 77 ER 1294 at 1296, in which the court
observed, albeit obiter: 'So the King may dig in the land of the subject for treasure-trove,
for he hath property . . .' and continued (16 WR 439 at 440):

> 'According to the law as to treasure trove, it would seem that the property might
> become vested in the Crown before it was dug out of its place of concealment, and,
> therefore, before the particulars of the hidden treasure were ascertained for the
g > purpose of being described in the inquisition . . . it seems to me difficult to conceive
> why the forfeited goods and choses in action of a felon should become vested in the
> Crown immediately upon the forfeiture, and treasure trove should not be similarly
> vested immediately upon the finding.'

He went on to rule that the Act 4 Edw 1 (Office of Coroner (1276)), which established
h the jurisdiction of the coroner in relation to treasure trove, did not affect 'any right of the
Crown to the immediate property in treasure trove when discovered which the Crown
possessed irrespective of that Act of Parliament . . .' (16 WR 439 at 441).

The approach of Pigot CB was cited with approval by Stirling J in *A-G v Moore* [1893]
1 Ch 676, [1891–4] All ER Rep 880, a case where there was no issue that the property in
j question was treasure trove, but it was claimed that the Crown had granted away its
entitlement to it under a grant of royalties. He said ([1893] 1 Ch 676 at 683, [1891–4]
All ER Rep 880 at 882):

> 'The jurisdiction of the coroner . . . is limited to an inquiry who were the finders
> and who is suspected thereof. I do not see, as at present advised, that he has any

jurisdiction to determine the title . . . That being so, I further think that according
to the authorities the title of the Crown is independent of the finding of the jury.' a

He went on to cite passages from Chitty Law of the Prerogatives of the Crown p 259 and
from Blackstone's Commentaries (3 Bl Com 259) and concluded ([1893] 1 Ch 676 at 684,
[1891–4] All ER Rep 880 at 883):

'I understand the meaning to be that although it may be proper that an inquest
should be held for the purposes of informing the Crown as to its rights, yet the b
finding of the jury is not essential to the title of the Crown to chattels.'

It was on the basis of the proprietary right of the Crown to treasure trove independently
of any coroner's inquisition that the court in R v Toole upheld the conviction of fraudulent
concealment of treasure trove. It is suggested by counsel for the Crown that some words
of Pigot CB towards the end of the judgment support his contention that the prosecution c
did not have to prove that the coins were treasure trove, merely that there was a real
possibility that they could be found to be treasure trove. We do not read Pigot CB's words
in that way. He was dealing with the difficulty or impossibility of holding a coroner's
inquisition when, before it could take place, the treasure trove had been converted into
another form or disposed of. In such a circumstance, he observed (16 WR 439 at 441):

'It may be difficult or perhaps impossible to procure testimony to specify or to d
enable an inquest jury to find the particulars of the goods for the purposes of an
inquisition, and yet it may be not difficult to obtain, for the purpose of prosecution,
evidence to show that some property capable of being in law the subject matter of
treasure trove was in fact found and was concealed by the culprit.' (Pigot CB's
emphasis.)
                                                                                    e
In our view, all that he was saying there was that, in a prosecution for concealment of
treasure trove, where the treasure had been disposed of or converted into another form,
the prosecution could call evidence that what had been found was within the category of
articles which in law were capable of constituting treasure trove. It was then for the jury
to decide whether it was satisfied that the property found, but no longer available, or
available in the same form, did in fact come within that category. The interpretation f
contended for by counsel for the Crown that the prosecution only had to show that the
Crown had a right to have the matter determined by a coroner's jury cannot stand with
the central point of Pigot CB's judgment that treasure trove vested in the Crown before
and independently of any verdict of a coroner's jury.

However, all that relates to the former offence of concealment of treasure trove, not
larceny, or its statutory successor, theft, of treasure trove. In R v Toole Pigot CB appears g
to have considered that a coroner's inquisition was a necessary prerequisite of a conviction
for larceny. He said (16 WR 439 at 440):

'It is true that before the Crown has acquired the possession of the treasure trove
(or before it is seised, as the phrase is, into the hands of the Sovereign by inquisition)
a person cannot be indicted for larceny of this species of property: [see 3 Co Inst 108, h
1 Hale PC 510 and 2 Hawk PC c 19, s 38]. But this is plainly a result of the nature of
the offence of larceny by which the asportation . . . from the possession actual or
constructive of the owner is an essential element.'

Whatever the position may have been for the offence of larceny, the lack of a coroner's
inquisition does not prevent a prosecution for and conviction of theft of treasure trove. j
That is because it is not necessary for the offence of theft that the property alleged to have
been stolen is in the possession, actual or constructive, of the owner at the time when it
is appropriated. Even at the time when Pigot CB was giving his judgment in R v Toole in
1867, the concept of ownership and special property in goods had begun to render the
old reliance on possession by the owner at the time of asportation somewhat academic:

see e g *R v Church* (1845) 5 LTOS 314, which concerned the buyer of undelivered goods.
a Now, by virtue of the replacement in s 3 of the Theft Act 1968 of appropriation for the
concept of asportation in the former offence of larceny, and the wider definition of
owership in s 5(1) of the 1968 Act than that in the offence of larceny, the distinction
drawn by Pigot CB between the mode of prosecution for concealment of treasure trove
and larceny cannot now preserve a coroner's inquisition as a prerequisite of a prosecution
for theft of treasure trove. The replacement of theft for larceny in the 1968 Act was the
b occasion for the abolition, in s 32(1)(*a*) of that Act, of the common law offence of
concealment of treasure trove, since many, if not all, such cases would now constitute
theft: see *Jervis* p 235.

    Any other view would lead to absurdity because it is now well established that a verdict
of a coroner's jury on the question whether certain property is treasure trove would not
be binding on another court in which the same issue arises: see *R v Toole* (1867) 16 WR
c 439, *A-G v Moore* [1893] 1 Ch 676, [1891–4] All ER Rep 880 and *A-G of the Duchy of
Lancaster v G E Overton (Farms) Ltd* [1982] 1 All ER 524 at 526, [1982] Ch 277 at 287,
where Lord Denning MR said 'That finding of the coroner's inquest is not binding on
the courts of law'.

    Accordingly, we are of the view that it was for the jury in the trial of this matter to
determine as part of their finding on the issue of guilt or innocence of the appellant
d whether the coins were in fact treasure trove and thus the property of the Crown. In
their determination of that issue they had to apply the ordinary criminal burden and
standard of proof, namely they could only convict the appellant if they were sure that
the coins in question were treasure trove, namely that they had been deposited by
someone who had intended to retrieve them. Whatever presumptions may be available
in civil disputes as to treasure trove (see *A-G v Trustees of the British Museum* [1903] 2 Ch
e 598 at 609 per Farwell J) or as to the Crown's entitlement to it (see *A-G v Moore* [1893] 1
Ch 676 at 683, [1891–4] All ER Rep 880 at 882 per Stirling J), they do not apply to
criminal proceedings.

    The judge did not direct the jury that they had to be sure that the coins in question
were treasure trove before they could convict. He told them, on a mistaken interpretation
of the law and, in particular, of the judgment of Pigot CB in *R v Toole*, that all they had
f to be sure about was that there was a real possibility of their being found to be treasure
trove. For the reasons that we have given that was a material misdirection. It is one in
respect of which we cannot apply the proviso to s 2(1) of the Criminal Appeal Act 1968,
since the highest to which the evidence for the prosecution went on the issue was only
that it was possible that the coins had been deposited at some time by someone who had
intended to retrieve them. On this ground alone we would allow the appeal.

g To that ruling we would add a footnote. Where there may be some doubt that property
found and kept by its finder is treasure trove, it may be possible to charge him or her in
the alternative with theft of the property from the owner of the land. We express
ourselves in that diffident way because the law relating to claims to the ownership and
possession of goods found on someone else's land is in an unsatisfactory state: see the
h Eighteenth Report of the Law Reform Committee on the *Law of Conversion and Detinue*
(Cmnd 4774 (1971)) and the Law Commission's publication *Treasure Trove: Law Reform
Issues* (September 1987) p 5. In such uncertainty, it may be difficult for the prosecution
to establish that an accused has been dishonest apart from anything else.

    The second ground of appeal is that the judge failed to direct the jury that before they
could convict they had to be sure that the defendant knew that the coins were gold or
j silver, or alternatively that they were composed substantially of gold or silver. As we
have indicated already, only articles made entirely or substantially of gold or silver
qualify as treasure trove.

    There is nothing in this complaint. It is true that the judge did not spell out to the jury
that they had to be sure that the coins were made at least substantially of gold or silver.
However, he did tell them that gold and silver coins concealed with a view to recovery

have the status of treasure trove before they are found. And, as we understand what
happened at the trial, it was not in issue that the coins were of silver.

The third ground of appeal is that the judge, having chosen to direct the jury on the
meaning of 'dishonesty', gave them the wrong direction. It is said that in purporting to
explain to them the two tests, objective and subjective, laid down by this court in R v
Ghosh [1982] 2 All ER 689, [1982] QB 1053, he correctly explained the objective test but
blurred his description of the subjective test so that it sounded like a repetition of the
objective test. The formula in R v Ghosh is straightforward enough, namely that the jury
should first consider whether the defendant had acted dishonestly by the standards of
ordinary and decent people and, if they find that he had, then they should consider
whether the defendant himself must have realised that what he was doing was by those
standards dishonest.

We doubt whether it was necessary for the judge to give a Ghosh direction at all. As
this court has said, in R v Roberts (1985) 84 Cr App R 117, there is no need to do so unless
the defendant has raised the issue that he did not know that anybody would regard what
he did as dishonest. Here, the appellant's case was that he did not find the coins himself
as alleged by the prosecution, but obtained them from his father. He accepted, as the
judge pointed out to the jury, that if he had found the coins, he would have known that
he should have handed them in. This is what the judge said:

> 'You ask yourselves this question: does a person who, knowing what this
> defendant knew, acted as this defendant we find acted, in our view act dishonestly?
> Is such behaviour, by our standards, dishonest? If you do not think that it is, well
> then he cannot be dishonest. But if you take the view that what he did in the
> circumstances was dishonest, *then ask yourselves whether he ought to be taken to share
> your view*? Is there something special about him which makes his standards of
> honesty and dishonesty different from yours, because it is him you are trying. If
> there is nothing special about him, and you think that the conduct was dishonest,
> well it was dishonest.' (Our emphasis.)

The use by the judge, when purporting to give the subjective part of the direction, of
the words, 'then ask yourselves whether he ought to be taken to share your view',
undoubtedly suggested a repetition of the objective part of the test. The following words
revert to a subjective approach, but they are not as clear as they could have been. The
overall effect of the direction on the jury must have been muddling. In our view, it was
a misdirection, but one in respect of which, if this were the only ground of appeal, we
would have applied the proviso. The jury's verdict of guilty means that they were
satisfied that the appellant had found the coins himself and that, therefore, on his own
account, he knew that in keeping them he had been dishonest.

However, for the reasons that we have given in relation to the first ground of appeal,
this appeal is allowed, and the conviction will be quashed.

Appeal allowed. Conviction quashed.

Solicitors: *Crown Prosecution Service*, Guildford.

Kate O'Hanlon   Barrister.

Naughton and another v O'Callaghan (Rogers and others, third parties)

QUEEN'S BENCH DIVISION

WALLER J

30, 31 JANUARY, 9 FEBRUARY 1990

Contract – Damages for breach – Misrepresentation – Misrepresentation not discovered until value of article had fallen by reason of defect – Measure of damages – Plaintiffs purchasing racehorse at thoroughbred sale – Horse's pedigree misdescribed – Misrepresentation as to pedigree not discovered until horse proving to be a failure on racetrack – Whether measure of damages difference between purchase price and actual value at time of purchase – Whether measure of damages difference between purchase price and value at time misrepresentation discovered.

In September 1981 the plaintiffs bought a thoroughbred yearling colt for 26,000 guineas at the Newmarket thoroughbred sales. The colt was put into training in Ireland and England for two seasons but was unplaced in all its six races. By reason of its lack of success on the racecourse the colt's value was then only £1,500. In June or July 1983 the plaintiffs discovered that the colt's pedigree had been incorrectly described in the sales catalogue because of an error at the stud where the colt had been foaled. Further training expenses were incurred after the discovery of the colt's true pedigree. One year after the discovery of the mistake in the colt's pedigree the plaintiffs wrote to the defendant, the vendor of the colt at the thoroughbred sales, claiming to repudiate the contract and seeking to recover the purchase price of £31,500 and training fees and expenses amounting to £14,734. When no reply was received from the defendant the plaintiffs issued a writ claiming damages for breach of contract and misrepresentation. The defendant issued a third party notice against the stud where the colt had been foaled and judgment was entered by default against the defendant and the third party for damages to be assessed. At the hearing to assess damages there was evidence that if the colt had been correctly described it would have fetched about 23,500 guineas at the sales. The defendant and the third party contended (i) that the plaintiffs had bought a horse of practically the same value as the horse they intended to buy and therefore the only damages recoverable for the misdescription was the small difference in value and (ii) that the plaintiffs would have incurred the training fees and expenses in respect of whatever horse they had bought.

Held – Where an article purchased as the result of a misrepresentation could have been sold immediately after the sale for the price paid but by the time the misrepresentation was discovered its value had fallen by reason of a defect in it which had by then become apparent the appropriate measure of damages could be the difference between the purchase price and its value at the time the misrepresentation was discovered and not the difference between the purchase price and its actual value at the time of purchase, provided that the article purchased was altogether different from that which had been expected. Accordingly, since (i) the plaintiffs had purchased an animal altogether different in reliance on the misrepresentation in the sales catalogue, (ii) they could, had they discovered the misrepresentation immediately, have resold the colt for its then value, (iii) their decision to keep the colt and race it was what the defendants would have expected and (iv) the fall in the colt's value because it did not win races was special to the colt and not due to a general fall in the market for racehorses, the plaintiffs were entitled to recover the difference between the colt's purchase price and its present-day value. The plaintiffs were also entitled to the training fees and costs of the upkeep of the colt up to the date on which they discovered its true pedigree (see p 197 *b c j* to p 198 *c e g h*, post).

Dictum of Winn LJ in *Doyle v Olby (Ironmongers) Ltd* [1969] 2 All ER 119 at 123–124 applied.

Twycross v Grant (1877) 2 CPD 469 and dictum of Lord Wilberforce in *Johnson v Agnew* [1979] 1 All ER 883 at 896 considered.

Notes
For damages for misrepresentation, see 31 Halsbury's Laws (4th edn) paras 1107–1108, and for cases on the subject, see 34 Digest (Reissue) 383–385, 3126–3140.

Cases referred to in judgment
Doyle v Olby (Ironmongers) Ltd [1969] 2 All ER 119, [1969] 2 QB 158, [1969] 2 WLR 673, CA.
Hickman v Haynes (1875) LR 10 CP 598.
Johnson v Agnew [1979] 1 All ER 883, [1980] AC 367, [1979] 2 WLR 487, HL.
Ogle v Earl Vane (1867) LR 2 QB 275; *affd* (1868) LR 3 QB 272, Ex Ch.
Radford v De Froberville [1978] 1 All ER 33, [1977] 1 WLR 1262.
Twycross v Grant (1877) 2 CPD 469, CA.
Waddell v Blockey (1879) 4 QBD 678, CA.

Assessment of damages
The plaintiffs, Thomas Joseph Naughton and Vincent Lawrence Kilkenny, by a writ issued on 20 March 1985, claimed damages against the defendant, Gay O'Callaghan, for breach of contract and/or warranty and/or for negligence or misrepresentation relating to the sale of a yearling at Tattersalls Premier Yearling Sales in Newmarket. On 7 October 1985 the defendant issued a third party notice against Sonia Rogers, John Byrne, Conor Crowley and Liam McGonagle claiming an indemnity on the grounds of breach of contract and/or warranty and/or for negligence or misrepresentation in the description of the breeding of the yearling when the defendant had bought the yearling from the Airlie Stud. By an order dated 16 October 1985 made by the deputy district registrar in the Reading district registry judgment was entered for the plaintiffs against the defendant for damages to be assessed and by a consent order dated 17 December 1985 judgment was entered for the defendant against the third parties for damages to be assessed. The facts are set out in the judgment.

William Norris for the plaintiffs.
Thomas Brudenell for the defendant and the third parties.

Cur adv vult

9 February. The following judgment was delivered.

WALLER J. In September 1981 the first plaintiff (Mr Naughton) and the second plaintiff (Mr Kilkenny) were intent on buying a yearling at the September sales at Newmarket. Their intention was to put such yearling in training in Ireland with Mr Adrian Maxwell with whom they had had previous horses in training, and it was Mr Maxwell who was to bid and advise on the purchase of the horse. No one remembers precise details of the way the purchase came about, but in conformity with normal practice it would seem that the catalogue would arrive with Mr Maxwell and he would consider in relation to various clients, including the plaintiffs, what horses might be suitable for his various clients to be purchased at the sale. He would mark in the catalogue those horses which he would be prepared to advise the plaintiffs to buy.

In the catalogue, lot 200 to be sold on Wednesday evening, 30 September 1981, was a chestnut colt named Fondu. A full description of the colt and its predigree is set out in

the agreed documents, but in particular the description was of a colt whose sire was
a Nonalco and whose dam was Habanna whose sire in turn was Habitat.

Habanna, as the description in the catalogue confirms, was itself a good class racehorse
having won two races including a listed race and having been placed second in a group 2
race. As the evidence before me showed, for the purposes of a description in the catalogue,
races have been categorised in order of merit, Group 1, Group 2, Group 3 and listed races.
The indication 'LR' or 'GR1' or 'GR11' or 'GR111' appears in black type, and it is common
b ground that the black type is of significance to anyone reading the catalogue and selecting
a horse for which to bid at auction.

Mr Maxwell picked out Fondu in the catalogue as suitable for the plaintiffs because of
the Habitat line in the pedigree. He may well have discussed the matter with the first
plaintiff who was also attracted by the Habitat line. There is no question, and it is
common ground, that the Habitat line was an attractive one in 1981, both because of
c Habanna's own record and because Habitat was itself building up an increasing reputation
as a sire of winners or class horses. Furthermore, Habitat was beginning, but only
beginning, to build up a reputation as a sire of brood mares, that is to say a sire of mares
themselves producing foals that turned out to be successful racehorses.

As I have said, Mr Maxwell was acting for various clients at the September sales, and
he went over early in order to confirm what recommendation to give to his clients. He
d went and inspected Fondu and confirmed that it was the horse for his particular clients,
the plaintiffs, but there is no doubt that he relied particularly on the pedigree as described
in the catalogue.

In the event, the first plaintiff and Mr Maxwell attended the sale at Newmarket and
Mr Maxwell bid for Fondu. The second plaintiff arrived late and may have been there
when the hammer fell, but it matters not. Mr Maxwell actually did the bidding and
e Fondu was purchased for the sum of 26,000 guineas.

In the bar after the sale, Mr Maxwell suggested to the plaintiffs that he should 'keep a
leg' (ie 25%) of the horse and that was agreed. That this arrangement had taken place
only came out during the trial and, for reasons which I gave earlier, I allowed Mr Maxwell
to be joined as a party having regard to his original interest in Fondu. Ultimately, it is
f right to say that Mr Maxwell gave his 25% to the first plaintiff, which is no doubt why
the action was brought originally only in the names of the original plaintiffs. This further
demonstrated, as I said when giving my reasons, that there was no injustice in allowing
Mr Maxwell to be joined for entirely technical reasons.

In any event, Fondu was taken to Ireland and put into training with Mr Maxwell. The
first race for which Fondu was entered was in September 1982 in Ireland, and it raced
three times that year, all in Ireland. Fondu was not a success on the racecourse during
g that season, it being placed seventh in its first race, twelfth in its second race and fourth
in its third race.

At the end of 1982 Mr Maxwell left Ireland to go and train in the United States of
America, and it was at this stage, judging Fondu to be no good, that Mr Maxwell gave his
25% to the first plaintiff. A decision was taken to put Fondu in training in England at
h Upper Lambourne near Newbury in Berkshire with Mr Charles Nelson. In 1983 Fondu
was entered for three races in England, but fared no better than it had done in Ireland. It
was placed eleventh in its first race at Bath, seventeenth in its second race at Bath, and in
its third race in May 1983 it was placed eighteenth. This third race was indeed only a
trainers' invitation race, ie one in which the trainers were jockeys. Mr Nelson rode Fondu
in that race, and it is really the fact that the colt was entered for such a race at all that is
j relied on as being an indication that Fondu was not likely to be any success at all on the
racecourse.

Discovery of Fondu's true pedigree

In about June or July 1983 the plaintiffs discovered that they had not bought a colt as
described in the catalogue at all. It appears that at the stud where Fondu was produced as
a foal, being the stud of the third parties in this action, some error had been made. Fondu

was not the son of Habanna at all. The fact was that Fondu's dam was Moon Min (USA) whose sire was First Landing whose dam was Capelet and the page of the catalogue should have looked much more nearly that produced before me dated 30 November 1979 in so far as that page describes the pedigree of Moon Min. No explanation of how this error occurred has been given, and certainly no justification for the error has been put forward.

Having discovered this error, one might have thought that there would have been an immediate reaction from the plaintiffs, either themselves or from advisers on their behalf. But the sequence of events thereafter is that Fondu was kept in training with Mr Nelson until October 1983, and the second plaintiff then kept Fondu at home from 1 November 1983 to 4 April 1984. Thereafter Fondu was placed by the first plaintiff (as he explained in the hope that it would be a point-to-point horse for his son) with Rodney Simpson's racing stables from about 5 April 1984. The first plaintiff received invoices for training fees and keep right through 1984 from Rodney Simpson, up until 31 July 1984. Thereafter he received a further invoice for Fondu's keep from Jane Webber of Great Shefford near Newbury in August 1984. It also appears from documents in the bundle relating to charges made to the first plaintiff by Weatherbys that Fondu actually continued to be entered for races during 1984, the last race being on 30 June 1984, but Fondu never in fact raced during 1984. These entries, it was suggested, must have been due to some overzealousness on the part of an employee of Mr Simpson.

Only on 7 June 1984 did solicitors on behalf of the plaintiffs write to the defendant, the seller of Fondu at the Newmarket sales. In that letter the solicitors, having referred to the purchase by their client of Fondu, stated that their clients had discovered midway through the 1983 season that the dam line was not as shown in the catalogue. The letter then suggested that the horse was taken out of training and that it had been of no use or interest to the plaintiffs since. It further stated that they would not have bid for Fondu if they had known the true breeding, since they were impressed by what the catalogue showed. They set out the loss suffered by their clients at £31,500, that being the purchase price plus VAT, and the training fees and expenses of £14,734. That figure appears to be the fees and expenses charged by Mr Maxwell in 1981 and the charge by Mr Nelson from November 1982 to October 1983, plus the cost of keeping Fondu at home for a period from 1 November 1983. The letter invited the defendant to take the horse back and settle with the plaintiffs by paying the purchase price plus the training fees. In default the letter suggested that the plaintiffs would sell the horse at public auction and look to the defendant for the difference between the net sale proceeds and the aforesaid figures. The horse was not taken back by the defendant and nor has it in fact been sold at public auction. It remained after 1984 with the second plaintiff, where it still is.

I have not seen any correspondence between 7 June 1984 and the issue of a specially indorsed writ, which took place on 20 March 1985. That specially indorsed writ claimed damages for breach of contract and misrepresentation, negligent or innocent, in the description of the horse. Judgment in default was entered on 16 October 1985 as against the defendant. A third party notice had been issued claiming damages again for breach of contract and/or for negligent or innocent misrepresentation. The defendants themselves entered judgment in default as against the third parties on 17 December 1985. The reference to negligent or innocent misrepresentation in both pleadings clearly included a claim under s 2(1) of the Misrepresentation Act 1967. The first date fixed for the assessment of damages was on 21 January 1986, some four years ago. That hearing was adjourned, I am told, because no documentation had by that time been produced in support of the plaintiffs' claim. Whatever the reason be, it is unhappy on any view that it has taken four years for this assessment of damages to come before the court.

The defendant and the third parties (who were represented by the same counsel at the hearing before me) not surprisingly have sought to make something of the delays in this case. In particular, the delay between discovery of the true pedigree and the writing of the letter of June 1984 needed some explanation. The explanation given for that delay

was to the effect that it was initially left to the trainer to take action, and he failed to do
a so. I will return to that delay in a moment for it could be said to be of some relevance.

In relation to the delay since the proceedings were issued, I am told that there were
two sides to the story, but rightly time was not taken up at the trial exploring that aspect
since in relation to the decision I have to take at this stage delay since the proceedings
were commenced is not relevant. It may become relevant in relation to questions of
interest on which I have still to hear full argument.

b   To return to the delay prior to the sending of the letter of June 1984. The plaintiffs are
not claiming to be entitled to reject the horse, if they had ever had any right, such delay
would have been a complete answer, but the delay could be relevant to a factual issue
with which it is convenient to deal here. The defendant has suggested as a possibility that
the plaintiffs having discovered the true pedigree of Fondu did not worry too much, and
indeed still thought they might have a good horse. This, it was suggested, is why it was
c kept on at Mr Nelson until October 1983, then put back in to training with Rodney
Simpson in April 1984.

I am satisfied that there is no substance in those suggestions. It is common ground that
by May/June 1983, when the true pedigree was discovered, Fondu by virtue of its record
on the track was worth about £1,500. Fondu was never raced after May 1983 and the
failure to take up the complaint was, as it seems to me, due to a rather casual approach to
d the whole matter at a time when Fondu was already thought to have proved useless.
Attitudes would have been very different indeed, in my view, if on the day following the
auction the true position had been made known. In my judgment, if the true pedigree
had become known before Fondu was raced, there is no question that the plaintiffs would
have sought to reject Fondu or otherwise dispose of the colt. I say that because albeit
Moon Min had a good pedigree, so far as Mr Maxwell was concerned that related in the
e main to horses which had been successful on the dirt tracks in America, rather than on
the turf in Europe. It equally follows that I am quite clear that if Fondu had been
described in the catalogue as out of Moon Min, there is no question of Mr Maxwell
having advised the plaintiffs to bid for the horse and no question thus of this horse having
been purchased with its true description in the catalogue.

It is also right to say however, and it is this that makes for the difficult point of law,
f that if Fondu had been correctly described in the catalogue as out of Moon Min, it would
have had a substantial value to persons other than the plaintiffs. On the defendant's side,
Major Philipson gave evidence that the value of Fondu correctly described would, in his
opinion, have been at least the price paid for Fondu incorrectly described in September
1981. On the plaintiffs' side, Mr Anderson confirmed that if he had been advising a
buyer who wanted to buy Fondu as correctly described out of Moon Min, he would have
g advised them to go to something in the region of £5,000 less than the price that he
would advise a buyer to go in relation to Fondu as incorrectly described.

The problem is thus a neat one. (1) The price paid for Fondu as it was described was
26,000 guineas, and no one suggested that that was other than a reasonable price. (2) The
price that might have been obtained for Fondu as it ought to have been described was
h about the same or, as I find, slightly less than the 26,000 guineas, say 23,500 guineas.
(3) The price of Fondu when it was discovered that it had been incorrectly described in
June/July 1983 and after it had proved a failure on the racecourse was (as agreed) £1,500.

The plaintiffs thus claim (a) the difference between 26,000 guineas and £1,500 and (b)
the cost of training and keeping Fondu up until discovery of the true pedigree and some
reasonable period thereafter.

j   The answer of the defendant and third parties is on the following lines. They say that
the plaintiffs, unbeknown to them, bought a horse of practically the same value and
whether damages are to be assessed for breach of contract or for misrepresentation the
normal measure is that difference in value. They further say that what reduced Fondu's
value was the lack of ability on the racecourse and there is no reason to apply some
different measure. They further say that the plaintiffs would always have incurred fees

for the training and upkeep in relation to whatever horse they had bought, and that those expenses do not flow naturally or at all from any breach of contract or from any misrepresentation.

The plaintiffs' response to the above is as follows. (1) If Fondu had been what they thought from the description given, ie that it was out of Habanna, and if it had then been trained by Mr Maxwell it *might* have won races and thus paid for its training out of prize money and become immensely valuable for stud purposes. They say that they do not make any claim for loss of that chance, but they say that that should be taken into account when assessing their claim in effect to have the money back which they expended in reliance on the misrepresentation. (2) They further say that the misrepresentation in effect continued from September 1981 right up until May/June 1983. If the description had been corrected in, for example, October 1981, the plaintiffs could have gone out into the market and obtained whatever value Fondu properly described would have fetched, and saved themselves the fees of training Fondu. Discovery in only June/July 1983 left them with a horse worth only £1,500 and the fees already expended.

The plaintiffs' argument makes plain that they are not seeking any loss of bargain damages. This, as it seems to me, makes it simpler to examine first the principles applicable to their claim in tort, or under s 2(1) of the Misrepresentation Act 1967. The basic principle is that an award of damages should put the plaintiffs in the position they would have been in if the representation had not been made to them, but it must be remembered that rescission is not the remedy; damages alone are being assessed and that means that some credit must be given for the value of whatever has been retained. The question that arises is at what date should the value for which credit is being given be ascertained. That question has been considered in many cases most of which have been concerned with the purchase of shares. In *McGregor on Damages* (15th edn, 1988) paras 1723–1728 some of those cases are discussed. As *McGregor* para 1724 says in relation to shares: 'The normal measure of damages is the purchase price of the shares less their actual value if any *at the time of acquisiton.*' (My emphasis.) As one would expect, this is not a special rule applicable to shares. That appears from the cases cited, eg *Waddell v Blockey* (1879) 4 QBD 678 was concerned with rupee paper purchased in reliance on a fraudulent misrepresentation and whose value deteriorated over a period of six months before it was sold by the plaintiff.

Furthermore, in one of the share cases, *Twycross v Grant* (1877) 2 CPD 469 at 544–545, Cockburn CJ cites an example actually relating to a racehorse. He said:

'If a man is induced by misrepresentation to buy an article, and while it is still in his possession, it becomes destroyed or damaged, he can only recover the difference between the value as represented and the real value at the time he bought. He cannot add to it any further deterioration which has arisen from some other supervening cause. If a man buys a horse, as a racehorse, on the false representation that it has won some great race, while in reality it is a horse of very inferior speed, and he pays ten or twenty times as much as the horse is worth, and after the buyer has got the animal home it dies of some latent disease inherent in its system at the time he bought it, he may claim the entire price he gave; the horse was by reason of the latent mischief worthless when he bought; but if it catches some disease and dies, the buyer cannot claim the entire value of the horse, which he is no longer in a condition to restore, but only the difference between the price he gave and the real value at the time he bought.'

The 'normal measure', as I see it, is not intended to lay down any rigid rule, any more than s 53(3) of the Sale of Goods Act 1979 lays down a rigid rule that the difference in value at the time of delivery is the difference in market value; that is only a prima facie rule. It happens in individual cases to have accurately reflected a plaintiff's loss. Where goods are purchased for the purpose of resale, eg rupee paper, and it is the plaintiff's decision not to sell for six months, it is appropriate that any loss produced by a fall in the

market should not be borne by the defendant. The normal measure is not however
a applied so as to enable the defendant to benefit from his fraud by being able to rely on
some market value at the time of purchase itself affected by the representations being
made. Furthermore, in cases such as *Doyle v Olby (Ironmongers) Ltd* [1969] 2 All ER 119,
[1969] 2 QB 158, where the plaintiff was buying a business which he had no intention of
selling immediately, the starting point was not, so far as I can see, the 'normal measure'
and then a consideration of the consequential damage. The principle, as Winn LJ
b described it is as follows ([1969] 2 All ER 119 at 123–124, [1969] 2 QB 158 at 168):

> 'It appears to me that in a case where there has been a breach of warranty of
> authority, and still more clearly where there has been a tortious wrong consisting of
> a fraudulent inducement, the proper starting point for any court called on to
> consider what damages are recoverable by the defrauded person is to compare his
c > position before the representation was made to him with his position after it,
> brought about by that representation, always bearing in mind that no element in
> the consequential position can be regarded as attributable loss and damage if it be
> too remote a consequence: it will be too remote not necessarily because it was not
> contemplated by the representor but in any case where the person deceived has not
> himself behaved with reasonable prudence, reasonable common sense or can in any
d > true sense be said to have been the author of his own misfortune. The damage that
> he seeks to recover must have flowed directly from the fraud perpetrated on him.'

Winn LJ then assessed the damages in that case by reference to precisely what the plaintiff
had done after acquiring the business including selling the business at some later time
and giving credit for that sale price. (I should perhaps make clear that *Doyle v Olby
(Ironmongers) Ltd* was concerned with fraud, but in relation to a claim for damages under
e the Misrepresentation Act 1967 the approach is the same: see *McGregor* paras 1742–1749,
esp para 1745 and the cases there referred to.)
    It is perhaps also helpful to mention at this stage, albeit I am not dealing with damages
for breach of contract, *Johnson v Agnew* [1979] 1 All ER 883 esp at 896, [1980] AC 367 esp
at 400–401, where Lord Wilberforce said:

f > 'The general principle for the assessment of damages is compensatory, ie that the
> innocent party is to be placed, so far as money can do so, in the same position as if
> the contract had been performed. Where the contract is one of sale, this principle
> normally leads to assessment of damages as at the date of the breach, a principle
> recognised and embodied in s 51 of the Sale of Goods Act 1893. But this is not an
> absolute rule; if to follow it would give rise to injustice, the court has power to fix
g > such other date as may be appropriate in the circumstances. In cases where a breach
> of a contract for sale has occurred, and the innocent party reasonably continues to
> try to have the contract completed, it would to me appear more logical and just
> rather than tie him to the date of the original breach, to assess damages as at the date
> when (otherwise than by his default) the contract is lost. Support for this approach
> is to be found in the cases. In *Ogle v Earl Vane* (1867) LR 2 QB 275; *affd* (1868) LR 3
h > QB 272 the date was fixed by reference to the time when the innocent party, acting
> reasonably, went into the market; in *Hickman v Haynes* (1875) LR 10 CP 598 at a
> reasonable time after the last request of the defendants (the buyers) to withhold
> delivery. In *Radford v de Froberville* [1978] 1 All ER 33, [1977] 1 WLR 1262, where
> the defendant had covenanted to build a wall, damages were held measurable as at
> the date of the hearing rather than at the date of the defendant's breach, unless the
j > plaintiff ought reasonably to have mitigated the breach at an earlier date.'

    What, as it seems to me, makes this case different from the norm is, first, that what
the plaintiffs in fact purchased in reliance on the representation in the catalogue was a
different animal altogether; second, if they had known of the misrepresentation within
a day or so they could, and as I have found would, have sold Fondu for its then value;

third, their decision to keep Fondu and race it was precisely what the sellers would have expected; Fondu was not a commodity like, for example, rupee paper, which it would be *a* expected that the defendants would go out and sell; fourth, the fall in Fondu's value if it did not win races was not due to a general fall in the market in racehorses, but was special to Fondu and to be expected if Fondu did not win. It might well not have happened if Fondu had been the different animal as it had been originally described.

Accordingly, in my judgment it would be unjust if the plaintiffs were not entitled to recover the difference between 26,000 guineas and £1,500, and on that aspect of the case *b* accordingly I award that sum.

Consequential losses

It seems to me that there can be no question of the plaintiffs being entitled to recover anything for the training and upkeep of Fondu past the date on which they discovered the true pedigree of Fondu, other than a reasonable figure for the horse's keep until it *c* could have been disposed of. If any sum is recoverable I assess it at £9,820. That figure is calculated as follows. It includes charges made by Weatherbys to the plaintiffs for the years 1982/83, ie £602·63. It includes 75% of the training fees of Mr Maxwell in 1982 as claimed. Mr Maxwell was a 25% owner during the period up to the end of 1982 and has made no claim on his own behalf for costs during that period and the appropriate figure accordingly is £5,673·33. It includes the training and keep charged by Kingsdown Ltd, *d* which I am satisfied was charged to the plaintiffs equally, up to 30 June 1983, ie a figure of £3,544·14. There has been no allowance for any element of keep thereafter. Since the plaintiffs have in fact made the choice just to keep the horse it does not seem to me that they should be entitled on any view to charge that element or any part of that element to the defendant.

Is the £9,820 recoverable at all? It seems to me that in relation to this particular horse, *e* applying Winn LJ's test in *Doyle v Olby (Ironmongers) Ltd* [1969] 2 All ER 119 at 123–124, [1969] 2 QB 158 at 168, the cost of training and keeping Fondu should be recoverable. But is it right to apply blinkers and consider the purchase of this particular animal and the expenditure on him? The defendant says that expenditure would have been incurred anyway on some yearling purchased at those September sales. To which the plaintiffs retort that that may be so, but if they bought the horse described by the defendant it *f* *might* have paid for its keep and reaped for them rich rewards.

I have concluded that the plaintiffs are entitled to ask the court to look simply at the contract they made in reliance on the representation which induced them to enter into that bargain. They are entitled to say that there must be no speculation one way or the other about what would have happened if they had not purchased this horse and if no misrepresentation had been made to them. They are entitled to say (putting it in broad *g* terms) we bought one horse and we spent money training it and entering it for races. We discovered two years after the purchase that it was not the horse we thought we had bought; it is not the horse on which we would have spent any money training or keeping, and therefore that is money only spent in reliance on the representation made. The figure I award under this head is thus £9,820.

As regards damages for breach of contract, I can now take that matter very shortly. *h* Section 53 of the Sale of Goods Act 1979 seems to me to be the appropriate section and not s 51 as contended for by the plaintiffs. Section 53 provides:

'...(2) The measure of damages for breach of warranty is the estimated loss directly and naturally resulting, in the ordinary course of events, from the breach of warranty. *j*

(3) In the case of breach of warranty of quality such loss is prima facie the difference between the value of the goods at the time of delivery to the buyer and the value they would have had if they had fulfilled the warranty...'

Subsection 3 is only a prima facie rule and in accordance with Lord Wilberforce's speech
a in *Johnson v Agnew* [1979] 1 All ER 883 at 896, [1980] AC 367 at 400–401, which I have
already quoted above, if it is unjust to apply that rule it will not be applied.

It seems to me that in the circumstances of this case it would have been unjust to apply
that prima facie rule for all the reasons I have given in relation to my assessment of
damages for misrepresentation. In the circumstances I would have awarded the difference
between 26,000 guineas and £1,500 as the difference in value. It further seems to me
b that if my reasoning in relation to the figure for training being recoverable for
misrepresentation is right, then the training fees and expenditure would be losses directly
and naturally resulting in the ordinary course of events from the breach of contract, and
I would have awarded those figures as well.

Accordingly, I give judgment for the two figures, the difference, £25,800, and £9,820.

c *Judgment accordingly.*

Solicitors: *Pitman McCloy*, Newbury (for the plaintiffs); *Campbell Hooper* (for the
defendant); *Crossman Block* (for the third parties).

K Mydeen Esq   Barrister.
d

Post Office v Union of Communication
e   Workers

COURT OF APPEAL, CIVIL DIVISION
LORD DONALDSON OF LYMINGTON MR, BUTLER-SLOSS AND FARQUHARSON LJJ
19 JANUARY, 1 FEBRUARY 1990

Trade dispute – Acts done in contemplation or furtherance of trade dispute – Ballot before
f *industrial action – Question on voting paper – Union seeking authorisation of action up to and*
including strike – Whether question asking voter whether he is prepared to take part in industrial
action up to and including strike satisfying legislative requirements – Whether voting paper
required to ask voter both whether he is prepared to take part in strike and whether he is prepared
to take part in action short of strike – Trade Union Act 1984, s 11(4).

g *Trade dispute – Acts done in contemplation or furtherance of trade dispute – Ballot before*
industrial action – Industrial action authorised or endorsed by ballot – Whether action required
to continue without substantial interruption if authority or endorsement of ballot to be relied on –
Whether change in workforce over period of action rendering ballot ineffective – Trade Union
1984.

h The requirements of s 11(4)[a] of the Trade Union Act 1984, as substituted by the
Employment Act 1988, Sch 3, para 7, as to the question or questions on a voting paper in
a ballot before industrial action are not satisfied by a single question asking the voter
whether he is prepared to take part in industrial action 'up to and including a strike'.
Instead, where a trade union seeks the authorisation of its members of industrial action
j up to and including a strike the voting paper must contain two questions, one asking the
voter whether he is prepared to take part in a strike and the other asking whether he is
prepared to take part in action short of a strike (see p 204 *b* to *e*, p 205 *g h* and p 206 *g*,
post).

---

a   Section 11(4) is set out at p 203 *j* to p 204 *a*, post

It is implicit in the 1984 Act that, once begun, industrial action by members of a trade union shall continue without substantial interruption if reliance is to continue to be *a* placed on the authority or endorsement of the members of the action given in a ballot. It is a question of fact and degree in each case whether an interruption in industrial action exhausts the protection of the ballot, a distinction being drawn between suspension of action for a specific and limited purpose and cessation of action (see p 204 *g h*, p 205 *g* and p 206 *d e g*, post); *Monsanto plc v Transport and General Workers' Union* [1987] 1 All ER 358 followed. *b*

It is a question of fact and degree whether industrial action over a long period is sufficiently continuous and self-contained for it to be capable of being supported by a single ballot (see p 205 *c g* and p 206 *g*, post).

Quaere. Whether a change which is more than de minimis in the relevant workforce over the period of industrial action will render ineffective the ballot which authorised or endorsed the action (see p 205 *e* to *g* and p 206 *g*, post). *c*

Notes

For secret ballots before industrial action, see Supplement to 47 Halsbury's Laws (4th edn) para 584A.

For the Trade Union Act 1984, s 11, see 16 Halsbury's (4th edn) (1990 reissue) 512.
d

Case referred to in judgments

Monsanto plc v Transport and General Workers' Union [1987] 1 All ER 358, [1987] 1 WLR 617, CA.

Interlocutory appeal

By notice of appeal dated 18 January 1990 the plaintiff, the Post Office, appealed against *e* the order of Turner J made in chambers on 17 January 1990 refusing the Post Office's application for orders that (i) until trial or further order the defendant, the Union of Communication Workers, be restrained whether by itself, its servants, agents or otherwise howsoever from inducing, enticing or encouraging employees of the Post Office to break their contracts of employment by taking strike or other industrial action save with the *f* lawful support of a ballot validly conducted in accordance with Pt II of the Trade Union Act 1984 and (ii) the union forthwith withdraw its authorisation of strike or other industrial action on or about 18 January 1990 and take all such action as might be necessary to countermand any instruction, advice or request which it had issued to its branches and/or members to take strike or other industrial action on or about 18 January 1990. The facts are set out in the judgment of Lord Donaldson MR.
g

Jeffrey Burke QC and *David Griffith-Jones* for the Post Office.
Gregory Mitchell for the union.

At the conclusion of the argument the court announced that the appeal would be allowed for reasons to be given later. *h*

1 February. The following judgments were delivered.

LORD DONALDSON OF LYMINGTON MR. This is an appeal by the Post Office against the refusal by Turner J to grant it an injunction restraining further industrial action by the unions in support of a long-running dispute concerning Crown post offices. *j*

At the conclusion of the hearing we indicated that in our judgment any further industrial action by the union would be unlawful, absent a further ballot, but that, as issues of some general importance had been raised, we wished to take time to put the reasons for reaching this conclusion into writing. The union, for its part, readily undertook not to promote any such action pending the giving of those reasons.

May I say at once that the union has throughout acted in the wholly genuine belief that it was entitled to take the industrial action which it did and there has not been, and is not, the slightest intention on its part to depart from its strict legal rights. May I also say that, although I have no doubt about the correctness of our conclusions, this legislation is a minefield in which it is all too easy to stray from the paths of safety and legality. Happily, the Post Office has said that if the union, on reflection, decides to treat this appeal as the hearing of the action, which would not of course preclude an appeal to the House of Lords if so advised and subject to obtaining leave, it would undertake not to seek an award of compensation.

The broad chronology is important, but not difficult to state.

Late 1987 or early 1988. The Post Office began to formulate what was known as a network conversion policy (NCP). The details do not matter, save to say that a large number of Crown post offices would be converted to 'agency status'. The union is, and has always been, implacably opposed to this policy for reasons which may or may not be sound, but are quite immaterial for present purposes.

August 1988. The union decided to ballot, and did ballot, all its members who were postal officers or postal assistants inquiring whether they were—

'willing to take Industrial Action up to and including Strike Action, in support of the UCW decision to oppose all aspects of the Post Office Board's decision to close up to 750 Crown Office Counters.'

September. The ballot result, on a 62% turn out, was 51% in favour of a 'Yes' answer to the question.

12 October–30 November. A series of selective 24-hour strikes took place in different parts of the country.

12 December. In a circular letter dated 6 December, Mr Tuffin, the general secretary of the union, informed branch secretaries that:

'As a result of the conclusion of the rolling programme of Strike Action, the Strike Committee have met and you are now instructed under National Rule 19 to ensure that *all Postal Officers and Postal Assistants in your Branch cease work for the whole of Monday 12 December 1988.* Returning to work at their scheduled time on Tuesday 13 December 1988. Postal Officers and Postal Assistants on Night Work should cease work for 24 hours from the commencement of their night shift on Sunday 11 December.' (Mr Tuffin's emphasis.)

This 24-hour strike duly took place. The extent to which it was effective is immaterial for present purposes and, inevitably, is a matter of dispute between the parties.

January–April 1989. No industrial action was taken, but the union mounted a public relations campaign in opposition to NCP. There were some discussions, in which a representative of the union was present, as to the personnel implications of NCP, but the union remained wholly opposed to that policy and no negotiations took place.

April. Crown post office closures began.

23 May. The union's annual conference took place at Bournmouth and there was a debate on the subject of Crown post office closures. Mr Ernest Dudley, the assistant general secretary of the union, has deposed that:

'In that debate in reply to an attempt to extend the Industrial action to the Uniform grades I said that the campaign is to continue and that the Union would authorise official industrial action in relation to the 1988 "YES" vote to any Branch. By making that promise I was able to persuade the Conference not to extend the industrial action further. I personally informed (on dates I do not remember) Mr. Peaple and Mr. Peter Curtis of Management of my comments and they could not have been in any continuing doubt either of the intention of the Union to continue to implement the ballot if and when necessary or of the view of the Union that the dispute would continue until agreement on the closure programme was reached.'

28 September. A 24-hour strike by postal officers and postal assistants took place at the Harrow Crown post office, of which notice had been given to the Post Office on 22 *a* September.

9 October–16 October. The Post Office asserted, and the union denied, that (a) the result of the ballot in August 1988 no longer provided any legitimisation of industrial action and (b) the wording of the ballot question itself had been defective.

19 October. The union notified the Post Office of its intention to call a half-day strike at Aldridge on 24 October and, in reply, the Post Office asked for an assurance that there *b* would be no further industrial action. This the union refused to give.

20 November. The solicitor to the Post Office wrote formally to the union asserting that any further industrial action would be unlawful.

12 January 1990. The union gave instructions for a 24-hour strike in the London south-east counters district on 18 January. The Post Office complained that it received no or no adequate notice, but, whilst formal notification is clearly desirable, it is not required *c* by law.

15 January. The Post Office heard of the proposal to strike and sought confirmation that this was authorised by the union. The union confirmed that it was indeed so authorised.

16 January. The Post Office told the union that it was applying to the court.

17 January. The Post Office applied to Turner J ex parte, but on notice to the union, *d* for an interlocutory injunction. The union attended the hearing and declined the offer of an adjournment.

Turner J refused to grant an injunction on the following grounds: (a) the Post Office has failed to take all reasonable steps with a view to securing that notice of their application, and an opportunity of being heard with respect thereto, had been given to the union (see s 17(1) of the Trade Union and Labour Relations Act 1974); (b) he thought *e* it to be well arguable that the union's defences would succeed at the trial (see s 17(2) of that Act).

Before us it was rightly accepted that, whether the judge was right or wrong as to ground (a) above, which was debatable, at the present juncture it was open to this court to grant an injunction if it was satisfied that, contrary to the judge's second ground of decision, the union would be acting unlawfully if it called for any further industrial *f* action. Accordingly, it is to that issue that I now turn. It has two aspects. The first concerns the form of the question asked in the ballot. The second concerns the time which has elapsed and the events which have and have not occurred between the ballot and the call for strike action in January 1990.

The question asked in the ballot   *g*
    Prior to the passing of the Trade Union Act 1984, trade unions which, in furtherance or contemplation of an industrial dispute, took industrial action which induced a breach of the contracts of employment of their members were protected from claims for damages or injunctive relief by s 13 of the 1974 Act. The 1984 Act introduced the further requirement that this protection only subsisted if the action was supported by a *h* ballot. This was achieved by s 10(1) and (3), which was (and is) in the following terms:

> '*Industrial action authorised or endorsed by trade union without support of a ballot.*—(1) Nothing in section 13 of the 1974 Act shall prevent an act done by a trade union without the support of a ballot from being actionable in tort (whether or not against the trade union) on the ground that it induced a person to break his contract of employment or to interfere with its performance . . .   *j*
> (3) For the purposes of subsection (1) above, an act shall be taken as having been done with the support of a ballot if, but only if—(a) the trade union has held a ballot in respect of the strike or other industrial action in the course of which the breach or interference referred to in subsection (1) above occurred; (b) the majority of those

a   voting in the ballot have answered "Yes" to the appropriate question; (c) the first
authorisation or endorsement of any relevant act, and in the case of an authorisation
the relevant act itself, took place after the date of the ballot and before the expiry of
the period of four weeks beginning with that date; and (d) section 11 of this Act has
been satisfied in relation to the ballot . . .'

These subsections were followed by sub-s (4), which has since been amended by the
b   Employment Act 1988. This, in its unamended form, provided:

'In subsection (3)(b) above "appropriate question" means—(a) where the industrial
action mentioned in subsection (3)(a) above is, or includes, a strike, the question
referred to in subsection (4)(a) of section 11; and (b) in any other case, that referred
to in subsection (4)(b) of that section.'

c   The key word here was the word 'includes'. As in the present case the union was
seeking support for industrial action which included strike action, although it also
extended to industrial action short of a strike, it may not unreasonably have thought that
it was required to base the question which it put to its members in the ballot on s 11(4)(a).
Paragraph (a) and (b) of s 11(4) were in the following terms:

d   '(a) a question (however framed) which requires the voter to say, by answering
"Yes" or "No", whether he is prepared to take part, or as the case may be to continue
to take part, in a strike involving him in a breach of his contract of employment; (b)
a question (however framed) which requires the voter to say, by answering "Yes" or
"No", whether he is prepared to take part, or as the case may be to continue to take
part, in industrial action falling short of a strike but involving him in a breach of his
e   contract of employment.'

I am not entirely sure that the question as framed by the union would have passed
muster under the unamended Act, but the union could certainly have been forgiven for
thinking that it would. This may indeed have been the position when the question was
framed. Most unfortunately, from the point of view of the union, the 1988 amendment
of the 1984 Act took effect on 26 July 1988, only a few days before the ballot was held.
f   We have therefore to consider whether the 1984 Act as amended, and in particular the
slightly amended s 11, was satisfied in relation to the ballot which took place in the
following month. The amendments were of crucial importance.
The first relevant amendment consisted of replacing s 10(4), which I have already set
out, with a new subsection and adding a new subsection (4A). These read:

g   '(4) Subject to subsection (4A) below, in this section and section 11 of this Act
references to the appropriate question are references to whichever of the questions
set out in subsection (4) of section 11 of this Act is applicable to the strike or other
industrial action in question.
(4A) Where both the questions mentioned in subsection (4) above are applicable
in relation to any industrial action, an act inducing a breach or interference such as
h   is mentioned in subsection (1) above shall be treated as an act for the purposes of
which the requirement of paragraph (b) of subsection (3) above is satisfied if but
only if that paragraph (or, as the case may be, that paragraph as it has effect by virtue
of subsection (3A) above) is satisfied in relation to the question applicable to that part
of the action in the course of which the breach or interference occurred.'

j   The questions set out in s 11(4) were amended so that they read:

'The voting paper must contain at least one of the following questions—(a) a
question (however framed) which requires the person answering it to say, by
answering "Yes" or "No", whether he is prepared to take part or, as the case may be,
to continue to take part in a strike; (b) a question (however framed) which requires

the person answering it to say, by answering "Yes" or "No", whether he is prepared to take part or, as the case may be, to continue to take part in action short of a strike.' *a*

The combined effect of these amendments, read with the unamended s 10(3)(*b*) was to require that the majority of those voting should have answered 'Yes' to the strike question set out in s 11(4)(*a*) if the union was calling for a strike and should have answered 'Yes' to the question set out in s 11(4)(*b*) if the union was going to call for industrial action short of a strike. If, as was the case here, the union contemplated both such types of action, it had to secure a 'Yes' vote in response to both questions. No longer was it even arguable *b* that a majority 'Yes' vote for strike action would authorise industrial action falling short of a strike on the grounds that the greater included the less.

If an Act of Parliament is unambiguous, as this one now is at least in this respect, the policy underlying it may not be directly relevant. However, it is reasonably clear that Parliament took account of the fact that some union members who might be prepared to take action short of a strike might not be prepared to take strike action or vice versa *c* and it considered that the union should be required to respect their wishes.

The single question, as framed by the Union, 'Are you willing to take Industrial Action up to and including Strike Action', does not permit its members to make this distinction. In effect, they have to say 'Yes' or 'No' to both questions set out in s 11(4) and this is contrary to the requirements of the amended Act, which clearly contemplate that, where both questions are asked, the members should be in a position to answer 'Yes' to one and *d* 'No' to the other.

It follows from the fact that the majority of those voting in the ballot answered 'Yes' to an inappropriate and not to the appropriate question (s 10(3)(*b*)) that the action of the union in calling for strikes was not in law an act done with the support of a ballot. As a result, the union is unable to rely on s 13 of the 1974 Act as a defence to the Post Office's *e* complaint.

This conclusion renders it unnecessary to consider two other objections to the union's reliance on the August 1988 ballot as a defence to claims for an injunction or damages based on industrial action in January 1990. As, however, they are of general importance, it may be helpful to the unions if I express a view.

f

The effect of discontinuity of industrial action

The intention of Parliament was quite clear that industrial action, whether taking the form of a strike or of industrial action short of a strike or both, should be begun, or its continuance endorsed, within a short period after the date of the ballot (see s 10(3)(*c*)). The reason is clear. Industrial relations are essentially fluid and attitudes change quickly. Accordingly, authority obtained from a ballot may in fact, as distinct from law, become *g* invalid within a relatively short time. Although the Act in terms only requires the action to be begun in the specified period of four weeks, it is implicit that, once begun, it shall continue without substantial interruption, if reliance is to continue to be placed on the verdict of the ballot. This is a question of fact and degree, but the question which the court has to ask itself is whether the average reasonable trade union member, looking at the matter at or shortly after any interruption in the industrial action, would say to *h* himself, 'The industrial action has now come to an end', even if he might also say, 'The union may want to call us out again if the dispute continues.' This is to be contrasted with a situation revealed in *Monsanto plc v Transport and General Workers' Union* [1987] 1 All ER 358, [1987] 1 WLR 617, where industrial action was 'suspended' for a short period (14 days) in order to enable active negotiations to take place. The negotiations failed and any reasonable union member would have said, and this court did say, that the *j* termination of the period of suspension restored the original and authorised industrial action.

On the facts of the present case, it is quite clear that the all-out one-day strike on 12 December 1988 ended the industrial action contemplated and authorised by the a August 1988 ballot and that this is why no further such action took place for over nine months. Applying the analysis of the traditional firework display, various rockets and bangers were discharged between 12 October and 30 November 1988 with the set-piece finale on 12 December 1988. This was followed by a complete change of tactics, namely the mounting of a public relations campaign, with a reversion to a policy of industrial action only in September 1989, even if a decision or tentative decision to adopt this course was taken in May 1989. This represented entirely new and disconnected action

b which needed the support of fresh ballot.

The effect of changes in the work force with the passage of time

The Post Office alleges, whether or not correctly, that between August 1988 and January 1990 there had been a 30% change in the relevant workforce and that this, of itself, would render the August 1988 ballot ineffective to support industrial action in

c January 1990. For my part, I do not see why, in principle, continuous industrial action over a period of over 18 months should necessarily be incapable of being supported by a single ballot, but two matters would require consideration.

The first is whether the action was sufficiently continuous and self-contained to constitute the particular strike or other industrial action contemplated by the ballot. Spasmodic and irregular action might not always qualify. It will be a question of fact and

d degree.

The second arises out of the terms of s 11(1) of the 1984 Act which requires the union to accord an entitlement to vote—

'to all those members of the trade union who it is reasonable at the time of the ballot for the union to believe will be induced to take part or, as the case may be, to continue to take part in the strike or other industrial action.'

e

The union clearly cannot identify and ballot those of its members who are not employees of the employer at the time of the ballot but who will, in the event, join the workforce at a later date. It would seem to follow that any call for industrial action following a ballot should expressly be limited to those who were employed by the employer, and given an opportunity of voting, at the time of the ballot. For the avoidance of doubt, let

f me say at once that I am not concerned, I do not think that any court would be concerned, at small changes in the workforce but, de minimis apart, this point may repay consideration.

For these reasons, I consider that the appeal should be allowed.

BUTLER-SLOSS LJ. I agree that this appeal should be allowed for the reasons given

g in the judgment of Lord Donaldson of Lymington MR, which I have had an opportunity to read in draft. Since we are differing from the judge, I shall however add a few observations of my own.

Whatever may have been the correct interpretation of s 10(3) of the Trade Union Act 1984 in its original form, I have no doubt that by the amendments in the Employment Act 1988 the present state of the law requires a specific question to be asked in respect of

h each of the two possible courses of action specified in s 11(4). Consequently, the 'rolled up' question which might have been acceptable before the coming into force of the 1988 Act on 26 July 1988 does not now comply with the statutory requirements and it is not therefore a valid notice. It is, of course, clear that this was an entirely innocent oversight by the union, which sent out the ballot papers on 15 August 1988, without being aware of the amendments to the Act and has the misfortune to find itself on a highly technical

j point without essential protection against the consequences of calling a strike. None the less, the fact that this point has been taken at a late stage and that the earlier calls to strike in 1988 and 1989 were not called into question by the Post Office as to the legality of the ballot paper does not, in my view, validate an invalid ballot paper. It might in other circumstances have a marked effect on the time allowed for a union to put its house in order if, for example, its members were at the time on strike. I should, however, have been very sad to be obliged to allow this appeal on this technical point alone.

I turn now to the question of the time lag between the holding of the ballot and the second wave of strikes starting in September 1989. It would appear to be clear that, as a result of the ballot in support of industrial action up to and including strike action, the union organised a rolling programme of one-day strikes in different areas from October 1988 until the end of November 1988 and a national one-day strike on 12 December which was the culmination and conclusion of that series of strikes.

Thereafter, between December and May 1989 no further strikes were planned or, it appears, in the immediate contemplation of the union. It appears to have sought to achieve its aims by other means. The union remain in dispute with the Post Office over the network conversion policy. In April the Post Office began to close Crown offices. At the union's annual conference in May 1989 the matter of further strikes was raised for the first time in that year, in the speech of Mr Ernest Dudley, deposed to in his affidavit. After that conference, arrangements were made for the strikes which started in September 1989, the notification of the latest of which on 18 January 1990 led to the application for an injunction, which was refused by Turner J on 17 January. The question is whether the second wave of strikes from September 1989 formed part of a continuous process deriving from and supported by the ballot in August 1988. Section 10(3) requires strike action to begin within a short period of the authorisation by the ballot, and it is implicit in the Act that the action should be continuous rather than discontinuous. It is clear from *Monsanto plc v Transport and General Workers' Union* [1987] 1 All ER 358, [1987] 1 WLR 617 that the process can be interrupted, albeit briefly. On the facts of that case the interruption was by way of suspension for the limited period of 14 days and for the specific purpose of negotiations between the parties in dispute. A distinction has to be drawn between suspension for a specific and limited purpose and cessation of action. It will, however, always be a matter of degree whether on the particular facts of each case the protection of the ballot has, in fact, been or not been exhausted.

On the present facts, in my view, the series of strikes authorised by the ballot started in October 1988 and was concluded on 12 December 1988. After 12 December 1988, in the absence of any contemplated arrangements for the next five months and without a strike for nine months, that authorisation was exhausted. The revival of the strike weapon in 1989 was a new decision and another change of tactics by the union, although manifestly in support of the continuing campaign by the union against the Post Office plans. It was fresh industrial action and consequently required the support of a fresh ballot.

The 1989–90 strikes were therefore unlawful and this was industrial action authorised or endorsed by a trade union without the support of a ballot (s 10(1)).

I would allow this appeal.

FARQUHARSON LJ. I agree.

Appeal allowed. Each party to pay its own costs in Court of Appeal below. Leave to appeal to the House of Lords refused.

Solicitors: *Brian A Holland*, Croydon (for the Post Office); *Simpson Millar* (for the union).

Frances Rustin   Barrister.

Quietlynn Ltd and another v Southend-on-Sea Borough Council

(Case C-23/89)

COURT OF JUSTICE OF THE EUROPEAN COMMUNITIES (SIXTH CHAMBER)

JUDGES KAKOURIS (PRESIDENT OF CHAMBER), SCHOCKWEILER, MANCINI, O'HIGGINS AND DÍEZ DE VELASCO

ADVOCATE GENERAL LENZ

27 MARCH, 3 MAY, 11 JULY 1990

European Economic Community – Imports – Reduction in volume of imports – Quantitative restriction on imports from another member state – Measures having equivalent effect – Control of sex establishments – Local authority having power to control sex shops in its area by requiring premises selling sex articles to a significant degree to be licenced – Retailer selling sex articles from unlicensed shop premises – Retailer attempting not to contravene legislation and thereby selling less material imported from other member states – Whether restriction on availability of articles from other member states a 'measure' having equivalent effect to quantitative restriction on imports – Whether restriction justifiable – Local Government (Miscellaneous Provisions) Act 1982, s 2(1), Sch 3, paras 6(1), 20(1) – EEC Treaty, arts 30, 36.

The respondent council resolved under s 2(1)[a] of the Local Government (Miscellaneous Provisions) Act 1982 that Sch 3 to that Act, which contained provisions for the licensing of sex shops, should apply to its area, with the consequence that a licence was required if premises were used as a business which consisted to a significant degree of selling and displaying sex articles. The appellants, who operated retail shops within the council's area, continued to sell such articles despite the refusal of a licence although they reduced their stock to avoid contravening the 1982 Act and, consequently, sold less material imported from other member states than they would otherwise have done. The council brought proceedings against the appellants in the magistrates' court alleging that they were using their premises without a licence contrary to paras 6(1)[b] and 20(1)[c] of Sch 3 to the 1982 Act. The appellants were convicted. They appealed to the Crown Court against their convictions. They admitted that they had used their premises without a licence contrary to the 1982 Act but contended that the provisions of that Act relating to the licensing system for sex establishments and offences against that system were incompatible with art 30[d] of the EEC Treaty inasmuch as they constituted a measure having an effect equivalent to a quantitative restriction on imports from other member states and did not fall within any of the exceptions provided for by art 36[e] of the Treaty or any other

---

a Section 2(1), so far as material, provides: 'A local authority may resolve that Schedule 3 to this Act is to apply to their area; and if a local authority so resolve, that Schedule shall come into force in their area on the day specified in that behalf in the resolution . . .'

b Paragraph 6(1), so far as material, provides: 'Subject to the provisions of this Schedule, no person shall in any area in which this Schedule is in force use any premises . . . as a sex establishment except under and in accordance with the terms of a licence under this Schedule by the appropriate authority . . .'

c Paragraph 20(1), so far as material, provides: 'A person who—(a) knowingly uses, or knowingly causes or permits the use of, any premises, vehicle, vessel or stall contrary to paragraph 6 above . . . shall be guilty of an offence . . .'

d Article 30 provides: 'Quantitative restrictions on imports and all measures having equivalent effect shall, without prejudice to the following provisions, be prohibited between Member States.'

e Article 36, so far as material, provides: 'The provisions of Article 30 . . . shall not preclude prohibitions or restrictions on imports, exports or goods in transit justified on grounds of public morality, public policy or public security . . . Such prohibitions or restrictions shall not, however, constitute a means or arbitrary discrimination or a disguised restriction on trade between Member States.'

derogation. The Crown Court considered that the appeal raised questions relating to the interpretation of Community law and therefore referred to the Court of Justice of the *a* European Communities for a preliminary ruling the questions (1) whether the prohibition on the sale of lawful sex articles without a licence where the effect was to enable the local authority to control sex establishments in its area and to restrict the appellants from selling goods from other member states in an attempt not to contravene the Act was a measure having equivalent effect to a quantitative restriction on imports within the meaning of art 30, (2) if it was, whether the prohibition was justified under *b* art 36 and (3) if the prohibition contravened art 30 and was not justified under art 36, whether it was totally unenforceable against a trader in the member state or only to the extent that it prohibited transactions involving goods manufactured or imported from other member states.

Held – National legislation which prohibited the sale of sex articles from unlicensed sex *c* establishments and which applied without distinction to imported and domestic products was merely a rule governing the distribution of such products by regulating the outlets through which the products might be marketed and, therefore, was not of such a nature as to impede trade between member states. Furthermore, the prohibition had no connection with intra-Community trade since the products covered by the 1982 Act could be marketed through licensed shops and other channels, including shops in which *d* sex articles accounted for an insignificant proportion of the sales and which were therefore not required to be licensed, or by mail order. Moreover, the provisions were not intended to regulate trade in goods in the Community and were therefore not of such a nature as to impede trade between member states. It followed therefore that they did not constitute a measure having an effect equivalent to a quantitative restriction on imports and accordingly did not contravene art 30 of the EEC Treaty (see p 221 *b c e* to *g j*, post). *e*

Notes

For control of sex establishments and the requirement for licences, see 45 Halsbury's Laws (4th edn) paras 1019–1020.

For the free movement of goods in the European Economic Community and *f* justifications for restrictions of trade between member states, see 52 ibid paras 388, 398, 412.

For the Local Government (Miscellaneous Provisions) Act 1982, s 2, Sch 3, paras 6, 20, see 45 Halsbury's Statutes (4th edn) 506, 521, 527.

For the EEC Treaty, arts 30, 36, see 50 ibid 276, 278.

Cases cited *g*

Blesgen v Belgium Case 75/81 [1982] ECR 1211.

Cinéthèque SA v Fédération Nationale des Cinémas Français Joined cases 60 and 61/84 [1985] ECR 2605.

Conegate v Customs and Excise Comrs Case 121/85 [1986] 2 All ER 688, [1987] QB 254, [1986] ECR 1007, CJEC.

Direction générale des impôts and Procureur de la République v Forest Case 148/85 [1986] ECR *h* 3449.

Duphar BV v Netherlands State Case 238/82 [1984] ECR 523.

EC Commission v Federal Republic of Germany Case 178/84 [1987] ECR 1227.

EC Commission v French Republic Case 152/81 [1980] ECR 2299.

EC Commission v French Republic Case 216/84 [1988] ECR 793.

EC Commission v Italian Republic Case 193/80 [1981] ECR 3019. *j*

Fabriek voor Hoogwaardige Voedingsproduckten Kelderman BV, Criminal proceedings against Case 130/80 [1981] ECR 527.

Fietje, Criminal proceedings against Case 27/80 [1980] ECR 3839.

GB-INNO-BM v Confédération du Commerce Luxembourgeois Case C-362/88 (7 March 1990, unreported), CJEC.

Krantz GmbH v Ontvanger der direkte Belastingen von Kerrasde and the Netherlands Case C-
a   69/88 (7 March 1990 unreported), CJEC.
Ministère Public v Gauchard Case 20/87 [1987] ECR 4879.
Nederlandse Bakkerij Stichting v Edah BV Joined cases 80 and 159/85 [1986] ECR 3359.
Oebel, Summary proceedings against Case 155/80 [1981] ECR 1993.
Oosthoek's Uitgeversmaatschappij BV, Criminal proceedings against Case 286/81 [1982] ECR
      4575.
b *Prantl, Criminal proceedings against* Case 16/83 [1984] ECR 1299.
Procureur du Roi v Dassonville Case 8/74 [1974] ECR 837.
R v Bouchereau Case 30/77 (1977) [1981] 2 All ER 924, [1978] QB 732, [1978] 2 WLR 250,
      [1977] ECR 1999, CJEC.
R v Henn, R v Darby [1980] 2 All ER 166, [1981] AC 850, [1980] 2 WLR 597, [1979] ECR
      3795, CJEC.
c *Rau (Walter) Lebensmittelwerke v De Smedt PvbA* Case 261/81 [1982] ECR 3961.
Rewe-Zentral v Bundesmonopolverwaltung für Branntwein Case 120/78 [1979] ECR 649.
3 Glocken GmbH v USL Centro-Sud and Provincia autonoma di Bolzano Case 407/85 [1988]
      ECR 4233.
Torfaen BC v B & Q plc Case 145/88 [1990] 1 All ER 129, [1990] 2 WLR 1330, CJEC.
van Bennekom, Criminal proceedings against Case 227/82 [1983] ECR 3883.
d

Reference

By order dated 7 September 1988 the Crown Court at Chelmsford referred to the Court
of Justice of the European Communities for a preliminary ruling under art 177 of the
EEC Treaty three questions (set out at p 220 g to j, post) on the interpretation of arts 30
and 36 of the Treaty in order to determine whether national legislation prohibiting the
e   sale of lawful sex articles from unlicensed sex establishments was compatible with those
provisions. The questions were raised in the course of an appeal by Quietlynn Ltd and
Brian James Richards, its managing director, against their conviction by Rochford and
Southend-on-Sea Magistrates' Court on 11 February 1986, on the prosecution of Southend-
on-Sea Borough Council, for contravening paras 6(1) and 20 of Sch 3 to the Local
Government (Miscellaneous Provisions) Act 1982 by using their retail shop premises at
f   Southend-on-Sea within the council's area without a licence on 13 March and 11 April
1985 contrary to that Act. Quietlynn Ltd, Mr Richards, Southend-on-Sea Borough
Council, the United Kingdom and the Commission of the European Communities
submitted written observations to the court. The language of the case was English. The
facts are set out in the report for the hearing presented by the Judge Rapporteur.

g   **The Judge Rapporteur (Diez de Velasco)** presented the following report for the
hearing.

I—LEGAL BACKGROUND
      1. Section 2 of the Local Government (Miscellaneous Provisions) Act 1982 provides
h   local authorities in England and Wales with the power to control sex cinemas and sex
shops in their area. In particular, it empowers those authorities to bring the provisions of
Sch 3 to the Act into force in their area by passing a resolution to that effect.
      2. Under paras 2, 4 and 6(1) of that schedule, a licence is required if the premises are
used for the business which consists to a significant degree of selling or displaying articles
made or intended for use in connection with, or for the purpose of stimulating or
j   encouraging, sexual activity. The definition embraces all forms of publications and
records of sound or vision, and excludes only articles which primarily relate to birth
control. Any person trading without a licence where the Act is in force is liable to a fine
not exceeding £20,000 (£10,000 at the time when the offences were committed).

II—FACTS AND PROCEDURE BEFORE THE NATIONAL COURT
      1. Southend-on-Sea Borough Council (the council) brought those provisions into force

in its area with effect from 23 June 1983. Quietlynn Ltd and Brian James Richards (the
appellants) operate retail shop premises at Southend-on-Sea, within the council's area. Mr *a*
Richards is the managing director of Quietlynn Ltd.

2. The council brought a prosecution against the appellants for using their premises
without a licence, contrary to paras 6(1) and 20 of Sch 3 to the Act, on 13 March and
11 April 1985. They were found guilty of two offences by Rochford and Southend-on-
Sea Magistrates' Court on 11 February 1986, fined £1,000 in respect of each offence and
ordered to pay costs.   *b*

3. The appellants appealed to the Crown Court at Chelmsford against the convictions.
From the outset of the appeal, they acknowledged that they had used their premises
without a licence, contrary to the Act, on 13 March and 11 April 1985. Their sole defence
is that the provisions of the Act relating to the licensing system for sex establishments
and offences against that system are incompatible with art 30 of the EEC Treaty inasmuch
as they constitute a measure having an effect equivalent to a quantitative restriction on *c*
imports from other member states and fall within neither one of the exceptions provided
for in art 36 nor any other derogation.

4. The appellants sell sex articles manufactured or supplied both in the United
Kingdom and abroad from other member states.

At the material times, the appellants were endeavouring to maintain sufficiently low
stocks at their premises to avoid infringing the relevant provisions. They claim that *d*
imported articles, for example rubber dolls and dildos, are noticeably more conspicuous
than similar items supplied from within the United Kingdom. Consequently, the
numbers that they felt they could sell were very small. The goods offered for sale in the
shop in question were at the material times lawfully on sale, apart from the operation of
the Act.

5. It therefore follows, according to the national court, that the effect of the Act is to *e*
reduce indirectly in absolute terms the quantity of sex articles imported into the United
Kingdom for the appellants to be able to sell.

6. The Crown Court at Chelmsford therefore requests the Court of Justice to give a
preliminary ruling on the following questions:

'1. Where a Member State (once a Local Authority has resolved that the legislation *f*
is to apply to their area subject to the requirement for premises which are sex
establishments to be licensed) prohibits the sale (*inter alia*) of lawful sex articles from
unlicensed sex establishments, and where the effect of such a prohibition is to enable
the Local Authority to exercise control over sex establishments within their area,
and where the effect is to have restricted the Appellants from selling goods from
other Member States since they have been attempting not to contravene the Act by *g*
their stocking policy and in doing so have been selling less imported material from
Member States than would otherwise have been the case and thus to restrict the
availability of sex articles manufactured in other Member States; is such a prohibition
a measure having equivalent effect to a quantitative restriction on imports within
the meaning of Article 30 of the Treaty?

2. If the answer to Question 1 is in the affirmative, does such a measure benefit *h*
from the justification set out in Article 36?

3. If the prohibition referred to in Question 1 contravenes Article 30 and is not
justified under Article 36, is it totally unenforceable against a trader in the Member
State or only unenforceable to the extent that it prohibits transactions involving
goods manufactured in or imported from other Member States?'   *j*

7. The order for reference was received at the court registry on 30 January 1989.

8. In accordance with art 20 of the Protocol on the Statute of the Court of Justice,
written observations have been submitted by the appellants in the main proceedings,
represented by N Peters, barrister, instructed by Kaye Tesler & Co, solicitors, by the
respondent in the main proceedings, represented by S Reid, barrister, instructed by the
borough solicitor of Southend-on-Sea Borough Council, by the United Kingdom,

represented by N Paines, barrister, instructed by S J Hay, Treasury Solicitor's Department,
a and by the Commission, represented by E L White, a member of its legal department,
acting as agent.

9. On hearing the report of the Judge Rapporteur and the views of the Advocate
General, the court decided to open the oral procedure without any preparatory inquiry.

By a decision of 6 December 1989, taken pursuant to art 95(1) and (2) of the rules of
procedure, the court assigned the case to the Sixth Chamber.
b

III—WRITTEN OBSERVATIONS SUBMITTED TO THE COURT

1. *Quietlynn Ltd and Mr Richards*, the appellants in the main proceedings, consider that
the effect of the legislation in question and in particular the words 'significant degree'
and their interpretation constitute a measure having an effect equivalent to a quantitative
restriction and therefore an infringement of art 30 of the EEC Treaty, since the effect or
c hindrance is direct, though the ambit of that article is very wide (see, for example,
Procureur du Roi v Dassonville Case 8/74 [1974] ECR 837).

Although they can still import certain sex articles, they are gravely restricted, they
claim, in the amount they can sell. The Act and Sch 3 itself may restrict the availability
of lawfully imported sex articles inasmuch as they give a local authority the power to
deny licences. The effect in this case, they submit, is to place imported goods at a
d disadvantage. Furthermore, the operation of the Act does in practice restrict importations
whether or not the appellants are guilty of the offences.

In the appellants' submission, the definition of sex article is very wide and therefore it
cannot be said that in any event the legislation is an 'equally applicable' measure. It is not
here an 'equally applicable' measure that may be justified on the ground that it is
necessary to satisfy some mandatory requirement relating in particular to consumer
e protection and fair trading (the 'rule of reason'). As the Act does not purport to prohibit
or legislate for sex articles per se, the cases in the line of *Blesgen v Belgium* Case 75/81
[1982] ECR 1211 and *Cinéthèque SA v Fédération Nationale des Cinémas Français* Joined
Cases 60 and 61/84 [1985] ECR 2605 cannot apply.

They submit, moreover, that the provisions of art 36 of the EEC Treaty cannot be used
f to derogate from art 30, since the Act constitutes a means of arbitrary discrimination or
disguised restriction on trade between member states. Nor, in their view, can there be
any justification in the interests of public morality, because public morality does not
come within the province of a local authority's powers, and the Act is in force in certain
areas but not in others. Furthermore, sex articles may be sold throughout the member
state, and they are lawful.

g The appellants therefore make the following submissions with regard to the answers
to be given to the questions raised by the national court:

'*Question 1* It is submitted that the answer to question 1 should be in the
affirmative because the appellants reduced their stock of imported goods to stay
within the law. The only safe course for the appellants is to cease selling the
imported goods in question so as to avoid any future prosecution. This would in
h itself be against the permissiveness of the Act as well as a restriction on the
importation and availability of goods from other member states.

Question 2 If the answer to question 1 is in the affirmative then it is submitted
that for the reasons advanced the answer should be in the negative.

Question 3 The Act is unenforceable only to the extent that it prohibits
(indirectly) transactions involving goods manufactured in or imported from other
j member states. The potential importation of lawful sex articles is threatened by the
Act. Where the Act has been adopted, there is power for a local authority to refuse
licences throughout its localities. This, together with a narrow interpretation of
"significant degree" in respect of any trader who sought to trade in such an area
would result in a new absolute restriction on imported sex articles. This may
amount to a means of arbitrary discrimination against traders in such an area. Other
areas may have licensed premises, whilst in yet other areas the Act may not be in

force and imported sex articles may be freely traded without hindrance. The court is asked to pronounce on the possible means of arbitrary discrimination or disguised *a* restriction on the trade between other member states and the United Kingdom in respect of lawful sex articles. This therefore affects any trader within the member states.'

2. *Southend-on-Sea Borough Council*, the respondent in the main proceedings, considers that the legislation forms no obstacle to intra-Community trade since it does not *b* constitute a quantitative restriction or measure having equivalent effect. The legislation is concerned with the control of sex shops as outlets to the consumer, and applies to the shops, not the goods sold therein.

In its submission, although the undisputed facts might show a restriction in the 'availability of sex articles imported from other member states', there is no allegation or evidence that intra-Community trade in such articles has been reduced. The goods in *c* question remain capable of importation and sale. There is no evidence to show that the presence of sex shops stimulates a demand for sex articles, and that their restriction reduces the demand for such goods. The demand can be adequately satisfied by the trade from unlicensed premises. In addition, such goods can be sold by mail order and are unaffected by the Act. Furthermore, the trade in lawful sex articles by its nature lends itself to mail order sale. It cannot be said that the consumer is therefore permanently *d* deprived of the goods.

Although there may be some disadvantage to an individual trader because sales of that sort of goods may pass to a competitor, that is not enough of an obstacle to intra-Community trade in the absence of a total diminution in imports of that sort. It cannot have been in the contemplation of the signatories of the Treaty that such an obstacle to 'personal' imports would render national legislation subject to detailed scrutiny by the *e* court. The concern of the Common Market is that goods are to move freely, not that all individuals have the right to move goods freely. Since no overall reduction in imports has been proven, the actual or potential reduction of the imports in question is not to be considered significant because of the de minimis principle.

The council submits that the 'sex shop' legislation is closely analogous to that in a number of previous cases (inter alia, *Summary proceedings against Oebel* Case 155/80 [1981] *f* ECR 1993, *Duphar BV v Netherlands State* Case 238/82 [1984] ECR 523, *Blesgen v Belgium* Case 75/81 [1982] EC 1211 and *Direction générale des impôts and Procureur de la République v Forest* Case 148/85 [1986] ECR 3449), although it is not as wide since it is concerned only with outlets. Sales to consumers can still occur irrespective of licensed outlets. The trade in such goods can continue and as long as the legislation makes no discrimination between national and imported goods there is no infringement. There is no such *g* discrimination either because the goods are not 'affected' within the meaning of art 30 or, alternatively, because they are equally restricted irrespective of their origin.

The council further submits that the provisions in question are to be recognised as being necessary in order to satisfy mandatory requirements. It points out that the sale of sex articles is a lucrative business and that such a sanction as the threat of the removal of a licence provides protection to the consumer. *h*

In its view, the control of sex shops is a purpose in the general interests which should take precedence over the free movement of goods. While the articles sold therein are lawful there is still a need for control of some sort to be exercised over their sale wherever and whenever they are displayed for sale in and sold from premises where there is a concentration of such articles. The quality and quantity of such articles condone a sexual attitude which is widely regarded as immoral or perverted. Without such controls such *j* attitudes could become commonplace. The council denies that such legislation is disproportionate in its restriction. It submits that the restrictions are no more than is necessary for the protection of the consumer.

Alternatively, it submits that the provisions of the Act can be justified by art 36 on the grounds of public morality, public policy and public safety. They are not more restrictive

than is necessary to achieve their legitimate objective and do not constitute a disguised
a   restriction on trade or arbitrary discrimination.
The council proposes that the national court's questions should be answered as follows:

'1. Article 30 of the EEC Treaty is not to be interpreted as meaning that the
prohibition against the sale of sex articles from sex shops (within the meaning of the
Act) which are unlicensed is a measure having equivalent effect to a quantitative
b   restriction on imports.
2. Question 2 does not require a reply (if, contrary to the council's submissions,
the court answers question 1 in the affirmative; the above-mentioned prohibition is
justified by art 36).
3. If the court answers questions 1 and 2 in the negative, the prohibition is only
enforceable to the extent that it prohibits goods manufactured in or imported from
c   other member states.'

3. The *United Kingdom* submits that the licensing system in question does not have the
effect of reducing the overall volume of imports of sex articles into the United Kingdom.
The case law of the court shows that measures which prevent the opening of a particular
outlet in a particular place, or which restrict the types of goods which may be sold in a
d   particular outlet, are not to be regarded as measures having an effect equivalent to
quantitative restrictions because of their effect on the turnover of the outlet or proposed
outlet in question.
Furthermore, the United Kingdom legislation on sex shops is in a similar category to
the Belgian law considered in *Blesgen v Belgium* Case 75/81. Neither of those rules is
capable of preventing the marketing of any imported product. They regulate the outlets
e   through which products may be marketed, but do so in a way which does not discriminate
between domestic and imported goods.
In the United Kingdom's view *EC Commission v French Republic* Case 152/78 [1980]
ECR 2299, *Blesgen v Belgium* Case 75/81 cited above, *Nederlandse Bakkerij Stichting v Edah
BV* Joined cases 80 and 159/85 [1986] ECR 3359, *Direction général des impôts and Procureur
de la République v Forest* Case 148/85, and *Ministère Public v Gauchard* Case 20/87 [1987]
f   ECR 4879 are examples of the principle that measures which affect products only by
placing restrictions on businesses processing or selling them are not measures within the
meaning of art 30 unless they are discriminatory as between domestic and imported
goods. The court has consistently and rightly maintained discrimination as the test of
the compatability of such measures with art 30.
In the alternative, the United Kingdom submits that the contested legislation is
g   justified by mandatory requirements or pursuant to art 36.
The objectives pursued by the contested legislation have to do with public morality,
public policy and justifiable social considerations. Controlling the manner of sale and
display of sex articles is a matter relating to public morality. Preventing unsuitable
persons from being concerned in trade in these articles is a matter relating to public order
h   and the defence of the consumer, and protecting the general public from the undesirable
intrusion of sex shops into inappropriate sites or areas is an objective which both falls
within the scope of public morality and is an objective which is justified with regard to
Community law, as the court held in *Cinéthèque SA v Fédération Nationale des Cinémas
Français* Joined cases 60 and 61/84 [1985] ECR 2605.
The United Kingdom government further submits that there is no principle of
Community law to the effect that discretion in matters of public policy must be exercised
j   by central government and not by local authorities. There is no principle that a system
in which such discretion is given to local authorities thereby constitutes a means of
arbitrary discrimination or a disguised restriction on trade.
Indeed, the court has already recognised in *Conegate Ltd v Customs and Excise* Case 121/
85 [1986] 2 All ER 688, [1987] QB 254 that a member state may have different legislation
relating to public morality in its different constituent parts.

The United Kingdom submits that the questions raised in the order for reference should be answered as follows:

'1. Article 30 is not to be interpreted as meaning that a rule requiring shops selling sex articles to be licensed by a local authority if they trade in such articles to a significant degree is a measure of equivalent effect to a quantitative restriction within the meaning of that article.

2. Questions 2 and 3 do not require a reply.'

4. The *Commission* remarks, first of all, that a licensing requirement for shops is by its nature a restriction on the freedom of establishment, a matter which is regulated by art 52 of the EEC Treaty. Since nothing in the present reference indicates that the appellants are nationals of another member state, it appears to the Commission that there can be no grounds for considering the contested measures to be contrary to the Treaty, as the court stated in the *Gauchard* case.

With regard to the compatibility of the provisions in question with art 30 of the EEC Treaty, the Commission considers, first, that even if unlicensed shops were prohibited from selling sex articles, that would still not necessarily affect the overall volume of imports. Disparities between indistinctly applicable national rules which merely regulate the circumstances in which goods may be sold or used do not create obstacles to trade. It is the very existence of the rules in the importing member state which may reduce the level of imports by reducing the outlets or uses for the goods in general and thus the demand for the goods.

In the Commission's opinion, the reduction in imports is completely independent of the existence or not of similar or differing rules in other member states. Consequently, the Commission submits, the court has not held indistinctly applicable measures which merely regulate in a general and neutral manner the circumstances in which goods may be used or sold to fall under art 30, as demonstrated by its judgments in the *Oebel, Blesgen, Forest* and *Gauchard* cases.

With regard to the applicability of art 30 to the licensing requirements which are the subject of the present reference, the Commission observes that those requirements are indistinctly applicable. The requirements of the Act merely regulate in a general and neutral manner the circumstances in which sex shops may be used and thus indirectly the circumstances in which sex articles may be sold.

In the Commission's view, therefore, they are not contrary to art 30, and they constitute a legitimate element of socio-economic policy.

Furthermore, if the measures involved in this case did fall under art 30, the Commission considers that they would in any case be justified by the protection of public morality pursuant to art 36 of the EEC Treaty. Public morality and public policy need not be viewed nationally, that is to say be uniform throughout a member state, as is clear from the court's judgment in *R v Henn, R v Darby* Case 37/79 [1980] 2 All ER 166, [1981] AC 850.

Finally, for the Commission, the impracticality of the effects of an incompatibility of the licensing requirements for sex shops selling products imported from other member states constitutes confirmation of its belief that art 30 cannot be applicable to non-discriminatory measures of that kind.

The Commission proposes that the answer to the national court's question should be in the following terms:

'Article 30 of the EEC Treaty is to be interpreted as not prohibiting a national rule which, in a general and non-discriminatory manner, restricts the sale of sex articles from unlicensed sex shops.'

Nigel Peters for the appellants.
Sebastian Reid for the council.
Nicholas Paines for the United Kingdom.
Eric L White for the Commission.

3 May. **The Advocate General (C O Lenz)** delivered the following opinion.[1] Mr
President, Members of the Court,

A *Facts*
 1. In the proceedings on which I now give my opinion the court is once again called
on to interpret the expression 'quantitative restrictions on imports and all measures
having equivalent effect' contained in art 30 of the EEC Treaty and to construe, if
appropriate, art 36 thereof.
 2. The interpretation is requested by the Crown Court at Chelmsford in order to
enable it to assess the validity under Community law of the Local Government
(Miscellaneous Provisions) Act 1982 in force in England and Wales. To put it briefly at
this stage, the Act covers trade in so-called sex articles (which are defined in detail), and it
gives local authorities the power to decide that Sch 3 to the Act shall apply with the
consequence that trade in those articles, if it reaches a significant degree, may only be
carried on with a licence from the appropriate authority.
 3. A resolution to that effect (similar action was taken by some other local authorities
but not throughout the Act's area of application) was adopted by the respondent in the
main proceedings with effect from 23 June 1983. The appellants in the main proceedings
are affected thereby as they, apparently in addition to other traders, some of whom are
licensed, carry on within the respondent's area such a trade in domestic and imported
products. Since the appellants continued to carry on this trade despite the refusal of a
licence, proceedings were brought against them in the Rochford and Southend-on-Sea
Magistrates' Court which resulted in their conviction in February 1986. They appealed
to the Crown Court at Chelmsford. In those proceedings they submitted in support of
their appeal, inter alia, that the 1982 Act was not compatible with Community law since
it led to a restriction on imports within the meaning of art 30 of the EEC Treaty (I shall
go into the details of that argument later). Since the national court was not unimpressed
by the force of this argument, it stayed the proceedings and referred the following
questions to the Court of Justice for a preliminary ruling:

 '1. Where a Member State (once a Local Authority has resolved that the legislation
 is to apply to their area subject to the requirement for premises which are sex
 establishments to be licensed) prohibits the sale (*inter alia*) of lawful sex articles from
 unlicensed sex establishments, and where the effect of such a prohibition is to enable
 the Local Authority to exercise control over sex establishments within their area,
 and where the effect is to have restricted the Appellants from selling goods from
 other Member States since they have been attempting not to contravene the Act by
 their stocking policy and in doing so have been selling less imported material from
 Member States than would otherwise have been the case and thus to restrict the
 availability of sex articles manufactured in other Member States; is such a prohibition
 a measure having equivalent effect to a quantitative restriction on imports within
 the meaning of Article 30 of the Treaty?
 2. If the answer to Question 1 is in the affirmative, does such a measure benefit
 from the justification set out in Article 36?
 3. If the prohibition referred to in Question 1 contravenes Article 30 and is not
 justified under Article 36, is it totally unenforceable against a trader in the Member
 State or only unenforceable to the extent that it prohibits transactions involving
 goods manufactured in or imported from other Member States?'

 4. On the basis of the written and oral observations submitted to the court, my
assessment is as follows.

B *Analysis*
 5. (1) If one proceeds on the basis of the *formula* which was set out in relation to art 30
in the judgment in *Procureur du Roi v Dassonville* Case 8/74 [1974] ECR 837 and appears

---
 1 Translated from the German

again and again in cases concerning that article (cf, for example, the judgments in *Blesgen v Belgium* Case 75/81 [1982] ECR 1211 and *Krantz GmbH v Ontvanger der direkte Belastingen von Kerkrade and the Netherlands* Case C-69/88 (7 March 1990, unreported)), that is to say if consideration is given to the question whether the provisions at issue are 'capable of hindering, directly or indirectly, actually or potentially intra-Community trade', there can be little doubt that this is the case.

6. It is indeed conceivable that, *without* the Act and the local authority resolutions adopted pursuant thereto, that is if so-called sex articles could be sold without hindrance, sales would be more extensive and imports therefore greater. For it may be assumed that the unrestricted growth of sex shops would create new demand and also lead to an increase in existing demand because that demand could more readily be satisfied than in a situation in which a potential customer has to travel to a different place (having licensed sex shops) or has to engage in the more complicated process of mail order. Regulating the sale of sex articles may therefore, it can safely be assumed, lead to a reduction in imports and thus justify the application of art 30.

7. (2) However, a *comprehensive appraisal of the relevant case law* makes clear that this consideration is not in itself sufficient. In fact, that formula is merely a starting point for the requisite examination. Further factors must then also be taken into account and, as the Commission and other parties have shown, each case must be decided on its own merits.

8. (a) Accordingly, if the case law is looked at more closely and it is borne in mind that in the present case there is no outright prohibition on the sale of certain products but rather that marketing rules apply which, under certain circumstances, preclude those products from being sold in certain places (where sales reach a significant degree), comparable situations may readily be encountered in earlier cases also concerning only the *nature and method of marketing* of products, in respect of which it was found that art 30 did not apply (although some impact on imports could not be ruled out).

9. I would cite, for example, *Summary proceedings against Oebel* Case 155/80 [1981] ECR 1993 concerning the sale of bakers' wares which, at certain times of the night, could not be sold to individual consumers and retail outlets but only to wholesalers and dealers. A central feature of this case was the finding that intra-Community trade nevertheless remained possible, and, consequently, there was held to be no infringement of art 30.

10. I would also cite the judgment in *Blesgen v Belgium* Case 75/81 [1982] ECR 1211 (concerning the prohibition on the sale of certain alcoholic beverages in Belgian public houses). An important factor in that case was that the rules in question did not apply to other forms of sale and it was, therefore, found that art 30 of the EEC Treaty did not apply since in reality the connection with imports was non-existent.

11. In this regard attention was also correctly drawn to *Ministère Public v Gauchard* Case 20/87 [1987] ECR 4879 concerning French provisions relating to authorisations to operate supermarkets which can result in a restriction of sales of goods including imported products. On this point the question as to the relevance of art 30 was examined during the proceedings. The Advocate General concluded that it was not relevant and pointed out that, as a result of the provisions in question, sales on the domestic market of imported goods and those produced domestically were affected to the same extent. The court evidently shared that assessment. In any event it is noteworthy that in the judgment art 30 is not examined at all; there is only an appraisal in the light of art 52 of the Treaty (right of establishment).

12. The quite recent judgment in *Torfaen BC v B & Q plc* Case 145/88 [1990] 1 All ER 129, [1990] 2 WLR 1330 is also not without some relevance. That case concerned the prohibition on the sale of certain goods on Sundays and is of interest because, in the first paragraph of the judgment containing the court's assessment, it is pointed out that, regard being had to the fact that the rules in question apply to imported and domestic products alike, the marketing of products imported from other member states is not in principle made more difficult than that of domestic products.

13. In the light of this case law it has been suggested, in my view not without some

justification, that a similar conclusion should be arrived at in the present case and it should be found that the provisions at issue in the main dispute are not within the scope of art 30 of the Treaty. In fact, in this case as well there are good reasons for stating that the Local Government (Miscellaneous Provisions) Act 1982 has nothing to do with international trade because the sale of the articles contemplated is in any case possible by means other than sex shops, in particular through businesses which require no licence (because the sale of sex articles does not reach a significant degree) or by means of mail order, even if in this case, as was stated at the hearing, certain restrictions apply (irrespective of the origin of the products).

14. (b) *The other judgments mentioned in the proceedings* are, it has to be said, basically not relevant and therefore provide no grounds for arriving at a different assessment in the present case.

15. Those judgments concern cases in which provisions were applicable without distinction to domestic and imported goods and the decisive question was whether imported products were in actual fact placed at any *disadvantage*, in which case art 30 came into play. The Commission correctly pointed out that those cases mainly concerned provisions relating to the *conditions which the products themselves* had to comply with (and where consequently the need to adapt imported products accordingly could constitute a hindrance to trade: cf the cases listed by the Commission its written observations (*Rewe-Zentral AG v Bundesmonopolverwaltung für Branntwein* Case 120/78 [1979] ECR 649, *Criminal proceedings against Fabriek voor Hoogwaardige Voedingsproduckten Kelderman BV* Case 130/80 [1981] ECR 527, *3 Glocken GmbH v USL Centro-Sud and Provincia autonome di Bolzano* Case 407/85 [1988] ECR 4233, *Walter Rau Lebesmittelwerke v De Smedt PvbA* Case 261/81 [1982] ECR 3961, *Criminal proceedings against Prantl* Case 16/83 [1984] ECR 1299, *Criminal proceedings against van Bennekom* Case 227/82 [1983] ECR 3883, *Criminal proceedings against Oosthoek's Uitgeversmaatschappij BV* Case 286/81 [1982] ECR 4575, *EC Commission v Italian Republic* Case 193/80 [1981] ECR 3019, *EC Commission v Federal Republic of Germany* Case 178/84 [1987] ECR 1227, *Criminal proceedings against Fietje* Case 27/80 [1980] ECR 3839, *EC Commission v French Republic* Case 216/84 [1988] ECR 793, *Cinéthèque SA v Fédération Nationale des Cinémas Français* Joined Cases 60 and 61/84 [1985] ECR 2605)) or at least cases involving a restriction on the advertising of certain products (cf the judgments in *EC Commission v French Republic* Case 152/78 [1980] ECR 2299 and *GB-INNO-BM v Confédération du Commerce Luxembourgeois* Case C-362/88 (7 March 1990, unreported)), to which the facts of this case are likewise not comparable.

16. However, if the criteria developed in the above-mentioned judgments are nevertheless included in an examination of the present case, which may be appropriate in the light of the indication by the national court that the appellants in the main proceedings have been restricted in the sale of products imported from other member states, in the final analysis this should indeed make no difference to the assessment of the applicability of art 30 of the EEC Treaty.

17. In this connection, it will be recalled, the appellants argue as follows. It is clear that, where the Act is applied and a sex shop is refused a licence, trade in the relevant articles cannot be carried on to a significant degree. That affects imported goods in particular, in so far as they are conspicuous in appearance which does not permit them to be exhibited and sold in smaller shops. They are also particularly affected because the business arrangements made necessary by the refusal of a licence allow only a small stock to be held, whereas it is beyond dispute that imports can only be profitable if they achieve a considerable volume.

18. On this point it should in fact be said that the first-mentioned argument (conspicuous appearance of imported products) was evidently not taken up by the national court in its comments on the assessment of the present case and, consequently, may be disregarded. Perhaps the reason was that it was not satisfied that imported goods are characterised by their particularly conspicuous appearance. The United Kingdom did state on this point that the production structure is not in fact different in this respect in the member states, and 'conspicuous' sex articles are certainly also produced in the United

Kingdom. Another factor might have been that the criterion of 'significant degree' used in the 1982 Act is merely to be construed as catching businesses which are engaged *principally* (and not merely on a secondary basis in addition to the sale of newspapers and magazines) in the sale of sex articles (on which point a number of cases were cited in the United Kingdom's written observations). This, however, in no way precludes conspicuous sex articles from also being sold in non-licensed businesses as long as that is not the principal object of the business.

19. On the other hand it should be noted, with regard to the second part of the appellants' arguments, that no mention was made in the proceedings of a reduction in *overall* imports of sex articles (this was emphatically contested by the United Kingdom by reference to the fact that sales by means of outlets other than sex shops are possible); rather it was merely presumed that the appellants' imports were reduced. For the purposes of art 30, however, it is plainly the former kind of reduction which is relevant. Moreover, justified doubts were also expressed as regards the alleged trend in the appellants' import activities. Those doubts stem from the fact that the appellants carry on business on a large scale (because they apparently belong to a group of companies which, according to the observations made at the hearing, operate more than 50 sex shops in the United Kingdom). For the appellants, therefore, imports in worthwhile quantities are certainly possible, not least because, as the respresentative of Southend-on-Sea Borough Council convincingly explained, the 1982 Act does not in any way relate to the holding of *stock* and the extent thereof. The Act can therefore hardly be said to entail a specific hindrance of imports.

20. (c) Accordingly, following examination of all the factors which, on the basis of the past cases, are relevant to art 30 of the EEC Treaty, the only conclusion which may be drawn is that the 1982 Act should not be held to be incompatible with art 30 of the EEC Treaty.

21. (3) If that is correct, there is in actual fact no longer any need to examine the further question of whether such a measure may be *justified*, in particular with reference to art 36 of the Treaty. But for the sake of completeness, in the unlikely event that the court should arrive at a different assessment on the application of art 30, allow me to make the following comments.

22. (a) In the first place, reference may be made to the principles regarding observance of '*mandatory requirements*', affording justification, developed in the case law, with respect to marketing rules applicable without distinction to domestic and imported products. Relevant factors are 'in particular' (which indicates that the list is not exhaustive) the fairness of commercial transactions and consumer protection (cf the judgments in *Rewe-Zentral v Bundesmonopolverwaltung für Branntwein* Case 120/78 [1979] ECR 649 and *Criminal proceedings against Prantl* Case 16/83 [1984] ECR 1299). Environmental protection is also mentioned in the judgement in *EC Commission v Denmark* Case 302/86 [1988] ECR 4607, and the judgment in the *B & Q* case Case 145/88 [1990] 1 All ER 129, [1990] 2 WLR 1330 refers generally to the legitimate pursuit of economic and social policy objectives.

23. In the present case, it is evidently particularly appropriate to assess whether there is justification from the point of view of *consumer protection*.

24. Although the goods in question are not in themselves excluded from sale, consumer protection could be relevant because under the Act marketing may be restricted in certain areas (where it is deemed appropriate in order to protect young persons or particularly vulnerable sections of the population) and also because, by limiting the number of sex shops, certain areas may be saved from saturation by such articles which could give rise to a deterioration in morals. However, these aspects ought rather to be raised, in my view, under art 36 (restrictions on imports on grounds of public morality).

25. Furthermore, the Act may help to ensure the defence of the consumer by making a certain degree of supervision of licensed business premises possible. In this way, and by

means of periodic checks, sales to under-age persons (who are banned from entering sex shops) may be prevented, and also the threat of the withdrawal of a licence may exert an influence on the conduct of business in such a way as to eliminate improper practices (as regards prices and quality).

26. Moreover, it would be recognised that the legislation does not disregard the principle of proportionality (whose importance was underlined, for example, in the judgment in *EC Commission v Denmark* Case 302/86 [1988] ECR 4607) because local authorities' licensing practice, which remains of course subject to review by the courts, may in fact have regard to an appropriate level of trade in articles which cannot exactly be regarded as common commercial wares. On the other hand, I would not attach any major importance to the fact that consumer protection, as I have described it, is not uniform throughout the whole country, since such a requirement is not to be found in the case law and is not implicit in the nature of the matter.

27. (b) Regard may, however, also be had to the application of art 36 of the EEC Treaty whereby, inter alia, restrictions on imports may be justified on grounds of public morality, and for public policy and public security reasons.

28. The former clearly plays a role inasmuch as the contested legislation may afford a certain degree of protection for young persons and vulnerable sections of the population. The latter reasons may be relevant in so far as the legislation may serve to prevent sex shops from being set up in certain areas (for example in residential districts in which high levels of trade would be regarded as disruptive).

29. In this connection, it was correctly pointed out, notwithstanding the arguments to the contrary raised by the appellants in the main proceedings, that there is no requirement that there should be a uniform yardstick applicable to the whole country (as may in particular be deduced from the judgments in *R v Henn, R v Darby* Case 34/79 [1980] 2 All ER 166, [1981] AC 850 and *Conegate Ltd v Customs and Excise Comrs* Case 121/85 [1986] 2 All ER 688, [1987] QB 254). Therefore, no objection may be raised against the fact that the application of the 1982 Act is left to local authorities, who are in the best position to assess the relevant circumstances. It was also correctly observed that the court has held (cf the judgment in the *Henn and Darby* case, Case 34/79) that it is for each member state to determine in accordance with its own scale of values and in the form selected by it the level of protection necessary in this area and that, in the maintenance of public order, the member states are granted an area of discretion (cf the judgment in *R v Bouchereau* Case 30/77 [1981] 2 All ER 924, [1978] QB 732), which may result in situations which differ from one period to another and from one place to another.

30. Moreover, those defending the legislation at issue are surely right in saying that the confining of the licensing requirement to businesses which trade in sex articles to a significant degree is to be indorsed in the interests of the principle of proportionality, even if, in consequence, the appraisal may be subject to some uncertainty which is only gradually disappearing as a result of definition on a case-by-case basis.

31. (c) Since, finally, there is no indication that the last sentence of art 36, which is intended to preclude arbitrary discrimination and disguised restrictions on trade, might be applicable (it was, of course, not argued that the Act itself brings about arbitrary discrimination but merely that it could be *operated* in an arbitrary manner), the only possible conclusion is that the legislation in issue, even were it to be caught by art 30 of the Treaty, could in any event be justified by means of the considerations set out above.

C   *Conclusion*

32. On the basis of the foregoing I propose that the court should reply as follows to the questions raised by the Crown Court at Chelmsford:

'Interpretation of art 30 of the EEC Treaty in accordance with the relevant case law reveals no facts to support the assumption that the application of the Local

Government (Miscellaneous Provisions) Act 1982 in an area of a local authority leading to the prohibition on the sale of sex articles in non-licensed sex shops could be regarded as a measure having equivalent effect to a quantitive restriction on imports within the meaning of art 30.'

11 July. **THE COURT OF JUSTICE** delivered the following judgment.

1. By order dated 7 September 1988 which was received at the court on 30 January 1989, the Crown Court at Chelmsford referred to the court for a preliminary ruling under art 177 of the EEC Treaty three questions on the interpretation of arts 30 and 36 of the EEC Treaty in order to determine whether national legislation prohibiting the sale of lawful sex articles from unlicensed sex establishments was compatible with those provisions.

2. Those questions were raised in proceedings brought against Quietlynn Ltd and Brian James Richards, its managing director (the appellants), who operate retail shop premises selling, inter alia, sex articles, by Southend-on-Sea Borough Council.

3. Section 2 of the Local Government (Miscellaneous Provisions) Act 1982 provides local authorities in England and Wales with the power to control sex shops in their area. In particular, it empowers them to resolve that Sch 3 to the Act, which provides for the sale of such articles to be subject to licensing, is to apply to their area.

4. The council exercised that power, with effect from 23 June 1983. It subsequently brought a prosecution against the appellants for using their premises without a licence on 13 March and 11 April 1985. They were found guilty of two offences by the Rochford and Southend Magistrates' Court on 11 February 1986, fined £1,000 in respect of each offence, and ordered to pay costs.

5. The appellants appealed to the Crown Court at Chelmsford against the convictions, their sole defence being that the provisions of the 1982 Act relating to the licensing system for sex establishments were incompatible with art 30 of the EEC Treaty inasmuch as they constituted a measure having an effect equivalent to a quantitative restriction on imports from other member states and fell neither within one of the exceptions provided for in art 36 nor under any other derogation.

6. The Crown Court at Chelmsford considered that the dispute raised questions relating to the interpretation of Community law and has therefore asked the court for a preliminary ruling on the following questions:

'1. Where a Member State (once a Local Authority has resolved that the legislation is to apply to their area subject to the requirement for premises which are sex establishments to be licensed) prohibits the sale (inter alia) of lawful sex articles from unlicensed sex establishments, and where the effect of such a prohibition is to enable the Local Authority to exercise control over sex establishments within their area, and where the effect is to have restricted the Appellants from selling goods from other Member States since they have been attempting not to contravene the Act by their stocking policy and in doing so have been selling less imported material from Member States than would otherwise have been the case and thus to restrict the availability of sex articles manufactured in other Member States; is such a prohibition a measure having equivalent effect to a quantitative restriction on imports within the meaning of Article 30 of the Treaty?

2. If the answer to Question 1 is in the affirmative, does such a measure benefit from the justification set out in Article 36?

3. If the prohibition referred to in Question 1 contravenes Article 30 and is not justified under Article 36, is it totally unenforceable against a trader in the Member State or only unenforceable to the extent that it prohibits transactions involving goods manufactured in or imported from other Member States?'

7. Reference is made to the report for the hearing for a fuller account of the relevant provisions, the facts of the case in the main proceedings, the course of the procedure and

the written observations submitted to the court, which are referred to hereinafter only in so far as is necessary for the reasoning of the court.

Question 1

8. By its first question the national court seeks to ascertain whether provisions prohibiting the sale of lawful sex articles from unlicensed sex establishments constitute a measure having an effect equivalent to a quantitative restriction within the meaning of art 30 of the EEC Treaty.

9. First, it must be noted that national legislation prohibiting the sale of sex articles from unlicensed sex establishments applies without distinction to imported and domestic products. It thus does not constitute an absolute prohibition on the sale of the products in question, but merely a rule regarding their distribution, regulating the outlets through which the products may be marketed. In principle, therefore, the marketing of products imported from other member states is not rendered any more difficult than that of domestic products.

10. It must be pointed out that in similar cases concerning rules governing the marketing of certain products the court has held art 30 of the Treaty not to be applicable. In *Summary proceedings against Oebel* Case 155/80 [1981] ECR 1993 the court held that national rules governing working hours in bakeries and the hours of delivery and sale of baker's wares were compatible with art 30 of the Treaty since trade within the Community remained possible at all times. Likewise, in *Blesgen v Belgium* Case 75/81 [1982] ECR 1211 the court considered that a legislative provision that concerned only the sale of strong spirits for consumption on the premises in all places open to the public and did not concern other forms of marketing the same drinks had in fact no connection with the importation of the products and for that reason was not of such a nature as to impede trade between member states.

11. It must also be pointed out that the provisions prohibiting the sale of sex articles from unlicensed sex establishments have in fact no connection with intra-Community trade, since the products covered by the 1982 Act may be marketed through licensed sex establishments and other channels, that is to say through shops in which sex articles account for only an insignificant proportion of sales and which are therefore not required to be licensed, or by mail order. Moreover, those provisions are not intended to regulate trade in goods within the Community and they are therefore not of such a nature as to impede trade between member states.

12. The answer to the first question must therefore be that art 30 of the Treaty should be construed as meaning that national provisions prohibiting the sale of lawful sex articles from unlicensed sex establishments do not constitute a measure having an effect equivalent to a quantitative restriction on imports.

Questions 2 and 3

13. In view of the answer to the first question, the second and third questions do not require an answer.

Costs

14. The costs incurred by the United Kingdom and the Commission of the European Communities, which have submitted observations to the court, are not recoverable. Since these proceedings are, in so far as the parties to the main proceedings are concerned, in the nature of a step in the proceedings pending before the national court, the decision on costs is a matter for that court.

On those grounds, the court (Sixth Chamber), in answer to the questions referred to it by the Crown Court at Chelmsford by order of 7 September 1988, hereby rules that art 30 of the EEC Treaty should be construed as meaning that national provisions prohibiting the sale of lawful sex articles from unlicensed sex establishments do not constitute a measure having an effect equivalent to a quantitative restriction on imports.

Agents: *Kaye Tesler & Co* (for the appellants); *David G Preddy*, Southend-on-Sea (for the council); *Susan Hay*, Treasury Solicitor's Department (for the United Kingdom); *Eric L White*, Legal Adviser, EC Commission (for the Commission).

Mary Rose Plummer   Barrister.

Burgess v Stafford Hotel Ltd

COURT OF APPEAL, CIVIL DIVISION
GLIDEWELL LJ AND SIR DENYS BUCKLEY
27 FEBRUARY 1990

Court of Appeal – Notice of appeal – Striking out – Jurisdiction of court – Inherent jurisdiction – Grounds on which notice of appeal may be struck out – Notice frivolous, vexatious or abuse of process of court – Exercise of jurisdiction – Notices to be struck out only in clear and obvious cases and where inquiry into facts not necessary.

Court of Appeal – Ground of appeal – Point not raised in court below – Discretion of court to allow new point to be raised – Abuse of process of court to raise point not raised below.

Costs – Order for costs – Costs of appeal – Appeal having no chance of success – Appeal pursuant to right of appeal conferred by statute – Whether appellant behaving disgracefully or deserving moral condemnation for taking advantage of right of appeal – Whether respondent's costs should be awarded on indemnity basis or standard basis.

The Court of Appeal has power under its inherent jurisdiction to strike out a notice of appeal on the ground that it is frivolous, vexatious or an abuse of the process of the court, and, although such a notice is not a pleading and therefore cannot technically be struck out under RSC Ord 18, r 19, the inherent jurisdiction will be exercised on precisely the same basis as if that rule strictly applied to notices of appeal. Furthermore, once the issue as to striking out has been raised, even if formally it requires amendment, the court is properly seised of all the grounds on which it can strike out a notice of appeal. However, the jurisdiction to make an order striking out a notice of appeal is one that is just as capable of abuse as is the power to put in a hopeless notice of appeal; it should therefore be confined to clear and obvious cases and should not be utilised, nor should an order to strike out be made, where any extensive inquiry into the facts is necessary (see p 227 *a* to *d*, p 228 *b* and p 229 *a*, post); *Aviagents Ltd v Balstravest Investments Ltd* [1966] 1 All ER 450 applied.

The fact that a point has not been raised in the court below does not depend on evidence. Once it is apparent that it is the case, then it can only be raised in the Court of Appeal if that court, wholly as a matter of discretion, allows it to be raised, if necessary after amendment or after fresh evidence. Since as a general rule the Court of Appeal will not allow a new point to be argued, as it would mean a rehearing, it follows that once it becomes apparent that a point has not been raised in the court below it is properly to be regarded as an abuse of the process of the court to seek to raise it on an appeal to the Court of Appeal (see p 227 *j* to p 228 *a* and p 229 *a*, post).

A person who takes advantage of a right of appeal conferred by statute cannot be said to be behaving disgracefully or deserving of moral condemnation, so as to justify an order for costs against him on an indemnity basis rather than the standard basis, merely because the appeal has no chance of success. In the case of such an appeal the respondent's remedy is to apply for an order to strike it out or to apply for an order for security for costs or to make both applications (see p 228 *g* to *j* and p 229 *a*, post).

Notes

For striking out notices of appeal, see 37 Halsbury's Laws (4th edn) paras 442, 686, 693, and for a case on the subject, see 37(3) Digest (Reissue) 156, 3773.

For raising on an appeal a point not taken below, see 37 Halsbury's Laws (4th edn) para 693, and for cases on the subject, see 37(3) Digest (Reissue) 192–195, 4009–4027.

For the right of appeal in general, see 37 Halsbury's Laws (4th edn) para 677.

For payment of costs on an indemnity basis, see ibid para 744.

Cases referred to in judgments

Aviagents Ltd v Balstravest Investments Ltd [1966] 1 All ER 450, [1966] 1 WLR 150, CA.
Deerslade Ltd v Hilton International Hotels (UK) Ltd [1989] CA Transcript 565.
Ghadami v Petticoat Lane Rentals Ltd [1986] CA Transcript 432.
Hives v Dawson (1927) 138 LT 238, DC.

Appeal and application

The plaintiff, Desmond Burgess (the tenant), appealed against the order of his Honour Judge Simpson sitting in the Westminster County Court on 30 October 1989 whereby, on the trial of a preliminary issue, the judge (i) granted the defendant, Stafford Hotel Ltd (the landlord), a declaration that the landlord was entitled to rely on the ground specified in s 30(1)(*f*) of the Landlord and Tenant Act 1954 to oppose an application by the tenant under s 25 of that Act for a new tenancy of premises at 21, 22 and 25 Blue Ball Yard, London SW1, (ii) dismissed the tenant's application for a new tenancy and (iii) ordered the tenant to pay the landlord's costs on scale III. By a notice dated 29 December 1989 the landlord applied for an order that the tenant's notice of appeal be struck out for failure to set down the appeal as required by RSC Ord 59, r 5 and as disclosing no reasonable ground of appeal pursuant to Ord 59 and Ord 18, r 19 and under the inherent jurisdiction of the court and that the costs of the landlord's application be paid by the tenant. The facts are set out in the judgment of Glidewell LJ.

Gavin Hamilton for the tenant.
Jonathan Brock for the landlord.

GLIDEWELL LJ. The defendant company (the landlord) is the owner of premises, 9–25 Blue Ball Yard, London SW1, which adjoin the Stafford Hotel on the east side. The landlord purchased those premises in December 1986. The plaintiff, Mr Burgess (the tenant), then held the tenancy of 21, 22 and 25 Blue Ball Yard. Number 21 is a residential flat in which he lives, no 22 is a bookstore and no 25 is an office and showroom from which he conducts a bookselling business.

Not long after the landlord purchased those premises the tenant's lease expired. The landlord wishes to occupy the whole of the premises for the extension of the hotel and to that end to carry out works of conversion which require planning permission.

When the tenant's lease expired he applied for a new tenancy under the Landlord and Tenant Act 1954. The landlord had applied for planning permission on 14 April 1987, but when the tenant's application for a new tenancy came to be heard on 24 May 1988 that planning permission had still not been granted. Accordingly, in its absence, the court ordered a new tenancy of the tenant's holding for six years but with a six-month break clause. That clause provided that the term could be determined—

> 'at any time by the Landlord giving to the Tenant not less than six months notice in writing terminating this tenancy on the grounds that it requires possession of the demised premises because it intends to demolish or reconstruct the whole or a substantial part of the demised premises or to carry out substantial work of construction on the whole or part of them and cannot reasonably do so without obtaining possession thereof . . .'

That wording is taken verbatim from s 30(1)(f) of the 1954 Act.

On 6 October 1988 the planning permission which the landlord had sought was granted by Westminster City Council. It related to nos 9 to 22 inclusive Blue Ball Yard. It was permission for:

'Alterations in connection with use as 12 suites for adjoining Stafford Hotel, one self-contained residential unit, also residential and hotel garaging.'

Then there was another permission of the same date for:

'Works of alteration in connection with use for hotel accommodation, self-contained maisonette and garaging.'

Those permissions referred to a number of plans which had been submitted with parts of the application.

Having obtained that permission, on 9 January 1989 the landlord served a new notice to terminate the tenancy under s 25 of the 1954 Act. Solicitors on behalf of the tenant on 2 February 1989 served a counter-notice, and on 5 May an application was made for a new tenancy. The landlord throughout indicated that it would oppose on the ground specified in s 30(1)(f) of the Act, ie the ground on which in the clause in the lease to which I have referred it was entitled to terminate, namely:

'that on the termination of the current tenancy the landlord intends to demolish or reconstruct the premises comprised in the holding or a substantial part of those premises or to carry out substantial work of construction on the holding or part thereof and that he could not reasonably do so without obtaining possession of the holding.'

The issue whether or not the landlord could make out that ground was ordered to be tried as a preliminary issue. It came on for hearing before his Honour Judge Simpson in the Westminster County Court on 30 October 1989, and he found in favour of the landlord and dismissed the tenant's application for a new tenancy.

The tenant had been advised by solicitors until shortly before the hearing in the county court, but in the county court he appeared in person and he put in his notice of appeal in person. The grounds for the appeal were shortly stated:

'1. Planning Permission by Westminster Council is not valid 2. Present Development Plans are not Major Redevelopment 3. The Judgment infringes the Plaintiff's rights under the Rent Act.'

The landlord riposted on 29 December 1989 by making an application to strike out the notice of appeal. That application read:

'. . . that the Notice of Appeal . . . be struck out for failure to set down the Appeal as required by Order 59 r. 5 of the Rules of the Supreme Court and as disclosing no reasonable ground of appeal pursuant to Order 59 and Order 18 r. 19 of the Rules of the Supreme Court and under the inherent jurisdiction of the Court . . .'

It is now conceded that the first basis of that application was misconceived. The landlord's solicitors did not know it, but in fact the tenant had set down his appeal immediately, so nothing turns on that.

The appeal and the application to strike out were both intended to be listed for hearing on Wednesday, 24 January 1990, but by the preceding day the tenant had not filed either a note of the judgment or any note of the evidence given in the county court. I make no comment why it was he had not obtained them. It seems that on 23 January he visited the Civil Appeals Office, said that the documents were not ready and was informed that accordingly the appeal would not proceed. A muddle then arose whether or not the application to strike out should properly be listed. In the event, as I understand it, it did not initially appear in the printed list but was added in manuscript.

The tenant handed in to the landlord's solicitors a letter on 23 January saying that the
matter was being taken out of the list. They promptly sought to serve on him a letter
saying that they intended to go ahead on 24 January with the application to strike out. It
seems, for whatever reason, that he never received that letter. Accordingly on 24 January,
when the landlord by counsel appeared to pursue the application to strike out, the tenant
did not appear and the application was therefore adjourned.

It was relisted to be heard on 6 February. The tenant says, but without any justification,
that the Civil Appeals Office had informed him that the matter was again being taken
out of the list. Be that as it may, he again did not appear. This time all that was in the list
was the hearing of the application to strike out. Again that was adjourned until today. So
today we have for hearing both the landlord's application to strike out and the tenant's
appeal.

At the opening of the hearing this morning counsel for the tenant consented to the
appeal being dismissed and to an order being made for the costs of the appeal against his
client. Counsel for the landlord, however, wants more than that. He applies for two
further orders. First, he applies for the costs also of the application to strike out; and,
second, he applies that any order for costs we make should in the circumstances of this
case be on an indemnity basis as opposed to the standard basis.

Where a tenant's application for a new tenancy under the 1954 Act is dismissed, the
tenant is entitled to appeal under s 77 of the County Courts Act 1984, assuming that the
matter has proceeded in the county court, on questions of both fact and law. By s 64(1)
of the 1954 Act the effect of entering an appeal is to extend the tenancy until a date three
months after the decision on the appeal is given. So it follows that even an appeal which
has no hope of success keeps a tenancy alive until it has been disposed of. Inevitably,
therefore, landlords of premises who have secured the defeat of tenants' applications for
new tenancies under the 1954 Act are concerned to stop hopeless appeals in their tracks
as early as possible. But there is no express provision in the Rules of the Supreme Court
for striking out a notice of appeal. However, this court as long ago as 1966 had before it
an application to strike out in a case under the 1954 Act. That was *Aviagents Ltd v
Balstravest Investments Ltd* [1966] 1 All ER 450, [1966] 1 WLR 150. At that stage there
was no right of appeal in a Landlord and Tenant Act case to this court on a point of fact.
The issue in that case was purely what was the proper rent, because it was conceded that
there should be a new tenancy. The tenants then sought to appeal against the rent which
was fixed by the county court judge on the ground that the judge misdirected himself
and that his order was against the weight of the evidence. The landlords applied for an
order that the tenants' notice of appeal be struck out on the ground that the only ground
of appeal contained therein related to a question of fact. It was held that the Court of
Appeal had inherent power to control its own proceedings by striking out a notice of
appeal in a case where an appeal was plainly incompetent, and that where the only
question for decision was one of fact the appeal clearly was not competent and so the
application succeeded. Willmer LJ said ([1966] 1 All ER 450 at 452, [1966] 1 WLR 150
at 154):

> 'Counsel for the tenants has contended that there is no power in this court to take
> the drastic step of striking out the notice of appeal. He has contended that we are
> limited to saying that the appeal might amount to an abuse of the process of the
> court, which would be a ground for making an order only for security for costs. No
> authority was cited for the proposition that this court has no power to strike out a
> notice of appeal. The only authority cited on the other side was an old Divisional
> Court case of *Hives* v. *Dawson* ((1927) 138 LT 238). In that case it sought to appeal
> on a question of law in relation to a sum of less than £20, and to do so without
> leave; and the Divisional Court came to the conclusion that it was not a competent
> appeal and took the course, which it is suggested that we should take, of striking out
> the notice of appeal. It appears to me inconceivable that this court should not have

inherent power to control its own proceedings by striking out a notice of appeal in a case where an appeal is plainly not a competent appeal.'

Davies LJ, after referring to the submission of counsel for the tenants that security for costs was the proper remedy, said ([1966] 1 All ER at 453, [1966] 1 WLR at 155):

'[The cases cited in *The Annual Practice 1966* p 1680 in the notes to RSC 1883 Ord 58, r 9] are cases in which there was a right of appeal, but the prospects of the appellant were so demonstrably hopeless that this court thought it proper to make an order for security. That is not this case. This case is not concerned with an appeal which is frivolous or vexatious or an abuse of the process of the court; it is a case in which there is no right of appeal at all, and it would be quite wrong to allow this appeal to proceed and merely to order security.'

Russell LJ gave a short judgment concurring with Willmer LJ.

There, so far as counsel's researches go, the matter rested. Certainly we have had no other authority cited to us until two recent decisions. The first is a decision in this court in *Ghadami v Petticoat Lane Rentals Ltd* [1986] CA Transcript 432, decided by a court comprising Parker, Woolf LJJ and Sir Denys Buckley. The second, to which Sir Denys was also a party, is *Deerslade Ltd v Hilton International Hotels (UK) Ltd* [1989] CA Transcript 565. The first judgment in that case was given by Staughton LJ. We have the advantage of a transcript in the *Deerslade* case. In the course of his judgment, with which Sir Denys agreed, Staughton LJ said:

'I turn then to the second and third points raised on this application, that this appeal is frivolous, vexatious and an abuse of the process of the court.'

That is the very point with which Davies LJ had said they were not dealing in *Aviagents Ltd v Balstravest Investments Ltd* [1966] 1 All ER 450 at 453, [1966] 1 WLR 150 at 155. Staughton LJ continued:

'There is jurisdiction to strike out an appeal on that ground. It may be that it is part of the inherent jurisdiction of the court, or else it is derived from RSC Ord 59, r 10(1): "In relation to an appeal the Court of Appeal shall have all the powers and duties as to amendment and otherwise of the High Court . . ." That there is such power, for one reason or another, appears from the judgment of this court in *Ghadami v Petticoat Lane Rentals Ltd* [1986] CA Transcript 432. There Parker LJ said: "This application for an order that the appeal be struck out succeeds, in my view, on two grounds: (a) because the notice of appeal is itself not in compliance with the rules and (b) because the matters raised are matters which, as grounds of appeal on the material we have before us, I regard as plainly frivolous." Woolf LJ and Sir Denys Buckley agreed. The test whether an appeal should be struck out on that ground was stated by [counsel] for the tenants as follows. He accepts that, if there is no possibility that the grounds are capable of argument and no possibility that the court would entertain new grounds relating to matters which had not been raised in the court below, then there is power to strike out the notice of appeal. [Counsel], who appears for the landlords, did not contend for any other test.'

The court then went on to consider the particular aspects of the grounds of appeal in that case and struck them out.

Should we decide that it would have been right if the appeal had not been conceded to strike it out here? In a sense, of course, the decision has become otiose except in relation to costs, but it has been argued in relation to that matter.

Counsel for the tenant refers us to the actual wording of the application to strike out and points out that this ground was an application that the notice of appeal be struck out as disclosing no reasonable ground of appeal pursuant to RSC Ord 59 and Ord 18, r 19. He argues that this is not a notice which raises the issue whether the appeal is frivolous or vexatious or an abuse of process.

For my part, once the issue as to striking out has been raised, even if formally it requires an amendment, I take the view that the court can properly be seised of all the grounds on which it can strike out a notice of appeal. Since, albeit the point was not taken in the initial notice, it was made quite clear in correspondence and, indeed, by counsel for the landlord at an early stage that he was seeking to rely on a wider jurisdiction than merely that the notice of appeal itself contained no reasonable ground, I would hold that that objection should not be sustained.

Counsel for the tenant also argues that, albeit he must concede on the authorities that this court has an inherent jurisdiction, it does not derive its jurisdiction strictly from the Rules of the Supreme Court. He points out that although Ord 59, r 10(1) gives this court 'all the powers and duties as to amendment and otherwise of the High Court', when one comes to look at Ord 18, r 19, which is the rule which gives the court power to strike out pleadings, that rule cannot apply to a notice of appeal because a notice of appeal is not a pleading.

For myself, I think that strictly that is a correct reading of the rules, and it is noticeable that Staughton LJ in the extract from his judgment which I read did not say categorically that the application could be made under the combined effect of those two rules. Nevertheless, although I believe that to be a correct interpretation of the rules, I regard it also as a technicality because it seems to me that the inherent jurisdiction of the court would be exercised on precisely the same basis as if r 19 of Ord 18 strictly applied to notices of appeal.

I have already read the grounds of appeal. I go back to them briefly. Number 1 is that the planning permission granted by Westminster City Council is not valid. To that counsel for the landlord submits that there is a simple answer, and I agree with him, ie that a grant of planning permission is valid unless and until it has been set aside by an order of a court. The only way in which a planning permission can be set aside is by an application in the Crown Office list for an order of certiorari quashing it or by means of a successful appeal under the provisions of the Town and Country Planning Act 1971. Neither having happened in this case, it follows automatically that the two planning permissions are valid and that ground is therefore bad on its face.

As to the third ground, that the judgment infringes the plaintiff's rights under the Rent Act, counsel for the landlord submits, and again I agree with him, that that disregards the provisions of s 24(3) of the Rent Act 1977. That subsection provides as follows:

'A tenancy shall not be a regulated tenancy if it is a tenancy to which Part II of the Landlord and Tenant Act 1954 applies . . .'

So, since it is conceded that Pt II of the 1954 Act applies to the whole of the tenant's tenancy, it is not a regulated tenancy within the Rent Acts and he had no right under the latter Act.

The only ground of appeal which presented on the face of it a little more difficulty was the second, 'Present Development Plans are not Major Redevelopment'. Consideration of that ground did not show that on its face it was necessarily bad. On the face of it it might involve examination of the facts and of the evidence given in the court below to decide whether or not it was a proper ground. However, we are told, without objection, so it is accepted as a fact, that this matter was not raised in the court below. Indeed, from the note we now have of the evidence given in the court below there is no suggestion that the matter was raised by way of cross-examination and we are told, and accept, that the tenant did not raise it in any representations he made.

The fact that a point has not been raised in the court below does not depend on evidence. Once it is apparent that it is the case, then it can only be raised in this court if this court allows it so to be raised, if necessary after amendment, if necessary after calling fresh evidence, and it is wholly a matter of discretion. As a general proposition this court would not allow this point to be argued since it would mean a rehearing. Once, therefore, it became apparent that the point had not been raised in the court below, it was in my view properly to be regarded as an abuse of the process of the court to seek to raise it on *a* this appeal in this court.

It follows therefore, in my judgment, that in the particular circumstances of this case it was right that an application to strike out the appeal should have been made, and for my part, had we still had power to deal with that application, I would have allowed it.

However, I do want to sound a word of warning. The jurisdiction to make orders striking out notices of appeal is one that is just as capable of abuse as is the power to put *b* in hopeless notices of appeal. In my view the power to strike out should be confined to clear and obvious cases. It should not be utilised, and an order to strike out should not be made, where any extensive inquiry into the facts is going to be necessary. But in this case that situation does not arise. I would therefore have granted the application made by the landlord to strike out had the matter come before me in a court of which I was a member at an earlier stage. *c*

It follows, therefore, that in my view the landlord should have its costs of the application to strike out. The only doubt I had about that concerned the costs of the hearing of 24 January. It does appear, to put it neutrally, that there was a possibility of a misunderstanding by the tenant whether or not any part of the hearing on 24 January was proceeding. Nevertheless, had he been properly advised, he would no doubt have been told that, even if he was not ready to proceed with the appeal, the absence of the *d* judgment and the notes of evidence was no reason why the landlord's application to strike out should not proceed. Indeed, if he had been available to receive the letter which the landlord's solicitors attempted to serve on him the afternoon before, he would have been apprised of the fact that they certainly had every intention of continuing with the application. Accordingly, since it clearly was not the landlord's solicitors' fault in any sense that that application proceeded, after consideration I take the view that we should *e* make no differentiation between the costs of the hearing on that day and on any other day, and Sir Denys Buckley agrees with me. I therefore propose that we simply make an order for the costs of the application to strike out including all hearings which resulted from that application.

That leaves to be decided the basis of the orders for costs which we should make. The *f* application is that we should order that they should be on an indemnity basis.

It is, I think, apparent that the tenant has 'played the system', ie he has taken advantage of the provisions in the Landlord and Tenant Act 1954 to extend his tenancy so far as he can. In the end he has patently accepted advice that his appeal had no chance of success, because his counsel has this morning in his presence consented to the appeal being dismissed on his behalf.

On the other hand, as has been argued to us on his behalf, Parliament has thought it *g* right to give him the rights contained respectively under s 64 of the 1954 Act and the right of appeal under s 77 of the County Courts Act 1984. One cannot say that a person who is granted such rights and takes advantage of them is behaving disgracefully or is deserving of moral condemnation. The landlord's remedy, if he takes the view that the appeal should not proceed, is either to apply for an order to strike out once it becomes *h* apparent that in appropriate circumstances he can do so, or to apply for an order for security for costs, or to make both applications. Some of the restrictions on orders for security for costs at first instance do not apply to the security for the costs of an appeal. Accordingly, in my view the tenant's conduct in this case is not such that we ought to depart from the normal basis of costs, and I would order that the costs be taxed in relation to both matters on the standard basis. *j*

The effect of that, if Sir Denys Buckley agrees with me, is that the order will be that the appeal is dismissed with costs and the landlord's application to strike out the appeal is the subject of no order save that the landlord have its costs of that application, both those orders being on the standard basis.

SIR DENYS BUCKLEY. I entirely agree with the judgment which Glidewell LJ has
a delivered in all its aspects. I do not think that I can usefully add anything further to what
he has already said, but I would like to associate myself with the word of warning which
he voiced in respect of the use of the jurisdiction to strike out a notice of appeal on the
ground of the court's general jurisdiction in any but cases which are clear and obvious
and do not involve inquiry into the facts underlying the decision appealed from.

b *Appeal dismissed by consent. No order on landlord's application to strike out save costs to
respondents; landlord to have its costs of all previous hearings in respect of application to strike
out notice of appeal.*

Solicitors: *Gamlens* (for the tenant); *Saunders Sobell Leigh & Dobin* (for the landlord).

c
                                                    L I Zysman Esq   Barrister.

Re consecrated land in Camomile Street

d
LONDON CONSISTORY COURT
CHANCELLOR G H NEWSOM QC
6, 7 NOVEMBER 1989, 10, 18 JANUARY 1990

e *Ecclesiastical law – Consistory court – Jurisdiction – Disposal of issues arising in and consequent
on exercise of faculty jurisdiction – Diversion of money received as consideration for grant of
licence executed under authority of faculty – Parish granted faculty authorising it to grant
company certain facilities over disused burial ground – Consideration received for grant of
facilities too large to be employed usefully by parish – Whether court having jurisdiction to divert
some of consideration to diocesan fund and neighbouring parish.*

f *Ecclesiastical law – Church – Property – Consecrated and unconsecrated land and chattels –
Ownership – Incumbent and churchwardens owners on behalf of parish and not beneficial owners.*

In March 1989 the consistory court granted a faculty on the petition of the incumbent,
churchwardens and parochial church council of a parish and a company authorising the
execution of a licence under which certain facilities were granted to the company by the
g incumbent over and in respect of a disused burial ground believed by the petitioners to
be vested in the incumbent. The licence was executed in consideration of £425,000,
which sum was paid into court to await consideration of its distribution. Since the parish
had very few parishioners and held very few services, the archdeacon submitted that the
whole of so large a sum could not be employed usefully by paying it to the parochial
church council. He therefore suggested that some of the money should be given to the
h diocesan fund, which, among other things, was responsible for paying the salary and
allowances of the incumbent, and some to a neighbouring parish which had a large and
thriving congregation and a full programme of services. The chancellor made an order
diverting some of the money to the diocesan fund and some to the neighbouring parish.
Before the order had passed the seal the question arose whether the court had the
j necessary jurisdiction to make the order, and the matter was reopened to hear argument.

Held – Notwithstanding that the burial ground had been closed for burials, it was
nevertheless within the jurisdiction of the consistory court since it had been consecrated,
and the court had jurisdiction to grant a faculty for the desired facilities which stemmed

from the exercise by the court of its jurisdiction over the land. It was obvious that there was jurisdiction in someone to decree the destination of the money, since it would be absurd to leave it permanently in court, and because the issue arose in duly constituted faculty proceedings and was consequential on the faculty it followed that the jurisdiction was vested in the consistory court, which once it had seisin of a cause of faculty was bound to dispose of the cause and to decide all questions which arose incidentally to, in and from the cause with regard not only to questions of title but to any and every incidental matter the decision of which was necessary for justice to be done in the cause and including the making of all conditions which were just and expedient. Furthermore, since there was jurisdiction to divert consecrated land from one ecclesiastical purpose to another, it followed that money resulting from the granting of a faculty relating to consecrated land could likewise be diverted to other ecclesiastical purposes. The court would accordingly affirm its earlier order (see p 232 *a b d e*, p 233 *e*, p 234 *a b d e g h*, p 235 *a d j* and p 236 *c d*, post).

Re St John's, Chelsea [1962] 2 All ER 850 and Re St Mary of Charity, Faversham [1986] 1 All ER 1 applied.

St John the Baptist, Cardiff (vicar and churchwardens) v Parishioners [1898] P 155 distinguished.

Per curiam. Although the life interest in consecrated land and the whole of the legal fee simple in unconsecrated curtilage is in the incumbent, while the chattels belong in law to the churchwardens, the incumbent and the churchwardens are not beneficial owners but owners on behalf of the parish, in reality both the consecrated and the unconsecrated land and the chattels being parish property held for the benefit of the parish church and its congregation (see p 233f to j, post).

Notes

For the use of consecrated ground for secular purposes, see 14 Halsbury's Laws (4th edn) para 1073, and for cases on the subject, see 19 Digest (Reissue) 381, 2989–2990.

For the faculty jurisdiction, see 14 Halsbury's Laws (4th edn) paras 1306–1318, and for cases on the subject, see 19 Digest (Reissue) 442–458, 3519–3603.

Cases referred to in judgment

All Hallows, Berkyngechirche, Re (5 July 1972, unreported), London Con Ct.
Christ Church, Chislehurst (incumbent and churchwardens) v Parishioners (1897) [1980] 1 All ER 283n, [1980] Fam 104n, [1980] 3 WLR 247n, Comm Ct.
Corke v Rainger and Higgs [1912] P 69, Arches Ct.
Gould v Gapper (1804) 5 East 345, 102 ER 1102.
Liverpool (Rector), Ex p (1870) LR 11 Eq 15, V-C.
Morley BC v St Mary the Virgin, Woodkirk (vicar and churchwardens) [1969] 3 All ER 952, [1969] 1 WLR 1867, York Ch Ct.
St Andrew's, North Weald Bassett, Re [1987] 1 WLR 1503, Con Ct.
St Benet Fink, Tottenham, Re (4 December 1975, unreported), London Con Ct.
St Botolph without Aldgate (vicar and one of the churchwardens) v Parishioners [1892] P 161, Con Ct.
St Gregory's, Tredington, Re [1971] 3 All ER 269, [1972] Fam 236, [1971] 2 WLR 796, Arches Ct.
St Gregory's, Tredington, Re [1971] 3 All ER 269, [1972] Fam 236, [1971] 2 WLR 796, Arches Ct.
St John the Baptist, Cardiff (vicar and churchwardens) v Parishioners [1898] P 155, Con Ct.
St John's, Chelsea, Re [1962] 2 All ER 850, [1962] 1 WLR 706, Con Ct.
St Mary Aldermary, Re [1985] 2 All ER 445, [1985] Fam 101, [1985] 3 WLR 113, Con Ct.
St Mary Magdalene, Paddington, Re [1980] 1 All ER 279, [1980] Fam 99, [1980] 3 WLR 243, Con Ct.
St Mary le Bow, Re [1984] 1 WLR 1363, Con Ct.
St Mary of Charity, Faversham, Re [1986] 1 All ER 1, [1986] Fam 143, [1985] 3 WLR 924, Comm Ct.

St Pancras Burial-Ground, Re (1866) LR 3 Eq 173, V-C.
St Stephen Walbrook (rector and churchwardens) v Sun Fire Office Trustees (1883) Trist 103, Con Ct.
Shotter v Friend (1690) 3 Mod Rep 283, 87 ER 188.

Petition for faculty

On 28 March 1989 the London Consistory Court granted a faculty on the petition of the Rev Alan John Tanner, the incumbent of the parish of St Botolph without Bishopsgate in the Diocese of London, Esmond Patrick Thomson Roney and Philip Frederick Allday, churchwardens, the parochial church council of the parish and Prudential Assurance Co Ltd (the Prudential) authorising the execution of a licence under which certain facilities were granted to the Prudential by the incumbent over and in respect of a disused burial ground believed by the petitioners to be vested in the incumbent. The licence was executed in consideration of £425,000, which sum was paid into court to await consideration of its distribution. The Archdeacon of London submitted that the whole of so large a sum of money could not be employed usefully by paying it to the parochial church council of St Botolph's since St Botolph's had very few parishioners and very few services. The archdeacon therefore suggested that some of the money should be given to the London Diocesan Fund, which (among other things) was responsible for paying the salary of the incumbent of St Botolph's. Evidence was given that the salary and allowances of the incumbent cost the London Diocesan Fund an annual sum considerably in excess of the amount paid by St Botolph's in respect of the diocesan quota to the common fund of the diocese. The archdeacon also suggested that some of the money should be given to the neighbouring parish of St Helen Bishopsgate, which had a large and thriving congregation and a full programme of services. It appeared moreover in the course of investigation that in 1962 the respective incumbents and parochial church councils of St Botolph's and St Helen's had agreed to divide between them the rents then arising from the burial ground (which was then let as an open space) in the proportions of 52:48. It later appeared, in consequence of the title being more fully investigated, that by virtue of a series of legislative enactments it was arguable that the title to the burial ground was in fact in the incumbent of St Helen's and not in the incumbent of St Botolph's, but that issue was never fully pleaded and, though it was to some extent argued at the hearings, it was not necessary in the event for the court to resolve it and it remained unresolved. The question of the distribution of the money was argued before the Chancellor on 27 April 1989 on the footing that all those present accepted that he had jurisdiction to make an order diverting the money from the parish of St Botolph's (a diversion order), and judgment was given in June 1989 on that basis. Shortly afterwards, but before the order which the court had directed by the June judgment had passed the seal, the St Botolph's petitioners were advised by counsel that there was an arguable question whether the court had the necessary jurisdiction to make the diversion order. The court allowed the matter to be reopened on the basis of *Re Harrison's share under a settlement, Harrison v Harrison* [1955] 1 All ER 185, [1955] Ch 260 and proceeded in chambers to hear full argument by counsel on the issue of jurisdiction. The case is reported by leave of the court. The facts are set out in the judgment.

Spencer G Maurice for the original petitioners other than the Prudential.
Robert Wakefield for the incumbent, churchwardens and parochial church council of St Helen Bishopsgate.
Thomas Coningsby QC and *Andrew Lloyd-Davies* for the archdeacon and the London Diocesan Fund.

Cur adv vult

18 January. The following judgment was delivered.

THE CHANCELLOR. These proceedings arise in connection with an area of land in Camomile Street in the City of London. It is 51 feet long and 27 feet wide at the east, and

19 feet 6 inches wide at the west. It appears to have been a burial ground, consecrated in 1539 for the benefit of the parishioners of St Martin Outwich. I shall call it 'the burial ground'. It was a detached piece of land, not near the church of St Martin, Outwich or any other church nor even in the parish of St Martin Outwich. I was told that it was closed for burials in 1852, but I have not seen a copy of the Order in Council. I shall, however, assume that burials in it have long been prohibited by law. None the less it is within the jurisdiction of the court, having been consecrated.

The proceedings were started by an undated petition lodged on 20 January 1989 by the incumbent, churchwardens and parochial church council of St Botolph without Bishopsgate. The burial ground has, since a scheme of 1954, made under the Reorganisation Areas Measure 1944, been situate in the parish of St Botolph. The basis of the petition was therefore that the incumbent claimed, and has continued to claim, that the freehold of the burial ground was and is vested in him as a burial ground for the use of his parishioners. He and his churchwardens and the parochial church council sought a faculty to authorise him and them to execute a document, in which Prudential Assurance Co Ltd (to which I refer as 'the Prudential') was the other party, granting to the Prudential certain facilities over the burial ground by way of licence. Correctly, the Prudential was also joined as a petitioner, pursuant to the directions given in *Re St Mary Aldermary* [1985] 2 All ER 445, [1985] Fam 101. When, or soon after, the petition was lodged, the solicitors for the petitioners represented to the court that it was of the utmost urgency that the Prudential should have the desired facilities, for which the parties had agreed that the Prudential should pay £425,000. There was no doubt that I had jurisdiction to grant a faculty for the facilities: see *Re St John's, Chelsea* [1962] 2 All ER 850, [1962] 1 WLR 706. I decreed citation; no one entered appearance in opposition, but I invited the Archdeacon of London to intervene in the proceedings for the purpose of the court's consideration of what was to be done with the money. He therefore did so.

I granted the faculty on 28 March 1989 as a matter of urgency on condition that the £425,000 should be paid into court 'in order that it may be the subject of a further application as for the distribution of the monies'. The deed was executed the next day under my authority thus given, and the money was duly paid into court, where it still is, swelled by accumulations of interest.

On 27 April 1989 there came before me in chambers the petitioner Mr Roney (a churchwarden of St Botolph), who is a solicitor. He appeared for the petitioners (other than the Prudential) and was accompanied by his incumbent. The Archdeacon of London appeared in person, and he invited me to hear evidence from persons representing two candidates which he wished to put forward as possible recipients of the benefit of the fund in court or some of it, viz the London Diocesan Fund and the incumbent, churchwardens and parochial church council of St Helen Bishopsgate with St Martin Outwich. Mr Monroe, a solicitor, appeared for these last. The Prudential, not being concerned with the destination of the money, was not summoned and did not attend. On 15 June 1989 I gave a written judgment, the broad effect of which was to give one-third of the fund to St Botolph's, one-third to St Helen's and the rest to the London Diocesan Fund.

The case was again brought before me in chambers on 6 and 7 November 1989 and on 10 January 1990. At these further hearings, Mr Spencer Maurice appeared for the original petitioners (other than the Prudential), Mr Robert Wakefield for the group of parties from St Helen's, and Mr Coningsby QC, with Mr Lloyd-Davies, for the Archdeacon of London and the London Diocesan Fund. Mr Wakefield asked that he should be regarded as representing separately Mr Lucas, the incumbent of St Helen's, and to that I assented.

Counsel for the original petitioners and counsel for the parties from St Helen's then contended that I had no jurisdiction to make a diversion order (ie to order that the money shall be applied elsewhere than in the parishes of St Botolph's and St Helen's) and each argued that I should, instead, make an order for the whole fund in court to be paid

out to whichever incumbent has the freehold of the graveyard, and counsel for the
original petitioners argued in the alternative that the whole fund should be paid to the
parochial church council of St Botolph's. Each of the incumbents claimed to be the
freeholder of the graveyard. Counsel for the archdeacon submitted that I had jurisdiction
to make a diversion order and that I should adhere to my decision of 15 June 1989, save
for one minor adjustment to which I agreed. If I confirm my previous directions, the
share of the money taken by the London Diocesan Fund will therefore be held as part of
the stipends fund. Counsel for the archdeacon submitted that the matter was regularly
before me at the April hearing, that the directions which I gave in June were fair and
reasonable and that (save on the one minor detail) there was no reason to disturb those
directions. But the amount of money at stake is large and the issue of jurisdiction has
been argued fully. Moreover, I was told that both the archdeacon and the London
Diocesan Fund would welcome a considered judgment, since they have other cases
awaiting the result of this one. In these circumstances, I propose to deal fully with the
issue of jurisdiction.

This petition instituted a cause of faculty for authorising physical acts relating to land
within the Diocese of London. These were acts for the doing of which a decree of faculty
was necessary, because the land is consecrated land. The petition is therefore within the
jurisdiction of the consistory court of that diocese under Ecclesiastical Jurisdiction
Measure 1963, s 6(1)(b). The court has granted authority for the execution of the deed
submitted in draft for approval and has directed that the money arising shall be paid into
court. As I said in Re St Mary Aldermary [1985] 2 All ER 445 at 447–448, [1985] Fam 101
at 104–105, the sort of relief which was asked for and granted here can either be given
by an extra-judicial document sanctioned by faculty or by the court itself in the faculty.
The form is a matter of convenience and indifference. But, whichever form is adopted,
the facilities granted stem from the exercise by the court of its jurisdiction over the land,
and from the faculty granted in exercise of that jurisdiction. The same would be true if
the subject matter of the cause were to be unconsecrated church curtilage, or chattels
being dealt with under the jurisdiction of the court as in Re St Gregory's, Tredington
[1971] 3 All ER 269, [1972] Fam 236. Like consecrated land and buildings, unconsecrated
land and parish chattels are in a broad sense ecclesiastical property. Technically, the
freehold, the life estate, in consecrated land or consecrated buildings is in the incumbent
(though the fee simple itself is an abeyance), but in the case of unconsecrated curtilage
the whole legal fee simple is usually in the incumbent. The chattels belong at law to the
churchwardens. Neither the incumbent nor the churchwardens are beneficial owners.
They are owners on behalf of the parishioners. The principles are in my judgment the
same for all these classes of property. The life interest in a consecrated burial ground is
held by the incumbent for the burial of the parishioners; but in this case fresh burials
have long been prohibited. No doubt, if the place had grass useful to sheep the incumbent
would be entitled to any grazing rents, and if the burial ground were to be open for
burials there would theoretically be a benefit to the incumbent from burial fees. But that
is academic nowadays because such rents and fees are deducted from the incumbent's
diocesan minimum stipend. In the past both these sorts of benefit must sometimes have
been of value; but that is no longer the case.

In reality both consecrated and unconsecrated land and chattels are parish property
held for the benefit of the parish church and its congregation. In former days the
parishioners, or congregation, acted through the vestry meeting. But the Arches Court
in Re St Gregory's, Tredington [1971] 3 All ER 269 at 272, [1972] Fam 236 at 240
recognised that the parochial church council is now the effective organ. In substance this
closed graveyard, though held by the incumbent at law, is held by him for the benefit of
the parochial church council and so for the congregation. The concept of 'parishioners' as
distinct from 'congregation' in the case of these two churches is artificial, since their
numbers are in each case derisory.

There must obviously be jurisdiction in someone to decree the destination of the money, since it would be absurd to leave it permanently in court. I hold that such jurisdiction is vested in this court, for the issue arises in faculty proceedings duly constituted and is consequential on the faculty. Once the consistory court has seisin of a cause of faculty, it is bound to dispose of the cause and to decide all questions which arise incidentally to, in and from that cause. For this proposition see *Phillimore's Ecclesiastical Law of the Church of England* (1st edn, 1873) p 1441 (a work of authority), which is as follows:

'. . . in case the principal matter belonged to the cognizance of the spiritual Court, all matters incidental (though otherwise of a temporal nature) are also cognizable there . . .'

The learned author cites *Gould v Gapper* (1804) 5 East 345, 102 ER 1102 and also the earlier case of *Shotter v Friend* (1690) 3 Mod Rep 283, 87 ER 188. These two decisions were referred to by Commissary General his Honour Judge John Newey QC in *Re St Mary of Charity, Faversham* [1986] 1 All ER 1 at 9, [1986] Fam 143 at 155. The point in that case was whether, incidental to a faculty application, the commissary court had jurisdiction to decide the title to a chattel. The Commissary General held that it had. It seems to me that the logic is inescapable: the consistory court or the commissary court has jurisdiction to deal with all matters arising incidentally in a cause of faculty. That cannot mean only questions of title but any and every incidental matter the decision of which is necessary for justice to be done in that cause and including the making of all conditions which are just and expedient. Conditions are very frequently imposed on faculties and are set out in them. Once the money has been paid, or is contracted to be paid, by the licensee under and by virtue of a faculty, its destination is incidental to the decision of this court to grant the faculty.

How wide, then, is my discretion? The proposals in the present case were that I should apply the money to other purposes which were purely ecclesiastical. Thus the problem here is essentially the same as that which arose in the Arches Court in *Corke v Rainger and Higgs* [1912] P 69, where the court was asked to allow the erection of a church school, to be run by its own body of trustees, on a piece of land near a church which had been consecrated either as part of the church site or as a churchyard. Since the land had not been used for burials, no question arose under the Disused Burial Grounds Act 1884. The court decided that because the church school was an ecclesiastical purpose there was jurisdiction to divert the land from its original purposes to the ecclesiastical purpose of a church school. If that can be done in relation to the consecrated land itself (and this was a decision of the Arches Court) I do not accept the submission that any money resulting from the granting of a faculty relating to consecrated land cannot likewise be diverted to other ecclesiastical purposes. The primary ecclesiastical purpose will normally be the parochial church council of the parish concerned. But if the money cannot all be employed usefully by that parochial church council for its statutory duties (as in effect I held here in my judgment last June) then one should look further, and a neighbouring parish or the diocese are obvious possibilities. I do not propose now to explore either the question of what ecclesiastical purposes would be admissible or how far (if at all) the power of diversion can go beyond ecclesiastical purposes. I shall deal only with the propositions which are before me.

But, it is argued, the land is vested in the incumbent and the only destination for the resulting money must be to the incumbent.

I dare say that that would have made good sense in the last century. In those days the value of the living had to be kept up, for the benefit of the patron and the incumbent. But it makes no sense now, when clerical stipends are uniform and are paid centrally. In deciding what to do, the court is, in my judgment, not only entitled but bound to consider what course is reasonable at the time when the decision has to be made.

It is argued that the money issues out of the land and that the land belongs to the
incumbent: so the money should go to him. I do not think that the former proposition
is right. For the consecrated status of the land puts it under the jurisdiction of the court
and the money in court stems from the exercise by the court of its own jurisdiction when
it grants the faculty. In the case of land the action of the court does not depend on the
consent of the incumbent: see Re St Andrew's, North Weald Bassett [1987] 1 WLR 1503 at
1507. Again, 'The final control of the church and chancel and of the churchyard is vested
in the chancellor, as ordinary for this purpose': per the Chancellor, Dr Tristram QC, in St
Botolph without Aldgate (vicar and one of the churchwardens) v Parishioners [1892] P161 at
167. This pronouncement of Dr Tristram is in any event binding on me, sitting in the
same court as that in which it was uttered. But I follow it without hesitation in view of
the great respect in which Dr Tristram's authority is held. Thus the consent of the
incumbent is not a condition of granting the faculty. It is merely a factor to be considered
by the court when it decides whether or not to grant it. (I pause here to say that some of
the phraseology used in Re St Gregory's, Tredington [1971] 3 All ER 269 at 272, [1972]
Fam 236 at 240 might be interpreted as meaning that a faculty cannot issue for the sale
of a church chattel without the consent of the vestry, now the parochial church council.
But what actually was said was that, if the parochial church council does consent, a faculty
can be granted, not that if there is no such consent a faculty cannot be granted. The
question whether the court could make an order authorising a sale against the wishes of
the churchwardens was not in issue in that case.)

So far, then, the broad authorities suggest that the court has jurisdiction to make a
diversion order in a proper case. Is there anything in the arguments put to me in
November or January to displace that provisional conclusion? It is said that Re St John the
Baptist, Cardiff (vicar and churchwardens) v Parishioners [1898] P 155 is an authority to the
contrary, since Chancellor Ollivant felt himself unable to agree to the sum of £500,
which was to be paid by the local authority for the creation of a footway across a
churchyard, being used as a repair fund for the church. He said that it was to be added to
the endowment of the benefice. This was a curious case in that the chancellor referred to
the way as if it was an easement and not a licence. However, his decision seems to have
turned on the supposed analogy with Ex p Rector of Liverpool (1870) LR 11 Eq 15. But
that was one of a group of cases about compulsory purchase, following Re St Pancras
Burial-Ground (1866) LR 3 Eq 173. From the St Pancras case it appears that the court was
in all these cases applying ss 69 and 70 of the Lands Clauses Consolidation Act 1845,
which covered the money in question. It seems to me that this line of decisions concerns
statutory construction in a case of compulsory purchase and that they have no relevance
to the point now before me, which is what is to be done with money arising from the
exercise by the court of its discretion; there is no compulsory acquisition.

On the other hand, there are two unreported cases of diversion orders fairly recently
in this diocese (Re All Hallows, Berkyngechirche (5 July 1972, unreported) and Re St Benet
Fink, Tottenham (4 December 1975, unreported)). Again, in Re St Mary le Bow [1984] 1
WLR 1363 a contingent diversion order was made. In all these cases counsel were
engaged and no one disputed that the court had jurisdiction to make such an order. In
each case all the churchwardens consented, they being cases about chattels. What is
perhaps more important is that a diversion order was made by Dr Tristram himself in
Christ Church, Chislehurst (incumbent and churchwardens) v Parishioners (1897) (reported as a
note to Re St Mary Magdalene, Paddington [1980] 1 All ER 279 at 283, [1980] Fam 99 at
104). In the Chislehurst case the incumbent owned a piece of unconsecrated church
curtilage which had been vested in him. Dr Tristram allowed him to sell the fee simple
and diverted the resulting £150 so that that sum could be used to pay debts incurred by
the incumbent and churchwardens, ie church debts and not the debts of the benefice.

I see no ground, so far as this point is concerned, to distinguish between a case of
consecrated land and one about unconsecrated curtilage. Similarly, though not quite on

the same point, in *St Stephen Walbrook (rector and churchwardens) v Sun Fire Office Trustees* (1883) Trist 103 Dr Tristram in effect dictated most of the terms, including all the money terms, of an agreement which he then proceeded to authorise.

Nor is any of this surprising. For the decisions are in line with the numerous cases, collected in *Re St John's, Chelsea* [1962] 2 All ER 850, [1962] 1 WLR 706, in which the consecrated land itself was diverted, wholly or partially, from its primary use as a place for burial, in some cases to purposes that were not ecclesiastical at all. *Morley BC v St Mary the Virgin, Woodkirk (vicar and churchwardens)* [1969] 3 All ER 952, [1969] 1 WLR 1867 is perhaps the most extreme example of the exercise of this power. The court in that case, being the appellate court of the northern province, followed *Re St John's, Chelsea*. *Corke v Rainger and Higgs* [1912] P 69 is on the other hand an example of a diversion to other ecclesiastical purposes. All that I now decide is what is currently before me, viz that a diversion order of money can be made to other ecclesiastical purposes.

How much further beyond ecclesiastical purposes such a diversion order can go (if at all) is a matter for some future decision. I am quite unable to see why a diversion order to other ecclesiastical purposes of money arising from a faculty relating to consecrated land can be an illegitimate exercise of the jurisdiction of the court. In my judgment, therefore, the order which I proposed to make in this case last June was within my jurisdiction. I therefore, affirm that order with the minor variation asked by counsel for the archdeacon; at the hearing on 10 January counsel for all parties agreed that, if I have jurisdiction, that order would be a proper one; there was no further argument on this issue.

Order affirmed with variation.

Solicitors: *Winckworth & Pemberton* (for the original petitioners other than the Prudential); *Monro Pennefather & Co* (for the incumbent, churchwardens and parochial church council of St Helen Bishopsgate); *Wedlake Bell* (for the archdeacon and the London Diocesan Fund).

N P Metcalfe Esq   Barrister.

a Knight and others v Home Office and another

QUEEN'S BENCH DIVISION

PILL J

31 OCTOBER, 1, 2, 3, 6, 7 NOVEMBER, 1 DECEMBER 1989

b *Negligence – Duty to take care – Prison hospital – Mentally ill prisoner – Suicide risk – Prisoner ordered to be detained in remand prison pending admission to hospital – Prisoner known to have suicidal tendencies – Prison medical staff deciding that prisoner should be observed in cell at 15-minute intervals – Prisoner committing suicide in between inspections – Whether standard of care provided for mentally ill prisoner in prison hospital required to be as high as standard of care provided in psychiatric hospital – Whether medical staff negligent in failing to keep prisoner*
c *under continuous observation.*

The deceased attacked a man and subsequently pleaded guilty to wounding with intent to cause grievous bodily harm and assault occasioning actual bodily harm. The court ordered that he be detained in hospital pursuant to s 60 of the Mental Health Act 1959 and further ordered that he be detained in a remand prison pending his admission to
d hospital. Because he was known to have suicidal tendencies he was subject to the prison's 'special watch' procedure but because he was also known to be violent it was not possible to put him in a ward in the prison hospital wing, where a continuous watch could be kept on him. Instead he was put in a cell where prison officers observed him at not less than 15-minute intervals. In between two 15-minute inspections the deceased committed suicide by hanging. His personal representatives brought an action against the Home
e Office claiming that the standard of care provided for the deceased in the prison hospital was inadequate.

Held – The standard of care provided for a mentally ill prisoner detained in a prison hospital was not required to be as high as the standard of care provided in a psychiatric hospital outside prison, since psychiatric and prison hospitals performed different
f functions and the duty of care in respect of each type of hospital had to be tailored to the act and function to be performed. Accordingly, the facilities and numbers of staff for the provision of medical care for persons detained in prison did not have to be the same as for the specialist function of psychiatric hospitals of treating and if possible curing mental illness. It followed that there had been no negligence on the part of the prison service in failing to provide in the hospital wing of the prison in which the deceased had been
g detained the patient/staff ratio which existed in psychiatric hospitals. Furthermore, applying the accepted test for medical negligence, the prison medical staff had not been negligent in failing to keep the deceased under continuous observation since their decision to observe him at 15-minute intervals was a decision which ordinary skilled medical staff in their position could have made. The action would therefore be dismissed (see p 243 *c* to *g*, p 245 *b* to *g* and p 246 *b*, post).
h *Bolam v Friern Hospital Management Committee* [1957] 2 All ER 118 and dictum of Mustill LJ in *Wilsher v Essex Area Health Authority* [1986] 3 All ER 801 at 813 applied.

Notes

For duty of care, see 34 Halsbury's Laws (4th edn) para 5, and for cases on the subject, see
j 36(1) Digest (Reissue) 17–32, 34–103.
 As from 30 September 1983 s 60 of the Mental Health Act 1959 was replaced by s 37 of the Mental Health Act 1983. For s 37 of the 1983 Act, see 28 Halsbury's Statutes (4th edn) 677.

Cases referred to in judgment

Bolam v Friern Hospital Management Committee [1957] 2 All ER 118, [1957] 1 WLR 582.
Daborn v Bath Tramways Motor Co Ltd [1946] 2 All ER 333, CA.
Hucks v Cole (1968) 112 SJ 483, CA.
Wilsher v Essex Area Health Authority [1986] 3 All ER 801, [1987] QB 730, [1986] 3 WLR
   425, CA; *rvsd* [1988] 1 All ER 871, [1988] AC 1074, [1988] 2 WLR 557, HL.

Action

The plaintiffs, Shani Teresa Knight and Olive Millicent Worrell, suing as administratrices
of the estate of Paul Barrington Worrell deceased, and Owen Paul Worrell, a minor suing
by the first plaintiff, his mother and next friend, by writ dated 10 January 1985, claimed
damages against the defendants, the Home Office and the Governor of Brixton Prison,
for breach of duty and negligence in, inter alia, failing to heed that the deceased presented
a serious risk of suicide, failing to keep the deceased under proper observation, failing to
institute any or any adequate system of care to prevent the deceased from killing himself,
failing to provide a proper system, proper staff and proper facilities for the care of the
deceased who presented a suicide risk and failing to take proper care of the deceased's
safety. The facts are set out in the judgement.

Oliver Thorold for the plaintiffs.
Timothy Stow QC and *Ian Burnett* for the defendants.

Cur adv vult

1 December. The following judgment was delivered.

PILL J. Paul Barrington Worrell, aged 21 years, committed suicide by hanging at
Brixton Prison, Brixton, on 12 January 1982. His personal representatives claim damages
from the Home Office and the governor of Brixton Prison on behalf of his estate. A claim
is also made on behalf of his infant son for loss of dependency.

On 17 September 1981 Mr Worrell attacked a man in a public house and on
18 September he was remanded in custody to Brixton, where he was detained in the
hospital wing until his death. On 22 December 1981 he pleaded guilty at Inner London
Sessions to an offence of wounding with intent to cause grievous bodily harm under s 18
of the Offences against the Person Act 1861 and an offence of assault occasioning actual
bodily harm.

On the basis of the medical evidence the court made an order under s 60 of the Mental
Health Act 1959 for his admission within 28 days and his detention in the Bethlem Royal
Hospital. It was ordered that until such admission he was to be detained in a place of
safety, namely HM prison. It has been agreed as a fact that the making of the hospital
order was a source of contentment to Mr Worrell.

The medical evidence before the court was from Dr H Gordon, senior registrar to Dr J
Mackeith at Bethlem Royal Hospital, and Dr G R Grant, senior medical officer at Brixton.
The opinion of both doctors was that Mr Worrell was suffering from mental illness, Dr
Gordon stating that 'the patient was suffering from mental illness, into which he shows
no insight'. Dr Gordon also stated in his report of 4 December 1981 that the patient had
recently been both a danger to himself and to others. In a covering letter of the same
date, Dr Gordon expressed a willingness to take Mr Worrell into the interim secure unit
at the hospital within 28 days of his court appearance on 22 December 1981. Before Mr
Worrell's death arrangements had been made to transfer him from prison to hospital on
15 January 1982, that is 24 days after the court order.

It is necessary to summarise the earlier medical history. On 28 August 1981 Mr
Worrell had jumped through a closed window in the upper storey of his parents' home,
where he lived. He reported hearing voices whose commands he obeyed. He was

detained in hospital for a few days. Physical injuries were minor. It was reported by Dr
a Timms, senior house officer to a consultant psychiatrist at the hospital, that Mr Worrell's
mental state had returned to normal. Dr Timms added that: 'As this seems to have been
an isolated, impulsive act follow-up has not been arranged.'

On 17 September 1981 Mr Worrell committed the criminal offence to which he later
pleaded guilty, and on appearance at the magistrates' court he was remanded to Brixton
for reports. There were differences of opinion between the doctors who examined him,
b but the medical advice to the court in December 1981 was that already stated. On
13 October 1981, Dr M S Lipsedge had diagnosed schizophrenia and offered admission
to Guys Hospital, provided an appropriate court order was made. That offer was
withdrawn on 28 October 1981. Dr Andrew Smith, by letter on 20 October 1981,
declined to take Mr Worrell into Bexley Hospital or the psychiatric unit at Greenwich
District Hospital.

c   Mr Worrell's conduct in the prison hospital wing gave cause for concern for his safety
and that of others. On 23 September 1981 he attacked another prisoner. On 10 October
he assaulted a prison officer. Disciplinary proceedings followed. On 16 October he
attempted to stab himself in the eye with a plastic fork. On 9 November he cut his face
with a razor blade. On 4 December a sheet was found tied in a noose around the window
bars in his cell. On 7 December he was noisy and very disturbed and banged and kicked
d his cell door.

Because of his violent conduct he was not kept in a ward with other prisoners. On five
occasions he was placed for short periods in a special medical room, sometimes known as
a strip cell because it was stripped of almost all furniture and amenities. For the
remainder of the time Mr Worrell was kept in an ordinary cell, which had a door with a
panel capable of being kept in the open position, and a barred aperture at about head
e height in another wall.

His parents, who are reliable people, became very concerned about him and solicitors
acting in the criminal proceedings wrote to the prison medical officer, expressing their
concern. Mr Worrell was refusing visits from his parents and they were offered the
opportunity to meet Dr Grant.

f   Prison standing orders then in force provided that where suicidal tendencies were
present the prisoner's hospital treatment card should be stamped with the letter 'F' in a
prominent place. That procedure has since been changed. Mr Worrell's card was marked
in that way and he was kept under what was known as 'Special Watch B'. Paragraph 60
of standing orders, as amended, provided:

g   'Prisoners exhibiting marked depression or emotion with or without suicidal
tendencies will if possible be located in association in the hospital under special
watch continuous supervision by hospital officers unless the medical officer considers
that because of a danger of violence to himself or others it is not safe to locate a
prisoner in association and orders him to be located in a room under special watch.
If no accommodation is available in the hospital for a prisoner exhibiting marked
depression or emotion or with known or expected suicidal tendencies who would
h   otherwise be suitable for location in association in the hospital he should be located
in a cell on the observation landing and observed at not less than 15 minute
intervals.'

'Special watch, continuous observation' was known as 'Special Watch A' following the
j categorisation in para 56 of the standing orders. Special watch A prisoners were normally
kept in wards in the prison hospital where continuous observation could be maintained
without the need for additional staff. In that minority of cases where a violent tendency
was present and the prisoner could not be in a ward, he would be kept under continuous
observation in a cell.

It is common ground between the doctors that, given staffing levels and arrangements in the prison hospital, it was not appropriate to keep Mr Worrell in a ward with other prisoners because of his violent tendency.

At about 8.15 am on 12 January 1982 the two patrolling officers in the medical wing heard another prisoner shout that a man was hanging in his cell. That other prisoner must have observed him through the open flap of the cell door. The officers went to the cell immediately and found Mr Worrell hanging by the neck. A shirt and towel had been tied together, one end placed around his neck and the other around a window bar in the cell. There was a chair under the window. Unsuccessful efforts were made to revive Mr Worrell. I accept the evidence of the officer who found him that Mr Worrell had been observed in a condition which did not give cause for concern within 15 minutes before the other prisoner's shout.

Brixton is the main remand prison for adult males in London. It was built in the 1860s. The prison population at the material time was about 700. In the course of a year 60,000 to 70,000 prisoners pass through the prison. There were up to 100 admissions or discharges a day. The hospital wing at the prison consisted of a wing for prisoners with physical conditions with 110 beds and a wing for prisoners with psychiatric conditions with 101 beds. B wing was being used for that purpose on a temporary basis while another wing was being renovated. The hospital was almost always full. B wing had 97 single rooms and four special medical rooms. The other wing housed prisoners mainly in dormitories but with some single rooms.

It was estimated in evidence that between 30 and 55 prisoners were at any one time classified as presenting a threat of suicide. The figure might be as high as 100 to 120. The principal medical officer at Brixton was Dr Blythe, the senior medical officer Dr Grant and there were four other medical officers. The nursing staff numbered 40. They were prison officers with training in this work and known as hospital officers. The training consisted of a course lasting between three and six months at one of three prison hospitals, followed by in-service training and refresher courses.

I have mentioned the staffing levels because the main thrust of the plaintiffs' case is that the defendants were in breach of duty to Mr Worrell because the general standard of care provided in the prison hospital was inadequate. The standard to be expected was the same as that in a psychiatric hospital outside prison, and the facilities available at Brixton fell far below that standard, it is submitted.

The allegation is put on the plaintiffs' behalf as starkly as that: failure to meet the much higher standards to be expected in psychiatric hospitals outside prison constitutes a breach of duty.

Save as to the points I consider later, it was not alleged that an intermediate standard or limited improvements to achieve it should have been adopted. An allegation is also made against the individual doctors, based on the decision they took not to put Mr Worrell on special watch A, that is continuous observation. That allegation is pursued with a lack of enthusiasm expressed by counsel and implicit in the evidence of Dr Mackeith, the plaintiffs' medical witness.

Allegations against individual doctors were at one stage of the trial abandoned, but the single allegation that Mr Worrell should have been under continuous observation was revived when the possibility of the provision of special watch A, that is continuous observation in a special cell, was mentioned in the course of the defendants' evidence. Dr Mackeith had experience at Brixton prison, and he believed that the choice available to the doctors was between placing Mr Worrell in a strip cell or placing him on special watch B. I gave leave to recall Dr Mackeith to give further evidence on the subject if the other possibility, which he did not believe was available, was in fact available.

The allegation that the doctors were negligent in failing to keep Mr Worrell in a special medical room or stripped cells was not revived. Dr Mackeith said that he would have kept the prisoner in a special medical room but accepted that the special medical room was a very deprived, indeed an inhuman environment. Taking that into account, the decision to remove Mr Worrell from the special medical room was not a negligent

decision, Dr Mackeith said. The longer a prisoner is kept in a special medical room, the
worse it is likely to be for him. Detention in an ordinary cell was rather less damaging.
a In an ordinary cell there was more contact with other people. Dr Mackeith also considered
that the decision not to keep Mr Worrell in a ward with other prisoners was justified
because of the violent tendency which was present.

I return to the plaintiffs' principal case, which is that the first defendants were negligent
because of the lack of facilities available in the prison hospital. Dr James Mackeith is a
b consultant forensic psychiatrist employed by the Bethlem Royal and Maudsley Hospitals.
The expertise of those hospitals in the psychiatric fields is, of course, well known. It
emerged in the course of the evidence of Dr Grant, who had apparently discussed the
matter with Dr Mackeith outside the court, that the staffing level at Bethlem was two
nursing staff to one patient. In other psychiatric hospitals where care was not as intensive,
the ratio was one to one or, in the worse case, o·8 staff to one patient.

c   Those figures were adopted on the plaintiffs' behalf to establish the proposition that
resources at Brixton were inadequate. Dr Mackeith said that the worse psychiatric
hospital he had ever visited was better staffed and resourced than Brixton's hospital wing.
Facilities were grossly and comprehensively inadequate. Because of insufficient staff at
Brixton, the patient would lack counselling, advice, support and therapy. In hospital Dr
Mackeith would try to deal with patients in open wards by medication and allocation of
d staff to disturbed patients. It was very important to help patients to engage in conversation
and interaction with other people.

What principally was required, it is submitted on the plaintiffs' behalf, was interaction
with skilled staff in a well staffed ward. If such interaction was limited, there was very
little scope for helping the patient. There were many other difficult patients to be dealt
with at Brixton; some of them, including Mr Worrell, had severe mental illnesses. They
e did not receive the standard of care at Brixton which should be and, said Dr Mackeith,
sometimes is available outside.

It is not suggested on behalf of the plaintiffs that any institution can offer a man a
guarantee against self-destruction.

Dr Mackeith was not able to compare facilities at Brixton with those at other prisons,
but that was not the relevant comparison, he said. Such evidence as there is of facilities at
f other prisons (and there has been no systematic comparison in the course of the evidence)
indicates that they were not, at the material time, very different from those at Brixton.

The prison doctors who gave evidence for the defendants were conscious of the limited
nature of the service which they were able to offer. They readily accepted that the type
of treatment contemplated by Dr Mackeith could not be provided in prison.

Counsel for the plaintiffs has taken the point that on the pleadings it is not open to the
g defendants to argue that the standard of care required is different from that for which he
contends. For the defendants it is submitted by counsel that the plaintiffs are not entitled
on the basis of the pleadings to argue that resources were inadequate. I cannot accept
either submission: neither statement of claim nor defence expressly pleads the standard
of care which is alleged to be appropriate in the circumstances. That is not unusual in
negligence actions. It does not prevent either side from arguing in the way they have
h what is alleged to be the appropriate standard.

As to the alleged deficiency in the particulars of the claim, an allegation of 'failing to
provide proper facilities' is made twice in the particulars of negligence. No further and
better particulars were sought.

In support of his contention that the appropriate standard of care is that in a psychiatric
j hospital outside prison counsel for the plaintiffs relies on s 7 of the Prison Act 1952.
Section 7(1) provides:

'Every prison shall have a governor, a chaplain and a medical officer and such
other officers as may be necessary.'

He relies on s 22(2) of the 1952 Act, which provides, inter alia:

'The Secretary of State may . . . if he is satisfied that a person so detained requires medical or surgical treatment of any description, direct him to be taken to a hospital *a* or other suitable place for the purpose of the treatment . . .'

Counsel relies on the fact that s 64 of the Mental Health Act 1959, which made provision for the accommodation of a patient pending his admission to a hospital under a hospital order, referred to his detention in a 'place of safety'. Section 73 of the 1959 Act empowers the Secretary of State to direct the transfer of a prisoner on remand to a hospital for *b* medical treatment.

Counsel also relies on r 17(1) of the Prison Rules 1964, SI 1964/388, which provides:

'The medical officer of a prison shall have the care of the health mental and physical of the prisoners in that prison.'

Rule 18 provides: *c*

'. . . (2) The medical officer shall pay special attention to any prisoner whose mental condition appears to require it, and make any special arrangements which appear necessary for his supervision or care.
(3) The medical officer shall inform the governor if he suspects any prisoner of having suicidal intentions, and the prisoner shall be placed under special observation.' *d*

The statute and rules contemplate a standard of care as high as that in a hospital outside prison, counsel submits.

Counsel for the defendants, of course, submitted that the s 60 procedure would be unnecessary if facilities available in psychiatric hospitals were also available in prisons. Reliance was placed by counsel for the plaintiffs on the speech of Mustill LJ in *Wilsher v* *e* *Essex Area Health Authority* [1986] 3 All ER 801 at 813, [1987] QB 730 at 750. In the context of considering the standard of care required in a hospital, where the skills of individual members of staff will vary according to their training and experience, Mustill LJ stated:

'To my mind, this notion of a duty tailored to the actor, rather than to the act *f* which he elects to perform, has no place in the law of tort.'

In *Wilsher's* case Sir Nicolas Browne-Wilkinson VC and Glidewell LJ clearly contemplated that a hospital authority could be held liable if it failed to provide staff of sufficient skill and experience to give the treatment offered at the hospital.

This is not a case where the general competence or experience of the doctors present at *g* Brixton is challenged. Indeed, Dr Mackeith expressed his high regard for Dr Grant's professional competence.

Counsel for the defendants referred me to a passage in the speech of Sir Nicolas Browne-Wilkinson V-C ([1986] 3 All ER 801 at 834, [1987] QB 730 at 778). Having posed the question:

h

'Given limited resources, what balance is to be struck in the allocation of such resources between compensating those whose treatment is not wholly successful and the provision of required treatment for the world at large? [the Vice-Chancellor stated] These are questions for Parliament not the courts.'

Counsel for the plaintiffs submits that it is not a defence to establish that the standard *j* of care was as good as that in other prisons or that it accorded with government circulars or standing orders in force at the time. While general practice in the prison service is a factor to be taken into account, I accept that the plaintiffs could succeed even if the current practice approved in the prison service had been followed in every respect. As Asquith LJ put it in *Daborn v Bath Tramways Motor Co Ltd* [1946] 2 All ER 333 at 336:

'In determining whether a party is negligent, the standard of reasonable care is
a   that which is reasonably to be demanded in the circumstances.'

It is for the court to consider what standard of care is appropriate to the particular
relationship and in the particular situation. It is not a complete defence for a government
department any more than it would be for a private individual or organisation to say that
no funds are available for additional safety measures.

b   I cannot accept what was at one time submitted by counsel for the defendants that the
plaintiffs' only remedy would be a political one. To take an extreme example, if the
evidence was that no funds were available to provide any medical facilities in a large
prison there would be a failure to achieve the standard of care appropriate for prisoners.
In a different context, lack of funds would not excuse a public body which operated its
vehicles on the public roads without any system of maintenance for the vehicles if an
accident occurred because of lack of maintenance. The law would require a higher
c   standard of care towards other road users.

In making the decision as to the standard to be demanded the court must, however,
bear in mind as one factor that resources available for the public service are limited and
that the allocation of resources is a matter for Parliament.

I am unable to accept the submission that the law requires the standard of care in a
d   prison hospital to be as high as the standard of care for all purposes in a psychiatric
hospital outside prison. I am unable to accept that the practices in a prison hospital are to
be judged in all respects by the standard appropriate to a psychiatric hospital outside
prison. There may be circumstances in which the standard of care in a prison falls below
that which would be expected in a psychiatric hospital without the prison authority
being negligent. Even in a medical situation outside prison, the standard of care required
e   will vary with the context. The facilities available to deal with an emergency in a general
practitioner's surgery cannot be expected to be as ample as those available in the casualty
department of a general hospital, for example.

Psychiatric hospitals perform a specialist function in treating mental illness and, where
possible, effecting a cure. Interaction with skilled staff is, on the evidence, a vital part of
the treatment in cases such as the present. The prison's central function is to detain
f   persons deprived of their liberty by operation of law. The prison authorities have a duty
to provide medical care where physical or mental illness is present. That includes a duty
to protect a mentally ill patient against himself. I bear in mind the statutory provisions,
but in my judgment the law should not and does not expect the same standard across the
entire spectrum of possible situations, including the possibility of suicide, as it would in
a psychiatric hospital outside prison. The duty is tailored to the act and function to be
g   performed.

There was no negligence in the failure to provide in the hospital wing of the prison
the patient/staff ratio present at Bethlem Royal Hospital and other psychiatric hospitals.
I am unable to find for the plaintiffs on the ground that the same facilities should have
been available in prison as would have been available in a psychiatric hospital.

Since no intermediate standard between that of a specialist psychiatric hospital and
h   that at Brixton has been advocated either in evidence or submissions, I do not consider
that it is open to me to speculate on what an appropriate standard might be. If necessary,
I would, however, be prepared to hold on the evidence before me as to conditions in
1981 and 1982 that even bearing in mind the number of prisoners and the condition of
many of them, the general standard of care was, on the information available, appropriate
to the function to be performed.

j   The irony of the present case, as Dr Mackeith recognised, is that an order for admission
to Bethlem Royal Hospital had been made and Mr Worrell was still in prison three weeks
after the order because the hospital, aware that he was a danger to himself, had been
unable to arrange earlier admission. I state that as a fact and not as a criticism of the
hospital because the reasons why there was no earlier admission have not been canvassed.
Section 64 of the 1959 Act does allow a period of up to 28 days before admission.

I accept that, on the balance of probabilities, Mr Worrell would not have died on
12 January had he been an in-patient at that Bethlem Royal Hospital on that date. That   *a*
does not fully deal with the question of causation, to which I will return. Nor can I find
negligence in the defendants' failure to transfer the prisoner to a psychiatric hospital.
There was a court order under s 60 of the 1959 Act requiring transfer. Failure to exercise
s 73 powers did not, in my view, constitute negligence in the circumstances. Dr Mackeith
and Dr Grant thought it right to pursue a s 60 disposal at the material time. Dr Grant's
evidence was that there was nothing which the prison authorities could do to expedite   *b*
the hospital admission under s 60.

I turn to the allegation against the doctors that Mr Worrell should have been watched
continuously. I accept as a fact that staff could have been made available for continuous
observation. I also accept the evidence of Dr Sethiamurthy that no patient's needs were
neglected in this respect. It was other less important work which, he said, would not be
done when resources were stretched. Had the doctors thought it appropriate, the   *c*
governor would have provided continuous observation, using disciplined staff, as distinct
from hospital staff, if that was necessary. Dr Mackeith expressed the opinion that if
facilities were available the doctors should have placed Mr Worrell on continuous
observation.

The doctors' conduct is to be judged by the *Bolam* standard: see *Bolam v Friern Hospital
Management Committee* [1957] 2 All ER 118 at 121, [1957] 1 WLR 582 at 586, where   *d*
McNair J stated:

> 'The test is the standard of the ordinary skilled man exercising and professing to
> have that special skill. A man need not possess the highest expert skill at the risk of
> being found negligent. It is well-established law that it is sufficient if he exercises
> the ordinary skill of an ordinary competent man exercising that particular art.'   *e*

The reasons given by the doctors for their decision should, however, be examined by the
court to see if they stand up to analysis: see *Hucks v Cole* (1968) 112 SJ 483 per Sachs LJ.
The doctors knew that the cell bar provided a usable suspension point, that Mr Worrell
had clothing, including shirt, sheet and towel and that he was a suicide risk. They were,   *f*
of course, aware of the regime under which he was detained in an ordinary furnished
cell.

In cross-examination of the defendants' witnesses, the system of medical and other
supervision and the significance of the entries in the treatment card and the hospital
occurrence book were analysed in detail in relation to the doctors' decision not to keep
Mr Worrell under continuous observation. A case based on such an analysis might have
been more persuasive if Dr Mackeith had given detailed evidence on it. I do not consider   *g*
that the absence of such evidence from him was accidental. He was critical of the lack of
facilities available to the doctors but was not minded to make a detailed criticism of their
actions during the weeks before 12 January 1982. Indeed, he was consistent in his view
that the main cause for complaint was lack of the general facilities for treating the
mentally ill. He expressed the view that resources used on continuous observation were   *h*
uneconomically used and should be deployed to the wards.

Counsel for the plaintiffs also criticised the lack of the system under which a single
doctor had overall responsibility for Mr Worrell throughout his time in prison. He
submits that the condition of the patient as noted in the records was such that he should
have been kept under continuous observation, bearing in mind the background and the
need to preserve life, especially after the noose incident and the absence of any proximate   *j*
warning of that. Counsel submits, as is the fact, that a suicide can be organised within
the period of 15 minutes between the observations made on special watch B.

The defendants' witnesses accepted that the discovery of the noose was an important
and serious matter. The risk of suicide was accepted as being fairly high. There was,
however, no evidence of an attempted suicide on that occasion and suicide gestures were

not uncommon in prison, they said and I accept. Dr Mackeith did say in evidence that
a the noose incident turned a serious situation into a very serious situation; but the weight
I can attach to his view of that incident is reduced by the fact that it was not singled out
for special comment by him in either of his two written reports. A real danger arises
from the benefit of hindsight in a situation such as the present. Tragically Mr Worrell
committed suicide, but on the evidence he was one of a considerable number of suicide
risks at Brixton and probably one of a smaller number, on the information available,
b presenting at least as high a risk as Mr Worrell did. Dr Grant put it at possibly five or six.
Dr Sethiamurthy said that there were others who were more ill.

While that is not decisive, because it may be that several men ought to have been on
special watch A who were not, Dr Mackeith's opinion on the point was, in my view,
influenced by the subsequent knowledge of what happened in the event. I am unable to
hold that the doctors were negligent in failing to keep Mr Worrell on special watch A
c during the weeks after 4 December. He was observed every 15 minutes in his cell. The
hospital wing was, in the words of Mr Pearson, the then prison governor, a hubub of
activity. Mr Worrell had opportunities for exercise daily, for visits and, of course, meals
and ablutions. Mr Worrell was placed on medication to stabilise his condition and the
dosage was somewhat increased shortly before his death. Appropriate records of his
behaviour and condition were kept. The hospital order was a source of contentment to
d him, and there was no reason to believe that a special risk arose by reason of the
imminence of his transfer to hospital. I accept the doctors' evidence that they consciously
exercised a clinical judgment in deciding not to place Mr Worrell on special watch A.
From the medical point of view, they considered that the action they took was the best
action.

I accept that the doctors and hospital staff were alert to the need to monitor Mr
e Worrell's condition. The doctors had discussions about his behaviour with the hospital
officers observing him. A doctor saw him daily. There was a weekly review. None of the
doctors involved between August 1981 and January 1982 expressed at that time the
opinion that continuous observation was required, other than on the occasions when it
was implemented for a short period.

The experience of 24-hour observation, which Dr Grant described as dehumanising,
f would have made treatment more difficult on transfer to Bethlem Royal Hospital.

I note recent expressions of opinion by doctors who have an increased workload at
Brixton now as compared with 1981 and 1982 that additional resources are required, but
I do not find that decisive of the question whether there was a breach of duty eight years
ago. I do not consider that the doctors' judgments can be classified as negligent, nor do I
consider that the absence of a single doctor with overall responsibility throughout the
g entire period constituted negligence by the defendants.

I add in parenthesis that I reject Mr Pearson's attempted justification of the absence of
any mention of the noose incident in the report into the death which was prepared. It
should have been reported. However, for present purposes I do not draw inferences
adverse to the defendants from the absence of a reference.

h There remains the allegation that the readily available suspension point provided by
the cell bars should have been removed or concealed. No criticism was made of the
supply to Mr Worrell of a shirt and sheet. I bear in mind that hanging is by far the most
common form of suicide in prisons. I bear in mind that there have been previous suicides
in Brixton: there were three in 1981 and a total of two in 1982. I also bear in mind the
evidence as to hanging from other possible suspension points. There was also evidence
j that shuttering provided to conceal the bars may itself provide a point of suspension, or a
material such as glass which may itself be used to injure. Security in prison is essential
and light and ventilation highly desirable in a prison cell. Dr Mackeith fairly accepted, as
did other witnesses, that they were not engineers and could not give expert evidence as
to the design of prison cells. He said that he was not an expert on containment. Dr
Mackeith did say that the cell design at Broadmoor removed this particular risk.

On the evidence as a whole, I am not able to hold that the presence and accessibility of the bars involved a breach of duty by the defendants. Even if it did, I would not hold on *a* the evidence that on the balance of probabilities a different window design would have prevented the death. Causation is not established. Continuous observation would have prevented the death while Mr Worrell was in prison, though it would have been likely to put him in a more dangerous frame of mind in the prison and on transfer to hospital. Accordingly, there must be judgment for the defendants.

b

Action dismissed.

Solicitors: B M *Birnberg & Co* (for the plaintiffs); *Treasury Solicitor.*

K Mydeen Esq   Barrister.

c

Kirkham v Chief Constable of the Greater Manchester Police

COURT OF APPEAL, CIVIL DIVISION   *d*
LLOYD, FARQUHARSON LJJ AND SIR DENYS BUCKLEY
5, 6, 20 DECEMBER 1989

Police – Negligence – Duty to take care – Person in custody – Suicide risk – Police taking person with suicidal tendencies into custody – Police having knowledge of prisoner's suicidal tendencies – Prisoner remanded in custody and taken to remand centre – Police not informing prison authorities *e* *of prisoner's suicidal tendencies – Prisoner committing suicide at remand centre – Whether police under duty to pass on to remand centre all available information relevant to risk of suicide by prisoner – Whether police owing duty of care to prevent prisoner committing suicide – Whether police in breach of duty of care – Whether cause of action barred by maxim ex turpi causa non oritur actio or public policy because claim arising out of suicide.*

f

The plaintiff's husband (the deceased) was an alcoholic with suicidal tendencies. After a suicide attempt he was admitted to hospital but was allowed to discharge himself the next day. The day after, following a domestic argument, he was arrested and charged with criminal damage. The plaintiff told the police that the deceased had recently tried to commit suicide. At his appearance before the magistrates the next day the police objected to bail and he was remanded in custody for his own protection. However, the *g* procedure for informing the prison authorities of a prisoner's suicidal tendencies, by completing the form for exceptional risk prisoners stating that the prisoner had suicidal tendencies, giving the relevant details, and handing that form to the magistrate's court gaoler for transmission to the prison authorities if the prisoner was remanded in custody, was not carried out in the case of the deceased. At the remand centre the deceased was *h* treated like a normal prisoner and placed in a cell alone, where he committed suicide by hanging. The plaintiff brought an action against the defendant chief constable claiming damages for negligence by the police in failing to pass on to the remand centre information relating to the deceased's suicidal tendencies. The defendant contended (i) that the police did not owe a duty of care to prevent the deceased inflicting harm on himself because they were in the position of mere bystanders and (ii) that the plaintiff's *j* cause of action was barred by the maxim ex turpi causa non oritur actio or some general ground of public policy because the claim arose out of an act of suicide. The judge held that the defendant did owe a duty of care to prevent the deceased committing suicide because the police had been expressly put on notice of the deceased's mental state and the risk of suicide and by taking him into custody and detaining him at the police station the

police had assumed a duty to take reasonable care of his safety, and that duty had not
_a_ ended when the deceased was taken to court and was passed over to the prison authorities,
since it was reasonably foreseeable on the part of the police that their actions would affect
the deceased after he passed out of their charge and their failure to pass on to the remand
centre all information available to them relevant to the risk of suicide by the deceased
amounted to a breach of their duty of care which was an effective cause of the deceased's
death. The judge accordingly awarded damages of £6,717. The defendant appealed,
_b_ contending that the failure of the police to pass on to the remand centre all information
available to them relevant to the risk of suicide by the deceased was a pure omission and
there was no duty of care to protect a person from the risk of injury created by himself,
that the deceased's voluntary act of suicide meant that the plaintiff's claim was defeated
by the defence of volenti non fit injuria and that a claim arising out of a suicide was
barred by the maxim ex turpi causa non oritur actio.

_c_
Held – The appeal would be dismissed for the following reasons—
    (1) When the police took the deceased into custody they assumed certain responsibilities
towards him, in particular the responsibility to pass on information which might affect
his well-being when he was transferred from their custody to the prison authorities, and
that assumption of responsibility imposed on the police a duty to speak. By failing to
_d_ complete the form for exceptional risk prisoners and thereby pass on to the remand
centre information relating to the deceased's suicidal tendencies the police had been in
breach of that duty (see p 250 _a c d_, p 253 _a c g_ to _j_ and p 255 _g_, post).
    (2) Since the deceased had been suffering from clinical depression and his judgment
was impaired at the time of his suicide his act had not been truly voluntary and he could
not be said to have waived or abandoned any claim arising out of his suicide. The defence
_e_ of volenti non fit injuria accordingly failed (see p 251 _b c_, p 254 _f_ to _h_, p 255 _g_ and p 256 _e_,
post).
    (3) Having regard to the changing public attitude to suicide, as evidenced by the
abolition of the crime of suicide by the Suicide Act 1961, the plaintiff's claim was not an
affront to the public conscience nor would it shock the ordinary citizen. The defence of
ex turpi causa non oritur actio therefore did not apply (see p 251 _g_ to _j_, p 252 _b c_, p 255 _d_
_f_ to _g_ and p 256 _d_, post); dictum of Lord Denning MR in _Hyde v Tameside Area Health
Authority_ (1981) Times, 16 April doubted.
    Per Lloyd LJ. Where a man of sound mind commits suicide his estate will be unable
to maintain an action against the hospital or prison authorities if he is in their care
because the maxim volenti non fit injuria will provide them with a complete defence
(see p 250 _h j_, post); dictum of Lord Denning MR in _Hyde v Tameside Area Health Authority_
_g_ (1981) Times, 16 April doubted.
    Per Farquharson LJ. The defence of volenti non fit injuria is inappropriate where the
act of the deceased relied on to support the defence is the very act which the duty cast on
the defendant required him to prevent (see p 254 _g h_, post).
    Decision of Tudor Evans J [1989] 3 All ER 882 affirmed.

_h_ **Notes**
For the duty of care generally, see 34 Halsbury's Laws (4th edn) para 5, and for cases on
the subject, see 36(1) Digest (Reissue) 17–32, 34–103.
    For the application of the maxim ex turpi causa non oritur actio, see 12 Halsbury's
Laws (4th edn) para 1136, and for cases on the subject, see 1(1) Digest (Reissue) 45–46,
310–315.
_j_   For the defence of volenti non fit injuria, see 34 Halsbury's Laws (4th edn) para 62.
    For the Suicide Act 1961, see 12 Halsbury's Statutes (4th edn) (1989 reissue) 311.

Cases referred to in judgments
Bank of Nova Scotia v Hellenic Mutual War Risks Association (Bermuda) Ltd, The Good Luck
    [1989] 3 All ER 628, [1990] QB 818, [1990] 2 WLR 547, CA.

Banque Financière de la Cité SA v Westgate Insurance Co Ltd [1989] 2 All ER 952, sub nom
   Banque Keyser Ullmann SA v Skandia (UK) Insurance Co Ltd [1990] QB 665, [1989] 3 WLR   a
   25, CA.
Beresford v Royal Insurance Co Ltd [1938] 2 All ER 602, [1938] AC 586, HL.
Euro-Diam Ltd v Bathurst [1988] 2 All ER 23, [1990] QB 1, [1988] 2 WLR 517, CA.
Hardy v Motor Insurers' Bureau [1964] 2 All ER 742, [1964] 2 QB 745, [1964] 3 WLR 433,
   CA.
Hyde v Tameside Area Health Authority (1981) Times, 16 April, [1981] CA Transcript 130.   b
McGhee v National Coal Board [1972] 3 All ER 1008, [1973] 1 WLR 1, HL.
Mackonochie v Lord Penzance (1881) 6 App Cas 424, HL.
Murphy v Culhane [1976] 3 All ER 533, [1977] QB 94, [1976] 3 WLR 458, CA.
Pigney v Pointers Transport Services Ltd [1957] 2 All ER 807, [1957] 1 WLR 1121, Assizes.
Saunders v Edwards [1987] 2 All ER 651, [1987] 1 WLR 1116, CA.
Selfe v Ilford and District Hospital Management Committee (1970) 114 SJ 935.   c
Smith v Littlewoods Organisation Ltd (Chief Constable, Fife Constabulary, third party) [1987] 1
   All ER 710, [1987] AC 241, [1987] 2 WLR 480, HL.
Thackwell v Barclays Bank plc [1986] 1 All ER 676.
Yuen Kun-yeu v A-G of Hong Kong [1987] 2 All ER 705, [1988] AC 175, [1987] 3 WLR 776,
   PC.

                                                                                        d
Cases also cited
Barnes v Nayer (1986) Times, 19 December, [1986] CA Transcript 1085.
Funk v Clapp (1984) 12 DLR (4th) 62, BC SC.
Lamb v Camden London Borough [1981] 2 All ER 408, [1981] QB 625, CA.

Appeal   e
The defendant, the Chief Constable of Greater Manchester Police, James Anderton,
appealed against the decision of Tudor Evans J ([1989] 3 All ER 882) given on
21 December 1988 at Manchester awarding the plaintiff, Margaret Rose Kirkham,
damages amounting to £6,717 in her action under the Fatal Accidents Act 1976 and the
Law Reform (Miscellaneous Provisions) Act 1934 on behalf of herself, her children and   f
the estate of her husband, John Joseph Kirkham deceased, against the Home Office, the
defendant and the Tameside and Glossop Area Health Authority for negligence in respect
of the death by suicide of her husband while in custody at Risley Remand Centre. The
action proceeded against the second defendant only. The facts are set out in the judgment
of Lloyd LJ.

Eric Shannon for the defendant.   g
Jonathan R Foster QC for the plaintiff.

                                                                     Cur adv vult ·

20 December. The following judgments were delivered.   h

LLOYD LJ. On 10 January 1980 John Joseph Kirkham committed suicide while on
remand at Risley Remand Centre. His widow brings an action against the police for the
benefit of his estate under the Law Reform (Miscellaneous Provisions) Act 1934 and for
the benefit of his dependants under the Fatal Accidents Act 1976. The judge, Tudor
Evans J, has found in favour of the plaintiff. He has awarded a total of £6,717, made up   j
as to £5,000 under the Fatal Accidents Act and the balance under the Law Reform Act.
The police, or more accurately Mr James Anderton, as Chief Constable of Greater
Manchester Police, now appeals both on liability and on quantum.
   The reason why the action has been pursued against the police, and not, as might have
been expected, against the prison authorities is as follows. The police were well aware of

Mr Kirkham's suicidal tendencies. They failed to pass this information on to the prison
a authorities. If they had, then the probability is, as found by the judge, that Mr Kirkham
would have been placed on the hospital wing on arrival at Risley, instead of in an
ordinary cell. If he had been placed on the hospital wing, the probability is that his
suicide would have been prevented. On these findings, the judge has held that the
negligence of the police in failing to pass on the information in their possession was an
effective cause of Mr Kirkham's suicide. The judge then went on to consider and reject a
b submission that the claim was barred under the principle ex turpi causa non oritur actio.
In so doing he felt free not to follow certain observations of Lord Denning MR in *Hyde v
Tameside Area Health Authority* [1981] CA Transcript 130. He drew no distinction between
the claim under the Law Reform Act and the claim under the Fatal Accidents Act.
     There was no dispute that the police knew that Mr Kirkham was a suicide risk. They
were told so by the plaintiff herself when he was arrested on a charge of criminal damage
c on 8 January 1980. Indeed he had made a serious suicide attempt only two days before,
on 6 January. On 9 January Mr Kirkham was taken before the Dukinfield magistrates.
The police objected to bail. The case summary prepared by the officer in charge stated
that Mr Kirkham had 'attempted suicide by hanging within the last week'. As a result
Mr Kirkham was remanded in custody, inter alia, for his own safety. So there is no doubt
that the police were well aware of Mr Kirkham's suicidal tendencies.
d   Were they negligent in not informing the prison authorities? The judge has found
that they were, and I agree with him. The police have a form, Pol 1, which they fill in
when a prisoner whom they regard as an exceptional risk is handed over to the prison
authorities. It is addressed to the prison governor. It is headed:

'PRISONER—EXCEPTIONAL RISK
e
FORM FOR COMPLETION BY POLICE HANDING OVER FOR PRISON CUSTODY A PRISONER WHO
PRESENTS SPECIAL RISKS.'

At the foot, in bold type, the form states:

f
'THIS FORM IS TO BE HANDED TO THE GAOLER AT THE MAGISTRATES' COURT OR TO THE
PRISON OFFICER AT THE CROWN COURT WHEN A PERSON, WHO HAS NOT BEEN PRODUCED
FROM PRISON, IS SENTENCED TO IMPRISONMENT OR REMANDED IN PRISON CUSTODY
IMMEDIATELY AFTER REMAND, COMMITTAL OR SENTENCE AS THE CASE MAY BE.'

There are a number of different reasons listed in the form why a prisoner might present
a special risk. One of them is 'may have suicidal tendencies'. Another is 'physical illness
or mental disturbance'. The police accepted in evidence that they should have filled in
form Pol 1 in the present case, as they clearly should. Otherwise the prison authorities
g had no means of knowing of Mr Kirkham's recent suicide attempt. Due to some
oversight, they failed to do so.
     Counsel for the defendant argued that the failure of the police to fill in form Pol 1 was
a pure omission. They owed Mr Kirkham no duty of care to pass on the information in
their possession. The purpose of filling in Pol 1 is not, so it is said, to protect the prisoner.
h It is to ensure that he is brought to trial. This is shown by the other reasons why a
prisoner might be regarded as a special risk, eg 'likely to try to escape' and 'being
associated with a dangerous gang who may attempt rescue'. Counsel for the defendant
relied on the speech of Lord Goff in *Smith v Littlewoods Organisation Ltd (Chief Constable,
Fife Constabulary, third party)* [1987] 1 All ER 710 at 728, [1987] AC 241 at 270 for the
proposition that there is as yet in English law no generalised duty to act positively so as
j to prevent harm to others. The common law does not impose liability for pure omissions.
'Otherwise', as Lord Keith said in *Yuen Kun-yeu v A-G of Hong Kong* [1987] 2 All ER 705 at
710, [1988] AC 175 at 192, 'there would be liability in negligence on the part of one who
sees another about to walk over a cliff with his head in the air, and forbears to shout a
warning.'
     Such was the argument of counsel for the defendant. I would, of course, accept his

general proposition. But there is an important qualification. The common law frequently imposes liability for a pure omission where the defendant is under a duty to act or, as the case case may be, a duty to speak. The Court of Appeal has had occasion to consider the existence of such a duty in two very recent cases, *Banque Financière de la Cité SA v Westgate Insurance Co Ltd* [1989] 2 All ER 952, sub nom *Banque Keyser Ullman SA v Skandia (UK) Insurance Co Ltd* [1990] QB 655 and *Bank of Nova Scotia v Hellenic Mutual War Risks Association (Bermuda) Ltd, The Good Luck* [1989] 3 All ER 628, [1990] QB 818. The question depends in each case on whether, having regard to the particular relationship between the parties, the defendant has assumed a responsibility towards the plaintiff, and whether the plaintiff has relied on that assumption of responsibility. In both cases the Court of Appeal held, on the facts, that the defendant was under no duty to speak, and was therefore not liable. But the principle is well established.

In the present case I have no difficulty in holding that the police assumed certain responsibilities towards Mr Kirkham when they took him into custody, and in particular assumed a responsibility to pass on information which might affect his well-being when he was transferred from their custody to the custody of the prison authorities. Nor have I any difficulty in inferring reliance. That is sufficient to impose on the police a duty to speak. They were not in the position of a mere bystander, as in the example given by Lord Keith in *Yuen Kun-yeu*'s case. That was the very language which the judge used in the present case. I find myself in complete agreement.

It follows that the police were under a duty to inform the prison authorities of Mr Kirkham's suicidal tendencies, and were in breach of that duty by failing to fill in form Pol 1.

As for causation, it would have been sufficient for the plaintiff to show that the failure to inform the prison authorities materially increased the risk of Mr Kirkham making a successful suicide attempt: see *McGhee v National Coal Board* [1972] 3 All ER 1008, [1973] 1 WLR 1. In fact the judge went further, and found that on the balance of probabilities Mr Kirkham would have been prevented from committing suicide if the prison authorities had been informed. I see no reason to interfere with that finding of fact.

I come now to the two defences which lie at the heart of this appeal. They are expressed, for convenience, in two Latin maxims, volenti non fit injuria and ex turpi causa non oritur actio.

I deal first with volenti non fit injuria. Where a man of sound mind injures himself in an unsuccessful suicide attempt, it is difficult to see why he should not be met by a plea of volenti non fit injuria. He has not only courted the risk of injury by another; he has inflicted the injury himself. In *Hyde v Tameside Area Health Authority* [1981] CA Transcript 130 the plaintiff, who had made an unsuccessful suicide attempt, brought an action for damages against the health authority alleging negligence on the part of the hospital staff. Lord Denning MR doubted whether a defence of volenti non fit injuria would be available in such a case 'seeing that [the plaintiff] did not willingly injure himself. He wanted to die.' I find that reasoning hard to follow. Any observation of Lord Denning MR is, of course, entitled to great weight; but the observation was obiter, since the court held that the hospital staff had not been negligent. Moreover we were told by counsel for the plaintiff, who happened to have appeared for the plaintiff in that case, as well, that the point was never argued.

So I would be inclined to hold that where a man of sound mind commits suicide, his estate would be unable to maintain an action against the hospital or prison authorities, as the case might be. Volenti non fit injuria would provide them with a complete defence. There should be no distinction between a successful attempt and an unsuccessful attempt at suicide. Nor should there be any distinction between an action for the benefit of the estate under the Law Reform Act and an action for the benefit of dependants under the Fatal Accidents Act. In so far as Pilcher J drew a distinction between the two types of action in *Pigney v Pointers Transport Services Ltd* [1957] 2 All ER 807, [1957] 1 WLR 1121, I would respectfully disagree.

But in the present case Mr Kirkham was not of sound mind. True, he was sane in the
a legal sense. His suicide was a deliberate and conscious act. But Dr Sayed, whose evidence
the judge accepted, said that Mr Kirkham was suffering from clinical depression. His
judgment was impaired. If it had been a case of murder, he would have had a defence of
diminished responsibility due to disease of the mind.

I have had some doubt on this aspect of the case in the light of Dr Sayed's further
evidence that, though his judgment was impaired, Mr Kirkham knew what he was
b doing. But in the end I have been persuaded by counsel for the plaintiff that, even so, he
was not truly volens. Having regard to his mental state, he cannot, by his act, be said to
have waived or abandoned any claim arising out of his suicide. So I would reject the
defence of volenti non fit injuria.

I turn last to ex turpi causa non oritur actio. This is the most difficult part of the case.
Prior to 1961 suicide was a crime. Although there appears to be no reported case directly
c in point, I do not doubt that a claim based on the failure of the authorities to prevent a
suicide would have failed. The courts would have declined to lend their aid to enforce
such a claim. But by s 1 of the Suicide Act 1961 the rule of law whereby it was a crime
for a person to commit suicide was abrogated. The question is whether that Act, by
abrogating the criminal nature of suicide, has taken away the defence of ex turpi causa.
d The judge took the straightforward line that the defence depends on some causally
related criminal activity. He referred to *Hardy v Motor Insurers' Bureau* [1964] 2 All ER
742, [1964] 2 QB 745 and *Murphy v Culhane* [1976] 3 All ER 533, [1977] QB 94 and
considered that, since suicide is no longer a crime, the defence ex turpi causa is no longer
available.

Unfortunately, the judge was not referred to three recent cases in which the scope of
the defence has been considered: *Thackwell v Barclays Bank plc* [1986] 1 All ER 676,
e *Saunders v Edwards* [1987] 2 All ER 651, [1987] 1 WLR 1116 and *Euro-Diam Ltd v Bathurst*
[1988] 2 All ER 23, [1990] QB 1. The last two cases contain an elaborate analysis of the
relevant principles by Kerr LJ. It would be superfluous to summarise the principles here.
It is sufficient to quote two sentences from Kerr LJ's judgment in the *Euro-Diam* case
[1988] 2 All ER 23 at 28–29, [1990] QB 1 at 35:

f   'The ex turpi causa defence ultimately rests on a principle of public policy that
          the courts will not assist a plaintiff who has been guilty of illegal (or immoral)
          conduct of which the courts should take notice. It applies if, in all the circumstances,
          it would be an affront to the public conscience to grant the plaintiff the relief which
          he seeks because the court would thereby appear to assist or encourage the plaintiff
          in his illegal conduct or to encourage others in similar acts . . .'

g
It is apparent from these authorities that the ex turpi causa defence is not confined to
criminal conduct. So we cannot adopt the simple approach favoured by the judge. We
have to ask ourselves the much more difficult question whether to afford relief in such a
case as this, arising, as it does, directly out of a man's suicide, would affront the public
conscience, or, as I would prefer to say, shock the ordinary citizen. I have come to the
h conclusion that the answer should be No. I would give two reasons.

In the first place the Suicide Act 1961 does more than abolish the crime of suicide. It
is symptomatic of a change in the public attitude to suicide generally. It is no longer
regarded with the same abhorrence as it once was. It is, of course, impossible for us to say
how far the change in the public attitude has gone. But that there has been a change is
beyond doubt. The fact that aiding and abetting suicide remains a crime under s 2 of the
j 1961 Act does not diminish the force of the argument.

The second reason is that in at least two decided cases courts have awarded damages
following a suicide or attempted suicide. In *Selfe v Ilford and District Hospital Management
Committee* (1970) 114 SJ 935 Hinchcliffe J awarded the plaintiff damages against a hospital
for failing to take proper precautions when they knew that the plaintiff was a suicide
risk. In *Pigney v Pointers Transport Services Ltd* [1957] 2 All ER 807, [1957] 1 WLR 1121,

to which I have already referred, Pilcher J awarded damages to the dependants of a suicide
under the Fatal Accidents Act 1846. Moreover, in *Hyde v Tameside Area Health Authority*,   *a*
another hospital case, the judge awarded £200,000 damages in respect of an unsuccessful
suicide attempt. The Court of Appeal allowed the defendant's appeal on the ground that
there had been no negligence on the part of the hospital, but not on the ground that the
plaintiff's cause of action arose ex turpi causa; the appeal was allowed. *Selfe's* case and
Pigney's case are not binding on us. But they are important for this reason. They show, or
appear to show, that the public conscience was not affronted. It did not occur to anyone   *b*
to argue in either case that the granting of a remedy would shock the ordinary citizen;
nor did it occur to the court.

For the above reason I would hold that the defence of ex turpi causa is not available in
these cases, at any rate where, as here, there is medical evidence that the suicide is not in
full possession of his mind. To entertain the plaintiff's claim in such a case as the present
would not, in my view, affront the public conscience, or shock the ordinary citizen. I   *c*
thus reach the same conclusion as the judge on this aspect of the case, but for somewhat
different reasons.

I come last to the judgment of Lord Denning MR in *Hyde v Tameside Area Health
Authority* [1981] CA Transcript 130. I have already quoted his observations on volenti non
fit injuria, with which I find myself in respectful disagreement. As to public policy, he
referred to the fact that suicide is no longer a crime, and continued (and I read from the   *d*
transcript):

> 'But it is still unlawful. It is contrary to ecclesiastical law, which was, and is still,
> part of the general law of England: see *Mackonochie v Lord Penzance* (1881) 6 App Cas
> 424 at 446 per Lord Blackburn. The suicide's body was not buried in the churchyard
> with Christian rites. You will remember the gravediggers' scence in *Hamlet* Act
> v.i.1: "Is she to be buried in Christian burial that wilfully seeks her own salvation?"   *e*
> I know this all sounds very out of date, but it has a useful lesson for us in modern
> times. I feel it is most unfitting that the personal representatives of a suicide should
> be able to claim damages in respect of his death. At any rate, when he succeeds in
> killing himself. And I do not see why he should be in any better position when he
> does not succeed. By his act, in self-inflicting this grievous injury, he has made   *f*
> himself a burden on the whole community. Our hospital services and our social
> welfare services have done, and will do, all they can to help him and his family in
> the grievous injury that he has inflicted on himself and on them. But I see no
> justification whatever in his being awarded, in addition, the huge sum of £200,000,
> because he failed in his attempt. Such a sum will have to be raised, in the long run,
> by society itself, a sum which it cannot well afford. The policy of law should be to   *g*
> discourage these actions. I would disallow them altogether, at the outset, rather than
> burden the community with them. Especially when, as this experience shows, they
> all fail in the end. At any rate, all failed before the trial judges until this one, and
> this one now fails before us.'

Since there was no argument on the application of public policy, or the maxim ex   *h*
turpi causa non oritur actio, the court was not referred to *Selfe's* case or *Pigney's* case. This
explains why Lord Denning MR thought that all previous cases at first instance had
failed. I accept, of course, that the ecclesiastical law is part of the law of England. But I
would not for that reason refuse all relief in the common law courts. In the end it comes
down to Lord Denning MR's view that to allow such an action as the present would be
unfitting. I have respect for that view. But I do not share it. The court does not condone   *j*
suicide. But it does not, in Bingham LJ's graphic phrase in *Saunders v Edwards* [1987] 2
All ER 651 at 666, [1987] 1 WLR 1116 at 1134, 'draw up its skirts and refuse all assistance
to the plaintiff'. I notice that neither Watkins LJ nor O'Connor LJ expressed agreement with that part of Lord Denning MR's judgment which I have quoted. Indeed,
O'Connor LJ clearly contemplated the possibility of a successful claim arising out of a

suicide. So I would not regard Lord Denning MR's judgment in *Hyde v Tameside Area*
a *Health Authority* as standing in the way of the view I have formed.

I would dismiss the appeal against liability.

As to quantum, the judge had first to decide on Mr Kirkham's expectation of life,
having regard to his general health and the chance that he would have made a further
attempt at suicide. Secondly, he had to arrive at a dependency, having regard to Mr
Kirkham's continuing capacity and willingness to earn.

b On the first, the judge accepted the evidence of Dr Sayed in preference to Dr Harkness,
and arrived at a multiplier of five. This may seem on the high side; but I am not disposed
to disagree with the very experienced judge who heard and saw the witnesses.

On the second, the judge accepted the evidence of the plaintiff herself. He found that
Mr Kirkham would have worked fairly consistently. Nevertheless, he regarded £30 a
week, which was the figure put forward by the plaintiff, as too high. Instead he took £20
c a week, or £1,000 a year, making £5,000 in all. I can see no basis for disturbing the
judge's decision on quantum.

On the case as a whole, I would dismiss the appeal.

FARQUHARSON LJ. The deceased, John Joseph Kirkham, had a long history of
excessive abuse of alcohol and had for some time prior to the month of January 1980
d been suffering from clinical depression. He had spent the first nine months of 1979 in
hospital suffering from this state, being discharged in the month of October. For a short
time thereafter he had been in work, but had given it up in the month of December.
During 1979 Mr Kirkham had made two apparent suicide attempts. On Sunday,
6 January 1980 he made two further attempts, one by an overdose of tablets and the
other by hanging. He was taken to hospital, where his doctor, Dr Sayed, described him
e as 'very depressed and suicidal . . . He is desperate and wants to do away with himself'.
Mr Kirkham discharged himself the following day, 7 January 1980, and that evening
had an argument with his wife, the plaintiff, because she refused to give him a bottle of
wine. Mr Kirkham went berserk and began to smash the furniture and their other
belongings. It was in these circumstances that the police were called, being officers under
f the command of the defendant, and Mr Kirkham was arrested.

There is no dispute that the police were told of Mr Kirkham's suicidal tendencies by
the plaintiff and of his specific attempts to kill himself as well as his alcoholism; further,
the defendant concedes that the form Pol 1 was not completed and sent to the authorities
at Risley, so that the latter were unaware of the risk created by Mr Kirkham's condition.

g *Did the defendant owe a duty of care to Mr Kirkham?*

The defendant argues that the judge was wrong in holding that such a duty existed,
more particularly that the duty was to prevent Mr Kirkham taking his own life. Counsel
submits that there can be no duty to safeguard a man from his own act of self-destruction,
on the principle that there is no duty of care to protect another from a risk of injury
h created by himself. The position must, in my judgment, be different when one person is
in the lawful custody of another, whether that be voluntarily, as is usually the case in a
hospital, or involuntarily, as when a person is detained by the police or by prison
authorities. In such circumstances, there is a duty on the person having custody of
another to take all reasonable steps to avoid acts or omissions which he could reasonably
foresee would be likely to harm the person for whom he is responsible. This is illustrated
j by the 'hospital' cases to which we have been referred by counsel for the defendant, such
as *Selfe v Ilford and District Hospital Management Committee* (1970) 114 SJ 935. Where, as in
the present case, the risk is specifically identified, then reasonable steps must be taken to
avoid that risk. It is conceded that the defendant's officers were aware that Mr Kirkham
was a suicide risk and it is not now contested that the failure to inform the authorities at
Risley of the existence of the risk amounted to a breach of that duty.

Was that breach causative of Mr Kirkham's suicide?

It was pointed out by counsel for the defendant that by the time Mr Kirkham killed *a* himself he was no longer under the defendant's control. Custody of him had passed to the officers at Risley. This issue really turned on what steps would have been taken by those officers had they been informed of Mr Kirkham's condition. On his arrival Mr Kirkham had been placed in a cell and it was while he was so confined and between inspections that he hanged himself with a torn blanket. The evidence was that if the proper information had been supplied by the police Mr Kirkham would have been *b* placed in the hospital wing at Risley, where he would have been under closer supervision. It was submitted that Mr Kirkham would still have had the opportunity, which he was likely to take, of killing himself. Dr Harkness, who subsequently became the principal medical officer at Risley, said in evidence that it is not possible to stop a man committing suicide if he is determined to do so. However, the question of whether the defendant's omission was causative of the suicide was a question of fact for the judge. He found that *c* Mr Kirkham was a high suicidal risk, that the failure to pass on all the information about him in Pol 1 considerably curtailed the full appreciation by the doctor at Risley of Mr Kirkham's mental state and the risk of suicide and that if the doctor had been given that information he would in all probability have put Mr Kirkham in the hospital wing. The judge concluded on these findings that, on a balance of probability, the standard of surveillance in the hospital would have prevented Mr Kirkham from commiting suicide. *d* On the evidence available to the judge he was entitled to come to that conclusion and there are no grounds on which this court could disturb those findings.

Volenti non fit injuria

Dr Sayed, who gave evidence for the plaintiff at the trial and was well acquainted with Mr Kirkham's medical history, agreed under cross-examination that Mr Kirkham's *e* suicide was a conscious and deliberate act. In those circumstances it is argued that the defendant could rely on the maxim volenti non fit injuria. In one sense there can be no better evidence of Mr Kirkham being volens than the fact that he died by his own hand. In my judgment this defence fails on two grounds. It is clear that Mr Kirkham was disturbed at the time of his death: quite apart from his recent medical history there was *f* his behaviour at home immediately before his arrest, and his shouting at the magistrates in court, when they remanded him in custody to Risley, that if he was sent there he would never come back. Dr Sayed gave evidence that Mr Kirkham was, at the time of his death, suffering from clinical depression. I have already cited his opinion that Mr Kirkham was desperate and wanted to do away with himself. In the light of those facts and that evidence, it seems to me quite unrealistic to suggest that Mr Kirkham was truly *g* volens. His state of mind was such that, through disease, he was incapable of coming to a balanced decision even if his act of suicide was deliberate. The second ground is that the defence is inappropriate where the act of the deceased relied on is the very act which the duty cast on the defendant required him to prevent. If in such circumstances the defendant could raise this defence, as counsel for the plaintiff submits, no action would ever lie in respect of a suicide or attempted suicide where a duty of care could be proved. *h*

Ex turpi causa non oritur actio

Perhaps the most formidable argument raised by counsel for the defendant is that such an action is barred by the rule ex turpi causa non oritur actio, or alternatively should be dismissed as being contrary to public policy. This stems from the general principle that nobody should benefit from his own wrong. Counsel for the defendant argues that the *j* rules still apply even where, as here, the suicide is not bringing the action but his widow under the Fatal Accidents Act 1976. Up till 1961 there may well have been no answer to the argument, at any rate so far as it affected the criminal himself, but in that year by the Suicide Act 1961 both suicide and attempted suicide were declared not to be crimes. The strongest support for the argument of counsel for the defendant is to be found in the

obiter dicta of Lord Denning MR in *Hyde v Tameside Area Health Authority* [1981] CA
Transcript 130 where he said:

'Before 1961 I cannot think that any such claim would have succeeded. Suicide
was then a crime. So was attempted suicide. And no one was allowed to benefit
from his own deliberate crime. Nor were his personal representatives: see *Beresford
v Royal Insurance Co Ltd* [1938] 2 All ER 602, [1938] AC 586. Is it any different now?
Under the Suicide Act 1961 suicide is no longer a crime. Nor is attempted suicide.
But it is still unlawful. It is contrary to ecclesiastical law, which was, and is still, part
of the general law of England: see *Mackonochie v Lord Penzance* (1881) 6 App Cas 446
per Lord Blackburn. The suicide's body was not buried in the churchyard with
Christian rites. You will remember the gravediggers' scene in *Hamlet* Act v.i.1: "Is
she to be buried in Christian burial that wilfully seeks her own salvation?" I know
this all sounds very out of date, but it has a useful lesson for us in modern times. I
feel it is most unfitting that the personal representatives of a suicide should be able
to claim damages in respect of his death. At any rate, when he succeeds in killing
himself.'

It is implicit in these observations that even where the turpis causa is not a crime the
action should still not lie if it is based on immoral conduct, at least if it is such as to merit
the condemnation of society at large. In this case Mr Kirkham committed no crime, but
would his act now be characterised in this way? For my part, I would regard the passing
of the 1961 Act as a mark of changing public attitudes to suicide. In times gone by an act
of suicide may well have met with universal condemnation and serious consequences,
but nowadays society has a different view. With the development of medical science a
much greater understanding has been achieved of those who are driven to act in this
way. In cases where grave mental instability on the part of the victim has been proved it
could hardly be said that any action brought in respect of the suicide, or for that matter
the attempt, is grounded in immorality. The position may well be different where the
victim is wholly sane, but I would respectfully differ from Lord Denning MR's view in
those cases where a serious mental instability has been proved. The same considerations
will apply if one is looking at the claim on public policy grounds. It is not necessary to
decide in these circumstances whether a claim by a widow under the Fatal Accidents Act
arising from her husband's suicide arises ex turpi causa or is against public policy.

I would dismiss this appeal against liability.

I agree with Lloyd LJ that for the reasons he gave the appeal against the quantum of
damages must likewise be dismissed.

SIR DENYS BUCKLEY. I agree with the conclusion reached by Lloyd and
Farquharson LJJ, and for the reasons which they have given. I only add a few words of
may own out of respect for Lord Denning MR, whose dictum in *Hyde v Tameside Area
Health Authority* [1981] CA Transcript 130, which has already been read, has been
criticised. That those observations of Lord Denning MR were obiter dicta is clear. The
claim with which he was concerned in that case was a claim against a hospital by a
plaintiff who, while in the care of the hospital, had made an unsuccessful suicide attempt.
He claimed damages for negligence against the hospital. The judge of first instance
awarded damages. Lord Denning MR allowed the appeal against that award, first on the
ground that the evidence did not justify a finding of negligence and second on the
ground that the suicide attempt was causally too remote from the conduct of the hospital
staff to support a claim in negligence.

Having thus disposed of the substance of the appeal, Lord Denning MR proceeded
thus: 'Seeing that this is the first case of its kind to come before the Court of Appeal, I
would add a few words on public policy.' He then referred to three unreported suicide
cases, all decided since the Suicide Act 1961 came into force, and continued with the
passage which Farquharson LJ has already read in full and which I shall not repeat.

Since we have only a transcript of the judgments in *Hyde v Tameside Area Health Authority*, we cannot be sure whether Lord Denning MR heard any argument relating to the subject matter of his observations contained in that passage. It seems to me to be most probable that he did not. He cannot, in any case, have been referred to *Selfe v Ilford and District Hospital Management Committee* (1970) 114 SJ 935 or *Pigney v Pointers Transport Services Ltd* [1957] 2 All ER 807, [1957] 1 WLR 1121, to which Lloyd LJ has referred. If he had been aware of those two cases, Lord Denning MR would surely have mentioned them.

Ecclesiastical law is a very specialised field. Although any excess of jurisdiction by an ecclesiastical court may be controlled by the ordinary courts of the land, the jurisdiction of the ecclesiastical courts is a distinct jurisdiction. The maxim ex turpi causa expresses a principle which for many centuries has been accepted by the common law courts as part of the common law of the land. I should need to be satisfied that the same is true of ecclesiastical courts and causes.

In these circumstances, although of course I recognise the respect in which any carefully framed dictum of Lord Denning MR (as this one clearly was) should be held, I feel at liberty to approach the present case without embarrassment from Lord Denning MR's observations.

On the broad question whether, since the enactment of the Suicide Act 1961, an act of suicide or an attempted suicide should be regarded as a turpis causa for the purpose of the doctrine expressed in the maxim, I am in entire agreement with what has been said by Lloyd and Farquharson LJJ, and I do not think that I can usefully add anything.

I also agree that on the facts of this case the dead man, although he died as a result of his own act, should not be treated as volens within the meaning of the maxim volenti non fit injuria.

For my part, I am not at present satisfied that a claim under the Fatal Accidents Act 1976 could be defeated by any turpitude on the part of the deceased. Although such a claim must under the statute be brought in the name of the deceased's legal personal representative, it is, as I understand it, in substance an action by the dependants for whose benefit it is brought. Should their statutory right to compensation be adversely affected by the deceased's conduct? This is not, I think, a point which requires resolution in the present case. I also would dismiss this appeal.

Appeal dismissed. Leave to appeal to the House of Lords refused.

Solicitors: *Lace Mawer*, Manchester (for the defendant); *Thompson & Cooke*, Stalybridge (for the plaintiff).

L I Zysman Esq   Barrister.

Attorney General v Barker and another

COURT OF APPEAL, CIVIL DIVISION

LORD DONALDSON OF LYMINGTON MR, PARKER AND NOURSE LJJ

31 JULY 1990

Injunction – Breach of covenant – Breach of undertaking – Contract of service – Undertaking expressed to be perpetual and worldwide – Employee employed in royal household on terms that he would not disclose information about his employment without authority to unauthorised persons or in a book – Employee planning to publish book about his employment in royal household – Attorney General bringing action against employee and Canadian publisher for worldwide restraint against publication – Whether Attorney General entitled to worldwide interlocutory injunction against employee and publisher restraining publication of book – Whether injunction should be limited to United Kingdom.

The first defendant was employed in the royal household between 1980 and 1983 on terms which included a contractual undertaking not to disclose, publish or reveal any incident, conversation or information concerning any member of the royal family or any visitor or guest which came to his knowledge during his employment or any information relating to his employment in the royal service unless duly authorised in writing to do so. The undertaking was perpetual and worldwide and the first defendant expressly acknowledged that it included an agreement on his part not to publish any such matter in any book. The second defendant, which was a Canadian company controlled by the first defendant, planned to publish in the United Kingdom a book written by the first defendant about his service in the royal household. The book was a flagrant breach of the first defendant's undertaking. The first defendant having refused to comply with the terms of his undertaking, the Attorney General issued a writ applying for worldwide injunctions against the defendants restraining publication of the book. The Attorney General was granted injunctions against both defendants pending trial of the action, the injunction against the first defendant applying within and outside the United Kingdom while the injunction against the second defendant was limited to the United Kingdom. The first defendant appealed against the order in so far as it had extra-territorial effect and the Attorney General cross-appealed seeking an order having extra-territorial effect against the second defendant.

Held – The Attorney General's claim was not based on a breach of confidentiality but on a breach of contract, the consideration for the covenant by the first defendant not to publish matter concerning his experiences in the royal household being the agreement to take him on the staff of the royal household and to pay him wages or a salary. Accordingly, the first defendant had for a consideration entered into a negative covenant which was limited neither territorially nor in time and such a covenant was enforceable provided it could not be attacked for obscurity, illegality or on public policy grounds such as being in restraint of trade. The covenant was not void on any ground of public policy or on the ground that it restricted the freedom of expression abroad contrary to art 10[a] of the Convention for the Protection of Human Rights and Fundamental Freedoms and in the circumstances the balance of justice required that an interlocutory injunction having extra-territorial effect be granted against both defendants. The appeal would therefore be dismissed and the cross-appeal allowed (see p 259 *j* to p 260 *c g*, p 261 *c e* to *h* and p 262 *c e* to *g*, post).

Notes

For injunctions to restrain breach of express negative covenants, see 24 Halsbury's Laws

---

Article 10, so far as material, is set out at p 260 *j* to p 261 *b*, post

(4th edn) paras 992–993, 995, and for cases on the subject, see 28(4) Digest (2nd reissue) 294–301, 6022–6078.

Cases referred to in judgments
A-G v Guardian Newspapers Ltd [1987] 3 All ER 316, [1987] 1 WLR 1248, HL.
A-G v Guardian Newspapers Ltd (No 2) [1988] 3 All ER 545, [1990] 1 AC 109, [1988] 3 WLR 776, HL.
American Cyanamid Co v Ethicon Ltd [1975] 1 All ER 504, [1975] AC 396, [1975] 2 WLR 316, HL.
Doherty v Allman (1878) 3 App Cas 709, HL.

Cases also cited
Babanaft International Co SA v Bassatne [1989] 1 All ER 433, [1990] Ch 13, CA.
Haiti (Republic) v Duvalier [1989] 1 All ER 456, [1990] QB 202, CA.

Interlocutory appeal
The first defendant, Malcolm John Barker, appealed against that part of the order of Wright J dated 27 July 1990 whereby in an action brought by the Attorney General against the first defendant and the second defendant, Fleetwood Publications Ltd, to restrain publication of a book entitled 'Courting Disaster' the judge granted the Attorney General an injunction having extra-territorial effect restraining the first defendant whether by himself, his servants or agents or otherwise howsoever from breaching the terms of his contract of employment dated 9 January 1980 in the royal household by causing or permitting or authorising the publication of or by publishing the book and by disclosing, publishing or revealing any incident, conversation or information concerning any member of the royal family or any guest or visitor which came to his knowledge during his employment in the royal service or any incident, conversation or information relating to his employment in royal service until judgment or further order. The Attorney General cross-appealed against the judge's order whereby he granted him a similar injunction against the second defendant but limited its effect to the United Kingdom. The facts are set out in the judgment of Lord Donaldson MR.

David Pannick for the defendants.
Charles Gray QC and *Heather Rogers* for the Attorney General were not called on.

LORD DONALDSON OF LYMINGTON MR. The first defendant, Mr Barker, was employed in the royal household, in what capacity has not been revealed, between 1980 and 1983. On entering that employment and as a condition of entering it, he signed the following undertaking:

> 'I HEREBY UNDERTAKE in consideration of my being employed on the terms set out in Part I that I will not, either during or after my service, disclose, publish or reveal to any unauthorised person any incident, conversation or information concerning any Member of the Royal family or any guest or visitor, which comes to my knowledge during my employment in the Royal Service, or any incident, conversation or information relating to my employment in Royal Service, unless duly authorised in writing to do so. I fully appreciate that this undertaking includes an agreement on my part not to publish any such matter in any book or article, by broadcasting or television, in any newspaper or periodical or by communication to any representative of the Press.'

Earlier on it said:

> '... I appreciate that I can ask for any explanation or further information. I understand these terms [of the contract] ...'

Fleetwood Publications Ltd, the second defendant, is a newly formed Canadian company of which Mr Barker is the sole director and company secretary and, we are told today, the sole beneficial owner. Indeed, in the absence of any evidence to the contrary, the inevitable inference would in any event have been that Fleetwood was merely Mr Barker in corporate form.

In June 1990 English solicitors acting for Fleetwood Publications asked the Treasury Solicitor if there was any legal objection to the publication in the United Kingdom of a book entitled 'Courting Disaster', of which the solicitors enclosed a copy. The Treasury Solicitor, not unnaturally, replied that it was not his function to give legal advice to those who were not engaged in the service of the Crown. However, he did pass the copy across to the solicitors acting for the Queen in her personal capacity, and as a result those solicitors replied saying that any publication would be a flagrant breach of Mr Barker's undertaking. In reply to that letter, the solicitors (it will be remembered that they were the solicitors acting for Fleetwood Publications at that stage and not Mr Barker) stated that Mr Barker was not prepared to comply with the terms of his undertaking and offered to accept service on behalf of Fleetwood. Subsequently, they agreed to accept service on behalf of Mr Barker as well.

The Attorney General, acting in his normal constitutional role of appearing as the plaintiff where the interests of the Queen in a personal capacity are involved, issued a writ and applied for injunctive relief against both defendants to restrain publication of this book, both within and outside the United Kingdom. Both defendants, by their solicitors, accepted service in accordance with the undertaking which the solicitors had given and, accordingly, submitted to the jurisdiction of the English court.

Wright J, on 27 July, granted the Attorney General an injunction against Mr Barker, which applied both within and outside the United Kingdom. He further granted the Attorney General a similar injunction against Fleetwood Publications, save that it was limited to the United Kingdom. Wright J also stayed the effect of his order against Mr Barker in respect of its extra-territorial effects, but only in so far as those extra-territorial effects related to the performance of existing contracts, and then only pending an appeal to this court. The existing contracts referred to concerned serialisation rights, which it is said that Fleetwood or Mr Barker had granted to various outside foreign bodies, such as 'Paris Match'.

Neither defendant seeks to appeal against the order in so far as it relates to the United Kingdom. In not seeking so to appeal they appear to have overlooked the fact that the jurisdiction of this court is limited to England and Wales, but nothing turns on that.

However, Mr Barker disputes the right of the judge to make an order having extra-territorial effect so far as he was concerned. The Attorney General, for his part, cross-appeals, seeking an order having extra-territorial effect against Fleetwood Publications, contending correctly that, when the matter came before Wright J, it was believed on the basis of statements by the defendants' solicitors that Fleetwood Publications was independent of Mr Barker, whereas it is now accepted that that was not correct. The error was a misunderstanding by the defendants' solicitors and very properly, and as one would expect, the solicitor concerned corrected it as soon as he became aware of the error.

I need not pause to consider whether the judge's judgment was right on the footing on which he thought he was giving it, namely that Fleetwood Publications was a foreign company entirely independent of Mr Barker because, of course, the facts are entirely different and it is for us to make up our own minds as to what should now be done.

It is, in my judgment, very important to notice that this is not a case such as *Spycatcher* (see eg *A-G v Guardian Newspapers Ltd (No 2)* [1988] 3 All ER 545, [1990] 1 AC 109), where the Attorney General is relying on a duty of confidentiality. His claim is based on a breach of contract, the consideration for the covenant by Mr Barker (that he would not publish matter true or false concerning his experiences in the royal household) being the agreement by those concerned to take him on the staff of the royal household and to pay him wages or a salary. It is not in principle in any way different from the case of someone who enters into a contract with a newspaper whereby the person concerned undertakes, in consideration of a money payment, not to give their story to anyone else for publication. The newspaper in those circumstances would be likely to publish, but they would not be obliged to publish. That is an exact analogy here: the royal household would be entitled to authorise publication if they wished but equally are fully entitled under the contract to refuse to allow it.

Nothing also turns, let me make it clear, on the fact that the plaintiff is the Queen or the royal household or the royal family. Exactly the same considerations would apply if the employer had been an ordinary citizen.

It is a simple case of someone who has entered into a negative covenant for a consideration where the covenant is not limited territorially and is not limited in time. As Nourse LJ pointed out in argument, in such circumstances the courts habitually enforce the covenant provided only that the covenant itself cannot be attacked for obscurity, illegality or on public policy grounds such as that it is in restraint of trade.

Neither defendant at this stage suggests that the conduct of Mr Barker has been other than a flagrant breach of contract, although counsel for the defendants reserves the right hereafter to submit that there may be circumstances which would excuse it or avoid that covenant. Neither now disputes the correctness of the judge's order, which was of course an interlocutory order, in so far as it relates to the United Kingdom or possibly to England and Wales. The sole issue in this appeal has been the extra-territorial effect of that court's order.

We were told that the book has been published in Canada, the United States and Australia and that 20,000 copies have been printed. Whether any have been sold we know not, but certainly we are invited to believe that a significant number have been sold. We were told that it has been serialised by 'Paris Match' but not 'Paris Match', for reasons which are not very difficult to divine, have thought it constitutionally highly imprudent to include the publication in copies distributed within this country.

This is, it is true, an interlocutory application which we are considering on this appeal and, to some extent, counsel for the defendants has to establish that there is a triable issue as to the defendants' defence. For my part, I am trying to say that I think this is unarguable and that, in a case such as this, on a final hearing it is inevitable that an injunction would be granted. However, it would be quite wrong for us so to rule, that will be a matter for the trial judge and, on the footing that this is an interlocutory application, the most that counsel for the defendants can say and all, to be fair, he does say is that there is a triable issue. Accordingly, we are concerned with the weighing of factors set out in Lord Diplock's speech in *American Cyanamid Ltd* [1975] 1 All ER 504, [1975] AC 396.

No one suggests or could suggest that damages would be an adequate remedy, and there may well be difficulties in calculating the damages if there were to be awarded. Then, we are concerned with where the balance of 'convenience' is the word used in the report but that may be misleading. Hearing, the balance of justice clearly dictates that some injunction be granted.

Indeed, counsel for the defendant does not dispute that. What he disputes is the extent of it. As I understand it, what he says is that freedom of speech, in the citizen there is a right to be informed which overrides contractual rights. As a startling proposition he relies in part on art 10 of the Convention for the Protection of Human Rights and Fundamental Freedoms (Rome, 4 November 1950; TS 71 (1953); Cmd 8969), which is conveniently set out in the speech of Lord Bridge in *Attorney General v Guardian Newspapers Ltd* [1987] 3 All ER 316 at 355, [1987] 1 WLR ... in these terms,

> '(1) Everyone has the right to freedom of expression. This right shall include freedom to hold opinions and to receive and impart information and ideas without interference by public authority and regardless of frontiers ...

(2) The exercise of these freedoms, since it carries with it duties and responsibilities, may be subject to such formalities, conditions, restrictions or penalties as are prescribed by law and are necessary in a democratic society, in the interests of national security, territorial integrity or public safety, for the prevention of disorder or crime, for the protection of health or morals, for the protection of the reputation or rights of others, for preventing the disclosure of information received in confidence, or for maintaining the authority and impartiality of the judiciary.'

Counsel for the defendants fastens on the exception of preventing the disclosure of information received in confidence and suggests that it is not for the English courts to decide whether the democratic rights of foreigners would be infringed by disclosure of information received in confidence.

For my part, I would have thought that much more relevant was the question of whether a man's word is his bond and whether contractual obligations freely entered into shall be maintained. It is not a question of what foreigners are entitled to read, but what somebody subject to the jurisdiction of this court is entitled to publish and it is an incidental result that, if he cannot publish, foreigners cannot read. I am bound to say, having read this book, I do not think they will miss anything at all, but that is merely a personal view. I cannot believe that there is a foreign country which would regard the sanctity of contract as not being of enormous importance and central to the necessities of a democratic society.

The only other point which counsel for the defendants makes is that there has been one month's delay in bringing these proceedings, from the moment when the Attorney General first learnt of the proposed publication and of the existing publication abroad. That cannot amount to acquiescence and that would be the only basis on which it would really be possible to rely on it as a defence and I attach no importance to it whatever.

My abiding impression of this case is that I have confirmed my admiration for counsel for the defendants as an advocate in his ability to dress up the wholly unarguable as if it had a scintilla of a basis of reason. I can see no reason whatever why Mr Barker should not be restrained worldwide from publishing this book, and I can see no reason why the same width of injunction should not be applied to Fleetwood Publications. Accordingly, I would allow the cross-appeal and dismiss the appeal.

PARKER LJ. I agree and do not wish to add anything.

NOURSE LJ. I also agree. Because I believe that the facts of this case are quite unexceptional, being governed by well-settled principles of contract law and practice which are not at all affected by any recent developments in regard to implied obligations of confidentiality and their effect on third parties, I add some observations of my own.

The first defendant, in consideration of his being employed on the terms set out in his contract of service, expressly undertook that he would not, either during or after his service, disclose, publish or reveal certain incidents, conversations or information unless he was duly authorised in writing to do so. He expressly acknowledged that the undertaking included an agreement on his part not to publish any such matter in any book. It is not suggested, it could not be suggested, that the undertaking was void for uncertainty. It is not suggested, it could not be suggested, that it was void on any ground of public policy which is recognised by the existing authorities. It is to be observed that the prohibited disclosures, publications and revelations were not limited either in point of time or geographically. The undertaking was perpetual and worldwide.

In this state of affairs the question whether an injunction to restrain the first defendant from publishing his book, either inside or outside the jurisdiction, ought or ought not to be granted would appear to be answered by the authoritative statement of principle made by Lord Cairns LC in *Doherty v Allman* (1878) 3 App Cas 709 at 720 which, because the argument for the defendants has effectively ignored it, deserves to be restated:

'If parties, for valuable consideration, with their eyes open, contract that a particular thing shall not be done, all that a Court of Equity has to do is to say, by way of injunction, that which the parties have already said by way of covenant, that the thing shall not be done; and in such case the injunction does nothing more than give the sanction of the process of the Court to that which already is the contract between the parties. It is not then a question of the balance of convenience or inconvenience, or of the amount of damage or of injury—it is the specific performance, by the Court, of that negative bargain which the parties have made, with their eyes open, between themselves.'

It has often been observed, no doubt correctly, that that is the principle which governs the grant or refusal of an injunction at trial. But in a case where the validity of the covenant cannot sensibly be attacked it is difficult to see what practical difference there can be at the interlocutory stage. Applying the converse of the *American Cyanamid* principles (see *American Cyanamid Co v Ethicon Ltd* [1975] 1 All ER 504, [1975] AC 396) to the present case, I would say that there is no real prospect that the first defendant will succeed in resisting the grant of a perpetual injunction at the trial. On that footing an injunction ought to be granted until that time.

What then is said to be so special about the present case? Counsel for the defendants submits that at the trial it will be open to the first defendant to contend that the undertaking is void on grounds of public policy. He submits that it is contrary to public policy for the English court to make an order whose effect would be to decide what people abroad may or may not read. That, he says, is something which ought to be left to the decision of the local courts.

I know of no principle of our law by which that submission can be supported. A valid covenant restricting freedom of expression abroad is just as much enforceable as a valid covenant restricting freedom of action abroad, for example a valid covenant in restraint of trade. True it is that the local courts may or may not enforce the covenant if it is sued on in the foreign country. But that has nothing at all to do with the question whether it is or is not right for the English court to grant an injunction to restrain a breach of a worldwide undertaking entered into in an English contract between persons who are amenable to the jurisdiction of the English court.

In the circumstances, I am of the opinion that no ground has been shown on which an interlocutory injunction could be refused. For these reasons, as well as for those given by Lord Donaldson MR, I too would dismiss this appeal. Now that it appears, contrary to what was said in evidence before Wright J, that the second defendant is only the alter ego of the first defendant, I also agree that the cross-appeal should be allowed.

Appeal dismissed. Cross-appeal allowed. Leave to appeal to the House of Lords refused.

Solicitors: *Jaques & Lewis* (for the defendants); *Farrer & Co* (for the Attorney General).

Mary Rose Plummer   Barrister.

a # Derby & Co Ltd and others v Weldon and others (No 6)

COURT OF APPEAL, CIVIL DIVISION
DILLON, TAYLOR AND STAUGHTON LJJ
24, 25, 26 APRIL, 10 MAY 1990

b
Practice – Pre-trial or post-judgment relief – Mareva injunction – Worldwide Mareva injunction – Pre-trial injunction – Extra-territorial effect of injunction – Injunction restraining foreign defendants from disposing of assets outside jurisdiction – Defendants having no assets within jurisdiction and likely to dissipate their assets to frustrate judgment or order against them – Receiver of foreign assets being appointed in aid of injunction – Receivership assets held on joint
c *account in Switzerland and including fiduciary deposits made by Swiss banks with banks outside Switzerland – Receiver obtaining ex parte injunctions restraining removal from jurisdictions in which they were held of assets deposited with banks outside Switzerland – Whether injunctions should be continued – Whether court having power to order transfer of receivership assets from one jurisdiction to another.*

d The plaintiffs were seven associated companies which were all part of a United States banking group. In 1981 the plaintiff group purchased a London commodity dealer, CML, from the first and second defendants, who were the directors and effective owners of CML. The sale of CML was made through the third and fourth defendants, a Panamanian company and a Luxembourg company, both of which were controlled by
e the first and second defendants. After the sale CML continued to be managed by the first and second defendants and while under their management CML offered very extensive credit to a Far Eastern commodity dealer which in 1984 became insolvent owing over £35m to CML. The plaintiff group recovered less than £1·5m in the insolvency and brought an action against the defendants alleging deceit, conspiracy to defraud, fraudulent breach of fiduciary duty and delivery up of secret profits. The plaintiffs were granted a
f worldwide Mareva injunction against the first and second defendants and later obtained similar relief against the third and fourth defendants and also receivership and disclosure orders in respect of their assets. The plaintiffs were then granted leave to join as defendants another six individuals and companies, including a Liechtenstein stiftung alleged to be the owner of the fourth defendant, the trustees of two other Liechtenstein trusts and two Panamanian companies owned by those trusts, on the basis that the added
g defendants had been parties to the conspiracy or had assisted in the commission of unlawful acts by the first four defendants or had received assets for which they were accountable. The plaintiffs also obtained worldwide Mareva injunctions against the added defendants and the appointment of a receiver of the assets of the added corporate defendants and the two Liechtenstein trusts. By agreement between the receiver and the fourth defendant's solicitors the assets (valued at £29m) of the fourth defendant and its
h subsidiaries were transferred into a Swiss account in the joint names of the receiver and the Swiss lawyer who acted for both the fourth defendant and the stiftung and who was himself subsequently joined as a defendant in the action. By November 1989 the receiver had joint control, either with the Swiss lawyer or with one of the trustees of the two Liechtenstein trusts, of assets amounting to £72m which were held on a joint account in Switzerland and included £47m (the external assets) deposited with banks outside
j Switzerland by the Swiss banks holding the joint account in order to obtain higher interest rates. The receiver was granted ex parte injunctions restraining removal of the external assets, then deposited in Europe, Canada and the United States of America, from the jurisdictions in which they were held. Those injunctions were later reinforced by orders of the courts in those countries. At the inter partes hearing of the receiver's application for the injunctions the receiver also sought directions whether the external

assets should be returned to Switzerland on maturity of the deposits, whether the
receivership assets in Switzerland should be transferred out of that country and whether
those assets should be transferred into the sole name of the receiver. The plaintiffs
contended that it was unlikely that the Swiss courts would recognise or enforce any
English judgment which might be obtained against the majority of the defendants, who
protested the English jurisdiction, so that for the plaintiffs to obtain relief in Switzerland
against those defendants all the relevant issues would have to be relitigated there. The
judge declined, having regard to the disingenuous conduct of the defendants, to release
the external assets from the restraint of the Mareva injunction to enable those funds to
be returned to Switzerland on maturity and refused to order that the assets held in
Switzerland be transferred into the sole name of the receiver or to order their transfer
out of Swtizerland into a joint account elsewhere. The plaintiffs appealed against the
judge's refusal to order the receivership assets to be transferred out of Switzerland or into
the sole name of the receiver, and the third to eleventh defendants appealed against the
continuation of the injunctions relating to the external assets.

Held – Given that the court's Mareva jurisdiction depended not on the territorial
jurisdiction of the English court over assets within its jurisdiction, but on its unlimited
jurisdiction in personam against any person properly made a party to proceedings
pending before it, the court had power to order the transfer of assets which were subject
to a worldwide Mareva injunction out of a jurisdiction in which that order would not be
recognised without a full retrial of the issues to a jurisdiction in which the order of the
English court after the trial of the action would be recognised, if the only connection of
the foreign jurisdiction with the matters in issue was that the assets had been placed there
for the sole purpose of making them safe against the enforcement of the court's order or
if that connection was financial in nature, i e a matter of controlling investments. In the
circumstances, the court would refuse to order the return of the external assets to
Switzerland on maturity of the deposits in view of the limited extent to which any
subsequent order of the court could be enforced against the defendants in the Swiss
courts and would continue the injunctions relating to those assets. The court would also
refuse to order the transfer of assets held in Switzerland out of that country because any
such order would be ineffective without the voluntary concurrence of those defendants
who were joint account holders with the receiver and such concurrence was unlikely to
be forthcoming, but the court would order the defendants to procure the transfer of the
external assets to the sole control of the receiver, since past experience indicated that the
local courts might be willing to make further orders in support of the court's order. The
third to eleventh defendants' appeal against continuation of the injunctions relating to
the external assets would therefore be dismissed while the plaintiffs' appeal would be
allowed in part (see p 272 *a b*, p 273 *f* to *h*, p 274 *c f* to *j*, p 275 *c*, p 276 *e* to *j* and p 277 *a
b*, post).

     Dictum of Lord Donaldson MR in *Derby & Co Ltd v Weldon (No 2)* [1989] 1 All ER
1002 at 1011–1012, 1014 applied.

     Ashtiani v Kashi [1986] 2 All ER 970 not followed.

Notes

For power of the court to appoint a receiver, see 37 Halsbury's Laws (4th edn) para 381,
and for cases on the subject, see 37(2) Digest (Reissue) 484–485, 3002–3007.

     For appointment of a receiver of foreign assets, see 39 Halsbury's Laws (4th edn)
para 855, and for cases on the subject, see 39(1) Digest (Reissue) 55, 650–663.

Cases referred to in judgments

Amin Rasheed Shipping Corp v Kuwait Insurance Co, The Al Wahab [1983] 2 All ER 884,
     [1984] AC 50, [1983] 3 WLR 241, HL.
Ashtiani v Kashi [1986] 2 All ER 970, [1987] QB 888, [1986] 3 WLR 647, CA.

Babanaft International Co SA v Bassatne [1989] 1 All ER 433, [1990] Ch 13, [1989] 2 WLR 232, CA.
British Nylon Spinners Ltd v Imperial Chemical Industries Ltd [1952] 2 All ER 780, [1953] Ch 19.
Chandler v Church (20 January 1988, unreported), Ch D.
Derby & Co Ltd v Weldon (No 1) [1989] 1 All ER 469, [1990] Ch 48, [1989] 2 WLR 276, CA.
Derby & Co Ltd v Weldon (No 2) [1989] 1 All ER 1002, sub nom *Derby & Co Ltd v Weldon (Nos 3 and 4)* [1990] Ch 65, [1989] 2 WLR 412, CA.
Derby & Co Ltd v Weldon (No 7) [1990] 3 All ER 161, [1990] 1 WLR 1156.
Hadmor Productions Ltd v Hamilton [1982] 1 All ER 1042, [1983] 1 AC 191, [1982] 2 WLR 322, HL.
Haiti (Republic) v Duvalier [1989] 1 All ER 456, [1990] 1 QB 202, [1989] 2 WLR 261, CA.
Henry v Geopresco International Ltd [1975] 2 All ER 702, [1976] QB 726, [1975] 3 WLR 620, CA.
Huinac Copper Mines Ltd, Re, Matheson & Co v The company [1910] WN 218.
Irish Shipping Ltd v Commercial Union Assurance Co plc, The Irish Rowan [1989] 3 All ER 852, [1990] 2 WLR 117, CA.
Maudslay Sons & Field, Re, Maudslay v Maudslay Sons & Field [1900] 1 Ch 602.
Ninemia Maritime Corp v Trave Schiffahrtsgesellschaft mbH & Co KG, The Niedersachsen [1984] 1 All ER 398, [1983] 1 WLR 1412, CA.
Nippon Yusen Kaisha v Karageorgis [1975] 3 All ER 282, [1975] 1 WLR 1093, CA.
Schemmer v Property Resources Ltd [1974] 3 All ER 451, [1975] Ch 273, [1974] 3 WLR 406.
Siskina (cargo owners) v Distos Cia Naviera SA, The Siskina [1977] 3 All ER 803, [1979] AC 210, [1977] 3 WLR 818, HL.

Cases also cited
Abidin Daver, The [1984] 1 All ER 470, [1984] AC 398, HL.
Cayne v Global Natural Resources plc [1984] 1 All ER 225, CA.
House of Spring Gardens Ltd v Waite [1990] 2 All ER 990, [1990] 3 WLR 347, CA.
Maclaine Watson & Co Ltd v International Tin Council (No 2) [1988] 3 All ER 257, [1989] Ch 286, CA.
X Ltd v Morgan-Grampian (Publishers) Ltd [1990] 1 All ER 616, [1990] 2 WLR 421, CA; affd [1990] 2 All ER 1, [1990] 2 WLR 1000, HL.

Interlocutory appeals
The plaintiffs, Derby & Co Ltd, Cocoa Merchants Ltd (CML), Phibro-Salomon Finance AG, Phibro-Salomon Ltd, Philipp Bros Inc, Philipp Bros Ltd and Salomon Inc (the holding company of the other plaintiff companies), by a writ issued on 25 June 1987 brought an action against (1) Anthony Henry David Weldon, (2) Ian Jay, (3) Milco Corp, a Panamanian company, and (4) CML Holding SA of Luxembourg, claiming damages for breach of contract, misrepresentation, negligence, deceit, conspiracy to defraud and fraudulent breach of fiduciary duty arising out of the trading activities of CML between June 1981 and February 1984 while under the management of the first and second defendants as executive directors of CML after it had been purchased by Salomon Inc from the liquidator of a subsidiary of the third defendant, which was itself a subsidiary of the fourth defendant. The statement of claim in the action was served on the four defendants on 4 December 1987 and on the same day Sir Nicolas Browne-Wilkinson V-C granted ex parte Mareva injunctions against the first and second defendants restraining them from removing their assets out of the United Kingdom or those countries which were parties to the Convention on Jurisdiction and the Enforcement of Civil and Commercial Judgments 1968 (Brussels, 27 September 1968, EC 46 (1978); Cmd 7395; and set out as amended in the Civil Jurisdiction and Judgments Act 1982, Sch 1) or from

dealing in any way with those assets except to the extent that they exceeded £25m and requiring the first and second defendants to file an affidavit disclosing the full value of their assets. On 27 June 1988 Mervyn Davies J granted, inter alia, a Mareva injunction restricted to the first and second defendants' assets in the United Kingdom but on appeal by the plaintiffs the Court of Appeal (May, Parker and Nicholls LJJ) ([1989] 1 All ER 469, [1990] Ch 48) granted a worldwide Mareva injunction against the first and second defendants. By notices of motion dated 16 August and 4 November 1988 the plaintiffs sought worldwide Mareva injunctions and receivership and disclosure orders against the third and fourth defendants which were granted by the Court of Appeal (Lord Donaldson MR, Neill and Butler-Sloss LJJ) ([1989] 1 All ER 1002, [1990] Ch 65) on 16 December 1988 and by Sir Nicolas Browne-Wilkinson V-C on 4 November 1988, respectively. On 8 March 1989 Vinelott J gave leave to join as defendants (5) Wollstein Stiftung, a Liechtenstein stiftung which was the ultimate owner of a Liberian company, Cocoa Merchants (Far East) Ltd, and therefore holder of profits made from foreign exchange dealings with CML and Derby & Co Ltd, (6) Tim Schneider, (7) Ernst Aeschbacher and (8) Peter Ritter, the trustees of two other Liechtenstein trusts (the Lagor trust and the Ralgo trust) and (9) Steelburg Management Inc and (10) Pilgrim Enterprises Inc, two companies owned by the two trusts, on the basis that they had been parties to the conspiracy or had assisted in the commission of unlawful acts by the first four defendants or had received funds for which they were accountable, and also granted an ex parte worldwide Mareva injunction against the added defendants and receivership orders in respect of the assets of the added corporate defendants and the two trusts. Vinelott J subsequently gave leave to the plaintiffs to join as defendant (11) Dr Louis Rohner, the Swiss lawyer for the fourth and fifth defendants. On 24 November 1989, with the leave of Sir Nicolas Browne-Wilkinson V-C granted on 20 November, the receiver, Christopher Morris, a partner in the chartered accountancy firm of Touche Ross & Co, applied ex parte to Vinelott J and was granted an ex parte injunction restraining the transfer out of the jurisdiction of the English court sums placed on fiduciary deposit by Swiss banks in London and leave to apply in the other jurisdictions to obtain similar relief. On 9 January 1990 at an inter partes hearing in respect of that order Sir Nicolas Browne-Wilkinson V-C (i) declined to direct the defendants to cause or procure that the receivership assets be vested under the sole control of the receiver or transferred out of Switzerland (save as provided under (ii)) and (ii) ordered that the injunctions in respect of the assets held outside Switzerland be continued. The plaintiffs appealed against (i) and the third to eleventh defendants appealed against (ii). The facts are set out in the judgment of Dillon LJ.

Michael Lyndon-Stanford QC, Charles Purle QC and *J Stephen Smith* for the plaintiffs.
Nicholas Chambers QC and *Mark Hapgood* for the first and second defendants.
Nicholas Stewart QC and *Terence Mowschenson* for the third to eleventh defendants.
Leslie Kosmin for the receiver.

Cur adv vult

10 May. The following judgments were delivered.

DILLON LJ. This court has before it an appeal by the plaintiffs in the action against an order of Sir Nicolas Browne-Wilkinson V-C dated 9 January 1990, and an appeal by the third to eleventh defendants against an order of Sir Nicolas Browne-Wilkinson V-C of the same date. Although, however, there are the two orders drawn up, each of which is stated to have been made on an application to the court by the receiver, the two were made after the one contested inter partes hearing and after one judgment on the substance of both applications had been delivered by Sir Nicolas Browne-Wilkinson V-C.

It is therefore convenient to treat the appeal by the third to eleventh defendants simply as a cross-appeal.

The appeal and cross-appeal represent the latest stage in the complex interlocutory proceedings in the action. The action is now set down for trial in the Chancery Division to commence early in October 1990 with an estimated duration of three to six months. The previous history is conveniently summarised in Sir Nicolas Browne-Wilkinson V-C's judgment under appeal; some of the matters out of which the plaintiffs' claims arise are set out in somewhat greater detail in a judgment of Vinelott J of the 12 March 1990 which is not the subject of this appeal (see *Derby & Co Ltd v Weldon (No 7)* [1990] 3 All ER 161, [1990] 1 WLR 1156).

The plaintiffs' claims against the various defendants are primarily claims for damages for deceit, breach of fiduciary duty and conspiracy to defraud, but there are also claims of a tracing nature in respect of alleged secret profits realised, directly or indirectly, by the first two defendants. There was a settlement agreement between certain of the parties entered into on certain matters in May 1984, and the plaintiffs claim to have that set aside on grounds of fraud.

The action was originally brought only against the first three defendants, Mr Weldon, Mr Jay and Milco Corp, a company incorporated in Panama. The other defendants were added as further information became available. Mr Weldon and Mr Jay are British subjects resident in this country and were served with the proceedings in this country in the normal way. The fourth defendant, CML Holding SA (CMI), is a company incorporated in Luxembourg which was properly served with the proceedings under the European Convention on Jurisdiction and the Enforcement of Civil and Commercial Judgments 1968 (which is set out in Sch 1 to the Civil Jurisdiction and Judgments Act 1982) and has submitted to the jurisdiction of the English court on that basis. The third and fifth to eleventh defendants were made parties to the action under RSC Ord 11. The third and fifth to tenth defendants, on being served with the proceedings, applied to set aside service under Ord 12, r 8; those applications failed and they then each entered a further acknowledgment of service, and they have since played a full part in the proceedings, serving defences, and in some cases even counterclaiming, but always asserting that they continue to protest the jurisdiction of the English court.

On 4 December 1987 Mareva relief was granted to the plaintiffs ex parte against Mr Weldon and Mr Jay in respect of their assets in the United Kingdom and in the EEC countries. At this stage leave was given for the fourth defendant, CMI, to be added as a party to the action. It seems that at this stage all the moneys which the plaintiffs wanted to secure by Mareva relief pending the outcome of the action were held by, or by subsidiaries of, the third and fourth defendants and the plaintiffs believed that the third and fourth defendants were controlled by Mr Weldon, with or without Mr Jay.

In the summer of 1988 the plaintiffs applied for worldwide Mareva relief against Mr Weldon and Mr Jay. This was refused by Mervyn Davies J on 20 June 1988, but allowed by this court on appeal on 29 July 1988: see *Derby & Co Ltd v Weldon (No 1)* [1989] 1 All ER 469, [1990] Ch 48; the judgments are important as indicating the basis on which worldwide Mareva relief may be granted. The order made by this court against Mr Weldon and Mr Jay in respect of their assets worldwide applied up to a total of £25m, that being the then estimated amount of the plaintiffs' claims.

Similar worldwide relief up to the same limit was granted, for a short term, by Mervyn Davies J on 11 August 1988 against the third and fourth defendants, Milco and CMI. That injunction was continued by Sir Nicolas Browne-Wilkinson on 4 November 1988 as against the fourth defendant, CMI, but not against the third defendant, Milco, since it was in the Vice-Chancellor's view important that there was no evidence that an injunction against Milco, a Panamanian company, would be enforced by the courts of Panama. On 7 November Sir Nicolas Browne-Wilkinson V-C appointed the receiver, Mr Morris, a partner in the firm of chartered accountants, Touche Ross & Co, to be receiver of the assets of CMI, but not of the assets of Milco. But he directed that no steps should be taken to enforce the appointment of the receiver as receiver of the assets of CMI by getting in those assets until after the courts of Luxembourg should have declared the order enforceable, or otherwise enforced it.

There were appeals against these orders of Sir Nicolas Browne-Wilkinson V-C and the decision of this court of 16 December 1988 is reported: see *Derby & Co Ltd v Weldon (No 2)* [1989] 1 All ER 1002, sub nom *Derby & Co Ltd v Weldon (Nos 3 and 4)* [1990] Ch 65. This court granted worldwide Mareva relief against Milco as well as against CMI and appointed the receiver receiver of the assets of Milco as well as of the assets of CMI. Moreover it deleted the proviso, mentioned above, which required the order to be recognised in relation to CMI by the courts of Luxembourg. Again, the judgments are of great importance in relation to the basis of worldwide Mareva relief. Plainly, the purpose of appointing the receiver was the same as the purpose of the Mareva injunctions, and in that sense the appointment of the receiver was in aid of the Mareva injunctions.

In the meantime in the course of the hearings before Sir Nicolas Browne-Wilkinson V-C in November 1988 there was disclosed for the first time the existence of the fifth defendant, Wollstein Stiftung, a stiftung established under the law of Liechtenstein. It appears that, at any rate on paper, CMI, the fourth defendant, is a wholly-owned subsidiary of a Panamanian company, Peripheria SA, which is wholly owned by Wollstein Stiftung.

It appears also that Wollstein Stiftung was in existence as long ago as 11 January 1975, which is well before any of the matters of which the plaintiffs complain in this action. It appears that the beneficiaries under the trusts of the stiftung were or included the descendants of Mr Weldon's grandfather, and it was envisaged in 1975 that the principal beneficiaries would be Mr Weldon's father, Max Weldon, uncle Henry Weldon and Mr Weldon himself. The principal function at that stage of Wollstein Stiftung seems to have been to receive, either directly or through Milco, dividends on shares in Cocoa Merchants Ltd, an English company, which is the second plaintiff in this action; as a matter of history it was the sale of the share capital of that company by, broadly, Mr Weldon and Mr Jay and their interests, to one of the other plaintiffs in June 1981 which set the scene for the matters of which the plaintiffs complain in the action. Max Weldon died before 1981, and there is an agreement of 27 January 1981 between Henry Weldon and Mr Weldon which appears to indicate that subject to a certain payment under that agreement being made Henry Weldon would have no further interest in the assets of the stiftung.

The receiver having been appointed by Sir Nicolas Browne-Wilkinson V-C in November 1988 in respect of CMI and the existence of the stiftung having been disclosed as above-mentioned, there was correspondence on 18 and 21 November between the receiver's solicitors, Messrs Cameron Markby, and the solicitors then acting for CMI, Messrs Theodore Goddard, whereby it was agreed that the assets of the subsidiaries of CMI by then identified by the receiver should be vested in a joint account in a Swiss bank in the names of the receiver and, as stated in the letter, Dr Peter Ritter, a Liechtenstein lawyer who is now the eighth defendant. The bearer shares of the subsidiaries were also to be held on joint account, except that the bearer shares representing the share capital of the top subsidiary, Dumaine Investment Corp (also a Panamanian company), were deposited with the receiver alone at the Zurich office of Touche Ross.

On 6 February 1989 the receiver, who was endeavouring to discover what further assets there were of CMI and, I think in particular, Milco, was told at a meeting in Zurich with Dr Rohner, the Swiss lawyer for CMI and the stiftung, who is now the eleventh defendant, of the existence of two Liechtenstein trusts called the Ralgo and Lagor trusts. Steps were thereupon taken, in extension of those taken in November 1988, to transfer the assets of those trusts into joint accounts in Switzerland in the joint names of the receiver and Dr Rohner. The assets so transferred were then valued at approximately £29m.

The sixth, seventh and eighth defendants, Mr Schneider, Dr Aeschbacher and Dr Ritter, all Liechtenstein citizens, are the trustees of the Ralgo and Lagor trusts, and the ninth and tenth defendants are the companies, again Panamanian, through which those trusts hold their underlying assets.

It is now conceded by the defendants that the Ralgo and Lagor trusts were formed in order, if possible, to render the assets held by the trusts, which were derived from Milco or CMI, proof against enforcement of any judgment which might be obtained by the plaintiffs in this action. By orders of Vinelott J of 8 March and 10 April 1989 the fifth to tenth defendants were added as parties to the action, worldwide Mareva injunctions were granted against them and the limit to be secured by Mareva relief was raised to £100m on a revised appreciation of the extent of the plaintiffs' claims. The receiver's appointment was also extended to cover the assets of the stiftung, the Ralgo and Lagor trusts and the two companies, the ninth and tenth defendants.

In an affidavit sworn on 24 November 1989 the receiver deposed that he had at that date joint control of assets presently valued at £72m-odd. These were assets held on joint account mainly with Dr Rohner but in part with Dr Ritter. These assets included fiduciary deposits of some £47m, being deposits made by the Swiss banks on behalf of the joint account holders with banks outside Switzerland. Those deposits outside Switzerland (the external assets) were made because substantially higher rates of interest can be obtained from banks in Britain, France, the United States of America and other countries outside Switzerland than can be obtained by keeping the deposits in Switzerland. The receiver was concerned, for reasons to be mentioned later, that the external assets should not be returned to Switzerland on the maturity of the deposits. He had also, by counsel, raised with Sir Nicolas Browne-Wilkinson V-C on 23 May 1989 and again in July, the issue of whether the joint account arrangements were satisfactory or whether further directions were required concerning the location of the assets which had been disclosed by the defendants and the manner in which they were held, viz on joint account. The orders which appointed the receiver had, as is usual, provided for the assets in question to be forthwith delivered up or transferred to the receiver.

Sir Nicolas Browne-Wilkinson V-C, with, as he said in his judgment of 9 January 1990, considerable hesitation because it would be contrary to the arrangements then currently made between the receiver and Dr Rohner, gave the receiver leave to apply to Vinelott J for injunctions in respect of the external assets. Vinelott J, on 24 November 1989, granted ex parte injunctions which were continued on 4 December 1989 pending an effective inter partes hearing. These injunctions in effect restrained the removal from the jurisdiction of the English court of the external assets currently deposited in London, and restrained the removal from the jurisdictions in which they were currently held of the external assets then deposited with banks in Brussels, Paris, Dusseldorf, Toronto, Luxembourg and New York. The order has been reinforced by orders made by the local courts in the countries where those deposits are made.

One matter therefore which came before Sir Nicolas Browne-Wilkinson V-C at the hearing which ended with his judgment of 9 January 1990 was whether or not the injunctions granted by Vinelott J in respect of the external assets should be continued. The other, and more fundamental matter, was whether, as the plaintiffs claim, the defendants should be ordered to cause or procure the receivership assets to be transferred out of Switzerland and/or into the control of the receiver. For reasons which will appear, there are two objectives: (1) that the receivership assets should be transferred out of Switzerland and (2) that they should be transferred into the sole name or under the sole control of the receiver. Accordingly, possible permutations include that the external assets be transferred into the sole name of the receiver and remain outside Switzerland while the other receivership assets be transferred out of Switzerland but remain in the joint names of the receiver and Dr Rohner, or that the external assets be transferred into the sole name of the receiver, as mentioned, while the other receivership assets remain in the joint names in Switzerland.

The receivership assets in Switzerland (being the difference between the total receivership assets of £72m-odd and the external assets of £47m) include, on the helpful schedules provided by the receiver, bonds, particularly Eurobonds, of £20·4m, convertible bonds of £2·4m and quoted shares of £1·7m.

There are two fundamental matters which underlie all the rival contentions and are the practicalities with which the court has to cope.

The first is that, though the Swiss courts will recognise and enforce any judgment which the plaintiffs may obtain in this action against Mr Weldon and Mr Jay and will probably, because of the European Convention, recognise and enforce any judgment obtained against CMI, they are unlikely to recognise or enforce any judgment which may be obtained against Milco, the third defendant, or any of the fifth to eleventh defendants, i e those defendants added in exercise of the extended jurisdiction claimed by the English court under RSC Ord 11 who have continued to protest the jurisdiction even though they are taking part in the proceedings. To get relief in Switzerland against the third and fifth to eleventh defendants the plaintiffs would have to relitigate all the relevant issues in proceedings in Switzerland, even though the plaintiffs had succeeded on those issues despite strenuous opposition of those defendants at the trial of this action in England. Qua those defendants the Swiss court would apparently not be bound by any finding of fact or ruling of law by the English court at the trial here. It is not surprising that the plaintiffs are perturbed at that prospect, and therefore wish to have the receivership assets held, or held as far as possible, outside Switzerland, since the receivership assets represent the only substantial moneys so far traced to which the plaintiffs could hope to look for satisfaction of a judgment against the defendants for such substantial amounts as are claimed. (I leave aside for present purposes the possibly formidable difficulties which the plaintiffs may in any event have if it becomes necessary for them, in order to enforce judgment, to pierce the corporate veils and identify CMI, Milco or the stiftung with Mr Weldon.)

The second and separate difficulty arises from art 271 of the Swiss Penal Code, which is set out (in translation) in Sir Nicolas Browne-Wilkinson V-C's judgment. This apparently makes it an offence punishable with imprisonment for the receiver to do on Swiss territory any act in his capacity as the receiver appointed by the English court and in the exercise of the powers conferred on him as an officer of that court. The seriousness of this is underlined by the threatening letter sent by Dr Rohner's firm on 8 November 1989 to the Zurich branch of Touche Ross in relation to the share certificates in Dumaine Investment Corp; notwithstanding Dr Rohner's disavowal of any desire to treat the English court with disrespect, the letter is unquestionably threatening and art 271 is a serious embarrassment to the receiver so long as receivership assets are held in Switzerland. It is apparently accepted that a transfer of assets out of Switzerland would not infringe art 271 if they continued to be held on joint account by the receiver and Dr Rohner, albeit out of Switzerland. It would seem that a transfer of assets which are out of Switzerland into the sole name of the receiver would not infringe art 271 since the article is not concerned with what happens outside Switzerland.

Against that background the conclusion of Sir Nicolas Browne-Wilkinson V-C embodied in his orders of 9 January 1990 was: (1) that he would not direct the defendants to cause or procure that the receivership assets be vested under the sole control of the receiver or (save as provided under 2 below) outside Switzerland; and (2) that he continued until judgment or further order the injunctions in respect of the external assets granted by Vinelott J.

Hence this court is faced with the appeal of the plaintiffs in respect of (1) and the cross-appeal of the third to eleventh defendants in respect of (2).

In relation to (2) Sir Nicolas Browne-Wilkinson V-C said that in the ordinary case he would have ordered the remission of the external assets to Switzerland. He said:

'They were locally situate there before the action was brought. The use of the Mareva relief to seize those assets because of the chance that they were here for investment purposes only and in circumstances where the seizure of the assets involved a breach of the arrangements then subsisting in Switzerland would have required that the assets be restored to Switzerland as a matter of comity and policy.'

He went on, however, to hold that there were very special circumstances which lead him not to make an immediate order to that effect. That was because he could see no escape from the conclusion that the court had been trifled with by the defendants. He referred to the transfer of assets to the Ralgo and Lagor trusts so as to remove assets in Switzerland from the liability to enforcement of any judgment which they would otherwise have been subject to. He referred also to the conduct of the defendants in dealing with the case having on occasion been tricky and verging on dishonesty; he referred to lack of candour when applications were made to allow costs to be paid out of funds in the hands of the receiver and to certain untruthful evidence which Mr Weldon himself had given to the Vice-Chancellor in November 1988.

Sir Nicolas Browne-Wilkinson V-C did not know, because the necessary research had not yet been carried out by the receiver, that funds had at all material times been invested in fiduciary deposits outside Switzerland. The amount of the funds so invested at 4 December 1987, when the first Mareva injunction was granted, and also at 4 November 1988, was over £56m, ie more than the amount secured by the order of Vinelott J.

Sir Nicolas Browne-Wilkinson V-C did order on 9 January 1990 that the receiver be authorised and directed to make further investigations as to the possibility of an application to the Swiss courts under art 10 of Switzerland's Private International Law Statute of 18 December 1987. Article 10, which I do not need to set out, apparently only came into force on 1 January 1989, and the practice of the Swiss courts under it has not yet been developed. From my feel of the present case, however, and from the evidence of the receiver's Swiss lawyer, Dr Bollmann, I regard any application to the Swiss courts under art 10 as unlikely to succeed without the support of Dr Rohner, and therefore unlikely to lead to anything except a blessing by the Swiss court of the present joint account arrangements which would remove, quoad the joint account arrangements, any possible threat under art 271 of the Penal Code, but would require the assets to be retained on joint account in Switzerland pending a final order of the Swiss court. I do not therefore regard art 10 as offering very attractive prospects.

It is plain, in my judgment, that the decisions of Sir Nicolas Browne-Wilkinson V-C against which the appeal and the cross-appeal are brought were decisions by him in the exercise of his judicial discretion. Any appeal is therefore faced with the well-known constraints on the interference by this court in the exercise of his discretion by a judge at first instance: see eg *Hadmor Productions Ltd v Hamilton* [1982] 1 All ER 1042, [1983] 1 AC 191.

But, in my judgment, with all respect to Sir Nicolas Browne-Wilkinson V-C, he misdirected himself in a material respect in the importance he attached to comity and the position of the Swiss court. He said, in what I regard as the key passage of his judgment:

'I think this court should hesitate long before taking steps, even though it may have power to do so under its right to act in personam, which require people to do things in foreign jurisdictions which may offend the sensibilities of the foreign jurisdiction in question, let alone requiring the doing of acts which may be unlawful by the law of the place where the act is to be done. In my judgment, the correct approach is to seek, if possible, to obtain the co-operation of the foreign court rather than seek to force people to do things in foreign countries under threat of penalty.'

That is similar to the view which I expressed in my own judgment in *Ashtiani v Kashi* [1986] 2 All ER 970, [1987] QB 888, when I favoured a limited territorial approach to the grant of Mareva injunctions. It is also the same as the view which Sir Nicolas Browne-Wilkinson V-C himself expressed when he made his order of 7 November 1988 appointing the receiver receiver of the assets of CMI but made the condition that no steps should be taken to enforce transfer of assets under the order until after the courts of Luxembourg had approved the order. He said: '. . . my own view is that each local court should co-operate with the other local courts to produce the results within its jurisdiction.'

But the more recent developments of the law in relation to Mareva injunctions show, in my judgment, that those views are wrong. The jurisdiction of the court to grant a Mareva injunction against a person depends not on the territorial jurisdiction of the English court over assets within its jurisdiction, but on the unlimited jurisdiction of the English court in personam against any person, whether an individual or a corporation, who is, under English procedure, properly made a party to proceedings pending before the English court. This is particularly underlined by the judgment of Lord Donaldson MR in *Derby & Co Ltd v Weldon (No 2)* [1989] 1 All ER 1002 at 1011–1012, esp at 1014, [1990] Ch 65 at 82, esp at 86 where he said in relation to CMI:

> 'In this situation I do not understand why the order that the assets vest in the receiver should only take effect if and when the order was recognised by the Luxembourg courts. True it is that CMI is a Luxembourg company, but it is a party to the action and can properly be ordered to deal with its assets in accordance with the orders of this court, regardless of whether the order is recognised and enforced in Luxembourg. The only effect of non-recognition would be to remove one of the potential sanctions for disobedience.'

Another potential sanction for disobedience that would remain is that a defendant who disobeyed an order of the court could be barred from defending the proceedings.

In truth the original, somewhat territorial, approach in *Ashtiani v Kashi* has been turned the other way round by the introduction of the so-called *Babanaft* proviso in *Babanaft International Co SA v Bassatne* [1989] 1 All ER 433, [1990] Ch 13. That was revised in *Derby v Weldon (No 2)* [1989] 1 All ER 1002, [1990] Ch 65, and as so revised is of course the basic order in the present case. Application to a foreign court to recognise the order or to declare it enforceable is only necessary in so far as the order purports to have effect outside England and Wales and it is sought to affect by the order a person to whom the order is not addressed and who is not in certain categories of person subject to the jurisdiction of this court.

To regard the grant of a Mareva injunction not as a matter of territorial jurisdiction to be exercised court by court throughout the various countries of the world where it may be appropriate but as a matter of unlimited jurisdiction in personam of the English court over persons who have properly been made parties, under English procedure, to proceedings pending before the English court is consistent with the approach of the English court to the appointment of receivers of the British and foreign assets of English companies. The court has always been ready to appoint a receiver over the foreign as well as the British assets of an English company, even though it has recognised that in relation to foreign assets the appointment may not prove effective without assistance from a foreign court: see *Re Maudslay Sons & Field, Maudslay v Maudslay Sons & Field* [1900] 1 Ch 602. Moreover, where a foreign court of the country where the assets are situate refuses to recognise the receiver appointed by the English court, the English court will, in an appropriate case, do what it can to render the appointment effective by orders in personam against persons who are subject to the jurisdiction of the English court: see the helpful decision of Neville J in *Re Huinac Copper Mines Ltd, Matheson & Co v The company* [1910] WN 218.

Conversely the English court is, international convention apart, unwilling to exercise its powers within this country in support of a receiver appointed by a foreign court, save on very strictly limited traditional principles of international law: see *Schemmer v Property Resources Ltd* [1974] 3 All ER 451, [1975] Ch 273. Indeed from the observations of Lord Diplock in *Siskina (cargo owners) v Distos Cia Naviera SA, The Siskina* [1977] 3 All ER 803, [1979] AC 210 it would seem that before the enactment of the Supreme Court Act 1981 there could have been problems of jurisdiction in some cases. But provided that third parties do not invoke the jurisdiction of the English court for the protection of their own rights, as in *British Nylon Spinners Ltd v Imperial Chemical Industries Ltd* [1952] 2 All ER a 780, [1953] Ch 19, the foreign court is free to achieve its objectives by making orders in personam against persons who are subject to its jurisdiction.

In my judgment, therefore, Sir Nicolas Browne-Wilkinson V-C misdirected himself in his deference to the Swiss court. This court is therefore free to exercise its own discretion on the appeal.

My own view, with all respect, is that Sir Nicolas Browne-Wilkinson V-C also misdirected himself in the weight he attached to the fact that amicable arrangements b had been made between the receiver and the defendants in November 1988 which had been supplemented in February 1989. As I read the correspondence in November 1988 between Cameron Markby and Theodore Goddard the receiver from the outset reserved his right to apply to the court for further directions, so that the agreement made was merely an interim arrangement. Moreover Theodore Goddard were obviously well aware of the receiver's obligations to the court as a receiver appointed by the court. c Beyond that, in November 1988, immediately after his first appointment, the receiver did not know of art 271, nor of the trickery over the Ralgo and Lagor trusts. In my judgment the court's concern should be to make the best practical order under the circumstances for the preservation of the receivership assets.

The object of a Mareva injunction is stated by Lord Donaldson MR in *Derby v Weldon (No 2)* [1989] 1 All ER 1002 at 1006–1007, 1009, [1990] Ch 65 at 76–77, 79, as being that d within the limits of its powers no court should permit a defendant to take action designed to ensure that subsequent orders of the court are rendered less effective than would otherwise be the case. That is in line with the statement by Kerr LJ in giving the judgment in this court in *Ninemia Maritime Corp v Trave Schiffahrtsgesellschaft mbH & Co KG, The Niedersachsen* [1984] 1 All ER 398 at 419, [1983] 1 WLR 1412 at 1422:

e '. . . the test is whether, on the assumption that the plaintiff has shown at least "a good arguable case", the court concludes, on the whole of the evidence then before it, that the refusal of a Mareva injunction would involve a real risk that a judgment or award in favour of the plaintiffs would remain unsatisfied.'

I see no reason why that should not extend, in principle and in an appropriate case, to ordering the transfer of assets to a jurisdiction in which the order of the English court f after the trial of the action will be recognised from a jurisdiction in which that order will not be recognised and the issues would have to be relitigated if, which may not be entirely the present case, the only connection of the latter jurisdiction with the matters in issue in the proceedings is that moneys have been placed in that jurisdiction in order to make them proof against the enforcement, without a full retrial in a foreign court, of any judgment which may be granted to the plaintiffs by the English court in this action g or indeed if the only connection with the latter jurisdiction is financial, as a matter of controlling investments.

In these circumstances, I would without any hesitation refuse to order the return of the external assets to Switzerland and I would therefore dismiss the cross-appeal.

What order to make on the appeal is more difficult.

So far as the receivership assets other than the external assets are concerned, no order h for them to be transferred out of Switzerland, whether into the sole name of the receiver or so as to remain in joint names, can be effective without the voluntary concurrence of Dr Rohner or, in so far as he is a joint account holder with the receiver, Dr Ritter. That voluntary concurrence is most unlikely to be forthcoming, and there is, as I see it, no possibility of the Swiss or Liechtenstein courts making any order against Dr Rohner, or j Dr Ritter, in aid of an order of the English court against them.

The only sanction for disobedience available would be an order of the English court which, while leaving Dr Rohner and Dr Ritter parties to the action, debarred them from defending. But that would serve no practical purpose. The position would be different if it could fairly be said that the consequence of a failure by the defendants collectively to comply with an order of the court against all the defendants to procure the transfer out of Switzerland of all the receivership assets located there would be that all the defendants would be debarred from defending the action. While, however, one may suspect that Dr *a* Rohner and Dr Ritter would transfer the assets in virtually any way that Mr Weldon really wants, I do not believe that it would be possible to establish, in advance of the trial in October, that Mr Weldon has such a degree of control as to warrant barring him and Mr Jay from defending the action because of Dr Rohner's failure to comply with the order. Most of the assets in question seem to have reached CMI, Milco or the stiftung legitimately, and without being traceable as fruits of wrongdoing on the part of Mr *b* Weldon and Mr Jay complained of in the action, and the question whether CMI, Milco and the stiftung are each to be regarded as the 'creature' or 'alter ego' of Mr Weldon (with such consequences, if any, as may follow from such conclusion) is a question for decision at the trial.

In all the circumstances, therefore, as a matter of discretion, I would for the present leave the assets in Switzerland where they are, held on joint account in Switzerland. *c*

In relation to the external assets the position is different in that past experience indicates that the local courts may be willing to make further orders in support of the order of this court. Moreover part of the external assets are held by banks in London, though to the order of Swiss banks acting on the joint mandate of the receiver and Dr Rohner.

In *Chandler v Church* (20 January 1988, unreported) Knox J, in my judgment rightly, applied the traditional view that receivership assets ought to be held solely by the receiver *d* appointed by the court, where the alternative proposed was that the assets in question should be held, on undertakings to the court, by an English solicitor of presumed integrity who was a partner in a large and well-known London firm. Experience shows that a solicitor's undertaking may be defeated by trickery, without any dishonesty on the solicitor's part. In the present case the funds deposited with the London banks are held by those banks to the order of Swiss banks on behalf of the receiver and Dr Rohner (or *e* Dr Ritter) on a joint account. But Dr Rohner professes respect, but does not owe allegiance, to the English court, and he regards his primary duty as being to his clients whoever they may actually be. His mandate to the Swiss banks pursuant to the orders of the English court is governed by Swiss law and so far as I am aware may be revoked by him at any time, if he is minded to cease to observe the English court order.

I do not regard that situation as satisfactory. Also I see no reason to differentiate *f* between the external assets on deposit with banks in London and the external assets on deposit with banks in the other countries I have mentioned. The risks are the same.

I see no reason to direct that the external assets in countries other than this should be brought back to this country. That is a mere matter of investment policy which can be dealt with subsequently on investment considerations; for the present they can remain in the countries where they are currently invested but they should be in the sole name of *g* the receiver.

I would therefore allow the appeal and I would order all the defendants to procure that the external assets are henceforth held to the sole order of the receiver and that each deposit and the interest is paid on maturity as the receiver shall direct. The order of Vinelott J which was extended by Sir Nicolas Browne-Wilkinson V-C shall continue to apply to each fiduciary deposit until it has been paid to the receiver, or as he shall direct, *h* on maturity.

TAYLOR LJ. I have had the advantage of reading the judgments of Dillon and Staughton LJJ. I agree with them and there is nothing I can usefully add.

STAUGHTON LJ. Fifteen years ago, in *Nippon Yusen Kaisha v Karageorgis* [1975] 3 All *j* ER 282, [1975] 1 WLR 1093, the Court of Appeal granted an injunction restraining the defendants from taking their assets out of the jurisdiction pending trial. Before long the Mareva injunction thus discovered was extended in other cases to dealing with assets in England and Wales, if it could be shown that there was a risk that they would otherwise

be dissipated so as to render any subsequent judgment unenforceable. Such an injunction
a was regarded as an exceptional measure, not to be granted as of course but only on
evidence which carried an appropriate degree of conviction.

   Some years later it was held that a Mareva injunction might be granted so as to restrain
dealing in assets which are outside the jurisdiction, as well as those that are here, subject
to what has been called the *Babanaft* proviso: see *Babanaft International Co SA v Bassatne*
[1989] 1 All ER 433, [1990] Ch 13. In *Republic of Haiti v Duvalier* [1989] 1 All ER 456,
b [1990] 1 QB2 202 I expressed the view that cases where such an order would be
appropriate must be rare, if not very rare indeed.

   A further development has been the appointment of a receiver, before trial, to take
charge of the assets of a defendant. I imagine that this too is a measure which will rarely
be appropriate. Now we are asked to take a further step, and order the transfer from one
country to another of assets that are outside the physical bounds of our jurisdiction. Like
c Dillon LJ I do not doubt that the court has power to make such an order, in the exercise
of its jurisdiction in personam against defendants who have been duly served with
process under our rules. The question is whether the order should be made in the exercise
of the court's discretion.

   The growth of pre-trial restraint over the past 15 years has had a number of
consequences. The most obvious, although not perhaps the most important, is an
d increasing demand on the time of the courts and judges. No doubt it is desirable that our
judicial system should include measures to ensure that judgments, when eventually
given, are enforceable; and it can be argued that the resources of the system must be
increased so as to make such measures available. But the amount that the country can
spend on courts and judges is finite, just as is the amount that it can spend on the national
health service. Since pre-trial business tends to have priority, an increase in it may result
e in additional delay for widows and orphans with claims for damages, and for persons
waiting to be tried for crime.

   One more significant consequence is the restraints that are placed on defendants in the
conduct of their affairs before there has been any determination of liability against them;
they may, after all, eventually be found to owe nothing. Another, which is relevant to
these appeals, is an increasing interference with transactions and property abroad. This
f should not in my view be regarded lightly. If it ever became common practice for
English courts not merely to assume jurisdiction over defendants abroad under RSC
Ord 11, but also to order them to transfer assets here so that any eventual judgment
could be more readily enforced, that would in my view justifiably be regarded as
unacceptable chauvinism by the international community. Of course a foreign plaintiff
may be ordered to bring assets here, by way of security for costs; but that is the price
g which he must pay if he chooses to invoke the English jurisdiction.

   It was perhaps for that reason that Parliament placed territorial limitations on ss 8 and
9 of the Drug Trafficking Offences Act 1986, which deal with restraint and charging
orders. A restraint order may prohibit the removal of property from Great Britain, by
s 8(7); and assets which may be subject to a charging order are broadly speaking confined
h to property in England and Wales. Parliament deliberately abstained from asserting a
worldwide jurisdiction for such orders and was no doubt mindful of what *Dicey and
Morris on the Conflict of Laws* (11th edn, 1987) p 101 describes as 'a well-established and
almost universal principle that the courts of one country will not enforce the penal and
revenue laws of another country'. But a welcome relaxation of that principle is to be
found in s 26, under which an Order in Council may make provisions for assistance to
j the courts of countries outside the United Kingdom.

   Against that background I turn to consider how the discretion to order the transfer of
assets which are situate abroad should be exercised. One can envisage cases which might
be plain enough, for example where the actual proceeds of fraud are on board a ship on
the high seas flying no national flag and subject to no country's local jurisdiction. Or
they may be in a country which has no effective system of law, or one which can only be

regarded as wholly uncivilised. In less obvious cases the English courts should proceed with great caution, particularly against defendants who have not been served here but *a* abroad under Ord 11.

The main argument for the plaintiffs in seeking an order for the transfer out of Switzerland of the assets that are there is based on the limited extent to which an English judgment can be enforced in Switzerland. As Dillon LJ has said, it is to be expected that a judgment against Mr Weldon and Mr Jay (who were served here) and against CMI (who have submitted to the jurisdiction) will be enforced in Switzerland. But it is not likely to *b* be enforced against other defendants who have protested, even though they are defending the action and have in some instances counterclaimed.

Sir Nicolas Browne-Wilkinson V-C, reciting the argument for some of the defendants, referred to this likely immunity in Switzerland as a 'legitimate juridical advantage'. That phrase comes from the law relating to service out of the jurisdiction and the doctrine of forum non conveniens. I would be inclined not to use it in the present context. The *c* question is whether the Swiss law on the enforcement of foreign judgments is or is not such as should encourage an English court to make a pre-trial order that the defendants move their assets elsewhere.

In my judgment a rule that someone may defend under protest without exposing himself to a risk that the resulting judgment can be enforced against him in another jurisdiction is not, per se, an uncivilised rule. I feel bound to reach that conclusion since *d* it is exactly the rule which prevails in this country with regard to arbitrations: see *Henry v Geopresco International Ltd* [1975] 2 All ER 702 esp at 718–719, [1976] QB 726 esp at 747–748 per Roskill LJ, where he contrasts the English rule as to submission to the jurisdiction of a foreign court with the rule in the case of arbitrations. I cannot think that the English rule as to foreign courts is the only one which can properly be held by a civilised system of law. *e*

Of course it is very inconvenient for the plaintiffs if they have to fight the case all over again in Switzerland before they can recover from some of the defendants there. The remedy might have been to sue in Switzerland in the first place. But I do not see that it is sufficient ground for ordering assets to be transferred from Switzerland elsewhere, at any rate pre-trial. It is a misfortune for the plaintiffs that Switzerland is not a party to the European Convention on Jurisdiction and the Enforcement of Civil and Commercial *f* Judgments 1968, so that neither pre-trial assistance under art 24 nor the mechanism for the enforcement of a judgment is available there. But that should not by itself lead the English courts to adopt what I would regard as a drastic and wholly expectional measure. Despite the plaintiffs' protests, it appears to me that the assets in Switzerland are safe from dissipation under the present regime.

If the assets in Switzerland are to remain there, the plaintiffs do not pursue their *g* application that they be transferred into the sole name of the receiver. That would, it seems, involve too great a risk that the receiver in dealing with them would infringe art 271 of the Swiss Penal Code.

As to the assets outside Switzerland, I agree that an order should not be made for their return to Switzerland. The court having concluded that some restraint on how the *h* defendants deal with their assets pending trial is justified, I do not see that it should assist the defendants by ordering assets to be transferred to Switzerland in order that they may be immune from enforcement there. I am not impressed by the argument that this would avoid multiple litigation in different jurisdictions. I would also refuse to discharge the orders which are designed to ensure that those assets stay in the several jurisdictions where they are presently located.

It remains to consider whether the assets outside Switzerland should be transferred *j* into the sole name of the receiver. This does not seem to me of great importance, since they appear to be safe from dissipation as they are. But one cannot be wholly sure of that. And it remains the fact that the Court of Appeal in *Derby & Co Ltd v Weldon (No 2)* [1989] 1 All ER 1002, sub nom *Derby & Co Ltd v Weldon (Nos 3 and 4)* [1990] Ch 65 ordered that the assets should be transferred to the receiver. So far as concerns the assets outside

Switzerland, where art 271 has no effect, nothing of significance has occurred which
a would justify a variation of that order. In particular, I am satisfied that the receiver's
bargain which led to assets being transferred into joint names expressly preserved his
right to ask for further directions.

In the result I would vary the orders of Sir Nicolas Browne-Wilkinson V-C by ordering
that the assets outside Switzerland be transferred into the sole name of the receiver. This
accords with the practice described by Knox J in *Chandler v Church* (20 January 1988,
b unreported); but I do not accept that, as a matter of law, this is the rule which must
invariably be applied. It is a matter of practical convenience, and the court should do
what is most suited to the circumstances of a particular case. Otherwise I would dismiss
the appeals.

Finally I would mention *Irish Shipping Ltd v Commercial Union Assurance Co plc, The Irish
Rowan* [1989] 3 All ER 853 at 866, [1990] 2 WLR 117 at 134, where I expressed a
c tentative view that we should regard our own conflict of laws rules as those which ought
to prevail in other jurisdictions (although frequently they do not). Having now
considered the speech of Lord Diplock in *Amin Rasheed Shipping Corp v Kuwait Insurance
Co, The Al Wahab* [1983] 2 All ER 884 at 891, [1984] AC 50 at 65, where he points out
that English law does not recognise in others the jurisdiction which we claim for
ourselves under RSC Ord 11, I realise that this generalisation was too wide. But, even if
d it were wholly accurate, one can still conclude (as I do) that the Swiss rule as to the
enforcement of foreign judgments, although different from our own rule, is one which
can reasonably be adopted by a civilised system of law.

*Plaintiffs' appeal allowed in part ; no order as to costs save as to receiver's costs. Third to eleventh
defendents' appeal dismissed. Leave to appeal to the House of Lords refused.*

e

Solicitors: *Lovell White Durrant* (for the plaintiffs); *Hopkins & Wood* (for the first and
second defendants); *Allen & Overy* (for the third to eleventh defendants); *Cameron Markby
Hewitt* (for the receiver).

Carolyn Toulmin   Barrister.
f

R v Coventry Magistrates' Court, ex parte Director of Public Prosecutions

g QUEEN'S BENCH DIVISION
WATKINS LJ AND POTTS J
30 APRIL, 1 MAY 1990

*Criminal law – Costs – Magistrates' court – Guilty plea – Prosecution's claim for costs – Case
disposed of without attendance of parties – Whether magistrates required to make separate
h adjudication on prosecution's claim for costs – Whether magistrates' clerk required to draw
prosecution's claim for costs to magistrates' attention – Whether prosecutor required to attend
court to ask for costs – Magistrates' Courts Act 1980, s 12 – Prosecution of Offences Act 1985,
s 18(1)(a).*

Where a guilty plea is entered by the defendant and the defendant has been notified in
j writing that the prosecution intends to claim costs against him, the disposal of the case
by the magistrates under the procedure laid down by s 12[a] of the Magistrates' Courts Act
1980 for disposal of guilty pleas without the attendance of the parties must include a
separate adjudication by the magistrates on the prosecution's claim for costs, and
accordingly the magistrates' clerk must draw the prosecution's claim for costs to the

---

a Section 12, so far as material, is set out at p 278 *j* to 279 *e*, post

attention of the magistrates so that they can decide whether to exercise their discretion
under s 18(1)(*a*)[b] of the Prosecution of Offences Act 1985 to order the prosecution's costs   *a*
to be paid by the defendant. In such a case it is not necessary for the prosecutor to attend
court to ask for costs (see p 281 *f* to p 282 *e g h*, post).

Notes
For disposal of a written plea of guilty in the absence of the accused, see 29 Halsbury's
Laws (4th edn) paras 338–339.   *b*
    For the Magistrates' Courts Act 1980, s 12, see 27 Halsbury's Statutes (4th edn) 180.
    For the Prosecution of Offences Act 1985, s 18, see 12 Halsbury's Statutes (4th edn)
(1989 reissue) 951.

Application for judicial review
The Director of Public Prosecutions applied, with the leave of Otton J given on 19 May   *c*
1989, for judicial review of the decisions of the Coventry magistrates on 7 February 1989
to refuse to cause the court clerk to read out the prosecution's application for costs in the
summary prosecution of Freda Basely, to refuse to adjudicate on the application and to
refuse to grant the application. The relief sought was declarations (a) that a claim for costs
by the prosecution against a defendant in a case proceeding according to the provisions
of s 12 of the Magistrates' Courts Act 1980 could be notified to the defendant in the same   *d*
document as contained the statement required to be made by the prosecution under
s 12(1)(*b*) thereof but, if so notified, did not form part of the statement, and (b) that if
such a claim for costs was so notified then when the document was before the court on
the day fixed for the hearing of the matter the claim had to be brought to the court's
attention and it was the duty of the court to adjudicate thereon. The facts are set out in
the judgment of Watkins LJ.   *e*

John Laws for the Director of Public Prosecution's.
The magistrates did not appear.

WATKINS LJ. This is an application by the Director of Public Prosecutions for judicial   *f*
review of a decision of the justices of the City of Coventry when sitting at Coventry
Magistrates' Court on 7 February 1989 whereby they refused to cause the court clerk to
read out the prosecutor's application for costs in an uncontested motoring case. The
director seeks the following declarations:

    '(a) A claim for costs by the Prosecution against the Defendant, in a case
    proceeding according to the provisions of s. 12 of the Magistrates Courts Act 1980,   *g*
    may be notified to the Defendant in the same document as contains the statement
    required to be made by the Prosecution under s. 12(1)(*b*) thereof, but, if so notified,
    does not form part of the said statement; (b) If such claim for costs is so notified,
    then when the document is before the Court on the day fixed for the hearing of the
    matter, the claim must be brought to the Court's attention, and it will be the duty
    of the Court to adjudicate thereon.'   *h*

Section 12 of the 1980 Act, so far as relevant, states:

    '(1) Subject to subsection (7) below, this section shall apply where a summons has
    been issued requiring a person to appear before a magistrates' court, other than a
    juvenile court, to answer to an information for a summary offence, not being an
    offence for which the accused is liable to be sentenced to be imprisoned for a term   *j*
    exceeding 3 months, and the clerk of the court is notified by or on behalf of the
    prosecutor that the following documents have been served upon the accused with

---

b   Section 18(1), so far as material, provides: 'Where—(*a*) any person is convicted of an offence before
    a magistrates' court . . . the court shall make such order as to the costs to be paid by the accused to
    the prosecutor as it considers just and reasonable.'

a the summons, that is to say—(a) a notice containing such statement of the effect of this section as may be prescribed; and (b) a concise statement in the prescribed form of such facts relating to the charge as will be placed before the court by or on behalf of the prosecutor if the accused pleads guilty without appearing before the court.

(2) Subject to subsections (3) to (5) below, where the clerk of the court receives a notification in writing purporting to be given by the accused or by a solicitor acting on his behalf that the accused desires to plead guilty without appearing before the

b court, the clerk of the court shall inform the prosecutor of the receipt of the notification and if at the time and place appointed for the trial or adjourned trial of the information the accused does not appear and it is proved to the satisfaction of the court, on oath or in such other manner as may be prescribed, that the notice and statement of facts referred to in subsection (1) above have been served upon the accused with the summons, then—(a) subject to section 11(3) and (4) above, the

c court may proceed to hear and dispose of the case in the absence of the accused, whether or not the prosecutor is also absent, in like manner as if both parties had appeared and the accused had pleaded guilty . . .

(4) Before accepting the plea of guilty and convicting the accused in his absence under subsection (2) above, the court shall cause the notification and statement of facts aforesaid, including any submission received with the notification which the

d accused wishes to be brought to the attention of the court with a view to mitigation of sentence, to be read out before the court by the clerk of the court.

(5) If the court proceeds under subsection (2) above to hear and dispose of the case in the absence of the accused, the court shall not permit any statement to be made by or on behalf of the prosecutor with respect to any facts relating to the offence charged other than the statement of facts aforesaid except on a resumption

e of the trial after an adjournment under section 10(3) above . . .'

That procedure has proved most beneficial in motoring cases, especially to defendants, prosecutors and the administration of justice generally, in its savings of time and the costs of proceedings in court. It is used in about 200,000 to 250,000 cases a year.

f Assuming that the costs of the prosecutor for preparation of a case dealt with without attendance by him and the defendant are £10 per case, the annual costs incurred in the application of the s 12 procedure would be something approaching £2,500,000. That figure would be multiplied many times if appearances had to be made before justices by either prosecutor, defendant or both. There is, therefore, manifestly a need for the procedure to be universally followed without appearances and the matter of the

g prosecution's costs dealt with, providing the defendants are clearly informed that the prosecutor has applied to the court for his, in the circumstances, modest costs.

There is no prescribed form for applying for costs, so that the prosecutor is free to choose an appropriate manner in which, without personal appearance, to make his application. To deny him that and so cause him to make a personal appearance for the sole purpose of applying for costs would, in my judgment, partly defeat Parliament's

h intention in introducing the s 12 procedure and obviously increase fairly substantially the burden of costs on a defendant. Common sense and simple justice demands that a defendant has notice of the prosecutor's intention to apply for costs and therefore that the prosecutor be enabled to make his application in writing.

There are prescribed forms which serve the purposes of (1) informing a defendant by summons of the information laid against him, (2) reciting the statement of facts relating

j to the offence charged relied on by the prosecutor, (3) causing or permitting a defendant to acknowledge receipt of those forms and to indicate his plea, guilty or not, to the charge and (4) allowing the defendant to make in writing a statement in mitigation which he wishes the court to consider when determining an appropriate penalty.

In the present case those forms were used to good effect. A cogent statement of facts was made under the heading 'Statement of Facts'. Beneath them a dotted line was drawn across the page separating that statement from the following typed words:

'Costs in the sum of £10 are claimed against you under section 18 of the
Prosecution of Offences Act 1985 by the Crown Prosecution Service for conducting   a
a review of the charge made against you. You must produce your driving licence
either by sending it to the court at least three days before the hearing or by having
it with you at the court. Failure to produce your licence may result in a fine of up to
£100 and its suspension until produced.'

The stage was set for the s 12 procedure to be followed without appearances, but the
Crown Prosecution Service scented trouble and sent to the hearing one of its solicitors,   b
Mr John Western of the Northampton branch of the Crown Prosecution Service. We
have from him an affidavit made under s 1 of the 1985 Act. In that he explains, inter
alia, that the Crown Prosecution Service had the conduct of the prosecution by virtue of
s 3(2)(a) of the 1985 Act, and he asserts:

'A large number of Clerks to the Justices in England and Wales have been refusing   c
to place prosecution costs applications before the Court in cases to which the Section
12 procedure applies. This therefore affects not only cases conducted by the Crown
Prosecution Service, but also the conduct by the police of proceedings which are
specified under the Prosecution of Offences Act 1985 (Specified Proceedings) Order
1985 [SI 1985/2010] and the Prosecution of Offences Act 1985 (Specified Proceedings)
Order 1988 [SI 1988/1121].'   d

There seems to be no doubt that his assertion is well founded. Yorkshire at least being
an exception, a practice seems to have grown of clerks refusing to put before the court a
written application by the prosecutor for his costs. Mr Western attended for the purpose
of persuading the Coventry justices that the practice was wrong, even contrary to law.

The background story of the present case and what happened at the hearing is as   e
follows.

On 30 October 1988 Mrs Freda Baseley committed the offence of driving without due
care and attention. On 16 January 1989 the appropriate forms, including the summons,
were sent to her. She returned the acknowledgment of service, stated she had pleaded
guilty and made a written statement in mitigation. On 7 February 1989 the hearing
took place before the justices. The statement of facts, of which Mrs Baseley had been   f
acquainted as I have said, relating to the offence was read out. Mr Western then asked the
clerk to read out the written application for costs to which I have already referred. The
court clerk did not wish to do that. He advised his justices that they should not cause
him to do so. The justices accepted his advice. Their reasons for doing so were, as stated
by them on a document before us, these:

'We are not going to cause the application for costs to be read out by our clerk   g
because we do not consider the application to be properly a part of the statement of
facts. We would also say that Section 12 Subsection 4 speaks of the court hearing the
statement of facts before deciding whether or not to accept the guilty plea. It does
not seem to us appropriate for a court to be dealing with the question of costs before
it has decided whether or not to accept a guilty plea. Also we would not expect our   h
clerk to make a costs application of his own volition without any statutory
requirement on him to do so. We believe that if a prosecutor wishes to obtain costs
then he should attend in person to make an application.'

We have from Mr Western a very carefully composed account of the submissions he
made to the justices in an endeavour to persuade them to come to a contrary decision.
Clearly he was unsuccessful. The clerk to the justices, Mr Kidner, explains in an affidavit   j
why the court clerk advised the justices, as plainly he did, not to accept Mr Western's
submission.

Neither the court clerk nor the justices have been represented before us. There is
sound reason for that. No provision exists for meeting the costs of justices or court clerks
should they be called on by this court to meet the costs of a successful party. That is
highly regrettable. It is a situation for which a remedy must be found.

Mr Kidner states:

a

'3 ... (a) That when a court deals with a case under S. 12 Magistrates' Courts Act 1980 then, by sub-section (5), the court may not permit any statement relating to the facts of the offence to be made by the prosecutor except those facts contained in the concise statement of facts relating to the charge provided for by sub-section (1)(b).

b

(b) That the obligation on the court clerk contained in sub-section (4) to read to the court information concerning the case includes the obligation to read the statement of facts mentioned above. (c) That sub-section (4) imposes a duty on the clerk to read and the court to consider, amongst other things, the statement of facts and the written representations of the accused before accepting a plea of guilty and convicting the accused. It would be out of order in criminal proceedings for the court to hear an application for prosecution costs before it had decided whether to accept the defendant's plea.

c

(d) That a claim for prosecution costs cannot be a fact "relating to the charge" or "relating to the facts of the offence" since it does not form part of the information required by statute to comprise the ingredients of the offence alleged against the defendant. (e) That since a claim for costs is considered a secondary issue and not properly a part of the statement of facts, the duty on the court and on the clerk described in sub-section (4) does not relate to such a claim.

d

4 ... It is not the duty of the clerk of the court to put forward any part of the prosecution or defence case save as may be stipulated by statute or Practice Direction ([1981] 2 All ER 831, [1981] 1 WLR 1163). It would be improper for the clerk of the court to "step into the arena" and put forward any aspect of the case of either the prosecution or the defence unless the clerk is acting under a duty so to do given with the express authority of Parliament.'

e

Counsel for the Director of Public Prosecutions made the following submissions to us. He contended that there is no doubt that the s 18 jurisdiction in the Prosecution of Offences Act 1985 to award costs applies in s 12 cases.

I agree. I think any argument to the contrary could not possibly be sustained. He also submitted that the claim for costs ascribed to a s 12(1) notice forms part of the statement

f of fact relating to the charge. Justices are, he said, bound by s 12(4) to cause it to be drawn to their attention, and it is their duty if they find the defendant guilty to adjudicate on the claim as in this case was submitted by Mr Western to the justices. The expression 'facts relating to the charge' in s 12(1)(b) is wider than 'facts relating to the offence charged' in s 12(5). The incurring of costs, he submits, is clearly a fact. Equally clearly, it relates to the charge.

g

I do not agree with that. The statement of facts referred to in s 12 refers, in my view, to the facts relating to the commission of the offence charged. They are set out specifically for the purpose of allowing a defendant proper opportunity to consider what plea to tender. They have no other purpose. The matter of costs is an entirely independent issue, and cannot, I think, by any stretch of the imagination, relate to the circumstances of the offence.

h

Counsel for the Director of Public Prosecutions, in the alternative, submitted that nothing in s 12 or in s 18 makes it a condition precedent to the consideration of an application for costs that the prosecutor should attend in person to make it. Of course in an ordinary case where the parties attend court any application for costs will be made orally; but the very purpose of s 12 is to obviate the need for personal attendance. It cannot have been the intention of Parliament that the s 12 procedure should only be

j capable of application in the absence of the prosecutor on condition that a claim for prosecution costs be not entertained; but the effect of the justices' decision here, he maintained, is to disapply s 18 unless the prosecutor attends the court.

He maintained that, if, as the justices held, the written claim for costs is not a statement of facts relating to the charge within s 12(1)(b), then s 12(5) cannot possibly operate to prohibit the clerk from drawing the justices' attention to the claim for costs.

Assuming, he said, there is no such prohibition the clerk is bound to put the claim for costs before the justices since not to do so would prevent them from carrying out what must be their duty, namely to adjudicate on an application which is properly before them.

If the justices entertain a policy never to have their clerk draw a claim for costs to their attention in s 12 cases they, he contended, unlawfully fetter their discretion, since the result of such a policy is that in effect such claims are systematically dismissed without exception.

Nothing in this is, he maintained, inconsistent with the terms of the practice direction referred to. Even if it was, a practice direction cannot justify a procedure whereby justices are disabled or disable themselves from considering and adjudicating on an application properly before them. I would add that there is nothing in that direction which relates to costs at all.

In the result, he submitted, whether or not the claim for costs constitutes part of the s 12(1)(b) statement, the clerk is bound to draw it to the justices' attention so as to enable them to decide whether or not to exercise their power under s 18.

Finally, he said that the justices' reasons, which I have already set out, disclose two further errors. (a) There was no question of the justices being asked to deal with the question of costs before deciding whether or not to accept a guilty plea; there can, he maintained, be no possible vice in the claim for costs being drawn to their attention before they adjudicate on the plea. (b) The clerk was not being asked to make a costs application 'of his own volition'. If the claim for costs was part of the s 12(1)(b) statement, the clerk was bound by sub-s (4) to read it out; if not, he was nevertheless bound to draw that to the justices' attention because not to do so would prevent them from carrying out their duty to adjudicate on a proper application.

In my judgment, counsel for the Director of Public Prosecutions is entirely right in every single one of those submissions.

The application for costs may be said, as made in the present case, to be inappropriately placed on the form requiring a statement of facts; but, even if that be so, the way in which the reference to costs appears on that form makes it absolutely clear that it was not meant to nor could it reasonably be taken to be part of the statement of facts relating to the offence. It may be, perhaps it ought to be, that a separate form should be contrived for the purpose of making an application for costs and any other matter which needs to be drawn to the attention of the court, such as the way drawn to the attention of the defendant before he or she responds to the invitation to make known to the court the plea to the charge. Such a form can easily be contrived. Indeed, the existing form headed 'Statement of fact' can be altered so as to make plainer that an application for costs made on that form cannot possibly be said to relate to the statement of facts which is there set out. The actual manner in which the necessary documents need be altered for achieving that purpose is clearly something which ought to be considered by the Crown Prosecution Service in consultation with the clerks to the justices. What is absolutely necessary forthwith is that the practice by clerks, wherever it is carried on, of not reading out to the justices a claim by the prosecution for costs when neither the prosecutor nor the defendant are appearing must cease. It is grossly improper not to bring that matter to the attention of the justices when the s 12 procedure has been followed.

For those reasons, I would allow the declaration sought by the Director of Public Prosecutions.

POTTS J. I agree.

Application allowed. Declarations accordingly.

Solicitors: *Crown Prosecution Service.*

Dilys Tausz   Barrister.

Sociedade Nacional de Combustiveis de Angola UEE and others v Lundqvist and others

COURT OF APPEAL, CIVIL DIVISION

SIR NICOLAS BROWNE-WILKINSON V-C, STAUGHTON AND BELDAM LJJ

5, 6, 7, 8, 11, 12 DECEMBER 1989, 31 JANUARY 1990

Practice – Pre-trial or post-judgment relief – Mareva injunction – Discovery in aid of injunction – Privilege against self-incrimination – Plaintiffs alleging conspiracy to defraud – Order requiring disclosure of value and whereabouts of defendants' overseas assets – Whether defendants entitled to claim privilege against self-incrimination in respect of information – Theft Act 1968, s 31.

The plaintiffs were three state-owned oil companies set up to explore, produce and market Angolan oil. The first plaintiff was registered in Angola and the second and third plaintiffs, which were wholly owned by the first plaintiff, were incorporated in England and Liberia respectively. The first defendant, an oil consultant who effectively ran the second plaintiff's operations in London, wholly owned and controlled the fourth defendant, a Liberian corporation which provided consultancy services for the plaintiffs. The plaintiffs claimed that the first defendant had conspired with others to defraud them of sums amounting to $US90m by arranging the sale of Angolan oil by the first plaintiff to companies controlled by him at less than the market price, and then arranging a resale at the market price so that the profit on the resale enured to the benefit of the first defendant or the companies controlled by him. In November 1987 the plaintiffs commenced proceedings to recover the sums lost and sought and obtained injunctions, disclosure orders and Anton Piller and Mareva orders restraining the disposal of assets by the defendants. On 19 May 1989 the plaintiffs applied ex parte for, and were granted, a worldwide Mareva injunction restraining the first and fourth defendants from disposing of or dealing with any assets outside England and Wales except to the extent that their value exceeded £US90m. Paragraph 2 of the order required the defendants to disclose by affidavit details of the value and whereabouts of their worldwide assets. The defendants applied, inter alia, to set aside para 2 of the order on the ground that they were entitled to claim privilege against self-incrimination in respect of the information which was the subject of the order. The judge held that the conduct alleged against the first defendant could give rise to criminal proceedings against him but, although the defendants might thereby be entitled to claim privilege, the claim to privilege had been insufficiently formulated. The judge accordingly dismissed the application. The defendants appealed.

Held – The privilege against self-incrimination could be invoked to resist the making of an order for discovery ancillary to a Mareva injunction where, on the facts alleged by the plaintiff, there was a reasonable apprehension on the part of the defendant that a prosecution for conspiracy to defraud might be brought in the United Kingdom and that, if the documents or information were produced, there was a real risk that they might incriminate the defendant. Accordingly, the court would uphold the claim for privilege in so far as the order of 19 May 1989 required the defendants to state the value of their assets overseas, since that information might form a link in the chain of proof against them on a criminal charge. However, the court would reject the claim in so far as it related to the nature or situation of those assets. The appeal would therefore be allowed to the extent of deleting from para 2 of the order the requirement that the defendants state the value of their overseas assets (see p 291 *f* to *j*, p 292 *a f* to *h*, p 294 *c*, p 297 *g j*, p 300 *f g*, p 301 *f g* and p 302 *c* to *e*, post).

Per Sir Nicolas Browne-Wilkinson V-C. If Parliament does not as a matter of urgency consider extending the provisions of s 31^a of the Theft Act 1968 so as to remove the privilege against self-incrimination in relation to all civil claims relating to property but on the terms that the statements made in documents disclosed are not admissible in any criminal proceedings, including conspiracy to defraud whether under statute or at common law, the effectiveness of civil remedies designed to redress fraud will be seriously impaired (see p 302 *j* to p 303 *a*, post).

Per Staughton LJ. Where a charge of conspiracy to defraud at common law or of a statutory conspiracy to commit an offence under the 1968 Act is laid the conspiracy itself will not be 'an offence under this Act' or 'proceedings for an offence under this Act' and therefore s 31 of the 1968 Act will not provide sufficient protection for the person charged with the conspiracy and will not remove the privilege against self-incrimination (see p 290 *h* and p 291 *b c*, post); *R v Cuthbertson* [1980] 2 All ER 401 applied.

Notes

For privilege from production of documents exposing a party to penalties, see 13 Halsbury's Laws (4th edn) para 92, and for cases on the subject, see 18 Digest (2nd reissue) 223–229, 1925–1988.

For the Theft Act 1968, s 31, see 12 Halsbury's Statutes (4th edn) (1989 reissue) 509.

Cases referred to in judgments

Adams v Lloyd (1858) 3 H & N 351, 157 ER 506.
Arab Monetary Fund v Hashim [1989] 3 All ER 466, [1989] 1 WLR 565.
A-G's Reference (No 1 of 1982) [1983] 2 All ER 721, [1983] QB 751, [1983] 3 WLR 72, CA.
A-G's Reference (No 1 of 1985) [1986] 2 All ER 219, [1986] QB 491, [1986] 2 WLR 733, CA.
Babanaft International Co SA v Bassatne [1989] 1 All ER 433, [1990] Ch 13, [1989] 2 WLR 232, CA.
Board of Trade v Owen [1957] 1 All ER 411, [1957] AC 602, [1957] 2 WLR 351, HL.
Brebner v Perry [1961] SASR 177, S Aust SC.
Derby & Co Ltd v Weldon (No 1) [1989] 1 All ER 469, [1990] Ch 48, [1989] 2 WLR 276, CA.
DPP v Doot [1973] 1 All ER 940, [1973] AC 807, [1973] 2 WLR 532, HL.
Genese, Re, ex p Gilbert (1886) 3 Morr 223, CA.
Haiti (Republic) v Duvalier [1989] 1 All ER 456, [1990] QB 202, [1989] 2 WLR 261, CA.
Khan v Khan [1982] 2 All ER 60, [1982] 1 WLR 513, CA.
Lamb v Munster (1882) 10 QBD 110, DC.
Osborn v London Dock Co (1855) 10 Exch 698, 156 ER 620.
Paxton v Douglas (1809) 16 Ves 239, 33 ER 975; *subsequent proceedings* (1812) 19 Ves 225, 34 ER 502.
R v Ayres [1984] 1 All ER 619, [1984] AC 447, [1984] 2 WLR 257, HL.
R v Boyes (1861) B & S 311, [1861–73] All ER Rep 172, 121 ER 730.
R v Cooke [1986] 2 All ER 985, [1986] AC 909, [1986] 3 WLR 327, HL.
R v Cox (Peter) [1968] 1 All ER 410, [1968] 1 WLR 88, CA.
R v Cuthbertson [1980] 2 All ER 401, [1981] AC 470, [1980] 3 WLR 89, HL.
R v El-Hakkaoui [1975] 2 All ER 146, [1975] 1 WLR 396, CA.
R v Garbett (Edmund) (1847) 1 Den 236, 169 ER 227, Ex Ch.
R v Governor of Brixton Prison, ex p Rush [1969] 1 All ER 316, [1969] 1 WLR 165, DC.
R v Governor of Pentonville Prison, ex p Osman [1989] 3 All ER 701, [1990] 1 WLR 277, DC.
R v Harden [1962] 1 All ER 286, [1963] 1 QB 8, [1962] 2 WLR 553, CCA.
R v Hornett [1975] RTR 256, CA.
R v Thompson [1984] 3 All ER 565, [1984] 1 WLR 962, CA.

---

a   Section 31, so far as material, is set out at p 290 *f g*, post

R v Tirado (1974) 59 Cr App R 80, CA.

a   *R v Tomsett* [1985] Crim LR 369, CA.

Rank Film Distributors Ltd v Video Information Centre [1981] 2 All ER 76, [1982] AC 380, [1981] 2 WLR 668, HL; *affg* [1980] 2 All ER 273, [1982] AC 380, [1980] 3 WLR 487, CA.

Reynolds, Ex p, re Reynolds (1882) 20 Ch D 294, [1881–5] All ER Rep 997, CA.

Rio Tinto Zinc Corp v Westinghouse Electric Corp [1978] 1 All ER 434, [1978] AC 547,
b   [1978] 2 WLR 81, HL; *affg* sub nom *Re Westinghouse Electric Corp Uranium Contract Litigation MDL Docket No 235 (No 2)* [1977] 3 All ER 717, [1978] AC 547, [1977] 3 WLR 492, CA.

Short v Mercier (1851) 3 Mac & G 205, 20 LJ Ch 289, 42 ER 239, LC.

Sidebottom v Adkins (1857) 29 LTOS 310.

Tarling v Government of the Republic of Singapore (1978) 70 Cr App R 77, HL.

c   *Treacy v DPP* [1971] 1 All ER 110, [1971] AC 537, [1971] 2 WLR 112, HL.

Triplex Safety Glass Co Ltd v Lancegaye Safety Glass (1934) *Ltd* [1939] 2 All ER 613, [1939] 2 KB 395, CA.

Cases also cited

Claridge v Hoare (1807) 14 Ves 59, 33 ER 443, LC.

d   *Green v Weaver* (1827) 1 Sim 404, 57 ER 630.

National Association of Operative Plasterers v Smithies [1906] AC 434, [1904–7] All ER Rep 961, HL.

Ninemia Maritime Corp v Trave Schiffahrtsgesellschaft mbH & Co KG, The Niedersachsen [1984] 1 All ER 398, [1983] 1 WLR 1412, CA.

e   *R v Governor of Brixton Prison, ex p Rush* [1969] 1 All ER 316, [1969] 1 WLR 165, DC.

Sitwell v Sun Engraving Co Ltd [1937] 4 All ER 366, CA.

Spokes v Grosvenor and West End Railway Terminus Hotel Co Ltd [1897] 2 QB 124, CA.

Symes, Ex p (1805) 11 Ves 521, 32 ER 1191.

Interlocutory appeal

f   The first defendant, Stellan Lundqvist, and the fourth defendant, SL Oil Executive Services AG (SLOES), appealed with the leave of the judge against the decision of Leggatt J dated 27 June 1989 whereby he held that the first and fourth defendants' claim to the privilege against self-incrimination in respect of compliance with para 2 of the order obtained by the plaintiffs, Sociedade Nacional de Combustiveis de Angola UEE, Sociedade Nacional de Combustiveis de Angola Ltd and Sociedade Nacional de Combustiveis de Angola SA, from Phillips J dated 19 May 1989 was insufficient and that the first and

g   fourth defendants were obliged to make the disclosure sought by para 2 of the order. The facts are set out in the judgment of Staughton LJ.

Anthony Clarke QC and Simon Rainey for the first defendant, Mr Lundqvist, and the fourth defendant, SLOES.

h   Alan Newman QC and Antony White for the plaintiffs.

Cur adv vult

31 January. The following judgments were delivered.

j   **STAUGHTON LJ** (giving the first judgment at the invitation of Sir Nicolas Browne-Wilkinson V-C). Sociedade Nacional de Combustiveis de Angola UEE is the national oil company of Angola and the first plaintiff in this action. I shall call them 'Sonangol UEE'. The second and third plaintiffs ('Sonangol Ltd' and 'Sonangol SA') are companies controlled by Sonangol UEE, incorporated in England and Liberia respectively. The role of Sonangol Ltd is that which is important for the purposes of this appeal. Between

January 1983 and February 1987 their task was to arrange the sale of oil exported from Angola.

During the same period the first defendant, Mr Stellan Lundqvist, effectively ran the operations of Sonangol Ltd. In point of form he acted as an employee of SL Oil Executive Services AG (SLOES), a company which he controlled and which is the fourth defendant in this action; SLOES in turn provided consultancy services for Sonangol Ltd.

The case for the Sonangol companies is that Mr Lundqvist conspired with others to defraud them of sums totalling at least $US88m. This is said to have been done by arranging the sale of Angolan oil or oil products at less than the market price, and then arranging a resale by the purchaser in such a manner that profit enured to the benefit of Mr Lundqvist or companies which he controlled.

The defence, in broad terms, is that these transactions were approved at the highest level in Angola, in order to provide funds for projects which would benefit Angola. That is the merest outline of the claim and the defence; I shall have to enter on more detail later.

The proceedings began with an ex parte order of Alliott J on 5 November 1987. This contained (i) an Anton Piller order, permitting representatives of the Sonangol companies to enter and search premises in England, and to copy and keep documents found there, (ii) an injunction restraining the defendants from destroying or removing documents, (iii) a Mareva order against Mr Lundqvist and another defendant in respect of assets within the jurisdiction, (iv) an order that Mr Lundqvist and four other defendants should answer by affidavit questions to be asked by the solicitors for the Sonangol companies and (v) an order that Mr Lundqvist disclose on affidavit his assets both in and out of the jurisdiction.

The writ was issued on 6 November 1987, and the Anton Piller order executed four days later. There followed a series of interlocutory battles which are only of indirect relevance to this appeal. On 23 November Hobhouse J gave directions as to the questions which the Sonangol companies required to be answered under the order of Alliott J. Their solicitors then served a formidable list of questions, including inquiries whether Mr Lundqvist had any beneficial ownership in 31 named companies.

Hobhouse J made a further order on 26 November. This restricted the order of Alliott J for disclosure to assets within the jurisdiction, in accordance with the view of the law and practice which prevailed at that time. It also made provision for Mr Lundqvist to claim the privilege against self-incrimination, if he wished, in respect of the questions required to be answered and the documents seized under the order of Alliott J.

Mr Lundqvist did claim the privilege against self-incrimination in certain respects, and Hobhouse J ruled on that claim by an order of 10 December 1987. The Anton Piller order was set aside in part; certain of the documents obtained under it were ordered to be returned, and any copies to be destroyed or delivered up. As to the questions required to be answered, Mr Lundqvist was content to answer in regard to two of the 31 companies, but claimed privilege in respect of the remainder. Hobhouse J upheld that claim. It was argued for the Sonangol companies that Mr Lundqvist was bound to assert separately, in respect of each of the remaining 29, that an answer would tend to incriminate him. That argument was rejected by the judge in these terms:

'The line of questioning as a whole is one where if the defendant were asked to pick and choose between the various companies or names and justify his position with regard to each individually, or specifically claim privilege with regard to each individually, that very exercise would tend to incriminate him beyond the mere fact of his claiming privilege.'

Pleadings were then served as between the Sonangol companies on the one hand and Mr Lundqvist and SLOES on the other; and on 19 April 1988 a summons was issued on behalf of the Sonangol companies seeking an interim order for an account. This was mentioned before Hobhouse J on 22 July 1988. The judge took the sensible course of

discouraging the application in plain terms, with the result that it was adjourned to the
a trial with liberty to apply and costs reserved. The Sonangol companies thus failed for the
second time to obtain interim disclosure of what had happened to the proceeds of resale
of their oil.

Then there was a pause so far as events material to this appeal are concerned.
Meanwhile decisions of this court in other cases revealed a different view of the law and
practice as to Marvea injunctions over assets abroad. As a result, on 19 May 1989 the
b Sonangol companies obtained ex parte from Phillips J an order restraining Mr Lundqvist
and SLOES from disposing of or dealing with any of their assets *outside* England and
Wales—

> 'whether such assets, property, money or goods be in their own names or jointly
> with any other persons or in the names of agents, nominees or trustees for them . . .'

c save in so far as the value exceeded $US90m. The order recited undertakings, amongst
others, by the Sonangol companies as follows:

> '(vii) That they will not, without first seeking and obtaining the leave of this
> Court, make any application to any foreign Court to enforce the provisions of this
> Order. (viii) That they will not, without first seeking and obtaining the leave of this
> d Court, make use of any information disclosed pursuant to the provisions of this
> Order in any proceedings in any foreign Court against the First or Fourth
> Defendants.'

At last I come to the topic which is the subject-matter of this appeal. Paragraph 2 of
the order of Phillips J read as follows:

> e 'The First Defendant and the Fourth Defendant by the First Defendant do within
> 28 days of service of this Order upon his Solicitors, Messrs Clyde and Co, make and
> file an Affidavit giving details of the value and whereabouts of all his assets, property,
> money and goods wherever situated including without prejudice to the generality
> of the foregoing all beneficial interests in any company or body wherever
> incorporated or established and any assets, property, money or goods held jointly
> f with any other person or in the names of agents, nominees or trustees, provided that
> if within 7 days of service of this Order upon Clyde and Co either Defendant gives
> notice to the Plaintiffs' Solicitors of an application to set aside this paragraph of this
> Order the obligation to comply with this paragraph shall be suspended until that
> application has been determined.'

g It is to be noted that the order relates to '*his* assets', i e Mr Lundqvist's. That may have
been a mistake for 'their', so as to include the assets of SLOES; but I am not convinced
that it was.

Mr Lundqvist and SLOES applied for an order that the ex parte order of Phillips J be
set aside or discharged on a number of grounds, which included the privilege against
h self-incrimination. Leggatt J on 27 June 1989 dismissed that application, thus upholding
both the injunction against dealing with assets outside the jurisdiction and the order for
disclosure of such assets. He did, however, leave it open to Mr Lundqvist and SLOES 'to
persist in the claim for privilege when responding on affidavit and to support it properly
by evidence on which the court may act'. The judge gave leave to appeal, with a stay of
execution, but only in respect of the order for disclosure and the privilege against self-
j incrimination.

On that topic the judge may be said to have directed himself in accordance with the
judgment of Lord Esher MR in *Re Genese, ex p Gilbert* (1886) 3 Morr 233 at 226–227,
where it was said that a witness 'must satisfy the Court that there is a reasonable
probability that his answer will or may criminate him'. The conclusion of Leggatt J was
in these terms:

'In relation, therefore, to para 2 of Phillips J's order, I conclude that in principle the defendants may well be entitled to claim privilege but that as a matter of form *a* they have not yet sufficiently done so. Potentially that part of para 2 of the order which refers to beneficial interests in companies might contain evidence of jeopardy to which the defendants would be exposed if they gave the information sought by identifying companies into which moneys were diverted. Even that is not a necessary consequence of the provision of information falling within that category. The remainder of the information, in any event, is in its form what Lord Esher MR *b* called perfectly innocent. The details of the value and whereabouts of the defendants' assets, property, money and goods wherever situate without more tells nothing of any conspiracy to defraud, nor does it give rise to any apparent risk of prosecution for such an offence. It requires, as Lord Esher MR said, something outside it to show that the answer of the witness might put him in jeopardy. It is not enough for the defendants or their solicitor to state, as they have, that they believe their answers *c* might tend to criminate the defendants. They are not by that means excused from answering at all. They must satisfy the court by factors outside the terms of para 2 of the order that their answers will or may put them in jeopardy.'

It is against that decision that this appeal is brought.

One other aspect of the judgment of Leggatt J needs to be mentioned. It had been *d* argued before him that the ex parte order of Phillips J was improperly obtained, because the affidavit evidence mentioned the previous claims of Mr Lundqvist to the privilege against self-incrimination, and suggested that these in themselves showed that the Sonangol companies had a strongly arguable case against him. Whilst Leggatt J rejected the suggestion that the ex parte order had been improperly obtained, he did accept that a claim for the privilege was not evidence of guilt: 'To comment adversely about a person *e* who claims privilege to avoid criminating himself is plainly wrong.' Although the point has not been directly in issue before us, and notwithstanding a dictum of Templeman LJ in *Rank Film Distributors Ltd v Video Information Centre* [1980] 2 All ER 273 at 291, [1982] AC 380 at 423 which might be thought on one view to suggest the contrary, I consider that the observation of Leggatt J was right. It has some indirect relevance at a later stage.

f

THE ISSUES

These can be listed as follows. (A) Would an English court have jurisdiction to try Mr Lundqvist on a charge of conspiracy to defraud? (B) Does s 31 of the Theft Act 1968 mean that he is in no danger of self-incrimination? (C) Could the fourth defendant, SLOES, be prosecuted here? (D) What standard of proof is required before the court will give effect to the privilege against self-incrimination? (E) Is proof to that standard *g* achieved in this case? (F) Are Mr Lundqvist and SLOES 'trifling with the court' in making their claim to privilege? It should be said at once that issues (A), (B) and (C) were not raised before Leggatt J or in the respondent's notice. As the judge said, it was accepted that the allegations made by the Sonangol companies would be capable of supporting not only a civil claim but also the prosecution of Mr Lundqvist should he render himself liable to such process by returning within the jurisdiction of the English court. (It *h* remains to be seen whether he *will* return, in order to give evidence in this action if it should ever come to trial.) Nevertheless, this court thought it right to inquire into the questions whether there could be a prosecution here, and if so for what offence.

(A) *Jurisdiction on a charge of conspiracy to defraud*   *j*
Section 14(1) of the Civil Evidence Act 1968 provides:

'The right of a person in any legal proceedings other than criminal proceedings to refuse to answer any question or produce any document or thing if to do so would tend to expose that person to proceedings for an offence or for the recovery of a penalty—(*a*) shall apply only as regards criminal offences under the law of any part of the United Kingdom and penalties provided for by such law . . .'

For this purpose offences 'under the law of ' England are treated, no doubt correctly, as
the same as offences which can be tried in an English criminal court. The question then
is whether the conduct alleged by the Sonangol companies is such that it could give rise
to a criminal trial of Mr Lundqvist in England.

It is necessary to consider in more detail how the scheme to defraud the Sonangol
companies is said to have worked. For this purpose I adopt the account given by Leggatt J:

> 'The description given by Mr Simons was to this effect. The first plaintiff, which
> is an Angolan national corporation, sold crude oil at a price instructed by the first
> defendant to customers who had no need to take physical delivery of the oil. Such
> customers frequently wish to sell the oil immediately. The first defendant from the
> office of the second plaintiff in London therefore arranged for the oil to be sold on
> by the customer. The vast majority of crude oil cargoes traced by the accountants
> was sold on by the initial purchaser either to Sonangol SA or to companies known as
> Beverley Inc and Beverley SA. The price of the onward sale by the customer was also
> fixed by the first defendant. Prior to arranging the sale from the first plaintiff to the
> customer and the onward sale by the customer to Sonangol SA or one of the Beverley
> companies, the first defendant would have agreed or been aware of a final sale by
> Sonangol SA or the Beverley companies or some other intermediate company to an
> end user of the product at a price considerably in excess of that for which the first
> plaintiff was to sell the oil. When the onward sale by the first plaintiff 's customer
> was to Sonangol SA that company would then assign its right to purchase and resell
> the oil, usually to one of the Beverley companies with which at that stage Mr Simons
> believed the first defendant had a connection. I put it in that way because it has
> since been established that there is such a connection. Mr Simons's account of the
> matter continued by saying that the assignee of Sonangol SA would then take
> advantage of the chain of transactions organised by the first defendant and take the
> profit on the sale to the end user which could and should have been available to the
> first plaintiff. When the onward sale by the first plaintiff 's customer was to one of
> the Beverley companies, the same interception of income would occur without need
> for the assignment by Sonangol SA. By arranging the price of sale to the end user
> prior to fixing the price for sale by the first plaintiff to its customer, the first
> defendant was able to ensure that a profit was available to an intermediate company
> in the chain of transactions. In this fashion, so it is said, the substantial sums the
> subject of the Mareva injunctions were syphoned off, which should have belonged
> or been accorded to the plaintiffs.'

There is nothing to indicate that anything done by Mr Lundqvist under such a scheme
was done otherwise than in England. The principal aspect of his conduct said to be
fraudulent may have been sending messages to Sonangol UEE in Angola, in order to
persuade them that a proposed sale price was in line with market levels and a good
bargain; or it may have been agreeing a price on their behalf with customers, in England
or abroad, if he had authority to do so; or it may have been arranging for the profit on
resale to remain with one of his companies and not to be remitted to Sonangol UEE. But
whatever he did was done in England.

On the other hand, it is said that any loss was suffered by Sonangol UEE in Angola. I
am by no means convinced that this is correct. Their banking arrangements have not
been explained in evidence before us, they may have kept dollar balances in New York,
or even (if they feared political trouble there) in London. Since the point was not raised
below, the full facts have not been investigated.

We have been referred to *Board of Trade v Owen* [1957] 1 All ER 411, [1957] AC 602,
R v Harden [1962] 1 All ER 286, [1963] 1 QB 8, *R v Cox (Peter)* [1968] 1 All ER 410,
[1968] 1 WLR 88, *Treacey v DPP* [1971] 1 All ER 110, [1971] AC 537, *R v Governor of
Brixton Prison, ex p Rush* [1969] 1 All ER 316, [1969] 1 WLR 165, *DPP v Doot* [1973] 1 All
ER 940, [1973] AC 807, *R v Hornett* [1975] RTR 256, *R v El-Hakkaoui* [1975] 2 All ER

146, [1975] 1 WLR 396 and *A-G's Reference (No 1 of 1982)* [1983] 2 All ER 721, [1983] QB 751 and to ss 1 and 5 of the Criminal Law Act 1977 as originally enacted. From that material I can see the argument that an English court might not have jurisdiction to try Mr Lundqvist, even on a conspiracy to defraud at common law. And the argument is stronger if the charge were of a statutory conspiracy.

There is another aspect of the problem. Prima facie Mr Lundqvist might be charged, on the facts alleged by the Sonangol companies, either with a common law conspiracy to defraud, or with a statutory conspiracy to commit an offence, which would no doubt be some offence under the Theft Act. But the combined effect of the decisions of the House of Lords in *R v Ayres* [1984] 1 All ER 619, [1984] AC 447 and *R v Cooke* [1986] 2 All ER 985, [1986] AC 909 might have the result that the prosecution would be obliged to charge only a statutory conspiracy to commit an offence under the Theft Act 1968. (The abrogation of the effect of those decisions by s 12 of the Criminal Justice Act 1987 did not come into operation until 20 July 1987 and does not affect things done before that date.)

An interlocutory appeal in a civil case, where the points were not argued below and the full facts are not available, is scarcely the right occasion to decide questions which may have important repercussions in the criminal law, unless it is essential to do so. For my part, I am content to accept what was agreed by the parties before both Hobhouse J and Leggatt J, that the conduct alleged against Mr Lundqvist could give rise to his being prosecuted here on a criminal charge if he were found in this country. In para 6 of his first affidavit, sworn on 1 December 1987, Mr Lundqvist said:

'. . . on the plaintiffs' case I am clearly exposed to criminal proceedings in England in respect of the same conspiracy to defraud which the plaintiffs are alleging in the action.'

That was not challenged in evidence or argument for two years. I think it right to decide this appeal on the basis that it is correct.

(B) *Section 31 of the Theft Act 1968*
    This provides:

'A person shall not be excused, by reason that to do so may incriminate that person . . . of an offence under this Act—(*a*) from answering any question put to that person in proceedings for the recovery or administration of any property, for the execution of any trust or for an account of any property or dealings with property; or (*b*) from complying with any order made in any such proceedings; but no statement or admission made by a person in answering a question put or complying with an order made as aforesaid shall, in proceedings for an offence under this Act, be admissible in evidence against that person . . .'

Does this section provide sufficient protection for Mr Lundqvist, and remove the privilege against self-incrimination? Whether the charge be of conspiracy to defraud at common law or of a statutory conspiracy to commit an offence under the 1968 Act, I do not think that the conspiracy itself would be 'an offence under this Act' or 'proceedings for an offence under this Act'. Exactly the same words occurring in the Misuse of Drugs Act 1971 were held in *R v Cuthbertson* [1980] 2 All ER 401 at 403, [1981] AC 470 at 480 per Lord Diplock not to embrace a conspiracy at common law or a statutory conspiracy under the Criminal Law Act 1977. In *Khan v Khan* [1982] 2 All ER 60, [1982] 1 WLR 513 it was suggested that the defendants might be liable to be charged under the Forgery Act 1913 as well as, or instead of, with offences under the 1968 Act. This court held that they were not protected by the privilege against self-incrimination. Stephenson LJ said that it was fanciful to suppose that the first defendant would be prosecuted for forgery alone, and that proceedings for theft and forgery would still be proceedings for an offence under the 1968 Act and added ([1982] 2 All ER 60 at 65, [1982] 1 WLR 513 at 519):

'But if an attempt were made to introduce any statement made by the first defendant in compliance with this order into proceedings for theft and forgery, the court would have to consider the substance of the proceedings and the real reason why he had not been excused from compliance with the order, and then the proceedings will be seen to be in substance proceedings for an offence under the Theft Act and so he could not have been compelled to incriminate himself except for an offence under that Act. Accordingly, any such statement would not be admissible in evidence against him in the proceedings.'

Without in any way seeking to depart from that decision, by which we are bound, I do not think that it extends to conspiracy or requires us to adopt a different construction of the 1968 Act than that laid down for the Misuse of Drugs Act 1971 in *R v Cuthbertson*. Accordingly, I would hold that s 31 of the 1968 Act does not provide adequate protection for Mr Lundqvist in the present case, or remove the privilege against self-incrimination.

(C) *Could the fourth defendant, SLOES, be prosecuted here?*
SLOES are also a Liberian corporation, and there may well be legal or practical difficulties in prosecuting them here. But the order that is challenged in this appeal requires SLOES to answer by Mr Lundqvist as to the value and whereabouts of *his* assets. Even if 'his' is altered to 'their' (or 'its'), I consider that Mr Lundqvist is entitled to claim privilege if he can show that compliance with that order would tend to incriminate him. In reaching that conclusion I do not think that I am departing from what Lord Diplock said in *Rio Tinto Zinc Corp v Westinghouse Electric Corp* [1978] 1 All ER 434 at 465, [1978] AC 547 at 637.
As will appear later, I am prepared to uphold the claim for privilege in part. It may be that the Sonangol companies, instead of the more limited order which I shall propose in respect of both Mr Lundqvist and SLOES, would prefer to have the order against SLOES be that they answer both as to the value and whereabouts of their assets *by their proper officer other than Mr Lundqvist.* I would be prepared to hear counsel on that alternative.

(D) *The standard of proof for a claim to the privilege against self-incrimination*
We were referred to a great many cases on this topic, extending over many years. Whilst there are differences in phraseology and emphasis, it is in my judgment possible to discern a theme which runs through most of them. It is stated by Cockburn CJ in *R v Boyes* (1861) 1 B & S 311 at 330, [1861–73] All ER Rep 172 at 174:

'. . . the Court must see, from the circumstances of the case and the nature of the evidence which the witness is called to give, that there is reasonable ground to apprehend danger to the witness from his being compelled to answer.'

The same test is to be found in *R v Garbett* (1847) 1 Den 236 at 257, 169 ER 227 at 235, *Ex p Reynolds, re Reynolds* (1882) 20 Ch D 294 at 299, 301, [1881–5] All ER Rep 997 at 999, 1001, *Lamb v Munster* (1882) 10 QBD 110 at 113, *Triplex Safety Glass Co Ltd v Lancegaye Safety Glass* (1934) *Ltd* [1939] 2 All ER 613 at 617, [1939] 2 KB 395 at 404, *Re Westinghouse Electric Corp Uranium Contract Litigation MDL Docket No 235 (No 2)* [1977] 3 All ER 717 at 721, [1978] AC 547 at 574 and *Khan v Khan* [1982] 2 All ER 60 at 64, [1982] 1 WLR 513 at 518. If there is a very small difference between that and the 'reasonable probability that his answer will or may criminate him' of *Re Genese, ex p Gilbert* (1886) 3 Morr 223 at 226–227, then I prefer reasonable ground to apprehend danger.
The other side of the coin appears from time to time. In the *Rio Tinto Zinc* case Lord Denning MR spoke of 'a remote or insubstantial risk', Roskill LJ 'no more than a fanciful possibility', Shaw LJ 'tenuous or illusory or so improbable as to be virtually without substance', Viscount Dilhorne 'not fanciful' and Lord Diplock also used the word 'fanciful' (see [1977] 3 All ER 717 at 722, 726, 728, [1978] AC 547 at 574, 579, 581, [1978] 1 All

ER 434 at 457, 465, [1978] AC 547 at 628, 637). In *Rank Film Distributors Ltd v Video Information Centre* [1981] 2 All ER 76 at 84, [1982] AC 380 at 446 Lord Fraser again used the phrase 'by no means remote or fanciful'.

The substance of the test is thus that there must be grounds to apprehend danger to the witness, and those grounds must be reasonable, rather than fanciful. Other points that emerge from the cases are these: (i) the affidavit claiming privilege is not conclusive (see *R v Boyes, Ex p Reynolds* and *Khan v Khan*); (ii) the deponent is not bound to go into detail, if to do so would itself deprive him of protection (see *Short v Mercier* (1851) 3 Mac & G 205 at 217, 42 ER 239 at 244 and the *Rio Tinto Zinc* case); (iii) '. . . if the fact of the witness being in danger be once made to appear, great latitude should be allowed to him in judging for himself of the effect of any particular question . . .' (see *R v Boyes* (1861) 1 B & S 311, [1861–73] All ER Rep 172 at 174, the *Rio Tinto Zinc* case and *Khan v Khan*); (iv) the privilege is not available where the witness is already at risk, and the risk would not be increased if he were required to answer (see *Brebner v Perry* [1961] SASR 177 and the *Rio Tinto Zinc* case); and (v) 'If it is one step, having a tendency to criminate him, he is not to be compelled to answer' (see *Paxton v Douglas* (1809) 16 Ves 239 at 242, 33 ER 975 at 976), '. . . as it is one link in a chain of proof' (see *Paxton v Douglas* (1812) 19 Ves 225 at 227, 34 ER 502 at 503). That last point recurs in other cases (eg the *Rio Tinto Zinc* case), and may be important. I am inclined to think that it refers to any fact which a prosecutor would wish to prove in order to establish the guilt of the witness on a criminal charge. In the *Rank Film Distributors* case [1981] 2 All ER 76 at 82, [1982] AC 380 at 443 Lord Wilberforce said that disclosure 'may set in train a process which may lead to incrimination or may lead to the discovery of real evidence of an incriminating character.' That may be thought to go rather further, and to protect a man from having to disclose the names of those who could give evidence against him, assuming that there was otherwise power to require that information. (See also *Short v Mercier* (1851) 20 LJ Ch 289 at 292, 'how evidence can be got'.) I am not presently convinced that the privilege, by virtue of the doctrine of links in a chain, extends as far as that. But the point need not be decided in this case.

(E) *Is the standard of proof achieved in this case?*

It is in my judgment plain that 'the fact of the witness being in danger', to quote from Cockburn CJ in *R v Boyes*, has been established in the case of Mr Lundqvist. The question is whether the value and whereabouts of his overseas assets would form a link in the chain of proof against him on a criminal charge. He is to be allowed 'great latitude' in judging that for himself. And it appears to me distinctly probable that the value of his assets may be such a link, not, I hasten to add, that it will be. Suppose, for example, that he has $US88m worth of assets overseas. I do not doubt that a prosecutor would wish to prove this on a charge of conspiracy to defraud. No doubt he would also wish to prove, if he could, that Mr Lundqvist was not a man of means before 1983, and did not have any other source of such wealth between 1983 and the present date. But his present assets, if of that order, would unquestionably be material for the jury to consider, as one link in the chain.

So I would uphold the claim for privilege in so far as Mr Lundqvist and SLOES are required to state the value of his assets overseas. But I cannot see that the same reasoning applies to the nature or situation of those assets. That information is surely innocuous; or at any rate I do not presently see reasonable grounds to apprehend danger to Mr Lundqvist if it is disclosed. And it will be of value to the Sonangol companies in enabling them to police the Mareva injunction. Counsel for Mr Lundqvist and SLOES submits that the Sonangol companies will be able to get information as to value from other sources once the nature and situation of the assets are disclosed. If that be right, it would be necessary to decide whether such information as to nature and situation qualifies as a link in the chain, and thus is protected from disclosure. But I do not think that counsel's submission is well founded. Bearing in mind undertakings (vii) and (viii) in the order of

Phillips J, which I have already set out, I do not see reasonable grounds for supposing that
a the Sonangol companies will be able to obtain information as to the value of assets abroad
to any significant extent, without first obtaining the leave of the English court, which
should be granted only if appropriate in the light of this judgment. In passing I would
mention that undertaking (viii) appears to me to be inappropriately worded: proceedings
in a foreign court may affect the interests of Mr Lundqvist and SLOES even if they are
proceedings against a third party, such as a bank where they may have an account.

b   There are two more points to be mentioned under this head. First, it was suggested
that Mr Lundqvist would be in no greater danger of incrimination if ordered to disclose
the value of his assets than he is in already, since the Serious Fraud Office has power to
require answers to questions, or at any rate would have that power if he came to this
country: see s 2 of the Criminal Justice Act 1987. However, apart from the question
whether the Serious Fraud Office is likely to exercise its powers under that section against
c Mr Lundqvist, it is to be observed that there is some degree of protection against use of
information thus obtained in criminal proceedings. As I understand s 2(8)(*b*) a person's
answers may be used, not to found a case against him on a criminal charge, but only to
rebut evidence which he may give inconsistent with his answers. So I would not regard
this case as coming within the doctrine of *Brebner v Perry*, that the privilege is not
available if disclosure would make the situation of the person at risk no worse than it is
d already.

Secondly, it is argued with some force that Mr Lundqvist must surely have *some* assets
abroad which were innocently obtained, and that he should not be allowed to make a
blanket claim to privilege in respect of all his assets abroad. There are occasions, as
Hobhouse J said at an early stage in this dispute, where a person should not be required
to pick and choose which questions he will answer, as 'that very exercise would tend to
e incriminate him beyond the mere fact of his claiming privilege'. On the other hand, the
general rule is, as Leggatt J said, that it is wrong to comment adversely about a person
who claims privilege. I do not see that Mr Lundqvist would be endangered if he were to
say, for example, that he owned a house in Sweden worth £500,000, but otherwise
declined to answer on the ground of privilege. And I cannot be confident that he has
f directed himself correctly in that respect. So it is arguable that he should be ordered to
swear a further affidavit in the light of this judgment. But seeing that he will in any
event have to disclose the location of all his assets abroad, although not their value, I do
not consider it necessary to take that course.

g (F) *'Trifling with the court'*
This topic takes its name from the judgment of Pollock CB in *Adams v Lloyd* (1858) 3
H & N 351 at 362, 157 ER 506 at 510:

> '... where the Judge is perfectly certain that the witness is trifling with the
> authority of the Court, and availing himself of the rule of law to keep back the
> truth, having in reality no ground whatever for claiming the privilege, then the
h > Judge is right in insisting on his answering the question.'

See also the *Triplex Safety Glass* case [1939] 2 All ER 613 at 617, [1939] 2 KB 395 at 403.
In this case a defence and counterclaim has been served on behalf of Mr Lundqvist and
SLOES, setting up an affirmative case as to the innocence of the transactions in question.
Furthermore that case has been verified to a large extent by their solicitor, in an affidavit
j of information and belief. It is said that there is inconsistency in Mr Lundqvist claiming
the privilege against self-incrimination.

I can see that a problem would arise if there were Ord 14 proceedings which did not
happen in this case, in which a defendant swore to facts consistent only with his
innocence, followed by an affidavit of the same person resisting discovery, in which he
positively stated that he would be incriminated by disclosure. One or other affidavit

would then be perjured. But here in para 6 of his fifth affidavit, which is the affidavit relevant to this appeal, as in his first which I have already quoted, Mr Lundqvist was careful to say that 'on the Plaintiffs' case' he was clearly exposed to criminal proceedings (my emphasis).

That, in my judgment, reveals the answer to this point. It is the Sonangol companies who say that Mr Lundqvist was fraudulent. So it cannot lie in their mouth to say that he is not telling the truth when he claims that he would be incriminated. Or if they do the inconsistency is theirs, not his. I am inclined to think that the answer would be the same if Mr Lundqvist had personally sworn affidavits saying that he had an innocent explanation of the transactions and also that he would in fact be incriminated, although whether the same legal adviser could have drafted both seems to me open to question. One or other of the affidavits would have been false and perjured, but the court would not know which; and it would not be open to the Sonangol companies to point to the affidavit of innocence and claim that one to be the truth.

Accordingly, I would allow this appeal to the extent of deleting the words 'value and' from the order of Phillips J. I would also make some amendment to undertaking (viii) in that order.

BELDAM LJ. The plaintiffs in these proceedings are three state-owned oil companies set up to explore, produce and market Angolan crude and fuel oil. They claim that the defendants have defrauded them of millions of dollars in oil revenues. The first plaintiff is registered in Angola, the second is an English company set up to arrange and organise trading transactions through its London offices. The third plaintiff, a company registered in Liberia, has undertaken some of the trading transactions. Both the second and third plaintiffs are wholly owned by the first plaintiff company.

The first defendant is a consultant in the oil industry. His services were provided by the fourth defendant to the plaintiffs for the purpose of advising them and arranging the marketing of their crude and fuel oil products worldwide. For this purpose the second plaintiff company was set up with headquarters in London to arrange sales for the first and third plaintiffs. He was in effective control of the London office of the second plaintiff.

Between February 1983 and February 1987 the first defendant arranged sales of the first plaintiff's products worldwide. In February 1987 the agreement by which he did this was brought to an end on terms agreed between him and the first plaintiff. Among other things they provided that he should receive a substantial sum of money (over £stg1m) and a continuing annual supply of oil, which would have produced a very substantial revenue for him.

After terminating the first defendant's services, the plaintiffs began inquiries and investigations. From these it emerged that a large number of contracts for the sale of their products had been arranged by the first defendant acting in concert with the other defendants in such a way that the price received by the first and third plaintiffs for their oil was substantially below that which could and should have been obtained. In all it is alleged that the defendants succeeded in depriving the first and third plaintiffs of revenues amounting to approximately $US90m. The plaintiffs therefore commenced proceedings in the courts of this country to try to recover the sums they had lost. In the course of these proceedings they have, since November 1987, sought a number of orders to try to ensure that any judgment they may obtain is not frustrated by the first and fourth defendants disposing of their assets.

The plaintiffs first sought and obtained from Alliott J an ex parte order in the usual Anton Piller and Mareva form to search six premises in London and Berkshire and two cars for documents, including contracts, telexes, contract notes etc, which they alleged had been removed from the offices of the second plaintiff by the first defendant and his secretary, the second defendant. They further sought an order restraining the defendants from altering, destroying or otherwise disposing of the documents in question.

In addition, however, they sought and were granted an order for discovery in very
a wide terms. They sought answers to questions concerning the conduct by the first
defendant of the first and third plaintiffs' affairs in London. The order obtained ex parte
was duly executed, but on 26 November 1987 the defendants applied to have part of it
set aside. It came before Hobhouse J inter partes. He varied the ex parte order by
requiring the plaintiffs to set out in writing the questions the first defendant was to
answer; he gave the defendants leave to object to them, or any of them, by 2 December.
b He ordered that any affidavit of assets which had been required under the terms of the
Mareva order be restricted to assets within the jurisdiction and further set aside that part
of the order which related to discovery of documents because it was contrary to the
principle that no person could be compelled to produce evidence which tended to
incriminate him. He ordered the return of all the documents and further ordered that
the first defendant identify those documents for which he claimed privilege.
c   In the result the first defendant declined to answer any of the questions of significance
on grounds that to do so would, or might, incriminate him and further claimed privilege
on the same ground in respect of the documents. Eventually Hobhouse J upheld the
general claim of privilege on 4 December 1987.
     In the meantime the pleadings in the action proceeded and were closed on 10 June
1988. It emerged in broad terms that the first defendant was prepared to admit many of
d the facts alleged by the first and third plaintiffs but he contended that the first and third
plaintiffs were at all times aware of those facts and of the conduct of which they now
complained. The schemes which they now contended amounted to conspiracy to defraud
were schemes set up under express instructions from the first plaintiff for the purpose of
concealing from the Bank of Angola the true nature and extent of the earnings from sales
of the products. Any moneys which were received by the first defendant or companies
e controlled by him had in fact been used in projects or schemes for investment in Angola
in political or commercial initiatives for Angolan national interests.
     On 27 April 1988 the plaintiffs applied for an account to be taken of all sums which
had been received by the defendants for and on behalf of the plaintiffs.
     Between May and July 1988 in three decisions, *Babanaft International Co SA v Bassatne*
f [1989] 1 All ER 433, [1990] Ch 13, *Republic of Haiti v Duvalier* [1989] 1 All ER 456, [1990]
QB 202 and *Derby & Co Ltd v Weldon (No 1)* [1989] 1 All ER 469, [1990] Ch 48, this court
held that where the plaintiff could establish that assets in England and Wales were
insufficient to meet the plaintiff's claim and that the defendant had substantial assets
overseas the court had jurisdiction to restrain a defendant who was not resident in the
jurisdiction from dealing with assets outside the jurisdiction. Further, where there was
evidence that a defendant appeared to have dealt with assets outside the jurisdiction in
g such a manner as to suggest that he was seeking to avoid the effect of an order or
judgment of the court, or might do so, there was jurisdiction to make an order to require
the defendant to disclose his assets to enable the plaintiff to 'police' the Mareva injunction.
Consequently on 15 May 1989 the plaintiffs sought ex parte from Phillips J an order,
which he made on 19 May 1989, that the first and fourth defendants be restrained from
h disposing of, or otherwise dealing with, any of their assets outside England and Wales
save in so far as the value of such assets, property, money or goods exceeded $US90m.
The plaintiffs also sought and obtained an order that within 28 days the first and fourth
defendants by the first defendant make and file an affidavit giving details of the value
and whereabouts of all assets, property, money or goods wherever situated but with the
proviso that the defendants could, by giving notice, apply to set aside the order requiring
j them to make and file such affidavit. The order also included the usual provisos
protecting those outside the jurisdiction who might be affected by the making of the
order.
     The first and fourth defendants retaliated by issuing a summons on 7 July 1989 to set
aside the order of Phillips J on the ground that the plaintiffs had failed to prove the
necessary exceptional circumstances to justify the making of a worldwide Mareva

injunction. They further sought to have set aside that part of Phillips J's order requiring them to file an affidavit giving details of the value and whereabouts of all their assets, property, money and goods on the ground that the first and fourth defendants were entitled to claim privilege against self-incrimination in respect of the information, the subject of the order.

The defendants' summons and applications were heard by Leggatt J on 27 June 1989. He concluded that in principle the defendants might well be entitled to claim privilege but that the claim which they had at that time made was insufficient in form. The disclosure by the first and fourth defendants of details of the value and whereabouts of their assets, property, money and goods would not, without more information, provide evidence of any conspiracy to defraud or give rise to any increase in the risk that the first and fourth defendants might be prosecuted. It was not enough for the defendants or their solicitors to state that they believed that their answers might tend to incriminate them. They were not by that statement excused from answering at all. Consequently he held that the first and fourth defendants should respond on affidavit though they would have the right in that affidavit to persist in a claim to privilege in support of any matter which they contended would expose them to jeopardy. Consequently he dismissed the defendants' application with costs. He gave leave to both the defendants and the plaintiffs to appeal against his order. That is the appeal which the defendants now pursue before the court.

The first and fourth defendants argue that if they are called on to give any information at all about their assets, including their whereabouts and value, they are being called on to give information which might tend to incriminate them. Even to give information about those of their assets which would not of itself tend to incriminate them would or might assist the plaintiffs to trace the whereabouts and thus the value of other assets, thus indirectly leading to a tendency to incriminate. The judge was therefore wrong to require the first and fourth defendants to go into any greater detail than they had already done in paras 47 to 49 of the eighth affidavit of Mr Thorp, a partner in the firm of solicitors acting for the defendants and in the fifth affidavit of the first defendant. Two questions were initially raised. The first was whether the court is bound to accept the statement of the defendants that to give details of the value and whereabouts of their assets would tend to incriminate them. The second was whether the defendants were justified in refusing to give details of assets which, though not themselves incriminating, might nevertheless lead to a course of inquiry which would or might assist the bringing of proceedings against them.

On these questions we were referred to numerous cases decided over the last two hundred years. Many of them were considered in *Ex p Reynolds, re Reynolds* (1882) 20 Ch D 294, [1881–5] All ER Rep 997. In *Ex p Reynolds* 20 Ch D 294 at 299, [1881–5] All ER Rep 997 at 999 Jessel MR accepted as stating the law correctly the decision of the Court of Queen's Bench in *R v Boyes* (1861) 1 B & S 311, [1861–73] All ER Rep 172 and cited with approval the passage from the judgment of Cockburn CJ in which he said (1 B & S 311 at 329–330, [1861–73] All ER Rep 172 at 173–174):

'It was also contended that a bare possibility of legal peril was sufficient to entitle a witness to protection: nay, further, that the witness was the sole judge as to whether his evidence would bring him into danger of the law: and that the statement of his belief to that effect, if not manifestly made malâ fide, should be received as conclusive. With the latter of these propositions we are altogether unable to concur. Upon a review of the authorities, we are clearly of opinion that the view of the law propounded by Lord *Wensleydale* in *Osborn* v. *The London Dock Company* ((1855) 10 Exch 698, 156 ER 620), and acted on by V.-C. *Stuart,* in *Sidebottom* v. *Adkins* ((1857) 29 LTOS 310), is the correct one; and that, to entitle a party called as a witness to the privilege of silence, the Court must see, from the circumstances of the case and the nature of the evidence which the witness is called to give, that there is reasonable ground to apprehend danger to the witness from his being compelled to answer. We indeed quite agree that, if the fact of the witness being in danger be once made to appear, great latitude should be allowed to him in judging for himself of the effect of any particular question: there being no doubt, as observed by *Alderson B.*, in *Osborn v. The London Dock Company*, that a question which might appear at first sight a very innocent one, might, by affording a link in a chain of evidence, become the means of bringing home an offence to the party answering. Subject to this reservation, a Judge is in our opinion, bound to insist on a witness answering unless he is satisfied that the answer will tend to place the witness in peril.'

Jessel MR went on:

'That decision, as it appears to me, states the law correctly and if it were necessary for the Court of Appeal to affirm it, we should, I think, be doing well and wisely in saying that we do affirm it.'

Later in his judgment he said (20 Ch D 294 at 300, [1881–5] All ER Rep 997 at 1000):

'Perhaps our law has gone even too far in the direction of protecting a witness from the chance of convicting himself. But without at all impugning the policy of the law, there must certainly be a larger policy which requires that a witness should answer when the Judge thinks that he is objecting to answer, not *bonâ fide* with the view of claiming privilege to protect himself, but in order to prevent other parties from getting that testimony which is necessary for the purposes of justice.'

More recently in *Re Westinghouse Electric Corp Uranium Contract Litigation MDL Docket No 235 (No 2)* [1977] 3 All ER 717 at 721, [1978] AC 547 at 574 Lord Denning MR, after referring to *Ex p Reynolds, re Reynolds*, said:

'It is for the judge to say whether there is reasonable ground or not. Reasonable ground may appear from the circumstances of the case or from matters put foward by the witness himself. He should not be compelled to go into detail because that may involve his disclosing the very matter to which he takes objection. But if it appears to the judge that, by being compelled to answer, a witness may be furnishing evidence against himself, which could be used against him in criminal proceedings or in proceedings for a penalty, then his objection should be upheld.'

I would therefore hold that the court is not simply bound by the statement of the defendants that to give the information requested would put them in peril of incrimination. The court is not only entitled but is bound to look further and to consider the merits of the claim which is advanced.

On the second question it will be observed that the passage from the judgment of Cockburn CJ in *R v Boyes* which Jessel MR approved in *Ex p Reynolds, re Reynolds* that if the information requested might, by affording a link in a chain of evidence, become the means of bringing home an offence to the party giving it, that that is a sufficient degree of peril to justify a refusal to answer. Following the *Sixteenth Report of the Law Reform Committee on Privilege in Civil Proceedings* (Cmnd 3472 (1967)), when the Civil Evidence Act 1968 was enacted, in dealing with the right of a person to refuse to answer any question or to produce any document or thing, Parliament used the words 'if to do so would tend to expose that person to proceedings for an offence or for the recovery of a penalty' (see s 14(1)). It is significant that Parliament referred to a 'tendency to expose' and to proceedings and not merely to conviction. Thus, in my judgment, it is sufficient to support a claim to privilege against self-incrimination that the answers sought might lead to a line of inquiry which would or might form a significant step in the chain of evidence required for a prosecution. I find support for this view in the judgments in the *Westinghouse Electric Corp* case and in *Rank Film Distributors Ltd v Video Information Centre* [1981] 2 All ER 76, [1982] AC 380. In the former case Lord Wilberforce accepted the proposition that the validation and connection of documents by sworn evidence with the RTZ companies would have a tendency to increase the risk of exposure to a penalty (see [1978] 1 All ER 434 at 445, [1978] AC 547 at 612). In the latter he said ([1981] 2 All ER 76 at 82, [1982] AC 380 at 443):

> 'Moreover, whatever direct use may or may not be made of information given, or material disclosed, under the compulsory process of the court, it must not be overlooked that, quite apart from that, its provision or disclosure may set in train a process which may lead to incrimination or may lead to the discovery of real evidence of an incriminating character. In the present case, this cannot be discounted as unlikely; it is not only a possible but probably the intended result. The party from whom disclosure is asked is entitled, on established law, to be protected from these consequences.'

Before Leggatt J it had been common ground that, for the purposes of considering a claim to privilege against incrimination, the fact that the first and fourth defendants might be liable to penalties under Angolan law was immaterial. That question had been considered by Morritt J in *Arab Monetary Fund v Hashim* [1989] 3 All ER 466, [1989] 1 WLR 565. He held that the privilege against self-incrimination did not extend to criminal offences and penalties under foreign law.

It was equally not in issue before the judge that the relevant proceedings in English law were proceedings for conspiracy to defraud. At that hearing it was not argued that the defendant could be in no peril of incrimination because the conspiracy to defraud had as its principal object defrauding the first and third plaintiffs in Angola, an offence for which they could not be convicted in England and Wales. However, when the court drew to the attention of the parties *A-G's Reference (No 1 of 1982)* [1983] 2 All ER 721, [1983] QB 751, the speech of Lord Tucker in *Board of Trade v Owen* [1957] 1 All ER 411 at 422, [1957] AC 602 at 634 and *R v Cox (Peter)* [1968] 1 All ER 410, [1968] 1 WLR 88, counsel for the plaintiffs argued that it was for the defendants to establish that they were at risk of criminal proceedings in this country and on the basis of the three cases referred to he contended that they had not done so.

It was further argued that, in the light of the decision in *R v Ayres* [1984] 1 All ER 619, [1984] AC 447, any prosecution to which the first and fourth defendants were exposed would be more likely to allege a statutory conspiracy under the Criminal Law Act 1977, s 1 on the basis that the conduct agreed on by the parties necessarily amounted to or involved the commission of an offence under the Theft Act 1968 by one or more of the parties. Since s 1(4) of that Act provides that for an offence of conspiracy under that Act to be triable in England and Wales, the offence contemplated must itself be an offence so triable, and since the probable offence was that of either theft or obtaining by deception, neither of those offences would have taken place in England and Wales. The basis of English criminal jurisdiction depends on proof of the last act necessary for the completion of the offence having been committed within the jurisdiction. The facts of the case therefore made it extremely unlikely that proceedings would be brought in England and Wales. Accordingly, there was no more than a theoretical possibility that the first and fourth defendants would be at risk of prosecution.

Counsel for the defendants countered these arguments by contending that since most if not all of the overt acts in pursuit of the conspiracy were done in England and Wales, the law was by no means settled that they could not be prosecuted here even though the principal object was to defraud the first and third defendants in Angola. Alternatively, counsel for the defendants contended that as the plaintiffs had conceded that there was a risk of proceedings in this country before the judge and the point had only arisen in the course of argument, the evidence was not directed to this issue and on the basis of the evidence and the pleadings the facts were insufficiently clear to establish that it was the principal purpose of the conspiracy to defraud the plaintiffs only in Angola. The second

plaintiff was an English company who on the evidence could have suffered loss as well as
a the first and third plaintiffs in Angola.

The question of exposure to criminal proceedings of the defendants, whether under
the Theft Act 1968 or for conspiracy to defraud, is a complicated one which would of
necessity depend on a detailed consideration of the facts of the particular transactions
carried out by the first and fourth defendants and whether any acts done by them in
England and Wales gave rise to a risk of their being prosecuted for a criminal offence
b committed within that jurisdiction. The question is further complicated by the law of
conspiracy. As a result of *R v Ayres* [1984] 1 All ER 619, [1984] AC 447, as modified by
the speeches in *R v Cooke* [1986] 2 All ER 985, [1986] AC 909, the choice by a prosecutor
of the appropriate charge is one of considerable complexity. Nevertheless, because of the
terms of s 1(4) of the Criminal Law Act 1977, the question whether it is an offence under
English law to conspire to commit a Theft Act offence abroad would still remain.

c Offences committed under the Thefts Acts themselves require careful analysis to
decide where they are committed. Save in exceptional cases such as murder, the
jurisdiction of the English criminal courts is territorial. It is based on proof of crimes
committed in England and Wales. Generally speaking it is based on the theory that an
offence occurs where the last act necessary for its completion occurs. Even the analysis of
the last act necessary for the completion of an offence has led to a number of complicated
d and sometimes seemingly inconsistent provisions: see, for example, *R v Harden* [1962] 1
All ER 286, [1963] 1 QB 8, *R v Tirado* (1974) 59 Cr App Rep 80, *R v Thompson* [1984] 3
All ER 565, [1984] 1 WLR 962, *R v Tomsett* [1985] Crim LR 369 and *R v Governor of
Pentonville Prison, ex p Osman* [1989] 3 All ER 701, [1990] 1 WLR 277.

Counsel for the defendants argued on the basis of the speeches in *DPP v Doot* [1973] 1
All ER 940, [1973] AC 807 that even if the principal object of a conspiracy was to defraud
e a victim who was abroad, nevertheless if overt acts in furtherance of the conspiracy were
carried out in England and Wales it was at least arguable that those responsible might be
subject to a risk of prosecution in this country. The issue in *DPP v Doot* was different
from that in the present case. It was whether those who enter into a conspiracy abroad to
commit an offence in England and Wales can be prosecuted for conspiracy here. The
House held that such a conspiracy was triable in England and Wales but it is not entirely
f clear from the speeches whether this was so only if an act was done in England and Wales
in pursuance of the conspiracy or whether such acts were regarded merely as evidence of
the existence of an agreement to commit a crime here. Whilst it is clear that an agreement
made abroad to commit an offence is indictable here as a conspiracy provided that the
offence is to be committed in England and Wales and while the agreement continues an
act in pursuance of it is done here, it in no way follows that because an act or acts are
g done in England or Wales in pursuance of an agreement to commit an offence abroad,
such a conspiracy is triable here.

A conspiracy formed in England and Wales to defraud persons abroad poses, in my
judgment, more formidable problems for any successful prosecution. Not only are there
the three decisions already referred to, *Board of Trade v Owen*, *R v Cox (Peter)* and *A-G's
h Reference (No 1 of 1982)*, but it is to be observed that in each of these cases overt acts had
in fact been done in England or Wales. Nevertheless in *R v Cox (Peter)* and *A-G's Reference
(No 1 of 1982)* the court found that an agreement made here to commit a crime abroad
was not an offence indictable under English law. Lord Diplock in his speech in *Treacey v
DPP* [1971] 1 All ER 110 at 123, [1971] AC 537 at 563, speaking of the judgment of the
House in *Board of Trade v Owen* [1957] 1 All ER 411, [1957] AC 602, said:

j 'The unanimous opinion of this House was given in the speech of Lord Tucker.
He treated the question correctly, not as one of jurisdiction but as to what were the
characteristics of the crime of conspiracy at common law. The conclusion reached
on examination of the authorities was that the common law crime of conspiracy did
not extend to an agreement to achieve an object which was unlawful in a foreign
country or to use means to achieve it which were unlawful in a foreign country.'

The crime of conspiracy at common law was abolished by the Criminal Law Act 1977 except for conspiracy to defraud and some instances of tending to corrupt public morals and outrage public decency. One of the main objections to the common law crime of conspiracy was that it rendered persons liable to conviction for agreeing with each other to do acts which would not have been criminal if done by them individually. The crime of conspiracy to defraud was retained because, if it had been abolished, a number of gaps would have been left in the criminal law: see *Conspiracy to Defraud* Law Commission working paper no 104 (1987). There is no general offence under English law of defrauding. Moreover, the crime of conspiracy to defraud is one which is unknown in countries whose criminal law is based on the civil law. It is therefore entirely possible that acts in pursuance of the agreement may be done in England and Wales which are punishable neither by the law of England and Wales nor by the law of the country where the object of the agreement is intended to be achieved. If therefore the object of the conspiracy in the present case was to defraud the first and third plaintiffs in Angola and elsewhere outside England and Wales, notwithstanding that acts were done in this country to achieve that object, I would entertain great doubt whether the first and fourth defendants were in peril of conviction in England and Wales on such a charge.

Further uncertainties arise from the nature of the claim made against the first and fourth defendants. Essentially, as I understood the allegation of fraud made by the plaintiffs, it is that the first and fourth defendants conspired to make a secret profit at the expense of the plaintiffs. It is by no means clear on the evidence whether the plaintiffs were induced to enter into contracts for the sale or transfer of oil products by any active representations made by the first defendant. There is considerable argument in the cases whether such conduct amounts to a criminal offence. Lord Wilberforce in *Tarling v Government of the Republic of Singapore* (1978) 70 Cr App R 77 at 110 was of the view that the making of secret profits in breach of fiduciary duty by itself did not amount to a criminal offence and was different from theft and fraud. An attempt to establish that such conduct amounted to an offence under the Theft Act 1968 failed in *A-G's Reference (No 1 of 1985)* [1986] 2 All ER 219, [1986] QB 491, though this decision and *Tarling's* case may now have to be reconsidered in the light of the decision of the House of Lords in *R v Cooke* [1986] 2 All ER 985, [1986] AC 909.

If, therefore, the question to be decided was whether the first and fourth defendants would be in peril of being convicted of an offence under English law, I would have considerable hesitation in deciding that they were. The question, however, is whether on the appropriate view of the facts the first and fourth defendants have established that in complying with the order of the court they would tend to expose themselves to prosecution. In this context I accept counsel's submission for the defendants that, unless the facts before the court and the state of the law are so certain that the court can come to the firm conclusion that the fear spoken to by the first defendant has no foundation, the claim to privilege is made out. Thus I would hold that the first defendant has established that there is at least a potential risk of exposure to prosecution in this country. However, in the case of the fourth defendant there are additional difficulties not only in proving complicity in any criminal offence but also of serving process on, and securing the appearance of, a foreign corporation which does not carry on business here before a court in England and Wales. Taking these difficulties into consideration with the others to which I have already referred, I would hold that the fourth defendant has failed to establish any more than a bare theoretical possibility that by complying with the order of the court to disclose its assets it would tend to expose itself to prosecution here. The company is registered in Liberia. Counsel for the defendants argued that the basis on which the fourth defendant claimed privilege was that if it was compelled to disclose its assets it might by doing so increase the risk of exposure of the first defendant to criminal proceedings.

The privilege claimed is a privilege against *self* incrimination and does not in my judgment extend in the case of a company to incrimination of its office holders. In *Rio*

Tinto Zinc Corp v Westinghouse Electric Corp [1978] 1 All ER 434, [1978] AC 547 it had
a been submitted that the RTZ companies, being entitled to withhold documents from
production, had a privilege in English law to require their officers to refuse to answer
questions which might provide evidence that would tend to expose the companies to a
penalty. Lord Diplock in his judgment said ([1978] 1 All ER 434 at 465, [1978] AC 547
at 637–638):

b   'At common law, as declared in s 14(1) of the Civil Evidence Act 1968, the
      privilege against self-incrimination was restricted to the incrimination of the person
      claiming it and not anyone else. There is no trace in the decided cases that it is of
      wider application; no textbook old or modern suggests the contrary. It is not for
      your Lordships to manufacture for the purposes of this instant case a new privilege
      hitherto unknown to the law.'

c   I would therefore reject the claim to privilege made on behalf of the fourth defendant
on this ground. However, as Staughton LJ has pointed out, the order of Phillips J was in
terms which required the fourth defendant by the first defendant to make and file an
affidavit giving details of the nature and whereabouts of all 'his' assets. Although it is not
clear, I would have assumed that the company was required to give details of its assets
and not merely of the first defendant's assets.
d   In swearing an affidavit on behalf of the company, the first defendant would be
entitled as deponent to claim, as any witness can claim, the right not to answer on
grounds of self-incrimination. If, therefore, the order were to stand in its present form,
it might prove ineffective to obtain details of the company's assets if in giving those
details the first defendant might incriminate himself.
      If the plaintiffs wished to overcome this difficulty they could, if they thought fit, seek
e a variation of the terms of the order so that it requires the fourth defendant 'by the first
defendant or other proper officer to make and file the affidavit'.
      Alternatively, if the order as a whole is, as later suggested, varied to delete the
requirement to state the value of the assets, the difficulty would disappear.
      To return to the claim of the first defendant, whilst I am satisfied that there is at least a
f potential risk of exposure to prosecution, I am not satisfied that this risk must necessarily
apply to disclosure of every one of his assets as is at present suggested.
      For example he may have assets acquired before 1983, when he undertook to serve the
plaintiffs, and which he still has. Furthermore, assets which he has acquired since 1987,
when he ceased to serve the plaintiffs, would not necessarily expose him to any risk.
      Even in the case of assets acquired between 1983 and 1987 merely to disclose the
location of assets without their value would not, in some countries at least, be likely to
g lead to discovery of the amount of such assets. I can see that to disclose the total value of
all his assets could of itself amount to an important link in evidence leading to a
prosecution. Nevertheless, I am unable to agree with counsel's argument for the
defendants that because the disclosure of the whereabouts and value of some of the first
defendant's assets might expose him to a risk of prosecution that therefore he can decline
h to answer in respect of all his assets.
      For the plaintiffs a further point was taken that since the substance of the case against
the first and fourth defendants amounted to a conspiracy to steal or to obtain by deception
under the Theft Acts, the first and fourth defendants could be required to give the
information requested notwithstanding that to do so might incriminate them. The
plaintiffs relied on s 31 of the Theft Act 1968 and on the decision of this court in *Khan v*
j *Khan* [1982] 2 All ER 60, [1982] 1 WLR 513.
      That case is clearly distinguishable on its facts. It had there been found to be very
unlikely that the defendant, if charged, would be charged with any offence other than an
offence under the Theft Acts though there was a possibility of an offence under the
Forgery and Counterfeiting Act 1981 being added to the indictment.
      In the present case the most likely charges would either be a charge of conspiracy to

defraud at common law or a charge of conspiracy under s 1 of the Criminal Law Act 1977. In neither case would the first and fourth defendants be deprived of the right to claim privilege by the terms of s 31(1) of the Theft Act 1968. The risk to the defendants would not be a risk of incrimination of an offence under the 1968 Act.

A provision depriving a person of such a fundamental right as the right to claim privilege against self-incrimination is undoubtedly to be strictly construed. It is clear from other similar provisions, for example s 72 of the Supreme Court Act 1981, s 434(5) of the Companies Act 1985, s 2(4) of the Criminal Justice Act 1987 and, more recently, s 98 of the Children Act 1989 that when on grounds of public policy Parliament decides that the public importance of certain inquiries overrides the private right to claim privilege against incrimination, it does so in clear and unequivocal terms confined to the particular circumstances in each case. I would therefore reject the argument based on the decision in *Khan v Khan.*

For these reasons I would uphold the judgment of Leggatt J subject to deletion from the order of the details of the value of the first defendant's assets and would allow the appeal only to this limited extent.

SIR NICOLAS BROWNE-WILKINSON V-C. I agree with the judgment of Staughton LJ. I also agree with the judgment of Beldam LJ, save that I prefer to express no view on the questions of criminal law which he discusses. I have no experience in the criminal field and, since we all reach the conclusion that there is a real risk of prosecution in this country, it is not necessary for me to reach any more detailed conclusions on those matters.

However, I must express great concern at the implications of our decision. Although we are allowing the appeal in part, our reasoning makes it clear that a properly formulated claim to privilege against incrimination can be put forward by the first defendant in this case. If he has a valid claim to privilege on discovery in aid of a Mareva injunction, it seems inescapable that he has an equally valid claim to privilege on discovery in the main action. We were told that he had in fact raised such a claim, though it is not before us. Now that this case has focused attention on the possibility of making such a claim for privilege, I fear that many defendants in fraud actions will be able to raise the same claim to privilege: the clearer the fraud alleged, the stronger will be the claim to privilege against self-incrimination. In my experience this is the first time in a fraud case that the claim to such privilege has been raised: now the point has been aired, it will certainly not be the last.

Cases involving frauds of the type alleged in this case are far from rare, and are increasing. In very many of them the proof of the fraud and the discovery of the assets against which any judgment can be enforced fundamentally depends on the court's ability to require the defendant to make disclosure. Although the privilege against self-incrimination is of great importance and should not be impaired, s 31 of the Theft Act 1968 has shown the way to protect both the rights of the defendant in relation to subsequent criminal prosecution and the rights of the plaintiff in pursuing his remedies under the civil law. The privilege against incrimination is removed but the statements and documents obtained in the civil proceedings are not admissible in subsequent criminal proceedings.

A similar problem arose in relation to discovery in aid of an Anton Piller order in a copyright case. In *Rank Film Distributors Ltd v Video Information Centre* [1981] 2 All ER 76, [1982] AC 380 the House of Lords held that the defendants in such a case were entitled to rely on the privilege. The point having emerged, Parliament promptly dealt with it by enacting s 72 of the Supreme Court Act 1981, which applied to such cases the solution contained in s 31 of the Theft Act 1968.

I express the hope that Parliament will consider, as a matter of urgency, extending the provisions of s 31 of the 1968 Act so as to remove the privilege against incrimination in relation to all civil claims relating to property (including claims for damages) but on the terms that the statements made in documents disclosed are not admissible in any criminal proceedings, including conspiracy to defraud whether under statute or at common law. If that is not done, I fear that the effectiveness of civil remedies designed to redress fraud will be seriously impaired.

Appeal allowed in part.

Solicitors: *Clyde & Co* (for the first and fourth defendants); *Simons Muirhead & Burton* (for the plaintiffs).

Celia Fox   Barrister.

Tate Access Floors Inc and another v Boswell and others

CHANCERY DIVISION

SIR NICOLAS BROWNE-WILKINSON V-C

17, 18, 21, 22, 23, 24 MAY, 13 JUNE 1990

Practice – Pre-trial or post-judgment relief – Mareva injunction – Ex parte application – Whether order must contain express undertakings not to start proceedings overseas or use information obtained in United Kingdom for purpose of overseas proceedings.

Practice – Pre-trial or post-judgment relief – Anton Piller order – Privilege against self-incrimination – Plaintiffs alleging conspiracy to defraud – Defendants reasonably apprehending that prosecution for conspiracy to defraud might be brought in United Kingdom and that documents produced or obtained under Anton Piller order might tend to incriminate them – Whether defendants entitled to claim privilege against self-incrimination in respect of disclosure of information – Whether defendants entitled to claim privilege against self-incrimination in respect of order requiring them to permit plaintiffs to enter, search and seize documents – Whether individual defendants entitled to claim privilege against self-incrimination on behalf of corporate defendants with whom they were connected.

Practice – Pre-trial or post-judgment relief – Ex parte application – Disclosure of material facts to court – Failure to disclose proceedings in other jurisdictions – Use of information obtained in English proceedings for collateral or improper purposes – Duty of applicant to disclose material facts – Whether urgency of matter precluding investigation of proceedings in other jurisdictions – Whether use of information obtained under English order in foreign proceedings for purpose of enforcing order of English court amounting to use for collateral or improper purpose – Whether injunction should be discharged because of plaintiffs' conduct in obtaining and executing order.

The first plaintiff, a company incorporated in Maryland, USA, and the second plaintiff, its United Kingdom subsidiary, alleged that the first three defendants (the individual defendants), who were former senior employees of the first plaintiff, had defrauded the plaintiffs by incorporating companies (the corporate defendants) which raised false invoices for payment by the second plaintiff and had then authorised the payments, which were made to those companies through off-shore bank accounts in the Isle of Man and the Channel Islands or through accounts in London. On 2 March 1990 the plaintiffs applied ex parte for, and were granted, worldwide Mareva injunctions and Anton Piller orders restraining the defendants from removing out of the jurisdiction or otherwise dealing with their assets except to the extent that they exceeded £1m, requiring the defendants to disclose and deliver up information and documents and to permit the plaintiffs to enter, search and seize documents, and requiring the defendants to verify on oath the information and documents disclosed and delivered up. In the same month the plaintiffs commenced proceedings against the individual and/or the corporate defendants in the Isle of Man, Jersey and Maryland. The individual defendants applied in the United Kingdom proceedings to have the Mareva and Anton Piller orders set aside on the grounds (i) that the Mareva order was oppressive because it did not contain express undertakings not to start proceedings overseas or to use information obtained in the United Kingdom proceedings for the purpose of overseas proceedings, (ii) that the Anton Piller order infringed the defendants' privilege against self-incrimination, and (iii) that in obtaining the orders the plaintiffs had failed to disclose to the judge that it would be necessary to start substantive proceedings in the Isle of Man and Maryland, that in executing the order the plaintiffs improperly used information obtained in the English proceedings for the collateral or improper purposes of bringing the Isle of Man proceedings without the leave of the court and claiming punitive damages of $US10m in the Maryland court when that relief had not and could not be claimed in the English proceedings and that the plaintiffs had obtained a freezing order from the Maryland court in reliance on evidence known by the plaintiffs to be false.

Held – (1) In any case where a worldwide Mareva order was made it was capable of being oppressive if the plaintiffs were free to start other proceedings in other jurisdictions thereby exposing the defendants to a multiplicity of proceedings and were free to use information obtained under the compulsion of the Mareva order for the purpose of pursuing remedies in other jurisdictions. However, although it would have been preferable to include express undertakings not to start proceedings overseas or to use information obtained in the United Kingdom proceedings for the purpose of overseas proceedings, the form of order granted by the judge imposed on the plaintiffs an implied undertaking not, without the leave of the court, to start proceedings overseas or use the information disclosed otherwise than for the purposes of the proceedings in which the information was obtained. It followed that the Mareva order itself was not oppressive (see p 310 h j and p 311 b to f, post).

(2) The privilege against self-incrimination precluded the making of an ex parte Anton Piller order where, on the facts alleged by the plaintiffs, there was a reasonable apprehension that a prosecution for conspiracy to defraud might be brought in the United Kingdom and that documents produced or obtained under such an order might tend to incriminate them on that charge. Furthermore, the privilege covered not only those parts of the order which required the defendants to produce and verify information and documents but also included that part of the order requiring them to permit the plaintiffs to enter, search and seize documents. Since there was a real risk that the execution of the Anton Piller order would incriminate them the order would be set aside as against the individual defendants, but it would not be set aside as against the corporate defendants since a person could not claim privilege against incrimination by a third party and therefore the individual defendants were not entitled to put forward the claim to privilege on behalf of the corporate defendants while at the same time denying that they were mere creatures of the individual defendants and taking advantage of the separate corporate identity when it suited them (see p 312 b to d g, p 313 f, p 314 d e j to p 315 a d to f h, post); *Sociedade Nacional de Combustiveis de Angola UEE v Lundqvist* [1990] 3 All ER 283 applied; *Rank Film Distributors Ltd v Video Information Centre* [1981] 2 All ER 76 explained; *Green v Weaver* (1827) 1 Sim 404 and *Robinson v Kitchin* (1856) 8 De GM & G 88 doubted.

(3) On the facts, there had been no failure to disclose material matters to the judge when applying for the orders since speed was of the essence in preventing the dissipation of overseas assets resulting from the fraud and there had not been time to investigate the position regarding proceedings in other jurisdictions before applying for the orders. Furthermore, the use of information obtained under the English orders in the Isle of

Man proceedings for the sole purpose of enforcing the orders of the English court did
a not amount to use for a collateral or improper purpose. Although there were false
statements in the affidavit sworn in support of the application to the Maryland court to
obtain the freezing order, that misconduct by the plaintiffs was not by itself sufficient
reason for the discharge of the whole order made by the judge since it could be rectified
by requiring the plaintiffs to disclose the full facts to the Maryland court forthwith (see
p 317 *g h* and p 318 *a c* to *e j*, post); *Behbehani v Salem* [1989] 2 All ER 143 considered;
b *Dormeuil Frères SA v Nicolian International (Textiles) Ltd* [1988] 3 All ER 197 doubted.

Notes
For Mareva injunctions and Anton Piller orders, see 37 Halsbury's Laws (4th edn) paras
362, 372, and for cases on the subject, see 37(2) Digest (Reissue) 474–476, 480–483,
2947–2962, 2978–2990.
c   For privilege from production of documents exposing a party to penalties, see
13 Halsbury's Laws (4th edn) para 92, and for cases on the subject, see 18 Digest (2nd
reissue) 223–229, 1925–1988.

Cases referred to in judgment
d *Babanaft International Co SA v Bassatne* [1989] 1 All ER 433, [1990] Ch 13, [1989] 2 WLR
    232, CA.
Behbehani v Salem [1989] 2 All ER 143, [1989] 1 WLR 723, CA.
Brink's-MAT Ltd v Elcombe [1988] 3 All ER 188, [1988] 1 WLR 1350, CA.
Derby & Co Ltd v Weldon (No 1) [1989] 1 All ER 469, [1990] Ch 48, [1989] 2 WLR 276,
    CA.
e *Derby & Co Ltd v Weldon (No 2)* [1989] 1 All ER 1002, sub nom *Derby & Co Ltd v Weldon*
    (Nos 3 and 4) [1990] Ch 65, [1989] 2 WLR 412, CA.
Dormeuil Frères SA v Nicolian International (Textiles) Ltd [1988] 3 All ER 197, [1988] 1
    WLR 1362.
Green v Weaver (1827) 1 Sim 404, 57 ER 630, V-C.
Haiti (Republic) v Duvalier [1989] 1 All ER 456, [1990] 1 QB 202, [1989] 2 WLR 261, CA.
f *Parkhurst v Lowten* (1819) 2 Swan 194, 36 ER 589.
R v Jones (1974) 59 Cr App R 120, CA.
Rank Film Distributors Ltd v Video Information Centre [1981] 2 All ER 76, [1982] AC 380,
    [1981] 2 WLR 668, HL; *affg* [1980] 2 All ER 273, [1982] AC 380, [1980] 3 WLR 487,
    CA.
Rio Tinto Zinc Corp v Westinghouse Electric Corp [1978] 1 All ER 434, [1978] AC 547,
g   [1978] 2 WLR 81, HL.
Robinson v Kitchin (1856) 8 De GM & G 88, 44 ER 322, LJJ.
Sociedade Nacional de Combustiveis de Angola UEE v Lundqvist [1990] 3 All ER 283, CA.
Sybron Corp v Barclays Bank plc [1985] Ch 299, [1984] 3 WLR 1055.

h **Cases also cited**
Altertext Inc v Advanced Data Communications Ltd [1985] 1 All ER 395, [1985] 1 WLR 457.
Anton Piller KG v Manufacturing Processes Ltd [1976] 1 All ER 779, [1976] Ch 55, CA.
Ashtiani v Kashi [1986] 2 All ER 970, [1987] QB 888, CA.
A-G v Liverpool Corp (1835) 1 My & Cr 171, 40 ER 342.
Bank Mellat v Nikpour [1985] FSR 87, CA.
j *Booker McConnell plc v Plascow* [1985] RPC 425, CA.
Columbia Pictures Industries Inc v Robinson [1986] 3 All ER 338, [1987] Ch 38.
Derby & Co Ltd v Weldon (No 6) [1990] 3 All ER 263, [1990] 1 WLR 1139, CA.
Distributori Automatici Italia SpA v Holford General Trading Co Ltd [1985] 3 All ER 750,
    [1985] 1 WLR 1066.
Helliwell v Piggott-Sims [1980] FSR 356, CA.
House of Spring Gardens Ltd v Waite [1985] FSR 173, CA.

International Electronics Ltd v Weigh Data Ltd [1980] FSR 423.
ITC Film Distributors v Video Exchange Ltd [1982] 2 All ER 241, [1982] Ch 431.   *a*
Khan v Khan [1982] 2 All ER 60, [1982] 1 WLR 513, CA.
Riddick v Thames Board Mills Ltd [1977] 3 All ER 677, [1977] QB 881, CA.
United States of America v McRae (1867) LR 3 Ch App 79.
Verrier v DPP [1966] 3 All ER 568, [1967] 2 AC 195, HL.

Motions   *b*
The first three defendants, Geoffrey Boswell, Graham Wall and Richard Johnson, by
notices of motion dated 20 March 1990, applied to set aside the order of Warner J made
on 2 March 1990 granting the plaintiffs, Tate Access Floors Inc and Tate Access Floors
Ltd, worldwide Mareva and Anton Piller relief restraining the defendants from removing
out of the jurisdiction or otherwise dealing with their assets except to the extent that
they exceeded £1m, requiring the defendants to disclose and deliver up information and   *c*
documents and to permit the plaintiffs to enter, search and seize documents, and
requiring the defendants to verify on oath the information and documents disclosed and
delivered up. The facts are set out in the judgment.

Terence Etherton QC and *Douglas Day QC* for the first defendant.
Christopher Gibbons for the second defendant.   *d*
Douglas Day QC and *Michael Briggs* for the third defendant.
James Goudie QC and *Geoffrey Vos* for the plaintiffs.
The fourth to thirteenth defendants did not appear.

                                                                    Cur adv vult
                                                                                      e
13 June. The following judgment was delivered.

SIR NICOLAS BROWNE-WILKINSON V-C. There are before me a number of
motions which raise questions relating to worldwide Mareva injunctions and Anton
Piller orders. In particular they raise in an acute form questions as to the impact of the
privilege against self-incrimination on the ability of the court to make Anton Piller   *f*
orders in a form which has become customary over the years.
    The first plaintiff, Tate Access Floors Inc (Tate Inc), is a corporation incorporated in
Maryland, USA. The second plaintiff, Tate Access Floors Ltd (Tate Ltd), is its United
Kingdom subsidiary.
    The first defendant, Mr Boswell, is a British citizen residing in the United States. He
held the position of vice-president for international operations of Tate Inc, reporting   *g*
directly to Mr Baker, its chief executive officer and president. He has been employed by
Tate Inc since 1983 and was the second most senior executive of Tate Inc. The complete
operational responsibility for Tate Ltd, of which he was a director, was delegated to him
and he was responsible to Tate Inc for its affairs.
    The second defendant, Mr Wall, was managing director of Tate Ltd responsible for its   *h*
day-to-day operations, reporting directly to Mr Boswell. He had been appointed managing
director of Tate Ltd in 1982. The third defendant, Mr Johnson, had been an employee of
Tate Inc since 1976 and until recently worked mainly from England. He had been
seconded to Tate Ltd since about 1983 and amongst other things he used to administer
the capital spending programmes. I will refer to Mr Boswell, Mr Wall and Mr Johnson
collectively as 'the individual defendants'.   *j*
    In late 1989 Mr Baker acquired certain information which led him to institute an
internal audit of Tate Ltd, which began on 5 February 1990. This audit immediately
disclosed, so it is alleged, that Mr Boswell had been obtaining the payment of large
personal expenses from Tate Ltd by procuring a public relations firm falsely to invoice
Tate Ltd for such private expenses. The amount of such private expenses was said to

amount to a sum in excess of £60,000. On 19 February 1990 the public relations firm in
a question admitted falsely invoicing Tate Ltd for those expenses. Mr Boswell was
interviewed on 22 February and admitted certain misappropriations. He was summarily
removed from office.

The internal audit continued and disclosed a far more serious state of affairs. It became
clear that the extent of the defalcations was far wider than had previously been believed
and involved Mr Wall as well as Mr Boswell. It involved a large number of what appear
b to be no more than 'invoicing companies' and other individuals. Investigations are still
continuing but a preliminary assessment is that Mr Boswell and Mr Wall instigated a
practice whereby they incorporated, or arranged to be incorporated, companies which
raised false invoices for payment by Tate Ltd. Mr Boswell and Mr Wall, it is alleged,
frequently authorised payments to those companies and individuals through off-shore
bank accounts in the Isle of Man and the Channel Islands or through accounts in London.
c The plaintiffs allege that none of the payments were for services rendered bona fide by
the invoicing company and that the moneys were almost certainly paid to or for the
benefit of the individual defendants.

The fourth defendant, Miss Nortier, is alleged to have submitted claims for sale fees
from Switzerland. The fifth defendant, Miss Graf, was, it is alleged, a girlfriend of Mr
Boswell, who corresponded from an address in Holland and was involved in the false
d invoicing and running of the companies. The remaining defendants are said to be false
invoicing companies incorporated for that purpose by the individual defendants. The
sixth defendant, Excel Tech, trades from Milan. The seventh defendant, Show Services
Ltd, is registered in Gibraltar and has correspondence addresses in London and
Switzerland. The eighth defendant, South American Management Inc, is registered in
Panama and has an address at 35 North Audley Street, London W1. The ninth defendant,
e Oxford Associates Ltd (Oxford), is registered in the Turks and Caicos Islands and is said
to have an address at Suite C, First Floor, 2–5 Old Bond Street, London W1. The tenth
defendant, Infolink Technology Ltd, is a Liberian company trading from an address in
Philadelphia and New York. The eleventh defendant, Guard Trading Ltd is a Channel
Islands company. As a result of information gained subsequently two further defendants
were joined but I am not immediately concerned with them. Each of the defendants,
f other than the individual defendants, are alleged to have carried on no real business
beyond submitting false invoices for services or goods never rendered or supplied to Tate
Ltd.

Mr Baker interviewed Mr Wall on 23 and 27 February asking him to explain the
position. He was unable to give any satisfactory response and was summarily dismissed.
On 1 March 1990 it emerged that Mr Johnson appeared to be seriously implicated with
g the eleventh defendant, Guard Trading Ltd, a Channel Islands company which also
appeared to be submitting false invoices to Mr Johnson's knowledge.

On 2 March 1990 the plaintiffs made an ex parte application to Warner J. The
application was supported by an affidavit from Mr Baker to the effect which I have
summarised, only in much greater detail, his evidence being supported by numerous
h documents. By an order dated 2 March 1990 Warner J granted Mareva and Anton Piller
relief. Paragraphs 1 to 11 of the order contained worldwide Mareva injunctions against
all the defendants in similar terms. The order against Mr Boswell restrained him until
after 23 March 1990 from—

j   'transferring or charging or disposing of or diminishing or (insofar as his assets
are within the jurisdiction of this Court) removing from the jurisdiction of this
Court or otherwise dealing with any of his assets wheresoever the same might be
situate and in particular without prejudice to the generality of the foregoing [three
identified properties or interests]   Save insofar as the value of such assets exceeds
the sum of £1,000,000·00 . . .'

Orders in similar terms were made against the other defendants, save that in relation to the fourth to eleventh defendants the value of assets to be retained varied according to the amounts alleged to have been received by each.

Paragraph 12 of the order provides:

'. . . that the Plaintiffs are to be at liberty to take such steps as they may be advised in the Courts in Australia the Isle of Man Italy Jersey the Netherlands Switzerland and the United States for the purposes of giving effect to the foregoing parts of this Order . . .'

Paragraph 13 required the defendants to swear the usual affidavit disclosing the full value of their assets within ten days of the service of the order. There were the usual provisos permitting the first to fifth defendants to draw £500 per week for living expenses and there was provision for them to draw for their legal costs. Finally, so far as the Mareva relief was concerned, there were the usual *Babanaft* provisos, as amended by *Derby & Co Ltd v Weldon (No 2)* [1989] 1 All ER 1002, sub nom *Derby & Co Ltd v Weldon (Nos 3 and 4)* [1990] Ch 65) (see *Babanaft International Co SA v Bassatne* [1989] 1 All ER 433, [1990] Ch 13. That was the end of the Mareva part of the order.

The Anton Piller part of the order provides as follows:

'(15) that the First Second Third Seventh Eighth and Ninth Defendants do upon service of this Order within the jurisdiction forthwith disclose to the persons serving this Order upon them the present location of any of the items specified in the Second Schedule hereto which each of them now has or has since 1985 had in their power possession custody or control and stating also what has become of all such documents and items (16) that the First Second Third Seventh Eighth and Ninth Defendants do upon service of this Order within the jurisdiction forthwith deliver up to the person who shall serve this Order upon them any such copy or document or item listed on the Second Schedule hereto which is within their possession power custody or control . . . (17) that the First Second Third Seventh Eighth and Ninth Defendants . . . do on any day other than a Sunday and at any hour between 9 a.m. and 5 p.m. permit a Solicitor serving this Order upon them and not more than 2 other persons authorised by the Plaintiffs Solicitors forthwith to enter the premises listed in the First Schedule hereto and any vehicles or other premises which are in the power possession custody or control of those Defendants for the purpose of searching for inspecting and taking into the Plaintiffs Solicitors custody all and any items or documents listed in the Second Schedule hereto or which appear to be such items or documents (18) that the First Second and Third Defendants and each of them do within 10 days of the service of this Order upon them make swear and serve upon the Plaintiffs Solicitors Affidavits verifying and confirming any and all information required to be disclosed to the Plaintiffs pursuant to paragraph 15 of this Order . . .'

The second schedule contained categories of documents relating to the plaintiff companies and the fourth to eleventh defendants, together with documentation relating to two other companies which are implicated in the story. The premises mentioned in the first schedule include Suite C, First Floor, 2–5 Old Bond Street, that is to say the premises said to constitute the London address of Oxford.

The Anton Piller order was executed against Mr Boswell at an address in Hampshire but no documents were found or removed. It was further executed against Mr Wall, where certain documents were removed. On 5 March the order was executed against the premises of Oxford at 2–5 Old Bond Street. In the course of the execution of the order a revolving drum was seen on the receptionist's desk, which contained cards of several companies including the sixth to eleventh defendants. In relation to the ninth defendant the words 'hold all mail and refer to Mr G Wall' were typed under the name of the company. Pursuant to a further order granted on 6 March, these card indexes were removed.

On 7 March 1990 the plaintiffs started proceedings in the Isle of Man against the same
a persons as are defendants to the English action but with the addition of International
Company's Services (ICS), the company which had been found to be operating at 2–5 Old
Bond Street as an accommodation address. These proceedings were taken pursuant to the
leave granted by the order. The plaintiffs were advised that that order could not be
directly enforced in the Isle of Man. It was necessary to start substantive proceedings in
the Isle of Man and then apply for interlocutory relief in those Isle of Man proceedings.
b Application was made in the Isle of Man for Mareva relief and for Anton Piller relief
against ICS and a bank. The evidence in support of the application to the Isle of Man
court included information obtained on 5 March from the premises of ICS at 2–5 Old
Bond Street. No leave to use this information was obtained from the English court. The
Mareva order made by the Isle of Man court was limited to assets in the Isle of Man. It
made no provision for living expenses or costs. The orders against ICS and the bank were
c complied with by them and documents supplied. These documents are central to the
point which I have to determine.

On 9 March proceedings were begun in Jersey against the eighth defendants, South
American Management Inc, and the eleventh defendant, Guard Trading Ltd, and certain
other parties. Mareva and Anton Piller relief was obtained and orders for production of
documents by two Jersey banks. Nothing turns on the Jersey proceedings on these
d motions.

On 14 March the plaintiffs commenced proceedings in the Maryland courts against
Mr Johnson and Mr Boswell. Again, the plaintiffs were advised that they could not
merely enforce the order of Warner J in the Maryland court but had to start substantive
proceedings. The complaint in the Maryland court included charges of fraud and deceit,
breach of duty and conspiracy. The plaintiffs claimed compensatory damages of $US2m
e plus punitive damages of $US10m. The plaintiffs made a successful application in the
Maryland court for a freezing order, the exact legal effect of which has not been explained
in evidence before me. The claim for interim relief was supported by an affidavit by Mr
Baker, which contained the following paragraphs:

f   '7. Geoffrey Boswell is an English citizen who up until the discovery of this
     scheme was residing in the State of Maryland. I have reason to believe that Geoffrey
     Boswell may have fled the jurisdiction of this court. Despite substantial efforts on
     the part of the Plaintiffs, Mr Boswell has not been located.
     8. Richard Johnson is an American citizen residing in Maryland and married to
     an English citizen with property in England. Mr Johnson's international ties,
     together with the disappearance of Mr Boswell, lead the plaintiffs to fear that Mr
g   Johnson may also flee the jurisdiction of this court.'

The time for compliance with the orders for disclosure made by Warner J was extended
to 23 March 1990. On that date there came before Millett J a notice of motion by the
plaintiffs to continue the relief granted by Warner J against all the defendants. In
addition, there was a notice of motion by the individual defendants claiming to set aside
h the orders of Warner J, extensions of time to comply with disclosure orders and an order
to restrain the continuation of the Isle of Man and Maryland proceedings. The short
evidence sworn in support by the individual defendants did not deal with the substantive
allegations made against them, nor did it disclose the whereabouts or value of their assets.
Each of the individual defendants claimed the privilege against self incrimination: Mr
Boswell and Mr Johnson also claimed increased living expenses.

j On 23 March Millett J stood over all the motions to come on as motions by order and
in the meantime continued the order of Warner J against the fourth to eleventh
defendants. The individual defendants gave undertakings in Mareva form. The plaintiffs
gave undertakings: (1) not without the leave of the court to take further steps in the Isle
of Man proceedings or the Maryland proceedings or to start further proceedings outside
the jurisdiction; and (2) to apply to the Isle of Man and Maryland courts to vary their

respective orders so as to make them no more extensive than the English order, to allow
the individual defendants to pay reasonable legal expenses and living expenses, to   a
discharge the disclosure requirements provided by those orders in respect of the
individual defendants and in particular to permit certain drawings by Mr Boswell and
Mr Johnson.

Those undertakings by the plaintiffs have been complied with and the orders of the
Isle of Man and Maryland courts varied accordingly.

On 25 April the plaintiffs obtained judgment in default of defence against Mr Wall.   b
He is not proposing to defend the proceedings and a post-judgment Mareva order was
made against him on 25 April in the same form as the previous order.

The plaintiffs have filed further evidence including documents produced as a result of
the Isle of Man discovery orders. So far, I have only heard argument on the motions by
the individual defendants to set aside the order of Warner J. The reason for this course is
as follows. The individual defendants claim that the order of Warner J is oppressive and   c
was obtained as a result of the failure by the defendants to disclose material facts. It is
further contended that the Isle of Man documents should not be looked at as the Isle of
Man order was improperly obtained by the use of information acquired as a result of the
Anton Piller order in England. In consequence, I have not so far looked at the documents
obtained in the Isle of Man. It was thought, rightly in my view, that I should first decide
whether the whole or certain parts of the ex parte order of Warner J should be set aside   d
since that might both affect the evidence I should look at on the plaintiffs' motion to
continue the Mareva injunction and also the exercise of my discretion in deciding
whether or not to grant the plaintiffs inter partes relief. This judgment is concerned
solely with the issues arising on the motions to set aside the ex parte order.

There are three main grounds on which the attack is mounted on the order of Warner
J by counsel for the first defendant with the support of counsel for the second and third   e
defendants: (a) that the Mareva part of the order was oppressive in that it did not contain
either an express undertaking not to start proceedings overseas or an express undertaking
not to use the information obtained in the United Kingdom proceedings for the purposes
of the overseas proceedings; (b) that the Anton Piller part of the order of Warner J
infringed the privilege of the individual defendants against self-incrimination and should
be set aside both as against the individual defendants and as against the other defendants;   f
and (c) that in obtaining the order from Warner J the plaintiffs failed to disclose to him
the need to start substantive proceedings in the Isle of Man and Maryland. Further, that
in executing the order the plaintiffs used information obtained in the English proceedings
for the purposes of the Isle of Man proceedings without the leave of this court, that the
plaintiffs had claimed punitive damages of $US10m in the Maryland court, and that they
had obtained the freezing order from the Maryland court in reliance on evidence known   g
by the plaintiffs to be false. In consequence, it is said, the ex parte order should be set
aside and no further relief granted to the plaintiffs. I will deal with each of these in turn.

(A) THE MAREVA PART OF THE ORDER
          It will be recalled that the Mareva order is a worldwide order. Counsel for the first   h
defendant submits, and I wholly accept, that in any case where a worldwide order is
made, it is capable of operating oppressively if the plaintiffs are free to start other
proceedings in other jurisdictions (thereby exposing the defendants to a multiplicity of
proceedings) and to use information obtained under compulsion in this jurisdiction for
the purposes of pursing criminal or civil remedies in other jurisdictions. It is for that   j
reason that the Court of Appeal has laid down that, as a term of any worldwide Mareva
relief, the order should contain undertakings not, without the leave of the court, to start
such proceedings or use such information: see *Derby & Co Ltd v Weldon (No 1)* [1989] 1
All ER 469 at 474–475, 477, 480, [1990] Ch 48 at 55, 57, 60, 64, *Babanaft International Co*

SA v Bassatne [1989] 1 All ER 433 at 455, [1990] Ch 13 at 46 and *Republic of Haiti v*
a *Duvalier* [1989] 1 All ER 456, [1990] 1 QB 202.

The question in the present case is not as to the existence of that principle, but whether
it was substantially observed in the order made by Warner J. For this purpose it is
necessary to consider the two undertakings separately. As to the undertaking not to start
foreign proceedings, such undertaking was not appropriate since the judge was being
asked for, and gave, his consent to proceedings in a number of foreign jurisdictions. All
b that is missing is any express undertaking not to start proceedings in other foreign
jurisdictions. The very fact that leave was sought and given for proceedings in certain
overseas jurisdictions shows that leave was required for proceedings in any other overseas
jurisdiction. In my judgment the form of order necessarily implies that proceedings in
other overseas jurisdictions would require leave. Looking at the matter with cool
hindsight rather than in the heat of an urgent ex parte application, it would obviously
c have been preferable to have included such an express prohibition. But in my judgment
it is impossible to characterise the order as oppressive for want of spelling out expressly
what is in any event clear by implication.

As to the omission of any express undertaking not without the leave of the court to
use the information (obtained by executing the English Anton Piller order) otherwise
than for the purpose of the proceedings, it would again have been desirable to include
d such express undertaking. But any order for discovery made by the court imposes an
implied undertaking to that effect. Such implied undertaking is usually expressed as
being not to use the information disclosed for a collateral or improper purpose and
authority clearly establishes that the use of information for the purpose of separate
proceedings is improper: see, for example, *Sybron Corp v Barclays Bank plc* [1985] Ch 299.
There was therefore in this case an implied undertaking by the plaintiffs not to use the
e documents obtained under the Anton Piller order improperly and for separate legal
proceedings. The risk of oppression through the lack of any such undertaking by the use
of the information for a collateral purpose was therefore not present. In my judgment
there is no authority that the undertaking has to be express, rather than implied, save
possibly for a dictum of Butler-Sloss LJ in *Derby & Co Ltd v Weldon (No 2)* [1989] 1 All ER
1002 at 1022, [1990] Ch 65 at 96–97, where the point was not in issue. I consider
f hereafter the question whether the use actually made of the information constituted a
breach of that implied undertaking.

In my judgment therefore the Mareva part of the order as made was not oppressive.

(B) THE ANTON PILLER PART OF THE ORDER

g (1) *Generally*

There are three elements in the Anton Piller part of the order. First, orders that the
defendants disclose and deliver up information and documents: paras 15 and 16. Second,
that the defendants permit the plaintiffs to enter, search and seize documents: para 17.
Third, that the defendants verify on oath the information and documents produced
h under paras 15 and 16: para 18.

The individual defendants contend that each of those aspects of the order infringes
their privilege against self-incrimination. They say that if the facts alleged by the
plaintiffs are true, the individual defendants have been guilty of either a statutory or
common law conspiracy to defraud and that the documents produced or obtained under
such an order might tend to incriminate them on that charge. In reliance on *Rank Film*
j *Distributors Ltd v Video Information Centre* [1981] 2 All ER 76, [1982] AC 380 they say that
the privilege extends not only to those parts of the order which require them or the
company defendants to produce and verify the information and documents (paras 15, 16
and 18) but also to the part which requires them to permit the plaintiffs to enter, search
and seize (para 17). They further say, in reliance on the *Rank Film* case, that since there

was a substantial risk that the effect of the order so made would have been to require
such self-incrimination, the order should not have been made at all: it should now be set   *a*
aside and the documents seized ordered to be returned to them. Finally, the individual
defendants say that even though the company defendants have not appeared or taken
any point on self-incrimination, the individual defendants are entitled to claim the
privilege since the plaintiffs allege that the company defendants are the mere creatures
of the individual defendants.

(2) *Was there a risk of self-incrimination?*
  The recent decision of the Court of Appeal in *Sociedade Nacional de Combustiveis de
Angola UEE v Lundqvist* [1990] 3 All ER 283 (the *Sonangol* case) disclosed that the privilege
against self-incrimination could properly be invoked in a case where, on the facts alleged
by the plaintiffs, there was a reasonable apprehension that a prosecution for conspiracy
might be brought in the United Kingdom and that, if the documents or information   *c*
sought were to be produced, there was a real risk that that might incriminate the
defendants. The *Sonangol* case itself was concerned with the risk of self-incrimination
arising from swearing an affidavit as to the defendant's assets pursuant to Mareva order.
But there is no doubt that the decision applies equally to all aspects of discovery in a fraud
action where there is a reasonable possibility of a prosecution for conspiracy.
  The claim to privilege against self-incrimination in relation to Anton Piller orders was   *d*
considered in the early days of such orders being made. In the *Rank Film* case, the House
of Lords upheld the claim to privilege in a case where the plaintiffs obtained an order in
aid of a claim for infringement of copyright. Parliament immediately legislated to deal
with the position by providing that defendants in intellectual property actions could not
resist production of documents on the grounds of self-incrimination but that the
documents so produced could not be used in any subsequent prosecution: see the   *e*
Supreme Court Act 1981, s 72. A similar position obtains where the danger apprehended
relates to a prosecution for a substantive crime under the Theft Act 1968. Discovery in
civil proceedings cannot be resisted in such a case but the documents produced may not
be used in aid of any prosecution for a substantive offence under the Act: see the 1968
Act, s 31. The position has therefore been reached where the right to resist discovery on
the grounds of self-incrimination only now applies where there is a serious risk of   *f*
prosecution for conspiracy.
  The individual defendants contend that in this case there is a real risk of the individual
defendants being prosecuted for conspiracy in this country. They do not, however,
contend that there is any risk that the defendant companies (all being overseas companies)
will be so prosecuted.
  In my judgment the claim that the individual defendants are in danger of prosecution   *g*
for conspiracy is made out. The facts alleged against them, if true, could plainly provide
the ground for a charge of conspiracy, whether statutory or at common law. The plaintiffs
submit that there is no such risk. First, they contend that the privilege against self-
incrimination does not extend to permit an agent, trustee or other fiduciary to claim the
privilege in an action brought against him for breach of that duty. Reliance is placed on   *h*
two nineteenth century cases, *Green v Weaver* (1827) 1 Sim 404, 57 ER 630 and *Robinson
v Kitchin* (1856) 8 De GM & G 88, 44 ER 322. In both those cases the plaintiff sought
redress from his brokers relating to their conduct of his affairs. The defendant brokers
(or some of them) had failed to obtain licences to act as brokers and were thereby exposed
to statutory penalties if they had so acted. On an application by the plaintiff for discovery,
the defendants claimed the privilege against self-incrimination by reason of the risk of   *j*
incurring such penalties if they were shown to have acted as unlicensed brokers. The
question whether or not they were licensed brokers was irrelevant to the claim made by
the plaintiff. The claimed privilege was refused in each case. In *Green v Weaver* Hart V-C
expressed himself in very wide terms to the effect that where a defendant agrees to act as

a fiduciary he impliedly contracts not to raise the claim to the privilege against self-
incrimination in any case brought by his principal to enforce the fiduciary duties.

In my judgment those cases do not establish any such wide proposition. It is doubtful
whether they are good law today. They are not referred to in any modern textbook and
were doubted by Bridge LJ in the *Rank Film* case [1980] 2 All ER 273 at 284, [1982] AC
380 at 414. In any event, in my judgment the decisions are limited to cases where the
defendant seeks to resist discovery because of some risk of a penalty arising by reason of
some matter wholly collateral to the plaintiff's claim. A defendant liable to account in
equity can in general claim the privilege: see *Parkhurst v Lowten* (1819) 2 Swan 194 at
212–214, 36 ER 589 at 594–595 and *Bray on Discovery* (1885) pp 337–339.

Second, the plaintiffs say that on the facts alleged the individual defendants are guilty
of substantive offences under the Theft Act 1968 and will therefore only be prosecuted,
if at all, for such substantive offences: privilege therefore cannot be claimed. They rely
on the Practice Direction of Lord Widgery CJ, which requires the prosecution to justify
the joinder of a conspiracy count with substantive counts and, in the absence of
justification, to elect which counts to pursue (see *Practice Note* [1977] 2 All ER 540, [1977]
1 WLR 537). But the rule is not an absolute one. For example, in a case such as this,
where each false invoice would have to be the subject of a separate substantive count, the
complexity of the prosecution would be enormous: therefore a single count of conspiracy
might well be justified: see *R v Jones* (1974) 59 Cr App R 120. In my judgment it is
impossible to say that in the present case the individual defendants' apprehension of the
risk that they might be charged with a criminal conspiracy is fanciful.

The plaintiffs further say that the evidence already available (before the Anton Piller
search) was so damning that there was no increased risk of self-incrimination by the
production of further documents. I wholly reject this submission. The plaintiffs
themselves are anxious for me to look at the evidence obtained as a result of the Anton
Piller order presumably in order to strengthen their case for continuing the Mareva
relief. In those circumstances it is impossible for me to say that any prosecutor would not
find those documents equally useful.

I therefore hold that if Warner J's mind had been directed to the risk of self-
incrimination by the individual defendants on the charge of conspiracy, he would have
been bound to hold that there was an appreciable risk of such prosecution.

(3) Does the privilege against self-incrimination apply to the 'search and seize' part of an Anton Piller order?

The basis of the privilege against self-incrimination is that a man is not bound to
provide evidence against himself by being forced to answer questions or produce
documents. Therefore, it does not necessarily follow that the privilege against self-
incrimination will apply to that part of an Anton Piller order which authorises the
plaintiff to enter and seize documents: documents seized by the police in the execution
of a search warrant can be used in evidence against the accused. It is not wholly clear
from the reports of the *Rank Film* case whether the Court of Appeal and the House of
Lords were holding that the privilege applied to the search and seize aspects of the Anton
Piller order.

In the *Rank Film* case the plaintiffs were alleging piracy of video tapes. The Anton
Piller order under consideration required the defendants: (1) to produce infringing
copies, information and documents; (2) to permit the plaintiffs to enter, search for and
seize (a) infringing copies and (b) documents relating thereto; and (3) to verify (2) and (3)
above on affidavit. It is clear that the House of Lords (who dismissed the appeal from the
Court of Appeal) held the privilege to apply to categories (1) and (3) above. It is also clear
that they held that the privilege did not apply to category (2)(a) since the privilege did
not override the property rights which the plaintiffs enjoyed in the infringing copies (see
[1980] 2 All ER 273 at 286–287, [1982] AC 380 at 415, 418 per Bridge and Templeman

LJJ; [1981] 2 All ER 76 at 80, [1982] AC 380 at 441 per Lord Wilberforce). What is not clear from the reports is whether the privilege was held to extend to category (2)(b) *a* above, i e to the documents which were the subject matter of the search and seize order. There is a passage in the judgment of Templeman LJ ([1980] 2 All ER 273 at 288, [1982] AC 380 at 418) which suggests that the privilege did not extend to the orders for 'discovery and interrogation' relating to the infringing copies (see also [1981] 2 All ER 76 at 83, [1982] AC 380 at 445 per Lord Fraser).

On the other hand, Bridge LJ appears to be expressing the contrary conclusion (see *b* [1980] 2 All ER 273 at 286, [1982] AC 380 at 416). The distinction between category (2)(a) and category (2)(b) does not appear to have been argued in the House of Lords: see the formulation of the relevant categories by Lord Wilberforce ([1981] 2 All ER 76 at 80, [1982] AC 380 at 440).

In those circumstances I asked to see the orders made by the Court of Appeal and House of Lords in the *Rank Film* case. Due to the industry of counsel these were obtained. *c* Although something has plainly gone wrong in the drafting of the Court of Appeal order, it is clear that the only part of the original ex parte Anton Piller order which was not set aside was the order to permit the search for and seizure of the infringing copies themselves (category (2)(a) above); the order permitting search for and seizure of the related documents (category (2)(b) above) was set aside. Therefore, in my judgment I am bound to hold that where the defendant's privilege against self-incrimination may arise *d* the making of an ex parte order for the seizure of documents from that defendant's premises is improper. That accords with my own sense of justice: if a man is entitled to refuse to produce documents, it would be strange if the law permitted an order to be made which forced him to admit others to his house for the purpose of seizing those documents.

(4) Taking the claim to privilege

In the ordinary case, it is up to the defendant to put forward the claim to privilege. However, the *Rank Film* case establishes that, where an ex parte order is sought which might in practice preclude the defendant from raising the claim to privilege before the order is executed, the judge should not have made the ex parte order at all (see [1980] 2 *f* All ER 273 at 286, 289, [1982] AC 380 at 416, 419 per Bridge and Templeman LJJ). The Court of Appeal set aside the ex parte order and the House of Lords upheld their decision. Therefore, in any case in which the *Rank Film* decision applies, an Anton Piller order should not be made at all.

(5) Can the individual defendants complain of the order against the company defendants?

The documents which the plaintiffs wish to put in evidence and the individual *g* defendants wish to exclude were all obtained in the Isle of Man as a result of the execution of the Anton Piller order against Oxford. The Isle of Man order against Oxford was obtained as a result of the order made by Warner J permitting search of the accommodation address of Oxford and the other defendant companies in London. Oxford, although served, has not raised any claim to privilege nor has it applied to set *h* aside the order of Warner J. Moreover, the individual defendants accept that Oxford could not claim the privilege against self-incrimination since, being an overseas company, there is no real risk of it being prosecuted for conspiracy in this country. Notwithstanding this, the individual defendants assert that they can claim the privilege in relation to the order made against Oxford.

They neither admit nor deny that Oxford is a mere creature of theirs. But they say *j* that it is the plaintiffs' case that Oxford is the mere creature of the individual defendants and, on that basis, they are entitled to claim that to require discovery by the companies is indirectly to require discovery by the individual defendants.

In my judgment this claim by the individual defendants is ill-founded. First, unless and until they accept that the company defendants are simply their creatures, there can

be no basis for the claim. The privilege is what it says it is: a privilege against *self-*
a *incrimination.* Even if it were possible to argue that a company which is the mere alter
ego of an individual faced with the risk of prosecution should not be required to give
discovery which might aid such prosecution, the foundation of such argument must be
that the company is in fact the mere alter ego of the individual who is at risk. The
individual defendants rely on certain remarks of Staughton LJ in the *Sonangol* case [1990]
3 All ER 283 as authority for the proposition that, since the plaintiffs are alleging the
b companies to be mere creatures of the individual defendants, the individual defendants
are entitled to claim privilege on that basis. Staughton LJ was there dealing with a
submission that the defendants were trifling with the court by denying the plaintiffs'
claim on the pleadings and simultaneously alleging that they were in danger of self-
incrimination. It was in that context that he said (at 294):

c   'It is [the plaintiff companies] who say that [the first defendant] was fraudulent.
       So it cannot lie in their mouth to say that he is not telling the truth when he claims
       that he would be incriminated. Or if they do the inconsistency is theirs, not his.'

       In my judgment those remarks have no application to the position where a defendant
is claiming that he will be incriminating himself if a third party gives discovery. In order
for a person to show that he has any privilege at all, the burden must be on him to show
d that he is being asked to incriminate himself: he has no privilege against incrimination
by a third party and must prove that the company is his creature.
       Even if, contrary to my view, the individual defendants are entitled to put forward the
claim to privilege on the basis that the defendant companies are their creatures, in my
judgment they are still not entitled to object to the discovery against the company
defendants. The privilege can only be claimed by the person who is likely to be
e incriminated: see *Rio Tinto Zinc Corp v Westinghouse Electric Corp* [1978] 1 All ER 434 at
465, [1978] AC 547 at 637 per Lord Diplock. If people choose to conduct their affairs
through the medium of corporations, they are taking advantage of the fact that in law
those corporations are separate legal entities, whose property and actions are in law not
the property or actions of their incorporators or controlling shareholders. In my
f judgment controlling shareholders cannot, for all purposes beneficial to them, insist on
the separate identity of such corporations but then be heard to say the contrary when
discovery is sought against such corporations.
       This conclusion is supported by the fact that in the *Sonangol* case discovery was ordered
against a company who was the mere creature of Mr Lundqvist, notwithstanding the
risk that this might incriminate Mr Lundqvist. Moreover, I was not referred to, nor have
g I found, any authority which supports the proposition advanced by the individual
defendants.

(6) Conclusion
       I therefore reach the conclusion on the Anton Piller part of the order that paras 15 to
18 of the order of Warner J must be set aside as against the first to third defendants on
h the grounds that there was a real risk that the execution of such order would incriminate
those defendants. However, I decline to set aside those orders as against the company
defendants (the seventh, eighth and ninth defendants) since in my judgment nobody has
shown any risk of those company defendants being incriminated.
       I reach this conclusion with regret. In the *Sonangol* case I pointed to the great difficulty
of proof in fraud cases if the privilege against self-incrimination could be invoked to
j resist discovery. I had not then foreseen the effect of that decision on Anton Piller orders:
if I had done, I would have asked for even more urgent consideration by Parliament with
a view to correcting the position. Anton Piller orders are only made when there is a
strong prima facie case of dishonest conduct by the defendants which indicates that they
are likely to destroy the evidence of their fraud. In such circumstances it is almost
inevitable that the judge asked to make the order will consider that there is a real risk of

prosecution for a criminal offence. If it is possible to say that the prosecution will be of a kind covered by s 31 of the Theft Act 1968 or s 72 of the Supreme Court Act 1981, that *a* will cause no trouble. But if, as is likely too often to be the case, there is a real risk of a conspiracy charge, the judge will not be able to make an Anton Piller order at all and in consequence vital evidence will be destroyed. As it seems to me, apart from cases falling within s 72 (proceedings relating to intellectual property and passing off), in the future it will normally only be proper for the court to make an ex parte Anton Piller order for the recovery of property belonging to the plaintiffs (without any related discovery as to *b* documents). To a large extent, the Anton Piller jurisdiction will become incapable of being exercised. It is for this reason that, for myself, I would welcome the early consideration of the problem by Parliament.

(C) THE CONDUCT OF THE PLAINTIFFS IN OBTAINING AND EXECUTING THE ORDER
c
(1) *Generally*
No rule is better established, and few more important, than the rule (the golden rule) that a plaintiff applying for ex parte relief must disclose to the court all matters relevant to the exercise of the court's discretion whether or not to grant relief before giving the defendant an opportunity to be heard. If that duty is not observed by the plaintiff, the court will discharge the ex parte order and may, to mark its displeasure, refuse the *d* plaintiff further inter partes relief even though the circumstances would otherwise justify the grant of such relief: see *Brink's-MAT Ltd v Elcombe* [1988] 3 All ER 188, [1988] 1 WLR 1350 and *Behbehani v Salem* [1989] 2 All ER 143, [1989] 1 WLR 723. In this case, the individual defendants contend that there was an innocent failure by the plaintiffs to discharge that duty of disclosure. As a result, they contend, the order of Warner J should be wholly set aside and the evidence obtained under it should be returned. They further *e* propose to contend hereafter that no fresh Mareva relief should be granted.
The individual defendants also contend that, in executing the order of Warner J, the plaintiffs have in certain respects acted improperly as a result of which the same consequences should ensue. I was not referred to any authority directly in point, but I accept that if in the course of executing a Mareva or Anton Piller order the plaintiffs fail *f* properly to observe any undertaking given to the court as a term of granting the ex parte order or otherwise act scandalously the court can and will take such conduct into account in deciding whether or not to set aside the ex parte order or grant further relief. Mareva and (especially) Anton Piller orders confer on one party to litigation draconian powers to interfere with the defendant's life and privacy without the party so interfered with being heard at all. The court in trying to protect as far as possible the absent party always imposes undertakings on the plaintiffs and expects the order to be carried out in good *g* faith. Failure to observe the undertakings or observe such good faith should not be tolerated.
In *Dormeuil Frères SA v Nicolian International (Textiles) Ltd* [1988] 3 All ER 197 at 200, [1988] 1 WLR 1362 at 1369 I said: '. . . save in exceptional cases, it is not the correct procedure to apply to discharge an ex parte injunction on the grounds of lack of full *h* disclosure at the interlocutory stage of the proceedings.' I expressed that view in the context of a growing practice of combing through large volumes of, often disputed, evidence with a view to showing that there had been some failure to make a material disclosure. I remain of the view that that type of application to discharge an ex parte injunction on the hearing of the inter partes motion to continue such injunction is inappropriate. But the decision in *Behbehani v Salem* shows that I expressed myself too *j* widely. That case (which was reported after my decision) shows that although the court has power to grant further interlocutory relief notwithstanding a failure to make proper disclosure at the ex parte stage, in deciding whether to grant such further relief the court has to consider all the circumstances of the failure to make proper disclosure and whether

a such failure was innocent or deliberate and to weigh the public interest in maintaining the golden rule as against the requirements of justice in granting the plaintiff inter partes relief to which he would otherwise be entitled.

It is clear that I was in error in thinking that normally the question whether or not there has been a failure to disclose is not appropriate to be dealt with at the interlocutory stage. If, as seems probable, my decision in this case is appealed, I (and I believe other first instance judges) would value guidance from the Court of Appeal as to how the test in
b *Behbehani v Salem* should be applied having regard to the practical problems which I set out in full in the *Dormeuil* case. There is no doubt that if the law requires the court at the interlocutory stage to consider in detail disputed evidence as to the failure to disclose, very long disputed interlocutory hearings are unavoidable to the detriment of the hearing of other cases brought by other litigants. It is to be noted that in *Behbehani v Salem* the plaintiffs admitted that there had been a failure to disclose material facts and that the ex
c parte order should be set aside, whereas in the *Dormeuil* case it was admitted that an inter partes injunction of some kind was appropriate whether or not there had been a failure to disclose. It may be that the reconciliation between the public interest in upholding the golden rule and the public interest in ensuring that the courts are not clogged with long interlocutory hearings is that the investigation of the circumstances in which the ex parte order was obtained should take place at an interlocutory stage only where it is clear
d that there has been a failure to make a material disclosure or where the nature of the alleged failure is so serious as to demand immediate investigation.

(2) Failure to disclose

The defendants first allege that in obtaining leave to start proceedings in overseas jurisdictions, the plaintiffs failed to inform the judge that it would be necessary in the
e Isle of Man and Maryland to start proceedings claiming substantive relief, thereby duplicating the relief claimed in the English proceedings. It is accepted by the defendants that this failure was not deliberate but due to the fact that at the time of the application to Warner J the legal position in the overseas jurisdictions had not been investigated by the plaintiffs. However, in reliance on *Behbehani v Salem* [1989] 2 All ER 143 at 154, 157,
f [1989] 1 WLR 723 at 734, 737, they submitted that before seeking leave to start overseas proceedings the plaintiffs should have researched the foreign law and placed it before the judge.

In my judgment this is a wholly unreal argument. The plaintiffs had recently discovered what they allege to be a serious fraud involving companies in many jurisdictions. Those alleged to be guilty of the fraud had been alerted to the fact that their conduct was under investigation. If the dissipation of overseas assets was to be
g prevented, speed was of the essence. In those circumstances it would be quite unreal to suggest that there was time for the plaintiffs to investigate the position in many foreign jurisdictions before applying to the court for leave to start proceedings. It was an emergency situation. Moreover, it was open to the defendants immediately to seek a stay of the foreign proceedings; they immediately applied for and obtained this relief. I can
h see here neither a failure to disclose nor any oppression to the defendants.

The second failure relied on by the defendants was a failure to disclose that it was wrong to grant Anton Piller relief when there was a risk of self-incrimination on a charge of conspiracy. It was said that the *Sonangol* case should have been drawn to the attention of Warner J. Counsel for the first defendant (in reply) did not persist in this allegation of a failure to disclose. It is not clear to me whether counsel for the third defendant also
j withdrew this head of objection. In any event, I find the suggestion as far-fetched as the first matter I dealt with. The *Sonangol* case had only been briefly reported in The Times at the time of the application to Warner J. Until the point was taken by the defendants in the present case, no one so far as I am aware had appreciated the interaction between the *Sonangol* case and the *Rank Film* case: I certainly had not. Indeed, the full impact of

the point could not be appreciated until the copies of the Court of Appeal order in the
Rank Film case were produced to me during the course of the argument.

I therefore find that there was no failure to disclose material matters to the judge.

(3) Method of execution of the order

Two matters were complained of. First the defendants say that by using information
obtained in London under the order of Warner J for the purpose of the Isle of Man
proceedings, the plaintiffs were in breach of the implied undertaking which I have held
was applicable to the information obtained in London, ie an undertaking not to use such
information otherwise than for the purposes of the proceedings in which the information
was obtained.

The Isle of Man proceedings were brought for the sole purpose for which they were
authorised, viz for the purpose of giving effect to the order of Warner J. In my judgment
the use of information obtained under English discovery in proceedings overseas (which
have been authorised by the judge) for the sole purpose of enforcing, directly or
indirectly, the order of the English court is not a breach of the undertaking. Any use of
such information for a wider or different purpose in overseas proceedings would plainly
be a breach of the implied undertaking. But use of the information for the sole purpose
of giving effect to the order made by the English court in the proceedings in which the
information was obtained is not, in my judgment, a use for a collateral or improper
purpose.

The other matter relied on by the defendants relates to the Maryland proceedings.
First, in those proceedings the plaintiffs claimed punitive damages of $US10m, being
relief neither claimed nor capable of being claimed in the English proceedings. By
seeking worldwide Mareva relief in the English court, the plaintiffs have elected to bring
their main action here, all other proceedings being merely ancillary to and in aid of the
English proceedings. In those circumstances the claim for punitive damages was quite
improper. However, it has not produced any harm to the defendants since the claim to
punitive damages can, and must, be abandoned if the plaintiffs intend to continue their
litigation here.

Second, and much more serious, the passages in the affidavit sworn by Mr Baker in
support of the application to the Maryland court to obtain the freezing order were false.
Counsel for the plaintiffs was constrained to admit that the statements I have read were
quite untrue. Far from the plaintiffs not knowing the whereabouts of Mr Boswell, he
was only served with the English proceedings by reason of the fact that he himself
collected the documents from the offices of the plaintiffs' solicitors on 9 March. His
English solicitors were in correspondence with the plaintiffs' English solicitors prior to
and at the time when Mr Baker swore his affidavit. As to Mr Johnson, he was to Mr
Baker's knowledge in Australia until 9 March on the plaintiff companies' business. He
returned to the United States at the request of Mr Baker and on 13 March (the day before
Mr Baker swore his affidavit) voluntarily attended a meeting at the offices of the plaintiffs'
lawyers in Baltimore at which Mr Baker himself was also present. It is impossible to say
whether or not the Baltimore court would have accepted jurisdiction in this case in the
absence of the false evidence put before them. I must make it clear that the English
solicitors acting for the plaintiffs were wholly unaware of what was being done in
Maryland.

I take a serious view of this matter. If, as in the present case, foreign proceedings are
being conducted under the authority of the English court it is important to ensure that
they are being properly and honestly conducted. However, in my judgment this serious
misconduct by the plaintiffs is not, in itself, sufficient to require the discharge of the
whole order made by Warner J. Until I have seen the other evidence, I am not able to say
what its impact will be on my decision whether or not to grant further Mareva relief. I
have already made it clear that a minimum requirement is that the plaintiffs apply

forthwith to the Baltimore court to disclose the misleading nature of part of the evidence
a on which the court was invited to act.

(D) CONCLUSIONS

I have already indicated that I will set aside the Anton Piller part of the order against
the individual defendants. The question remains whether, looking collectively at all the
factors that I have mentioned, in the exercise of my discretion I ought to set aside the
b whole order and thereby exclude the evidence obtained in the Isle of Man. Giving the
matter the best attention I can, I have reached the view that I should not do so. There was
not in my judgment any failure to disclose material facts. The only conduct of the
plaintiffs which is less than innocent and explicable relates to the Maryland proceedings,
the highly unsatisfactory nature of which can be marked by requiring the full facts to be
put before the Maryland court and by a suitable order for costs in due course. On the
c other side there is evidence which satisfied Warner J that the case merited Mareva and
Anton Piller relief; although I have not as yet heard full argument on the matter, I have
not yet seen anything which leads me to a different conclusion.

I will therefore set aside paras 15 to 18 of the order as against the first to third
defendants but otherwise decline to set aside the order of Warner J. It follows that it is
unnecessary for me to consider the question whether, if the order as a whole had been set
d aside, documents obtained under it ought to be returned or are admissible in any event.

I will, before deciding whether or not to continue the order of Warner J and the other
matters raised before me, look at the Isle of Man documents and hear counsels'
submissions on those matters.

Application allowed in part.
e

Solicitors: *Hopkins & Wood* (for the first defendant); *Paris & Co*, Birmingham (for the
second defendant); *Charles Russell Williams & James* (for the third defendant); *Travers
Smith Braithwaite* (for the plaintiffs).

Celia Fox   Barrister.

Practice Note

COURT OF APPEAL, CRIMINAL DIVISION
LORD LANE CJ, MANN LJ AND POTTS J
2 OCTOBER 1990

Crown Court – Distribution of court business – Serious and complex fraud cases – Places of trial – Supreme Court Act 1981, s 75(1) – Criminal Justice Act 1987, s 5(1).

LORD LANE CJ gave the following direction at the sitting of the court.

1. With the concurrence of the Lord Chancellor and pursuant to s 75(1) of the Supreme Court Act 1981 I make with effect from 2 October 1990 the following direction with regard to the place of trial for cases of serious and complex fraud transferred to the Crown Court under the Criminal Justice Act 1987.

2. The proposed place of trial specified in the notice of transfer under s 5(1) of the Criminal Justice Act 1987 shall be one of the following Crown Court centres:

Circuit	Centres
Midland and Oxford	Birmingham
	Leicester
	Nottingham
	Oxford
	Stafford
	Wolverhampton
North Eastern	Leeds
	Newcastle
	Sheffield
	Teesside
Northern	Liverpool
South Eastern	Aylesbury
	Central Criminal Court
	Chelmsford
	Guildford
	Isleworth
	Knightsbridge
	Maidstone
	Middlesex Guildhall
	Norwich
	Snaresbrook
	Southwark
	Wood Green
Wales and Chester	Cardiff
	Mold
	Swansea
Western	Bristol
	Exeter
	Portsmouth
	Southampton
	Winchester

3. The Practice Direction of 22 September 1988 (see *Practice Note* [1988] 3 All ER 733, [1988] 1 WLR 1161) is hereby revoked.

N P Metcalfe Esq   Barrister.

Al-Nakib Investments (Jersey) Ltd and another v Longcroft and others

CHANCERY DIVISION

MERVYN DAVIES J

5, 6, 9, 10 APRIL, 1 MAY 1990

Negligence – Information or advice – Knowledge that third party might rely on information – Company – Directors – Prospectus and company report – Liability of directors for inaccuracies in prospectus and report – Shareholder relying on prospectus and report when buying company's shares on stock market – Shareholder suffering loss on shares – Whether directors owing duty of care to shareholder or anyone else who relied on prospectus to purchase shares in company on stock market.

The plaintiff was a shareholder in the ninth defendant, CT plc, which developed an electronic information storage and retrieval system and incorporated a subsidiary, M Ltd, to exploit that system. CT plc decided to float M Ltd on the unlisted securities market and issued a prospectus inviting CT plc shareholders to subscribe for shares in both M Ltd and CT plc by way of a rights issue. The plaintiff subscribed for 400,000 M Ltd shares under the rights issue (the first transaction) and some months later made six purchases of CT plc and M Ltd shares through the stock market (transactions 2 to 6). The plaintiff subsequently brought an action against CT plc and its directors alleging that it had subscribed for and purchased shares in CT plc and M Ltd relying on the prospectus issued in connection with the rights issue and two interim reports issued by M Ltd, that both the prospectus and the interim reports contained misrepresentations that M Ltd's system was fully developed and marketable, that the defendants owed the plaintiff a duty of care in issuing the prospectus and the interim reports because it was reasonably foreseeable that the plaintiff might rely on the prospectus and the interim reports in deciding to purchase shares in CT plc and M Ltd, and that the plaintiffs had suffered damage as the result of subscribing for and purchasing shares in CT plc and M Ltd. The defendants applied to strike out the statement of claim in respect of transactions 2 to 6 on the grounds that it disclosed no reasonable cause of action.

Held – Although directors of a company owed a duty of care to persons who subscribed for shares in reliance on a prospectus they did not owe a duty of care to a shareholder or anyone else who relied on the prospectus for the purpose of deciding whether to purchase shares in the company through the stock market, because the prospectus was addressed to shareholders for the particular purpose of inviting a subscription for shares and if it was used by a shareholder for the different purpose of buying shares in the stock market there was not a sufficiently proximate relationship between the directors and the shareholder for a duty of care to arise on the part of the directors. It followed that any reliance on the part of the plaintiff on the prospectus or the interim report issued by the company in connection with a rights issue to buy shares in CT plc and M Ltd in the stock market did not give rise to a duty of care on the part of the defendants. It followed that the claims in the statement of claim arising out of transactions 2 to 6 would be struck out on the grounds that they disclosed no reasonable cause of action (see p 327 *f* to *h* and p 329 *b c*, post).

Caparo Industries plc v Dickman [1990] 1 All ER 568 and *Smith v Eric S Bush (a firm)* [1989] 2 All ER 514 applied.

Notes

For directors' liability for negligence, see 7(1) Halsbury's Laws (4th edn reissue) para 648 and for cases on misrepresentation by directors, see 9 Digest (Reissue) 109–124, 518–520, 546–666, 3098–3114.

For negligence in relation to statements by professional men, see 34 Halsbury's Laws (4th edn) para 53 and for cases on the subject, see 36(1) Digest (Reissue) 49–50, *149–158.*

Cases referred to in judgment
Andrews v Mockford [1896] 1 QB 372, CA.
Barry v Croskey (1861) 2 John & H 1, 70 ER 945.
Candler v Crane Christmas & Co [1951] 1 All ER 426, [1951] 2 KB 164, CA.
Candlewood Navigation Corp Ltd v Mitsui OSK Lines Ltd, The Mineral Transporter, The Ibaraki Maru [1985] 2 All ER 935, [1986] AC 1, [1985] 3 WLR 381, PC.
Caparo Industries plc v Dickman [1990] 1 All ER 568, [1990] 2 WLR 358, HL.
Hedley Byrne & Co Ltd v Heller & Partners Ltd [1963] 2 All ER 575, [1964] AC 465, [1963] 3 WLR 101, HL.
McKay v Essex Area Health Authority [1982] 2 All ER 771, [1982] QB 1166, [1982] 2 WLR 890, CA.
Peek v Gurney (1873) LR 6 HL 377, [1861–73] All ER Rep 116.
Scott Group Ltd v McFarlane [1978] 1 NZLR 553, NZ CA.
Smith v Eric S Bush (a firm) [1989] 2 All ER 514, [1989] 2 WLR 790, HL.
Williams & Humbert Ltd v W & H Trade Marks (Jersey) Ltd [1986] 1 All ER 129, [1986] AC 368, [1986] 2 WLR 24, HL.
Yianni v Edwin Evans & Sons (a firm) [1981] 3 All ER 592, [1982] QB 438, [1981] 3 WLR 843.

Summons
By a summons dated 2 May 1989 issued by the applicants, James George Stoddart Longcroft, Peter Brian Moody, Leon Joseph Staciokas, Jimmy Duane Stewart, Roger John Smith and Combined Technologies Corp plc, the first, second, third, fourth, fifth and ninth defendants respectively in an action brought against them by the plaintiffs, Al-Nakib Investments (Jersey) Ltd and Mrs Haya Al-Nakib, the applicants applied for an order that the statement of claim served on them on 18 November 1988 be struck out under RSC Ord 18, r 19, or under the inherent jurisdiction of the court, on the ground that it disclosed no reasonable cause of action. At the hearing of the summons the applicants applied for an order that paras 12 to 20 (inclusive), 23, 24.1, 24.4, 24.6.2, 24.6.3 and 24.7 (save for the reference to £236,924) be struck out. The summons was heard in chambers but judgment was delivered in open court. The facts are set out in the judgment.

Patrick Milmo QC and *Charles A H Gibson* for the plaintiffs.
Alan Steinfeld QC and *Lawrence Cohen* for the defendant applicants.

Cur adv vult

1 May. The following judgment was delivered.

MERVYN DAVIES J. I have before me a summons dated 2 May 1989 in an action in which the plaintiffs are Al-Nakib Investments (Jersey) Ltd (the Al-Nakib company) and Mrs Haya Al-Nakib and the defendants are (1) J G S Longcroft, (2) P B Moody, (3) L J Staciokas, (4) J D Stewart, (5) R J Smith, (6) F Mutch, (7) J A Pearman, (8) H C Butterfield and (9) Combined Technologies Corp plc. The summons was taken out by the first, second, third, fourth, fifth and ninth defendants (hereinafter called 'the applicants'). I am concerned only with para (2)(A) of the summons. Under para (2)(A) the applicants apply for an order that the statement of claim be struck out under RSC Ord 18, r 19 or under the inherent jurisdiction on the ground that it discloses no reasonable cause of action. Before me the application was not made in that wide form. The applicants asked for an order that paras 12 to 20 (inclusive), para 23 and paras 24.1, 24.4, 24.6.2, 24.6.3 and 24.7

(save the reference to £236,924) be struck out. If that order is made Mrs Al-Nakib would cease to be an effective plaintiff but the action would continue as respects some relief claimed by the Al-Nakib company. As is customary in a striking out application I will assume the matters stated in the statement of claim to be true and I will consider whether or not the challenged paragraphs disclose any causes of action.

The statement of claim was served on 18 November 1988 and was with consent amended before me. The amended statement of claim relies on the following matters.

(1) That at all material times the first to eighth defendants were directors of a Bermuda company called Mnemos Ltd that was incorporated on 14 April 1982. Mnemos was a subsidiary of the ninth defendant (Comtech), an English company.

(2) Comtech developed an electronic information storage and retrieval system (System 6000). Mnemos was incorporated to exploit System 6000.

(3) Application was made to The Stock Exchange for permission to deal in Mnemos shares, issued or to be issued, on the unlisted securities market. On 19 April 1983 (see para 4 of the statement of claim) 'There was published . . . a prospectus which invited persons to subscribe for 12,449,915 ordinary shares of 10 cents each in Mnemos at a price of 65p per share'. I was shown the prospectus referred to together with a circular letter dated 22 April 1983 referred to in para 11 thereof. In fact, in that letter the 'prospectus' is referred to as an 'Information Document'. The letter dated 22 April 1983 opens with these words:

> 'The directors of Comtech have decided that both Comtech and its subsidiary, Mnemos, should raise additional capital by means of issues respectively of 12,449,915 ordinary shares of 10p each of Comtech at 42p per share and 12,449,915 ordinary of 10 cents each of Mnemos at 65p per share, in each case by way of rights to Comtech's shareholders. In addition, certain institutional investors have agreed to subscribe an aggregate of 3,000,000 new ordinary shares of Mnemos at 65p per share.'

So the Mnemos shares were offered by the Comtech directors to the Comtech shareholders, the offer being associated with an offer of Comtech shares and with the fact that some Comtech shares were the subject of an agreed subscription by 'institutional investors'. The new Mnemos shares were offered to the Comtech shareholders at 65p per share on the basis of one Mnemos share for every five Comtech shares then held, and the Comtech shares at 42p per share on the basis of one for five. The action is concerned with shares taken up in response to the prospectus and the letter dated 22 April 1983 and with shares bought later in the market.

(4) The statement of claim (see, for example, paras 6 and 21) complains that a number of statements in the prospectus are untrue or misleading. In essence the principal complaint is of the untruth of a statement that System 6000 was a fully developed and marketable product. At the time of the issue of the prospectus the Al-Nakib company held 2,000,000 Comtech shares so that it was entitled to subscribe for 400,000 shares in Mnemos. In reliance on the prospectus Mr Talib Al-Nakib on behalf of the Al-Nakib company caused that company to subscribe for 400,000 Mnemos shares at a price of £260,000. As to that transaction (the first transaction) the Al-Nakib company, relying on inaccuracies in the prospectus, claims compensation pursuant to s 67 of the Companies Act 1895 and damages for negligence. The applicants do not seek to strike out those claims.

(5) In September 1983 Mnemos issued an interim report for the three months ended 30 June 1983 and in November 1983 another interim report for the six months ended 30 September 1983. Complaint is made of misrepresentations therein: see para 23.

(6) As well as the first transaction that I have mentioned the plaintiffs refer to six other transactions (said to have been entered into in reliance on the prospectus or the interim reports or both) concerning Mnemos or Comtech shares. Claims are made in respect of these other transactions and it is these claims which the applicants seek to strike out. The other six transactions are as follows. (i) The second transaction: the Al-Nakib company

acquired in the market (by numerous purchases through nominees) by 12 September 1983 3,000,042 Mnemos shares for £1,709,555 (see para 14.1). (ii) The third transaction: between 25 April and 15 May 1983 the Al-Nakib company acquired options on 1,050,000 shares in Mnemos for £95,608 (see para 14.3). (iii) The fourth transaction: by 12 September 1983 the Al-Nakib company increased its shareholding in Comtech by 6,489,271 extra shares in Comtech at a price of £2,390,422 (see para 14.2). (iv) The fifth transaction: the Al-Nakib company and Mrs Al-Nakib by 31 January 1984 acquired 3,795,000 Mnemos shares for £1,424,255 (see para 19.1). (v) The sixth transaction: on 17 October 1983 the Al-Nakib company acquired 400,000 Comtech shares for £97,779 (see para 19.2). (vi) The seventh transaction: the Al-Nakib company was allocated a shareholding in Comtech on applying for shares pursuant to the rights issue of Comtech shares referred to in the letter dated 22 April 1983. This transaction is not so clearly specified in the statement of claim (see para 12) as the others; but, as I understand, the plaintiffs complain that the transaction is affected by misrepresentations in the prospectus. The first, second, third, fourth and seventh transactions are said to be affected by misrepresentations in the prospectus; the fifth and sixth transactions are said to be affected by misrepresentations in the interim reports as read together with the prospectus. As I have said, the applicants do not seek to strike out the claims based on the first transaction. My understanding is that the seventh transaction is on the same footing in that that transaction relates to shares taken up in response to the rights issue. Accordingly, I propose to consider whether or not claims based on transactions 2 to 6 ought to be struck out.

The claims concerning transactions 2 to 6 are framed in negligence against Comtech and the Comtech directors, ie the applicants. Paragraphs 12 and 13 of the statement of claim are relevant to the prospectus claims. Those paragraphs read:

'12. Further or alternatively, at the time of issue of the prospectus the first, second, third and fifth defendants were directors of Comtech. They and Comtech knew or ought to have known that the first plaintiff had the shareholding referred to in para 10 hereof, which amounted to 2·3% or thereabouts of the ordinary shares in Comtech; that the first plaintiff was likely by reason of the issue of the prospectus to consider whether to acquire shares in Mnemos not only under the rights issue but also in the market, and whether to increase its shareholding in Comtech as the parent of Mnemos under a rights issue announced by the notice referred to in para 9 hereof and/or in the market; that persons, such as the second plaintiff, closely connected with the first plaintiff were likely by reason of the issue of the prospectus to consider whether to acquire shares in Mnemos in the market; and that the first plaintiff and persons such as the second plaintiff by themselves or by their agents would rely or were likely to rely upon the statements, the representations and the forecasts contained in the prospectus in deciding whether so to do.

13. By reason of the matters pleaded in para 12 hereof the first, second, third and fifth defendants and Comtech in considering the prospectus in draft form and in authorising its issue owed to the plaintiffs and each of them a duty of care.'

Paragraphs 17 and 18 are relevant to the claims based on the interim reports:

'17. At the time of the publications referred to in paras 15 and 16 hereof the first, second, third and fifth defendants were directors of Comtech as well as of Mnemos, and the third and fourth defendants were full time officers as well as directors of Mnemos. The first, second, third, fourth and fifth defendants and Comtech knew or ought to have known that Talib Al-Nakib on behalf of the first plaintiff following the publication of the prospectus and in reliance thereon had transacted the purchases set out in paragraphs 14.1, 14.2 and 14.3 hereof or otherwise had acquired large holdings of shares in Mnemos and in Comtech; that the first plaintiff by Mr Al-Nakib or otherwise was likely by reason of the said publications together with that of the prospectus to consider whether to buy further shares in Mnemos; that the second plaintiff by herself or by Mr Al-Nakib or otherwise was likely by reason of the said publications together with that of the prospectus to consider whether to buy shares in Mnemos; and that the first plaintiff by Mr Al-Nakib or otherwise and the second plaintiff by herself or by Mr Al-Nakib or otherwise would rely or were likely to rely upon the statements, the representations and the forecasts contained in the interim reports in deciding whether to do so. 18. By reason of the matters pleaded in paragraph 17 hereof the first, second, third, fourth and fifth defendants and Comtech in considering the interim reports in draft form and in authorising their publication owed to the plaintiffs and each of them a duty of care.'

There are further and better particulars of the statement of claim. In summary there is a pleading of duty, breach and damage thereby occasioned. The main question before me was whether any duty existed.

It is against this background that counsel for the applicants seeks to strike out the claims that derive from transactions 2 to 6. With the first transaction in mind he said that directors no doubt owe a duty of care in respect of statements in a prospectus to persons who subscribe for shares offered by that prospectus. But with transactions 2 to 6 in mind he said that it was otherwise. Before dealing with that approach I must consider some of the plaintiffs' submissions. Counsel for the plaintiffs said that no striking out should be ordered because it was inappropriate to consider the questions arising pursuant to an Ord 18, r 19 summons. In support of this view there were these observations.

(1) Order 18, r 19 is appropriate only for the disposal of simple cases: see *McKay v Essex Area Health Authority* [1982] 2 All ER 771 at 789, [1982] QB 1166 at 1191 where Griffiths LJ said:

'If on an application to strike out as disclosing no cause of action a judge realises that he cannot brush aside the argument, and can only decide the question after a prolonged and serious legal argument, he should refuse to embark on that argument and should dismiss the application unless there is a real benefit to the parties in determining the point at that stage.'

Griffiths LJ appears to have been there in a minority but his view accords with that of Lord Templeman in *Williams & Humbert Ltd v W & H Trade Marks (Jersey) Ltd* [1986] 1 All ER 129 at 139, [1986] AC 368 at 435–436:

'My Lords, if an application to strike out involves a prolonged and serious argument the judge should, as a general rule, decline to proceed with the argument unless he not only harbours doubts about the soundness of the pleading but, in addition, is satisfied that striking out will obviate the necessity for a trial or will substantially reduce the burden of preparing for trial or the burden of the trial itself.'

(2) In the present case striking out will not dispose of the action. There will in any event be a trial as respects the first transaction. At the trial much time will be spent on the issue as to breach or not of a duty of care, ie did the prospectus contain misrepresentations? The very same breach issue arises as respects transactions 2 to 6. It would be convenient to debate the issue as to breach along with the issue as to whether or not a duty of care arose as respects transactions 2 to 6. On the other hand, junior counsel for the applicants (who spoke in the absence of leading counsel) said that great time and expense would be saved if striking out were allowed in that there would be avoided a consideration of a multiplicity of share dealings engaged in by the plaintiffs after April 1983. Thus the first transaction appears to have been made up of no less than 25 separate packets of purchases of shares made through nominees. In the same way some of the other transactions are made up of numerous separate orders.

(3) The defendants ought to have proceeded by way of RSC Ord 33, r 3 rather than RSC Ord 18, r 19.

I see great force in these submissions. Indeed, I had myself referred to the *Williams & Humbert* case at an early stage. However, the submissions I have mentioned were made to me after I had heard detailed arguments of counsel for the applicants in favour of striking out. He raised in me such 'doubts' as Lord Templeman mentions in the *Williams & Humbert* case. As well I supposed that the trial might be shortened if there was a striking out. Thus it was that the application was not at that stage dismissed and I heard argument from both sides on the question raised by the summons, ie did the defendants owe to the plaintiffs a duty of care in respect of transactions 2 to 6? That question having been considered at length I must give it my consideration.

As to this question counsel for the applicants said that the directors of a company do not owe in respect of statements contained in a prospectus issued by the company (and/ or in interim reports published by the company) any duty of care to shareholders or others who might rely on those statements for the purpose of deciding to buy shares in the market. Counsel for the applicants said that in this case the Mnemos prospectus was issued for a particular purpose, that is to say to invite Comtech shareholders to subscribe for shares in Mnemos at 65p per share. That being the purpose of the prospectus it could not, it was said, be relied on in respect of a purchase of shares in the market. So in essence counsel says that transactions 2 to 6, being transactions in the market, cannot be related to the prospectus (or the interim statements) for the purpose of founding a negligence claim against the directors. I was referred to *Peek v Gurney* (1873) LR 6 HL 377, [1861–73] All ER Rep 116. The last holding in the headnote reads (6 HL 377 at 378):

'Held, that when the allotment was completed the office of the prospectus was exhausted, and that a person who had not become an allottee, but was only a subsequent purchaser of shares in the market, was not so connected with the prospectus as to render those who had issued it liable to indemnify him against the losses which he had suffered in consequence of his purchase.'

However, more particularly, counsel relied on the recent case of *Caparo Industries plc v Dickman* [1990] 1 All ER 568, [1990] 2 WLR 358. I was taken carefully through the speeches. Contract apart, there are circumstances in which a statement occasioning economic loss may be the subject of a negligence claim. Lord Bridge said ([1990] 1 All ER 568 at 576, [1990] 2 WLR 358 at 367–368):

'The salient feature of all these cases is that the defendant giving advice or information was fully aware of the nature of the transaction which the plaintiff had in contemplation, knew that the advice or information would be communicated to him directly or indirectly and knew that it was very likely that the plaintiff would rely on that advice or information in deciding whether or not to engage in the transaction in contemplation. In these circumstances the defendant could clearly be expected, subject always to the effect of any disclaimer of responsibility, specifically to anticipate that the plaintiff would rely on the advice or information given by the defendant for the very purpose for which he did in the event rely on it.'

So, as I understand, if X makes a statement and Y in reliance on the statement enters into a transaction which occasions a loss, Y can sue X if in the circumstances of the case X owes Y a duty of care. That duty of care exists only if X when making his statement knew or ought to have known that Y would rely on it for the purpose of such a transaction as Y did, in fact, enter into. In *Caparo Industries plc v Dickman* [1990] 1 All ER 568 at 578–579, [1990] 2 WLR 358 at 371 Lord Bridge quoted with approval the following extract from Richmond P in *Scott Group Ltd v McFarlane* [1978] 1 NZLR 553 at 566:

'All the speeches in *Hedley Byrne* seem to me to recognise the need for a "special" relationship: a relationship which can properly be treated as giving rise to a special

duty to use care in statement. The question in any given case is whether the nature
of the relationship is such that one party can fairly be held to have assumed a
responsibility to the other as regards the reliability of the advice or information. I
do not think that such a relationship should be found to exist unless, at least, the
maker of the statement was, or ought to have been, aware that his advice or
information would in fact be made available to and be relied on by a particular
person or class of persons for the purposes of a particular transaction or type of
transaction. I would especially emphasise that to my mind it does not seem
reasonable to attribute an assumption of responsibility unless the maker of the
statement ought in all the circumstances, both in preparing himself for what he said
and in saying it, to have directed his mind, and to have been able to direct his mind,
to some particular and specific purpose for which he was aware that his advice or
information would be relied on. In many situations that purpose will be obvious.
But the annual accounts of a company can be relied on in all sorts of ways and for
many purposes.'

In the *Caparo* case Lord Jauncey said ([1990] 1 All ER 568 at 607, [1990] 2 WLR 358):

'If the statutory accounts are prepared and distributed for certain limited purposes,
can there nevertheless be imposed on auditors an additional common law duty to
individual shareholders who choose to use them for another purpose without the
prior knowledge of the auditors? The answer must be No. Use for that other purpose
would no longer be use for the "very transaction" which Denning LJ in *Candler v
Crane Christmas & Co* [1951] 1 All ER 426 at 435, [1951] 2 KB 164 at 183 regarded
as determinative of the scope of any duty of care. Only where the auditor was aware
that the individual shareholder was likely to rely on the accounts for a particular
purpose such as his present or future investment in or lending to the company
would a duty of care arise. Such a situation does not obtain in the present case.'

Those words show that a duty of care is not fastened on to a situation when a statement
has been made for a particular purpose and the statement is used for another purpose.
That view also emerges, as I understand, from the words of Lord Bridge and of
Richmond P quoted above. In the present case we have the statements in the prospectus
made by the directors. It is said that the Al-Nakib company (acting by Mr Al-Nakib) in
reliance on the prospectus entered into transactions 2, 3 and 4. So does a duty of care exist
as between the directors and the Al-Nakib company? I would suppose that a duty of care
would not be regarded as arising because Mr Al-Nakib made use of the prospectus for a
purpose otherwise than that for which it was issued. The prospectus was given to
Comtech shareholders to enable them to consider whether or not to take up an offer of 1
Mnemos share for every 5 Comtech shares at a price of 65p per share. In these
circumstances there appears not to arise 'the special relationship' that is referred to in the
Scott Group case [1978] 1 NZLR 553: so that the facts pleaded do not suffice to ground
any duty of care as respects transactions 2, 3 and 4. On that footing my conclusion would
be the same (as respects the company and Mrs Al-Nakib) in respect of transactions 5 and
6. The interim reports (whether read alone or conjoined with the prospectus) were issued
for the purpose of informing the shareholders of Mnemos of the activities of the
company. Mr Al-Nakib used the reports for the purpose of making up his mind whether
or not to buy in the market.

I must not come to a conclusion without considering some of the submissions counsel
made for the plaintiffs. He referred to the words of Lord Bridge in the *Caparo* case [1990]
1 All ER 568 at 576, [1990] 2 WLR 358 at 368:

'Hence, looking only at the circumstances of these decided cases where a duty of
care in respect of negligent statements has been held to exist, I should expect to find
that the "limit or control mechanism . . . imposed on the liability of a wrongdoer
towards those who have suffered economic damage in consequence of his negligence"

(see *Candlewood Navigation Corp Ltd v Mitsui OSK Lines Ltd, The Mineral Transporter, The Ibaraki Maru* [1985] 2 All ER 935 at 945, [1986] AC 1 at 25) rested on the *a* necessity to prove, in this category of the tort of negligence, as an essential ingredient of the "proximity" between the plaintiff and the defendant, that the defendant knew that his statement would be communicated to the plaintiff, either as an individual or as a member of an identifiable class, specifically in connection with a particular transaction or transactions of a particular kind (eg in a prospectus inviting investment) and that the plaintiff would be very likely to rely on it for the purpose *b* of deciding whether or not to enter on that transaction or on a transaction of that kind.'

Counsel emphasised the words 'eg in a prospectus inviting investment', saying that the Mnemos prospectus invited investment. However that may be, I agree with counsel for the applicants that one still has to consider whether the prospectus which Lord Bridge *c* had in mind invites buying in the market or in the way of taking up a rights issue. Counsel for the plaintiffs said that the Mnemos prospectus was issued to encourage the Comtech shareholders (including the first plaintiff) to take up Mnemos shares either by taking up the rights issue or by buying in the market. Encouragement to buy in the market was said to be found in a statement appearing in the letter dated 22 April 1983:

'Any new ordinary shares of Mnemos or Comtech representing allocations not *d* taken up and which can be sold in the market at a net premium not later than the close of business on 17 May 1983, will be sold and the proceeds . . . will be remitted in due course to the persons to whom the Rights were originally allocated and whose allocations have not been taken up . . .'

I see no encouragement to buy in the market contained in those words nor from the *e* words with which the prospectus itself opens, 'Application has been made to the Council of the Stock Exchange for the grant of permission to deal in the ordinary shares of Mnemos . . . on the Unlisted Securities Market.' Then it was said that the document in the *Caparo* case, an auditor's report, was to be contrasted with the documents now under consideration, ie the prospectus and the interim reports. The documents, of course, do differ but the question whether statements in a document give rise to liability is the same *f* whatever may be the nature of the document; that is, was the document written for a particular purpose and to be communicated to a particular person or class of persons? Counsel for the plaintiffs relied on the words of Lord Griffiths in *Smith v Eric S Bush* [1989] 2 All ER 514 at 536, [1989] 2 WLR 790 at 815–816:

'I have come to the conclusion that Yianni's case (ie *Yianni v Edwin Evans & Sons (a firm)* [1981] 3 All ER 592, [1982] QB 438) was correctly decided. I have already *g* given my view that the voluntary assumption of responsibility is unlikely to be a helpful or realistic test in most cases. I therefore return to the question in what circumstances should the law deem those who give advice to have assumed responsibility to the person who acts on the advice or, in other words, in what circumstances should a duty of care be owed by the adviser to those who act on his *h* advice? I would answer: only if it is foreseeable that if the advice is negligent the recipient is likely to suffer damage, that there is a sufficiently proximate relationship between the parties and that it is just and reasonable to impose the liability.'

I respectfully adopt those words but, of course, they leave for further consideration what is a 'sufficiently proximate relationship'? As I understand that question, it is to be answered by considering by whom and to whom the advice is given: see, for example, *j* Lord Oliver in the *Caparo* case [1990] 1 All ER 568 at 589, [1990] 2 WLR 358 at 383–384.

There was then a reference to *Andrews v Mockford* [1896] 1 QB 372. There the plaintiff recovered damages in respect of false statements in a prospectus. After mentioning *Peek v Gurney* (1873) LR 6 HL 377, [1861–73] All ER Rep 116 and *Barry v Croskey* (1861) 2 John & H 1, 70 ER 945 A L Smith LJ said (at 381):

> 'In my opinion, without discussing the effect of these cases, neither decision governs the present one, which is a case of continued systematic fraud from its commencement to its end.'

For my part I do not accept that anything may be derived from that case, either by inference or by analogy, that is of help to the plaintiffs.

In the light of what I have said about counsel for the plaintiff's submissions it will be appreciated that I am confirmed in my view that the defendants did not owe to the plaintiffs a duty of care in respect of transactions 2 to 6; in that the prospectus (and the interim reports) having been addressed to the first plaintiff for a particular purpose (ie considering the rights issue) it was used by the plaintiffs for another purpose (ie buying shares in the market): see Lord Jauncey in the *Caparo* case [1990] 1 All ER 568 at 606, [1990] 2 WLR 358 at 404 where he refers to 'the fundamental question of the purpose'.

There remains the question whether or not striking out should nevertheless be refused for the reason that, in the circumstances of this case, an Ord 18, r 19 application was inappropriate or, at any rate, that the application ought to have been founded on Ord 33, r 3. A litigant ought not to launch an Ord 18, r 19 application when it is clear that the application will involve days of legal discussion. If he does so the application may be dismissed in accordance with Lord Templeman's words in *Williams & Humbert Ltd v W & H Trade Marks (Jersey) Ltd* [1986] 1 All ER 129 at 139, [1986] AC 368 at 435. However that may be, in the manner that I have set out above, the application was entertained and in the result I came to the firm conclusion that striking out was appropriate. Those events having happened it would, I think, be wrong to refuse relief on the ground that the defendants should have desisted from their application because it was likely to involve days of argument. I add that I agree with counsel for the plaintiffs in the view that if the application was to be made at all it should have been made under Ord 33, r 3. But now that the matter has been considered at length I think that little can be made of that point for reasons similar to those given by Lord Templeman in the *Williams & Humbert* case [1986] 1 All ER 129 at 139, [1986] AC 368 at 434.

It follows that a striking out will be ordered.

There will be struck out of the statement of claim paras 12, 14 to 20 (inclusive), 23, 24.4, 24.6.2, 24.6.3. In para 13 the reference to the plaintiffs should become a reference to the first plaintiff. In para 24.1 references to paras 14 and 19 should be deleted. There may in consequence be some consequential amendments to the statement of claim, e g para 12 may have to be rewritten to refer only to the seventh transaction. Leave is given for such consequential amendments.

Order accordingly.

Solicitors: *Kingsley Napley* (for the plaintiffs); *Norton Rose* (for the defendant applicants).

Jacqueline Metcalfe   Barrister.

Morgan Crucible Co plc v Hill Samuel Bank Ltd and others

CHANCERY DIVISION

HOFFMANN J

19, 20, 24 JULY 1990

Negligence – Information or advice – Knowledge that third party might rely on information – Take-over bid – Duty of care to bidder – Preparation of target company's financial statements and profit forecast – Duty to potential or actual bidder – Financial statements of company issued before announcement of bid for company – After announcement of bid target company issuing circulars and profit forecast – Circulars issued to and for guidance of shareholders – Whether board and advisers of target company owing duty of care to bidder – Whether sufficient proximity between bidder and board and advisers of target company to found action in negligence.

On 6 December 1985 the plaintiff company announced a take-over bid for another company, FCE. At that date the recent published financial statements of FCE were its report and accounts for the years ended 31 January 1984 and 1985, which had been audited by a firm of accountants, and an unaudited interim statement for the six months to July 1985. Before the bid the chairman of the plaintiff asked the chairman of FCE to confirm a profit forecast for the year to 31 January 1986 but received no reply. The formal offer document was sent on 17 December. On 19 December the chairman of FCE sent to FCE shareholders the first of a number of circulars, all of which were also issued as press releases by the merchant bank advising FCE. The chairman of FCE compared the profit record of the plaintiff unfavourably with that of FCE and recommended that the offer be refused. Further circulars followed on 31 December, 8 January 1986 and 17 January. All the documents expressly or impliedly referred to the earlier financial statements and the circular of 31 December announced that they were available for inspection. A circular dated 24 January 1986 forecast a 38% increase in profits before tax in the year to 31 January 1986. This document included a letter from the accountants stating that it had been properly compiled in accordance with FCE's stated accounting policies and a letter from the bank expressing the opinion that the forecast had been made after due and careful inquiry. On 29 January the plaintiff increased its bid and on 31 January 1986 the board of FCE sent a further circular recommending acceptance. On 14 February the bid was declared unconditional. The plaintiff subsequently claimed that the accounting policies adopted in the pre-bid financial statements and the profit forecast were negligently misleading and had the effect of grossly overstating the profits of FCE and that FCE was worthless at the time the bid was made with the result that if the plaintiff had known the true facts, it would never have made the bid, let alone increased it. The plaintiff issued a writ against the bank, the accountants, and the chairman and directors of FCE alleging that the plaintiff would foreseeably rely on the representations contained in the pre-bid financial statements and the profit forecast. The plaintiff subsequently applied to amend its statement of claim to allege that its actual materialisation as a bidder created the necessary relationship of proximity which gave rise to the duty of care owed by the defendants to the plaintiff. The defendants contended that the proposed amendments to the statement of claim disclosed no cause of action.

Held – The directors and financial advisers of the target company in a contested take-over bid owed no duty of care to a known take-over bidder regarding the accuracy of profit forecasts, financial statements and defence documents prepared for the purpose of contesting the bid since the reason such documents were prepared was to advise the shareholders of the target company whether to accept the bid and they were not meant for the guidance of the bidder. Accordingly, there did not exist sufficient proximity

between the directors and financial advisers of the target company and the bidder to give
a rise to a duty of care. It followed that the defendants did not owe a duty of care to the
plaintiff to ensure that FCE's pre-bid financial statements and the profit forecast were
accurate. The proposed amendments to the statement of claim disclosed no cause of
action and the application to amend would be dismissed (see p 335 j to p 336 a f h to
p 338 a, post).

Caparo Industries plc v Dickman [1990] 1 All ER 568 applied; Smith v Eric S Bush (a firm),
b Harris v Wyre Forest DC [1989] 2 All ER 514 considered.

Notes

For the duty of care generally and claims for economic loss, see 34 Halsbury's Laws (4th
edn) paras 5, 6, and for cases on the subject, see 36(1) Digest (Reissue) 17–32, 34–103.
For negligence in relations to statements by professional men, see 34 Halsbury's Laws
c (4th edn) para 53, and for cases on the subject, see 36(1) Digest (Reissue) 49–50, 149–158.

Cases referred to in judgment

Caparo Industries plc v Dickman [1990] 1 All ER 568, [1990] 2 WLR 358, HL.
Smith v Eric S Bush (a firm), Harris v Wyre Forest DC [1989] 2 All ER 514, [1990] 1 AC 831,
    [1989] 2 WLR 790, HL.
d

Summons

By a statement of claim served on 17 July 1987 the plaintiff, Morgan Crucible Co plc,
brought an action in negligence against the first to eighth defendants, namely Hill
Samuel Bank Ltd, Judkins & Co (a firm), Leslie John Connor, Howard Michael West,
John Laurence Harris, Kenneth Austin Broome, John Wilson Smith and John Victor
e Woollam, being respectively the bank, accountants, chairman and directors of First Castle
Electronics plc. On 19 July 1990 the plaintiff applied for leave to amend its statement of
claim. The application was heard in chambers but judgment was given by Hoffmann J
in open court. The facts are set out in the judgment.

   Stephen Suttle for Morgan Crucible.
f Michael Brindle for the bank.
   Thomas Lowe for the accountants.
   Leslie Kosmin for Mr Connor.
   Nigel Davis for the fourth and fifth defendants.
   Michael McLaren for the sixth to eighth defendants.

g   Cur adv vult

24 July. The following judgment was delivered.

HOFFMANN J. This is a summons for leave to amend which was heard in chambers.
It raises a point of very considerable importance for the City of London, namely whether
h the directors and financial advisers of the target company in a contested take-over bid
owe a duty of care to the bidder. For this reason, with the consent of the parties, I am
giving this judgment in open court.
   On 6 December 1985 the plaintiff (Morgan Crucible) announced a bid for First Castle
Electronics plc (the company). At that date the recent published financial statements of
the company were its report and accounts for the years ended 31 January 1984 and 1985,
j which had been audited by the second defendants (the accountants) and an unaudited
interim statement for the six months to July 1985. Before the bid the chairman of
Morgan Crucible asked the chairman of the company to confirm a profit forecast for the
year to 31 January 1986 but had received no reply.
   The formal offer document went out on 17 December. The usual exchange of boasts
and insults followed. Morgan Grenfell & Co advised the bidders and the first defendants,

Hill Samuel Bank Ltd (the bank), advised the company. On 19 December the third defendant (Mr Connor) as chairman of the company sent to shareholders the first of a number of circulars, all of which were also issued as press releases by the bank. Mr Connor compared the profit record of Morgan Crucible unfavourably with that of the company and recommended that the offer be refused. Further circulars followed on 31 December, 8 January and 17 January. All these documents expressly or impliedly referred to the earlier financial statements and the circular of 31 December announced that they were available for inspection. A circular dated 24 January 1986 forecast a 38% increase in profits before tax in the year to 31 January 1986. This document included a letter from the accountants stating that it had been properly compiled in accordance with the company's stated accounting policies and a letter from the bank expressing the opinion that the forecast had been made after due and careful inquiry. On 29 January Morgan Crucible increased its bid and on 31 January 1986 the board of the company sent a further circular recommending acceptance. On 14 February the bid was declared unconditional. A further recommendation of acceptance to shareholders who had not yet accepted was sent out by the board on 27 February.

This fairly commonplace history of a successful contested bid was followed, as occasionally happens, by disappointment and recrimination. Morgan Crucible says that the accounting policies adopted in the pre-bid financial statements and the profit forecast were negligently misleading and had the effect of grossly overstating the profits. Having paid about £50m for the company, Morgan Crucible now says that it was worthless. If it had known the true facts, it would never have made the bid, let alone increased it. A writ was issued on 6 May 1987, naming as defendants the bank, the accountants, Mr Connor and the rest of the board, both executive and non-executive. As originally pleaded, the statement of claim alleged that the accountants and the board were responsible for putting the financial statements into circulation and that they and the bank were responsible for the profit forecast and that a duty of care was owed to Morgan Crucible as a person who would foreseeably rely on them. Morgan Crucible did so rely on them in making and then increasing its offer and suffered loss in consequence. All these allegations were put in issue by the defendants. Discovery was huge and last year the action was set down for trial in January 1991 with an estimated length of 10 weeks.

On 8 February 1990 the House of Lords gave judgment in *Caparo Industries plc v Dickman* [1990] 1 All ER 568, [1990] 2 WLR 358. The House decided that auditors who certify a company's accounts for the purposes of the Companies Act 1985 owe no duty of care to a potential take-over bidder. It is not sufficient that it is foreseeable, even highly foreseeable, that there may be a bid and that the bidder will rely on the accounts. The House held that there was not the relationship of 'proximity' between auditors and bidder needed to found a duty of care.

Morgan Crucible recognised at once that *Caparo* was a blow to the way its case was originally pleaded. It had simply said that the financial statements and profit forecast had been published to the world at large and that Morgan Crucible was foreseeably a person who would rely on the representations which they contained. Now *Caparo* has decided that foreseeability is not enough. Something more is needed to create proximity. When the defendants said that in the light of *Caparo* they were considering a motion to strike out the action, Morgan Crucible asked them to wait while it formulated amendments to the statement of claim. It is the application to make these amendments which is now before me. Counsel for Morgan Crucible says that the amendments raise an arguable case for the existence of the necessary proximity. The defendants say that they do not. It is accepted that the test for whether I should allow the amendments is whether they would survive an application under RSC Ord 18, r 19 to strike them out as disclosing no cause of action.

In essence Morgan Crucible now says in its proposed amendments that what created a relationship of proximity was its actual materialisation as a bidder. Up to the moment when the bid was announced, it was merely someone in the market who might or might

not bid and *Caparo* shows that the auditors and, by parity of reasoning, the directors
a owed it no duty of care. But the announcement of the bid placed it in a relationship of
proximity and thereafter the board and its advisers owed it two duties. First, to take care
to correct any inaccurate pre-bid statements on which it would foreseeably have relied
and second, to take reasonable care in making statements in defence documents on which
it would foreseeably rely.

Counsel for Morgan Crucible, who valiantly defended his statement of claim against
b the combined attacks of five opponents, said that the announcement of the bid took him
out of the *Caparo* principle and brought him within that of the earlier decision of the
House of Lords in *Smith v Eric S Bush (a firm)* [1989] 2 All ER 514, [1990] 1 AC 831. In
that case the House had held that a surveyor carrying out a valuation for a building
society owes a duty of care to the intending purchaser, notwithstanding that the terms of
the valuation make it clear that it is intended only for the purposes of the building society
c in deciding whether to lend and that the purchaser is not to rely on it. In distinguishing
that case in *Caparo* [1990] 1 All ER 568 at 592, [1990] 2 WLR 358 at 387 Lord Oliver
said that it—

> 'provides no support for the proposition that the relationship of proximity is to
> be extended beyond circumstances in which advice is tendered for the purpose of
d > the particular transaction or type of transaction and the adviser knows or ought to
> know that it will be relied on by a particular person or class of persons in connection
> with that transaction.'

In this case, as in *Smith v Bush* but unlike *Caparo,* the defendants knew the particular
person who was likely to rely on the statements and the very transaction in which he
would do so. There was an announced bid by an identifiable bidder. The fact that the
e documents were formally addressed to the shareholders rather than the bidder made no
difference because, as Lord Oliver also explained, *Smith v Bush* makes it clear that—

> 'the absence of a positive intention that the advice shall be acted on by anyone
> other than the immediate recipient, indeed an expressed intention that it shall not
> be acted on by anyone else, cannot prevail against actual or presumed knowledge
f > that it is in fact likely to be relied on in a particular transaction without independent
> verification.'

(See [1990] 1 All ER 568 at 589–590, [1990] 2 WLR 358 at 384.)

Counsel for Morgan Crucible said that Morgan Crucible's case was in this respect much
stronger than in *Smith v Bush* because not only was there no disclaimer, but the pleaded
allegations showed a clear appreciation that Morgan Crucible would rely on the
g statements and the inference could be drawn that it was intended to do so. Thus on 17
January the company's chairman, Mr Connor, wrote to his shareholders:

> 'I will be writing to you next week with important news about First Castle's
> trading in the current year, and I believe that Morgan Crucible will thereafter be
> seriously considering increasing its offer to a more realistic level.'

h In a letter to the bank on 20 January, he said:

> '... the next circular ... has to be powerful, convincing but of course polite. It
> will form the basis on which Morgan Crucible may decide to increase their offer for
> our shares and perhaps will also flush out any other interested parties who may be
> watching from the touch-line.'

j This was a skilfully presented argument, but its weakness, as it seems to me, was that
it analysed the differences between *Caparo* and *Smith v Bush* solely in terms of the
knowledge, intentions and purposes of the parties. For the purposes of determining
whether or not a duty of care exists in a case of a negligent statement, they are an
impoverished set of concepts. Of course they are very important and are if I may

respectfully say so, rightly emphasised in various passages in the speeches in *Caparo* which contain general guidelines for whether or not a duty of care exists in cases of negligent statements. But they are by no means the only relevant factors. In distinguishing *Smith v Bush* by reference to knowledge and purpose, Lord Oliver guardedly said that it did not support an extension of proximity beyond cases in which the statement was intended for a particular person in a particular transaction. He did not suggest that liability would always exist when these conditions were satisfied.

In the recent cases on negligent statements in the House of Lords there is a strong current of emphasis on the importance of the specific situation in which the statement is made. The following passage from Lord Bridge in *Caparo* [1990] 1 All ER 568 at 573–574, [1990] 2 WLR 358 at 365 is typical:

'What emerges [from earlier authorities] is that, in addition to the foreseeability of damage, necessary ingredients in any situation giving rise to a duty of care are that there should exist between the party owing the duty and the party to whom it is owed a relationship characterised by the law as one of "proximity" or "neighbourhood" and that the situation should be one in which the court considers it fair, just and reasonable that the law should impose a duty of a given scope on the one party for the benefit of the other. But it is implicit in the passages referred to that the concepts of proximity and fairness embodied in these additional ingredients are not susceptible of any such precise definition as would be necessary to give them utility as practical tests, but amount in effect to little more than convenient labels to attach to the features of different specific situations which, on a detailed examination of all the circumstances, the law recognises pragmatically as giving rise to a duty of care of a given scope. Whilst recognising, of course, the importance of the underlying general principles common to the whole field of negligence, I think the law has now moved in the direction of attaching greater significance to the more traditional categorisation of distinct and recognisable situations as guides to the existence, the scope and the limits of the varied duties of care which the law imposes.'

In this passage pragmatism was not, I am sure, intended to be contrasted with principle but as meaning that, at least in cases of negligent statements, a principled decision requires finer discriminations than are possible with the aid of the high-level generalisations previously thought sufficient. The incremental approach recommended by the House of Lords requires one to analyse the factors which have been treated as relevant to the existence, scope or non-existence of a duty in earlier cases and deduce lower level principles which can be applied to new situations.

In a number of respects, the situations in *Caparo* and *Smith v Bush* were similar. First, the statements were in both cases obtained by the immediate recipients pursuant to a statutory obligation: in *Caparo* the auditor's certificate was required by the Companies Act 1985 and in *Smith v Bush* the valuation was required by the Building Societies Act 1986. In *Caparo* an analysis of the company legislation led to the conclusion that the statutory purpose of the auditor's certificate was to provide the shareholders and debenture holders with reliable information to enable them to exercise their rights as such and not to protect investors in the market. Likewise, in *Smith v Bush* it was plain that the purpose of the requirement of a valuation in the Building Societies Act 1986 was to ensure that the society did not lend on inadequate security and not to protect the purchaser.

Second, in neither case did the person making the statement actually have a wider purpose. In *Caparo* [1990] 1 All ER 568 at 593, [1990] 2 WLR 358 at 388, as Lord Oliver observed, there was no allegation that the auditors 'in certifying the accounts . . . did so for the purpose of assisting those who might be minded to profit from dealings in the company's shares.' Likewise, in *Smith v Bush* the valuer made it clear that he was giving

the valuation solely for the purposes of the building society and that the purchaser was
not to rely on it.

Third, in both cases reliance by the plaintiff was very foreseeable. In *Smith v Bush* there
was evidence that it was highly likely that the purchaser of a modest house would,
notwithstanding the disclaimer, rely on the valuation. In *Caparo* [1990] 1 All ER 568 at
579, [1990] 2 WLR 358 at 371 Lord Bridge was 'content to assume the high probability
of a take-over bid in reliance on the accounts . . .'

Why then was the House willing in *Smith v Bush* but not in *Caparo* to extend the duty
of care to a statement of which the statutory and declared purpose was different from
that for which it was used by the plaintiff? The differences between the cases appear with
great clarity in the speeches of Lord Templeman and Lord Griffiths in *Smith v Bush*. They
consist in the different economic relationships between the parties and the nature of the
markets in which they were operating.

First, Mr Smith had paid for the survey; although he had no contract with the
surveyor, the relationship was, as Lord Templeman said, 'akin to contract'. Economically
there was no distinction. Caparo Industries plc, on the other hand, had not paid for the
audit.

Second, the typical plaintiff in a *Smith v Bush* type case is a person of modest means and
making the most expensive purchase of his or her life. He is very unlikely to be insured
against the manifestation of inherent defects. The surveyor can protect himself relatively
easily by insurance. The take-over bidder, on the other hand, is an entrepreneur taking
high risks for high rewards and while some accountants may be able to take out sufficient
insurance, others may not. Furthermore, the take-over bidder is a limited liability
company and the accountants are individuals for whom, save so far as they are covered
by insurance, liability would mean personal ruin.

Third, the imposition of liability on surveyors would probably not greatly increase
their insurance costs and push up the cost of surveys because the typical buyer who relies
on a building society survey is buying a relatively modest house. Take-overs on the Stock
Exchange involve huge amounts and the effects on accountants' insurance and fees are
unpredictable.

I am conscious of the fact that courts do not have the information on which to form
anything more than a very broad view of the economic consequences of their decisions.
For this reason they are more concerned with what appears to be fair and reasonable than
with wider utilitarian calculations. For example, some might think that efficiency of the
economy requires that company management should be subject to the discipline of take-
overs and that take-overs should therefore be encouraged by reducing the risk that a
bidder relying on published financial statements will find that he has been misled. For
this purpose it may be necessary to bankrupt a few accountants to encourage the others.
On the other hand, if the decision in *Caparo* had gone the other way, firms of accountants
below a certain size may have been deterred by insurance costs from competing for the
audit work of public limited companies potentially liable to take-over bids. This would
have driven such companies into the hands of the largest firms. Such speculative
thoughts, while occasionally entertained by judges, tend to be left unarticulated and with
good reason: the courts are ill-equipped to evaluate them in any convincing fashion. If
the wider economic effects of a decision are contrary to the public interest, the legislature
must correct it. But that does not mean the economic realities which were mentioned in
Smith v Bush and which I have listed above do not enter into the consideration of what, as
Lord Bridge said, is 'fair, just and reasonable.' There is implicit in *Caparo* and explicit in
Smith v Bush a view about the significance of these matters and a principled decision
requires that I should accept that evaluation in this case.

If one has regard to the distinctions between *Caparo* and *Smith v Bush* which I have just
mentioned, it becomes very clear which side of the line the present case should fall. The
defence documents in this case, like the audit certificate in *Caparo* and the valuation in

Smith v Bush, have a regulatory background. In the present case, it was the City Code on Take-overs and Mergers (the code), an extra-statutory but none the less potent set of principles and rules by which the City regulates bids. It begins with a statement of general principles, which include the following:

'4. Shareholders must be given sufficient information and advice to enable them to reach a properly informed decision and must have sufficient time to do so. No relevant information should be withheld from them.

5. Any document or advertisement addressed to shareholders containing information or advice from an offeror or the board of an offeree company or their prospective advisers must, as is the case with a prospectus, be prepared with the highest standards of care and accuracy.

6. All parties to a take-over transaction must use every endeavour to prevent the creation of a false market in the securities of an offeror or the offeree company . . .'

Rule 30.2 requires the board of the offeree company to advise its shareholders of its views on the offer as soon as practicable after publication of the offer document. Rule 28.1 says:

'There are obvious hazards attached to the forecasting of profits: this should in no way detract from the necessity of maintaining the highest standards of accuracy and fair presentation in all communications to shareholders in a take-over. A profit forecast must be compiled with scrupulous care and objectivity by the directors, whose sole responsibility it is; the financial advisers must satisfy themselves that the forecast has been prepared in this manner by the directors.'

Under r 28.3(b):

'. . . the accounting policies and calculations for the forecasts must be examined and reported on by the auditors or consultant accountants. Any financial adviser mentioned in the document must also report on the forecasts.'

It is in my judgment clear from the tenor of these rules that the purpose of all the defence documents is to advise the shareholders whether or not to accept the bid and there is nothing to suggest that they are meant for the guidance of the bidder. The bidder has ex hypothesi already made his bid and under the terms of the code cannot withdraw it. The only effect which a defence document can have on him is to induce him to improve the bid if he thinks on reading it that, despite the counterblasts of his advisers, it is likely to persuade the shareholders that his offer is too low. All the defence documents were in fact addressed solely to the shareholders in the company. The reason why they were also released to the press was to comply with the principle that no false market should be created. The same information is released to everyone at exactly the same time and no advantage can be gained by being the first to receive a circular with an optimistic profit forecast. Counsel for Morgan Crucible placed some weight on the provisions in the code which require documents to be 'prepared with the highest standards of care and accuracy'. But this only concerns the standard of the duty. It does not affect the question of to whom the duty is owed.

Why then should the court be willing, any more than in *Caparo,* to extend the duty of care to a person relying on the documents for a purpose beyond that contemplated by the code? None of the economic distinctions between *Caparo* and *Smith v Bush* justify such an extension. The bidder has not paid for the information contained in the defence documents. The position of the bidder as a high risk entrepreneur and the accountants as professional men is the same. In relation to the shareholders the position of the accountants when reporting on the profit forecast may be different from what it was in *Caparo* because they are advising the shareholders individually on whether to sell their shares rather than collectively on the exercise of their rights in the management of the company. Accordingly, they may possibly owe individual duties to the shareholders to take reasonable care to ensure that they do not sell their shares too cheaply. But this has

nothing to do with whether they owe a duty to the bidder to take care that he does not
a pay too much. Similar reasoning applies to the bank and the case against a duty of care
owed by the directors is even stronger, since they would potentially be exposed to an
enormous liability against which they are very unlikely to be insured.

Should it make any difference that, unlike *Caparo,* the bid and bidder were, at the time
when the defence documents were issued, actual and known rather than potential and
foreseeable? I do not think so. Knowledge that a bid has actually been made is the
b limiting case on the scale of foreseeability. But in *Caparo* the degree to which a bid was
foreseeable was treated as irrelevant. During a bid, there is always the possibility that
another bidder (a 'white knight') may intervene with a higher bid. In deciding whether
or not to do so, he is also very likely to read the defence documents and the profit forecast.
On the distinction presently being advanced, the defendants would owe a duty of care to
the bidder who improved his offer on the strength of a defence document but not to
c another party who, no matter how foreseeably, made a counter-bid in reliance on the
same document. In my view it would be a mistake to base the existence of a duty of care
on subtle distinctions of knowledge and purpose rather than the realities of the economic
relationships between the parties and the market in which they are operating.

Nor does it matter that the documents and internal memoranda show that the board
and their advisers contemplated that Morgan Crucible would react to the statements in
d the defence documents. Of course there was a sense in which a purpose of the defence
documents was to persuade the bidder to improve his offer. It was highly foreseeable
that Morgan Crucible would take the defence documents into account in deciding
whether to increase the offer and the statements I have quoted are no more than frank
acknowledgements that their authors have foreseen the foreseeable. But it would seem
to me very odd that the existence of a duty of care, based on what is fair, just and
e reasonable, should depend on whether the defendants were sufficiently intelligent to
appreciate the realities of the situation and sufficiently honest to admit that they had
done so.

In my judgment, therefore, this case cannot be distinguished from *Caparo.* There is in
fact a sense in which the reasons for denying a duty of care are even stronger than in
f *Caparo.* In a contested bid, the interests of the bidder and the company's shareholders are
in conflict with each other. The duty of the board, with the professional assistance of its
advisers, is to ensure that the shareholders get as much as possible for their shares and the
interest of the bidder and his advisers is to ensure that he pays as little as possible. The
board cannot play safe by saying nothing because the code contains in r 30.2 a positive
duty to advise their shareholders. To impose on the board and its advisers a duty of care
g owed to the bidder would in my judgment put them in a difficult position. Counsel for
Morgan Crucible says that there is no problem: all that they have to do is to get their
profit forecasts right and their financial statements accurate and they will not be liable to
either side. But that is the case whenever one owes simultaneous duties to people with
conflicting interests. It can be done, but the position is nevertheless thought to be
uncomfortable and undesirable. The reality of a contested take-over bid is that you have
h to know which side you are on. Each side has its own advisers and everyone knows what
the rules are. In an agreed bid, the intending bidder can negotiate for access to more
information than is publicly available and even put in his own reporting accountant: see
r 19.1 of the code. But in a contested bid, he takes his chance on the information publicly
available. Counsel for the accountants, in a brief but telling submission, pointed out that
in the absence of an agreement under r 19.1, the code required that everyone in the
j market should be treated alike. In claiming a special duty of care requiring the furnishing
of additional information to itself alone, Morgan Crucible was seeking to subvert that
principle.

If there is no duty of care to the bidder in respect of the contents of the defence
documents, it must follow that there can plainly be no duty arising by reason of the bid
in relation to financial statements previously published. In my judgment, despite the

proposed amendments, the entire case based on the tort of negligence is bound to fail. Although a great deal had already been spent on legal costs before the decision in *Caparo*, it is still possible to save the huge costs of the preparation of expert and other evidence followed by a ten-week trial. The amendments will therefore be disallowed. Morgan Crucible will pay the defendants' costs in any event and there will be leave to appeal.

Order accordingly.

Solicitors: *Herbert Smith* (for Morgan Crucible); *Berwin Leighton* (for the bank); *Barlow Lyde & Gilbert* (for the accountants); *Reynolds Porter Chamberlain* (for Mr Connor); *McKenna & Co* (for the fourth and fifth defendants); *Allison & Humphreys* (for the sixth to eighth defendants).

Evelyn M C Budd   Barrister.

Gibbon v Mitchell and others

CHANCERY DIVISION

MILLETT J

20 FEBRUARY 1990

Dictum of MILLETT J at 343 applied in DENT v
DENT [1996] 1 All ER 659

Deed – Rectification – Gift – Mistake of law or fact – Transaction not having intended effect – Plaintiff executing surrender of life interest in marriage settlement fund with intention of vesting fund immediately and indefeasibly in his two children – Deed of surrender having effect of creating discretionary income fund during his lifetime and trust for capital for all his children after his death – Whether deed could be set aside.

The plaintiff was a beneficiary under a marriage settlement which created two funds for the plaintiff and his family and for his sister and her family. The value of the plaintiff's fund, in which the plaintiff had a protected life interest, was about £300,000. The plaintiff also had substantial assets of his own. In 1987, when the plaintiff was aged 69, he consulted accountants and solicitors to reduce the impact of inheritance tax on his estate on his death. On the mistaken advice of his professional advisers the plaintiff, without applying to the court under the Variation of Trusts Act 1958, executed a deed surrendering his life interest in his fund created by the marriage settlement and releasing his powers of appointment in respect of the fund with the intent that the fund should be vested immediately in his two children. However, because the surrender occasioned a forfeiture under the terms of the protective trusts the deed in fact had the effect of vesting an interest in possession in the fund's income in a discretionary class for the remainder of the plaintiff's life and after his death vesting the capital in all his children including any future children. When it was realised that the deed did not have the effect intended the plaintiff applied to the court to have the deed set aside.

Held – Whenever there was a voluntary transaction by which one party intended to confer a gift on another and the court was satisfied that the disponor did not intend the transaction to have the effect which it did the deed would be set aside for mistake of either law or fact so long as the mistake was as to the effect of the transaction itself and not merely as to its consequences or the advantages to be gained by entering into it. Since the evidence showed that the plaintiff had executed the deed in the clear belief that it vested the entire beneficial interest in both capital and income in his two children immediately and indefeasibly to the exclusion of himself and any one else whereas,

contrary to his instructions and intentions, it had the entirely different effect of creating
a a discretionary income fund during his lifetime and a trust for capital for all his children
after his death the court would grant the application and set aside the deed (see p 343 *b* to
h, post).

Walker v Armstrong (1856) 8 De GM & G 531, Re Walton's Settlement [1922] All ER Rep
439, Meadows v Meadows (1853) 16 Beav 401, Ellis v Ellis (1909) 26 TLR 166 and Phillipson
v Kerry (1863) 11 WR 1034 followed.

b
Notes
For setting aside deeds executed in error, see 12 Halsbury's Laws (4th edn) paras 1502–
1503.

Cases referred to in judgment
c Ellis v Ellis (1909) 26 TLR 166.
Meadows v Meadows (1853) 16 Beav 401, 51 ER 833.
Phillipson v Kerry (1863) 11 WR 1034.
Stone v Godfrey (1854) 5 De GM & G 76, 43 ER 798.
Walker v Armstrong (1856) 8 De GM & G 531, 44 ER 495.
Walton's Settlement, Re, Walton v Peirson [1922] 2 Ch 509, [1922] All ER Rep 439.
d Whiteside v Whiteside [1949] 2 All ER 913, [1950] Ch 65, CA.

Originating summons
By summons dated 1 August 1989 the plaintiff, Henry Gibbon, applied for (1) an order
that a deed dated 4 December 1987 executed by the plaintiff be rescinded and that the
trusts of and effecting the fund known as 'Henry's fund' as defined in a settlement dated
e 11 October 1946 made by the plaintiff's parents take effect as though the deed had not
been executed, and (2) an order pursuant to the Variation of Trusts Act 1958 varying the
trusts of the settlement. The defendants were Jane Mary Mitchell and David Henry
Gibbon, both of whom were entitled to the Henry fund in reversion expectant on the
death of the plaintiff, and Lionel Alfred White and Robin Bernard Jacomb Gibbon, who
were the trustees of the settlement. The facts are set out in the judgment.
f

Alan Steinfeld QC for the plaintiff.
Elizabeth Ovey for the defendants.

MILLETT J. This is an application by Mr Gibbon to set aside a deed which he executed
on 4 December 1987 by which he purported to surrender his protected life interest in a
g trust fund in favour of his two adult children, the first two defendants, whom I shall call
Jane and David, and to release a power of appointment in favour of his children and
remoter issue to the intent that Jane and David should take immediate beneficial interests
in the capital and income of the trust fund. Unfortunately, the deed was incapable of
having effect as intended and, accordingly, Mr Gibbon now applies to have it set aside on
h the ground that it was entered into in error.
The facts are not in dispute. Mr Gibbon was born on 1 August 1918. He is now
therefore 71 years old. Throughout his adult life he has been a successful farmer. He
carries on a farming business in partnership with Jane and David. They are his only
children, born of his first marriage. Jane, the elder, was born on 30 March 1945, so that
she is now almost 45 years old. She is married and has two children, aged 13 and 11.
j David was born on 23 March 1947, so that he is almost 43 years old. He is married and
has one very young child. Mr Gibbon's first wife died in 1978. He remarried in the
following year. There are no children of his second marriage.
On 11 October 1946, on the occasion of the marriage of Mr Gibbon's sister, May, his
parents made a marriage settlement. By that settlement, two funds were established,
May's fund, which was settled on trusts for Mr Gibbon's sister May and her family, and

Henry's fund, which was settled on similar though not identical trusts for the benefit of
Mr Gibbon and his family.

As far as Henry's fund was concerned, Mr Gibbon was given a protected life interest, *a*
but the persons who were to be included in the discretionary class of objects of the trust
which would arise in the event of forfeiture were expanded to include May and her issue.
Subject to his protected life interest and a limited power to appoint up to £500 a year to
a surviving spouse, the capital of Henry's fund was held in trust for such of his children
and remoter issue as he might by deed or deeds appoint, and in default of appointment *b*
for his children at 21, or in the case of females at 21 or earlier marriage, in equal shares.
In the event of there being no issue, there were cross-accruers between the two funds
which cannot of course now take effect.

The settlement contained an express clause (cl 13) which authorised May to surrender
her protected life interest so as to accelerate the interests of her children once they had
become vested. No similar provision was to be found in relation to Henry's fund.   *c*

In 1987 Mr Gibbon consulted his accountant and instructed him to review his estate,
both free and settled, with a view to advising what further steps he should take in order
to reduce the possible impact of inheritance tax on his death. He had a very substantial
free estate. In addition, Henry's fund was of a value of £300,000 or thereabouts.

In July 1987 the accountant reported and recommended that Mr Gibbon should   *d*
surrender his life interest in Henry's fund. His recommendation was expressly in terms
of Mr Gibbon surrendering his life interest in Henry's fund, 'the assets of which then
pass absolutely to David and Jane'. Mr Gibbon thereupon consulted a well known firm
of solicitors (not his present solicitors) who advised the execution of an appropriate deed.
They did not advise that there was any difficulty in relation to the surrender of Mr
Gibbon's protected life interest and, in particular, they did not advise that it could not be
done without incurring a forfeiture unless an order of the court was first obtained under   *e*
the Variation of Trusts Act 1958 which would remove the protection annexed to the life
interest. It is not clear how the error arose; it is possible that the fact that cl 13 of the
settlement was restricted to May's fund was overlooked.

Mr Gibbon's then solicitors also advised (correctly) that it was necessary for him to
release the limited power of appointment in favour of his widow and (incorrectly) that
he should release his special power to appointment in favour of future issue. They did so   *f*
expressly on the ground that this would enable Jane and David to take absolutely in equal
shares in default of appointment.

On receipt of his solicitors' advice, Mr Gibbon accepted their recommendations and
instructed them in the following terms:

> 'The various releases are to go ahead so that the fund passes immediately to David   *g*
> and Jane.'

In due course the solicitors prepared the deed of 4 December 1987. It accurately recites
the trusts of Henry's fund under the 1946 settlement and, in particular, that the fund is
held on protective trusts for the benefit of Mr Gibbon for the period of his life. Recital 4
is in these terms: *h*

> '[Mr Gibbon] has determined to release the powers of appointment hereinbefore
> recited and to surrender his life interest in the settlement so that his said protected
> life interest vests in his two children, namely Jane and David, absolutely.'

The operative part begins by the release of the powers of appointment in favour of   *j*
children and remoter issue, and in favour of the widow—

> 'to the intent that the said powers hereby released may henceforth be extinguished
> and so that [Mr Gibbon] may henceforth be precluded from exercising the said
> powers.'

Clause 2 is in the following terms:

a   '[Mr Gibbon] hereby surrenders, releases and assigns to Jane and David all that his protected life interest in the Henry fund, to the intent that such interest shall merge and be extinguished and that the entire interest therein shall become immediately vested in possession in Jane and David in equal shares absolutely.'

It is manifest from the very terms of the deed itself, let alone from the advice tendered
b by the solicitors which preceded it, that Mr Gibbon's object was to vest the entire capital and income of Henry's fund immediately in David and Jane to the exclusion of all other persons including himself. The deed did not, however, have that effect, because Mr Gibbon's life interest was subject to protective trusts. Accordingly, its purported surrender occasioned a forfeiture and brought into operation the discretionary trusts set out in s 33 of the Trustee Act 1925. Furthermore, the release of Mr Gibbon's power of
c appointment in favour of children and remoter issue, far from vesting the reversionary interest in capital in Jane and David exclusively, vested it in all Mr Gibbon's children including after-born children.

The consequence of these two errors is that so long as the deed stands there is an interest in possession in favour of a class of discretionary objects which will continue during the remainder of Mr Gibbon's life, and on his death the capital will vest in David
d and Jane together with any future children born to Mr Gibbon. Far from carrying out Mr Gibbon's intention to vest the capital immediately and indefeasibly in David and Jane, it has a totally different effect and one which will preclude effect being given to his intention. In those circumstances, Mr Gibbon applies to the court to have the deed set aside.

It is not, in my view, a case for rectification, but rather for setting aside for mistake.
e Mr Gibbon's intention could not be carried into effect by this deed or any other deed executed by him. What was required was an application to the court under the Variation of Trusts Act 1958. The equitable remedy of rectification, however, is only one aspect of a much wider equitable jurisdiction to relieve from the consequences of mistake.

My attention has been drawn to a number of authorities on the circumstances in
f which a voluntary disposition can be rectified, reformed or set aside where it has been entered into under a mistake, contrary to the intentions of the disponor, or in excess of his instructions.

In *Walker v Armstrong* (1856) 8 De GM & G 531, 44 ER 495 there was a series of errors which drew the criticism of Knight-Bruce LJ expressed in colourful and memorable terms, a series of errors which culminated in the drawing of a deed by solicitors who went far beyond their authority. Their instructions were to prepare an instrument for
g the limited purpose of restoring, confirming or assuring a life interest in certain estates, but the deed which they drew went further and inadvertently revoked a previous testamentary appointment. The solicitors had no instructions to prepare a document which revoked that appointment. The person who executed the document did not intend to revoke the appointment and the court relieved him from the consequences by
h declaring that in so far as the deed as executed went beyond his intentions and instructions it should not have effect.

That was a case where the disponor's intentions were carried out, but the document which he executed went further and had an effect which was beyond his instructions and outside his intentions. Knight-Bruce LJ found that so far as the deed exceeded the particular and restricted purpose for which the instructions were given, it was contrary
j to the wishes of the executing parties, opposed to their intention and executed by them in error.

In *Re Walton's Settlement, Walton v Peirson* [1922] 2 Ch 509, [1922] All ER Rep 439 in the events which had happened, funds settled by a husband and wife became held after the death of the husband in trust absolutely for the wife, subject only to an obligation that she should use the fund to purchase annuities for her own benefit. Being an elderly lady she did not wish to purchase annuities. She went to a solicitor and asked him to draw up whatever deed was necessary to relieve her from the obligation of purchasing *a* the annuities. He did not appreciate that his client, being solely entitled to the annuity when purchased, could call for a transfer for capital applicable for its purchase, and mistakenly advised her that she should revoke the trusts of the settlement. Unfortunately the effect of revoking them was to cause the trust fund to be held on a resulting trust for the settlors, and one half, therefore, revested in the husband's estate and not as intended in the wife. *b*

Following *Walker v Armstrong* Eve J held that it was a case where the solicitor had gone beyond his instructions in ignorance of the true legal position. His instructions and his client's intentions went no further than the revocation of the obligation to purchase annuities. Eve J said [1922] 2 Ch 509 at 513, [1922] All ER Rep 439 at 442:

> '. . . the client desirous only of putting an end to the trust for the purchase of the annuity and so instructing her adviser—the solicitor, in temporary forgetfulness of *c* the fact that the trust could be determined by a simple instruction to the trustees, preparing a deed which not only puts an end to the particular trust but revokes all the trusts of the settlement, and allowing the client to execute it without appreciating that it does a great deal more than give effect to her instructions. Can the client in these circumstances be held bound by the deed?'

d

On the authority of *Walker v Armstrong*, he held that she could not.

In *Meadows v Meadows* (1853) 16 Beav 401, 51 ER 833 a tenant in tail, wishing to mortgage the estate in order to borrow money, joined with his father, the tenant for life, in order to bar the entail so that appropriate security could be given to the mortgagee. The solicitors were instructed to draw the appropriate documentation which would bar the entail, secure the borrowing and then resettle the estate on the former trusts. They *e* took the opportunity to resettle the estate, cutting down the son's interest from a tenancy in tail to a life interest and resettling the estate on his children and remoter issue.

The court set the resettlement aside. In so far as the deed resettled the estate on new trusts, it was not authorised and was executed in ignorance of its true purport and effect. Romilly MR stated (16 Beav 401 at 404, 51 ER 833 at 834): *f*

> 'No person should be bound by a deed, unless he knew or had a fair opportunity of understanding its nature and operation before he executed it.'

He was, of course, talking about a voluntary transaction.

The present case, too, like the others is a case where the party executing the deed intended to achieve a specific purpose but through a mistake on the part of the professional advisers who drew the deed it either did not achieve it at all or achieved *g* something else in addition.

In *Ellis v Ellis* (1909) 26 TLR 166 a husband made a gift to his wife not realising that under the terms of her marriage settlement she had covenanted to settle all her after-acquired property. Warrington J, having described the mistake as a mistake of fact, held that the gift could be set aside. The mistake in fact was a mistake as to the effect of the after-acquired property clause in the marriage settlement. The husband, in evidence, said *h* that he knew of the settlement when he made the gift and that it contained an after-acquired property clause, but did not realise what the effect of the covenant was, and thought that it meant that the wife would have to settle anything that came to her from her own relations. Warrington J held that the gift could be set aside and stated that the requirements for setting aside a gift were not necessarily the same as those for setting *j* aside a transaction for value.

That case is, perhaps, not very different from the present, for here the principal mistake was either as to the effect of the provisions of s 33 of the Trustee Act 1925 or, more probably, a failure to appreciate that cl 13 of the 1946 settlement applied only to May's fund and not to Henry's.

Finally, in *Phillipson v Kerry* (1863) 11 WR 1034 a deed of gift was set aside on evidence
a that it was intended to be ambulatory. The finding which justified setting aside the gift
was that the consequences of the deed were not fully explained to the plaintiff and it did
not carry out her intentions.

In my judgment, these cases show that, wherever there is a voluntary transaction by
which one party intends to confer a bounty on another, the deed will be set aside if the
court is satisfied that the disponor did not intend the transaction to have the effect which
b it did. It will be set aside for mistake whether the mistake is a mistake of law or of fact,
so long as the mistake is as to the effect of the transaction itself and not merely as to its
consequences or the advantages to be gained by entering into it. The proposition that
equity will never relieve against mistakes of law is clearly too widely stated (see *Stone v
Godfrey* (1854) 5 De GM & G 76, 43 ER 798 and *Whiteside v Whiteside* [1949] 2 All ER
913 at 916, [1950] Ch 65 at 74).

c   I am satisfied on the internal evidence of the deed itself, as well as on the evidence
provided by the contemporaneous correspondence, that Mr Gibbon executed the deed in
the clear belief that it vested the entire beneficial interest in both capital and income in
Jane and David immediately and indefeasibly to the exclusion of himself and everyone
else. It did not; instead it brought into being a trust of income in favour of the
discretionary objects mentioned in s 33 of the Trustee Act 1925 during the remainder of
d his life, and a trust for capital for all his children, including future born children. That
was contrary to his instructions and intentions. It is true that if he were asked the narrow
question whether he intended to release his protected life interest or the power of
appointment in favour of his children, he must have answered 'Yes', for he was expressly
advised by his solicitors that both those steps were necessary in order to achieve his object.
But he did not intend to surrender his protected life interest or to release the power of
e appointment save for the purpose and with the effect that the beneficial interest in the
capital of the fund should forthwith vest indefeasibly in Jane and David. He did not have
the intention of releasing his protected life interest or the power of appointment in vacuo
or for its own sake, but solely to achieve the purposes I have stated.

Mr Gibbon did not merely execute the deed under a mistake of law as to the legal
consequences of his doing so. He executed it under a mistake as to its legal effect. The
f deed itself shows that to be the case. Since its effect was not that which he intended, he is
entitled to have it set aside. Equity acts on the conscience. The parties whose interest it
would be to oppose the setting aside of the deed are the unborn future children of Mr
Gibbon and the objects of the discretionary trust to arise on forfeiture, that is to say his
grandchildren, nephews and nieces. They are all volunteers. In my judgment they could
not conscionably insist on their legal rights under the deed once they had become aware
g of the circumstances in which they had acquired them.

I therefore relieve Mr Gibbon from the consequences of his mistake and set aside the
deed. I also accede to the consequential application under the Variation of Trusts Act
1958 to delete the protective nature of the protected life interest. I am quite satisfied this
is a proper case where I can exercise my discretion under the Act to do so.

h
Order accordingly. Plaintiff to pay costs of defendants on indemnity basis.

Solicitors: *Reynolds Porter Chamberlain* (for the plaintiff); *Gregory Rowcliffe & Milners* (for
the defendants).

Jacqueline Metcalfe   Barrister.

Pitts v Hunt and another

COURT OF APPEAL, CIVIL DIVISION

DILLON, BALCOMBE AND BELDAM LJJ

14, 15 MARCH, 4 APRIL 1990

Negligence – Duty of care – Joint illegal enterprise – Defence of ex turpi causa non oritur actio – Pillion passenger encouraging rider of motor cycle to drive recklessly and dangerously after both had been drinking together – Pillion passenger injured in collision between motor cycle and oncoming car – Car driver not to blame for accident – Whether motor cyclist owing pillion passenger duty of care – Whether plaintiff barred from recovering damages by public policy, maxim ex turpi causa non oritur actio or 100% contributory negligence – Whether volenti non fit injucia a defence to negligent driving – Law Reform (Contributory Negligence) Act 1945, s 1 – Road Traffic Act 1972, s 148(3).

The plaintiff, who was aged 18, and a friend, who was aged 16, spent the evening drinking at a disco before setting off home on the friend's motor cycle with the plaintiff riding as a pillion passenger. The plaintiff was aware that the motor cyclist was neither licensed to ride a motor cycle nor insured. On the journey home the motor cyclist, encouraged by the plaintiff, rode the motor cycle in a fast, reckless and hazardous manner deliberately intending to frighten members of the public. The motor cycle collided with an oncoming car and the plaintiff was severely injured. The motor cyclist, whose blood alcohol level was more than twice the legal limit for driving a motor vehicle, was killed. The plaintiff claimed damages in negligence against the personal representative of the motor cyclist and against the driver of the oncoming car. The judge found that there had been no negligence on the part of the driver of the car and held that the plaintiff could not recover damages against the motor cyclist's estate because the two were engaged on a joint illegal enterprise and the claim was barred by the maxim ex turpi causa non oritur actio and public policy. The judge further held that the claim would have been defeated by the defence of volenti non fit injuria but for the fact that s 148(3)[a] of the Road Traffic Act 1972, by providing that any 'agreement or understanding' between the driver and a passenger of a motor vehicle had no effect so far as it purported to negative or restrict the driver's liability to the passenger, precluded the defendants from relying on that defence in the context of a motor accident, and that in the event the plaintiff was 100% contributorily negligent. The plaintiff appealed against the dismissal of his claim against the motor cyclist's estate.

Held – Where one person was injured as the result of the actions of another while they were engaged in a joint illegal enterprise the issue whether the injured party was entitled to claim against the other person or whether his claim was barred by the maxim ex turpi causa non oritur actio was to be determined not according to whether there was any moral turpitude involved in the joint illegal enterprise but whether the conduct of the person seeking to base his claim on the unlawful act and the character of the enterprise and the hazards necessarily inherent in its execution were such that it was impossible to determine the appropriate standard of care because the joint illegal purpose had displaced the ordinary standard of care. Since the plaintiff had played a full and active part in encouraging the motor cyclist to commit offences which, had an innocent third party been killed, would have amounted to manslaughter by the commission of a dangerous act, the plaintiff ought not to be permitted to recover for the injuries which he sustained arising out of that unlawful conduct, on the grounds of the application of the maxim ex turpi causa non oritur actio, public policy and the fact that the circumstances precluded the court from finding that the driver owed any duty of care to the plaintiff. The appeal

---

a   Section 148(3) is set out at p 360 *c d*, post

would therefore be dismissed (see p 351 *j*, p 353 *e f*, p 355 *f g*, p 357 *e f j* to p 358 *b*, p 359
a *a e*, p 365 *h j* and p 366 *b c e*, post); dictum of Mason J in *Jackson v Harrison* (1978) 138
CLR 438 at 455–456 applied; *Thackwell v Barclays Bank plc* [1986] 1 All ER 676 and
Saunders v Edwards [1987] 2 All ER 651 not followed.

Per curiam (1) In the context of a plea of contributory negligence it is logically
unsupportable to find that a plaintiff was 100% contributorily negligent since the premise
on which s 1*b* of the Law Reform (Contributory Negligence) Act 1945 operates is that
b there is fault on the part of both parties which has caused the damage and that the
responsibility must be shared according to the apportionment of liability. Where (per
Dillon and Beldam LJJ) the parties have engaged in a joint illegal enterprise and the
parties are equally to blame the correct apportionment of liability is 50% each (see p 357
b d f g and p 359 *d e h j*, post).

(2) The effect of s 148(3) of the 1972 Act is that it is not open to the driver of a motor
c vehicle to say that the fact that his passenger could be said to have willingly accepted a
risk of negligence on the driver's part relieves the driver of liability for his negligence
since the defence of volenti non fit injuria is precluded by s 148(3) in the context of a
motor accident (see p 356 *h j*, p 359 *b* to *d* and p 360 *a b e f*, post); *Winnik v Dick* 1984 SLT
185 approved; dictum of Ewbank J in *Ashton v Turner* [1980] 3 All ER 870 at 878
disapproved.

d Per Dillon and Balcombe LJJ. Section 148(3) of the 1972 Act does not have the effect
that an express or tacit agreement by the parties to engage in a joint illegal enterprise
involving a motor vehicle cannot be relied on to negative or restrict liability for negligent
driving, since s 148(3) is concerned to preclude a defence of volenti non fit injuria but is
not concerned with any defence of illegality and the section does not contemplate an
illegal 'agreement or understanding' to carry out an illegal purpose (see p 359 *b* and p 366
e *c d*, post).

Per Beldam LJ. If the driver of a motor vehicle commits a road traffic offence so serious
that it would preclude the driver on public policy grounds from claiming an indemnity
under a policy of insurance statutorily required to be effected for the benefit of a
passenger, public policy will also preclude the passenger from claiming compensation if
f he is jointly guilty of that offence (see p 355 *f g*, post).

Notes

For the application of the maxim ex turpi causa non oritur actio, see 12 Halsbury's Laws
(4th edn) para 1136, and for cases on the subject, see 1(1) Digest (Reissue) 45–46, 310–315.

For the defence of volenti non fit injuria, see 12 Halsbury's Laws (4th edn) para 1142,
and for cases on the subject, see 36(1) Digest (Reissue) 242–255, 934–1001.

g For the Law Reform (Contributory Negligence) Act 1945, s 1, see 31 Halsbury's
Statutes (4th edn) 185.

As from 15 May 1989 s 148 of the Road Traffic Act 1972 was replaced by s 149 of the
Road Traffic Act 1988. For s 149 of the 1988 Act, see 38 Halsbury's Statutes (4th edn)
1002.

Cases referred to in judgments

h *Adamson v Jarvis* (1827) 4 Bing 66, [1824–34] All ER Rep 120, 130 ER 693.
Ashton v Turner [1980] 3 All ER 870, [1981] QB 137, [1980] 3 WLR 736.
Askey v Golden Wine Co Ltd [1948] 2 All ER 35.
Baker v Market Harborough Industrial Co-op Society Ltd [1953] 1 WLR 1472, CA.
Beresford v Royal Insurance Co Ltd [1938] 2 All ER 602, [1938] AC 586, HL.
j *Bondarenko v Sommers* (1968) 69 SR (NSW) 269, NSW CA.
Burrows v Rhodes [1899] 1 QB 816, [1895–9] All ER Rep 117, DC.

---

b   Section 1, so far as material, provides: 'Where any person suffers damage as the result partly of his
      own fault and partly of the fault of any other person or persons, a claim in respect of that damage
      shall not be defeated by reason of the fault of the person suffering the damage, but the damages
      recoverable in respect thereof shall be reduced to such extent as the court thinks just and equitable
      having regard to the claimant's share in the responsibility for the damage . . .'

Chettiar v Chettiar [1962] 1 All ER 494, [1962] AC 294, [1962] 2 WLR 548, PC.
Colburn v Patmore (1834) 1 Cr M & R 73, 149 ER 999.
Emery's Investments' Trusts, Re, Emery v Emery [1959] 1 All ER 577, [1959] Ch 410, [1969] 2 WLR 461.
Euro-Diam Ltd v Bathurst [1988] 2 All ER 23, [1990] 1 QB 1, [1988] 2 WLR 517, CA.
Everet v Williams (1725) *Lindley on Partnership* (15th edn, 1984) 149n, 9 LQR 197.
Godbolt v Fittock [1963] SR (NSW) 617, NSW Full Ct.
Gray v Barr (Prudential Assurance Co Ltd, third party) [1971] 2 All ER 949, [1971] 2 QB 554, [1971] 2 WLR 1334, CA.
Hardy v Motor Insurers' Bureau [1964] 2 All ER 742, [1964] 2 QB 745, [1964] 3 WLR 433.
Haseldine v Hosken [1933] 1 KB 822, [1933] All ER Rep 1, CA.
Henwood v Municipal Tramways Trust (South Australia) (1938) 60 CLR 438, Aust HC.
Hillen v ICI (Alkali) Ltd [1934] 1 KB 455, CA; *affd* [1936] AC 65, [1935] All ER Rep 555, HL.
Holman v Johnson (1775) 1 Cowp 341, [1775–1802] All ER Rep 98, 98 ER 1120.
Jackson v Harrison (1978) 138 CLR 438, Aust HC.
James v British General Insurance Co Ltd [1927] 2 KB 311, [1927] All ER Rep 442.
McCaig v Langan 1964 SLT 121, Ct of Sess.
Merryweather v Nixan (1799) 8 Term Rep 186, 101 ER 1337.
Murphy v Culhane [1976] 3 All ER 533, [1977] QB 94, [1976] 3 WLR 458, CA.
National Coal Board v England [1954] 1 All ER 546, [1954] AC 403, [1954] 2 WLR 400, HL.
Nettleship v Weston [1971] 3 All ER 581, [1971] 2 QB 691, [1971] 3 WLR 370, CA.
Progress and Properties Ltd v Craft (1976) 135 CLR 651, Aust HC.
R v Sheppard [1980] 3 All ER 899, [1981] AC 394, [1980] 3 WLR 960, HL.
Sajan Singh v Sardara Ali [1960] 1 All ER 269, [1960] AC 167, [1960] 2 WLR 180, PC.
Saunders v Edwards [1987] 2 All ER 651, [1987] 1 WLR 1116, CA.
Smith v Jenkins (1970) 119 CLR 397, Aust HC.
Smith v Selwyn [1914] 3 KB 98, [1914–15] All ER Rep 229, CA.
Thackwell v Barclays Bank plc [1986] 1 All ER 676.
Tinline v White Cross Insurance Association Ltd [1921] 3 KB 327.
Winnik v Dick 1984 SLT 185, Ct of Sess.

Cases also cited
Baddeley v Earl Granville (1887) 19 QBD 423, [1886–90] All ER Rep 374, DC.
Bankhead v McCarthy 1962 SC 263, Ct of Sess.
Boeyen v Kydd [1963] VR 235, Vic SC.
Dann v Hamilton [1939] 1 All ER 59, [1939] 1 KB 509.
Kirkham v Chief Constable of the Greater Manchester Police [1990] 3 All ER 246, [1990] 2 WLR 987, CA.
Owens v Brimmell [1976] 3 All ER 765, [1977] QB 859, [1977] 2 WLR 943.
Smith v Baker & Sons [1891] AC 235, [1891–4] All ER Rep 69, HL.
Wheeler v New Merton Board Mills Ltd [1933] 2 KB 669, [1933] All ER Rep 28, CA.
Wooldridge v Sumner [1962] 2 All ER 978, [1963] 2 QB 43, [1962] 3 WLR 616, CA.

Appeal
The plaintiff, Andrew James Pitts, appealed from that part of the order of his Honour Judge Fallon QC, sitting as a judge of the High Court in the Winchester District Registry of the Queen's Bench Division on 1 December 1988 ([1990] 1 QB 302) whereby he dismissed the plaintiff's claim for damages against the first defendant, John Edward Hunt, sued as the personal representative of Mark James Hunt deceased in respect of peresonal injuries received when he was travelling as a pillion passenger on a motor cycle ridden by the deceased which was in collision with a car driven by the second defendant, Richard Mark Jewell, on 10 September 1983. The facts are set out in the judgment of Beldam LJ.

John Peppitt QC and *Anthony Coleman* for the plaintiff.
a *William Barnett QC* and *Richard Methuen* for the first defendant.

Cur adv vult

4 April. The following judgments were delivered.

b **BELDAM LJ** (giving the first judgment at the invitation of Dillon LJ). The plaintiff, Andrew James Pitts, appeals against the judgment of his Honour Judge Fallon sitting as a judge of the High Court at Bristol on 1 December 1988 ([1990] 1 QB 302). The plaintiff claimed damages for personal injuries received when he was travelling as a pillion passenger on a motor cycle ridden by the deceased, Mark Hunt, which was in collision with a car driven by the second defendant on 10 September 1983. The question of *c* liability had been ordered to be tried as a preliminary issue. Having heard evidence on Wednesday, 26 to Friday, 28 October 1988, the judge dismissed the plaintiff's case against both defendants. From his dismissal of the claim against the first defendant, the plaintiff now appeals. The facts as found by the judge are not challenged.

The plaintiff at the time of the accident was 18 years old. He himself owned a motor cycle and was licensed to ride it. Mark Hunt, the deceased, whose personal representative *d* is the respondent to the appeal, was 16 years of age. He was the owner of a 250 cc Suzuki motor cycle, which he used as a trail bike. He was not, however, the holder of a licence, nor was he insured to use the motor cycle on a road. The plaintiff and the deceased were friends and used to go trail biking together. The plaintiff knew that the deceased was not the holder of a licence and that he was not insured to use the Suzuki motor cycle on the road. Together these two young men went to a disco at the *e* Boot Inn on 10 September 1983. They arrived there at about 7.30 pm and stayed until 11.15 pm. During that time they each drank far more than was good for them. After the accident samples taken from the deceased showed that the concentration of alcohol in his blood was over twice the permitted limit. In spite of this, the two young men set off together on the deceased's motor cycle with the deceased driving. Their journey home took them along the A338 road which leads from Shipton Bellinger to *f* Tidworth. They were travelling in a northerly direction towards Tidworth along a stretch of road which is approximately 8 metres wide and which passes the Tidworth Garrison cricket ground. The centre of the road is marked by painted hazard lines and cat's-eye studs. There is no street lighting on this section of the road and traffic is restricted to a speed of 60 mph. It is an 'A' class road with a good surface, which was wet at the time. Approaching the scene of the accident when travelling towards Tidworth, as the motor *g* cycle was, the road is virtually straight for 200 yards. It then rises to a crest and starts to bear to the left.

As these two young men rode home, no doubt in high spirits, the effects of intoxication began to exert themselves, and as is too frequently the case it caused them to throw caution to the wind; they began to behave in a reckless, irresponsible and idiotic way.

h Two Army non-commissioned officers whose car had broken down were walking towards Shipton Bellinger along the right-hand side of the road facing oncoming traffic when they heard the motor cycle approaching. They then saw its light and it was clearly in the middle of the road. The driver and pillion passenger were shouting as if they were having a good time and the horn was being blown. It then appeared to be driven straight towards them and passed them so closely that they moved onto the verge to get out of its *j* way. They noticed then that it was being driven from side to side of the road, weaving in and out of the white hazard lines. It was travelling at about 50 mph as it did so. They heard both the rider and pillion passenger shouting 'Hooray' and 'Yippee', as if enjoying the experience. They were clearly showing no concern for other users of the road and the judge drew the inference that they were deliberately riding in a way calculated to frighten others. The evidence of these two pedestrians clearly supported that inference.

The second defendant, a young man of 26, was driving his girlfriend home in his parents' Renault motor car. He was also giving a lift home to his brother's girlfriend. He was approaching the scene of the accident, travelling in a southerly direction at a reasonable speed, on his own side of the road. He was about to negotiate the bend in the road when he saw the motor cycle coming towards him on its wrong side of the road and travelling directly towards him in his path. Instinctively he moved to his offside in the hope that he would avoid a collision but, no doubt because the motor cycle was weaving down the centre of the road, it then seemed as if it swerved back onto its own side. So in response the second defendant steered towards his nearside but in the time available he was unable to avoid a collision. The motor cycle struck the Renault a severe but glancing blow on the front offside corner and then careered back onto its nearside verge for a distance of about 35 metres beyond the point of impact which appears to have been on or near the crown of the road. Tragically the injuries received by Mark Hunt were fatal. The plaintiff sustained injuries which have left him permanently partially disabled.

Such were the primary facts as the judge found them. He acquitted the second defendant of all blame and dismissed the plaintiff's claim against the first defendant on a number of grounds. Before considering them, it is necessary to state some further findings which the judge made. He found that the deceased had drunk so much that he was obviously unfit to drive and that if the plaintiff had been in a proper state he would have realised that. He found that the deceased, very much aided and abetted by the plaintiff, was deliberately trying to frighten others who were on the road. No doubt because they had drunk so much, they viewed it as a joke or a game but it was certainly reckless driving. He found that the plaintiff had supported or encouraged the deceased, whom he knew was under age, drunk and uninsured, and he added ([1990] 1 QB 302 at 312):

> 'On my findings the deceased was riding this motor cycle recklessly and dangerously and at the very least the plaintiff was aiding and abetting that driving. He was not manipulating the controls of the machine but he was fully in agreement with and was encouraging the way in which the deceased was manipulating the controls. Indeed, the eye-witness accounts which I have accepted demonstrate that both the plaintiff and the deceased were actually enjoying their experience, partly if not largely as a result of the very large amount they had drunk that night.'

The judge then considered the various defences which had been raised by the first defendant. Firstly he held that the plaintiff could not maintain an action which was based on or arose out of criminal conduct on his part, ex turpi causa non oritur actio. Secondly that on the grounds of public policy the law would not recognise in the circumstances of this claim that a duty of care was owed by the deceased to the plaintiff. Thirdly that, even if the plaintiff would ordinarily have been owed the normal duty of care, the risk of injury was so glaring and obvious that by the act of travelling as a pillion passenger on a motor cycle ridden by the deceased in a state of intoxication and in the manner which he himself encouraged and enjoyed, he must be taken to have willingly accepted any risk of injury involved, volenti non fit injuria. It had, however, been argued on the plaintiff's behalf that the provisions of s 148(3) of the Road Traffic Act 1972 precluded the first defendant from relying on such a defence.

Holding that the section did in fact have that effect, the judge then considered whether if there had been a breach of duty by the deceased the damages recoverable by him should be reduced having regard to his own fault and if so to what extent. On this basis he concluded that as the plaintiff was equally responsible for what had happened and was in effect a partner in a joint enterprise of stupidity with the deceased, that it would defy common sense to find that the plaintiff was not himself wholly to blame for his own injuries. Accordingly he held that the plaintiff was not entitled to recover any damages even on that basis.

The first two grounds on which the judge rejected the plaintiff's claim arose from the first defendant's reliance on public policy and, in particular, the policy expressed in the Latin maxim ex turpi causa non oritur actio.

Since the days of Lord Mansfield CJ it has been a rule of public policy that a court will
a not lend its aid to a man who founds his cause of action on an illegal or immoral act: see
Holman v Johnson (1775) 1 Cowp 341, [1775–1802] All ER Rep 98. The question there
arose in an action for goods sold and delivered, which it was alleged were supplied in the
knowledge that they were to be smuggled into England. The plaintiff, however,
recovered the price of the goods since mere knowledge on his part that they might be
unlawfully imported into England did not bar his claim.

b The same grounds of public policy were said to underlie the decision of Lord Kenyon
CJ in *Merryweather v Nixan* (1799) 8 Term Rep 186, 101 ER 1337 that a joint tortfeasor
who had alone been sued to judgment and had had to pay the whole damages could
claim no contribution from his fellow wrongdoer. This rule, finally abolished in 1935,
was narrowed in its effect by later decisions to cases in which the tortfeasor claiming
indemnity or contribution must have known that he was doing an unlawful act. In
c *Adamson v Jarvis* (1827) 4 Bing 66 at 72–73, [1824–34] All ER Rep 120 at 122 Best CJ
said:

> '. . . from the concluding part of Lord Kenyon's judgment in *Merryweather v.*
> *Nixan*, and from reason, justice, and sound policy, the rule that wrong-doers cannot
> have redress or contribution against each other is confined to cases where the person
> **d** seeking redress must be presumed to have known that he was doing an unlawful
> act.'

In *Colburn v Patmore* (1834) 1 Cr M & R 73 at 83, 149 ER 999 at 1003 Lord Lyndhurst
CB said:

> 'I know of no case in which a person who has committed an act, declared by the
> **e** law to be criminal, has been permitted to recover compensation against a person
> who has acted jointly with him in the commission of the crime. It is not necessary
> to give any opinion upon this point; but I may say, that I entertain little doubt that
> a person who is declared by the law to be guilty of a crime cannot be allowed to
> recover damages against another who has participated in its commission.'

f This principle was applied by Denning J in *Askey v Golden Wine Co Ltd* [1948] 2 All ER
35. He held that the plaintiff, who had been induced by the defendant's fraud to sell
liquor in breach of the Food and Drugs Act 1938 and who had been fined, could not
recover the amount of the fine from the defendant when he had himself at least been
guilty of gross negligence.

It is perhaps not surprising that few cases are to be found in the eighteenth and
nineteenth centuries in which joint participants in a tort, the facts of which also
g constituted a crime, are to be found seeking redress the one against the other. The
punishment meted out to the solicitors for the parties in the highwayman's case, *Everet v*
Williams (1725) *Lindley on Partnership* (15th edn, 1984) 149n, who were imprisoned and
fined £50 each, would not have encouraged the bringing of such proceedings (see 9 LQR
197) and until the rule in *Smith v Selwyn* [1914] 3 KB 98, [1914–15] All ER Rep 229 was
h abolished, no civil remedy could be pursued by the victim of a crime which amounted
to felony until the criminal had been prosecuted. Further, before 1870, if he was
prosecuted and convicted, the felon's property would be forfeited so that it was unlikely
that any claim against him would be satisfied.

The rule of public policy that a cause of action could not be based on an illegal act has
been held to extend to cases in which an insured has sought indemnity under a policy of
j insurance for liability caused through his own unlawful acts: see *Haseldine v Hosken* [1933]
1 KB 822, [1933] All ER Rep 1 and *Gray v Barr (Prudential Assurance Co Ltd, third party)*
[1971] 2 All ER 949, [1971] 2 QB 554. Such a rule was treated by Kennedy J in *Burrows v*
Rhodes [1899] 1 QB 816 at 828, [1895–9] All ER Rep 117 at 124 as having long been
settled law if the liability in respect of which a person seeks indemnity arises from an act
which is manifestly unlawful or which the actor knows to be unlawful as constituting
either a civil wrong or a criminal offence. However, the law has treated cases in which

an insured claims indemnity in respect of a liability arising out of the use of a motor
vehicle on the highway exceptionally in this respect. In *Tinline v White Cross Insurance*   *a*
Association Ltd [1921] 3 KB 327 an insured was held to be entitled to indemnity under a
policy of motor insurance in respect of an accident even though he had pleaded guilty to
manslaughter of a person killed as a result of his driving. Bailhache J acknowledged that
it was against public policy to indemnify a man against the consequences of a crime
which he knowingly commits and in the word 'crime' he included breach of any statutory
duty which rendered a man liable to a fine or imprisonment. In permitting recovery   *b*
under the policy the judge drew a clear distinction between accidents which occurred
through gross negligence and those which could be said to be the result of intentional
acts on the part of the insured in which case he would have been denied indemnity.

In *James v British General Insurance Co Ltd* [1927] 2 KB 311, [1927] All ER Rep 442 the
insured was drunk and had been convicted of manslaughter and sentenced to 12 months'
imprisonment. Roche J again drew the distinction between gross negligence or reckless   *c*
negligence, negligence of the kind which constitutes criminality but nevertheless
negligence as opposed to the wilful or advertent doing of the act. He said ([1927] 2 KB
311 at 323, [1927] All ER Rep 442 at 445):

> 'In such circumstances as these there is not, in my view, on the part of the person
> who does the act, that degree of criminality which in the doing of a known unlawful   *d*
> act makes it against public policy that the perpetrator should be indemnified in
> respect of it.'

The distinction between deliberate and intentional acts and those which are
unintentional though grossly negligent was maintained in *Hardy v Motor Insurers' Bureau*
[1964] 2 All ER 742, [1964] 2 QB 745. In that case a security officer had been intentionally
injured when he sought to prevent the driver of a van from driving off while he   *e*
questioned him. The security officer had obtained judgment for damages of £300 in
respect of his injuries. The driver of the van, who was uninsured, had been convicted of
maliciously inflicting grievous bodily harm to the security guard. The requirement of
malice in that office would have been satisfied by recklessness: see *R v Sheppard* [1980] 3
All ER 899, [1981] AC 394. Nevertheless it was clear that the driver had deliberately
driven off while the security guard was hanging on to the vehicle and had continued to   *f*
drive when it must have been obvious to him that he would cause some injury to the
guard. As the van driver was uninsured, the security guard sought to recover his damages
from Motor Insurers' Bureau, who, by the terms of their agreement with the Ministry of
Transport, had agreed to satisfy claims in respect of any judgment obtained for a liability
required to be covered under a policy of motor insurance issued under the Road Traffic
Acts. It was contended for the bureau that liability for a criminal act was not a liability   *g*
which the Road Traffic Acts required, or could require, to be covered by a policy of
insurance. This court held that it was not against public policy to allow the security guard
to recover under the agreement even though public policy would have precluded the
driver from claiming indemnity under a policy if he had had one. Diplock LJ said
([1964] 2 All ER 742 at 750–751, [1964] 2 QB 745 at 767):   *h*

> 'The rule of law on which the major premise is based, ex turpi causa non oritur
> actio, is concerned not specifically with the lawfulness of contracts but generally
> with the enforcement of rights by the courts, whether or not such rights arise under
> contract. All that the rule means is that the courts will not enforce a right which
> would otherwise be enforceable if the right arises out of an act committed by the
> person asserting the right (or by someone who is regarded in law as his successor)   *j*
> which is regarded by the court as sufficiently anti-social to justify the court's refusing
> to enforce that right.'

After holding that as the Road Traffic Act conferred on an injured third party a direct
right of action against insurers and that it was therefore within the agreement and that it

did not offend against the rule ex turpi causa non oritur actio to permit the injured
a person to recover, he went on ([1964] 2 All ER 742 at 752, [1964] 2 QB 745 at 769):

'No doubt, in the unlikely event of the assured himself discharging his liability to
the third party, the rule ex turpi causa non oritur actio would prevent his enforcing
his contractual right to indemnity against the insurers if the event which gave rise
to his liability to the third party were an intentional crime committed by the
assured.'
b

In *Gray v Barr* [1971] 2 All ER 949, [1971] 2 QB 554 an insured had been held liable
for injuries caused by discharging a shotgun when confronting his wife's lover. He
claimed indemnity under a policy of insurance covering him for personal liability for
accident. He had been charged with manslaughter of the wife's lover but had been
acquitted. This court unanimously held that in such a case he was not entitled to
c indemnity. The first ground of its decision was that the incident was not an accident
within the meaning of the policy, but the court went on to consider whether the claim
to indemnity was barred by public policy. Lord Denning MR drew the distinction
between manslaughter which could be categorised as 'motor manslaughter' on the one
hand, and manslaughter in which the conduct is wilful and culpable on the other. He
said ([1971] 2 All ER 949 at 957, [1971] 2 QB 554 at 569):
d

'If the death of Mr Gray was *caused* by the deliberate act of Mr Barr in going up
the stairs with a loaded gun, it was no accident, and it would, in any case, be against
public policy to allow him to recover indemnity for the consequences of it.' (Lord
Denning MR's emphasis.)

Salmon LJ thought that the cases which permitted an insured convicted of manslaughter
e for reckless and drunken driving to recover indemnity under a policy of insurance might
be sui generis. He went on ([1971] 2 All ER 949 at 965, [1971] 2 QB 554 at 581–582):

'In any event, although motor cars have sometimes been called lethal weapons,
these cases are not in my view akin to the cases in which injuries are caused in the
course of unlawfully threatening a man with a loaded gun. Public policy is not static
f   ... In any event, threatening violence with a loaded gun would, I am sure, now be
generally regarded as much more shocking and necessary to be deterred than what
the unfortunate Major Rowlandson did in *Beresford*'s case [*Beresford v Royal Insurance
Co Ltd* [1938] 2 All ER 602, [1938] AC 586]. I am confident that in any civilised
society, public policy requires that anyone who inflicts injuries in the course of such
an act shall not be allowed to use the courts of justice for the purpose of enforcing
g   any contract of indemnity in respect of his liability in damages for causing injury
by accident.'

Lord Denning MR drew attention to the distinction between manslaughter in which
the death of another may be the result simply of a reckless act, and manslaughter in
which the death arises from an unlawful and dangerous act done with the intention of
h frightening or harming someone or when the actor knows that it is likely to frighten or
harm someone and nevertheless goes on and does it regardless of the consequences (see
[1971] 2 All ER 949 at 956, [1971] 2 QB 554 at 568).
I have quoted at some length the considerations which have led courts to refuse on
grounds of public policy to permit a person to enforce a claim to indemnity for they
illustrate to my mind how the courts have adjusted the application of the maxim to
j changing social conditions and in particular to the policy underlying the Road Traffic
Acts. They establish, I believe, that it is the conduct of the person seeking to base his
claim on an unlawful act which is determinative of the application of the maxim.
Before leaving the question of public policy as it has been applied in cases of indemnity
or contribution, it is pertinent to point out that when in 1935 the rule in *Merryweather v
Nixan* (1799) 8 Term Rep 186, 101 ER 1337 was finally abolished by the Law Reform

(Married Women and Tortfeasors) Act 1935 a tortfeasor liable in respect of damage suffered by any person as a result of a tort (whether a crime or not) could recover contribution from any other tortfeasor liable in respect of the same damage. The rule was abolished as a result of the Law Revision Committee's third interim report (Cmd 4637 (1934)), which expressly considered whether an exception ought to be made in the case where a tort is also a crime. In its report the committee said (para 10):

> 'At first sight public policy might appear to demand that such an exception should be made at any rate when the crime is wanton and deliberate and not merely the result of inadvertence. We have, however, come to the conclusion that it is impracticable to draw such a distinction and that any attempt to exclude from our recommendation torts which are also crimes would produce anomalies (such as would result from the fact that libel is a crime while slander is not or that negligent driving may amount to felony) and uncertainties which it would be undesirable to introduce. Accordingly our recommendation is made without qualification.'

In defence to a claim in tort based on negligence or breach of statutory duty, public policy based on the rule ex turpi causa non oritur actio has not often been raised. It was raised in *National Coal Board v England* [1954] 1 All ER 546, [1954] AC 403. A mineworker who was injured in an explosion of a detonator in a colliery at Aberdare claimed damages for breach of statutory duty by the shotfirer who fired the shot without first ascertaining that all persons in the vicinity had taken shelter. The plaintiff had aided and abetted the shotfirer by coupling up the charges when he was not supposed to do so. It was contended that he could not recover because of his own illegal acts. Although the House of Lords had little difficulty in rejecting this contention, Lord Asquith said ([1954] 1 All ER 546 at 558, [1954] AC 403 at 428–429):

> 'Cases where an action in tort has been defeated by the maxim are exceedingly rare. Possibly a party to an illegal prize fight who is damaged in the conflict cannot sue for asault ... But it seems to me in principle that the plaintiff cannot be precluded from suing simply because the wrongful act is committed after the illegal agreement is made and during the period involved in its execution. The act must, I should have supposed, at least be a step in the execution of the common illegal purpose. If two burglars, A and B, agree to open a safe by means of explosives, and A so negligently handles the explosive charge as to injure B, B might find some difficulty in maintaining an action for negligence against A. But if A and B are proceeding to the premises which they intend burglariously to enter, and before they enter them B picks A's pocket and steals his watch, I cannot prevail on myself to believe that A could not sue in tort (provided he had first prosecuted B for larceny). The theft is totally unconnected with the burglary. There is, however, a surprising dearth of authority on this point.'

The case in which this question arose directly was *Ashton v Turner* [1980] 3 All ER 870, [1981] QB 137. The plaintiff was one of three young men who, after an evening's drinking, used a motor car belonging to one of them on a joint enterprise of burglary. Having stolen some radios and set off the alarm, they tried to make their escape in the car which, due to the negligent driving of the defendant, crashed and the plaintiff sustained injury. He sought to recover damages from the driver. Ewbank J dismissed the plaintiff's claim holding that as a matter of public policy the law would not recognise a duty of care owed by one participant in a crime to another. He held in the alternative that, even if a duty of care was owed, the plaintiff had willingly accepted as his the risk of negligence and injury resulting from it.

In arriving at this conclusion Ewbank J was much influenced by two decisions in the courts of Australia: *Godbolt v Fittock* [1963] SR (NSW) 617 and *Smith v Jenkins* (1970) 119 CLR 397. In the latter case the High Court of Australia held that no action would lie by the passenger in a motor vehicle to recover damages for injuries sustained by the careless

driving of the vehicle when the passenger and driver were at the time of the accident
a participating jointly in the offence of unlawfully using the motor vehicle. Although all
the judges were agreed that the plaintiff could not recover, there was a difference of
opinion about the legal basis for the decision. Kitto and Walsh JJ considered that in the
circumstances public policy would not recognise a right of action. Barwick CJ, Windeyer
and Owen JJ considered that the basis for dismissing the claim should be that the law
would not hold that a duty of care arose out of the relationship of joint participants in an
b illegal enterprise.

The question again came before the High Court of Australia in 1977 in *Jackson v
Harrison* (1978) 138 CLR 438. The respondent was injured when he was travelling as a
passenger in a motor car driven by a driver he knew to be disqualified. The two of them
were jointly participating in an offence under the Motor Vehicles Act 1959. The majority
distinguished *Smith v Jenkins* and held that the passenger was not disabled from recovering
c damages on the ground that the illegality did not bear on the standard of care reasonably
to be expected of the driver. Barwick CJ dissented and in the course of his judgment he
said (138 CLR 438 at 445):

> 'It seems to me that where there is a joint venture to do an act punishable by fine
> or imprisonment, no narrow or pedantic view should be taken of the nature and
> scope of the arrangement between the parties when applying the principle of *Smith*
d > v. *Jenkins* and that the consequence to one of the participants of any act done in
> furtherance of the arrangement or in obtaining the benefit of having carried it out
> should not give rise to a cause of action. The relationship of those participants should
> not be regarded as giving rise to relevant rights or duties. The public policy which
> the denial of a cause of action in such circumstances is designed to serve is not
e > satisfied if the miscreant is not denied rights against his co-participant in the
> commission of the offence in respect of acts related to that commission.'

Mason J said (at 455–456):

> 'If a joint participant in an illegal enterprise is to be denied relief against a co-
> participant for injury sustained in that enterprise, the denial of relief should be
f > related not to the illegal character of the activity but rather to the character and
> incidents of the enterprise and to the hazards which are necessarily inherent in its
> execution. A more secure foundation for denying relief, though more limited in its
> application—and for that reason fairer in its operation—is to say that the plaintiff
> must fail when the character of the enterprise in which the parties are engaged is
> such that it is impossible for the court to determine the standard of care which is
g > appropriate to be observed.'

Jacobs J based his conclusion on the fact that the type of offence in which they were
jointly engaged did not bear at all on the standard of care which was to be expected of
the driver in the circumstances.

In another jurisdiction nearer home in *Winnik v Dick* 1984 SLT 185, the Second
h Division of the Inner House also considered the question whether public policy would
preclude an action for damages by a passenger in a motor car which was being driven by
a driver with whom he had been drinking all day and knew that he was drunk. Lord
Hunter said (at 189):

> '. . . either because in law one joint participant would not in such circumstances
j > be held to owe a duty of care to the other joint participant or because on grounds of
> public policy, the court would not countenance nor adjudicate on a claim by one
> such joint participant against another. I see no reason why a Scottish court should
> not, on the basis of one or other or both of these principles, arrive in appropriate
> circumstances at a result the same as that reached in several cases in other
> jurisdictions, to which we were referred. See, e.g. *Smith* v. *Jenkins*; *Ashton* v. *Turner*.'

The Lord Justice Clerk (Wheatley), however, felt that such a defence would have far-reaching effects and could give rise to delicate decisions on what is embraced in 'crime' *a* in this context and he felt that in the circumstances of that case, since the pleadings did not raise the issue with clarity, the point should not be decided.

In opening his appeal on behalf of the plaintiff, counsel drew attention to *Saunders v Edwards* [1987] 2 All ER 651, [1987] 1 WLR 1116. This court, he said, had approved a test for determining whether in the circumstances the court would decline to allow the plaintiff to recover in cases of illegality. It was based on a helpful review of cases by *b* Hutchison J in *Thackwell v Barclays Bank plc* [1986] 1 All ER 676. The plaintiff in that case was a party to a fraudulent scheme under which a cheque had been made payable to him. The plaintiff's signature indorsing the cheque to a third party was forged and in reliance on the forgery the bank credited the third party. The plaintiff sued the bank for conversion. In defence the bank relied on the maxim ex turpi causa. The test applied by Hutchison J in that case and approved by the court in *Saunders v Edwards*—   *c*

> 'involved the court looking at the quality of the illegality relied on by the defendant and all the surrounding circumstances, without fine distinctions, and seeking to answer two questions: first, whether there had been illegality of which the court should take notice and, second, whether in all the circumstances it would be an affront to the public conscience if by affording him the relief sought the court *d* was seen to be indirectly assisting or encouraging the plaintiff in his criminal act.'

(See [1986] 1 All ER 676 at 687.)

Counsel for the plaintiff relied particularly on the passage in the judgment of Bingham LJ where he said ([1987] 2 All ER 651 at 665–666, [1987] 1 WLR 1116 at 1134):

> 'Where issues of illegality are raised, the courts have (as it seems to me) to steer a *e* middle course between two unacceptable positions. On the one hand it is unacceptable that any court of law should aid or lend its authority to a party seeking to pursue or enforce an object or agreement which the law prohibits. On the other hand, it is unacceptable that the court should, on the first indication of unlawfulness affecting any aspect of a transaction, draw up its skirts and refuse all assistance to the plaintiff, no matter how serious his loss or how disproportionate his loss to the *f* unlawfulness of his conduct.'

Bingham LJ went on to point out that the cases which had been referred to in the judgments of Kerr and Nicholls LJJ were valuable both for the statements of principle which they contained and for the illustrations which they give of the courses which courts had in fact steered in different factual situations. It was his view that, on the whole, the courts had tended to adopt a pragmatic approach to these problems, seeking *g* where possible to see that genuine wrongs were righted so long as the court did not thereby promote or countenance a nefarious object or bargain which it was bound to condemn. So counsel argued for the plaintiff that the court should take a pragmatic approach and, in deciding whether the public conscience would be shocked by allowing the plaintiff to recover damages in the circumstances of this case, the court should have *h* regard to the serious injuries which he had suffered and from which he would suffer for the rest of his life and should regard the public conscience as being as greatly shocked by the idea that he would recover no compensation for those injuries as it would be by the thought of allowing him to recover by basing his claim on the unlawful escapade in which he suffered the injuries.

The particular sphere of social behaviour and activity arising from the use of motor *j* vehicles in modern conditions is one in which Parliament has been continuously active during this century. It has produced codes designed to regulate and control the behaviour of drivers and for the contruction, maintenance and use of vehicles for the purpose of securing the safety of road users. It has also produced a code of requirements for motor insurance designed to make provision for compensating those who suffer injury from the use of vehicles on the road. Thus it seems to me that the primary source of public policy in this sphere must be the Acts of Parliament themselves. That policy is properly supplemented by taking into account the reasons given by the courts of this country for refusing to enforce rights based on conduct which has been regarded as sufficiently anti-social and contrary to the policy of the Acts. I would regard decisions in other jurisdictions which may have different social attitudes as of but secondary guidance, though of course entitled to respect and consideration. Although it is part of that policy that passengers carried on or in vehicles who sustain injury should be compensated, it is clear that Parliament did not regard it as essential that the driver of a vehicle who by his own fault injures himself should be required to insure against that risk. Parliament did however provide that, of the various offences specifically relating to the use of motor vehicles, causing death by reckless driving, reckless driving itself and driving when under the influence of drink and drugs were to be regarded as among the most serious of offences and were to be punishable by imprisonment. Parliament did not expressly provide that a passenger who took part with the driver in the commission of such offences should not be entitled to the benefit of the provisions designed to secure that he should receive compensation.

The policy underlying the provisions for compulsory insurance for passengers and others injured in road accidents is clearly one intended for their benefit; it does not follow that if an offence is committed jointly by the driver and passenger of a kind not regarded as so serious as to disentitle the driver from claiming indemnity for the benefit of an innocent passenger, the passenger who is a joint offender can, subject to questions of contributory negligence, recover compensation from the driver. If, however, the offence, or series of offences, is so serious that it would preclude the driver on grounds of public policy from claiming indemnity under a policy required to be effected under the Act for the benefit of a passenger, that public policy would in my judgment also preclude the passenger jointly guilty of that offence from claiming compensation.

On the facts found by the judge in this case the plaintiff was playing a full and active part in encouraging the young rider to commit offences which, if a death other than that of the young rider himself had occurred, would have amounted to manslaughter. And not just manslaughter by gross negligence on the judge's findings. It would have been manslaughter by the commission of a dangerous act either done with the intention of frightening other road users or when both the plaintiff and the young rider were aware or but for self-induced intoxication would have been aware that it was likely to do so and nevertheless they went on and did the act regardless of the consequences. Thus on the findings made by the judge in this case I would hold that the plaintiff is precluded on grounds of public policy from recovering compensation for the injuries which he sustained in the course of the very serious offences in which he was participating. On a question on which, as Bingham LJ said, the courts have tended to adopt a pragmatic approach, I do not believe that it is desirable to go further in an attempt to categorise the degree of seriousness involved in offences which will not preclude recovery of compensation. I would, however, add that the public attitude to driving a motor vehicle on a road when under the influence of drink has, I believe, changed markedly with the increasing number of serious accidents and the dreadful injuries which are the consequence of such driving. The public conscience is ever-increasingly being focussed not only on those who commit the offence but, in the words of recent publicity, those who ask the driver to drink and drive.

The second ground on which the judge held that the plaintiff's claim failed was because in the circumstances of the case the law would not recognise the existence of a duty of care owed by the rider to the plaintiff. As this ground is also based on public policy, it is not I think in the circumstances of this case significant. That both the plaintiff and rider owed a duty to other road users to exercise reasonable care is clear. I am not convinced of the wisdom of a policy which might encourage a belief that the duty to behave responsibly in driving motor vehicles is diminished even to the limited extent that they may in some circumstances not owe a duty to each other, particularly when those circumstances involve conduct which is highly dangerous to others.

As to the defence raised that the plaintiff voluntarily undertook to run the risk of injury by taking part in such a foolhardy, risky and illegal activity, I would have been prepared to say that it was obvious from the description of the plaintiff's behaviour whilst he was participating that he had done so. However the judge accepted that the effect of s 148(3) of the Road Traffic Act 1972 was that any agreement or understanding that the risk of injury would be the plaintiff's was of no effect.

Before the enactment of the Motor Vehicles (Passenger Insurance) Act 1971, a policy of insurance required to be effected under the provisions of s 203(4) of the Road Traffic Act 1960 was not required to cover:

'(a) liability in respect of the death of, or bodily injury to, persons being carried in or upon, or entering or getting on to or alighting from, the vehicle at the time of the occurrence of the event out of which the claims arise . . .'

unless such passengers were carried in a vehicle for hire or reward or in pursuance of a contract of employment.

It was this provision and proviso which were repealed by s 1(1) of the Motor Vehicles (Passenger Insurance) Act 1971. At the same time in sub-s (2) it was provided:

'. . . if any other person is carried in or upon the vehicle while the user is so using it, any antecedent agreement or understanding between them (whether intended to be legally binding or not) shall be of no effect so far as it purports or might be held— (a) to negative or restrict any such liability of the user in respect of persons carried in or upon the vehicle as is required by section 203 of that Act to be covered by a policy of insurance; or (b) to impose any conditions with respect to the enforcement of any such liability of the user; and the fact that a person so carried has willingly accepted as his the risk of negligence on the part of the user shall not be treated as negativing any such liability of the user. For the purposes of this subsection . . . the reference to an antecedent agreement is to one made any time before the liability arose.'

This is the provision now to be found in s 148(3) of the Road Traffic Act 1972. It is not at first sight easy to see a distinction between an understanding between the driver and passenger, whether legally binding or not, which is made at any time before the liability arises and the fact that the person so carried has willingly accepted as his the risk of negligence on the part of the user. If the former is of no effect, it would not negative any liability of the user. I can only think that the draftsman was drawing a distinction between agreements or understandings which negative or restrict liability by their terms on the one hand and, on the other, facts which would give rise to the defence of volenti non fit injuria, which, but for the provision, would be taken to negative the liability which is required to be recovered under a policy of insurance under s 145. That is to say, any liability which may be incurred by the driver in respect of death or bodily injury to any person caused by or arising out of the use of the vehicle on the road. I think therefore that the words of s 148(3) clearly mean that it is no longer open to the driver of a motor vehicle to say that the fact of his passenger travelling in a vehicle in circumstances in which for one reason or another it could be said that he had willingly accepted a risk of negligence on the driver's part relieves him of liability for such negligence. I am supported in this view by the decision of the Inner House of the Court of Session in *Winnik v Dick* 1984 SLT 185 and by the opinion of Lord Hunter and the Lord Justice Clerk (Wheatley) in that case. I do not believe that there is any difference of principle in the application of the doctrine of volenti in Scotland and England which would lead to a different result in England. This is a conclusion at which I arrive with some relief because the rights of a passenger under s 148 of the Road Traffic Act 1972, which applies to

Scotland as well as to England, ought not to suffer a change on his journey by car to
Scotland as it crosses the border.

   Although it is unnecessary in view of the decision to which I have come to express an
opinion on the judge's decision that the plaintiff should have his damages reduced to nil
by reason of his own fault, I would say that I was quite unpersuaded by the argument for
the plaintiff that this was a correct apportionment of responsibility. Although the court
when apportioning liability between two tortfeasors is given express power under s 6 of
the Law Reform (Married Women and Tortfeasors) Act 1935 to exempt a person from
liability to make contribution, or to direct that a contribution to be recovered from any
person liable in respect of the damage should amount to a complete indemnity, it seems
to me that the wording of s 1 of the Law Reform (Contributory Negligence) Act 1945 is
incapable of a similar interpretation. Section 1 begins with the premise that the person
suffers damage as a result partly of his own fault and partly of the fault of any other
person or persons. Thus before the section comes into operation, the court must be
satisfied that there is fault on the part of both parties which has caused damage. It is then
expressly provided that the claim shall not be defeated by reason of the fault of the person
suffering the damage. To hold that he is himself entirely responsible for the damage
effectively defeats his claim. It is then provided that the damages recoverable in respect
thereof (that is the damage suffered partly as a result of his own fault and partly the fault
of any other person) shall be reduced. It therefore presupposes that the person suffering
the damage will recover some damage. Finally reduction is to be to such extent as the
court thinks just and equitable, having regard to the claimant's share in the responsibility
for the damage. To hold that the claimant is 100% responsible is not to hold that he
shared in the responsibility for the damage.

   For these reasons I would not support the judge's conclusion. In the circumstances of
this case in which arguments can be advanced on the question of blameworthiness which
might suggest a greater degree of fault on the older as opposed to the younger boy, or as
to the rider as opposed to the passenger, I would not myself take any view which
attributed a greater share of responsibility to one or the other. They participated equally
in the illegal and dangerous escapade regardless of the safety of others and of themselves
and had they been jointly charged with the criminal offences they were jointly
committing they would have been charged and convicted as principals.

   Subject to the question of their ages, I doubt whether any distinction would have been
drawn for the purpose of any sentence imposed on them. In the circumstances, had the
plaintiff been entitled to damages, I would have held that they should have been reduced
by 50%. For the reasons I have given, however, I would dismiss the appeal.

BALCOMBE LJ. I have had the advantage of reading in draft the judgments of Beldam
and Dillon LJJ. The facts are fully set out in the judgment of Beldam LJ and I need not
repeat them.

   Three issues arise on this appeal and cross-appeal. (1) Whether the joint illegal
enterprise on which the appellant plaintiff and the deceased Hunt were engaged at the
time of the accident was such as to preclude the plaintiff from being able to sue the
deceased's representative (the first defendant) for damages? (2) Whether any defence of
volenti non fit injuria which might otherwise be available is excluded by s 148(3) of the
Road Traffic Act 1972. (3) Whether the plaintiff was 100% contributorily negligent. I
consider these issues separately below.

(1) The joint illegal enterprise
   In a case of this kind I find the ritual incantation of the maxim ex turpi causa non
oritur actio more likely to confuse than to illuminate. I prefer to adopt the approach of
the majority of the High Court of Australia in the most recent of the several Australian
cases to which we were referred, *Jackson v Harrison* (1978) 138 CLR 438. That is to

consider what would have been the cause of action had there been no joint illegal enterprise, that is the tort of negligence based on the breach of a duty of care owed by the deceased to the plaintiff, and then to consider whether the circumstances of the particular case are such as to preclude the existence of that cause of action. I find myself in complete agreement with the following passage from the judgment of Mason J in *Jackson v Harrison* (at 455–456):

> 'If a joint participant in an illegal enterprise is to be denied relief against a co-participant for injury sustained in that enterprise, the denial of relief should be related not to the illegal character of the activity but rather to the character and incidents of the enterprise and to the hazards which are necessarily inherent in its execution. A more secure foundation for denying relief, though more limited in its application—and for that reason fairer in its operation—is to say that the plaintiff must fail when the character of the enterprise in which the parties are engaged is such that it is impossible for the court to determine the standard of care which is appropriate to be observed. The detonation of an explosive device is a case of this kind. But the driving of a motor vehicle by an unlicensed and disqualified driver, so long as it does not entail an agreement to drive the car recklessly on the highway (see *Bondarenko* v. *Sommers* ((1968) 69 SR(NSW) 269), stands in a somewhat different position. In this case the evidence indicates that the participants contemplated that the vehicle would be driven carefully—an accident or untoward event might, as in fact it did, lead to discovery of their breach of the law. It is not suggested that either party lacked the experience or ability to drive carefully—that they were unlicensed was due to their having been disqualified as a result of earlier traffic offences . . . A plaintiff will fail when the joint illegal enterprise in which he and the defendant are engaged is such that the court cannot determine the particular standard of care to be observed. It matters not whether this in itself provides a complete answer to the plaintiff's claim or whether it leads in theory to the conclusion that the defendant owes no duty of care to the plaintiff because no standard of care can be determined in the particular case.'

The facts of the earlier case in the High Court of Australia, *Smith v Jenkins* (1970) 119 CLR 397, are set out in the judgment of Dillon LJ and I need not repeat them. Of those facts Jacobs J said in *Jackson v Harrison* (1978) 138 CLR 438 at 460:

> 'It appears to me that these facts lie at the basis of the conclusion that there was a relevant joint criminal enterprise. It was a jaunt, an escapade, a joy-ride even though of a most serious kind from the beginning to the end. How could a standard of care be determined for such a course of criminal activity? I doubt that the decision would have been the same if the accident had occurred days, weeks or months later when the circumstances of the taking of the vehicle had ceased to have any significant relationship to the manner in which the vehicle was being used.'

This approach seems to me to enable the court to differentiate between those joint enterprises which, although involving a contravention of the criminal law and hence illegal, eg the use of a car by an unlicensed and disqualified driver as in *Jackson v Harrison*, are not such as to disable the court from determining the standard of care to be observed, and those, such as the use of a get-away car as in *Ashton v Turner* [1980] 3 All ER 870, [1981] QB 137, where it is impossible to determine the appropriate standard of care.

Counsel for the plaintiff submitted that, however reprehensible the plaintiff's conduct may have been, his culpability involved neither dishonesty nor violence nor any moral turpitude such as is inherent in crimes of dishonesty or violence. Although an assessment of the degree of moral turpitude becomes unnecessary if one adopts, as I do, the approach of the majority of the High Court of Australia in *Jackson v Harrison*, I would not wish it to be thought that I accept this submission. It was only by good fortune that no innocent third party was injured by this disgraceful piece of motor cycle riding, in which the

judge found on the facts that the plaintiff was an active participant. If moral turpitude
a were relevant, here was moral turpitude of a high degree.

However, I prefer to found my judgment on the simple basis that the circumstances
of this particular case were such as to preclude the court from finding that the deceased
owed a duty of care to the plaintiff.

I agree with Dillon LJ, and for the reasons which he gives, that s 148(3) of the Road
Traffic Act 1972 does not affect the position under this head.
b

(2) *Volenti and s 148(3)*
Counsel for the first defendant sought to persuade us that the application of the volenti
doctrine is to extinguish liability and, if liability has already been extinguished, there is
nothing on which s 148(3) of the Road Traffic Act 1972 can bite. As Dillon LJ says, if this
argument were to be accepted, it would mean that s 148(3) could never apply to a normal
c case of volenti, although that was clearly its intention. For the reasons given by the judge
below, by both Beldam and Dillon LJJ and by the Inner House of the Court of Session in
Winnik v Dick 1984 SLT 185, I agree that the effect of s 148(3) is to exclude any defence of
volenti which might otherwise be available. On this issue I agree with the judge below
that Ewbank J's decision in *Ashton v Turner* [1980] 3 All ER 870 at 878, [1981] QB 137 at
148 was incorrect.
d

(3) *Contributory negligence*
I agree that the judge's finding that the plaintiff was 100% contributorily negligent is
logically unsupportable and, to use his own words, 'defies common sense'. Such a finding
is equivalent to saying that the plaintiff was solely responsibile for his own injuries,
which he clearly was not. For my part I prefer to express no opinion on how the liability
e should have been apportioned, had that been material.

I agree that this appeal should be dismissed.

DILLON LJ. I gratefully accept the account of the facts of this case contained in the
judgment of Beldam LJ.

On those facts the plaintiff accepts that if he is entitled to recover anything from the
f first defendant his award must be subject to a significant deduction for contributory
negligence. The judge's finding that the second defendant was not at fault is not
challenged by anyone. The first defendant says, however, that the plaintiff is not entitled
to recover anything at all, and the case was put in the court below on one or other or both
of the well-known Latin maxims ex turpi causa non oritur actio and volenti non fit
injuria.
g
The judge, in a very careful reserved judgment, held that because of s 148(3) of the
Road Traffic Act 1972 the maxim volenti could not provide the first defendant any
defence, but he also held that the plaintiff was not entitled to recover anything from the
first defendant on the ground of ex turpi causa and further that the plaintiff was 100%
contributorily negligent.
h
The judge's view on the extent of the plaintiff's contributory negligence was that the
plaintiff and the deceased boy, Mark Hunt, were jointly responsible for the reckless
driving of the motor cycle. So both were responsible for causing the accident and, on the
judge's view, 'logically at least' each was 100% to blame. With all respect I do not find
that logical nor has the judge approached the question correctly. In the context of the
plea of contributory negligence in the present case, the judge was required to apportion
j liability for the accident as between the deceased and the plaintiff. He does not affect any
apportionment by saying that each was 100% to blame. If they were equally to blame
the apportionment would be 50% to each. On the facts it would be impossible to
apportion more than 50% liability to the pillion passenger, the plaintiff, vis-à-vis the
driver, the deceased.

Another matter which can be disposed of quite shortly is the issue of volenti. We have

had argument whether the doctrine of volenti requires it to be shown, as Lord Denning
MR said in *Nettleship v Weston* [1971] 3 All ER 581 at 588, [1971] 2 QB 691 at 701, that *a*
the plaintiff had voluntarily agreed to waive any claim for any injury that might befall
him or whether the application of that doctrine is that it should be implied, from the
mere acceptance by the plaintiff of such an obvious risk, that there was no duty of care. I
find it unnecessary to explore this, since on any view the volenti defence is, in my
judgment, precluded by s 148(3) of the 1972 Act.

Section 148(3) (now replaced by s 149 of the Road Traffic Act 1988, which has entirely *b*
the same effect) provides as follows:

'(3) Where a person uses a motor vehicle in circumstances such that under section
143 of this Act there is required to be in force in relation to his use of it such a policy
of insurance or security as is mentioned in subsection (1) of that section, then, if any
other person is carried in or upon the vehicle while the user is so using it, any *c*
antecedent agreement or understanding between them (whether intended to be
legally binding or not) shall be of no effect so far as it purports or might be held—
(*a*) to negative or restrict any such liability of the user in respect of persons carried
in or upon the vehicle as is required by section 145 of this Act to be covered by a
policy of insurance; or (*b*) to impose any conditions with respect to the enforcement
of any such liability of the user; and the fact that a person so carried has willingly *d*
accepted as his the risk of negligence on the part of the user shall not be treated as
negativing any such liability of the user. For the purposes of this subsection
references to a person being carried in or upon a vehicle include references to a
person entering or getting on to, or alighting from, the vehicle, and the reference to
an antecedent agreement is to one made at any time before the liability arose.'

e
On that wording, the fact that the plaintiff has willingly, volens, accepted as his the
risk of negligence on the part of the deceased cannot be treated as negativing the liability
of the deceased, and the defence of volenti cannot apply. The Court of Session so held in
Winnik v Dick 1984 SLT 185 esp at 190–191 per Lord Hunter and I respectfully agree
with them. I see no significant difference between the English and Scottish doctrines of
volenti, taking the latter as explained by Lord Kilbrandon in *McCaig v Langan* 1964 SLT *f*
121, and I would reject arguments for the first defendant which would have the effect
that the provisions of s 148(3) could never apply to a 'normal' case of volenti.

The much more difficult aspect of this appeal arises from the first defendant's claim,
which the judge upheld, that the plaintiff is barred from recovering anything by the
application of the maxim ex turpi causa.

It so happens that the cases where a passenger has been injured by the 'negligence' of *g*
the driver when the vehicle in which the passenger was being carried was being used for
an illegal purpose in which the passenger was an accomplice have come before the High
Court of Australia more often than before the appellate courts in this country. The
factual situations in which the Australian courts have held that a passenger injured by
the 'negligence' of the driver in the course of a joint criminal enterprise cannot recover
damages from the driver are clear. But the reasoning by which the Australian courts *h*
have reached their conclusions from common law principles is, to me, very much less
clear, not least because of the extent to which the judgments in one particular decision of
the High Court, *Smith v Jenkins* (1970) 119 CLR 397, have been reinterpreted in later
decisions of the High Court. There is also the problem of how the Australian approach,
purportedly based on common law principles, is reconcilable with certain recent
developments in the English courts, also purportedly based on common law principles, *j*
in cases to which the judge below was not referred.

It is clear for a start that the fact that a plaintiff was engaged in an illegal activity which
brought about his injury does not automatically bring it about that his claim for damages
for personal injury as a result of the negligence of the defendant must be dismissed. (See
e g *Baker v Market Harborough Industrial Co-op Society Ltd* [1953] 1 WLR 1472, where, as in

many cases, the court apportioned liability for a road accident which had been caused by each driver, independently, driving negligently and without due care and attention. See also the judgment of Latham CJ in *Henwood v Municipal Tramways Trust (South Australia)* (1938) 60 CLR 438.) In that case a passenger on a tram, feeling ill, lent out of a window of the tram to be sick, and was killed because his head was struck in succession by two steel standards erected by the tram company to carry the overhead cables which supplied the current for the trams. It was an offence punishable by a fine under a byelaw having statutory force for any passenger in a tram to lean out of the window. But it was none the less held that the parents of the deceased could bring an action for negligence in respect of his death, and seemingly he himself could have brought the action if he had merely been injured and survived, on the grounds that the tram company had failed to take sufficient steps to protect passengers against a foreseeable, and indeed known, danger. Latham CJ said (at 446):

> 'But there are other considerations which are, in my opinion, sufficiently weighty to displace those to which I have referred. In the first place, there is no general principle of English law that a person who is engaged in some unlawful act is disabled from complaining of injury done to him by other persons, either deliberately or accidently. He does not become *caput lupinum*. Other persons still owe to him a duty to take care, the extent of that duty being determined by the circumstances of the case which create the duty. The person who is injured in a motor accident may be a child playing truant from school, an employee who is absent from work in breach of his contract, a man who is loitering upon a road in breach of a by-law, or a burglar on his way to a professional engagement—but none of these facts is relevant for the purpose of deciding the existence or defining the content of the obligation of a motor driver not to injure them. Thus, it cannot be held that there is any principle which makes it impossible for a defendant to be liable for injury brought about by his negligence simply because the plaintiff at the relevant time was breaking some provision of the law. The general principle stated will probably not be questioned . . .'

So much is common ground between the parties, but it raises questions which have been the subject of discussion in English and Australian judgments whether a line can be drawn between different grades of illegality, and whether there is a distinction, and if so, on what ground, between the ordinary case of negligence, albeit involving a criminal act, such as the two last cited, and cases where a passenger sues the driver for injuries sustained by reckless driving at the time of the accident when they were both engaged in a joint criminal enterprise of which the reckless driving was an inherent part .

Counsel for the plaintiff founds on certain recent authorities in this country which he relied on as establishing a 'conscience test' to be applied in cases of illegality.

The starting point is the judgment of Hutchison J in *Thackwell v Barclays Bank plc* [1986] 1 All ER 676. In that case the plaintiff claimed damages from the bank for having paid a cheque drawn in favour of the plaintiff to a third party in reliance on a forgery of the plaintiff's signature on an indorsement of the cheque. The claim was rejected on the ground that the cheque represented the proceeds of a fraud on a fourth party, to which the plaintiff, the drawer of the cheque and the forger of the indorsement were all parties. Hutchison J treated the case as one in which public policy would prevent the plaintiff suing just as it would prevent a burglar from whom the stolen goods were snatched by a third party just as the burglar left the victim's house from maintaining an action in conversion against the third party. The judge in reaching that conclusion seems to have accepted a submission from counsel for the defendants that there were two distinct but related lines of authority running through the cases on illegality, the second of which laid down the 'conscience test'. That test was put as follows (at 678):

> 'That test, he suggested, involved the court looking at the quality of the illegality relied on by the defendant and all the surrounding circumstances, without fine

distinctions, and seeking to answer two questions: first, whether there had been illegality of which the court should take notice and, second, whether in all the circumstances it would be an affront to the public conscience if by affording him the relief sought the court was seen to be indirectly assisting or encouraging the plaintiff in his criminal act.'

The context in which that submission was put forward in *Thackwell v Barclays Bank plc* [1986] 1 All ER 676 seems to have been one of the proximity of the illegality to the matters of which complaint was made in the action. There is authority in *Sajan Singh v Sardara Ali* [1960] 1 All ER 269, [1960] AC 167 that a person who has acquired property under an illegal contract and has been using it without a permit can none the less maintain an action for damages for conversion against a person, even the vendor of the property, who subsequently, on the facts some three or four years later, wrongly deprives him of that property. The suggestion seems to have been in *Thackwell v Barclays Bank plc* that it would be an affront to the public conscience to allow one thief to maintain an action because a second of the thieves had stolen the first's share in the course of the division of the swag.

The conscience test was approved by this court in *Saunders v Edwards* [1987] 2 All ER 651, [1987] 1 WLR 1116. That was again a case of the proximity, or relevance, of the illegality to the matters of which the plaintiff was complaining. The plaintiff claimed damages for fraudulent misrepresentation, which had induced him to purchase a flat from the defendant. The defendant sought unsuccessfully to defend himself by asserting that the contract for the sale of the flat, and presumably also the conveyance, were tainted with illegality in that in the apportionment of the purchase price in the contract between chattels and the flat itself the amount attributable to the chattels had been fraudulently inflated, and the amount attributable to the flat had been correspondingly reduced, in order to reduce the stamp duty payable to the Revenue. This court applied Hutchison J's test, to which Nicholls LJ added at the end of the formulation the words 'or encouraging others in similar criminal acts' (see [1987] 2 All ER 651 at 664, [1987] 1 WLR 1116 at 1132).

Saunders v Edwards was, it seems to me, a case where the alleged illegality over the stamp duty apportionment was independent of, or unrelated to, the wrong in the way of fraudulent misrepresentation for which the plaintiff was suing. Kerr LJ decided the case, however, on the basis that the cases 'show that there are no rigid rules for or against the ex turpi causa defence' and that the cases 'show that the conduct and relative moral culpability of the parties may be relevant in determining whether or not the ex turpi causa defence falls to be applied as a matter of public policy (see [1987] 2 All ER 651 at 660, [1987] 1 WLR 1116 at 1127). Bingham LJ used rather different language where he said ([1987] 2 All ER 651 at 666, [1987] 1 WLR 1116 at 1134):

'... I think that on the whole the courts have tended to adopt a pragmatic approach to those problems, seeking where possible to see that genuine wrongs are righted so long as the court does not thereby promote or countenance a nefarious object or bargain which it is bound to condemn. Where the plaintiff's action in truth arises directly ex turpi causa, he is likely to fail ... Where the plaintiff has suffered a genuine wrong, to which allegedly unlawful conduct is incidental, he is likely to succeed ...'

That passage was adopted by Kerr LJ in giving the leading judgment of this court in *Euro-Diam Ltd v Bathurst* [1988] 2 All ER 23 at 29, [1990] 1 QB 1 at 36. The latter part of it is sufficient to cover the decision in *Saunders v Edwards* [1987] 2 All ER 651, [1987] 1 WLR 1116.

I find a test that depends on what would or would not be an affront to the public conscience very difficult to apply, since the public conscience may well be affected by factors of an emotional nature, e g that these boys by their reckless and criminal behaviour happened to do no harm to anyone but themselves. Moreover, if the public conscience

happened to think that the plaintiff should be compensated for his injuries it might
a equally think that the deceased driver of the motor cycle, had he survived and merely
been injured, ought to be compensated, and that leads into the much-debated question
whether there ought to be a universal scheme for compensation for the victims of
accidents without regard to fault.

Beyond that, appeal to the public conscience would be likely to lead to a graph of
illegalities according to moral turpitude, and I am impressed by the comments of Mason
b J in *Jackson v Harrison* (1978) 138 CLR 438 at 455, where he said:

'. . .there arises the difficulty, which I regard as insoluble, of formulating a
criterion which would separate cases of serious illegality from those which are not
serious. Past distinctions drawn between felonies and misdemeanours, malum in se
and malum prohibitum, offences punishable by imprisonment and those which are
c not, non-statutory and statutory offences offer no acceptable discrimen.'

Bingham LJ's dichotomy between cases where the plaintiff's action in truth arises
directly ex turpi causa and cases where the plaintiff has suffered a genuine wrong to
which allegedly unlawful conduct is incidental avoids this difficulty, in that it does not
involve grading illegalities according to moral turpitude.
d   In the Australian courts it was held by the High Court of Australia in *Jackson v Harrison*
that the maxim ex turpi causa is a maxim of the law of contract which cannot apply in
the law of tort. This however is, as it seems to me, a matter of terminology and in the
present case rather a red herring. The most commonly cited anglicisation of the maxim
is that of Lord Mansfield CJ in *Holman v Johnson* (1775) 1 Cowp 341 at 343, [1775–1802]
All ER Rep 98 at 99 that 'No Court will lend its aid to a man who founds his cause of
e action upon an immoral or an illegal act'. Whether that is or is not (see per Windeyer J in
Smith v Jenkins (1970) 119 CLR 397 at 412) a correct translation of the maxim is now
beside the point since it has been applied continuously as the law of England for over 200
years. Moreover, it has been so applied not only in cases where the cause of action has
been laid in contract, but also in cases, such as *Chettiar v Chettiar* [1962] 1 All ER 494,
[1962] AC 294, where it was held that a person who was party to an illegal transaction
f could not be heard to claim that that transaction had given rise to an enforceable trust in
his favour. (See also *Re Emery's Investments' Trusts, Emery v Emery* [1959] 1 All ER 577,
[1959] Ch 410.)
    That a defence of illegality can be pleaded to a case founded in tort is, in my judgment,
clear, whether or not the defence is correctly called ex turpi causa. *Thackwell v Barclays
Bank plc* [1986] 1 All ER 676 is one instance. Another is *Murphy v Culhane* [1976] 3 All
g ER 533, [1977] QB 94. There the plaintiff as the widow and administratrix of the estate
of her deceased husband claimed damages from the defendant on the ground that the
defendant had unlawfully assaulted the deceased by beating him about the head with a
plank by which assault he was killed. The plaintiff did not have to plead any illegality as
part of her case, but on a preliminary issue the defendant was allowed by this court to
plead that the assault alleged occurred during and as part of a criminal affray initiated by
h the deceased and others with the joint criminal purpose of assaulting and beating the
defendant. Lord Denning MR considered that a man who took part in a criminal affray
might well be said to have been guilty of such a wicked act as to deprive himself of a
cause of action; alternatively, even if the plaintiff were entitled to damages, they might
fall to be reduced under the Law Reform (Contributory Negligence) Act 1945. Since the
case came before this court on a preliminary issue, it was unnecessary to decide between
j these alternatives.
    I find it, at this stage, both necessary and helpful to examine the principal Australian
cases.
    In *Smith v Jenkins* (1970) 119 CLR 397 a group of four youths all about 16 years of age,
who had been drinking, robbed a man, stole his car keys, and then, having found out
where his car was, stole the car and drove it off on a joyride. The plaintiff was the first

driver, but after a couple of changes of driver he was merely a passenger; a relatively few miles from the scene of the theft the car left the road at 80 or 90 mph and hit a tree. The plaintiff was seriously injured and sued the youth who had been the driver at the time of the accident; it was held that he could not recover anything.

In *Bondarenko v Sommers* (1968) 69 SR (NSW) 269 a decision of the Court of Appeal of New South Wales, a group of youths stole a car and proceeded to race the stolen car against a car one of them owned along a rough and fairly narrow road containing potholes and ruts. The result of such reckless driving was that the stolen car turned over. One of the youths who was a passenger in the stolen car at the time of that accident claimed damages for his injuries, but was held not entitled to recover.

Then in *Jackson v Harrison* (1978) 138 CLR 438 a passenger was injured through the negligent driving of a motor car by a driver who was at the time of the accident and to the passenger's knowledge disqualified from driving. It was held by the majority of the High Court, Barwick CJ dissenting, that the passenger was not thereby disabled from recovering damages from the driver. The view of the majority, Mason, Jacobs and Aicken JJ, was that the illegality did not bear on the standard of care reasonably to be expected of the driver. That followed from a further decision of the High Court in *Progress and Properties Ltd v Craft* (1976) 135 CLR 651, which was not a motoring case.

In that case the plaintiff, Craft, was a workman on a building site who, in breach of statutory regulations, was carried to the top floor of a building under construction in a goods hoist with the concurrence of the operator of the hoist, who was a fellow employee. As the hoist reached the top floor the operator's foot slipped off the brake, the hoist fell to the ground at a speed which exceeded the maximum permissible speed under the regulations, and the plaintiff was injured. He claimed damages from his employers because of the operator's negligence and the employers pleaded as a defence the illegality on which the plaintiff and the operator were jointly engaged. It was held by a majority of the High Court, Barwick CJ again dissenting, that the plea of illegality did not avail the employers. The reason given in the judgment of Jacobs J, with which the other members of the majority concurred, was that the duty of care owed by the operator was the same whether he was hoisting goods only or a man in the hoist. Therefore the illegality did not affect the standard of care that the plaintiff was entitled to expect. Both *Jackson v Harrison* and *Progress and Properties Ltd v Craft* can be regarded as cases within Bingham LJ's category, in *Saunders v Edwards* [1987] 2 All ER 651, [1987] 1 WLR 1116, of cases where the plaintiff had suffered a genuine wrong to which his allegedly unlawful conduct was merely incidental.

In *Smith v Jenkins* (1970) 119 CLR 397 Kitto J founded his judgment on a principle which he took from the judgment of Scrutton LJ in *Hillen v ICI (Alkali) Ltd* [1934] 1 KB 455 at 467 that if the whole transaction is known by each party to be illegal there is no contribution or indemnity between joint wrongdoers. He said (119 CLR 397 at 403):

'. . . it seems . . . clear that Scrutton L.J. perceived a general principle of law . . . namely that persons who join in committing an illegal act which they know to be unlawful (or, I should add in the language of the judgment in *Adamson* v. *Jarvis* ((1827) 4 Bing 66 at 73, [1824–34] All ER Rep 120 at 122), which they must be presumed to know to be unlawful) have no legal rights inter se by reason of their respective participations in that act.'

That principle cannot, however, have survived intact as a principle of English law since the enactment of s 6 of the Law Reform (Married Women and Tortfeasors) Act 1935.

Barwick CJ held in *Smith v Jenkins* 119 CLR 397 at 400 that the failure of the plaintiff to recover damages was to be attributed to a refusal of the law to erect a duty of care as between persons jointly participating in the performance of an illegal act, rather than to a refusal of the courts, on grounds of public policy, to lend their assistance to the recovery of damages for breach in those circumstances of a duty of care owed by the one to the other because of the criminally illegal nature of the act out of which the harm arose. The

other members of the High Court seem to have taken the same view. Owen J commented
a that it would be an odd state of affairs if in a case such as that put by Lord Asquith in
National Coal Board v England [1954] 1 All ER 546 at 558, [1954] AC 403 at 429 a court
was called on to consider and decide the standard of care to be expected in particular
circumstances of a prudent safebreaker, or whether in the case suggested by Scrutton LJ
in *Hillen v ICI (Alkali) Ltd* [1934] 1 KB 455 at 467 the smuggler who had not warned his
confederates of a defect in the rope which they were using in the course of hiding
b smuggled goods had acted with the degree of care to be expected in the circumstances of
a reasonable careful smuggler (see 119 CLR 397 at 425). The court considered that the
doctrine of volenti did not provide a satisfactory solution of the problem.

On the facts of *Progress and Properties Ltd v Craft* (1976) 135 CLR 651 it became clear
that merely to say that if the parties were engaging in a joint illegal act neither would
owe any duty of care to the other was to put the proposition too widely. The distillation
c of the law by the High Court of Australia rests therefore now on the judgment of Jacobs
J, with which the other members of the majority of the court concurred, in *Progress and
Properties Ltd v Craft* and in the judgments of Mason and Jacobs JJ with whom Aicken J
concurred in *Jackson v Harrison* (1978) 138 CLR 438. For relief to be derived on the
ground of the illegality, the circumstances of the joint illegal venture in the course of
which the accident which caused the plaintiff's injuries occurred must be such as to
d negate, as between the two of them, any ordinary standard of care. Thus Mason J said in
Jackson v Harrison (at 456):

'A plaintiff will fail when the joint illegal enterprise in which he and the defendant
are engaged is such that the court cannot determine the particular standard of care
to be observed.'

e And Jacobs J said in *Progress and Properties Ltd v Craft* (1976) 135 CLR 651 at 668:

'Where there is a joint illegal activity the actual act of which the plaintiff in a civil
action may be complaining as done without care may itself be a criminal act of a
kind in respect of which a court is not prepared to hear evidence for the purpose of
establishing the standard of care which was reasonable in the circumstances.'

f
This formulation would clearly cover the instances given in the authorities of the
careless smuggler or safebreaker, or the reckless driving, to escape capture, of the getaway
car after a robbery as in the English case of *Ashton v Turner* [1980] 3 All ER 870, [1981]
QB 137. It was regarded in *Jackson v Harrison* as also covering the factual situations in
Bondarenko v Sommers (1968) 69 SR (NSW) 269, where there was, in the words of Mason J
g in *Jackson v Harrison* 138 CLR 438 at 456, 'an agreement to drive the [stolen] car recklessly'
for the purpose of racing on the highway, and the factual situation in *Smith v Jenkins*. In
reference to *Smith v Jenkins*, Jacobs J said in *Jackson v Harrison* 138 CLR 438 at 460:

'It was a jaunt, an escapade, a joy-ride even though of a most serious kind from
the beginning to the end. How could a standard of care be determined for such a
h   course of criminal activity?'

I feel unable to draw any valid distinction between the reckless riding of the motor
cycle in the present case by the deceased boy, Hunt, and the plaintiff under the influence
of drink, and the reckless driving of the cars, albeit stolen, in *Smith v Jenkins* and *Bondarenko
v Sommers*. The words of Barwick CJ in *Smith v Jenkins* (1970) 119 CLR 397 at 399–400:

j   'The driving of the car by the appellant, the manner of which is the basis of the
respondent's complaint, was in the circumstances as much a use of the car by the
respondent as it was a use by the appellant. That use was their joint enterprise of the
moment.'

apply with equal force to the riding of the motor cycle in the present case. This is a case in which, in Bingham LJ's words, the plaintiff's action in truth arises directly ex turpi causa.

It remains, however, to consider whether the agreement or understanding between the plaintiff and the deceased to ride the motor cycle recklessly while under the influence of drink falls within s 148(3) of the Road Traffic Act 1972 and so is of no effect so far as it purports or might be held to negative or restrict any such liability of the deceased in respect of persons carried in or on the vehicle as is required by the Act to be covered by a policy of insurance.

It is fundamental to the distinction by the Australian courts between *Smith v Jenkins* and *Bondarenko v Sommers* (and the decision of the Full Court of the Supreme Court of New South Wales in *Godbolt v Fittock* [1963] SR (NSW) 617 on the one hand and *Jackson v Harrison* and *Progress and Properties Ltd v Craft* on the other hand) that the joint illegal purpose on which the parties were engaged at the time of the accident must have displaced the ordinary standard of care. Does s 148(3) have the effect that an express or tacit agreement by the parties to engage in such a joint illegal venture cannot be relied on to negative or restrict liability for negligent driving in the ordinary sense of those words?

My answer to that question is 'No' because s 148(3) is concerned to preclude a defence of volenti, but it is not concerned with any defence of illegality. The words 'agreement or understanding' in s 148(3) do not contemplate an illegal agreement, express or tacit, to carry out an illegal purpose, otherwise, since the words in s 148(3) are 'negative or restrict' liability, the passenger in the stolen getaway car driven recklessly from the scene of a robbery in order to escape interception and capture would be able to recover full damages from the Motor Insurers' Bureau, as representing the uninsured driver, without even any reduction or restriction of the damages for contributory negligence.

For the foregoing reasons I would dismiss this appeal.

Appeal dismissed. Leave to appeal to the House of Lords granted.

Solicitors: *Kenwright & Cox*, agents for *Talbot Davies & Copner*, Andover (for the plaintiff); *Lamport Bassitt*, Southampton (for the first defendant).

Carolyn Toulmin   Barrister.

Howard v Shirlstar Container Transport Ltd and another

COURT OF APPEAL, CIVIL DIVISION
LORD DONALDSON OF LYMINGTON MR, TAYLOR AND STAUGHTON LJJ
14, 16 MAY 1990

Contract – Illegality – Performance of contract illegal under foreign law – Enforcement of contract contrary to public policy – Criminal acts committed in performance of contract in order to escape danger to life – Owner of aircraft agreeing to pay plaintiff fee for successfully removing aircraft from Nigerian territorial airspace – Plaintiff removing aircraft without permission of Nigerian authorities and landing in Ivory Coast – Plaintiff believing life in imminent danger in Nigeria – Government of Ivory Coast returning aircraft to Nigerian authorities – Whether plaintiff entitled to fee – Whether contract unenforceable because tainted with illegality – Whether public conscience would be affronted if contract enforced.

The defendant company hired out two aircraft for private use in Nigeria. The hire instalments became overdue entitling the defendants to repossess the aircraft which were

then in Nigeria. The defendants engaged the plaintiff, a qualified pilot, to recover the
a aircraft under contracts which provided, by cl 1, for the payment of £25,000 to the
plaintiff 'for successfully removing [each] aircraft . . . from Nigerian airspace', £12,500
of which was to be paid as soon as the defendants received telex confirmation that the
plaintiff had removed the aircraft from Nigerian territorial airspace and the balance to be
paid within one month thereafter. The plaintiff flew to Lagos where he found one of the
aircraft parked at the airport and nine days later, having been warned by the head of the
b Federal Civil Aviation Department in Nigeria that the lives of himself and his wireless
operator were in imminent danger and that the government could not protect them, he
flew the aircraft out of Nigeria without obtaining air traffic control clearance, in breach
of Nigerian law. He evaded a military aircraft which he reasonably believed to be
interested in him and ultimately succeeded in landing in the Ivory Coast where he sent a
telex to the defendants stating that the aircraft had left Nigerian airspace. The defendants
c paid the first instalment of £12,500 on receipt of the telex. However, the Ivory Coast
government detained the aircraft and subsequently returned it to Nigeria while
permitting the plaintiff and his wireless operator to return to the United Kingdom. The
defendants refused to pay the plaintiff the second instalment and when the plaintiff
brought an action against the defendants claiming the second instalment and interest
they counterclaimed for the return of the first instalment. The judge held that the
d plaintiff was entitled to be paid both instalments and dismissed the counterclaim. The
defendants appealed, contending, inter alia, that the plaintiff was not entitled to the
second instalment because (i) he had not 'successfully' removed the aircraft from Nigerian
airspace within the meaning of cl 1 of the contract because he had not 'successfully and
finally' removed the aircraft but had only removed it temporarily, and (ii) the contract
had been performed illegally in Nigeria and was therefore unenforceable in England.
e

Held – (1) The word 'successfully' in cl 1 of the contract meant at most that the actual
flight out of Nigeria had to be completed without mishap or misfortune and end in a
safe landing. Since the plaintiff had succeeded in removing the aircraft from Nigeria and
landing it safely in the Ivory Coast and since payment of the first instalment was payable
irrevocably on completion of the flight out of Nigeria and the receipt of the telex he was
f entitled to both instalments of the fee (see p 370 *j* to p 371 *a* and p 375 *b c g*, post).

(2) Although the court would not normally enforce a contract which would enable a
plaintiff to benefit from his criminal conduct, since to do so would be an affront to the
public conscience, there were circumstances where it would be wrong to disqualify a
plaintiff from recovery, even though his claim was derived from conduct which
constituted a statutory offence. One such circumstance was where the plaintiff committed
g the criminal acts in order to escape danger to his life. Accordingly, although the plaintiff's
claim would otherwise be unenforceable in an English court because his breach of
Nigerian air traffic control regulations was central to his performance of the contract, the
public conscience would not be affronted if the contract was enforced against the
defendants because the plaintiff's criminal conduct was designed to free himself and his
h wireless operator from pressing danger. The appeal would therefore be dismissed (see
p 371 *e f h*, p 373 *d j* and p 375 *a d* to g, post); dicta of Kerr LJ in *Euro-Diam Ltd v Bathurst*
[1988] 2 All ER 23 at 28–29 and of Devlin J in *St John Shipping Corp v Joseph Rank Ltd*
[1956] 3 All ER 683 at 693 applied; *Thackwell v Barclays Bank plc* [1986] 1 All ER 676
approved.

j **Notes**
For contracts illegal at common law, see 9 Halsbury's Laws (4th edn) para 427, and for
cases on the subject, see 12 Digest (Reissue) 291–294, 2102–2118.

For performance of a contract which is illegal under foreign law, see 8 Halsbury's Laws
(4th edn) paras 603–607, and for cases on the subject, see 11 Digest (Reissue) 481–488,
876–911.

Cases referred to in judgments

Beresford v Royal Insurance Co Ltd [1938] 2 All ER 602, [1938] AC 586, HL; *affg* [1937] 2 All ER 243, [1937] 2 KB 197, CA.

Cleaver v Mutual Reserve Fund Life Association [1892] 1 QB 147, [1891–4] All ER Rep 335, CA.

Euro-Diam Ltd v Bathurst [1988] 2 All ER 23, [1990] 1 QB 1, [1988] 2 WLR 717, CA; *affg* [1987] 2 All ER 113, [1990] 1 QB 1, [1987] 2 WLR 1368.

Mackender v Feldia AG [1966] 3 All ER 847, [1967] 2 QB 590, [1967] 2 WLR 119, CA.

Marles v Philip Trant & Sons Ltd (Mackinnon, third party) (No 2) [1953] 1 All ER 651, [1954] 1 QB 29, [1953] 2 WLR 564, CA.

Pitts v Hunt [1990] 3 All ER 344, [1990] 3 WLR 542, CA.

St John Shipping Corp v Joseph Rank Ltd [1956] 3 All ER 683, [1957] 1 QB 267, [1956] 3 WLR 870.

Saunders v Edwards [1987] 2 All ER 651, [1987] 1 WLR 1116, CA.

Thackwell v Barclays Bank plc [1986] 1 All ER 676.

Case also cited

Ashmore Benson Pease & Co Ltd v A V Dawson Ltd [1973] 2 All ER 856, [1973] 1 WLR 828, CA.

Appeal

The defendants, Shirlstar Container Transport Ltd (Shirlstar) and their solicitor, Stanley Sherwin Beller, appealed against the judgment of his Honour Judge Gower QC, sitting as a judge of the High Court in the Queen's Bench Division, given on 9 May 1989 and entered on 9 June 1989 whereby he ordered the defendants to pay the sum of £27,250 to the plaintiff, Captain Michael Roy Howard, under an agreement dated 10 May 1984 by which Captain Howard undertook to remove an aircraft belonging to Shirlstar from Nigerian territorial airspace for the sum of £25,000. The facts are set out in the judgment of Staughton LJ.

Andrew Longmore QC for the defendants.
Nicholas Yell for the Captain Howard.

STAUGHTON LJ (giving the first judgment at the invitation of Lord Donaldson MR). In 1984 the first defendants (whom I shall call 'Shirlstar') were the owners of two aircraft which had been let out on hire. The hirers were British companies, but de facto the hire was in each case to a person of importance in Nigeria. The hire instalments were overdue, and Shirlstar wished to recover the two aircraft which were in Nigeria. In addition to any other difficulties they may have faced, there had been a coup d'état in Nigeria in December 1983, when the existing government was overthrown and replaced by a military junta.

In the result, Shirlstar made two contracts on 10 May 1984 with the plaintiff, Captain Howard. He was a qualified pilot. Each contract provided for him to attempt to recover one of the aircraft and fly it to Hurn airport near Bournemouth. He was to be paid a fee of £25,000 in two equal instalments, plus some expenses, on terms which I shall need to consider carefully. He secured the services of a young lady called Miss Spalding, to whom he was engaged, as a wireless operator. She took what the judge called a crash course in wireless operation, and obtained the necessary certificate.

Captain Howard and Miss Spalding flew to Lagos, arriving on 11 May. They found one of the two aircraft, with the signal letters G LORI, parked on grass at the airport. They were able to prepare it for take-off with the assistance of two British engineers who were there, and without becoming involved in any illegality as far as we are aware.

Meanwhile, they had various conversations with Mr Haslam, second secretary in charge of commercial affairs at the United Kingdom High Commission, and with Mr *a* Odigwe, the acting head of the Federal Civil Aviation Department. I shall have to return later to the substance of those conversations. Then, on 20 May in the evening, they took off in the aircraft, without obtaining permission from air traffic control at the airport. Captain Howard had not sought permission because he knew that it would not be granted. What followed was described by the judge and, although it is not essential to this judgment, the description bears repeating:

b 'Captain Howard became aware of a MIG fighter aircraft which he took to be interested in him and G LORI, and I doubt not that he is right in that assumption. He thought it likely that that aircraft would be armed with a heat sensitive missile, a missile being sensitive to the heat of the exhaust of a plane, and so what he did was to fly very low over the sea; indeed, he said at a height of 15 to 20 feet over the surface of the sea. The point of that was twofold: (a) because at that altitude the aircraft would not show up on a radar screen, and (b) because the sea in those *c* latitudes being very warm, the heat rising from the surface of the sea would confuse the missile by in effect masking the warmth from the exhaust. There was a further consideration which was that by flying at that very low altitude he would make it necessary for the MIG fighter, if it were minded to attack him using its guns to do so at a very sharp angle to the surface of the sea. He changed course several times *d* and eventually was able to take advantage of what he described as a slight rain squall. He flew behind the squall, evaded the fighter. He was listening over his radio to signals, conversations going on between air traffic controllers. There came a stage when he was in range of the airport at Accra. He received an invitation to land there from the Accra air traffic control authorities. They appeared to read out some kind of prepared statement from which it was clear that they were acting on the *e* instigation of the Nigerian authorities. He thought better of that notion and made for Abidjan, the principal airport on the Ivory Coast, and there he landed. His take-off was some time a bit before six o'clock in the evening: the flight as I understand it took half an hour. When he and Miss Spalding landed at Abidjan there was a reception awaiting them. Nigerian authorities had been in communication with the government of the Ivory Coast. Captain Howard and Miss Spalding were placed *f* under arrest and spent the night in a detention cell at the airport. The Ivory Coast, as I understand it on the evidence before me, was formerly a French colony, and those who are concerned with the running and management of that country have a civilised and Gallic approach to life, as I was informed, so it was not long before Miss Spalding and Captain Howard, having been interrogated, were removed from the rigours of the detention cell to the comparative comfort of the Hilton Hotel, and *g* there they stayed for some days. In the mean while a flurry of activity went on. The Nigerian authorities arrived in the form of a small team, one or two civilians and an airforce officer. In the mean time, in Lagos, a very unfortunate thing happened. The two engineers who helped to get the aircraft ready had been arrested and charged with conspiring with Captain Howard to steal the aircraft.'

h On 26 May Captain Howard was able to send a telex stating that the aircraft had left Nigerian airspace. This, under the terms of the contract, was relevant to payment of the first instalment of the fee. It was paid, either on 26 or 27 May.

The Ivory Coast government was urged by representatives of Shirlstar to allow Captain Howard, Miss Spalding and the aircraft to proceed to the United Kingdom, and by the Nigerian government to return all three to Nigeria. It adopted a middle course, *j* permitting Captain Howard and Miss Spalding to come here but handing the aircraft over to the Nigerian government. It has never been returned to Shirlstar. The two engineers in Lagos were tried and sentenced to long terms of imprisonment, but the Nigerian Court of Appeal quashed their convictions, and they too eventually returned to this country.

Captain Howard sues in this action for the second instalment of his fee, amounting to

£12,500. Shirlstar counterclaimed for the return of the first instalment. His Honour
Judge Gower QC, sitting as a judge of the High Court, held that the claim succeeded and   *a*
the counterclaim failed. Shirlstar now appeal against the judgment against them on the
claim, but they no longer pursue their counterclaim.

There are two issues. The first is whether, on the true meaning of the contract, the
second instalment of the fee has ever become due. It seems to me that Shirlstar's
argument would apply equally to the first instalment; but as I have just said, they no
longer claim that it should be returned. The second issue is whether, if Captain Howard   *b*
otherwise has a valid contractual claim, it is defeated by illegality under Nigerian law.

Construction

The material terms of the contract were as follows:

'1 THE Company will pay to Captain Howard the sum of TWENTY FIVE THOUSAND
POUNDS (£25,000) for sucessfully removing the aircraft or organising the removal of   *c*
the aircraft from Nigerian territorial airspace

2 THE said sum of £25,000 shall be paid by the Company into a joint account at
Lloyds Bank plc, 21 Station Avenue, Caterham, Surrey in the joint names of Nicholas
John Munns and Stanley Sherwin Beller, the respective parties' Solicitors on or
before the date hereof   *d*

3 THE Company hereby irrevocably authorises Stanley Sherwin Beller to sign a
release or transfer the sum of £12,500 to Captain Michael Roy Howard or as he may
direct as soon as they have in their possession a telex confirmation from Captain
Howard that he has removed the aircraft from Nigerian territorial airspace and to
release or transfer the balance of £12,500 as soon as either (a) the aircraft is delivered
to the United Kingdom a British protectorate or a country being a member of the   *e*
European Economic Community; or (b) one month after the date of the telex
confirming that the aircraft has been removed from Nigerian territorial airspace
[there is then a proviso about interest].

4 CAPTAIN HOWARD agrees that he will use his best endeavours to try and recover
possession of the said aircraft PROVIDED THAT he shall be entitled to abandon any
attempt to recover the said aircraft if he in his reasonable judgment feels that there   *f*
is an unacceptable personal risk to himself or his Co-Pilot.

5 CAPTAIN HOWARD agrees that once he has recovered possession of the aircraft to
ferry the aircraft from Nigerian territorial airspace to Hurn Airport or any other
U.K. airport or if necessary an airport in a British protectorate or E.E.C. country
without any delay whatsoever excepting serviceability and operational delays.'

The argument for Shirlstar depends on the word 'successfully' in cl 1. It is said that,   *g*
unless the aircraft has been removed from Nigerian territorial airspace sucessfully, no fee
is payable; and that this did not happen because the aircraft was detained at Abidjan and
subsequently returned to Nigeria.

If that be the correct interpretation of cl 1, it is difficult to reconcile with cl 3. That
provides for payment of the first instalment of Captain Howard's fee on telex confirmation   *h*
that he has removed the aircraft from Nigerian airspace without any requirement that
he shall have done so successfully; and the second instalment is payable one month later,
unless the aircraft has reached one of the destinations mentioned in cl 3(a) at some earlier
date. Payment of the first instalment is secured in a manner somewhat similar to a
documentary credit or performance guarantee: it is to happen irrevocably on receipt of
the telex. In those circumstances one would not ordinarily imply anything into the   *j*
clause which is not there. If that be right, the telex had to comply exactly with the
documentary requirement but, provided it did comply and was not fraudulent, the
deposit, to the extent of £12,500, had to be released.

In my judgment, the word 'successfully' means, at most, that the actual flight out of
Nigeria must be completed without mishap or misfortune and end in a safe landing.

Captain Howard could then send his telex. It may mean not even as much as that, but
a simply that Captain Howard must *succeed* in removing the aircraft from Nigerian
airspace. To the objection that the word is then unnecessary I would rely on the authority,
too well known to require citation, that the presumption against surplusage is of little
weight in the interpretation of commercial contracts. So I agree with the judge's
conclusion that both instalments of the fee became payable.

b *Illegality*
The argument under this head comprises a point on the conflict of laws, a point on
English domestic law and an issue as to Nigerian law.
The first question is as to when an English court will have regard to foreign law in
connection with the illegal performance of a contract. The topic was considered by the
Court of Appeal in *Euro-Diam Ltd v Bathurst* [1988] 2 All ER 23, [1990] 1 QB 1 on appeal
c from a judgment of mine at first instance (see [1987] 2 All ER 113, [1990] 1 QB 1).
Counsel for Captain Howard accepted before the judge that, if performance by him
involved illegal conduct in Nigeria, he could not enforce the contract here. In my view,
it is necessary to be a little more precise when one is dealing with a contract which is not
illegal in itself but involves illegality as performed, or is said to be tainted with illegality.
In such a case the contract will not in general be enforced by reason of illegality in a
d foreign country in the same circumstances as a contract for performance in England will
not be enforced by reason of illegality under English law.
I turn then to the second point, the effect of illegality under a contract of English
domestic law. This was dealt with in three propositions by Kerr LJ in the *Euro-Diam* case
[1988] 2 All ER 23 at 28–29, [1990] 1 QB 1 at 35. I can abbreviate them for present
purposes. (1) The ex turpi causa defence rests on a principle of public policy. It applies
e where the plaintiff has been guilty of illegal (or immoral) conduct, if in all the
circumstances it would be an affront to the public conscience to grant the plaintiff relief,
because the court would thereby appear to assist or encourage the plaintiff in his illegal
conduct or to encourage others in similar acts. (2) The main situations where the defence
will prima facie succeed are (i) where the plaintiff seeks, or is forced, to found his claim
on an illegal contract or to plead illegality in order to support his claim, either in the
f statement of claim or in a reply; (ii) where the grant of relief to the plaintiff would enable
him to benefit from his criminal conduct; (iii) where the situation is residually covered
by the general principle in (i) above. (3) However, the ex turpi causa defence must be
approached pragmatically and with caution, depending on the circumstances.
We were referred to *Pitts v Hunt* [1990] 3 All ER 344, [1990] 3 WLR 542 decided on
g 13 April. There Dillon LJ said that he did not find the 'public conscience' test satisfactory.
One reason was that appeal to the public conscience would be likely to lead to a graph of
illegalities according to moral turpitude. The difficulty of formulating a criterion for
separating cases of serious illegality from ones which were not so serious was insoluble.
However, Beldam LJ in that case recorded that, in *Saunders v Edwards* [1987] 2 All ER
651, [1987] 1 WLR 1116, the 'public conscience' test, first clearly set out by Hutchison J
h in *Thackwell v Barclays Bank plc* [1986] 1 All ER 676, was approved. We do not have a
complete transcript of the judgments in that case, nor do we know whether the *Euro-
Diam* case was cited. In the circumstances, it seems right to me for us to follow the
judgment of Kerr LJ in the *Euro-Diam* case.
In the present case it was, subject to an important point which will be mentioned later,
illegal by Nigerian law for Captain Howard to fly the aircraft out of Nigeria without
j obtaining permission from air traffic control. Counsel for the defendants contends that
it was also illegal by Nigerian law for other reasons, because there had been an order
grounding or confiscating the aircraft and a decree grounding all privately-owned
aircraft. The judge did not accept on the evidence that either the order or the decree had
been made. Counsel for the defendants sought to challenge that conclusion. However,
we did not hear him on that aspect of the case, since the second and third grounds of

illegality would not, in our view, and in the particular circumstances of this case, add anything of significance to the first ground, which the judge did find established, that is to say contravention of air traffic control regulations. *a*

If the case had stopped there, I would have no doubt that Captain Howard's claim would be unenforceable in an English court. To take off from a Nigerian airport in breach of regulations was central to his performance of the contract, as it was in fact performed. It was in no sense incidental illegality, like the example given by Russell LJ in the course of the argument in *Mackender v Feldia AG* [1967] 2 QB 590 at 595, or other *b* examples which I gave in the *Euro-Diam* case [1987] 2 All ER 113 at 118, [1990] 1 QB 1 at 13. Counsel for the defendants concedes that it would not come within proposition 2(i) of Kerr LJ because Captain Howard would not need to plead or prove illegality to support his claim. Whether or not that concession be rightly made, the case would plainly fall within proposition 2(ii), as to grant relief would enable Captain Howard to benefit from his criminal conduct. *c*

But there is another aspect of the case. Captain Howard and Miss Spalding gave evidence that, as time went by in Nigeria and during their conversations with Mr Odigwe, they were warned that their lives were in danger and that powerful people wished to prevent them taking the aircraft. There was much more in the same vein. Mr Odigwe's advice was that they should take off in the aircraft without delay. In addition, Captain Howard felt that it would be dangerous for him and Miss Spalding to attempt to *d* leave Nigeria on a scheduled flight.

Mr Odigwe did not himself give evidence. Mr Haslam, of the United Kingdom High Commission, was reluctant to accept that Mr Odigwe can have given the advice that he was said to have given, and did not share Captain Howard's apprehension about the danger of attempting to return on a scheduled flight. The judge had to find the facts on that evidence. He said: *e*

'My findings of fact are the following: that at the meetings in Lagos on the dates to which I have already referred, Mr Odigwe, acting head of the Civil Aviation Authority in Nigeria, warned the plaintiff and Miss Spalding that their lives were in danger; that that danger was an increasing one; that the government could not protect them at the airport. I find as a fact that those warnings intensified as the *f* meetings proceeded. I find also that Mr Odigwe was well aware of the dangers attendant on the flying of the aircraft G LORI out without clearance. So far as the flight was concerned, Miss Spalding herself described graphically her feelings whilst it was going on. I am wholly satisfied that Captain Howard also was well aware of the dangers attendant on unauthorised flight. I am satisfied that he would not and did not contemplate risking Miss Spalding's life, let alone his own, for £25,000 or *g* any other sum. It is no part of my function to decide whether or not Mr Odigwe's expressed forebodings were genuine or were unfounded and prompted by some oblique motive. I have no reason to think they were other than genuine. What I have to decide is their effect on Captain Howard. He had not only himself to consider but Miss Spalding. I am satisfied that he accepted these warnings as genuine; that he believed himself and Miss Spalding to be in danger of death. I am *h* well aware that it may appear to anyone who has not heard the evidence in this case, that to talk of danger of death may seem an over-dramatic way of looking at it. It came across to me in the court room in London as cold sober fact. I find also that faced with a choice of two evils Captain Howard chose the less. He flew the aircraft because he believed, as I find reasonably, that that was the only way of escaping *j* from the danger of which he had been warned by Mr Odigwe.'

Later he continued:

'I am certain that Captain Howard's anxieties and fears were genuine and that he had reasonable grounds for believing the warnings of Mr Odigwe to be genuine.

a   Those grounds are to be found not only in what Mr Odigwe himself said but also in Captain Howard's own knowledge and experience of Nigeria and what he had been told about [and then the judge mentions the name of one of the important persons in Nigeria who had been operating the aircraft, and that person's security company.] For those reasons I have come to the firm conclusion that Captain Howard believed, and had reasonable grounds for believing, that all the while he remained in Nigeria his life and that of Miss Spalding's were in imminent danger and the only way out
b   was to take the course suggested by Mr Odigwe which I find it to have been extremely risky, drastic and dramatic though that course was.'

Those findings have not been challenged on this appeal.

There are then two problems to be considered. First, even if it was still illegal to take off in the aircraft, should the court hold that there would be no affront to the public conscience if Captain Howard's claim is enforced, on the ground that his conduct was not
c   morally reprehensible? Second, did Captain Howard have an excuse in Nigerian law on the ground of pre-emptive self-defence, so that his conduct was not in fact illegal?

In answer to the first question, it is to be noted that proposition 2(ii) of Kerr LJ in the *Euro-Diam* case, dealing with the recovery of a benefit from the plaintiff's criminal conduct, is expressed to be an example of the main principle in proposition (1), that the
d   court will not assist a plaintiff if to do so would be an affront to the public conscience. Can there then be circumstances where the public conscience is not affronted, even though a plaintiff does recover a benefit from his criminal conduct? In my judgment, there can be. I find some support for that conclusion in the judgment of Devlin J in *St John Shipping Corp v Joseph Rank Ltd* [1956] 3 All ER 683 at 693, [1957] 1 QB 267 at 292:

e   'On counsel for the defendants' third point, I take the law from the dictum of FRY, L.J., in *Cleaver* v. *Mutual Reserve Fund Life Assocn.* ([1892] 1 QB 147 at 156, [1891–4] All ER Rep 335 at 340), that was adopted and applied by LORD ATKIN in *Beresford* v. *Royal Insurance Co., Ltd.* ([1938] 2 All ER 602 at 605, [1938] AC 586 at 596): ". . . no system of jurisprudence can with reason include amongst the rights which it enforces rights directly resulting to the person asserting them from the crime of that person." I observe in the first place that in the Court of Appeal in the
f   same case LORD WRIGHT, M.R., doubted whether this principle applied to all statutory offences ([1937] 2 All ER 243 at 254, [1937] 2 KB 197 at 220). His doubt was referred to by DENNING L.J., in *Marles* v. *Philip Trant & Sons, Ltd.* (No. 2) ([1953] 1 All ER 651 at 658, [1954] 1 QB 29 at 37). The distinction is much to the point here. The Merchant Shipping (Safety and Load Line Conventions) Act, 1932, imposes a penalty which is itself designed to deprive the offender of the benefits of
g   his crime. It would be a curious thing if the operation could be performed twice— once by the criminal law and then again by the civil. It would be curious, too, if in a case in which the magistrates had thought fit to impose only a nominal fine their decision could in effect be overridden in a civil action. But the question whether the rule applies to statutory offences is an important one which I do not wish to decide
h   in this case. The dicta of LORD WRIGHT, M.R., and DENNING, L.J., suggest that there are cases where its application would be morally unjustifiable; but it is not clear that they go as far as saying that the application would not be justified in law.'

That passage is plainly obiter, but it appears to me to contemplate that there may be cases where it would be wrong for a civil court to disqualify a plaintiff from recovery, even though his claim is derived from conduct which constituted a statutory offence.
j   If the court is free to take that view, as I think it is, this case is in my judgment plainly one where the plaintiff's claim should not fail, because the conscience of the court is not affronted. The offence, or offences, which Captain Howard committed were, on the judge's findings which are not now challenged, designed to free himself and Miss Spalding from pressing danger.

For the avoidance of doubt, I would add that I would have reached the same conclusion if a similar offence or offences had been committed in England under English law in *a* similar circumstances. It would have been for the criminal courts to consider what penalties should be imposed, and I say nothing as to whether they should have been substantial or lenient. But, if the offences had been committed to escape danger to life, I would not have held that Captain Howard was disqualified from claiming his fee in a civil action here.

That conclusion makes it unnecessary to consider at any length whether Captain *b* Howard's conduct was excused in Nigerian law on the ground of pre-emptive self-defence. We have been referred to two articles of the Nigerian criminal code as follows:

'Article 26: Subject to the express provisions of this code relating to acts done upon compulsion or provocation or in self-defence, a person is not criminally responsible for an act done or omission made under such circumstances of sudden *c* or extraordinary emergency that an ordinary person possessing ordinary powers of self-control could not reasonably be expected to act otherwise.

Article 32: A person is not criminally responsible for an act or omission if he does or omits to do the act under any of the following circumstances:—(1) in execution of the law; (2) in obedience to the order of a competent authority which he is bound by law to obey, unless the order is manifestly unlawful; (3) when the *d* act is reasonably necessary in order to resist actual and unlawful violence threatened to him, or to another person in his presence; (4) when he does or omits to do the act in order to save himself from immediate death or grievous harm threatened to be inflicted upon him by some person actually present and in a position to execute the threats, and believing himself to be unable otherwise to escape the carrying out of the threats into execution . . .' *e*

and then there is provision as to an exception.

We are told that art 26 was not relied on, perhaps because it was expressed to be subject to certain other provisions of the code. Nor does art 32(4) appear to have formed a defence, since it requires there to be an attacker who is actually present. By contrast, *f* art 32(3) does not expressly contain such a requirement.

Mr Nsugbe, who gave expert evidence for Shirlstar, was nevertheless at first of the opinion that a similar requirement applied in the case of art 32(3). However, in the course of his cross-examination, the judge asked this question:

'Q . . . A Nigerian Court would, in applying the code, find pre-emptive self-defence if the defendant reasonably and honestly believed that his life was in *g* immediate danger and that an otherwise unlawful act, falling short of killing, was his only way out. Is that a fair summary? A. That is a summary, but that appears to incorporate also duress. It seems to bring in duress.'

The judge repeated that summary in his judgment as the view of Nigerian law which *h* he was accepting. Counsel for the defendants submits that he was wrong to do so, or at any rate should have explained that the word 'immediate' required the physical presence of an attacker at the time when the crime was committed in order to prevent or escape from an attack. Having read that part of the cross-examination as a whole, I am not convinced that the judge was wrong.

Counsel also submits that, even on the view of Nigerian law which the judge accepted, *j* the danger was not immediate. There was an interval of two days between the last of the warnings given by Mr Odigwe and the departure of the aircraft. However, it is agreed that the test is subjective; and, on the judge's findings, Captain Howard reasonably believed that they were in imminent danger, although they were not actually face to face with an attacker. In my judgment, we would not be justified in departing from the

judge's conclusion that Captain Howard's conduct, whether it was said to involve one
a offence or more, was excusable in Nigerian law.
I would dismiss this appeal.

TAYLOR LJ. I agree. The defendants' case is that the word 'successfully' in cl 1 governs
the whole agreement and, in effect, means 'successfully and finally'. On this basis, unless
the aircraft was not merely removed from Nigerian airspace but was also successfully
b kept out of such airspace, the plaintiff would be entitled to neither half of his £25,000.
The telex which triggers payment of the first £12,500 under cl 3 could not, on the
defendants' contention, convey confirmation that the aircraft had successfully, in the
sense of finally, been removed from Nigeria. It might still be returned, as in fact
happened. Moreover, the trigger for the second £12,500 was not unequivocally the
successful arrival of the aircraft in the United Kingdom or other safe haven, but under
c cl 3(*b*) could be mere effluxion of time from the date of the telex.
I therefore agree with Staughton LJ that the word 'sucessfully' in cl 1 cannot have the
extensive effect claimed for it by the defendants and I consider the judge's construction
of the agreement was correct.
As to illegality, I consider the correct approach is that adopted by Hutchison J in
Thackwell v Barclays Bank plc [1986] 1 All ER 676, approved by this court in *Saunders v*
d *Edwards* [1987] 2 All ER 651, [1987] 1 WLR 1116. The test is set out in the judgment of
Nicholls LJ ([1987] 2 All ER 651 at 664, [1987] 1 WLR 1116 at 1132):

> '[It] involved the court looking at the quality of the illegality relied on by the
> defendant and all the surrounding circumstances, without fine distinctions, and
> seeking to answer two questions: first, whether there had been illegality of which
e > the court should take notice and, second, whether in all the circumstances it would
> be an affront to the public conscience if by affording him the relief sought the court
> was seen to be indirectly assisting or encouraging the plaintiff in his criminal act.'

Here, there clearly was illegality which the judge characterised as 'a very serious breach
indeed', flying out of Nigeria without first obtaining permission from the control tower.
f On the second limb of the test, however, I am satisfied that, in the perilous and life-
threatening circumstances found by the judge, it would not amount to an affront to the
public conscience to afford Captain Howard the relief he sought. Nor is there any reason,
in these highly exceptional circumstances, to think that allowing Captain Howard's claim
would be contrary to public policy.
In those circumstances, I find it unnecessary to consider the issue of pre-emptive self-
g defence under Nigerian law. I too would dismiss the appeal.

LORD DONALDSON OF LYMINGTON MR. I agree with both judgments which
have been delivered and, accordingly, that the appeal should be dismissed.

Appeal dismissed. Leave to appeal to the House of Lords refused.

Solicitors: *Holman Fenwick & Willan* (for the defendants); *Freed Stone Goodman* (for Captain
Howard).

Mary Rose Plummer   Barrister.

Express Newspapers plc v News (UK) Ltd and others

CHANCERY DIVISION

SIR NICOLAS BROWNE-WILKINSON V-C

8, 9, 12 FEBRUARY 1990

Action – Defence to action – Approbation and reprobation – Plaintiff obtaining summary judgment on claim for infringement of copyright – Defendant serving counterclaim which was exact mirror image of plaintiff's claim – Plaintiff advancing inconsistent cases on claim and counterclaim – Whether plaintiff entitled to put forward defence to counterclaim which was inconsistent with his own claim – Whether defendant entitled to summary judgment on counterclaim.

Copyright – Infringement – Newspaper – Mutual copying of news stories – Whether copyright in news story – Whether copyright in verbatim quotations.

The plaintiff newspaper instituted proceedings against the defendant newspaper for infringement of the plaintiff's copyright in the text of an exclusive interview which occurred when the defendant newspaper published a story based on the article in the plaintiff's newspaper, including verbatim quotations of the words used by the person interviewed, without any acknowledgement of the source of either the story or the quotations. The defendant served a defence and a counterclaim which was the exact mirror image of the plaintiff's claim, alleging that the plaintiff had, subsequent to instituting proceedings, infringed the defendant's copyright in the text of an exclusive interview with another person. The plaintiff obtained summary judgment under RSC Ord 14 on its claim on the basis that copyright subsisted in the whole of the plaintiff's article. The defendant then applied for summary judgment on its counterclaim, contending that since the plaintiff had succeeded in its claim on the basis that there was no defence it should not be allowed to put forward a defence to the counterclaim when the claim and counterclaim were legally indistinguishable.

Held – Although the plaintiff had an arguable defence to the counterclaim, namely an implied licence to publish arising out of the widespread newspaper practice of lifting stories from other newspapers, it had advanced wholly inconsistent cases on the claim and counterclaim and therefore, applying the principle that a person may not approbate and reprobate and adopt two inconsistent attitudes towards another person but must elect between those attitudes and, having elected to adopt one stance, he could not thereafter be permitted to go back and adopt an inconsistent stance, the defendant was entitled to summary judgment (see p 383 j to p 384 e, post).

Per curiam. (1) It is very improbable that the courts will hold that a newspaper can, by reason of the law of copyright, obtain a monopoly on a news story as opposed to copyright in the actual words used by its reporter in reporting that story (see p 380 b to d, post).

(2) The statutory requirement of originality does not imply inventive originality. It is enough that the work is the production of something in a new form as a result of the skill, labour and judgment of the reporter (see p 381 b c, post); *Sands & McDougall Pty Ltd v Robinson* (1917) 23 CLR 49 applied; *Walter v Lane* [1900] AC 539 followed.

Notes

For the principle of approbation and reprobation, see 16 Halsbury's Laws (4th edn) para 1507.

For infringement of copyright and the protection of original works or originality, see 9 Halsbury's Laws (4th edn) paras 909 and 831.

Cases referred to in judgment

a *Interlego AG v Tyco Industries Inc* [1988] 3 All ER 949, [1989] AC 217, [1988] 3 WLR 678, PC.

Lion Laboratories Ltd v Evans [1984] 2 All ER 417, [1985] QB 526, [1984] 3 WLR 539, CA.

Robertson v Lewis (trading as Virginia Music) (1960) [1976] RPC 169.

Sands & McDougall Pty Ltd v Robinson (1917) 23 CLR 49, Aust HC.

Walter v Lane [1900] AC 539, HL.

b *Walter v Steinkopff* [1892] 3 Ch 489.

Cases also cited

Jones v Lewis [1919] 1 KB 328, CA.

LB (Plastics) Ltd v Swish Products Ltd [1979] FSR 145, HL.

Mellor v Australian Broadcasting Commission [1940] 2 All ER 20, [1940] AC 491, PC.

c *Macmillan & Co Ltd v Cooper* (1924) 93 LJPC 113.

Application

By a summons dated 19 October 1989 the first defendant, News (UK) Ltd, applied for summary judgment under RSC Ord 14 on its counterclaim in an action against the plaintiff, Express Newspapers plc for breach of copyright. The facts are set out in the

d judgment of Sir Nicolas Browne-Wilkinson V-C.

Michael Burton QC and *Mary Vitoria* for the plaintiff.
Peter Prescott for the first defendant.

SIR NICOLAS BROWNE-WILKINSON V-C. This is an application by the

e defendant, News (UK) Ltd, for summary judgment under RSC Ord 14 on its counterclaim in this action against the plaintiff, Express Newspapers plc. The case is concerned with mutual copying of news stories appearing in the Daily Express and the Daily Star (both of which are owned by Express Newspapers), and the newspaper Today (which is owned by News (UK) Ltd).

The case, as it comes before me has a history which is relevant. Mrs Pamella Bordes is

f a lady who has enjoyed and is enjoying certain publicity value for her alleged relationships with people who are in the public eye. In April 1989 she was in Bali. The Daily Express and other newspapers, including Today, sent reporters to seek to get interviews with her. Mr Frame was the reporter from the Express, Mr Miles the reporter from Today.

On a flight on 2 April from Bali to Hong Kong, Mrs Bordes was accompanied by her solicitor and by what sounds like a substantial number of the press. Mr Frame from the

g Daily Express managed to sit next to her from time to time and obtained certain remarks from her. He made various manuscript notes of what she said. When he got to Hong Kong he wrote up the story, which contained verbatim quotations from what she had said. That story appeared prominently on the front page of the Daily Express, including quotations from Mrs Bordes, on 3 April 1989. The Express claimed that the interview

h was an exclusive interview.

On the same day, 3 April, the first edition of Today came out also carrying a story, by Mr Miles, about Mrs Bordes. It was not so sensational as that in the Daily Express. Having seen the Daily Express story, the second edition of Today was changed and appeared in quite a different form. The second edition carried the sensational story based on that which had appeared in the Daily Express that day, including quotations of what Mrs

j Bordes has said to Mr Frame, although there was no acknowledgement in Today of the source either of the story or of the quotations.

In consequence of that, Express Newspapers plc started these proceedings, claiming that Today had infringed the Daily Express's copyright in the story, claiming damages and additional damages under s 17(3) of the Copyright Act 1956, which is now s 97(2) of the Copyright, Designs and Patents Act 1988. The statement of claim was served on 23 June 1989. Express Newspapers applied for summary judgment.

Ten days before the hearing of that application for summary judgment on the claim, ie in October 1989, Mr Brough, a reporter on Today, obtained an exclusive interview with Miss Marina Ogilvy and her boyfriend. Miss Ogilvy was expecting a baby. She is a member of the royal family. In the course of an interview lasting some eight-and-a-half hours, Miss Ogilvy made certain allegations against her parents and other members of the royal family. The result of Mr Brough's labours was an article prominently featured in the edition of Today for Monday, 9 October carrying banner headlines and appearing on five other pages. The article in Today contained many quotations of the words actually used by Miss Ogilvy. Today made a major splash of the story. It was described by Today, with typical modesty, as being 'one of the most important scoops in popular journalism in modern times'.

On the following day, 10 October, a number of newspapers carried the Ogilvy story. Among them was the Daily Star, a newspaper also owned by the plaintiff, Express Newspapers plc. The Daily Star carried the Ogilvy story as a lead story on its front page and two other pages. A large part of the Daily Star's story was taken from the Today story of 9 October, including quotations. The evidence put in on behalf of the Daily Star, while suggesting that inquiries were made elsewhere, does not in terms allege that its reporters had interviewed Miss Ogilvy or her boyfriend. On the evidence before me, the only possible source of the quotations in the Daily Star article was the article in Today. Deeply embedded on an inside page of the Daily Star and after there had been a number of quotations of Miss Ogilvy's words, one quotation of her words was prefaced by words to the effect that she had spoken to Today newspaper. That was the only reference to the Today article.

Very shortly thereafter the defendants served their defence to the Daily Express's claim in this action relating to the Bordes article. They also served a counterclaim. The counterclaim is the exact mirror image of the claim made by the Express. In it Today alleges that Today has copyright in the Ogilvy story, that the copying by the Daily Star infringed Today's copyright, and claiming damages including additional damages under s 97(2) of the 1988 Act.

Unfortunately, the application for summary judgment on the Daily Express's claim relating to the Bordes story came before the court separately from the counterclaim brought by News (UK). The application for summary judgment on the claim came before Mr Blanco White QC sitting as a deputy judge of this division. The deputy judge gave the plaintiff summary judgment on the claim, including inquiries as to damages. Today has appealed against that summary judgment to the Court of Appeal. Now Today brings this application before me on the counterclaim relating to the Ogilvy article.

There is in the case a plain element of tit for tat. As Mr Montgomery, the editory of Today, says in his affidavit, what is sauce for the goose must also be sauce for the gander, and Express Newspapers plc, so he says, cannot be heard both to complain of breach of copyright by his article on the Bordes case and, at the same time, permit one of its newspapers, the Daily Star, to do exactly the same thing in relation to the Ogilvy article. The evidence discloses that there is a considerable degree of feeling running between the editors. Mr Lloyd, the editor of the Daily Express, says of the Bordes article that the decision to copy it was taken deliberately for the purpose of spoiling the Daily Express's coverage. He says that the incident is merely the latest of a number in which Today has engaged in a series of spoiling tactics. He points to two earlier occasions in which Today has, as he claims, poached the Express's ideas: one in relation to a travel promotion called Air Miles (which is the Express's name) which promptly led to Today launching a similar scheme called Air Smiles. That was restrained by an ex parte injunction in February 1989. In March 1989, the Express having produced a supplement under the name DX,

Today following with a supplement called TX. Today gave undertakings that the
a defendant would not use the name TX for its supplement.

Mr Lloyd says that what has happened in the Bordes case was blatant copying. Mr
Montgomery, the editor of Today, on the other hand, says that he would not have
bothered about what had happened in the Ogilvy case but for the Express's attitude to
the Bordes case. In the counterclaim it is alleged that the Express's conduct is cynical,
shameless and hypocritical.

b I am left with the strong impression that this is a dispute more concerned with
journalistic ethics and injuries to feelings than a genuine legal or commercial dispute.
Questions of journalistic ethics are, I would have thought, better dealt with by the Press
Council than by the courts, but, since the parties have chosen to bring the matters to
court, I must decide them. It is the less fortunate since the case raises legal points of some
importance not simply to these two warring newspaper groups but to the press generally
c and possibly to the general public.

Summary judgment under Ord 14 is a judgment given in the clearest cases before an
ordinary trial has taken place. Summary judgment is only given where it is clear that
there is no arguable defence to the claim. If there is an arguable issue to be tried, in
particular where there are matters of fact to be resolved which can only be resolved at
trial, the court gives leave to defend and the case goes to trial to be heard out. Summary
d judgment is a means of short-circuiting that system in the clear case where it is shown
that, even if it went to trial, the defence could not succeed.

Counsel for the defendant, News (UK) Ltd, says that whatever the underlying law
applicable in this case may be, as a matter of ordinary justice Express Newspapers cannot
be heard to say that there is a defence to the counterclaim relating to the Ogilvy article
since that is a mere mirror image of what Express Newspapers themselves claimed in
e relation to the Bordes article. He says that if the Express had established a claim to which
there was no defence in relation to the Bordes article, the reverse position must be the
same in relation to the Ogilvy article in the Daily Star, namely that it must be a clear
breach of copyright.

I have some sympathy with this attitude and will revert to it at the end of my
f judgment. But I do not think that it is possible for me to decide that in isolation without
first considering the ways in which the claims were advanced in the two cases.

There is one point of fundamental significance which applies both in the Bordes case
and the Ogilvy case. Each of the original stories is made up of two elements. First, there
is the news story as such; second, there are the quotations of the words used by the person
interviewed, Mrs Bordes or Miss Ogilvy, as the case may be. As to the news story, in each
g case the original journalist who wrote the original articles expresses the news story in his
own words. In the pirated article although the news itself is, in one sense, pirated, there
is no copying of the words used by the journalist responsible for the original article.
There is no verbatim quotation of the journalist's own words.

The position is different so far as the original article contains quotations of the actual
words used by Mrs Bordes or Miss Ogilvy, as the case may be. The original article quotes
h them verbatim. They are then also quoted verbatim in the pirated article. The only
source of the verbatim quotation of the words of Mrs Bordes and Miss Ogilvy to the
pirate reports were the quotations contained in the original articles.

Founding on that distinction, counsel for the plaintiff submits that, in the absence of
verbatim copying of the actual words, there is no copyright in the story as such. As to
the verbatim quotations of the words of Miss Ogilvy in the Daily Star, counsel for the
j plaintiff submits that on the evidence so far sworn Today has not shown that Today had
any copyright in the words of Miss Ogilvy. Therefore, it is said, Express Newspapers has
an arguable case and should be given leave to defend.

On the other side, counsel for the defendant submits that the dichotomy between the news story on the one hand and the quotations of Miss Ogilvy's words on the other is a false one. The only question is whether there has been a substantial copying of the article in Today relating to Miss Ogilvy. Counsel says that by repeating the verbatim quotations of Miss Ogilvy's own words, which run to some 154 words, the Daily Star has copied a substantial part of the whole of the Today article.

In my judgment, the submission of counsel for the defendant does not adequately confront the basic question which is: does copyright subsist in the whole of the article on Miss Ogilvy in Today or only in those parts of that article which are quotations of Miss Ogilvy's own words? For myself, I would hesitate a long time before deciding that there is copyright in a news story which would be infringed by another newspaper picking up that story and reproducing the same story in different words. Such a conclusion would strike at the root of what I think is the practice of the national press, namely to search the columns of other papers to find stories which they have missed and then using the story so found in their own newspaper by rewriting it in their own words. If it were the law that such practice constituted breach of copyright, the consequences, as it seems to me, would be that a paper that obtained a scoop from a confidential source would obtain a monopoly on that piece of news. That would not be in the public interest as it would prevent the wider dissemination of the news to the public at large.

I think, therefore, that it is very improbable that the courts would hold that a newspaper could, by reason of the law of copyright, obtain a monopoly on a news story as opposed to copyright in the actual words used by its reporter in reporting that story. To avoid reaching that conclusion there might be a number of different routes. It might be said that the case fell within the application of the fair dealing provisions in s 30 of the Copyright, Designs and Patents Act 1988 or by implying a licence to publish. I will consider both of these routes shortly hereafter but, in my judgment, there is plainly an arguable defence to a claim that the whole of the Today article (as opposed to quotations in that article from Miss Ogilvy) is entitled to copyright on the grounds that there is no copyright in a current news story corresponding to the copyright which a novelist, for example, enjoys in the plot of his novel in addition to the actual words used to express that plot.

What then of the position of the quotations of the exact words used by Miss Ogilvy? The law as to copyright in verbatim reports of the spoken words of another was settled by the House of Lords in *Walter v Lane* [1900] AC 539. In that case Lord Rosebery gave a public speech. A reporter from The Times newspaper attended and took down that speech verbatim in shorthand. A verbatim report was published in The Times. Subsequently the defendant compiled a book of Lord Rosebery's speeches and, without the consent of The Times, included the report of Lord Rosebery's speech, the source of such report being The Times newspaper. The question was, did the reporter of Lord Rosebery's words have any copyright in the report? The House of Lords held that he did. Lord Halsbury LC said (at 548):

> 'And though I think in these compositions there is literary merit and intellectual labour, yet the statute seems to me to require neither, nor originality either in thought or in language.'

Lord Davey said (at 552):

> 'It was of course open to any other reporter to compose his own report of Lord Rosebery's speech, and to any other newspaper or book to publish that report; but it is a sound principle that a man shall not avail himself of another's skill, labour, and expense by copying the written product thereof.'

As a result of that House of Lords decision it was established that the mere reporting of the words of another gives rise to a reporter's copyright so long as skill and judgment have been employed in the composition of that report.

The decision was made under the Copyright Act 1842, which contains no express
a requirement for the work in which copyright subsists to have been an original work.
From the Copyright Act 1911 onwards there has been an express statutory requirement
in relation to works of this kind that the work shall be an original work (see now s 1(1)(a)
of the 1988 Act). In *Robertson v Lewis (trading as Virginia Music)* (1960) [1976] RPC 169 at
174 Cross J suggested, obiter, that the statutory requirement that the work should be an
original work might mean that the decision in *Walter v Lane* was no longer good law. He
b was not referred to the decision of the High Court of Australia in *Sands & McDougall Pty
Ltd v Robinson* (1917) 23 CLR 49, where the court considered the impact of the
introduction into the 1911 Act of the requirement for the work to be original, dealt with
the matter very fully and reached the conclusion that *Walter v Lane* was still good law.
They held that the word 'original' in the statute does not imply inventive originality; it
is enough that the work is the production of something in a new form as a result of the
c skill, labour and judgment of the reporter.

I prefer the view expressed by the High Court of Australia. It seems to me sound. The
possibility of the continued existence of reporter's copyright is reflected in s 3(3) of the
1988 Act, which expressly refers to the possibility of the recorder of spoken words having
a copyright in the record of those words as distinct from the words recorded.

Counsel for the plaintiff also referred me to passages on the meaning of the word
d 'original' in the statutes in the speeches in *Interlego AG v Tyco Industries* [1988] 3 All ER
949, [1989] AC 217. It was, I think, suggested that that decision might have impliedly
modified the law as laid down in *Walter v Lane*. But *Walter v Lane* was not referred to in
argument, and the Privy Council were there considering quite a different point on
originality which does not, in my judgment, touch on *Walter v Lane*.

I therefore approach this case on the basis that *Walter v Lane* is undeniably still good
e law. On that footing, if skill, labour and judgment was put into the reporting of Miss
Ogilvy's words in the Today newspaper, copyright will subsist in the report of those
words even though the words themselves are Miss Ogilvy's.

Counsel for the plaintiff submitted that the evidence currently before the court did
not show that the quotations were the product of sufficient skill to create such reporters'
f copyright in Miss Ogilvy's words. He pointed out that there were no details given of the
interview with Miss Ogilvy. If there were any notes taken they had not been produced.
There was nothing to indicate how those quotations came into existence. Therefore, he
said, it had not been shown that there was sufficient skill, labour and judgment employed
in the preparation of those quotations to justify a holding at this stage that Today had
reporter's copyright.

I reject that submission. The evidence does show that there was an interview lasting
g over eight-and-a-half hours with Miss Ogilvy. The skills of the reporter in this case are
quite different and much greater than those shown regarding Lord Rosebery's speech in
Walter v Lane. It was not simply taking down the words of somebody who was already
going public by speaking publicly. Although Miss Ogilvy had approached the reporter,
the whole conduct of the interview and the selection of quotations involved at least as
h much (and in my view greater) skill and judgment than merely taking down the words
of a speaker at a public speech.

Therefore, in my judgment, in the absence of any other defence it has been shown
that Today does enjoy reporter's copyright in the words of Miss Ogilvy. It follows that,
in the absence of such defence, by copying those quotations from Today's article, the
Daily Star has infringed Today's copyright.

j The question then is whether there is any other defence. The first suggested defence is
fair dealing under s 30(2) of the 1988 Act, which reads:

'Fair dealing with a work (other than a photograph) for the purpose of reporting
current events does not infringe any copyright in the work provided that . . . it is
accompanied by a sufficient acknowledgement.'

'Sufficient acknowledgement' is defined by s 178 of the 1988 Act as meaning:

'... an acknowledgement identifying the work in question by its title or other *a*
description, and identifying the author unless—(*a*) in the case of a published work,
it is published anonymously; (*b*) in the case of an unpublished work, it is not possible
for a person to ascertain the identity of the author by reasonable inquiry ...'

The author in the case of the Ogilvy article was Mr Brough, whose name appeared above
it. His services are rendered to News (UK) under a contract of employment which vests *b*
the copyright in his work in his employers.

Counsel for the plaintiff appreciated the difficulty he had in relying on the fair dealing
defence since, even if the cursory reference in the Daily Star to one of the quotations
from Miss Ogilvy's words being given in answer to questions from Today otherwise
constituted fair dealing, such acknowledgement would not be sufficient to bring the case
within the fair dealing defence. At most it would be an acknowledgement of the right *c*
of the copyright holder, whereas the statute requires an acknowledgement of the
authorship of Mr Brough. Therefore the fair dealing defence does not apply in the case
of what, in my experience, is ordinary newspaper conduct, namely the acknowledgement
of the fact that the story originates with another newspaper. It is not the practice to
acknowledge the authorship in the sense of ascribing it to the particular journalist
involved.   *d*

Next, counsel for the plaintiff sought to rely on what he called the public interest
defence. This he founded on the evidence given by the Daily Star reporter, Mr Constable,
who said that the Ogilvy interview was a matter of public interest in the wider sense of
that word; it was a current newsworthy event. This was the first time that a member of
the immediate royal family had discussed that family's attitude towards unmarried
pregnancy. Its importance lay in exploring and contrasting the conflicting obligations of *e*
royalty towards state and family and the way in which their attitudes have changed with
the changing values of society. He says:

'My object in writing the article was not to regurgitate what had been said in the
Today articles. My interest lay in demonstrating the conflict between public and
private obligations and the Royal attitude to unmarried pregnancy revealed through *f*
the Ogilvy interview.'

If that was his object in writing it, he was ill-served by his sub-editors because the result
of his labours is sensational journalism, not a serious discussion of matters of public
interest.

Founded on that unpromising start, counsel for the plaintiff said that there was a
public interest defence. He relied on the decision of the Court of Appeal in *Lion* *g*
Laboratories Ltd v Evans [1984] 2 All ER 417, [1985] QB 526. That was a case concerned
with a disclosure both in breach of confidence and in breach of copyright. In relation to
breach of confidence, there is a well-known exception to the right of the confider to insist
on confidence, namely where the proposed breach is to disclose iniquity. It is said that
there is no confidence in iniquity. The Court of Appeal held that that principle applied *h*
as much to claims of breach of copyright as to breach of confidence. The Court of Appeal
further held that it was not only criminal offences which constituted iniquity but that
the defence could be invoked, both in relation to breach of confidence and breach of
copyright, if the information was such that it was in the public interest to know it.

In my judgment, that decision has no application to the present case. Where that type
of defence is put forward it permits the publication of secret information which it is in *j*
the public interest should be known. It does not apply to information of the kind which
it may be of interest to the public to know. Moreover, the basis of the defence being that
the public needs to know, the whole basis for the defence goes once such information has
been disclosed at all, ie by one paper. There is no further requirement of public interest
that another paper should be able to repeat the revelation of that information.

Finally, counsel for the plaintiff relied on a possible defence of implied licence. There
a is only an infringement of copyright if a work is copied without the consent of the owner
of the copyright. Counsel for the plaintiff relied on the well-known practice of newspapers
to which I have already referred, namely the practice of picking up news stories appearing
in other newspapers with a view to reproducing them in one's own. Such practice is
demonstrated by the evidence in this case. Following the appearance of the Ogilvy article
in Today, the story was picked up by many other papers. Many of those papers contained
b quotations of the exact words which Miss Ogilvy had used in response to Today. The
Guardian and The Times both ran the story, giving clear and express acknowledgement
to the fact that the news had originated with Today. So did the Daily Telegraph but it
referred only to an interview 'with another newspaper'. The Daily Express referred to
the story and referred to Today's involvement, albeit in scathing terms. The Daily Mail
carried the story and, like the Daily Star, buried a reference to Today's contribution to it
c deep in the text. Only Today's sister paper, which was also owned by News (UK),
managed to carry the story without any reference whatsoever to the intervention of
Today. However, it does show that there is a wide practice of taking up stories appearing
in other newspapers either with or without some acknowledgement.

It is therefore possible that at trial a custom in the press could be established under
which each newspaper accepted that this is what was going to happen. If so, in my
d judgment, such a custom might found a defence that in publishing a newspaper each
paper accepts and impliedly consents to the others picking up the story and using it in a
way which was proper. It might also be said that there was acquiescence in such conduct
since the practice has gone on for a very long time.

In my judgment, the decision in *Walter v Steinkopff* [1892] 3 Ch 489 is not inconsistent
with the establishment of such an implied consent. In that case North J held that there
e was not, and could not be, any consent implied from the customs of the press permitting
the verbatim copying of the words used by a reporter in one newspaper and reproducing
them in another newspaper. That decision was nearly 100 years ago and the press is now
a very different institution. More important, North J was not dealing with the use of
quotations of words, being the words of a third party (for example, Miss Ogilvy) in
f whom the copyright of the words as opposed to the report of the words was vested. In
my judgment, it may well be that the case is different when the only relevant verbatim
copying is not the copying of the reporter's words but the words of the interviewee.

Therefore, apart from the mirror-image aspect of this case, I would have given Express
Newspapers plc leave to defend the counterclaim so as to enable them to lead evidence of
press custom relating to the reproduction of press articles with a view to establishing a
defence based on implied licence granted by Today to the conduct of Express Newspapers
g in the Daily Star reproducing the story and quotations.

However, I come back to the first point raised by counsel for the defendant, which
greatly impresses me. Express Newspapers applied for and obtained summary judgment
against Today in relation to the Bordes article on facts which, in my judgment, are legally
indistinguishable from the facts of the Ogilvy case. Counsel for the plaintiff sought to
h draw a distinction between the two cases on the grounds that the Today copying of the
Bordes article involved the changing of the newspaper story between the first and second
editions so as to appear on the same day as the article on Mrs Bordes appeared in the Daily
Express. He contrasted that with the position where the Daily Star copying of the Ogilvy
story occurred on the following day and was merely picked up in the ordinary course of
press activity. In my judgment, the fact that Today were more efficient pirates than the
Daily Star has no legal significance.
j The fact is that if the defences now being put forward by News (UK) in relation to the
Daily Star article are good defences to the Ogilvy case, they were and are equally good
defences to the claim by the Daily Express against Today newspaper relating to the
Bordes claim. I think that what Mr Montgomery describes as 'what is sauce for the goose
is sauce for the gander' has a rather narrower legal manifestation. There is a principle of

law of general application that it is not possible to approbate and reprobate. That means you are not allowed to blow hot and cold in the attitude that you adopt. A man cannot adopt two inconsistent attitudes towards another: he must elect between them and, having elected to adopt one stance, cannot thereafter be permitted to go back and adopt an inconsistent stance.

To apply that general doctrine to the present case is, I accept, a novel extension. But, in my judgment, the principle is one of general application and if, as I think, justice so requires, there is no reason why it should not be applied in the present case. Express Newspapers obtained a judgment in this action against News (UK) which requires News (UK) to pay damages on the basis that the Today article on Mrs Bordes was an infringement of the whole of the Daily Express article, ie not only of those parts which were quotations from Mrs Bordes. That can only be a judgment rightly applied for and rightly obtained if the Daily Express had copyright in the whole of the Bordes article, and that there could be no implied consent to be derived from the custom of the press granted by the Daily Express to such copying. For the Daily Express now to say that there was not copyright in the whole of the Ogilvy article in Today and that Today had impliedly consented to its being copied, is a wholly inconsistent position. It is true that on the Ord 14 application relating to the Bordes article, Today did not raise the defence of implied consent. But the fact remains that the case advanced by the Daily Express on the claim and the case advanced by the Daily Express on the counterclaim are wholly inconsistent.

I therefore rule that in these proceedings the Express is not entitled to put forward two inconsistent cases. I propose therefore, accordingly, to give judgment under Ord 14 on the counterclaim brought by News (UK) Ltd. I trust that if the parties do not come to some sensible compromise the Court of Appeal will soon be able to make sense of this matter by hearing both the appeals from Mr Blanco White and from this judgment at the same time.

Order accordingly.

Solicitors: *Mishcon de Reya* (for the plaintiff); *Farrer & Co* (for the first defendant).

Celia Fox   Barrister.

Sandwell Metropolitan Borough Council v Bujok

HOUSE OF LORDS

LORD KEITH OF KINKEL, LORD TEMPLEMAN, LORD GRIFFITHS, LORD ACKNER AND LORD LOWRY

11 JULY, 11 OCTOBER 1990

Nuisance – Statutory nuisance – Complaint to justices – Proceedings against local authority – Abatement notice – Whether person entitled to lay information against local authority without first serving abatement notice – Public Health Act 1936, s 99.

Nuisance – Statutory nuisance – Complaint to justices – Proceedings against local authority – Costs – Mandatory award of costs against defendant – Whether magistrates required to award costs against local authority if nuisance order made against local authority in proceedings brought against it without abatement notice first being served – Whether costs in discretion of magistrates – Public Health Act 1936, s 94(3).

The respondent council tenant laid an information against the appellant council alleging that the defective state of her council house gave rise to a statutory nuisance as defined by s 92(1)(*a*)[d] of the Public Health Act 1936 and that the council as the owner of the premises was the person by whose default the nuisance had arisen. The respondent sought a nuisance order pursuant to s 99[b] of the 1936 Act. The respondent did not serve an abatement notice on the council before laying the information and the council was unaware of the alleged nuisance until served with the information. Under s 94[c] of the 1936 Act a local authority had power to lay an information alleging that premises gave rise to a statutory nuisance but before it could do so it was required by s 93[d] of that Act to serve an abatement notice on the owner of the premises requiring him to abate the nuisance. Under s 99 any person aggrieved by a statutory nuisance could make a complaint to a magistrate 'and thereupon the like proceedings shall be had . . . as in the case of a complaint by [a] local authority'. In regard to the costs of hearing and determining an information alleging a statutory nuisance the magistrates' court was required by s 94(3) to order the defendant to pay the local authority's reasonable costs if it was proved that the nuisance existed when the abatement notice was served and also when the complaint was made. At the hearing of the respondent's complaint the magistrates held that she was not required to serve an abatement notice on the council before laying the information and on the basis that the condition of the respondent's council house gave rise to a statutory nuisance the magistrates issued a nuisance order against the council and awarded costs of £491·18 against it. The council appealed by way of case stated to the Divisional Court, which dismissed the appeal, holding that a council tenant was not required to ensure that the council had been made aware of the state of the property prior to laying an information alleging a statutory nuisance. The council appealed to the House of Lords, contending that the 'like proceedings' referred to in s 99 denoted proceedings against a person who had been served with an abatement notice and therefore the respondent was required to serve an abatement notice on the council or at least ensure that the council was aware of the defects before laying the information.

Held – Since s 99 of the 1936 Act did not in terms place an obligation on an 'aggrieved person' to serve an abatement notice before commencing proceedings for a nuisance order and since the 'like proceedings' was limited to those proceedings which followed

---

a   Section 92(1), so far as material, is set out at p 388 *f*, post.
b   Section 99 is set out at p 389 *b c* post
c   Section 94, so far as material, is set out at p 388 *h* to p 389 *b*, post.
d   Section 93, so far as material, is set out at p 388 *g*, post

the complaint, rather than the procedure that had to be observed by a local authority before it made a complaint, an individual could commence proceedings under s 99 in a magistrates' court in respect of a statutory nuisance without first requiring the proposed defendant to abate the nuisance and allowing him a reasonable time to do so, although it would normally be advisable to give him proper notice before commencing proceedings. It followed that the appeal would be dismissed (see p 386 *j* to p 387 *a*, p 389 *d h*, p 390 *c d j* to p 391 *b* and p 392 *f* to *h*, post).

> *R v Newham Justices, ex p Hunt* [1976] 1 All ER 839 approved.
> *Coventry City Council v Doyle* [1981] 2 All ER 184 overruled.

Per curiam. The mandatory provision as to the award of costs against the defendant contained in s 94(3) of the 1936 Act does not apply to proceedings brought by an aggrieved person under s 99, since it is confined to proceedings brought by local authorities. The costs of proceedings under s 99 are therefore in the discretion of the magistrates, who are entitled to take into account whether notice of the nuisance was given to the defendant and whether if notice had been given the defects might have been remedied without the necessity of recourse to proceedings (see p 386 *j* to p 387 *a* and p 392 *c* to *h*, post).

Notes

For proceedings by a person aggrieved in respect of a statutory nuisance, see 38 Halsbury's Laws (4th edn) para 412.

For the Public Health Act 1936, ss 92, 93, 94, 99, see 35 Halsbury's Statutes (4th edn) 184, 185, 186, 190.

Cases referred to in opinions

Cocker v Cardwell (1869) LR 5 QB 15.
Coventry City Council v Doyle [1981] 2 All ER 184, [1981] 1 WLR 1325, DC.
R v Newham Justices, ex p Hunt [1976] 1 All ER 839, [1976] 1 WLR 420, DC.
Salford City Council v McNally [1975] 2 All ER 860, [1976] AC 379, [1975] 3 WLR 87, HL.
Warner v Lambeth London BC (1984) 15 HLR 40, DC.

Appeal

Sandwell Metropolitan Borough Council appealed with the leave of the Appeal Committee of the House of Lords given on 19 February 1990 against the decision of the Divisional Court of the Queen's Bench Division (Watkins LJ and Hutchison J) (88 LGR 521) on 2 November 1989 dismissing the council's appeal by way of case stated against the decision of the Warley magistrates on 15 November 1988, on an information laid by the respondent, Jean Edith Bujok, a council tenant to issue a nuisance order against the council requiring them to abate a nuisance existing at premises at 100 Slatch House Road, Smethwick, Warley, within ten weeks and that the council pay the respondent £491·18 costs. The facts are set out in the opinion of Lord Griffiths.

John Cherryman QC and *Douglas Readings* for the council.
David Neuberger QC and *Elizabeth Norman* for the respondent.

Their Lordships took time for consideration.

11 October. The following opinions were delivered.

LORD KEITH OF KINKEL. My Lords, I have had the opportunity of considering in draft the speech to be delivered by my noble and learned friend Lord Griffiths. I agree with it, and for the reasons he gives would dismiss the appeal, while holding that the magistrates were not required to award the costs of the proceedings to the appellant council.

LORD TEMPLEMAN. My Lords, for the reasons to be given by my noble and learned friend Lord Griffiths, I agree that an aggrieved person is not required to give warning of his intention to bring proceedings complaining of a statutory nuisance. I agree also that the magistrates are not required to award the costs of such proceedings to the appellant council.

LORD GRIFFITHS. My Lords, the first question raised by this appeal from the Divisional Court ((1989) 88 LGR 521) is whether under s 99 of the Public Health Act 1936 an individual may commence proceedings before a magistrates' court in respect of a statutory nuisance without first requiring the proposed defendant to abate the nuisance and allowing him a reasonable time to do so. The second question is whether under s 94(3) of that Act the magistrates are compelled to award costs to a complainant if at the time of his complaint a statutory nuisance existed, even though the defendant may have been unaware of the nuisance until he received the summons and has taken steps to abate the nuisance by the time of the hearing before the magistrates.

The relevant facts are found in the judgment of Hutchison J (88 LGR 521 at 523–524):

'The material facts, which I take from the case stated by the justices, are as follows: 1. [The respondent] and her family live in a house, 100 Slatch Road, Warley, as tenants of the council. 2. Among the written terms of the tenancy is an obligation on the part of the tenant to give immediate notice to the Director of Housing of any defect or damage to the premises; and one entitling the council by their officers, etc., and after giving reasonable notice, to enter and inspect the state of repair, etc., of the premises and to execute any repairs therein. 3. On 26 September 1988 [the respondent] laid an information against the council alleging the existence and continuance on the premises of a statutory nuisance as defined by Section 92(1)(a) of the Public Health Act 1936. The information alleged that the council, being owners of the premises, were the persons by whose act, default or sufferance that statutory nuisance arose and continued, and sought a nuisance order pursuant to Section 99 of the same Act. 4. [The respondent] had not, prior to the laying of the information, served an abatement notice upon the council or informed them of the alleged defects in the premises. It is implicit in the justices' findings that at the date of the information the council were unaware of the defective state of the premises. 5. The information was served by post, the letter of 28 September 1988 which accompanied it enclosing also a copy of an inspection report by the Sandwell Housing Aid Centre recording the results of an inspection on 12 September 1988. 6. It will be apparent therefore that what happened was that, having had the premises inspected on 12 September and received a report about their condition, [the respondent] (who was of course being advised at the time) did not take any steps to inform the council of the condition of the premises or the nature of her complaints but on 26 September laid the information which, with the report enclosed with it, constituted the first the council knew of the alleged statutory nuisance. The justices stated the following question for the opinion of this court whether "the tenant should be required to ensure that the council had been made aware of the state of the property prior to laying an information alleging a statutory nuisance as defined by section 92(1)(a) of the Public Health Act 1936 as under section 93 of the said Act the tenant must prove that the statutory nuisance has arisen as a result of the Council's act, default or sufferance?" The justices, after hearing argument and being referred to authority, had given a negative answer to that question. [Counsel for the council] contends that they were wrong.'

The Divisional Court upheld the judgment of the magistrates following previous decisions of the Divisional Court which had decided that a private individual could bring proceedings without first serving an abatement notice (see *R v Newham Justices, ex p Hunt* [1976] 1 All ER 839, [1976] 1 WLR 420 and *Warner v Lambeth London BC* (1984) 15 HLR

40) and, on the authority of the Divisional Court in *Coventry City Council v Doyle* [1981] 2 All ER 184, [1981] 1 WLR 1325, that the magistrates were compelled to award costs against the local authority. The council now challenge the correctness of these decisions of the Divisional Court.

Part III of the Public Health Act 1936 places a duty on a local authority to detect statutory nuisances within its district and provides a procedure by which the local authority is required to deal with them. In broad outline this procedure requires a local authority to serve an abatement notice on the person responsible for the nuisance requiring him to abate it. If that person fails to abate the nuisance then the local authority makes a complaint to the magistrates who issue a summons requiring the person served with the abatement notice to appear before a court of summary jurisdiction. If at the time the complaint is heard by the magistrates the nuisance has not been abated, the magistrates will make a nuisance order requiring the defendant to abate the nuisance and may also impose a fine. Thereafter if the defendant fails to comply with the order there is provision for further fines to be imposed on him and for the local authority to carry out the necessary work and recover the costs from the defendant.

Under this procedure no one will be taken to court by a local authority and accused of being responsible for a statutory nuisance unless he has first been given notice of the statutory nuisance and given an opportunity to abate it. It is only if he fails to act on the abatement notice that the sanction of the law will be used against him. This seems to be an eminently sensible procedure and it is the submission of the council that on its true construction the 1936 Act requires an individual to follow the same procedure.

In his judgment Hutchison J cited the relevant statutory provisions. Those provisions are:

'**91.** It shall be the duty of every local authority to cause their district to be inspected from time to time for the detection of matters requiring to be dealt with under the provisions of this Part of this Act as being statutory nuisances within the meaning of the next succeeding section.

92.—(1) Without prejudice to the exercise by a local authority of any other powers vested in them by or under this Act, the following matters . . . are in this Part of this Act referred to as "statutory nuisances," that is to say:—(a) any premises in such a state as to be prejudicial to health or a nuisance . . .

93. Where a local authority are satisfied of the existence of a statutory nuisance, they shall serve a notice (hereafter in this Act referred to as "an abatement notice") on the person by whose act, default or sufferance the nuisance arises or continues, or, if that person cannot be found, on the owner or occupier of the premises on which the nuisance arises, requiring him to abate the nuisance and to execute such works and take such steps as may be necessary for that purpose: Provided that—(a) where the nuisance arises from any defect of a structural character, the notice shall be served on the owner of the premises . . .

94.—(1) If the person on whom an abatement notice has been served makes default in complying with any of the requirements of the notice . . . the authority shall cause a complaint to be made to a justice of the peace, and the justice shall thereupon issue a summons requiring the person on whom the notice was served to appear before a court of summary jurisdiction.

(2) If on the hearing of the complaint it is proved that the alleged nuisance exists . . . then, subject to the provisions of subsections (4) and (5) of this section the court shall make an order (hereafter in this Act referred to as "a nuisance order") . . . (a) requiring the defendant to comply with all or any of the requirements of the abatement notice, or otherwise to abate the nuisance, within a time specified in the order, and to execute any works necessary for that purpose . . .

(3) Where on the hearing of a complaint under this section it is proved that the alleged nuisance existed at the date of the service of the abatement notice and that

at the date of the making of the complaint it . . . still existed . . . then, whether or not at the date of the hearing it still exists . . . the court shall order the defendant to pay to the local authority such reasonable sum as the court may determine in respect of the expenses incurred by the authority in, or in connection with, the making of the complaint and the proceedings before the court . . .

(6) If it appears to the court that the person by whose act or default the nuisance arises, or the owner or occupier of the premises, cannot be found, the nuisance order may be addressed to, and executed by, the local authority . . .

99. Complaint of the existence of a statutory nuisance under this Act may be made to a justice of the peace by any person aggrieved by the nuisance, and thereupon the like proceedings shall be had, with the like incidents and consequences as to the making of orders, penalties for disobedience of orders and otherwise, as in the case of a complaint by the local authority, but any order made in such proceedings may, if the court after giving the local authority an opportunity of being heard thinks fit, direct the authority to abate the nuisance.'

The argument of the council is founded on the phrase 'the like proceedings' in s 99. They submit that as the local authority may only bring proceedings against a person on whom an abatement notice has been served and who will therefore be given notice of the nuisance, it follows that 'the like proceedings' should be construed as proceedings against a person who has been served with an abatement notice or alternatively at least has knowledge of defects in the premises which are alleged to constitute the nuisance.

In support of this submission the council rely on the following passage from the speech of Lord Edmund-Davies in *Salford City Council v McNally* [1975] 2 All ER 860 at 865, [1976] AC 379 at 391:

'But, as a local authority may fall down in its duty to deal with statutory nuisances within its area, s 99 enables "any person aggrieved by the nuisance" to make complaint to a justice of the peace, and thereafter the procedure follows that already indicated in the case of a complaint made by the appropriate local authority. Accordingly, in (for example) December 1937, the occupier of a house could inform her landlord that it was in such a condition as to constitute a "statutory nuisance" because of certain specified defects, she could call on him to abate the nuisance within a specified reasonable time, and, if he defaulted, she could lay a complaint before a court of summary jurisdiction.'

Lord Edmund-Davies was not, however, considering the question that arises in this appeal and was merely illustrating the ability of a tenant to take proceedings against a landlord pursuant to s 99 and no doubt in framing his illustration of the procedure it did not occur to him that the tenant would be so unreasonable as to start proceedings without first notifying the landlord of the defects in the premises and asking for them to be repaired. I cannot therefore regard the decision as an authority on the construction of the section.

I regret that I am unable to accept the council's construction of s 99. I say 'regret' because, like the judges in the Divisional Court, I deplore the advice given to council tenants to commence proceedings without first notifying the council of the defects in the premises and asking them to carry out repairs. I entirely agree with the following passage from the judgment of Watkins LJ (88 LGR 521 at 534–535):

'. . . it is surely repugnant to common sense that in the area of legal activity a local authority should be prosecuted by one of its tenants without first being given the opportunity by that tenant to remedy the consequences of a neglect to repair the dwelling that tenant occupies. In law there is no doubt that [the respondent] was entitled to commence proceedings without giving notice of the state of the dwelling to the local authority. But in every other conceivable way I regard that action as entirely wrong. Endless trouble to many people in courts and local authority offices and much money could be saved by the giving of notice of disrepair which it is to be supposed a local authority would appropriately react to. If they did not, then would be the time for a tenant to exercise the right to prosecute. I doubt whether there is anyone, a ratepayer especially, giving proper thought to such a situation as we have been confronted with who would disagree with that approach to what surely is a commonplace problem.'

I hope that, in the light of what I say at a later stage on the question of costs, tenants and their lawyers will in future be discouraged from taking such action. But first I must give my reasons for rejecting the council's construction of the section.

In the first place s 99 does not in terms place an obligation on an 'aggrieved person' to serve an abatement notice as a condition precedent to the commencement of proceedings; and, if such was the intention, I would not have expected it to be introduced by so oblique a route as the use of the phrase 'the like proceedings'. I do not believe it would occur to any person, other than a most astute lawyer, that s 99 imposed an obligation on an individual to serve an abatement notice or to give any other form of notice to a proposed defendant before commencing proceedings. Not only is there an absence of an explicit obligation to serve any form of notice, the use of the word 'thereupon' which precedes 'the like proceedings' is significant. The section first enables an aggrieved person to make a complaint and 'thereupon the like proceedings shall be had', thus limiting the 'like proceedings' to those that follow the complaint, rather than the procedure that has to be observed by a local authority before it may make a complaint.

Furthermore, the whole weight of judicial authority is against the council's construction. In *Cocker v Cardwell* (1869) LR 5 QB 15 the court held that the effect of s 13 of the Act 23 & 24 Vict c 77 (removal of nuisances and the prevention of diseases (1860)) when construed with the Nuisances Removal Act for England 1855 and the Sanitary Act 1866 imposed no duty on an individual to serve a notice before commencing proceedings. Blackburn J said (at 17–18):

'The first Act empowers the local authority to take proceedings before justices, the second gives the same power to a private individual, and the justices are to proceed as if the local authority had made the complaint. Then the third Act says that the nuisance authority shall give notice before taking proceedings; and I cannot see why the notice should not be equally necessary in the case of a private individual. I can only suppose that the legislature had forgotten him, and that this is a casus omissus. At all events, we can put but one construction on the statutes, that no notice is necessary on the part of an individual.'

Hannen J said (at 18):

'I am entirely of the same opinion as to the construction that must be put upon these statutes. I only wish to add, that though this may be but another instance of clumsy and inartificial legislation, yet I do think that reasons may be imagined why the legislature may have intentionally omitted to require a notice in the case of a private person. Other and greater powers are given to the nuisance authority than are given to a private individual. They have, for instance, a right of entry to inspect premises, and it may well be that a public body having such powers should be required to give a previous notice, whereas a private individual knowing of a nuisance may be allowed to proceed without a notice, subject only to the risk of having to pay costs if he unnecessarily put the law in motion.'

Although Parliament had the matter drawn to their attention in these judgments they enacted s 105 of the Public Health Act 1875 in similar terms to s 13 of the 1860 Act and again repeated the same formula in s 99 of the present Act. I can only conclude that, for reasons I do not understand, Parliament has decided not to impose an obligation on an individual to give notice to a defendant before commencing proceedings.

Two recent decisions of the Divisional Court have construed s 99 as not requiring an individual to serve an abatement notice or give any other form of notice prior to commencing proceedings see *R v Newham Justices, ex p Hunt* [1976] 1 All ER 839, [1976] 1 WLR 420 and *Warner v Lambeth London BC* (1984) 15 HLR 40. I am satisfied that they are rightly decided, as is the decision of the Divisional Court in this case.

The council in their written case raised the question of whether a tenant who had given no notice of the defect to the landlord was a 'person aggrieved' within the meaning of s 99. However, the matter was not pressed in oral argument and I am satisfied that an individual who is adversely affected by a statutory nuisance is a 'person aggrieved' within the meaning of the section whether or not he has given notice of the nuisance to the proposed defendant.

I turn now to the question of costs and for convenience I set out s 94(3) again:

> 'Where on the hearing of a complaint under this section it is proved that the alleged nuisance existed at the date of the service of the abatement notice and that at the date of the making of the complaint it . . . still existed . . . then, whether or not at the date of the hearing it still exists . . . the court shall order the defendant to pay to the local authority such reasonable sum as the court may determine in respect of the expenses incurred by the authority in, or in connection with, the making of the complaint and the proceedings before the court.'

In *Coventry City Council v Doyle* [1981] 2 All ER 184, [1981] 1 WLR 1325 it was held that the mandatory provision for the payment of costs in s 94(3) of the 1936 Act was not limited to proceedings brought by a local authority and any person aggrieved was entitled to the expenses of the proceedings before the justices provided that they established that a statutory nuisance had existed at the date when the information was laid. In the course of his judgment Hodgson J said ([1981] 2 All ER 184 at 190, [1981] 1 WLR 1325 at 1338):

> 'The second question we are asked to consider is whether, where the council is defendant, the mandatory provision as to costs in s 94(3) applies. Section 94(3) in terms refers to an order that "the defendant . . . pays to the local authority such reasonable sum as the court may determine in respect of the expenses incurred by the authority". Section 99 refers to "the like proceedings" with the like incidents and consequences as to the making of orders, penalties for disobedience of orders and otherwise, as in the case of a complaint by the local authority. Obviously these two provisions cannot sensibly be read together. The position contemplated by s 94(3) is, as I have pointed out, one where, because the nuisance has been abated at the date of hearing, there is no order or conviction on which the magistrates could hang an order for costs. I think s 99 was intended to put "any person aggrieved" as nearly as possible in the same position as the local authority when the authority brings proceedings, and accordingly, I would hold that the mandatory provisions as to payment of expenses applies to "a person aggrieved" who establishes that at the date of the information the nuisance (since abated) existed.'   ·

In *Doyle's* case the council were at all times fully aware of the state of their premises and I feel certain that in so construing the section Hodgson J did not have in mind the situation of a council being sued in respect of defects of which it had no knowledge. If, however, as a matter of construction there is a mandatory obligation to award costs it will encourage wholly unnecessary litigation and it will involve local authorities in the expenditure of large sums of money in legal costs which would be far better spent on repairing their properties.

Section 94(3) is directed specifically to dealing with the situation where an abatement notice served by the local authority is ignored. The local authority is then required by s 94(1) to incur the expense of commencing proceedings before the justices. If the defaulter then under the threat of proceedings takes steps to abate the nuisance so that by the time of the hearing he has done the work, it is only just that he should be required to pay the costs of the unnecessary legal proceedings caused by his failure to comply with the abatement notice.

I can, however, see no sensible reason to apply this mandatory provision to the wholly different situation with which we are concerned in this appeal. There was no abatement notice in this case nor even any notification of the defect prior to the issue of proceedings. The decision to incur the costs of legal proceedings was not forced on the tenant but taken on advice for which she must take responsibility. The council had no opportunity to rectify the defects prior to the complaint, and, as I say, I very much doubt if so unreasonable a state of affairs was in the mind of Hodgson J when he gave his judgment in *Doyle's* case.

If *Doyle's* case is correctly decided it has exceedingly serious consequences for local authorities. We were told that this local authority had, since June 1988, been served with 632 summonses under s 99 involving expenditure of £122,264 in costs and in the present case the sum of £491·18 was awarded against the council.

In my opinion s 94(3) has no application to a complaint brought by an aggrieved person under s 99 and is confined to proceedings brought by local authorities.

The costs of proceedings under s 99 will therefore be in the discretion of the magistrates. If a tenant has given notice to a local authority of defects in his premises and has allowed a reasonable time for them to be repaired before commencing proceedings, it will of course lie within the magistrates' discretion to award costs to the tenant if by the time of the hearing the work has been carried out. If the proper conclusion is that it was only the threat of proceedings that jolted the landlord into action, the award of costs to the tenant will clearly be justified. If, on the other hand, no notice of the defects is given before the commencement of proceedings and the magistrates are of the view that if notice had been given the work would have been carried out without the necessity of recourse to proceedings, I would not expect them to exercise their discretion to award costs to the tenant. I will not say more because the circumstances of cases are infinitely variable and I have confidence in the magistrates to exercise their discretion wisely. They are however freed from the fetter placed on them by *Coventry City Council v Doyle* [1981] 2 All ER 184, [1981] 1 WLR 1325, which I consider to have been wrongly decided on the question of the proper construction of s 94(3). In future I hope that those advising tenants will realise that they will not automatically be entitled to the costs of s 99 proceedings and the advisability of giving proper notice to the landlord before commencing proceedings.

The council on this appeal do not seek to alter the award of costs in the lower courts; accordingly the appeal will be dismissed.

LORD ACKNER. My Lords, I agree that, for the reasons given by my noble and learned friend Lord Griffiths, this appeal should be dismissed. I also agree that the magistrates are not required to award costs to the tenants of proceedings under s 99 of the Public Health Act 1936.

LORD LOWRY. My Lords, I have had the advantage of reading in draft the speech of my noble and learned friend Lord Griffiths. I agree with it and, for the reasons given by my noble and learned friend, I, too, would dismiss this appeal.

Appeal dismissed.

Solicitors: *Sherwood & Co*, agents for M R Neale, West Bromwich (for the council); Michael Arnold, Oldbury (for the respondent).

Mary Rose Plummer   Barrister.

a Oladehinde v Secretary of State for the Home Department
Alexander v Secretary of State for the Home Department

b
HOUSE OF LORDS

LORD KEITH OF KINKEL, LORD BRANDON OF OAKBROOK, LORD TEMPLEMAN, LORD GRIFFITHS AND LORD ACKNER

23, 24, 25, 26 JULY, 18 OCTOBER 1990

c *Immigration – Deportation – Decision to deport – Delegation of power to make decision – Secretary of State authorising immigration inspectors to act on his behalf in reaching decision whether to deport person – Whether Secretary of State having power to authorise immigration inspector to act on his behalf in deciding whether to deport – Whether Secretary of State entitled to devolve exercise of power to issue notices of intention to deport – Immigration Act 1971, s 3(5)(a).*

d
Immigration – Appeal – Deportation – Function of immigration adjudicator – Power to inquire into decision to deport – Whether adjudicator entitled to inquire whether person making decision to deport had power to do so – Whether adjudicator entitled to inquire whether decision to deport invalid – Immigration Act 1988, s 5(1).

e The appellants, A and O, were given leave to enter the United Kingdom but O breached a condition preventing him from seeking employment in the United Kingdom and A overstayed his leave. Immigration inspectors who had been authorised by the Secretary of State for the Home Department to act on his behalf issued notices of intention to deport them under s 3(5)(a)[d] of the Immigration Act 1971 after receiving oral reports of interviews by immigration officers with the appellants. The inspectors were equivalent f in grade to senior executive officers of the Civil Service and had considerable experience in immigration matters. The appellants appealed against the orders to an adjudicator, who allowed O's appeal but dismissed A's appeal. On appeal by A and by the Secretary of State in O's case the Immigration Appeal Tribunal allowed the Secretary of State's appeal but dismissed A's appeal. The appellants applied for and were granted orders of certiorari by the Divisional Court quashing the tribunal's decisions on the ground that the Secretary g of State was not entitled to delegate his power to authorise service of a notice of intention to deport to immigration inspectors. The Secretary of State appealed to the Court of Appeal, which allowed his appeal on the grounds that, although the Secretary of State had no power to delegate his powers with regard to deportation under the 1971 Act to an immigration officer acting as such, he was entitled to devolve his power to make a decision to deport to an immigration inspector provided the inspector had not been h involved in the case as an immigration officer. The appellants appealed to the House of Lords, contending, inter alia, (i) that the Secretary of State could not validly authorise inspectors to take decisions to deport on his behalf and (ii) that the question whether the person who made the decision to deport had power to do so could be determined under the procedure for appeals to an immigration adjudicator set out in s 5(1)[b] of the j Immigration Act 1988.

a   Section 3(5) provides, so far as material: 'A person who is not a British subject shall be liable to deportation from the United Kingdom—(a) if, having only a limited leave to enter or remain, he does not observe a condition attached to the leave or remains beyond the time limited by the leave . . .'

b   Section 5(1) is set out at p 402 g h, post

Held – (1) Since immigration officers and inspectors were civil servants they fell within the principle that when a statute placed a duty on a minister it could generally be exercised by a member of his department for whom he accepted responsibility. Accordingly, the Secretary of State could validly authorise immigration inspectors to take on his behalf decisions to deport persons from the United Kingdom under s 3(5)(a) of the 1971 Act (see p 395 c d, p 396 f, p 399 f, p 401 e h j, p 402 a to d f and p 403 g h, post); *Carltona Ltd v Comrs of Works* [1943] 2 All ER 560 approved.

(2) The Secretary of State's delegation to inspectors of the power to take decisions to deport and the question whether such decisions were in fact taken by immigration officers and not by the inspectors were matters relating to the exercise rather than the existence of the power to make deportation orders and as such were properly the subject of judicial review and were not within an immigration adjudicator's jurisdiction under s 5(1) of the 1988 Act (see p 395 c d, p 396 f, p 402 j and p 403 c d g h, post); *R v Secretary of State for the Home Dept, ex p Malhi* [1990] 2 All ER 357 applied.

(3) Since the Secretary of State had lawfully authorised the inspectors to issue the notices to deport, the appeals would be dismissed (see p 395 c d, p 396 f and p 403 d g h, post).

Decision of the Court of Appeal sub nom *R v Secretary of State for the Home Dept, ex p Oladehinde* [1990] 2 All ER 367 affirmed.

Notes

For powers of the Secretary of State and immigration officers to refuse leave to enter the United Kingdom and liability for deportation of non-British citizens, see 4 Halsbury's Laws (4th edn) paras 1003, 1011, and for cases on the subject, see 2 Digest (Reissue) 203–214, 1160–1224.

For the Immigration Act 1971, s 3, see 31 Halsbury's Statutes (4th edn) 52.

Cases referred to in opinions

Carltona Ltd v Comrs of Works [1943] 2 All ER 560, CA.
R v Secretary of State for the Home Dept, ex p Malhi [1990] 2 All ER 357, [1990] 2 WLR 932, CA.

Conjoined appeals

Oladehinde v Secretary of State for the Home Dept

Shamusideen Aranji Oladehinde, a citizen of Nigeria, appealed against the decision of the Court of Appeal (Lord Donaldson MR, Stocker and Mann LJJ) ([1990] 2 All ER 367, [1990] 2 WLR 1195) on 15 March 1990 allowing the appeal of the Secretary of State for the Home Department against the decision of the Queen's Bench Divisional Court (Woolf LJ and Pill J) ([1990] 2 All ER 367, [1990] 2 WLR 1195) on 21 February 1990 granting the appellant judicial review by way of an order of certiorari to quash the determination of the Immigration Appeal Tribunal (D L Neve chairman) ([1989] Imm AR 461) dated 12 May 1989 allowing the Secretary of State's appeal against the decision of an adjudicator (I M S Donnell) on 8 November 1988 allowing the appellant's appeal against the decision of the immigration officer (C M Crowe) and/or the immigration inspector (D J Barrell) dated 25 August 1988 to deport the appellant under s 3(5)(a) of the Immigration Act 1971. The facts are set out in the opinion of Lord Griffiths.

Alexander v Secretary of State for the Home Dept

Julius Cornell Alexander, a citizen of St Vincent, appealed against the decision of the Court of Appeal (Lord Donaldson MR, Stocker and Mann LJJ) ([1990] 2 All ER 367, [1990] 2 WLR 1195) on 15 March 1990 allowing the appeal of the Secretary of State for the Home Department against the decision of the Queen's Bench Divisional Court (Woolf LJ and Pill J) ([1990] 2 All ER 367, [1990] 2 WLR 1195) on 21 February 1990 granting the appellant judicial review by way of an order of certiorari to quash the determination of the Immigration Appeal Tribunal (D L Neve chairman) dated 9 June 1989 dismissing

the appellant's appeal from the decision of an adjudicator (I M S Donnell) on 20 February
a 1989 dismissing the appellant's appeal against the decision of the immigration officer
(H M Crawford) and/or the immigration inspector (T McCormack) taken on
23 September 1988 to serve a notice of deportation on the appellant under s 3(5)(a) of the
Immigration Act 1971. The facts are set out in the opinion of Lord Griffiths.

Stephen Sedley QC and *Nicholas Blake* for Mr Alexander.
b *Ian A Macdonald* QC and *Richard Scannell* for Mr Oladehinde.
Michael Beloff QC and *David Pannick* for the Secretary of State.

Their Lordships took time for consideration.

c 18 October. The following opinions were delivered.

LORD KEITH OF KINKEL. My Lords, I have had the opportunity of considering in
draft the speech to be delivered by my noble and learned friend Lord Griffiths. I agree
with it, and for the reasons he gives would dismiss these appeals.

d **LORD BRANDON OF OAKBROOK.** My Lords, I have had the advantage of
reading in draft the speech prepared by my noble and learned friend Lord Griffiths. I
agree with it and for the reasons which he gives I would dismiss these appeals.

LORD TEMPLEMAN. My Lords, by s 4 of the Immigration Act 1971 an immigration
e officer could decide whether to grant or refuse leave to enter the United Kingdom. By
r 78 of the immigration rules the Home Secretary proposed and Parliament approved
that the refusal of leave to enter should require the authority of a chief immigration
officer or of an immigration inspector: see Statement of Changes in Immigration Rules
(HC Paper 1982–83) no 169). Thus an immigration officer can only report with a
recommendation that leave to enter be refused. That report is considered by a chief
f immigration officer or by an immigration inspector who then authorises and directs
leave to be granted or refused. Leave to enter would normally be refused if an
immigration officer considered and a chief immigration officer or an immigration
inspector agreed that the immigrant intended to overstay or intended to breach a
condition against employment.
By s 5 of the 1971 Act the Secretary of State decides whether to deport. Amongst the
g grounds for deportation are overstaying or breach of a condition not to take employment.
By rr 156 and 158 (now rr 164 and 166 of HC Paper (1989–90) no 251), where an
immigrant is an overstayer or has breached a condition of staying, deportation is normally
the proper course subject to full account being taken of all relevant circumstances
including compassionate circumstances.
Where an immigrant is suspected of overstaying or being in breach of a condition, the
h immigrant is interviewed by an immigration officer who makes a report. That report
will set out the ascertained information relevant to the accusation of overstaying or
breach of condition and any circumstances including compassionate circumstances
discovered by the immigration officer or urged by the immigrant and relevant to a
decision with regard to deportation. The report of the immigration officer relating to
deportation was originally considered by a member of the deportation department of the
j Home Office, who alone could authorise the service of a notice of intention to deport.
The report of the immigration officer relating to deportation is now considered by one
of the specified number of immigration inspectors, members of the Home Office, who
alone can sanction service of notice of intention to deport. Formerly and now, the
immigrant may appeal against the intention to deport but since the Immigration Act
1988 the adjudicator and the Immigration Appeal Tribunal have no power to allow an
appeal against an intention to deport an immigrant who is proved to be liable to be

deported and to have been guilty of overstaying or breach of condition. If an appeal is not made or if an appeal is unsuccessful, the report of the immigration officer and the intention to deport are reviewed by the deportation department at the Home Office (taking into account any fresh representations or development) and with the advice of the department and with the advice of the Minister of State, the Secretary of State decides whether to sign a deportation order and thus to exercise the power conferred on him by the 1971 Act.

No one contends that it is illegal or improper for deportation procedures to be initiated by an interview and report by an immigration officer. It is contended that it is illegal or improper for an immigration inspector approved by the Secretary of State and apprised of that report to direct the service of notice of intention to deport. There is no express or implied statutory prohibition on the employment of immigration inspectors selected by the Secretary of State with due regard to their seniority and experience to authorise the service of a notice of intention to deport. As to impropriety, if an immigration inspector may decide to refuse leave to enter I see no reason why he should not be allowed to authorise the service of notice of intention to deport. The intention to deport will in any event be reviewed by the deportation department, by the Minister of State and by the Secretary of State. Some attempt was made to equate the members of the immigration service (including immigration inspectors) with the role of policemen and to equate members of the deportation department with the role of judges. In my opinion the analogy is false. All members of the Home Office who are concerned with entry or deportation or both are bound to use their best endeavours to ensure that persons lawfully seeking to enter are treated fairly, that persons lawfully entitled to remain are permitted to remain and that persons who have acted unlawfully are nevertheless permitted to enter or allowed to remain if in all the circumstances their unlawful conduct ought fairly to be excused.

The position of immigrants who have overstayed or are in breach of condition is said to have been weakened because a decision to deport now rests with the Secretary of State alone, whereas prior to the Immigration Act 1988 an adjudicator or the Immigration Appeal Tribunal might on appeal against a notice of intention to deport rule against deportation. But this possibility does not affect the present question.

In full agreement with the speech to be delivered by my noble and learned friend Lord Griffiths, I would dismiss these appeals.

LORD GRIFFITHS. My Lords, the appellant Shamusideen Aranji Oladehinde is a citizen of Nigeria. On 17 September 1983 the appellant was granted leave to enter the United Kingdom for 12 months as a student with a condition restricting him from taking employment. This leave was extended, subject to the condition restricting employment, until 31 May 1988. On 31 May 1988 the appellant applied for further leave to remain in the United Kingdom as a student. On 25 August 1988, before that application for further leave had been determined, the appellant was arrested. He was interviewed by an immigration officer. After some initial prevarication the appellant admitted during the course of the interview that he had worked under an assumed name for two security firms in breach of the condition restricting his taking employment attached to his leave to enter the United Kingdom as a student. The immigration officer reported the result of the interview on the telephone to an immigration inspector who, acting on behalf of the Secretary of State, decided that the appellant should be deported and authorised the immigration officer to serve a notice of intention to deport on the appellant on the ground that he had taken employment in breach of the condition attached to his leave to enter. The notice was served forthwith by the immigration officer on 25 August.

The appellant appealed against the decision to deport him and his appeal was allowed by an adjudicator on 8 November 1988 on the ground that the Secretary of State had not acted fairly in deciding to deport the appellant. On 12 May 1989 the Immigration Appeal Tribunal allowed an appeal by the Secretary of State.

The appellant Julius Cornell Alexander is a citizen of St Vincent. On 7 October 1984
a he was given leave to enter the United Kingdom as a visitor for two months. His leave to
remain was extended to 7 April 1985. The appellant did not apply for a further extension
of his stay but remained in the United Kingdom without leave. On 23 September 1988
the appellant was arrested and interviewed by an immigration officer. The immigration
officer reported the result of the interview on the telephone to an immigration inspector
who acting on behalf of the Secretary of State decided that the appellant should be
b deported and authorised the immigration officer to serve a notice of intention to deport
on the appellant on the ground that he had overstayed his leave to enter the United
Kingdom. On 20 February 1989 the appellant's appeal against the decision to deport him
was dismissed by the adjudicator. On 9 June 1989 the appellant's further appeal was
dismissed by the Immigration Appeal Tribunal.

The Divisional Court granted orders of certiorari to quash each of the decisions to
c deport on the ground that the Secretary of State could not validly authorise immigration
inspectors to make decisions to deport immigrants from the United Kingdom (see [1990]
2 All ER 367, [1990] 2 WLR 1195).

The Court of Appeal allowed appeals by the Secretary of State and granted the
appellants leave to appeal to your Lordships' House (see [1990] 2 All ER 367, [1990] 2
WLR 1195).

d   These appeals raise three issues. First, can the Secretary of State validly authorise
immigration inspectors to take on his behalf decisions to deport persons from the United
Kingdom? Second, did the inspectors in fact take the decisions or did they merely rubber-
stamp decisions already taken by the immigration officers? Third, is a submission that a
decision to deport has been taken by a person who has no power to make it within the
appellate jurisdiction created by s 15 of the Immigration Act 1971 as amended by s 5 of
e the Immigration Act 1988?

The statutory framework

Each of the appellants, one a citizen of Nigeria, the other a citizen of St Vincent, is
subject to immigration control under the Immigration Act 1971.

f   The first appellant took employment and so did not observe the condition on which
he was given leave to enter the United Kingdom as a student, the second appellant has
been an overstayer since 7 April 1985. Therefore each appellant is liable to deportation
pursuant to s 3(5)(a) of the 1971 Act, as amended by s 39(6) of and Sch 4 to the British
Nationality Act 1981, which provides:

g   'A person who is not a British citizen shall be liable to deportation from the
United Kingdom—(a) if, having only a limited leave to enter or remain, he does not
observe a condition attached to the leave or remains beyond the time limited by the
leave . . .'

Section 5(1) provides for the making of the deportation order:

h   'Where a person is under section 3(5) or (6) above liable to deportation, then
subject to the following provisions of this Act the Secretary of State may make a
deportation order against him, that is to say an order requiring him to leave and
prohibiting him from entering the United Kingdom; and a deportation order
against a person shall invalidate any leave to enter or remain in the United Kingdom
given him before the order is made or while it is in force.'

j However, before the deportation order is made the immigrant is given an opportunity
to appeal against the decision to make it (see s 15(1)(a)); and s 15(2) provides that a
deportation order shall not be made until the time for appealing has expired or until the
appeal is determined.

Under the 1971 Act the scope of the appeal was very wide. Section 19(1) provided:

'Subject to . . . any restriction on the grounds of appeal, an adjudicator on an

appeal to him under this Part of the Act—(a) shall allow the appeal if he considers—
(i) that the decision or action against which the appeal is brought was not in
accordance with the law or with any immigration rules applicable to the case; or
(ii) where the decision or action involved the exercise of a discretion by the Secretary
of State or an officer, that the discretion should have been exercised differently; and
(b) in any other case, shall dismiss the appeal.'

The Immigration Act 1988, however, has imposed a considerable restriction on the
appellate jurisdiction of the adjudicator. Section 5 provides:

'(1) A person to whom this subsection applies shall not be entitled to appeal under
section 15 of the principal Act against a decision to make a deportation order against
him—(a) by virtue of section 3(5)(a) of that Act (breach of limited leave) . . . except
on the ground that on the facts of his case there is in law no power to make the
deportation order for the reasons stated in the notice of the decision.
(2) Subsection (1) above applies to any person who was last given leave to enter
the United Kingdom less than seven years before the date of the decision in question
but the Secretary of State may by order exempt any such persons from that
subsection in such circumstances and to such extent as may be specified in the
order.'

I turn now to some of the provisions relating to immigration officers for it is with
their status that this appeal is primarily concerned. Section 4 of the 1971 Act provides:

'(1) The power under this Act to give or refuse leave to enter the United Kingdom
shall be exercised by immigration officers, and the power to give leave to remain in
the United Kingdom, or to vary any leave under section 3(3)(a) (whether as regards
duration or conditions), shall be exercised by the Secretary of State; and, unless
otherwise allowed by this Act, those powers shall be exercised by notice in writing
given to the person affected, except that the powers under section 3(3)(a) may be
exercised generally in respect of any class of persons by order made by statutory
instrument.
(2) The provisions of Schedule 2 of this Act shall have effect with respect to—
(a) the appointment and powers of immigration officers and medical inspectors for
purposes of this Act; (b) the examination of persons arriving in or leaving the United
Kingdom by ship or aircraft, and the special powers exercisable in the case of those
who arrive as, or with a view to becoming, members of the crews of ships and
aircraft; and (c) the exercise by immigration officers of their powers in relation to
entry into the United Kingdom, and the removal from the United Kingdom of
persons refused leave to enter or entering or remaining unlawfully; and (d) the
detention of persons pending examination or pending removal from the United
Kingdom; and for other purposes supplementary to the foregoing provisions of this
Act.'

Schedule 2, para 1 deals with the appointment of immigration officers and their duty
to act in accordance with instructions given them by the Secretary of State:

'(1) Immigration officers for the purposes of this Act shall be appointed by the
Secretary of State, and he may arrange with the Commissioners of Customs and
Excise for the employment of officers of customs and excise as immigration officers
under this Act.
(2) Medical inspectors for the purposes of this Act may be appointed by the
Secretary of State or, in Northern Ireland, by the Minister of Health and Social
Services or other appropriate Minister of the Government of Northern Ireland in
pursuance of arrangements made between that Minister and the Secretary of State,
and shall be fully qualified medical practitioners.

a   (3) In the exercise of their functions under this Act immigration officers shall act
in accordance with such instructions (not inconsistent with the immigration rules)
as may be given them by the Secretary of State . . .'

The remainder of Sch 2, which runs to 33 paragraphs, is primarily concerned with the
powers to be exercised by immigration officers over the control of entry of immigrants
into the United Kingdom and the arrest and removal of illegal immigrants, that is to say
immigrants who have not at any time been given leave to enter the United Kingdom.
b The two appellants are not illegal immigrants and if they are to be removed from the
United Kingdom it must be through the deportation procedure. The 1971 Act does not
bestow the power to deport on an immigration officer. That power is reserved to the
Secretary of State: see ss 4(1) and 5(1).

The immigration rules referred to in para 1(3) are rules laid down by the Secretary of
c State as to the practice to be followed in the administration of the Act which he is
required to lay before Parliament for approval: see ss 1(4) and 3(2). The rules lay down in
considerable detail the approach to their work to be adopted by immigration officers and
the way in which they are to carry it out; by way of example only r 2 of the 1983 rules
(HC Paper (1982–83) no 169) provides:

'Immigration officers will carry out their duties without regard to the race, colour
d   or religion of people seeking to enter the United Kingdom.'

And r 87 provides:

'Before removal a passenger should be given the opportunity to telephone friends
or relatives in this country, or his High Commission or Consul, if he wishes to do
so.'
e

The practice
It is obvious that the Secretary of State cannot personally take every decision to deport
an immigrant who is in breach of his condition of entry or who is an overstayer. The
decision must be taken by a person of suitable seniority in the Home Office for whom
the Home Secretary accepts responsibility. This devolution of responsibility was
f recognised as a practical necessity in the administration of government by the Court of
Appeal in *Carltona Ltd v Comrs of Works* [1943] 2 All ER 560 and has come to be known
as the *Carltona* principle.

Before August 1988 the practice was as follows. An immigration officer who had
interviewed the immigrant would report the results of that interview to a civil servant
in the deportation department of the Home Office whose duty it was to decide whether
g or not the immigrant should be deported. In arriving at his decision the officer in the
deportation department would have regard to the guidance contained in the immigration
rules which provide that where a person is an overstayer or has breached a condition of
stay, deportation is normally the proper course subject to full account being taken of all
relevant circumstances including compassionate circumstances: see rr 156 and 158 of
h Statement of Changes in Immigration Rules (HC Paper (1982–83) no 169) (now rr 164
and 166 of HC Paper (1989–90) no 251). This decision was taken by a civil servant of not
less than senior executive officer grade and there is no suggestion that this was not a
proper exercise of the devolution of responsibility within the Home Office.

If the decision was taken to deport the immigrant, the immigration officer would be
instructed to serve a notice of intention to deport on the immigrant which gave the
j grounds on which the decision had been taken and notified the immigrant of his rights
of appeal and of the availability of the United Kingdom Immigrants' Advisory Service
which, if he wished, would assist him in an appeal. In the event of an unsuccessful appeal
or after the time for appealing had expired the case would again be reviewed in the
deportation department, taking into account any additional relevant material that had
come into existence since the decision to deport was first made. The decision might then

be reversed but if it was not, a report on the case would be prepared and submitted to the Minister of State and then if he approved to the Home Secretary who signed the deportation order personally unless he was not available for a long period in which case it was signed by a junior Home Office minister.

On 1 August 1988 after the passing of the 1988 Act the Home Secretary took the decision which gives rise to these appeals. It was decided that the initial decision to deport an immigrant liable to deportation under s 3(5)(a) of the 1971 Act, that is because he has not observed the condition attached to leave to enter or is an overstayer, should in future be taken by an inspector of the immigration service and not by a civil servant in the deportation section. The first three grades in the immigration service are directly equivalent to administrative grades in the Civil Service: an immigration officer is equivalent to an an executive officer, a chief immigration officer equivalent to a higher executive officer, an inspector is equivalent to a senior executive officer. An inspector is of the equivalent grade to those in the deportation section who had previously been taking the decision to deport in s 3(5)(a) cases. At the same time inspectors were also authorised to exercise the powers of the Secretary of State contained in Sch 3 to the 1971 Act relating to restriction orders, detention and supervised departure. Not all inspectors were given this authority. It was limited to 14 out of a total of 52 inspectors and their authority was further limited to cases in which they had not previously been involved as immigration officers. Those nominated were all persons of long service and experience in the immigration service. Mr Barrell, the inspector in Mr Oladehinde's case, had 24 years' experience and Mr McCormack, who made the decision in Mr Alexander's case, had 22 years' experience.

Since the introduction of this new power there has been a considerable increase in the number of immigrants deported for being in breach of their conditions or for overstaying. The appellants attributed this to a less scrupulous examination of the circumstances of an immigrant by inspectors before taking the decision to deport than had hitherto been the case when the deportation section had taken the decision. I am in no position to judge the truth of this assertion; there is certainly no evidence that the inspectors involved in these cases neglected their duty and it seems to me that the increase may equally have been affected by the fact that adjudicators are no longer entitled to reverse a decision on compassionate grounds.

There is no dispute that both appellants were liable to be deported, the one for breach of condition, the other as an overstayer, and Parliament has approved a rule that says that in such circumstances deportation should generally follow. Furthermore, the initial decision to deport is in a sense provisional as the case is again reviewed before the Home Secretary is invited to sign the deportation order. I appreciate, however, that the initial decision is a serious matter setting in motion the deportation procedure which will gather a momentum that may be difficult to reserve.

Such is the background against which the appellants' submissions must be examined. I will deal first with the submission that the decision to deport was taken by the immigration officers concerned and not by the inspectors. There is no evidence to support this submission which is based on the suspicion that there cannot be a full appreciation of the circumstances of the case as a result of a telephone conversation. I confess myself to some unease about the practice of taking the decision to deport in this way, but it was not a practice introduced as a result of giving inspectors the power to take the decision. It was first introduced in 1986 when decisions were still taken in the deportation section. It seems to me that it would be much more satisfactory if whoever is responsible for taking the decision had the opportunity to consider a written report including any representations on behalf of the immigrant before taking the decision. It is after all a grave decision affecting the future welfare of the immigrant and although it will be reviewed again in the deportation section, I have already commented on the momentum of the initial decision. There is however a practical difficulty in that the power to detain only arises after service of the notice of intention to deport (see Sch 3,

para 2(2) to the 1971 Act), so unless the immigrant is held in custody for the purpose of
a taking criminal proceedings against him, he cannot be detained for a short period whilst
the written report is being considered and by the time a written report has been
considered and a decision taken the immigrant may well have disappeared. What seems
to me to be required is a power to detain for a short period while the report is considered.
However that may be, both inspectors swore affidavits that they received full oral reports
of the results of the interviews with the immigrants and that they personally took the
b decision in the light of those reports to authorise service of the notice to deport. No
application was made to cross-examine the inspectors and I can see no grounds on which
it would be right to reject their sworn evidence that the decision to deport was theirs and
not that of the immigration inspectors. Nor in these cases is there any challenge to the
fact that both appellants were liable to deportation. On this issue the appellants must fail.

I turn now to the principal issue. The appellants submit that immigration officers are
c the holders of a statutory office and as such they are independent of the executive arm of
government and cannot have devolved on them any of the executive's powers. Therefore
it is said that the Carltona principle cannot extend to cover the exercise of the Secretary of
State's powers by an immigration inspector.

Alternatively, it is submitted that if immigration officers are civil servants in the
Home Office the structure of the Act, which differentiates between the powers of the
d immigration officers, which are primarily concerned with entry control and subsequent
policing of illegal immigrants, and the powers of the Secretary of State in relation to
deportation, carries with it a clear statutory implication that the powers of the Secretary
of State are not to be exercised by immigration officers.

I cannot accept either of these submissions. I have no doubt in my mind that
immigration officers have been civil servants since they were first employed under the
e Aliens Act 1905. The fact that nowhere in the 1971 Act is there any reference to an
immigration service, or the structure of such a service, is only explicable in terms that it
was recognised that it had evolved as part of the Home Office expanding over the years.
The status of immigration officers is not that of statutory office holders such as
adjudicators or members of appeal tribunals who are referred to in the Act as office
holders: see Sch 3, paras 2 and 8. Immigration officers are civil servants in the Home
f Office to whom are assigned specific statutory duties under the Act. Apart from a small
pay lead in recognition of their statutory responsibilities, their conditions of service and
grading are in all respects comparable to other Home Office civil servants. The Act makes
no provision for the management of the immigration service, for that is the function of
the Home Office of which the service is a part. Immigration inspectors are senior line
managers and as such will rarely exercise the specific powers given to immigration
g officers by the Act. The only mention of a duty to be carried out under the Act by an
immigration inspector is to be found in r 78 of the 1983 immigration rules, which reads:

'The power to refuse leave to enter is not to be exercised by an immigration
officer acting on his own. The authority of a Chief Immigration Officer or of an
h Immigration Inspector must always be obtained.'

As there are many more chief immigration officers than inspectors I would expect the
power only occasionally to be exercised by an inspector.

It is well recognised that when a statute places a duty on a minister it may generally be
exercised by a member of his department for whom he accepts responsibility; this is the
j Carltona principle. Parliament can of course limit the minister's power to devolve or
delegate the decision and require him to exercise it in person. There are three examples
of such a limitation in the 1971 Act. Section 13(5) provides:

'A person shall not be entitled to appeal against a refusal of leave to enter, or
against a refusal of an entry clearance, if the Secretary of State certifies that directions

have been given by the Secretary of State (and not by a person acting under his authority) . . .'

and see also ss 14(3) and 15(4).

There is no such limitation in respect of the decision to deport, nor would the Act be workable if there was such a limitation.

Where I find in a statute three explicit limitations on the Secretary of State's power to devolve I should be very slow to read into the statute a further implicit limitation.

The immigration service is comprised of Home Office civil servants for whom the Home Secretary is responsible and I can for myself see no reason why he should not authorise members of that service to take decisions under the *Carltona* principle providing they do not conflict with or embarrass them in the discharge of their specific statutory duties under the Act and that the decisions are suitable to their grading and experience.

It has been recognised that it would not be right to authorise an inspector to take a decision to deport in any case on which he had been engaged as an immigration officer, for to do so would be too much like asking a prosecutor to be judge in the same cause. But in a case in which he has been in no way personally involved I am unable to see any good reason why the decision to deport in a s 3(5)(a) case should not be left to an immigration inspector. He will be a person of comparable grade to those who previously took the decision and equally experienced in immigration matters. There was a suggestion that because immigration officers were primarily concerned with control of entry and policing functions in respect of illegal immigrants there might be an ethos in the service that would lead too readily to a decision to deport. There was no evidence to support this suggestion and I can see no reason why senior members of the service should be tarred with this image, and in any event their decisions are reviewed in the deportation department before the order is signed by the Home Secretary. It is also to be remembered that direct transference may take place within the Home Office between those working in the immigration service and the deportation section and the evidence is that training of all those in the Home Office concerned with the implementation of immigration control is closely co-ordinated.

On this issue my Lords I am in agreement with the Court of Appeal that there is no legal impediment to the Home Secretary authorising immigration inspectors to take the decision to deport immigrants who are in breach of their conditions of entry or who are overstayers.

The final question concerns the scope of the appeal against the decision to deport provided by s 5(1) of the 1988 Act which, for convenience, I will set out again:

'A person to whom this subsection applies shall not be entitled to appeal under section 15 of the principal Act against a decision to make a deportation order against him—(a) by virtue of section 3(5)(a) of that Act (breach of limited leave); or (b) by virtue of section 3(5)(c) of that Act as belonging to the family of a person who is or has been ordered to be deported by virtue of section 3(5)(a), except on the ground that on the facts of his case there is in law no power to make the deportation order for the reasons stated in the notice of the decision.'

In *R v Secretary of State for the Home Dept, ex p Malhi* [1990] 2 All ER 357, [1990] 2 WLR 932 the Court of Appeal held that on the true construction of s 5(1) an adjudicator hearing an appeal under s 15 of the 1971 Act was not entitled to investigate the propriety of the procedures leading up to the Secretary of State's decision to make a deportation order but could only inquire whether the facts of the applicant's circumstances were such that the Secretary of State had power to make a deportation order for the reasons stated in the notice of intention to deport.

The appellants submit that this decision can be distinguished or, alternatively, was wrongly decided. In my opinion the case cannot be distinguished and it was rightly decided.

In passing the 1988 Act Parliament took the decision to curtail the appellate powers of
a adjudicators which had under s 19(1) of the 1971 Act enabled an adjudicator to substitute
his own discretion for that of the Secretary of State. This the adjudicator can no longer
do. I read s 5(1), as did the Court of Appeal in *Malhi's* case, as confining the adjudicator to
considering whether or not in a given case the evidence establishes that the immigrant is
liable to deportation on the grounds stated in the notice of the decision to deport. There
is no question in these appeals that there is in law power to make deportation orders
b because Mr Oladehinde had breached his condition of entry and Mr Alexander is an
overstayer. What is in issue in these appeals is whether the power is being correctly
exercised by the Secretary of State. As Stuart-Smith LJ pointed out in *Malhi's* case [1990]
2 All ER 357 at 366, [1990] 2 WLR 932 at 943, the adjudicator is concerned with the
existence of the power and not with the exercise of the power. The procedures of judicial
review exist to enable litigants to challenge the allegedly improper exercise of power and
c to have the matter tested in the High Court, as has been done in these appeals. It would
be an unnecessary and potentially embarrassing overlap of jurisdiction if the adjudicator
also had similar powers. In my opinion the adjudicator had no jurisdiction to inquire
into the propriety of the Secretary of State's decision to allow immigration inspectors to
take the decision to deport, nor had he jurisdiction to inquire into whether the decision
had been taken by the immigration officers and not the inspectors. These are matters
d relating to exercise of the power and not with the existence of the power and are properly
the subject of judicial review.

I agree with the judgments in the Court of Appeal in *Mahli's* case and am prepared to
adopt their reasoning as my own.

I would therefore dismiss both appeals.

e **LORD ACKNER.** My Lords, the essential issue in this case is whether immigration
inspectors are entitled to take the initial or preliminary decision to serve a notice of
intention to deport, on behalf of the Secretary of State, on persons who have entered this
country lawfully but who are alleged to have broken the rules or conditions relating to
their stay. The issue is not whether such immigration inspectors in the instant appeals
f broke the rules of natural justice in making their decisions. During the course of
submissions I expressed concern both at the apparent failure to give the appellants any
opportunity to make representations to the inspectors prior to their making their
decisions and the apparent failure to ensure that the appellants knew precisely what
material the immigration officers had put before the inspectors as the basis on which to
decide whether or not to make the decision. The Immigration Act 1988 seriously
restricted the immigrant's right of appeal. It has therefore become even more important
g that the decision-maker has all the relevant material before him and that this material is
accurate. However, the procedure which was or should have been adopted by the
immigration inspectors is not the subject matter of this appeal. The essential issue is
whether the inspectors had lawful authority to make the decisions which they made. For
the reasons given by my noble and learned friend Lord Griffiths I am satisfied that the
h inspectors had such authority and I too would dismiss these appeals.

Appeals dismissed.

Solicitors: *Alison Stanley* (for Mr Alexander); *Lewis Silkin* (for Mr Oladehinde); *Treasury
Solicitor.*

Mary Rose Plummer   Barrister.

Kuwait Asia Bank EC v National Mutual Life   *a*
Nominees Ltd

PRIVY COUNCIL

LORD KEITH OF KINKEL, LORD BRANDON OF OAKBROOK, LORD TEMPLEMAN, LORD GOFF OF CHIEVELEY AND LORD LOWRY

28, 29, 30 NOVEMBER 1989, 21 MAY 1990   *b*

Practice – Service out of the jurisdiction – New Zealand – Service of proceedings without leave – Appearance of defendant under protest – Whether court retaining inherent discretion to decline jurisdiction – Whether defendant's submission of forum non conveniens may be raised on application by defendant to set aside service – High Court Rules (NZ), rr 219(a)(h), 131.

                                                        c

Company – Director – Duty – Breach of duty – Director nominated by major shareholder – Shareholder's liability for nominee director's breach of duty – Bank nominating and employing two of five directors of money-broking company – Trustee appointed to protect depositors of company – Company covenanting in trust deed to furnish trustee with certificates of financial position on behalf of directors – Directors nominated by bank not signing certificates – Company becoming insolvent – Whether bank's nominee directors owing duty of care to company and trustee   *d* *in relation to certificates – Whether bank vicariously liable for breach of duty by its nominee directors – Whether nominee directors acting as agent of bank in carrying out duties as directors – Whether bank a director on basis that nominee directors accustomed to act on its direction or instruction – Companies Act 1955 (NZ), s 2.*

A New Zealand company (AICS) carried on business as a money broker in New Zealand   *e* and took deposits in the course of that business. In order to protect depositors the respondent company was appointed trustee for the depositors in March 1988 pursuant to the requirements of the New Zealand Securities Act 1978. Under the trust deed AICS covenanted with the respondent as the trustee to furnish it with monthly and quarterly certificates of AICS's financial position on behalf of the directors of AICS and signed by two of them. The appellant, a Bahrein bank which operated internationally but had no   *f* place of business in New Zealand, was beneficial owner of about 40% of the shares of AICS and nominated two of its employees to be two of the five directors of AICS. The bank's nominees did not sign any certificates of AICS's financial position sent to the respondent. In August 1986 AICS went into liquidation and its depositors were unable to recover their deposits in full. One of the depositors brought a representative action against the respondent for breach of trust, alleging that it had failed to perform its duties   *g* under the trust deed with diligence and competence. The respondent settled the action and then sought contribution from several defendants, including the directors of AICS. In July 1988 it obtained leave to join the bank as sixth defendant in the proceedings and served the writ on the bank outside New Zealand. The respondent alleged against the directors of AICS that they were in breach of the duty of care which they owed to the   *h* respondent, as trustee for the unsecured depositors, to exercise due diligence to ensure that the statements in the monthly and quarterly certificates were correct, that the certificates contained fraudulent or negligent misrepresentations regarding AICS's financial position and that the directors were in breach of the duties owed to the respondent and other creditors of AICS under the New Zealand Companies Act 1955 to keep proper accounting records of AICS and to refrain from allowing the company to   *j* contract debts without reasonable prospect of repayment. The respondent alleged against the bank that, as the employer of two of the directors of AICS, it was vicariously liable for acts or omissions committed by them in the course of their employment, that the relationship between the bank and the two directors was that of principal and agent and therefore the bank was responsible for all acts or omissions by them in respect of their

office as directors which were within the scope of their authority as agents of the bank,
a that as a substantial shareholder in the holding company of AICS the bank owed a duty
of care to the respondent as trustee for the unsecured depositors of AICS and to the
unsecured depositors themselves to ensure that the business of AICS was not conducted
negligently or recklessly and was in breach of that duty and that since the two directors
were accustomed to act in accordance with the bank's instructions the bank was a director
of AICS within the meaning of s 2^a of the 1955 Act. The bank entered an appearance
b under protest and applied under r 131^b of the New Zealand High Court Rules to set aside
service of the writ on the ground that the court had no jurisdiction to hear and determine
the proceeding. The respondent relied on r 219(a) and (h)^c of the rules to justify service,
contending, inter alia, that the acts or omissions for or in respect of which damages were
claimed were done or occurred in New Zealand, and that the bank was a necessary and
proper party to a proceeding properly brought against another person duly served or to
c be served within New Zealand. The judge refused the bank's application on the ground
that the service of the writ fell within r 219 and that the respondent's claims could not
be said to disclose no cause of action. On appeal by the bank the New Zealand Court of
Appeal affirmed the judge's decision, holding further that the test of a good arguable case
had to be satisfied before the court would accept jurisdiction and that the respondent had
satisfied that test. The bank appealed to the Privy Council.
d
Held – The appeal would be allowed for the following reasons—
    (1) Notwithstanding the right conferred by r 219 to serve proceedings without leave
outside New Zealand and the ostensibly narrow grounds of objection embodied in r 131,
the court retained an inherent discretion to decline jurisdiction on grounds such as forum
non conveniens or the fact that the plaintiff had not made out a good arguable case.
e Furthermore, although a defendant's submission that the plaintiff's choice of venue was
forum non conveniens could be presented as an application for a stay, forum non
conveniens, like any other discretionary objection, could be raised on an application by a
defendant under r 131 to set aside service, although it was for the New Zealand courts to
follow their own preferred procedure in that respect (see p 408 c, p 414 h, p 416 a to c,
p 419 h to p 420 c, post); dicta of Lindley LJ in *Société Générale de Paris v Dreyfus Bros*
f [1886–90] All ER Rep 206 at 210 and of Arnup JA in *Singh v Howden Petroleum Ltd* (1979)
100 DLR (3d) 121 at 132–133 adopted.
    (2) Any duty of care owed by the two directors could only be sought in the trust deed
entered into between AICS and the respondent. Although under that deed a duty of care
in relation to the certificates was only assumed by the directors who signed the certificates,
the respondent had by its statement of claim established an arguable case (a) that since
g the two directors knew that the certificates were being furnished on behalf of all the
directors they had assumed a special duty owed to the respondent and the depositors to
take reasonable care to see that the certificates were accurate and (b) that they were in
breach of that duty and consequently liable to contribute to the liability incurred and
settled by the respondent (see p 408 c, p 421 h j and p 422 c to f, post).
    (3) However, if the two directors were in breach of their duty to the respondent or
h AICS to see that the certificates were accurate or their duty to the bank to exercise
reasonable diligence and skill, those duties were separate and distinct and different in
scope and nature, with the result that the bank was not responsible for a breach of the
duties owed by the two directors to AICS or the respondent. Furthermore, if the two
directors had committed a breach of trust to AICS or the respondent they had done so as
individuals and as directors of AICS and not as employees of the bank, notwithstanding
j that the bank had allowed them to perform their duties to AICS in the bank's time and
at its expense. Moreover, in the performance of their duties as directors and under the

---

a   Section 2, so far as material, is set out at p 424 j, post
b   Rule 131 is set out at p 411 c to j, post
c   Rule 219, so far as material, is set out at p 409 j to p 410 a, post

trust deed, the two directors had been bound to ignore the interests and wishes of their employer, the bank, and could not plead any instructions from the bank as an excuse for breach of their duties to AICS and the respondent. If the bank had exploited its position as employer to obtain an improper advantage for itself or to cause harm to the respondent it would be liable for its own misconduct but its employment of the two directors did not make it responsible for their negligence in the discharge of their duties under the trust deed (see p 408 c, p 423 h to p 424 c, post).

(4) The two directors of AICS appointed by the bank were not agents of the bank in carrying out their duties to AICS but were agents of AICS for the purpose of the trust deed and, by the express terms of the trust deed, accepted responsibility for the accuracy of the certificates as directors of AICS (see p 408 c and p 424 c d, post).

(5) The bank did not owe a personal duty of care to the respondent since no duty of care was imposed by the trust deed or by supplemental agreement on employers, shareholders or any other third parties for the acts or omissions of the directors, who were the only persons who were charged by the trust deed with the duty to see that the figures were accurate. Furthermore, an employer who as a shareholder of a company nominated an employee to be a director did not owe a duty to the company unless the employer interfered with the affairs of the company. It followed therefore that the bank was not vicariously liable to the respondent either as employer or as principal nor was it personally liable in negligence (see p 408 c and p 424 f g, post).

(6) The bank was not a director of AICS within the meaning of s 2 of the 1955 Act since the bank's two appointees were two out of five directors and there was no allegation that in those circumstances the directors were accustomed to act on the directions or instruction of the bank. Since the bank was not a director and had never accepted or assumed any duty of care towards the respondent, in the absence of fraud or bad faith on its part no liability attached to the bank in favour of the respondent for any instructions or advice given by the bank to its two nominees. It followed therefore that the statement of claim disclosed no cause of action against the bank, and the pleading would therefore be struck out (see p 408 c, p 424 j to p 425 e g, post).

Notes

For service out of the jurisdiction generally, see 37 Halsbury's Laws (4th edn) paras 171– 195, and for cases on the subject, see 37(2) Digest (Reissue) 308–319, 326–332, 1941– 1993, 2026–2068.

For liability of directors, see 7(1) Halsbury's Laws (4th edn reissue) paras 643–655, and for cases on the subject, see 9(2) Digest (2nd reissue) 154–172, 4376–4491.

Section 2 of the New Zealand Companies Act 1955 corresponds to s 741 of the Companies Act 1985. For s 741 of the 1985 Act, see 8 Halsbury's Statutes (4th edn) 674.

Cases referred to in judgment

Belan v Neumeyer (1960) 33 WWR 48, Man CA; affg sub nom Selan v Neumeyer (1959) 29 WWR 542, Man QB.

City Equitable Fire Insurance Co Ltd, Re [1925] Ch 407, Ch D and CA.

Cockburn v Kinzie Industries Inc (1988) 1 PRNZ 243, NZ HC.

Equiticorp Finance Group Ltd v Cheah [1989] 3 NZLR 1, PC.

Ewing (John) & Co Ltd v Pullmax (Canada) Ltd (1976) 13 OR (2d) 587, Ont HC.

Ferguson v Wilson (1866) LR 2 Ch App 77, LJJ.

Gartside v Sheffield Young & Ellis [1983] NZLR 37, NZ CA.

Grandmaitre (Roger) Ltd v Canadian International Paper Co (1977) 15 OR (2d) 137, Ont HC; affd 18 OR (2d) 175n, Ont CA.

Great Australian Gold Mining Co v Martin (1877) 5 Ch D 1, CA.

Hagen, The [1908] P 189, [1908–10] All ER Rep 21, CA.

Hedley Byrne & Co Ltd v Heller & Partners Ltd [1963] 2 All ER 575, [1964] AC 456, [1963] 3 WLR 101, HL.

Johnson v Taylor Bros & Co Ltd [1920] AC 144, HL.

a *Kingsway Industries Ltd v John Holland Engineering Pty Ltd* (14 May 1986, unreported), NZ HC.

Kloeckner & Co AG v Gatoil Overseas Inc [1990] 1 Lloyd's Rep 177.

McConnell Dowell Constructors Ltd v Lloyd's Syndicate 396 [1988] 2 NZLR 257, NZ CA.

Mackender v Feldia AG [1966] 3 All ER 847, [1967] 2 QB 590, [1967] 2 WLR 119, CA.

Maclaine Watson & Co Ltd v Dept of Trade and Industry [1989] 3 All ER 523, [1989] 3
b WLR 971, HL.

Metall und Rohstoff AG v Donaldson Lufkin & Jenrette Inc [1989] 3 All ER 14, [1990] 1 QB 391, [1988] 3 WLR 563, CA.

Monro (George) Ltd v American Cuanamid and Chemical Corp [1944] 1 All ER 386, [1944] KB 432, CA.

Pemberton v Chappell [1987] 1 NZLR 1, NZ CA.

c *Petersen v Ab Bahco Ventilation* (1979) 107 DLR (3d) 49, BC SC.

Rainham Chemical Works Ltd v Belvedere Fish Guano Co Ltd [1921] 2 AC 465, [1921] All ER Rep 48, HL.

Ryde Holdings Ltd v Sorenson [1988] 2 NZLR 157, NZ HC.

Salomon v Salomon & Co Ltd [1897] AC 22, [1895–9] All ER Rep 33, HL.

Scott v Scott [1943] 1 All ER 582.

d *Shaw (John) & Sons (Salford) Ltd v Shaw* [1935] 2 KB 113, [1935] All ER Rep 456, CA.

Singh v Howden Petroleum Ltd (1979) 100 DLR (3d) 121, Ont CA.

Siskina (cargo owners) v Distos Cia Naviera SA, The Siskina [1977] 3 All ER 803, [1979] AC 210, [1977] 3 WLR 818, HL.

Société Générale de Paris v Dreyfus Bros (1885) 29 Ch D 239; rvsd (1887) 37 Ch D 215, [1886–90] All ER Rep 206, CA.

e *Spiliada Maritime Corp v Cansulex Ltd, The Spiliada* [1986] 3 All ER 843, [1987] AC 460, [1986] 3 WLR 972, HL.

Takaro Properties Ltd v Rowling [1978] 2 NZLR 314, NZ CA.

Tyne Improvement Comrs v Armement Anversois SA, The Brabo [1949] 1 All ER 294, [1949] AC 326, HL.

Vitkovice Horni a Hutni Tezirstvo v Korner [1951] 2 All ER 334, [1951] AC 869, HL.

f *Wendell v Club Mediterranee NZ* (25 March 1987, unreported), NZ HC; affd [1989] 1 NZLR 216, NZ CA.

Wilson v Lord Bury (1880) 5 QBD 518, CA.

Wincham Shipbuilding Boiler and Salt Co (Poole, Jackson and Whyte's Case) (1878) 9 Ch D 322, CA.

g
Appeal

Kuwait Asia Bank EC (the bank), a Bahrain exempt joint stock company which was the sixth defendant in proceedings brought in the New Zealand High Court by the respondent, National Mutual Life Nominees Ltd (NMLN), a company incorporated in Victoria, Australia, appealed with final leave to appeal granted by the Court of Appeal of
h New Zealand on 24 August 1989 against the decision of that court (Cooke P, Somers, Casey, Hardie Boys and Wylie JJ) ([1989] 2 NZLR 50) on 7 June 1989 dismissing its appeal against the judgment of Henry J ([1989] 2 NZLR 43) in the High Court of New Zealand dated 8 March 1989 refusing the bank's application under r 131 of the High Court Rules for an order that proceedings served on the bank outside the jurisdiction by NMLN should be dismissed and that the bank's appearance under protest should be set
j aside on the ground that the New Zealand courts had no jurisdiction over the bank. The facts are set out in the judgment of the Board.

Howard Page QC and *Robert S Chambers* (of the New Zealand Bar) for the bank.
James Farmer QC and *J W Turner* (both of the New Zealand Bar) for NMLN.

At the conclusion of the argument the Board announced that the appeal would be
allowed for reasons to be given later.

_a_

21 May. The following judgment of the Board was delivered.

LORD LOWRY. This is an appeal by Kuwait Asia Bank EC (the bank) from a judgment
of the Court of Appeal of New Zealand (Cooke P, Somers, Casey, Hardie Boys and
Wylie JJ) ([1989] 2 NZLR 50) delivered on 7 June 1989, whereby that court dismissed _b_
the bank's appeal from a judgment given on 8 March 1989 by Henry J ([1989] 2 NZLR
43), who had refused the bank's application to the High Court under r 131 of the New
Zealand High Court Rules for an order that proceedings served on the bank outside the
jurisdiction by the plaintiff, National Mutual Life Nominees Ltd (NMLN), the present
respondent, should be dismissed. At the conclusion of the hearing their Lordships
announced that they had agreed humbly to advise Her Majesty that the appeal ought to _c_
be allowed for reasons which they would deliver later. This they now do.

AIC Securities Ltd (AICS) was a New Zealand company which carried on business in
Auckland as a money broker. Part of its business was the taking of deposits and, in order
to protect the depositors, by a deed of trust dated 5 March 1985 NMLN was appointed
trustee for AICS's depositors pursuant to the statutory requirements of New Zealand law _d_
contained in the Securities Act 1978. Under the trust deed AICS covenanted with NMLN,
as the trustee, to furnish it with monthly and quarterly certificates on behalf of the AICS
directors.

In August 1986 AICS became insolvent and went into liquidation and its unsecured
depositors have been unable to recover in full their deposits and interest from AICS. One
of the depositors, a Mr Fletcher, brought a representative action against NMLN for breach _e_
of trust, alleging that NMLN had failed to perform its duties under the trust deed with
diligence and competence. The sum claimed by the depositors amounted to $14·5m, and
NMLN thought it prudent to dispose of the litigation by paying $6·75m on the basis
that, when added to recoveries already made, the settlement payment would return to
each depositor a sum equal to 75 to 80 cents in the dollar excluding interest and costs.
The legal expenses of NMLN incurred in connection with the litigation brought against _f_
it by the depositors amounted to $503,555 plus interest and costs.

In these proceedings NMLN seeks contribution from several defendants towards the
sum of $6·75m and $503,555 plus interest and costs. Originally its claim was in third
party proceedings against Deloittes Haskins & Sells, the auditors of AICS. Later it started
separate actions against Messrs Worn, Wright, Scott, House and August, the directors of
AICS, and Mr Gilmour, the company secretary. That action was subsequently consolidated _g_
with the original proceedings. Later still, in July 1988, NMLN obtained leave to join the
bank as sixth defendant in the consolidated proceedings. That leave was granted and it is
the subsequent service of proceedings on the bank outside New Zealand that is the
subject of the present appeal.

The bank is incorporated under the laws of Bahrain. It operates internationally but has
no branch or place of business in New Zealand. Its connection with the action against _h_
NMLN and with these proceedings arises from the fact that the bank had a 49·9%
shareholding in a New Zealand company called Australasia Investment Corp Ltd (AICL)
incorporated in 1982. The other shares in AICL, amounting to 50·1%, were held by
Kumutoto Holdings Ltd (Kumutoto), a New Zealand company. AICL then became the
owner of between 75% and 81% of the shares in a company originally called AIC Finance
Ltd and subsequently renamed AIC Corp Ltd (AICC). One of AICC's wholly-owned _j_
subsidiaries was AICS, already mentioned. The bank was therefore beneficially interested
in about 40% of the shares in AICS. By agreement between the bank and Kumutoto
there were five directors of AICS, three nominated by Kumutoto and two by the bank.
They were Messrs House and August, both of whom were employed by the bank.

As against the five directors, NMLN pleaded four causes of action: (1) that the directors

owed a duty of care to NMLN as trustee for the unsecured depositors of AICS to exercise
a due diligence in relation to the provision of certain monthly and quarterly certificates to
ensure that the statements in those certificates were correct in so far as they related to
matters of fact and were reasonably and honestly made in so far as they related to matters
of opinion, which duty they breached; (2) that these certificates contained various express
or implied representations as to AICS's financial position, and that the representations
were false and misleading, and made fraudulently and/or negligently; (3) that the
b directors owed a statutory duty to NMLN and to other creditors of AICS pursuant to the
provisions of ss 151 and 319 of the Companies Act 1955 to keep proper accounting
records of AICS, which duty was breached; and (4) that the directors owed a duty to
NMLN and to other creditors of AICS pursuant to the provisions of s 320 of the 1955 Act
to refrain from allowing AICS to contract debts without any reasonable prospect of
repayment and to refrain from allowing AICS to carry on any business in a reckless
c manner, which duty was breached.

As against the bank, NMLN also pleaded four causes of action: (1) that House and
August were employees of the bank and that their acts or omissions (as summarised
above) were committed or omitted by them in the course of their employment, and
accordingly that the bank was vicariously liable for those acts or omissions as their
d employer; (2) that the relationship of the bank to House and August in respect of their
appointment to and performance of the office of directors of AICS was such as to amount
in law to a relationship of principal and agent so that the bank was responsible for all acts
of or omissions by House and August in respect of their office as directors of AICS, the
acts or omissions being within the scope of their authority, whether actual, implied or
ostensible, as agents for the bank; (3) that the bank, 'a substantial shareholder in AICL
e which was the holding company which exercised power of ownership and control over
AICS', owed a duty of care to NMLN as trustee for the unsecured depositors of AICS and
to the unsecured depositors themselves to ensure that the business of AICS was not
conducted negligently or recklessly or in such manner as to materially disadvantage the
interests of those unsecured depositors, which duty the bank breached; and (4) that
House and August were persons occupying a position of directors of AICS who were
f accustomed to act in accordance with the bank's directions, and that therefore the bank
was a director of AICS within the meaning of s 2 of the Companies Act, and was
accordingly liable for any loss occasioned to NMLN by the acts or omissions of House
and August.

The bank being resident outside New Zealand, NMLN had to justify the service which
had been effected and for that purpose originally relied on three grounds: (1) an act or
g omission for or in respect of which damages were claimed was done or occurred in New
Zealand (r 219(a)); (2) the subject matter of the proceeding is land, stock or other property
situated in New Zealand, or any act, deed, will, instrument or thing affecting such land,
stock or property (r 219(e)); (3) where any person out of New Zealand is a necessary or
proper party to a proceeding properly brought against some other person duly served or
to be served within New Zealand (r 219(h)). In the Court of Appeal and before the Board
h NMLN relied only on the first and third grounds as set forth in paras (a) and (h).

The disposal of the appeal involves two main questions. The first was concerned with
the proper interpretation of the relevant High Court Rules; and, in the light of the rules
as so interpreted, the second question was whether NMLN, as plaintiff, had made out a
case against the bank, as the defendant outside New Zealand, which justified the court in
entertaining the plaintiff's claim against that defendant.

j   The question whether service of the proceedings on the bank outside New Zealand
ought to be set aside has to be considered against the background of the new High Court
Rules which came into operation on 1 January 1986. Rule 219, so far as directly relevant,
reads:

'*When allowed without leave*—Where in any proceeding a statement of claim or
counterclaim and the relevant notice of proceeding or third party notice cannot be

served in New Zealand under these rules, they may be served out of New Zealand
without leave in the following cases: (a) Where any act or omission for or in respect *a*
of which damages are claimed was done or occurred in New Zealand ... (h) Where
any person out of New Zealand is a necessary or proper party to a proceeding
properly brought against some other person duly served or to be served within New
Zealand ...'

This rule for the first time allowed service out of the jurisdiction of the statement of
claim (which replaced the writ of summons as the originating document) in 13 specified *b*
cases, two of which are now relied on by NMLN, and replaced the procedure contained
in rr 48, 49 and 50 of the old Code of Civil Procedure which, like the English RSC
Ord 11, rr 1 and 4, required leave for such service to be obtained and which, so far as
material, provided:

'**48.** *When allowed*—The writ of summons may be served out of New Zealand by *c*
leave of the Court or a Judge—(a) Where any act for which damages are claimed
was done in New Zealand: (b) Where the contract sought to be enforced or rescinded,
dissolved, annulled, or otherwise affected in any action, or for the breach whereof
damages or other relief is demanded in the action—(i) Was made or entered into in
New Zealand: or (ii) Was made by or through an agent trading or residing within
New Zealand: or (iii) Was to be wholly or in part performed in New Zealand: or *d*
(iv) Was by its terms or by implication to be governed by New Zealand law:
(c) Where there has been a breach in New Zealand of any contract, wherever made
... (h) Where any person out of New Zealand is a necessary or proper party to an
action brought against some other person duly served or to be served in New
Zealand ...

49. *How discretion to be exercised*—Upon any application to serve a writ of *e*
summons under paragraph (b) or paragraph (c) [this is why those paragraphs are
included above] of the last preceding rule, the Court or a Judge in exercising its or
his discretion as to granting leave to serve such writ shall have regard to the amount
or value of the property in dispute or sought to be recovered, and to the existence,
in the place of residence of the defendant, of a Court having jurisdiction in the
matter in question, and to the comparative cost and convenience of proceeding in *f*
New Zealand or in the place of such defendant's residence; and in the above-
mentioned cases no such leave shall be granted without an affidavit stating the
particulars necessary for enabling the Court or a Judge to exercise its or his discretion
in manner aforesaid, and all such particulars (if any) as it may require to be shown.

50. *Applications to be supported by evidence*—Every application for an order for
leave to serve a writ out of New Zealand shall be supported by evidence, by affidavit *g*
or otherwise, showing in what place or country the defendant is or probably may be
found, and whether such defendant is a British subject or not, and the grounds on
which the application is made.'

It will be noted that r 49, which was directed towards the question of forum conveniens,
referred to only two kinds of case (both arising out of contract) out of a total of ten. *h*
Rule 50, on the other hand, was comprehensive and required in all cases what might be
called an affidavit of merits: see *Great Australian Gold Mining Co v Martin* (1877) 5 Ch D 1.
The new r 220 provides:

'*When allowed with leave*—(1) In any other proceeding which the Court has
jurisdiction to hear and determine, any document may be served out of New *j*
Zealand by leave of the Court.

(2) An application for leave under this rule shall be made on notice to every party
other than the party intended to be served.

(3) A sealed copy of every order made under this rule shall be served with the
document to which it relates.

a
(4) Upon any application for leave under this rule, the Court, in exercising its discretion, shall have regard to—(a) The amount or value of the property in dispute or sought to be recovered; and (b) The existence, in the place of residence of the person to be served, of a Court having jurisdiction in the matter in question; and (c) The comparative cost and convenience of proceeding in New Zealand or in the place of residence of the person to be served.

(5) Every application for leave under this rule shall be supported by an affidavit—
b
(a) Stating the particulars referred to in subclause (4); and (b) Showing—(i) In what place or country the person to be served is or possibly may be found; and (ii) Whether or not the person to be served is a New Zealand citizen.'

In cases to which this rule applies the old r 49 criteria with regard to forum conveniens are applied generally.

c
Rule 131, which has an affinity with the English Ord 12, r 8, provides:

'*Appearance under protest to jurisdiction*—(1) A defendant who objects to the jurisdiction of the Court to hear and determine the proceeding in which he has been served may, within the time limited for filing his statement of defence and instead of so doing, file and serve an appearance stating his objection and the grounds thereof.
d
(2) The filing and serving of an appearance under subclause (1) shall not be or be deemed to be a submission to the jurisdiction of the Court in the proceeding.

(3) A defendant who has filed an appearance under subclause (1) may apply to the Court to dismiss the proceeding on the ground that the Court has no jurisdiction to hear and determine it.

e
(4) On hearing an application under subclause (3), the Court—(a) if it is satisfied that it has no jurisdiction to hear and determine the proceeding, shall dismiss the proceeding; but (b) If it is satisfied that it has jurisdiction to hear and determine the proceeding, shall dismiss the application and set aside the appearance.

(5) At any time after an appearance has been filed under subclause (1), the plaintiff may apply to the Court by interlocutory application to set aside the appearance.

f
(6) On hearing an application under subclause (5), the Court—(a) If it is satisfied that it has jurisdiction to hear and determine the proceeding, shall set aside the appearance; but (b) If it is satisfied that it has no jurisdiction to hear and determine the proceeding, shall dismiss both the application and the proceeding.

(7) The Court, in exercising its powers under this rule, may do so on such terms and conditions as may be just and, in particular, on setting aside the appearance may
g
enlarge the time within which the defendant may file and serve a statement of defence and may give such directions as may appear necessary regarding any further steps in the proceeding in all respects as though the application were an application for directions under rule 437 or rule 438.

(8) Where the appearance set aside has been filed in relation to a proceeding in which the plaintiff has applied for judgment under rule 136 or rule 137, the Court—
h
(a) Shall enlarge the time within which the defendant may file and serve—(i) A notice of opposition; and (ii) An affidavit by or on behalf of the defendant in answer to the affidavit by or on behalf of the plaintiff; and (b) May, under subclause (7), give such other directions as appear necessary regarding any further steps in the proceeding.'

j
This is the rule pursuant to which the bank appeared and applied under sub-cl (3) to dismiss NMLN's proceeding. It may be noted that, once a defendant outside the jurisdiction has appeared under protest in accordance with sub-cl (1), there are two courses open: either, as happened in the present case, the defendant may apply under sub-cl (3) to dismiss the proceeding or the plaintiff may apply under sub-cl (5) to set aside the defendant's appearance. If the latter application succeeds, the appearance is set aside

and the defendant will be given a time within which to serve a statement of defence.
Either way, according to the wording of sub-cll (4) and (6), the court's duty is to decide　a
whether it has or has not jurisdiction and to proceed accordingly; the rule does not deal
with any other question.

The judgment of the Court of Appeal, delivered by Cooke P, shows how the court
dealt with the procedural issue. Pointing out that the defendant can apply under r 131,
Cooke P said ([1989] 2 NZLR 50 at 52):

> 'On hearing such an application the Court, if satisfied that it has no jurisdiction,　b
> shall dismiss the proceeding but, if satisfied that it has jurisdiction, shall dismiss the
> application and set aside the appearance.'

Having described the English procedure under RSC Ord 11, r 1, he continued:

> 'That is not so under the New Zealand R 219 and the English cases about what
> must be shown to obtain leave in the first place are not directly in point. But they　c
> provide help, we think, in deciding how far the New Zealand Court should go
> under R 131 in considering the strength of the plaintiff's case.'

(Their Lordships note that the Court of Appeal there recognised as relevant a point which
does not on the face of it go to jurisdiction, namely the strength of the plaintiff's case.)

Cooke P noted a second difference from the English procedure: RSC Ord 12, r 8　d
('which is the equivalent of the New Zealand R 131 in so far as it enables a defendant
who wishes to dispute jurisdiction to apply to the court for an order setting aside the
service of the writ') expressly empowers the court to give directions for the disposal of
the matter in dispute including directions for its trial as a preliminary issue, but r 131
does not. The judgment continued (at 52–53):

> 'It happens in the present case, for the reasons appearing hereinafter, that the
> question arising under R 219(a), whether any act or omission for or in respect of
> which damages are claimed was done or occurred in New Zealand [it may be noted
> that the word is 'claimed', and not 'claimable'], is another way of putting what will
> be a major issue at the trial if the Kuwait Bank is a party. That issue is whether the
> bank is responsible for the acts or omissions in New Zealand of the fourth defendants.　f
> Similarly, as to R 219(h), although that paragraph has the less [sic] exacting language
> "proper party" and "properly brought", the matters falling for consideration go to
> the heart of the case against the bank. So we now have to decide how far the Court
> should go at this preliminary stage towards determining major issues in the
> litigation . . . We accept that if the necessary facts are sufficiently before the Court a
> foreign defendant may be able to satisfy the Court that on the true view of the law　g
> there cannot possibly be jurisdiction over him. For instance it may be plain that the
> action cannot succeed against the local defendants, as in The Brabo ([1949] 1 All ER
> 294, [1949] AC 326). In that event the foreign defendant can obtain an order
> dismissing the proceeding if service abroad has to be based on (h). Again, if the bank
> here could show that in law the acts or omissions of the fourth defendants in New
> Zealand could plainly not be attributed to the bank, the Court could and should　h
> determine that there is no jurisdiction under (a). Where the case is not plain at the
> preliminary stage the test to be applied by the Court in deciding whether it will accept
> jurisdiction has been variously stated.' (Our emphasis.)

Cooke P then referred to Tyne Improvement Comrs v Armement Anversois SA, The Brabo
[1949] 1 All ER 294, [1949] AC 326, Vitkovice Horni a Hutni Teẓirstvo v Korner [1951] 2　j
All ER 334, [1951] AC 869 and Metall und Rohstoff AG v Donaldson Lufkin & Jenrette Inc
[1989] 3 All ER 14, [1990] 1 QB 391, all well-known RSC Ord 11 authorities. He went
on (at 54):

> 'It has to be remembered that in New Zealand the issue arises on an application to
> dismiss the proceeding, whereas in England it can arise on an application for leave,

a but probably that makes no significant difference; in England it commonly arises on applications to set aside service. Neither the question of forum conveniens nor that of lis alibi pendens, questions dealt with in this Court in *McConnell Dowell Constructors Ltd v Lloyd's Syndicate 396* ([1988] 2 NZLR 257), arise in the present case.'

b (Their Lordships must later make further reference to the point that the question of forum conveniens, of which lis alibi pendens is a particular example, does not raise the issue of jurisdiction.)

Having adverted to the 'established principle' that a foreigner resident abroad will not lightly be subjected to the local jurisdiction, Cooke P said:

c 'Finally, the two-fold tests posed by the English Court of Appeal, a good arguable claim on the merits and a strong probability that the claim falls within the letter and spirit of the rule about service abroad, relate to questions that at least under R 221(1)(a) [this must be r 219(a)] merge into one in the present case. At least under that paragraph, on which the argument in this Court was mainly centred, whether the New Zealand Court *has jurisdiction depends on the strength* of the plaintiff's case *against the bank on the merits* . . . The ultimate issue under R 131 is whether the Court is satisfied that there are sufficient grounds for it properly to *assume jurisdiction*. The

d strength of the plaintiff's case against the party served abroad and all the circumstances of the case have to be weighed.' (Our emphasis.)

There is in this passage an unresolved contrast between the two phrases 'has jurisdiction' and 'assume jurisdiction' (the latter, but not the former, involving the exercise of a discretion).

e Having commented on the rival submissions of the parties, Cooke P came back to the point of principle, saying (at 55–56):

'As explained earlier in this judgment, the good arguable case test seems to us right; and we have no doubt that the plaintiff satisfies it for the purposes of R 219(a). The argument . . . is sufficiently strong to warrant the New Zealand Court in accepting jurisdiction under that paragraph.'

f At first instance the approach of Henry J had been different. Having described the new regime, he said ([1989] 2 NZLR 43 at 46):

g 'The important change made by the High Court Rules is that the existence of jurisdiction over a person served outside New Zealand does not now necessarily depend upon the exercise of the Court's discretion on application, but will arise if the particular case falls within one or more of the categories enumerated in R 219. That is not to say a plaintiff has an absolute right to have the Court exercise jurisdiction simply by invoking or purporting to invoke R 219; a defendant may still challenge the validity of such invocation because clearly if the case on proper consideration is shown not to come within one of the specified categories, then

h service outside New Zealand in reliance on the rule would be ineffective for jurisdictional purposes. It is also clear that the Court's power to consider the principle of forum non conveniens and if appropriate to stay or to decline jurisdiction on that ground remains, as has been discussed by the Court of Appeal in *McConnell Dowell Constructors Ltd v Lloyd's Syndicate 396* ([1988] 2 NZLR 257) where the dual questions of jurisdiction arising from R 219 and forum non conveniens were considered.'

j Having contrasted RSC Ord 11 with the current New Zealand procedure and having questioned the value of considering the English practice for the purpose of construing r 219, he continued (at 47):

'In my judgment there is no obligation on a plaintiff who invokes R 219 to satisfy the Court by affidavit evidence that factually there is a meritorious claim. On the contrary the merits are I think in such a case irrelevant to the issue of jurisdiction,

and to embark on a consideration of the factual basis for the claim in the way
envisaged is quite inappropriate and contrary to the intent of the rule. In each case   *a*
coming within R 219 there is a strong territorial content to the proceeding, and as I
apprehend it the philosophy of the new rule is to vest jurisdiction in the Court in
such cases as a matter of course rather than as a matter of discretion.'

The judge held that the 'good arguable case' test applied only when considering the
question whether the claim came under r 219 and that the question whether the plaintiff
had a good arguable case on the factual and legal merits did not arise. He went on (at 48):   *b*

'It would therefore appear at first sight that this issue is really whether the
proceeding should be struck out because no cause of action is disclosed, which is
something not related directly to the issue of jurisdiction to hear and determine.
However, on balance I think the issue could be appropriate for consideration on an
application under R 131(3) for two reasons. First, it can be argued that if the claim   *c*
has no proper basis in law, there is in a broad sense no jurisdiction to entertain it.
Secondly, and perhaps of more importance, the Courts have always regarded as
serious the question whether a "foreigner should be brought to contest his rights in
this country" (*Société-Générale de Paris v Dreyfus Bros* ((1885) 29 Ch D 239 at 242). If
it is clear the claim is ill-founded, or in the words of Lord Simonds in *The Brabo*
([1949] 1 All ER 294 at 304, [1949] AC 326 at 348), bound to fail, then to decline   *d*
jurisdiction may perhaps be proper. Such an inquiry may involve a detailed
consideration of the relevant law, as is sometimes conducted for example on an
application to strike out (*Gartside v Sheffield Young & Ellis* ([1983] NZLR 37)) or on
an application for summary judgment (*Pemberton v Chappell* ([1987] 1 NZLR 1)).'

The judge then considered the submission that all the plaintiff's causes of action   *e*
against the bank were demonstrably bad in law and, although sceptical of the propositions
advanced by the plaintiff, decided that it would be inappropriate, in the absence of full
knowledge and findings on the facts, to embark on a detailed consideration of the
arguments in an endeavour to reach a conclusion on the questions of law involved. He
concluded (at 48–49):

'I do not think that the claims although arguable are so unlikely to succeed as to   *f*
warrant the Court as a matter of overall discretion (if that power were available)
now renouncing jurisdiction in respect of this foreign defendant, whose admitted
employees are properly before the Court on this very proceeding, and whose actions
as such are brought in question as against Kuwait.'

(It seems that 'arguable' in this context must mean 'questionable' or 'debatable'.)   *g*
Thus the position reached on the bank's application was that Henry J ruled against it
because the plaintiff had come within r 219 and its claims could not be said at that stage
to *disclose no cause of action.* The Court of Appeal, while observing that there would be *no
jurisdiction* under para (a) if the bank could show that in law the acts or omissions of the
fourth defendants could plainly not be attributable to the bank and also *no jurisdiction*
under para (h) if the action could not succeed against House and August (as in *The Brabo*),   *h*
set up (despite the strict wording of r 131(4)) an additional hurdle for the plaintiff,
namely that the test of a good arguable case must be satisfied before the court will *accept*
jurisdiction. There is another point not covered by this summary: under para (h) not
only must the action be viable against the parties within the jurisdiction, but the party
outside the jurisdiction has to be 'a necessary or proper party'; if there were *no cause of
action* against the bank, grounded on its *own* negligence, there would again, according to   *j*
both Henry J and the Court of Appeal, be *no jurisdiction* under para (h).

As was said recently in *Equiticorp Finance Group Ltd v Cheah* [1989] 3 NZLR 1 their
Lordships would be most reluctant to differ from the Court of Appeal on a matter of
procedure under the New Zealand rules and indeed, since they consider that the plaintiff

has no cause of action under any heading against the bank, they need not for present
a purposes try to resolve the difference of opinion as to the right test between the Court of
Appeal and Henry J. It may, however, prove helpful to consider further the powers of
the court under r 131.

That rule expressly deals with jurisdiction and nothing else; yet the Court of Appeal
contemplated that jurisdiction would not be accepted if the plaintiff did not make out a
good arguable case, and both Henry J and the Court of Appeal recognised the principle
b (which in England has often involved the exercise of the court's discretion) 'that a
foreigner resident abroad will not lightly be subjected to the local jurisdiction'. The
authority cited by Henry J for this proposition was, not surprisingly, *Société Générale de
Paris v Dreyfus Bros* (1885) 29 Ch D 239, in which Pearson J, after carefully considering
the merits of the claim, refused to discharge an order, based on the plaintiff's claim for
an injunction, giving leave under RSC 1883, Ord 11, r 1(f) (now RSC Ord 11, r 1(b)) for
c service of a writ out of the jurisdiction. The judge there said (at 243–244):

> 'It is urged on one side that whenever a case occurs that comes within any one of
> the sub-sections of the rule the Court really has no discretion, but is bound to order
> the writ to be served. It is urged on the other side, and as I think correctly, that the
> Court has discretion whether or not a writ shall be served even in those cases; and,
d > as in the old cases, the Court looked through the bill in order to see whether or not
> the statements in the bill shewed a reasonable case for granting the writ, so I conceive
> on the present occasion, when I am dealing simply with the granting of an
> injunction, I am bound to look into the circumstances of the case to see whether or
> not there is any sufficient justification to authorize the Court in its discretion to
> allow service out of the jurisdiction. I am perfectly aware that when I lay down the
e > rule in that way I am laying it down most indistinctly and most indefinitely, but I
> cannot help doing so. It is said, and said I have no doubt with perfect accuracy, that
> in these cases you cannot go into the merits of the case, that all you have to do is to
> ascertain properly whether or not the jurisdiction for the trial of the action is here
> or elsewhere. But I do not see how in a great number of cases you can go into that
> question without ascertaining, to some degree at all events, what appear to be the
f > merits of the case.'

The Court of Appeal reversed this decision, the French court having by that time decided
the action, but did not differ in principle. Lindley LJ said ((1888) 37 Ch D 215 at 225,
[1886–90] All ER Rep 206 at 210):

> '... Order XI enumerates certain circumstances under which, and under which
g > alone, the Court can give leave to serve writs out of the jurisdiction. It does not say
> that when those circumstances occur the Court is bound to give leave. On the
> contrary, the language is that service out of the jurisdiction "may be allowed by the
> Court or a Judge" in certain specified events. This shews that the Court has a
> discretion and is bound to exercise its discretion. This becomes still plainer by
> turning to rule 2, which states certain matters which the Court is bound to have
h > regard to when it is asked for leave to serve a writ in *Ireland* or *Scotland*. It is not that
> you are entitled to have leave simply because you bring your case within one or the
> other of the eleven rules of Order XI. You cannot get the leave unless you do, but it
> does not follow if you do you are to have the leave. The Court has a discretion, and
> that discretion must of course be exercised judicially, and upon proper grounds.
> Then it is said you cannot go into the merits. That is quite true. Of course you
j > cannot properly upon an application to serve a writ try the action. The object in
> giving leave to serve the writ is to put the parties in a position to try the action bye-
> and-bye, but at the same time a judge cannot perform the duty imposed upon him
> by this Order unless he so far look into the matter as to see whether the plaintiff has
> a probable cause of action or not.'

Their Lordships agree with the approach which commended itself to the Court of Appeal and consider that, notwithstanding the right conferred by r 219 to serve _a_ proceedings without leave out of New Zealand and the ostensibly narrow ground of objection embodied in r 131, the court retains a discretion to set aside service on the same principles as governed the granting of leave under the former r 48 and the setting aside of service before 1986. Their Lordships have been assisted towards this conclusion, which happily accords with the Court of Appeal's view of New Zealand procedure, by a number of considerations.   _b_

The English Ord 11, which has served as the model in most Commonwealth countries for service of process out of the jurisdiction, does not spell out the entirety of the court's discretion to refuse leave, even where the case falls within r 1, but that the discretion exists is not in doubt: see _Johnson v Taylor Bros & Co Ltd_ [1920] AC 144 at 153 per Lord Birkenhead LC and Viscount Haldane, and per Lord Dunedin where he said (at 154):

> 'I think it is legitimate to begin by considering the genesis of the rule. I understand _c_ that jurisdiction according to English law is based on the act of personal service and that if this is effected the English law does not feel bound by the Roman maxim "Actor sequitur forum rei". It is far otherwise in other systems where service is in no sense a foundation of jurisdiction, but merely a sine qua non before effective action is allowed. Now service being the foundation of jurisdiction, it follows that _d_ that service naturally and normally would be service within the jurisdiction. But there is an exception to this normal rule, and that is service out of the jurisdiction. This however is not allowed as a right but is granted in the discretion of the judge as a privilege, and the rule in question here prescribes the limits within which that discretion should be exercised.'

For further statements of princple one may refer to _The Brabo_ [1949] 1 All ER 294, [1949] _e_ AC 326, _Vitkovice Horni a Hutni Tezirstvo v Korner_ [1951] 2 All ER 334, [1951] AC 869, _Siskina (cargo owners) v Distos Cia Naviera SA, The Siskina_ [1977] 3 All ER 803, [1979] AC 210, _The Hagen_ [1908] P 189, [1908–10] All ER Rep 21 and _Spiliada Maritime Corp v Cansulex Ltd, The Spiliada_ [1986] 3 All ER 843, [1987] AC 640 and, for a recent example, see _Kloeckner & Co AG v Gatoil Overseas Inc_ [1990] 1 Lloyd's Rep 177.

An application to discharge an order giving leave to serve the writ out of the _f_ jurisdiction is brought under RSC Ord 12, r 8(1)(c), which reads:

> 'A defendant who wishes to dispute the jurisdiction of the court in the proceedings by reason of any such irregularity as is mentioned in rule 7 or on any other ground shall give notice of intention to defend the proceedings and shall, within the time limited for service of a defence, apply to the Court for . . . (c) the discharge of any _g_ order giving leave to serve the writ on him out of the jurisdiction . . .'

It is, however, recognised that not only the question of forum conveniens (which does not affect jurisdiction) but all the factors relevant to the grant or refusal of the order are to be canvassed on the hearing of this application: see _The Supreme Court Practice 1988_ vol 1, para 11/4/10. It is noteworthy that both Cooke P in his judgment and _McGechan on_ _h_ _Procedure_ (1988) have regarded r 131 as comparable to Ord 12, r 8. _McGechan_ also states:

> 'Rule 131 empowers a defendant who objects to the jurisdiction of the court to enter an appearance under protest and it will be in the context of that rule that forum non conveniens questions will become relevant.'

Their Lordships are grateful to have been furnished with a copy of 'The First Report to _j_ the Rules Committee by the Supreme Court Procedure Revision Committee' (April 1978) but the report contains only one reference to the proposed new procedure for service abroad, which does not assist the interpretation of either r 219 or r 131. Nor is any real help to be found in New Zealand cases decided under the new regime. Because it had been mentioned in both courts below, their Lordships carefully considered *McConnell Dowell Constructors Ltd v Lloyd's Syndicate 396* [1988] 2 NZLR 257, in which the Court of Appeal applied *The Spiliada* but, although the judgment of Cooke P contains a most instructive discussion of forum conveniens, the report does not assist for present purposes. In *Cockburn v Kinzie Industries Inc* (1988) 1 PRNZ 243 a statement of claim was served under r 220 by leave (although it might have been served under r 219) on helicopter manufacturers in Oklahoma, USA. The report contains a valuable historical survey by Hardie Boys J and their Lordships take note of the fact that, the defendant Kinzie's objection to jurisdiction being refused, its appearance under r 131 was set aside and that, its objection on the ground of forum non conveniens being upheld, the plaintiff's action against it was stayed.

It can be seen that the analogy with RSC Ord 12, r 8 provides what may be the answer to a narrow interpretation of the court's power on an application under r 131, but that still leaves the effect of r 219 for consideration. New Zealand, however, is not the only English-derived jurisdiction to have adopted service abroad without leave and, with *McGechan on Procedure* again pointing the way, their Lordships have had the benefit of reading a most helpful article by Elizabeth Edinger, a member of the Faculty of Law of the University of British Columbia, in that university's Law Review (see 'Discretion in the assumption and exercise of jurisdiction in British Columbia' (1982) 16 U Br Col LR 1), in which the author notes the adoption in British Columbia, Manitoba, Ontario and Nova Scotia, being common law provinces of Canada, of the new procedure of serving process 'ex juris' without leave and considers, inter alia, 'the existence of a discretion after service "ex juris" as of right'.

As at the date of the article the position appeared uncertain. In Manitoba the Court of Appeal in 1960 affirmed without reasons the judge's decision that no discretion exists, the court's only function being to see whether the facts fall within the prescribed grounds (see *Belan v Neumeyer* (1960) 33 WWR 48). The British Columbia Supreme Court in 1979 came down on the side of discretion in *Petersen v Ab Bahco Ventilation* (1979) 107 DLR (3d) 49, but the value of this decision as a guide is minimised by a rule which virtually decides the issue. That is r 14(6) of the British Columbia Supreme Court Rules, which provides:

> 'Where a person served with an originating notice has not entered an appearance and alleges that (*a*) the process is invalid or has expired, (*b*) the purported service of the process was invalid, or whether or not he has entered an appearance, alleges that (*c*) the Court has no jurisdiction over him in the proceeding or should decline jurisdiction, he may apply to the Court for a declaration to that effect.'

The most valuable discussion of the principles, and also the clearest guidance, is found in Ontario, where the Court of Appeal ruled clearly in favour of discretion in *Singh v Howden Petroleum Ltd* (1979) 100 DLR (3d) 121, in which the headnote reads:

> 'The intended effect of the 1975 amendments (O. Reg. 106/75) to the Ontario Rules relating to service *ex juris* was merely to remove as unnecessary the initial *ex parte* application before the Master for leave to serve out of Ontario. This procedural change does not alter or remove from the Court the discretion to control its own process. The Court retains the power and discretion, in addition to the question of *forum conveniens*, to set aside service *ex juris* in appropriate cases. While the realities of interprovincial and international trade are such that businessmen are constantly engaged in commercial activities which cross borders, Courts must respect the sovereignty of independent States with the same solicitude and care that was exercised prior to 1975.'

The judgment of the court was delivered by Arnup JA, who began as follows (at 122):

> 'In 1975 the Rules of Practice respecting service out of Ontario were drastically

changed. On this appeal we are asked to decide whether the amendments were merely intended to simplify the procedure, or to both simplify the procedure and change the principle underlying its application. The Divisional Court took the latter view.'

He then traced the history of the old procedure, which closely resembled that of RSC Ord 11 and the old New Zealand r 48, referring en route to *Société Générale de Paris v Dreyfus Bros* (1887) 37 Ch D 215, *Johnson v Taylor Bros & Co Ltd* [1920] AC 144 at 153 and *George Monro Ltd v American Cuanamid and Chemical Corp* [1944] 1 All ER 386, [1944] KB 432.

The new Ontario r 25 closely resembles r 219 and Ontario r 29 allows the parties served to apply for an order setting aside service. This rule, unlike British Columbia r 14(6), provides no clue as to the discretionary powers of the court hearing the application. Having noted the new procedure, Arnup JA referred to *John Ewing & Co Ltd v Pullmax (Canada) Ltd* (1976) 13 OR (2d) 587 at 590, in which Southey J, referring to the court's discretion under the old practice, said:

'The weight to be attached to those considerations under the circumstances in which international and interprovincial business is now conducted has been questioned in recent cases. It appears that the persons enacting the 1975 amendments decided that such considerations should give way completely to the need for simplifying our procedure and avoiding time-consuming and wasteful interlocutory proceedings. The party served out of Ontario may still move to set aside service under Rule 29, as amended (O. Reg. 106/75, s. 8), but that Rule, in my judgment, does not restore the judicial discretion which formerly existed under Rule 25. Such a motion would succeed in a case in which it could be shown that the claim did not fall within any of the subclauses of Rule 25(1). The absence of an affidavit, verifying the essential facts in the plaintiff's claim is not now, in my judgment, a ground for setting aside service outside Ontario.'

Robins J took a different view in *Roger Grandmaitre Ltd v Canadian International Paper Co* (1977) 15 OR (2d) 137 at 140–141:

'I do not construe the amended Rules as removing the discretion which the Court has long exercised in matters in this nature. In my view, even if the facts disclose a case which falls within the terms of Rule 25, the Court is not bound to allow service to stand. *Forum conveniens* is a common law doctrine applying generally to cases involving problems of conflict of laws. I do not understand how a change in Rules of Practice and Procedure can operate to modify the Court's power to exercise a discretion founded on this doctrine. Rule 29 does not purport to limit or restrict the principles on which service may be set aside and it seems to me that those factors which were taken into consideration on applications for *ex parte* orders for service out of Ontario or on applications to set aside or rescind such *ex parte* orders remain relevant to applications under Rule 29. In other words there is, in my opinion, no distinction to be drawn between the cases in which service *ex juris* required leave of the Court and those in which service *ex juris* may be effected without a Court order—in either situation the plea of *forum conveniens* may be invoked and the Court may, notwithstanding that jurisdiction is conferred by the Rules, still exercise its discretion to determine whether jurisdiction should be assumed or declined.'

Forum conveniens was the actual point in issue and the Court of Appeal affirmed the judge's decision to set aside service. Estey CJO said in a brief oral judgment (18 OR (2d) 175 at 176):

'It became apparent during the argument of this appeal, however, that a judgment of the Ontario Supreme Court by Southey, J., in *John Ewing & Co. Ltd. v. Pullmax (Canada) Ltd. et al.* ((1976) 13 OR (2d) 587), had not been drawn to the attention of

a
the learned Justice sitting in Weekly Court. We have had the advantage of examining the reasons of Southey, J., in that case, and of hearing an explanation put upon that case by all counsel on this appeal, and, none the less, we see no reason to dispose of this matter otherwise than has been done by Mr. Justice Robins sitting in Weekly Court.'

b
After referring to two other judgments in the High Court and setting out the facts of the case under appeal, Arnup JA stated his conclusion on the question of principle (100 DLR (3d) 121 at 132–133):

c
'In my view the Rules Committee did not intend to remove from the Court its discretion to control its own process, and to place that control solely in the hands of the bar. The contrary view, in my respectful opinion, is tantamount to saying that if the solicitor drawing the documents uses all the right words, no judicial officer has any right to interfere with the service of the process out of the jurisdiction. All of the repeated warnings as to the "great care" which is to be exercised by the Court in permitting its process to be served anywhere else in the world would, on the basis of the judgment of the Divisional Court, become obsolete. Moreover, there is no express language in either the old or the new Rule dealing with the question of

d
forum conveniens, but that question, as already noted, was constantly dealt with on motions to set aside service of Ontario process outside the jurisdiction, yet no one has suggested in this or any of the other cases decided after the amendments that consideration of forum conveniens has been abolished. Since that consideration formed a part of the exercise of the former discretion, its acknowledged continuance strengthens my view that the discretion of the Court survived the amendments. I quite agree with the view of Southey, J., that the realities of interprovincial and

e
international trade are such that businessmen are constantly engaged in commercial activities which cross our borders, and as a matter of course, cross continents and oceans as well. The fact is, however, that there are now more independent States in the world than there ever were, and the Courts of this Province must respect their sovereignty with the same solicitude and care that was exercised prior to 1975.

f
Form 3 is not a command of the Queen of Canada, as a writ of summons is, but although signed by the plaintiff's solicitor only, it notifies the defendant to come into the Ontario Court or suffer the consequences. Without saying that this Court is in terms bound by the earlier judgment of the Court of Appeal in the Roger Grandmaitre case, I find it difficult to believe that the Court would have passed over in silence the observations of Robins, J., as to the effect of the 1975 changes if they

g
had been of the view that those observations were wrong. In my respectful view, the judgment of Robins, J., was correct, and John Ewing & Co. Ltd. v. Pullmax (Canada) Ltd. was wrongly decided in its holding as to the effect of the 1975 amendments. In the result, I am of the opinion that the Divisional Court erred in the approach that it took and that the service out of Ontario in this case must be looked at by the Court having in mind the same principles which governed the scrutiny by the Court of

h
process issued under the old Rules when the Court was hearing an application to set aside the order allowing service ex juris.'

Their Lordships find these observations to be strong and convincing arguments in support of the approach of the New Zealand Court of Appeal to r 131.

A defendant's submission that the plaintiff's choice of venue is forum non conveniens

j
can of course be presented as an application for a stay. This method was adopted in McConnell Dowell Constructors Ltd v Lloyd's Syndicate 396 [1988] 2 NZLR 257 and Cockburn v Kinzie Industries Inc (1988) 1 PRNZ 243. Indeed, in Wendell v Club Mediterranee NZ (25 March 1987, unreported; affd [1989] 1 NZLR 216) and Kingsway Industries Ltd v John Holland Engineering Pty Ltd (14 May 1986, unreported) Hillyer J took the view that a forum conveniens objection must be so dealt with and not under r 131. Their Lordships

consider that, as with RSC Ord 11 and Ord 12, r 8 (see *Mackender v Feldia AG* [1966] 3 All ER 847, [1967] 2 QB 590), and consistently with the view of the Court of Appeal of Ontario, forum conveniens (like every other discretionary objection) *can* be raised on a r 131 application, but also think that it is for the courts of New Zealand to follow their own preferred procedure in this respect.

The fact that, unlike RSC Ord 11, r 219 does not require a supporting affidavit is partly offset by the need under that rule for a statement of claim, and not merely a writ; and the absence from r 131 of power to direct trial of a preliminary issue contrasts much more in theory than in practice with the RSC Ord 12, r 8 procedure. Their Lordships therefore do not regard these points as strong indications against the continuing existence of discretion on an application under r 131. That rule and r 219 have not abrogated the court's inherent discretion to decline jurisdiction.

Their Lordships now proceed to consider the causes of action pleaded by NMLN against the bank. Two general principles may first be stated. (1) A director does not by reason only of his position as director owe any duty to creditors or to trustees for creditors of the company. (2) A shareholder does not by reason only of his position as shareholder owe any duty to anybody.

In *Ferguson v Wilson* (1866) LR 2 Ch App 77 at 89–90 Cairns LJ said:

'What is the position of directors of a public company? They are merely agents of a company. The company itself cannot act in its own person, for it has no person; it can only act through directors, and the case is, as regards those directors, merely the ordinary case of principal and agent. Wherever an agent is liable those directors would be liable; where the liability would attach to the principal, and the principal only, the liability is the liability of the company. This being a contract alleged to be made by the company, I own that I have not been able to see how it can be maintained that an agent can be brought into this Court, or into any other Court, upon a proceeding which simply alleges that his principal has violated a contract that he has entered into. In that state of things, not the agent, but the principal would be the person liable.'

In *Re Wincham Shipbuilding Boiler and Salt Co (Poole, Jackson and Whyte's Case)* (1878) 9 Ch D 322 three directors paid the amounts due on shares issued to them into the overdrawn account of the company which had been guaranteed by the directors. The liquidator of a company failed in an action against the directors for breach of their fiduciary duties. In the Court of Appeal Jessel MR, reversing Bacon V-C, said (at 328–329):

'The Vice-Chancellor decided the question on this ground, that the directors were trustees of all their powers. So, no doubt, they were. But it is further said that they exercised their powers in breach of trust and for their own benefit, and, therefore, that the act which they did was nugatory. But it appears to me that the question is, for whom were they trustees? It does not appear that the Vice-Chancellor considered this point; but it makes all the difference whether they were trustees for the persons who were injured by what had been done in this case, namely, the other creditors of the company. It has always been held that the directors are trustees for the shareholders, that is, for the company. They are the managing partners of the company, and if they abuse their powers, which they hold in trust for the company, to the damage of the company, for their own benefit, they are liable to make good the breach of trust to their *cestuis que trust* like any other trustees. But directors are not trustees for the creditors of the company. The creditors have certain rights against a company and its members, but they have no greater rights against the directors than against any other members of the company. They have only those statutory rights against the members which are given them in the winding-up.'

In *Wilson v Lord Bury* (1880) 5 QBD 518 a company borrowed £1,000 from the plaintiff
a and covenanted to secure payment by assigning a mortgage to him. The mortgage was
paid off and the redemption moneys paid into the funds of the company, which then
became insolvent. The plaintiff sued the directors of the company alleging negligence on
their part. Brett LJ said (at 525–526):

> '. . . it is clear that there was at least a contract between the company and the
> plaintiff, that the company would on payment off of the mortgage debt . . . to the
b > company give to the plaintiff another mortgage security . . . that such contract had
> been broken by the company, that the plaintiff would at least have been entitled to
> sue the company, if it had remained solvent, for such breach . . . It is clear that there
> was no contract between the plaintiff and the defendants personally to the like effect.
> It is equally clear that there was no contract of principal and agent between the
> plaintiff and the defendants personally. These matters have been too often decided
c > to require further discussion. It was strenuously urged on behalf of the plaintiff that
> the defendants were as a necessary consequence of their position as directors of the
> company, personally trustees of the plaintiff and had been guilty of a breach of trust.
> Being clearly of opinion, as above stated, that there was no contract between the
> plaintiff and the defendants . . . the question is whether there was the relation
> between the cestui que trust and trustee. I know of no principle or authority for
d > saying that such a relation can be constituted by any agreement or any intercourse
> between the parties less direct than the agreement or intercourse, which forms the
> relation of principal and agent. As the agent of an agent is not thereby the agent of
> the original principal, so is neither the agent or trustee of a trustee thereby the
> trustee of the original cestui que trust.'

e After citing the views of Cairns LJ in *Ferguson v Wilson*, Brett LJ continued (at 527):

> 'This seems to me to shew that Lord Cairns, dealing with the procedure of a Court
> of Equity, was of opinion that the same want of direct intercourse which prevents
> any remedy at common law by the dealer with a company against the directors
> personally of such company, on the mere ground of their being directors, equally
f > prevents any remedy against them by the same party in respect of the same relation
> in a Court of Equity.'

But, although directors are not liable *as such* to creditors of the company, a director
may by agreement or representation assume a special duty to a creditor of the company.
A director may accept or assume a duty of care in supplying information to a creditor
analogous to the duty described by the House of Lords in *Hedley Byrne & Co Ltd v Heller*
g *& Partners Ltd* [1963] 2 All ER 575, [1964] AC 456. In that case, but for an express
disclaimer of liability, a bank which supplied a reference of creditworthiness in respect
of a customer of the bank would have been under an implied duty of care towards the
person who sought and relied on the reference.

In the present case, a duty of care owed by House and August to the trustees can only
h be sought in the trust deed entered into between AICS and NMLN. The statement of
claim contains the following allegations:

> '10. PURSUANT to the provisions of clause 3.5.1. of the Trust Deed, AICS was
> required to furnish NMLN with monthly reports certified as true and correct by
> two of its directors in relation to the matters set out in the said clause 3.5.1. ("the
> Monthly Certificates") . . .'

j
The statement of claim annexes particulars of the names of the directors of AICS who
signed monthly certificates. House and August did not sign any of the monthly
certificates. A duty of care in relation to the monthly certificates was only assumed by
the directors who signed the certificates. The statement of claim continues:

'11. PURSUANT to the provisions of clause 3.5.2. of the Trust Deed, AICS was
required within twenty business days after the end of each financial quarter to *a*
furnish to NMLN a report by two directors of AICS on behalf of all of its directors
relating to the matters set out in the said clause 3.5.2. ("the Quarterly Certificates")
...

15. EACH of the Quarterly Certificates . . . contained a statement or statements by
or on behalf of all the Defendants (by virtue of the express provisions of Clause
3.5.2. of the trust deed), that (inter alia): (i) AICS had duly observed and performed *b*
all of the covenants, conditions, agreements and provisions binding upon it under
the Trust Deed; (ii) No event had happened which had caused or could have caused
the deposits placed with AICS to become repayable.'

NMLN intends at the trial to show that House and August must have known or ought
to have known that the quarterly certificates were furnished on behalf of all the directors *c*
of AICS including House and August, and that in those circumstances House and August
assumed and accepted a special duty owed to NMLN and the depositors to take reasonable
care to see that the statements in the quarterly certificates were accurate. NMLN also
proposes to show that House and August did not exercise reasonable care, the quarterly
certificates were not accurate and NMLN relied on the quarterly certificates and therefore
did not take timely action under the trust deed to protect the interest of the depositors *d*
and is entitled to a contribution from House and August to meet the liability incurred
and settled by NMLN for the sum of £6·75m.

Of course, NMLN may fail to show either the existence or the breach of the duty
alleged to have been accepted by House and August. It may be that House and August
relied, and were entitled to rely, on information received from their co-directors or from
Deloittes. House and August might be able to show that NMLN received sufficient *e*
information and that the loss to the depositors could have been averted or reduced if
NMLN had properly evaluated the information and facts supplied to them. There are
other allegations against House and August in the statement of claim, and there may be
other defences open to House and August. There is no doubt that NMLN, by its statement
of claim, has established an arguable case against House and August arising out of the
fact that the quarterly certificates were furnished on behalf of all the directors of AICS. *f*

As against the bank, the statement of claim pleaded that the bank was liable to
contribute to the loss suffered by NMLN in settling the claims of the depositors against
NMLN for all or any of the following reasons. (1) House and August were appointed to
the board of directors of AICS by the bank, were employed by the bank and carried out
their duties as directors in the course of their employment by the bank. (2) House and
August were, as directors of AICS, the agents of the bank, which was the principal. (3) As *g*
a substantial shareholder in AICL, which was the holding company that controlled AICS,
the bank owed a duty of care to NMLN and to the depositors 'to ensure that the business
of AICS was not conducted negligently or recklessly, or in such a manner as to materially
disadvantage the interests of those unsecured depositors'. (4) House and August were
persons occupying a position of directors of AICS who were accustomed to act in *h*
accordance with the bank's directions, and therefore the bank was a director of AICS
within the meaning of s 2 of the Companies Act 1955.

As to (1), the power of appointing a director of a company may be exercised by a
shareholder or a person who is not a shareholder by virtue of the articles of association of
the company, or by virtue of the control of the majority of the voting shares of the
company, or virtue of the agreement or acquiescence of other shareholders. In the present *j*
case, the bank and Kumutoto, who together controlled AICS, decided that the bank
should nominate two directors. In the absence of fraud or bad faith (which are not alleged
here), a shareholder or other person who controls the appointment of a director owes no
duty to creditors of the company to take reasonable care to see that directors so appointed
discharge their duties as directors with due diligence and competence. One shareholder

may lock away his paid-up shares and go to sleep. Another shareholder may take an
a active interest in the company, insist on detailed information and deluge the directors
with advice. The active shareholder is no more liable than the sleeping shareholder. In
Salomon v Salomon & Co Ltd [1897] AC 22 at 35, [1895–9] All ER Rep 33 at 39 Lord
Watson said:

> 'Any person who holds a preponderating share in the stock of a limited company
> *b* has necessarily the intention of taking the lion's share of its profits without any risk
> beyond loss of the money which he has paid for, or is liable to pay upon, his shares
> . . .'

In *Rainham Chemical Works Ltd v Belvedere Fish Guano Co Ltd* [1921] 2 AC 465 at 475,
[1921] All ER Rep 48 at 52, where it was argued that shareholders were liable for a tort
committed by a company, Lord Buckmaster LC said:
c
> 'It not infrequently happens in the course of legal proceedings that parties who
> find they have a limited company as debtor with all its paid-up capital issued in the
> form of fully-paid shares and no free capital for working suggest that the company
> is nothing but an alter ego for the people by whose hand it has been incorporated,
> and by whose action it is controlled. But in truth the Companies Acts expressly
> *d* contemplate that people may substitute the limited liability of a company for the
> unlimited liability of the individual, with the object that by this means enterprise
> and adventure may be encouraged.'

The liability of a shareholder would be unlimited if he were accountable to a creditor
for the exercise of his power to appoint a director and for the conduct of the director so
appointed. It is in the interests of a shareholder to see that directors are wise and that the
e actions of the company are not foolish; but this concern of the shareholder stems from
self-interest, and not from duty. The House of Lords, in the recent case of *Maclaine
Watson & Co Ltd v Dept of Trade and Industry* [1989] 3 All ER 523, [1989] 3 WLR 971
(the International Tin Council case), reiterated that a corporation is a legal person, that no
one can sue on a contract save the parties to the contract and that therefore the members
of a corporation are not liable as members for the debts of the corporation. It does not
f make any difference if the directors appointed by a shareholder are employed by the
shareholder and are allowed to carry out their duties as directors while in the shareholder's
employment. House and August owed three separate duties. They owed in the first place
to AICS the duty to perform their duties as directors without gross negligence; the
liability of a director to his company is set forth in the judgment of Romer J in *Re City
Equitable Fire Insurance Co Ltd* [1925] Ch 407. They owed a duty to NMLN to use
g reasonable care to see that the certificates complied with the requirements of the trust
deed. Finally, they owed a duty to their employer, the bank, to exercise reasonable
diligence and skill in the performance of their duties as directors of AICS.

If House and August did not exercise reasonable care to see that the quarterly
certificates were accurate, they committed a breach of the duty they owed to NMLN and
h may have committed a breach of the duty they owed to AICS and a breach of the duty
they owed to the bank to exercise reasonable diligence and skill. But these duties were
separate and distinct and different in scope and nature. The bank was not responsible for
a breach of the duties owed by House and August to AICS or to NMLN any more than
AICS or NMLN were responsible for a breach of duty by House and August. If House
and August committed a breach of the duty which was imposed on them and the other
j directors of AICS and was owed to NMLN under and by virtue of the trust deed they did
so as individuals and as directors of AICS and not as employees of the bank; House and
August were not parties to the trust deed, nor was the bank. House and August were
allowed by the bank to perform their duties to AICS in the bank's time and at the bank's
expense. It was in the interests of the bank that House and August should discharge with
diligence and skill the duties which they owed to AICS, but these facts do not render the

bank liable for breach by House and August of the duty imposed on them by the trust deed. In the performance of their duties as directors and in the performance of their duties imposed by the trust deed, House and August were bound to ignore the interests and wishes of their employer, the bank. They could not plead any instruction from the bank as an excuse for breach of their duties to AICS and NMLN. Of course, if the bank exploited its position as employers of House and August to obtain an improper advantage for the bank or to cause harm to NMLN then the bank would be liable for its own misconduct. But there is no suggestion that the bank behaved with impropriety. Its duty to refrain from exploiting its influence over its employees is not different in principle from the duty of a father not to exploit his influence over a son who is a director or the duty of a businessman not to exploit his influence over a business associate who is a director. The employment of House and August could have given the bank the opportunity to injure AICS and NMLN but it did not make the bank responsible for negligence of House and August in the discharge of their duties under the trust deed.

(2) Then it is said that House and August were the agents of the bank. But, as directors of AICS, they were the agents of AICS and not of the bank. As directors of AICS, House and August were agents for AICS for the purposes of the trust deed and, by the express terms of the trust deed, responsibility for the accuracy of the quarterly certificates was assumed by the directors of AICS. House and August accepted responsibility for the quarterly certificates as directors of AICS and not as agents or employees of the bank.

(3) Next it was said that the bank owed a personal duty of care to NMLN. For the protection of the depositors NMLN stipulated for and obtained by the trust deed a duty of care in the preparation of the quarterly certificates by the directors of AICS. NMLN may or may not have known that two of the directors of AICS were employed by the bank and that the bank would allow those two directors to carry out their duties as directors while in the employment of the bank. Any of these circumstances, even if known, could change at any time. NMLN may or may not have known that the bank was beneficially interested in 40% of the shares of AICS. That circumstance also could change at any time. NMLN did not rely on any of these circumstances. By the terms of the trust deed or by agreement supplemental to the trust deed NMLN might have attempted to impose a duty of care on third parties such as the bank, but NMLN neither intended nor attempted expressly or by implication to impose on employers, shareholders or any other third parties liability for the acts or omissions of the only persons who by the trust deed were charged with the duty to see that the quarterly certificates were accurate. An employer who is also a shareholder who nominates a director owes no duty to the company unless the employer interferes with the affairs of the company. A duty does not arise because the employee may be dismissed from his employment by the employer or from his directorship by the shareholder or because the employer does not provide sufficient time or facilities to enable the director to carry out his duties. It will be in the interests of the employer to see that the director discharges his duty to the company but this again stems from self-interest and not from duty on the part of the employer. NMLN's counsel referred to *Ryde Holdings Ltd v Sorenson* [1988] 2 NZLR 157, but in that case the employer interfered with the affairs of the company by *instructing* the director to sell the assets of the company to a subsidiary company of the employer at an undervalue. None of the other authorities cited, New Zealand, English or Australian, supported the submission that the bank is vicariously liable to NMLN either as employer or as principal or personally liable for its own negligence. In two authorities, *John Shaw & Sons (Salford) v Shaw* [1935] 2 KB 113, [1935] All ER Rep 456 and *Scott v Scott* [1943] 1 All ER 582, it was held that majority shareholders are not liable to creditors of a company: management is vested in the directors, who are liable to the company for gross negligence.

(4) Finally, NMLN relied on s 2 of the Companies Act 1955, in which a 'director' is defined as 'a person in accordance with whose directions or instructions the persons occupying the position of director of a company are accustomed to act'. In the present case House and August were two out of five directors, the other three being appointees

of Kumutoto. And there is no allegation (and it is also inherently unlikely) that the
a directors in these circumstances were accustomed to act on the direction or instruction
of the bank.

The only rights and remedies of NMLN were against AICS for breach of contract and
against the directors of AICS who owed a duty to NMLN. By the trust deed, the quarterly
certificates were rendered on behalf of the directors and nobody else. Even if NMLN
knew that House and August had been appointed by the bank, that the bank controlled
b a substantial shareholding in AICS and that House and August were bound to perform
their duties as directors of AICS while employed by the bank, NMLN by the trust deed
was only entitled to be furnished with quarterly certificates on behalf of the directors.
House and August were directors but the bank was not a director. The bank never
accepted or assumed any duty of care towards NMLN. In the absence of fraud or bad
faith on the part of the bank, no liability attached to the bank in favour of NMLN for
c any instructions or advice given by the bank to House and August. Of course, it was in
the interests of the bank to give good advice and to see that House and August
conscientiously and competently performed their duties both under the trust deed and
as directors of AICS. But such advice is not attributable to any duty owed by the bank to
NMLN, which was only entitled to the protection which the trust deed provided, namely
quarterly certificates furnished on behalf of all the directors of AICS. By the trust deed
d the directors of AICS accepted and assumed responsibility for the quarterly certificates,
and the directors did not include the bank. The Companies Act 1955 cannot alter the
construction of the trust deed or impose on the bank a duty assumed by House and
August but never assumed by the bank.

Thus the statement of claim does not disclose any cause of action against the bank. The
pleading would therefore be fit to be struck out on the application of the defendant. It
e complies, in their Lordships' opinion, with the test enunciated in *Takaro Properties v
Rowling* [1978] 2 NZLR 314 at 316–317, namely that the cases pleaded as causes of action
are so clearly untenable that they cannot possibly succeed. The fact that applications to
strike out may raise difficult questions of law requiring extensive argument does not
exclude the jurisdiction to do so (*Gartside v Sheffield Young & Ellis* [1983] NZLR 37 at 45),
and the same principle applies to applications under r 131 of the High Court Rules and
f RSC Ord 12, r 8. There is no need for the circuity of procedure which would be involved
in an application to strike out the statement of claim in a case like the present, since 'no
cause of action' provides the ultimate example of failing to show a good arguable case.
Having regard to their Lordships' conclusions and to the terms of r 131, the appropriate
order, by analogy with successful applications to set aside service under RSC Ord 12, r 8
(which is on its face concerned with absence of jurisdiction), is to dismiss the proceeding
g as against the bank.

Finally, there is the matter of costs. In the light of the conclusions which they have
reached on the appeal, their Lordships are of the opinion that the bank is entitled against
NMLN to its costs in the courts below and before their Lordships' Board. And, because
for good reasons the date of trial of the action was fixed for the month of February 1990,
h the bank will also receive all its costs necessarily incurred in preparing for that trial, but
not the costs of preparing and presenting a petition to this Board for leave to appeal.

Appeal allowed.

Solicitors: *Macfarlanes* (for the bank); *Wray Smith & Co* (for NMLN).

Mary Rose Plummer   Barrister.

Whitfield v H & R Johnson (Tiles) Ltd

COURT OF APPEAL, CIVIL DIVISION
PURCHAS, BELDAM LJJ AND SIR ROGER ORMROD
25 JANUARY, 2 MARCH 1990

Factory – Lifting excessive weights – Person not to be employed to lift, carry or move excessive weight – Load so heavy as to be likely to cause injury to employee – Likely to cause injury 'to' employee – Likely – Female employee employed to lift and move tiles – Employer not knowing that employee suffering from congenital back condition making her specially vulnerable to back injury – Employee performing her job over long period without difficulty before sustaining back injury – Whether employee's back condition and predisposition to injury relevant in determining whether employer liable for employing her to lift load so heavy as to be likely to cause injury to her – Factories Act 1961, s 72.

The plaintiff had suffered since birth from a congenital back condition which affected the strength and durability of her back and made her vulnerable to back injuries. In about 1973 the plaintiff started work at the defendant employer's tile factory and was employed, as were other women in the factory, to lift and load tiles from a trolley onto a conveyor belt. The defendant neither knew nor had it reason to suspect that the plaintiff suffered from a congenital back condition. From April 1984 the plaintiff was required to lift and move heavier tiles than before but despite her back condition she experienced no difficulty in performing her job until she injured her back on 4 December 1984 while bending to lift a stack of tiles from a trolley. The plaintiff was forced to stop work and although she returned to work after a period of rest she found she could no longer do the job of loading tiles and left the defendant's employment. She brought an action against the defendant claiming negligence and breach of the defendant's statutory duty under s 72[a] of the Factories Act 1961 not to employ a person 'to lift, carry or move any load so heavy as to be likely to cause injury to him'. The judge dismissed the negligence claim on the ground that the defendant operated a safe system of work in respect of lifting and moving tiles. The judge also dismissed the plaintiff's claim for breach of statutory duty even though he found that it was inevitable, having regard to her back condition, that sooner or later she would suffer a back injury through lifting the tiles. The plaintiff appealed against the dismissal of her claim for breach of statutory duty, contending that the defendant had employed her to lift and move a load which was so heavy as to be 'likely to cause injury to [her]', within s 72, that the defendant had to take her as it found her, ie with her back condition, and that accordingly, having regard to her back condition and susceptibility to injury, it was likely that she would sustain injury in lifting and moving the tiles as had in fact happened and it was immaterial that the defendant was unaware of her back condition.

Held – Section 72 of the 1961 Act was to be construed according to its natural meaning and, so construed, the likelihood of injury related to the weight of the load. Accordingly, whether a person was employed to lift or move loads so heavy as to be 'likely' to cause injury to him depended on whether the weight of the particular load was likely to cause injury. The reference in s 72 to the injury being caused 'to him' meant that, if the employer was to be liable under s 72, the weight of the particular load had to be likely, having regard to the nature of the load, the relevant surrounding circumstances and the particular employee's obvious and known characteristics, to cause injury to the particular employee employed to lift or move it. Once it was proved that, having regard to the employee's obvious characteristics and the relevant surrounding circumstances, the

---

a   Section 72 is set out at p 430 j, post

weight of the load he was employed to lift was likely to cause injury to him, a breach of
s 72 was established. It followed that any unknown weakness or predisposition to injury
from which the employee suffered was irrelevant in determining the likelihood of injury
since otherwise an employer would be in breach of s 72 whatever the weight of the load
if, due to some unknown characteristic of the employee, lifting the load would be likely
to injure him. Since the plaintiff had been lifting and moving the heavier tiles for several
months without any difficulty before she sustained her injury and it was her back
condition rather than the weight of the tiles that was likely to cause her injury, it could
not be said that she had been employed to lift or move a load so heavy as to be likely to
cause injury to her, within s 72 of the 1961 Act. The appeal would therefore be dismissed
(see p 432 b c, p 434 h to p 435 c j, p 436 c d f to h, p 437 b, p 439 h to p 440 a, post).
    Bailey v Rolls Royce (1971) Ltd [1984] ICR 688 considered.

Notes
For the prohibition on employers employing persons to lift excessive weights, see 20
Halsbury's Laws (4th edn) para 642.
    For the Factories Act 1961, s 72, see 19 Halsbury's Statutes (4th edn) (1990 reissue) 499.

Cases referred to in judgments
Bailey v Rolls Royce (1971) Ltd [1984] ICR 688, CA.
Brown v Allied Ironfounders Ltd [1974] 2 All ER 135, [1974] 1 WLR 527, HL.
Brutus v Cozens [1972] 2 All ER 1297, [1973] AC 854, [1972] 3 WLR 521, HL.
Kinsella v Harris Lebus Ltd [1963] CA Transcript 327.

Appeal
The plaintiff, Susan Jane Whitfield, appealed against the judgment of Hobhouse J given
in the Queen's Bench Division at Birmingham on 7 March 1989 dismissing the plaintiff's
action against the defendant, H & R Johnson (Tiles) Ltd, claiming damages for breach of
statutory duty under s 72 of the Factories Act 1961 and for common law negligence
regarding an injury the plaintiff sustained to her back in the course of her employment
with the defendant. The facts are set out in the judgment of Beldam LJ.

Nicholas Worsley for the plaintiff.
Roger S Giles for the defendant.

Cur adv vult

2 March. The following judgments were delivered.

BELDAM LJ (giving the first judgment at the invitation of Purchas LJ). On 1 March
1989 in the Queen's Bench Division at Birmingham Hobhouse J gave judgment in this
action in favour of the defendant. The plaintiff now appeals to this court. The defendant
is a well-known company in the pottery industry specialising in the production of tiles.
It has nine factories in the Stoke-on-Trent area and employs about 3,000 people. As in
most other industries, the production of tiles has in part at least become automated and
the sorting and packing of tiles is done by a process using a conveyor belt. In some of the
defendant's factories tiles were brought to the conveyor belt on another conveyor belt; in
others they were stacked in rows on trolleys which were placed at the end of the belt.
Each trolley contained about 6,000 tiles. In the factories where the tiles were brought on
trolleys it was necessary to unload them from the trolleys by hand and place them on the
conveyor belt. The work of sorting and packing was done by teams of five workers, one
of whom was allocated the task of unloading the trolleys. Some teams consisted of men
and some of women, and some were mixed. The work of unloading the tiles from the

trolleys was more arduous than the work of sorting and packing. In the teams consisting entirely of men one man would be employed throughout a shift unloading and *a* transferring the tiles to the conveyor belts. The teams of women organised the work so that they took it in turns during the shift to unload the tiles. Thus each member of the team would be doing unloading work for about one and a half hours.

The teams were paid on a piece-work basis but, because at least one of the objects of the process was quality control, the sorting of the defective from the good tiles generally controlled the rate of progress. Nevertheless, the member of the team who unloaded the *b* tiles from the trolley to the conveyor belt was expected to keep pace with the rest of the team.

According to Mr Brindley, the defendant's health and safety adviser, the task of unloading tiles onto the conveyor belt had been done by women for at least 35 years at one or other of the defendant's factories. At the time when he joined the defendant in the early 1950s, women were doing the work in two of the defendant's factories. By *c* 1984 there was only one team which consisted entirely of women. In those teams where there were both men and women, men did the work of unloading the tiles. From about April 1984 the tiles with which the plaintiff had to deal were 6-inch tiles. Previously they had been 4¼-inch tiles. Although the 6-inch tiles were heavier than the 4¼-inch tiles, each 6-inch tile weighing about ½ lb, the change in size is of no particular significance because it was left to the unloaders themselves to select a comfortable and convenient number to *d* place onto the conveyor belt at any given time. The unloader would start unloading from the top of the load and, in the case of men, would select about 80 tiles at a time and transfer them to the conveyor belt. The work involved picking up the tiles using both arms and turning through approximately 135°–180° and placing the tiles on the conveyor belt. The women, including the plaintiff, would select fewer tiles, probably about 50. As they weighed ½lb each the total weight was some 25 lb. The rate of work was such that *e* the plaintiff would, on average, place three or four armfuls on the conveyor belt each minute.

The tiles, arranged in rows, were divided by hardboard separators. An armful of tiles was referred to as 'bung'. Each trolley contained four rows of tiles, each about six tiles high. When the loader reached the last row he would have to bend down and across the *f* trolley in order to lift them and place them on the conveyor belt. It was the practice for the loaders to move the tiles towards them on the bed of the trolley before lifting. But nevertheless the lifting of the last row of tiles was more awkward than lifting those nearer to the conveyor belt. On the evidence the judge found that approximately 150 tiles would be moved each minute and so it would take about 40 minutes to clear a trolley. *g*

By 1984 the plaintiff had worked for the defendant for some 11 years. She was 36 years of age and 5 ft 2 in tall. She had, since birth, suffered from a condition of incomplete formation of the lower spinal column which reduced the load bearing strength and durability of her back. One of the major ligaments was missing and extra stress was placed on the facets of the vertebrae. Degenerative changes were present in the small *h* joints of the lumbar spine and there was some wasting of her right leg. The judge found that the congenital condition of the plaintiff's back made her specially vulnerable to injury. Later in his judgment he described the condition as being one in which almost any incident of everyday life might trigger the osteo-arthritis that sooner or later she was going to suffer in any event owing to the congenital weakness of her spine. It was common ground that the defendant neither knew nor had any reason to suspect this weakness. *j*

In spite of the condition of her back, it was the plaintiff's evidence that she had had no trouble in doing the job of unloading the tiles onto the conveyor belt. She picked up the number of tiles that suited her and she knew that she could cope with, and she had had no problems in lifting the tiles and no problems with her back. If the load was too heavy, she would put it back on the truck and take a smaller quantity. She had not found it difficult or awkward to lift an appropriate quantity of tiles from the back of the truck.

At about 11 am on 4 December 1984 the plaintiff was loading tiles from the trolley onto the conveyor. She had dealt with the majority of the load and bent down to lift the last stack of tiles. As she bent forward and took hold of them, she had only lifted them a few inches when she felt a pain in her back and right leg. She was unable to continue work and reported to the defendant's first aid post. Three days later, on 7 December, she consulted her doctor. After a period of rest she felt sufficiently recovered to return to work but six or seven weeks later it was clear that she could no longer continue. Consequently she left the defendant's employment. Fortunately she was eventually able to get work which did not involve her in any continuing loss of earnings.

In these proceedings the plaintiff claims that the accident to her and the onset of pain which she suffered was caused by breach of statutory duty and negligence of the defendant. At common law she claimed that the defendant had exposed her to an unnecessary risk of injury by employing her to lift and carry the bungs of tiles from the truck to the conveyor belt. They failed to instruct or supervise her properly and required her to operate a system of work which was unsafe. She also contended that the defendant was in breach of duty under s 72 of the Factories Act 1961 because it required her to move or lift a load which was so heavy as to be likely to cause injury to her. The judge rejected both claims. Although he found on the evidence that the job did involve a risk of injury that was foreseeable, he held that a reasonably prudent employer would not regard it as necessary to take precautions to guard against it. He drew attention to the fact that, following the introduction of the 6-inch tiles, 15 women had done the plaintiff's job every day for about eight months without any accident or complaint. Since the accident the same or a lesser number of women had been lifting bungs of tiles every day, again without any accident or injury being suffered. The only accident that had occurred was the one in which the plaintiff was involved and she was a person with a congenital condition of her back which made her specially vulnerable. In addition Mr Brindley gave evidence that women had been doing the job for some 35 years. He had made inquiries back to 1981 and there had been no record of any complaints of stress or strain, injury or accident. So the judge held:

> 'On these facts there is no adequate basis for holding that the defendant failed to act reasonably and failed to take reasonable care. The system of work proved itself and the explanation of the occurrence of this accident is not want of reasonable care on the part of the defendant but the congenital weakness of the back of the plaintiff which manifested itself on this occasion.'

The judge also said that if he had found that the system of work was not safe, it would have been comparatively simple for the defendant to have avoided the risks involved by ensuring that only men did the work of unloading the tiles from the trolley to the conveyor belts. Before us it was argued that the judge's finding that the job involved a risk of injury which was foreseeable was inconsistent with his finding that there was no adequate basis for holding that the defendant had failed to act reasonably and failed to take reasonable care. To see if this argument is well founded, it is necessary to look more closely at the evidence and his judgment.

Expert witnesses called by the plaintiff had pointed out that there were risks in lifting in the way in which the plaintiff did. They described the method as dangerous but the judge considered that their expressions of opinion had to be assessed and tested against what had actually happened. He evidently preferred the approach of the defendant's expert who did not deny an element of risk but said that the practice since the 1930s, in industry as a whole, had shown that where an employee had control over the size of his load and the way he chose to lift it, that was an effective system for avoiding the imposition of excessive strains. So in this case the plaintiff and other employees who unloaded the trolleys could choose not only the size of the bung but the way in which they chose to lift. Thus the judge held that the system of work was safe and that it was *a* legitimate to expect employees in simple situations to select a size of load that did not impose excessive strains on themselves. Even on the plaintiff's own evidence the system worked in her case.

The judge's review of the evidence clearly justified his findings and the way in which he expressed them. The fact that the plaintiff with her predisposition to injury had been able to carry on the work without difficulty for as long as she did must provide further *b* support for the judge's finding that the defendant was not negligent.

It was further argued for the plaintiff that the judge paid insufficient attention to the fact that she was employed on a repetitive task, that she might in doing such a task select a load which was too heavy for her and that she was lifting the last tiles from the bed of the trolley at the time when she felt the onset of pain.

But the plaintiff in evidence did not suggest that the rate at which she had to unload *c* the tiles had caused her to select more tiles than she could manage or that she felt uncomfortable in keeping up the ordinary rate of progress. On the contrary, it was her evidence that she experienced no difficulty with the work. She made no mention of the bung she was lifting at the time being any larger or heavier than usual.

I would therefore uphold the judge's finding that there was no negligence on the part of the defendant. On the evidence I do not see how he could have reached any other *d* conclusion.

After stating his finding on this issue the judge added:

'. . . and the explanation of the occurrence of this accident is not want of reasonable care on the part of the defendant but the congenital weakness of the back of the plaintiff which manifested itself on this occasion.'   *e*

The nature of that weakness he further described when he came to consider what the effects of the accident had been on her . He said:

'. . . almost any incident of everyday life might trigger the osteo-arthritis that sooner or later she was going to suffer in any event owing to the congenital weakness of her spine.'   *f*

Those findings, indicative of the degree to which the plaintiff's back was susceptible to injury, are of considerable significance to the question whether there was a breach by the defendant of s 72 of the Factories Act 1961.

Section 72 of the 1961 Act was originally enacted as s 56 of the Factories Act 1937. It was under Pt IV of that Act, 'Health, Safety and Welfare (Special Provisions and *g* Regulations)', and provided:

'(1) A young person shall not be employed to lift, carry or move any load so heavy as to be likely to cause injury to him.

(2) The Secretary of State may make special regulations prescribing the maximum weights which may be lifted, carried or moved by persons employed in factories; *h* and any such regulations may prescribe different weights in different circumstances and may relate either to persons generally or to any class of persons or to persons employed in any class or description of factory or in any process.'

Section 20 of the Factories Act 1959 amended sub-s (1) by deleting the word 'young'. In sub-s (2) the power to prescribe different weights in different circumstances by regulation was removed. In 1974 sub-s (2) was repealed altogether so that s 72 now reads *j* simply:

'A person shall not be employed to lift, carry or move any load so heavy as to be likely to cause injury to him.'

The judge was referred to *Bailey v Rolls Royce (1971) Ltd* [1984] ICR 688. He said of
that decision:

> 'That Court of Appeal authority lays down a number of propositions. The
> criterion is not one of negligence. Therefore the knowledge or ignorance of the
> defendant of any weakness of the plaintiff is irrelevant. The defendant, for the
> purpose of the statutory duty, must take the plaintiff as she is. It is also established
> by that authority that the word "likely" is a reference to probability. It must be
> proved that the load was so heavy as to be likely, that is probable, to cause injury to
> the plaintiff. Mere risk is not sufficient. Thirdly, it is clear that in any case one must
> assess the likelihood or probability having regard to all the surrounding
> circumstances, including the position in which the plaintiff is going to have to lift
> or move the load, and that includes the relationship of the plaintiff to the load and,
> in my judgment, it must include such elements as stress or elements of fatigue if
> they are material. In the present type of case is it likely? Here, unlike any other case
> to which I have been referred, there is a simple repetitive job that is being done by
> the plaintiff, and it is a situation where, as I find on the facts, it is not likely that in
> any individual operation or, indeed, any individual day's work, she will on that day
> suffer an injury.'

If the judgment of the judge had ceased at this point it would have given rise to no
difficulty. However, he said that in a case such as the present it was necessary to decide
what was meant by 'likely' in the context of likely to injure this plaintiff. He said that it
was necessary to consider three possible meanings. (i) Was it likely at any time before the
accident actually occurred? (ii) In the case of repetitive employment, was it likely when
the plaintiff was committed to the employment on which she was engaged, that is to say
when she first began in April 1984 to unload trolleys containing the 6-inch tiles? (iii) Was
it likely at the start of the shift on the morning of 4 December when the plaintiff
embarked on work of unloading the trolley on that day?

The judge rejected the first way of looking at the meaning of the word 'likely' as
'unrealistic and inappropriate for a statutory provision of this kind'. He rejected the third
way because he said no one would be able to say at the start of work or the start of the
shift on 4 December that the plaintiff would suffer injury. There was no more than a
risk and according to the decision in *Bailey v Rolls Royce (1971) Ltd* a risk was not enough.

Although the plaintiff had expressly declined his invitation to argue the case on the
basis of his second way of looking at the meaning of the word 'likely', the judge went on
to say that:

> '... on the findings of fact that I have made it will be appreciated that there is in
> my judgment a likelihood, using that test, that there would be an injury caused to
> the plaintiff. She had a congenital weakness in her back and, viewed over a prolonged
> period on the medical evidence and, indeed, the expert evidence, in my judgment
> the combination of that weakness and the weight she was employed to lift or move
> meant that sooner or later she would suffer an injury to her back. The likelihood in
> that sense existed and, indeed, did materialise.'

Before us it was therefore argued that on the basis of the judge's findings he should
have found that there was a breach of s 72 of the 1961 Act. Further, the plaintiff argued
that she was employed to lift and move the tiles and viewing the matter objectively it
was likely that with her condition she would sustain injury. Accordingly, on the
interpretation of the words 'likely to cause injury to him' in the judgments in *Bailey's*
case, it was immaterial that the defendant was unaware of the weakness in the plaintiff's
back which made her particularly susceptible to injury.

With respect to the judge, I confess I found it difficult to follow the reasoning of his
threefold approach. If in April 1984 the lifting and moving of a bung of tiles gave rise to

more than a 'risk' of injury so that it was 'likely', it is difficult to see why at the start of the plaintiff's work on 4 December it was no more than a 'risk'.

The judge may have been misled by the analogy which he introduced into his judgment that, whereas on one toss of a coin it is not likely to 'come down heads', if you toss it ten times it is strongly likely it will come down heads at least once. Whilst on probability theory this is undoubtedly correct, it is of no assistance in deciding the meaning of 'likely' in s 72. It assumes that, on each occasion the plaintiff lifted a bung of tiles, it was equally probable (likely) that she would suffer injury as that she would not. Yet the facts of this case clearly show that this was not the case.

The words used in s 72 are ordinary English words and there is no suggestion that they are used in any unusual sense. It is, of course, essential to construe the words of the section but, unless it can be said that they have some unusual meaning in the context in which they are found, the task of the tribunal which decides the case is—

'to consider, not as law but as fact, whether in the whole circumstances the words of the statute do or do not as a matter of ordinary usage of the English language cover or apply to the facts which have been proved.'

(See *Brutus v Cozens* [1972] 2 All ER 1297 at 1299, [1973] AC 854 at 861 per Lord Reid.)

The plaintiff's second argument was founded on the observations made in the course of the judgments in *Bailey v Rolls Royce (1971) Ltd* and in particular on the emphasis placed by the court on the use of the words 'to him' at the end of s 72(1). They undoubtedly led the judge in the present case to his conclusion that 'the defendant for the purposes of the statutory duty must take the plaintiff as she is'. And that is the argument advanced for the plaintiff on this appeal.

The plaintiff in *Bailey v Rolls Royce (1971) Ltd* claimed damages against his employers, Rolls Royce, for an injury to his back which occurred when he was positioning a heavy component on a turntable. To the knowledge of his employers, he had injured his back on previous occasions. The county court judge had held that the employers were negligent in failing to give the plaintiff advice about lifting. He had also held that they were in breach of s 72 of the 1961 Act. The defendants appealed and their appeal was allowed. On the facts the Court of Appeal held that they were not negligent. The employers argued that they had not been in breach of s 72 because—

'the use of the word "likely" involved an element of foresight: that before a defendant employer could be held to have committed a breach of his statutory obligation, which after all would involve the commission of a criminal offence, it must be shown that he has been guilty of some fault: it must be shown that he knew, at least of the possibility of injury to the employee.'

(See [1984] ICR 688 at 697.)

The court was referred to cases decided under different sections (ss 4 and 63) of the 1961 Act and it was argued that the word 'likely' should be given the same meaning as it had in those sections. This construction of s 72 was rejected by the court. After considering the question of fact whether the plaintiff had been employed to move the casing in question, May LJ went on to consider the second part of s 72(1). He said (at 699):

'The second part requires one, as I think, to ask the question: Was the load so heavy as to be likely to cause injury to the particular person concerned? The reference to "him" at the end of the subsection in my judgment clearly directs attention to the particular employee that one is considering at any particular time. In my opinion, one has to approach the construction of this subsection, and the meaning of its provision, giving the words used their ordinary and natural English meaning. In my view, "likely" is the equivalent of "probable" or "more probable than not"; it is certainly more than merely "possible". On this point the judge

CA   **Whitfield v H & R Johnson (Tiles) Ltd (Beldam LJ)**   433

certainly found this particular plaintiff to be predisposed to back injury; but he
made no finding that it was more likely than not that for this particular plaintiff to
move this particular casing this would cause injury to him; indeed, in my opinion
there was no evidence to support any such finding. The plaintiff had done this job,
including lifting and moving these casings, for a number of years. It may be that,
with his weak back, when he did so there was a risk that he would suffer an injury,
just as with such a back as he probably had, there was risk of injury when he lifted a
suitcase, bent down to tie up his shoelace or did any other twisting or bending
movement which one has to do so frequently in the course of everyday life. That is
not, however, the same as finding that when he had to do the particular job of
moving this particular casing it was probable that an injury to the back would occur.
If that had been the position, I would have expected this plaintiff to have sustained
an injury to his back doing this particular job much earlier than November 1976,
when the relevant accident occurred. There was clearly a risk that injury might
occur, but I do not think that one can say that it was "likely," or "probable," or "more
probable than not." In those circumstances I reach the conclusion, again with respect
to the judge, that the claim based upon a breach of section 72(1) of the Act was not
made out.'

Slade LJ also referred to the construction of s 72(1). He drew attention to the words 'to
him' at the end of the subsection as showing that the duty owed under the subsection to
one employee may be different from that owed to another ([1984] ICR 688 at 700). After
rejecting the defendant's submission that the words 'likely to cause injury' meant
foreseeably likely, he said (at 700–701):

'I confess that I was at one stage much attracted by that argument. If correct, it
would avoid the need to construe the subsection in a manner which might otherwise
give rise to a statutory offence even in a case where the employer could not
reasonably have foreseen the relevant injury and was not at fault in any way. One
can conceive hypothetical cases where the plaintiff's construction of the subsection
could, at least at first sight, cause considerable hardship—for example, in a case
where an employee has, before the start of his employment suffered serious spinal
injury but has told his employer nothing of the injury. Nevertheless, like May L.J.,
I have been driven to the conclusion that [counsel for the plaintiff] is right in
submitting that one must take the words of the subsection simply as they stand.
They make no express reference to what the employer knew or ought to have
known. Nor, I think, can any such reference be implied from the words "likely to
cause injury to him." In deciding whether a particular employee has been "employed
to lift, carry or move any load so heavy as to be likely to cause injury" to that
employee, within the meaning of the subsection, it seems to me that the court must
apply an objective test of likelihood (or otherwise) as at the date of the injury,
without regard to the employers' actual or constructive knowledge of the
circumstances of the particular employee.'

After agreeing, with May LJ that 'likely' meant 'more probable than not', he continued
(at 701):

'We can surely take judicial knowledge of the fact that there are innumerable
persons in this country who, to a greater or lesser extent, suffer from what may be
loosely described as back trouble. Many such sufferers may be exposed to some
slight risk of physical injury through lifting almost anything. However, fortunately
for them, as well as for their employers, the mere fact that a particular job may
involve some lifting operations does not necessarily render them unemployable for
such purposes. The statutory embargo falls on their employers only when the lifting
which would be involved in the job in question is "*likely*" to cause the particular

employee injury. I do not think that in construing and applying the subsection it would be in the interests of employers or employees, when viewed generally, that *a* the likelihood of injury should be assessed by a test more onerous to employers than the test of probability indicated by May L.J., or that Parliament would have intended otherwise. The very fact that, if our construction is right, liability under the subsection may arise without any fault at all on the part of the employer, seems to me a good reason for not giving the word "likely" a meaning wider than that which it fairly bears.'

b

Stephenson LJ, agreeing with the judgments of both May and Slade LJJ, posed the question in a different way (at 701):

'Was the plaintiff's back in such a condition on 28 November 1976 as to make it likely that the casing which he was employed to lift or move, and did then lift or move, was so heavy as to be likely to cause injury to him?'

c

After rejecting the employer's construction of s 72 Stephenson LJ said (at 702):

'If I look at the words of the section in their natural meaning, I conclude, as do May and Slade L.JJ., that the first question is: Was the casing in fact likely to cause injury to the plaintiff himself? That is irrespective of two matters; first of all, irrespective of the question whether the defendants knew, or ought to have known, *d* that it might cause injury to him, a question which I am not satisfied that the judge ever considered separately; and secondly, irrespective of the question whether it was likely to cause injury to other employees who were fit or in reasonably good health and without the back trouble from which the plaintiff suffered.'

On the basis that 'likely' meant 'probable', he held that the plaintiff had failed to *e* establish a breach of statutory duty.

It is argued in the present case that, to use Slade LJ's words, the statutory embargo falls on the defendant because the lifting involved in the plaintiff's job was likely to cause injury to the particular employee having regard to the disability which she had. The plaintiff's back, to use Stephenson LJ's words, was in such a condition on 4 December as to make it likely that the tiles she had to lift would cause injury to her. *f*

The basis of the decision in *Bailey v Rolls Royce (1971) Ltd* was that there could be a risk of injury from lifting which fell short of rendering it 'likely' that an injury would occur and on the facts of that case no injury was likely to be done to the plaintiff even with his predisposition.

The difficulty caused by the further observations suggesting that the likelihood of injury has to be assessed having regard to any individual weakness or predisposition of *g* the employee is that the more severe the inherent and latent weakness, the more likely it is that any risk in lifting or moving any load will cause injury to him. On the hypothetical case referred to by Slade LJ, and on the facts of the case before us, the likelihood of injury does not arise from the weight of the load at all. Lifting or moving an object of virtually any weight would have been likely to cause injury to the plaintiff sooner or later. So it is said that, because of the use of the words 'to him', the occupier of a factory or an employer *h* would be in breach of s 72 if he employed a person on work which involved lifting even the lightest of load if, for example, the employee suffered from an unsuspected aneurism and the strain of lifting caused it to burst. Thus a breach would be established in such circumstances, whatever the weight of the load, because it would be likely to cause injury 'to him'. So, too, an employee may be employed one week to lift or move a load without *j* any risk of injury but on the following Monday, due to a strain sustained by him over the weekend which diminished his ability to withstand the strain imposed by lifting, the same load could on this hypothesis be said to be likely to cause injury to the employee. I am unable to agree that Parliament, by adding those two words, intended so unreasonable or unlikely a result. I consider that full meaning can be given to those words read in the context of the section as a whole by holding that they were intended to make sure that

the weight of the load was appropriate to the sex, build and physique, or other obvious
a characteristic, of the employee in question. To construe the section in this way does not
detract from the strict nature of the prohibition against employing persons to lift loads
which are so heavy that they are likely to cause injury. Nor does it depart from an
objective standard. Once it is shown that the weight of the load he is employed to lift is
likely to cause injury to the particular employee, having regard to his obvious
characteristics, a breach would be established. It would be no defence to an occupier or
b employer to argue that he personally did not foresee the likelihood of injury.

In short, it seems to me clear from the language of this section that the mischief at
which it was aimed was employing persons to lift or move objects of excessive weight, or
put in another way, that the likelihood of injury to the employee must arise from his
being employed to lift an object of a weight which in all the circumstances, including
the nature of the object, the grip he can take of it, the foothold he has, the space available
c and all the other relevant circumstances, is excessive for him.

I find support for this approach in the full transcript of the judgment of this court in
Kinsella v Harris Lebus Ltd [1963] CA Transcripts 327. The short report in the Solicitors
Journal (108 SJ 14) does not mention this aspect of the judgments. Willmer LJ,
considering identical words to those of s 72 as they appeared in s 56 of the Factories Act
d 1937, as amended by the 1959 Act, said:

'When one looks at the section, it is to my mind clear that it is a section designed
to give protection against excessive weight and excessive weight only. If that be the
correct construction of it, I should be disposed to agree with the judge that the
weight involved here, which she found was 145 lbs is not, as a matter of weight
alone, such a weight as is likely to cause injury to a man of experience such as this
e plaintiff was, a man accustomed to moving weights of this sort.'

Pearson LJ said:

'I agree also as to the effect of s 56 of the Factories Act 1937, as amended by the
1959 Act, and I think it reappears in the same form in s 72 of the new Factories Act
1961. The emphasis of that section is on weight as such. It seems reasonable to
f suppose that you have to take into account to some extent also the other
circumstances affecting the question whether the weight, in view of all the
circumstances, is excessive or not. But, as I have said, the whole emphasis of the
section is on weight. One finds that in sub-s (1) of the section, which mentions only
weight, and in sub-s (2) in the provision that "the Secretary of State may make
special regulations prescribing the maximum weights which may be lifted, carried
g or moved". It is quite true that the section goes on to say "and any such regulations
may prescribe different weights in different circumstances", and so on. Thus the
surrounding circumstances are not wholly without importance. But it still remains
that if any prosecution were launched under s 56 it would have to be proved that
the weight itself was too great in the particular circumstances, and, in my view,
there were reasonable grounds on which the judge could come to the conclusion
h that the offence against s 56 was not proved.'

Diplock LJ, the third member of the court, did not express any dissent from that view
of the construction of the section. Insofar as these views differ from those expressed in
Bailey v Rolls Royce (1971) Ltd, I would prefer them.

On the judge's findings of fact in this case I believe the only view to which the court
j can come is that no breach of s 72 was proved. It is quite clear that, but for the condition
of the plaintiff's back, the weight of the tiles which she lifted or moved in the course of
her employment was not likely to cause injury to her and I would dismiss this appeal.

SIR ROGER ORMROD. I have had the opportunity of reading the judgments of
Purchas and Beldam LJJ and I agree with them. On the issue of negligence there is
nothing which I can usefully add.

Section 72 of the Factories Act 1961 is a short and apparently simple statement but in fact it is deceptive. On closer examination it becomes increasingly difficult to construct, *a* if it is not to be a potential cause of injustice, clearly not intended by Parliament. Beldam LJ, in his judgment, has pointed out some of these possibilities and I need not repeat them. The explanation for this situation emerges from the legislative history. The words of what is now s 72 originally appeared in s 56 of the Factories Act 1937, but qualified in two ways: (a) by the word 'young' before 'person', which immediately introduced a qualitative distinction; and (b) by being subject to the power of the Secretary of State to *b* make regulations prescribing the relevant weights and classes of person to whom the section was to apply. By subsequent amendment in 1959 and 1974 both these qualifying provisions were deleted, leaving only a rump of the original provision to be construed.

As it stands, s 72 is prohibitory. An offence is committed by an employer if he employs a person to 'lift, carry or move any load so heavy as to be likely to cause injury to him'. So the offence is complete before the load is touched, if it is likely to cause injury to the *c* employee. It follows, in my judgment, that, if the plaintiff is to succeed in her claim based on breach of statutory duty, she would have to show that in April 1984 when she was first employed to move 'bungs' of 6-inch tiles from the trolley to the conveyor, it was likely to injure her health. There is no evidence to support such an allegation, nor was there evidence of any subsequent change, either in the character of the plaintiff, or in the nature of the task. *d*

The construction of this section has not been made any easier by the observations in the judgments of this court in *Bailey v Rolls Royce (1971) Ltd* [1984] ICR 688, which lay emphasis on the two concluding words of the section 'to him' and conclude that they require the court to take into account, in assessing likelihood, idiosyncracies of the employee, even if unknown to him or the employer. It seems, with respect, most unlikely that Parliament would have intentionally exposed employers to the risk of *e* prosecution in such circumstances, especially as it would be a new risk arising out of the deletions from the original provision in the 1937 Act. In fact the words 'to him' simply complete the sentence and should not, in my respectful opinion, be overemphasised.

In my judgment the gravamen of the section lies in the words 'so heavy as to', and I am therefore most grateful to Beldam LJ for calling attention to the full transcript of the judgments in *Kinsella v Harris Lebus Ltd* [1963] CA Transcript 327. With respect to the *f* judgments in *Bailey v Rolls Royce (1971) Ltd*, I prefer the views of Willmer and Pearson LJJ in that case. It is perhaps rather easier than it might have been to take this line because it appears from May LJ's judgment that the emphasis on the particular person concerned in all three judgments may have been obiter since there was no finding of fact by the trial judge that it was more probable than not that moving the component would cause injury to that plaintiff by reason of his defective back. *g*

At the same time I am conscious that all the above observations may also be obiter because in my judgment this case can be decided empirically on its facts. The evidence was that the task of lifting bungs of tiles had been done in identical circumstances on innumerable occasions by many different women and very many times since April 1984 by the plaintiff without difficulty. The load cannot therefore have been so heavy as to be *h* likely to cause injury to the plaintiff, notwithstanding the abnormality of her back. I would therefore dismiss this appeal.

PURCHAS LJ. The circumstances and statutory provisions with which this appeal is concerned have been set out in the judgment already delivered by Beldam LJ, whose exposition I gratefully adopt. On the facts as found by him the trial judge was clearly *j* entitled to find that the plaintiff had failed to establish a case in negligence or breach of common law duty on the part of the defendants which would enable the plaintiff to recover damages. There is nothing that I wish to add to the judgment already delivered on this aspect of the case.

I now turn to consider the allegation of breach of statutory duty based on s 72 of the
a Factories Act 1961, which reads simply:

'A person shall not be employed to lift, carry or move any load so heavy as to be
likely to cause an injury to him.'

With respect to the judge I do not consider that this section, which is simply worded,
requires any gloss and may be construed by a reading of the ordinary meaning of the
b word 'likely'. In its context the word 'likely' delimits the weight of the load before there
can be a breach of this provision. The words 'to him' mean that when applying the word
'likely' to any given load which the employee is employed to lift, carry or move, regard
must be had to the particular characteristics and capacity of the person employed.

In his judgment Hobhouse J referred to *Bailey v Rolls Royce (1971) Ltd* [1984] ICR 688
as an authority for a number of propositions. These were that the defendant must take
c the plaintiff 'as she is', that the word 'likely' is a reference to probability, namely that it
must be proved that the load was so heavy as to be likely, that is probable, to cause injury
and, thirdly, that in any case the likelihood or probability, having regard to all the
surrounding circumstances including the position in which the plaintiff is going to have
to lift or move the load, must include such elements as stress or fatigue if they are
material. In considering the word 'likely' the judge considered three different meanings,
d which included, in the case of a repetitive process, one likely to occur at any time during
the process; referring to this latter approach the judge said:

'The position in this case is that the plaintiff, by her counsel, has expressly
declined, despite my invitation, to advance any argument based on that proposition.
If he had chosen to advance that argument then it would have to be considered
whether the formulation of the statutory duty could stand with the Court of Appeal
e   decision in *Bailey v Rolls Royce (1971) Ltd* [1984] ICR 688. I have not had to deal with
that proposition; therefore I have not had to consider whether or not it can stand
with the *Bailey* case. In view of the concession I will say no more, save that on the
findings of fact that I have made it will be appreciated that there is in my judgment
a likelihood, using that test, that there would be an injury caused to the plaintiff.
f   She had a congenital weakness in her back and, viewed over a prolonged period, on
the medical evidence and, indeed, the expert evidence, in my judgment the
combination of that weakness and the weight she was employed to lift or move
meant that sooner or later she would suffer an injury to her back. The likelihood in
that sense existed and, indeed, did materialise.'

Although, as appears from the judgment, this approach was not argued below counsel
g for the plaintiff in presenting the appeal adopted this approach and relied on the
judgments in *Bailey*'s case. He submitted that the judge had found as a fact that an
accident was likely to occur and did occur and that, therefore, 'taking the plaintiff as she
was' the requirements of s 72 were satisfied. Before accepting *Bailey*'s case as an authority
for 'taking the plaintiff as you find her' it is necessary to look a little closer at the
h judgments. In that case the plaintiff had been employed by the defendants as a paint-
sprayer working on metal components. The defendants' medical staff had known that
the plaintiff had injured his back on previous occasions but had not given any specific
advice to the defendants about his load-lifting capabilities. The plaintiff had consulted
his own doctor who had advised him to be careful but had not mentioned the matter to
the defendants. The plaintiff's work on the day of the accident included placing and
j positioning components on a hydraulically-operated turntable. He sprained his back,
although not seriously, while loading a heavy, circular component weighing 192½ lb and
trying to pull it into position on the turntable. The trial judge, after hearing conflicting
medical evidence, found that the plaintiff had a weak back, that the defendants knew of
that condition and that they had been negligent and in breach of statutory duty under

s 72(1). On appeal the Court of Appeal allowed the appeal on the basis that there was conflicting medical evidence and that there were no grounds for preferring one of the *a* conflicting views held by equally qualified practitioners on whether there had been a need before the plaintiff's injury to take measures to protect him from the risk of such injury and, therefore, held that no case had been made out in negligence. On the question of breach of statutory duty the court came to the conclusion that if the plaintiff had been employed to lift the particular load and in so doing it was likely he personally would suffer injury, that 'likely' in the subsection was to be construed as 'probable' or 'more *b* probable than not', and since there was no evidence that the plaintiff in lifting the particular object and placing it on the turntable would probably suffer injury the defendants were not in breach of their statutory duty. However, in the judgments of Stephenson and Slade LJJ it was said that the court had to consider the likelihood of injury to the particular employee irrespective of the question of whether the employers knew, or ought to have known, that the work was likely to cause that employee injury. *c*

In his judgment May LJ ([1984] ICR 688 at 698–699) referred to the speech of Lord Kilbrandon in *Brown v Allied Ironfounders Ltd* [1974] 2 All ER 135, [1974] 1 WLR 527:

'In the end, I think that the question is one of the proper construction of section 72(1) of the Act. This thereafter throws up two questions of fact. First, was the plaintiff "employed to lift . . . or move" the relevant casing? When one is considering *d* that part of the subsection, the emphasis is on the word "employed." This was extensively considered by the House of Lords in *Brown v. Allied Ironfounders Ltd.* ([1974] 2 All ER 135, [1974] 1 WLR 527). That was a case in which a woman employee had to turn a heavy stillage. It was accepted that if she had to do that without assistance it was likely to cause her injury, and the only question which then arose was whether she had been "employed . . . to move" the stillage on her *e* own within the meaning of section 72(1) of the Act of 1961. For present purposes I think it only necessary to refer to three passages from the speech of Lord Kilbrandon, where he said ([1974] 2 All ER 135 at 140, [1974] 1 WLR 527 at 533): "In the course of the day-to-day operation of a factory the employees are constantly moving weights as part of their duties under their contracts. Employers are not required or expected *f* to be on a constant watch to see that no one moves a weight which is too heavy for him, nor would such solicitude be well received, however kindly intentioned. It is clearly not called for by the terms of section 72. Often it must be left to the employee to make up the load he is to move; if the work does not necessarily involve the moving of injuriously heavy weights, but is quite compatible with the selection by the employee of a safe load for individual movement, the employer cannot be said *g* to have employed him to move a weight which was not safe." A little later, having given two factual examples, Lord Kilbrandon continued: ". . . I cannot believe that section 72 involves this, that whenever a man in the course of his employment lifts a load which is too heavy for him, then unless he had been forbidden to lift that load, he has been employed to lift that load." Finally, Lord Kilbrandon referred to the unusual paucity of decisions on the provisions of section 72(1), which after all *h* relate to a process, as he described it, which is of the essence of all industrial work, the lifting and moving of loads. He said ([1974] 2 All ER 135 at 141, [1974] 1 WLR 527 at 534): "The employer will not normally order dangerous loads to be handled, and the employee is too skilled and sensible to do it off his own bat. In any event, this is not the class of case in which the multiplication of citations is profitable." So much, then for the first part of section 72(1).' *j*

May LJ then continued to consider the meaning of the word 'likely' in the passage already cited in the judgment of Beldam LJ.

In his judgment Slade LJ said ([1984] ICR 688 at 700–701):

a
'Nevertheless, like May L.J., I have been driven to the conclusion that [counsel for the plaintiff] is right in submitting that one must take the words of the subsection simply as they stand. They make no express reference to what the employer knew or ought to have known. Nor, I think, can any such reference be implied from the words "likely to cause injury to him." In deciding whether a particular employee has been "employed to lift, carry or move any load so heavy as to be likely to cause injury" to that employee, within the meaning of the subsection, it seems to me that

b
the court must apply an objective test of likelihood (or otherwise) as at the date of the injury, without regard to the employers' actual or constructive knowledge of the circumstances of the particular employee. Nevertheless, the burden of proof must still rest on a plaintiff relying on the subsection to show that, on the evidence and on an application of this objective test, the defendant employer has broken the statutory duty owed to him; and in view of the use of the word "likely" in the

c
subsection, this involves showing not just a possibility but a likelihood of injury occurring at the date of the actual injury.'

Stephenson LJ agreed with the judgments of May and Slade LJJ emphasising that the two questions were not relevant to the consideration of s 72, namely whether the defendants knew or ought to have known that the load might cause injury to the plaintiff

d
and whether or not the load was likely to cause injury to other employees who were fit or in reasonably good health and without the back trouble from which the plaintiff suffered. In his submissions in support of the appeal counsel for the plaintiff relied on the judgments in this case for the proposition that 'the employer had to take the employee in the condition in which he was at the material time'. He relied in particular for this proposition on the inclusion of the words 'to him' at the end of the section. It is clear

e
from the judgments which I have cited that this court took the view in *Bailey v Rolls Royce (1971) Ltd* that the question whether a given load was likely, ie more probable than not, to cause injury to the employee was not an objective test but was subjective to the employee concered. However, it is quite obvious that there must be limits to the unbridled application of this concept. I do not read the judgments in *Bailey v Rolls Royce (1971) Ltd* as intending to go anything like the distance counsel for the plaintiff invited

f
the court to go, namely that however weak or sensitive the employee happened to be at the moment when the accident occurred, if the accident occurred then that was evidence that the load was likely to cause the injury. As Beldam LJ has pointed out in his judgment, this would place a hopelessly impractical burden on the employer who would be held absolutely liable for breach of statutory duty which has with it a criminal content if, owing to some transient injury sustained away from the place of work, a load which

g
previously would not have been likely to cause injury suddenly achieved that quality because of the change in the condition of the employee. I do not believe that Parliament could have intended such an irrational result when enacting s 72.

In my judgment the solution is to be found in a natural interpretation of the words 'likely to cause injury to him'. The closing words 'to him' must introduce the particular condition of the employee when he is given the task. If taking the employee with his

h
known characteristics it was likely that injury would be caused by the load which as part of his employment he was required to lift or move then the breach is established. But if the injury is occasioned because of some latent condition unknown to anyone or a transient change in condition, as I have already indicated, then the load could not be said to be 'likely to cause injury' because the word 'likely' imports a reasonable anticipation that the event will happen. Without the necessary information to form this conclusion

j
even on a subjective basis I cannot see that a breach of the statute would be occasioned. As I have said, with respect to the judgments in *Bailey v Rolls Royce (1971) Ltd*, this question did not really arise for determination in that appeal since the court came to the conclusion that it was not established, even with the condition of the plaintiff's back, that the load was likely to cause injury.

For these reasons I agree that the appeal should be dismissed.

Appeal dismissed.

Solicitors: *Tinsdills*, Stoke-on-Trent (for the plaintiff); *William F Hatton & Co*, Dudley (for the defendant).

Wendy Shockett Barrister.

Re St Bartholomew's, Aldbrough

YORK CONSISTORY COURT

CHANCELLOR THOMAS CONINGSBY QC

30 JANUARY, 21 FEBRUARY 1989

Ecclesiastical law – Faculty – Sale of chattel – Monument – Helmet – Funeral accoutrement associated with tomb – Helmet – Jurisdiction to grant faculty – Ownership of helmet – Helmet owned by heir-at-law of person commemorated – Heir-at-law agreeing to transfer ownership of helmet to parish in return for parish accepting responsibility for upkeep of tomb – Parish finances in chronic state of crisis – Whether consistory court having jurisdiction with respect to item remaining property of heir-at-law – Whether agreement between heir-at-law and parish giving sufficient interest in helmet to bring it within faculty jurisdiction – Whether faculty should be granted – Faculty Jurisdiction Measure 1964, s 3(4).

Ecclesiastical law – Church – Repairs and maintenance – Evidence as to repairs needed – Expert evidence to be given personally by fully-informed architect.

The incumbent, church treasurer, church secretary and parochial church council petitioned for a faculty to permit the sale of an ancient helmet. The helmet, which was English and dated from the fourteenth century, had been associated with the tomb commemorating Sir John de Melsa, who died in 1377, which was in the church. The helmet was part of the funerary armour placed with the monument at or shortly after death. The helmet was not complete but was historically a very important item. It had remained in the church until 1978, when largely for security reasons it was lent to the armoury at the Tower of London, where it had been put on public display. The church was in a small village in a sparsely populated part of a deeply rural coastal area of Yorkshire. It had an electoral roll of 30 and average attendances at services of 22 or 23. Many of the congregation were retired and/or without any great financial resources. By the late 1980s the parish had become unable to pay its diocesan quota and accordingly it lost its entitlement to a diocesan grant to meet the cost of repairs to the fabric of the church, some of which were urgently required. It was accepted that the ownership of the helmet was the same as that with regard to the tomb, and that accordingly, by virtue of s 3(4)[a] of the Faculty Jurisdiction Measure 1964, the owner of the helmet was the heir-at-law of the person commemorated. In 1988 the heir-at-law agreed to a transfer of ownership of the helmet to the church, followed by a sale by the church if a faculty were obtained. The parish agreed in return to accept responsibility for the upkeep of the tomb. The questions arose whether the consistory court had jurisdiction to grant a faculty authorising the sale of the helmet and, if so, whether it ought to grant such a faculty.

Held – (1) An item which remained the property of heirs-at-law (such as a tomb) and in respect of which there had been no agreement with the parish for any transfer of

---

[a]   Section 3(4), so far as material, is set out at p 443 *a b*, post

ownership was not an item within the court's jurisdiction in so far as an application by
a the parochial church council for sale was concerned. However, the agreement whereby
the heir-at-law and owner of the helmet had agreed that the ownership of the helmet
should pass to the church in exchange for the church accepting responsibility for the
tomb gave a sufficient interest in the helmet to bring it within the faculty jurisdiction.
The correct persons to whom the gift should be made were the churchwardens of the
parish, as it was they who held chattels as quasi-trustees for the parish (see p 445 *a* to *c*,
b post).

(2) The question which the court had to decide was whether there was an emergency
in the finances of the parochial church council due to the condition of the fabric and the
small congregation of the church, coupled with the question whether there were any
overriding policy considerations pointing against the grant of a faculty. On the evidence
the finances of the church could be described as being in a chronic state of crisis, with
c some work required to be done to the church urgently. There were accordingly good
and sufficient grounds for granting a faculty subject to any convincing points of principle
to the contrary. On the basis that it might be possible to sell the helmet for £20,000, an
income of £1,500 per annum could be produced by sensible investment, such a sum
making an appreciable contribution to the parish's income. The factors against granting
a faculty, namely the undesirability of separating articles with a close or artistic
d connection, the fear of establishing a precedent for the alienation of connected items, the
difficulty of arranging loans to museums and similar institutions such as the Royal
Armouries where an application for purchase might follow, and the need to look after
national treasures in church possession, were however of insufficient weight in the
circumstances to justify refusal of a faculty, provided substantial conditions were imposed
to ensure, inter alia, that the helmet remained in England and was kept on display to the
e public. A faculty would be granted accordingly (see p 446 *g*, p 447 *e f*, p 449 *a*, p 450 *d*
to *f*, p 451 *d f* to *j*, p 453 *j* to p 455 *b g*, p 456 *f* to *h* and p 457 *h*, post); dictum of the
deputy Dean of the Arches in *Re St Gregory's, Tredington* [1971] 3 All ER 269 at 272
applied; *Re St Gregory's, Tredington* [1971] 3 All ER 269 followed; *Re St Helen's, Brant
Broughton* [1973] 3 All ER 386, *Re St Mary's, Broadwater* [1976] 1 All ER 148 and *Re St
f Andrew's, Thornhaugh* [1976] 1 All ER 154 distinguished.

Per curiam. Expert evidence as to repairs needed to the fabric of a church should not
be given in an indirect way, such as by correspondence between an architect and the
parochial church council, but personally by a fully-informed architect (see p 450 *b*, post).

Notes

g For property in monuments, see 14 Halsbury's Laws (4th edn) para 1085.

For faculties relating to monuments, see ibid para 1316, and for cases on the subject,
see 19 Digest (Reissue) 451, 3559–3560.

For faculties relating to the contents of churches, see 14 Halsbury's Laws (4th edn) para
1318.

For the Faculty Jurisdiction Measure 1964, s 3, see 14 Halsbury's Statutes (4th edn)
h 340.

Cases referred to in judgment

St Andrew's, Thornhaugh, Re [1976] 1 All ER 154, [1976] Fam 230, [1976] 2 WLR 123,
Con Ct.

St Gregory's, Tredington, Re [1971] 3 All ER 269, [1972] Fam 236, [1971] 2 WLR 796,
j Arches Ct.

St Helen's, Brant Broughton, Re [1973] 3 All ER 386, [1974] Fam 16, [1973] 3 WLR 228,
Arches Ct.

*St Mary, Northolt (vicar and churchwardens) v St Mary, Northolt (parishioners), St George-in-
the-East (rector and churchwardens) v St George-in-the-East (parishioners)* [1920] P 97, Con
Ct.

St Mary's, Broadwater, Re [1976] 1 All 148, [1976] Fam 222, [1976] 2 WLR 116, Con Ct.
St Mary's, Gilston, Re [1966] 2 All ER 408, [1967] P 125, [1966] 2 WLR 697, Con Ct.
St Mary's, Westwell, Re [1968] 1 All ER 631, [1968] 1 WLR 513, Comm Ct.

Petition for faculty
By a petition dated 24 January 1984 the Aldbrough Parochial Church Council, George
Crawforth, Clarice Jackson and the Rev K G Skipper, the vicar of the parish of Aldbrough
in the Diocese of York, sought a faculty permitting the sale of the Great Basinet Skull, an
English helmet of the fourteenth century which was on loan to the Royal Armouries at
the Tower of London for a period of five years expiring on 28 December 1983. The
petition was not formally opposed but the Council for the Care of Churches and the
Royal Armouries both submitted written evidence to the court in opposition to the
petition and gave oral evidence as judge's witnesses. The facts are set out in the judgment.

The petitioners appeared in person.

Cur adv vult

21 February. The following judgment[1] was delivered.

THE CHANCELLOR. These proceedings were commenced by a petition dated
24 January 1984 by the incumbent, church treasurer, church secretary and parochial
church council of the parish of St Bartholomew's, Aldbrough in the diocese of York. The
petition asks for a faculty to permit the sale of an ancient helmet known as the Great
Basinet Skull, described in the petition as being 'English 15th century'. This helmet has
been associated for many years with a tomb commemorating Sir John de Melsa, who
died in 1377, which is in St Bartholomew's Church. Research has clarified the position so
that it is now clear that the helmet must have been part of the funerary armour placed
with the monument at or shortly after the death of Sir John de Melsa. The helmet is not
complete because it has lost its vizor and its chin-piece (if it originally had one), it has a
rust hole above the rear rim and it is generally corroded. Historically it is a very important
item but its defective condition is such that it would not be of great interest to a private
collector. It remained in the church until December 1978, when largely for security
reasons it was lent to the armoury of the Tower of London and since then it has been on
public display continuously at the Tower of London armoury. Before it went to the
armoury it had been kept in a safe for security reasons. Prior to that it had been in a
position in the church suspended over the de Melsa tomb. In the seventeenth and
eighteenth centuries it had not been properly looked after; at the time when part of the
church building was used as a school the tomb itself was moved into the belfry of the
church and the helmet was allowed to deteriorate. Now that it is being looked after by
the Tower of London armoury its condition is being preserved and, since it is the
petitioners' proposal that if a faculty is granted the basinet should be sold to the Tower of
London armoury, but that if it is not sold it should remain there on permanent loan, its
future preservation may be considered to be secure.
   In considering whether or not to grant a faculty the court has to be concerned not only
with whether or not the petitioners have made out a case for allowing the disposal of a
valuable and historic item but also with the question of its ownership. Since it is accepted
that this helmet must have been part of the funerary accoutrements of Sir John de Melsa,
deposited in the church at the time of the erection of the de Melsa monument, the
principle with regard to ownership of the helmet is the same as that with regard to the

---

1   Those parts of the judgment relating to a narration of the course of the proceedings and the
    evidence submitted to the court have been summarised by the Chancellor for the purposes of this
    report.

tomb, and the appropriate principle is that the owner of these items is the heir-at-law of
a the person commemorated. Section 3(4) of the Faculty Jurisdiction Measure 1964
provides:

'. . . owner means the person who erected the monument in question and, after
his death, the heir or heirs at law of the person or persons in whose memory the
monument was erected . . .'

b (See *Re St Andrew's, Thornhaugh* [1976] 1 All ER 154 at 159, [1976] Fam 230 at 235.)
As a result of research carried out early in 1987 by Mr C B L Barr of York Minister
library (to whom I am extremely indebted) it became clear that the heir-at-law in the
present case is the 15th Earl of Huntingdon and I will make reference to the
correspondence which there has been with members of his family, he now being an
elderly gentleman unable to deal personally with correspondence.

c
Course of the proceedings
When the York Diocesan Advisory Committee considered the petition in July 1984 it
decided to support it but subject to a recommendation that the basinet should remain in
England, either at the Tower of London or in some other secure place, and that it should
be on view to the public. In February 1985 I gave a direction that the petition should be
d referred to the Council for the Care of Churches and on 7 March 1985 the council
provided its first report. This was prepared by Mr Claude Blair, who has carried out an
immense amount of research into the history of the helmet and I am most indebted to
him. The report also included a description of the church itself and its situation. The
church is sited about one mile from the Yorkshire coast, approximately ten miles north-
east of Hull. The arch of one doorway is Norman, the lower part of the west tower is
e early thirteenth century, the top stage of the tower is fifteenth century, the chancel is
fourteenth century and the nave arcades are nineteenth century. Apart from the tomb of
Sir John de Melsa there is another tomb on which lies the effigy of a lady, dating from
the late fourteenth century. Because of its association with the de Melsa monument Mr
Blair was satisfied that the helmet must date from before 1377 and it is therefore one of
f the earliest helmet-forms of its type. It is one of three dating from before 1400 which
can be associated with specific monuments, the other two being the achievements of the
Black Prince of Canterbury and the helmet of Sir Richard Pembridge (which formerly
hung over his monument in Hereford Cathedral). Because of its poor condition the
basinet is not likely to be particularly attractive to private collectors and he concluded (in
1985) that its value was in the region of £15,000. He noted that the Tower of London
g Armouries had provided the church with a convincing replica of the helmet, which is in
fibreglass and which hangs over the de Melsa monument. Mr Blair was concerned that a
sale in the present case might be treated as a precedent for other applications for the sale
of items placed with museums. At the hearing Mr Blair gave evidence, and two further
reports were presented by him. The Council for the Care of Churches opposes the
petition. I should, however, mention that in a letter dated 19 March 1985 (which
h accompanied Mr Blair's first report) the Council for the Care of Churches (as then
constituted) was prepared to accept the possibility of a private treaty sale to the Tower of
London Armouries (now called the Royal Armouries) if the financial circumstances of
the church made this necessary, and the main concern of the council as expressed in that
letter was that there should be no sale by public auction or in any other way which would
lead to the basinet disappearing from public view. The letter indicated that the council
j as a whole took a slightly different view of the petition from that of Mr Blair. In his
evidence Mr Blair explained that since the letter of March 1985 the membership of the
Council for the Care of Churches had substantially altered and the new council took a
more stringent view than its predecessor.
In March 1985 I gave a direction designed to ascertain the views of the Master of the
Armouries and this led to a letter from the then master, Mr A V B Norman, in May

1985. He said that the Royal Armouries were not in a position to make an offer but that, in the event of a sale being permitted by faculty, the Royal Armouries would have to consider a purchase of the helmet. He did not wish the Royal Armouries to be in a position where, following a loan of an item by a church, the Royal Armouries felt virtually compelled to purchase the item in question.

In May 1985 I gave a direction that the petitioners should seek to identify the heir-at-law of Sir John de Melsa and this led to the approach to Mr C B L Barr. He was able to establish the line of succession from Sir John de Melsa to the present Earl of Huntingdon and he suggested that the problem of ownership of the helmet could be dealt with either by the Earl renouncing ownership in favour of the parish or by the Earl making a present of the helmet to the Royal Armouries. There was then correspondence between the petitioners and the Earl of Huntingdon and this resulted in a letter dated 25 January 1988 from Lady Selina Hastings, the Earl's daughter, saying that Lord Huntingdon did not wish to stand in the way of the parish and would waive his rights to ownership of the helmet. Later, on 5 December 1988, Lady Selina Hastings wrote: 'I am writing to let you know that my father, Lord Huntingdon, has no objection to sale of the Aldbrough Helmet.' In its context that clearly meant a transfer of ownership from Lord Huntingdon to St Bartholomew's, followed by a sale by the church if a faculty were obtained. In other correspondence the parish agreed to accept responsibility for the upkeep of the tomb of Sir John de Melsa and also of the other medieval tomb to which I have referred.

On 1 August 1987 the then Archdeacon of the East Riding, the Ven Michael Vickers, provided a letter drawing attention to the need of the parish for funds for the restoration of its church and his letter is generally supportive of the petition. Subsequently his successor as archdeacon, the Ven Hugh Buckingham, visited the church and advised the parish that it would need to demonstrate to the court in detail its financial problems and fabric needs. He did not express any view contrary to the merits of the petition and when he gave evidence at the Consistory Court hearing on 13 January 1989 he said that he was sympathetic towards the petitioners' application.

Following a letter from the registrar inquiring whether the diocesan advisory committee wished to give evidence at the hearing, the secretary of the committee (the Rev Edwin Newlyn) wrote to the registrar confirming that in 1984 the committee had supported the sale of the basinet subject to the terms of the sale being made known and that the basinet would remain in this country, preferably at the Tower of London. That position was maintained by the committee at the hearing.

In November 1988 a letter was received from Mr G M Wilson, the current Master of the Armouries. He confirmed the view of his predecessor that if a sale were to be permitted the Royal Armouries would be the most appropriate body to ensure that the helmet would be preserved. He said that the valuer to the Royal Armouries felt that the helmet was now worth a figure in the region of £20,000 as an insurance valuation. For purposes of a purchase price he would expect the figure to be in the range of £15,000 to £20,000.

The hearing took place on 30 January 1989 in the Consistory Court Room of York Minster. I make a finding that the heir-at-law of Sir John de Melsa is the 15th Earl of Huntingdon and I have reached a clear conclusion, on a balance of probabilities, that the helmet was a funeral accoutrement associated from the outset with the tomb. Therefore the owner of the helmet is Lord Huntingdon. On the correspondence to which I have referred I find that Lady Selina Hastings has authority to act on behalf of her father and that she, on his behalf, has clearly stated her father's willingness to give the basinet to St Bartholomew's, with the knowledge that St Bartholomew's will endeavour to sell the basinet to the Royal Armouries and to have the benefit of the proceeds of sale, subject to such directions as I may give in relation to those proceeds.

The petitioners' interest

In law it is only open to me to make a decision on the petition if the petitioners have a

sufficient interest in the helmet to bring it within my jurisdiction. An item which
a remains the property of heirs-at-law (such as the tomb) and in respect of which there has
been no agreement with the parish for any transfer of ownership is not an item within
my jurisdiction at least in so far as an application by these petitioners for sale is concerned.
However, in the present case there has clearly been an agreement, arising from the
correspondence with Lady Selina Hastings, whereby Lord Huntingdon has expressed his
agreement for the ownership of the helmet to pass to St Bartholomew's in exchange for
b St Bartholomew's accepting responsibility for the de Melsa tomb and the other tomb (of
which it is quite likely that Lord Huntingdon is also the heir-at-law). That agreement
gives a sufficient interest in the helmet to these petitioners to bring it within faculty
jurisdiction. I consider however that the correct persons to whom the gift should be
made by Lord Huntingdon are the churchwardens of the parish as it is churchwardens
who hold chattels as quasi-trustees for the parish. If a faculty is to be granted it will be
c necessary to join the churchwardens as petitioners. I see from the petition that one of the
churchwardens has signed it but the signature is obscure and it is not clear to me that
this churchwarden is actually one of the petitioners named at the head of the petition. In
any event if there are two churchwardens both of them should be parties to the
proceedings.

I heard evidence at the hearing from Mr Barr (in confirmation of his written evidence).
d I then heard from the Rev Kenneth Skipper, the incumbent, and from Mr Jackson, the
church treasurer (on behalf of the petitioners). I heard Mr Claude Blair on behalf of the
Council for the Care of Churches. I heard Mr Wilson, the Master of the Royal Armouries,
and I heard the Rev Edwin Newlyn (secretary of the diocesan advisory committee) and
Canon Buckingham, the archdeacon. As I have said, there were no formal objectors, but
since the Council for the Care of Churches and the Royal Armouries were basically
e opposed to the parish being allowed to alienate a historic item such as this helmet I gave
Mr Blair and Mr Wilson the opportunity to put questions to the other witnesses. I also
gave them the opportunity to address me after the evidence was concluded, but in the
event the only address was that of Mr Skipper. There was no legal representation, but I
do not comment adversely on this. In view of the existing financial problems at St
Bartholomew's it would clearly have been a considerable additional burden on them to
f have legal representation and I consider that they made the right decision in not doing
so. This, however, did mean that I did not have the benefit of any reference to legal
authorities on the question of the sale of valuable items by a church, or on the question
of ownership by the heir-at-law, and I therefore indicated through directions at an early
stage that I would need to reserve my judgment in order to do some legal research
myself.
g

Previously decided cases

Re St Gregory's, Tredington [1971] 3 All ER 269, [1972] Fam 236 is a decision of the
Arches Court of Canterbury (G H Newsom QC, Deputy Dean of the Arches). The decision
was in October 1970 and it was by way of appeal from the Coventry Consistory Court,
h where Chancellor Gage had refused a faculty for churchwardens to sell on the open
market two sixteenth century silver livery pots or flagons. The deputy dean allowed the
appeal and granted a faculty permitting the sale of the flagons, subject to certain
conditions. The reason given by the petitioners for wanting to sell the flagons was that
the parish was faced with a financial emergency caused by the condition of the fabric of
the church. The flagons were made and given in 1591 and 1638 respectively and were
j valued at £35,000. The flagons had at one time been used as communion plate but had
not been used in recent years as the church was otherwise provided with adequate plate.
At least £16,000 was required for immediate work on the fabric of the church. As in the
present case there were no formal objectors to the petition but the chancellor received
evidence from a member of the Council for the Care of Churches, from the diocesan
advisory committee and also from the Archdeacon of Warwick, and it was on the basis of

the evidence from these witnesses that he refused the faculty. These witnesses could not be professionally cross-examined because the petitioners were not legally represented. During the course of his judgment the deputy dean suggested that in those circumstances the court should ask the archdeacon to enter a formal appearance to the proceedings and to be ready either to cross-examine witnesses himself or to engage a solicitor or counsel to do so. Applying those considerations to the present case, I do not feel that it would have materially affected the overall evidence if Mr Blair and Mr Wilson had been professionally cross-examined on behalf of the parish. Mr Skipper was able to put appropriate questions to them and I felt it useful for the archdeacon to remain in a neutral position rather than becoming a protagonist on either side.

In *Re St Gregory's* the deputy dean went on to deal with the chancellor's jurisdiction to grant a faculty for sale and said that in his view it was clear that there was such jurisdiction. After a reference to *The Ecclesiastical Law of the Church of England* (1st edn, 1873) pp 1792, 1797, by Sir Robert Phillimore, Dean of the Arches, the deputy dean said ([1971] 3 All ER 269 at 272, [1972] Fam 236 at 240–241):

> 'These passages recognise that while church goods are not in the ordinary way in commerce or available for sale and purchase, yet the churchwardens with the consent of the vestry (now the parochial church council) and the authority of a faculty may sell them or even give them away. Without such consent and authority the churchwardens cannot pass the legal interest which is vested in them. To obtain a faculty some good and sufficient ground must be proved. In the case of a sale, one of the grounds suggested by Sir Robert Phillimore is redundancy. It is not an essential ground or the only possible ground. But some special reason is required if goods which were given to be used in specie are to be converted into money. This is not a jurisdiction to authorise changes of investment. Like all faculties, of course, this kind is a matter for the chancellor's judicial discretion, and the evidence will mainly be directed to helping him with its exercise. The existence of the jurisdiction has been recognised since Sir Robert Phillimore wrote in at least four reported cases: *St Mary, Northolt (Vicar and Churchwardens) v St Mary, Northolt (Parishioners)* [1920] P 97, *Re St Mary's, Gilston* [1966] 2 All ER 408, [1967] P 125, and *Re St Mary's, Westwell* [1968] 1 All ER 631, [1968] 1 WLR 513.'

In the present case we are, of course, not dealing with communion plate but with armour and there may be some differences of principle in the approach which should be adopted. Nevertheless, I consider that the broad principles of what is said by the deputy dean apply in the present case and in particular the statement that 'To obtain a faculty some good and sufficient ground must be proved'. I would add that before a faculty can be granted there ought not to be any substantial reason of policy which would indicate against the granting of a faculty and I will return to that aspect later.

The facts of *Re St Gregory's* are of interest in that it was a case of financial need. St Gregory's Church, Tredington, was a fairly large country church which had reached its present shape by the end of the fifteenth century. The parish had 573 names on the roll of parliamentary electors and there was a church electoral roll of 67. The living was held in plurality with another living. Church attendances at Holy Communion averaged about eight and at matins they averaged about 28. It was a small worshipping community relative to the population of the parish and it was on the worshipping community that the expense of keeping up the church rested. There were nine members of the parochial church council all of whom voted in favour of the proposal to sell the flagons. The accounts of the church council for four years before the hearing were in evidence and showed a considerable effort on the part of the congregation to make ends meet. The deputy dean found that there was an immediate need for £3,150 and he said that in his judgment, taking together the figures of church attendance, the accounts and the evidence of the architect, there was a financial crisis in the affairs of Tredington church. He clearly took the view that the church could not make ends meet because at one stage

he discussed the possibility of declaring the church redundant under the Pastoral Measure
a 1968, although he did accept that it was right for the church to be retained for pastoral
reasons. The deputy dean found that the chancellor had exercised his discretion wrongly
in that he had given weight to certain matters which were either irrelevant or to which
little weight should have been given. He said that the responsibility for the future of the
church lay on the parochial church council and the members of the congregation rather
than those members of the parish who did not attend church. With regard to a proposal
b that the flagons could be placed in a museum on loan, he said that in a museum the
flagons would not be used for their original purpose and that their presence there would
not help with the problem of the upkeep of the church. In response to an argument that
the flagons were part of the local history of the church he pointed out that, while that
was undoubtedly so, the value of selling the flagons would be that the church itself would
be preserved, the church being a more important part of local history than any items of
c its contents. He felt that, as the items had been in a museum for some time, they had in
fact been diverted from their original purpose. He felt that the proceeds of sale would be
more useful to the church (in both senses of that word) than the flagons had been over
recent years. In response to an argument that to sell the flagons would be contrary to the
intentions of the donor he said that to keep them in a bank or museum was also contrary
to those intentions. He said that the grounds for granting the faculty were that the
d flagons were redundant to the needs of the church and that there was an emergency in
the finances of the parochial church council due to the state of the fabric and the small
congregation of the church. Finally he said that he did not wish to be understood as
saying that these were the only grounds for exercising a discretion in favour of sale but
that other kinds of cases might be considered as and when they arose, but that in all cases
the jurisdiction should be sparingly exercised. *Re St Gregory's* being a decision on appeal
e I must clearly give primary weight to it and I consider that the central question for me
to decide is whether there is 'an emergency in the finances of the parochial church
council due to the state of the fabric and the small congregation of the church', coupled
with the question of whether there are any overriding considerations of policy which
point against granting a faculty.

In *Re St Helen's, Brant Broughton* [1973] 2 All ER 386 at 388, [1974] Fam 16 at 18 Sir
f Harold Kent, Dean of the Arches, also deciding a case in the appellate jurisdiction,
referred to *Re St Gregory's, Tredington* as 'setting out the general principles of law
applicable' in a case involving the sale of chattels. In *Re St Helen's* the chattel was a
painting worth between £10,000 and £40,000. Sir Harold Kent said that he was 'in
agreement' with the statement of the law as set out in *Re St Gregory's*. In *Re St Helen's*,
which was an appeal from Chancellor Goodman (Diocese of Lincoln), the Dean of the
g Arches refused to disturb the decision of the chancellor that the petitioners had failed to
discharge the onus of proving a good and sufficient ground for a faculty for sale. The
application had been made on the basis, inter alia, of financial need but the Dean of the
Arches found that while there were certain financial pressures on the parish it had been
able to meet its expenses up to the present time and there was 'no immediate financial
h crisis' and that there were no grounds for supposing that a crisis would necessarily arise
in the future. The accounts for the parish for the past few years showed a small deficit in
one year and a small surplus in another, but the basic picture was of a parish which could
meet its obligations. Another ground for asking for sale was that the picture had become
expensive to insure, but the Dean of the Arches took the view that it need not be insured
for its full value, but only on the basis that enough money should be available to provide
j a replacement 'of some distinction' and there was evidence that the insurance premium
for the first year was available and could be met out of parish funds in future years.

There are two decisions at first instance reported in 1976 and each of them relates to
an application for the sale of a helmet, being an accoutrement of a tomb. The first is *Re
St Mary's, Broadwater* [1976] 1 All ER 148, [1976] Fam 222, a decision of the Chichester
Consistory Court in 1974. The chancellor allowed the petition. There was no formal

opposition to the petition but the Diocesan Art Council opposed the sale and
recommended that the helmet should be placed on loan at the royal armoury in the *a*
Tower of London. The witness who gave evidence for the Diocesan Art Council said that
he disapproved of the disposal of the helmet because one should not dissociate associated
objects and this helmet formed part of the funeral accoutrements which should be
associated with the tomb of Lord De La Warr. The church did not put forward a financial
need in relation to maintenance of its fabric but it wished to sell the helmet in order to
finance the employment of an additional curate, for which the parish had a need. It was *b*
a parish of some 24,000 persons and the church provided five services each Sunday at
which attendances were good. There were also four services at the daughter church of St
Stephen. The staff of the church consisted of the incumbent, two curates (one attached to
St Stephen's) and a parish worker. The chancellor granted the faculty for sale on the open
market, having reached a conclusion that the Royal Armouries were unlikely to be able
to match the market price for the helmet, but he directed that there should be a reserve *c*
price. He further directed that the proceeds of sale should be applied, after costs, for the
provision of a stipend for a new assistant curate, the capital fund to be held by the
Chichester diocesan board of finance.

In *Re St Andrew's, Thornhaugh* [1976] 1 All ER 154, [1976] Fam 230 a faculty for the
sale of a helmet was refused. The petition was opposed by the diocesan advisory
committee, the Master of the Armouries of the Tower of London, the Church of England *d*
Council for Places of Worship (now the Council for the Care of Churches) and one
parishioner. The first ground for dismissing the petition was that the ownership of the
tomb in the church and its accoutrements (the helmet) remained in the heir-at-law of the
deceased and that as the chancellor had not received any evidence as to who the heir-at-
law might be, he did not have jurisdiction to grant the petition. However, he went on to
deal with the position which would have arisen if the question of ownership had been *e*
resolved, and he said that a monument and its accoutrements should be separated only
in exceptional circumstances since a monument and it accoutrements should be regarded
as one entity and should not normally be separated. He accepted that a factor would be
the problem of security but in the case of St Andrew's he did not regard the element of
risk in leaving the helmet hanging above the tomb as particularly high. He said that it
was clearly the intention of those who originally placed the helmet in that position that *f*
it should remain there and that such intention should not lightly be interfered with. He
did not accept a suggestion that the helmet should be kept in safe custody and replaced
by a replica in fibre glass. He held that the petitioners had failed to establish a case which
would justify an order for sale. There were formal objections to the petition by the
Archdeacon of Oakham on behalf of the diocesan advisory committee, the Dean of
Peterborough on behalf of the Council for Places of Worship, Mr Dufty, the Master of *g*
the Armouries and a parishioner, Mrs Dorothy Ellison. A little evidence was given to the
chancellor that the church was having difficulty in meeting its diocesan quota, but it had
only had difficulty in one year, and this case does not seem to have been developed in
detail. The sum to be realised on a sale of the helmet would have been in the order of
£700 to £1,000. There was no appeal against the chancellor's decision.

The facts of the present case differ in certain substantial respects from those of *Re St* *h*
Andrew's. In particular I received more detailed evidence about the financial position of
the parish and I would not think it right to hold that the de Melsa helmet could properly
be restored to its place in St Bartholomew's church because of the risk of theft. Also I
heard evidence from the incumbent and church treasurer as to substantial repair work
which is needed to St Bartholomew's, but evidence of that nature was not adduced in *Re* *j*
St Andrew's. It is further to be noted that in that case there was active opposition from
the diocesan advisory committee, the archdeacon and a parishioner, whereas that is not
so in the present case. The resolution in the present case in support of the petition was
carried by eight votes in favour, none against and one abstention, and later when the
question of taking responsibility for the de Melsa Tombs arose the parochial church
council was unanimous.

Summary of evidence

a   It is clear from citing these authorities, and particularly those in the Court of the Arches, that I have to weigh carefully the evidence given to me on behalf of the petitioners as to their financial needs on the one hand and the points of principle raised by the Council for the Care of Churches and the Master of the Armouries on the other. I will therefore summarise the evidence which was given to me. Mr Skipper, the incumbent, told me that the church was in a poor financial position and that a great deal

b   of work needed to be done on the fabric. If sale of the helmet is permitted the capital sum received will be retained but the interest from this will be used for fabric repairs and maintenance. The parish owes £3,373 to the York Diocesan Board of Finance Ltd by way of unpaid quota. This debt has been built up over a period of years. By 31 December 1985 the sum owing was already £1,215. For the year to 31 December 1986 there was default to the extent of £947 (being six out of twelve monthly payments). In the year

c   1987 there was a default in respect of four months. In the year 1988 the default was in respect of three months; there was therefore no year after 1984 when the parish could meet its quota. There has been very little money available to spend on fabric. In the relevant years between 1985 and 1988 the total receipts of the parish were approximately £4,000 per annum and the church had to rely heavily on gift days, fetes and bazaars, since its covenanted giving and collections produced an income of only about £1,000 per

d   annum. In one year the income was somewhat larger when there was an urgent need for more maintenance and repair work. An architect's report in 1985 listed some 60 items of repair to the church (and the churchyard walls) which needed to be done. Of these 39 items are urgent matters. At the date of the hearing it had not been possible for any of the items in the 1985 report to be carried out except for some work on rainwater goods. The items outstanding include such matters as repointing, attention to tiles, further work

e   to rainwater goods, treatment of exposed rafters and removal of certain banks of earth resting against the lower part of the church walls. The electoral roll consists of 30 names. The population of the village is a little over 1,000. Average attendances at St Bartholomew's are 22 or 23. If the parish were able to pay its diocesan quota in full the diocese would provide a grant of 10% of the cost of fabric repairs. Due to non-payment of quota the parish had lost its entitlement to this grant. Mr Skipper is responsible for

f   two other parishes, each of which has financial difficulties but not of the same gravity as St Bartholomew's. The other parishes have two churches each. Mr Skipper has given thought to ways of 'making ends meet' at St Bartholomew's but feels that very little more could be done. Each special fundraising event will raise no more than between £60 and £120.

g   Mr Skipper told me that the accounts for the year ended 31 December 1988 would be available soon and I therefore asked that these should be sent to me, so that if possible I could consider them before giving judgment. I received them on 23 February 1989 and will treat them as part of the evidence. They do not show any significant change in the financial position of the parish. Total income was £4,368·41 against total expenditure of £4,440·96, a deficit of £72·55. Diocesan quota amounting to £1,368·21 was paid, but

h   the monthly payments for October, November and December (as in earlier years) were not paid due to absence of funds. The largest item of income was 'gift days, fetes and bazaars: £1,269·51'. The regular income amounted to only £1,297·48. There was a small excess of income over expenditure of £147·64 from the Stamford Hall. During the year only £178·37 was spent on the church fabric, leaving a small sum of £379·58 in the fabric fund at the end of the year. There was also at that date £860·73 in the ordinary

j   account, a sum which I calculate to be about enough to cover the regular outgoings of the church for some two months. Over the four-year period for which I have the figures the gross income of the parish has only increased by £700 in spite of what I consider to be substantial fund-raising efforts.

    Mr Jackson, a resident of Aldbrough, is the treasurer of the parochial church council. He listed the various fabric repairs which were needed and pointed out that these had been outstanding for three and half years. He submitted a letter from the church's new architect (Mr Blackmore), which I admitted in evidence without objection. This expressed concern about the rotten state of certain pew platforms and it listed the particularly urgent repair works needed. Dampness penetrates through the walls of the church because of the raised level of earth on the outside. There is a need for electricial rewiring and replacement of the flue of the boiler. As he had only recently taken over as church architect he had not yet had an opportunity of inspecting the tower but understood from his predecessor that work was needed there. He estimated that no less than £20,000 would be needed for fabric work. I consider it to be unsatisfactory that expert evidence as to these matters is being given in an indirect way through the letter from Mr Blackmore and through the church treasurer, Mr Jackson, and in future cases the court will require such evidence to be given personally by a fully-informed architect. However, in this particular instance the parish is in difficulty over the fact that its previous architect, Mr Tooley, retired shortly before the hearing in November 1988. I find that there are a number of urgent repair works needed in this church. The boiler flue will need to have about £450 spent on it. The wooden platforms under the pews and the floors beneath them need considerable work and the problem is of long standing. The last electrical wiring was in 1947 or 1948 and rewiring is needed. External walls need to be repointed. The north-east roof is leaking. There are sections of the churchyard wall which need to be rebuilt or repaired. The ground level outside the church walls needs to be reduced and a new lightning conductor needs to be installed. My general impression of the cost of repairs needed does not differ substantially from the estimate of £20,000 in Mr Blackmore's letter, although I am able to make a definite finding as to costings. I am satisfied that this church has substantial expenditure to meet in the very near future and its existing resources are inadequate. Its accounts show that it has not been able to spend any substantial sums on its fabric in the last five to ten years.

The crucial factors in this case as far as the church's needs are concerned are the smallness of its congregation (no more than 23 on average, with 30 on the electoral roll), the fact that many of these people are retired and/or without any great financial resources and the evidence from the accounts and diocesan record of quota payments, all of which indicate that the church has been in serious financial difficulty for some time. This is a congregation which had become unable by the late 1980s to pay its way in terms of the quota obligation coupled with the obligation to maintain a quite substantial church building (and also a church hall). It does not surprise me that its resources are inadequate. The church is in a relatively small village in a rather sparsely populated part of a deeply-rural coastal area. I inquired if there was anyone in the parish, or who had an interest in this church, to whom any special approach for financial support could be made, but the answer was in the negative. My findings about this church are based not only on its own accounts and the position given to me about its financial situation, but on the evidence of Mr Skipper as to the financial difficulties he is experiencing in his two other parishes (and four other churches), coupled with the indications given to me by the present Archdeacon of the East Riding (and his predecessor) as to the state of affairs generally in this rather remote part of the diocese. When the Ven Hugh Buckingham gave evidence he said that this part of Yorkshire (known as Holderness) is the part of the diocese which is having the greatest financial difficulty. The churchpeople there are faithful but there are simply less of them. He spoke of the problems in Holderness being similar to those in other sparsely populated rural areas of the country where there is little or no national support for local people in the maintenance of their churches and where diocesan quotas have increased very steeply in recent years. The diocease itself does not have funds available since, if it were to provide more money for the maintenance of churches, it would simply have to increase quota. He confirmed that in principle it would not be possible for St Bartholomew's to be given any special treatment by the diocese. He raised a question whether St Bartholomew's might be eligible for a grant from English Heritage, but Mr Skipper had already given evidence that this had been investigated under the previous Archdeacon of the East Riding, and that the church had not been considered to

be of sufficient importance to be eligible. In any event English Heritage will grant 40%
a of the cost of major repairs, but will not contribute towards maintenance. Electrical
rewiring and some of the other outstanding works would not be reckoned as repair work.
The archdeacon's assessment of St Bartholomew's was that it had continued to default in
its quota to some extent year by year. He was asked if there was any scope for reducing
the quota but indicated that this was highly unlikely as the allocation was made within
the deanery, which would be fully aware of the problems of St Bartholomew's and of
b other churches in the area. The archdeacon said that the overall shortfall on quota in the
diocese as a whole was only 1·5%. Out of that a very high proportion related to churches
in Holderness. He concluded by saying that he had considerable sympathy for the
incumbent and the other petitioners over their financial plight and that he agreed with
their proposition that a helmet is an item which is only marginally concerned with the
Christian faith and is not to be looked on as in the same category as an item such as a
c chalice.

Conclusions as to financial state of parish
    I have reached the conclusion that the financial affairs of St Bartholomew's can be
d described as in a state of 'crisis'. It is a state of affairs which has been in existence for a
number of years and can therefore be described as a chronic state and I accept and adopt
the view of the archdeacon that the church's inability to meet its quota in full will
continue for the foreseeable future. It is the parochial church council of the church
which has responsibility for the financial affairs of the church, but with an electoral roll
of as few as 30, it is understandable that the parochial church council is unable to meet
e its legal responsibilities. Matters have become more difficult since the cases reported in
1976 to which I have referred were decided, because of (a) steep increases in quota since
then and (b) increases in real terms in the cost of repair and maintenance work for
churches arising from the fact that this is a labour-intensive area. I think that some of the
work which is required to be done to this church can properly be described as urgent. I
f place the work to the platforms under the pews and the removal of soil from the outside
walls as in this category, with possibly the electrical rewiring and the boiler work in
addition. In any event, even if the work is not to be regarded as urgent, I would still have
to find that there was a financial crisis in the church and, following the decision in *Re St
Gregory's, Tredington* [1971] 3 All ER 269, [1972] Fam 236, I would find that there was a
'good and sufficient ground' for a faculty subject to any convincing points of principle to
the contrary. If St Bartholomew's does not receive additional funds from some source I
g fail to see how it will be able to prevent the eventual closure of the church. This would
come about either by the diocese having to introduce a pastoral scheme to declare the
church redundant because the church was unable to pay its diocesan quota, or because
the church was becoming dilapidated through non-repair. Those events might be some
time away, but there is a powerful argument on the side of the petitioners that it is right
h to enable them to obtain some income from the proceeds of sale of the helmet in order
to prevent these events occurring. Seen in that light the petitioners are acting prudently
in seeking to obtain income from an available source. Indeed, if they were to make no
effort to try to do this they might fall under criticism.
    Another factor in the equation is that I have to be satisfied that the exercise of selling
the helmet is a sufficiently worthwhile one in financial terms. On the basis that it may
j be possible to obtain £20,000 my conclusion is that the sum obtained will be far from
negligible and that the exercise is worth while. Invested in a sensible way it should
produce about £1,500 per annum and, in terms of an annual income at present of about
£5,000, such a sum can be seen as making an appreciable contribution. The income
available may well be sufficient to enable the parish to carry out the repairs which are
necessary and to put the parish back into a financially viable state.

The case for the opponents

However, I have to consider the arguments made to me both by Mr Blair and by Mr **a**
Wilson against the granting of a faculty because these raise important points of principle
which could prevail against the arguments of the petitioners. Mr Blair is a member of
the metalworks sub-committee of the Council for the Care of Churches, and has held
that post for many years. He impressed me as a man of great expertise and he is not
unsympathetic to the plight of the petitioners. I have already referred to his first and
second reports and there is a third report dated 21 January 1989. This report is mainly **b**
confirming the attribution of a clear connection between the helmet and the de Melsa
tomb, which means that the helmet is a very early one. Mr Blair said that it would be
worth about £50,000 if it was in fine condition, but that unfortunately it is really hardly
more than a 'rather large fragment'. It is therefore worth between £15,000 and £20,000.
He said that the Council for the Care of Churches was concerned that if a faculty in the
present case is allowed a precedent might be established for other parishes to say that **c**
because an article had been away from the parish for some years the connection with the
parish had been severed. He pointed out that if such applications were to be made in any
numbers it will then become difficult to arrange loans of precious items to museums
because museums will fear the possibility of being virtually forced into purchasing the
items at a later stage. He explained the position with regard to export licences, but in the
event I do not think that evidence is relevant to the present case. Mr Blair said that in his **d**
view care should be taken not to breach the principle lying behind the ecclesiastical
exemption from listed building control. The Church of England has committed itself to
a proper system for ensuring the care of national treasures and it is important that no
impression should be given that it is failing to live up to what it has promised. He
confirmed that St Bartholomew's was not a church which would be likely to be eligible
for a grant from English Heritage. He agreed that it was hard on an individual parish to **e**
be faced on the one hand with a policy on the part of the church that church buildings
and their contents should be fully maintained and the contents not alienated, while at
the same time no financial help was forthcoming for individual parishes in meeting
those commitments.

Mr Wilson, Master of the Armouries, said that his solution was that the existing loan **f**
to the Armouries should continue, since he agreed that the helmet could not be returned
to the church for reasons of safety. If the Earl retained ownership rather than giving the
helmet to the church he would suggest that the Earl should present it to the Royal
Armouries. If however the helmet was given to the parish and a faculty was granted for
sale, it would then be for the trustees of the Royal Armouries to decide whether or not to
purchase the item. In this respect he said that there were problems both of principle and
of finance involved. On the financial side the Royal Armouries had funds of £300,000 **g**
available in 1989 for purchases but was already committed to purchases amounting to
£360,000. Other items had been offered to the Royal Armouries and the Armouries had
already agreed to purchases amounting to £30,000. There were, however, a number of
ways in which extra money could be made available over and above the grant of
£300,000 per annum. These included application for adjustment in the amount of the **h**
grant from the Department of the Environment and an appeal to the National Heritage
Memorial Fund, which was established in 1983, being a central fund for the preservation
of objects of national importance. Mr Wilson could not say whether or not funds could
be made available for the purchase of the de Melsa helmet by these means, although he
did not rule this out. He said that the de Melsa helmet had been on continuous display
since it went on loan to the Royal Armouries and it was an item which was important in **j**
the collection. He said that £20,000 was the absolute limit which might be paid for the
helmet. The point of principle involved as far as the Royal Armouries are concerned is
that if the de Melsa helmet becomes available for sale and is in fact purchased by the
Royal Armouries that might encourage other churches who have helmets on loan to the
Royal Armouries to seek faculties for sale and, if such faculties were granted, the Royal

a   Armouries would be presented with a flood of items which it would be under considerable pressure to purchase, not only to retain them in its collection, but more significantly to prevent them, in the national interest, from being sold to an overseas buyer. If there was a flood of applications to the Royal Armouries its funds would not enable it to purchase all the items which were on the market and the result would be that items would be sold abroad.

b   When questioned by Mr Skipper Mr Wilson accepted that it was a term of the loan agreement in 1979 (renewed in 1984) that:

> 'If at any time during the period of the loan it becomes necessary [for the parish] to sell the object lent [the parish would] give the Armouries first refusal and allow them reasonable time in which to complete the purchase.'

c   Mr Wilson accepted that this term had been mentioned to a parish representative when he (Mr Wilson) came to the parish to collect the helmet in late 1978 or early 1979. He agreed that there was an inference from this term in the agreement that the Armouries were not averse to purchasing items which originally came to them by way of a loan, and it was pointed out to him that there was no question in the loan agreement that the Armouries would be reluctant to be forced into a position of having to purchase an item.

d   Mr Skipper suggested to Mr Wilson that there was a clear difference between an item of spiritual significance such as communion plate and other items, such as this helmet, which were of historical (but secular) importance. Mr Wilson said that to a fourteenth century man the helmet might well have had spiritual significance and it had to be taken into account that it was placed in the church as an act of devotion and in commemoration of the deceased.

e   *Diocesan advice*

The Rev Edwin Newlyn, secretary of the diocesan advisory committee, said that the committee felt that this was a case which was fairly finely balanced but that in the end the committee would support the petitioners on the grounds of need and on the ground that the helmet had already been alienated from the tomb during its period of ten years'

f   loan (and the previous period when it had been kept in a safe). He confirmed that St Bartholomew's was having greater financial difficulties than most other churches in the diocese. To owe £3,500 in unpaid quota accumulated over a period of five years was unusual and indicated a serious state of affairs. The committee had not altered its position in the case since it first considered the matter in 1984. Mr Wilson suggested to Mr Newlyn that a helmet lent to the Tower of London was no more alienated from its church than a chalice which because of its value was kept in a bank and was only used on

g   rare occasions, but Mr Newlyn did not agree with this and considered that there were far greater difficulties in making any arrangement for the helmet ever to be on display in the church than there would be in the case of the occasional use of a chalice.

Points of principle

h   I come therefore to consider these various points of principle which have been raised against the granting of a faculty.

(a) *Undesirability of alienation*

I accept that it is highly desirable that an item which has a close historical or artistic connection with another article in the same place should not be separated from that

j   article. However, there are obvious limitations to this principle. For reasons of security it is no longer possible to keep the helmet on display in the church, so that it must be in some museum or other safe place. It is quite undesirable that it should remain in a bank or a safe locked up where no one can see it, so that one is forced to the conclusion that the right place for it is in a museum such as the Royal Armouries. Realistically it must remain there on an indefinite basis. I do not accept that in realistic terms there is any possibility that it will ever return to the church. If it did return there it could not be displayed and nothing would be achieved other than a nominal re-establishment of a connection between the helmet and the tomb. It would be purely nominal because they could not be displayed together. I feel it is also relevant that the tomb and the helmet do not have any artistic or aesthetic connection, as might be the case with a pair of paintings or a pair of flagons. The connection is a historical one which, though clearly important, does not include an aesthetic element. I consider it is also relevant that the helmet is basically a secular item rather than an item of spiritual significance and I accept the distinction made by Mr Skipper between an item such as a chalice and an item such as this helmet. In many ways the Royal Armouries is a more natural place in which to display this helmet than a church. I agree with the diocesan advisory committee's view that there has already been a substantial degree of alienation between the helmet and the tomb. In terms of the argument of principle that there ought not to be an alienation except in the most exceptional circumstances I cannot avoid a conclusion that a substantial degree of alienation has already occurred. If there was any real prospect of the item going back to the church in such a way that it could be seen there or used there I would not take that view, but on the evidence in the present case I conclude that the degree of alienation which has already occurred is great. By severing the ownership of the helmet from the ownership of the tomb there is, of course, a further step in the separation, but this I think can be mitigated by appropriate records being made of the provenance of both items and their historical connection. This can be done at both ends, by a suitable notice, or plaque, stating the history of each item.

(b) *Fear of establishing a precedent for the alienation of connected items*
I understand this fear but each faculty application has to be considered on its merits and it will only be in a case, such as the present, where the parish can prove to the court's satisfaction that there is a genuine financial crisis that the court will consider giving leave to sell. Even then there will be other considerations to be taken into account. If it appeared to a chancellor that the case before him was one of a flood of similar applications, he would presumably take into account the undesirability of allowing too many applications for sale to be granted. The Council for the Care of Churches would no doubt alert him to the number of such applications which had been made recently or which were pending.

(c) *Difficulty of arranging loans where application for purchase might follow*
Mr Blair raised this as a general problem if an indication is given in the present case that the existence of a loan might be used as a springboard for a subsequent faculty for sale. He feels that it might be difficult to arrange loans with museums or treasuries if those places are in fear of being placed under pressure to purchase later. I understand this point, but it is not suggested that at the present time this is a major problem. If it were to become a problem at a later stage it is a matter which a chancellor would take into account. A chancellor would presumably not grant a faculty for sale unless he was satisfied on the evidence that there was at least a probability that the item would be purchased by a museum or other body where it could be kept in England and would be on show to the public. He would take into account any evidence which he had from the museum concerned that if it felt forced to purchase the item in question that might affect its future policy in relation to taking such items on loan, and this factor might be of such weight as to cause him to refuse the faculty. In the present case I have not received any evidence from Mr Wilson that if I grant a faculty the Royal Armouries will alter their policy with regard to taking items on loan from churches. I regard Mr Blair's point as one which needs to be kept under consideration but one which, on the evidence before me, is not sufficiently made out for me to use it as an argument for refusing a faculty.

(d) *The need to look after national treasures in church possession in relation to preservation of*
a *the ecclesiastical exemption*

The ecclesiastical exemption relates to buildings rather than to contents and, while I think it is necessary for the church to maintain a policy that historical and valuable items in the possession of the church should not be alienated except in cases of financial crisis or where some other powerful case is made out, I do not think that the granting of a faculty for sale in the present case will have any detrimental effect on the essential policy
b of the church or on the maintenance of the ecclesiastical exemption in particular.

(e) *The Royal Armouries' funds*

The Royal Armouries have limited funds available and will have to decide as a matter of policy whether to purchase the helmet. My conclusion from the evidence of Mr Wilson as a whole is that there is a good prospect that the Royal Armouries will want to
c purchase this item for a figure in the region of £20,000. He described the item as a most important part of the Royal Armouries collection. His description of the various ways in which further sums of money can be available from the government and from other sources to purchase important items leads me to conclude that it is probable that the necessary money will be available. Possibly it will not be available in 1989, in respect of which the whole of the £300,000 quota has been earmarked, but there does not seem to
d be any compelling reason why it should not be purchased within the 1990 budget. Obviously it is important to St Bartholomew's that the money should be available as soon as possible, but timing is not wholly critical. As far as policy is concerned the written statement of Mr Wilson prepared recently and which I admitted in evidence in addition to his oral evidence given during the hearing shows that there are 26 pieces of church armour from 20 different churches deposited on loan with the Royal Armouries. There
e are apparently no other applications for sale in relation to those items at the present time. Therefore as things stand it does not seem to me that there is any immediate risk of the Royal Armouries being flooded with applications to purchase items on loan and I do not think that there are serious risks in this area which are likely to prevent the Royal Armouries from purchasing the de Melsa helmet. Of course I am not concerned with whether or not a sale will actually take place, since my part is only to say whether or not
f a faculty should be granted facilitating such a sale. If I grant a faculty and the sale does not go through the end result will be that the helmet will be retained on loan to the Royal Armouries and nothing will have changed. I do have to be satisfied that there is a reasonable prospect that the sale will go through; otherwise it would be pointless for me to grant a faculty. I have reached the conclusion that there *is* a reasonable prospect of it and I go so far as to say that I think it is desirable that there should be a sale because of the
g financial needs of the church.

(f) *Should the item be presented by the Earl of Huntingdon or given by him to the church and then sold to the Royal Armouries?*

I am satisfied that the Earl of Huntingdon, through his daughter as his agent, has now
h fully understood the church's wish to sell and retain the proceeds of sale, and that he has agreed to this. I do not agree with Mr Wilson that there is any reason for preferring the alternative method of presentation of the helmet to the Royal Armouries. That was a course originally suggested by Mr Barr at a time when he was probably not fully aware of the parish's intention and of its financial needs. Because it was mentioned to Lord Huntingdon and his daughter it was a proposition which was taken up by them, but
j again I conclude that at the time they did not really understand what was in the mind of the parish. When it was explained to them that the parish was in need of money and wished to sell, they readily concurred in that method of dealing with the matter. I do not agree with Mr Wilson that anything has occurred during the course of the correspondence to justify the conclusion that presentation is the appropriate method of

dealing with the matter. I consider that the appropriate method is that Lord Huntingdon should give the item to the churchwardens, in exchange for an undertaking by the *a* parochial church council to maintain the de Melsa tombs, and that the church should then be at liberty to offer the helmet for sale, subject to the strict limitations which I propose.

Further consideration

There are some further considerations which relate to my decision. As far as Lord *b* Huntingdon is concerned, I think that it is significant that when he was first written to by the petitioners his response was that he had no knowledge whatever of the de Melsa tomb or the helmet and had no interest in the matter. In those circumstances I think it is quite appropriate that he should fall into line with the parish's proposals that the item should be disposed of in such a way as to provide moneys for the parish. The parish has been looking after the de Melsa tombs for several hundred years and has had responsibility *c* for making appropriate decisions about the helmet. The helmet has been in the de facto possession of the parish since the fourteenth century and it has at least a considerable moral claim to express a view as to what should happen to it now, subject of course to my ruling under the faculty jurisdiction.

I do not think that I can give weight to the argument put forward on behalf of the Royal Armouries that it ought not to be put under any pressure to purchase items which *d* are already on loan to it. This is because of cl 7 of the conditions in the loan agreement. It seems to me that if the Armouries have the benefit of a condition that they are to be given first refusal in relation to any sale, the Armouries must be anticipating that possibility. The condition seems almost to welcome the possibility. It also seems to recognise that sale may 'become necessary'; and, in relation to an item on loan from a church, one would expect that to cover the sort of circumstances which have in fact *e* occurred in the present case. I conclude that because of cl 7 I ought not to give any weight to that particular argument on behalf of the Royal Armouries.

Final conclusions

In the end I have reached the firm conclusion that none of the points of principle, or other matters, raised by Mr Wilson and Mr Blair (on behalf of the Council for the Care of *f* Churches) is of sufficient weight to justify me in refusing a faculty in a case where I have already concluded that the church is in the middle of a financial crisis and faces very considerable further financial problems with regard to the repair and maintenance of its fabric. I have come to the conclusion that the church has made out its case for a faculty enabling it to sell the helmet, but it will be necessary to impose substantial conditions. The sale must be to the Royal Armouries or to some other museum which will agree to *g* keep the helmet in England and to keep it on display to the public. I set the price at £20,000 with liberty to apply to review this. The arrangements for the sale, once provisionally agreed, must be submitted to the registrar of the consistory court for his approval. With regard to the costs of the proceedings I am not in a position to call for any contribution by any person or body other than the petitioners because the other bodies *h* which were represented before me attended as judge's witnesses and not as parties who had entered an appearance or lodged formal objection. It was necessary to hold a court because of the complex issues involved in the case and because the Council for the Care of Churches wished to give evidence and to have a hearing. They are a central church body with a responsibility to place their views before the court and they have done so carefully and helpfully in the present case. The fact that in the end I have decided to *j* grant the faculty in spite of the reservations of the Council for the Care of Churches does not mean that I disagree with the essential points which they placed before me. In the circumstances the court fees involved in the hearing and the preparation for the hearing must be paid by the petitioners. I will direct that payment be postponed until the helmet has been sold and that they will be paid out of the proceeds of sale. If for any reason there

is no sale within 12 months of the drawing up of my order I will give a fresh direction as
a to how these court fees are to be paid. The proceeds of sale will therefore be applied first
in recouping to the petitioners their court costs. The balance of the proceeds of sale will
be paid to the diocesan board of finance for the diocese of York to be held by that board
in appropriate investments and with power from time to time to vary the investments
and on trust to pay the income to the parish church council of St Bartholomew,
Aldbrough for the maintenance and care of the church fabric. In any year in which the
b sum received from the fund is not all used for fabric maintenance or repair, the church
(which already keeps a fabric fund) should add the balance to its fabric fund so that it will
be available for expenditure on the fabric in future years. It seems likely that there will
be a need in the first few years for more money to be released to the parish from the fund
for major items such as the pew platforms. The parish is therefore to have the right to
apply to the diocesan board of finance for capital to be released and the board is to have
c an unfettered discretion whether or not to release it. If capital is released in that way the
income to be paid to the parish in subsequent years shall be reduced to half the income
resulting from the remaining fund until such time as the amount of the capital advance
has been discharged by retention in the capital fund of the other half of the income
which has been retained in the intervening period. There is to be a small plaque placed
near to the de Melsa tomb in the church explaining that the helmet now hanging there
d is a replica and that the original helmet has been sold, under faculty, to the Royal
Armouries, where it is on public display, and there should be an explanation that the
proceeds of sale are being used for the upkeep of the fabric. The wording of this plaque
should be submitted to the diocesan advisory committee for agreement, and to me if
necessary.
There will be liberty to the Archdeacon of the East Riding to apply to the consistory
e court to be joined as a party in these proceedings so as to enable him to intervene if
necessary to secure the due execution of my order. The order will be expressed as a
faculty 'until further order' to enable the consistory court to supervise the carrying out of
the order. The petitioners are to have liberty to apply to me in relation to the carrying
out of the order. If the Council for the Care of Churches or the Royal Armouries wish to
make any application to me they should do so through the archdeacon as they are not
f strictly parties to the proceedings.
The transfer of the helmet from the Earl of Huntingdon to the churchwardens should
be properly recorded in a document which should be in a form agreed with the registrar.
The churchwardens, in so far as they are not already parties to the petition, should be
joined as petitioners. The parochial church council must give a written undertaking to
the Earl of Huntingdon and his successors to maintain the two de Melsa tombs and this
g should be in a form of words agreed with the registrar. My order proceeds on the
assumption that the Earl of Huntingdon will indeed transfer the helmet to enable it to
be sold by the parish (ie the churchwardens). I cannot, of course, make any order against
the Earl of Huntingdon, but because of what his daughter has written I am able to
assume that this is the course which the matter will follow. The faculty will include leave
h for the churchwardens to take the gift of the helmet from the Earl of Huntingdon, for
the parochial church council to give the proposed undertaking with regard to the de
Melsa tombs, and then for the churchwardens to sell the helmet, but only to the Royal
Armouries or some other English museum which will give undertakings to keep the
item in England and to keep it on display, and which will pay the reserved price.

j *Petition granted.*

N P Metcalfe Esq   Barrister.

Practice Direction

SUPREME COURT TAXING OFFICE

Costs – Taxation – Misconduct, neglect etc – Notice of intention to make application – Allegation that costs have been unreasonably or improperly incurred – Procedure for making application – Drawing up of order – Dissatisfaction with taxing officer's decision – Appeals – Appeal direct to judge in chambers – Enforcement proceedings – RSC Ord 42, rr 4, 5, Ord 58, Ord 62, rr 10(1), 11(1)(a), 28(4A), 33–35.

RSC Ord 62, r 28 confers on taxing masters and registrars certain powers. Where it appears that anything has been done or that any omission has been made unreasonably or improperly by and on behalf of any party in the taxation proceedings or in the proceedings which gave rise to the taxation proceedings, the taxing officer 'may exercise the powers conferred on the Court by rule 10(1)'.

Where it appears that (a) any costs have been incurred unreasonably or improperly in the taxation proceedings or in the proceedings which gave rise to the taxation proceedings or (b) any costs have been wasted by failure to conduct those proceedings with reasonable competence and expedition or (c) there has been a failure to procure taxation, the taxing officer may 'exercise the powers conferred on the Court by rule 11(1)(a)'.

This change in jurisdiction has meant that provision has had to be made for procedures for dealing with such issues. To this end Ord 62, r 28 is being amended to provide for appeals direct to a judge in chambers[1].

Henceforth any party wishing to make any application under Ord 62, r 28 in the Supreme Court Taxing Office should do so in writing. The Practice Direction of 26 June 1990 ([1990] 3 All ER 24, [1990] 1 WLR 1089) will apply to all such applications. The party making the application must indicate the time required for the application or, if it be preferable, request a (short) directions hearing. If possible a date and time of hearing will be given immediately; if that is not possible the applicant will be notified of the time and date as soon as possible. Once an order has been made Ord 42, r 4 will apply. The order must normally be drawn up and it is the responsibility of the applicant to do so (Ord 42, r 5). In Chancery Division proceedings it will be the responsibility of the parties to draw up the order unless the master directs otherwise. Three copies of the order must be prepared, one for sealing and return, one for filing at the Supreme Court Taxing Office and one for filing in room 81 (Queen's Bench Division) or the Chancery Registry as the case may be. The order must be taken for sealing to the Central Office or Chancery Chambers and a copy of the sealed order must be brought to the master's clerk in the Taxing Office (room 745) for filing in the Taxing Office file.

The party having carriage of the order must serve a copy of the order on any opposing party.

In the event of either party being dissatisfied with the taxing officer's decision under Ord 62, r 28 an appeal lies to the judge in chambers in accordance with Ord 58 (Ord 62, r 28(4A)). This must not be confused with the carrying in of objections and summons for review before the judge, which continues to apply to all taxations (Ord 62, Pt VI, rr 33–35).

Any enforcement proceedings will be in the Queen's Bench Division or Chancery Division as the case may be.

This Practice Direction will take effect from 1 October 1990.

P T HURST
Vacation Master for
Chief Taxing Master.

20 August 1990

1   See r 29 of RSC (Amendment No 2) 1990, SI 1990/1689, made on 23 August 1990 and coming into force on 1 October 1990

Eldan Services Ltd v Chandag Motors Ltd

CHANCERY DIVISION

MILLETT J

5 MARCH 1990

Injunction – Breach of contract – Interlocutory injunction to protect payment made under contract pending hearing – Jurisdiction – Plaintiffs purchasing business stock from defendants by means of postdated cheque – Cheque presented pursuant to solicitors' undertaking – Plaintiffs bringing action against defendants to recover alleged overpayment – Plaintiffs also applying for injunction to restrain defendants from presenting postdated cheque for payment prior to trial – Whether injunction should be granted – Whether plaintiffs' action amounting to personal claim for money had and received or proprietary claim.

In 1989 the plaintiffs entered into an agreement for the sale and purchase of a business together with stock valued according to the total cost prices shown on the defendants' computer print-out, which produced a figure of £68,302·15. The parties agreed on delayed payment for the stock and, in addition, the defendants agreed to give the plaintiffs a credit of £20,000 for six months on terms under which the £68,302·15 would be paid on 7 March 1990 by a postdated cheque drawn by the plaintiffs' solicitors. A postdated cheque was duly delivered to the defendants and the £20,000 credit was given against an undertaking by the plaintiffs' solicitors to pay the defendants that sum together with interest on the £68,302·15 for the six months. Shortly after completion a dispute arose over the amount payable under the contract because the plaintiffs claimed, inter alia, that the stock was not worth the figure produced by the computer print-out since it included dead stock with no net realisable value which ought to have been excluded, thereby reducing the amount payable by some £20,000. The plaintiffs brought an action against the defendants to recover the alleged overpayments and applied inter partes for interlocutory relief, seeking orders (i) restraining the defendants from presenting the postdated cheque or, alternatively, an order which would safeguard the proceeds of the postdated cheque pending the hearing of the action and (ii) varying the undertaking by the plaintiffs' solicitors to pay the £20,000 to an undertaking to pay that sum after judgment in the action and then only if the defendants succeeded.

Held – Where payment under a contract was made by means of a postdated cheque the court would not intervene in a dispute over the true sum payable on completion by way of granting an injunction restraining the recipient of the cheque from presenting it for payment or disposing of the proceeds prior to trial of the action or by ordering the disputed sum to be paid into court or into a joint account in the name of the parties' solicitors, since the plaintiffs' claim amounted to a personal claim for money had and received rather than a proprietary claim. Moreover, the mere fact that the money was still identifiable, since it was still in transit between the payer and the recipient, did not of itself form the basis on which a proprietary remedy could be made available by imposing a constructive trust. The court would therefore refuse to grant an injunction and, since the court had no jurisdiction to vary or discharge a solicitor's undertaking which had been given to a third party rather than to the court, the plaintiffs' application would be dismissed (see p 461 *f* to *j* and p 462 *c* to *f*, post).

Chase Manhattan Bank NA v Israel-British Bank (London) Ltd [1979] 3 All ER 1025 considered.

Notes

For the principles governing the grant of interlocutory injunctions, see 24 Halsbury's Laws (4th edn) paras 953–956, and for cases on the subject, see 28(4) Digest (2nd reissue) 152–187, 4957–5221.

Case referred to in judgment

Chase Manhattan Bank NA v Israel-British Bank (London) Ltd [1979] 3 All ER 1025, [1981] *a*
Ch 105, [1980] 2 WLR 202.

Motion

The plaintiffs, Eldan Services Ltd, brought an action against the defendants, Chandag
Motors Ltd, to recover alleged overpayments made in connection with the sale and
purchase of a business, and prior to the hearing applied inter partes for interlocutory *b*
relief, seeking (i) an order restraining the defendants from presenting a cheque for
£68,302·15 postdated 7 March 1990 or, alternatively, that some other order might be
made safeguarding the proceeds of the cheque pending the hearing and (ii) an order
varying an undertaking made by the plaintiffs' solicitors to pay a sum of about £20,000,
so that it was an undertaking to pay that sum after judgment in the action, and then only
if the defendants succeeded. The facts are set out in the judgment.   *c*

Jill Gibson for the plaintiffs.
Stephen Moverley Smith for the defendants.

MILLETT J. In 1989 the plaintiffs, Eldan Services Ltd, agreed to buy, and the
defendants, Chandag Motors Ltd, agreed to sell, a garage premises together with the *d*
business and goodwill and stock. The date fixed for completion was 1 September 1989.
The price was agreed in relation to most items sold, but the stock was to be valued by an
independant valuer as at the date of completion at cost or market value, whichever was
the lower, and was to be paid for separately.

The defendants held a Volkswagen-Audi franchise with VAG (UK) Ltd, which was not
assignable. The contract was not in any way conditional on the plaintiffs being able to *e*
secure a similar franchise. They applied for a franchise but were unable to obtain one.
That gave rise to a dispute whether the stock, which included a lot of Audi stock, was still
to be acquired.

On 31 August there was a meeting between the parties, as a result of which it was
agreed that the plaintiffs would take over the VAG Audi stock on the basis, not of an
independent valuation, but at the prices shown on the defendants' computer print-out. *f*
That produced a figure of £68,302·15. It was, strictly speaking, a little more than that
but the parties agreed that that figure should be taken to represent the total. The
computer print-out was a print-out of cost prices and it was not in any sense a valuation.

The parties agreed on delayed payment for the VAG Audi stock. In addition the
defendants agreed to give the plaintiffs a credit of £20,000 for six months provided that
the £68,302·15 should be paid by a postdated cheque payable on 7 March 1990, and *g*
drawn by the plaintiffs' solicitors. Such a cheque was duly drawn and delivered it to the
defendants, who hold it and are proposing to present it on Wednesday of this week. The
£20,000 credit was also given against a solicitor's undertaking to the defendants given by
the plaintiffs' solicitors, to pay a sum of £20,000, together with interest on the £68,302·15
at an agreed rate of interest for the six months.

The parties are now in dispute as to the true sums payable on completion. Completion *h*
took place on 7 or 8 September 1989. Most of the disputed items are relatively minor
and would not justify any kind of interlocutory intervention. There is, for example, a
dispute as to the correct rate of interest, but the sum involved is less than £1,000. Two
substantial items, however, are in contention. First, the plaintiffs contend that the VAG
Audi stock was not worth anything like £68,000. The computer print-out, it is alleged, *j*
included items of stock which had no net realisable value, and the plaintiffs claim that
those items ought to have been excluded. This would reduce the figure by some £20,000.

Second, it is alleged that the value of the stock should be taken as at 1 September 1989,
at which time in fact the plaintiffs had been refused a Volkswagen-Audi franchise, and
that the net realisable value of the stock was significantly affected by the failure to obtain

the franchise. It should have been valued, the plaintiffs contend, as effectively bankrupt

a stock or on the basis of a non-continuing franchise, and that would produce a very much lower valuation of some £12,000 only.

Third, it is alleged that the value added tax of about £13,000, which was charged by the defendants to the plaintiffs on top of the overall purchase price and included in the figures, was not in fact chargeable because this was a transfer of a business as a going concern. That is conceded, but the value added tax was charged and the defendants have

b acccounted to the Customs and Excise for it. It is now recoverable, and the defendants have undertaken to assist the plaintiffs should their assistance be necessary in order to obtain recovery from the authorities.

The plaintiffs have issued a writ alleging that the true sums payable on completion were considerably less than the sums actually paid and they claim to recover the overpayment. They now apply inter partes for interlocutory relief. They do not seek

c Mareva relief. The circumstances would not warrant such relief. This is not a case where the defendants are alleged to have obtained money by fraud, or where there is any evidence that they are likely to dissipate their assets or make themselves judgment proof or anything of that kind. This is a straightforward dispute about the true sum payable on completion of a contract.

Instead, the plaintiffs seek two sorts of relief: first, an order to restrain the defendants

d from presenting the postdated cheque dated 7 March or, alternatively, some other order safeguarding the proceeds of that cheque; and, second, an order varying the plaintiffs' solicitors' undertaking to pay the sum of £20,000-odd so that it is an undertaking to pay that sum after judgment in the action and then only if the defendants succeed.

The application comes before me inter partes at a time when the evidence is not complete, and it is agreed that the motion should be adjourned to come on as a motion

e by order. The defendants, however, refuse to give any undertakings in the meantime, and accordingly the plaintiffs seek to safeguard the position pending the hearing of the motion. They ask me, inter alia, to restrain the defendants from presenting the postdated cheque until the hearing of the motion. It would not, in my judgment, be right to do so. On the hearing of the motion, it would not be right to restrain the defendants from presenting the cheque until judgment in the action, for the cheque would cease to be

f payable after three months. That would not be right. Accordingly, it would not be right to restrain presentation until the motion. I was asked, as an alternative, to authorise the solicitors to stop the cheque. They would not be prepared to stop it without the leave of the court, since it is a solicitor's cheque; but the circumstances in which a cheque can be stopped are very limited, and if they did stop it there is nothing the court could do to prevent the defendants from bringing an action against the plaintiffs' solicitors on the

g cheque. That would not provide a solution to the present problem. If any solution is to be found it must, I think, lie in granting an injunction against the defendants requiring them to pay the proceeds of the cheque either into court or into a joint account in the names of the two solicitors.

Similar considerations apply to the solicitors' undertaking to pay the balance of

h £20,000. In my judgment the court has no jurisdiction to vary or discharge a solicitor's undertaking given not to the court but to a third party. While the court can of course decline to enforce a solicitor's undertaking it cannot intervene to vary or discharge it. That must be a matter for the person to whom the undertaking is given. But again, if it were appropriate to do so, I would intervene by restraining the defendants from disposing of the proceeds of the cheque otherwise than by payment into court or into a joint

j account.

So the question is whether or not this is a case where the court should intervene in order to protect the property in dispute, and that at once raises the real question in the case: is this property in dispute? In my judgment it is not. The plaintiffs rely on the decision of Goulding J in *Chase Manhattan Bank NA v Israel-British Bank (London) Ltd* [1979] 3 All ER 1025, [1981] Ch 105, where the plaintiff was granted a proprietary remedy in circumstances where it had paid money under a mistake of fact. But that was a case where the plaintiff had paid the defendant twice over as a result of a clerical error and there was no intention to make the second payment at all. The defendant had notice of the mistake, and the court held that the conscience of the recipient was affected to the extent that a constructive trust could be imposed. But in the present case the true analysis of the transaction appears to be that the parties agreed on a variation of the terms of the contract, and substituted for the contractual right to payment for the stock on the basis of an independent valuation the payment of the sum shown on a computer print-out. Unless and until that variation agreement is set aside it stands and the payment was made in accordance with the terms of the contract as varied. The plaintiffs have not yet pleaded any grounds for setting aside the variation, but, assuming that some such grounds exist, nevertheless the claim is to recover the sums paid under the contract as varied as money had and received. There is no question of the defendants' having notice of an overpayment, or of their conscience being affected by the circumstances of the payment. They have received a payment to which they are prima facie entitled, and they resist the claim to repayment. The plaintiffs' claim is a personal claim only, and I cannot see any similarity between such a claim and the circumstances in which a proprietary remedy can be made available by imposing a constructive trust.

Counsel submitted to me that while the funds were still identifiable, as they are here, the court should step in and prevent them being mixed or their identity lost. That would certainly be right if there were any kind of proprietary claim, but the mere fact that the moneys are still identifiable and are, as it were, in transit between payer and recipient does not of itself form a basis for any proprietary claim. In my judgment this is a straightforward action for the setting aside of a variation of a contract in order to leave the original unvaried contract in being and to recover moneys paid in accordance with the contract as varied, but in excess of those payable in accordance with the original contract. The only unusual feature about the case is that the moneys were paid by postdated cheques or solicitor's undertakings so that they have not yet been paid but are about to be paid. In the absence of grounds which would entitle the court to intervene by way of a Mareva injunction, in my judgment it would be wrong for the court to intervene at all.

Accordingly, even in advance of the motion coming on as a motion by order, I decline to grant any relief.

Motion dismissed.

Solicitors: *Singh & Choudry* (for the plaintiffs); *Middleton & Upsall*, Warminster (for the defendants).

Jacqueline Metcalfe   Barrister.

Swingcastle Ltd v Gibson

COURT OF APPEAL, CIVIL DIVISION

NEILL, FARQUHARSON LJJ AND SIR JOHN MEGAW

24, 25 JANUARY, 16 MARCH 1990

Damages – Measure of damages – Negligence – Surveyor – Surveyor negligently valuing property for mortgage – Finance company making advance on security of property in reliance on valuation – Advance secured by mortgage which included default rate of 45% – Mortgagor defaulting on mortgage – Finance company selling house for less than amount lent and accrued interest – Finance company claiming damages against surveyor – Whether surveyor liable for interest accruing under mortgage at default rate.

The plaintiff finance company specialised in making high-risk mortgage loans. In 1985 it agreed to make a loan of £10,000 to mortgagors on the basis of a valuation of their house carried out by the defendant surveyor, who negligently valued the house at £18,000 on a forced sale with vacant possession. The interest payments under the mortgage were 37% with a default rate of 45% if the mortgagors fell into arrears. In 1986 the mortgagors fell into arrears and the finance company sought and obtained a possession order and sold the house in February 1987 for £12,000, leaving a shortfall, including interest accrued under the mortgage at the default rate, of £7,136·41. The finance company brought an action against the defendant seeking to recover that sum on the ground that it was a loss caused by his negligence. The judge gave judgment for the amount claimed. The defendant accepted liability but appealed on the ground that accrued interest at the default rate should not have been included in the amount of damages because the correct method of assessing damages was to award such damages as would place the finance company in the same position as if it had never entered into the mortgage contract and that to include the accrued interest at the default rate amounted to the defendant warranting or guaranteeing the mortgagors' performance of their obligations.

Held – Where a surveyor's negligent valuation of a mortgaged property caused the mortgagee to suffer a loss on a mortgagee's sale of the property following the mortgagor's default, the surveyor was liable for the total amount of the mortgagee's loss, including any unpaid interest at a default rate stipulated in the mortgage. It followed that the defendant's appeal would be dismissed (see p 468 b j, p 470 a and p 472 d to f, post).

Baxter v F W Gapp & Co Ltd [1939] 2 All ER 752 followed.

Notes

For the measure of damages, see 12 Halsbury's Laws (4th edn) paras 1127–1144, and for cases on the subject, see 17 Digest (Reissue) 101–119, 109–208.

Cases referred to in judgments

Baxter v F W Gapp & Co Ltd [1939] 2 All ER 752, [1939] 2 KB 271, CA; *affg* [1938] 4 All ER 457.

Corisand Investments Ltd v Druce & Co (1978) 248 EG 315.

Dolby v Olby (Ironmongers) Ltd [1969] 2 All ER 119, [1969] 2 QB 158, [1969] 2 WLR 673, CA.

JEB Fasteners Ltd v Marks Bloom & Co (a firm) [1983] 1 All ER 583, CA.

Livingstone v Rawyards Coal Co (1880) 5 App Cas 25, HL.

London and South of England Building Society v Stone [1983] 3 All ER 105, [1983] 1 WLR 1242, CA; *affg* (1981) 261 EG 463.

Lowenburg Harris & Co v Wolley (1895) 25 SCR 51, Can SC.
Perry v Sidney Phillips & Son (a firm) [1982] 3 All ER 705, [1982] 1 WLR 1297, CA.
Philips v Ward [1956] 1 All ER 874, [1956] 1 WLR 471, CA.
Scholes v Brook (1891) 64 LT 674, CA; *affg* 63 LT 837.
Seeway Mortgage Investment Corp v First Citizens Financial Corp (Realtex Appraisals Ltd and von Doelln, third parties) (1983) 45 BCLR 87, BC SC.
Singer & Friedlander Ltd v John D Wood & Co (1977) 243 EG 212.
Smith Kline & French Laboratories Ltd v Long [1988] 3 All ER 887, [1989] 1 WLR 1, CA.
Yianni v Edwin Evans & Sons (a firm) [1981] 3 All ER 592, [1982] QB 438, [1981] 3 WLR 843.

Cases also cited

Brandeis Goldschmidt & Co Ltd v Western Transport Ltd [1982] 1 All ER 28, [1981] QB 864, CA.
Brown & Davis Ltd v Galbraith [1972] 3 All ER 31, [1972] 1 WLR 997, CA.
Dodd Properties (Kent) Ltd v Canterbury City Council [1980] 1 All ER 928, [1980] 1 WLR 433, CA.
Ford v White & Co [1964] 2 All ER 755, [1964] 1 WLR 885.
Greenwood v Bennett [1972] 3 All ER 586, [1973] QB 195, CA.
Johnson v Agnew [1979] 1 All ER 883, [1980] AC 367, HL.
Radford v De Froberville [1978] 1 All ER 33, [1977] 1 WLR 1262.
Simple Simon Catering Ltd v Binstock Miller & Co (1973) 228 EG 527, CA.
Testabridge Investments Ltd v Davis (19 March 1985, unreported), QBD.

Appeal

The defendant, Alastair Gibson, a chartered surveyor, appealed against the judgment of his Honour Judge Harris QC sitting in the Westminster County Court on 19 May 1989 whereby he gave judgment for the plaintiffs, Swingcastle Ltd (the finance company), for £7,136·41 together with interest, as damages for loss suffered by the finance company in advancing a mortgage loan in reliance on a negligent valuation carried out by the defendant on a property 36 North Road, Audenshaw, Manchester. The facts are set out in the judgment of Neill LJ.

Peter Wulwik for the finance company.
Roger Toulson QC and *Roger Stewart* for the surveyor.

Cur adv vult

16 March. The following judgments were delivered.

NEILL LJ. This is an appeal by Mr Alastair Gibson, a chartered surveyor (the surveyor), against the order of his Honour Judge Harris QC dated 19 May 1989 in the Westminster County Court whereby judgment was entered for the plaintiff company, Swingcastle Ltd (the finance company), for the sum of £7,136·41, together with interest and costs.

The appeal raises a question as to the correct measure of damages where money has been lent in reliance on the negligent valuation of property.

At the beginning of 1985 Mr and Mrs Clarke were living at 36 North Road, Audenshaw in Manchester. At that time the property was charged to a building society and also to a finance company, Cedar Holdings. Mr and Mrs Clarke wished to obtain a loan in order to repay the charges. They approached a firm of brokers, Richard Murtagh & Co. Murtagh instructed the surveyor to make a survey and to prepare a valuation. On 25 January 1985 the surveyor gave a written valuation of the property.

The valuation was addressed to 'the lending principals of Richard Murtagh & Co'. The valuation stated the accommodation at the property and gave other particulars, including

the form of construction. Paragraph 4(a) of the valuation was in these terms: 'Forced Sale
a Value for easy sale with vacant possession . . . £18,000.'

On 11 February 1985 the finance company, who are licensed under the Consumer
Credit Act 1974, lent Mr and Mrs Clarke the sum of £10,000. This loan was secured on
the property. The loan was applied as to £1,700 for the repayment of the moneys due to
Cedar Holdings and as to £2,000 to pay the fee of the brokers.

By the agreement dated 11 February 1985 between Mr and Mrs Clarke and the finance
b company it was provided that the repayment period for the loan would be ten years, that
the total interest charged would be £23,000, that the annual percentage rate would be
36·51%, but that in the event of any default the rate would be increased to 45·619%. It
was further provided that there should be 120 instalments payable of £275 each, the first
payment to be made on 11 March 1985 and thereafter on the eleventh day of each
month.

c Mr and Mrs Clarke fell into arrears with their repayments almost at once. On 11 April
1985 they failed to pay the instalment due on that date and thereafter interest became
payable at the higher rate of 45·619%. On 29 June 1985 the finance company issued
proceedings for possession and on 22 October 1985 they obtained a suspended order for
possession.

On 30 June 1986 Mr and Mrs Clarke gave up possession of the property, which was
d then placed on the market for sale.

In February 1987 the finance company sold the property to a third party for £12,000.

It is now common ground that at the date of the sale of the property in February 1987
the following sums were due from Mr and Mrs Clarke to the finance company:

		£
e	unpaid principal	9,474·59
	unpaid interest	7,802·92
	disbursements	344·99
	interest on disbursements	129·31
	selling agents' commission	401·35
f	legal costs relating to sale	983·25
	total	19,136·41
	less	12,000·00
		7,136·41

g It is also now common ground (a) that the valuation made by the surveyor was made
negligently and (b) that had the finance company known that the property would only
realise £12,000 on resale they would not have made any loan to Mr and Mrs Clarke on
the security of the property. It is the policy of the finance company not to make loans on
properties of a forced sale value of less than £15,000.

h On 4 September 1987 the finance company issued a writ indorsed with a statement of
claim against the surveyor claiming damages. The statement of claim was subsequently
amended, but these amendments are of no importance for the purposes of this appeal.

In due course the action was transferred to the Westminster County Court, where it
was tried by Judge Harris. At the trial the sum claimed by the finance company was
£9,297·56. This sum included a sum of £2,161·15 claimed by the finance company as
j redemption interest. The judge, however, disallowed the claim for redemption interest
on the basis that this interest was not owing on 27 February 1987 when the property was
sold. He gave judgment, however, for £7,136·41, being the balance of the sum claimed
by the finance company. This sum is made up in the way which I have already set out
and represents the sum which was due from Mr and Mrs Clarke to the finance company
on 27 February 1987, the date of the sale.

The judge was referred, as we were, to a number of authorities, including in particular *Baxter v F W Gapp & Co Ltd* [1939] 2 All ER 752, [1939] 2 KB 271; *affg* [1938] 4 All ER   *a* 457 and *London and South of England Building Society v Stone* [1983] 3 All ER 105, [1983] 1 WLR 1242. In *Baxter's* case the defendants, a firm of estate agents, valued a property in Maidenhead for the purpose of an advance by way of mortgage. The valuation was £1,800. The defendants advised an advance of £1,200 on first mortgage and subsequently advised an advance of £150 on second mortgage. After a short time, however, the mortgagor made default and in April 1937 Mr Baxter, the mortgagee, retook possession.   *b* He had some difficulty in selling the property, which was finally sold for £850. He then brought an action against the estate agents claiming damages.

At the trial before Goddard LJ, sitting as an additional judge of the King's Bench Division, it was the case for Mr Baxter that had a careful valuation been made the property would have been valued at a considerably lower sum. In that event he would not have entered the first mortgage transaction. He left open the question whether he   *c* might have advanced £800 or £1,000. The judge made no finding as to the actual value of the property, considering that it was unnecessary for him to do so, but was clearly satisfied that there had been a serious overvaluation and that Mr Baxter would not have entered into this transaction had the property been valued carefully.

Having decided the issue of liability in favour of the plaintiff, the judge turned to consider the question of damages. He came to the conclusion that the plaintiff was   *d* entitled to recover the whole loss which he had suffered as a result of entering into the transaction. He was, therefore, held to be entitled to recover not only the expenses which he had incurred following the repossession, namely the expenses of abortive sales, insurance premiums paid, the builder's account for the upkeep of the property and his expenses and disbursements in connection with the ultimate sale, but also the principal sum which he had advanced to the mortgagor and the interest which had not been paid   *e* by the mortgagor under the mortgage since the last payment in February 1986.

The defendants then appealed to the Court of Appeal, where it was argued on their behalf that the damages should be limited to the difference between the valuation figure and the true value of the property at the time of valuation. This argument was rejected, however, and the Court of Appeal approved the method of assessment adopted by Goddard LJ. MacKinnon LJ stated ([1939] 2 KB 271 at 274, cf [1939] 2 All ER 752 at   *f* 758): '. . . the measure of damages in such a case as the present is that which the plaintiff has lost by being led into a disastrous investment . . .'

I come next to the decision of the Court of Appeal in *London and South of England Building Society v Stone* [1983] 3 All ER 105, [1983] 1 WLR 1242. The facts in that case were unusual. The defendant valuer was instructed by a building society to inspect a house which the borrowers wished to purchase. The valuer recommended that the   *g* property would be a suitable security for a loan of £12,800 repayable over 25 years. In reliance on this recommendation the building society lent £11,880 to the borrowers, the size of the loan being limited by the policy of the building society not to lend more than 80% of the purchase price (£14,800). Soon after the transaction had been completed it was found that the house was subject to subsidence and that unless repairs were carried   *h* out part of the house would collapse. The borrowers approached the building society, who agreed to repair the house, having warned the valuer that they proposed to take proceedings against him. The cost of the repairs, however, proved to be no less than £29,000. In the subsequent proceedings against the valuer the building society put forward their claim for damages in alternative ways. Their actual loss was £29,000 because, although the borrowers had kept up their repayments under the mortgage and   *j* had repaid the original advance when the repaired house was sold, the building society had spent that sum on the repairs and had decided not to enforce the personal covenants in the mortgage to try to recover any part of this expenditure from the borrowers.

The judge decided, however, that it was unreasonable to have spent so much money on repairing the house (see 261 EG 463). He assessed the damages by reference to the

sum advanced (£11,880) less a discount of £3,000 to take account of the possibility that
a the building society, if they had chosen to enforce their rights, might have recovered this
sum from the borrowers on the personal covenants. He also included in the damages the
sum of £253·13 as the reasonable costs incurred by the building society in investigating
the matter and a further sum by way of interest of about £3,455. The report does not
make clear what rate of interest was used for the purpose of the calculation.

In the Court of Appeal the arguments were directed to the question whether the judge
b was right to reduce the award by a discount to allow for the possibility of recovery under
the personal covenants. The building society succeeded on this issue, but this is not a
matter which arises for consideration in this case. Nevertheless the decision in *London and
South of England Building Society v Stone* is of importance to the present appeal for the
following reasons: (a) it was there held that the decision in *Baxter v FW Gapp & Co Ltd*
was binding on the court; and (b) it was agreed between counsel that the measure of
c damages was the difference between the sum the plaintiff advanced on the negligent
valuation and the sum he would have advanced on a true valuation (see [1983] 3 All ER
105 at 110, 119, [1983] 1 WLR 1242 at 1249, 1260 per O'Connor and Stephenson LJJ).
In that case the relevant figures were £11,880 and nil. The majority of the Court of
Appeal seem to have accepted that this was in general the correct measure of damages,
but Stephenson LJ treated the decision in *Baxter's* case as binding authority for the
d proposition that 'the loss of the money advanced may be increased by expenses and
reduced by receipts'.

The point at issue in the present appeal is whether the finance company are entitled to
recover interest at the default rate stipulated in the mortgage or whether they are
restricted to the ordinary commercial rate of interest.

It was argued on behalf of the surveyor as follows.
e   (1) It was wrong in principle to allow the finance company to recover interest at the
mortgage rate because to do so had the same effect as if the surveyor had warranted the
performance by the borrowers of their mortgage obligations.

(2) The true measure of damages was the net loss suffered by the finance company
together with any expenses incurred by them as a result of making the loan, less any
sums recovered either from the borrowers or from the proceeds of the sale of the
f property. In this context the net loss meant the amount lent by the finance company.
Interest would be recoverable on this sum but only at the ordinary rate. In addition the
finance company were entitled to recover the expenses they had incurred.

(3) If the finance company were to recover any additional sum to represent the loss of
the use of the money for lending elsewhere it would have been necessary for them to
plead and to prove that the money lent to Mr and Mrs Clarke could and would have been
g lent to another borrower. In the present case there was no evidence to support this
additional loss.

(4) The decision in *Baxter's* case was of no assistance on the question of the proper rate
of interest because: (a) the question of the rate of interest was never argued before
Goddard LJ (indeed in the report it was said that 'The loss which [Mr Baxter] suffered is
h not challenged in this case as a figure' (see [1938] 4 All ER 457 at 466)); (b) it was not
surprising that the question of the rate of interest was not investigated in that case
because the difference between the rate allowed under the mortgage and the rate of
interest which would otherwise have been recoverable was of little importance at that
time; and (c) the rate of interest was not considered when the matter reached the Court
of Appeal. Furthermore, as was noted by O'Connor LJ in *London and South of England
j Building Society v Stone* [1983] 3 All ER 105 at 115, [1983] 1 WLR 1242 at 1255,
MacKinnon LJ misapprehended the effect of the judgment of the Supreme Court of
Canada in *Lowenburg Harris & Co v Wolley* (1895) 25 SCR 51 when treating that case as
some support for the decision of Goddard LJ at first instance.

I see the force of these criticisms. Moreover, I have not been able to derive any
assistance from the reports of the decision in *Scholes v Brook* (1891) 64 LT 674, which was

regarded as binding by du Parcq LJ in *Baxter's* case [1939] 2 All ER 752 at 760, [1939] 2 KB 271 at 275 as to the correct principle to be applied. Nevertheless, I am quite satisfied *a* that this court is bound by the decision in *Baxter's* case and that one cannot treat that decision as having been reached per incuriam. In the Court of Appeal detailed argument was directed to the measure of damages, and, even if no reference was made to the rate of interest, it seems to me to be impossible to exclude this one element of the award from the general approval given to the judge's method of assessment.

In these circumstances I would dismiss the appeal on the short ground that this court *b* is bound by authority and that the judge was right to assess the damages in the way that he did.

In deference to the full and careful arguments which were addressed to us, however, I propose to examine a little further the basis on which the damages should be assessed in a case such as the present if the matter were free from authority.

In the course of argument our attention was drawn to the statement of principle by *c* Lord Blackburn in *Livingstone v Rawyards Coal Co* (1880) 5 App Cas 25 at 39, where he said:

> '. . . where any injury is to be compensated by damages, in settling the sum of money to be given for reparation of damages you should as nearly as possible get at that sum of money which will put the party who has been injured, or who has *d* suffered, in the same position as he would have been in if he had not sustained the wrong for which he is now getting his compensation or reparation.'

In seeking to apply this statement of principle to cases where, in reliance on a negligent valuation by B, A has lent money to C on mortgage for the purchase of property it is necessary to distinguish between two types of case.

In the first type of case the evidence may establish that had a proper valuation been *e* made A would still have lent the money to C though he would have lent a smaller sum. In such a case it seems clear that the measure of damages will be the difference between the sum lent and the sum which would have been lent had the valuation been a proper one. Thus in *Singer & Friedlander Ltd v John D Wood & Co* (1977) 243 EG 212 Watkins J awarded damages of £491,250, being the difference between the sum actually lent and the sum which the bank would have lent on a proper valuation of the property. And a *f* year later in *Corisand Investments Ltd v Druce & Co* (1978) 248 EG 315 Gibson J awarded damages of £34,625 to a moneylending company on the basis of the difference between the sum which the company had lent (£60,000) less the sums repaid (£9,075) and the sum which the judge considered they would have lent (£16,300) on a proper valuation.

It is to be noted that in each of these cases the actual loss sustained by the lenders was greater than the sum awarded. In the *Singer & Friedlander* case the security was worth *g* £900,000 less than the sum lent. In the *Corisand* case the security was worthless to the lenders because on the borrowers' default the property had been taken by the first mortgagees. In both cases, however, the lenders would have made a loan in any event so that the losses attributable to the default of the borrowers had not been caused by the negligence of the valuers.

In the second type of case, however, the evidence may establish that had a proper *h* valuation been made the lenders would not have made a loan at all to the particular borrowers to whom they in fact made the loan. This was the position in *Baxter v F W Gapp & Co Ltd* and in the present case. In such a case the prima facie measure of damages would seem to be the same as in the first type of case, namely the difference between the sum advanced (£X) and the sum which would have been advanced (£nil).

This was the general approach which appealed to O'Connor and Stephenson LJ in *j* *London and South of England Building Society v Stone*. But if the claim is for damages for negligence and the actual loss suffered by the lender exceeds the prima facie measure of damages, I see no reason in principle why, subject to proof, the lender should not recover the actual loss which he has suffered as a result of making the loan. Recovery on this

alternative basis would seem to be in accord with the general rules relating to the measure
a of damages in tort. Thus, in *JEB Fasteners Ltd v Marks Bloom & Co (a firm)* [1983] 1 All ER
583 at 587, where the plaintiffs had taken over a manufacturing company and had
reached a decision to do so in reliance on the accounts prepared by the defendants as
auditors, Donaldson LJ, referring to the measure of damages recoverable by the plaintiffs,
said:

b   'The plaintiffs did not take the usual precaution of requiring the directors . . . to
     warrant the accuracy of the audited accounts and the fact that there had been no
     material change in the profitability of the company since the end of the period
     covered by those accounts. Accordingly, they cannot sue the directors for breach of
     warranty but must rely on a claim against the defendant auditors for negligent
     misstatement. Furthermore, the measure of damage is different. It is not the
c   difference between the value of the company if the facts had been as stated in the
     accounts and its actual value, but the loss which the plaintiffs have sustained as a
     result of acting in reliance on the accuracy of the accounts.'

   On this basis the lender would be awarded (a) the amount advanced less the aggregate
of any sum recovered from the borrower and any sum recovered on the realisation of the
security and (b) any expenses incurred by the lender in realising the security or in
d maintaining the value of the security until disposal.

   It remains to consider, however, whether, in this second type of case, the lender can
recover in addition any sum for the loss of the use of the money during the period before
the security can be realised. This is a matter of importance for those who advanced
money at the high-risk (or, as it is called, the non-status) end of the market and where it
may be possible to claim that the high rates of interest charged are no more than a
e reflection of the perils of the business undertaken.

   A number of approaches are possible, including the following. (a) The lender could be
awarded the unpaid interest owed by the borrower at the date when the security was
realised. This was the method adopted in *Baxter v F W Gapp & Co Ltd* [1939] 2 All ER
752, [1939] 2 KB 271. But to award damages on this basis is in effect to treat the valuer
as the guarantor of the contract of loan. In the absence of authority I would for my part
f reject this solution. (b) The lender could be awarded a sum equivalent to the amount he
would have earned by way of interest on another loan if he had had the money available
for this purpose. In my view, however, such an award should not be made in the absence
of evidence that the money lent would have been used for another transaction. This
evidence would have to be directed to proving an unsatisfied demand for loans and I
anticipate that such evidence might seldom be forthcoming. Moreover, even if evidence
g of a lost transaction were available, I see no reason why the interest should be at the
default rate rather than at the ordinary rate provided for in a standard contract for this
type of business. (c) The lender could be awarded a sum equivalent to the interest which
would have been earned if the sum had been placed on deposit. (d) The lender could be
awarded a sum to represent the loss of the opportunity to invest the money elsewhere.
h This was the solution adopted by the Supreme Court of British Columbia in *Seeway
Mortgage Investment Corp v First Citizens Financial Corp (Realtex Appraisals Ltd and von
Doelln, third parties)* (1983) 45 BCLR 87 at 101, where it was said:

     'What the plaintiff lost then was the opportunity to invest its $50,000 in a security
     which had the same risks except that the appraisal would be accurate.'

j   I do not propose to express any concluded view about these methods of assessment. I
do not consider that any one of the last three methods of assessment would necessarily be
right to suit all cases. It would depend on the evidence. I would, however, also observe
that it may be necessary in some future case to examine whether any valid distinction
can be drawn between damages awarded for a negligent misstatement and damages
awarded in deceit. In the latter case the measure of damages is that laid down by *Doyle v*

Olby (Ironmongers) Ltd [1969] 2 All ER 119, [1969] 2 QB 158 and *Smith Kline & French Laboratories Ltd v Long* [1988] 3 All ER 887, [1989] 1 WLR 1.

In the present case, however, for the reasons which I have stated, I consider that the court is bound by the decision in *Baxter v F W Gapp & Co Ltd.*

I would dismiss the appeal.

FARQUHARSON LJ. The respondents, Swingcastle Ltd (the finance company), finance mortgage agreements at the high-risk, or, as it is called, the non-status end of the market. The appellant, Mr Alastair Gibson (the surveyor), carries on business as a surveyor. In January 1985 a Mr and Mrs Clarke applied to the finance company through mortgage brokers for a loan of £11,000 on their house at 36 North Road, Audenshaw, Manchester. The surveyor was asked to give the finance company a valuation of the house, and he did so giving a figure of £18,000 on a forced sale with vacant possession. The valuation was admittedly made negligently. The house was not worth anything like so much.

On the faith of the valuation the finance company advanced the sum of £10,000 secured on a mortgage of the house. The interest rates under the mortgage were very high, being 37% per annum while the borrowers made payments in accordance with the agreement and 45% if they fell into arrears. The Clarkes defaulted very quickly. Proceedings for possession were launched by the finance company in the county court and possession was obtained on 30 June 1986. On 27 February 1987 the finance company sold the house to a third party for £12,000.

In this action against the surveyor the finance company sought to recover damages flowing from the surveyor's negligence under the following heads: (1) the principal sum advanced less such repayment as were made by the Clarkes, (2) general disbursements and interest on them, (3) legal costs arising out of the possession proceedings, (4) estate agents' commission on sale of the property and (5) interest accrued under the mortgage contract.

Bringing into account the £12,000 recovered on the sale of the house, the finance company claimed damages amounting to £7,136·41 with interest and the judge gave judgment for that amount.

The surveyor concedes that the finance company are entitled to recover all the above items of damages, save the last, and this appeal is brought against the judge's award of the sum of £7,808·92, being the interest which was due under the mortgage contract and which the Clarkes failed to pay.

The basis of the argument of counsel for the surveyor against this award starts with the general proposition on the measure of damages enunciated by Lord Blackburn in *Livingstone v Rawyards Coal Co* (1880) 5 App Cas 25 at 39:

'. . . where any injury is to be compensated by damages, in settling the sum of money to be given for reparation of damages you should as nearly as possible get at that sum of money which will put the party who has been injured, or who has suffered, in the same position as he would have been in if he had not sustained the wrong for which he is now getting his compensation or reparation.'

Counsel submits that so far from putting the finance company in the position they would have been in if they had not entered into the mortgage agreement, they are in a much better one by recovering interest payments at an extremely high rate. He admits that all the general expenses in preparing the mortgage, the legal costs of obtaining possession and the sale of the property are recoverable as being in the category of damages naturally flowing from the surveyor's negligence, but the contractual interest is a benefit resulting from the finance company's entering into the mortgage contract. If they are to be placed in the same position as they would have been in if they had never entered into the mortgage contract the finance company clearly cannot recover moneys only payable under that contract. The finance company's claim, he argues, in effect puts them in the

same position as if the surveyor had warranted or guaranteed the performance by the
a Clarkes of their contractual obligations, which he had not. Neither had he warranted the
correctness of his valuation. Counsel concedes that the finance company could properly
recover as damages any loss they sustained by reason of losing the use of the £10,000
advanced under the mortgage, but that there would have to be evidence, which there
was not, that the finance company could have applied the £10,000 in another mortgage
investment or at the very least to have earned interest by placing it on deposit.

b   As a matter of principle, I would, for my part, find these arguments hard to resist, but
it is submitted by counsel for the finance company that the weight of authority shows
that the judge's decision as to the measure of damages is correct.

The textbook writers have drawn a distinction as to the proper measure of damages
between cases where a person has purchased a house on the basis of a negligent valuation
and suffered damage as a result and cases, such as the present, when a mortgagee has
c advanced money on a loan on the same basis, when but for the negligent valuation it
would not have advanced any money at all, or not so much. In the former category a line
of cases from *Philips v Ward* [1956] 1 All ER 874, [1956] 1 WLR 471 to *Perry v Sidney
Phillips & Son (a firm)* [1982] 3 All ER 705, [1982] 1 WLR 1297 has shown that the correct
measure of damages is the difference in value between the purchase price and the market
value of the house at the time of the purchase. In the case of a mortgagee who would not
d have made any advance but for the negligent valuation the measure of damages will be
the difference between the sum advanced and the sum recovered on sale of the property
plus any consequential loss and expenses (see *Clerk and Lindsell on Torts* (16th edn, 1989)
para 11–45). This definition does not, of course, answer the present problem and it is
necessary to look at the authorities on which it is based.

The first case is *Scholes v Brook* (1891) 63 LT 837, where Romer J gave damages to a
e mortgagee in an action against a negligent surveyor representing the whole loss he had
sustained through the deficiency of the security. Although his decision was upheld in
this court (see 64 LT 674), the report is too short to be satisfactory and again does not deal
directly with the present problem.

The most important case is *Baxter v F W Gapp & Co Ltd* [1938] 4 All ER 457. Here
again the mortgagee would not have advanced money on a house but for a negligent
f survey. Goddard LJ, sitting as an additional judge of the King's Bench Division, held that
the measure of damages was the whole loss sustained by the mortgagee and included the
expenses of abortive sales, insurance premiums, a builder's account for upkeep of the
property, the mortgagee's expenses and disbursements and the selling agent's commission
on the ultimate sale of the property, in addition to the principal advanced and the interest
unpaid by the mortgagor. The decision of Goddard LJ was also upheld by this court
g ([1939] 2 All ER 752, [1939] 2 KB 271). Counsel for the surveyor seeks to discount the
weight of that authority by pointing to the fact that Goddard LJ says that 'The loss which
he has suffered is not challenged in this case, as a figure' (see [1938] 4 All ER 457 at 466),
and says this issue was not argued. However, I think counsel for the finance company is
right when he submits that the reference is to the mathematics of calculating the figure
h rather than to the measure of damages which was clearly in dispute. While this case is
authority for the submission of counsel for the finance company in the present case, once
again the principle involved does not seem to have been argued, ie whether the interest
should be the contractual amount in the mortgage deed or what represents the loss of use
of the capital sum.

Corisand Investments Ltd v Druce & Co (1978) 248 EG 315 was a case where the
j mortgagees lent a greater sum than they would have done but for the negligent valuation.
Gibson J rejected the argument that the mortgagees were entitled to the 30% interest
they would have got if the borrowers had performed their contractual obligations.

However, in *London and South of England Building Society v Stone* [1983] 3 All ER 105 at
116, [1983] 1 WLR 1242 at 1256 O'Connor LJ, in referring to that decision, said: 'For
some reason which is not clear to me, Gibson J rejected the plaintiffs' claim for interest

. . .' In *Stone's* case the issue was whether the plaintiff mortgagee was obliged to pursue its rights against the mortgagors and take any amount recovered into account when suing *a* the negligent valuer, so the decision is not in point. Nevertheless O'Connor LJ held that *Baxter's* case was binding on the Court of Appeal (see [1983] 3 All ER 105 at 116, [1983] 1 WLR 1242 at 1255). Furthermore, Stephenson LJ said ([1983] 3 All ER 105 at 120, [1983] 1 WLR 1242 at 1261):

> 'Though the identity of the borrowers was of no interest or relevance to the valuer *b* or his duty to the lender, the amount of the advance and the length of time for repayment were. Though the mortgage deed by way of legal charge gave the lender a right to foreclose for other breaches of covenant, the object of securing the loan by charging the property was to secure repayment of the sum lent with interest under the covenant to repay. The borrowers' obligation to repay was therefore not so collateral or remote as to be disregarded altogether in measuring the lender's loss, *c* and although the valuer was not a party to the mortgage, and the mortgage was literally res inter alios acta, it was a transaction with which the valuer's report and valuation and breach of duty were closely connected, as now demonstrated by the decision of Park J in *Yianni v Edwin Evans & Sons (a firm)* [1981] 3 All ER 592, [1982] QB 438.'

These observations evidently weaken the argument of counsel for the surveyor that *d* the valuer is not concerned with or responsible for the acts of the mortgagor.

In the result, although the authorities are not entirely satisfactory in resolving the question whether a mortgagee in these circumstances is entitled to recover loss of contractual interest under the mortgage from the negligent valuer, they are binding on this court.

I would accordingly dismiss this appeal. *e*

SIR JOHN MEGAW. Despite the cogent arguments of counsel for the surveyor, I think that we are bound to dismiss this appeal on the authority of the decision of this court in *Baxter v F W Gapp & Co Ltd* [1939] 2 All ER 752, [1939] 2 KB 271.

However, lest that view of the effect of *Baxter's* case should be wrong, I think it is desirable to indicate why, if the issue were free from authority, I should not feel able to *f* accept the submission by counsel for the surveyor as to the correct approach to the assessment of damages in this case.

There is no doubt what the law is, at any rate so far as this court is concerned, where a negligent valuation has been provided to the potential purchaser of a house, with the result that the house has been bought at a price above the market value. *Perry v Sidney Phillips & Son (a firm)* [1982] 3 All ER 705, [1982] 1 WLR 1297 confirms that in such a *g* case the measure of damages is the difference between the inflated, negligent valuation at which the house was bought, in reliance on the valuation, and the true market value of the house at the date of the purchase. (The question did not arise in that case; but presumably, if there had been a lapse of time between the date of the valuation and the date of the purchase, the relevant market value might have to be adjusted, if there had *h* been a material change between the two dates, due to extraneous circumstances.)

The issue decided in *Perry's* case was as to the date by reference to which the damages were to be calculated. The answer was that it was the date when the loss was actually incurred. The loss was incurred when, as a result of the surveyor's negligence, the purchaser became the owner of a house for which he had paid £X, whereas the market value of that house was £(X − Y). This is consonant with the general principle in tort. *j* The tort is committed when loss is incurred as a result of negligence, whether or not the fact of the negligence or of the loss is known as at that moment.

As it appears to me, the analogy of the principle laid down in *Perry's* case, the purchase of a house on a negligent valuation, applies to a case such as the present. The damages have to be calculated by reference to the date when the loss is incurred. No loss is

incurred, nor can anyone foretell whether any loss is going to be incurred, as a result of
a the surveyor's negligent valuation, unless and until the third party, the borrower under
the loan contract with the lender, defaults on the payments due under the loan contracts,
the lender seeks to exercise his right to enforce the security and the proceeds of the
security prove to be less than the total amount which the lender is then entitled to
recover from the borrower under the terms of the loan contract. Up to that time, or at
any rate up to the time when the lender decides to enforce the security, there may be a
b potential loss; but there is no actual loss.

There is no 'market value', so far as I am aware, ascertainable by reference to the bundle
of rights contained in a loan contract secured against property, varying according as the
value of the security is £X or £Y. In any case, unlike the purchase of a house, the value
of a loan contract to the lender, if it could be assessed in the market or otherwise, depends
on other elements besides the value of the security. If the loan contract proceeds to
c normal completion in accordance with its terms the lender suffers no loss. I can see no
practical basis for any distinction in the assessment of damages according to whether the
lender, if he had not been misled as to the value of the security, would not have entered
into a loan contract with that borrower or, alternatively, would have entered into a loan
contract but with a loan of a smaller amount. It might, depending on the figures, affect
d the amount recoverable; but why should it affect the method of assessment, at any rate
in a case where, as here, the error in the valuation is not known until the occasion has
arisen for realisation of the security?

In the absence of authority to the contrary, I should regard the correct principle of
damages as being that the claim for damages arises when the loss is incurred. The loss is
incurred if and when the lender, validly under the loan contract, realises the security,
and the amount realised is less than the amount due under the loan contract, including
e expenses properly incurred, and allowing for all payments made by the borrower. There
is one important qualification. The surveyor should not be liable for a greater amount
than the amount of his original overestimate of the value compared with the true market
value as at the date of the valuation. Any shortfall in the proceeds of the realisation above
that amount should not be regarded as being caused by the negligent valuation.

f Subject, possibly, to that qualification, which did not arise in *Baxter v F W Gapp & Co
Ltd*, it appears to me that the principle which I have suggested above is wholly in accord
with *Baxter's* case.

Application dismissed. Leave to appeal to the House of Lords refused.

g *6 June. The Appeal Committee of the House of Lords gave leave to appeal.*

Solicitors: *Brand Montague*, Harrow (for the finance company); *Reynolds Porter Chamberlain*
(for the surveyor).

Raina Levy   Barrister.

Practice Direction

SUPREME COURT TAXING OFFICE

Solicitor – Remuneration – Taxation of solicitor's bill of costs – Procedure – Originating summons – Drawing up of order – Appeals – Appeal to judge in chambers – Fees payable – Applications to which direction applies – Solicitors Act 1974, Pt III, ss 57(5), 61(1)(3)(5), 62, 63, 64(3), 68, 69, 70(1)(2)(3), 73 – RSC Ord 28, r 1A(1), Ord 32, Ord 42, rr 4, 5, Ord 58, Ord 106, r 3(1)(2), App A.

RSC Ord 106 gives to taxing masters the power to exercise the jurisdiction of the High Court under Pt III of the Solicitors Act 1974 in the Queen's Bench and Family Divisions.

All applications to the taxing master under the 1974 Act are by originating summons and must be in Form 10 in App A to the Rules of the Supreme Court. The proceedings will be issued in room 745. A solicitor who applies for an order under the Act for taxation of his bill of costs must lodge with his application a certificate that all the relevant requirements of the Act have been satisfied.

RSC Ord 28 applies to all originating summons procedure in the Supreme Court Taxing Office, save that where application is made for taxation of a solicitor's bill of costs the requirements of Ord 28, r 1A(1) (as to the filing of affidavit evidence) will not be implemented unless it is known that the application will be contested, the Taxing Master so directs or a certificate as to special circumstances is sought.

Every application for taxation of a solicitor's bill of costs must be accompanied by the original or a copy (certified by the solicitor to be a true copy) of the original bill or bills.

If during the course of an application under Pt III of the 1974 Act it is necessary for any interlocutory application to be made this should be done on summons which should be taken to room 745 for issue in accordance with Ord 32 by the clerk in charge of Solicitors Act applications. The party issuing the summons must indicate the time required for the application or, if it be preferable, request a (short) directions hearing. If possible a date and time of hearing will be given immediately; if that is not possible the party issuing the summons will be notified of the time and date as soon as possible. It is the responsibility of the party issuing the summons to serve it on any opposing party.

Once an order has been made Ord 42, r 4 will apply. The order must normally be drawn up and it is the responsibility of the party having custody of the summons on which the order is indorsed to do so (Ord 42, r 5). Two copies of the order are required, one for sealing and return and one for filing at the Supreme Court Taxing Office. The order must be taken for sealing to room 745. The party having carriage of the order must serve a copy of it on any opposing party.

In the event of either party being dissatisfied with the master's decision on either the substantive application or on an interlocutory summons, appeal lies to the judge in chambers in accordance with Ord 58.

With regard to the fees payable, if the application is for 'a solicitor's bill to be taxed' the fee payable is £10; if the application is for any other relief under Pt III of the 1974 Act the fee will be £60.

SCHEDULE OF APPLICATIONS

Set out below are the applications under RSC Ord 106 and Pt III of the Solicitors Act 1974 to which this Practice Direction applies.

i. Under RSC Ord 106, r 3(1) for an order for: (a) the delivery by the solicitor of a cash account; (b) the payment or delivery up by the solicitor of money or securities; (c) the delivery to the plaintiff of a list of the moneys or securities which the solicitor has in his possession or control on behalf of the plaintiff; (d) the payment into or lodging in court of any such moneys or securities.

ii. Under RSC Ord 106, r 3(2), a solicitor's application for such order for taxation and payment, or securing the payment of costs and the protection of his lien, if any, as the court thinks fit.

iii. Under s 57(5) of the Solicitors Act 1974, where a non-contentious business agreement is relied on by the solicitor and objected to by the client as unfair and unreasonable, for inquiry and certificate whether the agreement should be set aside.

iv. Under s 61(1) of the 1974 Act in relation to a contentious business agreement, as to the enforcement or setting aside of the agreement and questions as to its validity and effect.

v. Under s 61(3) of the 1974 Act for a contentious business agreement to be examined as to its fairness and reasonableness.

vi. Under s 61(5) of the 1974 Act, where the amount agreed under a contentious business agreement has been paid, for the agreement to be reopened and the costs taxed.

vii. Under s 62 of the 1974 Act, where a client who makes a contentious business agreement makes it as a representative of a person whose property will be chargeable with the amount payable under the agreement, for the agreement to be laid before a taxing master before payment.

viii. Under s 63 of the 1974 Act, where after some business has been done under a contentious business agreement, but before the solicitor has wholly performed it, (a) the solicitor dies or becomes incapable of acting or (b) the client changes his solicitors.

ix. Under s 64(3) of the 1974 Act, where an action is commenced on a gross sum bill, for an order that the bill be taxed.

x. Under s 68 of the 1974 Act, for the delivery by a solicitor of a bill of costs and for the delivery up of, or otherwise in relation to, any documents.

xi. Under s 69 of the 1974 Act for an order that the solicitor be at liberty to commence an action to recover his costs within one month of delivery of the bill.

xii. Under s 70(1) of the 1974 Act, by the party chargeable, for taxation.

xiii. Under s 70(2) of the 1974 Act, by either party, for taxation.

xiv. Under s 70(3) of the 1974 Act for taxation showing special circumstances.

xv. Under s 71(1) of the 1974 Act for taxation by a person, other than the party chargeable with the bill.

xvi. Under s 71(3) of the 1974 Act for taxation by any person interested in any property out of which a trustee, executor or administrator has paid or is entitled to pay a solicitor's bill.

xvii. Under s 73 of the 1974 Act for a charging order.

This Practice Direction will take effect from 1 October 1990.

P T Hurst
Vacation Master for
Chief Taxing Master.

20 August 1990

The Bowbelle

QUEEN'S BENCH DIVISION (ADMIRALTY COURT)
SHEEN J
8, 13 MARCH 1990

Shipping – Limitation of liability – Limitation fund – Notice of limitation fund – Prevention of arrest of other vessels – Notice of limitation fund to be filed in Admiralty Registry – Merchant Shipping Act 1979, Sch 4, Pt I, art 13(1).

A shipowner whose vessel has been involved in a collision and who wishes to avoid dislocation of trade caused by the arrest of other vessels of his by persons claiming in respect of damage arising out of the collision after he has set up a limitation fund under art 13(1)[a] of the Convention on Limitation of Liability for Maritime Claims 1976, which has the force of law in the United Kingdom and is set out in Pt I of Sch 4 to the Merchant Shipping Act 1979, and which provides that a person who has a claim against a limitation fund set up by a shipowner may not arrest any ship in the same ownership, should file in the Admiralty Registry a notice signed by his solicitor undertaking to acknowledge service of the writ in any action begun against the shipowner and stating that a limitation fund in respect of damage arising from the relevant incident has been constituted by payment into court of the appropriate amount. Thereafter any person who has a claim arising out of the same incident and who wishes to contend that the shipowner's conduct bars his right to limitation may pursue that allegation but without the security provided by the arrest of a ship (see p 480 *e* to *g*, post).

Notes

For limitation of liability under the Merchant Shipping Act 1979, see 43 Halsbury's Laws (4th edn) paras 1121–1130.

For the Merchant Shipping Act 1979, s 17, Sch 4, Pt I, art 13, see 39 Halsbury's Statutes (4th edn) 909, 961.

Case referred to in judgment

Wladyslaw Lokietek, The [1978] 2 Lloyd's Rep 520, DC.

Appeal

The owners of the vessel Bowbelle and of five named sister ships, who were the first defendants in an action in rem commenced by an amended writ issued on 20 January 1990 by the plaintiff, Sally Ann Smith, who sued on her own behalf and on behalf of other dependants and as administratrix of the estate of Jane Louise Bourke, against the first defendants and against the second defendants, the owners of the vessel Marchioness and of three named sister ships, appealed against the decision of the Admiralty Registrar refusing to give leave to file in the Admiralty and Commercial Court Registry a praecipe requesting that a caveat against an issue of a warrant to arrest any of the 14 ships named in the praecipe be entered in the praecipe book. The appeal was heard in chambers but judgment was given by Sheen J in open court. The facts are set out in the judgment.

Simon Rainey for the owners of the Bowbelle.
The plaintiff and the second defendants did not appear.

Cur adv vult

---

a Article 13, so far as material, is set out at p 478 *j* to p 479 *b*, post

13 March. The following judgment was delivered.

SHEEN J. On 20 August 1989 there was a collision between the ship Bowbelle and the ship Marchioness in the river Thames. It was a disastrous collision, which resulted in the loss of many lives and many persons suffered injury and loss. It is common knowledge that the collision occurred during the hours of darkness but in good visibility. The court is not aware of any facts relevant to liability for the collision.

The court has before it an appeal by the owners of Bowbelle against a decision of the Admiralty Registrar refusing to give leave to file in the registry a praecipe requesting that a caveat against the issue of a warrant to arrest any of the 14 ships named in the praecipe be entered in the caveat book. The praecipe requests a caveat against arrest by reason of the payment into court of the limitation fund of the owners of the Bowbelle in respect of damage resulting from the collision. The solicitors for the owners undertake to acknowledge service of the writ in any action arising out of the collision against any of the named ships. I decided to give judgment in open court because the application raises a matter of practice which is not covered by the Rules of the Supreme Court.

The only rule which enables a shipowner to give warning that one of his ships ought not to be arrested is RSC Ord 75, r 6, which provides:

'(1) A person who desires to prevent the arrest of any property must file in the registry a praecipe, in Form No. 5 in Appendix B, signed by him or his solicitor undertaking—(a) to acknowledge issue or service (as may be appropriate) of the writ in any action that may be begun against the property described in the praecipe, and (b) within 3 days after receiving notice that such an action has been begun, to give bail in the action in a sum not exceeding an amount specified in the praecipe or to pay the amount so specified into court; and on the filing of the praecipe a caveat against the issue of a warrant to arrest the property described in the praecipe shall be entered in the caveat book.

(2) The fact that there is a caveat against arrest in force shall not prevent the issue of a warrant to arrest the propery to which the caveat relates.'

The owners of the Bowbelle contend that by virtue of the provisions of the Merchant Shipping Act 1979 they cannot be compelled to give bail or any other security beyond that provided by the limitation fund which has been constituted by them. They contend that if any ship owned by them were to be arrested in respect of a claim arising out of the collision the court would be bound to order the release of that ship without further security being provided. For this reason they contend that they are entitled to give warning to any person contemplating such an arrest that the arrest would be pointless and that it might result in a claim for damages.

They contend that the appropriate way of giving such a warning is to enter a caveat in the caveat book. RSC Ord 75, r 7, provides:

'Where any property with respect to which a caveat against arrest is in force is arrested in pursuance of a warrant of arrest, the party at whose instance the caveat was entered may apply to the Court by motion for an order under this rule and, on the hearing of the application, the Court, unless it is satisfied that the party procuring the arrest of the property had a good and sufficient reason for so doing, may by order discharge the warrant and may also order the last-mentioned party to pay to the applicant damages in respect of the loss suffered by the applicant as a result of the arrest.'

The law

On 1 December 1986 by the Merchant Shipping Act 1979 (Commencement No 10) Order 1986, SI 1986/1052, there was a profound change in the law which gives shipowners and others the right to limit their liability in respect of certain claims. On that date there came into force those parts of the 1979 Act dealing with limitation of liability. Section 17 of the Act provides:

'(1) The provisions of the Convention on Limitation of Liability for Maritime Claims 1976 as set out in Part I of Schedule 4 to this Act (hereafter in this section and in Part II of that Schedule referred to as "the Convention") shall have the force of law in the United Kingdom.

(2) The provisions of Part II of that Schedule shall have effect in connection with the Convention, and the preceding subsection shall have effect subject to the provisions of that Part.'

Part II of Sch 4 to the Act contains the text of the Convention on Limitation of Liability for Maritime Claims 1976 (London, 1–19 November 1976; TS 13 (1990); Cm 955), of which the following parts are relevant:

'ARTICLE 1

Persons entitled to limit liability

1. Shipowners and salvors, as hereinafter defined, may limit their liability in accordance with the rules of this Convention for claims set out in Article 2 . . .

7. The act of invoking limitation of liability shall not constitute an admission of liability.

ARTICLE 2

Claims subject to limitation

1. Subject to Articles 3 and 4 the following claims, whatever the basis of liability may be, shall be subject to limitation of liability: (a) claims in respect of loss of life or personal injury or loss of or damage to property occurring on board or in direct connexion with the operation of the ship . . . and consequential loss resulting therefrom . . .

ARTICLE 4

Conduct barring limitation

A person liable shall not be entitled to limit his liability if it is proved that the loss resulted from his personal act or omission, committed with the intent to cause such loss, or recklessly and with knowledge that such loss would probably result . . .

ARTICLE 11

Constitution of the fund

1. Any person alleged to be liable may constitute a fund with the Court or other competent authority in any State Party in which legal proceedings are instituted in respect of claims subject to limitation. The fund shall be constituted in the sum of such of the amounts set out in Articles 6 and 7 as are applicable to claims for which that person may be liable, together with interest thereon from the date of the occurrence giving rise to the liability until the date of the constitution of the fund. Any fund thus constituted shall be available only for the payment of claims in respect of which limitation of liability can be invoked . . .

ARTICLE 13

Bar to other actions

1. Where a limitation fund has been constituted in accordance with Article 11, any person having made a claim against the fund shall be barred from exercising any right in respect of such a claim against any other assets of a person by or on behalf of whom the fund has been constituted.

2. After a limitation fund has been constituted in accordance with Article 11, any ship or other property, belonging to a person on behalf of whom the fund has been

constituted, which has been arrested or attached within the jurisdiction of a State Party for a claim which may be raised against the fund, or any security given, may be released by order of the Court or other competent authority of such State. However, such release shall always be ordered if the limitation fund has been constituted: (a) at the part where the occurrence took place . . .

3. The rules of paragraphs 1 and 2 shall apply only if the claimant may bring a claim against the limitation fund before the Court administering that fund and the fund is actually available and freely transferable in respect of that claim . . .'

In considering the effect of those provisions on shipowners and in order to appreciate the dramatic change which has been brought about by the enactment of the 1976 convention it is helpful to have in mind the state of the law immediately preceding the coming into force of that part of the 1979 Act.

On 10 October 1957 there was signed at Brussels an International Convention relating to the Limitation of the Liability of Owners of Sea-going Ships (TS 52 (1968); Cmnd 3678). The preamble to the 1957 convention states that the high contracting parties have recognised the desirability of determining by agreement certain uniform rules relating to the limitation of the liability of owners of seagoing ships. In that convention the British system of limitation of liability was adopted and by art 5 an attempt was made to ensure that when and wherever claims were made against a shipowner who had the right to limit his liability that shipowner would be able to give bail or satisfactory security or establish one limitation fund against which all claims arising out of one incident would be brought. The 1957 convention started with the statement that the owner of a seagoing ship may limit his liability in accordance with this convention in respect of claims arising from certain stated occurrences 'unless the occurrence giving rise to the claim resulted from the actual fault or privity of the owner'. Those last few words are the time honoured words which were found in s 503 of the Merchant Shipping Act 1894.

For the purpose of giving effect to art 5 of the 1957 convention s 5 of the Merchant Shipping (Liability of Shipowners and Others) Act 1958 was enacted. The opening words of that section are:

'(1) Where a ship or other property is arrested in connection with a claim *which appears to the court* to be founded on a liability to which a limit is set by section five hundred and three of the Merchant Shipping Act, 1894 . . .'

In respect of any claim arising before 1 December 1986 a shipowner who claimed that he was entitled to limit his liability by virtue of s 503 had to discharge the burden of proving that the occurrence giving rise to the claim occurred without his actual fault or privity. In 1976 a collision between a German ship and a Polish ship took place in fog in the Baltic Sea. The owners of the Polish ship constituted a limitation fund in a court in Poland. In May 1977 the ship Wladyslaw Lokietek, which was a sister-ship of the Polish ship in collision, was arrested in this country. After security had been given the ship was released from arrest. Her owners applied for the release of the security, relying on s 5 of the 1958 Act. In the *Wladyslaw Lokietec* [1978] 2 Lloyd's Rep 520 Brandon J held that on such an application the shipowner had to show that there was no serious question to be tried in relation to the absence of actual fault or privity on his part and it was not enough for him merely to show that he had a prima facie case or a reasonably arguable case on that issue. That decision frustrated the use of s 5. It appears to me that art 13 of the 1976 convention was drafted with the intention of overcoming the effect of that decision and of ensuring that shipowners would only be compelled to provide one limitation fund, in respect of any one incident giving rise to claims.

I return to consider the 1976 convention, under which shipowners agreed to a higher limit of liability in exchange for an almost indisputable right to limit their liability. The effect of arts 2 and 4 is that the claims mentioned in art 2 are subject to limitation of liability unless the person making the claim proves (and the burden of proof is now on him) that the loss resulted from the personal act or omission of the shipowner committed with the intent to cause such loss, or recklessly and with knowledge that such loss would *a* probably result. This imposes on the claimant a very heavy burden.

But, regardless of whether a claimant contends that he can prove that the shipowner was guilty of conduct barring limitation, the combined effect of arts 2 and 13 is that a shipowner can only be compelled to constitute one fund in accordance with art 11. Article 2 sets out the categories of claims which are subject to limitation of liability. The claims against the owners of the Bowbelle come within para 1(*a*). I turn now to art 13. It *b* is clear that any claimant may bring a claim against the limitation fund in court. Therefore by virtue of para 3 the rules set out in paras 1 and 2 apply.

Paragraph 1 makes it clear that any person who has made a claim against the fund in court is not entitled to arrest any ship in the same ownership as the Bowbelle.

Any person who has a claim against the owners of the Bowbelle (but has not yet made a claim against the fund) has 'a claim which may be raised against the fund'. The fund *c* has been constituted in London, which is 'the port where the occurrence took place'. Accordingly, if one of the ships named in the praecipe were to be arrested the court would be bound to order its release. The fund has been constituted by the owners of the Bowbelle in accordance with art 11 in 'respect of claims subject to limitation'. Those last six words clearly refer to the categories set out in art 2. The draftsman has omitted the words '*which appears to the court* to be founded on a liability to which a limit is set' which *d* led to the decision in *The Wladyslaw Lokietek* [1978] 2 Lloyd's Rep 520. The court is not required to investigate the question whether the shipowner has been guilty of conduct barring limitation. In these circumstances common sense dictates that there should be some machinery by which warning can be given to would-be arresters that they should not arrest any of the ships belonging to the owners of the Bowbelle. The current Rules of *e* the Supreme Court have not made provision for this situation. Until such provision is made, shipowners who wish to provide some protection against unnecessary dislocation of trade caused by the arrest of their ships should file in the Admiralty and Commercial Registry a praecipe which must be signed by their solicitor who must undertake to acknowledge service of the writ in any action which may be begun against the owners of the ship in question and state that a limitation found in respect of damage arising from *f* the relevant incident has been constituted by payment into court of the appropriate amount.

Any person who has a claim arising out of the same incident and who wishes to contend that the conduct of the shipowner bars his right to limitation may nevertheless pursue that allegation but he will not have the security provided by the arrest of a ship.

Appeal allowed. *g*

Solicitors: *Hill Taylor Dickinson* (for the owners of the Bowbelle).

N P Metcalfe Esq   Barrister.

Armour and another v Thyssen Edelstahlwerke AG

HOUSE OF LORDS

LORD KEITH OF KINKEL, LORD GRIFFITHS, LORD OLIVER OF AYLMERTON, LORD GOFF OF CHIEVELEY AND LORD JAUNCEY OF TULLICHETTLE

25, 26, 27, 28 JULY, 18 OCTOBER 1990

Sale of goods – Passing of property – Vendor retaining property in goods – Contract reserving property in goods to vendor until payment of all debts due to vendor – Purchaser becoming insolvent – Goods transferred to purchaser pursuant to contract of sale – Whether property in goods remaining property of vendor or forming part of assets of purchaser – Whether reservation of property clause effective to create right of security over goods without transfer of possession – Sale of Goods Act 1979, ss 19(2), 62(4).

The appellants, a German steel manufacturing company, sold and supplied to C Ltd, a Scottish engineering company, quantities of steel strip for use in its manufacturing processes. The contracts of sale were subject to a condition that the property in the goods would not pass to C Ltd until all debts due from the purchaser to the vendor had been paid. Subsequently, the respondents were appointed joint receivers of C Ltd and a dispute arose between them and the appellants whether the steel strip remained the property of the latter or formed part of the assets of C Ltd available to its creditors. The respondents raised an action against the appellants in the Court of Session in Scotland claiming, inter alia, a declarator that C Ltd were the owners of the steel and that they were entitled to take possession of it and sell it. The Lord Ordinary held that the reservation of property clause in the contract constituted an ineffective attempt to create a right of security over the steel strip without transfer of possession, contrary to Scottish law and therefore the property in the steel strip had passed to C Ltd on delivery. The Second Division of the Inner House of the Court of Session affirmed the decision. The appellants appealed to the House of Lords, contending that by virtue of s 19(1)[a] of the Sale of Goods Act 1979 the reservation of the right of disposal until all debts had been paid had the effect that the property in the goods did not pass until the condition was fulfilled. The respondents contended that the word 'conditions' in s 19(1) was to be construed as excluding any condition which had the effect of creating a right of security over the goods.

Held – A condition in a contract for the sale of goods reserving title to the seller until the contract price and all other debts had been paid did not constitute an exception to the general rule in Scottish law that a right of security over goods was incapable of being created without transfer of possession, since the essence of a right of security was that the debtor retained the ultimate right to the goods and until the condition was satisfied the title to the goods remained in the creditor. Accordingly, the appellants had not created a right of security over the steel. The reservation of property condition in the contract was not a separate transaction in the form of a contract of sale but was simply one of the conditions of what was a genuine sale and therefore s 62(4)[b] of the 1979 Act, which excepted contracts by way of mortgage, pledge, charge or other security from the operation of the Act, had no application to the transaction. It followed that the respondents were not entitled to possession of the steel. The appeal would therefore be allowed (see p 484 g to p 485 a c f to j, p 486 d to p 487 b, post).

Emerald Stainless Steel Ltd v South Side Distribution Ltd 1982 SC 61 and *Deutz Engines Ltd v Terex Ltd* 1984 SLT 273 overruled.

---

a   Section 19(1) is set out at p 485 d e, post
b   Section 62(4) is set out at p 486 b c, post

Notes

For retention of title clauses in contracts for the sale of goods, see 41 Halsbury's Laws (4th
edn) paras 707, 731, and for cases on the transfer of property from seller to buyer in
general, see 39(2) Digest (Reissue) 255–263, 2042–2069.

For the Sale of Goods Act 1979, ss 19, 62, see 39 Halsbury's Statutes (4th edn) 124, 151.

Cases referred to in opinions

Clough Mill Ltd v Martin [1984] 3 All ER 982, [1985] 1 WLR 111, CA.
Cowan v Spence (1824) 3 S 42 (new edn 28), Ct of Sess (Outer House).
Deutz Engines Ltd v Terex Ltd 1984 SLT 273, Ct of Sess (Outer House).
Emerald Stainless Steel Ltd v South Side Distribution Ltd 1982 SC 61, Ct of Sess (Outer House).
Macartney v Macredie's Creditor (1799) Mor App (Sale) 1, Ct of Sess (Outer House).
Murdoch (John G) & Co Ltd v Greig (1889) 16 R 396, Ct of Sess (Outer House).

Appeal

Thyssen Edelstahlwerke AG, a company incorporated under the laws of the Federal
Republic of Germany, appealed against the interlocutor of the Second Division of the
Inner House of the Court of Session, Scotland (the Lord Justice Clerk (Ross), Lords
McDonald and Wylie) (1989 SLT 182) dated 6 July 1988 refusing a reclaiming motion
by the appellants against an interlocutor pronounced by the Lord Ordinary (Mayfield)
(1986 SLT 452) dated 4 February 1986 to the effect that the respondents, Peter Hamish
Armour and Frank Hutchison Mycroft, joint receivers of the property and undertaking
of Carron Co Ltd, were entitled to take possession of a quantity of steel on the ground
that the property in it passed to Carron on delivery. The facts are set out in the opinion
of Lord Keith.

Jonathan Mance QC and *J W McNeill* (of the Scottish Bar) for the appellants.
J E Drummond Young QC and *N F Davidson* (both of the Scottish Bar) for the respondents.

Their Lordships took time for consideration.

18 October. The following opinions were delivered.

LORD KEITH OF KINKEL. My Lords, the appellants are a company carrying on
business in West Germany as manufacturers and suppliers of steel. The respondents are
the joint receivers of the assets of Carron Co Ltd (Carron), appointed on 3 August 1982
under powers contained in a floating charge in favour of two banks. Carron carried on
business at Falkirk as manufacturers of metal, plastic and general engineering products.

For a considerable period prior to 3 August 1982 the appellants and Carron engaged in
a course of dealing under which the appellants sold and supplied to Carron steel strip for
use in their manufacturing processes. The contracts of sale between them were expressed
as being subject to the appellants' general conditions of delivery and payment. At the
time of the respondents' appointment as receivers there were lying in Carron's works at
Falkirk some 67,423 kg of steel strip which had been delivered in pursuance of such
contracts. Part of the steel had been cut into sheets and a further part was in course of
being so cut, but most of it was in the state in which it had been delivered. The invoice
price of the 67,423 kg was £71,769, no part of which had been paid.

Clause I(3)(1) of the appellants' general conditions of delivery and payment provided,
according to an agreed translation from the German:

'All goods delivered by us remain our property (goods remaining in our
ownership) until all debts owed to us including any balances existing at relevant
times—due to us on any legal grounds—are settled. This also holds good if payments

are made for the purpose of settlement of specially designated claims. Debts owed
a   to companies, being members of our combine, are deemed to be such debts.'

Following the respondents' appointment as receivers, a dispute arose between them
and the appellants whether the 67,423 kg of steel strip remained the property of the
latter, by reason of cl I(3)(1), or whether they formed part of the assets of Carron available
to their preferred or other creditors. By telex dated 12 August 1982 the respondents
b   informed the appellants that if they were able to prove retention of title the steel strip
would be returned or paid for if used. In February 1983 the respondents raised an action
against the appellants in the Court of Session claiming a number of declarators, the only
one that remains relevant for purposes of this appeal being a declarator that Carron were
the owners of all steel supplied to them by the appellants and delivered to Carron's
premises. The appellants lodged a counterclaim concluding for payment by the
c   respondents personally of the invoice price of 67,423 kg of steel strip, namely £71,769.

The case went to proof before Lord Mayfield, who on 4 February 1986 decided in
favour of the respondents (see 1986 SLT 452). A considerable amount of the proof was
taken up with competing expert evidence about German law, which was claimed by the
appellants to govern the contracts of sale. At the end of the day the Lord Ordinary was
unable to reach any clear view about the nature and effect of the relevant German law, so
d   he proceeded on the presumption that it was the same as the applicable law of Scotland.
He was further of the opinion that in any event Scots law, as the lex situs, governed the
ownership of the goods. According to that law, cl I(3)(1) amounted to an ineffective
attempt to create a right of security over the steel strip without transfer of possession.
The property in the steel strip passed to Carron on delivery. In reaching this conclusion
the Lord Ordinary followed two decisions of Lord Ross in the Outer House, namely
e   *Deutz Engines Ltd v Terex Ltd* 1984 SLT 273 and *Emerald Stainless Steel Ltd v South Side
Distribution Ltd* 1982 SC 61.

The appellants reclaimed, and the reclaiming action was heard by the Second Division
(the Lord Justice Clerk (Ross), Lords McDonald and Wylie). No attempt was made to
found on the law of West Germany. On 6 July 1988 the Second Division found in favour
of the respondents on substantially the same grounds as had the Lord Ordinary, namely
f   that cl I(3)(1) constituted an attempt, ineffective under the law of Scotland, to create a
right of security over corporeal moveables without transfer of possession, and that the
property in the steel strip had passed to Carron on delivery (see 1989 SLT 182). The
appellants now appeal to your Lordships' House.

It is well settled in the law of Scotland that a condition in a contract for the sale of
corporeal moveables which provides that, notwithstanding delivery, ownership of the
g   goods shall not pass to the buyer until the price had been paid is valid and effective. This
was accepted in the opinion of the Lord Justice Clerk, referring to *Stair's Institutions* (5th
edn, 1832 (More)) I.XIV.4, *Gloag and Irvine on the Law of Rights in Security* (1897) p 241,
Macartney v Macredie's Creditor (1799) Mor App (Sale) 1, *John G Murdoch & Co Ltd v Greig*
(1889) 16 R 396 and *Cowan v Spence* (1824) 3 S 42 (new edn 28).

Cowan v Spence was a case where the petitioner had granted to a partnership a sublease
h   for a period of years of certain houses and lands and also of a paper mill situated on the
lands. The petitioner was the owner of certain moveable machinery in the paper mill
and elsewhere on the lands, and this was delivered to the partnership for their free use
and benefit during the currency of the sublease, subject to a provision that at its expiry—

j   'at the term of Whitsunday 1828, and upon all the rents or subtack duties hereby
contracted to be paid, and which may then be due, being fully paid up and
discharged the said . . . machinery shall be held to be the absolute and exclusive
property'

of the partnership. The latter was taken bound to pay, in addition to the rents, the further
sum of £450 annually as remuneration for the use of the machinery during the currency

of the sublease. The partnership was sequestrated under the Bankruptcy Act in 1822 and
the respondent, having been appointed trustee, claimed the machinery for behoof of the *a*
creditors. The First Division decided that the petitioner was entitled to the machinery,
on the ground that it was to belong to the partnership only in the event of the rents and
other prestations being duly paid and on the expiration of the sublease, which period had
not arrived. It is a feature of the case that the contract did not specifically fix any price for
the machinery, though the provision for payment of the annual sums of £450 may
perhaps warrant the case being regarded as an early instance of a hire-purchase agreement. *b*
It is to be noted, however, that transfer of the property in the machinery was expressed
as being conditional not only on payment of these sums but also on payment of all rents
due under the sublease of the heritable property.

The Lord Justice Clerk took the view that the validity of a provision in a contract for
the sale of goods that the property in the goods should not pass until the price had been
paid constituted a particular exception to the general rule that security over corporeal *c*
moveables is incapable of being created without transfer of possession. That rule is thus
expressed in *Gloag and Irvine on the Law of Rights in Security* (1897) pp 188–189:

> 'It is a cardinal rule of the common law of Scotland that no real right to corporeal
> moveable subjects can be transmitted by a voluntary conveyance, assignation, or
> other transfer, unless and until the transfer is completed by delivery of the subjects *d*
> in question to the transferee ... The rule that a security over moveables *retenta
> possessione* is of no effect is so well settled that the cases where it has been attempted
> to uphold an express security resting merely on a verbal or written assignation, have
> not been very numerous.'

In the Lord Justice Clerk's opinion an 'all debts' provision such as cl I(3)(1) is designed
to provide security without possession and thus falls foul of the general rule. It is to be *e*
observed, however, that at the outset of the chapter in which the general rule is expressed
Gloag and Irvine p 187 states:

> 'It is proposed in this and the succeeding chapters to consider by what methods a
> party in possession of [corporeal moveable] property may convey or transfer it in
> security; that is, by what methods he may, while retaining the ownership in, or at *f*
> least the ultimate right to, the subject, confer on a particular creditor a right over it,
> which will enable that creditor to vindicate that subordinate right in a question
> with the general creditors of his author, with particular creditors attaching the
> subject by diligence, or with a third party to whom it may have been transferred.'

In the present case the appellants, the owners of the steel strip, transferred possession *g*
of it to Carron under what was unquestionably a contract of sale. There was no question
of the appellants creating a right of security. They were not in the position of debtors
seeking to give a right of security to a creditor. They were themselves creditors of Carron
for the price of the steep strip and it may be for other debts also. Carron obtained
possession of the steel strip on delivery, subject to a condition that they should not obtain
the property until they had paid all debts due to the appellants. Can it be said that Carron *h*
somehow attempted to create a security over the goods in favour of the appellants? In
order that it might do so it would require to have both the ownership and the possession,
actual or constructive, of the goods. The essence of a right in security is that the debtor
retains at least what *Gloag and Irvine* calls the ultimate right to the goods. Can it be said
that Carron obtained anything which gave them the capacity to retain an ultimate right
to the goods? That could be so only if the contract of sale gave them the property in the *j*
goods, but the contract of sale said that the property in the goods was not to pass until all
debts due to the appellants had been paid. We are here very far removed from the
situation where a party in possession of corporeal moveables is seeking to create a
subordinate right in favour of a creditor while retaining the ultimate right to himself. It
is true that by entering into the contract of the sale Carron agreed that they should

receive possession of the goods on delivery but should not acquire the property until all
a debts due to the appellants had been paid, and thus agreed that the appellants would in
effect have security over the goods after they had come into Carron's possession. But at
that stage Carron had no interest of any kind whatever in any particular goods. Carron
were never in a position to confer on the appellants any subordinate right over the steel
strip, nor did they ever seek to do so.

Section 17 of the Sale of Goods Act 1979 provides:

b
'(1) Where there is a contract for the sale of specific or ascertained goods the
property in them is transferred to the buyer at such time as the parties to the
contract intend it to be transferred.

(2) For the purpose of ascertaining the intention of the parties regard shall be had
to the terms of the contract, the conduct of the parties and the circumstances of the
c case.'

In the present case the parties in the contract of sale clearly expressed their intention
that the property in the steel strip should not pass to Carron until all debts due by them
to the appellants had been paid. In my opinion there are no grounds for refusing to give
effect to that intention.

d Further, s 19(1) of the same Act provides:

'Where there is a contract for the sale of specific goods or where goods are
subsequently appropriated to the contract, the seller may, by the terms of the
contract or appropriation, reserve the right of disposal of the goods until certain
conditions are fulfilled; and in such a case, notwithstanding the delivery of the
goods to the buyer, or to a carrier or other bailee or custodier for the purpose of
e transmission to the buyer, the property in the goods does not pass to the buyer until
the conditions imposed by the seller are fulfilled.'

Here the appellants, by the terms of the contract of sale, have in effect reserved the
right of disposal of the steel strip until fulfilment of the condition that all debts due to
them by Carron have been paid. By virtue of this enactment, that has the effect that the
property in the goods did not pass to Carron until that condition had been fulfilled.
f Counsel for the respondents argued that the word 'conditions' in s 19(1) must be read as
excluding any condition which has the effect of creating a right of security over the
goods. I am, however, unable to regard a provision reserving title to the seller until
payment of all debts due to him by the buyer as amounting to the creation by the buyer
of a right of security in favour of the seller. Such a provision does in a sense give the seller
security for the unpaid debts of the buyer. But it does so by way of a legitimate retention
g of title, not by virtue of any right over his own property conferred by the buyer.

In all cases where a right of security is conferred the debtor retains an ultimate right
over the subject matter in question. The creditor, having realised out of that subject
matter a sufficient sum to meet the debt, is obliged to account to the debtor for any
surplus. Where, however, the seller of goods retains title until some condition has been
h satisfied, and on failure of such satisfaction repossesses them, then he is not obliged to
account to the buyer for any part of the value of the goods. Where the condition is to the
effect that the price of the goods shall have been paid and it has not been paid, then in
the situation where the market price of the goods has risen, so that they are worth more
than the contract price, the extra value belongs to the unpaid seller. That is clearly the
position where the condition relates to payment of the price of the actual goods, and goes
j to show that the retention of title provision is not one creating a right of security forming
an exception to the general rule requiring possession by the creditor. The same is true, in
my opinion, where the provision covers not only the price of the very goods which are
the subject of the particular contract of sale, but also debts due to the seller under other
contracts.

In *Clough Mill Ltd v Martin* [1984] 3 All ER 982, [1985] 1 WLR 111 it was held that a retention of title provision in a contract for the sale of goods did not constitute the creation of a charge conferring a security over the property of the purchasing company such as required to be registered under what was then s 95 of the Companies Act 1948. The judgments of the Court of Appeal contain interesting discussions of the problems which might arise where the goods, the subject matter of the contract of sale, had been partially paid for before being repossessed by the seller. In that case the court did not find it necessary to form a concluded view as to the solution of these problems, nor is it necessary in this case.

The judges of the Second Division placed some reliance on s 62(4) of the Sale of Goods Act 1979, which provides:

'The provisions of this Act about contracts of sale do not apply to a transaction in the form of a contract of sale which is intended to operate by way of mortgage, pledge, charge or other security.'

The view seems to have been that the transaction here could be treated as being both a sale of goods and an attempt to create security without possession. In so far as the transaction was a contract of sale it was good but the provisions of cl I(3)(1) were struck at by s 62(4). However, quite clearly cl I(3)(1) in itself is not a transaction in the form of a contract of sale. It is simply one of the conditions of what is a genuine contract of sale. In my opinion s 62(4) has no application to this case.

My Lords, I am of opinion that the reasoning of the Lord Ordinary and of the judges of the Second Division was erroneous, as was that of Lord Ross in *Emerald Stainless Steel Ltd v South Side Distribution Ltd* 1982 SC 61 and in *Deutz Engines Ltd v Terex Ltd* 1984 SLT 273. Clause I(3)(1) is valid and effective.

I would therefore allow the appeal and recall the interlocutors of the Second Division and of the Lord Ordinary, and find that the respondents are not entitled to any of the declarators concluded for in their action, but that the appellants are entitled to decree for payment as concluded for in their counterclaim.

LORD GRIFFITHS. My Lords, I have had the advantage of reading in draft the speech of my noble and learned friend Lord Keith and for the reasons he has given I would allow the appeal.

LORD OLIVER OF AYLMERTON. My Lords, I have had the opportunity of reading in draft the speech of Lord Keith. I agree with it and for the reasons he has given I would allow the appeal.

LORD GOFF OF CHIEVELEY. My Lords, I have had the opportunity of reading in draft the speech of my noble and learned friend Lord Keith. I agree with it and for the reasons he has given, I would allow the appeal.

LORD JAUNCEY OF TULLICHETTLE. My Lords, I have had the advantage of reading in draft the speech prepared by my noble and learned friend Lord Keith. I agree with it and for the reasons he has given and I would allow the appeal.

I consider that the courts below were in error in failing to appreciate the true nature of the transaction between the parties. A right in security is a right over property given by a debtor to a creditor whereby the latter in the event of the debtor's failure, acquires priority over the property against the general body of creditors of the debtor. It is of the essence of a right in security that the debtor possesses in relation to the property a right which he can transfer to the creditor, which right must be retransferred to him on payment of the debt. The Second Division took the view that cl I(3)(1) amounted to an ineffective attempt to create a right of security over moveables without the transfer of possession thereof. This conclusion presupposed that Carron were in a position to transfer

the title to the steel to the appellants, this being the only right available to them to
a transfer so long as they retained possession.

My Lords, in terms of the contract of sale Carron never acquired title to the steel. They
acquired possession thereof on delivery but would only have acquired dominium in and
hence title to it on fulfilment of the conditions in cl I(3)(1). It follows that they never
acquired any right under the contract, other than a right of possession, which they were
in a position to transfer in security to the appellants. The contract of sale did not attempt
b to create a right in security in favour of the appellants, rather did it operate to transfer
possession and dominium in two stages. Until the conditions of cl I(3)(1) were satisfied
dominium remained in the appellants.

Appeal allowed.

c Solicitors: *Pritchard Englefield & Tobin*, agents for *Bird Semple Fyfe Ireland WS*, Edinburgh
(for the appellants); *Masons*, agents for *MacRoberts*, Edinburgh (for the respondents).

Mary Rose Plummer   Barrister.

d
R v Bow Street Stipendiary Magistrate, ex parte Roberts and others

QUEEN'S BENCH DIVISION
e WATKINS LJ AND POTTS J
10 MAY 1990

*Judicial review – Application for judicial review – Application for leave to apply for judicial
review – Leave granted on some grounds but not on others – Whether necessary to seek additional
f leave to pursue further grounds – Whether applicant granted leave on some grounds entitled to
rely on other grounds at substantive hearing of application.*

The applicant was one of a number of defendants charged with mortgage frauds who
were committed for trial by a stipendiary magistrate. The defendants applied for leave
to apply for judicial review of the magistrate's decision. The judge granted leave in
respect of one of the grounds on which leave was sought but did not give leave on the
g other grounds. The applicant renewed his application before the Divisional Court in
order to obtain additional leave in respect of two of the grounds on which the judge had
declined to grant leave.

Held – An applicant for judicial review who wished to rely at the substantive hearing of
h the application on grounds other than those for which leave to apply was granted did not
need to renew his application for the purpose of obtaining leave in respect of those other
grounds but instead had to give notice to the respondent that he intended to rely on the
other grounds at the substantive hearing. The respondent could then file any affidavit on
which he wished to rely. It followed that since the defendants did not need leave in
respect of the grounds on which they had been refused their application would be
j dismissed (see p 489 *b* to *f*, post).

Notes
For applications for leave to move for judicial review, see 37 Halsbury's Laws (4th edn)
para 568.

Application for leave to apply for judicial review
Jonathan Howard Roberts, Janet Ann Thain, Michael John Digby Row and Jane Alison   *a*
Knapton applied for leave to apply for judicial review by way of an order of certiorari to
quash the decision of Ronald Bartle, a metropolitan stipendiary magistrate sitting at Bow
Street Magistrates' Court on 14 September 1989, committing the applicants to stand trial
at the Crown Court at Southwark on charges alleging offences contrary to s 17(1)(a) of
the Theft Act 1968. On 13 December 1989 Rose J granted the applicants leave to apply
for judicial review on one of the six grounds on which leave had been sought. Mr Roberts   *b*
and Mr Row renewed their applications for leave to apply for judicial review on two of
the other grounds on which they had originally sought leave. The facts are set out in the
judgment of Watkins LJ.

The applicants Roberts and Row appeared in person.
                                                                                          c
WATKINS LJ. These are renewed applications for judicial review. They are made by
Jonathan Howard Roberts, Janet Ann Thain, Michael John Digby Row and Jane Alison
Knapton. The origins of this affair were in the Bow Street Magistrates' Court where Mr
Bartle, a metropolitan stipendiary magistrate, conducted committal proceedings. They
affected the whole of the applicants, who faced five charges of breaches of the provisions
of s 17(1) of the Theft Act 1968. The following is a specimen of those charges: *d*

> 'That you Jonathan Howard Roberts with Janet Thain [who, incidentally, is his
> wife] on or about 13th August 1985 dishonestly and with a view to gain for
> yourselves or others, or with intent to cause loss to another, falsified a document
> required for accounting purposes, namely an application form to the Halifax
> Building Society for a mortgage in the sum of £39,900 in respect of a property   *e*
> known as 69 Woodbridge Hill, Guildford, Surrey.'

What is alleged is the commission of what are commonly known as mortgage frauds.
In the course of the committal proceedings a number of submissions were made by the
applicants, particularly by Mr Roberts himself, to the magistrate, all of which he rejected.
Notably he refused to accept that there had been an abuse through delay of process.
There was another submission made of no case to answer, which he rejected.   *f*
    The proceedings having terminated with the committal of the applicants for trial,
applications for judicial review were launched. They came before Rose J. He, having
considered them, gave leave to move to all the applicants in respect of ground (2) for the
relief sought. The relief sought was an order for certiorari to remove into this court for
the purpose of its being quashed the decision of the magistrate to commit the applicants
to stand trial at the Crown Court at Southwark. The grounds relied on are these: *g*

> '(1) that the learned Magistrate erred in law in rejecting a submission that there
> had been an abuse of Court process by reason of the delays in the mounting of the
> prosecution
> (2) that the learned Magistrate erred in law in not following the mandatory
> requirements of section 102(5) of the Magistrates' Court Act 1980 [that is the ground   *h*
> on which leave was given by the single judge]
> (3) that the learned Magistrate erred in law in not directing the Crown to
> particularise the charges against the Applicants
> (4) that the principles of natural justice were not adhered to by the failure of the
> Crown to supply each of the Applicants with a copy of the charges relating to each
> of the other Applicants   *j*
> (5) that the principles of natural justice were not adhered to by the failure of the
> learned Magistrate to allow to the Applicants and each of them facilities in his court
> for writing and the laying out of documents equal to those afforded to the Crown.'

The sixth ground affects Mr Row and Miss Knapton only:

'(6) that the learned Magistrate erred in law in failing to make any determination at all on an application by Michael John Digby Row that parts of certain written statements tendered in evidence under section 102 of the Magistrates' Courts Act 1980 were inadmissible in expressly leaving it to the discretion of the Crown as to whether it should rely upon such evidence at a later stage so that he was not thereby in a position to fulfil the obligation imposed upon him by rule 70(5)(a) of the Magistrates' Courts Rules 1981 [SI 1981/552]...'

The object of the renewal of the applications for leave to move is so that this court may give additional leave, so to speak, in respect of grounds (1) and (3), that is abuse of due process and failure to particularise charges against the applicants. Grounds (4), (5) and (6) have been expressly abandoned before us by all the applicants.

The practice as to reliance on grounds other than those which have formed the basis for the leave to move given by the single judge to an applicant for judicial review needs to be explained in the present context. It is this. Where an applicant has made an application for leave to apply for judicial review on a number of grounds and is given leave to move expressly on one of them, for example, it is unnecessary for him to renew his application to this court for the purpose of relying on the other grounds on which he has not specifically been given leave to move provided, and this is of the utmost importance, that he gives notice to the respondent whoever he may be, and if there is more than one then each of them, that he intends at the substantive hearing to rely on one or more of the other grounds on which he has not expressly been given by the single judge leave to move. That is so that the respondent shall have ample opportunity to consider his position in respect of the other grounds on which the applicant seeks to rely.

If that is not generally known and so as to remove all doubt about it for the future, I emphasise that any applicant who seeks to rely on grounds specified in his notice and in respect of which the single judge has not expressly given leave and who intends to rely on one or more of those other grounds should within 21 days of the service of his notice of motion serve on the respondent a notice which specifies that or those other grounds. It is not necessary to make formal renewal on Form 86B.

Thus in the instant case what the applicants have to do in respect of grounds (1) and (3) is within the next 21 days to give notice to the respondents of the intention to rely on those grounds. Because the normal period for filing affidavits has already elapsed the respondents will have from the day of the receipt of the notice from the applicants 56 days in which to file any affidavit or affidavits on which it is intended to rely. After the expiry of that 56-day period the matter can be listed before this court for hearing.

POTTS J. I agree.

Order accordingly.

Dilys Tausz   Barrister.

R v Secretary of State for the Environment, ex parte Simms
R v Secretary of State for the Environment, ex parte Burrows and another

COURT OF APPEAL, CIVIL DIVISION

PURCHAS, GLIDEWELL AND RUSSELL LJJ

26, 27 OCTOBER, 23 NOVEMBER 1989

Highway – Classification – Definitive map – Conclusive evidence of classification – Reclassification – Review – Review consequent on discovery of evidence showing highway wrongly described on map or that no public right of way existing over land – Bridleways shown on maps – Discovery of evidence after maps prepared showing one bridleway should be downgraded to footpath and that no right of way existing over land shown as bridleway – Whether after discovery of further evidence bridleway can be downgraded to footpath or right of way can be deleted on review of map – Whether map conclusive of existence of bridleways – Wildlife and Countryside Act 1981, ss 53(2)(3)(c)(ii)(iii), 56(1).

In two separate appeals the appellant sought modification of definitive maps recording public rights of way by the redefinition and deletion of bridleways. In the first case the appellant sought the downgrading to the status of a footpath of a right of way described on the definitive map prepared under the National Parks and Access to the Countryside Act 1949 as a bridleway, on the ground that the way was incorrectly recorded. In the second case the appellant sought the deletion of two rights of way described as bridleways on the map prepared by the county council, on the ground that they had never been rights of way of any description. The respective county councils refused to modify the maps as requested and the Secretary of State refused to entertain appeals by the appellants from those refusals, on the ground that s 56(1)[a] of the Wildlife and Countryside Act 1981 provided that a definitive map was 'conclusive evidence as to the particulars contained' in the map and therefore entry of a right of way on a definitive map as a bridleway was conclusive of the existence of the bridleway and conclusive against any future downgrading or deletion of it from the map, thereby preventing the county council from exercising its power under s 53(2)[b] of the 1981 Act to review the map by deleting or downgrading a right of way shown on the map. The appellants applied for judicial review of the Secretary of State's decision but leave to apply was refused by the judge in one case and the application was dismissed by the Divisional Court in the other case. In the first case the appellant renewed his application for leave before the Court of Appeal and the application was granted. The appellants appealed to the Court of Appeal in the second case. The appeals on the substantive issues were heard together.

Held – On their true construction the 1949 and 1981 Acts were concerned with the limited purpose of enabling the preparation and maintenance of an authoritative record in the form of a definitive map and statement of public rights of way and so were concerned with the ascertainment and not the creation of rights of way. Furthermore, the Acts imposed a duty on surveying authorities to keep the definitive map and statement under review so as to incorporate evidence discovered after the preparation of the map showing that the status of a right of way was incorrectly recorded or that no right of way of any description existed over the land, thereby producing the most reliable map and statement that could be achieved. Accordingly, the purpose of the conclusive provisions in s 56(1) of the 1981 Act was to make, until any subsequent review took

---

a Section 56(1) is set out at p 504 *e* to *j*, post

b Section 53 is set out at p 503 *e* to p 504 *b*, post

place, a definitive map and statement conclusive evidence of the rights shown on the map in any dispute occurring between a landowner and users or between different users of rights of way recorded on the map. However, when evidence was discovered subsequent to the preparation of the map which proved that no right of way existed where one was recorded or that a right of way was incorrectly described and should be downgraded, the map was not conclusive and could be corrected under the review procedure contained in s 53(2) of the 1981 Act. It followed that there could be a review of a definitive map pursuant to s 53(2) and (3)(c)(ii) and (iii) of the 1981 Act consequent on the discovery of evidence after the preparation of the map, in order to modify the map by downgrading a bridleway to the status of a footpath or by deleting a right of way previously recorded on the map as a bridleway. The appeals would therefore be allowed (see p 505 e to g j to p 506 a, p 509 a g h, p 510 c to e, p 511 b c, p 513 b, p 514 j and p 515 d to g, post).

Dictum of Browne LJ in R v Secretary of State for the Environment, ex p Hood [1975] 3 All ER 243 at 250, R v Secretary of State for the Environment, ex p Stewart (1978) 37 P & CR 279 and dicta of Lord Diplock and Lord Morris in Suffolk CC v Mason [1979] 2 All ER 369 at 374, 377 applied.

Rubinstein v Secretary of State for the Environment (1989) 57 P & CR 111 overruled.

Notes

For the contents of a definitive map as evidence and for the revision of maps, see 21 Halsbury's Laws (4th edn) paras 271–275, and for cases on the subject, see 26 Digest (Reissue) 602–603, 4188–4191.

For the Wildlife and Countryside Act 1981, ss 53, 56, see 20 Halsbury's Statutes (4th edn) 528, 532.

As from 28 February 1983 the 1981 Act made fresh provision with respect to the ascertainment of public rights of way in place of that made in the National Parks and Access to the Countryside Act 1949.

Cases referred to in judgments

Dawes v Hawkins (1860) 8 CBNS 848, 141 ER 1399.
Morgan v Hertfordshire CC (1965) 63 LGR 456, CA.
R v Secretary of State for the Environment, ex p Hood [1975] 3 All ER 243, [1975] QB 891, [1975] 3 WLR 172, CA; rvsg [1975] 1 All ER 102, [1974] 1 WLR 1479, DC.
R v Secretary of State for the Environment, ex p Stewart (1978) 37 P & CR 279, DC.
Rubinstein v Secretary of State for the Environment (1989) 57 P & CR 111.
Suffolk CC v Mason [1979] 2 All ER 369, [1979] AC 705, [1979] 2 WLR 571, HL.

Appeal

R v Secretary of State for the Environment, ex p Burrows and anor

Richard John Burrows and Chapman Estates (Leicester) Ltd appealed from the order of the Divisional Court of the Queen's Bench Division (Neill LJ and Pill J) on 30 June 1989 dismissing their application for an order of mandamus to compel the respondent, the Secretary of State for the Environment, to entertain an appeal under para 4 in Sch 14 to the Wildlife and Countryside Act 1981 from the refusal of Leicestershire County Council to make an order modifying the definitive map for Cropston, Leicestershire by downgrading Bridleway J75 shown on the map to the status of footpath. The grounds of the appeal were that the Divisional Court was wrong in law to hold that (1) the Secretary of State had no jurisdiction to entertain an appeal from refusal of the county council in the exercise of its powers under s 53(2) and (3)(c)(ii) of the 1981 Act to order downgrading of the bridleway to a footpath, (2) the effect of s 56(1)(b) of the 1981 Act was to prevent a footpath mistakenly designated as a bridleway under the National Parks and Access to the Countryside Act 1949 from being subsequently downgraded to its proper status of footpath, (3) s 56 of the 1981 Act did not take effect subject to the review provisions of s 53 and (4) s 53(3)(c)(ii) did not permit the status of a way to be modified both upwards and downwards. The facts are set out in the judgment of Purchas LJ.

Application for judicial review
                    R v Secretary of State for the Environment, ex p Simms
On 14 June 1989 the Court of Appeal (Lord Donaldson MR, Balcombe and Nicholls LJJ) on the renewed ex parte application of Roger Simms for leave to apply for judicial review of a decision of the Secretary of State given on 20 July 1988, refusing to entertain Mr Simms's appeal against Buckingham County Council's decision not to order modification of their definitive map by deleting bridleways BR 21 and BR 21A, the original application having been refused by Simon Brown J on 23 November 1988, ordered that the renewed application for leave to apply for judicial review by way of an order of mandamus requiring the Secretary of State to hear and determine the applicants' appeal from Buckinghamshire County Council's decision be granted and that the substantive application be heard by the Court of Appeal. The facts are set out in the judgment of Purchas LJ.

By consent of the parties the appeal and the application were heard together.

George Laurence for Mr Burrows and his co-appellant.
Peter Birts for Mr Simms.
Duncan Ouseley for the Secretary of State.

Cur adv vult

23 November. The following judgments were delivered.

PURCHAS LJ. There are two causes before the court. The first one is a substantive motion for judicial review by Roger Simms of Denham Farm, Quainton, Buckinghamshire brought by order of the Court of Appeal (Lord Donaldson MR, Balcombe and Nicholls LJJ) of 14 June 1989 to be heard by the Court of Appeal (the Simms application). The second is an appeal from the refusal to grant an order for judicial review by the Queen's Bench Divisional Court (Neill LJ and Pill J) of an application by Richard John Burrows and Chapman Estates (Leicester) Ltd (the Burrows appeal). I shall hereafter, albeit inaccurately, refer to both causes as appeals. Both raise the same important issue of principle, namely the true construction of ss 53 and 56 of the Wild Life and Countryside Act 1981. With the consent of the parties, both appeals have been heard together and this judgment covers both.

In the Burrows appeal the applicants sought an order of mandamus directed to the Secretary of State for the Environment to entertain and decide an appeal brought by them under para 4 of Sch 14 to the 1981 Act from a refusal of the Leicestershire County Council to make a draft modification order in relation to the definitive map for Leicestershire. The application sought the redefinition of a highway, J75, shown as a bridleway in the plan, which had been prepared under the provisions of Pt IV of the National Parks and Access to the Countryside Act 1949. The applicants contended that it was incorrectly recorded and should have been described as a footpath. In a report to the planning and recreation sub-committee of the environment committee of Leicestershire County Council, which was considered by that sub-committee on 17 October 1985, the officers recommended that the definitive map should be amended by altering bridleway J75 to a footpath. This recommendation was not accepted by the committee. The applicants then appealed to the Secretary of State. In his decision letter dated 11 April 1988 the Secretary of State dismissed the appeal without considering the merits of the case. Paragraph 3 of his letter stated:

'The Department takes the view that the decision [*Rubinstein v Secretary of State for the Environment* (1989) 57 P & CR 111] not only precludes the making of orders under Section 53 of the [1981] Act which seek to delete a right of way from a definitive map and statement by reference to the provisions of Section 53(3)(c)(iii), but also orders which purport to downgrade a right of way shown on the map and statement by reference to Section 53(3)(c)(iii) eg from bridleway to footpath.'

The Simms application seeks an order of mandamus directed to the Secretary of State in similar terms to that in the Burrows appeal, namely to consider an appeal against a decision by the Buckinghamshire County Council refusing to make an order modifying the definitive map and statement prepared by them under s 53 of the 1981 Act by deleting two bridleways, numbers 21 and 21A, under the provisions of s 53(3)(c)(iii) of the 1981 Act. Counsel for Mr Simms informed the court, and he was not challenged in any way, that his client, Mr Simms, had available a substantial body of evidence to show that the inclusion of bridleways 21 and 21A on the definitive map for Buckinghamshire was an administrative error for which there was no historical or factual justification. As he submitted, his client seeks the opportunity to redress this injustice.

Mr Simms's case is that bridleways BR21 and BR21A, far from being used as a bridleway, have never been used to his recollection or that of his father even as footpaths. It is not necessary in this judgment to go into further details except to record that in March 1980 solicitors acting for the Simms family made formal objections to Buckinghamshire County Council and were informed by a letter of 11 November 1980 that a public inquiry would be held into their objections. This was overtaken by the passing of the 1981 Act. The matter was, however, pursued to the point where an appeal under the 1981 Act was made to the Secretary of State. This received from the Secretary of State in his decision letter of 20 July 1988 a similar reference to the judgment of Taylor J in *Rubinstein v Secretary of State for the Environment* (1989) 57 P & CR 111. Thus, the argument before the court in both causes was directed to the justification, or otherwise, of the Secretary of State's refusal to hear the appeals under the provisions of the 1981 Act because of the decision in *Rubinstein's* case.

The case in the Burrows appeal was first presented by counsel for Mr Burrows. The procedure, which was agreed between the parties and seemed appropriate to the court, was that after counsel for Mr Burrows had concluded his submissions then counsel presenting the Simms application should follow and that counsel who appeared for the Secretary of State should then respond to both. I turn to consider the statutory provisions which are relevant to both appeals. Before proceeding I would wish to acknowledge the gratitude of the court for the skilful presentation of the statutory provisions and the authorities by all three counsel in presenting their respective cases. These have been of great assistance. In order properly to achieve the construction of ss 53 and 56 of the 1981 Act it is necessary first to have regard to the general history which led up to the passing of the 1981 Act.

At common law the rule was and remains 'once a highway, always a highway'. There is no extinctive presumption or prescription arising from the non-exercise of rights of passage; saving only when this arises from natural causes such as inroads of the sea or landslips: see *Dawes v Hawkins* (1860) 8 CBNS 848, 141 ER 1399. Apart from the old procedure by way of writ ad quod damnum, in order to extinguish or even vary a right, intervention by statute has always been necessary. There are numerous examples of such statutes in connection with compulsory purchase powers etc. The general powers are now contained in the provisions of the Highways Act 1980.

The 1949 Act
The title to the 1949 Act, so far as is relevant, reads:

'... to make further provision for the recording, creation, maintenance and improvement of public paths and for securing access to open country, and to amend the law relating to rights of way ... and for matters connected with the purposes aforesaid.'

Notwithstanding the reference in the title to 'creation . . . of public paths', the relevant parts of Pt IV of the 1949 Act (ss 27 and 28) appear under the subheading 'Ascertainment of footpaths, bridleways and certain other highways'.

Sections 27 and 28 provided for the preparation of a draft map after a comprehensive investigation to ascertain the existence of footpaths, bridleways etc. Sections 29 and 30 provided for representations and objections by interested parties to the draft maps and statements. Section 31 provided for the judicial determination of disputes between landowners and others by legal process in the quarter sessions. Section 32 provided for the initial recording of the results of the processes under ss 27 to 31 in the form of a 'definitive map and statement'. Section 33 provided that thereafter at five yearly intervals, or sooner as appeared appropriate to the authority, the map and statement should be reviewed having regard to 'events' as therein defined. There can be no dispute that an object of the Act was to avoid tiresome and expensive litigation between individuals over disputed rights of way. Thus, in s 32(4) the Act provided that the definitive map and statement should be conclusive 'as to the particulars contained therein' in accordance with the provisions of the subsections of that section to which I shall have to refer in greater detail later. One of the central questions raised in these appeals is the degree and area over which the map and statement is to be 'conclusive' having regard to the provisions in s 33 for periodical review of the map and statement themselves.

Section 27(1), so far as is relevant, provided:

'Subject to the provisions of this Part of this Act, the council of every county in England or Wales shall . . . prepare a draft map of their area, showing thereon a footpath or a bridleway, as may appear to the council to be appropriate, wherever in their opinion such a right of way subsisted, or is reasonably alleged to have subsisted at the relevant date.'

Section 27(2) provided that the map should also show 'a road used as a public path' (RUPP).

Section 27(6) contained the following important definitions:

'In this Part of this Act the following expressions have the meanings hereby respectively assigned to them, that is to say,—"footpath" means a highway over which the public have a right of way on foot only, other than such a highway at the side of a public road; "bridleway" means a highway over which the public have the following, but no other, rights of way, that is to say, a right of way on foot and a right of way on horseback or leading a horse, with or without a right to drive animals of any description along the highway; "horse" includes pony, ass and mule, and "horseback" shall be construed accordingly; "public path" means a highway being either a footpath or a bridleway; "right of way to which this Part of this Act applies" means a right of way such that the land over which the right subsists is a public path; "road used as a public path" means a highway, other than a public path, used by the public mainly for the purposes for which footpaths or bridleways are so used.'

Section 32(4) provided:

'A definitive map and statement prepared under subsection (1) of this section shall be conclusive as to the particulars contained therein in accordance with the foregoing provisions of this section to the following extent, that is to say—(a) where the map shows a footpath, the map shall be conclusive evidence that there was at the relevant date specified in the statement a footpath as shown on the map; (b) where the map shows a bridleway, or a road used as a public path, the map shall be conclusive evidence that there was at the said date a highway as shown on the map, and that the public had thereover at that date a right of way on foot and a right of way on horseback or leading a horse, so however that this paragraph shall be without

a
prejudice to any question whether the public had at that date any right of way other than the rights aforesaid; and (c) where by virtue of the foregoing paragraphs of this subsection the map is conclusive evidence, as at any date, as to a public path, or road used as a public path, shown thereon, any particulars contained in the statement as to the position or width thereof shall be conclusive evidence as to the position or width thereof at the relevant date, and any particulars so contained as to limitations or conditions affecting the public right of way shall be conclusive evidence that at

b
the said date the said right was subject to those limitations or conditions, but without prejudice to any question whether the right was subject to any other limitations or conditions at that date.'

It is convenient to note at this stage in relation to the above provisions the qualification contained in sub-s (4)(b) (any right of way other than the rights aforesaid) and in sub-s

c
(4)(c) (without prejudice to any other limitations or conditions at that date). Section 32(5) and (6) provided for the receipt in evidence in proceedings of a definitive map and statement.

I now turn to the provisions of s 33, which provides:

'*Periodical revision of maps and statements*—(1) The authority . . . shall from time to time review the particulars contained [in the definitive map and statement] having

d
regard to *events* which have occurred at any time between the relevant date . . . and such date as may be determined by the authority for the purposes of the review . . .

(2) The *events* so occurring as aforesaid to which an authority shall have regard in carrying out a review under the last foregoing subsection shall include the following events, that is to say—(a) the coming into operation of any enactment or instrument, or any other event, whereby a highway required to be shown, and shown, on the

e
map has been authorised to be stopped up, diverted, widened or extended; (b) the coming into operation of any enactment or instrument, or any other event, whereby a highway shown on the map as being a highway of a particular description required to be shown thereon has ceased to be a highway of that description; (c) the coming into operation of any enactment or instrument, or any other event, whereby a new right of way has been created, being a right of way to which this Part of this Act

f
applies; (d) the expiration, in relation to a way in the area of the authority, of any period such that the enjoyment by the public of the way during that period raises a presumption that the way has been dedicated as a public path; and (e) the discovery by the authority of *new evidence such that, if the authority were then preparing a draft map* under the foregoing provisions of this Part of this Act, they would be required by those provisions to show on the map, *as a highway of a particular description, a way*

g
not so shown on the definitive map, or on the revised map last prepared in accordance with the following provisions of this section, as the case may be.'

Section 33(4) and (5) deals with the revision of the map and statement in consequence of s 33(1) and (2) and in the case of any alterations the notice to be given to persons affected thereby. The proviso to s 33(5) provides for the consideration by the surveying

h
authority of representations made by such persons who are given a right of appeal to the minister against decisions made by the authority. For the purposes of this appeal, however, the important provision in this section is that in sub-s (2)(e), which provides for the action to be taken on 'the discovery . . . of new evidence' which would have affected the preparation of the map and statement had the authority then been carrying out the exercise of preparing a draft map and statement under s 27(1). Section 33 is relied on by

j
the appellants as indicating that under the 1949 Act there was an unrestricted power to revise the particular description of highways shown on the map and contained in the statement. It was not possible, however, to construe from the terms of s 33(2)(e) a power to delete a highway altogether as a result of the discovery of 'new evidence'. This led to a provision included in Sch 3 to the Countryside Act 1968, to which I must now refer.

The 1968 Act

As counsel for Mr Burrows informed the court in his excellent submissions, the brave *a* new world envisaged in the immediate post-war legislation relating to planning control etc did not in practice come to pass. Along with the timely preparation of plans under the town and country planning legislation so with the quinquennial reviews under s 33 of the 1949 Act local authorities fell woefully behind the envisaged programme. In fact in many areas by 1968 the initial draft plan under s 27(1) of the 1949 Act had not been approved or published. This unsatisfactory state of affairs was recognised by Parliament *b* in the 1968 Act. The relevant part of the title to this Act read:

'An Act . . . to make other provision for the matters dealt with in the Act of 1949 . . . and to amend the law about . . . footpaths and bridleways, and other public paths.'

Section 31 provided for the enactment of amendments to the 1949 Act contained in *c* Sch 3 to the 1968 Act. Part I of Sch 3, so far as is relevant, made the following amendment to the 1949 Act:

'Section 33 (revision of maps and statements)
In carrying out a review under section 33(1) the authority shall have regard to the discovery by the authority, in the period mentioned in that subsection, of any new *d* evidence, or of evidence not previously considered by the authority concerned, showing that there was no public right of way over land shown on the map as a public path, or as a road used as a public path, or that any other particulars in the map or statement were not within the powers of Part IV of the Act of 1949, and their powers of preparing a revised map and statement under subsection (4) or as the case may be proviso (*d*) to subsection (5), of the said section 33 may be exercised *e* accordingly: Provided that the authority shall not take account of the evidence if satisfied that the person prejudiced by the public right of way, or his predecessor in title, could have produced the evidence before the relevant date mentioned in the said section 33(1) and had no reasonable excuse for failing to do so . . .'

The appellants submit, in my judgment with considerable force, that the amendment to *f* the 1949 Act, providing, as it did, powers for the deletion of public paths without reference to the reclassification of public paths, indicated that Parliament considered that the existing powers in s 33 of the 1949 Act as originally drafted already provided for revision of the map and statement by reclassifying public paths.

The unsatisfactory performance under the 1949 Act in many areas is underlined by the special provisions included in Pt III of Sch 3 to the 1968 Act, which provided for a special review of RUPPs. I do not propose to set out at length the provisions of Pt III of *g* Sch 3 although they formed part of the argument on the appeals. The purpose of the special review was to bring to an end the use of the expression 'road used as a public path' and to substitute by way of reclassification of RUPPs one of three descriptions: (a) a 'byway open to all traffic'; (b) a 'bridleway'; (c) a 'footpath'.

It is now necessary to turn to three authorities in which the provisions of the 1949 and *h* 1968 Acts were considered. In *Morgan v Hertfordshire CC* (1965) 63 LGR 456 the definitive map showed a highway as 'carriage road bridleway'. Without the matter coming to the attention of the landowner, the full procedure under Pt IV of the 1949 Act was completed and a definitive map and statement produced. The relevant date would appear to have been in 1953. The landowner, at some date not recorded in the report but described by Harman LJ in terms as being hopelessly out of time, applied under the *j* provisions of Pt III of Sch 1 to the 1949 Act questioning the validity of the definitive map on the ground that the requirements of Pt IV of the 1949 Act had not been complied with. As appears from the judgments, this was a hopeless approach to the problem. The landowner did not seek a review or revision of the map under s 33. This is referred to in the judgment of Lord Denning MR (at 458) (the reference to s 35 is clearly a mistake for s 33):

'The applicant is disposed to acknowledge that the map is conclusive evidence,
a   but he says: "Surely, when the map is revised, as it has to be every five years, I can
get the matter put right and I can show there is no public way there at all." We have
looked at the provisions for review which are in section 35. They show that, if new
evidence is discovered showing that there is a public way which ought to be inserted
in the map it can be added. But there is no provision to enable a public way (once it
has become conclusive) to be *deleted* from the map. Even if new evidence is
b   discovered showing that there never was a public way there, nevertheless there is no
machinery for deleting it. The map is conclusive evidence of a highway, no matter
how inappropriate it may be. On a review a new path can be added but an existing
path cannot be deleted.' (Lord Denning MR's emphasis.)

It is, in my judgment, fair to notice that the reference to the powers under s 33 are to the
insertion or deletion from the map of a 'public way'. There is no critical discussion
c   directed to reclassification.

R v Secretary of State for the Environment, ex p Hood [1975] 3 All ER 243, [1975] QB 891
concerned an application in relation to a 'road used as a public path'. On the definitive
map the highway in question was classified as 'road used as a public path'. Subsequently
it was reclassified as a result of a 'special review' under the provisions of Pt III of Sch 3 to
d   the 1968 Act as a footpath. The reclassification was confirmed by the Secretary of State;
the applicant applied for an order of certiorari to quash the Secretary of State's decision
on the ground that the classification as a RUPP raised a conclusive presumption that
rights of footway and bridleway existed. The application was refused by the Divisional
Court but an appeal against this refusal was allowed by the Court of Appeal on the basis
that s 32(4)(b) of the 1949 Act was conclusive of the status of the highway as being one
e   over which the public had a right of way on foot and a right of way on horseback etc.
The case involved, therefore, a challenge to the powers of the local authority acting in
relation to the duty imposed on them by Pt III of Sch 3 to the 1968 Act to abolish RUPPs
and to substitute for them one of the three categories listed in the schedule. This was not
a case in which the local authority were acting under their revising duties in s 33 of the
1949 Act as amended by Pt I of Sch 3 to the 1968 Act. There are, however, relevant
f   passages in the judgments which are of assistance in the resolution of the issues raised in
this appeal.

Counsel for Mr Burrows in his submissions relating to *Hood*'s case correctly submitted
that Lord Denning MR when referring to *Morgan*'s case 63 LGR 456 was mistaken. After
citing s 32(4)(b) of the 1949 Act Lord Denning MR turned to the case before him in these
terms ([1975] 3 All ER 243 at 246–247, [1975] QB 891 at 898):
g
'In 1952 the way at Herne Bay was shown on the definitive map as a "road used as
a public path". The map was, therefore, conclusive evidence that in 1952 the public
had a right of way on foot and on horseback or leading a horse. The question is
whether the local authority can now downgrade the way into a public footpath
only. There was certainly no means of doing so under the 1949 Act. That Act
h   provided for periodical reviews every five years. On those periodical reviews the
highway authority could upgrade a way, if they had new evidence. So it could be
upgraded, say from a footway to a bridleway (see s 33(2)(e)), but there was no
machinery by which the owner of land could get it downgraded. This court so held
in *Morgan v Hertfordshire CC* (1965) 63 LGR 456.'

j   The reference by Lord Denning MR to *Morgan*'s case is, regrettably, inaccurate. As I
have already indicated in this judgment, *Morgan*'s case, in which Lord Denning MR
himself gave the leading judgment, was dealing with the deletion of a highway from the
map and did not consider the question of reclassification. Referring to the 1968 Act Lord
Denning MR again inaccurately referred to the amendment to s 33 of the 1949 Act by
Pt I of Sch 3 to the 1968 Act ([1975] 3 All ER 243 at 247, [1975] QB 891 at 898):

'This brings me to the Countryside Act 1968. In that Act Parliament put in a

special provision so as to reverse *Morgan's* case. It enabled an owner to come and ask
for a way to be downgraded. It is in Part I of Sch 3 and is described as an amendment
to s 33 of the 1949 Act. The owner could come in and get it downgraded if he had
got new evidence which he could not reasonably have been expected to produce
before.'

Here again, as counsel for Mr Burrows rightly submitted, Lord Denning MR has once
again confused the amendment to s 33 of the 1949 Act effected by Pt I of Sch 3 to the
1968 Act, which related solely to the deletion of a highway on the definitive map, with
the reclassification of RUPPs provided for in Pt III of Sch 3 to the 1968 Act. Lord
Denning MR does, however, refer to the reclassification of RUPPs as a separate matter in
the next ensuing paragraph of his judgment. The remainder of Lord Denning MR's
judgment is directed to the central issue of the appeal, namely the powers afforded to the
local authority in carrying out the reclassification exercise under Pt III of Sch 3 to the
1968 Act. The conclusion reached in the judgment, from which there has been no
dissent, is that on the reclassification of RUPPs the only matter to be considered is the
degree of use of the public path by vehicles or, alternatively, its suitability for such use
and whether any hardship would be caused if the use were to be determined (see Sch 3,
Pt III, para 10). These considerations do not assist the resolution of the issues which arise
on this appeal. However, Lord Denning MR returns to the general question ([1975] 3 All
ER 243 at 248, [1975] QB 891 at 899–900):

> 'Those are the only grounds of review on a reclassification. There is no machinery
> to enable the local authority to reopen the whole question once more of whether or
> not the way was shown properly in the 1952 definitive map. I cannot think that
> Parliament ever contemplated that there should be such a reopening. The definitive
> map in 1952 was based on evidence then available, including, no doubt, the evidence
> of the oldest inhabitants then living. Such evidence might well have been lost or
> forgotten by 1975. So it would be very unfair to reopen everything in 1975. In the
> present case there is no evidence whatever to justify any change in the original
> classification. To my mind, the conclusive presumption in s 32(4)(b) of the 1949 Act
> remains unimpaired. There is nothing in the 1968 Act which enables it to be
> displaced. It shows that at December 1952 there was a right of way on foot and a
> right of way on horseback or leading a horse. That right remains. It must be shown
> as such on the review. The description must be as "a bridleway". It must appear on
> the new classification as a bridleway, that is a right for man on foot and on horse.'

Counsel for Mr Burrows submitted that this passage must be read in its proper context,
namely that the main issue on the appeal related to reclassification of RUPPs. He further
submitted that the mistaken view of the position in *Morgan's* case, to which I have just
made reference must put a question mark over the validity of the other comments made
by Lord Denning MR in which he considered the effect of *Morgan's* case in the context
of reclassification. I agree with this submission.

Counsel for Mr Burrows relied on certain passages in the judgment of Browne LJ
([1975] 3 All ER 243 at 250–251, [1975] QB 891 at 903). In the earlier part of his
judgment Browne LJ had considered what powers there were under the paragraphs of
Sch 3 to the 1968 Act relating to the reclassification of RUPPs but he turned to more
general considerations after referring to the presumption to be found in s 32(4)(b) of the
1949 Act and said ([1975] 3 All ER 243 at 250–251, [1975] QB 891 at 903–904):

> 'In my judgment this presumption could only be displaced on the reclassification
> by such subsequent events as are specified in s 33(1) and (2) of the 1949 Act or by
> new evidence admissible under Part I of Sch 3 to the 1968 Act. In my view, the only
> powers to alter public rights in reclassifying given by Part III of Sch 3 are those given
> by para 10 of that schedule. In certain cases, of course, the other powers to alter
> rights conferred by the 1949 Act as amended may arise. The only question to be

a
considered under para 10 is whether public rights extend to rights of vehicular traffic; and if they do, whether they ought to be extinguished. If it is decided that the way should not be classified as a "byway open to all traffic", I agree with Ackner J ([1974] 1 All ER 102 at 108, [1974] 1 WLR 1479 at 1485) *that there is no power to downgrade it further, except in cases covered by s 33(1) and (2) or by Part I of Sch 3 to the 1968 Act.* In my view, s 32(4)(b) requires the way to be shown as a bridleway, which by definition includes a footway, unless it is shown by material admissible under

b
s 33 as amended to be only a footpath, in which case it can and should be shown as such under para 9 of Sch 3.' (My emphasis.)

Counsel for Mr Burrows relied on this passage for support for his submission that, whilst Browne LJ held that downgrading from bridleway to pathway was not open under the reclassification of RUPPs under paras 9 and 10 of Pt III of Sch 3 to the 1968 Act, this was

c
without prejudice to the right to reclassify a bridleway to footpath available under s 33(1) of the 1949 Act and para 9(2) of Pt III of Sch 3 to the 1968 Act or by Pt I of Sch 3 to the 1968 Act amending s 33 of the 1949 Act to delete a highway altogether.

R v Secretary of State for the Environment, ex p Stewart (1978) 37 P & CR 279 concerned a definitive map for the county of Wiltshire the relevant date of which was 1 May 1953 and on which was contained a highway shown as a footpath. The first review was

d
1 September 1958 and a second and special review was dated 31 May 1972. As a result of the latter the status of part of the highway was altered to that of a bridleway. There were objections followed by a public inquiry. The evidence accepted by the inspector and the Secretary of State was that, although there had been no use of the highway as a bridleway since the first definitive map, evidence had become available at the time of the second review which established that the highway had been used as a bridleway prior to the date

e
of the definitive map. The Divisional Court (Lord Widgery CJ, Talbot and Ackner JJ) held that the discovery of this evidence constituted an 'event' within s 33(2)(e) of the 1949 Act which should have been considered with a view to reclassifying the highway as a bridleway. Delivering the judgment of the court, Talbot J dealt with the impact of s 33(2)(e) in the following terms (at 285):

f
'The authority, therefore, has to consider on a review events that have occurred at any time between the relevant dates. One of the events to which the authority must have regard is the *discovery* of new evidence. The nature of that new evidence must be such that, if the authority were then preparing a draft map, they would be required by the Act to show on the map a highway of a description that was not so shown on the definitive map or on the revised map last prepared. The draft map is

g
that which has to be prepared by the authority under section 27 of the Act of 1949; it is then followed by a provisional map required under section 30. It was, therefore, submitted by [counsel for the applicant] that the event in this case was the discovery by the authority between the relevant dates of new evidence as a result of the information provided by [the applicant] and that that new evidence had to be considered by the authority as if they were then preparing the draft map under the

h
relevant provisions of the Act. If that is the proper construction, then it would have been relevant, when considering the draft map, to consider that evidence that [the applicant] produced as to the user of this path as a bridleway. In the view of this court, the submissions of [counsel for the applicant] are correct. It seems quite clear from the wording of the section that there was between the relevant dates an "event" in the discovery by the authority of new evidence, and that the evidence should

j
have been considered as if the authority were then preparing the draft map; in that case, the evidence excluded by the inspector was wrongly excluded and the Secretary of State was in error in accepting the inspector's conclusions.' (Talbot J's emphasis.)

It is to be noted that the court in *Stewart's* case was referred to the leading authority of *Suffolk CC v Mason* [1979] 2 All ER 369, [1979] AC 705, to which I now turn. In that case

on a definitive map published by the council a lane giving access to land later acquired
by the defendants was shown as a footpath. Subsequent research having established that
the lane had long ago been used as a public cartway, the defendants sought to use the lane
for vehicular access to their land. The council, relying on the definition of footpath in
s 27(6) and the provisions of s 32(4)(a) of the 1949 Act, claimed a declaration that the lane
was a highway over which the public had a right of way on foot only. By a majority
(Lord Hailsham and Lord Fraser dissenting) the House of Lords upheld the contentions
of the council. There are, however, a number of valuable observations to be found in the
various speeches to which reference in this judgment will be useful. It must be
remembered that the issues raised did not concern the powers to revise the definitive
map and statement under s 33 of the 1949 Act but cross-declarations relating to the map
and statement under s 31(1). The speech of Lord Diplock contains the following
comments and passages which, in my judgment, are of relevance. He referred to the
provisions of s 32(4) of the 1949 Act ([1979] 2 All ER 369 at 373, [1979] AC 705 at 713):

'The probative effect of the particulars of rights of way contained in it [ie the
definitive map] are dealt with in s 32(4) . . .'

Thereafter he cited the subsection in extenso and continued ([1975] 2 All ER 369 at 374,
[1979] AC 705 at 713):

'On a literal reading of para (a), if one interpolates the whole of the definition of
"footpath" from s 27(6), as the paragraph directs, it seems plain that the showing of
a right of way as a "footpath" on the definitive map is as conclusive of the negative
element in that definition as it is of the positive element: there was on the relevant
date a right of way on foot, there was not then any more extensive public right of
passage. In contrast with this, para (b) does not direct one to interpolate the definition
of "bridleway" from s 27(6) and so make the entry of a "bridleway" evidence of the
negative element in that definition.' (Lord Diplock's emphasis.)

Subsequently in his speech Lord Diplock emphasised that the negative element in the
definition of 'footpath' is of importance to protect the interests of ramblers against the
incursion of riders. He did this in one of six conclusions which were set out towards the
end of his speech ([1979] 2 All ER 369 at 375, [1979] AC 705 at 715):

'(1) The only classes of users of highways who are intended to be benefited by the
recording of public rights of way are those who may conveniently be referred to as
ramblers and riders; they go on foot or horseback. Motorists are not among the
intended beneficiaries, nor are cattle drovers. (2) Consequently, the only kinds of
highways with which the relevant provisions of the Act are concerned are those
which are exclusively, or mainly, used either by ramblers alone or by both riders
and ramblers. Footpaths are much commoner than bridleways and a much larger
part of the electorate are ramblers than are riders. (3) The way in which ramblers
and riders are to be benefited is by providing them with an easy and conclusive way
of proving their rights to walk or ride on particular routes. (4) The interests of
ramblers and of riders as users of a public path are liable to conflict, not simply in
their simultaneous use of a limited width of passage but as a consequence of the
poaching of the surface by hoofmarks in wet weather. It is in the interests of
ramblers that riders as well as motorists should be excluded from the paths they use.
(5) Regard must be had too to the considerations (a) that there are provisions for
careful investigation of all claims by members of the public that rights of way of
any of three descriptions existed on the relevant date, (b) that the procedure is biased
in favour of the recognition of the more extensive claims unless the owner of the
soil carries his opposition as far as quarter sessions (now the Crown Court), and
(c) erroneous entries on a definitive map which fail to recognise fully all existing
rights of passage do not have permanent consequences, since they can be corrected

a after a lapse of time which it was contemplated by the Act should not exceed five years. These, and particularly the last, are in my view sufficient to explain a parliamentary purpose to ensure, *at least for the time that a* particular definitive map remains in force, that ramblers should enjoy what is shown on the map as a "footpath" without disturbance by either riders or motorists. (6) I find it regrettable but cannot stigmatise it as irrational that the same parliamentary tenderness is not extended to riders in their use of "bridleways". The entry of a highway as a
b "bridleway" is no evidence that there are not more extensive rights of way over it: but here the conflicting interest is that of motorists, and they form a larger part of the electorate than riders. *For these reasons I see no escape from the conclusion that in the instant case the first revised definitive map is conclusive evidence of a fact which it is now conceded has always been untrue, and that the Suffolk County Council are entitled to the declaration claimed.* I would dismiss the appeal.' (My emphasis.)

c It is to be remembered that this was involved with cross-declarations sought by the council on the one hand and the landowners on the other hand, the council claiming a declaration that the highway was as defined on the map, namely a footpath only, whereas the landowners were claiming for a wider use, namely a public cartway. This case did not concern the powers of revision under s 33 of the 1949 Act. Referring to these powers
d in the context of the issues raised in the appeal Lord Diplock said ([1979] 2 All ER 369 at 374–375, [1979] AC 705 at 714):

'The entry on the definitive map does not necessarily remain conclusive evidence for ever. Section 33 makes provision for quinquennial revisions, though these do not appear in practice to have been carried out punctually. On a revision, entries on the definitive map which require modification as a result of events that have
e occurred since the date of the last revision may be modified accordingly. Among the subsequent events which call for a modification of an entry is the discovery by the county council of new evidence which, if it had been known to them at the time of the last revision, would have resulted in their being required to enter it on the definitive map as a highway of a different description. *So an entry made by mistake because of lack of historical knowledge would, if the Act were administered in accordance*
f *with its terms, endure for a maximum of five years after the error was discovered. These provisions for revision have since been amended by the Countryside Act 1968; but this cannot affect the construction of the National Parks and Access to the Countryside Act 1949 as it was originally enacted.'* (My emphasis.)

I find no basis disclosed in this speech for the proposition that the provision for
g quinquennial revision is in any way limited by the presumptions to be found in s 32(4)(*a*) to (*c*), the only qualification, namely the absence of power to delete a highway altogether, being imported into the Act as recorded in the last sentence of the extract from Lord Diplock's speech cited above by the 1968 Act.

Turning now to the speech of Lord Morris, there is in this speech strong support for the contention that the conclusiveness afforded by the definitive map is valid only so
h long as that map remains unrevised as a result of subsequent revisions. After reciting s 32(4)(*a*) he said ([1979] 2 All ER 369 at 377, [1979] AC 705 at 717):

'The definition of "footpath" must again be applied. "Conclusive evidence" that there was a "right of way on foot only" must negative or preclude any evidence that there was a right of way on a horse or in a motor car or that Marsh Lane was a road
j used a public path. It seems to me that the clear purpose and policy of Parliament in prescribing the elaborate procedures set out in the various sections was that when the stage of having a definitive map was reached (and thereafter until later reviews) the stage of conclusion should be reached and (until later reviews) should be adhered to. If the map showed that Marsh Lane was a footpath it would then be impossible

for anyone to assert that it was a bridleway or a carriageway, or was anything other
than a footpath.'

In this part of his speech Lord Morris is emphasising the negative aspect of the definition
of 'footpath' as being an element to be preserved for the protection of the rambler rather
than for the benefit of the landowner himself: see the passage appearing subsequently in
the speech ([1979] 2 All ER 369 at 377, [1979] AC 705 at 718:

> 'So if the definitive map shows a footpath and if Parliament has decreed that in
> such event the map must be regarded as "conclusive evidence" it follows in my view
> that Parliament has said that no one must be heard to attack the truth of that which
> is "conclusive". It was a necessary and inevitable consequence of what Parliament
> enacted and in my view it must have been the policy and intention of Parliament
> that any unknown or undiscovered right of way, which, had it existed, might
> destroy the status of a footpath, should be regarded as being non-existent unless or
> until some opportunity for revision later arose.'

There is nothing in the speech of Lord Morris to suggest that when the review is made it
should be in any way biased in favour of one class of user to the detriment of either
another class of user or indeed the landowner.

In the speech of Lord Hailsham the emphasis is again on the evidential value of the
map and statement, there being no reference to any limitations to the scope of the
revision provisions of the 1949 Act (after the 1968 amendment). The issue is between
the evidential status of the definitive map and statement as established by s 32(4)(a) and
(b) on the one hand and the scholarly researches which had disclosed the use of the
highway as a cartway in the distant past.

The speech of Lord Fraser does not refer to s 33 of the 1949 Act either in its original
form or as amended. It is concerned, however, with the effect of the definitive map and
statement as defined in s 32(4)(a) to (c). It is not necessary to rehearse this analysis in this
judgment. I wish only to refer to the concluding paragraphs of the speech ([1979] 2 All
ER 369 at 386–387, [1979] AC 705 at 730–731):

> 'The Act provides elaborate procedure for preparing first a draft map, then a
> provisional map, and finally a definitive map of the public paths etc in the area. I do
> not find that the procedure laid down is of much assistance in determining the
> present question except in so far as it seems to make it rather unlikely that the Act
> was intended to benefit ramblers by enabling them to establish conclusively that a
> highway which had been or might reasonably have been shown on the draft map as
> a road used as a public path or bridleway, was really only a footpath. If that had been
> intended, I think that express provision would have been made. But the only
> provision for any person to take steps to have a highway reclassified (either upwards
> or downwards) is in s 31(1)(b) where the right is conferred only on "the owner, lessee
> or occupier, of any land shown on the map to which the notice relates." He is
> permitted then to apply to quarter sessions for a declaration, inter alia—"(b) that the
> rights conferred on the public at that date by the public right of way over the land
> were such rights as may be specified in the application, and not such rights as are
> indicated in the provisional map and statement . . ." No doubt he would generally
> seek to have the public rights declared to be more limited than those indicated in
> the provisional map and statement, but the procedure is not available to ramblers.
> For all these reasons I have reached the conclusion that there is no sufficient reason
> for attributing to the definitive map under the 1949 Act the effect of extinguishing
> or otherwise affecting public rights of cartway. It was in my opinion simply not
> concerned with such rights, and I am, with respect, unable to agree with the
> observation to the contrary by Browne LJ in *R v Secretary of State for the Environment,
> ex parte Hood* [1975] 3 All ER 243 at 249, [1975] QB 891 at 901. Its whole emphasis
> is on recording and preserving rights which might otherwise be lost. That is also in

a
my view the reason why the definitive map is not required to show ordinary roads over which of course there must be a public right of way on foot and on horseback. Such roads are entirely outside the scope of the Act. A footpath at the *side* of a public road is expressly excluded from the definition of footpath in s 27(6) and it may well have been assumed that the right of way on foot *along* a public road was so clearly outside the Act as not to call for express mention.' (Lord Fraser's emphasis.)

b
The speech of Lord Fraser is concerned with the evidential effect of the map and statement in connection with the preservation of the negative rights of the rambler under s 32(4)(a) to (c) of the 1949 Act in the event of evidence becoming available to show that the map may be incorrect and is wholly without reference to the revision provisions in s 33 of the 1949 Act (as amended). The reference to s 31(1) as a vehicle for reclassifying a highway is related to the initial provisions under which the final definitive map is produced and also ignores the revision proceedings. As I said earlier in this judgment, the speeches in that case do contain useful passages but the issues directly raised in the appeal, namely cross-declarations as to the effect of s 32, do not directly touch on the powers of revision under s 33.

c

The 1981 Act

d
The wording of the title makes it clear that this is once again an amending Act so far as it relates to the public rights of way and connected purposes. I can pass immediately to cite the relevant sections, which are to be found in Pt III under the subheading 'Ascertainment of public rights of way'. Section 53 provides:

e
'*Duty to keep definitive map and statement under continuous review.*—(1) In this Part "definitive map and statement", in relation to any area, means, subject to section 57(3),—(a) the latest revised map and statement prepared in definitive form for that area under section 33 of the 1949 Act; or (b) where no such map and statement have been so prepared, the original definitive map and statement prepared for that area under section 32 of that Act; or (c) where no such map and statement have been so prepared, the map and statement prepared for that area under section 55(3).

f
(2) As regards every definitive map and statement, the surveying authority shall—(a) as soon as reasonably practicable after the commencement date, by order make such modifications to the map and statement as appear to them to be requisite in consequence of the occurrence, before that date, of any of the events specified in subsection (3); and (b) as from that date, keep the map and statement under continuous review and as soon as reasonably practicable after the occurrence, on or after that date, of any of those events, by order make such modifications to the map

g
and statement as appear to them to be requisite in consequence of the occurrence of that event.

(3) The events referred to in subsection (2) are as follows—(a) the coming into operation of any enactment or instrument, or any other event, whereby—(i) a highway shown or required to be shown in the map and statement has been

h
authorised to be stopped up, diverted, widened or extended; (ii) a highway shown or required to be shown in the map and statement as a highway of a particular description has ceased to be a highway of that description; or (iii) a new right of way has been created over land in the area to which the map relates, being a right of way such that the land over which the right subsists is a public path; (b) the expiration, in relation to any way in the area to which the map relates, of any period such that

j
the enjoyment by the public of the way during that period raises a presumption that the way has been dedicated as a public path; (c) the discovery by the authority of evidence which (when considered with all other relevant evidence available to them) shows—(i) that a right of way which is not shown in the map and statement subsists or is reasonably alleged to subsist over land in the area to which the map relates, being a right of way to which this Part applies; (ii) that a highway shown in

the map and statement as a highway of a particular description ought to be there shown as a highway of a different description; or (iii) that there is no public right of way over land shown in the map and statement as a highway of any description, or any other particulars contained in the map and statement require modification.

(4) The modifications which may be made by an order under subsection (2) shall include the addition to the statement of particulars as to—(a) the position and width of any public path or byway open to all traffic which is or is to be shown on the map; and (b) any limitations or conditions affecting the public right of way thereover ...'

The marginal note to s 54 reads 'Duty to reclassify roads used as public paths'. This section provides for the cessation of the use of the expression 'roads used as public paths' and their reclassification under the three classes defined in Sch 3 to the 1968 Act. Section 54(3) provides:

'A road used as a public path shall be shown in the definitive map and statement as follows—(a) if a public right of way for vehicular traffic has been shown to exist, as a byway open to all traffic; (b) if paragraph (a) does not apply and public bridleway rights have not been shown not to exist, as a bridleway; and (c) if neither paragraph (a) nor paragraph (b) applies, as a footpath.'

Section 55 provides that no new surveys or reviews should be undertaken under the 1949 Act. I now turn to the second of the two important sections of the 1981 Act. Section 56 provides:

'Effect of definitive map and statement.—(1) A definitive map and statement shall be conclusive evidence as to the particulars contained therein to the following extent, namely—(a) where the map shows a footpath, the map shall be conclusive evidence that there was at the relevant date a highway as shown on the map, and that the public had thereover a right of way on foot, so however that this paragraph shall be without prejudice to any question whether the public had at that date any right of way other than that right; (b) where the map shows a bridleway, the map shall be conclusive evidence that there was at the relevant date a highway as shown on the map, and that the public had thereover at that date a right of way on foot and a right of way on horseback or leading a horse, so however that this paragraph shall be without prejudice to any question whether the public had at that date any right of way other than those rights; (c) where the map shows a byway open to all traffic, the map shall be conclusive evidence that there was at the relevant date a highway as shown on the map, and that the public had thereover at that date a right of way for vehicular and all other kinds of traffic; (d) where the map shows a road used as a public path, the map shall be conclusive evidence that there was at the relevant date a highway as shown on the map, and that the public had thereover at that date a right of way of foot and a right of way on horseback or leading a horse, so however that this paragraph shall be without prejudice to any question whether the public had at that date any right of way other than those rights; and (e) where by virtue of the foregoing paragraphs the map is conclusive evidence, as at any date, as to a highway shown thereon, any particulars contained in the statement as to the position or width thereof shall be conclusive evidence as to the position or width thereof at that date, and any particulars so contained as to limitations or conditions affecting the public right of way shall be conclusive evidence that at the said date the said right was subject to those limitations or conditions, but without prejudice to any question whether the right was subject to any other limitations or conditions at that date ...'

Section 66 provides the interpretation of the rights for the purposes of Pt III of the 1981 Act:

'(1) In this Part—"bridleway" means a highway over which the public have the following, but no other, rights of way, that is to say, a right of way on foot and a right of way on horseback or leading a horse, with or without a right to drive animals of any description along the highway; "byway open to all traffic" means a highway over which the public have a right of way for vehicular and all other kinds of traffic, but which is used by the public mainly for the purpose for which footpaths and bridleways are so used . . . "footpath" means a highway over which the public have a right of way on foot only, other than such a highway at the side of a public road . . . "public path" means a highway being either a footpath or a bridleway . . .'

Before turning to *Rubinstein v Secretary of State for the Environment* (1989) 57 P & CR 111 and the judgment under appeal, I must mention in general terms the rival contentions proposed on the one hand by counsel for Mr Burrows and counsel for Mr Simms and on the other hand by counsel for the Secretary of State. The former submitted that the 1981 Act was a further step in the progressive adjustment in favour of the landowner from the immediate post-war rigour of the 1949 Act. On the other hand, counsel for the Secretary of State referred to the passage of 13 years since the amendment to the 1949 Act which allowed for the deletion of pathways erroneously shown on the map and said that this supported the suggestion that the highways and their categories shown on the definitive map should now finally be determined subject only to upgrading in favour of the user of the highway. This argument is to be found echoed in the judgment of Taylor J in *Rubinstein v Secretary of State for the Environment* (at 116) where after mentioning the 1968 provisions he said:

'However, in 1981 we have moved on a number of years, and at that time the legislature passed the new Act which contains the relevant provisions in section 53.'

It can at least be said in favour of the arguments for the appellants that in the 1949 Act, as with the 1981 Act, the relevant provisions are in each case under the heading 'Ascertainment of footpaths, bridleways and certain other highways' or 'Ascertainment of public rights of way' and the object of the preparation or revision of the plan is to show on its surface or in the wording of the statement where the highway, of whatever quality, 'subsisted or is reasonably alleged to have subsisted' (the 1949 Act). Appearing, as they do, under the heading 'Ascertainment' etc and from their own wording, in my judgment the clear inference to be drawn from the sections themselves is that the process envisaged by Parliament is the full investigation, so far as is practicable at the time, of the existence, or otherwise, of a highway and if one is established or is alleged to exist its definition as to status. Once this has been done the object must be to create documents in the form of a map and statement which would be conclusive as evidence in any dispute which would otherwise be litigated between landowner and user, whether rambler or rider, and indeed as between two classes of users, rambler or rider, themselves.

Although the title to the 1949 Act referred to the 'creation' as well as the 'recording . . . maintenance and improvement' of public paths etc, for Parliament to have provided for the creation of a highway where none existed at common law clear and express terms would be expected, and such terms are conspicuously absent from Pt IV of the 1949 Act. The preparation of the definitive map and statement under the 1949 Act is the statutory datum point for all ensuing legislation and again this is of some significance when interpreting the 1981 Act. Section 33(2)(e) of the 1949 Act related back to the provisions of the original draft map under s 27 of that Act. The 1968 Act merely provided amendments to the provisions of the 1949 Act: see s 31. Section 53(1) of the 1981 Act defines 'definitive map and statement' initially by reference to s 33 of the 1949 Act or, in the absence of a revision, the original definitive map prepared under s 32(1) of that Act and where no map or statement had been prepared at all a map produced under the provisions of s 55(3) of the 1981 Act. Here I sense no express statutory provision which would indicate that the original intention of Parliament was to achieve anything other than the production of a map and statement recording, so far as could be ascertained from information available at the relevant date, the highways and their respective qualities as proved to exist at that date. I see no provision in the 1981 Act specifically empowering the local authority to create a right of way by continuing to show it on the map, after proof had become available that it had never existed, any more than a power to extinguish a right of way, proof of the existence of which had been discovered.

It is necessary in this context to proceed to a more detailed study to ascertain the intention of Parliament in relation to what may be called the revision provisions in s 53 of the 1981 Act in the context of s 56 of that Act. The expression used in s 56(1) is the same as that used in s 32(4) of the 1949 Act, namely that the definitive map and statement 'shall be conclusive as to the particulars contained therein', except that in s 56 of the 1981 Act the phrase has the added word 'evidence'. This reads 'shall be conclusive evidence as to the particulars contained therein'. The language of the section is concerned with 'evidence'. Section 33 of the 1949 Act provided for 'periodical revision of maps and statements', whereas s 53 provides a duty 'to keep definitive map and statement under continuous review'.

If anything is to be derived from the differences in language between these two sections, then the duty on the surveying authority under the 1981 Act would appear to call for a more detailed and specific ascertainment of existing rights than under the 1949 Act. Section 53(2) provides that the authority shall 'make such modifications . . . requisite in consequence of the occurrence' on or after the date of the existing map and statement of any of a number of specified events.

The events referred to in s 53(3)(a) are changes of status as a result of enactment or instrument which have occurred during the relevant period. Section 53(3)(b) is concerned with the acquisition of prescriptive rights occurring during the relevant period. Section 53(3)(c) provides that the discovery of new evidence which ex hypothesi must relate to conditions existing prior to, or at, the relevant date shall in certain circumstances constitute 'an event'. In these appeals attention has only to be directed to the discovery by the authority of 'new evidence' (the 1949 Act) or 'evidence which (when considered with all other relevant evidence available to [the authority])' (the 1981 Act). It would, in my judgment, be strange if the detailed and extensive provisions of s 53 were to be inhibited in important or material respects from achieving an accurate, up-to-date record. This would be particularly so if, notwithstanding the discovery of new evidence, an error which had been detected on the definitive map or in the statement would nevertheless be perpetuated. In view of the speeches in *Suffolk CC v Mason* [1979] 2 All ER 369, [1979] AC 705, I am not including in the interesting categories the drivers of carts or the drovers of cattle. For the purposes of this appeal it is sufficient to concentrate on those categories which Lord Diplock considered were the object of the intentions of Parliament under this legislation, namely the ramblers and riders.

I appreciate that this approach runs contrary to the submission made by counsel for the Secretary of State which rested at the basis of his argument, namely that s 56 deals with and preserves for all times what existed at the relevant date, whereas s 53 deals with what happens since the relevant date. Based on this argument and the brocard 'once a highway always a highway' counsel for the Secretary of State submitted that the provisions of s 53 dealt solely with events occurring since the relevant date by virtue of which the absence of a highway on the definitive map and from the statement could be corrected, if such was shown to have existed or to have come into existence as a result of events occurring subsequently, but that nothing under s 53 would allow the surveying authority to modify the map and statement so as to 'downgrade' or delete a right of way shown on the definitive map.

I must now turn to *Rubinstein v Secretary of State for the Environment* (1989) 57 P & CR 111. In that case the surveying authority made an order modifying a definitive map by deleting a footpath. In deciding whether to approve the order an inspector acting on behalf of the Secretary of State received evidence from a landowner that no path had ever existed and that, therefore, it ought not to have been shown on the definitive plan. The Secretary of State confirmed the decision. The applicants, who represented the Ramblers Association, challenged the decision. As counsel for the Secretary of State frankly confessed, at the time the Secretary of State's attitude towards s 53 was that it empowered the surveying authority to delete or downgrade a highway on evidence becoming available to them under s 53(3)(c) but that now he found himself supporting the decision which had gone against him in *Rubinstein's* case. Taylor J was sitting as a single judge in the Queen's Bench Division. As I have already mentioned in this judgment, the court considering *Rubinstein's* case had *Morgan v Hertfordshire CC* (1965) 63 LGR 456 and *R v Secretary of State for the Environment, ex p Hood* [1975] 3 All ER 243, [1975] QB 891 cited in argument but no reference was made to *Suffolk CC v Mason* [1979] 2 All ER 369, [1979] AC 705. In his judgment Taylor J recited part of the judgment of Lord Denning MR in *Morgan's* case, then referred to the provisions of Sch 3 to the 1968 Act and continued (57 P & CR 111 at 115):

> 'Two things are to be noted from those provisions. First, the new or other evidence referred to was to be evidence "showing that there *was* no public right of way." [Counsel], for the applicants in this case, contrasts that word "was" with the word "is" in section 53(3)(c)(iii) of the 1981 Act. Secondly, the proviso excluded evidence which could have been produced before the relevant date. Those provisions certainly modified to an extent the stringency of section 32(4) of the 1949 Act, but only within the terms of the proviso. In *R. v. Secretary of State for the Environment, ex p. Hood* the Court of Appeal had to consider the provisions in relation to a case where a road shown on a definitive map was reclassified as a footpath upon a special review under section 33 of the 1949 Act as amended.'

Taylor J then cited parts of the judgment of Browne LJ and referred to the argument then being proposed by counsel for the applicant, which was based on the relaxation of the stringency of the 1949 Act in relation to the deletion of highways by the 1968 Act amendments but which, of course, in the circumstances of *Rubinstein's* case did not refer to downgrading as such. Taylor J continued (at 116):

> 'However, in 1981 we have moved on a number of years, and at that time the legislature passed the new Act which contains the relevant provisions in section 53. There, although there is no limit on the evidence which can be adduced (that is to say, no limit in regard to a relevant date being the deadline for going back), the extent to which there can be a deletion from the map is very much restricted. It seems to me that one does have to read section 53 and section 56 together. Section 56 is in very positive and strict terms: that where a footpath is included in a definitive map, then that is conclusive evidence that there was at the relevant date a footpath at least in regard to that right of way. Evidence would not be excluded that it might have been a bridleway or more, but one cannot go back, as I read section 56, before the relevant date to expunge a right of way. The provision in the relevant subsection, that is to say, 53(3)(c)(iii), is framed in the present tense. It provides that the discovery by the authority of evidence which shows that there is no public right of way over land shown in the map can be used in modifying the map. But that word "is," it seems to me, has to be contrasted with the word "was" that appeared in the schedule of the 1968 Act.'

Taylor J then considered the arguments which had been presented by counsel who appeared for the Secretary of State. These were in support of a power to delete and were based on three points: first, that without the power to delete ss 56 and 53 would be in conflict; second, that if there was not a power to delete then the provisions in s 53(3)(c)(iii) were really 'beating the air'; and, third, that it was legitimate to read the word 'is' in s 53(3)(c)(iii) as 'was and is'. Dealing with these three submissions Taylor J said (at 117–118):

'There need not be any conflict, it seems to me, if one reads section 56 as governing the situation up to the relevant date and to regard section 53 as imposing an obligation, certainly in relation to deletions, to review the situation only after the relevant date. It is true the field in regard to additions or upgradings may cover the whole period, but as to deletions, it [seems] to me that section 53 and section 56 can ride together only if one accepts, as section 53 requires, that the possibility of review in regard to deletions is after the relevant evidence coming to light in regard to the period after the relevant date. [Counsel for the Secretary of State's] second point concerns the purpose of the Act. He submits that if the applicants are right, then the provisions in 53(3)(c)(iii) are really beating the air. They have no likely situation upon which they could bear. He submits that once a highway, always a highway. Therefore, if there was a highway at the relevant date, there is no reason to think that anything will have diminished it unless, if his submission is correct, one can go back and correct matters which were wrongly decided when the definitive map was drawn up. The only specific instance which either counsel, or I am bound to say I, have been able to envisage in which, on the applicants' contention, subsection (iii) would apply would be a situation where the land had fallen away, perhaps due to the erosion of the sea, and there could physically be no public right of way over the land, an event which would have had to occur since the relevant date. That situation is clearly one that on the applicants' submissions subsection (iii) would be apt to cover. But the words, in my judgment, of section 56 and the contrast between the use of the word "is" in (iii) of section 53 as against the word "was" in the schedule to the 1968 Act are so strong that I see no reason not to read the words in their ordinary, plain and natural meaning. It seems to me, therefore, despite [counsel for the Secretary of State's] submission as to the limited application of (iii) as contended for by the applicants, the applicants' interpretation of it is correct. That really decides the issue raised by [counsel for the Secretary of State] on his third point, which is whether it is legitimate to read the word "is" in (iii) of section 53(3)(c) as "was and is." In my judgment there is no reason to add words which Parliament has not added, which Parliament could well have added, and which Parliament has declined to add, notwithstanding the previous provision, which must have been well in the draftsman's mind containing the word "was." I therefore conclude in this case that the applicants' submissions are correct, and that the policy of the 1981 Act is, as Browne L.J. said some considerable time ago in dealing with the provisions as from 1968, to try to avoid reopening all the matters which were thoroughly gone into under the 1949 Act. In my judgment the 1981 Act seeks to go forward from there, certainly in regard to any deletions which anyone proposed to make from the relevant map. For those reasons, I conclude that this application should succeed.'

With the assistance of the comprehensive and skilful analysis both of the statutes and authorities presented by counsel before us I have reached, with the greatest respect, the firm conclusion that Taylor J was not entitled to reject the submissions made on behalf of the Secretary of State by counsel as he is reported to have done in the passage which I have just cited from his judgment. The minister was, in my opinion, correct in his initial view of the intention of the 1981 Act and from which he only departed as a result of the judgment in *Rubinstein's* case. With deference to the judge, I venture to surmise that had he had the advantage of the submissions which have been made to us, including especially the reference to the speech of Lord Diplock in *Suffolk CC v Mason* [1979] 2 All ER 369, [1979] AC 705 and the emphasis on the fact that the judgments in *R v Secretary of State for the Environment, ex p Hood* [1975] 3 All ER 243, [1975] 1 QB 891 related to the special problems arising in connection with the reclassification of RUPPs under Pt III of Sch 3 to the 1968 Act rather than under s 33(1) of the 1949 Act as amended by Pt I of Sch 3 to the 1968 Act, the decision in *Rubinstein's* case might well have been different and should now be considered as having been given per incuriam.

I have reached this conclusion for a number of reasons which I will attempt to set out.

1. The whole emphasis and purpose of the provisions with which we are concerned is the 'recording' rather than the 'creation' of rights of way. Although both words appear in the title to the 1949 Act, all the sections under consideration are grouped under the heading of 'ascertainment' in both the 1949 and 1981 Acts.

2. The conclusions reached by Lord Diplock contain an important aspect which may well have been overlooked, namely the conflict of interest between ramblers and riders with the necessity to protect both from the drivers and drovers and the one from the other. The preservation of the exclusive rights arising in favour of ramblers under a highway defined as a footpath indicates that the use of the words 'downgrading' and 'upgrading' are not really appropriate to describe the relative interests as between the ramblers and the riders. Ramblers might well consider the conversion of a bridleway to a footpath as upgrading rather than downgrading. Although the saving in s 65(1)(a) of 'other rights' than a right of way on foot in the context of the definition of footpath in s 66 may be said to derogate from the exclusive or negative element in the latter, I do not think that this prejudices Lord Diplock's approach to the rambler/rider conflict of interest on my overall view of the intention of the 1981 Act.

3. As Lord Diplock recorded in his first conclusion, the provisions of the 1949 and 1968 Acts with which these appeals are concerned are directed to the interests of the ramblers and riders, rather than to the interests of other users, such as the drivers of motor vehicles, riders in carriages or even the drovers of cattle. The provisions of Pt III of Sch 3 to the 1968 Act and s 54 of the 1981 Act provide for the reclassification of RUPPs by means of a special review under Pt III of Sch 3 to the 1968 Act or under the provisions of s 54 of the 1981 Act. These provisions in turn, ie the 1968 and 1981 Acts, were designed to classify RUPPs either as 'byways open to all traffic' or 'highways' not open to traffic at all. Thus, the right to 'downgrade' from the first category, ie byway open to all traffic, is made subject to negative analysis under s 54(3), ie if it has not been shown that the right of way is for vehicular traffic then it shall be classified as a bridleway unless it is shown as a negative fact that it did not exist as a bridleway, in which case it is to be classified as a footpath. This process of reclassification is not affected by any of the presumptions as to the evidential effect of the existing definitive map under s 56.

4. The exercise being considered by the Court of Appeal in *Hood's* case was, of course, the reclassification of RUPPs under Pt III of Sch 3 to the 1968 Act. This involved considering what use there had been by vehicular traffic, the suitability of the way for vehicular traffic having regard to the position of the existing right of way, the condition and state of the repair of the way and the nature of the soil, and where the way had been used by vehicular traffic whether the extinguishment of vehicular rights of way would cause any undue hardship. As with the 1981 Act it is to be noticed that there is no saving or reference to the provisions of s 32(4) of the 1949 Act. The classification, survey and review is not to be inhibited in any way by the provisions of that section.

5. The duty under s 53 of the 1981 Act is a continuous one to keep the map and statement up to date and, where evidence becomes available which would indicate that there was an error in the definitive map or any subsequent revision thereof, the surveying authority are under a duty to revise the map and statement accordingly.

6. I do not, with respect to the judgments both in *Rubinstein's* case (1989) 57 P & CR 111 and of Pill J in the judgment under appeal, find difficulty in the use of the word 'was' in Pt I of Sch 3 to the 1968 Act and 'is' in s 53(3)(c)(iii) of the 1981 Act. Part I of Sch 3 to the 1968 Act was amending the provision of s 33 of the 1949 Act. The material provision is s 33(2)(e), which required the authority having discovered new evidence to act as if the evidence had become available to them when preparing a draft map under the provisions of s 27 of the 1949 Act or on the occasion of the last revision as the case might be. The use of the past tense in this context seems to me to be of no particular significance except that it fits in with the hypothetical exercise on which the authority were called to embark under s 33(2)(e). In contrast, however, the use of the word 'is' in

s 53(3)(c)(iii) is consistent with the ongoing duty to keep the definitive map and statement under continuous review. If the evidence shows that at the time it is discovered and when considered with all other relevant evidence that there is no public right of way then, by virtue of the brocard, there never could have been a right of way. Any event which otherwise would prevent a pre-existing right of way from existing at the time of the discovery of the evidence would come within the provisions of s 53(3)(a) and, therefore, cannot be within the contemplation of s 53(3)(c)(iii). The strained explanation called on in argument in *Rubinstein's* case to justify the inclusion of sub-para (iii), ie landslip or erosion, is so remote in my judgment as to be an unrealistic explanation of the ordinary language of the section. I do not believe that the possibility of such eventualities would justify the special inclusion of a provision of this sort in this kind of Act.

There is no difficulty in reconciling ss 53 and 56 of the 1981 Act once the comparatively restricted purpose of the legislation as a whole is understood, namely the preparation and maintenance of an authoritative record in the form of a definitive map and statement showing those highways over which the public have rights of way whether as 'ramblers' only or as 'ramblers and riders'. As Lord Diplock commented, the drivers of vehicles or drovers of cattle or other users play only a minor part when after 1968 Parliament decided to rationalise the classification of RUPPs. Once prepared, however, and until subsequently revised, the map and statement is to be conclusive evidence in rights of way disputes between landowners and the various categories of persons exercising rights of way. Parliament never removed the duty to revise and keep the record up to date, so that not only changes of status caused by supervening events, eg the stopping up of a highway under statute or otherwise, or the creation of prescriptive rights, but also changes in the original status of highways or even their existence resulting from recent research or discovery of evidence should all be taken into account in order to produce the most reliable map and statement that could be achieved.

In this process the passage of time still has a part to play, not by way of perpetuating errors but by refining and updating the evidential content of the map and statement. Clearly, with the passage of time, 'events' within s 53(3)(c) will become less and less frequent. However, when they do occur, full cognisance of the result must be taken whether by addition under s 53(3)(c)(i), adjustment under sub-para (ii) or deletion under sub-para (iii). In this way equal weight can be given to the three sub-paragraphs of s 53(3)(c) and a strained construction avoided. The progress over the years from the 1949 Act, through the 1968 Act to the 1981 Act, merely represents the recognition by Parliament of a defect in the 1949 Act (deletion of highways) and the recognition in 1981 of the importance of maintaining, as an up-to-date document, an authoritative map and statement of the highest attainable accuracy.

I now turn to the judgment of the Divisional Court from which these appeals have been brought. I hope it will not be considered discourteous if I summarise the judgment by saying that Pill J cited and adopted the reasoning and conclusion of the judgment in *Rubinstein's* case (1989) 57 P & CR 111. For the reasons which I have given earlier in this judgment when dealing with *Rubinstein's* case, I cannot agree with Pill J where he said:

> 'Section 53 of the 1981 Act imposed a duty on surveying authorities to keep the definitive map and statement under continuous review. It provided a new review procedure. By virtue of s 56, however, the possibility of review by way of downgrading a bridleway is limited to a consideration of events after the relevant date.'

The events under consideration in these appeals are, of course, the discovery of evidence tending to negative the existence of bridleways not only at the time when the evidence is discovered but also by virtue of the doctrine ('once a highway always a highway') at the relevant date or at the date of any immediate preceding review under the 1949 Act. I do not think that downgrading (and I have already indicated why I think that this is an

inappropriate word to use in the context of changing a bridleway to a footpath) is
a prevented because s 53 relates to evidence which comes to hand after the relevant date.
The evidence is or may be still critical in ascertaining the presence or absence of a
highway in the first place and if established the quality of that highway, namely either as
a footpath only or as both a footpath and a bridleway. In order to maintain the accuracy
of the evidence which is to be 'conclusive' as long as it appears unrevised on the map and
statement it must, unless there is strong and specific provision to the contrary, be capable
b of revision of all kinds in order to ascertain the true state of affairs on the ground.

For these reasons I have come to the conclusion that *Rubinstein's* case, as I have already
said, was wrongly decided and that, therefore, the judgment of the Divisional Court
which was based on it must be flawed. For these reasons I would allow the appeal in the
Burrows application and grant the relief sought in the Simms application that orders for
judicial review should be granted as prayed.

c

GLIDEWELL LJ. I have had the advantage of reading in draft the judgment of
Purchas LJ. I agree with him that the appeal in Burrows's case should be allowed and that
the relief sought by Mr Simms should be granted. I set out my own reasoning shortly,
not least because we are differing not merely from the judgment of the Divisional Court
in Burrows's case but also from the decision of Taylor J in *Rubinstein v Secretary of State for*
d *the Environment* (1987) 57 P & CR 111.

Purchas LJ has set out the facts of these two matters, which I therefore need not repeat.
He has also rehearsed the relevant legislation, which again I therefore need not set out in
full. However, I do think it helpful to start by repeating the words of part of s 53 of the
Wildlife and Countryside Act 1981. These provisions are:

e   '... (2) As regards every definitive map and statement, the surveying authority
shall ... (b) ... keep the map and statement under continuous review and as soon as
reasonably practicable after the occurrence ... of any of those events [ie the events
specified in sub-s (3)] by order make such modifications to the map and statement
as appear to them to be requisite in consequence of the occurrence of that event.
(3) The events referred to in subsection (2) are as follows—(a) the coming into
f   operation of any enactment or instrument, or any other event, whereby—(i) a
highway shown or required to be shown in the map and statement has been
authorised to be stopped up, diverted, widened or extended; (ii) a highway shown
or required to be shown in the map and statement as a highway of a particular
description has ceased to be a highway of that description; or (iii) a new right of way
has been created over land in the area to which the map relates, being a right of way
g   such that the land over which the right subsists is a public path; (b) the expiration,
in relation to any way in the area to which the map relates, of any period such that
the enjoyment by the public of the way during that period raises a presumption
that the way has been dedicated as a public path; (c) the discovery by the authority
of evidence which (when considered with all other relevant evidence available to
them) shows—(i) that a right of way which is not shown in the map and statement
h   subsists or is reasonably alleged to subsist over land in the area to which the map
relates, being a right of way to which this Part applies; (ii) that a highway shown in
the map and statement as a highway of a particular description ought to be there
shown as a highway of a different description; or (iii) that there is no public right of
way over land shown in the map and statement as a highway of any description, or
any other particulars contained in the map and statement require modification ...'

j   I agree with the suggestion made to us in argument that paras (a) and (b) of s 53(3)
relate to events which have happened since the definitive map was prepared. These
events may have resulted in a right of way coming into existence where none existed
before, or the upgrading of an existing right of way to a right of a wider sort, eg by
express dedication under para (a)(iii) or by prescription under para (b). Paragraph (a)(i)

relates to the happening of an event which results in the extinguishment of a previously existing right of way, shown on the definitive map. Since the common law maxim is 'once a highway, always a highway', such a result can only be achieved by statute, and the events to which sub-para (i) refers as authorising the stopping up or diversion of a highway can therefore only take place under statute.

On the other hand, s 53(3)(c) differs from the preceding sub-paragraphs in that the use of the word 'discovery' suggests the finding of some information which was previously unknown, and which may result in a previously mistaken decision being corrected. This information will normally, if not always, relate to a fact or situation which already existed at the time when the definitive map was prepared. In this way, para (c) is to be distinguished from its predecessors.

If I am right in my view that para (c) is concerned with the correction of mistakes as the result of newly discovered information, in order to be comprehensive, the power of correction must cover three different situations: (i) the addition of a right of way not shown on the definitive map: para (c)(i) achieves this; (ii) the upgrading or downgrading of rights of way shown on the map, but so shown in a wrong category: para (c)(ii) covers both these situations; (iii) the deletion of a right of way which the latest information proves should not have appeared on the map at all: para (c)(iii) by its terms achieves this.

It follows that on its face s 53(3)(c) is both comprehensive and coherent.

The problem is to reconcile the downgrading and deletion provisions with the terms of s 56 of the 1981 Act. Both the matters we are currently considering are concerned with what are shown on the respective definitive maps as bridleways. It is therefore only necessary to refer directly to that part of s 56 which deals with bridleways, namely:

'(1) A definitive map and statement shall be conclusive evidence as to the particulars contained therein to the following extent, namely . . . (b) where the map shows a bridleway, the map shall be conclusive evidence that there was at the relevant date a highway as shown on the map, and that the public had thereover at that date a right of way on foot and a right of way on horseback or leading a horse, so however that this paragraph shall be without prejudice to any question whether the public had at that date any right of way other than those rights . . .'

There are two alternative ways in which the deletion and downgrading provisions in s 53(3) may be reconciled with the provisions of s 56.

The first is that adopted by Taylor J in Rubinstein's case, namely by treating s 56 as pre-eminent and as limiting the operation of s 53(3). The alternative course is to interpret s 56 as not applying to the review process in s 53 at all so that the review starts from what is shown in the definitive map, but does not for its purposes treat the definitive map as conclusive. For all other purposes within the limits laid down by s 56(1) the definitive map is conclusive. In particular it is conclusive evidence in any dispute that may arise between a landowner over whose land a bridleway is shown on the definitive map and those who may wish to ride horses along the way, or between riders of horses and pedestrians on that bridleway.

It was suggested to us in argument that para (c)(iii) of s 53(3) is dealing with two separate matters, which could really more conveniently have been turned into two separate sub-paragraphs, i e: '(iii) that there is no public right of way over land shown in the map and statement as a highway of any description, or [(iv) that] any other particulars contained in the map and statement require modification.'

I agree with this, and concern myself only with the first phrase of sub-para (iii).

If, as Taylor J held in Rubinstein's case and the Divisional Court has held in Burrows's case, s 56 limits the operation of s 53(3) so that the evidence in the definitive map of the existence of a bridleway is conclusive against deletion of, or downgrading of, the bridleway in future, the only factual situation which anybody in any of these cases has been able to suggest comes within the first phrase of sub-para (iii) is the example of the cliff-top path disappearing because of sea erosion. In my view that illustration, while not totally unknown, is so rare an occurrence as to make it entirely unlikely that Parliament

would have devoted a part of a separate sub-paragraph of the statute to it. In any case, as
a has been pointed out to us, by ordinary operation of law the right of way would disappear:
see 21 Halsbury's Laws (4th edn) para 143. Moreover, it would be probable in such a case
that the relevant authority would take steps to make a path diversion order so as to ensure
that a continuous right of way continued to exist along the new edge of the cliff (always
assuming this was safe). Section 53(3)(a)(i) would then apply to permit the path as so
diverted to be shown as the modified map. By ordinary principles of statutory
b construction, it is in my view much more likely that s 53(3)(c) is intended in appropriate
circumstances to permit the downgrading of a right of way or its complete deletion from
the definitive map if evidence justifying this course has come to light.

   I have therefore considered whether such an interpretation is consistent with the
wording of the statutes which preceded the 1981 Act, and of such decisions of the courts
on those statutes as are relevant. Section 33(2)(a) to (d) of the National Parks and Access
c to the Countryside Act 1949 covered exactly the same ground as s 53(3)(a) and (b) of the
1981 Act. Section 33(2)(e) of the 1949 Act related to the coming into existence of new
highways and of the upgrading or downgrading of highways. However, s 33 did not
permit the complete deletion of a highway shown on the map. This court so held in
Morgan v Hertford CC (1965) 63 LGR 456.

   No doubt as a result of the decision in *Morgan's* case, a power in appropriate
d circumstances to delete completely from the definitive map a way shown on the map as
a public path or a road used as a public path was added by Sch 3 to the Countryside Act
1968. Counsel for the Secretary of State accepts that after the 1968 Act a complete
deletion under the provisions of Sch 3 was possible, despite s 32(4) of the 1949 Act. He
maintains, however, that there was a material alteration in wording between s 32(4) of
the 1949 Act and s 56(1) of the 1981 Act, which had the effect that the power to delete a
e way shown on the definitive map was removed by the 1981 legislation. In other words,
he submits that Parliament, having recognised that there was no power to delete and
thought it right to add one, 13 years later thought it right to remove that power in the
latest legislation. To my mind such a thought process is basically unlikely, but if I am
compelled by the wording of the two respective sections to the conclusion that it is the
f process through which Parliament went then, unlikely or not, I must accept the
submission.

   Before considering this, I look shortly at what I consider the two most relevant
authorities. They are the decision of this court in *R v Secretary of State for the Environment,
ex p Hood* [1975] 3 All ER 243, [1975] QB 891 and the decision of the House of Lords in
Suffolk CC v Mason [1979] 2 All ER 369, [1979] AC 705. In neither case did the problem
with which we are concerned arise directly, but both contained brief dicta which bear on
g the point. It must, of course, be remembered that both decisions fell during the period
when the relevant legislation was contained in the 1949 Act as amended by the 1968 Act.

   Hood's case was concerned with another provision of the 1968 Act, to which I have so
far not referred. This provided that, for the future, what had in the 1949 Act been shown
as a 'road used as a public path' should be reclassified into one of three separate categories,
h namely 'a byway open to all traffic' or 'a bridleway' or 'a footpath'. In his judgment in
that case Browne LJ said ([1975] 3 All ER 243 at 249, [1975] QB 891 at 901–902):

   'It seems to me that the intention of the 1949 Act was that all questions as to the
   extent, nature and incidents of footpaths, bridleways and roads used by the public
   for other purposes should be fully investigated and decided before the definitive
   maps were drawn up under that Act, and that the definitive maps should finally
i decide these questions, subject only to the exception at the end of s 32(4)(b) to which
   Lord Denning MR has referred, namely that although the map should be conclusive
   evidence of the matters therein specified, this is to be without prejudice to any
   question whether the public had at the relevant date any right of way other than a
   footpath or a bridleway. And the decisions made under the 1949 Act were, of
   course, all subject to the provisions as to review contained in the 1949 Act itself in
   s 33.'

Later Browne LJ said ([1975] 3 All ER 243 at 250–251, [1975] QB 891 at 903):

'It seems to me that when the authority or the Secretary of State is approaching *a*
the problem of reclassification under the 1968 Act, one starts with the presumption
that there was in 1952 a right of way for horses and on foot. In my judgment this
presumption could only be displaced on the reclassification by such subsequent
events as are specified in s 33(1) and (2) of the 1949 Act or by new evidence
admissible under Part I of Sch 3 to the 1968 Act. In my view, the only powers to
alter public rights in reclassifying given by Part III of Sch 3 are those given by para *b*
10 of that schedule. In certain cases, of course, the other powers to alter rights
conferred by the 1949 Act as amended may arise. The only question to be considered
under para 10 is whether public rights extend to rights of vehicular traffic; and if
they do, whether they ought to be extinguished. If it is decided that the way should
not be classified as a "byway open to all traffic", I agree with Ackner J ([1975] 1 All
ER 102 at 108, [1974] 1 WLR 1479 at 1485) that there is no power to downgrade it *c*
further, except in cases covered by s 33(1) and (2) or by Part I of Sch 3 to the 1968
Act.'

It follows that Browne LJ was clearly of the view that the bridleway could be
downgraded under s 33(1) and (2) of the 1949 Act, despite the effect of s 32(4) of that Act.
The decision of the House of Lords in *Suffolk CC v Mason* [1979] 2 All ER 369, [1979] *d*
AC 705 was to the effect that on a proper interpretation of s 32(4)(*a*) of the 1949 Act,
where the definitive map showed a footpath, the map was conclusive evidence that there
was a footpath, but no greater or lesser public right. Thus, the map was conclusive that
there was no right of way to ride or lead horses over the path. In this respect, the wording
of s 32(4)(*a*) of the 1949 Act differs from that of s 56(1)(*a*) of the 1981 Act. Thus *Suffolk
CC v Mason* was not directly concerned with the question whether on a review there *e*
could be a deletion or downgrading. However, in his speech Lord Diplock said ([1979] 2
All ER 369 at 374–375, [1979] AC 705 at 714):

'The entry on the definitive map does not necessarily remain conclusive evidence
for ever. Section 33 makes provision for quinquennial revisions, though these do
not appear in practice to have been carried out punctually. On a revision, entries on *f*
the definitive map which require modification as a result of events that have
occurred since the date of the last revision may be modified accordingly. Among
the subsequent events which call for a modification of an entry is the discovery by
the county council of new evidence which, if it had been known to them at the time
of the last revision, would have resulted in their being required to enter it on the
definitive map as a highway of a different description. So an entry made by mistake *g*
because of lack of historical knowledge would, if the Act were administered in
accordance with its terms, endure for a maximum of five years after the error was
discovered. These provisions for revision have since been amended by the
Countryside Act 1968; but this cannot affect the construction of the National Parks
and Access to the Countryside Act 1949 as it was originally enacted.'

Counsel for Messrs Burrows and Simms respectively submit that this expression of *h*
opinion by Lord Diplock applies logically to the question of the deletion or downgrading
of a right of way on a review just as it did to the possible upgrading of a right of way
despite the provisions of s 32(4)(*a*) of the 1949 Act.

I agree with those submissions. In my view the dicta to which I have referred in *Hood's*
case and *Suffolk CC v Mason*, though not conclusive, are an indication that both Browne LJ *j*
and Lord Diplock were of the view that on a review the conclusive provisions that were
in s 32 of the 1949 Act and are now in s 56 of the 1981 Act did not and do not operate so
as to prevent what proves to have been a mistake of any kind in the definitive map from
being rectified.

The argument to which I have already referred which counsel for the Secretary of State

advances based on the difference between the wording of the 1949 and 1981 Acts can be
a illustrated as follows. In s 32(4)(b) of the 1949 Act, as I have said, the relevant wording is:

'where the map shows a bridleway . . . the map shall be conclusive evidence that
there was at the said date a highway as shown on the map . . .'

Counsel for the Secretary of State submits that under the 1981 Act it is not permissible to
consider whether there was at the time when the definitive map was prepared a right of
b way. All that the review is now concerned with is the situation at the date of the review.
In my view this reasoning is fallacious. If the evidence now shows that there is at the
time of the review no public right of way over the relevant land, and if there has been no
stopping up or diversion under statutory powers, then it can only be that there never was
a public right of way. If there had been such a right, then it would still be in existence.
Thus the change of tense makes no difference to the substantive effect of s 53 of the 1981
c Act as compared with s 32 of the 1949 Act in my view.
    It is with great diffidence that I differ from the decision of Taylor J. I observe, however,
that he was not referred to Suffolk CC v Mason, and thus had no guidance from the speech
of Lord Diplock. If he had read this speech, it might have altered his decisions.
    Nevertheless, for the reasons I have sought to express, in addition to those contained in
the judgment of Purchas LJ, I would hold that Taylor J came to a wrong decision in
d Rubinstein's case. It follows that I would allow the appeal of Mr Burrows and order the
Secretary of State to entertain the appeal to him in the case. In Mr Simms's case I would
grant him the relief he seeks by making a similar order against the Secretary of State.

RUSSELL LJ. Having regard to the very comprehensive and closely reasoned judgments
of Purchas and Glidewell LJJ, which I have read and with which I respectfully agree,
e there is very little that I can usefully add.
    I would, however, wish to emphasise that sub-ss (2) and (3) of s 53 of the Wildlife and
Countryside Act 1981 provide scope for the modification of the map and statement to
keep pace with the reality of changing circumstances. In particular I am satisfied that
s 53(3)(c), with its use of the word 'discovery', embraces the situation where a mistaken
decision has been made and its correction becomes possible because of the discovery of
f information which may or may not have existed at the date of the definitive map.
    It is the reconciliation of s 53 with s 56 that has led to difficulty. In this context I find
the words of Lord Diplock in Suffolk CC v Mason [1979] 2 All ER 369 at 374–375, [1979]
AC 705 at 714 provide the true analysis, albeit that they were directed to the earlier
legislation. In agreement with Purchas and Glidewell LJ I too am left in no doubt but
that Rubinstein v Secretary of State for the Environment (1989) 57 P & CR 111 was wrongly
g decided. It follows that the appeal of Mr Burrows must be allowed and that in the case of
Mr Simms he is entitled to the relief claimed.
    I reach these conclusions with a measure of satisfaction, for, unless the wording of a
statute drives one irresistably to the conclusion that a wrong cannot be righted, a
construction which enables the real justice of the case to be met is always to be welcomed.
h Without doing any violence to the language of the 1981 Act, I believe that the
construction of ss 53 and s 56 as developed in the judgments of Purchas and Glidewell LJJ
achieves this purpose.

Appeal allowed. Application granted.

j Solicitors: *Sharpe Pritchard*, agents for *Straw & Pearce*, Loughborough (for Mr Burrows
and his co-appellant); *Boyle & Ormerod*, Aylesbury (for Mr Simms); *Treasury Solicitor*.

Wendy Shockett   Barrister.

R v Brentwood Justices, ex parte Nicholls

QUEEN'S BENCH DIVISION
WATKINS LJ AND POTTS J
25 APRIL, 14, 16 MAY 1990

Magistrates – Summary trial – Offence triable summarily or on indictment – Several defendants jointly charged with single offence triable either way – Magistrates determining that offence suitable for summary trial – One defendant electing trial on indictment – Whether magistrates required to commit all defendants for trial by jury – Whether co-defendant entitled to elect to have other offence or offences tried summarily – Interpretation Act 1978, s 6(c) – Magistrates' Courts Act 1980, ss 19(1), 20(3).

Where a number of defendants appearing before a magistrates' court are jointly charged with a single offence which is triable either way but which the court determines under s 19(1)[a] of the Magistrates' Court Act 1980 to be more suitable for summary trial than for trial on indictment and one of the defendants elects to be tried on indictment when asked, in accordance with the procedure set out in s 20(3)[b] of that Act, whether 'the accused ... consents to be tried summarily or wishes to be tried by a jury', the court must then commit all the defendants for trial on indictment, irrespective of whether the other defendants have consented to summary trial, since the words 'the accused' in s 20(3), although expressed in singular terms, are to be read as including the plural by virtue of s 6(c)[c] of the Interpretation Act 1978 (see p 521 e to h and p 522 c e, post); *Chief Constable of West Midlands Police v Gillard* [1985] 3 All ER 634 considered.

Where a defendant is charged with two or more offences he may exercise his right under s 20(3) of the 1980 Act to elect his preferred mode of trial in respect of each offence, with the result that where the defendant has his right to summary trial denied because a co-defendant elects to be tried on indictment that fact will not affect his right to elect to have the remaining offence or offences tried summarily (see p 522 *a b e*, post).

Notes

For mode of trial proceedings for offences triable either way, see 29 Halsbury's Laws (4th edn) para 303, and for cases on the subject, see 33 Digest (Reissue) 99–108, 564–637.

For the Interpretation Act 1978, s 6, see 41 Halsbury's Statutes (4th edn) 902.

For the Magistrates' Courts Act 1980, ss 19, 20, see 27 ibid 186, 187.

Cases referred to in judgments

Chief Constable of West Midlands Police v Gillard [1985] 3 All ER 634, [1986] AC 442, [1985] 3 WLR 936, HL.

R v Brentford Magistrates' Court, ex p O'Neill (26 March 1990, unreported), DC.

R v Liverpool Justices, ex p CPS, Liverpool (1990) 90 Cr App R 261, DC.

R v St Helens Magistrates' Court, ex p Critchley [1988] Crim LR 311, DC.

R v Southend Magistrates' Court, ex p Wood (1988) 152 JP 158, DC.

R v Telford Justices, ex p Darlington (1988) 87 Cr App R 194, DC.

Application for judicial review

Mark Ernest Nicholls applied, with the leave of Macpherson J given on 31 January 1990, for judicial review by way of (i) an order of certiorari to quash the decision of justices sitting at Brentwood Magistrates' Court on 16 January 1990 whereby they committed

---

a Section 19(1) is set out at p 517 h, post
b Section 20(3) is set out at p 518 c, post
c Section 6 is set out at p 521 g, post

him jointly with two co-defendants for trial in the Crown Court at Chelmsford on a
a charge of affray contrary to s 3(1) of the Public Order Act 1986, (ii) an order of prohibition
preventing the applicant's committal to the Crown Court and (iii) an order of mandamus
requiring the justices to try the applicant summarily in accordance with s 20(3) of the
Magistrates' Courts Act 1980. The grounds of the application were that after the mode of
trial had been concluded in accordance with s 19 of the 1980 Act and the applicant had
elected summary trial the justices were required to proceed to summary trial. The facts
b are set out in the judgment of Watkins LJ.

Michael M Wood for the applicant.
Andrew Williams for the Crown.
John Laws as amicus curiae.

c   *Cur adv vult*

16 May. The following judgments were delivered.

WATKINS LJ. The applicant, Mark Ernest Nicholls, moves with the leave of
d Macpherson J for judicial review of a decision of justices sitting at Brentwood Magistrates'
Court on 16 January 1990 whereby they committed him, jointly with Michael Anthony
Willbourne and Ernest Carr, for trial in the Crown Court at Chelmsford for the offence
of affray contrary to s 3(1) of the Public Order Act 1986. He seeks an order of certiorari
to remove into this court and to quash the order that he be tried on indictment, an order
of prohibition preventing his committal to the Crown Court and an order of mandamus
e requiring the justices to try the applicant summarily in accordance with s 20(3) of the
Magistrates' Courts Act 1980. The grounds on which this relief is sought are that the
order was wrong in law and is contrary to the provisions of ss 20 to 25 of the 1980 Act,
in that after the mode of trial procedure had been concluded in accordance with s 19 and
the applicant had elected summary trial the justices were required to proceed to summary
trial. They erred in that they had no power to change from a summary trial to committal
f proceedings pursuant to s 25 because they had not begun to try the information
summarily and they failed to follow a number of well-known authorities in this context.
    Affray is an offence triable either way. The applicant and Carr, represented at the
magistrates' court by the same solicitor, Mr Brice, wished to be tried summarily.
Willbourne, represented by another solicitor, Mr Witherspoon, wished to be tried by a
jury. We have affidavits from Mr Brice, Mrs Werrett, a member of the Bar appearing for
g the Crown Prosecution Service, and Mrs Batchelor, the clerk to the court.
    In determining the mode of trial of an either way offence justices are governed by the
provisions of ss 19 to 25 inclusive of the 1980 Act. Those sections as relevant state:

    '**19.**—(1) The court shall consider whether, having regard to the matters
    mentioned in subsection (3) below and any representations made by the prosecutor
h   or the accused, the offence appears to the court more suitable for summary trial or
    for trial on indictment.
        (2) Before so considering, the court—(a) shall cause the charge to be written
    down, if this has not already been done, and read to the accused; and (b) shall afford
    first the prosecutor and then the accused an opportunity to make representations as
    to which mode of trial would be more suitable.
j   (3) The matters to which the court is to have regard under subsection (1) above
    are the nature of the case; whether the circumstances made the offence one of
    serious character; whether the punishment which a magistrates' court would have
    power to inflict for it would be adequate; and any other circumstances which appear
    to the court to make it more suitable for the offence to be tried in one way rather
    than the other . . .

20.—(1) If, where the court has considered as required by section 19(1) above, it appears to the court that the offence is more suitable for summary trial, the *a* following provisions of this section shall apply (unless excluded by section 23 below).

(2) The court shall explain to the accused in ordinary language—(*a*) that it appears to the court more suitable for him to be tried summarily for the offence, and that he can either consent to be so tried or, if he wishes, be tried by a jury; and (*b*) that if he is tried summarily and is convicted by the court, he may be committed for sentence to the Crown Court under section 38 below if the convicting court, on *b* obtaining information about his character and antecedents, is of opinion that they are such that greater punishment should be inflicted than the convicting court has power to inflict for the offence.

(3) After explaining to the accused as provided by subsection (2) above the court shall ask him whether he consents to be tried summarily or wishes to be tried by a jury, and—(*a*) if he consents to be tried summarily, shall proceed to the summary *c* trial of the information; (*b*) if he does not so consent, shall proceed to inquire into the information as examining justices.

21. If, where the court has considered as required by section 19(1) above, it appears to the court that the offence is more suitable for trial on indictment, the court shall tell the accused that the court has decided that it is more suitable for him to be tried for the offence by a jury, and shall proceed to inquire into the information *d* as examining justices . . .

25.—(1) Subsections (2) to (4) below shall have effect where a person who has attained the age of 17 appears or is brought before a magistrates' court on an information charging him with an offence triable either way.

(2) Where the court has (otherwise than in pursuance of section 22(2) above) begun to try the information summarily, the court may, at any time before the *e* conclusion of the evidence for the prosecution, discontinue the summary trial and proceed to inquire into the information as examining justices and, on doing so, may adjourn the hearing without remanding the accused.

(3) Where the court has begun to inquire into the information as examining justices, then, if at any time during the inquiry it appears to the court, having regard *f* to any representations made in the presence of the accused by the prosecutor, or made by the accused, and to the nature of the case, that the offence is after all more suitable for summary trial, the court may, after doing as provided in subsection (4) below, ask the accused whether he consents to be tried summarily and, if he so consents, may subject to subsection (3A) below proceed to try the information summarily . . .'

g

We heard on two occasions submissions on the important issues raised in this application. On the first of them counsel for the applicant and counsel for the Crown Prosecution Service were so much at odds how they should be resolved, there was a lack of any or any firm authority on the construction of s 20 and the practice being adopted about the application of that section seemed to differ from one magistrates' court to another, that we decided to ask for the assistance of an amicus curiae. Thus on the second *h* occasion we heard both counsel again and the amicus curiae. We were referred to the following cases: *Chief Constable of West Midlands Police v Gillard* [1985] 3 All ER 634, [1986] AC 442, *R v Southend Magistrates' Court, ex p Wood* (1988) 152 JP 158, *R v St Helens Magistrates' Court, ex p Critchley* [1988] Crim LR 311, *R v Telford Justices, ex p Darlington* (1988) 87 Cr App r 194, *R v Liverpool Justices, ex p CPS, Liverpool* (1990) 90 Cr App R 261 and *R v Brentford Magistrates' Court, ex p O'Neill* (26 March 1990, unreported). *j*

In *Gillard's* case the short facts, so far as they need to be referred to, were these. The respondent was brought before a magistrates' court charged with an offence which was triable either summarily or on indictment. The justices decided to accept summary jurisdiction and when put to his election the respondent elected summary trial and

entered an unequivocal plea of guilty. He was remanded in custody and appeared for
a sentence before a different bench, who acceded to a prosecution application to discontinue
the summary proceedings and to commit the respondent to the Crown Court for trial on
indictment. Judicial review proceedings ensued. It was held in the House of Lords that
once a magistrates' court allowed an accused to elect summary trial of an offence which
was triable either way and the accused's plea of guilty was accepted, the court could not
thereafter exercise its power under s 25(2) of the 1980 Act to discontinue the summary
b trial and act as examining justices in committal proceedings for the trial of the accused
on indictment.

Lord Bridge in his speech, having referred to the construction of s 25(2), went on to
say ([1985] 3 All ER 634 at 640, [1986] AC 442 at 454):

'I recognise that in cases where two or more accused are jointly charged the
c situation may sometimes present difficulties. It would be inappropriate to discuss
those difficulties or their possible resolution in this case, since there may be issues
for decision in such a case on the true construction of ss 19 and 20 which do not
presently arise. However, it is, I think, proper to observe that, in a case like the
present where, of two accused jointly charged, one is content to accept summary
trial and plead guilty and the other exercises his right to be tried by jury, the fact
d that, if the second is in the event convicted, they will be sentenced by different
courts is not necessarily inimical to justice. To put the matter in another way, in a
relatively trivial case where justices are told in advance that one of two co-accused
intends, if given the opportunity, to accept summary trial and plead guilty but that
the other would in any event elect to be tried on indictment, the later circumstances
cannot, by itself, amount to an overriding reason for committing both for trial.'

e
All counsel agree that that was an obiter dictum. The construction of s 20 did not arise
for consideration in Gillard's case, but counsel for the applicant contended that what Lord
Bridge said assisted him in his submissions to this court.

The issue before us was stated on behalf of the applicant at one time to be: when does
a magistrates' court begin to try an information for the purposes of s 25(3)? It was the
f issue referred to in a number of the cases I have mentioned, but, as will appear later in
this judgment, it is not, I think, apt to the circumstances of this case which involve the
joint trial of three men on a single charge. That was not so in any of the cases referred to
us.

What happened in the magistrates' court was, broadly stated, this. When the case was
called on the defendants were identified, the charge was read to them and the mode of
g trial procedure commenced. Mrs Werrett outlined the facts to the justices and submitted
that the case was suitable for summary trial. Mr Brice made representations on behalf of
the applicant and Carr that the matters were suitable for summary trial. Mr Witherspoon
made no representations at that time. The justices decided that the matter was suitable
for summary trial. Mrs Werrett then asked the clerk to the court to put the defendants
to their election under s 20(3) and to address in that context Willbourne first. All the
h defendants were cautioned, as was usual, and then Willborne asked where he wished to
be tried and he stated he wished to be tried on indictment.

Thereupon Mrs Werrett asked the justices to reconsider their decision with regard to
the mode of trial in respect of the applicant and Carr. The clerk advised the justices that
it would be more suitable for all three defendants to be dealt with by the same court. Mr
Brice, however, strongly demurred. He submitted that his clients, having expressed a
j preference for summary trial, should be so tried.

The clerk then put the election to both the applicant and Carr. Both of them consented
to have the matter tried summarily. No pleas were taken at that stage. Further
representations were made by Mr Brice and either then or at some other stage the justices
were informed that all pleas were not guilty.

Mrs Werrett then submitted to the justices that they should reconsider the mode of trial. There was further argument. The justices, very wisely, allowed all legal *a* representatives time to consider their respective positions and to take the opportunity of a short adjournment to look at legal textbooks, including *Stone's Justices' Manual* (122nd edn, 1990). That opportunity having been taken, submissions to the justices were resumed. Mr Brice submitted that since the justices had already determined the mode of trial under s 19 they were functus in that respect and could not return to that subject. He went on to submit that the only power which the justices had was to consider their *b* position under s 25, assuming that they had begun a summary trial of the applicant and Carr. He drew the justices' attention to a number of cases, including *Chief Constable of West Midlands Police v Gillard* [1985] 3 All ER 634, [1986] AC 442, *R v Southend Magistrates' Court, ex p Wood* (1988) 152 JP 158 and *R v St Helens Magistrates' Court, ex p Critchley* [1988] Crim LR 311.

Mrs Werrett submitted that the procedure under s 19 had not been complied with *c* because although the charge had been written down the accused themselves had not had the opportunity to make representations. She also said that the common sense of the matter dictated that where one defendant elected trial and the others summary trial all should be sent for trial and that in any event where there was a divergence of choice of mode of trial all should be tried on indictment.

The justices retired. They received advice from the clerk during retirement and *d* returned to say: 'We agree with the prosecution with the age-old custom and practice whatever the words of the statute might say.' They indicated that they would commit all the defendants for trial and thereupon adjourned the proceedings until some time in February.

It is quite clear that there was in the magistrates' court some confused appreciation of the application of ss 19, 20 and 25 and no proper concentration on the precise construction *e* of s 20. Moreover, there was the somewhat delphic reference to age-old custom by the justices which likewise seemed to ignore an appreciation of the effect of s 20 and assisted to create the impression that strict construction of this section has been avoided in some magistrates' courts, perhaps because of the apparent obscurity of the provisions of s 20 or perhaps because those provisions, on one possible construction of them, appear at times *f* to be unjust to a defendant who wishes to be tried summarily. For example, suppose out of 20 people charged with affray 19 express a wish to be tried summarily and one expresses the wish to be tried on indictment, on the construction contended for by counsel appearing as amicus curiae all must be committed for trial. That, he said, and counsel for the Crown agreed with him, is an unavoidable consequence of a proper construction of s 20. That is not so, counsel for the applicant argued. He pointed to what *g* Lord Bridge said in *Gillard's* case. He also urged us to consider the use of the word 'shall' both in ss 20 and 21. That, he said, is indicative of the mandatory nature of the provisions both in ss 20 and 21. Thus if defendants consent to summary trial justices cannot proceed other than to try them summarily. It is impermissible for them to commit for trial those defendants no matter that one of the persons jointly charged with them elects to be tried on indictment. Two forms of trial, he said, where a number of defendants are jointly *h* charged involving witnesses having to testify on two or more occasions, is unavoidable. Every defendant is entitled to be tried where he wishes to be. Justices are forced to decide initially under s 19 what the mode of trial should be, but that decision under s 19 cannot prevail once s 20 comes into play and a defendant will not consent to be bound by it. At that stage the provisions of s 25(2) simply do not enter into the matter because the justices will not then have embarked on a summary trial.

Moreover, counsel for the applicant strongly urged that it would be iniquitous if *j* defendants elected summary trial and they were not to be allowed that form of trial. Take the case, he said, of a defendant who has elected summary trial, he being one of a number of defendants on a joint charge and he is not legally assisted, is he to be put to the expense of going where he does not want to go, namely to the Crown Court to be

tried on indictment, dragged there, so to speak, by that person or those persons who have
a   elected not to be tried summarily?
    Clearly the time has come, I think, if it is not overdue, for such a vital issue as arises
here to be resolved.
    Counsel appearing as amicus curiae submitted, and counsel for the Crown wholly
supported him and save as to s 20 counsel for the applicant too, that the relevant sections
must be construed and have effect as follows, no matter that the consequences may be
b   inconvenient, unjust perhaps, time wasting and apparently needlessly expensive.
    Under s 19(1) justices are required to form their view as to mode of trial with in mind
not the defendants but the offence, so that if there is more than one offence before the
court the justices may in principle arrive at different views concerning the mode of trial
in respect of each offence. Here, of course, there was but one. Once the justices reach a
view under s 19(1) they proceed to s 20 or s 21 as the case may be. These sections both
c   begin to apply on the premise that the s 19 exercise has been concluded. Reconsideration
of the decision-taker under s 19 is not permissible. There is no question of the court at
any stage thereafter going back and thinking again about what it was they decided under
s 19. Such an issue arose in R v Southend Magistrates' Court, ex p Wood (1988) 152 JP 158
and was resolved in the way in which the amicus would have us resolve it. I entirely
agree with him in that respect: justices may not return to s 19 once they have determined
d   what the mode of trial shall be.
    As to s 20, what the justices are called on to do is to reach a determination having
regard to the procedures outlined in that section where the defendants shall in fact be
tried, that is to say whether they shall be tried summarily or on indictment.
    The question in the present case, the amicus submitted, arises strictly under s 20(3).
Thus where, as here, there is only one offence before the court and a number of
e   defendants are jointly charged, and one of those defendants elects jury trial but the others
elect summary trial or one elects summary trial and the others elect jury trial, it cannot
matter who is in the majority or whether an equal number elect a different form of trial.
The words 'the accused' in s 20(2) and (3) apply to the person accused of the offence
referred to in s 19 and further referred to in s 20(1). In a case such as the present, where
f   more than one person is accused, regard has to be had to a proper construction of the
whole of the terms of s 20 and there must be invoked for that purpose the provisions of
s 6(c) of the Interpretation Act 1978. Section 6 states:

> 'In any Act, unless the contrary intention appears,—(a) words importing the
> masculine gender including the feminine; (b) words importing the feminine gender
> include the masculine; (c) words in the singular include the plural and words in the
g   > plural include the singular.'

    It is the last of those provisions which is of course of particular relevance in the present
case. Counsel appearing as amicus submitted that when justices, having proceeded step
by step under s 20, arrive at s 20(3)(a) and (b), they must where necessary read the
h   singular, for that appears in both provisions, as the plural in accordance with the 1978
Act.
    This approach, the amicus submitted, does not involve treating s 20 as directory only
because manifestly it is not. He accepted that each defendant is entitled to be put to his
election. But, he said, once one defendant has elected jury trial it is nugatory to put the
others to their election, since jury trial for all is inevitable. The proper procedure to be
j   adopted under s 20(2) cannot depend on the chance that a defendant who is first addressed
elects trial on indictment and it is always possible that that defendant, hearing his co-
defendants consent to summary trial, will change his mind. The amicus agreed with the
counsel for the Crown that the common sense of the matter assists in such a construction
of this part of s 20. This construction implicitly acknowledges, he went on, that the
position would be different where justices are considering more than one offence. That

was the situation in many of the cases which were referred to us and others which we have examined which were not.

Clearly if a defendant is charged with two or more offences he may, the amicus said, elect in respect of each. If, in respect of any one of those offences, another charged jointly with him of that offence elects jury trial, then in relation to that offence they must both be committed for trial but in relation to the other offence or offences he will if he so elects be tried summarily. The amicus concluded by submitting that Lord Bridge was not called on to attempt in *Gillard's* case [1985] 3 All ER 634, [1986] AC 442 any construction of s 20. Thus what he rather tentatively said in the course of his speech as to that section has to be regarded an an obiter dictum and cannot, therefore, possibly be said to be binding on this or any other court. With that I agree.

In my judgment the submissions of counsel appearing as amicus on the construction to be placed on s 20 are irresistible. It seems to me, there being nothing in the 1980 Act especially within ss 19 to 25, to disapply the 1978 Act, that Act must be brought to bear as to s 6 on the construction of s 20.

In a case where a number of defendants in a magistrates' court are jointly charged with one offence and one of them elects to be tried on indictment the others, though they will have consented to be tried summarily, must also be committed for trial. That, I recognise, leads in certain situations to an unsatisfactory state of affairs for those who would, if they could, be tried summarily. That is the effect of what Parliament had enacted. If it is possible in the future for some reconsideration of this section to be made by Parliament it will have to be looked at in the light of the difficulties which inevitably arise when persons jointly charged with one offence differ as to their choice of trial.

For those reasons I see no alternative but to refuse the applicant the relief which he seeks and to dismiss this application because, in my judgment, the justices here, albeit for entirely the wrong reasons, came to the right decision which was that the applicant and the other two defendants be tried on indictment.

POTTS J. I agree.

Application dismissed.

Solicitors: *Gepp & Sons*, Chelmsford (for the applicant); *Crown Prosecution Service*, Essex; *Treasury Solicitor*.

Dilys Tausz   Barrister.

Cambridge Nutrition Ltd v British Broadcasting Corp

COURT OF APPEAL, CIVIL DIVISION
KERR, RALPH GIBSON LJJ AND EASTHAM J
24, 25, 26 NOVEMBER 1987

Injunction – Interlocutory – Grant or refusal effectively ending action – Monetary compensation irrelevant to both parties – Transmission of broadcast or publication of article – Impact and value depending on timing of transmission or publication – Whether interlocutory injunction should be granted if plaintiff able to show good arguable case and that balance of convenience lay in granting injunction – Whether court should assess relative strength of parties' cases before deciding whether injunction should be granted.

The plaintiffs manufactured and marketed a very low calorie diet which was very widely used. The BBC, in co-operation with the plaintiffs, prepared a television programme about very low calorie diets which focused particularly on the plaintiffs' diet because of its very high market share. In the course of the making of the programme the plaintiffs became concerned about the tone and content of the programme and before it was broadcast the plaintiffs applied for an injunction to prevent it being broadcast until after publication of a report by a government committee which was investigating the medical aspects of very low calorie diets. The plaintiffs claimed that the BBC had agreed as a condition of the plaintiffs co-operating in the making of the programme that they would not transmit the programme until after publication of the report. The BBC denied that they were contractually bound not to transmit the programme until after publication of the report. The nature of the programme was such that it was only appropriate for transmission in its existing form before publication of the report. The judge granted the injunction sought on the grounds, inter alia, that the plaintiffs had established a plausible case that there was a contract between the parties preventing transmission until after publication of the committee's report, that the balance of justice required an injunction to be granted and that the BBC could be adequately compensated in damages if it turned out that the injunction should not have been granted. The BBC appealed.

Held – The appeal would be allowed and the injunction discharged for the following reasons—

(1) Where neither side was interested in monetary compensation and the decision on an application for an interlocutory injunction would be the equivalent of giving final judgment and, in particular, where the subject matter of the application for an interlocutory injunction was the transmission of a broadcast or the publication of an article the impact and value of which depended on the timing of the transmission or publication, the court should not grant an interlocutory injunction restraining transmission or publication merely because the plaintiff was able to show a good arguable case and the balance of convenience lay in granting an injunction. Instead, the court should assess the relative strength of the parties' cases before deciding whether the injunction should be granted. Furthermore (per Kerr LJ), given that, all other things being equal, a doubtful contract should never prevail over the right of free speech, it would be wrong to restrain publication on the strength of nothing more than a plausible allegation of an agreement not to publish (see p 534 *j*, p 535 *b* to *e*, p 536 *a c d*, p 538 *g* to p 539 *a*, p 542 *g* and p 544 *d e*, post); *American Cyanamid Co v Ethicon Ltd* [1975] 1 All ER 504 distinguished.

(2) In carrying out the balancing exercise between the parties the judge had been wrong to conclude that the BBC could be adequately compensated by damages if the plaintiffs' claim failed, since although the BBC would be able to recover their production costs they would have been permanently deprived of their right to transmit a programme

on a topic of public interest in the form and at the time of their choice. He had also been
wrong to hold that the BBC's right of free speech was counterbalanced by the plaintiffs' a
assertion of a contract between the parties preventing transmission until after publication
of the committee's report, since the plaintiffs had not established the existence of such a
contract but only that it was arguable that there was such a contract. In view of the
judge's misdirection the court was entitled to exercise its own discretion, and having
regard to the relative strength of the parties' cases and the importance of the BBC being
allowed to broadcast programmes on matters of public interest the court would refuse an b
injunction (see p 532 a to e, p 533 j to p 534 b, p 535 gj, p 537 a to cj, p 539 de, p 540 a,
p 541 $cefh$ and p 543 gj to p 544 bfg, post); Schering Chemicals Ltd v Falkman Ltd [1981]
2 All ER 321 distinguished.

Notes
For the grant of interlocutory injunctions, see 24 Halsbury's Laws (4th edn) paras 953, c
955–956, and for cases on the subject, see 28(4) Digest (2nd reissue) 152–186, 4957–
5221.

Cases referred to in judgments
A-G v BBC [1980] 3 All ER 161, [1981] AC 303, [1980] 3 WLR 109, HL.
A-G v Guardian Newspapers Ltd [1987] 3 All ER 316, [1987] 1 WLR 1248, HL. d
Addis v Gramophone Co Ltd [1909] AC 488, [1908–10] All ER Rep 1, HL.
American Cyanamid Co v Ethicon Ltd [1975] 1 All ER 504, [1975] AC 396, [1975] 2 WLR
   316, HL.
Bestobell Paints Ltd v Bigg [1975] FSR 421.
Bonnard v Perryman [1891] 2 Ch 269, [1891–4] All ER Rep 965, CA.
Cayne v Global Natural Resources plc [1984] 1 All ER 225, CA. e
Dunhill (Alfred) Ltd v Sunoptic SA [1979] FSR 337, CA.
Eagil Trust Co Ltd v Piggott-Brown [1985] 3 All ER 119, CA.
Hadmor Productions Ltd v Hamilton [1982] 1 All ER 1042, [1983] 1 AC 191, [1982] 2 WLR
   322, HL.
NWL Ltd v Woods [1979] 3 All ER 614, [1979] 1 WLR 1294, HL.
Schering Chemicals Ltd v Falkman Ltd [1981] 2 All ER 321, [1982] QB 1, [1981] 2 WLR f
   848, CA.
Slater v Raw [1977] CA Transcript 374C.
Trevor (J) & Sons v Solomon (1977) 248 EG 779, CA.
Wakefield v Duke of Buccleuch (1865) 12 LT 628.
Woodward v Hutchins [1977] 2 All ER 751, [1977] 1 WLR 760, CA.
X (a minor) (wardship: restriction on publication), Re [1975] 1 All ER 697, [1975] Fam 47, g
   [1975] 2 WLR 335, CA.

Appeal
The defendants, the British Broadcasting Corp, appealed against the decision of his
Honour Judge Tibber, sitting as a judge of the High Court on 29 October 1987, granting h
an interlocutory injunction in favour of the plaintiffs, Cambridge Nutrition Ltd,
restraining the BBC from publishing or transmitting a programme on very low calorie
diets prior to the publication by the Committee on Medical Aspects of Food of a report
on such diets. The facts are set out in the judgment of Kerr LJ.

David Eady QC and Manuel Barca for the BBC. j
Gavin Lightman QC and John Whittaker for the plaintiffs.

KERR LJ. The plaintiffs manufacture and market a very low calorie diet (VLCD)
known as the Cambridge Diet. This was launched in 1984 and is designed to assist people
to lose weight. It is mainly taken in the form of a powder in a range of 11 or so flavours,

containing an intake of no more than 330 calories per day. It has been medically researched for many years and enjoys some distinguished medical support.

It is marketed through counsellors, as they are called, who are paid on a commission basis and are, or have been, themselves users of the diet and experienced in its characteristics.

It is common ground that the merits, or possible dangers, of VLCDs are matters of great public interest. The Cambridge Diet appears to have been taken by no less than about two million people. Since March 1986 VLCDs have been under consideration by the government Committee on the Medical Aspects of Food (COMA). This is now expected to report in December and its recommendations are due to be published. In close co-operation with the plaintiffs, representatives of the British Broadcasting Corp (the BBC) have for some months been preparing a television programme about VLCDs. This focuses on the Cambridge Diet, bearing in mind in particular that the plaintiffs appear to have a preponderant market share in VLCDs said to be, I think, in excess of 70%.

That programme has now been completed. In its complete form it is ready for transmission, and it is common ground that it is what has been called a pre-COMA programme, in the sense that it is only appropriate for transmission before publication of the COMA report.

The main issue of fact is as follows. The plaintiffs contend, and the BBC deny, that when the possibility of the making of this programme was first discussed over the telephone in March 1987 with a respresentative of the plaintiffs' public relations consultants, it was agreed as one of two conditions that the programme would not be broadcast until after COMA had published its report. On the plaintiffs' side it is also said that the representative of the BBC agreed to confirm this and another condition in writing. But it is common ground that no such confirmation was ever given, and indeed there was no further reference to either condition when both parties began to co-operatate in the preparation of the programme, from about April 1987 onwards.

By August it became evident that there were signs of strain between the parties about the tone and content of the programme and that the plaintiffs were beginning to have second thoughts about its desirability from their point of view.

On 21 August the plaintiffs wrote a letter raising for the first time the allegation that this oral agreement had been made in March, together with various other matters concerning the content and nature of the programme.

On 11 September the BBC wrote back denying that any such agreement, oral or written, had ever been made, and responded to the plaintiffs' other complaints.

On 18 October the plaintiffs brought the present action, claiming various injunctions relating to the programme, including injunctions to the effect that it could not be broadcast at all. However, these have not been pursued, and the relevant injunction for present purposes is solely concerned with an order that the programme should not be transmitted until after the publication of the COMA report. No point is taken on delay in relation to the institution of the proceedings or in any other respect.

On 29 October his Honour Judge Tibber, sitting as a judge of the High Court in the Queen's Bench Division, granted this injunction. The order which he made, and which is under appeal, is that the BBC—

> 'be restrained . . . from publishing or transmitting in any manner any programme containing material or information provided only by or whose provisions was in any manner facilitated by the Plaintiff after 23 March 1987 [that was the date of the telephone call], prior to the trial of this action or earlier publication by the Government of a report by the Committee on Medical Aspects of Food on the use of very low calorie diets.'

On 12 November (a Thursday) the BBC appealed, and we began hearing their appeal on 24 November.

I should say in passing that the programme features in the Radio Times for this week, scheduled I think for Saturday, 28 November, that is the day after tomorrow. This is *a* because the preparations for the layout and printing of the Radio Times have to be made long in advance. But the fact that the programme is featured in the Radio Times is of course entirely irrelevant for the purposes of this appeal, although it shows its urgency.

In that connection I must add another parenthesis which should be noted generally. This case had originally been listed before a division of this court consisting of two members, because it is interlocutory. However, it is not a suitable case for such a court in *b* view of its urgency, the danger of a possible disagreement is too great, or of a feeling on the part of members of the court of being under some pressure to reach agreement, which is also undesirable. As the argument has shown, the case is of some general importance. It so happened that I read enough of the papers towards the end of last week to realise that it was inappropriate for the case to be heard by a court of-two. It then proved possible, on Friday of last week, to make arrangements at short notice for a court *c* of three in co-operation with the Master of the Rolls and the Registrar of Civil Appeals. I mention this because it is necessary to remind counsel, as shown by this case, that they must resolutely and critically consider in every case which may be heard by a Court of Appeal of two members under the provisions of the Supreme Court Act 1981 whether it is appropriate for such a court. If counsel on either side then consider that the case may not be appropriate for that purpose they should notify the Registrar of Civil Appeals. A *d* decision will then be taken whether in all the circumstances the appeal should be heard before a court of three, even though it is one which may be heard by a court of two.

I turn now to the evidence which must be reviewed fairly fully in the circumstances. All the dates refer to 1987.

On 22 March an article about the Cambridge Diet appeared in the Sunday Times. It purported to leak parts of the COMA report, saying that this was expected to be published *e* within the next few weeks. As sometimes happens, reality proved to be different.

In the result, however, there was an important telephone conversation, or possibily two in rapid succession, between Carys Howell, a research worker employed by BBC East, based in Norwich, and a Miss Ione Nurdin, a director of Communication Group plc in London, who had been retained by the plaintiffs to handle their public relations with *f* the media. Miss Nurdin's account of the telepone call is in the following terms:

> 'Carys Howell informed me that the Defendants wished to do a programme on the Plaintiff and asked whether the Plaintiff would agree to co-operate in order to facilitate the production of the programme. I told her that agreement could not be given as the Plaintiff had determined that it would not comment to the media about the COMA report on VLCD prior to publication of the Report. (The reason for this *g* policy was twofold, firstly because the company could not possibily comment on a Report which it had not seen and secondly, because it was in the process of compiling new evidence to put before the COMA sub committee). Carys Howell, however, stated that the programme that the Defendants were considering producing was a feature on "before and after" the Cambridge Diet, and after further discussion during which Carys Howell offered to agree that the programme would not be *h* broadcast until after the publication of the COMA Report and, following persuasion by her, I eventually agreed to the Plaintiff giving its co-operation to facilitate the production of the programme on the basis that: a) it was a programme featuring dieters "before and after" the Cambridge Diet and b) the programme would not be broadcast until after publication of the COMA Report. This latter condition, as Carys Howell fully appreciated, was absolutely fundamental to my giving the *j* Plaintiff's agreement to co-operate and as a consequence she volunteered to confirm this in writing.'

Miss Nurdin then exhibited two contemporaneous memoranda concerning this telephone call, which were in the following terms:

a

'*Media Contact*   Following a discussion with BBC TV Norwich, a meeting was arranged with CNL [the plaintiffs] to progress a feature film on the Cambridge Diet. This is subject to a written agreement that it will not be released pre Coma.'

In another memorandum dated 24 March, which appears to be the date of the telephone call, unless it was on the previous day, Miss Nurdin wrote:

b

'BBC TV Norwich considering production of "before and after" feature film on the Cambridge Diet. Have agreed to arrange a meeting next week (please advise possible timing) on basis a letter confirms programme will not appear pre COMA report.'

c

Another employee of these consultants, Amanda Riddle, said that she was aware of the COMA condition when she later arranged a meeting on 14 July between Miss Howell and a BBC producer, Mr Meadows, and others, because she had heard about this condition from Miss Nurdin in March.

Finally, a public relations officer of the plaintiffs, Maria Piggot, said that she knew about this condition, probably from Miss Nurdin, round about 24 March. She participated in the making of the programme, but she also said in her affidavit:

d

'It is also my understanding at that time that what was being envisaged was a short programme (about 10 minutes) by BBC TV East in Norwich featuring the Cambridge Diet as a success story by a local company.'

That was certainly never the nature of the programme which had been envisaged.

Dr Wallace, the marketing director of the plaintiffs, said that he had not been aware of any condition concerning transmission only after the COMA report, until August of this year.

e

No explanation was ever given by any of the plaintiffs' professional public relations advisers why the elementary precaution of ensuring some written confirmation of an alleged oral agreement was simply ignored.

The evidence of Carys Howell in this connection is as follows:

f

'I told Ms Nurdin that we wanted to make a programme about low calorie diets and the Cambridge Diet. I said that this was an initial enquiry about the making of such a programme and the possibility of the plaintiffs co-operating in its filming; and that the content of the programme would depend upon whether or not it was made with the co-operation of the Plaintiffs. As I expected, Ms Nurdin said that she would have to find out from the Plaintiffs whether they wanted to take part in the making of the programme. She said that there was a report due out about very low

g

calorie diets, and I said that I knew that that was so. I added that that was what made the matter topical. Ms Nurdin said that neither Dr Howard [the Chairman of the plaintiffs] nor anybody from the Plaintiffs would be able to comment directly on that report because it had not yet been published. I indicated that I understood that, but I stressed that we would want to talk to Dr Howard during the filming about

h

the Diet and scientific research into it. There was no question of a formal decision being arrived at during that conversation, let alone of a binding contract between the Plaintiffs and the BBC being agreed. The conversation only lasted a few minutes. Ms Nurdin promised to ask her client Company whether they would consider taking part in the programme. She later telephoned me to say that she had arranged for me to meet with the Company to discuss the matter further. I asked whether I

j

should put the request I had made into writing but Ms Nurdin said that that would not be necessary. What happened afterwards seems to me to be entirely consistent with the account I have given of my telephone conversation with Ms Nurdin, and entirely inconsistent with the suggestion now advanced on behalf of the plaintiffs that a contract was made during the conversation, under the terms of which, in consideration of the BBC receiving the Plaintiffs' co-operation, it was obliged not to

broadcast this programme until after publication of the COMA report, and
furthermore to make a programme "featuring" . . . or "only" featuring . . . people *a*
"before and after" they had been on the Cambridge Diet.'

There is also lengthy evidence from Mr Meadows, the producer, explaining how the
programme was put together in co-operation with the plaintiffs. To summarise part of
the contents, the position is that filming at the plaintiffs' factory at Corby took place in
April; there was further filming in Cambridge and Norwich in May and June, and
filming of the plaintiffs' annual conference for 1987 which was held in Dublin. The *b*
filming in this country was completed around the middle of July.

Mr Meadows then said:

'There was never any suggestion from any of the Plaintiffs' representatives that
we had met, including Dr. Howard, Dr. Marks [who was the senior medical
consultant] Ms. Piggott and Ms. Riddle of their public relations consultants either *c*
that the programme was to be limited to a "before and after" treatment of obese
people taking the Cambridge Diet, or that it was a programme which could not be
broadcast until after the COMA report was published. We have not been able to
obtain any information as to the likely date of the publication of the COMA report;
indeed, on July 14 1987 at a meeting which I am about to describe, Dr. Wallace of
the Plaintiffs said that it might never be published. What was taking shape was a *d*
substantial programme about very low calorie diets which it would be appropriate
and topical to broadcast in advance of the publication of the COMA report.'

The Cambridge Diet was manufactured and marketed in the United States under
licence. Towards the end of July interviews were also conducted by the BBC
representatives with persons in the United States. I should add that the condition about *e*
featuring users of the diet 'before and after', which was also alleged to have been agreed
in the original telephone conversation, has not been pursued in these proceedings, nor in
the statement of claim which was served after the notice of appeal had been issued.

Next there is a lengthy transcript of an important meeting on 14 July, which I have
already mentioned, between representatives of the two parties, Miss Howell and Mr
Meadows on the side of the BBC and Dr Wallace and Miss Riddle, and possibly others, on *f*
the side of the plaintiffs, for the purpose of discussing the programme. This shows that
tensions about the content and tone of the programme were beginning to make
themselves felt. There were references to the possibility of defamation and litigation.
There were also references to the uncertainties concerning the COMA Report, and Dr
Wallace said at one point that there 'could be no COMA at all with the way things are
going'. *g*

In that connection Mr Meadows said:

'I have read what purports to be a copy of an affidavit sworn herein by Ms. Riddle,
in which she concludes by saying of that meeting on July 14 1987 that: "Nothing
was said which led me to believe that the programme would be broadcast before
publication of the COMA report". This I cannot accept. Dr. Wallace said that the *h*
COMA report might never be published; but no-one suggested that, in consequence,
the programme might never be broadcast.'

We have no affidavits from Dr Howard or Dr Marks.

The final part of the evidence with regard to the alleged oral agreement is to be found
in the letters which I have already mentioned and from which I must read a few extracts.
On 21 August 1987 Miss Nurdin wrote to Mr Meadows as follows: *j*

'I write further to the meeting which took place on 14 July, which you were
asked to attend because of both our and Cambridge Nutrition Limited's mounting
concern over the programme you intend to broadcast. When BBC TV East first
approached Cambridge Nutrition on or around 23 March in relation to the possible

production of a programme concerning the company, I told Carys Howell, who
a   telephoned me, that due to the circumstances surrounding the publication of the
forthcoming COMA report, the company could not agree to assist. Carys, however,
persisted and after discussion we eventually agreed that Cambridge Nutrition would
co-operate fully on the basis that the programme would feature only "before and
after" of dieters who were on, or had been on, the Cambridge Diet and that, most
importantly, the programme would not be broadcast until after the publication of
b   the COMA report, which Carys volunteered to confirm in writing. Cambridge
Nutrition's co-operation, as you are well aware, has always been on the basis that the
programme would not go out before publication of the COMA report as its
publication renders it an extremely sensitive time for the company. This, as you
also know, was a fundamental condition to Cambridge Nutrition agreeing to
become involved in the programme at all. In the circumstances, we would be
c   grateful for your confirmation that the programme will not, as agreed, be broadcast
until after publication of the report . . . More recently, however, it has begun to
appear to both ourselves and those at Cambridge Nutrition, that your intentions for
the programme have radically altered. This was firmly brought home at the meeting
on 14 July when you said that the programme objective was to try and tell the story
of the Cambridge Diet in the context of very low calorie diets in general and to
d   reflect accurately the climate of opinions surrounding them. You will appreciate
that this is fundamentally different to the original basis of the programme in respect
of which Cambridge Nutrition agreed to co-operate. This is regarded with
considerable concern by Cambridge Nutrition in view of the current sensitive
position in relation to the COMA report . . .'

e   There was then a suggestion that there should be co-operation in considering a transcript
of the programme to ensure its accuracy and fairness.
      The reply to that letter, dated 11 September, was addressed to Amanda Riddle:

      'Firstly, I must make it quite clear that no verbal or written promise has been
made by or on behalf of the BBC to the effect that we shall transmit our programme
f   after publication of the COMA Report. Secondly, it was made plain from the outset
that all aspects of the Cambridge Diet would be referred to. To ignore any part of
the history of the diet would greatly affect the honesty of the programme. In
addition, to produce a programme along the lines to which you allude, would
amount to nothing more than a free advertisement for Cambridge. This would
constitute a breach of the terms of the BBC's-Charter . . . Finally, the programme is
g   far from complete as editing is likely to continue for some weeks yet. It will
therefore be quite impossible for me to produce a script at this stage . . .'

and then it goes on to say that it would be inconsistent with editorial independence if a
script were provided in advance.
      Leaving that topic, I must refer to the evidence about the likely damage to the parties,
h   depending on whether or not the injunction was granted. In that regard Dr Wallace said:

      'This threatened action [ie, the transmission of the programme before publication
of COMA] is a matter of great concern to the Plaintiff. It is reasonably to be
anticipated that the COMA Report will make what will be perceived to be definitive
statements as to very low calorie diets which may well lead to statutory regulations.
j   The showing now of the Defendants programme before it is known what the
COMA Report says (either pro or anti VLCD) could (and I think most probably
would) be extremely damaging to the Plaintiff. Indeed it could be catastrophic. The
underlying reason behind this is that the Cambridge Diet is marketed and sold
through a Counsellor System. It is not sold on a retail or wholesale basis at all. The
Counsellor system is a method of sales whereby users of the diet themselves

determined to sell the product to others in return for which they are paid a
commission. The Cambridge Diet is sold in this way as the Plaintiff wishes to ensure *a*
that those taking the diet receive suitable counselling and advice in relation to it and
dieting generally and the Counsellors are trained to give this advice. However, the
consequence is that 80% of the Counsellors are housewives and approximately 53%
purchase less than £200 of the Cambridge Diet per month. Particularly this latter
group, who have no business experience and are simply selling the diet because they
believe it will assist others and for a small amount of side money, are highly *b*
susceptible to influence from publicity. Once the COMA Report has been published,
which from the information available to me seems most likely to occur in November
1987 (although I should say that there is no guarantee of this or that it will be
published at all), it will be possible for interested parties fully to evaluate the contents
of the Report which has taken in excess of eighteen months for the COMA sub
committee to compile, and make a sensible and considered judgment on VLCD and *c*
particularly the Cambridge Diet.'

In fairness to Dr Wallace I should read another passage, in a later affidavit, in which he
said:

'The Plaintiff has at all times been confident that the COMA Report, which will
be the Report of detached and balanced experts, will not be adverse to the Plaintiff *d*
and that any recommendations made by the Report will be capable of being
implemented by the Plaintiff without counsellor or customer resistence. Adverse
publicity after the Report (by, for instance, the showing of a programme by the
Defendants) will be capable of being measured and evaluated against the findings of
the Report; and it will be those findings and not the message of the Defendants
which will determine the degree of confidence in the Plaintiff and the Cambridge *e*
Diet on the part of counsellors and customers. It was this reasoning that lay behind
the original stipulation that the programme should only be shown [after] the
publication of the Report and why the Plaintiff is insisting on the performance of
their obligation by the Defendants.'

Counsel for the BBC commented on that paragraph by pointing out that in another *f*
passage Dr Wallace has said that he himself had been unaware of the alleged condition
until August.

Mr Meadows, the producer of the programme, dealt with this aspect from the point of
view of the BBC as follows:

'As the programme was being made, it was never clear to us when we could *g*
expect that the COMA report would be published. If the COMA report had been
published in the summer while the programme was being made, then the report's
recommendations would have been included in the programme and discussed with
contributors to the programme including Dr. Howard and Dr. Marks of the
Plaintiffs. In the event, the report was not published and is still not published, and
the programme is almost ready. It is, accordingly, a programme which it is *h*
appropriate to broadcast in advance of and only in advance of the publication of the
COMA report; and the timing of the proposed programme centres upon the fact
that the contents of the Report commissioned by the DHSS have been leaked and
are therefore in the public domain and also upon the fact that it may be officially
published in the near future. There never was any contract under the terms of
which the BBC was obliged to limit the content of this programme, and/or obliged *j*
not to broadcast it until after publication of the COMA report. In co-operating with
us in the making of the programme, the Plaintiffs have acted in a manner quite
inconsistent with the existence of any such obligations on our part. If the injunctions
sought were granted, the effect would be to oblige the BBC to consign this nearly
completed programme to the waste-bin, and to consider making another programme

a on the basis of the existing material, but excluding all material and information obtained as a result of the co-operation which these Plaintiffs have given us. Accordingly, I cannot accept the assertion made by Dr. Wallace, the Plaintiffs' Marketing Director, in his Affidavit of which I have read what purports to be a copy, that the BBC will suffer no damage if the injunction is granted. It will suffer damage, but this will be difficult or impossible to quantify in money terms. The likelihood is that the true cost of the programme lies between £25,000 and £50,000.'

b I think that was said because of a passage which I have not read in an affidavit by Dr Wallace as to the probable cost of the programme.

Mr Meadows went on:

'Not only would the BBC suffer financial damage, but the public interest would be injuriously affected by such a restriction of the Corporation's freedom of speech c and discussion. The Cambridge Diet as currently marketed involves consumption of 330 calories of energy a day. Our extensive enquiries have indicated that the COMA report will recommend an increase in this figure. Dr. Wallace has told me that the COMA report may recommend such an increase, and that he for his part would hope that the Plaintiffs would respond by increasing the calorie content of their Diet food. In that event there would no longer be any current public interest d in the merits or alleged de-merits of 330 calorie regime. It is with the merits and the alleged de-merits of such a regime that the programme deals. The programme is a carefully researched and, I believe, a balanced examination of that regime. If the injunctions sought are granted, the public will almost certainly be deprived of the opportunity of seeing such a programme about the diet which is currently being marketed. Dr. Wallace, in his paragraph 13, asserts that the Cambridge Diet is sold e by counsellors, and that the broadcast of the programme will be damaging to the Plaintiffs through its impact upon those counsellors who are apparently, despite their training, highly susceptible to influence from publicity. His further suggestion appears to be that the programme will cause this damage if it is broadcast before publication of the COMA report, but not after publication of that report; for my own part I am unable to understand why that could be so. It might be possible for a f limited form of injunction to be granted, whereby I could perhaps re-make the programme omitting all the fruits of the Plaintiffs' co-operation—the filmed interviews, and the information and documents provided. But the result would be a programme which was unbalanced, to the disadvantage of the Plaintiffs, on account of its omission of their defence of their diet.'

g   That is the relevant evidence. I should only add that the plaintiffs have provided a bank guarantee of £100,000 to cover their cross-undertaking in damages in the event of it being held subsequently at a trial that the injunction should not have been granted.

I turn to the judgment. The first issue, which was hotly debated below and in this court, was whether the grant or refusal of an interlocutory injunction in this case should be determined according to the guidelines laid down by the House of Lords in the well-h known speech of Lord Diplock in *American Cyanamid Co v Ethicon Ltd* [1975] 1 All ER 504, [1975] AC 396. The judge reviewed the plaintiffs' contentions in favour of, and the BBC's contentions against, the application of that case. He then quoted the second paragraph of the headnote of the decision of this court in *Cayne v Global Natural Resources plc* [1984] 1 All ER 225, which I need not set out. That case arose from an exceptional situation in which the grant of the injunction would have been the equivalent of giving j final judgment in favour of the plaintiffs. He went on as follows:

'That [referring to the *Global Natural Resources* case] seems to me to be far from the facts in the instant case where, although the plaintiffs will attain their objective if the injunction is granted, the [BBC] will not be prevented from making a programme about the Cambridge Diet without the co-operation of the plaintiffs and can, in fact, be adequately compensated in damages if it turns out to be wrong to grant the injunction.'

a

Pausing there, I entirely agree that the *Global Natural Resources* case was a very different case. But I find it astonishing that the judge felt able to conclude, as he evidently did, that if the injunction were granted and it should thereafter turn out that the BBC had never been bound by the alleged condition, and had therefore been free to broadcast the programme as and when they had planned, they could 'in fact, be adequately compensated *b* in damages'. It is hardly necessary to point out that it is part of the statutory function, and indeed the duty, of the BBC to broadcast on matters of public interest and concern. This programme certainly lies within that field of the BBC's responsibilities. The programme was planned and made over the last six months or so because it was judged to be right, and in the public interest, to transmit it at the present time. This had not been disputed. It was, and remains, entirely appropriate and in the public interest to *c* broadcast a programme on this topic now. As was pointed out in the affidavits, the diet is being marketed extensively and used every day by many thousands of people. Although it had originally been uncertain whether the COMA report would be published while the programme was being made, in which case the report would obviously have had to feature as a major part of the programme, in its final form it is now only suitable for transmission before publication by COMA. The consequence of a wrongly granted *d* injunction would therefore be that the BBC would have been excluded from the proper exercise of their functions in this respect, and incidentally also to deprive them of their right of free speech on a topic of public interest. I cannot accept that these consequences could be adequately compensated by a sum of money equivalent to the cost of the cancelled programme, or anything of that kind. Nor can I accept, despite the judge's clear language, and making every allowance for the difficulties which he faced when *e* giving his judgment, to which I refer again later, that he must have had in mind additional uncompensatable damage when he expressed himself as he did. Indeed, looking at the judgment as a whole, it seems clear that he did not have in mind any uncompensatable damage. This is the first point where I part company from the judge, and where he clearly appears to have misdirected himself in his approach to the balancing exercise which he had to carry out.   *f*

Then he went on as follows:

'I therefore intend to deal with this application on *Cyanamid* principles, as modified in later cases, but will later consider the result of a "broad brush" approach.'

I pause there to say that his conclusion in favour of the grant of an injunction was based both on the application of the *Cyanamid* test and on what he refers to as the 'broad brush' *g* approach, to which he referred briefly at the end of his judgment.

The judgment went on to conclude that the plaintiffs had an arguable case for contending that the BBC were contractually bound not to transmit this programme until after COMA, so that there was a triable issue of breach of contract. The judge did not examine its strength; he merely said in that regard, 'I find that the plaintiffs have a case which is sufficiently plausible to be taken seriously'. I shall return to that point. He went *h* on:

'Where does the balance of justice lie? If the injunction is not granted and the [BBC] broadcast their programme, the plaintiffs' alleged right is gone forever and they are left to a right in damages which will be difficult if not impossible to quantify: *Schering Chemicals Ltd v Falkman Ltd* [1981] 2 All ER 321 at 347, [1982] QB *j* 1 at 38 per Templeman LJ. If the injunction is granted, the broadcast is merely deferred until after the publication of the COMA report in four weeks' time. Good sense may require the programme to be amended in the light of that report, but the [BBC] can still, if they wish, use their interviews with the plaintiffs' advisers and use a the information provided by them. The balance of justice seems to me to require the granting of the injunction.'

I differ from the judge in two respects in these passages, although I recognise that it might go too far in a review of the exercise of his discretion to regard the judge's differing conclusions as being capable of amounting to a misdirection.

The reasons why I differ from him are briefly as follows.

b First, the reference to the analogy of the *Schering Chemicals* case is in my view inappropriate. The *Schering Chemicals* case was concerned with a film about a product of the plaintiffs in circumstances which amounted to a gross breach of trust and confidence. The court saw the film. Shaw LJ appears to have regarded it as a gratuitous onslaught in the guise of a crusade. Templeman LJ said that the film contained harmful publicity to Schering. The sentence from the judgment of Templeman LJ, which the judge clearly had in mind, was the following well-known sentence, characteristically concise ([1981] 2 c All ER 321 at 339, 348, 346, [1982] QB 1 at 29, 40, 38): 'It is impossible to quantify the damage caused by bad publicity.' In my judgment that is not relevant to the plaintiffs' alleged contractual right in the present case; at any rate, I am not satisfied that any sufficient case to that effect has been made out. Apart from the fact that there is no evidence that the programme would be harmful for the plaintiffs' publicity, they have d no right, according to the contract which they allege, to seek to ban the transmission of this programme, nor any basis for complaining about its provenance or contents. That is radically different from the situation in the *Schering Chemicals* case. The plaintiffs' only claimed right is to control the timing of the programme in relation to the COMA report. If it were shown the day after the COMA report they could have no complaint; if it were shown the day before, any damages might well be merely nominal. No question of e damages for breach of confidence arises in this case, as it did in the *Schering Chemicals* case and many other cases on which counsel for the plaintiffs relied. They have nothing to do with the situation in the present case.

My second reason for differing from the judge is that in my view he seriously understated the effect on the programme if it now has to be postponed beyond the publication of the COMA report. It seems clear that its contents would then be largely f outdated and that there could be no question of amending it, at any rate within a reasonable time.

I then come to the second passage in the judgment where I part company with the judge to the extent of concluding that he has misdirected himself in carrying out the balancing exercise, which on any view, whatever test is to be applied, has to be performed in cases such as the present.

g He referred to the points raised by counsel for the BBC. In relation to the first he said:

'First [counsel for the BBC] says that the balance is tipped in favour of the [BBC] because the grant of an injunction will restrain freedom of speech in a matter of public interest. The matter is of public interest because the evidence shows that there are two million users of the Cambridge Diet. This is balanced, in my view, by h the submission of the plaintiffs that it is not in the public interest that the BBC can publish despite contracting to the contrary. In *Schering Chemicals Ltd v Falkman Ltd* it was held, despite the dissenting judgment of Lord Denning MR that in very similar circumstances to the instant case, the injunction did not interfere with the freedom of the press to inform the public because there was "nothing to prevent any ... television company ... from making a film about Primodos provided that they do j not employ the services of [one] who can only give those services by making use of information which he ... voluntarily debarred himself from [using]" (see [1981] 2 All ER 321 at 347, [1982] QB 1 at 40).'

In my view that passage contains two material misdirections. First, the correct approach on the facts of this case is to put on one side of the balance the admitted public interest in the transmission of the programme, but not, on the other side, 'the public interest that the BBC can publish despite contracting to the contrary'. It hardly needs to *a* be pointed out that the evidence is far from clear that the BBC in fact contracted not to transmit this programme until after the COMA report had been published. There is merely a triable issue that there may have been a contract of that nature, or at any rate a reference to such a condition subject to written confirmation, in the original telephone conversations. It follows that the balancing exercise reflected in this passage of the judgment is erroneous. In my view the whole case would be different if the BBC had in *b* fact entered into a binding contract from which they now sought to resile. In that event, but only in that event, would there have to be a competing balance of public interest against contract, such as that which the judge envisages.

Second, as already indicated, I cannot accept that the *Schering Chemicals* case arose 'in very similar circumstances to the instant case'. Both lie to some extent in the same field of the law, but the circumstances were wholly different. As I have already indicated, the *c* film which was the subject matter of the *Schering Chemicals* case was made in circumstances of a blatant breach of trust and confidence. The judgments of the majority of the court, Shaw and Templeman LJJ, use highly derogatory terms in describing the conduct of the defendants. Templeman LJ said expressly that but for the breach of confidence there would have been no adequate grounds for the grant of an injunction (see [1981] 2 All ER 321 at 348, [1982] QB 1 at 40). In the present case the evidence cannot support more *d* than a triable issue as to whether or not an agreement was made as the result of a short introductory telephone conversation, to the alleged terms of which the plaintiffs made no further reference for five months, despite close and active co-operation between the parties throughout that period. There is no similarity between the circumstances of the two cases.

There is no need to refer to the last part of the judgment, in which the judge expressed *e* the view that *Woodward v Hutchins* [1977] 2 All ER 751, [1977] 1 WLR 760 would now be decided differently in the light of the decision in the House of Lords in the *Spycatcher* case (see *A-G v Guardian Newspapers Ltd* [1987] 3 All ER 316, [1987] 1 WLR 1248). I express no view about that.

The judge concluded his judgment as follows: *f*

> 'If I am wrong in applying the *Cyanamid* test, I think that the same result would be achieved if the "broad brush" approach were adopted and for much the same reasons. I am very conscious that I have not embarked on an exhaustive examination of all the authorities cited by counsel, but this is an interlocutory application and the parties are anxious to receive the reasons for the decision which I made at 5.45 pm on Friday.'   *g*

I naturally bear in mind the high respect to which the exercise of discretion by a judge of first instance is entitled. The difficulties which he faced, as indicated in that last sentence, must also be borne in mind in judging the way in which he expressed himself. But in the light of the misdirections to which I have referred, it appears to me that this court must carry out the balancing exercise afresh and apply its own discretion to the question *h* whether or not to grant an interlocutory injunction.

On that basis I would unhesitatingly refuse such an injunction in this case, and I summarise my reasons as briefly as I can.

First, I do not consider that the question whether or not an injunction should be granted should in this case be tested simply by reference to the guidelines laid down in the *American Cyanamid* case. I accept that the judge was entitled to conclude that he *j* should be guided by that case, but in my view it is not suitable for that purpose. Although *Cayne v Global Natural Resources plc* [1984] 1 All ER 225 was clearly an exceptional case, I would reiterate without repeating what I then said (at 234–235) and I refer equally to the tenor of the judgments of Eveleigh and May LJJ in that case, which are much to the same effect. It is important to bear in mind that the *American Cyanamid* case contains no

principle of universal application. The only such principle is the statutory power of the
a court to grant injunctions when it is just and convenient to do so. The *American Cyanamid*
case is no more than a set of useful guidelines which apply in many cases. It must never
be used as a rule of thumb, let alone as a strait-jacket. Admittedly, the present case is
miles away on its facts from the *Global Natural Resources* case, and it is also much weaker
than *NWL Ltd v Woods* [1979] 3 All ER 614, [1979] 1 WLR 1294, where Lord Diplock
himself recognised the limitations of the *Cyanamid* guidelines. But nevertheless, I do not
b consider that it is an appropriate case for the *Cyanamid* guidelines because the crucial
issues between the parties do not depend on a trial, but solely or mainly on the grant or
refusal of the interlocutory relief. The *American Cyanamid* case provides an authoritative
and most helpful approach to cases where the function of the court in relation to the
grant or refusal of interlocutory injunctions is to hold the balance as justly as possible in
situations where the substantial issues between the parties can only be resolved by a trial.
c In my view, for reasons which require no further elaboration, the present case is not in
that category. Neither side is interested in monetary compensation, and once the
interlocutory decision has been given, little, if anything, will remain in practice.

But for present purposes the point can be put more narrowly. It seems to me that cases
in which the subject matter concerns the right to publish an article, or to transmit a
broadcast, whose importance may be transitory but whose impact depends on timing,
d news value and topicality, do not lend themselves easily to the application of the *Cyanamid*
guidelines. Longer term publications, such as films or books, may not be in the same
category. I think that it would be an inappropriate test for the grant or refusal of
interlocutory injunctions in such cases if the transmission of a broadcast, or the
publication of an article, whose value and impact depended on their timing, could be
prevented merely by the plausible, or not implausible, allegation of a term alleged to
e have been agreed orally in an informal conversation. In such cases it *should* matter
whether the chances of success in establishing some binding agreement are 90% or 20%.
I use that phraseology because counsel for the plaintiffs referred us to the decision of this
court in *Alfred Dunhill Ltd v Sunoptic SA* [1979] FSR 337 at 373, where Megaw LJ said that
in the application of the *Cyanamid* test it did not matter whether the chances of success
in establishing liability were 90% or 20%. The *Dunhill* case, like *Cyanamid* itself, was a
f typical case in which the *Cyanamid* guidelines are of great value, because everything
depended on the trial and the long-term rights of the parties. The present type of case is
not in the same category.

Accordingly, since I would not follow the structured approach of the *American
Cyanamid* case in the present case, in carrying out the necessary balancing exercise I would
g have some regard to the relative weakness of the plaintiffs' case in establishing the
contract on which they rely. Counsel for the plaintiffs conceded that clearly no contract
of any kind had been made in the telephone conversations themselves. It is obvious that
neither party was bound to anything at that stage. The conversations were no more than
preliminary discussions. At most, as suggested by counsel for the plaintiffs, they resulted
in a statement of terms which would apply if the BBC went ahead with the programme
h and the plaintiffs co-operated in making it. Even then, either side could no doubt have
resiled from the project; for some time at least. The whole situation was by its nature
undefined, and not easily definable in legal terms. Moreover, the alleged conditions were
to be confirmed in writing, but never were. The second alleged condition, concerning
the featuring of users of the diet 'before and after' was never pursued. And no reference
to the existence of any condition was made for five months or so, despite all that
j intervened.

In my view it would be highly undesirable if, on evidence of that nature, which the
judge rightly characterised as being no more than 'plausible' in support of the alleged
condition, the court were driven to grant an injunction because of the application of the
Cyanamid guidelines. In situations of this kind, quite apart from the alleged express
reference to a written confirmation in the original telephone calls, it is essential that there

should indeed be written confirmation of any fetter on transmission or other publication. In the absence of clear evidence of a contract having been made, I consider that the court should be extremely slow to grant an interlocutory injunction in such situations. And if the application of the *Cyanamid* test were to lead to a different conclusion, then that would demonstrate that it is not appropriate in these situations.

However, in the same way as the judge, I do not think that it makes any difference whether this case is decided in accordance with the *Cyanamid* test or not. On either basis the answer is the same. The judge and I agree about that, even though our answers are different. That in itself serves to demonstrate that one must be careful not to lose sight of the real demands of justice in any given case by attaching too much importance to the *Cyanamid* guidelines. The only real difference of substance in the court's approach concerns the extent to which it is permissible or otherwise to have some regard to the relative strength of the parties' contentions on the merits. But in that connection it should also be remembered that the speech of Lord Diplock in the *American Cyanamid* case [1975] 1 All ER 504 at 511, [1975] AC 396 at 409 itself contains a later passage where he appears himself to qualify to some extent the earlier passage on this aspect. I can summarise the position by saying that in a context such as the present a doubtful contract should never prevail over the right of free speech, all other things being even. Leaving aside the *Schering Chemicals* case, which was sui generis for the reasons already mentioned, the only case to which we were referred which involved on the one hand the right of free speech and on the other an alleged contractual right which fettered it, though in substantially different circumstances from the present, was the unreported decision of this court in *Slater v Raw* [1977] CA Transcript 374C. All three members reached the same conclusion and refused an injunction, though for slightly different reasons. But I think that it is worth citing a brief passage from the judgment of Lord Denning MR as follows:

'But I go on from there. Supposing every one of these stipulations [they were the stipulations in the contract], including the one about a "balanced and comprehensive account" is workable, and supposing that the series which is published in the Sunday Times does not comply with those stipulations, what is the remedy of Mr Slater and Mr Walker? It seems to me that the only remedy would be one in damages . . . Just as it will not in a libel case grant an injunction to restrain the publication when the defendant says it is justified, so also in a case such as this, it will not grant an injunction on the suggestion that there was a breach of a contract or a breach of a stipulation except in the clearest possible case. I would like to quote the words of Lord Coleridge CJ in *Bonnard v Perryman* [1891] 2 Ch 269 at 284, [1891–4] All ER Rep 965 at 968: "The right of free speech is one which it is for the public interest that individuals should possess, and, indeed, that they should exercise without impediment, so long as no wrongful act is done; and, unless an alleged libel is untrue, there is no wrong committed; but, on the contrary, often a very wholesome act is performed in the publication and repetition of an alleged libel." The matters discussed in this series of articles are of great public interest. It is of the highest importance that the press should be free to publish their comments on matters of public interest. No court should grant an injunction to restrain a newspaper from doing so except in the most extreme circumstances.'

The great reluctance of the courts to fetter free speech by injunction is supported by many other cases. Illustrations of this principle, to which counsel for the BBC referred, are found in *Bestobell Paints Ltd v Bigg* [1975] FSR 421, a decision of Oliver J, *Re X (a minor) (wardship: restriction on publication)* [1975] 1 All ER 697, [1975] Fam 47, a decision of this court, *J Trevor & Sons v Solomon* (1977) 248 EG 779, a decision of this court which made it clear that *Cyanamid* did not affect the principle of *Bonnard v Perryman* [1891] 2 Ch 269, [1891–4] All ER Rep 965 and, generally, an important passage in the speech of Lord Scarman in *A-G v BBC* [1980] 3 All ER 161 at 183–184, [1981] AC 303 at 362.

Finally, I should mention that in carrying out the balancing exercise in this case I have attached some importance to the facts that the topic to which this programme is directed is very much under discussion at present and that the plaintiffs are actively participating in this discussion. The contents of the COMA report, whether accurate or not, have evidently been leaked to a large extent. There have been numerous articles in the press about its likely conclusions. And on the evidence which we have seen in this court, which was admitted without objection but had not been before the judge, the plaintiffs have commented freely and extensively on the expected contents of the COMA report in the context of their own Cambridge VLCD.

In these circusmtances it seems to me to be obviously contrary to the public interest that the plaintiffs should be entitled to an order which has the effect of suppressing similar discussion of this topic by the BBC in a programme made with the plaintiffs' full co-operation, merely on the basis of a shadowy claim of an oral agreement concerning the timing of this programme alleged to have been made on the telephone some eight months ago.

I would allow this appeal and lift the injunction.

RALPH GIBSON LJ. I agree that this appeal should be allowed.

Before examining the arguments it is useful to look to the end result of the judge's order. I have in mind what has been called the 'great object' of the court in hearing an application for an interlocutory injunction, namely to abstain from expressing any opinion on the merits of the case until the hearing: see per Lord Diplock in *American Cyanamid Co v Ethicon Ltd* [1975] 1 All ER 504 at 510, [1975] AC 396 at 408, citing *Wakefield v Duke of Buccleuch* (1865) 12 LT 628 at 629.

The judge found that the plaintiffs had a good arguable case, and for my part I agree with him. Nevertheless, on the material before the court, without such information as discovery and cross-examination may provide, the plaintiffs' case is not obviously a strong case. Since it turns on findings as to what was said in a telephone conversation and on construction of the meaning of the words found to have been used, and since no documents passing between the parties refer to, or confirm, the making of the agreement until the dispute arose, the case is plainly one which may well fail on the view as to the probability of the assertions either way. As everybody knows, of course, when the evidence is in, such a case may, and not seldom does, succeed. Comments such as these, by this court, will of course have no effect on the trial of the action, because the judge who tries it will make up his or her mind on the evidence, and my comments contain nothing which will not have been obvious to the plaintiffs before they heard them.

So, looking to the end result of the judge's order, the position is, if his order were to stand, that for the protection of an alleged right in the plaintiffs to prevent broadcasting of the programme before publication of the COMA report, a programme prepared for broadcasting before that publication must be withheld from the public, including the large number of people interested in, and possibly affected by, the issues to be discussed in the programme, and must be discarded or amended to take note of the report and then broadcast at a later date.

The risk of damage, which damage the plaintiffs fear they will suffer if the programme is broadcast before the report, is, I accept, a real risk against which the plaintiffs would be entitled to be protected if their right to that protection were sufficiently clear, or of sufficiently probable success. But on the material before the court, the injunction which has been granted is based on an uncertain claim. I do not think that it should have been granted for the reasons which follow. The judge held that on the evidence before him the plaintiffs had shown a good arguable case. Counsel for the BBC had argued that it is impossible to find in the plaintiffs' evidence allegations of fact which, if true, amount to an enforceable contract. Having in her first affidavit described the making of the oral agreement with Miss Howell in March 1987, to which Kerr LJ has referred, Miss Nurdin in a later affidavit says that it was understood that the agreement she had concluded with

Miss Howell was subject to the plaintiffs' not declining to participate. That
acknowledgment that the plaintiffs were not at once bound to provide co-operation, so   *a*
that the alleged agreement was effectively conditional on the plaintiffs' later agreeing to
take part, demonstrates, said counsel for the BBC, that there could in law be no contract.
He referred the court to *Chitty on Contracts* (25th edn, 1983) vol 1, para 160:

> 'Consideration would again be illusory where it was alleged to consist of a promise
> the terms of which left performance entirely to the discretion of the promisor.'   *b*

I do not accept that submission. It seems obvious to me that at the stage at which the
alleged agreement was made, both Miss Nurdin and Miss Howell knew that the former
was not committing the plaintiffs to co-operate in the making of a programme, and that
the latter was not committing the BBC to make the programme. If Miss Nurdin's account
of the conversation should be accepted at trial it would be open to the court, in my view,
to find that the parties had agreed that if thereafter the plaintiffs did co-operatate in the   *c*
making of a programme, the terms agreed between Miss Nurdin and Miss Howell should
have contractual force. The consideration to support the promise of the BBC would be
the act of the plaintiffs in co-operating to facilitate the production of the programme.
    The next main submission made for the BBC by counsel was that the judge was wrong
to apply the *Cyanamid* principles in this case. The injunction, it was said, permanently
deprives the BBC of the opportunity ever to show the programme made because it was   *d*
made to be shown before publication of the COMA report and could not be shown after
publication of that report. Further, since the grant of the injunction gave to the plaintiffs
the full extent of the relief sought in the writ and thus effectively disposed of the action,
the judge should have refused the injunction. Reliance was placed on *NWL Ltd v Woods*
[1979] 3 All ER 614, [1979] 1 WLR 1294 and *Cayne v Global Natural Resources plc* [1984]
1 All ER 225.   *e*
    It is convenient to refer to a case as being within or without the principles of the
American Cyanamid case, because it is a useful form of shorthand for the principles listed
there by Lord Diplock. He was not, however, stating an exhaustive list of relevant
considerations. He said that it would be unwise to attempt even to list all the various
matters which may need to be taken into consideration in deciding where the balance of   *f*
convenience, or of justice, lies, let alone to suggest the relative weight to be given to them
which, he said, would vary from case to case (see [1975] 1 All ER 504 at 511, [1975] AC
396 at 408–9). He added:

> 'I would reiterate that, in addition to those to which I have referred, there may be
> many other special factors to be taken into consideration in the particular
> circumstances of individual cases.'   *g*

    In *NWL Ltd v Woods* [1979] 3 All ER 614 at 625, [1979] 1 WLR 1294 at 1306 Lord
Diplock said that there was nothing in the decision in the *American Cyanamid* case to
suggest that in considering whether or not to grant an interlocutory injunction the judge
ought not to give full weight to all the practical realities of the situation to which the
injunction will apply. *NWL Ltd v Woods* was exceptional, he said, in that the grant or   *h*
refusal of an injunction at that stage would in effect dispose of the action finally in favour
of whichever party was successful on the application, because there would be nothing
left on which it was in the unsuccessful party's interest to proceed to trial. In such an
exceptional case Lord Diplock said that there is brought into the balance of convenience
an important additional element: when the grant or refusal of the interlocutory
injunction will have the practical effect of putting an end to the action because the harm   *j*
that will have been already caused to the losing party by its grant or its refusal is complete,
and of a kind for which nothing can constitute any worthwhile recompense, then the
degree of likelihood that the plaintiff would have succeeded in establishing his right to
an injunction if the action had gone to trial is a factor to be brought into the balance by
the judge in weighing the risks that injustice may result from his deciding the application

one way rather than the other (see [1979] 3 All ER 614 at 625–626, [1979] 1 WLR 1294 at 1307). I do not regard Lord Diplock's words in *NWL Ltd v Woods* as modifying principles established by the decision in the House of Lords in the *American Cyanamid* case; but I do, with respect, regard them as pointing out the true meaning of that decision when, as Lord Diplock said, 'properly understoood' (see [1979] 3 All ER 614 at 625, [1979] 1 WLR 1294 at 1306).

The judge in this case did not, as I read his judgment, and for the purposes of applying the principles I am quite certain that he did not, assess the prospects of success of the plaintiffs in succeeding in their claim. He took the view on the facts, I think, that this was not an exceptional case of the sort referred to by Lord Diplock, on the ground that the grant of the injunction would not produce a situation in which the action would thereby be finally disposed of in favour of the plaintiffs, or in which there would be nothing left on which it would be in the unsuccessful party's interests to proceed to trial; or in which harm suffered by the BBC by the grant of the injunction would be both complete and of a kind for which money could not constitute any worthwhile recompense. In one sense the injunction would finally decide the point in the case against the BBC because, as now appears certain, the COMA report will be published before this case could come on for trial; but the BBC could proceed to trial in order to demonstrate the plaintiffs' inability to prove that the alleged contractual term was ever agreed, and to recover the financial damages which they would suffer in having been prevented from using a completed programme. Those damages would not cover the uncompensatable and unquantifiable loss which, as I think, the BBC would suffer by not being able to publish their programme at the time chosen by them, but I see no reason to hold that the judge was bound on the evidence before him to regard this case as falling within the exceptional sort of case described by Lord Diplock. The damages to be awarded to the BBC would not, in my view, be complete recompense for what the BBC would suffer from the injunction; I must return to that matter later in this judgment. But that does not necessarily mean that the entire harm caused by the injunction would be such as for which money could not constitute any worthwhile recompense. I am not saying that I would necessarily have formed the same view. I do not think that I would. That, of course, is not the point; it is not open to this court to substitute our view of the facts, or as to the way in which the court's discretion should be exercised, if the decision of the judge on the point in question was open to him on the evidence, and he is not shown to have misdirected himself, or to have misapprehended the evidence in reaching his decision: see *Hadmor Productions Ltd v Hamilton* [1982] 1 All ER 1042, [1983] 1 AC 191.

The judge was pressed to regard this case as covered by the reasoning of this court in *Cayne v Global Natural Resources plc* [1984] 1 All ER 225 but he declined to do so. He said that the facts in that case were very special, in that if the plaintiffs there had obtained the injunction sought the plaintiffs would control the defendant company, and neither the plaintiffs nor the defendants would pursue the action. For that reason he decided that he would approach this case in accordance with the principles or guidelines of *Cyanamid*. For my part I do not think he is shown to have been wrong in so directing himself.

This court should, I think, examine with care a suggestion that a judge has gone wrong in law because on the facts he selected the wrong category of guiding principles. He cannot be treated as having gone wrong in law in that way if his view of the facts which caused him to make the selection he did was open to him on the evidence. I also reject the suggestion that because in this case the trial could not be held before the likely date of publication of the COMA report, the judge was therefore bound to treat the case as covered by this court's reasoning in the *Global Natural Resources* case. In that case if the injunction were granted there would be no trial of the issue whether before the date of the decision, or after that date, for the purpose of enforcing a claim to damages. In this case there would be such a trial unless the BBC chose, for some reason, not to pursue the matter.

The judge therefore set himself to consider the case on *Cyanamid* principles; he did not follow the order of questions set out by Lord Diplock, but that is of no separate importance. Before doing so, he expressed the view that if it turned out to be wrong to grant the injunction the defendants could be adequately compensated in damages. Like Kerr LJ I also think that that finding was in error because it was not open to the judge on the evidence. I shall return to that later.

He asked himself first where the balance of justice lies in this case. It is common ground that each side is capable of paying any damages which might be awarded under an undertaking in damages. He was satisfied that the plaintiffs had a good arguable case. He then considered whether, if the injunction were refused, the plaintiffs would be adequately compensated by an award of damages. He held that they would not be, because they would lose for ever their right to prevent publication of the programme containing their material, and would be left with a right in damages which would be difficult, if not impossible, to quantify.

Counsel for the BBC has submitted that the judge was wrong to reach that conclusion. It was said that the plaintiffs' assertion of damage rested on the commercial consequences to them which would result from injury to their reputation; that such damage does not fall to be recovered in contract and ought properly to be claimed in an action for defamation. Reference was made to *Addis v Gramophone Co Ltd* [1909] AC 488 at 496, [1908–10] All ER Rep 1 at 5. Any loss caused by the premature broadcast of the programme would, it was said, either be nominal, in which case no injunction would be justified, or would be for such substantial damages as could be proved to have been caused by the premature broadcast, and for such injury damages would be an adequate remedy.

I do not accept that the judge's view on this point is shown to have been wrong. If the plaintiffs' case were to be upheld, they were from the start concerned about the damaging effect which in their opinion would be caused to their trading operation by the broadcasting of a programme by the BBC before the authoritative findings of the COMA report were available. The plaintiffs feared the consequences on the confidence and enthusiasm of their counsellors. They asked for and, on their case obtained, a promise that the programme, if they co-operated in the making of it, would not go out before publication of the COMA report.

I confess that I am not confident that a premature broadcast of the programme would have the grave effect which the plaintiffs feared; but that, in my view, is nothing to this point. The plaintiffs know their business. The judge was entitled to accept that in all probability damage would be caused to the plaintiffs in their trade by a premature broadcast of the programme, and that an award of damages at trial, which damages would be difficult to prove and to quantify, would not be adequate compensation. The points of law with reference to the recovery of damages in an action of contract for injury to reputation seem to me to have no force. It is not necessary to decide the point, but for my part I do not think that the decision in *Addis v Gramophone Co Ltd* is a bar to the recovery of damages for injury to reputation in an action for breach of contract, where the contractual provision proved to have been broken had as its purpose, or one of its purposes, the protection of the claimant against the sort of damage suffered.

Further, as counsel for the plaintiffs pointed out, if the substantial damage which, on their case, would be caused to the plaintiffs by a premature broadcast of the programme could not be recovered at law as damages, there is thereby established the more reason for holding that damages would not be an adequate remedy to the plaintiffs.

Returning now to the judgment of the judge, he next considered what the position of the BBC would be if the injunction were granted. He had already expressed the view that they could be adequately compensated in damages if it should turn out that the injunction should not have been granted. He held that—

'the broadcast is merely deferred until after the publication of the COMA report in four weeks' time. Good sense may require the programme to be amended in the light of that report, but the defendants can still, if they wish, use their interviews with the plaintiffs' advisers and use the information provided by them.'

Criticism was directed at that holding. It was said that the judge had not had proper regard to the fact that the making of the injunction would cause the BBC to lose the opportunity of ever showing the programme as made, since it would be out of date and inept if shown after the publication of the COMA report. The judge, by his holding, showed that he assessed the impact on the BBC of the making of the injunction, in so far as it concerned the need to modify the programme before it could be shown, as of less gravity than the BBC by their evidence attributed to it. Again, I do not accept that the judge in that regard was shown to have been wrong; he was entitled, in my view, to hold that view on the evidence.

In so far, however, as the judge found that the BBC would be adequately compensated under the plaintiffs' undertaking as to damages for the loss which the BBC would sustain as a result of the grant of the injunction, if it should turn out to have been wrongly granted, then in my view the judge was wrong. On the evidence before him, that view was in my judgment one which he could not reasonably form.

I have very great sympathy for the judge over this matter. I think that the loss to the BBC caused by the denial of free speech, that is to say the loss of the right to broadcast a programme in the form prepared by them and at the time selected by them, became swept up in, and considered as part of, the BBC's contentions, which included contentions about the overriding importance of the right to free speech on the matter of public importance. It is not clear to me that this particular point of misdirection was put to the judge as it has now been raised in this court in the course of argument by Eastham J; it did not, for example, appear in the notice of appeal.

But once the point is raised in its proper place, namely is the loss which the BBC would suffer from the grant of the injunction if the plaintiffs should fail to prove the right to it adequately compensated by an award of damages, and in particular for the money thrown away by the unusable parts of the programme and by other financial loss, coupled with such estimate as the court could make in respect to the loss of the right to publish at the time chosen by them, then, as it seems to me, the answer must be that the BBC's loss would not be adequately compensated. Counsel for the plaintiffs contended that the judge must be treated as having recognised that the BBC would suffer uncompensatable loss in respect of being denied the right to broadcast, but to have assessed it as of such minor importance that payment of financial loss would be adequate compensation. I cannot so read this judgment although, of course, in reading it I have had in mind the admonitions of Griffiths LJ in *Eagil Trust Co Ltd v Pigott-Brown* [1985] 3 All ER 119, to which counsel for the plaintiffs drew our attention.

The judge considered freedom of speech under a separate heading and disposed of it by reference to *Schering Chemicals Ltd v Falkman Ltd* [1981] 2 All ER 321, [1982] QB 1, as Kerr LJ has described. I agree with what Kerr LJ has said with reference to that part of the judge's judgment.

The judge therefore, in my view, is shown to have misdirected himself in the application of the principle by reference to which he was analysing the case, and this court must itself exercise the discretion which the law entrusts to the court.

It is necessary to go back to the *Cyanamid* principles as set out by Lord Diplock. The judge had reached the point that the plaintiffs had a good arguable case for the injunction sought, and that the plaintiffs would not be adequately compensated by an award of damages at trial. The finding that the BBC would be adequately compensated by an award of damages, which the plaintiffs could pay, could have been regarded by the judge as sufficient to establish that, in the absence of any other relevant factor, there could be no reason to refuse an interlocutory injunction: see the *American Cyanamid* case [1975] 1 All ER 504 at 510, [1975] AC 396 at 408 per Lord Diplock. The judge in fact went on to consider the balance of justice or convenience, as I have said, and it is important to note that in my view it was essential that that balance be considered, because on the evidence, contrary to the judge's view, the remedy in damages was not adequate to compensate for the loss which would be suffered by either party if the injunction was wrongly granted or wrongly withheld.

Since neither party would be adequately compensated by an award to damages, the guidance offered in the following paragraph in Lord Diplock's speech was of crucial importance (Kerr LJ has referred to it and it was the passage to which Eastham J drew attention) ([1975] 1 All ER 504 at 511, [1975] AC 396 at 408–409):

> 'Save in the simplest cases, the decision to grant or to refuse an interlocutory injunction will cause to whichever party is unsuccessful on the application some disadvantages which his ultimate success at the trial may show he ought to have been spared and the disadvantages may be such that the recovery of damages to which he would then be entitled either in the action or under the plaintiff's undertaking would not be sufficient to compensate him fully for all of them. The extent to which the disadvantages to each party would be incapable of being compensated in damages in the event of his succeeding at the trial is always a significant factor in assessing where the balance of convenience lies; and if the extent of the uncompensatable disadvantage to each party would not differ widely, it may not be improper to take into account in tipping the balance the relative strength of each party's case as revealed by the affidavit evidence adduced on the hearing of the application. This, however, should be done only where it is apparent on the facts disclosed by evidence as to which there is no credible dispute that the strength of one party's case is disproportionate to that of the other party. The court is not justified in embarking on anything resembling a trial of the action on conflicting affidavits in order to evaluate the strength of either party's case.'

It is clear that what is there said is the setting out of guidelines for the assistance of the judges. I quote this passage again:

> '. . . if the extent of the uncompensatable disadvantage to each party would not differ widely, it may not be improper to take into account in tipping the balance the relative strength of each party's case . . .'

For my part, I would hold that on the evidence before the judge this case was at best for the plaintiffs clearly within that principle. The uncompensatable disadvantage of each party in this case is difficult to assess separately for this purpose, and therefore even more difficult to compare with any confidence that one is more grave than the other.

This is a case, therefore, in which I think that the relative strength of the parties' cases should be taken into account, and this can be done by reference to the undisputed evidence on the affidavits and documents.

I have already referred to the nature of the plaintiffs' claim. A contract is proved if the court finds that words were said which, properly construed in the context in which they were used, would be understood by a reasonable man or woman as the exchange of contractual promises. The making of a contract does not turn on the unstated intentions or understandings of a party. It follows that a contract may be proved to have been made in the telephone conversation in March 1987; or the court may hold that no contract was then made, despite the respective beliefs, honestly held, by the parties to that conversation that a contract was or was not then made. On the evidence as it now stands, it seems clear to me that in probability those concerned in the making of the programme on behalf of the BBC were unaware, until the letter was sent in August 1987, that the plaintiffs were alleging that a contract to the present effect had been made. It seems likely that, whichever way the ultimate decision goes, this is a case of honest misunderstanding and not of an attempt to avoid a promise given or confirmed after deliberation.

There is one further matter to be taken into account on the balance of justice. Since I am following the judge through the principles stated in the *American Cyanamid* case, I should point out that it comes under the heading: '. . . many other special factors to be taken into consideration in the particular circumstances of individual cases' (see [1975] 1 All ER 504 at 511, [1975] AC 396 at 409). I refer to the public interest in the exercise by the BBC of their rights and duties in communication to the people of this country.

The judge refused to regard the BBC as possessed of any right which would entitle them, in the circumstances of this case, to override a clear obligation of confidence, or the clear obligation not to broadcast assumed by contract; in that, for my part, I agree with him. It is not in my view necessary to examine in detail, or to decide on, the submissions of counsel for the BBC to the effect that because of the public importance of the concept of free speech it was the duty of the judge, or that it was open to him, to refuse the injunction if otherwise the plaintiffs had proved their right to it under the principles by reference to which the judge was directing himself; or to the effect that the plaintiffs, who had commented in the press on the issues raised with reference to VLCDs, and thereby sought publicity for their views, should be, or could properly be, denied relief under the principles discussed in *Woodward v Hutchins* [1977] 2 All ER 751, [1977] 1 WLR 760; or to the effect that, since the true nature of the plaintiffs' complaint is that premature publication will injure their reputation, the court should refuse an injunction on the principles stated in *Bonnard v Perryman* [1891] 2 Ch 269, [1891–4] All ER Rep 965.

For my part, I do not think that, if the plaintiffs had otherwise established a right to the injunction, after proper consideration of all the relevant factors, the court could have declined to grant the injunction on any of those grounds.

Counsel for the plaintiffs contended that if the judge had gone wrong at any point in applying the *Cyanamid* principles, he had also, as an alternative, considered and applied what he called the 'broad brush' approach, namely that derived from the reasoning of this court in *Cayne v Global Natural Resources plc* [1984] 1 All ER 225 and that there was no ground on which that alternative conclusion could be faulted.

The passage, at the end of the judge's judgment, reads as follows:

'If I am wrong in applying the *Cyanamid* test, I think the same result would be achieved if the "broad brush" approach were adopted and for much the same reasons.'

I do not accept this submission. That which I think has been shown to be erroneous in the judge's assessment of the case requires the court to reject also the alternative conclusion of the judge.

I would allow this appeal.

EASTHAM J. I agree that this appeal should be allowed. In view of the fact that we are differing from the judge in the present case, I wish very briefly to state my prinicpal reasons for reaching the conclusion that the injunction granted by him should be discharged.

For my part, I am not prepared to find that the judge's conclusion that he should apply the guidelines contained in the speech of Lord Diplock in *American Cyanamid Co v Ethicon Ltd* [1975] 1 All ER 504, [1975] AC 396 was wrong; I think that his conclusion that the plaintiffs' claim was sufficiently plausible to be taken seriously was right.

However, like Kerr LJ, I think that he was wrong in three respects. Firstly, when he came to the conclusion that the BBC could be adequately compensated in damages if it turned out that it was wrong to grant the injunction. If that was a permissible finding, the judge ought to have granted the injunction at that stage, because there would have been nothing further to consider. As Lord Diplock points out in *American Cyanamid Co v Ethicon Ltd* [1975] 1 All ER 504 at 510, [1975] AC 396 at 408, it is where there is doubt as to the accuracy of the respective remedies or damages available to either party, or to both, that the question of balance of convenience arises. It is perfectly true that if this action continues and the plaintiffs' claim fails, the BBC will be entitled to recover damages in *a* respect of programme production costs, whether by way of adaptation of the present programme or by making a new programme; but they would have been permanently deprived of their right to transmit their programme on very low calorie diets, including the plaintiffs' diet, in the form and at the time of their choice. In that important respect they would be placed at an uncompensatable disadvantage.

I also take the view that the judge was wrong in holding, as he did, that the *b* circumstances in *Schering Chemicals Ltd v Falkman Ltd* [1981] 2 All ER 321, [1982] QB 1 were very similar to the circumstances in the instant case; and that he was also wrong, on the facts before him, in holding that the freedom of speech aspect was completely balanced by the assertion by the plaintiffs of the existence of a contract.

I accept that in the case of a clear contract, probably in writing, under which one party had agreed quite clearly not to publish or transmit until after the happening of some *c* particular future event, a court would most likely reach a conclusion that the breach of such a contract would balance any freedom of speech aspect in the case.

As in my judgment the judge was wrong in the three aspects that I have mentioned, this is one of the cases in which this court is entitled, indeed, is under the duty, to review the exercise of his discretion. Ralph Gibson LJ has already read as part of his judgment the speech of Lord Diplock in the *American Cyanamid* case [1975] 1 All ER 504 at 511, *d* [1975] AC 396 at 409, where he was pointing out that although one cannot try and decide disputed questions of fact in considering whether or not the application is a serious application, nevertheless, if one gets to the stage at which there is an uncompensatable disadvantage to each party, and the court cannot reach any clear conclusion as to whether it is more heavy on one side than it is on the other, it is permissible, or is not improper, to take into account in tipping the balance the relative strengths of each party's case. *e*

I consider that in this case, in reviewing the judge's decision, it is proper to consider the respective strengths of the cases and, for the reasons which have been advanced by Kerr LJ, in my view it is absolutely clear that the BBC's case is substantially stronger than that of the plaintiffs.

Furthermore, in my view, although the freedom of speech aspect was overstated by *f* the BBC, both in this court and in the court below, the right of someone like the BBC to produce and to show programmes on matters of public interest is of considerable, but not overriding, importance and in my view that considerably important matter is not balanced by the mere assertion on weak grounds of a contractual obligation to defer transmission.

For those reasons, in my judgment, the appeal should be allowed and the injunction discharged. *g*

Appeal allowed. Injunction discharged.

Solicitors: *Glenn Del Medico* (for the BBC); *Peter Carter-Ruck & Partners* (for the plaintiffs).

Dilys Tausz   Barrister.

Rosseel NV v Oriental Commercial and Shipping (UK) Ltd and others

COURT OF APPEAL, CIVIL DIVISION
LORD DONALDSON OF LYMINGTON MR AND PARKER LJ
31 JULY 1990

Practice – Pre-trial or post-judgment relief – Mareva injunction – Worldwide Mareva injunction – Foreign judgment or arbitration award – Whether court will grant worldwide Mareva injunction in support of foreign judgment or arbitration award.

Only in very exceptional circumstances will the court grant a worldwide Mareva injunction in support of a foreign judgment or arbitration award which the court is being asked to enforce. Normally, any Mareva injunction granted in such cases will be limited to assets within the jurisdiction (see p 546 c d f and p 547 a, post).

Republic of Haiti v Duvalier [1989] 1 All ER 456 distinguished.

Notes
For Mareva injunctions, see 37 Halsbury's Laws (4th edn) para 362, and for cases on the subject, see 37(2) Digest (Reissue) 474–476, 2947–2962.

Cases referred to in judgments
Babanaft International Co SA v Bassatne [1989] 1 All ER 433, [1990] Ch 13, [1989] 2 WLR 232, CA.
Haiti (Republic) v Duvalier [1989] 1 All ER 456, [1990] 1 QB 202, [1989] 2 WLR 261, CA.

Ex parte appeal
The plaintiffs, Rosseel NV, a Belgian corporation, appealed against the judgment of Hirst J dated 31 July 1990 refusing their ex parte application for an order (i) that the second and third defendants, Abdul Hamed Bokhari and Oriental Commercial and Shipping Ltd, a Saudi Arabian company, be restrained whether by their servants, agents or, in the case of the third defendant, its officers or otherwise howsoever until an arbitration award dated 20 June 1990 obtained by the plaintiff against the defendants in New York had been enforced and satisfied in full from disposing of, transferring, charging, diminishing or otherwise howsoever dealing with any of their assets wheresoever situated outside the jurisdiction, subject to the usual provisos as to amount and as respects third parties, and (ii) that the second defendant swear and serve on the plaintiffs' solicitors an affidavit on his own behalf and on behalf of the third defendant stating precisely what assets each of them had outside the jurisdiction wherever situated, their whereabouts and their value. The judge granted the plaintiff a Mareva injunction against the second and third defendants in respect of their assets within the jurisdiction. The first defendant, Oriental Commercial and Shipping (UK) Ltd, was a defunct English company. The facts are set out in the judgment of Lord Donaldson MR.

Richard Millett for the plaintiffs.

LORD DONALDSON OF LYMINGTON MR. This is an appeal from a refusal of Hirst J to grant worldwide Mareva relief in support of a New York arbitration award made last month which the plaintiffs are seeking to enforce in this country under s 3 of the Arbitration Act 1975, the United States of America being a convention country.

There was no difficulty so far as the judge was concerned in granting a Mareva injunction in respect of assets of the defendants in this country but, when it came to granting a wider injunction, he said:

'With regard to the application for a worldwide Mareva, the court clearly has power (*Babanaft International Co SA v Barsatne* [1989] 1 All ER 433, [1990] Ch 13) to make such an order. If it was a case of enforcing an English judgment it would have followed the *Babanaft* case. If it were an English arbitration award then it would seem the same applies but this concerns the 1975 Act. What has been asked is to enforce the award in England and Wales and I am not persuaded to enforce a New York arbitration award beyond England and Wales. The appropriate court is the New York court or the foreign court where assets are to be found and therefore I will not carry this order beyond [the jurisdiction]. I will however order an affidavit of all the United Kingdom assets.'

That was an exercise of discretion and that, of course, is an obstacle to an appeal against the judge's decision. But I am bound to say that, in my view, he was abundantly right. I say that because, as it seems to me, there is all the difference in the world between proceedings in this country, whether by litigation or by arbitration, to determine rights of parties on the one hand, and proceedings in this country to enforce rights which have been determined by some other court or arbitral tribunal outside the jurisdiction.

Where this court is concerned to determine rights then it will, in an appropriate case, and certainly should, enforce its own judgment by exercising what would be described as a long arm jurisdiction. But, where it is merely being asked under a convention or an Act of Parliament to enforce in support of another jurisdiction, whether in arbitration or litigation, it seems to me that, save in an exceptional case, it should stop short of making orders which extend beyond its own territorial jurisdiction.

I say that because, if you take a hypothetical case of rights being determined in state A and assets being found in states B to M, you would find a very large number of subsidiary jurisdictions (in the sense that they were merely being asked to enforce the rights determined by another jurisdiction) making criss-crossing long arm jurisdictional orders with a high degree of probability that there would be confusion and, indeed, resentment by the nations concerned at interference with their jurisdictions.

It seems to me that, apart from the very exceptional case, the proper attitude of the English courts (and, I may add, courts in other jurisdictions) is to confine themselves to their own territorial area, save in cases in which they are the court or tribunal which determines the rights of the parties. So long as they are merely being used as enforcement agencies they should stick to their own last.

Counsel for the plaintiffs, while disappointed at the preliminary indication that that was our view, referred us to *Republic of Haiti v Duvalier* [1989] 1 All ER 456, [1990] 1 QB 202, where it is certainly correct that this court did exercise an extra-territorial jurisdiction, and it appears that it did so in support of French proceedings. The actual jurisdiction to do so arises under s 25(1) of the Civil Jurisdiction and Judgments Act 1982, which, of course, applies to European countries only. But it is not without significance that even s 25(2) of that Act expressly confers a discretion to refuse relief if the fact that the court has no jurisdiction apart from the section in relation to the subject matter of the proceedings makes it inexpedient for the court to grant it. So it seems reasonably clear that the authors of the convention or Parliament, as the case may be, had well in mind this problem of interlocking and competing and confusing orders to which I have already referred.

Haiti v Duvalier was very unusual because, quite apart from the scale of the alleged operation, part of it was being undertaken through an English solicitor. This is not a criticism of the English solicitor, who was acting perfectly properly on the instructions of his client to act not only as an investment adviser but an investment executive. So that there were very special reasons for tracing the assets through the English solicitor, and in so far as he had deposited those assets in the Channel Islands, there was every ground for granting an extra-territorial injunction relating at least to the Channel Islands. So that was a very special case.

a   It may very well be that this court has jurisdiction, but I entirely agree with Hirst J that there are no sufficiently exceptional features in this case to justify our exercising it. Accordingly, I would dismiss the appeal.

PARKER LJ. I agree.

Appeal dismissed.

b

Solicitors: *Baker & McKenzie* (for the plaintiffs).

Mary Rose Plummer   Barrister.

c

North West Water Ltd v Binnie & Partners (a firm)

QUEEN'S BENCH DIVISION
d DRAKE J
I I, I 2, I 3 OCTOBER, 9 NOVEMBER 1989

Estoppel – Res judicata – Negligence – Same issue in separate proceedings between different parties arising out of identical facts and dependent on same evidence – Plant designed by consultant engineers built by contractors for water authority – Explosion at plant killing and
e *injuring visitors – Victims or personal representatives bringing action against water authority, contractors and consultant engineers – Consultant engineers held to be solely to blame – Water authority bringing action against consultant engineers for negligence and breach of contract – Whether consultant engineers estopped from denying negligence.*

    A water authority commissioned a firm of consultant engineers to design and supervise
f the construction by contractors of an underground tunnel link and valve house to take water from one river to another by means of 12-km tunnel and pumping system. The scheme prompted protests from local residents which caused the plaintiff to arrange a meeting of the local residents at the valve house in order to demonstrate the operation of the scheme. During the meeting an explosion occurred because, unknown to anyone, the valve house had filled with methane gas which ignited. Six people were killed and
g the rest injured. A number of victims or their personal representatives brought an action (the first action) claiming damages for personal injury or death against the water authority, the contractors who constructed the system and the consultant engineers. By their defence the water authority claimed that the explosion had been caused by the consultant engineers' negligence. At the trial of the action the judge held that all three
h defendants were to blame and apportioned liability between them as to 55% against the consultant engineers, 30% against the water authority and 15% against the contractors. All three defendants appealed to the Court of Appeal, which allowed the appeals of the water authority and the contractors and held that the consultant engineers were wholly to blame. In separate proceedings (the second action) the water authority issued proceedings against the consultant engineers seeking to recover the damage to the tunnel
j system caused by the explosion, estimated to be £2m. The water authority alleged that the damage had been caused by the consultant engineers' negligence and/or breach of contract in designing and/or constructing and/or supervising the link system and further alleged that as between the water authority and the consultant engineers the issue of negligence had been decided in the first action and was res judicata and that the consultant engineers' defence denying negligence was an abuse of process and should be

struck out. The question whether the consultant engineers were estopped from denying
negligence and whether their defence should be struck out was tried as a preliminary   *a*
issue.

Held – Where an issue had for all practical purposes been decided in a court of competent
jurisdiction the court would not allow that issue to be raised in separate proceedings
between different parties arising out of identical facts and dependent on the same
evidence, since not only was the party seeking to relitigate the issue prevented from   *b*
doing so by issue estoppel but it would also be an abuse of process to allow the issue to be
relitigated. It followed that since the issue of negligence had already been determined
against the consultant engineers in the first action they were estopped from denying
negligence and further it would be an abuse of process if they were to be permitted to
deny negligence. Their defence denying negligence would accordingly be struck out (see
p 552 c, p 553 f g, p 555 a b, p 558 b c and p 561 b to g, post).   *c*

Marginson v Blackburn BC [1939] 1 All ER 273, Bell v Holmes [1956] 3 All ER 449,
Randolph v Tuck [1961] 1 All ER 814, Wood v Luscombe (Wood, third party) [1964] 3 All ER
972, Craddock's Transport Ltd v Stuart [1970] NZLR 499 and Hunter v Chief Constable of
West Midlands [1981] 3 All ER 727 considered.

                                                                                          d
Notes
For the doctrine of res judicata and issue estoppel, see 16 Halsbury's Laws (4th edn) paras
1526–1530, and for cases on the subject, see 21 Digest (Reissue) 40–62, 260–390.

Cases referred to in judgment
Arnold v National Westminster Bank plc [1988] 3 All ER 977, [1989] Ch 63, [1988] 3 WLR   *e*
   1229.
Bell v Holmes [1956] 3 All ER 449, [1956] 1 WLR 1359, Assizes.
Bragg v Oceanus Mutual Underwriting Association (Bermuda) Ltd [1982] 2 Lloyd's Rep 132,
   CA.
Carl-Zeiss-Stiftung v Rayner & Keeler Ltd (No 2) [1966] 2 All ER 536, [1967] 1 AC 853,
   [1966] 3 WLR 125, HL.   *f*
Carl-Zeiss-Stiftung v Rayner & Keeler (No 3) [1969] 3 All ER 897, [1970] Ch 506, [1969] 3
   WLR 991.
Clyne v Yardley [1959] NZLR 617, NZ HC.
Craddock's Transport Ltd v Stuart [1970] NZLR 499, NZ CA.
Croston v Vaughan [1937] 4 All ER 249, [1938] 1 KB 540, CA.
Eckersley v Binnie (1988) 18 Con LR 1, QBD and CA.   *g*
Hunter v Chief Constable of West Midlands [1981] 3 All ER 727, [1982] AC 529, [1981] 3
   WLR 906, HL; affg sub nom McIlkenny v Chief Constable of West Midlands Police Force
   [1980] 2 All ER 227, [1980] 1 QB 283, [1980] 2 WLR 689, CA.
Jackson v Goldsmith (1950) 81 CLR 446, Aust HC.
Ladd v Marshall [1954] 3 All ER 745, [1954] 1 WLR 1489, CA.
Marginson v Blackburn BC [1939] 1 All ER 273, [1939] 2 KB 426, CA.   *h*
Mills v Cooper [1967] 2 All ER 100, [1967] 2 QB 459, [1967] 2 WLR 1343, DC.
Neenan v Woodside Astoria Transportation Co Inc (1932) 235 AD 9, NY SC App Div; rvsd
   [1933] 261 NY 159, NY Ct of Apps.
Phosphate Sewage Co v Molleson (1879) 4 App Cas 801, HL.
Randolph v Tuck [1961] 1 All ER 814, [1962] 1 QB 175, [1981] 2 WLR 855.
Reichel v MaGrath (1889) 14 App Cas 665, HL.   *j*
Stephenson v Garnett [1898] 1 QB 677, CA.
Tebbutt v Haynes [1981] 2 All ER 238, CA.
Wood v Luscombe (Wood, third party) [1964] 3 All ER 972, [1966] 1 QB 169, [1965] 3 WLR
   998, Assizes.
Yat Tung Investment Co Ltd v Dao Heng Bank Ltd [1975] AC 581, [1975] 2 WLR 690, PC.

Preliminary issue

a By writ issued on the 23 December 1985 the plaintiffs, North West Water Ltd (as successor to the North West Water Authority) (the water authority), claimed against the defendants, Binnie & Partners (a firm) (Binnies), damages for negligence and breach of contract. Binnies served a defence denying liability. The water authority applied by summons under RSC Ord 18 r 19 and the inherent jurisdiction of the court to strike out the defence as disclosing no reasonable defence or as being otherwise an abuse of the *b* process of the court or because Binnies were estopped from denying liability because the issue of negligence on their part had already been decided against them in an action brought on behalf of the victims of an explosion which occurred at a valve house at Abbeystead, Lancashire in 1984 against the water authority, Binnies and a further defendant, Edmund Nuttall Ltd, which was tried by Rose J in the Queen's Bench Division at Lancaster and by the decision of the Court of Appeal on appeal therefrom (see *Eckersley* *c* *v Binnie* (1988) 18 Con LR 1). The facts are set out in the judgment.

Timothy Stow QC for the water authority.
D H Gardam QC and *David Streatfeild-James* for Binnies.

Cur adv vult

d
9 November. The following judgment was delivered.

DRAKE J. This is a preliminary issue in an action brought by North West Water Ltd (the water authority) against Binnie & Partners (a firm). The action arises out of the Abbeystead disaster of May 1984.

e Prior to 1980 the water authority commissioned Binnies to design and supervise the construction of a system of piping, tunnels and pumps so as to take water from the River Lune to the River Wyre in Lancashire. The total length of the link system of pipeline and tunnelling was about 12 km.

At Abbeystead at the River Wyre end of the link near to where the water was discharged into the river, and as part of the system, a valve house was constructed.

f It was necessary for there to be a vent from the tunnelling so as to permit air to be drawn into or to be allowed to escape from the tunnelling when water was flowing into or out of the tunnel. Normally such a vent is taken up into the open air in the form of a chimney. But the end of this system at the River Wyre is in an area of outstanding natural beauty. So the valve house and vent were designed to be underground. There was a vent chamber next to the valve house and the exit to the vent was into part of the *g* valve house.

By 1984 a number of local residents had become concerned over the possibility of flooding in their area as a result of the operation of the new link system. The water authority, wishing to relieve their anxiety, invited a number of them to visit the valve house for a demonstration of the working of the system. On 23 May 1984 a number of *h* these residents, together with some of the water authority officials, gathered in the valve house for this purpose.

There had been a period of drought just before that date and for that reason no water had been pumped along the link for some 16 days. However, a small quantity of water always entered the tunnelling from the surrounding ground, and the water authority had deliberately left the exit valve from the tunnel very slightly open (the technical term is 'cracked open') so as to allow the small quantity of water to pass through into the river. *j* This is a desirable practice so as to prevent silt and impurities building up inside the tunnel and then being discharged when the link system is activated to pump quantities of water along it. However, due to the non-operation of the link for a period of 16 days, the River Wyre end of the tunnel was virtually empty.

Unknown to anyone a large quantity of methane gas had entered the tunnel and collected at the valve house end.

When the visitors were in the valve house the demonstration was started by some of the pumps being turned on. Water flowed along the tunnel and started to fill the void at *a* the valve house end. The methane gas was expelled through the exit vent into the valve house. The quantity and concentration was sufficient to be explosive. Something, perhaps a match lit by a smoker amongst those present, ignited the gas and led to a very violent explosion. The valve house and parts of the equipment were wrecked, and of the 44 people present in the building six were killed and the rest injured.

Twenty eight of the victims or their personal representatives brought proceedings *b* claiming damages in respect of the deaths or injuries. They sued (1) the water authority, (2) the contractors who constructed the system, who were Edmund Nuttall Ltd, and (3) Binnies as the designers and consultant engineers. The action was heard before Rose J at Lancaster over a period of about seven weeks starting in January 1987. On 13 March 1987 he gave judgment (see *Eckersley v Binnie* 18 Con LR 1). He found all three defendants to blame. I will refer to the trial as 'the Lancaster action' to distinguish it from the present *c* proceedings.

At the trial it was common ground that the explosion had resulted from the collection of methane gas in an explosive concentration. One of the important issues was the source of this gas. On one view it was 'reservoir' methane, that is to say it originated from a large natural reservoir of gas of the kind which exists in various places, sometimes in commercially exploitable quantities, as in the fairly nearby Morecambe Bay area. On *d* another view it was 'stress relief' methane, which exists only in comparatively small pockets which may be released by numerous means, such as by blasting of rocks.

'Stress relief' methane may not be detectable during the construction of works such as this link system and once released disperses into the atmosphere within a comparatively short time, that is to say days or weeks rather than years. 'Reservoir' methane involves a very large quantity. It should much more readily be detected and once the reservoir is *e* punctured it may continue to be released over a period of years.

Rose J found that this was 'reservoir' methane and he held that Binnies were negligent in that they should have foreseen the probability that methane would enter the tunnel and affect the works, and that they shared responsibility for inadequate testing for methane during the construction of the tunnel. Further, they should not have designed *f* the system so that the vents led into the valve house.

In the pleadings all three defendants had denied liability. The water authority by their defence denied any negligence on their part. They further stated that they had entrusted the design of the scheme to Binnies as consultant engineers and had relied on Binnies to ensure that the scheme was safe and to warn them of any special risk or hazard that might be associated with the construction and/or operation of the scheme. By para 3 of *g* their defence they pleaded:

'Further or in the alternative in so far as the explosion was caused by the negligence of anyone it was caused by the negligence of the First Defendants their servants or agents, and these Defendants will reply upon any allegations in Paragraph 11 of the amended Statement of Claim which may be established at the trial.'

h

Paragraph 11 of the statement of claim (ultimately the rereamended statement of claim) runs to some nine pages of very detailed allegations of negligence against the first defendants, Binnies.

Binnies and Nuttalls each denied negligence but neither made any allegation against another defendant. No contribution notices were served by any defendant on a co-defendant, and at the trial none of the defendants sought an apportionment of liability *j* for such negligence as might be found. However, when Rose J held that all three defendants were liable, he also apportioned blame, 55% against Binnies, 30% against the water authority and 15% against Nuttalls.

All three defendants appealed against his judgment. After a hearing lasting about six weeks the Court of Appeal unanimously allowed the appeal of the water authority and

Nuttalls and held that they were not liable to the plaintiffs (see *Eckersley v Binnie* (1988)

a 18 Con LR 1). But by a majority (Russell and Fox LJJ, Bingham LJ dissenting) it dismissed the appeal of Binnies and held Binnies soley to blame. Bingham LJ would have allowed Binnies' appeal so that the plaintiffs would have failed against all three defendants. A petition to the House of Lords for leave to appeal was refused.

The writ in the Lancaster action was issued on 4 June 1985. The present proceedings were started by a writ issued on 23 December 1985. The water authority sue Binnies for

b damage caused by the explosion, I understand the claim is in the order of £2m. They allege that Binnies were negligent and/or in breach of contract in designing and/or constructing and/or supervising the link system. In the statement of claim served in 1988, after the judgments of Rose J and the Court of Appeal in the Lancaster action, they contend that as between themselves and Binnies the issue of negligence is res judicata and/or Binnies are estopped from denying liability. By an amendment for which I gave

c leave by consent at the outset of the present hearing, the water authority add the allegation that the attempt by the Binnies to reopen the issue of negligence is frivolous and vexatious and an abuse of the process of the court. On these grounds the defence should be struck out under the RSC Ord 18, r 19 and/or under the inherent jurisdiction of the court.

Binnies deny negligence and deny that the issue of negligence is res judicata or that

d they are estopped from contesting negligence or that their defence on negligence is an abuse of the process of the court. Further, Binnies propose at the trial of this action to adduce fresh evidence in the form of an expert report prepared by Exploration Consultants Ltd (referred to as the 'ECL report'). This report was commissioned by the water authority before the Lancaster trial; but although disclosed before the trial it had never been agreed and no directions had been sought or leave given to call the makers of

e the report as experts. The water authority having obtained the report had decided not to apply to call the experts to give evidence along the lines of the report. However, Binnies wanted that evidence and did apply to Rose J on the ninth day of the trial for leave to call the experts. The application was opposed by the plaintiffs in that action and Rose J held that because the application had been made so late and because, in his view, the evidence was not necessary for the fair determination of the issues between the parties, the

f application should be refused. He considered that to admit it so late would prejudice the plaintiffs in the action.

Binnies say that that decision cannot prevent them from adducing the evidence in the present action and that this entitles them to overcome any issue estoppel and to avoid being held to have abused the process of the court if, which they deny, such issue estoppel or abuse exist. Furthermore, they may wish to amend their defence so as to plead

g contributory negligence, and they say that if they do so this will introduce a fresh issue which has not yet been determined between them and the water authority.

Terminology

In many of the older cases the terms 'res judicata', 'issue estoppel' and 'cause of action

h estoppel', 'estoppel by record' or 'collateral estoppel' were sometimes used loosely and the distinction between them was not always clear. The modern tendency has been to use 'res judicata' comprehensively to cover all those terms of estoppel. Cause of action estoppel is confined to cases where the cause of action and the parties are the same in the second suit as they were in the first suit.

In the present proceedings both parties agree that I am not concerned with cause of

j action estoppel (otherwise called estoppel by record) despite the fact that both parties were parties to the first suit, that is to say the Lancaster action. The judgment in that action was for individual victims or their personal representatives and not directly between the water authority and Binnies, despite the fact that Rose J did apportion liability between them. Furthermore, the cause of action in the Lancaster suit was undoubtedly negligence, in tort. In the present action the claim of the water authority is in contract as well as negligence, even if there may in fact be no practical difference involved.

a

Issue estoppel

In the present proceedings the water authority rely on issue estoppel. They submit that the *issues* between them and Binnies were decided in the first action, and that for all practical purposes the present action would involve going over precisely the same points as were investigated at great length and in great detail and decided on by Rose J and *b* subsequently by the Court of Appeal.

Much of the argument before me turned on the limits which should be put on the application of issue estoppel. Consideration of the authorities reveals two schools of thought on this. One approach is what I will call the broad one which holds that the true test of an issue estoppel is whether for all practical purposes the party seeking to put forward some issue has already had that issue determined against him by a court of *c* competent jurisdiction, even if the parties to the two actions are different. The conflicting approach is to confine issue estoppel to that species of estoppel per rem judicatam that may arise in civil actions between the same parties or their privies: see, for example, Lord Diplock in *Hunter v Chief Constable of West Midlands* [1981] 3 All ER 727, [1982] AC 529.

These conflicting approaches can be illustrated by considering a question which I put to counsel for Binnies during argument. A motor vehicle leaves the road and runs into *d* and injures a crowd of 100 people standing on the pavement. One of the 100 injured persons succeeds in an action for negligence against the driver. There are no facts to distinguish the position of any of the 100 injured. If the other 99 bring separate actions, is the driver to be permitted to defend each action, calling the same evidence on each occasion? Counsel for Binnies did not flinch from answering in the affirmative. The parties to each action would not be the same and the duty owed by the driver to each *e* plaintiff would be a distinct duty albeit in each case a similar one. Therefore, with different parties *and* different duties owed to each, no issue estoppel could arise.

That situation which I put to counsel for Binnies is of course one considered by Lord Denning MR in *McIlkenny v Chief Constable of the West Midlands* [1980] 2 All ER 227 at 237, [1980] 1 QB 283 at 320. Lord Denning MR had no doubt that an issue estoppel would operate against the driver. But it is clear that Goff LJ, dissenting on this matter, *f* thought it would not. So also, as I have said, did Lord Diplock on the appeal, reported in the House of Lords sub nom *Hunter v Chief Constable of West Midlands*, to which I have already referred.

The water authority contend that the broader approach is the correct one, and on that approach I should find that the issues between them and Binnies have all been fully litigated in the Lancaster trial, notwithstanding that that action was by plaintiffs who are *g* not parties to the present proceedings, and there were no contribution notices or other pleadings between the defendants, including the water authority and Binnies. Binnies contend that the narrow definition of issue estoppel is correct. On this basis issue estoppel cannot here be applied against Binnies since they have not been parties to any action in which they were directly against the water authority.

I understand that counsel for the water authority submits that even on the narrow *h* approach issue estoppel should apply, because despite the lack of any contribution notices the parties did in fact fully litigate every matter arising out of the Abbeystead explosion; and Rose J and subsequently the Court of Appeal did consider the degree of negligence of all three defendants. As I have said, much of the argument before me turned on the true limits of issue estoppel. I will return to consider this later.

j

The need for caution

Whether or not the broader or narrower definition of issue estoppel is correct I think it is clear that the power to strike out and, also, the finding of an issue estoppel, are matters on which the court should proceed with very great caution before debarring a party, whether plaintiff or defendant, from putting forward his case in another action.

In my judgment it is obvious that great caution is required because it is a drastic step
a for whatever reason to deprive a litigant of the opportunity to put forward either his
claim or defence. But if authority were required for the need to exercise great caution it
is readily available: see, for example, per Chitty LJ in *Stephenson v Garnet* [1898] 1 QB
677, where it was held that there was an abuse of process, per Buckley J in *Carl-Zeiss-
Stiftung v Rayner & Keeler Ltd (No 3)* [1969] 3 All ER 897 at 908, [1970] Ch 506 at 537,
per Goff LJ in *McIlkenny v Chief Constable of West Midlands Police Force* [1980] 2 All ER 227
b at 246, [1980] 1 QB 283 at 331 and per Sir Nicolas Browne-Wilkinson V-C in *Arnold v
National Westminster Bank plc* [1988] 3 All ER 977 at 982–983, [1989] Ch 63 at 70.

The power to strike out all or part of a party's case as an abuse of process of the court,
whether under Ord 18, r 19 or under the inherent jurisdiction of the court, may be
applied in much wider circumstances than issue estoppel; but it can be and sometimes
has been used for reasons similar to those which give rise to issue estoppel. Indeed, it is
c clear that, in circumstances where the narrower definition of issue estoppel is applied and
the court rejects a plea of issue estoppel, it may nevertheless have no doubt that the issues
between the parties have already been decided so that it would amount to an abuse of
process to permit the party seeking to relitigate them to do so. This is well illustrated by
McIlkenny's case. Despite the differences of opinion on the limits of issue estoppel, Goff
LJ in the Court of Appeal and Lord Diplock in the House of Lords, supported by the
d other Lords of Appeal, had no doubt that the attempt to relitigate was an abuse of process.

As the scope for finding abuse of process appears to be wider than issue estoppel, I
propose to consider it first.

e *Abuse of process*
In each of two early cases, *Reichel v MaGrath* (1889) 14 App Cas 665 and *Stephenson v
Garnett* [1898] 1 QB 677, a party was debarred from litigating an issue which had already
been decided by a court of competent jurisdiction. In *Stephenson v Garnett* the Court of
Appeal did not find the issue to be res judicata apparently, as I read the judgments,
because the cause of action was not the same, albeit it found the issue raised in the later
f proceeding was identical. In *Reichel v MaGrath* the House of Lords held that the appellant
should be debarred from relitigating an issue identical to that which had been decided
between him and a different party. The speeches do not mention res judicata. I suspect
that this was because there was no cause of action estoppel and the law on issue estoppel
was not then developed as it is today. On the broader approach to issue estoppel, which I
believe is the correct one, I think that today both issues would be decided on that basis.
g But if I am wrong in applying the broad approach to issue estoppel I see no reason why
Reichel v MaGrath should not be decided today as it was in fact decided then, on the
grounds that to permit the same issue to be litigated, albeit between different parties,
would be an abuse of the process of the court.

I have already referred to *McIlkenny v Chief Constable of West Midlands Police Force* in
which Goff LJ and Sir George Baker both found an abuse of process on the grounds that
h the plaintiffs were attempting to relitigate an issue already decided against them. The
House of Lords unanimously upheld the finding of abuse of process.

Counsel for Binnies does not dispute the jurisdiction of the court to find abuse of
process in an appropriate case. He referred to *Bragg v Oceanus Mutual Underwriting
Association (Bermuda) Ltd* [1982] 2 Lloyd's Rep 132 at 137, where Kerr LJ said: '. . . it is
clear that an attempt to relitigate in another action issues which have been fully
j investigated and decided in a former action *may* constitute an abuse of process . . .' (Kerr
LJ's emphasis). But as to the onus of proof, counsel for the defendants relied on the
judgment of Sir David Cairns, where he said ([1982] 2 Lloyd's Rep 132 at 138–139):

> 'I do not accept the proposition advanced by Counsel for the appellant Heath that
> when an issue has already been decided in proceedings between A and B it is prima
> facie an abuse of the process of the Court for B to seek to have the issue decided

afresh in proceedings between himself and C and that in such circumstances there is an onus on B to show some special reason why he should be allowed to raise the *a* issue against C. On the contrary, I consider that it is for him who contends that the retrial of the issue is an abuse of process to show special reason why it is so . . . The facts that the first action had been fairly conducted and that the issue had been the subject of lengthy evidence and argument could not, in my view, be sufficient in themselves to deprive the defendant of his normal right to raise any issue which he is not estopped from raising.'   *b*

I entirely accept that. It is really another way of saying that consideration of a suggested abuse of process must be exercised with great caution.

Counsel for Binnies submits that (1) the issues raised in the present action have never been decided between the water authority and Binnies and (2) no special reason or exceptional circumstances are shown by the water authority so as to justify depriving *c* Binnies of their normal right to raise any issue which they are not strictly estopped from raising.

As to the latter point the water authority contend that they have already been put to enormous trouble and expense in defending themselves in the Lancaster action. Their defence there included the allegation that Binnies were solely to blame; and, if the plaintiffs in that action were to succeed, the realities were that all issues affecting the *d* possible negligence of each of the three defendants had to be tried. Both Binnies and the water authority called extensive evidence and their experts were examined and cross-examined at length so that every possible aspect of the case was considered in very great detail. To put them to the expense of relitigating the same issues now that $5\frac{1}{2}$ years has already elapsed since the explosion, and $3\frac{1}{2}$ years after the trial at Lancaster, would be intolerable and wholly unjustified, and involve unwarranted disruption to their business. *e*

If the issues have indeed already been litigated in the sense that Binnies have already had a fair and full opportunitiy of showing that they were not negligent, then I agree that the trouble and expense to which the water authority would be put, and the anxiety which would be suffered by the individual officers against whom negligence is alleged, is a sufficient reason to debar Binnies from proceeding. But this leaves the question: have the issues in fact, in practical terms, already been litigated?   *f*

It was only at the start of the hearing of this preliminary issue that I gave leave to amend the statement of claim to plead abuse of process of the court. So I gave notice to counsel for Binnies at that stage, and before he began his submissions in reply to counsel for the water authority, that I would like him to tell me what practical as opposed to theoretical differences there would be in the two sets of litigation. He pointed out in due course that the issue between the Lancaster plaintiffs and Binnies was in tort, whereas the *g* action between Binnies and the water authority lies in contract, it may be in contract and tort, but Binnies will say only in contract. But I asked to be shown the contract and to have pointed out to me any way in which the contract in practice would modify or give rise to different issues from liability in tort. I was given no, or no satisfactory, answer.

Next Binnies rely on the fact that there were no contribution notices between any of the three defendants in the Lancaster action, nor was Rose J asked to apportion liability, *h* although he did in fact do so. In my judgment Rose J was entitled to do that.

In *Croston v Vaughan* [1937] 4 All ER 249, [1938] 1 KB 540 the Court of Appeal had held that the trial judge had jurisdiction at the end of proceedings, in which it had been held that the plaintiff was entitled to recover, to entertain an application to apportion blame between two defendants without the necessity of formal legal proceedings being instituted and served. Furthermore, Scott LJ said ([1937] 4 All ER 249 at 262, [1938] 1 *j* KB 540 at 565):

'I am inclined to think that it was open to the judge, even if one of the parties had dissented, to exercise the jurisdiction [to apportion] if he thought fit.'

I respectfully agree with that view, and I believe that it was open to Rose J to apportion
a liability as he did.

But, irrespective of any procedural technicalities or defects, I agree with the water
authority that the reality is that the respective liability of each party was litigated, and
very fully litigated, before Rose J at Lancaster. Furthermore, it was then reconsidered by
the Court of Appeal, which differed from Rose J and substituted its own conclusion that
Binnies were 100% to blame.

b Counsel for Binnies said that Binnies might wish to apply for leave to amend their
defence so as to allege contributory negligence on the part of the water authority. No
firm application for leave to amend has been made and no proposed form of amendment,
even in rough draft form, has been put forward. Counsel for the water authority in his
reply poured scorn on this as amounting to no more than a tactical move by Binnies to
try to create the shadow of a fresh issue not decided in the Lancaster action, and that in
c any event it would be unfair to the water authority to give leave for such an amendment
to be introduced at this late stage.

Counsel for Binnies wished to make a further submission in response to this; but as
we had already passed the normal end of the court's day and I had another engagement
to attend I said I would have to hear Binnies' counsel the next day. Neither of the parties
wished to return for what was to be only a brief submission, so it was agreed that counsel
d for Binnies would put his further submission on the matter in writing. I have received
and carefully taken into account his written submission on this point.

Counsel for Binnies states that the proposed plea of contributory negligence is not
merely a 'tactical' defence but one that Binnies will seriously consider in this action, in
which the Lancaster plaintiffs are not present. As to the alleged lateness of the application
to amend he points out that leave to amend the statement of claim was only given on 11
e October 1989 and against the history of the water authority's delay in prosecuting the
present action it would be quite wrong to hold that the application is made too late.

Although there is some substance in these submissions I do not think it would be right
to give leave to amend at this stage. The allegation of contributory negligence does not
arise out of the water authority's recent amendment of the statement of claim, and could
have been made at the time of the existing defence, which was served on 16 December
f 1988, some ten months before. Further, I would have expected the application for leave
to amend to have been made well in advance of the hearing of this preliminary issue. As
it is, even now there is no firm commitment to seek leave to amend nor any form of
draft amendment to show the particulars on which Binnies would seek to rely.

It is correct to say that in his written submission counsel for Binnies does say:

g   'In the changed tactical situation created in this action in the absence of the
      Lancaster plaintiffs, Binnies should consider whether, when the North-West Water
      Authority allege against them that Binnies should have foreseen reservoir methane,
      they should not reply that, if that is so, North-West Water Authority's engineers
      ought also to have foreseen it and, by failing to do so, failed to take reasonable care
      for the safety of the permanent works.'

h
That, counsel says, is something which Binnies are to consider. No decision has yet
been made that any such allegation will in fact be made. But even if it is put forward I
am of the view that it will raise no new matter which was not fully explored in the
Lancaster action. Accordingly, I decline to accept that this introduces a new issue into the
present action, and (a) I would refuse leave for it to be introduced on the grounds that it
j is made too late and (b) even if it were introduced I do not think it would in fact raise any
new matter not already decided in the Lancaster action.

New evidence
Binnies further submit that the issue in the present action will not be precisely the

same as in the Lancaster action because they propose in this action to call fresh evidence, a report of a seismic investigation by ECL. The ECL report was in existence before the *a* Lancaster trial but Rose J refused to allow Binnies to adduce it in evidence in the following circumstances.

The report had been commissioned by the water authority after the explosion in order to try to discover the cause thereof and decide what might be done to avoid further risk. It was disclosed to the parties and the report was included in the papers given to the judge before the trial. Counsel for Binnies told me that at that time Binnies assumed that the *b* report would become an agreed document. However, the report had not in any way been admitted by the Lancaster plaintiffs, and neither the water authority nor Binnies had asked for any order for directions so as to obtain leave to adduce the report in evidence or call the makers of the report as experts.

During his opening of the case at Lancaster, counsel for the plaintiffs referred to the ECL report to say that it was not admitted, that no directions had been given to permit it *c* to be adduced in evidence and that the plaintiffs objected to it being used in any way at the trial. The water authority did not want to use it, so they took no action. Binnies did wish to use it, but having wrongly assumed that it would become an agreed document they had taken no steps to have the authors of the report available to give evidence. They proceeded to take such steps and seven days later (that is to say on the ninth day of the trial) they applied to Rose J to call two of the authors as additional experts. The plaintiffs *d* objected. The order for directions giving leave to each party to call four expert witnesses had been made on 4 March 1986 and amended on 9 July 1986 only in respect of the date on which those reports were to be exchanged, which became 11 August 1986. The ECL report was made available by the water authority to the other parties on 16 September 1986.

Against that background Rose J refused the application by Binnies to call additional *e* experts to produce the ECL report. In his ruling he held (1) that it was not necessary for the fair determination of the issue between the parties that leave to adduce this evidence should be given and (2) that it would be seriously prejudicial to the plaintiffs to give such leave. He observed that counsel for Binnies had not suggested that the report was necessary to the presentation of Binnies' case, and that if it had been he would have expected an application to adduce the evidence to have been made at an earlier date, and *f* not left until the ninth day of the trial. He further took into account the fact that if he now gave leave to adduce the evidence he would consider it right to give the plaintiffs time to obtain expert evidence of a similar nature and this would involve a very lengthy adjournment of the trial.

With that history, should Binnies be permitted to adduce the evidence in the present action, and, if so, will the effect be to introduce new issues so as to alter the position from *g* what would otherwise amount to an abuse of process or give rise to an issue estoppel?

Counsel for Binnies submits that the ECL report is vital to Binnies' defence in the present action and he relies on the judgment of Rose J and of Russell LJ to demonstrate this. Counsel for Binnies disagrees and submits that it is at best very questionable whether the report would be directly relevant to the issues between Binnies and the *h* water authority.

What is the correct test to be applied to consider whether fresh evidence should be admitted which will have the effect of overcoming issue estoppel or what would otherwise amount to an attempt to relitigate the same issue and thus amount to an abuse of process?

Counsel for the water authority relies on the test propounded by Earl Cairns LC in *j* *Phosphate Sewage Co v Molleson* (1879) 4 App Cas 801 at 814, that is to say the new evidence must be such as 'entirely changes the aspect of the case . . . and was not and could not by reasonable diligence have been ascertained before . . .'

Counsel for Binnies denies that this is the correct test. He submits that the court

should look at the new evidence and the reasons why it was not adduced in the previous
a proceedings and decide whether the new facts are such that circumstances make it fair
and just that the decided issues between the parties should be reopened. For that
proposition he relies on a passage in the judgment of Lord Denning MR in *Tebbutt v
Haynes* [1981] 2 All ER 238 at 242 and the observations of Sir Nicolas Browne-Wilkinson
V-C in *Arnold v National Westminster Bank plc* [1988] 3 All ER 977 at 982, [1989] Ch 63 at
69 where he said:

b
        '. . . there are circumstances in issue estoppel where the injustice of not allowing
    the matter to be relitigated outweighs the hardship to the successful party in the
    first action in having to relitigate the point. The rules applicable to issue estoppel
    and the proper exceptions to it are in course of development: see *Carl-Zeiss-Stiftung v
    Rayner & Keeler Ltd (No 2)* [1966] 2 All ER 536 at 554, [1967] 1 AC 853 at 917. The
c   authorities show that the exception applying to "special circumstances" is designed
    to ensure that where justice requires the non-application of issue estoppel, it should
    not apply: see *Yat Tung Investment Co Ltd v Dao Heng Bank Ltd* [1975] AC 581 at 590.
    In the *Carl-Zeiss* case [1966] 2 All ER 536 at 573, [1967] 1 AC 853 at 947 Lord
    Upjohn said: "All estoppels are not odious but must be applied so as to work justice
    and not injustice, and I think that the principle of issue estoppel must be applied to
d   the circumstances of the subsequent case with this overriding consideration in
    mind."'

I have no doubt that, in every case where issue estoppel or an abuse of process is being
considered against the wish of a party to introduce fresh evidence, the overall justice of
the decision to be made should be an important, and it may be, an overriding
e consideration. But I do not think that Lord Denning MR or Sir Nicolas Browne-
Wilkinson V-C in either of the cases I have just referred to was suggesting that a general
test of fairness or hardship should be substituted for the long-standing test stated by Earl
Cairns LC in the *Phosphate Sewage* case. Indeed in *Tebbutt v Haynes* Lord Denning MR, in
making the observations relied on by counsel for Binnies had, in the very same passage,
referred to his observations in *McIlkenny v Chief Constable of West Midlands Police Force*
f [1980] 2 All ER 227 at 237, [1980] 1 QB 283 at 319 where he had expressly relied on the
Phosphate Sewage test and observed that this test is a much stricter one than is applied
when considering fresh evidence on an appeal, that is to say that the fresh evidence must
be such that, if given, it would probably have an important influence on the result of the
case, although it need not be decisive (see *Ladd v Marshall* [1954] 3 All ER 745 at 746,
[1954] 1 WLR 1489 at 1491).
g   Counsel for Binnies also referred to observations by Lord Diplock in *Hunter v Chief
Constable of West Midlands* [1981] 3 All ER 727, [1982] AC 529 where he reaffirmed what
he said about issue estoppel in *Mills v Cooper* [1967] 2 All ER 100 at 104, [1967] 2 QB 459
at 469, where he had stated that a previously decided issue is binding on the parties—

        'unless further material which is relevant to the correctness or incorrectness of the
h   assertion and could not by reasonable diligence have been adduced by that party in
     the previous proceedings has since become available to him.'

In *Mills v Cooper* fresh evidence was not directly in issue. But in *Hunter's* case Lord
Diplock directly considered the circumstances in which fresh evidence may be admitted
so as to make an exception to what otherwise would amount to an abuse of process of the
j court. Agreeing with what Goff LJ had stated in the Court of Appeal he stated clearly
that the test to be applied is the more rigorous *Phosphate Sewage* test rather than that
derived from *Ladd v Marshall*.
    So in this case I think it right to apply the *Phosphate Sewage* test. Doing so, I find that
Binnies fail. I do not think that they can show that the ECL report entirely changes any

aspects of the case. On the contrary, I am satisfied by the submissions for the water authority that it does not do so.

In my judgment Binnies also fail on the other limb of the *Phosphate Sewage* test. I think it is clear that the ECL report was available to them at the Lancaster trial *and* that it was solely due to their own default in not applying before the trial for leave to adduce that evidence that their application, made only on the ninth day of the trial, failed.

Thus I hold (1) that the attempt by Binnies to relitigate issues already decided is an abuse of the process of the court, (2) that the ECL report does not enable them to avoid that decision and (3) that they should not be permitted now to plead contributory negligence which, in any event, has been covered by the Lancaster trial and the subsequent appeal.

Having made that judgment it may not strictly be necessary for me to deal with issue estoppel. However, this was argued before me very fully and, until I gave leave to amend the statement of claim so as to plead abuse of process, it was on issue estoppel alone that the water authority relied. I think it right, therefore, to deal with this matter, albeit perhaps not quite as fully as I might otherwise have done.

Issue estoppel

I referred earlier to the conflicting views about the extent to which issue estoppel should be applied. It seems to me that these differing views were very clearly illustrated in *McIlkenny's* case. The narrow approach was favoured by Goff LJ in his dissenting judgment in the Court of Appeal and by Lord Diplock on the appeal to the House of Lords. The broader approach was that of Lord Denning MR supported by Sir George Baker.

This difference of approach can be traced back well before *McIlkenny's* case. Both counsel relied on a number of older authorities, notably *Marginson v Blackburn BC* [1939] 1 All ER 273, [1939] 2 KB 42, *Bell v Holmes* [1956] 3 All ER 449, [1956] 1 WLR 1359 and *Wood v Luscombe (Wood, third party)* [1964] 3 All ER 972, [1966] 1 QB 169 by counsel for the water authority and *Randolph v Tuck* [1961] 1 All ER 814, [1962] 1 QB 175 and *Craddock's Transport Ltd v Stuart* [1970] NZLR 499 following the Australian case of *Jackson v Goldsmith* (1950) 81 CLR 446 by counsel for Binnies.

These cases do indeed show the two schools of thought as to the limits of issue estoppel. But I observe that, when Lord Denning MR and Goff LJ arrived at their sharply differing conclusions on issue estoppel in *McIlkenny's* case, not one of those cases is referred to in the judgments, and only one, *Marginson v Blackburn BC*, was cited in argument.

The differences in approach to be found in the older English cases cited to me by both counsel were in fact very extensively reviewed by North P in the New Zealand Court of Appeal in *Craddock's Transport Ltd v Stuart*, and a broad but very clear summary of these differences was made on that appeal in the dissenting judgment of McCarthy J. He said ([1970] NZLR 499 at 521):

'There are, very broadly, two schools of thought relating to the use of issue estoppel in actions arising out of motor vehicle collisions, especially when one of the two actions under consideration is a claim by a passenger in one of the vehicles. On the one hand, there are those who in the general run of such cases favour seeking what they see as the substantial question involved—who caused the collision? This approach has been called, with no complimentary intention, the "robust" approach: it being hinted that it fails to recognise the refinements which are apparent on deeper examination. It is the approach which as the President has demonstrated has been favoured in most of the English decisions and by Shorland J in our Supreme Court in *Clyne v Yardley* ([1959] NZLR 617). On the other hand there are those whose approach is dominated by the question—often highly theoretical—what in law were the respective duties of care? They say that if the two duties cannot be formulated in precisely identical terms, no issue estoppel can arise. The extension of

this approach has led to it being held that the duty owed by X., a driver of one
a vehicle, to Y., a passenger in another, is not to be equated to the duty owed by him
to Z., another passenger in the same car. The critics of this approach suggest that it
departs from reality and pursues a tidy legal theory at the expense of the rule that
an end should be brought to litigation. This approach has found strong favour in
Australia, a country not generally regarded as insensitive to reality. One may suspect
too from a reading of the judgments and writings on this topic that many legal
b minds can be classified under two opposing heads: those to whom estoppels are
generally odious, and those who think that the administration of justice requires
more than lip service of the maxim *interest reipublicae ut sit finis litium*.'

I will return later to the facts of that case.

In *Marginson v Blackburn BC* [1939] 1 All ER 273, [1939] 2 KB 426 a collision took place
between a bus belonging to the defendant corporation and a car belonging to the plaintiff
c M in which he was being driven by his wife. She was killed, he was injured, and the bus
ran into and damaged two houses. The house-owners brought a county court action for
damage to the houses alleging negligence against each of the two drivers, suing M and
the council as the respective principals or employers of the drivers. The council and M
both denied liability and blamed the other driver. Each served a third party notice on
d the other claiming an indemnity or contribution; and the council further claimed
£66 16s 0d from M for damage to their bus. The county court judge held both drivers
equally to blame. M then brought an action in the High Court against the council
claiming (a) on his own behalf damages for personal injuries and (b) on behalf of his
deceased wife for damages under the Law Reform (Miscellaneous Provisions) Act 1934
and the Fatal Accidents Act 1846. The Court of Appeal held that the decision of the
e county court judge estopped M from maintaining his claim in respect of his own personal
injuries but not from pursuing the claims on behalf of his wife.

That case was decided before the Law Reform (Contributory Negligence) Act 1945,
hence the decision to debar M entirely from pursuing his own claim against the council.
Furthermore, M was not the driver of his car, although he was deemed to be the principal
and therefore to be treated in the same way as if he had been driver.

f The case is considered to be the first in which the court applied issue estoppel to
prevent an issue being relitigated. The terminology used by Slesser LJ in drawing a
distinction between 'estoppel by record' and 'estoppel by res judicata' is confusing today,
but nevertheless the case does appear to be an application by the Court of Appeal of issue
estoppel as opposed to cause of action estoppel. On the other hand, both M and the
council had served on each other third party notices in the earlier proceedings so that the
g issue of negligence had been litigated between them in the county court.

In *Bell v Holmes* [1956] 3 All ER 449, [1956] 1 WLR 1359 there had been a collision
between two vehicles driven by P and D respectively. The passenger in D's car sued both
drivers. The county court judge held both to blame. Although there were no contribution
notices both P and D asked him to apportion blame and he did so: P five-sixths and D
one-sixth to blame. In an action by P against D McNair J held that P was estopped by the
h earlier proceedings from denying that he was five-sixths to blame. He said ([1956] 3 All
ER 449 at 454–455, [1956] 1 WLR 1359 at 1366–1367):

> 'It was said that the issues in the county court action and the issues in the present
> action were not the same because in the county court action the matter in issue
> between Miss Elsworth [the passenger in D's car] and the two defendants to that
j > action was whether or not there had been a breach of their respective duties towards
> her, whereas in the present action the question was whether there had been a breach
> of the duties: (i) owed by the defendant to the plaintiff, and (ii) owed by the plaintiff
> to the defendant. Those are different legal issues of course, in a sense, but I do not
> feel that the fact that they are technically different should prevent effect being given
> to the plea of estoppel in a case where, having examined the pleadings in the county

court action and compared them with the pleadings in the present action, I am
satisfied that the issues of fact, and the evidence to support them in respect of
liability, would be identically the same . . . The conclusion which I have reached on
that point seems to me to be wholly consistent with the views expressed by the
Court of Appeal in *Marginson* v. *Blackburn Borough Council* ([1939] 1 All ER 273,
[1939] 2 KB 426) . . .'

McNair J then referred briefly to the decision of the High Court of Australia in *Jackson v
Goldsmith* (1950) 81 CLR 446 but added that (because he was out on assize) he had seen
only a short citation of the judgment and not the actual judgment itself.

In *Randolph v Tuck* [1961] 1 All ER 814, [1962] 1 QB 175 Lawton J did consider the
full judgment in *Jackson v Goldsmith* and also the American case of *Neenan v Woodside
Astoria Transportation Co Inc* (1932) 235 AD 9. Lawton J in a reserved judgment declined
to follow McNair J in *Bell v Holmes* and held that the fact that the duties of two defendants
to each other was a different one to that owed by them to the plaintiff was fatal to a
finding of an estoppel. In *Randolph v Tuck* two drivers had been in collision. In the county
court it was held that one was wholly to blame. In an action brought by a passenger in
one of the cars against both drivers Lawton J held that the county court proceedings did
not estop the driver who had been found wholly to blame for denying liability to the
passenger, as the duties owned by each driver to the other driver and their duty to the
passenger were separate and distinct.

The different approaches of McNair and Lawton JJ in those cases seem to me to be the
same as the differences of Lord Denning MR and Goff LJ in *McIlkenny v Chief Constable of
West Midlands Police Force* [1980] 2 All ER 227, [1980] 1 QB 283 to which I have already
referred.

Wood v Luscombe (*Wood, third party*) [1964] 3 All ER 972, [1966] 1 QB 169 was another
running down case. There was a collision between two motor cyclists, one of whom had
a pillion passenger. In proceedings in the High Court between the two motor cyclists
both parties were found equally to blame. The pillion passenger subsequently brought
an action against one motor cyclist, L, who joined the other, W, as third party, claiming
contribution. In his third party notice the defendant L claimed that the third party W
was estopped from denying that he was equally to blame with L. Streatfeild J held that
the issue to be determined in the third party proceedings was the same as that in the
previous action between L and W, namely who was to blame for the accident? and, as
the evidence would support both suits, the issue of liability between L and W was res
judicata. So he followed *Bell v Holmes* but disagreed with the judgment of Lawton J in
Randolph v Tuck.

Counsel for Binnies relies heavily on the New Zealand Court of Appeal majority
judgment in *Craddocks Transport v Stuart* [1970] NZLR 499. In that case there was a
collision between a car driven by Mr S in which Mrs S was a passenger and a lorry owned
by Craddocks Transport driven by their servant K. Mrs S was injured and sued Craddocks,
who joined Mr S as third party. The jury found K negligent and Mr S *not* negligent in a
manner causing or contributing to Mrs S's injury. Mr S then sued Craddocks for the
damage to his car, and his statement of claim pleaded issue estoppel. Craddocks pleaded
contributory negligence by Mr S. The parties in effect agreed that the preliminary issues
of issue estoppel should go straight to the Court of Appeal. On appeal Craddocks argued
that there was no issue estoppel because (1) the parties in the second action were different,
in that in the first action Craddocks had been compelled to entrust the conduct of the
action to insurers, whereas this was not the case in the second action, and (2) the issues
were different, because a different duty of care was owed by each driver towards Mrs S as
passenger to that owed by them towards each other. North P, with whom Turner J
agreed, accepted this second submission and observed that one particular difference
between the issues raised in each action was that the defence of contributory negligence
was not available to Craddocks in the first action.

a   North P gave a very full review of the English, Australian and New Zealand authorities and followed the decision of Lawton J in *Randolph v Tuck* in preference to those of McNair J in *Bell v Holmes* and Streatfeild J in *Wood v Luscombe*. In the circumstances North P found it unnecessary to decide Craddocks' submission that the fact that they were compelled to entrust the conduct of the earlier action to insurers meant that the parties were not identical, but he doubted whether this submission was valid, as also did Turner J. That does not arise in the present case.

b   In his dissenting judgment McCarthy J preferred the broader approach and considered that the issues raised in the two actions under consideration were for all practical purposes the same.

In my judgment, this broader approach to a plea of issue estoppel is to be preferred. I find it unreal to hold that the issues raised in two actions arising from identical facts are different *solely* because the parties are different or because the duty of care owed to c   different persons is in law different. However, I at once stress my use of the word 'solely'. I think that great caution must be exercised before shutting out a party from putting forward his case on the grounds of issue estoppel or abuse of process. Before doing so the court should be quite satisfied that there is no real or practical difference between the issues to be litigated in the new action and that already decided, and the evidence which may properly be called on those issues in the new action.

d   I have already decided, when considering abuse of process, that in the present case no such real or practical difference does exist.

Thus on the broader approach to issue estoppel, which in my judgment should be applied, I hold that Binnies are estopped from denying negligence in the present action.

Even if I am wrong about the limits to issue estoppel and the true limit is in fact the narrower one, that is to say that favoured by Goff LJ in *McIlkenny v Chief Constable of West* e   *Midlands Police Force* [1980] 2 All ER 227, [1980] 1 QB 283 and Lord Diplock on the appeal to the House of Lords ([1981] 3 All ER 727, [1982] AC 529), I would still hold that Binnies are in this case caught by issue estoppel. This is because I find that the issues arising in the present action have already been decided and that in practical terms they have been decided between the same parties, the water authority and Binnies. The absence of third party or contribution notices does not affect my finding on this for I f   think the reality is that all issues concerning negligence were in fact litigated before Rose J and decided by him and subsequently by the Court of Appeal.

For these reasons I find in favour of the water authority and hold that Binnies' denial of negligence should be struck out as an abuse of the process of the court under RSC Ord 18, r 19, alternatively under the inherent jurisdiction of the court. I further hold that Binnies are estopped from denying negligence on the ground that the issue has already g   been decided against them in the Lancaster action.

In my judgment the proceedings between these two parties have reached the stage where it can emphatically be said that it is in the public interest that there should be a finish to this litigation.

h   *Order accordingly.*

Solicitors: *Davies Arnold Cooper* (for the water authority); *Beale & Co* (for Binnies).

K Mydeen Esq   Barrister.

R v Secretary of State for the Home Department, ex parte K

COURT OF APPEAL, CIVIL DIVISION

SLADE, BALCOMBE AND McCOWAN LJJ

13, 14 JUNE, 3 JULY 1990

Mental health – Patient – Recall to hospital – Recall of conditionally discharged patient by Secretary of State – Patient having history of sexual offences and ordered to be detained in secure hospital – Patient conditionally discharged from hospital by mental health review tribunal – Uncontroverted medical evidence that patient not suffering psychopathic disorder – Secretary of State issuing warrant for recall of patient – Whether Secretary of State required to act on medical opinion when exercising power – Whether Secretary of State acting reasonably in issuing warrant for recall of patient – Mental Health Act 1983, ss 42(3), 73(2).

The appellant had a history of sexual offences and in 1966 was sentenced to three years' imprisonment for rape. In 1970, six weeks after being released from prison, he raped and killed a 12-year-old girl, for which he was convicted of manslaughter. He was ordered to be detained in a secure hospital on the ground that he was suffering from psychopathic disorder and a restriction order was made restricting his discharge without limit of time. In March 1985 a mental health review tribunal decided that he was not suffering from any mental disorder and ordered that he be conditionally discharged from hospital under s 73(2)[a] of the Mental Health Act 1983. Under a conditional discharge a patient was entitled to be released from hospital while remaining liable to be recalled for further treatment. Six months after being discharged he attacked and assaulted two young women in separate incidents for which he was sentenced to six years' imprisonment. In June 1986 the appellant applied for his case to be considered by a mental health review tribunal so that the conditions under which he had been discharged could be lifted. After hearing uncontroverted medical evidence from the doctors at the hospital where the appellant had been detained that he was not suffering from psychopathic disorder the tribunal decided in December 1986 that he was not suffering from any mental disorder and ordered that he should remain conditionally discharged but that the conditions imposed in 1985 should be suspended until his release from prison on the expiry of his sentence, which was due to end on 24 October 1989. On 1 September 1989 the Secretary of State issued a warrant under s 42(3)[b] of the 1983 Act recalling the appellant to hospital on the ground that he presented a danger to the public. The appellant applied for judicial review of the Secretary of State's decision to issue the warrant, contending that it was to be implied that the Secretary of State could only exercise his power to recall a patient to hospital on the recommendation of a medical practitioner and that the Secretary of State could not exercise his power of recall in circumstances where a mental health review tribunal was obliged to order his conditional discharge because he was not suffering from any mental disorder. The judge dismissed the application and the appellant appealed.

Held – There was no requirement in s 42(3) of the 1983 Act that the Secretary of State could only issue a warrant to recall a patient who had been conditionally discharged if there was medical evidence that the patient was then suffering from mental disorder. The nature of the power conferred on the Secretary of State by s 42(3) was such that, subject to recognised public law constraints and to balancing the interests of the patient against those of public safety, he had a discretion to recall a patient to hospital at any time while a restriction order continued in force in respect of that patient. On the facts, the

---

a   Section 73(2) is set out at p 565 a, post

b   Section 42(3) is set out at p 565 d e, post

Secretary of State had taken into account the appellant's mental condition as well as the
a interests of public safety and his decision to recall the appellant had not been unreasonable.
The appeal would therefore be dismissed (see p 569 h j, p 570 a b e f h j and p 571 f, post).
Decision of McCullough J [1990] 1 All ER 703 affirmed.

Notes
For the power of a mental health review tribunal to order the discharge of a patient from
b detention, see 30 Halsbury's Laws (4th edn) para 1970.
For the Mental Health Act 1983, ss 42, 73, see 28 Halsbury's Statutes (4th edn) 686,
714.

Cases referred to in judgment
Associated Provincial Picture Houses Ltd v Wednesbury Corp [1947] 2 All ER 680, [1948] 1
c KB 223, CA.
Padfield v Ministry of Agriculture Fisheries and Food [1968] 1 All ER 694, [1968] AC 997,
[1968] 2 WLR 924, HL.
R v Merseyside Mental Health Review Tribunal, ex p K [1990] 1 All ER 694, CA.
R v Secretary of State for the Home Dept, ex p Brind [1990] 1 All ER 469, [1990] 2 WLR 787,
CA.
d X v UK (1981) 4 EHRR 188, E Ct HR.

Cases also cited
Ashingdane v UK (1985) 7 EHRR 528, E Ct HR.
Pickering v Liverpool Daily Post and Echo Newspapers plc [1990] 1 All ER 335, [1990] 2
e WLR 494, CA.
R v Haberdashers' Aske's Hatcham School Governors, ex p Inner London Education Authority, R
v Inner London Education Authority, ex p Brunyate and Hunt (1989) Independent, 28
February, CA.
Tower Hamlets London BC v Chetnik Developments Ltd [1988] 1 All ER 961, [1988] AC 858,
HL.
f Winterwerp v Netherlands (1979) 2 EHRR 387, E Ct HR.

Appeal
K, a restricted patient under the Mental Health Act 1983, appealed against the decision
of McCullough J ([1990] 1 All ER 703, [1990] 1 WLR 168) given on 23 October 1989
dismissing his application for judicial review by way of an order of certiorari to quash
g the warrant issued by the Secretary of State for the Home Department under s 42(3) of
the 1983 Act on 1 September 1989 recalling the appellant to hospital on the ground that
the warrant was issued unlawfully. The facts are set out in the judgment of the court.

Alan Newman QC and Oliver Thorold for the appellant.
h Nigel Pleming for the Secretary of State.

Cur adv vult

3 July. The following judgment of the court was delivered.

j **McCOWAN LJ.** This is an appeal from the decision of McCollough J ([1990] 1 All ER
703, [1990] 1 WLR 168) given on 23 October 1989 that the Secretary of State for the
Home Department had not acted unlawfully in issuing a warrant pursuant to ss 42(3)
and 73(4)(a) of the Mental Health Act 1983 that the appellant be recalled to Broadmoor
Hospital.
The appellant was born on 13 June 1945. He has been convicted in the criminal courts

on many occasions, of which the following are relevant. In July 1962 for indecent assault on a girl aged 13 he was fined £15. In December 1963 he was convicted of having sexual *a* intercourse with a girl aged between 13 and 15 and conditionally discharged. In January 1966, when he would have been 20, he was convicted of rape and sent to prison for three years. On 6 November 1970, when he was aged 25, he killed the 12-year-old daughter of a neighbour, the condition of her body when found indicating that she had been raped, asphyxiated, cut with a sharp instrument and bitten. He was charged with murder but, on 5 January 1971, in the Crown Court at Liverpool, he pleaded guilty to manslaughter *b* on the ground of diminished responsibility and this plea was, in the light of the medical reports, acceptable to the prosecution and the court. The medical evidence was that the appellant was suffering from a psychopathic disorder and on that basis the court made him the subject of a hospital order and a restriction order without limit of time under the provisions of ss 60 and 65 of the Mental Health Act 1959 (the equivalent sections in the Mental Health Act 1983 being ss 37 and 41).	*c*

The appellant was admitted to Broadmoor Hospital in February 1971 and transferred to Park Lane Hospital in November 1981. The Secretary of State has ever since been consistently and strongly opposed to the appellant's discharge from hospital, expressing the view that the appellant's motivation for the offence in respect of which the hospital order was made has not been satisfactorily established and that he felt continuing concern *d* at the pattern of violence in the appellant's behaviour.

It is necessary at this point to have regard to a number of the provisions of the Mental Health Act 1983. Section 1(1) of that Act reads:

> 'The provisions of this Act shall have effect with respect to the reception, care and treatment of mentally disordered patients, the management of their property and other related matters.'	*e*

'Mental disorder' is defined in s 1(2) as follows:

> 'In this Act—"mental disorder" means mental illness, arrested or incomplete development of mind, psychopathic disorder and any other disorder or disability of mind and "mentally disordered" shall be construed accordingly.'

'Psychopathic disorder' is defined in the same subsection as follows:	*f*

> '"psychopathic disorder" means a persistent disorder or disability of mind (whether or not including significant impairment of intelligence) which results in abnormally aggressive or seriously irresponsible conduct on the part of the person concerned.'

Section 73(1) reads:	*g*

> 'Where an application to a Mental Health Review Tribunal is made by a restricted patient who is subject to a restriction order, or where the case of such a patient is referred to such a tribunal, the tribunal shall direct the absolute discharge of the patient if satisfied—(a) as to the matters mentioned in paragraph (b)(i) or (ii) of section 72(1) above; and (b) that it is not appropriate for the patient to remain liable *h* to be recalled to hospital for further treatment.'

The matters mentioned in s 72(1)(b)(i) and (ii) are as follows:

> '(b) the tribunal shall direct the discharge of a patient liable to be detained otherwise than under section 2 above if they are satisfied—(i) that he is not then suffering from mental illness, psychopathic disorder, severe mental impairment or *j* mental impairment or from any of those forms of disorder of a nature or degree which makes it appropriate for him to be liable to be detained in a hospital for medical treatment; or (ii) that it is not necessary for the health or safety of the patient or for the protection of other persons that he should receive such treatment.'

Section 73(2), (3) and (4) reads:

'(2) Where in the case of any such patient as is mentioned in subsection (1) above the tribunal are satisfied as to the matters referred to in paragraph (a) of that subsection but not as to the matters referred to in paragraph (b) of that subsection the tribunal shall direct the conditional discharge of the patient.

(3) Where a patient is absolutely discharged under this section he shall thereupon cease to be liable to be detained by virtue of the relevant hospital order, and the restriction order shall cease to have effect accordingly.

(4) Where a patient is conditionally discharged under this section—(a) he may be recalled by the Secretary of State under subsection (3) of section 42 above as if he had been conditionally discharged under subsection (2) of that section; and (b) the patient shall comply with such conditions (if any) as may be imposed at the time of discharge by the tribunal or at any subsequent time by the Secretary of State.'

Section 42(2) and (3) reads:

'(2) At any time while a restriction order is in force in respect of a patient, the Secretary of State may, if he thinks fit, by warrant discharge the patient from hospital, either absolutely or subject to conditions; and where a person is absolutely discharged under this subsection, he shall thereupon cease to be liable to be detained by virtue of the relevant hospital order, and the restriction order shall cease to have effect accordingly.

(3) The Secretary of State may at any time during the continuance in force of a restriction order in respect of a patient who has been conditionally discharged under subsection (2) above by warrant recall the patient to such hospital as may be specified in the warrant.'

Section 75(1) provides:

'Where a restricted patient has been conditionally discharged under section 42(2), 73 or 74 above and is subsequently recalled to hospital—(a) the Secretary of State shall, within one month of the day on which the patient returns or is returned to hospital, refer his case to a Mental Health Review Tribunal . . .'

In this case the tribunal, on 19 March 1985 on an application by the appellant, ordered that he be conditionally discharged from Park Lane Hospital, the conditions being that:

'1. we shall reside at accommodation approved by Dr MacCulloch, his RMO [we interpolate there that those initials stand for "responsible medical officer"]; 2. he shall attend for such out-patient treatment as shall be prescribed by Dr MacCulloch and at such place as shall be directed by Dr MacCulloch; 3. he shall be supervised by an appropriate probation officer; 4. he shall accept and act on the advice of Dr MacCulloch and such probation officer. And further such discharge shall be deferred until accommodation approved by Dr MacCulloch is available for [the appellant].'

The reasons for the decision of the tribunal are stated as follows:

'The Tribunal is satisfied:—That [the appellant] is not suffering from mental illness, psychopathic disorder, severe mental impairment or mental impairment. The Tribunal is of the view that it is appropriate for the [appellant] to remain liable to be recalled to hospital for further treatment.'

In the light of those findings, the tribunal had no option but to order a conditional discharge. The record continues:

'The Tribunal is satisfied about these reasons because The Tribunal heard a substantial body of evidence which subscribed to the view that the [appellant] is not suffering from mental disorder. Such evidence was firmly expressed and unshaken by cross-examination on behalf of the Home Secretary. There was no evidence at all from any source that [the appellant] was at present suffering from mental disorder.' *a*

The record then shows that the evidence emanated from a large body of witnesses and reports, most of the witnesses being psychiatrists. It is only necessary to refer to some of those witnesses. One, Dr Tennant, a former consultant to special hospitals, is referred to and it is said of him that his 'impressive evidence that "there is no evidence of psychosis . . . I don't feel [the appellant] is a danger to himself and others" carried particular weight with us . . .' Then another witness was mentioned, 'Dr Blackburn, the Chief Psychologist *b* of Park Lane Hospital whose evidence was that [the appellant] "is functioning now at a normal level"'. Then reference was made to Mr McVey, 'a nursing officer with considerable experience, well acquainted with [the appellant] who stated his confidence in the patient's ability to live outside hospital . . .' And again reference was made to Mr Sorrell, a charge nurse of experience, who had given evidence that he would 'welcome him as a next door neighbour'. *c*

By reason of that decision the appellant was released on 9 April 1985, but with very unhappy results. On 20 October 1985 he made an unprovoked attack on a girl aged 16 whom he saw walking along a road in the afternoon. He put both hands round her throat and squeezed, pushed her against a fence and told her to get over it or he would 'do her'. Eventually she managed to bend one of his thumbs back and he ran off. The *d* next night at about 11.30 pm, again without provocation, he attacked a woman aged 21. After speaking to her he held her neck in an armlock, put his hand over her mouth, pulled her into an entry and pushed her to a crouching position. She then pretended to weaken and flopped down; he began to let her go, and when she screamed he ran off. Neither of these victims was in any way known to him. Obviously these attacks were extremely frightening for the two victims concerned, but fortunately they were not *e* seriously hurt. When interviewed five days after the second attack, he said: 'I attacked a girl . . . I don't know why I did it.'

It is right to point out that, during his period of conditional release, both the RMO and the probation officer had made reports on their periodic visits to see him but none had contained a hint of impending violence.

Understandably a sexual motive for each assault was suspected but there was judged to *f* be insufficient evidence of it in either case and in consequence the prosecution accepted pleas from him of assault occasioning actual bodily harm in respect of the first victim and unlawful wounding in respect of the second victim. His pleas of guilty to those offences were given at the Crown Court on 14 April 1986.

In his plea in mitigation, very experienced leading counsel appearing for him had this, among other things, to say on his behalf: *g*

'Your Honour knows the history; it is terrible. He was subject to a life committal order under the Mental Health Act 1959 then in force, and a decision was ultimately taken that he should be let out on licence from Park Lane. Of course, he is for life subject to recall. It is now clear that a tragic and no doubt entirely genuine mistake was made by those who came to that decision . . . he is severely mentally disturbed. *h* He committed the offences, and there is no defence to them, but in considering sentence your Honour will no doubt wish to have in mind the moral and personal and public responsibility that lies on the defendant before you who is to be sentenced. In this case it is a man who, although not insane and therefore subject to legal responsibility, is so disturbed mentally that he cannot control the impulses from which he suffers . . .' *j*

A time came during the plea in mitigation when the judge asked:

'Am I right in thinking that there is no medical recommendation from any source available for me today? *Counsel:* There is no medical recommendation because, as your Honour will know, such a recommendation is only available if a there is treatment available and a place available for treatment and such treatment is regarded as being likely to be successful. I have a medical report which indicates that this man suffers from a severe personality disorder which is thought to be untreatable at the moment . . .'

That report was in fact dated 10 April 1986 from Dr Perera, a consultant forensic psychiatrist at Rampton Hospital. We have had a copy of it and the conclusion reached b by that doctor is as follows:

'[The appellant] certainly has a severe personality disorder, probably with some psycho-sexual involvement and alcohol problem. This, however, in my opinion, cannot be equated with a psychopathic disorder which needs or which would respond to treatment, and is not of a nature or degree which makes it appropriate for him to receive medical treatment in a hospital. In conclusion therefore, it is my c opinion that [the appellant] does not suffer from a mental disorder within the meaning of the Mental Health Act 1983. I do not believe that there is any treatment which could be offered to him in Rampton Hospital.'

In sentencing the appellant, the judge said:

d '. . . it is obvious from everything that I have been told about you and from what I have read about you that you are a very dangerous man, and you are dangerous in particular to young girls and to young women.'

The judge went on to describe what he had done as amounting to 'very serious assaults indeed'. The sentence was one of three years' imprisonment on each count consecutive, making a total of six years' imprisonment.

e On 30 June 1986 the appellant applied for his case to be considered again by a mental health review tribunal. That was held on 18 December 1986. He sought lifting of the conditions, which would have meant his absolute discharge. The Secretary of State made observations to the tribunal, including the following:

f 'The Home Secretary does not accept Dr MacCulloch's conclusion, in his report of 7 October 1986, that [the appellant] is no longer suffering from psychopathic disorder or any other form of mental disorder within the meaning of the Mental Health Act 1983. The Home Secretary had grave misgivings about Dr MacCulloch's contention (supported by other doctors) made at [the appellant's] previous Tribunal that [the appellant] was not then suffering from psychopathic disorder and considers that those misgivings have been fully confirmed by the two offences of which [the g appellant] has been convicted following his conditional discharge by that Tribunal . . . The Home Secretary considers that, in view of the circumstances of [the appellant's] index offence, the most recent offences and his previous history, restrictions upon his discharge should not be terminated so that, if it is deemed necessary in the interests of public safety, he can be recalled to hospital at the expiration of his current sentence of imprisonment or subsequently. In conclusion, h the Home Secretary urges the Tribunal to consider the evidence before it with the utmost caution. For the reasons already given, the Home Secretary believes serious doubts remain and that in a case of this gravity full weight should be given to considerations relating to the protection of the public.'

The tribunal's decision was that—

j 'no direction be made, save that the conditions of discharge be varied to provide that conditions as to residence, attendance for out-patient treatment, and supervision by a Probation Officer and Consultant Psychiatrist be suspended until the day of the applicant's release from prison.'

Their reasons for the decision were stated to be as follows:

'The Tribunal is satisfied that the Applicant is not suffering from any mental disorder. The Tribunal is of the view that it continues to be appropriate for the applicant to remain liable to be recalled to hospital for further treatment.'

The record goes on to say that the tribunal was satisfied about these reasons because:

'The Tribunal accept the views expressed in all the medical reports that the applicant does not suffer from psychopathic disorder.'

The appellant then challenged the tribunal's decision in the Divisional Court on the ground that, having found him not to be suffering from any form of mental disorder, he should no longer be subject to any of the provisions of the Mental Health Act 1983. Reliance in particular was placed on the definition of 'patient' in s 145 of the Act, namely that it means 'a person suffering or appearing to be suffering from mental disorder'. The challenge was unsuccessful, and the subsequent appeal to the Court of Appeal was dismissed in June 1989: see *R v Merseyside Mental Health Review Tribunal, ex p K* [1990] 1 All ER 694. In giving the first judgment, Butler-Sloss LJ said (at 699–700):

'The 1983 Act lays down a framework for the admission and detention, inter alia, of those convicted of crimes who are suffering from mental disorder and capable of being treated. There is thereafter a procedure designed to give them the opportunity of discharge into the community by application to an independent body, the mental health review tribunal. At the time the offender is detained under a hospital order he is a patient within the interpretation in s 145. By s 42(3)(a) a restricted patient continues to be liable to be detained until discharged under s 73 and, in my judgment, remains a patient until he is discharged absolutely, if at all, by the tribunal. Any other interpretation of the word "patient" makes a nonsense of the framework of the 1983 Act and the hoped-for progression to discharge of the treatable patient, treatable being a prerequisite of his original admission. Section 73 gives to the tribunal power to impose a conditional discharge and retain residual control over patients not then suffering from mental disorder or not to a degree requiring continued detention in hospital. This would appear to be a provision designed both for the support of the patient in the community and the protection of the public, and is an important discretionary power vested in an independent tribunal, one not lightly to be set aside in the absence of clear words. In my judgment, the appellant remains a patient in the context of this part of the 1983 Act until absolutely discharged.'

The appellant continued to serve his prison sentence at Albany Prison. His earliest date of release was 24 October 1989. Facing that prospect, the Secretary of State issued a warrant on 1 September 1989 that as soon as the appellant was released from prison he be taken to and detained in Broadmoor Hospital. A letter of the same date informing the appellant of the decision gave the following reasons for it:

'The Home Secretary, having considered the nature of your further offences of assault occasioning actual bodily harm and wounding, of which you were convicted on 14 April 1986, has concluded that he cannot be satisfied that you no longer present a serious risk to public safety, and he has therefore authorised your recall to Broadmoor Hospital under section 42(3) of the Mental Health Act 1983 when your prison sentence expires on 24 October 1989. Following your recall the Home Secretary is obliged under section 75(1)(a) of the Mental Health Act 1983 to refer your case to a Mental Health Review Tribunal no later than one month from the date of your return to hospital. When the case has been referred you will be notified by the Tribunal. The Tribunal will then decide, in accordance with criteria laid down in the 1983 Act, whether you should remain liable to be detained or whether you are entitled to be absolutely or conditionally discharged.'

The appellant then brought the present proceedings seeking an order of certiorari to quash the Home Secretary's warrant on the ground that it was issued unlawfully. McCullough J heard the application and gave judgment refusing it on 23 October 1989, the day before the appellant was due to be released from prison.

The first point taken by counsel for the appellant was that unless there was evidence of mental disorder at the time of the recall the appellant was not a 'patient' within the meaning of the expression in s 42(3), and the Secretary of State had no power to order his recall. He sought to distinguish the position here from that considered by this court in R v Merseyside Mental Health Review Tribunal, ex p K on the ground that the court was there considering the word 'patient' in s 73(2), which is in Pt V of the 1983 Act, while here the court is concerned with s 42(3) in Pt III of the Act. The Court of Appeal decision, he argued, only governs the word 'patient' when used in Pt V and he drew attention to the opening words of the definition section, s 145, namely: 'In this Act, unless the context otherwise requires . . .' In s 42(3), he submitted, there was nothing in the context requiring that a 'patient' be someone other than 'a person suffering or appearing to be suffering from mental disorder'.

However, it is to be noted that s 42(3) only has application in this case at all because s 73(4), which is of course in Pt V, says it shall. We see no reason to interpret 'patient' in s 42(3) in a different sense from 'patient' in s 73(2). Moreover, if one did, it would also be necessary to read s 42(2) in a different sense, which would make a nonsense of it, since the Secretary of State would then have power under it to discharge a person from hospital if he were suffering from mental disorder but not if he were not. Counsel for the appellant saw the force of that and did not pursue the point further.

Counsel's second point for the appellant is that s 42(3) should be construed so as to accord with art 5 of the European Convention on Human Rights (Convention for the Protection of Human Rights and Fundamental Freedoms (Rome, 4 November 1950; TS 71 (1953); Cmd 9869)). So far as material this reads:

'(1) Everyone has the right to liberty . . . No one shall be deprived of his liberty save in the following cases . . . (e) the lawful detention . . . of persons of unsound mind . . .'

He further placed reliance on various decisions of the European Court of Human Rights, the effect of which, he says, is that in this context detention cannot be lawful in the absence of evidence that the person detained is of unsound mind, which evidence was not available to the Secretary of State at the time he issued the warrant.

To consider this argument we look again at the words of s 42(3). It reads:

'The Secretary of State may at any time during the continuance in force of a restriction order in respect of a patient who has been conditionally discharged under subsection (2) above by warrant recall the patient to such hospital as may be specified in the warrant.'

It has been held by this court in R v Secretary of State for the Home Dept, ex p Brind [1990] 1 All ER 469, [1990] 2 WLR 787 that where the words of an English statute are plain and unambiguous it is not open to the courts of this country to look to the convention for assistance in their interpretation. The words of s 42(3) are in our judgment plain and unambiguous. There is no requirement there that the Secretary of State cannot by warrant recall a patient who has been conditionally discharged unless he has medical evidence that the patient is then suffering from mental disorder.

Counsel for the appellant submitted that if the section is given this literal interpretation the Secretary of State would be provided with an unbridled power at his whim and without cause to deprive a conditionally discharged patient of his liberty. That is only so, however, if one ignores the public law constraints recognised by the decisions in Associated Provincial Picture Houses Ltd v Wednesbury Corp [1947] 2 All ER 680, [1948] 1 KB 223 and Padfield v Ministry of Agriculture Fisheries and Food [1968] 1 All ER 694, [1968] AC 997.

Counsel for the appellant argues that, even if the convention cannot assist him, *Padfield*'s case should. The discretion given to the Secretary of State by s 42(3) can only be *a* used to promote the policy and objects of the Act, which are, according to his submission, that persons should not be deprived of their liberty unless they are shown, on the basis of objective medical evidence, to be suffering from mental disorder of such a degree as to warrant their compulsory confinement. In our judgment, that defines the policy and objects of the Act on far too narrow a basis. We prefer the view of McCullough J ([1990] 1 All ER 703 at 709, [1990] 1 WLR 168 at 174):   *b*

> 'These are to regulate the circumstances in which the liberty of persons who are mentally disordered may be restricted and, where there is conflict, to balance their interests against those of public safety.'

Counsel for the appellant relied on *X v UK* (1981) 4 EHRR 188. This decided that the United Kingdom was in breach of art 5(4) of the European Convention on Human Rights *c* because the power of recall under s 66(3) of the Mental Health Act 1959 was not accompanied by a provision which enabled the person thereby deprived of his liberty to take proceedings in which the lawfulness of his detention could speedily be determined by a court. That defect was in fact remedied by the inclusion of s 75(1) in the Mental Health Act 1983, and it is to be presumed that in framing the 1983 Act Parliament had the decision in *X v UK* in mind. None the less, it chose not to include a provision in *d* s 42(3) that the Secretary of State could only recall a patient if he acted on medical advice.

There are many powers in the 1983 Act which cannot be exercised save on the recommendation of one or more doctors. A good example is s 47(1), where the Secretary of State is empowered to direct by warrant that a person serving a sentence of imprisonment be removed to and detained in a hospital, but he can only do this if he is satisfied by reports from at least two doctors that 'the said person is suffering from mental *e* illness, psychopathic disorder, severe mental impairment or mental impairment'. It is, in our judgment, no accident or omission on the part of the legislature that under s 42(3) there is no requirement that the Secretary of State be satisfied by medical evidence that the person is suffering from mental illness, etc. The clear intention is that the Secretary of State be empowered in his discretion at any time during the continuance of a restriction order in respect of a patient to recall the patient to hospital. In exercising that *f* discretion, the Secretary of State will no doubt find it necessary to balance the interests of the patient against those of public safety. The intention of the 1983 Act is that the interests of the patient shall be safeguarded by the provision in s 75(1) that within one month of the patient being returned to hospital the Secretary of State must refer his case to a mental health review tribunal. Indeed, the very presence of that provision in the Act strengthens our belief that counsel for the appellant is wrong in his contention that by *g* reason of the policy and objects of the Act s 42(3) is to be construed as permitting the Secretary of State to recall a patient only if he is in possession of medical evidence that it is appropriate, or in any emergency, for example, if the patient is threatening violence.

For all these reasons counsel for the appellant has failed to persuade us that the Secretary of State has acted contrary to *Padfield* principles.

Counsel for the appellant asserts, however, that even so the Secretary of State's decision *h* is flawed because, judging by the terms of his letter of 1 September 1989, he addressed his mind only to the aspect of public safety and not also to the appellant's mental condition. We cannot accept that argument. It is quite apparent from the history of the Secretary of State's representations to successive tribunals and from para 13 of the affidavit of Nicholas Jordan, a civil servant in the Home Office, sworn on 19 October 1989, that *j* the Secretary of State has throughout had the appellant's mental condition very much in mind.

Finally, counsel for the appellant argues that the Secretary of State's decision to recall the appellant was *Wednesbury* unreasonable because: (1) there had been no change of circumstances since the decision of the tribunal in December 1986; (2) the Secretary of

State had no medical evidence that the appellant was now suffering from any mental
disorder; and (3) had the Secretary of State any doubts on that score his only proper
course would have been, well in advance of the appellant's earliest date of release, to ask
the appellant to subject himself to another psychiatric examination.

   Against these arguments the following factors must, in our judgment, be weighed.
(1) The appellant's record of offences of violence to women prior to the index offence.
(2) The nature of the index offence and the manner in which it was dealt with by the
court. (3) From 1970 to 1985 the diagnosis of the appellant was that he was suffering
from psychopathic disorder. (4) His commission of two further serious offences of
violence to women six months after his release from hospital. (5) The report of Dr Perera
from Rampton Hospital dated 10 April 1986. (6) What was said by the appellant's counsel
in his plea in mitigation on 14 April 1986. (7) When the tribunal made its decision on
18 December 1986 there was no question of the appellant's being released to the public
in general and young women in particualr for some years to come. (8) The unsatisfactory
nature of the RMO's report which was before the tribunal on 18 December 1986, notably
his apparent acceptance of the account that the appellant had given him of why he had
committed the offences of October 1985, the first being attributed to anger because the
girl (aged 16) had spoken to him in a hostile and aggressive manner and the second
because the young women had gone berserk when he no more than tapped her on the
shoulder, neither of which accorded with what prosecution counsel had, without dissent
from the defence, told the Crown Court judge were the facts of the offences. (9) The very
fact that no tribunal had seen fit to discharge the appellant absolutely meant that they
thought there was a danger of the appellant suffering a relapse. (10) Nearly three years
had in fact passed since a tribunal last looked at the case, during which time the appellant
had been in prison. (11) The best method of coming to an up-to-date conclusion on the
appellant's mental state and his possible danger to the public would be by another
reference to a tribunal which would base its conclusion on a number of recent psychiatric
reports on the appellant made in hospital rather than prison. (12) The Secretary of State
believed that such a tribunal might well conclude that the appellant is suffering from
psychopathic disorder.

   Taking account of all those factors, we find ourselves quite unable to say that the
Secretary of State's decision was irrational.

   Accordingly, we dismiss this appeal.

   We should add that, had we seen force in the contentions of counsel for the appellant,
we would none the less have exercised our discretion against granting the relief sought,
because of a report on the appellant dated 24 November 1989 from Dr Dooley, a
consultant forensic psychiatrist, which the court has looked at, in which the opinion is
expressed that the appellant continues to suffer from psychopathic disorder.

Appeal dismissed. Leave to appeal to the House of Lords refused.

Solicitors: *Irwin Mitchell*, Sheffield (for the appellant); *Treasury Solicitor*.

                                                          Celia Fox   Barrister.

Dance and another v Welwyn Hatfield District Council

COURT OF APPEAL, CIVIL DIVISION

SIR NICOLAS BROWNE-WILKINSON V-C, NOURSE AND McCOWAN LJJ

7, 8, 29 MARCH 1990

Housing – Local authority houses – Tenant's right to buy – Exclusion of right – Order for possession of property – Right to buy exercised before possession order sought – Local authority's duty to convey – Council tenants applying to exercise right to buy council house – Tenants paying deposit and exercising right to defer completion for three years – Council resolving to demolish house for redevelopment – Tenants requesting completion of purchase – Council serving notice on tenants seeking possession – Whether tenants having right to enforce sale of house – Whether council entitled to possession order – Housing Act 1985, ss 121(1), 138(1)(3).

On 11 June 1987 the plaintiffs, who were council tenants, applied to exercise their right to buy their council house under s 118(1)(a) of the Housing Act 1985 at the price proposed by the council. On 6 August the council's legal officer wrote to the plaintiffs informing them that he had been instructed to proceed with the sale. On 15 August the council's housing committee resolved that all buildings in the area of the plaintiffs' house should be demolished as part of a redevelopment scheme but the existence of the resolution was not then made known to the plaintiffs. On 29 September 1987 the plaintiffs paid a deposit of £150 and served notice on the council claiming the right to defer completion for three years, as they were entitled to do under s 142 of the 1985 Act. On 29 October the council's legal officer wrote to the plaintiffs acknowledging that the plaintiffs had chosen to defer the purchase for three years and confirming that the council had no plans for the compulsory purchase of any properties in the area. On 7 July 1988 the council informed the plaintiffs that it intended to demolish the plaintiff's house and that their deposit would be refunded. On 2 September the plaintiffs wrote to the council requesting completion of the purchase on 26 September. On 30 September the council served a notice on the plaintiffs seeking possession of the house under ground 10[a] to Sch 2 to the 1985 Act, ie on the ground that the council intended to demolish it. In November the plaintiffs issued county court proceedings to obtain an injunction under s 138(3)[b] of the 1985 Act directing the council to convey the house to them. By its defence the council contended that the plaintiffs' right to buy ceased to be exercisable if an order was made under s 121(1)[c] requiring the tenant to give up possession of the house, and it counterclaimed for possession of the house. The judge adjourned the plaintiffs' claim for an injunction and directed that the claim and counterclaim should be heard together. The plaintiffs appealed, contending that they were entitled to an immediate conveyance of the house to them.

Held – The council's letter of 6 August 1987 informing the plaintiffs that it would proceed with the sale amounted to an acknowledgment that all matters relating to the grant of a fee simple estate had been agreed and determined as contemplated by s 138(1) of the 1985 Act and accordingly the council was under a duty by virtue of s 138(1) to convey the freehold to the plaintiffs if and when it was requested to do so, which it was on 2 September 1988. That duty was enforceable by an injunction under s 138(3) and gave rise to a right vested in the plaintiffs which was analogous to the right to specific performance to enforce a contract for the sale of land. Accordingly, as from 2 September 1988 or at the latest 26 September, being the requested completion date, the plaintiffs became the equitable owners of the freehold by virtue of being entitled to enforce the

---

a Ground 10, so far as material, is set out at p 575 *g*, post

b Section 138, so far as material, is set out at p 574 *g* to *j*, post

c Section 121(1) is set out at p 574 *d e*, post

council's duty by injunction and had thus exercised their right to buy before any order
a was made under s 121(1) of the 1985 Act requiring the tenant to give up possession of
the house. The plaintiffs' appeal would be allowed and an order granted in a form
corresponding to an order for specific performance of an uncompleted contract (see p 577
b to *e g* to *j*, p 578 *d e j* to p 579 *a d f* to *h*, post).
   Enfield London BC v McKeon [1986] 2 All ER 730 distinguished.

b **Notes**
For local authority tenants' right to buy their homes, see 27 Halsbury's Laws (4th edn)
paras 886–905.
   For the Housing Act 1985, ss 118, 121, 138, 142, Sch 2, ground 10, see 21 Halsbury's
Statutes (4th edn) (1990 reissue) 148, 150, 168, 171, 579.

c **Cases referred to in judgments**
Enfield London BC v McKeon [1986] 2 All ER 730, [1986] 1 WLR 1007, CA.
London and South Western Rly Co v Gomm (1882) 20 Ch D 562, [1881–5] All ER Rep 1190,
   CA.

Cases also cited
d *Close v Steel Co of Wales* [1961] 2 All ER 953, [1962] AC 367, HL.
Grimshaw v Dunbar [1953] 1 All ER 350, [1953] 1 QB 408, CA.
Miller-Mead v Minister of Housing and Local Government [1963] 1 All ER 459, [1963] QB
   196, CA.
Norway's (State) Application (Nos 1 and 2), Re [1989] 1 All ER 745, [1990] 1 AC 723, HL.
Quinn v Leatham [1901] AC 495, [1900–3] All ER Rep 1, HL.
e *Sutton London BC v Swan* (1985) 18 HLR 140, CA.
Walsh v Lonsdale (1882) 21 Ch D 9, CA.

Appeal
The plaintiffs, Cyril Dance and Joan Dance, appealed against the order of his Honour
Judge John Hamilton made on 10 July 1989 in the Hertford County Court adjourning
f the plaintiffs' claim for an injunction requiring the defendants, Welwyn Hatfield District
Council, to convey to the plaintiffs the freehold of 29 Ravenfield Road, Welwyn Garden
City. The facts are set out in the judgment of Nourse LJ.

David Watkinson and *Stephen Cottle* for the plaintiffs.
John Haines for the defendants.
g

                                                                    Cur adv vult

29 March. The following judgments were delivered.

h **NOURSE LJ** (giving the first judgment at the invitation of Sir Nicolas Browne-
Wilkinson V-C). It is natural to expect that 'the right to buy', which was introduced by
the Housing Act 1980 and is now governed by Pt V of the Housing Act 1985, will bear a
strong resemblance to an option to purchase. In some respects it does. But because it is a
statutory and not a contractual right, from whose perfection the purchaser can desist at
any time before he has acquired the property, the resemblance is far from complete.
j Furthermore, allied to the right to buy is a right to a mortgage, in exercising which the
purchaser may be able to defer completion for up to three years. On the other side, the
rights cannot be exercised if the purchaser is obliged, whether immediately or
prospectively, to give up possession of the property under an order of the court, or if he
is bankrupt or in danger of becoming so.
   The interaction of these provisions and the problems to which they can give rise were
considered by this court in *Enfield London BC v McKeon* [1986] 2 All ER 730, [1986] 1

WLR 1007, a decision to which close consideration must be given in this case, whose
facts are not the same. Here the matter has reached the stage contemplated by s 138 of a
the 1985 Act (s 16 of the 1980 Act). The question is whether the defendants' duty under
that section to convey the property to the plaintiffs is modified by the claim for possession
which they have made, but in furtherance of which they have not obtained an order of
the court. The question largely depends on whether the right to buy has by that stage
been 'exercised' or not.

The plaintiffs, Mr Cyril Dance and his wife Joan, are the joint tenants of No 29 b
Ravenfield Road, Welwyn Garden City, a three bedroomed house of which the landlords
and freehold owners are the defendants, Welwyn Hatfield District Council. It is agreed
that for the purposes of the 1985 Act as amended, to which I shall henceforth refer
simply as 'the Act', the property is a dwelling-house of which the plaintiffs are the secure
tenants. It is also agreed that the right to buy the property, ie to acquire the freehold of
it, has arisen in their favour under s 118(1)(a) of the Act. c

The material provisions of the Act are lengthy and intricate. With two exceptions, I
propose to summarise their effect as briefly as I can.

Apart from s 138, the section on which the outcome of this case most depends is s 121,
which sets out the circumstances in which the right to buy, although it has arisen, cannot
be exercised: d

'(1) The right to buy cannot be exercised if the tenant is obliged to give up
possession of the dwelling-house in pursuance of an order of the court or will be so
obliged at a date specified in the order.

(2) The right to buy cannot be exercised if the person, or one of the persons, to
whom the right to buy belongs—(a) has a bankruptcy petition pending against him,
(c) is an undischarged bankrupt, or (d) has made a composition or arrangement with e
his creditors the terms of which remain to be fulfilled.'

Sections 122 to 125 provide for the tenant's exercise of the right to buy, for the landlord's
admission or denial of the right and, where the right is established, for notice to be given
of the purchase price which the landlord proposes and other matters. Sections 126 to 128
provide that the purchase price shall be the equivalent of the open-market value of the
dwelling-house, determined in the case of a dispute by the district valuer, less any f
discount to which the tenant is entitled under ss 129 to 131. Sections 132 to 137 make
provision for the tenant's right to a mortgage.

Section 138, so far as material, is in these terms:

'(1) Where a secure tenant has claimed to exercise the right to buy and that right
has been established, then, as soon as all matters relating to the grant and to the g
amount to be left outstanding or advanced on the security of the dwelling-house
have been agreed or determined, the landlord shall make to the tenant—(a) if the
dwelling-house is a house and the landlord owns the freehold, a grant of the
dwelling-house for an estate in fee simple absolute . . . in accordance with the
following provisions of this Part.

(2) If the tenant has failed to pay the rent or any other payment due from him as h
a tenant for a period of four weeks after it has been lawfully demanded from him,
the landlord is not bound to comply with subsection (1) while the whole or part of
that payment remains outstanding.

(3) The duty imposed on the landlord by subsection (1) is enforceable by
injunction.'
j

Section 139 provides for the terms and effect of the conveyance or grant and the
mortgage, if there is one. Sections 140 and 141 empower the landlord to serve two
successive notices to complete on the tenant, subject to the tenant's right to defer
completion, and so that if the tenant does not complete the landlord is no longer bound
to do so. Section 142 provides that in a case where he is not entitled to a full mortgage

the tenant is entitled to defer completion, provided that he has served an appropriate
a notice and deposited the sum of £150 with the landlord.

In the present case the plaintiffs' right to buy was admitted by the defendants, who
proposed a price which was acceptable to the plaintiffs. The plaintiffs then claimed the
right to a mortgage and they were notified of the amount which, in the opinion of the
defendants, they were entitled to leave outstanding on the security of the property. That
was not the full amount of the purchase price and so the plaintiffs became entitled to
b defer completion. By a letter dated 6 August 1987 the defendants' chief legal officer
informed the plaintiffs' solicitors that he had received instructions to proceed with the
sale. By a notice dated 29 September 1987 the plaintiffs, within the time allowed to
them, claimed the right to defer completion in accordance with s 142 of the Act. They
also deposited the sum of £150 with the defendants. It is agreed that, by virtue of
s 140(3)(c) of the Act, the effect of that was to entitle the plaintiffs to defer completion
c until 5 February 1990, being three years after the service of the plaintiffs' notice claiming
to exercise the right to buy under s 122(1). By a letter dated 29 October 1987 the
defendants' chief legal officer acknowledged that the plaintiffs had chosen to defer their
purchase for three years.

The letter of 29 October 1987 also confirmed that there was no planned compulsory
purchase by the defendants of any properties in Ravenfield Road. The true position was
d that on 15 August 1987 the defendants' housing committee had resolved to demolish all
buildings in the area in order to make way for a redevelopment scheme. That was not
made known to the plaintiffs until they received a letter from the defendants dated 7 July
1988, in which they were informed that the defendants intended to carry out demolition
in the area and that the proposals included No 29 Ravenfield Road. They were also told
that it was proposed to refund their deposit of £150 to them as soon as possible. However,
e by a letter dated 2 September 1988 the plaintiffs' solicitors wrote to the defendants as
follows:

> 'We refer to previous correspondence in this matter, and our Clients would like
> to complete this purchase on Monday, the 26th September. Accordingly, we enclose
> herewith the Transfer duly signed by our Clients, for sealing by the Council. If this
f > date is not convenient, please let us know as soon as possible.'

On 30 September the defendants served on the plaintiffs a notice seeking possession of
the property on ground 10 in Pt II of Sch 2 to the Act, which, so far as material, reads:

> 'The landlord intends, within a reasonable time of obtaining possession of the
> dwelling-house—(a) to demolish or reconstruct the building or part of the building
g > comprising the dwelling-house . . . and cannot reasonably do so without obtaining
> possession of the dwelling-house.'

No accommodation having been reached between the parties, on 24 November 1988
the plaintiffs issued proceedings in the Hertford County Court claiming an injunction
pursuant to s 138(3) of the Act directing the defendants to convey the property to them
h as required by sub-s (1)(a) of that section. By their defence and counterclaim the
defendants asserted their right to possession of the property and contended that the
plaintiffs' right to buy ceased to become exercisable 'if an Order is made pursuant to
section 121(1) of the said Act.' They requested that the plaintiffs' claim for injunctive
relief should be adjourned until the defendants' claim for possession had been determined.

In due course the matter came on for hearing before his Honour Judge John Hamilton.
j On 10 July 1989 the judge delivered a full and careful judgment, to which this court is
indebted for its consideration of the material provisions of the Act and their bearing on
the facts of this case. If left to himself, the judge would have held that the defendants'
duty to convey the freehold under s 138(1)(a) had arisen. But he thought that the decision
in *Enfield London BC v McKeon* [1986] 2 All ER 730, [1986] 1 WLR 1007 obliged him to
decide to the contrary. In the end he acceded to the defendants' request to adjourn the

plaintiffs' claim for an injunction until the merits of the defendants' claim for possession
had been determined. He directed that the two claims should be heard together. The   *a*
plaintiffs now appeal to this court, renewing their claim for an immediate injunction.

Enfield London BC v McKeon was decided under the 1980 Act as amended by the
Housing and Building Control Act 1984. For the sake of convenience, I will continue to
refer to the corresponding provisions of the 1985 Act. The material facts of that case
were these. The tenant served on the council a notice claiming to exercise the right to
buy under s 122(1). The council then served a notice admitting the right to buy under   *b*
s 124. The next thing which happened was that the council served on the tenant a notice
indicating its intention to seek possession of the property on ground 16 in Pt III of Sch 2
to the Act, namely that the accommodation was more extensive than was reasonably
required by the tenant. Some seven weeks later the council, pursuant to the obligation
imposed on it by s 125, served on the tenant a notice containing the particulars required
by that section. Two months later the council issued proceedings, claiming possession on   *c*
ground 16. Although it is not clear whether the price proposed by the council had been
accepted by the tenant, it is, I think, clear that a stage had not been reached when, for the
purposes of s 138(1), all matters relating to the grant and to the amount to be left
outstanding or advanced on the security of the property had been agreed or determined.
The facts accordingly differed from those of the present case in an important respect.

It was argued on behalf of the tenant that the right to buy had been 'exercised' for the   *d*
purposes of s 121(1) when she had served her notice under s 122(1). As to that, Slade LJ,
with whose judgment the other member of the court, Eastham J, agreed, said ([1986] 2
All ER 730 at 736, [1986] 1 WLR 1007 at 1014):

> 'According to usual legal terminology, an ordinary option to purchase is, I think,
> commonly regarded as being exercised at the moment when notice is first given of   *e*
> the donee's intention to exercise the option. Correspondingly, on a first reading of
> s [121(1)], I was inclined to think that the tenant's right to buy must be "exercised"
> for the purpose of that subsection at the moment when he serves his notice under
> s [122(1)] (which is also the "relevant time" for ascertaining the purchase price
> payable (see s [125(2)(a)], and at no other time. Nevertheless, I am now satisfied that
> this is not the correct way to read the word "exercised" in the particular context of   *f*
> s [121]. In my judgment, the right is "exercised" each and every time when the
> tenant takes any step towards the implementation of his right to purchase.'

Slade LJ then said that he was particularly fortified in that conclusion by three
considerations, the third of which was that, if the tenant's submissions were correct, the
right to compel completion would not be affected in any way if at the date of completion   *g*
a bankruptcy petition was pending against her. He continued ([1986] 2 All ER 730 at
737, [1986] 1 WLR 1007 at 1015):

> 'In my judgment, the short answer to the tenant's point of law is that, for the
> purpose of applying s [121] (on the true construction of which her case depends) the
> [Act] treats a tenant as purporting to exercise his right to buy at any time and from   *h*
> time to time when he takes steps towards implementation of that right, up to and
> including completion of the purchase. If, therefore, any of the circumstances set out
> in [s 121] subsist at any time between the time when he serves his s [122(1)] notice
> and completion, his right to buy ceases to be exercisable.'

Counsel for the defendants submitted that the decision in Enfield London BC v McKeon   *j*
is binding on this court and, moreover, that it is decisive of this case. He relied particularly
on the view of Slade LJ that the Act treats a tenant as purporting to exercise his right to
buy at any time and from time to time when he takes steps towards implementation of
that right 'up to and including completion of the purchase'. Although others might have
preferred the simple view of s 121(1) which had been urged on Slade LJ and Eastham J

by the tenant, we must certainly accept that their decision is binding on us. I do not,
however, think that it is decisive of this case. Although the words of Slade LJ on their
face apply here, the decision is only a binding authority for cases where the facts are the
same. As I have already pointed out, the facts of this case are different. Indeed, the facts
of the *McKeon* case were such that it never became necessary to consider s 138, to whose
effect on the facts of this case I now turn.

By his letter of 6 August 1987 the defendants' chief legal officer informed the plaintiffs'
solicitors that he had received instructions to proceed with the sale of the property.
Subject perhaps to a notification by the plaintiffs that the amount to be left outstanding
on the mortgage was acceptable to them, that was effectively an acknowledgment that
all matters relating to the grant and to the amount to be left outstanding or advanced on
the security of the dwelling house had been agreed or determined as contemplated by
s 138(1). Accordingly, as recognised by that letter, the defendants had already come
under a duty to convey the freehold to the plaintiffs if and when they were requested to
do so. No request was made at that time, because on 29 September 1987 the plaintiffs
exercised their right to defer completion. But that deferment was brought to a premature
end by their solicitors' letter of 2 September 1988 requesting completion on 26 September
following. At that stage, by virtue of s 138(3), the defendants' duty to convey the freehold
became enforceable by injunction.

What was the effect of the coming into operation of s 138(3)? There was some debate
as to the intention of Parliament in making the duty to convey enforceable by injunction.
It was suggested that it was in order to make good the inability of the county court to
grant an order by way of mandamus. I do not think that the reason is important. What
is important is that the tenant's remedy is an injunction, that is to say an order that the
landlord shall convey to him the legal estate in the property. The right to an injunction
in a case where there is no contract cannot be any different in its incidents from the right
to an order for specific performance in a case where there is a contract, as to which I need
only cite a passage from the well-known judgment of Jessel MR in *London and South
Western Rly Co v Gomm* (1882) 20 Ch D 562 at 581, [1881–5] All ER Rep 1190 at 1193:

> 'The right to call for a conveyance of the land is an equitable interest or equitable
> estate. In the ordinary case of a contract for purchase there is no doubt about this,
> and an option for repurchase is not different in its nature. A person exercising the
> option has to do two things, he has to give notice of his intention to purchase, and
> to pay the purchase-money; but as far as the man who is liable to convey is
> concerned, his estate or interest is taken away from him without his consent, and
> the right to take it away being vested in another, the covenant giving the option
> must give that other an interest in the land.'

Although that was a case of a contractual option to purchase, the principle is the same.
Here the equitable interest in the property is acquired by the tenant directly the landlord's
duty to convey arises and becomes enforceable by injunction under s 138. Subject to
payment of the purchase price and execution of the mortgage, if there is one, by the
tenant, the landlord is bound to convey to him the legal estate in the property.

Although neither s 142 nor s 140(3)(c) contains any express provision bearing on the
point, it was not suggested by counsel for the defendants that the three-year deferment
period could not be prematurely determined by the tenant. I am in no doubt that that is
a correct view of the matter. I therefore conclude that as from 2 September or, at the
latest, 26 September 1988 the plaintiffs, being entitled to enforce the defendants' duty by
injunction, became the equitable owners of the freehold in the property. At that stage, if
not beforehand, they must, on any natural use of language, have 'exercised' their right to
buy for the purpose of s 121(1). At that stage there was no order of the court obliging
them to give up possession of the property. Nor had any proceedings been commenced.
Nor had the plaintiffs ever been served with a formal notice requiring them to give up
possession. In the circumstances, I do not see how s 121(1) can be said to affect the matter.

I should add that I was at one time, although I am no longer, troubled by s 122(3), which provides that the tenant's notice claiming to exercise the right to buy under *a* sub-s (1) of that section 'may be withdrawn at any time by notice in writing served on the landlord'. The effect of sub-s (3), as I understand it, is that the tenant may withdraw from the purchase at any time up to actual completion. It was suggested by counsel for the defendants that the tenant's ability to withdraw his notice showed that the right to buy had not been exercised. I do not think that that suggestion is correct. If the right to withdraw is relied on by a tenant who has already become entitled to enforce the *b* landlord's duty under s 138(1), admittedly the right to buy will cease to be *enforceable*. But that does not mean that it has not already been *exercised*. That is a distinction which was correctly made by Judge Hamilton.

Counsel for the defendants submitted that the judge's decision to adjourn the plaintiffs' claim for an injunction can in any event be supported on the ground that an injunction is a discretionary remedy. That may or may not be correct in this context, but, if it is, it *c* is correct only to a limited extent. I have already compared the injunction which is available under s 138(3) with an order for specific performance. The comparison may or may not be exact, but the injunction cannot be *less* readily available than an order for specific performance, which, although it is a discretionary remedy, is refused only on well settled grounds, for example hardship to the party against whom it is granted. No such grounds are alleged by the defendants in this case. There is no ground on which the *d* injunction can properly be refused.

I fully recognise that to distinguish this case from the *McKeon* case will leave the law in a somewhat unsatisfactory state. It is perhaps inevitable that novel legislation of this kind will give rise to difficulties which can only be identified on a case-by-case process. Be that as it may, I am in no doubt that the distinction ought to be made and we in this court are in a better position to make it than was Judge Hamilton in the court below. *e*

I would allow the appeal and make an order in a form corresponding with an order for specific performance of an uncompleted contract.

McCOWAN LJ. In this case it is not in dispute that the position had been reached by the beginning of September 1988 where under s 138(1)(a) of the Housing Act 1985 the plaintiffs were entitled as against the defendants to 'a grant of the dwelling-house for an *f* estate in fee simple absolute'. There was, moreover, no question of the plaintiffs having 'failed to pay the rent or any other payment' due from them within the terms of sub-s (2). Accordingly, the plaintiffs were entitled, pursuant to sub-s (3), to enforce the duty imposed on the defendants by sub-s (1)(a) by injunction.

The plaintiffs' solicitors, as was therefore their right, wrote to the defendants on 2 September 1988 saying: *g*

'... our Clients would like to complete this purchase on Monday, the 26th September. Accordingly, we enclose herewith the Transfer duly signed by our Clients, for sealing by the Council.'

The defendants did not complete on 26 September 1988. In fact they did not reply to *h* that letter. Instead, on 30 September 1988 they wrote to the plaintiffs enclosing a notice seeking possession of the house on the ground that they intended to demolish it.

From receipt of the letter of 2 September the defendants were under a duty to convey the house to the plaintiffs on or before 26 September. It follows that from that date the defendants were in breach of their statutory duty to convey the house, and the plaintiffs were entitled to an injunction to enforce that duty. It would, in my view, be very *j* regrettable if the defendants could, by refusing or failing to carry out their statutory duty, improve their position. Therefore, unless I am obliged by the words of the statute or by authority to decide otherwise, I would hold that, certainly by the time 26 September 1988 had passed, it was too late for the defendants to take steps to defeat the plaintiffs' entitlement to completion.

Section 121(1) of the Act could not assist the defendants at the hearing before the judge
a because at that date it was not possible to say that 'the tenant is obliged to give up
possession of the dwelling-house in pursuance of an order of the court or will be so
obliged at a date specified in the order'.

What then of the decision of this court in *Enfield London BC v McKeon* [1986] 2 All ER
730, [1986] 1 WLR 1007? I agree with the judge in the present case that—

b   'the *Enfield* case could have been decided on the narrow ground that the tenant
there had no right to enforce her right since the relevant matters still fell to be
determined or agreed, and thus the right could not have been said to have been
exercised to the point where it became enforceable.'

However, considering the basis on which the case was in fact decided and adapting Slade
LJ's words ([1986] 2 All ER 730 at 737, [1986] 1 WLR 1007 at 1015) to the corresponding
c sections of the later Act, they would read:

'If, therefore, any of the circumstances set out in [s 121] subsist at any time
between the time when he serves his [s 122] notice and completion, his right to buy
ceases to be exercisable.'

When the present case was before his Honour Judge John Hamilton, the plaintiff was
d there and then indefeasibly entitled to completion, and none of the circumstances set out
in s 121 subsisted. Hence the present case is, in my judgment, distinguishable from that
of *McKeon*.

Before us, counsel for the defendants put the matter in this way: 'I accept the judge
had a discretion to grant the plaintiffs the injunction they sought. Had he done so, I
could not have complained. But he chose to exercise his discretion by adjourning the
e application in order to hear at the same time the defendants' claim for possession. Unless
it can be said that that exercise of discretion was wholly wrong, this court should not
interefere.'

In my judgment, the judge had, in the circumstances of this case, no discretion to
refuse the plaintiffs an injunction, and no question therefore arose, as the judge thought,
of a 'balancing exercise required to exercise the discretion either to grant or refuse an
f injunction and consequently to grant or refuse an order for possession'. Accordingly, I do
not consider that he had a discretion to adjourn the matter to allow the defendants to get
their claim for possession before the court.

If, contrary to that view, the judge had a discretion, his exercise of it was, in the light
of the following circumstances, plainly wrong: (1) the due date for completion had
passed before the defendants served their notice of seeking possession; (2) the defendants
g came before the judge admittedly in breach of their statutory duty to convey; (3) the
plaintiffs were entitled when the case came before the judge to the injunction they
sought; (4) the plaintiffs were not then under any of the disabilities set out in s 121 of the
Act; and (5) the defendants' reason for seeking an adjournment was purely in order to
get before the court an application for relief which might enable the defendants, despite
their breach of duty to the plaintiffs, to defeat their claim.
h I would, therefore, allow this appeal and grant the plaintiffs the order they seek under
s 138(3) of the 1985 Act.

SIR NICOLAS BROWNE-WILKINSON V-C. I agree with both judgments.

j *Appeal allowed. Leave to appeal to the House of Lords refused.*

Solicitors: *Graham Fear & Co*, Enfield (for the plaintiffs); *W J Anderson*, Welwyn Garden
City (for the defendants).

Celia Fox   Barrister.

Re F (a minor) (adoption order: injunction)

FAMILY DIVISION

DOUGLAS BROWN J

24, 25 APRIL 1990

Adoption – Order – Terms and conditions which may be imposed – Injunction restraining natural parents from making contact with child and adoptive family – Whether court having jurisdiction to grant injunction as term of order – Adoption Act 1976, s 12(6) – Supreme Court Act 1981, s 37(1).

A baby girl, whose natural parents suffered from chronic schizophrenia and had spent long periods under psychiatric care, was taken into care soon after her birth and placed in foster care. The natural parents had intermittent access to the child when she was with short-term foster parents. However, when she was placed with long-term foster parents access to the natural parents was terminated. The natural father subsequently discovered the address of the foster parents and visited their home and wrote aggressive letters to them opposing any adoption. As a result an injunction was granted restraining him from communicating with the child or the foster parents or from going within 500 yards of their home. When the foster parents applied to adopt the child the natural father opposed the application because he wished to resume contact with the child. There was professional evidence supporting the adoption and indicating that a close bond had developed between the child and the foster parents. The question arose whether the court could grant an injunction as a 'term' of any adoption order made under s 12(6)[a] of the Adoption Act 1976. The father contended that although under s 12(6) the court could make an adoption order subject to such terms and conditions as it thought fit an injunction could not be 'a term or condition' of an order.

Held – Since it was clearly in the child's best interests to make an adoption order in favour of the foster parents and since from the point of view of the hypothetical reasonable parent the child's welfare and her sense of security and stability would be best achieved by the adoption, an adoption order would be granted and the consent of the natural parents dispensed with on the ground that they were withholding their consent unreasonably. On the question of whether an injunction should issue the court had a wide discretion under s 12(6) of the 1976 Act to grant an injunction as a term of the adoption order in appropriate cases where it was necessary to safeguard and promote the welfare of the child. Alternatively, the court had a discretion under the wide jurisdiction conferred by s 37(1)[b] of the Supreme Court Act 1981 to grant a final injunction at the end of the proceedings. Since the child's welfare demanded the security of an injunction in order to keep the natural father from her home an injunction would be granted, either as a term of the adoption order or under s 37(1), restraining the father from communicating with the child or the foster parents or from going within 500 yards of their home (see p 585 g to j, p 586 a b g and p 588 c to e, post).

Re C (a minor) (adoption: conditions) [1988] 1 All ER 705 followed.

Notes

For the making of adoption orders, see 24 Halsbury's Laws (4th edn) paras 654–663, and for cases on the subject, see 28(3) Digest (2nd reissue) 360–395, 3213–3375.

For the Adoption Act 1976, s 12, see 6 Halsbury's Statutes (4th edn) 450.

For the Supreme Court Act 1981, s 37, see 11 ibid 792.

---

a   Section 12(6) is set out at p 587 f, post

b   Section 37(1) is set out at p 587 h, post.

Cases referred to in judgment

a C (a minor) (adoption order: conditions), Re [1988] 1 All ER 705, [1989] AC 1, [1988] 2 WLR 474, HL.
C (a minor) (wardship: adopted child), Re [1985] FLR 1114.
V (a minor) (adoption: consent), Re [1988] 1 All ER 757, [1987] Fam 57, [1986] 3 WLR 927, CA.

b Application
The husband and wife applied to adopt a young girl born in 1982. The natural parents opposed the application. The Official Solicitor, as guardian ad litem of the mother, a patient under a disability, whilst not consenting on her behalf, did not oppose the application. The application was heard and judgment was given in chambers. The case is reported by permission of Douglas Brown J. The facts are set out in the judgment.

c Anthony Radevsky for the applicants.
Richard H Bond for the guardian ad litem of the natural mother.
Rozanna Malcolm for the natural father.
Alison Ball for the guardian ad litem of the child.

d DOUGLAS BROWN J. This is an application made under the confidential serial number procedure by a husband and wife for the adoption of a young girl, F, who was born on 15 May 1982, and who is therefore eight next month. Her parents do not consent to the adoption, although in reality the opposition has come from the father as the mother is a patient under disability within the meaning of rules of court, and the Official Solicitor, as her guardian, whilst not consenting on her behalf because that would e be directly contrary to her wishes, has not actively opposed the application and has left it to the court's discretion.

The parents are JF (the mother) and RF (the father). F became a ward on 9 July 1982 because of serious concerns as to the mother's ability to care for her. In fact, a few weeks earlier, on 23 June a place of safety order was applied for by the local authority and granted by the magistrates. The mother, most unhappily, has suffered for many years f from severe chronic schizophrenia. She has spent long periods in psychiatric hospitals suffering from persecutory delusions, auditory hallucinations and thought disorders.

The father, who is also a chronic schizophrenic, was until very recently (about a month ago) represented by a guardian ad litem himself. He is at present in remission and able to instruct solicitors and counsel, which he has done.

F was placed with two sets of foster parents and was with each foster parent for a g considerable time. The move from one to the other was traumatic and disturbing, and that is an important part of the history of this little girl, and her move to the applicants in March 1985 was again far from easy because she had successfully bonded with the second foster parents, but she has been with the applicants now from that time, from the age of three. That is approximately five years.

h Access to her parents took place at approximately fortnightly intervals from August 1982 until April 1984, since when no access has taken place of any structured kind. In October 1984 Ewbank J gave leave for F to be placed with long-term foster parents, ie the applicants, and ordered that there be no access in the future for the parents. There was access of a brief and unsanctioned nature in 1986 when the father discovered where the applicants lived and he went to their home. Exactly what transpired on that occasion, j and what happened between him and F, is certainly not clear in the evidence and I make no finding about it, but what there is no doubt about is that in 1986 the father wrote two letters to the applicants purporting to come from both himself and his wife. I read them in full because, together with evidence that the father went to the house and that telephone calls were made on a number of occasions which disturbed the applicants until they changed their telephone number (those calls not being directly attributed to either the mother or the father), because of those concerns and those events there is an application for continued injunctive relief ordering the father and the mother (although it is principally the father) not to go to the applicants' home and not to communicate with F. Those letters are in these terms. The first of them is dated 7 March 1986 but was in fact delivered in October, addressed to the applicants and it clearly comes from the parents because their address on a printed sticker is at the top of the letter:

'We are [F's] parents. We strongly object to an arrangement that has kept [F] away from us and urge you to decline from applying to adopt our child as this concept is totally against our wishes. If [F] was old enough to understand, it would be rejected by her, and we must say will be fought daily by ourselves with no restraint until [F] is in her rightful place with us, however long it may take. We must also point out to you that should [F] be adopted there will be reprisals from us and [F] which will make you regret the day you took custody of our little daughter. Your involvement with [F] would prove to be financially, emotionally and psychologically disabling to you, your greatest mistake. From, Mr and Mrs [F].'

Then there is a postcript:

'We suggest you have your own child or adopt an orphan.'

Then there is a letter dated 18 September 1986 to the applicants:

'Further to our March '86 letter to you, if we do not have [F] returned to us before she reaches the age of five years and there is no indication that you intend to release her from your household, with written confirmation of this intention sent to us at the above address before the start of October '86, we will take unrelenting appropriate action against you which would include reprisals for which there was justification. Eventually our daughter will know the truth directly from us. Yours vengefully, Mr and Mrs [F].'

Those letters are also very important to the submissions of the applicants and the view of the guardian ad litem of F that the father is a man who does put his own interests first regardless of any effect that this conduct might have on the child.

At the date of those letters there had only been one appearance of any note before a judge of this division, but in 1987 the matter came before Swinton Thomas J. By then a brother had been born for F on 26 May 1986. He was made a ward very soon after birth and placed with foster parents. His future as well as F's was considered before Swinton Thomas J. Both the mother and father were represented and they called psychiatric evidence as well as their own, and the judge heard (and indeed preferred) the evidence of other consultant psychiatric witnesses that were called. The judge did not accept that either parent would be able to give either child the degree of care they required. I refer only briefly to part of the judgment of the judge. He said:

'I have to evaluate the risks which would be attendant on an order which involved the return of one or other or both of these two children to their parents, and against that the risks which are involved in not returning them to their parents and placing them with foster parents, or in the case of [F], leaving her with foster parents with whom she has now been living for a period of time. I have to try and evaluate the level of care which the children would receive in the parents' home or in the alternatives' home. I believe, based on the evidence I have heard in this case, that there must be a real risk that the health of the mother and of the father (particularly the mother) may break down from time to time in the future. The proposed return of the two children, one now aged nearly five, and the other aged nearly one, would inevitably impose considerable stress and strain on them, and it is highly likely that the children, particularly the older child, would be considerably disturbed (at least at the outset). The stress, if it was imposed on the parents, would involve the risk of further breakdown in their health. Based on the evidence which I have heard, I do

not believe or accept that the parents would be able to give either child the degree
of care that they require.'

He then proceeded to make the order, having said:

> 'Placing as I do at the very forefront of my mind the concept that it must be best
> in the ordinary circumstances of the children to be cared for by their own parents,
> and weighing that particular factor very heavily in the balance, I must take the
> course with these two children which is in *their* best interests. They will need a good
> deal of security and stability in the future. They need now one home where they
> will remain and where they will be settled. It is absolutely vital that their emotional
> needs should be met. I do not believe that the parents will be able to supply those
> much-needed and necessary requisites to these children.' (Swinton Thomas J's
> emphasis.)

He goes on to express a view of very great sympathy with these two parents.

At the time of the hearing before the judge the mother was pregnant with a third
child by the father, a girl who was born on 11 May 1987. She was warded at birth or very
shortly afterwards, and has been placed with the same foster parents as the boy. The
evidence is that there has been no access to those children for the parents since the end of
1988. Indeed, these foster parents themselves have been granted leave to commence
adoption proceedings in respect of the two children.

Turning to F herself, she is a child of mixed race, ie of white and West Indian
extraction. The male applicant is white and the female applicant is of West Indian
extraction. The male applicant is 44 years of age and the female applicant some 10 years
older. She was married before and has a son who is now grown up. The male applicant
was not previously married and he, of the two, gave evidence before me. They are clearly
a mature, sensible couple. He is a professional man and she is a personal secretary. All
the evidence points to F being very closely bonded with them and thriving with them.
There has been no meaningful contact with either parent for some six years, and very
little before that. The father has never at any time had the care of F.

The guardian ad litem for this child strongly supports the adoption as being in F's best
interests. The local authority as well, in their material presented to the court in the usual
way, again support the adoption. The Official Solicitor, representing the mother, having
obtained psychiatric evidence and indeed having considered evidence from Dr Helene
Palasidou, senior registrar on psychiatry at Kings College Hospital, Denmark Hill, who
gave evidence on behalf of the father before me, but who is also the psychiatrist having
the care of the mother, came to the conclusion that there was no basis on which she could
realistically oppose the application to dispense with the mother's consent.

The father's former guardian ad litem, Mr Ian Israel, a very experienced court welfare
officer, formed the same opinion and that would have been his evidence and opinion to
Eastham J, before whom this hearing was to have taken place in March but it was
adjourned then because the father was able to present evidence of a psychiatric nature to
indicate that he was now able to conduct his own affairs so far as litigation was concerned,
and he now, as I have said, appears by counsel. He also has the support of the organisation
MIND and I have had a letter put before me (but not the evidence) of an official of that
organisation, Mr Benton, who has very clearly set out the case for the father, the case
which the father himself repeated, and which certainly in part was repeated by the
psychiatrist who gave evidence on behalf of the father.

The father accepts, or certainly accepts now (whether he did in the past is another
matter), that there is no realistic prospect of him being able to care for F, and certainly
not for his wife caring for her, and he therefore supports long-term fostering to the
applicants but he opposes adoption for a number of reasons.

He gave evidence at length. He has provided an affidavit and before Eastham J his
solicitor exhibited some reasons shortly and concisely setting out his case. I summarise
the father's case. The strength of the blood tie is something that he very much stresses

before me and it is something that in his 13 points, as they have been called, features
strongly. He wants to play a part, and, if she is able to, his wife, in F's upbringing, and as   *a*
he puts it, 'to help the applicants raise the child'.

As there is a measurable risk of F herself suffering from schizophrenia, which Dr
Palasidou put it at between 30% to 36%, and indeed there is no serious contest that there
is a risk of that disorder, then, says the father, he ought to be on hand to help and give
his daughter informed care and assistance which only a fellow sufferer can give, and he
can see in her someone who has survived and is able to lead, under medication, a   *b*
reasonable life.

The evidence seems to be, although it was not something canvassed with the
psychiatrist when she gave evidence, that the condition in a child will not show itself. It
is only when the child becomes a young person in late teens or even in the early twenties
that the condition will manifest itself. What the father says is that before that situation is
reached then not only ought the child to be made aware of her mother and father by   *c*
contact with them but also she ought to be made aware of the nature of schizophrenia
and, when she is older, made fully aware of what it can do so that she is prepared for
either herself having it or her brother and sister.

He wants her to have access to her brother and sister now and that is a point where
there is no dispute between the parties because the applicants say that it is their intention
soon to introduce F to her brother and sister.   *d*

The 13 points I need not read out in any detail but it is worth, I think, referring to
point B, because in it the father refers to his condition and to his medication and he says
this: the doctors have said that as long as he remains on medication there is no need for
him realistically ever to have a breakdown again. Indeed, that is absolutely true.

The difficulty in the father's case is that he does not always take his medication. If he
does take it, and it can be difficult and distressing to take, involving two visits a week to   *e*
hospital for injections, then there is a very small risk of hallucinations and delusions
breaking out, but, if he does not take it and if he breaks down in his medication, then
there is a very strong risk of his condition returning. This was something that was
actively considered in the hearing before Swinton Thomas J and it is apparent from the
judgment that the father had told the judge that he was taking his medication regularly
and had every intention of continuing to do so in the future. Indeed that is what the   *f*
father has told me, and indeed it is right to say that Dr Palasidou has noted in the six
months she has had him as a patient a very considerable improvement.

I think everyone connected with this case is pleased to hear that the father is making
some progress, but one must not be too starry-eyed about this; although he has made
progress, he has made promises before about keeping to his medication. There was
exhibited to Mr Israel's affidavit earlier this year a letter from Dr O'Brien, who is registrar   *g*
to the consultant psychiatrist who had charge of the father, and in that letter he said:

> 'As to prognosis this is difficult to judge because [the father's] medical condition
> and insight may stay at its current level, improve or worsen, and this fact is largely
> determined by the extent to which he carries on complying with medication on   *h*
> discharge. However, as past performance is often the best predictor of future events,
> it seems highly likely that [the father] will default from medication and become ill
> again in the future.'

Dr O'Brien was there reviewing a long psychiatric history, going back some 19 or 20
years, and looking not just at a six-month period but at the history which he used as a   *j*
predictor.

I sincerely hope that the father's condition will now remain as it is, and indeed
improve, and that he will continue to take his medication and that the optimism of
Dr Palasidou is justified. But, if it is not, then it has to be recognised that his condition is
one which would bar him from contact with his daughter completely. There is no doubt

that he has had serious delusions and hallucinations and when he is suffering from
a schizophrenia he suffers in a considerable way.

But the father says, 'I do not want to see her if I am suffering from schizophrenia in an active way.' The proposal that is put forward is that he should only see his daughter when the psychiatrist says that it is safe for him to do so, that a few days or so before an arranged access visit (which itself should be supervised) he should see his psychiatrist, who should give him the all-clear (or the contrary) whether it would be all right for him to see his
b daugher, ie that he continued to be in remission.

The other matter, which is not unimportant, is in relation to religion. The father is of the Jewish faith and he is very anxious that his daughter be brought up with a full awareness of the fact that she is Jewish.

The father's case is that he is opposed to adoption; he wants the fostering to continue, and he wants contact to be renewed, but, if the court orders otherwise and contrary to
c his wishes an adoption order is made, then he wishes the court as a condition attached to that order to order that there be access to him, and indeed, although the mother does not ask for it, he says the mother should have access as well, and that the access should be of the kind that I have mentioned, infrequent (perhaps four times a year), supervised and prefaced by a visit to his psychiatrist to see that he is still in a fit condition to see his daughter. The advantages of F seeing the father would be numerous. She would be able
d to have firsthand knowledge, not just from a story book, which he accepts is being kept (although not in a particularly adequate or detailed way), that he would be able to counsel her, as he puts it, in relation to schizophrenia and that he would be able to help the foster parents (or, in this alternative case, the adopting parents) in bringing up his daughter. He would be able to talk to her about important things, help her with her education and help her with any problems that she had.

e He does not see that there would be any harm or stress caused to his daughter in his reappearing on the scene and indeed in this he is supported by Dr Palasidou. Dr Palasidou, who is not a child psychiatrist, and she acknowledged that when she made this comment, says that it could be for the benefit not only of her patient (and it would be undoubtedly for his benefit) but it could be for F's benefit to see her father.

f Her lack of knowledge of F's situation really prevented her from taking the matter further than that. She has seen virtually none of the papers in this matter; she only saw the two letters when they were produced to her in court; there has been no application for the wardship papers to be released to her; she has not seen F and has no idea at all of the circumstances as to her first foster parents and this change to the second foster parents, or how she has progressed during the time that she has been with the applicants; above all, her speciality is not child psychiatry. But she offered that view and I have to take
g account of it.

At the end of the day I have to say that I agree with counsel for the applicants that the evidence in support of an adoption order being made is really overwhelming. All the professional evidence points in the direction that that is an order which is overwhelmingly in F's best interests.

h As to the withholding of consent, having every sympathy for the position of the mother and the father, I have to say that, in the words of the statute, they are withholding their consent unreasonably. Looking at the matter from the point of view of a hypothetical reasonable parent, such a person would be driven to the view that it is in F's best interests for her security and stability to be achieved by the adoption order being made.

j I can see how it is an attractive idea to the father that from his point of view an adoption order would take away much that is precious to him, but I have to put myself in the shoes of the objective reasonable parent, and the evidence really is overwhelming that in F's interests this order should be made. She is living with an admirable family, who have given her love and stability and security now for some five years. Her connection with her parents is now sadly extremely tenuous, if not non-existent. Indeed, all that probably remains is the blood tie and what is contained in her life story book, which tells her that she does have natural parents, that they are ill and that they have not *a* been able to look after her for most of her life.

I am satisfied that if an adoption order was not made (and this is something that must have impressed the hypothetical objective parental observer) this young girl would lose a considerable amount of her security. She is aware of these proceedings; she is aware that an adoption order is being sought, and, although she may not fully understand what is involved, she knows that it is sealing her relationship and her place in the applicants' *b* home. I accept that she is terrified of being removed from the applicants and anything which reassures her on those lines must be in her interests, and indeed on the evidence in this case nothing less than adoption will do.

So far as access is concerned, access is strongly opposed by the adopting parents, it is strongly opposed by the guardian ad litem on behalf of F herself, even supervised access. I need only refer to this short passage in a draft proof of evidence adopted by the guardian *c* ad litem of F, and put in today, where she says this:

'I have not discussed the specific question of supervised access visits from her natural parents with [F] because since she has no memory of her parents this would probably generate a great deal of anxiety for her and feed her existing insecurities, whilst contributing nothing, to my understanding of her preferences in this matter.' *d*

Then she says this:

'Supervised access from [Mr and Mrs F] would in my view threaten [F's] fragile but growing sense of security. As a result, I do not believe supervised access from [F's] natural parents is in her best interests.' *e*

I completely agree with that. I think it would be wholly wrong, where the adopting parents opposed access and where there has been no effective contact between F and her parents for years, it would be completely wrong to impose on her now a regime of access. Again, distressing though that may be for the father and (if she learns of it) the mother, I have no doubt, looking at it from the child's point of view, that that is the correct course. *f* So I decline to add to the adoption order which I will make any order as to access.

There remains the question of an injunction. After the events in 1986, the letters, the visit, there was an injunction imposed in wide terms and there was some evidence of a breach of it; although committal proceedings were dealt with by way of undertakings, there has been no effective breach of the injunction for some three years, but I have no doubt that both these parents, particularly the father, should be restrained in future from *g* interfering with the applicants in any way and, I regret to say, from communicating with F or coming within 500 yards of any place where she may live with her adoptive parents.

The father, I strongly suspect, still has a deep obsession about his child and her adoption. That is the fear of the applicants and I think that it is justified. There are protestations from him in evidence that he has behaved himself, that he will continue to *h* do so. It may be, when he is fully in control of himself, that that is the stance to which he will adhere. But I have considerable doubts whether he will remain fully in control of himself, and the letters show that he is quite insensitive to the interests of the applicants and F. I have seen and heard him and I have some doubts as to how capable he is of appreciating how an attack on the security of the applicants would be likely to affect the peace of mind of the child. I have no doubt that that would be the direct effect of any *j* attempt by the father to reintroduce himself into F's life. I am far from certain that he has given up the struggle. The matter is put very clearly in the supplementary report of the guardian ad litem and I can do no better than quote from it in a very short passage:

'It is clear however that the fear of [the father] visiting is both real and justified. I a   am concerned about the effect of such anxieties on [F], who as I have already noted, is a somewhat insecure child.'

She then goes on to discuss how a condition might be attached to the adoption order.

I am grateful to all four counsel for their help in resolving the question of how such an order should be made. I am told, and indeed there is authority referred to, that a practice in similar cases has been for the wardship to continue after the adoption order has been made but with most of the restraints of wardship inconsistent with full parental
b   rights being removed, but within the wardship an injunction being granted, and a bar being placed on applications to the court in the wardship by the natural parents.

An example of that, which in fact arose some time after the adoption order had been made, can be seen in Re C (a minor) (wardship: adopted child) [1985] FLR 1114, where Bush J made an order giving the adopters general liberty to exercise all normal parental duties and directing that no application should be made in the wardship by the natural
c   mother save with the leave of the court and that such application should not be served on the adopters save with the leave of the court. But the applicants in this case are concerned that following that practice will give rise to dangers and risks of the wardship being reactivated with the accompanying disturbance, distress and worry to the applicants, which without doubt would in some way find itself communicated to the
d   child. Adoption really should put an end to worries of that kind.

Of course, if leave is required, leave would have to be applied for, but the practical approach of experienced counsel, with which I am bound to say I agree, is that when applications are made ex parte to the applications judge, however cautious and careful he might be, there may be occasions when he has not before him all the material he should have to arrive at a correct conclusion on an application for leave of this sort. It might be
e   that applications for leave would be granted and then the whole matter might be reopened, certainly until a judge fully seised of the matter was able to bring it to an end. That is not a fanciful fear on the part of the applicants, and indeed on the part of the guardian ad litem, who, after some considerable heart-searching as to the state of the law, now supports the applicants in this solution, a solution to be found from the very wide discretion given to the court under s 12(6) of the Adoption Act 1976, repeating provisions
f   already enacted in the Children Act 1975. That subsection reads in this way: 'An adoption order may contain such terms and conditions as the court thinks fit.'

Counsel for the father, who has taken every legitimate point with skill on his behalf says that an injunction does not fall within the description of 'terms'. It is clearly not a condition, neither is it (she says) a term, and the statute provides no justification for an injunction being made under that provision.
g   As to the suggestion that s 37 of the Supreme Court Act 1981 might be invoked, that (she says) has to attach to something, to some proceedings, and the proceedings (she says) are at an end when the adoption order is made. Section 37(1) reads thus:

'The High Court may by order (whether interlocutory or final) grant an injunction or appoint a receiver in all cases in which it appears to the court to be just and
h   convenient to do so.'

Counsel says that if an injunction has to be imposed here it should be done within the wardship, which should be kept in being.

Counsel for the applicants, supported by counsel for the guardian ad litem, referred me to Re C (a minor) (adoption: conditions) [1988] 1 All ER 705 at 712, [1989] AC 1 at 17, the principal speech being that of Lord Ackner. My attention was drawn to Lord Ackner's
j   speech where it deals with the very wide nature of the discretion contained in s 12(6). The passage referred to begins:

'Counsel for Mrs B conceded that the terms of s 8(7) of the 1975 Children Act (now replaced by s 12(6) of the Children Act 1976) were unambiguous and on the face of the subsection there was jurisdiction to impose any terms or conditions that the court thought fit. She, however, in essence, repeated the unsuccessful submission made in *Re V (a minor) (adoption: consent)* [1986] 1 All ER 752, [1987] Fam 57 ... *a* that the subsection only enabled the attachment of such terms and conditions as the court could see would be immediately fulfilled or met and not conditions which involved the intervention or supervision of the court in the future. Thus in her submission the decisions of the Court of Appeal which, expressly or by necessary implication, decided the contrary were wrong. I cannot agree. It seems to me essential that, in order to safeguard and promote the welfare of the child throughout *b* his childhood, the court should retain the maximum flexibility given to it by the Act and that unnecessary fetters should not be placed on the exercise of the discretion entrusted to it by Parliament.'

Emboldened by Lord Ackner's description of the section and his emphasis on the words 'maximum flexibility' it does seem to me that in an appropriate case where it is necessary to safeguard and promote the welfare of the child the Act is wide enough to *c* justify the grant of an injunction. This is such a case. This child's welfare, it seems to me, demands the security of an injunction to keep away from the home where she will live with her adoptive parents a father who can only bring, sadly, intrusion and stress into her life, if not directly on her, then on those who care for her. In those circumstances I propose to make an injunction in the same terms as has been previously granted under *d* s 12(6). The injunction will be a term of this adoption order.

If that is held to be a wrong view, then in my judgment the wording of s 37(1) of the Supreme Court Act 1981 is by its very wide terms apt to cover this situation. It does seem to me just and convenient to grant a final injunction at the end of these adoption proceedings, and I do so in the alternative, in the same terms as the parents have been restrained heretofore. In the result I make an adoption order, an order that the name be *e* recorded in the register of adopted names as the child's name with the applicants' surname.

Order accordingly.

Solicitors: *Glazer Delmar* (for the applicants); *Official Solicitor*; *Hornby & Levy* (for the *f* natural father); *Hilarie Clifford & Co* (for the guardian ad litem of the child).

Bebe Chua   Barrister.

Hammersmith and Fulham London Borough Council v Secretary of State for the Environment
and other appeals

QUEEN'S BENCH DIVISION

LEGGATT LJ, McCULLOUGH AND ROCH JJ

5, 6, 7, 8, 11, 15 JUNE 1990

COURT OF APPEAL, CIVIL DIVISION

LORD DONALDSON OF LYMINGTON MR, RALPH GIBSON AND TAYLOR LJJ

19, 20, 21, 22, 25, 26, 27 JUNE, 3 JULY 1990

HOUSE OF LORDS

LORD BRIDGE OF HARWICH, LORD BRANDON OF OAKBROOK, LORD OLIVER OF AYLMERTON, LORD GOFF OF CHIEVELEY AND LORD JAUNCEY OF TULLICHETTLE

10, 11, 12, 16, 17 JULY, 4 OCTOBER 1990

Local government – Community charge – Charge capping – Power of Secretary of State to charge cap local authorities – Whether Secretary of State's decision to charge cap local authorities susceptible to judicial review – Local Government Finance Act 1988, s 100.

The Local Government Finance Act 1988 replaced the rating system of local government finance and taxation with a new system commencing on 1 April 1990. A central feature of the new system was the community charge which local authorities that were charging authorities were entitled to set under the 1988 Act and which was payable by adult residents to raise part of its annual revenue, the balance being provided by central government by revenue support grant and a payment out of non-domestic rates. The scheme for local finance under the 1988 Act provided for each local authority to be notified by the Secretary of State of the amount it would receive by way of revenue support grant and non-domestic rates and the amount of its standard spending assessment, ie the amount which it was estimated that the authority would require to spend in the year to maintain a level of services to a common standard determined by reference to the total amount available for spending by all authorities. The authority could then set its community charge to make up the balance, but if it set its budget at a level which the Secretary of State considered was excessive in accordance with principles determined by him under s 100(4)^a of the 1988 Act he was empowered under the Act to 'charge cap' the authority by designating it under s 100 and specifying its maximum expenditure for the year. After local authorities had set their budgets for the year beginning on 1 April 1990 the Secretary of State charged capped 21 local authorities. In doing so the Secretary of State made no distinction between the different classes of authorities. Nineteen of the charge-capped authorities challenged the legality of his action in proceedings for judicial review. The Divisional Court dismissed the applications and the Court of Appeal affirmed its decision. Sixteen of the authorities appealed to the House of Lords, contending, inter alia, that the Secretary of State's action contravened the 1988 Act because (i) before designating a particular authority the Secretary of State was required to decide on an ad hoc basis whether that authority's budget was excessive, taking into account all the individual circumstances affecting the authority, and in forming his opinion whether the budget was excessive he was not entitled to determine what the norm of local authority expenditure ought to be and then decide according to that norm that the

---

a   Section 100, so far as material, is set out at p 631 *e* to *h*, post

budget was excessive, (ii) the Secretary of State had acted unreasonably in charge capping individual authorities according to the norm of local authority expenditure, (iii) the *a* designation notices did not comply with the requirements of the 1988 Act because the principles on which a particular authority's expenditure was determined under s 100(4) to be excessive were not the same for all authorities of the same class, (iv) the Secretary of State's action in designating the authorities was irrational and procedurally irregular and (v) it was to be implied in the 1988 Act in the interest of fair procedure that the Secretary of State was under an obligation to consult local authorities before determining the *b* principles on which he would act under s 100(4) in relation to designation and that, having determined those principles, he was required to announce them before authorities set their budgets so that those budgets could be set at a level which avoided charge capping.

Held – An administrative decision taken by the Secretary of State to charge cap a local *c* authority by designating it pursuant to s 100 of the 1988 Act and to set a maximum amount for the authority's budget lower than the amount which the authority thought it appropriate to raise by way of community charge was essentially a matter of political judgment of what was the appropriate level of expenditure justifying designation, since under the 1988 Act the ceiling levels of expenditure to which local authorities had to conform had to be set by the Secretary of State according to criteria of general application *d* and not ad hoc on a case-by-case basis and the decision was dictated by the principles formulated under s 100(4) of the Act, which were designed to ensure even-handed treatment of different authorities in the same class and to settle the norm which would provide the basis of the opinion of the Secretary of State as to what constituted excessive budgeting. Accordingly, provided the Secretary of State's decision was taken in good faith within the four corners of the 1988 Act and he complied with the procedural *e* requirements of the Act his decision was not susceptible to judicial review. Furthermore, the designation notices complied with the Act, notwithstanding that the principles determined under s 100(4) were not the same for all authorities in the same class, because although the principles to be applied to all authorities were the same the Act did not require that every principle should be capable of application to every authority. There was, moreover, no basis on which to imply a statutory obligation to consult local *f* authorities before determining the principles on which the Secretary of State proposed to act in relation to designations under s 100, and therefore the fact that the Secretary of State made no prior announcement of the principles did not render his decision unlawful. Since the procedure laid down by the Act had been duly followed and there was no suggestion that the Secretary of State had acted in bad faith there were no grounds for judicial review of his decision. The appeals would accordingly be dismissed (see p 633 *f* *g* to *h*, p 634 *c* to p 635 *a*, p 636 *e* to *g*, p 637 *b* to *e*, p 638 *b f h* to p 639 *b d j* to p 640 *b e* to *g*, post).

Nottinghamshire CC v Secretary of State for the Environment [1986] 1 All ER 199 applied.

Secretary of State for Education and Science v Tameside Metropolitan Borough [1976] 3 All ER 665 distinguished.

h

Notes

For the Secretary of State's powers to limit the amount which a charging or precepting authority intends to raise from its community charges or precept, see Supplement to 28 Halsbury's Laws (4th edn) para 1260B.

For the Local Government Finance Act 1988, s 100, see 25 Halsbury's Statutes (4th *j* edn) (see below) (1990 reissue) 1031.

Cases referred to in judgments and opinions

A-G v Ryan [1980] AC 718, [1980] 2 WLR 143, PC.

A-G of Hong Kong v Ng Yuen Shiu [1983] 2 All ER 346, [1983] 2 AC 629, [1983] 2 WLR 735, PC.

Associated Provincial Picture Houses Ltd v Wednesbury Corp [1947] 2 All ER 680, [1948] 1
a KB 223, CA.
Council of Civil Service Unions v Minister for the Civil Service [1984] 3 All ER 935, [1985] AC
   374, [1984] 3 WLR 1174, HL.
Durayappah v Fernando [1967] 2 All ER 152, [1967] 2 AC 337, [1967] 3 WLR 289, PC.
Hillingdon London BC v Commission for Racial Equality [1982] AC 779, [1982] 3 WLR 159,
   HL.
b Hoffmann-La Roche (F) & Co AG v Secretary of State for Trade and Industry [1974] 2 All ER
   1128, [1975] AC 295, [1974] 3 WLR 104, HL.
Kanda v Government of the Federation of Malaya [1962] AC 322, [1962] 2 WLR 1153, PC.
Liverpool Taxi Owners' Association, Re [1972] 2 All ER 589, sub nom R v Liverpool Corp,
   ex p Liverpool Taxi Fleet Operators' Association [1972] 2 QB 299, [1972] 2 WLR 1262,
   CA.
c McInnes v Onslow Fane [1978] 3 All ER 211, [1978] 1 WLR 1520.
Nottinghamshire CC v Secretary of State for the Environment [1986] 1 All ER 199, [1986] AC
   240, [1986] 2 WLR 1, HL.
Padfield v Minister of Agriculture Fisheries and Food [1968] 1 All ER 694, [1968] AC 997,
   [1968] 2 WLR 924, HL.
Payne v Lord Harris of Greenwich [1981] 2 All ER 842, [1981] 1 WLR 754, CA.
d Pergamon Press Ltd, Re [1970] 3 All ER 535, [1971] Ch 388, [1970] 3 WLR 792, CA.
Preston v IRC [1985] 2 All ER 327, [1985] AC 835, [1985] 2 WLR 836, HL.
Public Service Board of New South Wales v Osmond [1987] LRC (Const) 681, Aust HC.
R v Brent London BC, ex p Gunning (1985) 84 LGR 168.
R v Gaming Board for GB, ex p Benaim [1970] 2 All ER 528, [1970] 2 QB 417, [1970] 2
   WLR 1009, CA.
e R v Secretary of State for the Environment, ex p Brent London BC [1983] 3 All ER 321, [1982]
   QB 593, [1982] 2 WLR 693, DC.
R v Secretary of State for Transport, ex p Factortame Ltd Case C-213/89 [1990] 3 WLR 818,
   CJEC and HL.
Ridge v Baldwin [1963] 2 All ER 66, [1964] AC 40, [1963] 2 WLR 935, HL.
Secretary of State for Education and Science v Tameside Metropolitan Borough [1976] 3 All ER
f 665, [1977] AC 1014, [1976] 3 WLR 641, CA and HL.
Wiseman v Borneman [1969] 3 All ER 275, [1971] AC 297, [1969] 3 WLR 706, HL.

Application for judicial review
Nineteen local authorities, viz Hammersmith and Fulham London Borough Council,
Derbyshire County Council, Islington, Greenwich, Camden and Southwark London
g borough councils, Doncaster and Rotherham metropolitan borough councils, Bristol City
Council, Lambeth London Borough Council, North Tyneside Metropolitan Borough
Council, Avon County Council, St Helens, Calderdale and Rochdale metropolitan
borough councils, Brent London Borough Council, Basildon District Council, Haringey
London Borough Council and Barnsley Metropolitan Borough Council each applied with
h the leave of Hodgson J given on 24 April 1990 (in respect of applications made in open
court) and on 30 April 1990 (in resepct of applications dealt with on the documents) for
judicial review by way of (i) an order of certiorari to quash the designation of the local
authority by the Secretary of State for the Environment under s 100 of the Local
Government Finance Act 1988 for the financial year beginning 1 April 1990,
(ii) alternatively, a declaration that the designation by the Secretary of State was ultra
j vires and of no effect, (iii) an order of certiorari to quash the notice of designation and (iv)
a declaration that the Secretary of State was obliged before exercising his powers under
s 104(2) of the 1988 Act to provide to a council designated by him the reasons why he
proposed the amount he did under s 102(1)(c) and/or any potentially adverse information
received by him under s 110(8) of the 1988 Act from a source other than the council
itself, and related matters. The National Union of Teachers, Michael Heiser, chairman of
the governors of William Gladstone Community School, Brent, and Maureen Parris,

chairman of the governors of Brentfield Junior and Infant School, Brent, were given leave
to be heard. The facts are set out in the judgment of the court.

a

Roger Henderson QC and *Timothy Mould* for Haringey, Islington and St Helens.
James Goudie QC and *Nigel Giffin* for Avon, Barnsley, Brent, Bristol, Lambeth and North
  Tyneside.
Roger Henderson QC and *Alan Wilkie* for Camden, Doncaster and Rotherham.
Roger Henderson QC for Greenwich.

b

Alan Newman QC and *Philip Engelman* for Derbyshire.
Anthony Scrivener QC and *Ian Croxford* for Basildon, Calderdale and Hammersmith and
  Fulham.
Anthony Scrivener QC and *Tobias Davey* for Rochdale.
Stephen Sedley QC and *Anthony Bradley* for Southwark.
Eldred Tabachnik QC and *Gavin Millar* for the National Union of Teachers.

c

Lord Gifford QC and *Kate Markus* for the chairmen of the Brent school governors.
John Laws, Presiley Baxendale and *Paul Walker* for the Secretary of State.

Cur adv vult

d

15 June. The following judgment of the court was delivered.

LEGGATT LJ.

INTRODUCTION

All the applicants complain of having been designated. That is the first stage of a
statutory process designed by Parliament to further twin policies of reducing local
government expenditure and protecting community charge payers. The statutory process
is intended to result in what has become known as 'charge capping'. The applicants have
sought to invoke the intervention of the court to avoid apprehended hardship. Without
the authority of the House of Commons the Secretary of State cannot carry the proposed
charge capping into effect. He has stated that he will not before 18 June 1990 ask the
House for approval of the order that he needs. So we have accepted to give our judgment
before that date. The result is that, although we are clear in our conclusions, the
presentation of them may not be felicitous.

e

f

The nature of the applications

On 3 April 1990 the Secretary of State for the Environment designated 20 English
councils pursuant to s 100(2) of the Local Government Finance Act 1988 in relation to
the financial year 1990–91, and by notice of the same date made under s 102(1) of the
Act he communicated to each of them the fact that he had done so. On 10 April 1990 he
made a further such designation and notice in respect of one further council. Each of the
councils designated (except Wigan) applied, pursuant to leave, for an order of certiorari
to remove into this court and quash the decision to designate and the notice of
designation, together with consequential declarations and orders. Since proceedings were
instituted, Hillingdon London Borough Council has desisted in its application. In
addition, the National Union of Teachers (the NUT) and two school governors (in the
London borough of Brent) were heard by leave. They have an interest in opposing the
charge capping of local education authorities, lest in consequence schools budget shares
be cut.

g

h

j

With the co-operation of all the applicants attempts were made to co-ordinate the
efforts of the lawyers, and in particular to counsel, so as to avoid duplication. In the
result, the burden of presenting the applications in this court has been divided between
counsel who represent applicants either in combination or individually.

a Material to these applications are five of the classes of council identified by s 100(5) of the Act, namely (a) county councils, and the councils of (b) metropolitan districts, (c) non-metropolitan districts, (d) inner London boroughs and (e) outer London boroughs. Between these classes the applicants are distributed as follows: (a) Avon and Derbyshire; (b) Barnsley, Calderdale, Doncaster, North Tyneside, Rochdale, Rotherham and St Helens; (c) Basildon and Bristol; (d) Camden, Greenwich, Hammersmith and Fulham, Islington, Lambeth and Southwark; and (e) Brent and Haringey.

b Save for Avon and Derbyshire, which are precepting authorities, all of the applicants are charging authorities.

It is convenient at the outset to summarise the applicants in a table showing in relation to each its class for purposes of s 100(5), its community charge, its budget figure and the amount of the cap proposed by the Secretary of State:

COMMUNITY CHARGES

c

Authority	Class	Community charge	Budget	Proposed cap
Avon	a	—	£533·700m	£507·1m
Derbyshire	a	—	£560·568m	£520·6m
Barnsley	b	£329	£141·952m	£132·0m
d	Basildon	c	£478	£27·884m	£23·7m
Brent	e	£498	£249·285m	£241·7m
Bristol	c	£490·23	£64·217m	£56·6m
Calderdale	b	£296·57	£132·866m	£125·4m
Camden	d	£534	£181·433m	£177·0m
Doncaster	b	£334	£190·068m	£178·5m
e	Greenwich	d	£408	£213·021m	£203·0m
Hammersmith	d	£424·22	£167·521m	£155·8m
Haringey	e	£572·89m	£216·530m	£206·5m
Islington	d	£498·62	£189·501m	£185·8m
Lambeth	d	£547·89	£293·924m	£285·1m
f	North Tyneside	b	£399	£129·744m	£122·9m
Rochdale	b	£386	£152·018m	£144·0m
Rotherham	b	£334	£165·441m	£157·5m
Southwark	b	£390	£241·037m	£226·9m
St Helens	b	£410	£126·745m	£122·8m

Budgets and charge capping

g Counsel have aptly described these processes, starting with s 95(4) of the Act which imposes on each local authority the duty to calculate how much it needs to raise by way of community charge. Section 90 identifies the collection fund as the fund into which all income from community charges, non-domestic rates and revenue support grant has to be paid, and out of which it is to meet precepts issued to it and, through its general fund, its own budgetary requirements. The authority is obliged by s 97 to transfer from its
h collection fund to its general fund the amount equal to that calculated under s 95(4). Each charging authority is also obliged to set an amount for its personal community charge so as to secure that the total amount yielded is sufficient, after allowing for income from other collection fund transactions, to provide for any precept issued to it and the amount of its s 95(4) calculation.

j The Secretary of State is given the power to designate an authority by reference, inter alia, to his view of its s 95(4) calculation. He has to be of the opinion that the calculation by that authority is 'excessive' within the meaning of s 100(1)(a). By s 100(4) the Secretary of State has to decide whether or not to designate in accordance with principles determined by him. Those principles must be the same for all authorities within the same class, the classes being those set out in s 100(5). There is an exemption from designation for authorities whose s 95(4) calculation is (for this year) less than £15m. If the Secretary of State decides to designate he must, at the same time, notify the authority *a* under s 102(1) of (a) his decision, (b) the principles determined in relation to it under s 100(4) and (c) the amount he proposes shall be the maximum to be calculated by it under s 95(4) (the cap). There is an appeal or review procedure which under s 102(5)(*a*) the authority may invoke within 28 days of notification by informing the Secretary of State of the amount it states should be the maximum and its reasons for so stating. The authority may instead do nothing or it may inform the Secretary of State under s 102(5)(*b*) *b* that it accepts the proposed cap.

The level of revenue support grant (RSG) and its distribution derive from reports which the Secretary of State is obliged to make pursuant to ss 78 and 80 of the Act. The starting-point for this exercise is the Secretary of State's assessment of the total sum which would be appropriate for the local authorities to incur in 1990–91 on revenue expenditure in providing a standard level of service, which in this year is £32·8bn, as announced on *c* 19 July 1989. This is known as total standard spending (TSS). Roughly speaking, one-third of local authorities' expenditure is financed by grants from central government (principally RSG) and one-third from non-domestic rates (now shared nationally), leaving the remaining one-third to be raised by community charges. Part of the means used by the Secretary of State to distribute grant is the standard spending assessment (SSA). It postulates a common standard consistent with local authorities as a whole spending *d* £32·8bn. The Secretary of State distributed his RSG to local authorities by reference to an SSA. The local authorities prepared their budgets and calculated their s 95(4) amounts which they submitted to the Secretary of State in March 1990.

The Secretary of State then considered whether to exercise his power to designate local authorities. He in fact chose to divide local authorities into three groups and to apply slightly different principles to each. These groups are inner London boroughs, the *e* councils of the city of London and the rest. The principles for each group contain substantial common elements, including in particular a test for excessiveness and also a 'de minimis' rule. The Secretary of State decided that the test for excessiveness would have a 'combined criterion' comprising two components: (i) a percentage overspend against SSA (12½%) and (ii) a per adult overspend against SSA (£75 per head), both of *f* which had to be satisfied before spending could be characterised as 'excessive'. The 'de minimis' rule was that no local authority be designated unless chargepayers would be saved at least £26 per head.

The statutory framework

It is necessary to examine the statutory framework (as Mr Griffin helpfully did in *g* grounds for relief drafted by him) in a little more detail. The system for financing local government in England and Wales has been substantially changed from 1 April 1990 through the coming into effect of the relevant provisions of the Act. A main element of the new system is the community charge. This is a system of taxing individuals, as opposed to the former rating system, which taxed properties. Further, the old rate support grant system has been replaced by the new RSG. *h*

For each chargeable financial year, a charging authority must set as its personal community charge an amount or amounts in accordance with ss 32 and 33 of the Act.

So far as material, s 32 provides:

'. . . (3) In setting any amount the authority must secure (so far as practicable) that the total amount yielded by its community charges for the year is sufficient to *j* provide for the items mentioned in subsection (4) below, to the extent that they are not to be provided for by other means.

(4) The items are—(*a*) any precept issued to the authority for the year, (*b*) the authority's estimates of the aggregate of the payments to be set from its collection fund in the year under section 90(2)(*b*) to (*g*) below or section 90(4)(*b*) and (*c*) below (as the case may be), (*c*) the amount calculated (or last calculated) by the authority in

a   relation to the year under section 95(4) below, and (d) the authority's estimate of the
amount to be transferred from its collection fund in the year under section 98(4)
below . . .'

Pursuant to s 89 of the Act, each charging authority established a collection fund into
which and out of which all income and expenditure relevant to these applications are to
be paid.

b   For each chargeable financial year a precepting authority must issue precepts to the
charging authorities within its area in accordance with s 68 which provides for precepts
to be issued corresponding with the sums to be calculated by authorities under s 95(2)
that are set out later in this judgment.

The new RSG system is established by Pt V of the Act. Part V itself, however, provides
only the barest framework. Pursuant to s 78, the Secretary of State determines (subject to
c   the approval of the House of Commons) the global amount for distribution. Pursuant to
s 80(1) he makes a report (the distribution report) setting out the basis on which he
proposes, subject to any report under s 84 (special provision for transitional years), to
divide the global amount between authorities. By s 80(3) the distribution report is to be
laid before the House of Commons. If the House of Commons approves the distribution
report by resolution, it comes into force on the day stated in the report.

d   There is no statutory requirement that the principles by which the RSG is distributed
should be principles applicable to all authorities. Pursuant to s 82(1) of the Act the
Secretary of State calculates what sum is to be paid to each authority by way of RSG, in
accordance with the basis of distribution set out in the distribution report. That sum is
then payable under s 83.

Before a charging authority can calculate the amount to be set by way of community
e   charge, as required by s 32, there are certain prior calculations which must be made,
pursuant to s 95 of the Act, as amended by Sch 5, para 63 to the Local Government and
Housing Act 1989.

So far as material, s 95 provides:

'. . . (2) The authority must calculate the aggregate of—(a) the expenditure the
f   authority estimates it will incur in the year in performing its functions in the year
and will charge to a revenue account for the year; (b) such allowance as the authority
estimates will be appropriate for contingencies in relation to expenditure to be
charged to a revenue account for the year; (c) the financial reserves which the
authority estimates it will be appropriate to raise in the year for meeting the
estimated expenditure referred to in subsection (2A) below; (d) such financial
reserves as are sufficient to meet so much of the amount estimated by the authority
g   to be a revenue account deficit for any earlier financial year as has not already been
provided for; and (e) any amounts it estimates will be charged to a revenue account
in respect of the authority's general fund or City fund, as the case may be, by virtue
of a transfer,—(i) pursuant to regulations under section 89(5) above, of such an
additional sum as is referred to in subsection (3)(d) of section 98 below; or
h   (ii) pursuant to a direction under subsection (5) of that section, of such an amount as
is referred to in that subsection.

(2A) The estimated expenditure referred to in subsection (2)(c) above is—(a) that
which the authority estimates that, in the financial year following the year in
question, it will incur, will charge to a revenue account and will have to defray
before sums to be transferred as regards that year from its collection fund to its
j   general fund or to the City fund (as the case maybe) become sufficiently available;
and (b) that which the authority estimates it will incur in the financial year referred
to in paragraph (a) above or any subsequent financial year in preforming its
functions and which will be charged to a revenue account for that or any other year.

(2B) References in subsection (2) and (2A) above to expenditure incurred by the
authority shall be construed in accordance with section 41(3) of the Local
Government and Housing Act 1989.

subsection (5) above, the Secretary of State may decide whether to exercise his powers, and how to perform his functions, under this Part on the basis of such *a* assumptions and estimates as he sees fit.

(8) In deciding whether to exercise his powers, and how to perform his functions, under this Part the Secretary of State may also take into account any other information available to him, whatever its source and whether or not obtained under a provision contained in or made under this or any other Act.'

b

The government's approach

The government's approach to charge capping is best seen from the affidavit sworn on behalf of the Secretary of State by Paul Rowsell, who is an assistant secretary in the Department of the Environment. He says:

'. . . the Government sought the legislation enacted in the 1988 Act to secure that local authorities would be properly accountable to their electorate. It is the policy of *c* the Government that, to promote local accountability, the level of an authority's budget ought to be a matter between the authority and its electorate; that the authority ought to be responsive to that electorate; that the electorate ought to have sufficient information to make informed judgments; and that the electorate ought to be able adequately to express its wishes to the authority. The Government *d* considered that the new system of local government finance which it was seeking to introduce would secure these aims. The Government also considered that such a system with effective mechanisms for local accountability would exert a firm and continuous pressure on local authorities to hold spending down, to improve the economy and efficiency of their operations, and to set community charges at appropriate and affordable levels. Local authority spending and the level of local *e* taxation is of considerable importance to the Government as part of its strategic management of the national economy: (i) as part of its concern about the public sector's share of the economy, the Government has an interest in the aggregate level of local authority revenue expenditure; (ii) as part of its fiscal policy the Government is concerned about the overall and relative levels of taxation, which include the community charge; and (iii) at the centre of the Government's economic strategy is *f* the fight against inflation; community charges are an element of cost in the economy reflected in the Retail Prices Index. The Government would therefore be concerned if local authorities budgeted excessively and set community charges correspondingly. Whilst the Government considered that the new system established by the 1988 Act when fully in place would result in the majority of authorities avoiding excessive budgets, it recognised given past experience which had led it to seek the powers in *g* the Rates Act 1984 . . . that a few authorities might decide on excessive spending policies and set their charges accordingly notwithstanding the possible consequences for those councils. The Government concluded that it should therefore seek powers which would enable it to take rapid action to secure reductions in such excessive budgets and to bring rapid relief to those chargepayers burdened with high charges as a result of excessive budgets. It considered that in the first years of the new system *h* when due to the various transitional arrangements . . . the accountability pressures would not be fully in place there might be a greater need for it to exercise its powers to secure reduction in excessive budgets and the resulting charges. The Government accordingly sought the powers for selective charge-capping which it has been given in Part VII of the 1988 Act. Selective charge-capping is a process of securing reductions in both budgeted expenditure and charges of individual authorities *j* whose budgets are excessive. For its management of the national economy the Government wishes to curb excessive spending by any authority, and it is also concerned to protect chargepayers from the effects of excessive budgeting.'

On 19 July 1989 the Secretary of State sent to local authorities a letter informing them of his announcement that the government considered that it would be appropriate for

local authorities to spend £32·8bn in total in 1990–91 by way of revenue expenditure in
a providing services. In order to distribute grant he stated his intention to calculate an
assessment for each authority of what he considered would be an appropriate level of
expenditure for the authority to incur to provide services locally to a common standard,
consistent with local authorities as a whole spending £32·8bn. These assessments were
called standard spending assessments, or SSAs.

On 6 November 1989 under cover of a consultation paper the Secretary of State sent to
b local authorities a draft of his proposed distribution report. He invited comments and
made it clear that he would consider them before making the report itself. In his
statement of 6 November 1989 the Secretary of State said that the SSA for each authority
would be based on an assessment for each of the main services for which it is responsible.
It would be calculated using information for each authority about factors which lead to
differences in the costs of providing services to a common standard and would in this
c way take account of variations between authorities in the costs they face. For each
authority, each SSA element would be consistent with a total for the service concerned,
known as the control total. The aggregate of these totals would represent the total
amount of revenue expenditure (apart from revenue expenditure from specific grants),
which the Secretary of State considered it appropriate for all authorities to incur in the
year. It is this total together with revenue expenditure financed by specific grants that is
d known as TSS.

The proposals of 6 November 1989 took account of recent research and extensive
discussions between officials and officers of the local authorities. These are summarised
in a lengthy report of the Local Government Finance Needs Assessment Sub-Group. The
Secretary of State's statement also emphasised that the relationship between an authority's
budget and its SSA determines the community charge for that area. He said that under
e his proposals for RSG, if authorities were to spend at the level of their SSA, the community
charge before transitional arrangement would in each area be about £278. He described
this figure, which he called the community charge for standard spending, as 'the
benchmark of accountability'.

By letter of 7 November 1989 to the borough treasurer of Southwark Mr Rowsell said:

f   'It would not be appropriate for me to speculate what procedure and timetable
the Secretary of State might adopt if he were to designate any local authorities for
capping in 1990/91 ... Ministers have made it clear that ideally, there will be no
need to use the charge capping provisions. They have said that authorities must
realise the importance of keeping expenditure under control and budget sensibly.
But Ministers have made it equally clear that if some authorities fail to set sensible
g   budgets and instead budget excessively they will not hesitate to cap them to bring
chargepayers rapid relief from the excessive spending plans of their local authority.'

The Secretary of State considered all the comments that he had received. Having done
so, he made five reports called respectively the Revenue Support Grant Report (England)
1990–91, the Revenue Support Grant Distribution Report (England), the Population
h Report (England), the Special Grant Report and the Revenue Support Grant Transition
Report (England). On 20 and 21 December 1989 these reports were published. They
were laid before the House of Commons on 11 and 12 January 1990. On the same days
copies of the reports were sent to local authorities in England; and on the following day
they were sent detailed figures underlying the calculations of authorities' SSAs and
entitlements to revenue support grant. On 18 January 1990 the reports were approved
j by the House. On 25 January 1990 the Secretary of State duly notified authorities of his
calculation of the amounts due to each receiving authority pursuant to the distribution
report.

During consultation on the grant settlement the Secretary of State received many
requests for some indication of how he was minded to fix the criteria for designating
authorities under Pt VII. The Secretary of State nevertheless considered that announcing
possible criteria before budgets were set could give the criteria the status of a norm or

target which would distort the very accountability the new system was designed to promote. This could encourage authorities to spend up to that target figure, thereby *a* leading to an overall increase in local authority spending. It was for this reason that the decisions on designation for rate limitation had always been taken after the budgets for the preceding year had been set.

On 9 February 1990 the Secretary of State notified local authorities of the information, nearly all of which he required not later than 18 March, in order to do what was demanded of him under Pt VII of the Act. On 16 February 1990 there was sent to local *b* authorities a report setting out the assumed community charge and the assumed rate poundage for each charging authority for the purposes of the community charge transitional relief scheme, generally known as the 'safety net'.

This prompted the officers of the local authorities to prepare reports for their consideration such as are exemplified by those before the court from the County Treasurer of Avon, for Hammersmith and Fulham, and for North Tyneside. These *c* reports analysed the budget proposals, considered the risk of charge capping and speculated on possible criteria for determining the levels at which capping might occur.

Under s 100(4) of the Act the Secretary of State determined principles, to which it will be necessary to return later in this judgment. He than applied those principles to the information obtained by him under s 100 and decided to designate 18 charging authorities under s 101(1)(a) and two precepting authorities under sub-s (2)(a). On 3 April *d* 1990 he notified these 20 authorities of their designation and of his principles together with the proposed maximum amounts, as required by s 102(1) of the Act. Lambeth's revised budget having been delayed, the Secretary of State designated that authority on 10 April 1990. Designation prompted several of the authorities, such as Basildon, to ask the Secretary of State to provide a detailed explanation and justification for his proposal to cap the authority. It also prompted the NUT and the National Association of Head *e* Teachers to tell local education authorities (LEAs) that the education element in their budgets could not be cut in response to charge capping.

Notices of designation

The notices of designation served on the local authorities were all similar. Each started by declaring the Secretary of State's decision to designate the council under s 100 of the *f* Act as regards the financial year beginning in 1990 in accordance with princples determined by him under s 100(4) of the Act. The principles were stated to be applicable to the specified classes. Each notice then defined 'relevant population' as meaning 'the population of the area of the authority calculated by the Secretary of State for the year in accordance with the rules set out in the Population Report' and defined 'standard spending assessment' as meaning 'the authority's standard spending assessment calculated by the *g* Secretary of State using principles established by him and set out in the Distribution Report'. By the terms of the notice authorities were designated in accordance with the following principles:

'(1) The first principle is that an authority is to be designated if in the opinion of the Secretary of State the amount calculated by it in relation to the year under *h* Section 95(4) of the 1988 Act is excessive in that: (i) the amount exceeds the authority's standard spending assessment by at least $12\frac{1}{2}\%$, and (ii) the amount divided by the authority's relevant population exceeds by at least £75 a sum equal to the authority's standard spending assessment divided by the authority's relevant population.

(2) The second principle is that an authority is not to be designated *j* notwithstanding that it falls to be designated under the first principle if in its case the product of the following formula is less than £26. The formula is: $\dfrac{(A-B)}{R}$

where—A is the amount calculated by the authority in relation to that year under

section 95(4) of the 1988 Act; B is the greatest of—(i) the authority's standard
spending assessment plus an amount equal to 12½% of that standard spending
assessment, (ii) an amount equal to the product of £75 and the authority's relevant
population, plus the authority's standard spending assessment, (iii) £15 M; and R is
the relevant population.'

Finally, the notice informed the authority of the amount which the Secretary of State
proposed should be the maximum for the amount calculated by the authority in relation
to the year under s 95(4) of the Act.

Professor Harvey Goldstein has analysed these principles and their effect. He remarks
that all of the 31 local authorities with SSAs over £100m which satisfy the first half of
the first principle also satisfy the second half, whereas only four out of 18 local authorities
with SSAs under £100m which satisfy the first half of the first principle also satisfy the
second half. Because for two local authorities with the same percentage increase over SSA
and the same population, the amount per head over SSA is directly proportional to the
SSA itself, it follows that any criterion additional to a simple percentage criterion, such as
that set out in para (1)(ii), favours local authorities with small SSAs. So, although
Bournemouth and Hammersmith have similar populations and similar increases over
SSA of about 20%, because their increases per head are £23 and £239 respectively
Hammersmith is designated but Bournemouth is not.

Professor Goldstein reformulates the second principle by saying that a local authority
is not capped if either of the two amounts is less than £26: (i) the percentage excess over
its SSA less 12½% (expressed as an amount per head), or (ii) the amount per head less £75.
This reformulation may be expressed affirmatively by saying that a local authority is
capped if the amount per head exceeds both (a) its SSA plus 12½% (expressed as an amount
per head) by at least £26 and (b) £101. Professor Goldstein makes the point that because
£75 equals 12½% of £600 if an SSA per head is £600 or more only the first part of the
relevant principle applies, and if it is less than £600 only the second part applies. So of
the 18 local authorities with an SSA of not more than £600 only Bristol is capped whereas
of the 31 local authorities with an SSA of more than £600, 20 are capped.

The use of SSAs

Because SSAs constitute a pivotal feature of the capping process, it is important to see
how the SSA and its use are explained and justified in the Secretary of State's evidence.
The Secretary of State's proposed method for making the SSAs was set out in the
document he circulated on 6 November 1989, to which we have earlier referred. The
actual content is best seen from the distribution report. That shows that an SSA, which
will be calculated annually for each notifiable authority, is built up from separate
elements for what are termed 'major service blocks' consisting of education, personal
social services, police, fire and civil defence, highway maintenance, all other services and
capital financing. To each block and sub-block a monetary weight is attributed for the
purpose of calculating the SSA.

The Secretary of State's proposal for TSS was £32·8bn. The element of the total for a
service to be allocated to each authority would be calculated by a formula containing
factors reflecting the physical, social, and demographic characteristics of the authority's
area in so far as they were relevant to the costs of providing the service concerned. In this
way, there would be calculated for each authority an assessment of a benchmark level of
expenditure. The benchmark would be the appropriate level of expenditure to provide
services to a particular standard; the standard would be that standard consistent with
authorities in total spending at a certain amount proposed by the Secretary of State.

The SSA for an authority (except the City of London to which special considerations
apply) for a year is thus intended to prepresent the amount of revenue expenditure which
it would be appropriate for the authority to incur in that year to provide a standard level
of service consistent with the Secretary of State's view of the amount of revenue

expenditure (TSS) which it would be appropriate for all local authorities to incur. Thus, the SSA is also intended to represent the amount it would be appropriate for an authority to raise by way of precept (if a precepting authority) or by a calculation under s 95(4) of the Act (if a charging authority) on the basis that it makes no use of financial reserves beyond that allowed for in net TSS.

In some parts of England parish councils provide services which would otherwise be provided by charging authorities. A single SSA is calculated for each charging authority to cover the range of services provided by themselves and parish councils. The distribution of functions between a district council and the parish councils in its area varies significantly both between districts and even within a single district. It would thus be wholly impracticable to have several SSAs within each district and the 8,000 odd parishes tailored to the particular distribution of functions in each case.

In his answer to a parliamentary question on 11 January 1990, the Secretary of State stated his belief that authorities would now have all the information they needed to press ahead with their budget setting and charge setting. He stated his firm belief that authorities should be able to keep their spending down in line with TSS of £32·8bn. He noted that any extra spending would fall on community charge payers and would have to be justified to them and expressed his hope that charge payers would take the opportunity of the introduction of the new more accountable system to take a good look at what their authorities are spending. He believed that it was right to that, where this was more than the SSA, charge payers should be able to seek an explanation and that it was right that authorities should bear in mind the effects on charge payers when they made their budget decisions.

Even though the Secretary of State did not think it right to consult about possible definitions of excessiveness he had, in the distribution report and in his regulations for the community charge bill, made it plain that he considered that SSAs represented his view of the appropriate level of spending for authorities. By implication any level of spending in excess of an SSA might, therefore, potentially be viewed by him as being excessive. The Secretary of State considered that SSAs should form the benchmark for excessive spending (in the same way as grant-related expenditure (GRE) had under the Rates Act 1984) not least given the considerations he had expressed on 11 January 1990. The SSAs were the measure of spending need which had been devised following extensive consultations with local authority associations and had been adopted by him for the purpose of distribution and approved by the House of Commons under s 80 of the Act for that purpose.

The SSA was also the criterion he had required to be identified for the purposes of comparison of community charge bills. He decided that the SSA was an appropriate touchstone against which to consider whether the exercise by an authority of its discretion had resulted in a budget that was, in his opinion, excessive. The Secretary of State therefore considered that SSAs were the most appropriate measure by reference to which he could reach an opinion about whether authorities' budgets were excessive. In his consideration of principles for designation the Secretary of State, taking account of the fact that he had already established SSAs for the purposes of distribution of grant and as the benchmark for accountability, further considered that forming an opinion about excessive spending without reference to its SSA could be the subject of criticism.

[His Lordship then considered the applicants' objections to the use by the Secretary of State of SSAs as a basis for determining whether a local authority's spending in 1990–91 was excessive, and continued:]

THE MAIN ARGUMENT

The scope of judicial review

By s 100(1) the Secretary of State may designate a charging authority 'if in his opinion ... the amount calculated by it ... under section 95(4) above is excessive'. The amount calculated consists of the difference between expenditure and income other than that

from the community charge, that is to say that sum which the local authority will have
to raise from its community charge payers. About s 100(1) there are two things to be
noted: (a) the appraisal of the amount is subjectively for the Secretary of State alone and
(b) the appraisal is of whether the amount is 'excessive'. Although an opinion reached by
the Secretary of State could be impugned on the ground of bad faith or improper motive,
no such allegation is made here.

The marshalling of the argument of counsel for the applicants in this case is rendered
difficult by the fact that they inevitably overlapped, as do the grounds for seeking judicial
review themselves. But it is convenient to adopt the structure formulated by Lord
Diplock in *Council of Civil Service Unions v Minister for the Civil Service* [1984] 3 All ER 935
at 950–951, [1985] AC 374 at 410–411 in a classic passage in which he identified the
three main types of abuse of power as illegality, irrationality and procedural impropriety.
These most commonly occur by mistake of law in misconstruing the nature or extent of
statutory powers; by unreasonableness in the *Wednesbury* sense (see *Associated Provincial
Picture Houses v Wednesbury Corp* [1947] 2 All ER 680, [1948] 1 KB 223); and by failure
to observe the rules of natural justice. All three types are here invoked to impugn the
Secretary of State's actions.

This case, like *Nottinghamshire CC v Secretary of State for the Environment* [1986] 1 All ER
199, [1986] AC 240, is a case in which the separation of powers between the legislature,
the executive and the judiciary is relevant and important. In that case the minister had a
statutory discretion to give guidance to local authorities in relation to the rate support
grant. The guidance given differentiated between high-spending and low-spending
authorities, that for high-spending authorities being based on the previous year's guidance
rather than on the authorities' grant-related expenditure. Although the guidance had
been approved by the House of Commons, it was sought to establish by judicial review
both that the guidance was unlawful because it was not framed by reference to principles
applicable to all local authorities and that it was unreasonable. The House of Lords held
that the guidance was not unlawful and that it was inappropriate for the courts to
intervene on the grounds of 'unreasonableness'. As Lord Scarman said in that case ([1986]
1 All ER 199 at 202, [1986] AC 240 at 247):

> 'We are in the field of public financial administration and we are being asked to
> review the exercise by the Secretary of State of an administrative discretion which
> inevitably requires a political judgment on his part and which cannot lead to action
> by him against a local authority unless that action is first approved by the House of
> Commons.'

He added ([1986] 1 All ER 199 at 204, [1986] AC 240 at 250–251):

> 'Judicial review is a great weapon in the hands of the judges; but the judges must
> observe the constitutional limits set by our parliamentary system on their exercise
> of this beneficent power.'

Mr Goudie sought to distinguish this case on the ground that designation is an act
distinct from capping and is not itself subject to parliamentary approval. It is therefore
outwith the principle of the *Nottinghamshire CC* case which would have to be extended,
not applied, if it were to operate here. He sought to argue that the distribution of grant
which involves economic policy is different from capping with its serious impact on the
local authority concerned. Mr Goudie also argued that designation is not of the same
character as distribution because it involves a decision to intervene in matters not
exclusively within the Secretary of State's own province, but in one primarily within the
purview of the local authorities.

Although designation is not directly subject to parliamentary approval, it will be open
to the House of Commons when considering the capping order to conclude that the
Secretary of State should not have designated the relevant authorities. In our judgment
designation and the selection of principles by which local authorities are to be designated

involve considerations of national economic policy, and the Secretary of State's decision constituted a political judgment which remains within the political domain since the proposed maxima have yet to be approved by the House of Commons. It is true that designation cannot cause a local authority's budget to be capped unless it accepts the proposed maximum, or the House of Commons approves the draft order stating the maximum. The House of Commons can, however, decline to do so because it disagrees with the Secretary of State's decision to designate, or the principles determined under s 100(4) of the Act in relation to it, or the amount which he proposes should be the maximum for the amount calculated under s 95(4). In short, the scheme of the Act is that no local authority should be capped without its consent unless the approval of the House of Commons is given.

Public financial administration is a matter peculiarly within the province of Parliament to the exclusion of the courts. Parliament has here enacted that the limitation of charges by local authorities following their designation by the Secretary of State is not to be carried into effect without the approval, first obtained, of the House of Commons. The courts have the task of interpreting the legislation and they are concerned in a case like this to investigate whether the Secretary of State has abused his power by exceeding the limits of the statute, or by committing a procedural error. The reasonableness in the *Wednesbury* sense and the consistency with the conferring statute of his exercise of power in seeking, as he has, to designate the applicant authorities are different aspects of a policy and the implementation of it that must be adjudged good, indifferent or bad by the House of Commons. For that assessment the House of Commons is answerable to the electorate, without, however, having in the meanwhile been subject to review by the courts. But notwithstanding that in our judgment the applicants are therefore confined for present purposes to attacks on the legality and on the procedural propriety of what has been done, we shall consider on their merits all the main arguments relied on by the applicants, including those based on irrationality.

Illegality

'*Excessive*'

The *Nottinghamshire CC* case does not preclude the courts from considering whether there has been an abuse of power by reason of illegality. Section 100(4) of the Act provides: 'A decision whether to designate an authority shall be made in accordance with principles determined by the Secretary of State . . .' By s 102(1): 'If the Secretary of State decides under section 100 above to designate an authority he shall notify it in writing of . . . (b) the principles determined under section 100(4) above in relation to it . . .' The Secretary of State's notices of designation each identified the two principles determined under s 100(4). They were the same, not only for all authorities falling within each class, but for all classes referred to in s 100(5). Of the principles only the first was material for present purposes. That was the principle that propounded a twofold test of whether the calculated amount was 'excessive', namely whether it exceeded by at least $12\frac{1}{2}\%$ the authority's SSA and whether it exceeded by at least £75 the SSA per head. The main attack on the legality of the decision to designate was based on the construction of the term 'excessive', in s 100(1), and on the validity of the principles determined under s 100(4).

Mr Henderson boldly argued that on a proper construction of s 100 the first stage of the designation process is the formation of an opinion whether the amount is excessive; and the second stage is the decision whether to designate if the Secretary is of the opinion that the amount calculated by a particular charging authority in relation to a particular year is excessive. It is to the decision 'whether to' designate that the principles relate and not to the opinion as to excessiveness. According to this argument it is plain from his evidence that the Secretary of State has misapplied the principles to the first stage by determining excessiveness by principles rather than by forming his opinion as to excessiveness on an individual or ad hoc basis, and he has misdirected himself in law.

In our judgment this argument is more ingenious than realistic. A decision to *a* designate an authority is not a two-stage process. Although the Secretary of State has power to designate in the event that a budget is in his opinion excessive, he may not decide to do so except in accordance with principles. The principles are not at large: it is by reference to them that the decision to designate on the ground that a budget is excessive must be taken. Mr Henderson's construction would absolve the Secretary of State from the need to notify designated authorities under s 102(1) of the basis on which *b* he regarded their budgets as excessive. Not only was the argument advanced late in this case, it was never advanced at all in relation to the corresponding provisions of the Rates Act 1984. In our judgment it is wrong.

One purpose of the contention is to support the argument that 'excessive' is a measure of the spending needs of individual authorities. For the authorities it was submitted that a judgment of excessiveness must necessarily have regard to the spending needs of each *c* authority. We do not agree. The approach laid down by s 100 is in two stages: first, the setting of principles by which excessiveness is to be adjudged, these principles being common for each authority in any specific class; second, the determination of the amount of the cap proposed for each authority. Because the second stage is specific to authorities, the approach at the first stage will probably be more general, but that is for the Secretary of State to decide. The omission from the Act of the words 'having regard to general *d* economic considerations', which were present in s 2(2) of the Rates Act 1984, indicates, in our judgment, that Parliament intended his determination of the principles to be unfettered. The fact that a judgment of excessiveness under s 100(1)(b) will necessarily take into accounts the needs, at least in the previous year, of an individual authority is no warrant for saying that in selecting principles for the purpose of s 100(1)(a) those needs must be considered. The matter is at large. The Secretary of State may, at the first stage, *e* take into account such considerations as he thinks right. In all probability he will have regard to national economic considerations, but that is for him. He may, or may not, also have regard to needs, as he sees them, of individual authorities. Again that is for him. If so, it is for him to decide what weight to give to those words. In this instance he took such account as he thought right of both national and local needs. SSAs to some extent reflect individual authorities' needs. The fact that they are, as he realised, an imprecise, *f* and in some respects inadequate, measure of those needs does not render unlawful his use of them.

There were various submissions about the meaning of the word 'excessive'. Lighting on an answer given on behalf of the government in the House of Lords, Mr Scrivener argued that it means 'irrational'. This led to a blurring between the argument that in failing to equate 'excessive' with 'irrational' the Secretary of State had misconstrued s 100 *g* and the argument that because the Secretary of State acted as no reasonable Secretary of State properly directing himself as to the law could have done, what he did was open to criticism as 'irrational' in the *Wednesbury* sense. But in reply Mr Scrivener explained the point as confined to interpretation. It was Mr Henderson's contention that 'excessive' connotes a criticism of profligacy or inordinate extravagance.

h In our judgment, the phrase 'if in his opinion [the s 95(4) amount] is excessive' means 'if he thinks it is more than it should be'. But the Secretary of State must act responsibly and can only come to that conclusion by reference to the principles of which he notifies a designated local authority at the same time as his decision. The decision cannot be arbitrary because the principles have to be the same at least for all the other authorities in the same class as the designated authority. Taking account of national economic policy *j* is not inconsistent with giving some weight to the needs of individual local authorities by using SSAs or indeed to factors of which local authorities do not take account.

Retrospectivity

The only other argument exclusive of law concerned what was called 'retrospectivity'. It is convenient to consider it here. Mr Newman remarked that other provisions of the

Act require acts to be done by 1 or 11 March or 1 April. Because the Act and powers under it should be interpreted so as not to frustrate good administration, and because historically and actually local government finance is conducted on an annual basis, he argued that the discretion to designate under s 100 cannot validly be exercised after 1 April when a local authority, having set its budget, embarks on a new financial year. Since all the relevant notices were served on 3 or 10 April 1990, all are invalid. To that Mr Laws responded that the requirement to revise budgets in-year renders the term 'retrospectivity' inapt.

A reading of Pt VII of the Act makes it clear that the Secretary is empowered to set the maximum amount and require reconsideration by a local authority of its budget during the current financial year. By contrast with the Rates Act 1984 which referred in s 2(1) to acts 'in the preceding financial year' there is no such limitation here. Indeed, if the Secretary of State could not designate after 31 March, the absurd result would follow that if a budget were preferred late the local authority concerned could not be capped. We find that service of a notice of designation within a few days of 1 April is not invalid. There is no magic in the passing of midnight on 31 March. Whether an authority be designated before or after 1 April the consequential uncertainties are the same.

Illegality or irrationality

Class by class

Some arguments were advanced compendiously or by reference to one or other of these types of abuse of power. Mr Sedley, for example, contended that Parliament has by s 100(5) of the Act intended to differentiate between classes, because there are real distinctions between classes such as are exemplified by differences in function. Even if there are no legal differences there may be factual differences such as 'physical, social and demographic'. Section 100(5) in effect enjoins the Secretary of State not to collapse differentials but to consider separately what principles to adopt class by class. This, Mr Sedley argues, he has not done. We are inclined to the view that the subsection does not impose any such duty on the Secretary of State; but it is not necessary to decide that question, because even if Mr Sedley's submission were right, there is no evidence that the Secretary of State did not give separate consideration to each of the several classes.

Under the same head Mr Sedley argues in the alternative that what the Secretary of State has done, by using each of the local authorities' individual SSAs as a base line, is to distinguish between local authorities not by principle class by class, but local authority by local authority by relationship of budget to SSA, which is forbidden by s 100(4) of the Act. Mr Sedley further argues that the Secretary of State, by applying a single principle to all seven classes, has failed to consider or respect classified differences in function and in other respects. Further, he has covertly applied a distinction which is not authorised by Parliament. In effect there are two tests which have a consequent unequal impact on authorities depending on the size of their SSAs, that is to say whether the SSA per head is more or less than £600. The Secretary of State has thus ignored the real differences under s 100(4) and (5).

Looking at the words of s 100(4), it is plain that each of the designated authorities falls within one of the classes specified in s 100(5) and that in relation to each designated authority the principles are the same for all authorities falling within the class into which each designated authority falls. The terms of the statute are therefore complied with. It does not require the principles to be different for each of the prescribed classes; nor that there should be any particular relationship between the principles applicable to one class and those applicable to another; nor that the effect on authorities in one class should be the same as their effect on those in another; nor even that their effect, as distinct from their application, should be the same in relation to all the authorities in the same class. The Secretary of State is obliged to determine principles in accordance with which the decision whether to designate is to be made, which are the same for all authorities in each class. In our judgment, he has done so in this case.

Use of SSAs

The suitability of the principles for this purpose is challenged by reference to the use of SSAs. Mr Scrivener argues that the use in this context by the Secretary of State of SSAs is exceptionable because they were designed for use in the distribution of grant; they cannot pay attention to individual needs; they represent the amount which it would be appropriate for local authorities to incur to provide a standard level of service overall; they include matters which would not be considered by a charging authority lawfully exercising its discretion under s 95(4) of the Act and it would have been easy for the Act to provide that SSAs (like GREs) should be used as criteria if Parliament had so intended. Other counsel supported these criticisms, Mr Newman contending that SSAs disregard local authority discretions and previous year's budgets and Mr Henderson criticising them as formulaic.

To be of general application the principles were bound to be formulaic: see *R v Secretary of State for the Environment, ex p Brent London BC* [1983] 3 All ER 321 at 345, [1982] QB 593 at 635. Although the Secretary of State did not consult local authorities about the use of SSAs as a component of the principles, he had consulted the various local authority associations extensively about the content of the SSAs as a measure of spending need. Their use as an aid to distribution of grant had been adopted by the House of Commons. The SSAs pay regard to all 'major service blocks' and to facts reflecting the physical, social and demographic characteristics of each authority's area in so far as they are relevant to the costs of providing services. SSAs were therefore used as a benchmark for excessive spending, much as GREs had been under the Rates Act 1984.

Criticism of the content of the SSAs does not constitute a valid ground for objecting to their use in the Secretary of State's principles. The main objection to their use is that they do not reflect the spending needs of individual local authorities. But they do so to such extent as the Secretary of State thought appropriate. His use of them for that purpose was unexceptionable. Once the principles had been determined, it was on them alone that designation was to depend.

The 12½% and £75 tests

The other main assault on the principles is based on the argument that, because it is of £600 that £75 is 12½%, the principles result in the application of different tests according to whether an authority's SSA is up to or more than £600 per person. On account of this dichotomy the principles are said to fail the requirement that they should be the same for all authorities falling within any given class. But this is not so. The tests applied are identical. What vary are their effects according to the circumstances of the authorities concerned. The fact that the application of the tests to different local authorities in the same class produces different results does not mean that the principles are not the same for all local authorities in the same class: it means that some which fail the 12½% test are not designated, because they do not also fail the £75 test. Because £75 is 12½% of £600, the latter is the figure above which a local authority will automatically fail the £75 test. But the reality is that those spending at more than 12½% over SSA will not be designated, if the actual amount by which the SSA per head is exceeded is not more than £75. Thus the twin principles or tests effectually reproduce the twin purposes of the Act, to cut local government expenditure and to protect the charge payer.

None of the arguments about the meaning of 'excessive' or about the formal content of the principles leads to the conclusion that the Secretary of State has misdirected himself in law.

Irrationality

The £75 test

Mr Newman made several submissions based exclusively on allegations of unreasonableness in the *Wednesbury* sense. First, he submitted that the Secretary of State has given no rational explanation for the £75 measure of excessiveness. That is what Mr Newman

characterises as 'the heart of darkness'. According to him, it can have no other basis than
an intention to discriminate against large authorities, which consist of the London *a*
boroughs, metropolitan district councils and all but three county councils. But the
Secretary of State's purpose in including the £75 test as part of his principles was plainly
to avoid the capping of authorities whose proposed expenditure did not have the effect
of requiring the charge payer to pay more than £75 above the SSA per head. The
complaint made is not that by this means the applicants have been rendered amenable to
charge capping where otherwise they would not have been, but that other authorities *b*
have been exonerated from charge capping which would have been designated but for
the £75 test. Mr Newman also argues that the use of the £75 test is objectionable because
the Secretary of State has failed to give any explanation for its use other than that a
payment by an individual charge payer of about £1·50 a week above the SSA per head
was as much as was tolerable. But this is simply an example of the legitimate application
by the Secretary of State of the economic policy that seems good to him, and there is no *c*
available inference from the choice of the amount of £75 that the Secretary of State has
acted arbitrarily or improperly. As Mr Laws said, Mr Newman's criticism of the adoption
of a per capita test overlooked the fact that the Act for the first time introduced a per
capita charge. Mr Newman himself acknowledged that £75 was a figure that could
reasonably have been chosen.

d

One and two tiers

Finally, there is a group of criticisms which are all alleged to involve a failure to take
account of relevant considerations. First, it is said that there was a failure to distinguish
between one- and two-tier authorities: for example, by fixing a £75 threshold for all
authorities without regard to the fact that metropolitan authorities carry out the
functions both of non-metropolitan district councils and of county councils. In answer *e*
to this complaint, Mr Rowsell asserts the Secretary of State's power to treat different
classes of authority differently, and in particular to divide between tiers the £75 excess
over SSA per head, and acknowledges that, for reasons that seemed good to the Secretary
of State, he has refrained from doing so this year. But the essential point is that the
Secretary of State has not treated local authorities differently within the same class. By
applying his £75 test he has not designated any authorities that would not otherwise *f*
have been designated: he has avoided designating others that might have been designated.
This is unobjectionable.

Parish councils

Second, it is said that there was a failure to distinguish between other categories of
local authority, such as those which do, and those which do not, incorporate parish *g*
councils. Again, it is argued that, because SSAs allow for parish expenditure whereas
budgeted spending does not, an unfair advantage is given to those authorities which do
not incorporate parish councils. Apart from the fact that the spending of parish councils
is only a tiny proportion of the whole, this argument protests at the advantage being
given to other local authorities, rather than a disadvantage to the applicants, and is a *h*
protest best advanced in the House of Commons.

Cuts in-year

Third, the Secretary of State is accused of failing to recognise the difficulty, if not
impossibility, of making the cuts demanded in-year, especially for LEAs, since the
budgets of each of them represent a high proportion of its total budget, much of which *j*
is outwith its control. The difficulty of making such cuts in-year, which are a feature of
the community charge system, also constitutes a basis for inviting the Secretary of State,
and if need be the House of Commons, to increase the maximum amounts proposed. It
does not constitute a basis for inviting the court to intervene on the ground that the
Secretary of State has failed to take account of relevant considerations.

Unfairness

a   We would add that Mr Henderson relies separately on what he calls 'substantive unfairness' as distinct from 'procedural unfairness'. As Mr Laws submitted, there is no separate category from illegality, irrationality or procedural impropriety. Unfairness merely describes what the applicants say results from the illegality or irrationality which they allege. They do not allege any breach of contract or of representation such as the House of Lords contemplated in *Preston v IRC* [1985] 2 All ER 327, [1985] AC 835 could

b   properly be described as unfairness amounting to abuse or excess of power.

Procedural impropriety

Legitimate expectation and unfairness

Mr Henderson started his submission on these issues by saying that designation of a local authority is tantamount to an accusation that the local authority intends to be

c   profligate in its spending. Moreover, designation itself will have serious financial consequences for the local authority designated: it will have to reassess its budgets, to consider whether to challenge the Secretary of State's proposed maximum amount calculated under s 95(4) and, if it does, to produce its own figure and give reasons in support of it. The local authority will also have to meet the cost of issuing fresh

d   community charge bills. Mr Henderson also submitted that in fixing its original budget the local authority will have exercised its own judgment. It is improper for the Secretary of State to overturn this judgment by reference to principles unknown to the local authority when it fixed its budget.

Proper procedure requires, submitted Mr Henderson, that the local authority will be accorded notice of the principles on which the decision to designate will be made and an

e   opportunity to comment on those principles. He relied on *Secretary of State for Education and Science v Tameside Metropolitan Borough* [1976] 3 All ER 665 at 671, [1977] AC 1014 at 1025, where Lord Denning MR said:

> 'To my mind, if a statute gives a Minister power to take drastic action if he is satisfied that a local authority have acted or are proposing to act improperly or
> f   unreasonably, then the Minister should obey all the elementary rules of fairness before he finds that the local authority are guilty or before he takes drastic action overruling them. He should give the party affected notice of the charge of impropriety or unreasonableness and a fair opportunity of dealing with it.'

Mr Henderson also relied on a passage in *R v Secretary of State for the Environment, ex p Brent London BC* [1983] 3 All ER 321 at 354, [1982] QB 593 at 642 in which Ackner LJ

g   indicated that the principles of natural justice should apply where the Secretary of State's decision involved taking away an existing right. Procedural propriety therefore required that the legitimate rights of those affected or likely to be affected by the exercise of the discretionary power should be respected in that they should be given an opportunity of being heard before the decision is made. These submissions were based on the principle that a person exercising a discretionary statutory power must act fairly, or on a legitimate

h   expectation that such powers would be exercised fairly by allowing the person affected by the decision an opportunity to present his case before it is taken.

Mr Henderson accepted that there was no legitimate expectation of prior consultation arising from practice under the Rates Act 1984. Legitimate expectation arose, it was claimed, in two ways: first, because the Secretary of State had made earlier statements which implied that local authorities would be consulted before the decisions referred to

j   in s 102(1) were taken by the Secretary of State and, second, because of the requirement for procedural fairness.

Lord Fraser said in *Council of Civil Service Unions v Minister for the Civil Service* [1984] 3 All ER 935 at 944, [1985] AC 374 at 401:

> 'Legitimate, or reasonable, expectation may arise either from an express promise

given on behalf of a public authority or from the existence of a regular practice
which the claimant can reasonably expect to continue.'

a

In the present case it was conceded that there is no such regular practice. Further, the
evidence discloses no express promise given on behalf of the Secretary of State that any
local authority would be consulted before the Secretary of State reached any decision or
exercised any of his functions under Pt VII of the Act. Thus, in our judgment, no
argument can succeed in this case based on a legitimate expectation that the views of
local authorities would be taken before decisions were made by the Secretary of State.

b

Has there been procedural impropriety on the ground that there was a failure to act
with procedural fairness towards a local authority that will be affected by the Secretary of
State's decision? It cannot be, and has not been, suggested that he has failed to observe
the procedures expressly prescribed by the Act. Section 102(2)(a) of the Act provides that
a designation is to be invalid unless s 102(1) is complied with. The implication is that
designation shall be valid if the procedures required by ss 100 and 102(1) have been
followed. We accept the submission of Mr Laws that the whole structure of Pt VII of the
Act is inconsistent with an intention on the part of Parliament that the Secretary of State
should consult local authorities or that local authorities should be given the opportunity
to be heard, before the Secretary of State decides to designate or puts forward his proposed
maximum for the s 95(4) calculated amount. Where Parliament intended that there be
consultation it has so provided: see e g ss 76(5), 78(5) and 80(2).

c

d

Neither the basic rules of natural justice nor a requirement to act with procedural
fairness give rise to any obligation for the Secretary of State to 'hear' a local authority at
that stage. It has to be remembered that under s 102(5) the local authority can submit a
counter-proposal accompanied by reasons for the maximum to be calculated under
s 95(4), that this step leads to the procedures laid down in s 104, and that before making
an order under s 104(2) of the Act, the Secretary of State has to consider any 'information
he thinks is relevant'.

e

Lord Denning MR's comments in the *Tameside* case are to be distinguished on two
grounds. First, under the statutory wording the Secretary of State had to be satisfied on
complaint by any person or otherwise that an LEA had acted unreasonably with respect
to the exercise of the power conferred or the performance of a duty imposed by or under
the Act. Second, no drastic action of overruling the local authority on its s 95(4)
calculation can occur without the approval of the House of Commons.

f

Equally, we do not consider the observations of Ackner LJ in the *Brent* case to be
applicable because the decision to designate and the proposed maximum under s 102(1)
are not decisions which take away some existing right or position of the local authority.

g

Failure to give reasons

At this point the applicants contend that the Secretary of State's failure to give reasons
for the amounts he has proposed as the maxima under s 95(4) when notifying the local
authorities in writing pursuant to s 102(1) was a procedural irregularity. They say that it
placed any local authority wishing to challenge the proposed figure in an impossible
position, because s 102(5)(a) requires it to inform the Secretary of State by notice in
writing of the maximum amount which the local authority believes to be correct, for
reasons stated in the notice. It was submitted that a local authority could not submit a
properly reasoned counter-proposal if it was unaware of the grounds on which the
Secretary of State had arrived at his proposed maximum sum. If the local authority did
not know the case it had to meet, its reasons could not respond to the reasoning of the
Secretary of State.

h

j

We reject the challenge for procedural irregularity under this heading. The first reason
is that s 102(1) of the Act sets out the matters that the Secretary of State has to notify to
the local authority in writing when designating the local authority. Paragraph (c) refrains
from placing on the Secretary of State a requirement to give reasons for the amount

which he proposes as the maximum under s 95(4). This is to be contrasted with para (b)
a which requires the principles for determining excessiveness under s 95(4) to be stated in
the notice. It is also to be contrasted with s 102(5)(a) which requires the local authority to
give reasons for its counter-proposal. Parliament would have indicated if it had been its
intention that the Secretary of State should give reasons for the amount which he
proposed as the maximum under s 95(4).

Do the general principles of administrative law require the Secretary of State to give
b reasons where it is clear that Parliament has deliberately refrained from imposing such
an obligation on him? In our judgment, looking at the description of 'procedural
impropriety' in Lord Diplock's speech in the Council of Civil Service Unions case [1984] 3
All ER 935 at 951, [1985] AC 374 at 411, neither the basic rules of natural justice nor a
requirement for procedural fairness oblige the Secretary of State to include in his written
notification, under s 102(1) of the Act, any reasons for the maximum figure he proposes
c under s 95(4). In our view the local authority can make a reasoned counter-proposal
without knowing the Secretary of State's reasons.

We would, however, add that if the Secretary of State had available to him information
from a source other than the local authority itself which he intended to take into account
in determining the figure for insertion into the draft order under s 104(2) of the Act and
of which the authority did not know (as s 110(8) makes possible) procedural fairness
d would, in our view, require him (subject to any proper claim to privilege) to make that
information known to the local authority in time for it to respond should it so desire.

Maximum amounts
This topic requires separate treatment. Once an authority's maximum amount has
e been proposed by the Secretary of State by notice under s 102(1)(a) it has a right of
challenge under s 106 by informing the Secretary of State by notice under s 102(5)(a) that
'for reasons stated in the notice, it believes the maximum amount stated under subsection
(1)(c) above should be such as the authority states in its notice . . .' Mr Sedley contends
that a right of this sort carries with it a right to know the reasons for what is proposed in
sufficient detail to be able to challenge them intelligibly. In relation to the written notice
f he relies on Kanda v Government of the Federation of Malaya [1962] AC 322 and R v Brent
London BC, ex p Gunning (1985) 84 LGR 168. In addition, the Secretary of State received
oral representations, in relation to which Mr Sedley relies on Re Liverpool Taxi Owners'
Association [1972] 2 All ER 589, [1972] 2 QB 299 and A-G of Hong Kong v Ng Yuen Shiu
[1983] 2 All ER 346, [1983] 2 AC 629. In these circumstances he submits that not to
vouchsafe any explanation of how the maximum amount was arrived at until Mr
g Rowsell's affadavit was sworn on 21 May 1990, after the notice and oral representations
had been given and made, was contrary to the purposes of the Act and frustrated the
legitimate expectations of the local authorities concerned.

To this Mr Laws responds that, having regard to Nottinghamshire CC v Secretary of State
for the Environment [1986] 1 All ER 199, [1986] AC 240, the proper place to object to the
maximum amount is the House of Commons, since the Secretary of State's proposal for
a maximum amount is, unless agreed, incapable of having effect without the approval of
h the House of Commons. In any event, s 102(5) provides a statutory mechanism for
seeking a review of the maximum amount proposed, and that that method of challenge
be exhausted before applying for judicial review. Mr Sedley's retort is that if the
applicants are right in their contention that the obliquity of the Secretary of State has
prevented them from exercising their statutory rights, it is meaningless to require them
j to wait and to allow the Secretary of State to seek parliamentary approval following a
procedure unlawfully conducted.

This reasoning seems to us to ignore the statutory purpose of the capping procedure.
It is, as Mr Laws submitted, not to give the Secretary of State an opportunity to accuse
local authorities of misconduct, to which they must therefore be accorded a right of

reply: it is to allow him to impose as a matter of policy an expenditure regime which ex hypothesi will be at variance with the local authority's own, no doubt lawful, expenditure *a* policy. This distinguishes the cases cited. Thus the opportunity under s 102(5)(a) of the Act to notify the Secretary of State that for reasons stated the authority believes the maximum amount should be more is not an answer to a case against it: it is a response by the authority to a provisional requirement. Knowing that the maximum amount was proposed using the SSA as a benchmark, the local authority can contend for a higher maximum by reference to its own particular circumstances. This therefore is an example *b* of an administrative decision in respect of which public law does not require reasons to be given. As Gibbs CJ observed in *Public Service Board of New South Wales v Osmond* [1987] LRC (Const) 681 at 687, citing several English cases:

'There is no general rule of the common law, or principle of natural justice, that requires reasons to be given for administrative decisions, even decisions which have *c* been made in the exercise of a statutory discretion and which may adversely affect the interests, or defeat the legitimate or reasonable expectations, of other persons. That this is so has been recognised in the House of Lords . . .'

That principle applies here and no exception from it is warranted by the language of the Act.
d

Main argument fails
It follows that the applicants' submissions on the main argument fail. We decline to grant the relevant relief sought. We are conscious that we have not mentioned all of the subsidiary matters raised. That has not been through any failure to consider them but in the interests of an economical presentation of our response to the main issues. We *e* proceed to analyse, necessarily in more detail, the point of statutory interpretation raised by the education argument.

[His Lordship then considered an argument under the Education Reform Act 1988 as to the rights of LEAs to make reductions to the general schools budgets, granted them a declaration clarifying their rights but refused to grant them declaratory relief to the effect that before reducing its general school budget in-year an LEA must consult the governing *f* bodies and head teachers, and continued:]

CONCLUSION
Many people may be disappointed by the effect of this judgment. How, they may ask, can the court allow substantial in-year reductions to be made to budgets (school budgets in particular) which have been set by elected local authorities with all the consequences that may follow? The answer is that the consequences flow from the legislation. Our role *g* has been to interpret it. In operating the statutory process of charge capping the Secretary of State has not, in our judgment, acted unlawfully and so warranted the intervention of the court. That local authorities which have been designated will be adversely affected by the requirement to reduce budgets in-year is a consequence inherent in the statutory process. It is still open to the Secretary of State, or in default the House of Commons, to *h* relieve against any apprehended hardship or unfairness.

Order accordingly.

Dilys Tausz   Barrister.
j

Appeal
The applicants appealed. Michael Heiser, chairman of the governors of William Gladstone Community School, Brent, and Maureen Parris, chairman of the Brentfield Junior and Infant School, Brent, were given leave to be heard on the appeal.

Anthony Scrivener QC, Roger Henderson QC, James Goudie QC, Alan Wilkie, Ian Croxford, John
a   *Howell* and *Timothy Mould* for the applicants other than Southwark and Derbyshire.
Stephen Sedley QC and *Anthony Bradley* for Southwark.
Alan Newman QC and *Philip Engelman* for Derbyshire.
Lord Gifford QC and *Kate Markus* for the chairmen of the Brent school governors.
John Laws, Presiley Baxendale and *Paul Walker* for the Secretary of State.

b   At the conclusion of the argument their Lordships stated that the appeal would be
dismissed for reasons to be given later.

3 July. The following judgment of the court was delivered.

LORD DONALDSON OF LYMINGTON MR. This judgment, of which the three
c   members of the court are joint authors, constitutes the judgment of the court.

INTRODUCTION
   The applicants for judicial review appeal against the refusal of relief by a Divisional
Court consisting of Leggatt LJ, McCullough and Roch JJ. As is well known, the subject
matter is the Secretary of State's invocation of his powers under the Local Government
d   Finance Act 1988 to 'cap' or limit the amount of the community charge or precept which
particular charging and precepting authorities designated by him can levy. The matter
is of considerable urgency since the timetable is such that, subject to House of Commons
approval of a draft order, the Secretary of State would wish to make orders under the Act
on 48 hours' notice to the applicants. Once such orders are made the authorities concerned
will be involved in significant expenditure which would be wasted if relief were
e   subsequently to be granted. It is also of very considerable importance in that our decision,
like that of the Divisional Court, will affect 19 local authorities and something of the
order of four million residents in the areas concerned, both in their capacity as community
charge payers and users of the services provided by the authorities.
   The Divisional Court gave judgment on Friday, 15 June after an expedited hearing
f   dictated in part by the fact that the Secretary of State had said that he would not seek
parliamentary approval of a draft charge-capping order before 18 June, but might feel
obliged to seek such approval on or shortly after that date. In the light of indications that
the applicants might wish to appeal, we began the prereading of relevant papers on the
same day and continued the process on Monday, 18 June and the morning of 19 June,
oral argument beginning at 2 pm on that day and ending at noon on Wednesday,
g   27 June. After a short adjournment we announced that the appeals would be dismissed
and undertook to give our reasons as soon as possible. This we now do.
   It is customary for judgments in the Court of Appeal to begin by 'setting the scene'
before moving on to an examination of the arguments and an expression of the court's
conclusions. We do not propose to do so in this instance for three reasons. The first is the
time factor. To do so would be time-consuming, for the whole system of local
h   government finance is complex and the legislation with which we are concerned could
not have been expected to, and has not, simplified matters. Second, those immediately
concerned are fully familiar with the background and issues, whilst those more remotely
concerned, notably the community charge payers, are much more interested in the result
than how it is arrived at. Third, notwithstanding Leggatt LJ's expressed fears that, whilst
the Divisional Court had reached clear conclusions, pressure of time might have led to
j   the presentation of those conclusions and of the reasons for them being less than
felicitous, the judgment of the Divisional Court is in fact a model of clarity on which we
could not possibly improve. Instead, therefore, of ourselves seeking to 'set the scene', we
propose in this instance to treat the Divisional Court's account of the statutory and factual
background as incorporated as a preface to our judgments or at least to assume that all

who wish to refer to our judgments will have read the Divisonal Court's judgment, studied it carefully and appreciated that, in default of so doing, our own judgments may not be fully intelligible.

a

THE MAIN ARGUMENT

The scope of judicial review

This received consideration in the Divisional Court's judgment. We agree with the judges of that court that this is a case in which the separation of powers between the legislature, the executive and the judiciary is relevant and important. It is no less important that the nature of this separation and the precise role of the judiciary should be understood by politicians, press and public alike. In particular they should appreciate that we are not concerned with whether the new system of local taxation is or is not 'a good thing'. Nor are we concerned with the merits or demerits of particular aspects of this system or with the wisdom or lack of wisdom displayed by the Secretary of State in taking the actions which we have been called on to examine. These are matters for Parliament and not for us.

b

c

The role of the judiciary is essentially that of a referee. In saying this we do not suggest for one moment that the Secretary of State and the local authorities are involved in any sort of game. But the powers and duties of each of them are governed by rules. In the Football World Cup, which is engaging the attention of so many at the present time, the moves made by the players and the tactics employed by the teams are matters entirely for them. The referee is only involved when it appears that some player has acted in breach of the rules. The referee may then stop play and take some remedial action but, tempting though it may be, it is not for him to express any view on the skill of the players or how he would have acted in their position. Still less, following a breach of the rules, does he take over the position of one of the players. So too with the judiciary.

d

e

The role of the referee in the World Cup is somewhat simpler than that of the judiciary to the extent at least that he is applying the same set of rules to every game. In our field, the rules are made by Parliament supplemented by and against the background of rules of the common law, but the complication lies in the fact that Parliament, understandably and indeed inevitably, tends to lay down different rules for different situations. We are therefore continually being faced with the need to study, interpret and apply new versions of the rules. Indeed, the problem is usually not so much finding out what has happened on 'the field of play', as deciding whether what happened was or was not in breach of the rules. That is certainly true of the present dispute, the Secretary of State's powers and duties being derived from a brand new and politically controversial statute, namely the Local Government and Finance Act 1988.

f

In general we agree with the analysis of the Divisonal Court. Thus allegations of illegality, procedural impropriety and, which is not alleged, bad faith or improper motive are clearly within our purview. Where we differ from the Divisional Court is in relation to its exposition of a limitation on our jurisdiction under the head of 'irrationality', which, basing itself on *Nottinghamshire CC v Secretary of State for the Environment* [1985] 1 All ER 199, [1986] AC 240, it thought was imposed on, or should be accepted by, the courts when confronted with disputes concerning public financial administration where the decision impugned has been or will be subject to approval by one or both Houses of Parliament. We think that the Divisional Court misunderstood that decision which, like this case, was concerned with local taxation. If the House of Lords had so decided, it would have been inconsistent with *F Hoffmann-La Roche & Co AG v Secretary of State for Trade and Industry* [1974] 2 All ER 1128 esp at 1140, 1159, [1975] AC 295 esp at 349, 372 per Lord Morris and Lord Cross.

g

h

j

The constitutional position is clear. Subject only to a recent pronouncement by the Court of Justice of the European Communities (see *R v Secretary of State for Transport, ex p Factortame Ltd* Case C-213/89 [1990] 3 WLR 818), the significance of which has yet to

be worked out, Parliament has a limitless right to alter or add to the law by means of
a primary legislation, enacted by the full constitutional process of debate and decision in
both Houses on first and second readings of the Bill, committee and report stages and
third readings, followed by royal assent. The result is a statute and in relation to statutes
the only duty of the judiciary is to interpret and apply them.

Such a statute can, and often does, confer on the executive the right to legislate or,
which can amount to much the same thing, by direction to alter the rights and duties of
b others. In relation to such action by the executive, the judiciary has a wider role. It still
has to interpret the (subordinate) legislation or direction. But the validity of that
legislation or direction is open to challenge on the grounds that it was not authorised by
the enabling statute. The limits of the authority conferred by the statute will be partly
expressed and partly implied. Consultative and other procedures may be laid down by
the statute and must be strictly observed, if its authority is to be relied on. But further
c procedures, not inconsistent with the express terms of the statute or with the furtherance
of its apparent objectives, may be implied by the common law requirement of natural
justice or fairness in action as it has been described. In the event of a challenge to the
validity of subordinate legislation or executive action, based on an alleged breach of the
express or implied terms of the enabling statute, the challenge may fall to be considered
by the courts under the general headings of 'illegality' or 'procedural impropriety' and it
d has not been suggested that this aspect of our jurisdiction is in any way limited by the
fact that the action sought to be reviewed may concern financial administration or be
subject to parliamentary approval. It is solely in relation to the third of the heads of the
judicial review jurisdiction enumerated by Lord Diplock in *Council of Civil Service Unions
v Minister for the Civil Service* [1984] 3 All ER 935, [1985] AC 374, namely 'irrationality',
that any question has arisen.

e This head is relevant if it is alleged that the decision taker has had regard to matters
which are legally irrelevant or has failed to have regard to matters which are legally
relevant or that his decision would frustrate the policy of the Act on which he relies for
his authority (see *Padfield v Minister of Agriculture Fisheries and Food* [1968] 1 All ER 694,
[1968] AC 997). There is nothing in the judgments in the *Nottinghamshire CC* case to
suggest that this aspect of the jurisdictional head of 'irrationality' has no application to
f decisions concerning public financial administration, whether or not they are also subject
to review by one or both Houses of Parliament and no principle dictates that this should
be the case.

This leaves only the other limb of the 'irrationality' jurisdiction, namely a decision 'so
unreasonable that no reasonable authority could ever have come to it' (per Lord Greene
MR in *Associated Provincial Picture Houses Ltd v Wednesbury Corp* [1947] 2 All ER 680 at
g 685, [1948] 1 KB 223 at 234). It was to this that Lord Scarman referred in the
Nottinghamshire CC case [1986] 1 All ER 199 at 202, [1986] AC 240 at 247 when he said:

'. . . I refuse in this case to examine the detail of the guidance or its consequences.
My reasons are these. Such an examination by a court *would be justified* only *if a
prima facie* case were to be shown for holding that the Secretary of State had acted in
h bad faith, or for an improper motive, or *that the consequences of his guidance were so
absurd that he must have taken leave of his senses.* The evidence comes nowhere near
establishing any of these propositions.' (Our emphasis.)

From this and other passages in the speeches, we have concluded that the *Nottinghamshire
CC* case does not deny the 'irrationality' jurisdiction. It asserts it, but at the same time
j warns against the risk of the courts exceeding that jurisdiction by considering not
whether the decision was irrational in the sense of being perverse (no reasonable authority
properly acting in good faith and within its powers, applying its mind to all relevant
considerations and refraining from taking account of irrelevant considerations, could
ever have come to it) but the wholly different question of whether the decision was

reasonable, in the sense of being sensible or politic. To consider the latter question would be an abuse of power by the judiciary itself, for, within whatever the ambit of the *a* authority given to the decision maker by Parliament, the decision maker is sovereign.

This warning is particularly apposite in cases which involve public financial administration. One of the principal responsibilities of the government of the day is the formulation and execution of fiscal and economic policies. Accordingly, those are areas in which traditionally Parliament gives the executive a wide discretion and a fortiori where Parliament reserves to itself a power to review the political wisdom of particular *b* decisions by requiring that they, or some aspect of them, be subject to approval by one or both Houses. But, just as political wisdom and policy is for Parliament and not for the courts, so the extent of the decision taker's authority is for the courts and not for Parliament. Were it otherwise a parliamentary motion of approval could validate action taken without authority and Parliament would in effect be legislating otherwise than by the full statutory procedure. This, as things stand at present, would be wholly *c* unconstitutional. What can be said, and should be said, is that, where Parliament has retained a right to review a decision made under its authority, it is likely that the discretion which has been conferred on the decision taker will be wider than might otherwise be the case and that this should be borne in mind by the courts in determining the limits of his authority and in considering whether he has exceeded that authority.

It may be convenient to mention at this point, although logically it comes later, that *d* the applicants complain that the Divisional Court misappreciated the role of the House of Commons in approving or disapproving a draft order laid before it pursuant to s 104(8) or s 106(4) preparatory, and as a condition precedent, to making an operative order under s 104(2) or s 106(3), that being the order which definitively fixes the amount of the 'cap'. The Divisional Court expressed the view that:

'. . . it will be open to the House of Commons when considering the capping order to conclude that the Secretary of State should not have designated the relevant authorities.'

(See p 603, ante.)

The applicants sought to persuade us that the House of Commons would be fettered *f* by its own rules from so deciding. In our judgment, it is not for us to consider the scope of debate or decision by the House of Commons, but only the effects of its decision. We therefore decline to express any view on this point.

What is, however, clear as a matter of law is that, if the House of Commons does not approve the relevant draft order when it is laid before it, the Secretary of State will be unable to make a valid order under s 104 or s 106 imposing a cap of a defined amount. What is also clear, as a matter of law, is that, in the absence of further parliamentary *g* action, the authorities who have received notices of designation under s 102 will remain designated whatever the fate of any draft order and, in theory at least, could be the subject of separate principles when the Secretary of State comes to consider exercising his powers under s 100 in the next financial year. The political and practical consequences of this are not for us.

The power to designate authorities

This power arises under s 100(1) in the case of charging authorities and s 100(2) in the case of precepting authorities. In each case the Secretary of State's power arises in two different situations. The first is where the amount calculated by a charging authority in relation to the year under s 95(4) is, or the aggregate amount of precepts issued by a *j* precepting authority are, in the opinion of the Secretary of State, 'excessive'. In either or both cases s 100(4) applies and a decision whether to designate has to be—

'made in accordance with principles determined by the Secretary of State and, in the case of an authority falling within any of the classes specified in subsection (5)

below, those principles shall be the same either for all authorities falling within that
class or for all of them which respectively have and have not been designated under
this Part as regards the preceding financial year.'

The nature of the power

It was submitted that the power to designate constituted a power akin to judicial
review. The Secretary of State was obliged to ask himself whether a local authority,
circumstanced as was the particular local authority, could, acting reasonably and within
the proper scope of its discretion, have calculated the amount which it did under s 95(4)
or could have issued the aggregate amount of precepts which it did issue. In order words,
he was required by Parliament to apply *Wednesbury* standards. We reject this submission.
Whilst it would not be impossible for Parliament to have created an ad hoc quasi-judicial
review system, with the possibility of the result itself being subject to true judicial review
(see, for example, *Secretary of State for Education and Science v Tameside Metropolitan Borough*
[1976] 3 All ER 665, [1977] AC 1014), it would be unusual. Looking at Pt VII of the
1988 Act as a whole, we have no doubt that something quite different was intended,
namely that the Secretary of State should review the actions of the local authorities and,
exercising his own discretion afresh as contrasted with reviewing *their* exercise of
discretion, should decide whether or not to designate.

'Excessive'

The Divisional Court has been much criticised for saying 'if in his opinion the [s 95(4)]
amount is excessive' means 'if he thinks it is more than it should be'. In saying this, the
Divisional Court was not treating the Secretary of State as if he were Humpty Dumpty
in *Through the Looking Glass* ch 6: 'When I use a word . . . it means just what I chose it to
mean.' It is the natural and ordinary meaning of the words 'if in his opinion . . . the
amount is excessive'. But it does, of course, involve him in making a comparison. The
s 95(4) amount must be excessively more than something. In the case of s 100(1)(*a*), the
basis of comparison is left to the Secretary of State to determine. In the case of s 100(1)(*b*),
Parliament has specified that basis, namely the 'increase in the amount so calculated by it
in relation to the preceding year under section 95(4)' and the Secretary of State's task is
simply to form an opinion on whether any such increase can properly be described as
'excessive'. Analogous provisions covering precepting authorities are to be found in
s 100(2). Although there has been no preceding year the transitional provisions of s 103
enable a notional previous year's s 95(4) amount or aggregate amount of precepts to be
calculated.

The applicants would very much have preferred the Secretary of State to have relied
on s 100(1)(*b*) and (2)(*b*), because the basis of comparison would then have been what in
relation to the preceding year they had themselves considered to be a reasonable and
proper level of expenditure taking full account of the needs of their respective areas. In
other words, such a basis would have eliminated the effect of historic overspend, if any.
This is understandable, but Parliament has said that the Secretary of State may designate
on either basis and the choice is his. He has chosen to rely on s 100(1)(*a*) and (2)(*a*).

The principles governing designation

There was some argument whether, as the Divisional Court held, the Secretary of
State, in forming a view whether an amount was excessive, could only come to that
conclusion by reference to the principles which he is obliged to determine under s 100(4)
for purposes of deciding which, if any, authorities he would designate. These are also
principles which he is obliged to notify to the authorities concerned when designating
them (see s 102(1)). Whilst the Act does not in terms require this, the Secretary of State,
in forming an opinion that amounts were excessive, had, of course, to do so on some
rational basis. It would be surprising if the principles governing designation were not
the same as, or a refinement of, those which he adopted in forming an opinion on

excessiveness. In fact, as we know from paras 107 to 109 of the first affidavit of Mr Rowsell (an assistant secretary in the Department of the Environment), the Secretary of *a* State decided to adopt standard spending assessments (SSAs) as the benchmark or touchstone for the determination of whether there would be 'excessive spending' and an authority's budget could be regarded as 'excessive' and then measured that excess by reference to percentage and per adult overspend against SSA for the purpose of deciding which, if any, authorities should be designated. He was thus using the same *principles* for purposes of sub-ss (1) and (2) of s 100 as for sub-s (4), although their application under *b* s 100(4) was limited by additional criteria. Whether or not the Secretary of State was, as we think, obliged to do this, he was clearly entitled to do so.

The point was taken that what the Secretary of State had to consider was whether the s 95(4) amount in the case of a charging authority and the aggregate amount of precepts in the case of a precepting authority were 'excessive' and that this was not the same as 'spending'. It is quite true that there is a difference in that the two types of amount which *c* the Secretary of State was called on to consider could, for example, include or reflect budgetary provision for the use or creation of reserves and for defined contingencies. Transfers to and from reserves do not involve spending and the contingencies may never happen. Whilst Mr Rowsell's words may be open to this criticism, we are quite satisfied from the evidence as a whole and, in particular, Mr Rowsell's fourth affidavit that the Secretary of State was well aware of what amounts he had to characterise as being or not *d* being 'excessive'. The relationship between 'spending' in popular parlance and the amounts with which he was concerned is very close.

The use of SSAs

It was said that it was inappropriate for the Secretary of State to base his designation principles on SSAs. Once again, it has to be said that it is not for us to decide whether the *e* Secretary of State could have found a more appropriate basis. What we have had to consider was whether they were a permissible basis in the light of the Secretary of State's statutory mandate. The main criticisms were that (a) they reflect the government's macro-economic policy as applied to local authorities and, as such, took no or no sufficient account of local needs, (b) they took no account of paras (b), (c) and (d) of s 95(2), which feed through into the calculation called for by s 95(4), and (c) they were devised for a *f* different purpose, namely determining the proper distribution of revenue support grant.

As a matter of policy the Secretary of State determined a figure for the total spending by local authorities during the year 1990–91 (TSS). That figure was £3,280m. It included his estimate of revenue expenditure financed by specific grants. If these were deducted, a figure of £2,980·53m (net TSS) resulted. Under s 80 of the 1988 Act the Secretary of State was required to prepare a report containing the basis on which he proposed to *g* distribute revenue support grant and to lay that report before Parliament. He did so and the distribution report defined 'net TSS' as—

> 'the amount of revenue expenditure falling to be financed via the Collection Fund which he considers appropriate for all local authorities in England to incur to finance a standard level of service [subject to the special position of the City of London] and *h* is equal to the sum of the S.S.A.'s for all authorities.'

It is thus right to say that SSAs reflect the government's macro-economic policy. It is not, however, right to say that individual SSAs took no account of local needs. As part of the process leading to the distribution report, there was extensive consultation between the Secretary of State and representatives of classes of local authorities in which there was *j* fierce competition for larger slices of the fixed cake of net TSS on the basis of local needs.

The total of the grant-related expenditure (GRE) determined under the previous legislation, the equivalent of TSS, took account of national economic policy, this being a factor specified in the relevant statute. This particular provision is not reproduced in the

1988 Act, but we can see no possible reason for holding that the Secretary of State was
a not entitled to take it into account even if he was no longer bound to do so. In view of
the importance of local authority expenditure to the economy of this country, it would
be astonishing if he could not. So far as local needs are concerned, it is not for us to decide
whether individual SSAs adequately reflected them, this being a matter which quite
clearly falls within the scope of the Secretary of State's discretion.

This leaves the complaint that individual SSAs are not comparable with amounts
b calculated under s 95(4) because, it was said, they took no account of s 95(2)(b), (c) and
(d). It would appear that this point was not raised in the court below and we admitted
further evidence to deal with it. On the evidence, and in particular that contained in Mr
Rowsell's fourth affidavit, this complaint is misconceived. We do not think it helpful,
and it would add very considerably to the length of this judgment, if we set that evidence
out in full. Much of it is now common ground, and it would appear that the applicants'
c real grievance concerns the Secretary of State's treatment of reserves and contingencies.
The need to take account of contingencies is undoubtedly reflected in the SSAs and it is
not for us to consider whether this reflection is or is not adequate. That was for the
Secretary of State. As to reserves, the Secretary of State decided that, whilst no doubt
some authorities in the light of their individual circumstances would draw from or add
to reserves, the appropriate aggregate figure for movement in reserves was 'nil'. He also
d decided that the appropriate amount to be included in the aggregate for contribution to
reserves in order to meet deficits for earlier years was 'zero'. Both these decisions were
made within the legitimate scope of his discretion. There was a subsidiary complaint
that some local authorities were in a worse position than others, because they had
outstanding loans which had to be serviced and those loans had been approved by the
Secretary of State in previous years. Individual SSAs should, they submitted, take account
e of this fact. The facts underlying this complaint appear to be mistaken in that the
Secretary of State approves borrowing in general terms, but is not concerned to approve
the specific purposes for which the borrowing is undertaken or the specific needs which
gave rise to it.

Against this background it is not correct to assert that SSAs take no account of these
f matters. They do take account of them, but give them no weight. The applicants say that
this renders the SSAs an inappropriate yardstick both for judging excessiveness and for
designation. In our judgment, it was open to the Secretary of State in the exercise of his
discretion to say:

'Your s 95(4) amount is excessive and indeed so excessive that I intend to designate.
In so far as this excess arises out of historic commitments or difficulties peculiar to
g your authority, such as an unusual unwillingness on the part of your tenants to pay
their rents, this renders your s 95(4) amount no less excessive. All that it does is to
explain wholly or in part why it is excessive. I appreciate that it would be wrong to
make an order restricting the amount calculated under s 95(4) to a level which is
not reasonably achievable and I have taken these special factors into account in
making my proposal under s 102(1)(c). Further I will reconsider this figure if you
h challenge it under s 102(5)(a).'

This in substance is precisely what the Secretary of State has done. It was a policy decision
entrusted to him by Parliament.

The use of the same principles for all classes of authority
j   It was argued that this contravened s 100(4), which, by implication, required a separate
decision to be made in relation to each class. Even if this was correct, it is not clear to us
why the Secretary of State should not, in the exercise of his discretion, reach the
conclusion that the same principles were appropriate to each class. In fact, we do not
consider that there is any such implication. All that s 100(4) does is to require the

Secretary of State (a) to designate in accordance with principles determined by him and (b) to apply the same principles to all authorities within the same class which respectively *a* have and have not been designated as regards the preceding financial year.

Leaving this point, which turns on the construction of s 100(4), the applicants then argued that the functions of the various classes of authority were so disparate that there could be no rational basis for applying the same principles to all classes. Whilst we accept that the Secretary of State's selection of principles must have some rational basis, we reject this submission. SSAs take some account of these disparities and whether they do so *b* sufficiently to enable them to be used as a basis of designation is well within the limits of the Secretary of State's discretion. In fact, he did apply a modified principle in the case of the Inner London boroughs by excluding expenditure inherited from the Inner London Education Authority. Some or all of the authorities would have wished him to apply modified principles in the case of other classes. He did not do so. That was one of the many matters which Parliament has left to be decided in the exercise of his discretion. *c*

The £600 point

The applicants argue that by using a double test of eligibility for designation, 12½% above SSA and £75 above the SSA level of charge per charge payer, the Secretary of State is in fact using different tests for different authorities in the same class. The factual basis for this argument is that an authority whose SSA is more than £600 per head of its *d* relevant population will reach the £75 limit before it reaches the 12½% limit and only the latter will be decisive in its case. By contrast one whose SSA is less than £600 per head will reach the 12½% limit before it reaches the £75 limit and only the latter will be decisive in its case.

This too we reject. The test is a composite one and both limbs apply to all authorities within the class. That in some cases it is one 'trigger' which is pulled first and in other *e* cases the other is quite immaterial, since nothing happens until both have been pulled. Thereafter the second principle comes into play. This is designed to exclude authorities whose 'overspend' is less than £15m or £26 per head. The Secretary of State introduced it in order to avoid designating and capping authorities where the financial benefit to charge payers would or might be outweighed by the costs of implementation. The *f* decision to adopt both principles seems to us to be well within the scope of the Secretary of State's discretion.

The £75 point

The complaint here is that the Secretary of State has used the £75 criterion separately for precepting authorities and for charging authorities. As a result, it is said, charge payers could theoretically be exposed to a £150 excess and that the extent of the *g* protection in fact afforded to charge payers depends on the mix of original and precepted expenditure.

The Secretary of State's answer is that he considered apportioning the £75, but concluded that any apportionment would involve arbitrary judgments and that it was not desirable to do so. This is a judgment for the Secretary of State in the exercise of his *h* discretion and is not one which it is appropriate for us to review.

The parish councils point

This is a connected complaint. SSAs have been calculated so as to take account of precepts by parish councils, but expenditure leading to the s 95(4) calculations does not include the precepted sums. This, it is said, gives an advantage to the authorities which *j* are exposed to parish council precepts, in the sense that they can 'overspend' to a greater extent than other councils without risk of being designated. The facts are admitted, but the Secretary of State has taken the view that whilst in a marginal situation the fact that parish precepts are not part of a district council's s 95(4) calculation could lead to its budget escaping being judged excessive, whereas otherwise it would be so judged, the

problem was not of such a magnitude as to justify the making of any special provision.
a This again was a judgment for the Secretary of State in the exercise of his discretion.

Retrospectivity
    The Divisional Court dealt with this aspect of the case in its judgment. It received a
passing mention in argument before us and we think that we will do it no injustice if we
say only that we agree with the reasoning of the Divisional Court.
b
Cuts in-year
    The Divisional Court dealt with this in its judgment. The difficulty is real, but it was
one of the many factors for consideration by the Secretary of State in fixing the proposed
maxima under s 102(1)(c) and for reconsideration, if the authority relies on it, following
a challenge under s 102(5). Nothing in the evidence suggested that he has not considered
c it. Whether the weight which he attached to it was or was not adequate in particular
cases is not something which we are entitled to review. For that he is answerable to
Parliament and not to the court.

Procedural impropriety
    All the applicants contend that, in seeking to implement the scheme of the 1988 Act,
d the Secretary of State has been guilty of procedural impropriety. It is variously put as a
failure to consult the local authorities, to inform them and to meet their legitimate
expectations. These alleged failures are said to have occurred in regard to three different
matters: (1) the principles he was minded to apply under s 100(4); (2) the exercise of his
discretion to designate under s 100(1); (3) proposing the maximum amount or cap
pursuant to s 102(1)(c).
e   1. *The principles*   The applicants contend that fairness required the Secretary of State
to tell local authorities the criteria by which he proposed to judge excessiveness. They
would then have had an opportunity to comment on them or would at least have been
forewarned before setting their budgets. The labour, expense and confusion involved in
recalculation after capping might thereby have been avoided. Contrary to the view of
the Divisional Court, it is argued that designation of an authority does remove certain
f rights and irrevocably affects it interests. The right and duty to fix its own budget is
removed. It is put in a separate category in the following year under s 100(4). Its standing
is likely to be damaged in the eyes of financial institutions and others. Even if Parliament
declines to approve the Secretary of State's draft order under s 104(8), the authority
remains designated.
    There is no requirement in the detailed procedures expressly laid down in the 1988
g Act for the Secretary of State to consult or inform authorities as to the principles he
proposes to adopt under s 100(4). There are in other contexts sections of the Act which
specifically show and implement Parliament's intention that there must be consultation.
The Divisional Court pointed to ss 76(5), 78(5) and 80(2). The applicants say those
sections are not in Pt VII of the Act and relate only to consultation with representatives
h of local government. But s 102, which *is* in Pt VII and is crucial to the scheme for
designation and capping, imposes a duty on the Secretary of State to tell the authority his
proposed figure and provide for a reasoned response by the authority in a specified time
before, having taken all relevant information into account, he makes his order. The
absence of any similar provision for consultation in s 100 is in conspicuous contrast.
    More cogent still is the effect of s 102(1)(b). That requires the Secretary of State, once
j he has decided to designate an authority, to notify it not only of that decision but of the
principles under s 100(4) by which he has reached it. If the Secretary of State were under
a duty to inform the authority what those principles are, before the latter decides its
budget, there would be no need to set them out again.
    The applicants assert that the mere absence of an express requirement to consult in the
Act does not absolve the Secretary of State of a duty to act fairly. The common law will

supplement the statute in requiring consultation unless the latter clearly shows the contrary. We agree with the Divisional Court that the whole structure of Pt VII does *a* show the contrary. Not only is there no requirement to consult in advance in s 100. There is by contrast a detailed scheme for consultation under s 102 and the requirement, *after designation*, to notify the authority of the principles.

Does this lead to unfairness? Whether the principles of natural justice apply to supplement a statutory scheme and the extent to which consultation is necessary in the interests of fairness depend on the subject matter (see *R v Gaming Board for GB, ex p* *b* *Benaim* [1970] 2 All ER 528 at 533, [1970] 2 QB 417 at 430 and *Payne v Lord Harris of Greenwich* [1981] 2 All ER 842 at 845, 850, 852, [1981] 1 WLR 754 at 757, 764, 766).

The applicants relied in the Divisonal Court on dicta of Lord Denning MR in *Secretary of State for Education and Science v Tameside Metropolitan Borough* [1976] 3 All ER 665 at 671, [1977] AC 1014 at 1025 where he said:

> 'To my mind, if a statute gives a Minister power to take drastic action if he is *c* satisfied that a local authority have acted or are proposing to act improperly or unreasonably, then the Minister should obey all the elementary rules of fairness before he finds that the local authority is guilty or before he takes drastic action overruling them. He should give the party affected notice of the charge of impropriety or unreasonableness and a fair opportunity of dealing with it.' *d*

However, the immediately preceding passage should also be noted:

> 'Much depends on the matter about which the Secretary of State has to be satisfied. If he is to be satisfied on a matter of opinion, that is one thing. But if he has to be satisfied that someone has been guilty of some discreditable or unworthy or unreasonable conduct, that is another.' *e*

Here the statute specifically provides in s 100(1) that the decision *is* to depend on the 'opinion of the Secretary of State'.

Reliance was also placed on *R v Secretary of State for the Environment, ex p Brent London BC* [1983] 3 All ER 321 at 354, [1982] QB 593 at 642, where Ackner LJ, in reviewing the reasoning in *McInnes v Onslow Fane* [1978] 3 All ER 211, [1978] 1 WLR 1520, indicated *f* that the principles of natural justice apply when the Secretary of State's decision involves taking away an existing right. Again, however, the immediately preceding passage is in point. Ackner LJ said:

> 'It is not possible to lay down rigid rules as to when principles of natural justice are to apply, nor as to their scope and extent. Everything depends on the subject matter (*R v Gaming Board for Great Britain, ex p Benaim* [1970] 2 All ER 528 at 533, *g* [1970] 2 QB 417 at 430 per Lord Denning MR). It is clear that different classes of cases were recognised in *Ridge v Baldwin* [1963] 2 All ER 66 at 74, [1964] AC 40 at 72 per Lord Reid.'

Before us Mr Henderson relied additionally on *A-G v Ryan* [1980] AC 718 at 727 and *Hillingdon London BC v Commission for Racial Equality* [1982] AC 779 at 787 to show that, *h* where there is power to affect an individual's rights, the person or body exercising the power must apply the principles of natural justice and give the individual an opportunity to be heard.

Clearly, cases in which there is an application by an individual, e g for a licence (*McInnes v Onslow Fane*) or for registration as a national (*A-G v Ryan*) or in which allegedly discreditable conduct is being investigated (e g the *Hillingdon London BC* case and *Re* *j* *Pergamon Press Ltd* [1970] 3 All ER 535, [1971] Ch 388), import a requirement to apply natural justice principles, because of the subject matter. But there is an important distinction between such cases in which a public body has power to affect the rights of an individual in the application of statutory provisions or of an established principle or

policy and a case, such as is before the court, where what the minister has to decide is the
a principle or policy itself.

Here, the Secretary of State had to decide what principles would govern designation
and adopted, as he was free to do, similar criteria for judging excessiveness in s 95(4)
calculations. The principles he adopted were based on SSAs. The process of arriving at
the SSA for each authority included extensive and thorough consultation. Once the SSA
was established, it represented not only the 'benchmark of accountability' to charge
b payers (who were to have it set out on their demand notices) but also a benchmark by
which the Secretary of State would measure actual budgets. Mr Henderson concedes that
local authorities might reasonably have expected SSAs to play some part in calculating
what the Secretary of State considered to be excessive. The complaint is that they were
not told the formula.

In *Wiseman v Borneman* [1969] 3 All ER 275 at 277, [1971] AC 297 at 308 Lord Reid
c said:

> 'For a long time the courts have, without objection from Parliament, supplemented
> procedure laid down in legislation where they have found that to be necessary for
> this purpose. But before this unusual kind of power is exercised it must be clear that
> the statutory procedure is insufficient to achieve justice and that to require additional
> *d* steps would not frustrate the apparent purpose of the legislature.'

It is the Secretary of State's view that to have revealed his criteria for designation to the
authorities in advance of their budgets *would* have frustrated one purpose of the
legislature.

Mr Rowsell in his first affidavit said that the Secretary of State bore in mind the
possibility that in some instances disclosing of criteria might prove a restraining influence
e on budgeting. It was also recognised that under the rate limitation system designation
was in advance of the relevant year so that authorities had time to adjust their budgets
before billing their ratepayers. However in his affidavit Mr Rowsell said:

> '91. [The Secretary of State] considered that announcing possible criteria before
> budgets were set could give the criteria the status of a norm or target which would
> *f* distort the very accountability the new system was designed to promote. This could
> encourage authorities to spend up to that target figure, thereby leading to an overall
> increase in local authority spending. It was for this reason that the decisions on
> designation for rate limitation had always been taken after the budgets for the
> preceding year had been set. He concluded that on balance there would be serious
> disadvantages in giving an indication of, or announcing criteria before budgets were
> *g* set. It could run counter to the very essence of the new system which is designed to
> let accountability operate between a local authority and its electorate.
> 92. In contrast to the grant system under Part V of the 1988 Act where there is a
> clear statutory scheme of consultation and notification of intentions, there is no such
> scheme for the exercise of powers of designation under Part VII of the Act. Nor was
> there any promise or practice of consultation on designation under the 1988 Act,
> *h* just as there had been no promise or indeed practice of consultation under the 1984
> Act.'

One may disagree with that view but it cannot in our judgment be said to be irrational
or contrary to the purpose of the statute, which aims to control spending and to achieve
accountability. Nor do we think it unfair, bearing in mind the full consultation there
j had already been over SSAs and the clear indication that budgeting substantially in excess
of them carried a risk of designation.

Mr Henderson next argued that the principles of designation and the test of
excessiveness chosen by the Secretary of State were contrary to the legitimate expectation
of the authorities. He does not base this on either of the grounds propounded by Lord

Fraser in *Council of Civil Service Unions v Minister for the Civil Service* [1984] 3 All ER 935 at 943–944, [1985] AC 374 at 401, ie express promise or regular practice. He relies on an implied promise to be inferred from statements in the speeches of ministers, especially those indicating that councils budgeting sensibly have nothing to fear. Apart from the difficulty of spelling out a legitimate expectation from general remarks in a ministerial speech, the word 'sensibly' involves a question of judgment and cannot be regarded as setting a standard. It must under the statute be for the minister's opinion what is sensible and what excessive. Again, reliance is placed on ministerial remarks that the SSA is not a target at which authorities should aim or a level to which they are obliged to reduce but that it was for local government to determine what it will spend on its services, being answerable to the electorate for the resulting charges. Carried to its logical conclusion, the authorities' argument that this gave rise to a legitimate expectation would preclude the minister from capping them at all. Finally, Mr Henderson relied on the 'assumed personal community charge' calculated for the purposes of transitional relief. He asserted that the calculation and use of this figure by the Secretary of State raised a legitimate expectation that no authority setting a charge at or below that figure would be capped. Haringey was chosen as an example of an authority allegedly misled. But it is clear from Haringey's own documents that it realised its assumed personal community charge might well be considered excessive. In the result we do not consider there is any merit in the arguments based on legitimate expectation.

2. *The discretion to designate* Having decided under s 100(1) that an authority's s 95(4) figure is excessive, the Secretary of State ought, it is said, to have told the authority he was minded to designate it before doing so. The authority could then have had an opportunity to persuade him not to designate or voluntarily to reduce its calculation pursuant to s 96.

Again, the detailed scheme of the 1988 Act does not provide for any consultation at that stage although it does at others. Nevertheless, it is argued, the common law requires such consultation to supplement the statutory scheme in the interests of fairness.

In our judgment, this contention is misconceived. The Secretary of State established principles under s 100(4) and decided to apply them both for the purposes of testing excessiveness and of designation as he was entitled to do. Once, therefore, he decided a figure was excessive, the authority fell to be designated under the principles. Since they have to be the same for all authorities within a class, it would be wrong for the Secretary of State to enter into individual negotiation, authority by authority, whether, where the principles bite, he should designate or take a more lenient view. Were he to do so he would be substituting a case-by-case discretion for the principles in deciding whether to designate.

3. *Proposing the cap under s 102(1)(c)* At this stage of the procedure, attention is concentrated not on general principles, nor on local authorities at large or even class by class, but on the appropriate figure for each individual authority. Clearly, on this issue, the views of each authority need in fairness to be heard. Section 102(5) provides for it. The Secretary of State under s 102(1) notifies the authority of the maximum figure he proposes. The authority may either accept that figure or within 28 days give written notice, for reasons stated therein, of its counter-proposal. Where there is such a counter-proposal, s 104 requires the Secretary of State, after considering any information he thinks relevant, to make an order fixing the cap. The order has to be approved by resolution of the House of Commons and the Secretary of State has then to serve notice on the authority stating the amount of the cap.

Notwithstanding the clear and precise procedure set out in those sections, counsel for Southwark argues that fairness requires the Secretary of State additionally to give reasons for this proposed figure. Without such reasons it is said that the local authority cannot properly present a reasoned counter-proposal. Failure by the Secretary of State to give them therefore frustrates the statutory right of an authority to present its reasoned

response and frustrates its legitimate expectation that the Secretary of State would explain
his proposals.

a   Because of the 28-day period, the argument of counsel for Southwark would necessarily
require the Secretary of State to give reasons for his proposed figure at or about the same
time as his s 102(1) notice. But this would mean rewriting s 102(1), which is not only
specific in its requirement but is enforced by the sanction in s 102(2) that, unless it is
observed precisely, the designation is invalid. Under s 102(1) the Secretary of State must
b   notify his decision to designate and the principles in relation to it (ie his reasons for
finding excessiveness and designating). He must also notify the cap he proposes but no
mention is made of giving reasons for his figure. In fact, the principles indicate clearly to
the authority on what basis he considered its calculation to be excessive. If, as was the
case with a number of authorities, the cap proposed was at the level dictated by the
principles (ie SSA plus 12½% or £75 per adult overspend against SSA) the authority knew
c   exactly how the figure was reached. If, as occurred in other cases, the Secretary of State's
proposed cap allowed some latitude above that level on grounds of achievability, there is
no reason why an authority should not be able to respond with a counter-proposal
explaining why the Secretary of State's figure is not achievable.

No doubt the statutory procedure was devised to take full account of the time factor,
which is crucial under the scheme. Local authority budgets were submitted in March
d   1990 for the financial year starting in April. The Secretary of State's decisions to designate
were made on 3 and 10 April. Clearly, the longer the process thereafter culminating in
orders approved by Parliament and notified to each authority, the greater the problems
in recalculating and reissuing demands for community charge payments and their
collection. The scheme is that the local authority puts forward its budget. The Secretary
of State supplements all the information he gained during consultation over SSAs by
e   seeking further and updated information (s 110(8)). He then in the designation notice
indicates his criteria of excessiveness to the authority and puts to them his proposed
figure. This is the statutory provision for consultation. The authority can then challenge
his figure for reasons which are specially within its own knowledge. In the end,
Parliament has to approve the order. We do not consider there is any unfairness in this
scheme requiring further provisions for consultation to be implied.

f   Counsel for Southwark relied on a number of cases in support of his argument.
However, as already indicated, the subject matter is all-important in considering the
application and scope of natural justice principles. *Kanda v Government of the Federation of
Malaya* [1962] AC 322 and *Durayappah v Fernando* [1967] 2 All ER 152, [1967] 2 AC 337
were both cases involving accusations against individuals. In *R v Brent London BC, ex p
Gunning* (1985) 84 LGR 168 the decision turned on the nature of the consultation about
g   education proposals and the adequacy of the consultative documents in the particular
case. Hodgson J seems to have accepted four basic principles suggested by counsel for
Southwark (set out at 189). The second of these was: 'That the proposer must give
sufficient reasons for any proposal to permit of intelligent consideration and response.'
In the context of this case, the SSAs, the principles of designation and the proposed cap
figure were, in our judgment, sufficient to permit of intelligent consideration and
h   response. The proof is that authorities have been able to put in detailed reasons to support
their counter-proposals. It may well be that an explanation from the Secretary of State
why and how his proposed figure was achievable would have been of assistance to each
authority, but that is a matter for him. We do not consider he was under a legal duty to
provide it.

j

The Derbyshire point
The Divisional Court, after rejecting the arguments based on procedural impropriety
said (see p 611, ante):

'We would, however, add that if the Secretary of State had available to him information from a source other than the local authority itself which he intended to take into account in determining the figure for insertion into the draft order under s 104(2) of the Act and of which the authority did not know (as s 110(8) makes possible) procedural fairness would, in our view, require him (subject to any proper claim to privilege) to make that information known to the local authority in time for it to respond should it so desire.'

Clearly, that passage caused all parties to re-examine their positions. The Secretary of State's policy, without accepting it as a legal obligation, had always been as a matter of grace to do what the Divisional Court enjoined. On re-examining their material, attention was focused in the department on a letter relevant only to Derbyshire's case. Hence, 'the Derbyshire point'. The letter, dated 14 March 1990, was from the leader of the minority Conservative group in the Derbyshire County Council to the Minister for Local Government. It criticised the Derbyshire budget and suggested that economies could be made under a number of heads which would have reduced the budget by a total of some £58m. The Secretary of State believed that the Derbyshire County Council knew of this information because of press reports and because of a meeting between members of the council and a minister on 15 March. However, following the Divisonal Court's judgment on 15 June, ex abundanti cautela, the Secretary of State sent a copy of the Conservative group's letter to the authority on 19 June indicating that he had taken its contents into consideration. It then emerged that the county council had not been aware of those contents. Moreover, the leader of the Conservative group has subsequently apologised by letter for substantial inaccuracies in the figures he gave originally.

There is no suggestion of any bad faith. Indeed, Mr Rowsell's first affidavit on 21 May 1990 expressly stated that information put forward by opposition parties had been taken into account (para 134). No point was taken as to non-disclosure before the Divisional Court.

Relying on the dicta of the Divisional Court, counsel for Derbyshire contends that there has been a procedural irregularity. Derbyshire should have had an opportunity to respond to the information from the Conservative group. Failure to give that opportunity should lead the court to strike down the Secretary of State's proposal of the cap figure for Derbyshire and, since s 102(1) requires a single notice, to strike down the notice of designation as a whole.

To summarise the facts, the notice of designation was issued on 3 April 1990. Derbyshire had 28 days in which to put in its s 102(5) notice. That period had therefore expired before the letter of 19 June drew attention to the Conservative group's letter. However, the Secretary of State has not yet proceeded under s 104(2) to make an order containing the cap figure and no order has therefore been laid before Parliament. Meanwhile, Derbyshire has had full opportunity to respond to the disclosed letter and, indeed, the Secretary of State is now aware of its challenge to its contents and the author's apology for them.

In our judgment, the Divisional Court was right. But the stage it referred to was after the notice under s 102(1) and before the making of a draft order under s 104(2), ie the period when the local authority has the opportunity of putting its proposals and reasons before the Secretary of State reaches his final conclusions. That is consistent with our holding that there was no duty on the Secretary of State to consult before designation. On this basis, there are no grounds for striking down the notice under s 102(1). Had the process advanced, before the letter was disclosed, to the point of an order being laid before Parliament or beyond, it may well have been open to Derbyshire to challenge the s 104 order. The success of such a challenge would depend, inter alia, on how significant the undisclosed information was and the part it played in the decision. Here, however, matters had not gone that far and there has been and still is time for Derbyshire's response to the letter to be taken into account by the Secretary of State in reaching his final figure.

Counsel for Derbyshire says that, since the 28-day period had passed before disclosure
a of the letter, it was too late for amends to be made. The statutory consultation period was
over. But the statute does not place any embargo on the giving or receiving of further
information between the expiry of the 28 days and the Secretary of State inserting a final
figure in his draft order. It merely states the period within which an authority may give
notice of its proposed figure with reasons. Even if failure to disclose the letter before
expiry of the 28 days did constitute a flaw in the procedure, as a matter of discretion the
b court would not interfere since in the circumstances no injustice will have resulted.

We therefore conclude that the challenges, general and particular, based on procedural
impropriety fail.

[The court then dealt with an argument based on the provisions of the Education
Reform Act 1988 directed to the legal relationship between the applicant authorities
which were local education authorities and the governors of schools in respect of which
c schemes for the local management of schools had been made under that Act. The
contention was that the budget of any school to which financial management had been
delegated under a scheme could not lawfully be reduced after the start of the financial
year to which that budget related, that accordingly the Secretary of State had misdirected
himself in making his decisions and that therefore the notices of designation could not
stand. The court rejected that argument, and continued:]

d

IN CONCLUSION

We, and probably counsel, have been very greatly assisted by the travaux préparatoires
constituted by the Divisional Court's judgment. We are no less grateful to all concerned
for the very considerable, and largely successful, efforts which they made to avoid
duplication of arguments whilst ensuring that every conceivable point was made in the
e interests of their respective clients. Nevertheless, and we make no complaint on this
account, the arguments were wide ranging and complex. If this judgment, in the
interests of brevity, might make it appear that some have not received the consideration
which those who put them forward may feel was their due, we can assure them and their
clients that each received the most careful consideration. Whether we have given them
due weight is for others to say.

f Finally, may we commend to the applicants the words of Lord Templeman in
Nottinghamshire CC v Secretary of State for the Environment [1986] 1 All ER 199 at 217,
[1986] AC 240 at 267:

'Judicial review is not just a move in an interminable chess tournament . . . I hope
that in future local authorities will bite on the bullet and not seek to persuade the
g courts to absolve them from compliance with the Secretary of State's guidance. If
for any particular city or for any group of cities guidance is set too low, having
regard to their peculiar needs, then persuasion should be offered not to the judges,
who are not qualified to listen, but to the department, the minister, all members of
parliament and ultimately to the electorate.'

h Appeals dismissed. Southwark's application for a declaration refused. Local authorities granted
leave to appeal to the House of Lords. Brent School governors refused leave to appeal to the House
of Lords.

Frances Rustin   Barrister.

j Appeals
Sixteen of the local authorities, viz Avon County Council, Barnsley Metropolitan Borough
Council, Basildon District Council, Brent London Borough Council, Bristol City Council,
Camden London Borough Council, Derbyshire County Council, Doncaster Metropolitan
Borough Council, Hammersmith and Fulham, Islington, Lambeth London borough

councils, North Tyneside, Rochdale, Rotherham and St Helens metropolitan borough
councils, appealed.

a

Roger Henderson QC, John Howell and *Timothy Mould* for all the councils other than
Derbyshire.
Alan Newman QC and *Philip Engleman* for Derbyshire.
John Laws, Presiley Baxendale and *Paul Walker* for the Secretary of State.

b

At the conclusion of the hearing their Lordships dismissed the appeals stating that they
would give their reasons for judgment later.

4 October. The following opinions were delivered.

LORD BRIDGE OF HARWICH. My Lords, the Local Government Finance Act   *c*
1988, as amended by the Local Government and Housing Act 1989, introduces a radically
reformed system of local government finance and local taxation in place of the long
familiar rating system. As is well known, the central feature of the new system, the
community charge, is a matter of acute political controversy. Scarcely less controversial
in a political sense is the control which the 1988 Act enables the Secretary of State for the
Environment to exercise over the finances of individual local authorities, subject to   *d*
approval by the House of Commons, by setting a maximum which an authority's budget
may not exceed and thereby limiting the amount which those liable to the community
charge in that authority's area can be required to pay. The process is colloquially referred
to as 'charge capping' or simply 'capping' and this is a convenient terminology to adopt
for brevity when referring to the statutory process. The current financial year,
commencing on 1 April 1990, is the first year of the operation of the new system. After   *e*
local authorities had set their budgets for the year the Secretary of State proposed to cap
21 authorities, 19 of which challenged the legality of the action taken by the Secretary of
State in proceedings for judicial review. These applications, together with certain others,
were argued extensively by a galaxy of counsel appearing for the different authorities,
first before the Divisonal Court of the Queen's Bench Division (Leggatt LJ, McCullough
and Roch JJ), which gave judgment dismissing the applications on 15 June, and, second,   *f*
before the Court of Appeal (Lord Donaldson MR, Ralph Gibson and Taylor LJJ), which
dismissed the authorities' appeals on 27 June but gave leave to appeal to your Lordships'
House. The Court of Appeal gave reasons for its decision in a reserved judgment on
3 July. Only 16 authorities, all but one now represented by the same counsel, availed
themselves of the leave to appeal which had been granted. Your Lordships were able to
report to the House on 17 July your unanimous opinion that the appeals should be   *g*
dismissed so that an order to that effect might be made without delay, but then indicated
that reasons for the decision would be given later.
     I would like, if I may, at the outset to express my unqualified admiration for the
thoroughness and the speed with which both courts below adjudicated on the issues
raised before them in these proceedings. The importance of an early determination was
obvious. Both courts had to consider a formidable volume of documentary material and   *h*
heard many days of oral argument, but were able within a very short time following the
conclusion of the argument to deliver lengthy reserved judgments dealing comprehensively with every issue raised. I agree entirely with the conclusions which they reached
and, in large measure, would be content to indorse the detailed reasoning in both
judgments. Some of the points argued below were not pursued in your Lordships' House   *j*
and of the many points which were argued I shall find it neither necessary nor useful to
examine every one in detail. But having the opportunity, which the courts below were
denied, for reflection at leisure in the formulation of my reasons, I hope it may be
possible to examine from a rather broader perspective the legitimacy of the grounds on
which the local authorities seek to challenge the action taken by the Secretary of State.

It is necessary first to consider the broad scheme of the legislation. In the explanations
a that follow I acknowledge my indebtedness to the helpful guidence through the
complexities of the 1988 Act provided by the affidavit of Mr Paul Rowsell, an assistant
secretary in the Department of the Environment and the head of its Finance Local
Authority Expenditure and Revenues Division. Local authorities are divided into
charging authorities, which are also referred to as receiving authorities, and precepting
authorities. Among the appellants the charging authorities are either district councils or
b London borough councils and the precepting authorities are county councils. The income
of both classes of authority is derived from three main sources, the revenue support
grant, non-domestic rates and the community charge. It is the responsibility of the
charging authorities to set and collect the community charge. Charging authorities also
receive from central government their share of the revenue support grant and of the
national pool of non-domestic rates. From this income charging authorities must fund
c the services they provide and meet the precepts of precepting authorities. Precepting
authorities derive their income from the precepts they serve on charging authorities.

The amount of the revenue support grant for any financial year is determined by two
reports required to be made by the Secretary of State to, and approved by, the House of
Commons. The first, under s 78 of the 1988 Act, determines the global amount of grant,
the second, under s 80, determines the amounts to be distributed to individual receiving
d authorities. The Act provides for consultation with representatives of local government
before the Secretary of State determines the amount of the global grant.

Non-domestic rates are payable by occupiers of non-domestic property according to a
national rate poundage set by the Secretary of State. The rates are collected by charging
authorities but accounted for entirely to the Secretary of State and then distributed by
him to receiving authorities in proportion to their relevant population.

e Thus it will be seen that the amount of income which a local authority will receive in
any year from these two central sources is directly determined by the central government
and in the case of the revenue support grant is subject to the approval of the House of
Commons.

It is through the community charge alone that a local authority is able in some degree
to determine its own local expenditure and taxation policies. Again, as is now well
f known, at whatever rate the community charge is set by the authority it is payable,
subject to reliefs and exemptions, at that rate by each adult resident in the local authority's
area, representing broadly speaking the local electorate. As explained in the affidavit of
Mr Rowsell, the political thinking which underlies the new system is that it will operate
to secure that local authorities are properly accountable to their electorate.

At the centre of the budgeting process prescribed for charging authorities are the
g calculations required to be undertaken for each financial year by s 95 of the 1988 Act, as
amended by paras 1 and 63 of Sch 5 to the 1989 Act. Section 95(2) lists the main heads of
revenue expenditure and certain other items for which funds must be provided on
revenue account. Section 95(3) lists certain sources of funds available to meet the
requirements under s 95(2), not including the three main sources of income. Having
h estimated these amounts, a charging authority must then calculate the difference between
them under s 95(4), which is, in substance, the aggregate of estimated expenditure falling
to be met out of the three main sources of income, revenue support grant, non-domestic
rates and the community charge. I shall refer to this for brevity and convenience as the
authority's annual budgeted expenditure. A parallel budgeting process is prescribed by
s 68 for precepting authorities. A precepting authority's annual budgeted expenditure
j represents the amount it requires to raise by precepts which will reflect its own share of
the revenue support grant and non-domestic rates included in the sums allocated to
receiving authorities and also the additional amount which charging authorities require
to raise by their community charge to meet the balance of the precepting authority's
annual budgeted expenditure.

The amounts of the annual budgeted expenditure of precepting and charging authorities are the focal points of the whole system. It is by reference to these amounts that the Secretary of State's powers of capping are exercisable and it is by reference to *a* these amounts that community charges are set. The statutory programme is such that before authorities set their budgets they will know how much they are to receive by way of revenue support grant and non-domestic rates and thus what is the balance required to be raised by way of community charge. Precepting authorities set their budgets before charging authorities, which therefore also know how much they require to raise to meet precepts. Thus when a charging authority sets its community charge it is determined by *b* the amount required to meet precepts made on it, so far as that amount exceeds the precepting authority's relevant share of revenue support grant and non-domestic rates and the amount by which the charging authority's own annual budgeted expenditure exceeds its own share of revenue support grant and non-domestic rates.

I have not included in this very much abbreviated and necessarily over simplified account of the main provisions of the 1988 Act any reference to transitional arrangements *c* or to the so-called 'safety net', which are complex and do not, I think, throw any light on the issues falling for determination in the appeals. But before turning to the capping provisions themselves I must summarise, as briefly as I can, the steps taken by the Secretary of State in the operation of the statutory machinery generally which form the essential background to his subsequent operation of the capping machinery in relation *d* to the appellant authorities.

The Secretary of State announced in July 1989 that the amount the government considered appropriate as the global total of local authority revenue expenditure on services in the year 1990–91 was £32·8bn. This becomes the figure referred to in various reports as total standard spending (TSS), which plays a key role in determining the amount to be distributed by way of revenue support grant, the amount to be raised from non-domestic rates and the amount considered by the Secretary of State as appropriate to *e* be raised by the community charge. The other key concept which features in the Secretary of State's calculation of these amounts and in the breakdown of TSS is the standard spending assessment (SSA). A local authority's SSA is the amount which it is estimated that the authority would require to spend in the year to maintain a level of services to a common standard determined by reference to TSS as the total available for spending by all authorities. The calculation of SSAs is a matter of great complexity in *f* detail but the basic principles which govern it are simple. The services which local authorities provide are divided into seven major blocks as follows: education, personal social services, police, fire and civil defence, highway maintenance, all other services and capital financing. Each major service block is allocated a control total representing the share of TSS available countrywide to fund that service or those services. A local *g* authority's individual SSA is built up from separate elements calculated for each of the major services for which that authority is responsible. Each separate element is calculated by a formula reflecting the physical, social and demographic characteristics of the authority's area in so far as they are relevant to the cost of providing the service concerned. The objective is that an authority's SSA should provide a benchmark of the level of expenditure appropriate to enable the authority to provide services to a common standard *h* consistent with authorities in total spending to the level dictated by TSS.

The detailed basis on which SSAs were eventually calculated was the outcome of extensive consultation throughout 1989 between officials of the Department of the Environment and officers of the local authority associations. On 6 November 1989 the Secretary of State issued a consultation paper setting out his proposals for grant determination and a draft of his proposed distribution report, indicating a proposed *j* calculation of SSAs, to the English local authority associations and local authorities, inviting the comments of the associations and indicating that he would consider any representations made by individual authorities. In a statement to the House of Commons announcing the consultation paper the Secretary of State made clear that his principal

objective in the proposed grant distribution was to ensure that, in general, if each
a authority spent so as to provide a common standard of services, the community charge
could be set at the same level in every area before allowing for the transitional
arrangements.

After considering comments and representations made in response to the consultation
paper relating, inter alia, to the proposed total of the revenue support grant, the proposed
control total for different services and the proposed methodology for calculating SSAs,
b the Secretary of State submitted his definitive proposals to the House of Commons in the
Revenue Support Grant Report (England) 1990–91 and the Revenue Support Grant
Distribution Report (England) under ss 78 and 80 of the Act respectively. These reports
were approved by the House of Commons on 18 January. The report under s 78
determined the total amount of the revenue support grant at £9·647bn and determined
the rate poundage for non-domestic rates at a level estimated to yield a distributable
c amount of £10·428m. The report under s 80 set out the definitive basis on which SSAs
were to be calculated. The opening paragraph of the section of the report, headed
'Distribution of Grant' states, that the revenue support grant is to be distributed so that if
each authority were to spend at the level of its SSA then, subject to certain qualifications,
all charging authorities could set the same personal community charge. During January
1990 local authorities were notified individually of the amounts of their SSAs, the
d amounts they were to receive in revenue support grant and of their relevant population
(determined as required by Sch 12A to the Act) which would determine their share of
non-domestic rates and were thus furnished with all the information they required to set
their budgets and their community charges.

I turn now to the capping machinery in Pt VII of the 1988 Act under the heading
'Limitation of Charges etc' and set out the relevant provisions of ss 100 to 102:
e

'**100.** *Power to designate authorities.*—(1) As regards a chargeable financial year the
Secretary of State may designate a charging authority if in his opinion—(a) the
amount calculated by it in relation to the year under section 95(4) above is excessive
. . .

f   (2) As regards a chargeable financial year the Secretary of State may designate a
relevant precepting authority if in his opinion—(a) the aggregate amount of precepts
issued by it for the year is excessive . . .

    (4) A decision whether to designate an authority shall be made in accordance
with principles determined by the Secretary of State and, in the case of an authority
falling within any of the classes specified in subsection (5) below, those principles
shall be the same either for all authorities falling within that class or for all of them
g which respectively have and have not been designated under this Part as regards the
preceding financial year.

    (5) The classes are—(a) county councils, (b) councils of metropolitan districts,
(c) councils of non-metropolitan districts, (d) councils of inner London boroughs,
(e) councils of outer London boroughs, (f) metropolitan county police authorities
h and the Northumbria Police Authority, and (g) metropolitan county fire and civil
defence authorities . . .

    101. *Restriction on power to designate.*—(1) An English authority shall not be
designated under section 100 above as regards a financial year unless the amount
calculated by it in relation to the year under section 95(4) above or the aggregate
amount of precepts issued by it for the year (as the case may be) is equal to or greater
j than £15 million or such greater sum not exceeding £35 million as the Secretary of
State may specify by order . . .

    102. *Designation of authorities.*—(1) If the Secretary of State decides under section
100 above to designate an authority he shall notify it in writing of—(a) his decision,
(b) the principles determined under section 100(4) above in relation to it, and (c) the

amount which he proposes should be the maximum for the amount calculated by
it in relation to the year under section 95(4) above or the maximum for the aggregate *a*
amount of precepts issued by it for the year (as the case may be) . . .'

It will be appreciated that, in relation to a charging authority, the phrase 'the amount
calculated by it in relation to the year under section 95(4)' and, in relation to a precepting
authority, the phrase 'the aggregate amount of the precepts issued by it for the year' refer
in each case to what I have earlier described as the authority's annual budgeted *b*
expenditure and it will be remembered that the amount which a charging authority
may set as its community charge is directly determined by its own annual budgeted
expenditure and the amount of the precepts made on it by precepting authorities, so that
the capping of the budget of either a charging authority or a precepting authority
precepting on it will result in the resetting of the community charge.

The procedure which follows the service of a notice under s 102(1) on a local authority *c*
depends on the local authority's response to the notice. The authority has 28 days
following receipt of the notice within which it may give notice to the Secretary of State
either accepting the maximum proposed by the Secretary of State for its annual budgeted
expenditure or stating an alternative higher maximum and giving reasons for its belief
that the higher maximum is appropriate (s 102(5)). If the authority accepts the maximum
proposed by the Secretary of State, the Secretary of State serves a further notice confirming, *d*
in effect, that the maximum he proposed in his notice under s 102(1)(c) is to be the
maximum amount of the authority's annual budgeted expenditure (s 105). If the
authority gives notice proposing an alternative maximum, the Secretary of State, after
considering any information he thinks relevant, makes a draft order specifying the
amount which is to be the maximum amount of the authority's annual budgeted
expenditure, which may be either greater or smaller than the maximum amount he *e*
originally proposed in his notice under s 102(1)(c), and this takes effect when the order is
approved by resolution of the House of Commons (s 104). If the authority makes no
response within 28 days to the notice served on it under s 102(1), the Secretary of State
makes a draft order specifying that the maximum originally proposed in his notice under
s 102(1)(c) is to be the maximum amount of the authority's annual budgeted expenditure *f*
and this again takes effect when the order is approved by resolution of the House of
Commons (s 106). Section 110 provides for authorities to supply to the Secretary of State
whatever information he requires for the purpose of deciding whether to exercise his
powers and how to perform his functions under Pt VII of the Act and, in default,
authorises the Secretary of State to act on the basis of such assumptions and estimates as
he thinks fit. Section 110(8) provides that in deciding whether to exercise his powers and *g*
how to perform his functions the Secretary of State may take into account any other
information available to him, whatever its source and whether or not obtained under
any statutory provision.

Under the 1988 Act precepting authorities are required to set their budgets before
1 March and charging authorities before 11 March. Community charges are required to
be set by 1 April. In 1990 all the appellant authorities except Lambeth London Borough *h*
Council had complied with this timetable and had supplied to the Secretary of State all
the information he required about their budgets by 18 March. On 3 April the Secretary
of State served designation notices on all the appellant authorities except Lambeth, whose
budget was set late and which was served on 10 April.

In determining, as required by s 100(4), the principles in accordance with which the
decisions to designate were to be made, the Secretary of State made no distinction *j*
between the different classes of authorities listed in s 100(5) save in respect of the councils
of inner London boroughs. These councils were to be the subject of special treatment in
so far as they had inherited liabilities from the former Inner London Education Authority.
Subject to this, which has no relevance for present purposes, all authorities were to be
designated in accordance with the same principles as follows. The first pinciple was that

an authority was to be designated if its budget exceeded its SSA (1) by at least 12½% and
a (2) by at least £75 per adult of its relevant population. The second principle operated by
way of exception to the first in that an authority was not to be designated if the
elimination of the excess referred to in the first principle, ie the reduction of the budget
to an amount not exceeding 12½% or £75 per adult above SSA, or the reduction of the
budget to £15m, the statutory minimum for designation prescribed by s 101, would
effect a saving of less than £26 per adult of the relevant population. Specifying in his
b notices under s 102(1)(c) the amount which he proposed to be the maximum amount for
each authority's annual budgeted expenditure, the Secretary of State proposed, in the case
of 8 of the 16 authorities which were appellants before the House, reduction by the full
amount necessary to eliminate the excess referred to in the first principle, but in the case
of the other 8 authorities, taking account of what he considered that the authorities could
in practice achieve in their individual circumstances, he specified a less stringent
c maximum allowing some expenditure above the level of 12½%/£75 per adult in excess
of SSA.

At the heart of the appellant authorities' attack on the Secretary of State's decisions to
designate them are two submissions relating to the construction of s 100 of the 1988 Act.
First, it is submitted that in making a decision to designate an authority under s 100
there are two steps to be taken which are independent of each other. The Secretary of
d State must first form the opinion under s 100(1) that the authority's budget is excessive.
This is to be decided on an ad hoc basis taking account of all the individual circumstances
affecting that authority and without regard to the principles to be formulated under
s 100(4). It is only after forming the opinion that an authority's budget is excessive that
the Secretary of State is required or permitted under s 100(4) to formulate the principles
which will determine whether or not that authority is in fact to be designated. The
e second submission is that, in taking the first step and forming his opinion that the
authority's budget is excessive, the Secretary of State is not entitled to determine what
the norm of local expenditure ought to be. The norm, it is said, is what a 'sensible' local
authority in the particular circumstances obtaining in its area may reasonably decide to
be the appropriate level of expenditure and the Secretary of State may only form the
opinion that an authority's budgeted expenditure is excessive if it exceeds that norm as
f being so profligate and extravagant that no 'sensible' authority could have approved it.

I have no hesitation in rejecting both these submissions. The decision to designate is
clearly a single decision dictated by the princples formulated under s 100(4), which are
to ensure even-handed treatment of different authorities in the same class and to settle
the norm which will provide the basis of the opinion of the Secretary of State as to what
g constitutes excessive budgeting. This is emphasised by s 102(1) requiring the Secretary
of State to notify his decision to designate and the princples determined under s 100(4)
'in relation to' that decision. Moreover, if a decision 'whether to designate' is to be made
'in accordance with principles' as s 100(4) requires, those principles can only be directed
to the determination of the question what level of expenditure is to be treated as excessive
to a degree justifing designation. To construe s 100 as requiring the Secretary of State to
h form an opinion ad hoc on a case-by-case basis as to what budgets are excessive without
regard to principle would be to defeat the plain purpose of the section.

The second submission is so clearly related to the first that it must fall with it, but even
if considered independently it is fatally flawed. The second submission presupposes that
every decision to designate an authority as having set a budget which in the opinion of
the Secretary of State is excessive is a decision made ad hoc, having regard only to the
j circumstances affecting that authority and having regard to some notional objective
standard of what a 'sensible' authority might properly budget to expend. The aim of this
second submission is to bring the decisions made by the Secretary of State to designate
the appellant authorities within the ambit of a familiar line of authority of which the
leading case is *Secretary of State for Education and Science v Tameside Metropolitan Borough*
[1976] 3 All ER 665, [1977] AC 1014. That case concerned the exercise by the Secretary

of State for Education and Science of a power under s 68 of the Education Act 1944
authorising him to give directions to a local education authority as to how it should   *a*
perform its statutory functions if he was satisfied that the authority was 'proposing to act
unreasonably with respect to the exercise of any power conferred or the performance of
any duty imposed by or under this Act'. The House held that this did not empower the
Secretary of State for Education and Science to substitute his own opinion for that of the
local education authority as to the course of action which it should take, but that he could
only give directions if, on the material before him, he was entitled to be satisfied that no   *b*
reasonable local education authority would act as the authority in question was proposing
to act. This was a decision on different statutory language in a wholly different statutory
context and it has no relevance whatever to the construction of s 100 of the 1988 Act. If
one asks in the circumstances of an individual case whether a local education authority
has acted unreasonably in the discharge of its statutory functions, this is clearly a question
which admits of an objective answer. If one asks, however, even in the circumstances of   *c*
an individual case, whether a local authority's budgeted expenditure for a year is
excessive, it is plain that there can be no objective criterion by which to determine the
answer. What is the appropriate level of public expenditure and public taxation is, and
always has been, a matter of political opinion. At one end of the political spectrum it
may be thought proper for 90% of the national income to be levied in taxation and
redistributed to the citizens in the form of free services designed to meet nearly all their   *d*
needs. At the other end it may be thought that taxation should be kept to the barest
minimum level necessary to provide minimal public services. Differences of political
opinion within this spectrum obviously apply at local as well as at national level. Thus
there can be no objective norm by which it would be possible to determine that a local
authority's budget was excessive. If the Secretary of State's powers under Pt VII of the Act
were limited to restraining excesses in budgetary expenditure beyond what any 'sensible'   *e*
authority might determine to be appropriate to its own circumstances, they would, in
effect, be wholly nugatory. The setting of a norm of local government expenditure is
essentially a matter of political opinion. That is precisely why the Act, in entrusting to
the Secretary of State the function of determining the norm and imposing a ceiling level
of expenditure to which local authorities must conform, does so by requiring him to   *f*
spell out the criteria of excessive expenditure in terms of principles of general application,
which is the very antithesis of subjecting the budgets of individual authorities to the ad
hoc review which is suggested to be the basis of the capping power in the submissions
made on behalf of the appellant authorities.

As an alternative to the submissions directed to the construction of s 100, it was
submitted that various pronouncements by the Secretary of State and other government
ministers in the House of Commons and elsewhere had induced in local authorities a   *g*
'legitimate expectation' that the Secretary of State's powers of capping would only be
exercised to restrain excesses going beyond the limits of such budgets as a 'sensible'
authority might properly set and that this legitimate expectation could, if necessary, be
relied on as imposing a limitation on the power otherwise exercisable under s 100 to the
same effect as that which would follow from acceptance of the authorities' submissions   *h*
on the true construction of the section. I need only say that, in my opinion, this
submission is plainly misconceived.

The appellant authorities next submitted that the Secretary of State's designation
notices did not comply with the 1988 Act because the principles determined under
s 100(4) were not the same for all authorities in the same class. The basis of this
submission is that the principle determining that an authority's budget shall be treated   *j*
as excessive only if it exceeds the authority's SSA both by 12½% in the aggregate and by
£75 per adult of the relevant population is a principle which can only apply to those
authorities whose SSA divided by the relevant adult population is at least £600. This is,
of course, factually correct, but the fallacy in the submission is that it confuses a
requirement that the principles shall be the same for all authorities, which the statute
imposes, with a requirement that the principles shall be capable of application to all

a
authorities, which the statute does not impose. In the nature of the case the principles designed to govern the determination to designate will discriminate between authorities according to whether their budgets are or are not to be treated as excessive. The principles to be applied are the same, but to require that every principle should be capable of application to every authority would defeat the whole purpose of the exercise. Accordingly, this submission also is without substance.

b
I have now referred to all the grounds relied on by the appellant authorities to impeach the Secretary of State's action as contravening the Act either on its true construction or as falling to be applied in the light of the authorities' legitimate expectations. Adopting Lord Diplock's threefold classification of the grounds on which administrative decisions may be challenged as illegality, irrationality and procedural impropriety (*Council of Civil Service Unions v Minister for the Civil Service* [1984] 3 All ER 935 at 950, [1985] AC 374 at 410), the grounds of challenge so far considered would, if they had succeeded, have fallen

c
under the head of illegality. The remaining grounds of challenge fall under the heads of irrationality or procedural impropriety. Before turning to these grounds it is appropriate to consider whether any limitations on the scope of judicial review are imposed by the subject matter of the legislation. In this we are not without authoritative guidance.

In *Nottinghamshire CC v Secretary of State for the Environment* [1986] 1 All ER 199, [1986] AC 240 the House had to consider an earlier challenge to the action of the Secretary of

d
State under the Local Government, Planning and Land Act 1980 which had this in common with the action here in question, that the 'expenditure guidance' which the Secretary of State had there issued to local authorities and which the authorities sought to challenge had a directly restraining effect on the authorities' conduct of their financial affairs but before it could take effect required the approval by resolution of the House of Commons. The appellant authorities in that case had challenged the Secretary of State's

e
statutory expenditure guidance on the ground, inter alia, that it was unreasonable as contravening the principles expounded in the judgment of Lord Greene MR in *Associated Provincial Picture Houses Ltd v Wednesbury Corp* [1947] 2 All ER 680 at 682, [1948] 1 KB 223 at 229, which is the classic statement of the basis for a challenge to an administrative decision on the ground of irrationality. Adverting to this challenge in the *Nottinghamshire* case [1986] 1 All ER 199 at 202, [1986] AC 240 at 247 Lord Scarman said:

f
'The submission raises an important question as to the limits of judicial review. We are in the field of public financial administration and we are being asked to review the exercise by the Secretary of State of an administrative discretion which inevitably requires a political judgment on his part and which cannot lead to action by him against a local authority unless that action is first approved by the House of

g
Commons ... I cannot accept that it is constitutionally appropriate, save in very exceptional circumstances, for the courts to intervene on the ground of "unreasonableness" to quash guidance framed by the Secretary of State and by necessary implication approved by the House of Commons, the guidance being concerned with the limits of public expenditure by local authorities and the incidence of the tax burden as between taxpayers and taxpayers. Unless and until a

h
statute provides otherwise, or it is established that the Secretary of State has abused his power, these are matters of political judgment for him and for the House of Commons. They are not for the judges or your Lordships' House in its judicial capacity. For myself, I refuse in this case to examine the detail of the guidance or its consequences. My reasons are these. Such an examination by a court would be justified only if a prima facie case were to be shown for holding that the Secretary of

j
State had acted in bad faith, or for an improper motive, or that the consequences of his guidance were so absurd that he must have taken leave of his senses.'

Later he added ([1986] 1 All ER 199 at 204, [1986] AC 240 at 250–251):

'To sum it up, the levels of public expenditure and the incidence and distribution of taxation are matters for Parliament, and, within Parliament, especially for the

House of Commons. If Parliament legislates, the courts have their interpretative role: they must, if called on to do so, construe the statute. If a minister exercises a *a* power conferred on him by the legislation, the courts can investigate whether he has abused his power. But if, as in this case, effect cannot be given to the Secretary of State's determination without the consent of the House of Commons and the House of Commons has consented, it is not open to the courts to intervene unless the minister and the House must have misconstrued the statute or the minister has, to put it bluntly, deceived the House. The courts can properly rule that a minister *b* has acted unlawfully if he has erred in law as to the limits of his power even when his action has the approval of the House of Commons, itself acting not legislatively but within the limits set by a statute. But, if a statute, as in this case, requires the House of Commons to approve a minister's decision before he can lawfully enforce it, and if the action proposed complies with the terms of the statute (as your Lordships, I understand, are convinced that it does in the present case), it is not for *c* the judges to say that the action has such unreasonable consequences that the guidance on which the action is based and of which the House of Commons had notice was perverse and must be set aside. For that is a question of policy for the minister and the Commons, unless there has been bad faith or misconduct by the minister. Where Parliament has legislated that the action to be taken by the Secretary of State must, before it is taken, be approved by the House of Commons, *d* it is no part of the judges' role to declare that the action proposed is unfair, unless it constitutes an abuse of power in the sense which I have explained; for Parliament has enacted that one of its Houses is responsible. Judicial review is a great weapon in the hands of the judges; but the judges must observe the constitutional limits set by our parliamentary system on their exercise of this beneficent power.'

Lord Scarman's speech commanded the agreement of all members of the Appellate Committee participating in the decision, of whom I was one. I regard the opinions expressed in the passages quoted as an accurate formulation of an important restriction on the scope of judicial review which is precisely in point in the instant case. There is here no suggestion that the Secretary of State acted in bad faith or for an improper motive or that his decisions to designate the appellant authorities or the maximum amounts to *f* which he decided to limit their budgets were so absurd that he must have taken leave of his senses. Short of such an extreme challenge, and provided always that the Secretary of State has acted within the four corners of the Act, I do not believe there is any room for an attack on the rationality of the Secretary of State's exercise of his powers under Pt VII of the Act.

This accords with the view expressed by the Divisional Court, though it went on to *g* examine on their merits and to reject the grounds relied on by the applicant authorities including those challenging the rationality of the Secretary of State's decisions and orders. The Court of Appeal expressed a somewhat different view. Referring to irrationality as a ground for judicial review of the exercise of a statutory discretion it said (see p 615, ante):

'This head is relevant if it is alleged that the decision taker has had regard to *h* matters which are legally irrelevant or has failed to have regard to matters which are legally relevant or that his decision would frustrate the policy of the Act on which he relies for his authority (*Padfield v Minister of Agriculture Fisheries and Food* [1968] 1 All ER 694, [1968] AC 997). There is nothing in the judgments in the *Nottinghamshire CC* case [1986] 1 All ER 199, [1986] AC 240 to suggest that this aspect of the jurisdictional head of "irrationality" has no application to decisions *j* concerning public financial administration, whether or not they are also subject to review by one or both Houses of Parliament and no principle dictates that this should be the case.'

I think there is a danger of confusion in terminology here. If the court concludes, as the House did in *Padfield's* case, that a minister's exercise of a statutory discretion has

been such as to frustrate the policy of the statute, that conclusion rests on the view taken
a by the court of the true construction of the statute which the exercise of the discretion in
question is then held to have contravened. The administrative action or inaction is then
condemned on the ground of illegality. Similarly, if there are matters which, on the true
construction of the statute conferring discretion, the person exercising the discretion
must take into account and others which he may not take into account, disregard of those
legally relevant matters or regard of those legally irrelevant matters will lay the decision
b open to review on the ground of illegality.

The restriction which the *Nottinghamshire CC* case imposes on the scope of judicial
review operates only when the court has first determined that the ministerial action in
question does not contravene the requirements of the statute, whether express or implied,
and only then declares that, since the statute has conferred a power on the Secretary of
State which involves the formulation and the implementation of national economic
c policy and which can only take effect with the approval of the House of Commons, it is
not open to challenge on the grounds of irrationality short of the extremes of bad faith,
improper motive or manifest absurdity. Both the constitutional propriety and the good
sense of this restriction seem to me to be clear enough. The formulation and the
implementation of national economic policy are matters depending essentially on
political judgment. The decisions which shape them are for politicians to take and it is
d in the political forum of the House of Commons that they are properly to be debated and
approved or disapproved on their merits. If the decisions have been taken in good faith
within the four corners of the Act, the merits of the policy underlying the decisions are
not susceptible to review by the courts and the courts would be exceeding their proper
function if they presumed to condemn the policy as unreasonable.

One of the main grounds on which the appellant authorities attacked the basis on
e which the Secretary of State determined the principles under s 100(4) in accordance with
which they were designated was that the calculation of an authority's SSA does not take
account of all the factors which come into play under the terms of s 95, in the case of
charging authorities, or of s 68, in the case of precepting authorities, in the determination
of an authority's annual budgeted expenditure. In essence this ground complains that in
using SSAs as the criterion by reference to which an authority's budget is judged excessive
f under s 100 the Secretary of State is not comparing like with like. The Court of Appeal
examined this complaint on its merits and rejected it for reasons with which I agree. But
I would reject it also on the shorter ground that the complaint seeks to assert that the use
of SSAs as the basic criterion by which to determine the permissible level of local
government expenditure is unreasonable in the *Wednesbury* sense and for the reasons I
have explained I am of opinion that such a complaint is inadmissible.

g The remaining complaints advanced by the appellant authorities relate to matters of
procedure. Before I advert to these complaints individually, I must try to dispel a
misapprehension which underlay the arguments addressed to the House on behalf of the
appellant authorities on this part of the case. The arguments proceed from the assumption
that, as between the Secretary of State and any authority which may be or is the recipient
h of a notice of designation, the authority, or more accurately the majority party in control
of the budgeting process, is in the position of a person whose 'rights', in the broadest
sense, are liable to be detrimentally affected by any action taken by the Secretary of State
under Pt VII of the 1988 Act. This is the necessary assumption on which to base the
argument advanced by the appellant authorities that the court must supplement the
procedural requirements which the Act itself stipulates by implying additional
j requirements said to be necessary to ensure that the principles of natural justice are
observed in the procedures both leading to designation and following designation. The
decided cases on this subject establish the principle that the courts will readily imply
terms where necessary to ensure fairness of procedure for the protection of parties who
may suffer a detriment in consequence of administrative action. Clearly this principle
applies to decisions whereby citizens may be affected in their person, their property or
their reputation. The principle equally applies to public bodies or public authorities

affected by an administrative decision which is based on their having acted, or which necesssarily implies that they have acted, unlawfully or discreditably. Thus in *Durayappah* *a* *v Fernando* [1967] 2 All ER 152, [1967] 2 AC 337, the case primarily relied on by the appellant authorities, the Privy Council held that a minister, given power by statute to direct the dissolution of a municipal council on the ground that it 'is not competent to perform, or persistently makes default in the performance of, any duty or duties imposed upon it, or persistently refuses or neglects to comply with any provision of law', was not entitled to exercise the power without giving the council a fair opportunity to be heard *b* in its defence.

The administrative decision taken by the Secretary of State in designating a local authority and setting a maximum amount for the authority's budget lower than the amount which the authority thinks it appropriate to raise by way of community charge and to spend in the provision of local services is in one sense adverse to the authority, but it does not in any way impinge on the rights of members of the authority, either as *c* citizens or as councillors, nor does it impugn their collective conduct as either unlawful or discreditable. A difference of opinion between the Secretary of State and the designated authority as to what is the appropriate level at which their community charge and their expenditure should be set is purely a political difference. The parties affected by the capping process are the community charge payers and the consumers of local services. The payers gain, the consumers lose. The party in control of the council may be politically *d* frustrated by the restriction imposed on powers which they might otherwise exercise freely, but it is only in this sense that the Secretary of State acts to their detriment and they are perfectly at liberty to continue to claim that they were right and the Secretary of State was wrong and to make what political capital they may out of the dispute. In this statutory context I am very doubtful whether it would be appropriate for the court to imply terms in the statute derived from the doctrine of audi alteram partem. But it is *e* unnecessary to consider this point further because, at the only point in the process leading to capping at which it might be appropriate to insist that, as a matter of fair procedure, authorities should have the opportunity to be heard in opposition to the Secretary of State's proposed cap and to make a reasoned case in support of an alternative and less restrictive maximum for their budget, the Act itself by ss 102(5)(a) and 104 expressly prescribes a procedure precisely to this effect. This procedure was duly followed and in *f* addition all the authorities who had served notices under s 102(5)(a) proposing alternative maximum amounts for their annual budgeted expenditure were given the opportunity to make representations orally in support of their cases by delegations received by the Minister for Local Government and Inner Cities and the parliamentary under-secretary.

There are two further points at which the appellant authorities invite the House to conclude that terms must be implied in the statute in the interests of fair procedure. *g* First, it is said that the Secretary of State should be held under an obligation to consult local authorities before determining the principles on which he will act under s 104 in relation to designation and, having determined those principles, must announce them before authorities have set their budgets so that the authorities may have the opportunity to set them at a level which will avoid the necessity for designation. So far as consultation *h* is concerned, no obligation to consult is imposed by Pt VII of the Act. This is in contrast with Pt V, where s 78 imposes an express obligation to consult 'such representatives of local government as appear to [the Secretary of State] to be appropriate'. As I have recounted earlier, a very full process of consultation between the Department of the Environment and officers of local authority associations preceded the setting of local authorities' SSAs. I can see no basis whatever on which to imply a statutory obligation to *j* consult local authorities about the principles on which the Secretary of State proposed to base his designation decisions under s 100. The advantages of a prior announcement of ˰ what those principles are to be, enabling authorities to budget to avoid designation and the administrative expense and inconvenience necessarily consequent on designation, are obvious. Mr Rowsell in his affidavit carefully explains that the Secretary of State weighed

these advantages against the disadvantages which he saw in a prior announcement as
a presenting a temptation to authorities to budget to spend up the limit which the proposed
principles would allow and therefore as inimical to the achievement of economy in local
government expenditure which is the primary objective of government policy. The
Secretary of State concluded that the disadvantages outweighed the advantages and
therefore made no prior announcement of the principles. Whether or not this was a
politically wise decision is no concern of your Lordships. Here again I can see no basis on
b which to imply a term in the Act which would render it an unlawful decision.

A second point at which it is contended that additional obligations on the Secretary of
State must be implied in the statutory procedure is in any case where an authority is
minded, after receiving the Secretary of State's designation notice under s 102(1), to give
notice under s 102(5)(a) proposing an alternative maximum for its budget and giving
reasons in support of that alternative. It is accepted that the Secretary of State is under no
c initial obligation when he serves a designation notice to give reasons for the amount of
the cap which he proposes under s 102(1)(c), but it is said that he must do so on request
by an authority wishing to challenge the cap to enable it the better to formulate its
counter-proposal. I need only say that, in my opinion, the implication that it would be
necessary to make to sustain this proposition is plainly excluded by the very precise terms
in which the statute lays down the relevant procedure to be followed. The Secretary of
d State's notice under s 102(1) is in terms required to inform the authority of his decision,
the principles determined under s 100(4) in relation to it and the amount of the proposed
cap. An authority wishing to challenge the cap has 28 days in which to do so and is in
terms required to give reasons in support of its alternative proposal. If it were intended
that the Secretary of State should give reasons in support of the proposed cap, it is
inconceivable that this should not either be stated in terms as a requirement of the notice
e under s 102(1) or, if the reasons were only to be given on request, that the statute should
not prescribe a timetable for making the request and for the time to be allowed to the
authority after receipt of the Secretary of State's reasons for formulating and notifying its
counter-proposal.

Finally, it was submitted for the appellant authorities that the Secretary of State is
under a legal obligation before submitting a draft order for approval by the House of
f Commons under s 104 to disclose to the authority affected any information which he
intends to take into account received from a source other than the authority in question
and of which that authority might not be aware. Both courts below accepted the view
that the requirements of fair procedure imposed such an obligation, but the Court of
Appeal rejected the complaint, which only arose after the hearing in the Divisional
Court, that there had been any breach of the obligation. The position taken on behalf of
g the Secretary of State in relation to this submission was that it was the practice to inform
an authority of any factual information on which the Secretary of State proposed to act
which contradicted the case put forward by the authority, but that the reason for this
practice was simply to ensure so far as possible that the information on which the
Secretary of State proposed to act was accurate. It was not accepted that there was any
legal obligation in the matter.
h This is the only point where I take a view at variance with that of both courts below.
As I have pointed out, s 110 of the 1988 Act in terms provides that in performing his
functions under Pt VII the Secretary of State may take into account any information
available to him from whatever source it comes. In the nature of the case the Secretary of
State is bound to receive representations as to how he should exercise his power of
j capping from many quarters. Bodies speaking for community charge payers and political
opponents of those who have set the budget to be capped are likely to urge one view,
political supporters and bodies speaking for consumers of local services or employees
engaged in the provision of those services are likely to urge another. These representations
may be factual, argumentative or both. Against this background, to read into the statute
a legal obligation on the Secretary of State to disclose to an authority challenging his

proposed cap all relevant information before him and then to give the authority the
opportunity to comment on or counter that information (which would be the only *a*
purpose to be served by requiring disclosure) would introduce such delays into a
procedure which is meant to operate with the greatest expedition that I cannot believe
that this is what Parliament intended. Short of this, I do not think it is possible to spell
out, as a matter of legal obligation, a duty of disclosure confined to a particular narrow
category of factual information which it would be necessary to define with great
precision. Here again it is vital to remember that the procedure under the Act is not in *b*
any ordinary sense an adversarial one. The important objective of the procedure is that
the information on which the Secretary of State acts should be both full and accurate. In
this respect it is much better, in my opinion, to leave the attainment of that objective to
sound administrative practice than to attempt to achieve it by nice legal definitions.

As this is the first year of the operation of the new system of local government finance
it was predictable that there would be a challenge in the courts to any exercise by the *c*
Secretary of State of his capping power and in the light of the public importance and
sensitivity of the subject matter it was appropriate that the authorities which wished to
do so should be given leave to bring their case before your Lordships' House. But I hope
that your Lordships' decision will serve to make it clear for future years that no similar
challenge has any prospect of success unless an authority is in a position to show that the
Secretary of State has acted in bad faith or for an improper motive or can point to some *d*
failure to comply with the procedural requirements which the Act clearly spells out.

LORD BRANDON OF OAKBROOK. My Lords, I am in full agreement with the
reasons which have been given by my noble and learned friend Lord Bridge for
dismissing these appeals.

e

LORD OLIVER OF AYLMERTON. My Lords, I am in full agreement with the
reasons which have been given by my noble and learned friend Lord Bridge for
dismissing these appeals.

LORD GOFF OF CHIEVELEY. My Lords, I am in full agreement with the reasons *f*
which have been given by my noble and learned friend Lord Bridge for dismissing these
appeals.

LORD JAUNCEY OF TULLICHETTLE. My Lords, I am in full agreement with
the reasons which have been given by my noble and learned friend Lord Bridge for
dismissing these appeals.

g

Appeals dismissed.

Solicitors: *Sharpe Pritchard*, agents for *Alun G Phillips, Patricia A Hughes, David N Atkinson,
Francis Nickson, Clive L Grace, William R Bugler*, Doncaster, *Timothy C Mumford*, Rotherham,
Dudley W P Lewis, Bristol, *Arthur J George, Eric D Nixon*, North Shields, *Basil D Smith*, *h*
Bristol, *Vivienne Neale*, St Helens, *Michael Ellison*, Halifax, *David Shipp*, Rochdale, *Stephen
R Forster*, Wembley, *John L Knight*, Basildon, *Julia C Lomas* and *Michael B Kenny*, Barnsley
(for Hammersmith and Fulham LBC, Islington LBC, Greenwich LBC, Camden LBC,
Southwark LBC, Doncaster MBC, Rotherham MBC, Bristol City Council, Lambeth LBC,
North Tyneside MBC, Avon CC, St Helens MBC, Calderdale MBC, Rochdale BC, Brent
LBC, Basildon DC, Haringey LBC and Barnsley MBC); *Kingsford Stacey*, agents for *David* *j*
W Tysoe, Matlock (for Derbyshire CC); *G Clayton* (for the National Union of Teachers);
James A G Ritchie (for the chairmen of the Brent school governors); *Treasury Solicitor.*

Mary Rose Plummer   Barrister.

Cie Commerciale Sucres et Denrées v C Czarnikow Ltd
The Naxos

HOUSE OF LORDS

LORD BRIDGE OF HARWICH, LORD BRANDON OF OAKBROOK, LORD ACKNER, LORD OLIVER OF
AYLMERTON AND LORD JAUNCEY OF TULLICHETTLE

18, 19 JULY, 11 OCTOBER 1990

*Contract – Condition – Breach – Effect – Right of other party to terminate contract – Stipulation
as to time – Shipping contract incorporating rule requiring sellers to have cargo ready for delivery
at any time within contract period – Buyers giving proper notice of readiness to load – Sellers
failing to deliver cargo on presentation of buyers' vessel – Buyers regarding sellers as in breach of
condition of contract and treating contract as terminated – Whether buyers entitled to rescind
contract – Whether rule as to delivery imposing obligation on sellers to have cargo available for
loading immediately on presentation of vessel – Whether obligation amounting to condition of
contract.*

In 1985 the buyers agreed to purchase from the sellers 12,000 metric tons of sugar on
fob stowed terms. The contract of sale was on the standard Assuc Sugar Contract No 2
form used exclusively between dealers in sugar and incorporating the Rules Relating to
Contracts of the Refined Sugar Association of London (the RSA rules). Rule 14(1) and (2)[a]
of the RSA rules provided that in the case of fob stowed contracts 'the Seller shall have
the sugar ready to be delivered to the Buyer at any time within the contract period' and
that the buyer 'having given reasonable notice, shall be entitled to call for delivery of the
sugar between the first and last working day inclusive of the period of delivery'. Clause 7
of the contract provided that delivery was to be made to 'one or more vessels presenting
ready to load' during May/June 1986, and that the buyer was to give the seller 'not less
than 14 days' notice of vessel(s) expected readiness to load'. On 15 May the buyers gave
due notice to the sellers that their vessel would arrive at the agreed loading port to lift
the full 12,000 tons between 29 and 31 May 1986. The vessel presented itself ready for
loading on 29 May but, despite repeated calls by the buyers and a warning on 27 May
that if loading did not commence on 29 May the buyers would hold the sellers in default,
the sellers did not have the sugar ready to be delivered to the buyers. On 3 June the
buyers telexed the sellers setting out those facts, holding them in default for not providing
the cargo and informing them that the buyers were treating the contract as terminated
and had purchased a replacement cargo. The buyers made a claim for the difference
between the contract price of the cargo and the market price on 3 June represented by
the cost of the replacement cargo and for loss of despatch which would have been earned
had the vessel not remained idle while awaiting a cargo. The sellers denied liability,
maintaining that they had until the end of the delivery period set out in cl 7 of the
contract to deliver the cargo. The dispute was referred to the Council of the Refined
Sugar Association for arbitration. The council found in favour of the buyers on both
claims, holding that r 14 of the RSA rules imposed on the sellers an obligation to have
the sugar ready to be delivered to the buyers at any time within the contract period and
to deliver it when called for by the buyers after they had given the required notice, that
the obligation was a condition of the contract, that the sellers were in breach of that
condition and that the buyers were entitled to treat that breach as bringing the contract
to an end as they had done. The council accordingly awarded the buyers damages in

---

a   Rule 14 is set out at p 645 d to f, post.

respect of both claims. The sellers appealed to the Commercial Court, where the judge set aside the council's award on the ground that r 14(1) did not impose any further obligation on the sellers in addition to that of being able to give delivery in accordance with the terms of the contract when called on to do so, still less an obligation in the nature of a condition. The buyers appealed to the Court of Appeal, which dismissed the appeal, holding that, although r 14(1) did impose an additional obligation on the sellers, it could not be construed as a time clause and hence a condition of the contract, since the r 14(1) obligation to have the cargo 'ready to be delivered . . . at any time within the contract period' was so imprecise as to make it unlikely that the parties intended compliance with the obligation to be a condition of the contract. The buyers appealed to the House of Lords.

Held – (1) On its true construction, r 14(1) of the RSA rules imposed on the sellers an express additional obligation to have the sugar called for by the buyers in accordance with the contract terms available to begin loading without delay or interruption as soon as the vessel was ready to load the cargo in question, the justification for which was that mercantile contracts were often concluded with a reasonably long period of delivery and at a price which presupposed the buyers' rights to call for delivery at any time having given reasonable notice. That was a valuable option which the buyers would lose if the sellers were entitled to deliver whenever they were willing and able to do so within the delivery period. Accordingly, the sellers were in breach of their r 14(1) obligation when the buyers treated the contract as terminated on 3 June 1986 (see p 643 d f, p 648 b c f to h, p 649 c and p 651 f g, post); dictum of Donaldson J in *European Grain and Shipping Ltd v David Geddes (Proteins) Ltd* [1977] 2 Lloyd's Rep 591 at 602 applied.

(2) (Lord Brandon dissenting) Rule 14(1) could properly be described as a time clause since it imposed on the sellers an obligation to have the goods called forward available for loading at a definite point in time, ie at the expiration of notice of expected readiness to load given under cl 7 and as soon as the vessel presented itself ready to load within the contract period and, since r 14(1) also provided commercial certainty to a mercantile contract by ensuring to a very large extent that loading would be promptly commenced and speedily carried out thus enabling the buyers punctually to perform their own onward delivery obligations to their customers, it was to be regarded as a condition of the contract, breach of which would entitle the buyers to treat the contract as at an end. Accordingly, the buyers had been entitled to terminate the contract on 3 June 1986 following the sellers' failure to deliver the cargo in accordance with r 14(1) and were entitled to recover the difference between the market price of the replacement cargo as at 3 June and the original contract price and to loss of despatch. The appeal would therefore be allowed and the council's award reinstated (see p 643 d, p 649 g, p 650 f to h and p 651 c e to g, post); dicta of Bowen LJ in *Bentsen v Taylor Sons & Co (No 2)* [1893] 2 QB 274 at 281 and of Lord Wilberforce and Lord Lowry in *Bunge Corp v Tradax SA* [1981] 2 All ER 513 at 542, 545 applied.

Notes

For stipulations as to time in mercantile contracts, see 41 Halsbury's Laws (4th edn) para 686, and for cases on the subject, see 39(2) Digest (Reissue) 170–181, 1271–1355.

Cases referred to in opinions

Bentsen v Taylor Sons & Co (No 2) [1893] 2 QB 274, CA.
Bremer Handelsgesellschaft mbH v Vanden Avenne-Izegem PVBA [1978] 2 Lloyd's Rep 109.
Bunge Corp v Tradax SA [1981] 2 All ER 513, [1981] 1 WLR 711, HL.
European Grain and Shipping Ltd v David Geddes (Proteins) Ltd [1977] 2 Lloyd's Rep 591.
State Trading Corp of India Ltd v M Golodetz Ltd [1989] 2 Lloyd's Rep 277, CA.
Tradax Export SA v Italgrani di Francesco Ambrosio [1986] 1 Lloyd's Rep 112, CA; *affg* [1983] 2 Lloyd's Rep 109.

Appeal

a C Czarnikow Ltd (the buyers) appealed with leave of the Appeal Committee of the House of Lords given on 22 November 1989 against the decision of the Court of Appeal (Lloyd and Butler-Sloss LJJ, Sir Michael Kerr dissenting) ([1989] 2 Lloyd's Rep 462) on 13 July 1989 dismissing their appeal from a decision of Gatehouse J given on 3 November 1988 in favour of the respondents, Cie Commerciale Sucres et Denrées (the sellers), whereby he set aside an arbitration award dated 12 May 1988 of the Council of the Refined Sugar *b* Association (Mr M A J Cronk chairman) holding that the sellers were in breach of a condition under a contract between the parties for the sale of sugar and that the breach entitled the buyers to terminate the contract. The facts are set out in the opinion of Lord Ackner.

David Johnson QC and *Duncan Matthews* for the buyers.
c *Martin Moore-Bick QC* and *Stephen Males* for the sellers.

Their Lordships took time for consideration.

11 October. The following opinions were delivered.

d **LORD BRIDGE OF HARWICH.** My Lords, I have had the advantage of reading in draft the speech of my noble and learned friend Lord Ackner. I agree with it and, for the reasons he gives, I would allow the appeal.

LORD BRANDON OF OAKBROOK. My Lords, I have had the advantage of considering in draft the speech to be delivered by my noble and learned friend Lord *e* Ackner. I adopt gratefully his account of the material facts of the case and his formulation of the two questions which arise for decision on them.

The first question is whether paras 1 and 2 of r 14 of the Rules Relating to Contracts of the Refined Sugar Association of London imposed on the sellers an obligation to have the sugar available for loading immediately on the arrival of the ship after proper notice at the loading port ready to load. With regard to that question I agree with my noble and *f* learned friend's conclusion that it should be answered Yes and with the reasoning which leads him to that conclusion.

The second question is whether that obligation was a condition of the contract of sale, so that any breach of it, however insignificant and however much beyond the control of the sellers, would entitle the buyers, if they so elected, to treat the contract as at an end. My noble and learned friend concludes that this question should also be answered Yes. I *g* respectfully disagree with him on that. For the reasons which follow I am of the opinion that this second question should be answered No.

Breach by the sellers of the obligation concerned would cause delay in the loading of the sugar on the ship. It seems to me helpful, therefore, to consider what the contract provided in the case of breaches by either party of other contractual obligations which would also cause such delay.

h I consider, first, a breach by the buyers of their obligation under para 3 of r 14 to present the ship in readiness to load within five calendar days of the date contained in their notice calling for delivery of the sugar. That paragraph provided that, in the event of a breach of such obligation, the buyers should be responsible for any consequential loss incurred by the sellers. That provision made it clear that the obligation of the buyers concerned was not a condition of the contract but a warranty, for breach of which the *j* only remedy available to the sellers was damages.

I consider, second, a breach by the sellers of their obligation to complete loading within the permitted lay time, agreed to have been 16 weather working days. It is not in dispute that this obligation was not a condition but a warranty, for breach of which the only remedy available to the buyers was damages, such damages being liquidated damages in the form of demurrage.

It seems to me to be illogical to interpret the contract, with its incorporated rules, in such a way as to classify two obligations, the breach of which would cause delay in the *a* loading of the ship, as warranties, and another obligation, the breach of which would have the same effect, as a condition. In each case what matters to the party to whom the obligation is owed is the result of its breach, namely delay in the loading of the ship, and not the form or the nature of the obligation itself. It seems to me that the logical way to interpret the contract, with its incorporated rules, is to classify all obligations of either party, the breach of which would cause delay in the loading of the ship, in the same way, *b* that is to say as warranties and not as conditions.

My noble and learned friend, Lord Ackner, like Sir Michael Kerr in the Court of Appeal ([1989] 2 Lloyd's Rep 462 at 474), attaches great importance to the view of the arbitrators that the obligation imposed on the sellers by paras 1 and 2 of r 14 was a condition of the contract. I recognise that the view of the arbitrators is important and should be accorded proper respect by the courts. It seems to me, however, that the *c* arbitrators, in reaching their conclusion on this question, concentrated too much on the single obligation in issue, and not enough on the general scheme and tenor of the contract as a whole in relation to delays in the loading of the ship. In any case, as pointed out by Lloyd and Butler-Sloss LJJ in the Court of Appeal, the question is solely one of construction of a written contract, so that the courts are not only entitled but bound to exercise their own independent judgment on it. *d*

For my part I would dismiss the appeal.

LORD ACKNER. My Lords, on 11 December 1985 the appellants, referred to hereafter as the 'buyers', entered into a contract with the respondents, referred to hereafter as the 'sellers', on the Assuc Sugar Contract No 2 form for the purchase of 12,000 metric tons of *e* white crystal sugar at a price of 1,425 French francs net per metric ton net on fob stowed terms. This contract incorporated the Rules Relating to Contracts of the Refined Sugar Association of London, referred to hereafter as 'the rules'.

This appeal raises essentially only two questions, both of which are far easier to state than they are to answer. In short they are: (1) does r 14 impose on the sellers an obligation to have the sugar available to begin loading immediately on the arrival after proper *f* notice of the ship at the loading port ready to load; (2) if so, is this obligation a condition of the contract?

To these two questions, the arbitrators answered Yes, and the commercial judge Gatehouse J answered No. In the Court of Appeal, to question (1) Sir Michael Kerr, with Butler-Sloss LJ providing some, but not total support, answered Yes. Lloyd LJ dissented. As to the second question, Lloyd and Butler-Sloss LJJ answered No with Sir Michael Kerr *g* dissenting; hence this appeal by the buyers.

The relevant terms of the contract

It is only necessary to set out the following three clauses of the contract:

'7. DELIVERY:—To one or more vessels presenting ready to load during MAY/JUNE *h* 1986 Buyer to give Seller not less than 14 days' notice of vessel(s) expected readiness to load. Such notice to be given on a business day in Seller's Country prior to 16.00 hours London time to be effective that day.

8. PRICE:—FF1,425, – net per Metric Ton net FOB Stowed one nominated EEC port per vessel, Seller's quay(s).

9. LOADING:—The Seller shall load sugar at a rate of 750 MT per weather working *j* day of 24 consecutive hours basis 5 or more hatches . . . Demurrage and despatch as per Charter Party rate for Seller's account . . .'

It is common ground: (a) that the formula provided in cl 9 gave the seller 16 weather working days to load the sugar; and (b) that under the above terms the sellers were under

no obligation to have the sugar available to begin loading immediately on the arrival of
a the vessel at the loading port. If they did not load within the 16 weather working days,
then their liability was limited to the payment of demurrage. If, however, they failed to
load by the end of June that would amount to a repudiatory breach of the contract,
enabling the buyers to determine the contract forthwith.

The rules
b   The rules are set out under a number of headings such as 'Quantity', 'Packages',
'Weight', 'Supervision', 'Quality'. Under the heading 'Delivery' there first appears r 11,
which is in these terms:

> 'In c. & f. and c.i.f. contracts the Seller has the option of delivering the contract
> quantity in one or more lots during the contract period. In f.a.s., f.o.b. and free
> stowed in hold (f.o.b. stowed) contracts the Buyer has the option of taking delivery
c > of the contract quantity in one or more lots during the contract period.'

Rule 14 is from the point of view of this appeal the vital rule. It contains four
paragraphs and for ease of reference these have been numbered. The rule reads as follows:

> '[1] In cases of f.a.s., f.o.b., and free stowed in hold (f.o.b. stowed) contracts the
> Seller shall have the sugar ready to be delivered to the Buyer at any time within the
d > contract period.
> [2] The Buyer, having given reasonable notice, shall be entitled to call for delivery
> of the sugar between the first and last working day inclusive of the period of
> delivery.
> [3] If the vessel (or vessels) has presented herself in readiness to load within the
> contract period but has failed to be presented within 5 calendar days of the date
e > contained in the notice above calling for delivery of the sugar the Buyer shall be
> responsible for any costs incurred by the Seller by reason of such delay exceeding
> the 5 calendar days.
> [4] If the vessel (or vessels) has presented herself in readiness to load within the
> contract period, but loading has not been completed by the last working day of the
f > period, the Seller shall be bound to deliver and the Buyer bound to accept delivery
> of the balance of the cargo or parcel up to the contract quantity.'

The relevant facts giving rise to the dispute
    On 15 May the buyers gave notice to the sellers for the Naxos to lift the full contract
quantity, that is the 12,000 metric tons of sugar eta Dunkirk 29/31 May 1986. The vessel
g presented for loading on 29 May 1986 but despite repeated calls by the buyers and a
warning given on 27 May that if loading did not commence on 29 May the sellers would
be held in default, the sellers did not, to quote the words of r 14(1), 'have the sugar ready
to be delivered to the Buyer'. Not only did the sellers fail to commence delivery of the
sugar on that day, they failed at any time thereafter before 3 June 1986.
    On 3 June 1986 the buyers telexed the sellers setting out these facts, recording that the
h buyers had learned from agents in Dunkirk that morning that no sugar had been
available nor had a berth been nominated. They further recorded that in a telephone
conversation with the sellers' agent, Mrs Choisnet, the sellers had not been able to give
the buyers any assurance as to when the cargo would be forthcoming. In this telex the
buyers held the sellers to be in default for not having provided the cargo, informed them
that they treated the contract as terminated, and that they had purchased a replacement
j cargo at FFr11,500 per metric ton fob stowed per metric ton. The replacement cargo was
purchased for delivery to the Naxos presenting to load at Dunkirk on 4–5 June 1986. In
a further exchange of telexes the sellers contended that they had until the end of the
delivery period (May/June 1986) to deliver the cargo and accordingly the buyers had not
validly terminated the contract on 3 June 1986.

In due course the buyers' claim for the difference between the contract price and the market price on 3 June 1986, together with a claim for loss of despatch which they *a* alleged they would have earned had the Naxos not remained idle whilst waiting for a cargo from the sellers, was submitted to arbitration pursuant to r 4 of the Rules of the Refined Sugar Association. The arbitrators found in favour of the buyers both in relation to their claim for the difference between the contract price and the market price and their claim for loss of despatch.

In view of the summary of the facts which I have set out above, I need only quote para *b* 14 of the award which reads as follows:

'The Respondent's obligation under the Contract was to deliver "to one or more vessels presenting to load during May/June 1986". The Claimant had to give the Seller not less than 14 days' notice of the vessel's expected readiness to load. The effect of the Association's Contract Rule 14 was that the Respondent should have *c* had the sugar ready to be delivered to the Claimant at any time during the Contract period and that the Claimant, having given reasonable notice (in fact 14 days under the Contract) was, in the words of the Rule, "entitled to call for delivery of the sugar between the first and last working day inclusive of the period of delivery". If the Claiment was entitled to call for delivery, the corollary is that the Respondent was under an obligation to deliver upon the agreed notice. We find that time was of the *d* essence of this obligation which was therefore a condition of the Contract. We have come to this conclusion for a number of reasons.

(1) Time of delivery is of the greatest importance in commercial contracts and contracts in the sugar trade are no exception.

(2) We regard Contract Rule 14 of the delivery rules as being of the utmost importance and we consider that the wording of the relevant parts of Rule 14, in *e* particular the phrases "The seller shall have the sugar ready to be delivered" and "The Buyer . . . shall be entitled to call for delivery", as being emphatic.

(3) The reason why the Buyer under the Association's Rules must give reasonable notice (and why in the Contract it must give 14 days' notice) is precisely because this enables the Seller to perform its own very important obligation which is to ensure that sugar is available for the commencement of loading. When a vessel is presented *f* under Contract Rule 14, we consider a Buyer is entitled to prompt delivery of a cargo. We do not accept that the wording of the third and fourth paragraphs of this Rule affect the position, as the Respondent argued. The delays catered for in those paragraphs do not, in any event, apply in this case.

(4) We do not accept that the payment of demurrage would be adequate compensation for the Buyer in the circumstances. It is important to the Buyer that *g* the cargo will be available as called for in accordance with the contract terms in order to fulfill onward commitments. Contracts, as in the present case, are often concluded with a reasonably long period of delivery and at a price which presupposes the Buyer's rights to call for delivery at any time having given reasonable notice. This is a valuable option which the Buyer would lose if the Seller were entitled to deliver whenever it was willing and able to do so providing it was within the *h* delivery period. This would turn a Buyer's option into a Seller's option.

(5) Finally, we dismiss the argument that the position is any different in this particular Contract because of the long string between the Respondent and the ultimate Supplier. That is no concern of the Claimant who is entitled to look to the Respondent to honour the contractual obligation it has undertaken.'

j

It is clear from the award that the arbitrators were satisfied that r 14(1) imposed an additional contractual obligation on the sellers. The arbitrators did not accept the sellers' submission that r 14(1) added nothing to the buyers' obligations to be found in the contract, and was therefore merely a restatement in general terms of their obligations.

The construction of r 14(1)

a   It is common ground that r 14(1) falls to be construed against the background of the general law relating to fob contracts and in the context of the rules. It is quite clear that r 14 taken as a whole cannot be said to contain mere statements of general principle, adding nothing to the contractual obligations to be found in the form contract used by the parties. For instance, if the vessel (or vessels) which had been notified presented herself ready to load within the contract period, but not within five calendar days of the b date contained in the notice which the buyers had given calling for delivery of the sugar, then the buyers were responsible for any costs incurred by the sellers by reason of such delay exceeding those five days: see r 14(3). Rule 14(4) prevented the shutter coming down on the last day of the contract shipping period, ie at the end of June. True enough, if r 14(2) had stood alone it could be said that it would have added nothing to the contract, since cl 7 provided that the buyers' notice must not be less than 14 days of the vessel(s) c expected readiness to load. However, r 14(2) does not stand alone and indeed is not in itself a separate rule but part of r 14, to which the numbering has been added merely as a matter of convenience.

I turn now to the specific elements of r 14(1) which have been the subject matter of particular submissions.

d   (1) *The meaning of 'the sugar'*

Both in the Court of Appeal and before your Lordships, counsel for the sellers submitted that for the purposes of his argument that r 14(1) added nothing to the contractual obligations, the meaning of 'the sugar' raised a crucial question. If I followed correctly his argument it was that 'the sugar' in the context of r 14 meant the entire e contract goods, whether or not the buyers had exercised their option of taking delivery in one or more lots as provided by r 11. Accordingly, a construction of r 14(1) which imposed on the buyers an obligation to have the entirety of the sugar available to begin loading immediately on the arrival of the vessel at the loading port irrespective of whether or not the buyers had exercised their option under r 11 produced a wholly unreasonable and commercially quite undesirable situation.

f   Counsel's submission, however, overlooks that r 14(1), (2) and (3) are concerned with 'the sugar' specified in a 'notice . . . calling for delivery'. In view of the buyers' option in r 11 it seems to me quite clear that 'the sugar' must refer to the entire contractual quantity of sugar *or* to any lesser quantity for which the buyers may have called if they had exercised their option of taking delivery in one or more lots as provided by r 11. Lloyd LJ, while posing various meanings that could be ascribed to 'the sugar', said ([1989] g   2 Lloyd's Rep 462 at 474): 'No doubt workable answers can be given to all these questions.' The other questions relate to the following elements in r 14(1) to which I now refer.

(2) *The meaning of 'ready to be delivered'*

Counsel for the buyers does not suggest that this obliges the sellers to have physically stacked on the quay when the vessel comes alongside the sugar which has been called h forward. As to the meaning of this phrase, both Sir Michael Kerr and Lloyd LJ found that a statement by Donaldson J in the Commercial Court in *European Grain & Shipping Ltd v David Geddes (Proteins) Ltd* [1977] 2 Lloyd's Rep 591 helpful. In that case there was a provision in a sale contract that 'Sellers shall have the contracted goods available for delivery in good condition from the first day of the Delivery Period.' As to this, the judge said (at 602):

j   'But what *do* the words mean? In my judgment, they mean that the contracted goods must be in such a state of availability for delivery from and including the first day of the delivery period that they can be delivered to the buyer as soon, in a commercial sense, as the buyer requires the seller to deliver. A seller who can say no more than that he has entered into a contract to buy goods of the contract description and quantity does not have "the contracted goods" available for delivery in this *a* sense. The words "the contracted goods" indicate that the goods must be identified, even if only as a part of an identified bulk, and must be in a deliverable state.' (Donaldson J's emphasis.)

That was a contract for a sale 'ex-Store/Silo' and not fob. Accordingly, the words in the judgment 'that they can be delivered to the buyer as soon, in a commercial sense, as the buyer requires the seller to deliver' have to be adapted to refer to the readiness for loading *b* on a vessel nominated by the buyer as soon as the vessel is ready to load the cargo in question. I agree with Sir Michael Kerr that here 'ready to be delivered' in its context means that the sugar must be available for loading without delay or interruption in the event that the vessel is able to start loading at once and to continue without interruption (see [1989] 2 Lloyd's Rep 462 at 468). *c*

(3) *The meaning of 'at any time within the contract period'*
Since the whole purpose of the buyers' call, which must be given on reasonable notice, was to enable the sellers to make arrangements for the sugar to be 'ready to be delivered', counsel for the sellers submitted that it did not make sense to require the sellers to have such arrangements in place throughout the whole contractual period. But the requirement *d* is '*at any time* within the contract period' and *not* '*at all times*'. The particular time is when the vessel duly nominated by the buyers presents herself ready to load. In this context it is interesting to note that the arbitrators in their award, having highlighted the buyers' complaint 'that no sugar had been available nor berth nominated for the cargo' and recorded that the buyers had held the sellers in default 'for not having provided the cargo', stated the 'essential issue' in terms of the sellers' 'failure to provide a cargo to meet *e* the vessel Naxos when it presented for loading' (para 13 of the award) and referred later to the sellers' obligation to ensure that sugar 'is available for the commencement of loading': see para 14(3) set out above.

If I have thus correctly interpreted r 14(1) it can be restated in these terms: the seller shall have the sugar called forward available for loading without delay or interruption as soon as the vessel is ready to load the cargo in question. *f*

As thus expressed, this rule is not a statement of general principle which adds nothing to the terms of the contract. The reason for its existence is clearly expressed by the arbitrators in para 14(4) of their award, set out above, which it is convenient to quote once more:

> '... Contracts, as in the present case, are often concluded with a reasonably long *g* period of delivery and at a price which presupposes the Buyer's rights to call for delivery at any time having given reasonable notice. This is a valuable option which the Buyer would lose if the Seller were entitled to deliver whenever it was willing and able to do so providing it was within the delivery period. This would turn a Buyer's option into a Seller's option.'

Indeed, since r 14(4) removes the delivery deadline to be found in cl 7, it is even more *h* important that the buyers should have the right to call for delivery at any time, having given reasonable notice for the sugar called forward to be available to begin loading immediately on the arrival of the vessel at the loading port ready to load.

It is understandable that much time and intellectual energy was expended in the Court of Appeal in considering the decision both at first instance and in the Court of Appeal of *Tradax Export SA v Italgrani di Francesco Ambrosio* [1983] 2 Lloyd's Rep 109; *affd* [1986] 1 *j* Lloyd's Rep 112. The facts of that case are complicated but are conveniently summarised by Sir Michael Kerr when giving judgment in this appeal (see [1989] 2 Lloyd's Rep 462 at 469–470). Bingham J in the Commercial Court and the Court of Appeal were concerned essentially with the meaning of the words 'at Buyer's call'. Bingham J asked himself the question ([1983] 2 Lloyd's Rep 109 at 114):

'Are those words procedural only, indicating how the seller's delivery obligation
a is to be triggered and the running of time started? Or do the words express a more
peremptory stipulation, requiring the goods to be delivered by the seller when,
within the delivery period, the buyer calls for delivery?'

The judge as a matter of pure construction said he preferred the second view, observing:

'The words "at Buyer's call" mean, I think, something very close to "on Buyer's
b call" and have a flavour somewhat similar to, although weaker than, "on Buyer's
demand". I infer that the buyer's call is to be made in the confident expectation of a
prompt response.'

The Court of Appeal held that the judge had wrongly construed 'at Buyer's call.' I do
not consider it is helpful to debate to what extent that decision on the meaning of those
words assists in interpreting the words of r 14(1). I have concluded that on its proper
c construction it imposed on the sellers an express additional obligation of which they
were in breach by 3 June.

The second question: was the obligation imposed by r 14(1) a condition of the contract?
d   I start by reminding myself of the statements of principle made in this House in *Bunge
Corp v Tradax SA* [1981] 2 All ER 513 esp at 542, [1981] 1 WLR 711 esp at 716 per Lord
Wilberforce. Having stated that the courts should not be too ready to interpret contractual
clauses as conditions, Lord Wilberforce said:

'But I do not doubt that, in suitable cases, the courts should not be reluctant, if
the intentions of the parties as shown by the contract so indicate, to hold that an
e obligation has the force of a condition, and that indeed they should usually do so in
the case of time clauses in mercantile contracts.'

Lord Wilberforce then accepted as being correct the statement of the law in 9 Halsbury's
Laws (4th edn) paras 481–482 asserting:

'(1) that the court will require precise compliance with stipulations as to time
f wherever the circumstances of the case indicate this would fulfil the intention of
the parties, and (2) that broadly speaking time will be considered of the essence in
"mercantile" contracts...'

This clearly was a mercantile contract and r 14(1) can properly be described as a 'time
clause'. It imposes an obligation to have the goods called forward available for loading at
g a definite point of time: at the expiration of the notice given under cl 7 and as soon as the
vessel presents herself ready to load within the contract period. The performance by the
sellers of their obligations under r 14(1) does not involve questions of degree as in *Bremer
Handelsgesellschaft mbH v Vanden Avenne-Izegem PVBA* [1978] 2 Lloyds Rep 109, where the
relevant clause contained the obligation on the sellers to advise the buyers *without delay*
of certain causes of the shipment proving impossible.

h   I next consider the commercial significance of r 14(1). In the *Bunge Corp* case [1981] 2
All ER 513 at 545, [1981] 1 WLR 711 at 719 Lord Lowry observed:

'The treatment of time limits as conditions in mercantile contracts does not
appear to me to be justifiable by any presumption of fact or rule of law, but rather
to be a practical expedient founded on and dictated by the experience of
j businessmen...'

On the day before embarking on the hearing of the present appeal, the Court of
Appeal, identically constituted, gave judgment in *State Trading Corp of India Ltd v M
Golodetz Ltd* [1989] 2 Lloyd's Rep 277. The leading judgment was given by Kerr LJ and
was concurred in by Lloyd and Butler-Sloss LJJ. One of the questions to be decided in
that case was whether a particular obligation of the sellers was a condition of the contract.

Kerr LJ quoted from the classic judgment of Bowen LJ in *Bentsen v Taylor Sons & Co (No 2)* [1893] 2 QB 274 at 281:

> 'There is no way of deciding that question except by looking at the contract in the light of the surrounding circumstances, and then making up one's mind whether the intention of the parties, as gathered from the instrument itself, will best be carried out by treating the promise as a warranty sounding only in damages, or as a condition precedent by the failure to perform which the other party is relieved of his liability.'

Having referred to, amongst other authorities, the *Bunge Corp* case, Kerr LJ observed ([1989] 2 Lloyd's Rep 277 at 283–284):

> 'At the end of the day, if there is no other more specific guide to the correct solution to a particular dispute, the Court may have no alternative but to follow the general statement of Lord Justice Bowen in *Bentsen v. Taylor* which I have already quoted, by making what is in effect a value judgment about the commercial significance of the term in question.'

It will be recalled that in para 14 of the award set out above, the arbitrators considered r 14 as being 'of the utmost importance' and that under the rule the buyers were entitled 'to prompt delivery of a cargo' so that the cargo would be available to fulfill onward commitments. The arbitrators did not accept that payment of demurrage would be adequate compensation for the buyers. They considered that the buyers had paid for a valuable option which they would lose if the sellers were entitled to deliver whenever they were willing and able to do so providing it was within the delivery period. The arbitrators might well have added, in view of r 14(4), which extends the frustrating period beyond 30 June, providing loading is commenced by that date, that there could well be a lengthy period of many weeks for which the presenting vessel might otherwise be contractually required to wait for a cargo to be loaded. If the buyers are not then able to terminate the contract, then they may have to wait until the expiry of a frustrating period beyond the second month. In those circumstances it was therefore essential for the buyers to be able to terminate the contract and buy in elsewhere if, when the notice expired and the vessel arrived, the sellers had not then the sugar ready for delivery.

To my mind the evaluation by this experienced trade tribunal of the commercial significance of r 14(1) was wholly justified. Rule 14(1) was crucially important to the buyers since it removed the risk that the absence or insufficiency of cargo would be a cause of delay. Since it must be rare, if ever, for it to be in the sellers' interest to load a vessel very slowly, the rule ensures to a very large extent that loading will be promptly commenced and speedily carried out and thus enable the buyers punctually to perform their own obligations to their customers. The rule tends to provide certainty which is such an indispensable ingredient of mercantile contracts.

Lloyd LJ in his judgment was not persuaded that the parties intended to make readiness for delivery a condition of the contract. He based his decision very largely on his view that the language of r 14(1) and in particular the words or phrases 'the sugar', 'ready to be delivered' and 'at any time within the contract period' were so vague and lacking in precision as to make it unlikely that the parties intended the sellers' compliance with r 14(1) to be a condition of the contract. I have already expressed my view as to the true meaning of the words used in r 14(1) and have concluded that they are neither vague nor do they lack precision.

Lloyd LJ was also clearly impressed by the consequences, as he saw them, of construing r 14(1) as a condition. He said ([1989] 2 Lloyd's Rep 462 at 474):

> 'Suppose 11,000 tons were ready to be delivered on day one, and the remaining 1,000 tons on day two, so that on no view could the loading have been held up, could it really be said that the breach went to the root of the contract?'

With respect, Lloyd LJ was clearly in error, since, if looked at on day one, on no view
a could the loading have been held up by the absence of cargo: then the goods *were* ready
for delivery on day one and no question of breach arises.

In deciding whether r 14(1) was a condition Lloyd LJ relied to some extent on r 14(4),
observing (at 475):

> 'Even the obligation to load within the shipment period, which is usually a
b condition, is softened in the present contract by r 14(4), so that the sellers may
continue loading, if the vessel has presented herself in readiness to load within the
contract period. If the completion of loading is not in all circumstances a condition
of the contract, is it really to be supposed that an event prior to the commencement
of loading was intended to be a condition?'

But, in the light of the views expressed by the arbitrators in para 14 of their award
c referred to above, r 14(4) makes it even more important that the buyer has an option to
terminate the contract and buy in elsewhere if the seller is unable to give adequate
assurances that the absence of cargo is not going to be a cause of delay. As Bingham J
succinctly observed in his judgment at first instance in the *Italgrani* case [1983] 2 Lloyd's
Rep 109 at 115:

> 'If a vessel were duly tendered at the very outset of a contractual shipment period,
d and the market were falling sharply, it could well pay the seller to keep the vessel
waiting, on payment of demurrage, until shortly before the end of the period, only
then buying in the goods and making delivery. I find it hard to believe that parties
to this form of contract would regard such an outcome as permissible.'

A fortiori having regard to r 14(4), which could well extend the contractual shipment
e period certainly into July and maybe beyond. The short judgment of Butler-Sloss LJ
relies essentially on the reasoning of Lloyd LJ.

Accordingly, I would allow this appeal, set aside the orders of the Court of Appeal and
Gatehouse J and restore the award of the Council of the Refined Sugar Association.

f **LORD OLIVER OF AYLMERTON.** My Lords, I have had the advantage of reading
in draft the speech prepared by my noble and learned friend Lord Ackner. I agree with
it, and for the reasons he gives, I too would allow this appeal.

LORD JAUNCEY OF TULLICHETTLE. My Lords, I have had the advantage of
reading in draft the speech of my noble and learned friend Lord Ackner. I agree with it,
g and for the reasons he gives, I too would allow this appeal.

Appeal allowed.

Solicitors: *William A Crump* (for the buyers); *Richards Butler* (for the sellers).

Mary Rose Plummer   Barrister.

R v Immigration Appeal Tribunal and another, ex parte Secretary of State for the Home Department

COURT OF APPEAL, CIVIL DIVISION

GLIDEWELL, STUART-SMITH LJJ AND SIR DAVID CROOM-JOHNSON

16, 17 MAY 1990

Immigration – Leave to enter – Successive applications – Application on more than one ground – Applicant refused leave to enter as visitor – Applicant then applying for asylum while still in United Kingdom – Whether adjudicator having jurisdiction to entertain appeal from refusal of leave to enter as visitor – Whether applicant can make successive applications for leave to enter – Immigration Act 1971, s 13.

The two immigrants were Sri Lankan Tamils whose applications for leave to enter the United Kingdom as visitors had been refused. They were served with notices of refusal under the Immigration Act 1971. While still in the United Kingdom they applied for political asylum but those applications were also refused. They then returned to Sri Lanka, from where they exercised their statutory right of appeal under s 13[a] of the 1971 Act against the refusal of asylum. The adjudicator allowed their appeal. The Secretary of State appealed to the Immigration Appeal Tribunal but the tribunal declined to hear the appeal because the notice of appeal had been delivered out of time. The Secretary of State sought judicial review to quash the decisions of the adjudicator and the tribunal on the ground that the adjudicator had had no jurisdiction to hear the immigrants' appeals because the 1971 Act contemplated a single application for leave to enter and the immigrants had exhausted the right to apply for leave to enter when they had applied to enter as visitors and been refused. The Divisional Court dismissed the Secretary of State's application. The Secretary of State appealed to the Court of Appeal.

Held – Since neither the 1971 Act nor the statement of rules laid down by the Secretary of State under that Act, either expressly or by implication, restricted successive applications for leave to enter from a person seeking such leave or restricted an applicant from putting forward more than one ground for applying at any one time, the fact that the immigrants had already applied for and been refused leave to enter as visitors did not preclude them from applying for asylum while they were still in the United Kingdom. That application necessarily included an application for leave to enter, the refusal of which gave rise to a right of appeal under s 13 of the 1971 Act. The adjudicator accordingly had had jurisdiction to entertain their appeals. The Secretary of State's appeal would therefore be dismissed (see p 654 *h j*, p 655 *b c*, p 656 *e j*, p 657 *j* to p 658 *a*, p 659 *e g j* and p 660 *a* to *c j* to p 661 *a c f*, post).

Notes

For appeals against exclusion from the United Kingdom, see 4 Halsbury's Laws (4th edn) paras 1016–1017, and for cases on the subject, see 2 Digest (Reissue) 219–221, *1225–1235*.

For the Immigration Act 1971, s 13, see 31 Halsbury's Statutes (4th edn) 66.

Cases referred to in judgments

DPP v Bhagwan [1970] 3 All ER 97, [1972] AC 60, [1970] 3 WLR 501, HL.

R v Chief Immigration Officer, ex p Hazari (13 November 1975, unreported), DC.

R v Secretary of State for the Home Dept, ex p Amarasingham (12 May 1989, unreported), QBD.

---

a   Section 13, so far as material, is set out at p 654 *d e*, post

R v Secretary of State for the Home Dept, ex p Labiche (1989) Times, 17 July, DC.
a   *R v Secretary of State for the Home Dept, ex p Sivakumaran* [1988] 1 All ER 193, [1988] AC 958, [1988] 2 WLR 92, HL.

Case also cited
Ashraf v Immigration Appeal Tribunal [1989] Imm AR 234, CA.

b   **Application for judicial review**
The Secretary of State for the Home Department appealed against the decision of the Divisional Court (Lloyd LJ and Auld J) on 27 July 1989 dismissing his application for judicial review by way of (i) orders of certiorari to bring up and quash the determination of the first respondent, the Immigration Appeal Tribunal (D L Neve chairman), dated 19 April 1989 that the Secretary of State's appeal to the Immigration Appeal Tribunal against c   the determination of the second respondent, the adjudicator (R G Care) was out of time, (ii) a declaration that the Immigration Appeal Tribunal had jurisdiction to entertain the Secretary of State's appeal or in the alternative (iii) an order of certiorari to bring up and quash that part of the determination of the adjudicator dated 13 March 1989 whereby he held that he had jurisdiction to entertain appeals from Vythialingam Skandarajah and Nadarajah Vilvarajah (the immigrants) under s 13 of the Immigration Act 1971. The d   facts are set out in the judgment of Stuart-Smith LJ.

Robert Jay for the Secretary of State.
Ian A Macdonald QC and *Alper Riza* for the immigrants.
The respondents were not represented.

e   **STUART-SMITH LJ** (giving the first judgment at the invitation of Glidewell LJ). Vythialingam Skandarajah and Nadarajah Vilvarajah, who I shall refer to as 'the immigrants', are Sri Lankan Tamils. They arrived at Heathrow Airport on 11 June 1987. Each applied for leave to enter as visitors, presenting forged Malaysian passports. Their applications were refused and they were served with a notice of refusal in writing in f   accordance with s 4(1) of the Immigration Act 1971. Shortly thereafter each applied for political asylum. In accordance with the provisions of para 73 of the Statement of Changes in Immigration Rules (HC Paper (1982–83) no 169) those applications were referred to the Secretary of State. They were interviewed by immigration officers for the purposes of determining their applications. On 20 August 1987 the Secretary of State refused their applications for asylum. A letter of that date, signed by Mrs Underhill for the Secretary of State, was sent to the immigration officer and served by him on the g   immigrants. The immigrants were told that 'your application for asylum is refused. Since you do not otherwise qualify for leave to enter the United Kingdom, the Immigration Service have been instructed to arrange your removal to Sri Lanka.'
        The immigrants, together with three other Sri Lankan Tamils, sought judicial review of the Secretary of State's decision to refuse asylum. Their applications were refused by h   McCowan J, appeals to the Court of Appeal were allowed, but on 16 December 1987 the House of Lords restored the decision of the judge (see *R v Secretary of State for the Home Dept, ex p Sivakumaran* [1988] 1 All ER 193, [1988] AC 958). In February 1988 the immigrants returned to Sri Lanka and there they purported to exercise their statutory right of appeal to the adjudicator under s 13 of the 1971 Act. On 13 March 1987 the adjudicator, Mr Care, allowed the immigrants' appeal. He held that they should be j   treated as political refugees and granted asylum. He rejected a submission made on behalf of the Secretary of State that he had no jurisdiction to entertain the appeals.
        The Secretary of State appealed to the Immigration Appeal Tribunal, but the notice of appeal was delivered out of time and the Immigration Appeal Tribunal declined jurisdiction to entertain the appeals. The Secretary of State then sought judicial review. He challenged the decision of the Immigration Appeal Tribunal that the notice of appeal was out of time.

On 27 July 1989 the Divisional Court, consisting of Lloyd LJ and Auld J, rejected that submission and there is no appeal from the decision on that point. The Secretary of State *a* also challenged the adjudicator's decision that he had jurisdiction to entertain the immigrants' appeals. On this point the Divisional Court were divided. Lloyd LJ held that the adjudicator had no jurisdiction; Auld J held that he had. The adjudicator's decision remained and the Secretary of State now appeals to this court.

Counsel for the Secretary of State submits that once an application for leave to enter has been refused by a notice served on the immigrant, his application for leave to enter *b* has been determined and he cannot, while he physically remains in this country, make or require to be considered another application based on another ground: consequently, if he does make such an application and it is refused, he has no right of appeal. Counsel for the Secretary of State submits that the Act contemplates a single application, albeit based on a number of grounds. It does not contemplate two or more applications, refusal of which each attracts a right of appeal. He accepts that there is nothing in the Act which *c* expressly limits an immigrant to one application, but he submits that it is a necessary implication of the Act and that for good measure it would be unworkable if it were not so.

Counsel for the immigrants submits that there is no such necessary implication limiting an immigrant to one application and that the present case falls within the express words of s 13(1) of the 1971 Act, which confers the right of appeal. That *d* subsection reads as follows:

> 'Subject to the provisions of this Part of this Act, a person who is refused leave to enter the United Kingdom under this Act may appeal to an adjudicator against the decision that he requires leave or against the refusal.'

The question therefore is whether the immigrants are persons who have been refused *e* leave to enter the United Kingdom under the 1971 Act.

There is a certain amount of common ground. Counsel for the Secretary of State concedes, rightly in my judgment, that where an immigrant claims asylum at the outset, he is seeking leave to enter the country under the 1971 Act and that is so, even if he advances other grounds. Thus, if the immigrant on arrival seeks leave to enter as a visitor *f* and then, before that is refused, he also asks for asylum, counsel for the Secretary of State accepts that that is one application for leave to enter, albeit based on one or more grounds. Consequently, refusal attracts a right of appeal on either or both grounds.

Second, it is accepted by counsel for the Secretary of State, again correctly in my opinion, that if, after refusal of his application for leave to enter on one ground, the immigrant physically leaves the country, he may return as soon as he likes and apply *g* again on a different ground and he is entitled to have his application considered. If it is refused he has a right of appeal. But, says counsel for the Secretary of State, it makes all the difference if he is served with a written notice of refusal before making his second application on a different ground and he does not physically leave the country before making it.

For my part, I cannot see any reason in logic or policy why that should make all the *h* difference. If an application for asylum is an application for leave to enter the country and it is one of the grounds put forward in the first application, I have difficulty in seeing why it is anything else when it is made the ground of a second application. Moreover, I fail to see that there is any difference simply because the immigrant leaves the country between the first and the second application. In my judgment light is cast on this point by s 11(1) of the 1971 Act, which provides: *j*

> 'A person arriving in the United Kingdom by ship or aircraft shall for [the] purposes of this Act be deemed not to enter the United Kingdom unless and until he disembarks, and on disembarkation at a port shall further be deemed not to enter the United Kingdom so long as he remains in such area (if any) at the port as may be

a
approved for this purpose by an immigration officer; and a person who has not otherwise entered the United Kingdom shall be deemed not to do so as long as he is detained, or temporarily admitted or released while liable to detention, under the powers conferred by Schedule 2 to this Act.'

This means that a person who never gets beyond the immigration area does not enter the United Kingdom and continues to need leave to do so. If he remains there, he is in
b
the same position as one who gets on the next plane out of Heathrow, flies across the Channel or round the Isle of Wight and then presents himself again to the immigration officer and asks for leave to enter on a different ground from that previously refused.

Counsel for the Secretary of State argues, however, that it is the necessary implication of the Act that only one application can be made while the applicant remains physically in the United Kingdom. I can find nothing in s 3 or s 4 of the 1971 Act which supports
c
this view. So far as is relevant s 3(1) provides:

'Except as otherwise provided by or under this Act, where a person is not a British citizen—(a) he shall not enter the United Kingdom unless given leave to do so in accordance with this Act; (b) he may be given leave to enter the United Kingdom (or, when already there, leave to remain in the United Kingdom) either for a limited or for an indefinite period; (c) if he is given a limited leave to enter or remain in the
d
United Kingdom, it may be given subject to conditions restricting his employment or occupation in the United Kingdom, or requiring him to register with the police, or both.'

Section 4(1) provides:

e
'The power under this Act to give or refuse leave to enter the United Kingdom shall be exercised by immigration officers, and the power to give leave to remain in the United Kingdom, or to vary any leave under section 3(3)(a) (whether as regards duration or conditions), shall be exercised by the Secretary of State . . .'

That establishes the clear division between the functions of the immigration officer and the Secretary of State. Questions of asylum have to be referred to the Secretary of
f
State by the immigration officer under the rules. Paragraph 73 of the Statement of Charges in Immigration Rules (HC Paper (1982–83) no 169) which was in force at the material time (now para 75 of HC Paper (1989–90) no 251) provides as follows:

'Special considerations arise where the only country to which a person could be removed is one to which he is unwilling to go owing to well-founded fear of being persecuted for reasons of race, religion, nationality, membership of a particular
g
social group or political opinion. Any case in which it appears to the immigration officer as a result of a claim or information given by the person seeking entry at a port that he might fall within the terms of this provision is to be referred to the Home Office for decision regardless of any grounds set out in any provision of these rules which may appear to justify refusal of leave to enter. Leave to enter will not
h
be refused if removal would be contrary to the provisions of the Convention and Protocol relating to the Status of Refugees.'

But the actual leave to enter, or refusal of such leave, is given by the immigration officer to the immigrant, though the officer has to act in accordance with the instructions of the Secretary of State: see para 1(3) of Sch 2 to the 1971 Act. Counsel for the Secretary of State relied on certain provisions of Sch 2, which are administrative provisions as to
j
the control of entry. Paragraph 2(1) of Sch 2 reads as follows:

'An immigration officer may examine any persons who have arrived in the United Kingdom by ship or aircraft (including transit passengers, members of the crew and others not seeking to enter the United Kingdom) for the purpose of determining—(a) whether any of them is or is not a British citizen; and (b) whether, if he is not, he may or may not enter the United Kingdom without leave; and (c) whether, if he may not, he should be given leave and for what period and on what conditions (if any), or should be refused leave.'

To my mind there is nothing expressed in that paragraph to the effect that the officer can only examine a person once, or any necessary implication to that effect. It simply empowers the officer to conduct examinations for the stated purpose.

Next, counsel for the Secretary of State referred to para 6(1). That provides:

'Subject to sub-paragraph (3) below, where a person examined by an immigration officer under paragraph 2 above is to be given a limited leave to enter the United Kingdom or is to be refused leave, the notice giving or refusing leave shall be given not later than twelve hours after the conclusion of his examination (including any further examination) in pursuance of that paragraph; and if notice giving or refusing leave is not given him before the end of those twelve hours, he shall (if not a British citizen) be deemed to have been given indefinite leave to enter the United Kingdom and the immigration officer shall as soon as may be give him written notice of that leave.'

That paragraph is concerned with setting a time limit, now extended to 24 hours, after conclusion of the examination within which notification of refusal of leave is to be given. Counsel for the Secretary of State submits that it would be absurd if an immigrant was entitled to make any number of applications requiring an appropriate number of examinations and consequent risk that the immigration officer might fail to notify the immigrant in time of refusal to leave, with the consequence permitted by the paragraph. But, while I can see that from an administrative point of view it is much more convenient if all grounds of an application are considered together, I can see nothing absurd or unworkable in permitting successive applications. If the subsequent application is made on the same grounds, or on grounds which are quite inconsistent with facts previously stated, it is likely to get short thrift.

Paragraph 6(2) and (3) of Sch 2 to the Act deal with the position where the immigration officer has a change of mind. They are as follows:

'(2) Where on a person's examination under paragraph 2 above he is given notice of leave to enter the United Kingdom, then at any time before the end of twelve hours from the conclusion of the examination he may be given a further notice in writing by an immigration officer cancelling the earlier notice and refusing him leave to enter.

(3) Where in accordance with this paragraph a person is given notice refusing him leave to enter the United Kingdom, that notice may at any time be cancelled by notice in writing given him by an immigration officer; and where a person is given a notice of cancellation under this sub-paragraph, the immigration officer may at the same time give him a limited leave to enter, but in the absence of a notice giving a limited leave the notice of cancellation shall be deemed to be a notice giving him indefinite leave to enter.'

Counsel for the Secretary of State submits that sub-para (3) is a mirror image of sub-para (2), that this in some way shows that only one application can be made. To my mind the significance of these paragraphs is that it makes plain that the immigration officer can consider matters which come to light after the initial grant or refusal of leave. Where the grant of leave is to be refused, it must be done within twelve hours from the conclusion of the examination. There is no such time limit where the initial refusal is cancelled and leave to enter is granted. In my judgment para 6(3) supports the immigrants' contention and enables the immigration officer to change his mind if new matter is put before him as the result of a second application based on different grounds.

Finally counsel for the Secretary of State relied on para 16(1) and (2) of Sch 2. They
a provide:

'(1) A person who may be required to submit to examination under paragraph 2
above may be detained under the authority of an immigration officer pending his
examination and pending a decision to give or refuse him leave to enter.

(2) A person in respect of whom directions may be given under any of paragraphs
b 8 to 14 above may be detained under the authority of an immigration officer
pending the giving of directions and pending his removal in pursuance of any
directions given.'

Counsel for the Secretary of State argued that these two provisions are mutually
exclusive, in other words an immigrant who was detained under para 16(2), as these
immigrants were, after their initial application for leave to enter as visitors was refused,
c could not then be detained for the purpose of examination in relation to their second
application, and he points out that there are different provisions as to bail: see paras 22
and 29 of Sch 2.

I agree with Auld J that this argument is misconceived and I cannot improve on what
he said. He gave two reasons:

d   'First, where an unsuccessful applicant has been detained under para 16(2), an
immigration officer does not need to exercise his powers of detention under para
16(1) while he conducts an examination under para 2 of Sch 2 of any further
application. The applicant is not entitled to be detained under para 16(1) as soon as
he makes a further application. He does not, therefore, necessarily bring himself
within para 16(1) by making a further application. Accordingly, he need not become
e   subject to any conflict that there might be between the possibility of being granted
bail under para 16(1) but not under para 16(2). Second, an applicant who has been
refused leave to enter and detained under para 16(2), and whom an immigration
officer on a further application might unnecessarily choose to detain under para
16(1), does not become entitled to release on bail on a successful application under
para 22 when he makes a further application, any more than a man committed for
f   trial in custody on one offence becomes entitled to release on bail if committed for
trial on bail for another offence. The bail, if granted on the second application,
would simply not be operable. The reality is that an adjudicator would not grant it,
knowing that the applicant was also a person detained under para 16(2) as one who
had been refused leave to enter on his original application and who was subject to
removal directions.'

g   In answer to the question, 'Under what powers was the Secretary of State acting in
entertaining the applications of these respondents for asylum and refusing it, if not under
the Act?', counsel for the Secretary of State said that it was under the prerogative. But in
my judgment that will not do. The prerogative power is suspended by the 1971 Act, save
to the limited extent provided by s 33(5), which provides as follows:

h   'This Act shall not be taken to supersede or impair any power exercisable by Her
Majesty in relation to aliens by virtue of Her prerogative.'

These immigrants were not aliens. Sri Lanka is a member of the Commonwealth.
Before 1962, unlike aliens, they enjoyed the common law right, in common with all
British subjects, to come into and go from this country without let or hindrance. It is the
j   legislation passed in that year that restricted these rights and subsequent legislation,
including the 1971 Act that further restricted them: see per Lord Diplock in DPP v
Bhagwan [1970] 3 All ER 97 at 104–105, [1972] AC 60 at 80. I accept that it is s 3(1) of
the 1971 Act that takes away this right, but the Act as a whole abrogates the prerogative
power, save to the limited extent provided by s 33(5). Accordingly, in my judgment,
refusal of the second application, based on a claim for political asylum, is just as much a

refusal of leave to enter the United Kingdom under the Act within s 13(1) as a refusal of a first, and only application, made on such grounds.

As the Divisional Court recognised, there is little authority on the point and what there is I have not found of assistance. In *R v Secretary of State for the Home Dept, ex p Amarasingham* (12 May 1989, unreported) McCowan J said:

> 'In my judgment where there has already been a refusal of leave to enter on a non-asylum ground, as was the situation here, there does not have to be a further refusal of leave to enter if at some later stage an asylum application is refused.'

But the judge gave no reasons for this view and we are told by counsel for the Secretary of State that although there was some slight argument on the point, it was only a minor consideration in that case.

In *R v Secretary of State for the Home Office, ex p Labiche* (1989) Times, 17 July, which was decided on 11 July 1989 by the same Divisional Court as the present case, the two cases being argued consecutively, Lloyd LJ expressed the same view obiter as he did in the present case.

Counsel for the Secretary of State also referred the court to *R v Chief Immigration Officer, ex p Hazari* (13 November 1975, unreported), a decision of the Divisional Court, consisting of Lord Widgery CJ, Park and May JJ. In that case the applicant had arrived at Heathrow on 13 October 1975 and sought leave to enter on grounds of a proposed marriage to a man called Patel in the United Kingdom. While that claim was being investigated, it became clear that the marriage plans were breaking down and some question was raised by those representing her whether or not she should be given leave to enter as a visitor. However, it is important to notice that the applicant herself never made any such request. She made it plain that she only came for the purpose of marriage to Mr Patel and had no other interest in being here. Leave to enter was refused on 15 October, but on 16 October those representing the applicant wrote seeking leave to enter as a visitor. Lord Widgery CJ said:

> 'What in fact is happening in this court where counsel moves for an order of mandamus on behalf of the applicant is that it is being alleged that there were really here two applications for leave to enter the United Kingdom, and that although one has been fairly and completely and properly disposed of, the other has never been subject to a formal notice of refusal at all. So, argues counsel, the second application, if refused, has not been backed up by a formal notice as required by para 6 of Sch 2 to the 1971 Act and therefore his client has a deemed indefinite permission to enter the United Kingdom. He accordingly argues that he should be given an order of mandamus to require the immigration officer to allow her to enter. It is of course fundamental to this application that there are here two separate applications. True, there are two grounds: the first which was related to the fiancee rules and the second which related to the visitor rules. It is said by counsel that there are two applications and he claims that the second brings him home in his request for mandamus. For my part I am quite satisfied that this is a false concept, this idea of two applications, merely because two different reasons at one time or another had been canvassed. As I see it, when the Commonwealth immigrant arrives at Heathrow and has not automatic right of entry by virtue of being patrial, he or she presents him or herself to the immigration officer and says "I desire leave to enter" and the immigration officer, after appropriate investigation, says "Yes" or "No"; and if, which is very unusual one gathers, in fact the request to enter contains within it more than one ground, if the applicant seems to have more than one possible ground for seeking leave to enter, then both grounds, or all grounds, must be considered simultaneously. When the final decision is given either to admit or to refuse, then it must reflect all the matters which have been urged before the immigration officer. It seems to me therefore that in this case, although by the 16 October we find a formal letter of

a request from the applicant's solicitors asking for leave to enter as a visitor, the obligation of the immigration officer to listen to the applicant had already expired, and indeed it had expired when the refusal was made on the 15 of the month. There are discretionary powers in the Act for the immigration officer to re-open a refusal, but I see no principle which requires him to do that, and accordingly if his formal refusal, which I have read, was valid when made, that to my mind is an end of the whole case and there can be no question of the prerogative orders going with a view
b to re-opening the decision.'

He went on to consider whether or not the immigration officer had acted fairly.

Counsel for the Secretary of State relies on what was said in that case. But in the first place it seems to me that it is far from clear that the applicant ever in fact made an application for leave to enter as a visitor, or authorised her advisers to make one.
c Moreover, whether or not the immigration officer in that case had a discretion to entertain the second application, in the present case the Secretary of State did entertain the application based on asylum, as he was bound to do so. Paragraph 16 of the Statement of Changes in Immigration Rules (HC Paper (1982–83) no 169) provides:

'Where a person is a refugee full account is to be taken of the provisions of the
d Convention and Protocol relating to the Status of Refugees (Cmd 9171 and Cmnd 3096). Nothing in these rules is to be construed as requiring action contrary to the United Kingdom's obligations under these instruments.'

I have already referred to para 73 of the rules.

For these reasons I consider that the adjudicator and Auld J were right in holding that the respondents had a right of appeal. I would dismiss this appeal.
e

SIR DAVID CROOM-JOHNSON. The framework within which the Immigration Act 1971 works is that an immigrant is unable to enter the United Kingdom unless he has obtained leave in one form or another, which means that he can only enter if he has made an application for leave to enter. The statute contains no express provisions laying down when, where or how such an application is to be made, but clearly in the ordinary
f way it is effected by the immigrant presenting himself to the immigration officer at immigration control when he arrives and asking to come in. The immigration officer then has a duty to decide whether leave should be granted or refused.

There is nothing in the Act which states in terms that only one ground of application may be put forward at any one time, or that, if the original application is refused, a second application on a different ground may not be made while the applicant is still
g physically in this country.

In this appeal the most the Secretary of State can do is to seek to demonstrate that the provisions of the Act cannot work if a second application for leave to enter is made after the refusal of the first while the would-be immigrant is still physically in the country after arrival. What has been relied on to show unworkability is that para 16(1) and (2) of Sch 2 are framed in such a way that they necessarily lead to the conclusion that no second
h application can be made in those circumstances. Paragraph 16(1) deals with the detention of someone who is still awaiting a decision whether he may enter or not. Paragraph 16(2) deals with the detention of someone who has been refused entry and has not yet been removed. In the ordinary course of events an applicant could be one or the other, but not both. But there is no reason why, if a second application to enter is made, para 16(1) should not apply if it is appropriate, after a refusal has brought para 16(2) into play. I do
j not regard those two sub-paragraphs as mutually exclusive. They simply deal with different situations in normal circumstances. The Secretary of State's suggestion that they are mutually exclusive is sought from the provisions of Sch 2, para 6(2) and (3) which lay down the times within which an immigration officer, who has either granted or refused leave, may have second thoughts and change his mind. It is urged that these provisions

exclude the possibility that the same applicant should be covered by both. Again I do not so read them and I agree on this point with Stuart-Smith LJ. If Parliament's intention *a* had been that a second, separate application for leave to enter was to be excluded, I would have expected clear language to that effect. To allow an applicant to put forward a second application after the refusal of his first may be administratively inconvenient, but it would be illogical and unjust not to allow him that right. Accordingly, once it is open to the applicant to make a second application, as I think it is, and it is refused, s 13(1) of the 1971 Act gives him a right of appeal to the adjudicator, which is the real point of issue of *b* this appeal.

In my view the conclusion reached by Auld J in his careful judgment was correct, and I too would dismiss this appeal.

GLIDEWELL LJ. I agree with both Stuart-Smith LJ and Sir David Croom-Johnson that this appeal must be dismissed for the reasons they have given. I also agree with the *c* reasoning in the judgment of Auld J in the Divisional Court.

I add some observations of my own because the issues raised in this appeal are of some importance and because the members of the Divisional Court were unable to reach agreement about them.

The basis of the argument for the Secretary of State is that, in refusing the immigrants' application for asylum, he has nevertheless not refused them leave to enter the United *d* Kingdom. Alternatively, if in effect he has refused them leave to enter, he was not acting, when so doing, under the powers contained in the Immigration Act 1971. These alternative arguments raise four issues.

First, has a person who is not a British citizen, who has made an application for leave to enter the United Kingdom which has been refused, but who has not yet left the United Kingdom, 'entered' the United Kingdom? Such a person may be in detention under para *e* 16 of Sch 2 to the 1971 Act, or have been temporarily admitted to the United Kingdom under para 21 of Sch 2. In either case I agree with Auld J that the combined effect of ss 3(1), 4(1), (2)(c) and 11(1) of the 1971 Act is that a person in this situation is deemed not to have entered the United Kingdom.

Second, can such a person, after he has received a notice of refusal of his original *f* application for leave to enter the United Kingdom, but while he is still in the United Kingdom, make a further valid application for leave to enter? Counsel for the Secretary of State does not suggest that the Act contains any express provision which prevents such a further application being made, but he argues that by necessary implication this result must follow. As a result of the refusal of his original application, the status of the applicant has altered and his new status debars him from making a fresh application.

I am tempted to say that counsel for the Secretary of State puts the applicant in the *g* position of a 'refusenik', but that may be doing a disservice to his argument. Counsel accepts that an initial application may be made on more than one ground, for example to enter as a student or as a visitor, and that both must then be considered by the immigration officer. He also accepts that if the applicant, after receiving the notice of refusal, leaves the United Kingdom, however, briefly, and immediately returns, he does *h* so shorn of his altered status and thus is able to make a fresh, valid application for leave to enter on any ground. These concessions in my view underline that if the argument of counsel for the Secretary of State is correct the result seems to have little practical benefit to the administration of immigration control. Of itself this does not mean that the argument is incorrect, but it does require a close scrutiny of the Act to decide whether this result is to be implied. For the reasons which Stuart-Smith LJ and Sir David Croom- *j* Johnson have given in their judgments, in my view it is not. A person in the situation in which these immigrants were may, in my opinion, validly make a second application for leave to enter whilst still in the United Kingdom.

Third, does an application for asylum amount to, or necessarily include, an application for leave to enter? In my opinion the answer to this question can only be Yes. The

purpose of an application for asylum is to permit the applicant to stay in the United
a Kingdom. For that purpose he requires leave to enter. Therefore, if he has not already
entered, within the meaning of the 1971 Act, his application for asylum necessarily
includes an application for leave to enter.

Fourth, is such an application to be considered within or outside the Immigration Act
1971? Counsel for the Secretary of State argues that if on first arrival an applicant seeks
asylum, that application is to be treated as an application to enter under ss 3 and 4 and
b Sch 2 to the 1971 Act. However, an application for asylum made after an initial refusal
of leave to enter and (despite counsel's earlier arguments) considered and determined, as
with the applications for asylum made by these immigrants, is not considered and
determined under the 1971 Act but under the prerogative power. If I understand that
argument correctly, it can succeed only if counsel for the Secretary of State has already
succeeded in his earlier argument, that is that, after refusal of leave to enter, a second
c valid application for leave to enter may not be made while the applicant is still in the
United Kingdom. Since I have already said that in my view that earlier submission fails,
it follows also that I am against counsel for the Secretary of State on this question.

However, counsel for the immigrants provides another reason why the submission of
the Secretary of State on this issue fails. These two immigrants were, before the coming
into force of the British Nationality Act 1981, citizens of the United Kingdom and
d Colonies. They are now British overseas citizens: see s 26 of that Act. They are subject to
immigration control under the 1971 Act, but they are not aliens. Until the
Commonwealth Immigrants Act 1962 came into force, there was no restriction on their
right to enter the United Kingdom. I refer to the quotation from the speech of Lord
Diplock in DPP v Bhagwan [1970] 3 All ER 97 at 104–105, [1972] AC 60 at 80, to which
Stuart-Smith LJ has referred. Thus, I agree with him that these immigrants are not
e affected by s 33(5) of the 1971 Act. It follows that the only power to control their entry
into the United Kingdom is the power given by s 3 of the 1971 Act and any application,
on whatever ground, made by them for leave to enter must be an application made and
considered under the Act and, in so far as relevant, the Immigration Rules made under
the Act.

f For these reasons, in addition to those given by Stuart-Smith LJ and Sir David Croom-
Johnson and in agreement with the judgment of Auld J, I too am of the opinion that the
adjudicator did have jurisdiction to entertain the appeals to him, and I would therefore
dismiss the Secretary of State's appeal to this court.

Appeal dismissed. Leave to appeal to the House of Lords refused.

g
Solicitors: *Treasury Solicitor*; *Winstanley-Burgess* (for the applicants).

Carolyn Toulmin   Barrister.

Middleweek v Chief Constable of the Merseyside Police and another

COURT OF APPEAL, CIVIL DIVISION

ACKNER, SLADE AND GLIDEWELL LJJ

8, 9, 24 JULY 1985

False imprisonment – Conditions of imprisonment – Lawfully arrested person – Whether detention of lawfully arrested person is unlawful if person detained in intolerable conditions.

Police – Right of search – Arrested person – Good reason for search – Trespass to person – Police officer acting in accordance with standard procedure – Police officer required to have good reason to search detained person.

The respondent was a solicitor who was engaged by a former police officer to defend him on charges of perverting the course of justice while he was a member of the police force. At a bail hearing a police officer noticed that the respondent's file contained a general crime information sheet, which was a confidential internal police document the property of the chief constable. The police officer approached the respondent and asked him whether he had the document and where he had obtained it from. The respondent refused to discuss the matter and the officer arrested him on suspicion of theft at 10.45 am. He was then taken to an interview room where he produced the crime information sheet and explained that he had received it from his client. The interview ended at 11.22 am and the respondent was then searched in accordance with the standard procedure, his possessions were taken away and he was detained in a cell while the officer left to make further inquiries, in particular to find the respondent's client to check the respondent's story. The respondent was permitted to call a solicitor and after the arrival of the solicitor the respondent made and signed a statement, after which he was released on bail at 1.00 pm. The respondent brought an action against the chief constable and the police officer claiming damages for, inter alia, trespass and false imprisonment, alleging that the search and removal of the respondent's possessions was wrongful, that he had been detained for an unreasonably long time and that it was unreasonable to detain him in a cell. At the trial of the action the judge ruled that the arrest was lawful and directed the jury that they were to decide whether the period of the respondent's detention was unreasonably long, whether it was reasonable to detain the respondent in a cell and whether it was reasonable to search the respondent and take away his possessions. The jury found that the period of the respondent's detention was not unreasonably long but that it was not reasonable to detain him in a cell, for which they awarded him £500 damages. The jury further found that it had been reasonable to search the respondent and take away his possessions. The chief constable appealed against the award of damages on the ground that the detention of person in a cell at a police station following his lawful arrest could never be unreasonable provided the period of detention was not unreasonable and therefore the issue whether it was unreasonable to detain the respondent in a cell should never have been put to the jury. The respondent cross-appealed on the ground that liability on the issues whether the period of his detention was unreasonably long and whether it had been unreasonable to search him and take away his possessions should not have been left to the jury because a search undertaken merely in accordance with standard procedure and without good reason in the particular circumstances was unlawful and his continued detention after the conclusion of the interview was unreasonable.

Held – (1) Although a person lawfully detained ceased to be lawfully detained if the conditions of detention were so intolerable, eg because they were prejudicial to his health, as to render the detention unlawful, the conditions under which the respondent

had been detained had not been intolerable and therefore the issue whether it had been
a reasonable to detain the respondent in a cell should not have been put to the jury and no
award of damages should have been made on that issue. The chief constable's appeal
would accordingly be allowed (see p 668 *a* to *d*, post); dictum of Tudor Evans J in *Williams
v Home Office (No 2)* [1981] 1 All ER 1211 at 1227 not followed.

(2) Although a police officer had to have good reason to search a detained person, the
fact that at the time the officer was simply acting in accordance with standard procedure
b did not of itself render the search unlawful if there were in fact good reasons for the
search. Since the police had had good reasons to search the respondent and take away his
possessions, namely to safeguard his property, to protect themselves from false allegations
that they had stolen his property and to protect the respondent from injuring himself,
the issue whether it had been reasonable to search the respondent and take away his
possessions had been properly left to the jury. Furthermore, since the police were entitled
c to detain a person following his lawful arrest in order to make further inquiries, the issue
whether it had been reasonable to detain the respondent after the conclusion of the
interview in order to make further inquiries and whether the time spent in making
those inquiries had been reasonable had been properly left to the jury. It followed that
the respondent's cross-appeal would be dismissed (see p 670 *f* to p 671 *a e* to *j*, post).

d
Notes
For false imprisonment, see 45 Halsbury's Laws (4th edn) paras 1325–1338, and for cases
on the subject, see 46 Digest (Reissue) 307–311, 2675–2707.

For the power of police officers to search persons in police custody, see 36 Halsbury's
Laws (4th edn) para 324.

e
Cases referred to in judgment
Brazil v Chief Constable of Surrey [1983] 3 All ER 537, [1983] 1 WLR 1155, DC.
Cobbett v Grey (1850) 4 Exch 729, 154 ER 1409.
Lindley v Rutter [1981] QB 128, [1980] 3 WLR 660, DC.
Osborne v Milman (1886) 17 QBD 514; *rvsd* (1887) 18 QBD 471, CA.
f *R v Comr of Police of the Metropolis, ex p Nahar* (1983) Times, 28 May, DC.
R v Gartree Prison Board of Visitors, ex p Sears (1985) Times, 20 March.
Scavage v Tateham (1601) Cro Eliz 829, 78 ER 1056.
Williams v Home Office (No 2) [1981] 1 All ER 1211; *affd on other grounds* [1982] 2 All ER
     564, CA.
Yorke v Chapman (1839) 10 Ad & El 207, 113 ER 80.

g
Appeal and cross-appeal
The Chief Constable of the Merseyside Police, the first defendant in an action brought by
the plaintiff, Malcolm David Middleweek, against the chief constable and Det Insp
William Coady of the Merseyside Police claiming damages for trespass, wrongful arrest,
h false imprisonment and defamation, appealed against the judgment dated 19 December
1983 awarding Mr Middleweek £500 damages following trial of the action before
Eastham J and a jury at Manchester. Mr Middleweek cross-appealed against the dismissal
of his claim that following his arrest by Insp Coady it was unreasonable for the police to
search him and take away his possessions. The facts are set out in the judgment of the
court.

j
Andrew Rankin QC and *M S E Grime* for the chief constable.
Thomas Shields for Mr Middleweek.
Insp Coady did not appear.

Cur adv vult

24 July. The following judgment of the court was delivered.

ACKNER LJ. The respondent to this appeal, Mr Middleweek, is a partner in a firm of Manchester solicitors and he personally is concerned mainly with criminal cases. On 15 May 1980 he issued a writ against the appellant, the Chief Constable of the Merseyside Police, claiming damages for trespass, wrongful arrest, false imprisonment and defamation, all of which were alleged to have occurred on 25 April 1980 in Main Bridewell police station, Liverpool. His claim was heard over a number of days in December 1983 by Eastham J and a jury at the Manchester Courts of Justice and on 19 December 1983 he obtained judgment for the sum of £500, with an order that the chief constable should pay one-third of his costs. It is against that order that the chief constable now appeals, and Mr Middleweek cross-appeals.

The circumstances out of which Mr Middleweek's claims arose are as follows. One of Mr Middleweek's clients was a Mr B F Wylie. He had been a serving police officer with the rank of inspector in the Merseyside Police until he resigned when disciplinary proceedings were about to be initiated in 1977. It was the contention of the Merseyside Police that this former police officer had set about perverting the course of justice in a most dangerous manner, viz by arranging for false alibis, supported by false evidence and persuading witnesses who were prejudicial to the defence not to attend to give evidence. In 1980 there was a pending prosecution. Det Insp Coady was the senior officer in charge of those proceedings and responsible for making inquiries in regard to them. Police officers rely on getting information from other police forces on sheets which are called 'general crime information sheets'. Any senior officer such as Mr Coady can ask for the insertion on those sheets of particulars of the man he is investigating together with the nature of the inquiries which are being made in relation to him. At some time prior to 5 February Mr Coady made a request for an insertion in the general crime information sheet, and on sheet no 25 dated 5 February 1980 there appeared a photograph of Mr Wylie, together with particulars of offences which he was suspected of having committed. In the insertion Mr Coady sought further information concerning Mr Wylie.

Mr Wylie instructed Mr Middleweek to seek the relaxation of the strict conditions which had been imposed on the grant to him of bail. He was further instructed to apply for the six weeks' period of remand to be reduced. On 25 April 1980 there was a hearing in court 1 at the Liverpool Magistrates' Court, when Mr Middleweek made the appropriate applications, albeit unsuccessfully. Mr Coady, who was in court, happened to notice that in Mr Middleweek's file was a general crime information sheet. Those sheets are marked 'Confidential—for Police use only'. They should never be removed from the police station and are circulated to police stations for information of the police only. This particular sheet was the property of the chief constable.

When Mr Middleweek left court Mr Coady, who had moments before discussed the matter with Supt Robinson, introduced himself and Mr Robinson to Mr Middleweek in the ante-room to the court and asked if he could ask Mr Middleweek a few questions. This was agreed and they proceeded down the public foyer into the corridor. In the presence of Mr Robinson, Mr Coady asked the following three questions and received from Mr Middleweek the following answers:

'Q. I saw you in possession of a document which I suspect to be a general crime information sheet, which is the property of the chief constable. Have you got such a document? A. You say so, but have I? This is confidential [referring to the entire file].
Q. I suspect you do possess such a document, but I must ask you where you got it. A. I refuse to discuss what is in this [again pointing to his folder of papers].
Q. Have you got a confidential police document, the property of the chief constable in that folder? A. I will not discuss what is in this folder with you.'

Having heard the replies Mr Coady decided that he had reasonable cause to suspect
a that Mr Middleweek had committed the arrestable offence of theft and they moved away
to a private place, where at 10.45 am he arrested Mr Middleweek in the presence of Mr
Robinson.

The judge, having sought and obtained from the jury answers to certain questions
relating to disputed issues of fact, which we need not recount, concluded and so directed
the jury that the arrest was lawful. He further ruled, for reasons which are in no way
b criticised by Mr Middleweek, that the chief constable had no case to answer with regard
to the alleged libel and slander.

Although the judge had ruled that the arrest was lawful and had withdrawn from the
jury the claim in libel and slander, it was common ground between counsel who then
appeared for Mr Middleweek and counsel for the chief constable that the jury had to
decide whether or not Mr Middleweek was detained for longer than was necessary. If he
c was so detained, then he would have established that he had been falsely imprisoned.
The contention of counsel for Mr Middleweek was that he should have been released at
11.05 am, some 20 minutes after he had been arrested, because during that period he
had been taken to the constables' reading room where there was a short interview.
During that interview he produced the general crime information sheet, explained that
he had received it from his client Mr Wylie, and said, 'If you prove it is stolen I will give
d it to the chief constable'. Counsel further contended that if his client ought not to have
been released at the end of that interview when Mr Robinson left, then he should have
been released some 17 minutes later, at 11.22 am, when further questioning ceased.
However, at 11.25 am Mr Coady took Mr Middleweek before an inspector, informed
him that he had arrested him on suspicion of theft and that he wanted him to be detained
while he, Mr Coady, made further inquiries. Mr Coady then left to look for Mr Wylie.
e Mr Middleweek after a search, to which we will refer in more detail later, was allowed to
telephone a solicitor, a Mr Makin, and was then locked in a cell. It was not until some 20
minutes later when Mr Makin arrived that he was released from his cell. Following an
interview between Mr Makin and Mr Middleweek, which lasted approximately 25
minutes, Mr Middleweek informed the police that he wished to make a statement. At
12.24 pm he began the statement, at 12.44 pm the statement was completed and just
f before 1.00 pm he was bailed.

It was accordingly agreed between counsel that the first question the jury had to decide
at the conclusion of the judge's summing up was: 'Was the period of the plaintiff's
detention unreasonably long?' If the answer to that question was in the affirmative, then
there were supplemental questions as to when Mr Middleweek should have been released
and the sum which should be awarded to him by way of damages, compensatory,
g aggravated, exemplary or punitive.

At one stage, prior to the judge's ruling and when discussing the potential consequences
with counsel, he expressed the view that if Mr Middleweek was entitled to damages for
unlawful detention, then the jury could take into account, if they thought that it
aggravated the position, the fact that Mr Middleweek had been searched and subsequently
h locked up in a cell. However, immediately after making that observation he expressed
the view that a wrongful search would amount to a tort (presumably trespass to the
person) and 'that certainly would remain before the jury'. He further added: 'I think,
although there is no decided authority, there might be a tort about being put into a cell
if it is unnecessary.' Accordingly, with the concurrence of counsel, the jury were asked
the specific question: 'Was it reasonable to detain the plaintiff in a cell?' They were
j further informed that if the answer was in the negative, then they had to go on and
consider what sum they should award by way of compensatory and/or aggravated
damages.

As to the search, which apparently involved requiring Mr Middleweek to empty his
pockets and then checking that he had done so, counsel for Mr Middleweek submitted

that the search had been made pursuant to a standing practice, without having regard to the particular facts, accordingly it was unlawful and the only issue was the quantum of *a* damages. The judge took the view that the essential issue was whether or not the search was reasonable, and accordingly the jury were asked to answer the question: 'Was it reasonable to search the plaintiff and take away his possessions?' If they answered that question in the negative, then they would have to go on to consider the question of damages.

In due course the jury answered the questions as follows. (1) The period of Mr *b* Middleweek's detention was *not* unreasonably long. (2) It was *not* reasonable to detain Mr Middleweek in a cell. (3) For his detention in the cell they awarded aggravated damages of £500. (4) It was reasonable to search Mr Middleweek and take away his possessions.

There was no attempt to move in arrest of judgment and accordingly judgment was entered against the chief constable in the sum of £500, and he was ordered to pay one-third of Mr Middleweek's costs. Subsequent consideration has led the advisers of the *c* chief constable to conclude that the question 'Was it reasonable to detain the plaintiff in a cell?' should never have been put to the jury; hence this appeal.

Mr Middleweek has entered a cross-appeal, contending (1) that the issue of liability on search should have been withdrawn from the jury and they should only have considered the question of damages and (2) that the judge should have directed the jury that Mr Middleweek should have been released at 11.22 am when the final interview was *d* concluded and that any detention thereafter was unreasonable.

The appeal

Counsel for the chief constable submits that neither the tort of false imprisonment nor trespass to the person nor any other tort is committed where a person who has been lawfully arrested, and whose period of detention thereafter is not unreasonable, spends *e* part of that detention in a cell in a police station. To the question put to the jury, 'Was it reasonable to detain the plaintiff in a cell?' there could have been only one answer, an affirmative answer. Accordingly, the question should never have been put. The judge's first thoughts on this part of the case (as referred to above) were correct, namely if the initial arrest was unlawful, or became subsequently unlawful by reason of the excessive length of the detention, then in assessing the quantum of damages, the manner of the *f* false imprisonment then became relevant.

No complaint was made about the nature of the cells. They had in the past been inspected and approved by the Home Office and the Secretary of State had authorised their use for the detention of prisoners for up to a period of seven days. Except in very special cases, for example where a very old person was detained or someone obviously in need of drugs or medicine, it was standard practice for the police who wished to detain a *g* person after questioning and pending further inquiries, to lock him in a police cell. How could it then be said that Mr Middleweek's detention in the cell gave rise to an actionable wrong for which he was entitled to claim damages? Mr Middleweek's essential complaint when he came to give evidence was that the police were acting in bad faith, that they did not believe that he had stolen the document and that they knew full well that there was *h* no justifiable basis for keeping him in custody. However, this suggestion was rejected by the judge when he held that the arrest was lawful. Given therefore that the initial arrest was lawful, and bearing in mind the relatively serious nature of the offence which Mr Middleweek was reasonably suspected of having committed, there was no basis for suggesting that the police had acted unlawfully in following their ordinary procedure of detaining a person whom they had arrested in a cell.

The judge's attention was not drawn on this issue to any decided cases. Had this been *j* done, then it seems to us to be most unlikely that he would have dealt with the detention in the cell in the manner in which he did. In *Williams v Home Office (No 2)* [1981] 1 All ER 1211 Tudor Evans J had to consider, inter alia, the lawfulness of the plaintiff's being confined for a period of 180 days in a special control unit while serving a sentence of 14

years' imprisonment. He reviewed (at 1224–1227) a number of old cases, ie *Scavage v*
a *Tateham* (1601) Cro Eliz 829, 78 ER 1056, *Yorke v Chapman* (1839) 10 Ad & El 207, 113
ER 80, *Osborne v Milman* (1886) 17 QBD 514 and *Cobbett v Grey* (1850) 4 Exch 729, 154
ER 1409. The cases which he reviewed were all concerned with the detention of a
prisoner in a place not authorised by law. They all derived from a time when there were
particular prisons or types of prisons appropriate for the circumstances which caused the
prisoner to be sent there. He said (at 1224):

b   'Thus, if a civil debtor was committed to prison for non-payment of debt he had
       to be sent to a place of detention for civil debtors. He could not be placed in a prison
       for the detention of criminals. If he was, there could be no lawful justification for
       the detention, which was therefore unlawful. All the cases cited have this feature of
       detention in the wrong "place".'

c He accordingly held that there was 'no authority in modern law to support the plaintiff's
submission that although a detention may be lawful it can become unlawful if the nature
(meaning the conditions) of the imprisonment changes' (at 1227).
   This decision was followed recently by Mann J in *R v Gartree Prison Board of Visitors, ex*
p Sears (1985) Times, 20 March. That case concerned an application for judicial review in
which the applicant sought, inter alia, damages to compensate him in respect of the
d service by him of eight days cellular confinement and eight days loss of privileges which
he had been awarded by the board of visitors after finding him guilty of an offence
against good order and discipline while he was serving a sentence of 18 years'
imprisonment at Gartree Prison. The claim for damages was based on the tort of false
imprisonment. Mann J, in the course of giving his judgment, stated:

e   'If a person is imprisoned in the place where he is lawfully so imprisoned, then it
       does not seem to me that a variation in conditions of confinement can constitute the
       tort of false imprisonment at common law.'

He added that he was not concerned with other species of trespass to the person, for
example assault or battery.
f   Our attention was also drawn to the decision of the Divisional Court in *R v Comr of*
Police of the Metropolis, ex p Nahar (1983) Times, 28 May. In that case the two applicants
sought writs of habeas corpus. They had been remanded in custody by the Uxbridge
Magistrates' Court. The warrants of committal ordered the constables of the Metropolitan
Police force to convey each of the applicants to Brixton Prison and there to deliver each
applicant to the governor, together with the warrant. However, the applicants could not
be taken to Brixton Prison because of a restriction then operating on admission of
g prisoners, and instead they were taken to cells below the Camberwell Green Magistrates'
Court. It was accepted that s 6(2) of the Imprisonment (Temporary Provisions) Act 1980
authorised this detention in such circumstances, but it was contended that the conditions
in which the two applicants were detained were of such a character that the court should
consider their detention to be unlawful. Those conditions were considered in detail by
h the court and they were found to be far from satisfactory. Stephen Brown J observed that
s 6 of the Act did not lay down any particular standard. He added: 'There must be some
minimum standard to render detention lawful.' He concluded, however, that the
conditions described were not such as could give rise to a finding that the detention was
unlawful. McCullough J observed that despite the temporary nature of the detention
contemplated by the Act, there must be implied into s 6 of the Act some term which
j relates to the conditions under which a prisoner may lawfully be detained. He said:

       'I say so because it is possible to conceive of hypothetical circumstances in which
       the conditions of detention were such as to make that detention unlawful.'

He too concluded that the facts before the court were not such as might be said to render
the detention unlawful.

We agree with the views expressed by the Divisional Court that it must be possible to conceive of hypothetical cases in which the conditions of detention are so intolerable as *a* to render the detention unlawful and thereby provide a remedy to the prisoner in damages for false imprisonment. A person lawfully detained in a prison cell would, in our judgment, cease to be so lawfully detained if the conditions in that cell were such as to be seriously prejudical to his health if he continued to occupy it, eg because it became and remained seriously flooded, or contained a fractured gas pipe allowing gas to escape into the cell. We do not therefore accept as an absolute proposition that, if detention is *b* initially lawful, it can never become unlawful by reason of changes in the conditions of imprisonment.

On the facts of this case there was not a shred of evidence to suggest that the conditions of detention were in any respect below the ordinary standard to be expected of police cells. On the contrary, they were regulated, inspected and approved by the Home Office. There was accordingly no material to support the contention that the conditions of the *c* detention could render that lawful detention unlawful and thereby give rise to the tort of false imprisonment or trespass to the person.

It therefore follows that the question 'Was it reasonable to detain the plaintiff in a cell?' should not have been put to the jury and accordingly their answer and their assessment of damages based on that answer is of no significance and must be disregarded. Accordingly, we allow the appeal.   *d*

The cross-appeal

Counsel for Mr Middleweek, in his ably presented submission, has taken two points.

(1) *The search of Mr Middleweek*   That Mr Middleweek was in fact searched is admitted in the defence. The evidence was that he was asked to turn out his pockets and agreed to this request. While it was part of the routine that an officer would quickly check that the *e* pockets were empty, there was in fact no evidence that such a check had been made. Counsel for the chief constable very fairly conceded that if the request had not been acceded to by Mr Middleweek, the police would indeed have searched him and the very request must be taken to have carried the implied threat of a search if Mr Middleweek had not co-operated. We are therefore prepared to treat the situation as if the police had *f* in fact searched the pockets of Mr Middleweek and removed the property which they found into their custody.

It is contended by counsel for Mr Middleweek that this searching and the removal of his client's possessions constituted an unlawful and tortious act, the tort alleged being trespass to the person. The basis of this submission is: (1) that under the standing instructions issued to Liverpool police, all prisoners are searched, irrespective of their age, character and the nature of the offence alleged against them; (2) no regard was paid to *g* the circumstances of Mr Middleweek's particular case; (3) that on the authority of the Divisional Court's decision in *Lindley v Rutter* [1981] QB 128 such a search is, ipso facto, unlawful and accordingly it was not open to the jury to consider the question put to it by the judge namely, 'Was it reasonable to search the plaintiff and take away his possessions?'

As regards the standing instructions, counsel for Mr Middleweek has drawn our *h* attention to reg 22 of the Merseyside Police Internal Regulations, which reads:

> '*Searching prisoners on arrest*
> 22. Where practicable, a prisoner should be discreetly searched at the time of the arrest in order to trace any property subject to an alleged offence and any weapon with which the prisoner might injure himself or the arresting officer. This is especially necessary when the prisoner has been searched for an offence alleging that *j* he was found in possession of certain property or articles. Female prisoners should be searched by female officers.'

The comment is made that this regulation, subject to it being practicable, imposes a mandatory obligation on the police officer to search without regard being had to whether

there are special circumstances which would justify or demand a departure from the
a standard procedure. Counsel also relies on reg 60, which reads:

> 'Searching of prisoners
>   60. Should the Station Sergeant accept the charge, the prisoner must be searched
> and all monies and property recorded on the charge sheet.'

This regulation was not, however, applicable since Mr Middleweek was never in fact
b charged.

The police evidence was that they followed their normal procedure when a person is
arrested on suspicion of asking him to empty his pockets and to take off any personal
items of jewellery, watches and earrings. Then an officer would check to see there was
nothing left in the pockets.

Three reasons were given by the police to justify the search and removal of Mr
c Middleweek's property. These were as follows.

(1) The safety of the prisoner's own property. Although Mr Middleweek was put into
a cell which was empty, the officers did not know how long he would be detained and
there was always the possibility, having regard to the number of persons who were, from
time to time, detained in the police station, that another prisoner might be put in his
cell. If this occurred there was always the risk that a detained person might be robbed of
d any money or valuables he had on his person.

(2) The protection of the police from false allegations that they had stolen the detained
person's property. By removing his property at an early stage, recording item by item
what the property was, obtaining his signature to the inventory and then locking the
property away, the risk of false allegations was obviated.

(3) To protect the prisoner from using his property to injure himself.
e A particular complaint was made that Mr Middleweek was deprived of his watch and
his matches. As to the watch, this the police said was covered by all three of their reasons
for the search. As regards the third reason, the glass of a watch could be used by a prisoner
to injure himself. The matches could be used to set light to property in the cell.

Lindley v Rutter [1981] QB 128 concerned a woman who was arrested for disorderly
behaviour while drunk and removed to a police station where she was lodged in a cell.
f She refused to be searched by a police woman who attempted to search her and was met
by resistance. A second police woman was called to give assistance and both officers
searched the defendant and removed her brassiere. The police women believed that they
were acting in accordance with the chief constable's standing orders which they
understood required them to search every female prisoner and remove her brassiere for
her own protection. The woman was charged, inter alia, with and convicted of,
g unlawfully assaulting a police officer in the execution of her duty, contrary to s 51(1) of
the Police Act 1964.

Donaldson LJ in his judgment, with which Mustill J agreed, observed that the forceable
removal of the brassiere was understandably regarded by the defendant as peculiarly
offensive (at 135):

h   'Such conduct would require considerable justification. It was inherently unlikely
    that possession of the brassiere could lead to accidental injury. If it was to be used
    intentionally for this purpose, other clothing would probably have served as well.'

The justices had made no finding as to whether the removal of the brassiere was in fact
necessary for the defendant's own protection.
j The part of Donaldson LJ's judgment on which counsel for Mr Middleweek particularly
relies is in these terms (at 134–135):

    'It is the duty of the courts to be ever zealous to protect the personal freedom,
    privacy and dignity of all who live in these islands. Any claim to be entitled to take
    action which infringes these rights is to be examined with very great care. But such

rights are not absolute. They have to be weighed against the rights and duties of
police officers, acting on behalf of society as a whole. It is the duty of any constable   *a*
who lawfully has a prisoner in his charge to take all reasonable measures to ensure
that the prisoner does not escape or assist others to do so, does not injure himself or
others, does not destroy or dispose of evidence and does not commit further crime
such as, for example, malicious damage to property. This list is not exhaustive, but
it is sufficient for present purposes. What measures are reasonable in the discharge
of this duty will depend upon the likelihood that the particular prisoner will do any   *b*
of these things unless prevented. That in turn will involve the constable in
considering the known or apparent disposition and sobriety of the prisoner. What
can never be justified is the adoption of any particular measures without regard to
all the circumstances of the particular case. This is not to say that there can be no
standing instructions. Although there may always be special features in any
individual case, the circumstances in which people are taken into custody are capable   *c*
of being categorised and experience may show that certain measures, including
searches, are prima facie reasonable and necessary in a particular category of case.
The fruits of this experience may be passed on to officers in the form of standing
instructions. But the officer having custody of the prisoner must always consider,
and be allowed and encouraged to consider, whether the special circumstances of
the particular case justify or demand a departure from the standard procedure either   *d*
by omitting what would otherwise be done or by taking additional measures. So far
as searches are concerned, he should appreciate that they involve an affront to the
dignity and privacy of the individual. Furthermore, there are degrees of affront
involved in such a search. Clearly going through someone's pockets or handbag is
less of an affront than a body search. In every case a police officer ordering a search
or depriving a prisoner of property should have a very good reason for doing so.'   *e*

    Counsel for Mr Middleweek construes that part of the judgment as authority for the
following proposition. If there is a standing instruction or a standard procedure which is
followed without first giving consideration to the particular circumstances of each case,
it must follow that the search cannot be justified, is unlawful, and that the tort of trespass   *f*
to the person has been committed. We do not so understand the judgment. What has
been emphasised was that the existence of a standing instruction or an established
procedure, which had been faithfully complied with by a police officer, was in itself no
conclusive answer to the complaint that the search was unlawful. If the legality is
challenged, it is for the police to establish that the search and the way in which it was
carried out were justified in the circumstances of the particular case. To quote again the
final sentence of the paragraph relied on from *Lindley v Rutter*, 'in every case a police   *g*
officer ordering a search depriving a prisoner of property should have a very good reason
for doing so'. If the officer fails to establish that he had such a good reason, the search,
even though carried out in accordance with standing instructions, would be unlawful.
Whether the search was so justified is, however, a matter to be determined by the court
before whom the issue is raised. The fact that at the time of the search the police officer   *h*
was simply acting in accordance with general instructions does not, of itself, render the
search unlawful.

    Our attention was also called to a later decision of the Divisional Court, *Brazil v Chief
Constable of Surrey* [1983] 3 All ER 537, [1983] 1 WLR 1155, which followed *Lindley v
Rutter*. Again that was another extreme case, where the police officer formed the
suspicion that the defendant was in possession of prohibited drugs, but never told the   *j*
defendant that she was to be searched for that reason. When she declined to be searched,
she was held down by officers, her boots removed, her jeans taken down to her thighs
and her jumper raised to allow a visual check of her brassiere. We do not consider that
this later case adds any support to counsel's interpretation of *Lindley v Rutter*. Accordingly,
we conclude that the judge was right not to accede to the submission of Mr Middleweek's

counsel that the issue of liability for trespass to the person based on an unlawful search
a be withdrawn from the jury and that they should only consider the question of damages.
The judge properly left to them for their decision the question, 'Was it reasonable to
search the plaintiff and take away his possessions?' He properly directed them with
regard to the evidence that there was material which justified their answering this
question in the affirmative, and accordingly their decision on this issue must stand.

(2) *The length of the detention*   Counsel for Mr Middleweek submits that the judge
b should have directed the jury that the plaintiff should have been released at 11.22 am
when the interview concluded and that any detention thereafter was unreasonable. This
is a bold submission, which was not made in the court below, and which without
disrespect can be dealt with quite shortly. The justification given by the police for not
releasing Mr Middleweek after the conclusion of the interviews was that they wanted to
find and interview Mr Wylie and check with him Mr Middleweek's explanation with
c regard to the document, before Mr Middleweek had an opportunity of first seeing his
client. In short, they took the view that there was a risk that had Mr Middleweek been
released he would have got to Mr Wylie before the police and would have interfered with
the inquiries which they wished to make. Mr Wylie had been in court when Mr
Middleweek had made his applications; they therefore considered that he was likely to
be traced without much difficulty and within a reasonably short space of time. Having
d spent something under one hour looking for Mr Wylie, they returned to the police
station concluding that it was unreasonable to detain Mr Middleweek further. He was
not then immediately bailed, because he was in conference with his solicitor, Mr Makin,
and then on the latter's advice made his statement which was completed, as previously
stated, at 12.44 pm and bail was granted some ten minutes later.

Clearly the police were not obliged to accept the accuracy of the statements made to
e them by Mr Middleweek and were entitled to investigate the situation further by, inter
alia, interviewing Mr Wylie. The submissions of counsel for Mr Middleweek clearly
involve the following propositions: (1) the police were not entitled *as a matter of law* to
detain Mr Middleweek for any period at all, so as to ensure that he did not interfere with
their inquiries by getting to Mr Wylie before they did and frustrating, in one way or
another, the inquiries they wished to make of Mr Wylie, and/or (2) that *as a matter of law*
f the period of time they spent in making these inquiries was excessive.

We cannot accept either of these propositions. Once it was decided that the initial
arrest was lawful, the length of the detention raised two simple issues of fact, namely was
it reasonable to detain Mr Middleweek after the interviews were complete, in order that
he should have no opportunity to interfere with the further inquiries which the police
wished to make of Mr Wylie, and if so, did they act with reasonable expedition in seeking
g to make those further inquiries? These questions of fact were essentially matters for the
jury to decide and were properly encompassed in the agreed question, 'Was the period of
the plaintiff's detention unreasonably long?' Counsel for Mr Middleweek complains that
in summing up this matter to the jury, they were not told to take into account, when
judging the reasonableness of the length of the detention, that part of it was spent in the
h cells. He conceded that this point was never made on Mr Middleweek's behalf at the trial.
In our judgment Mr Middleweek's counsel was wholly correct in not making the point,
since if it was reasonable to ensure that Mr Middleweek did not have the opportunity to
interfere with the inquiries they wished to make immediately following his statement,
he had to be detained and the police cell was a proper and authorised place for such
detention.

j   Accordingly, we dismiss the cross-appeal.

In the result we order that the judgment and verdict be set aside and that judgment be
entered for the Chief Constable of the Merseyside Police, with costs in the court below.

As regards the costs in this court (as to which we have already heard argument), we
only award two-thirds of the cost of the appeal to the chief constable. We do so because
the questions which the jury were asked to answer with regard to the plaintiff's detention

in a cell were agreed questions, and at no stage was it apparently argued, either before or
after the jury had answered the questions relative to the detention in the cell, that those *a*
questions were irrelevant and the answers should be disregarded. As regards the costs of
the cross-appeal, these must be paid by Mr Middleweek.

Appeal allowed. Cross-appeal dismissed.

Solicitors: *A W Mawer & Co*, Manchester (for the chief constable); *Shammah Nicholls* *b*
Marson & Co, Manchester (for Mr Middleweek).

Mary Rose Plummer   Barrister.

c

Weldon v Home Office

COURT OF APPEAL, CIVIL DIVISION
FOX, PARKER AND RALPH GIBSON LJJ   *d*
27, 28 FEBRUARY, 28 MARCH 1990

*False imprisonment – Prisoner serving sentence – Residual liberty – Prisoner alleging he was
confined without lawful authority in punishment cell while in prison – Prisoner bringing action
for false imprisonment against prison authorities – Whether prisoner entitled to bring action for
false imprisonment – Whether tort of false imprisonment available to protect residual liberty of* *e*
*convicted prisoner – Whether statutory provision that prisoner might be 'lawfully confined in any
prison' a defence to prisoner's action for false imprisonment – Prison Act 1952, s 12(1).*

The plaintiff, who was a prisoner serving a four-year sentence, brought an action for false
imprisonment against the Home Office as the authority responsible for the prison in
which he was detained, claiming that after 5.30 pm on 9 May 1984 prison officers had, *f*
without lawful authority, dragged him out of his cell to a cell in the punishment block
and then removed him to a strip cell, where his clothes were taken from him and where
he remained until the following morning. He also claimed that he had been assaulted by
prison officers. The Home Office applied to strike out the plaintiff's claim for false
imprisonment on the ground that it disclosed no reasonable cause of action, contending
(i) that a prisoner could not claim that he had been deprived of his liberty because by *g*
definition he was not entitled to liberty, and (ii) that s 12(1)[a] of the Prison Act 1952,
which provided that a prisoner, whether sentenced to imprisonment or committed to
prison on remand or pending trial or otherwise, might be 'lawfully confined in any
prison', operated as a defence to an action of false imprisonment brought by a duly
sentenced prisoner and that the detention of a prisoner was not rendered unlawful by *h*
any variation in the regime or conditions of confinement. The registrar dismissed the
application to strike out, holding that the allegations of false imprisonment had not been
shown to be unarguable and should therefore go to trial. The judge upheld his decision
on appeal. The Home Office appealed to the Court of Appeal.

Held – A prisoner detained in prison retained such residual liberty within the prison as *j*
was left to him under the provisions of the Prison Rules 1964 and that residual liberty
would be protected by the availability of the tort of false imprisonment. Accordingly, a
prisoner lawfully detained in prison was entitled to bring an action for false imprisonment

---

a   Section 12(1) is set out at p 679 *d*, post

against the prison authority in respect of acts committed by prison officers which amounted to confinement of the prisoner without lawful authority in a punishment cell or his detention in conditions which the prison officers knew to be intolerable and which deprived the prisoner of his residual liberty within the prison. Moreover, although s 12(1) of the 1952 Act afforded a defence to the prison authority in respect of the confinement of a prisoner, it did not justify the conduct of prison officers who intentionally deprived a prisoner of his residual liberty within the prison without reasonable cause or in bad faith. Since the allegations of false imprisonment, whether based on interference with residual liberty or on the deliberate imposition of intolerable conditions, sufficiently alleged want of good faith on the part of the prison officers concerned, those allegations had not been shown to be unarguable and should therefore go to trial. The Home Office's appeal would therefore be dismissed (see p 677 j to p 678 b, p 680 g h, p 681 c d j to p 682 b and p 684 j to p 685 a j to p 686 c f, post).

Middleweek v Chief Constable of Merseyside [1990] 3 All ER 662 followed.

Dictum of Tudor Evans J in Williams v Home Office (No 2) [1981] 1 All ER 1211 at 1240–1241 considered.

Notes

For false imprisonment, see 45 Halsbury's Laws (4th edn) paras 1325–1338, and for cases on the subject, see 46 Digest (Reissue) 307–311, 2675–2707.

For prisoners' rights and privileges, see 37 Halsbury's Laws (4th edn) paras 1137–1147.

For the Prison Act 1952, s 12, see 34 Halsbury's Statutes (4th edn) 651.

For the Prison Rules 1964, see 18 Halsbury's Statutory Instruments (4th reissue) 10.

Cases referred to in judgments

Arbon v Anderson [1943] 1 All ER 154, [1943] KB 252, CA.
Becker v Home Office [1972] 2 All ER 676, [1972] QB 407, [1972] 2 WLR 1193, CA.
Bourgoin SA v Ministry of Agriculture Fisheries and Food [1985] 3 All ER 585, [1986] QB 716, [1985] 3 WLR 1027, CA.
Dallison v Caffery [1964] 2 All ER 610, [1965] 1 QB 348, [1964] 3 WLR 385, CA.
Furber v Kratter (1988) Independent, 9 August.
Leech v Parkhurst Prison Deputy Governor [1988] 1 All ER 485, [1988] AC 533, [1988] 2 WLR 290, HL.
Lister v Perryman (1870) LR 4 HL 521.
Lonrho plc v Fayed [1989] 2 All ER 65, [1989] 3 WLR 631, CA.
Meering v Grahame-White Aviation Co Ltd (1920) 122 LT 44, CA.
Middleweek v Chief Constable of the Merseyside Police (1985) [1990] 3 All ER 662, [1990] 3 WLR 481, CA.
Murray v Ministry of Defence [1988] 2 All ER 521, [1988] 1 WLR 692, HL.
Osborne v Milman (1886) 17 QBD 514; rvsd (1887) 18 QBD 471, CA.
R v Deputy Governor of Camphill Prison, ex p King [1984] 3 All ER 897, [1985] QB 735, [1985] 2 WLR 36, CA.
R v Deputy Governor of Parkhurst Prison, ex p Hague (1989) Independent, 11 August, DC.
R v Gartree Prison Board of Visitors, ex p Sears (1985) Times, 20 March.
R v Hull Prison Board of Visitors, ex p St Germain [1979] 1 All ER 701, [1979] QB 425, [1979] 2 WLR 42, CA.
R v Metropolitan Police Comr, ex p Nahar (1983) Times, 28 May, DC.
Raymond v Honey [1982] 1 All ER 756, [1983] 1 AC 1, [1982] 2 WLR 465, HL.
Solosky v R (1979) 105 DLR (3d) 745, Can SC.
Union Carbide Corp v Naturin Ltd [1987] FSR 538, CA.
Williams v Home Office (No 2) [1981] 1 All ER 1211; affd [1982] 2 All ER 564, CA.

Cases also cited

Congreve v Home Office [1976] 1 All ER 697, [1976] QB 629, CA.

R v Chief Immigration Officer, Heathrow Airport, ex p Salamat Bibi [1976] 3 All ER 843, [1976] 1 WLR 979, CA.

Interlocutory appeal
The Home Office appealed against the order of Mr D R Wood sitting as an assistant recorder at Leeds County Court on 22 November 1988 whereby he dismissed an appeal by the Home Office against the decision of Mr Registrar Bower made on 3 October 1988 in the same court refusing to strike out an action for damages for false imprisonment brought by the plaintiff, Kenneth Weldon, a prisoner serving a four-year sentence at HM Prison Leeds who claimed that on or about 9 May 1984 he had been falsely imprisoned in a strip cell where his clothes had been taken from him and where he remained until the following morning and unlawfully assaulted by certain prison officers. The facts are set out in the judgment of Ralph Gibson LJ.

John Laws and *J Scott Wolstenholme* for the Home Office.
D M Harris QC and *Timothy Owen* for the plaintiff.

Cur adv vult

28 March. The following judgments were delivered.

RALPH GIBSON LJ (giving the first judgment at the invitation of Fox LJ). This appeal by the Home Office raises the question whether it is possible in law for a prison officer to commit against a convicted prisoner, who is lawfully in custody in a prison, the common law tort of false imprisonment. The Home Office asks in this appeal that the claim made by the plaintiff, Kenneth Weldon, in his action against the Home Office, be struck out in so far as it is a claim in respect of false imprisonment.

The facts pleaded by the plaintiff are that the Home Office is the authority responsible for Leeds Prison and employed the prison officers there. The plaintiff was detained in the prison pursuant to a sentence of four years' imprisonment. He complains of two incidents which occurred on 9 and 10 May 1984. The first includes the claim in respect of false imprisonment and must be set out in full:

'2. On or about 9 May 1984, the Plaintiff was falsely imprisoned and unlawfully assaulted and battered by certain prison officers. PARTICULARS (i) Shortly after 5.30 pm on the said date, three prison officers burst into the Plaintiff's cell and without good cause dragged him onto the landing, where they were joined by three further prison officers; (ii) the Plaintiff was then dragged down the stairs (despite his request to walk) and placed in a cell in the punishment block; (iii) shortly afterwards, the Plaintiff was removed to a strip cell where his clothes were taken from him. He remained there till the following morning. During this time the Plaintiff was further assaulted by the same prison officers; (iv) the Plaintiff will allege that the unlawful treatment hereinbefore described converted pro tem a lawful detention into a false imprisonment.'

The incident of the following day, 10 May 1984, is alleged to have included various assaults and batteries on the plaintiff after a disciplinary hearing but alleges no further false imprisonment. There is, of course, no suggestion that the allegations of assault could be struck out and it is not necessary to describe them further.

The proceedings in the county court
The particulars of claim were dated 9 December 1987. As appears from the passage set out above, the allegations lack particulars in several respects. It would appear that the plaintiff alleges that he was left naked overnight in the strip cell. It is not clear whether there was a bed or bedding available to him. The defendants did not ask for particulars before making application for the claim in respect of false imprisonment to be struck

out. Their application was dismissed by the registrar on 3 October 1988. It is not clear
a why there was such long delay. The appeal by the Home Office from the registrar's
decision was heard by Mr D R Wood sitting as an assistant recorder on 22 November
1988 and was dismissed. The recorder was not satisfied that the allegations of false
imprisonment had no prospects of success and therefore ruled that they should go for
trial.

 For the purposes of the striking out application the allegations made by the plaintiff
b are to be taken as true. It it, nevertheless, right to mention the terms of the Home Office
defence. The defence was served on 17 November 1988. The allegations of assault are
denied. In brief, it is alleged that the plaintiff on 9 May 1984, when lying on his bed in
his cell, attacked a prison officer by kicking him in the face. Other officers were then
kicked by the plaintiff while the plaintiff was being removed from the cell. The plaintiff
was lawfully restrained. It is further alleged that the plaintiff on 25 May 1984 before the
c board of visitors at Leeds Prison pleaded guilty to assaulting the officers in the incident
of 9 May 1984.

 As to 10 May 1984 the Home Office asserts that, during a disciplinary hearing on that
day, the plaintiff became aggressive and the governor ordered that he be removed. The
plaintiff was then lawfully restrained, removed by prison officers and placed in a strip
cell.
d

The right to the jury trial

 Before considering the submissions made in this court one matter of procedural
background should be mentioned which the parties, no doubt, regard as important. By
s 66 of the County Courts Act 1984 it is provided that certain sorts of proceedings shall
be without a jury and then by sub-ss (2) and (3):
e
 '(2) In all other proceedings in a county court the trial shall be without a jury
unless the court otherwise orders on an application made in that behalf by any party
to the proceedings . . .
 (3) Where, on any such application, the court is satisfied that there is in issue . . .
 (b) a claim in respect of libel, slander, malicious prosecution or false imprisonment
f . . . the action shall be tried with a jury, unless the court is of opinion that the trial
requires any prolonged examination of documents or accounts . . .'

It is clear, and neither side has argued to the contrary, that the provisions of s 66, and the
effect of those provisions on the trial of this action if the claim in respect of false
imprisonment is sustainable in law, have no relevance to the questions which this court
g must decide.

The submissions for the parties on appeal

 Counsel for the Home Office submitted that the tort of false imprisonment consists of
complete deprivation of liberty for a period of time, however short, without lawful
excuse. Since a prisoner is not entitled to his liberty he cannot make a claim in respect of
h a loss of it. Further, it is provided by s 12(1) of the Prison Act 1952:

 'A prisoner, whether sentenced to imprisonment or committed to prison on
remand or pending trial or otherwise, may be lawfully confined in any prison.'

That provision operates, it was submitted, as a defence to an action of false imprisonment
brought by any duly sentenced prisoner. The detention of a prisoner is not rendered
j unlawful by any variation in the regime or conditions of confinement.

 It was conceded that a prisoner retains his ordinary rights in law so far as consistent
with his detention as a prisoner. If he suffers ill-treatment while in prison he may bring
an action for assault, or battery, or for damage caused by negligence. In respect of alleged
ill-treatment falling short of those torts, however, it was submitted that a prisoner's
remedy is by way of appeal to the governor, the visiting committee and, finally, the

Secretary of State, under the Prison Act 1952 and the Prison Rules 1964, SI 1964/388. The Secretary of State is subject to judicial review in the exercise of his duties under those *a* provisions.

Next it was submitted that no action lies in respect of a breach of the 1964 rules: see *Becker v Home Office* [1972] 2 All ER 676, [1972] 2 QB 407; and that neither breaches of the 1964 rules nor torts committed against a prisoner during a lawful imprisonment can render the imprisonment itself unlawful so as to found an action for false imprisonment: see *Williams v Home Office (No 2)* [1981] 1 All ER 1211 per Tudor Evans J and *R v Gartree* *b* *Prison Board of Visitors, ex p Sears* (1985) Times, 20 March per Mann J.

As to a detention becoming unlawful, although initially lawful, because of changes in the conditions of imprisonment, reference was made to *R v Metropolitan Police Comr, ex p Nahar* (1983) Times, May 28, *Middleweek v Chief Constable of the Merseyside Police* (1985) [1990] 3 All ER 662, [1990] 3 WLR 481 and *Furber v Kratter* (1988) Independent, 9 August. Counsel for the Home Office submitted that, in so far as those cases held that *c* there is a remedy in false imprisonment, they were wrongly decided. Alternatively, if those cases were correctly decided, they are, it was said, applicable only to a prisoner under arrest and not to a convicted prisoner; and false imprisonment in the case of a serving prisoner will only be made out if it is shown that the conditions of detention were intolerable or seriously prejudicial to health and no allegation to that effect is made by the plaintiff.   *d*

Counsel for the plaintiff conceded that the unlawful use of force against a prisoner could not by itself convert the confinement into a false imprisonment. He submitted, however, that the treatment of the plaintiff alleged in para 2 of the particulars of claim constituted false imprisonment. Counsel supported that contention in two ways. Firstly, he argued that a prisoner retains such residual liberty as is left to him under the provisions of the 1964 rules; and to confine such a prisoner, without lawful authority, in a *e* segregation cell, or in a strip cell, deprived the plaintiff of that residual liberty and was false imprisonment. Secondly, in reliance on *Middleweek v Chief Constable of the Merseyside Police*, he submitted that the treatment of the plaintiff on 9 May 1984, done in bad faith and with an improper motive or, at least, without lawful authority, rendered the conditions of detention of the plaintiff intolerable and thus made his detention during *f* that time unlawful.

Further, of course, counsel relied on the well-known rule that recourse should be had to the summary process of striking out only in plain and obvious cases when the action is one which cannot succeed or is in some way an abuse of the process or the case is unarguable: see per Dillon LJ in *Lonrho plc v Fayed* [1989] 2 All ER 65 at 70, [1989] 3 WLR 631 at 638.

It is necessary first to examine the contention that, by reason of the principles on which *g* the tort of false imprisonment is based, it cannot be available as a remedy to a convicted prisoner. If, contrary to that contention, the tort is available, a convicted prisoner might be unlawfully deprived of liberty, while in prison, in physical circumstances which could not be described as intolerable within the terms of the principles stated in *Middleweek*. If the tort is not available, the principle in *Middleweek* might still, if the necessary factual *h* basis is proved, require the court to order, as a matter of public law, that confinement of the claimant in the intolerable conditions must cease without affording to the claimant any right to damages based on false imprisonment.

False imprisonment of a prisoner: the nature of the tort

Counsel for the Home Office argued that false imprisonment is not available to a *j* convicted prisoner because it cannot be a matter of degree. It is not committed by a mere partial interference with freedom of movement: e g the closing of one way of leaving a place. A prisoner, who is already lawfully imprisoned, cannot be falsely imprisoned. He referred to the passages in *Clerk and Lindsell on Torts* (16th edn, 1989) paras 17-15–17-28.

To consider these contentions, and before considering the particular authorities on
a which the parties have relied, it is necessary to examine the nature of the tort as set out
in decisions of the courts. The law protects the right of the individual to be free of any
unjustified interference with his personal security and personal liberty. The general
heading of the remedies provided by the law is trespass to the person and there are three
varieties: assault, battery and false imprisonment (see 45 Halsbury's Laws (4th edn) para
1308). For false imprisonment it is not necessary that the plaintiff should be aware of the
b fact of the imprisonment (see per Atkin LJ in *Meering v Grahame-White Aviation Co Ltd*
(1920) 122 LT 44 at 53–54); although the damages might be diminished if the plaintiff
was unconscious of the imprisonment. Atkin LJ continued (at 54):

'If a man can be imprisoned by having the key turned upon him without his
knowledge, so he can be imprisoned if, instead of a lock and key or bolts and bars,
he is prevented from, in fact, exercising his liberty by guards and warders or
c policemen. They serve the same purpose. Therefore it appears to me to be a question
of fact. It is true that in all cases of imprisonment so far as the law of civil liability is
concerned that "stone walls do not a prison make," in the sense that they are not the
only form of imprisonment, but any restraint within defined bounds which is a
restraint in fact may be an imprisonment.'

d   It is clear that the policy of the law is jealously to protect personal liberty. Thus, it
appears that, if a man is without justification confined in a room, it would be no defence
to show that, if he had not been locked in, he would not in fact have had occasion to leave
the room during the period of time over which he was so confined, although, again, that
would be relevant to damages. The wrong done is the infringment of the right to the
ability to leave and go elsewhere. Further, it would appear to follow that, if a man should
e be under some restraint not to leave a particular place for a period of time, for example
because he does not have the means to leave, or because he has contracted to stay there to
guard the place, or because, as a soldier or policeman, he has been ordered to remain
there, he could, nevertheless, claim damages for false imprisonment if, without
justification, he should be imprisoned within that place. The immediate and wholly
unrestricted freedom and ability to go somewhere else are not, therefore, a precondition
f for asserting a claim in false imprisonment.
      Lord Griffiths in *Murray v Ministry of Defence* [1988] 2 All ER 521 at 528–529, [1988]
1 WLR 692 at 703, in a speech with which Lord Keith, Lord Templeman, Lord Oliver
and Lord Jauncey agreed, approved the passage which is cited above from Atkin LJ in
Meering's case and continued:

g   'The Restatement of the Law of Torts has now been changed and requires that the
person confined "is conscious of the confinement or is harmed by it" (Restatement
of the Law, Second, Torts 2d (1965) § 35, p 52). If a person is unaware that he has
been falsely imprisoned and has suffered no harm, he can normally expect to recover
no more than nominal damages, and it is tempting to redefine the tort in the terms
of the present rule in the American Law Institute's Restatement of the Law of Torts.
h On reflection, however, I would not do so. The law attaches supreme importance to
the liberty of the individual and if he suffers a wrongful interference with that
liberty it should remain actionable even without proof of special damage.'

The intention necessary for commission of the tort is intentionally to do the act which
causes the imprisonment. Added malice towards the imprisoned plaintiff is not necessary:
j see 45 Halsbury's Laws (4th edn) para 1325. It is not necesary for present purposes to
consider whether negligence would suffice.
      Further, and this seems to me to be important to the issue under consideration, it is
clear from the passage from *Meering's* case cited above that the tort of false imprisonment
can be committed without confinement of the plaintiff by walls or bars and locks. If a

man is prevented from exercising his liberty by guards and warders or policemen he
may thereby be falsely imprisoned. If, therefore, in a prison a prison officer intentionally   *a*
and without justification directs a prisoner to go to his cell, when the prisoner was
entitled, under the 1964 rules and the standing rules and regulations of the prison, to be
on exercise in association with other prisoners, the tort of false imprisonment would be
committed by the prison officer if, as counsel for the plaintiff submits, the tort is
applicable without modification to the residual liberty of a convicted prisoner.

   What may amount to jurisdiction for arrest and imprisonment, as a defence to a claim   *b*
for false imprisonment, will depend on the position in law of the person making the
arrest and causing the complainant to be confined. A police constable has the same
powers of arrest as a member of the public together with certain additional statutory
powers. In general, an arrest on suspicion is not lawful unless there exists reasonable
grounds for that suspicion (see *Dallison v Caffery* [1964] 2 All ER 610, [1965] 1 QB 348);
and, in an action for false imprisonment based on wrongful arrest, it is for the court to   *c*
judge the reasonableness of the suspicion (see 11 Halsbury's Laws (4th edn) para 101 and
Lister v Perryman (1870) LR 4 HL 521). The application of these principles to a prison
officer, who by his authority requires a prisoner to remain in a cell when the prisoner
under the rules and regulations of the prison was entitled to be in association with other
prisoners, and their application in particular to the exercise by such an officer of his
authority in good faith but in mistake and without actual justification under the 1964   *d*
rules, was not examined in argument in any detail. In the context of a prison, and by
analogy to the position of a police constable acting on reasonable suspicion, it seems to
me that, if a prison officer in good faith uses his authority to direct a prisoner to go to a
place, or to remain in a cell, that may properly be regarded as sufficient justification for
the direction or order given so as to provide a defence against an action for false
imprisonment.   *e*

The residual liberty of the convicted prisoner
   The retention by a prisoner of his ordinary rights in law, so far as consistent with his
detention as a prisoner, was considered in *Raymond v Honey* [1982] 1 All ER 756, [1983]
1 AC 1, in which one issue was concerned with a prisoner's right of access to the court in   *f*
order to advance a complaint of contempt against the governor of Albany Prison. It was
conceded in argument that 'a person confined to prison retains all his civil rights, other
than those expressly or impliedly taken from him by law' (see [1983] 1 AC 1 at 3). The
proposition was accepted by Lord Wilberforce, who referred to *Solosky v R* (1979) 105
DLR (3d) 745 at 760 in the Canadian Supreme Court per Dickson J and to *R v Hull Prison
Board of Visitors, ex p St Germain* [1979] 1 All ER 701 at 716–717, [1979] QB 425 at 455.   *g*
The reference to *St Germain's* case, which was a judicial review case, was to a passage in
the judgment of Shaw LJ which included the following:

   'Now the rights of a citizen, however circumscribed by a penal sentence or
   otherwise, must always be the concern of the courts unless their jurisdiction is
   clearly excluded by some statutory provision. The courts are in general the ultimate   *h*
   custodians of the rights and liberties of the subject whatever his status and however
   attenuated those rights and liberties may be as the result of some punitive or other
   process. Although r 7(1) impliedly enables a prisoner to petition the Secretary of
   State in respect of some grievance or deprivation, there is nowhere in the 1952 Act
   or the rules made under it any indication that such rights, however attenuated, as
   he may still possess are not cognisable in a court of law. Once it is acknowledged   *j*
   that such rights exist the courts have function and jurisdiction. It is irrelevant that
   the Secretary of State may afford redress where the rules have been infringed or
   their application has been irregular or unduly harsh. An essential characteristic of
   the right of a subject is that it carries with it a right of recourse to the courts unless

some statute decrees otherwise. What should be the nature and measure of the relief
accorded must be a matter for the courts.'

To determine what are the attenuated rights of liberty, if any, of a convicted prisoner,
it is necessary to consider the statutory framework under the provisions of which a
convicted prisoner is confined. Counsel for the plaintiff relied on the terms of the statute
and of the 1964 rules in support of his submission that a prisoner may be falsely
imprisoned within prison if the minimum standards of physical comfort and amenity
and of humane treatment are for a time not observed with reference to him. Counsel for
the Home Office relied on the same provisions as providing a defence for the minister to
any claim for false imprisonment as contrasted with other remedies.

The Prison Act 1952 entrusts the general superintendence of prisons to the Secretary
of State for the Home Department (s 4(1)); and his officers are required to visit all prisons
and to examine the state of buildings, the conduct of officers, the treatment and conduct
of prisoners and all other matters concerning the management of prisons and to ensure
that the provisions of the Act and of any rules made thereunder are duly complied with
(s 4(2)). By s 8 every prison officer while acting as such has all the powers, authority,
protection and privileges of a constable.

12: Provision is made for 'the confinement and treatment of prisoners' in ss 12, 13 and
14, on which counsel for the Home Office placed reliance.

By s 12:

> '*Place of confinement of prisoners.*—(1) A prisoner, whether sentenced to imprison-
> ment or committed to prison on remand or pending trial or otherwise, may be
> lawfully confined in any prison.
>
> (2) Prisoners shall be committed to such prisons as the Secretary of State may
> from time to time direct; and may by direction of the Secretary of State be removed
> during the term of their imprisonment from the prison in which they are confined
> to any other prison.'

By s 13:

> '*Legal custody of prisoner.*—(1) Every prisoner shall be deemed to be in the legal
> custody of the governor of the prison . . .'

The reference in s 4 to rules made under the Act is to rules made under s 47(1). Rules
so made are required to be laid before Parliament (s 52(2)).

The prison rules current in 1984 indicate the extent to which a prisoner may enjoy
some freedom of movement within the prison together with access to his permitted
possessions and association with other prisoners. Reference must be made to some of the
rules:

> '1. The purpose of the training and treatment of convicted prisoners shall be to
> encourage and assist them to lead a good and useful life.
>
> 2.—(1) Order and discipline shall be maintained with firmness, but with no
> more restriction than is required for safe custody and well ordered community life
> . . .
>
> (3) At all times the treatment of prisoners shall be such as to encourage their self-
> respect and a sense of personal responsibility . . .
>
> 3.—(1) Prisoners shall be classified . . . having regard to their age, temperament
> and record and with a view to maintaining good order and facilitating training . . .
>
> (3) Nothing in this Rule shall require a prisoner to be deprived unduly of the
> society of other persons . . .
>
> 15. Arrangements shall be made so as not to require prisoners of the Christian
> religion to do any unnecessary work on Sunday . . . or prisoners of other religions
> on their recognised days of religious observance . . .

20 ... (2) A convicted prisoner shall be provided with clothing adequate for warmth and health in accordance with a scale approved by the Secretary of State ... *a*

24. Each prisoner shall be provided with a separate bed and with separate bedding adequate for warmth and health ...

27.—(1) A prisoner not engaged in outdoor work, or detained in an open prison, shall be given exercise in the open air for not less than one hour in all, each day, if weather permits ...

28.—(1) A convicted prisoner shall be required to do useful work for not more *b* than ten hours a day, and arrangements should be made to allow prisoners to work, where possible, outside the cells and in association with one another ...

29.—(1) Every prisoner able to profit from the education facilities provided at a prison shall be encouraged to do so.

(2) Programmes of evening educational classes shall be arranged at every prison and ... reasonable facilities shall be afforded to prisoners who wish to do so to *c* improve their education by correspondence courses or private study ...

30. A library shall be provided in every prison and ... every prisoner shall be allowed to have library books and to exchange them ...

41 ... (2) Anything ... which a prisoner has at a prison and which he is not allowed to retain for his own use shall be taken into the governor's custody ...

43.—(1) Where it appears desirable, for the maintenance of good order or *d* discipline or in his own interests, that a prisoner should not associate with other prisoners, either generally or for particular purposes, the governor may arrange for the prisoner's removal from association accordingly.

(2) A prisoner shall not be removed under this Rule for a period of more than 24 hours without the authority of a member of the board of visitors, or of the Secretary of State. An authority given under this paragraph shall be for a period not exceeding *e* one month, but may be renewed from month to month ...

46.—(1) The governor may order a prisoner to be put under restraint where this is necessary to prevent the prisoner from injuring himself or others, damaging property or creating a disturbance ...

47. A prisoner shall be guilty of an offence against discipline if he ... (18) *f* disobeys any lawful order or refuses or neglects to conform to any rule or regulation of the prison ...

77.—(1) It shall be the duty of every officer to conform to these Rules and the rules and regulations of the prison, to assist and support the governor in their maintenance and to obey his lawful instructions ...'

It is apparent, in my judgment, from consideration of those rules that the legislative *g* intention is that a prisoner should, subject to any lawful order given to him and to any rules laid down in the prison, enjoy such liberty, his residual liberty, within prison as is left to him. The rules may be regarded as the detailed provisions designed to achieve the purpose stated in rr 1 and 2(1). If the first contention of counsel for the Home Office should be accepted, namely that the tort of false imprisonment is not by reason of its nature available to a convicted prisoner, the question arises whether the residual liberty *h* of the prisoner would be effectively protected by the law in accordance with the policy of jealous protection of liberty which the law has stated. The prisoner would be able to have recourse to the remedies mentioned by counsel for the Home Office, namely appeal to the governor, to the visitors and to the Secretary of State. If the impairment of residual liberty is caused by or accompanied with an assault or battery the prisoner could sue in respect of them. If he suffers personal injury through negligence he could sue. In *j* addition, counsel conceded, as I understood his argument, that if interference with residual liberty was caused by a governor or prison officer without justification, and with knowledge that there was no justification and that the action in question would injure the prisoner in his personal liberty, the prisoner could claim damages for the tort of

misfeasance in public office: see *Bourgoin SA v Ministry of Agriculture Fisheries and Food*
a [1985] 3 All ER 585, [1986] QB 716. For the plaintiff, junior counsel submitted that an
unjustified and invalid act by a prison officer could not form the basis of a claim for
misfeasance in public office and, in any event, such a cause of action could not be available
against a fellow prisoner.

It seemed to this court that these contentions could, to an extent, be tested by asking
whether the nature in law of the tort of false imprisonment precluded a claim by a
b convicted prisoner not only against the Secretary of State for the actions of prison officers
as his agents but also against a fellow prisoner who deliberately interfered with his
residual liberty. Counsel for the Home Office contended that it would preclude a claim
in both cases. If a prisoner is prevented by threats or other means by another prisoner
from enjoying his ability to associate with other prisoners, or to follow a permitted
activity, he would have no claim save to the extent that the threats amounted to an
c assault. If there was no assault, there could be, it was said, no claim. The loss, no doubt,
in almost all cases would be theoretical, because of the inability of most prisoners to pay
damages, but the analysis seems to be of some use. There is no reason, apparent to me,
why the nature of the tort, evolved by the common law for the protection of personal
liberty, should be held to be such as to deny its availability to a convicted prisoner whose
residual liberty should, in my judgment, be protected so far as the law can properly
d achieve unless statute requires otherwise. If, however, as counsel submits, the tort of false
imprisonment is not available to a convicted prisoner against a prison officer, I accept his
submission that it could not, for the same reasons, be available to a convicted prisoner
against a fellow prisoner.

Reference was made to the difficulties which could arise in the administration of
prisons and in the maintenance of order within prisons, if the tort of false imprisonment
e should be held to be available without modification in favour of a convicted prisoner in
respect of his residual liberty, and also to the discussion of those difficulties, in the context
of judicial review of disciplinary decisions by governors, in *R v Deputy Governor of*
Camphill Prison, ex p King [1984] 3 All ER 897, [1985] QB 735 and *Leech v Parkhurst Prison*
Deputy Governor [1988] 1 All ER 485, [1988] AC 533. The potential difficulties seem to
f me to be real.

The objective of a well ordered community life within a prison (r 2(1)) requires that
prison officers have the authority which is given to them by the rules. The prisoner is
required to obey any lawful order from a prison officer and to comply with any rule or
regulation of the prison (r 47(18)). It is the duty of the prison officer to preserve order
within the community of the prison and, I conceive, a prison officer must on occasion be
g required to act swiftly and firmly. By s 8 of the 1952 Act a prison officer is given all the
powers, authority, protection and privileges of a constable and, it may be added, no more.
It would be, I think, surprising and adverse to the maintenance of well ordered
community life within a prison and to the proper working of the prison rules if a prison
officer should be subjected to liability for false imprisonment of a prisoner by reason
only of some interference with the residual liberty of that prisoner caused by the acts of
h the prison officer done in good faith but without actual authority under the rules. This
aspect of the case also was not fully explored in argument.

In *R v Deputy Governor of Parkhurst Prison, ex p Hague* (1989) Independent, 11 August,
the Divisional Court, Nolan J and myself, in a passage of the judgment which was obiter
and not necessary for the decision, expressed the opinion that an act, unauthorised but in
good faith, which caused the prisoner to lose part of his remaining freedom as a prisoner
j and subjected him to the worsened conditions of segregation, was not an actionable
wrong of false imprisonment[1]. It is not necessary, in my judgment, on this appeal, for
this court to reach a final conclusion of that question. It is sufficient to say that it is not

---

1   Subsequent to the decision reported herein, *R v Deputy Governor of Parkhurst Prison, ex p Hague* was,
    apart from the granting of certain declaration, affirmed by the Court of Appeal: see p 687, post

clear to me, merely by reference to the nature of the tort of false imprisonment itself, having due regard to any appropriate policy considerations, that the court must hold on a an application to strike out that a convicted prisoner cannot in any circumstances claim against a prison officer for false imprisonment. The allegations made by the plaintiff sufficiently allege want of good faith on the part of the prison officers concerned, if that is, as I am disposed to think that it is, a necessary ingredient in the claim. It is preferable that, on such an issue, the law should be developed by reference to facts decided at trial rather than on the imprecise allegations in an unparticularised pleading: see per Slade LJ b in *Union Carbide Corp v Naturin Ltd* [1987] FSR 538 at 544, cited in *Lonrho plc v Fayed* [1989] 2 All ER 65 at 72, [1989] 3 WLR 631 at 641.

Some support for the view that an action for false imprisonment may be brought by a convicted prisoner is provided, I think, by *Osborne v Milman* (1886) 17 QBD 514. The plaintiff was committed to prison by order of the Queen's Bench Division under certain statutes for having practised as a solicitor though not duly qualified. He was conveyed to c Holloway Gaol on a warrant and there placed 'on the criminal side' and treated as a convicted criminal not sentenced to hard labour. He contended that, although lawfully committed to Holloway and confined therein, he was entitled to be treated as a 'misdemeanant of the first division' and he sued the governor of Holloway for false imprisonment. The issue whether, even if he was right in his contention that he was not a 'person convicted of a crime', it was impossible for the tort of false imprisonment to d have been committed against him, was not argued. The Attorney General, Sir Charles Russell, agreed that the plaintiff was entitled to £50 damages if he was right on the point of law. The plaintiff succeeded before Denman J but lost in the Court of Appeal (Lord Esher MR, Bowen and Fry LJJ) on the ground that he was in law a convicted criminal (see (1887) 18 QBD 471). No doubt was expressed at any stage by either court as to the availability of the remedy of false imprisonment to a person lawfully confined in a e prison.

The authorities

So far I have considered the submission of counsel for the Home Office based on the nature of the tort of false imprisonment. It is next necessary to consider the authorities f on which both sides have relied.

The starting point is *Williams v Home Office (No 2)* [1981] 1 All ER 1211. The claim was for damages for false imprisonment by a convicted prisoner who was transferred from a prison at Hull to a special control unit at Wakefield Prison established by the Secretary of State in 1974 as a means of containing and controlling prisoners regarded as subversive and disruptive. Confinement in this control unit was claimed to have been unlawful on g various grounds including the nature of the imprisonment, breach of the Prison Rules 1964, and in particular misuse of r 43, and the imposition of a punitive regime of confinement contrary to the Bill of Rights (1688) as being cruel or unusual. There was, however, and not surprisingly, no allegation that any of the officers of the Secretary of State concerned with the matter had been acting in bad faith. Tudor Evans J held that the confinement was neither cruel nor unusual in fact and, in addition, that the plaintiff's h sentence on conviction and s 12(1) of the 1952 Act justified his confinement in any prison, and that the Secretary of State had power to act under r 43. Counsel for the Home Office relied on the following passage in the judgment (at 1240–1241):

'Section 12(1) of the Act empowers the Secretary of State lawfully to confine a prisoner in any prison. Counsel for the plaintiff submits . . . that the subsection is j concerned only with the place of imprisonment and not with any tortious act done within it. This means that the subsection is not capable of justifying the detention of a prisoner when the nature of the imprisonment differs from that in the remainder of the system and where there is a breach of the Prison Rules. In my

judgment, the sentence of the court and the provisions of s 12(1) always afford a
a   defence to an action of false imprisonment. The sentence justifies the fact of
imprisonment and the subsection justifies the confinement of a prisoner in any
prison. How then can it be unjustifiable and unlawful to confine him there? I accept
the submission of counsel for the defendant that the sentence of the court and the
provisions of s 12(1) provide a defence to this action, subject to the arguments based
on the Bill of Rights and natural justice ... The next question is whether the
b   lawfulness of the detention can be affected by the conditions of the detention. I do
not think so. The question of the conditions of imprisonment is a matter for the
Secretary of State. The check or safeguard against unacceptable conditions ... lies in
the prisoner's rights under the rules to complain to the governor or the Secretary of
State. Counsel for the plaintiff submits that if this is right it means that a prisoner is
without remedy even though he is subjected to a regime which is harsh and
c   unpleasant. There is in fact in the administration of prisons ... ample safeguard
against abuse ... s 4(2) of the Act provides comprehensively for supervision of the
conduct of prison officers ... and all matters concerning the management of
prisons.'

The plaintiff in that case appealed but only on the ground that, contrary to *Arbon v*
d *Anderson* [1943] 1 All ER 154, [1943] KB 252 and *Becker v Home Office* [1972] 2 All ER
676, [1972] 2 QB 407, the plaintiff was entitled to damages for breach of r 43. Leave to
amend the statement of claim was necessary for that purpose and leave was refused (see
[1982] 2 All ER 564). This court, therefore, did not consider the grounds of decision of
Tudor Evans J.

In *R v Gartree Prison Board of Visitors, ex p Sears* (1985) Times, 20 March, Mann J,
e applying the reasoning of Tudor Evans J in *Williams v Home Office (No 2)*, held that a
variation in the conditions of confinement of a lawfully detained prisoner could not
constitute the common law tort of false imprisonment, whether the variation in
conditions of confinement was a result of a managerial decision of the governor or a
determination of the board of visitors which could be flawed for want of jurisdiction.

In *R v Metropolitan Police Comr, ex p Nahar* (1983) Times, 28 May, which was an
f application for habeas corpus, the applicants had been remanded in custody by magistrates
on charges relating to the illegal importation of controlled drugs. They could not be
confined in Brixton Prison in accordance with the warrant of committal because of a
restriction then in operation, and they were therefore confined in cells below Camberwell
Green Magistrates' Court pursuant to s 6(2) of the Imprisonment (Temporary Provisions)
Act 1980. It was contended that the conditions in which the applicants were detained in
g custody were such as to render their detention unlawful. Their complaints included the
size of the cell, the absence of daylight, inadequate electric light and ventilation etc. The
facts were considered by Stephen Brown J in detail. He held that the conditions described
in the affidavits could not give rise to a finding that the detention was unlawful. In
reaching that conclusion he held that art 3 of the European Convention for the Protection
of Human Rights and Fundamental Freedoms (Rome, 4 November 1950; TS 71 (1953);
h Cmd 8969) did not provide an appropriate standard for application and that the 1952 Act
itself did not apply directly or by implication to a prisoner held in custody under s 6 of
the 1980 Act, which did not lay down any standards. There was, however, implicit in his
judgment the opinion that conditions of confinement, if bad enough, could give rise to a
finding that the detention was unlawful. McCullough J made the point expressly. He
said (and I read from the transcript):
j

    '... there must be implied into s 6 of the 1980 Act some term which relates to
    the conditions under which a prisoner may lawfully be detained. I say so because it
    is possible to conceive of hypothetical circumstances in which the conditions of
    detention were such as would make that detention unlawful. I do not propose to

offer any formulation of that term. Were it broken in any particular case I would reject emphatically the suggestion that the matter would not be one for the exercise *a* of the court's jurisdiction to grant the writ of habeas corpus.'

One comment, I think, should be made. It would, I think, be possible for the court to order the release of the applicant from custody in the cells where they were confined, on the ground that such confinement was not authorised by s 6 of the 1980 Act, without necessarily acknowledging any right of the applicants to damages for false imprisonment *b* in respect of that confinement.

In *Middleweek v Chief Constable of the Merseyside Police* (1985) [1990] 3 All ER 662, [1990] 3 WLR 481 a claim to damages for false imprisonment was made by a solicitor who had been arrested on suspicion of theft of a document and detained in a cell for a period of time before being released. The trial judge rejected the plaintiff's claim that the police had acted in bad faith and ruled that the arrest was lawful, but the jury was *c* instructed to decide whether the plaintiff was detained for longer than was necessary on the basis that, if he was so detained, he would have established that he had been falsely imprisoned. The jury was also asked whether it was reasonable for the plaintiff to have been detained in a cell. The jury answered that the period of detention was not unreasonable but it had been unreasonable to detain the plaintiff in a cell. There was no complaint about the nature or condition of the cell. Ackner LJ, giving the judgment of *d* the court (himself Slade and Glidewell LJJ), held that, given that the initial arrest was lawful and the serious nature of the offence which the plaintiff was reasonably suspected of having committed, there was no basis for suggesting that the police had acted unlawfully in following their ordinary procedure of detaining the plaintiff in a cell. Ackner LJ considered the judgment of Tudor Evans J in *Williams v Home Office (No 2)* [1981] 1 All ER 1211 and his conclusion that there was no authority in law in support of *e* the contention that although a detention may be lawful it can become unlawful if the nature (meaning the conditions) of the imprisonment changes. Ackner LJ then referred to the decision of Mann J in *R v Gartree Prison Board of Visitors, ex p Sears* (1985) Times, 20 March and of the Divisional Court in *R v Metropolitan Police Comr, ex p Nahar* (1983) Times, 28 May and continued ([1990] 3 All ER 662 at 668, [1990] 3 WLR 481 at 487):

f

'We agree with the views expressed by the Divisional Court that it must be possible to conceive of hypothetical cases in which the conditions of detention are so intolerable as to render the detention unlawful and thereby provide a remedy to the prisoner in damages for false imprisonment. A person lawfully detained in a prison cell would, in our judgment, cease to be so lawfully detained if the conditions in that cell were such as to be seriously prejudicial to his health if he continued to *g* occupy it, eg because it became and remained seriously flooded, or contained a fractured gas pipe allowing gas to escape into the cell. We do not therefore accept as an absolute proposition that, if detention is initially lawful, it can never become unlawful by reason of changes in the conditions of imprisonment.'

No doubt or reservation was expressed over the reasoning of Tudor Evans J in *Williams* *h* *(No 2)* in reaching his conclusion that, in the absence of intolerable conditions, s 12 of the 1952 Act provides a defence to the Secretary of State to action of false imprisonment. It is, however, to be observed that the issue of interference with the residual liberty of a lawfully confined prisoner by actions otherwise than in good faith was not in issue in *Middleweek*.

For my part, I do not find the reasoning of Tudor Evans J in *Williams (No 2)* conclusive *j* of the plaintiff's case based on unlawful and unjustified interference with the plaintiff's residual liberty by acts done otherwise than in good faith. In particular, the terms of s 12(1) of the 1952 Act do not, in my judgment, afford a defence to the Secretary of State to an action based on false imprisonment of a convicted prisoner by such acts of prison officers for which the Secretary of State is vicariously responsible. The subsection affords

a defence to the Secretary of State in respect of confinement of a prisoner in any prison
a but it does not, in my judgment, extend to justify the conduct of prison officers who
intentionally deprive a prisoner of his residual liberty within the prison and who do so
without reasonable cause and with knowledge that they have no reasonable cause, or, in
short, in bad faith.

False imprisonment based on conditions of confinement
b   Whatever be the right view of the decision in *Middleweek's* case as an authority binding
on this court, there could be no arguable case based on 'intolerable conditions of detention'
unless the facts alleged are capable of being properly regarded as within that concept.
Counsel for the plaintiff developed a submission to the effect that imprisonment within
a prison of a convicted prisoner must be held to become unlawful if, in any respect, it
falls below the standards set by the Prison Rules 1964, the European Standard Minimum
c Rules for the Treatment of Prisoners of 1973 (Council of Europe Committee of Ministers
Resolution (73)5; now superseded by revised rules: see Recommendations R(87)3) and
the European Convention of Human Rights, whether the breach be in respect of the
physical conditions of confinement or of standards of treatment, for example with
reference to the quality of food, facilities for religious observance or access to educational
facilities. It is not necessary to decide on the validity of that submission and I would say
d only that it appears to me to be unsustainably wide. Neither the European Convention
on Human Rights nor the European Standard Minimum Rules can be directly applied
or administered by the courts of this country. Nevertheless, I have no doubt that the
allegations in the particulars of claim do include an assertion of fact capable of constituting
such 'intolerable conditions of detention' as to render the detention unlawful within the
principles stated by Ackner LJ in *Middleweek's* case. That assertion is that the plaintiff was
e put into a strip cell where his clothes were taken from him and that he was left naked in
the strip cell overnight and, as I think we must assume, without bed or bedding available
to him.

   As to the remaining submissions of counsel for the Home Office, I do not accept that
the principle stated by Ackner LJ in *Middleweek's* case was an obiter dictum and not part
of the court's decision. The submission made to the court was that, as an absolute
f proposition, if detention is initially lawful, it cannot become unlawful by reason of
changes in the conditions of imprisonment. That submission was rejected by the court
and its rejection required the court to consider the evidence directed to whether the cell
was below the ordinary standard to be expected of police cells. It was then held that the
evidence showed that the conditions of detention were not below the standard to be
expected. The consideration and rejection of the absolute proposition put before the
g court were, in my judgment, part of the court's decision.

   Lastly, it was submitted that the decision in *Middleweek's* case was directed to, and
should be restricted to, a prisoner under arrest and is not applicable to a convicted
prisoner. I do not accept that submission. I see no reason why the principles stated in
Ex p Nahar should not apply to the detention of a convicted prisoner who is confined in
h intolerable circumstances on the ground that Parliament cannot have intended the 1952
Act, and the 1964 rules made thereunder, to authorise confinement of a prisoner in
physical circumstances which are intolerable. The question whether a prisoner so
confined is entitled thereby to damages for false imprisonment, irrespective of the good
faith of those who have been responsible for his continued confinement, was not
considered in *Ex p Nahar*, which was not a case of false imprisonment. The prisoner's
j remedy in a particular case might not go beyond the making of an order that the prisoner
be no longer confined in those intolerable circumstances. For the reasons explained above
I think that the better view is that, to support a claim for false imprisonment on such a
ground, it would at least be necessary for the complainant to prove that the defendant
had continued the confinement of the prisoner in intolerable circumstances with
knowledge that the circumstances were intolerable. In this case, the allegation is that the

intolerable conditions were imposed on the plaintiff deliberately with knowledge of them. It is not necessary for the purpose of this case to deal more precisely with the *a* necessary elements of a claim based on this ground.

For the reasons given it seems to me that the assistant recorder was right in his ruling that the allegation of false imprisonment, whether based on interference with residual liberty or on the imposition of intolerable conditions, is not shown to be unarguable and should therefore go for trial.

I would dismiss the appeal.   *b*

PARKER LJ. I have had the opportunity to read in draft the judgment delivered by Ralph Gibson LJ. I agree that this appeal should be dismissed for the reasons set out in that judgment. I add some observations of my own only for the purpose of illustrating what appear to me to be the wholly unacceptable consequences of the case advanced on behalf of the Home Office.   *c*

Although the plaintiff may, in the end, fail to establish the facts, we must proceed for the moment on the basis that he was kept locked up naked overnight in a cell known as a strip cell. It is said that as he was lawfully detained in the prison this cannot amount to false imprisonment. If this be right it must I think follow that he could have had no claim for false imprisonment if his detention naked in that cell had continued for weeks. It would also seem to me to follow that if he had been locked up in a similar condition, *d* not by prison officers, but by fellow inmates, he would have no such claim.

It would follow, too, that, if a convicted criminal were confined in a prison in which he and his fellows were permitted, within the confines of a perimeter fence enclosing some acres of ground, to lead normal lives he would have no such claim if he were locked up, with or without clothes, in a shed in some remote part of the grounds, whether by fellow inmates or prison officers. To hold that such treatment could not amount to false *e* imprisonment offends in my judgment against common sense. The submission that it could not so amount is one which I could only accept if driven so to do by clear and binding authority. I am not so driven.

The facts alleged, in my judgment, disclose a clearly arguable case.

FOX LJ. I have read in draft the judgments of Ralph Gibson and Parker LJJ. I agree *f* with them and would dismiss the appeal accordingly.

Appeal dismissed. Leave to appeal to the House of Lords granted.

Solicitors: *Marklands*, Leeds, agents for *Treasury Solicitor*; *R M Broudie & Co*, Liverpool *g* (for the plaintiff).

Sophie Craven   Barrister.

a # R v Deputy Governor of Parkhurst Prison and others, ex parte Hague

COURT OF APPEAL, CIVIL DIVISION
SIR NICOLAS BROWNE-WILKINSON V-C, NICHOLLS AND TAYLOR LJJ
27, 28, 29, 30 MARCH, 2, 3 APRIL, 25 MAY 1990

b

Prison – Prison conditions – Removal from association – Prison governor ordering transfer of prisoner to another prison – Governor ordering prisoner to be segregated at other prison – Whether prison governor having power to order transfer and segregation – Prison Act 1952, s 12 – Prison Rules 1964, r 43.

c *False imprisonment – Prisoner serving sentence – Removal from association – Prisoner lawfully imprisoned – Breach of prison rules – No evidence of intolerable conditions – Whether prisoner could claim damages for false imprisonment.*

The appellant was sentenced to 15 years' imprisonment for a number of offences including robbery, using a firearm with intent to resist arrest and escape from custody
d while on remand. He was assessed as a category A prisoner having regard to his offences and his record. After periods in several prisons, he was transferred to Parkhurst Prison. On 8 July 1988 the deputy governor of Parkhurst decided to transfer the appellant to Wormwood Scrubs Prison pursuant to the provisions of prison department circular instruction 10/1974 because he had twice deliberately gone out on unauthorised exercise and had made it clear that he would continue such behaviour. In accordance with para 9
e of the circular the transfer of the appellant was made subject to r 43ᵃ of the Prison Rules 1964 (dealing with segregation of prisoners) and the deputy governor obtained authority from the regional director of the prison service in accordance with para 9 for segregation at Wormwood Scrubs to continue for up to 28 days. Under r 43 a prison governor had power to order the removal of a prisoner from association with other prisoners where it
f was considered desirable in the interests of good order and discipline for a period of 24 hours at his own discretion or up to one month with the approval of a prison visitor or the Secretary of State acting by the regional director. The appellant spent 28 days in segregation at Wormwood Scrubs Prison. He sought judicial review of the decisions made on 8 July to transfer and segregate him pursuant to the prison department circular instructions and to continue the segregation for 28 days and he also claimed damages for
g false imprisonment. The Divisional Court dismissed the appellant's application and claim. He appealed to the Court of Appeal, contending (i) that para 9 unlawfully fettered the discretion of the dispersal prison governor by obliging him to make all transfers subject to r 43 of the 1964 rules and that a prison governor had no power to order the segregation of a prisoner in another prison, (ii) that para 9 in stating that the necessary authority for the continued segregation 'will be obtained by the dispersal prison governor
h from the Regional Director' indicated that such authority would be routinely granted when in fact the regional director was required under r 43(2) to make a reasoned decision, (iii) that he had a right to make representations before the regional director made his decision and the right to be given the reasons for the decision and (iv) that because the decision to order his segregation at Wormwood Scrubs was flawed he had been falsely imprisoned, for which he was entitled to damages. The prison governor and the Secretary
j of State contended that the court's supervisory jurisdiction should only be invoked after the rejection of a complaint to a prison visitor or a petition to the Secretary of State and then only to review such rejection and that s 12ᵇ of the Prison Act 1952, which provided

---

a   Rule 43 is set out at p 691 c d, post
b   Section 12, so far as material, is set out at p 694 a, post

that a prisoner could 'be lawfully confined in any prison', was a complete defence to the action for false imprisonment.

Held – The appeal would be allowed in part for the following reasons—

(1) The court had jurisdiction to grant judicial review of managerial decisions relating to the transfer and segregation of prisoners, since the procedure for complaint to a prison visitor or a petition to the Secretary of State were not established appeal procedures which had to be exhausted before judicial review was invoked. However, because the grant of judicial review would interfere with the management of prisons the court would approach the exercise of the discretion to grant judicial review with great caution and would only exercise that discretion where a clear case was made out for relief (see p 700 h, p 701 e to g, p 708 g and p 710 f, post); Leech v Deputy Governor of Parkhurst Prison [1988] 1 All ER 485 applied.

(2) Paragraph 9 of the prison department circular instructions was contrary to r 43 of the 1964 rules since (a) a prison governor had no power to order a prisoner transferred to another prison to be segregated at the other prison under r 43 because the rule was clearly intended to apply to a prison governor's powers and management of the inmates in his own prison and (b) the regional director was required when giving authority under r 43(2) for segregation of a prisoner for up to 28 days to make a reasoned decision not only whether segregation should be ordered but also as to the length of time for which it should continue, whereas para 9 contemplated that authority to segregate for the full 28-day period would be granted routinely by the regional director without a reasoned decision. The appellant was entitled to declarations that para 9 was contrary to r 43 in those two respects (see p 695 d e h to p 696 b, p 699 c, p 701 h, p 708 f g and p 710 f, post); dictum of Tudor Evans J in Williams v Home Office (No 2) [1981] 1 All ER 1211 at 1228–1229 not followed.

(3) A prisoner had no right to be heard before a decision was made by the regional director to order his segregation under r 43 for an extended period and he had no right to be given the reasons for his transfer and segregation, since the object of r 43 was not punitive and the prisoner's rights were safeguarded by the procedure for obtaining a reasoned decision from the regional director and the right to complain to the governor or a prison visitor or to petition the Secretary of State. In those circumstances it would be inappropriate to apply the full measure of the rules of natural justice to a decision under r 43 to transfer and segregate a prisoner. Moreover, the appellant had been aware of why he was being transferred and segregated and he had suffered no injustice because the outcome would have been the same even if the procedure under para 9 had not been flawed since it was unlikely that the governor of Wormwood Scrubs would have been willing to place in association with his own prisoners an aggrieved troublemaker from another prison who had been deemed by the governor there to be in need of segregation and who was additionally aggrieved by being transferred. For that reason the decisions made on 8 July to transfer and segregate him pursuant to the prison department circular instructions and to continue the segregation for 28 days would not be quashed and an order of certiorari would be refused. It followed that, in so far as the claim for damages depended on those decisions being quashed, the damages claim failed in limine (see p 696 d, p 697 e to g, p 698 e to h, p 699 b g, p 700 b, p 702 a b, p 708 g and p 710 f, post); dictum of Tudor Evans J in Williams v Home Office (No 2) [1981] 1 All ER 1211 at 1247 approved; Leech v Deputy Governor of Parkhurst Prison [1988] 1 All ER 485 distinguished.

(4) Decisions made under the prison rules which were regulatory and bore on administrative action in the public law domain were open to judicial review and could give rise in an appropriate case to public law remedies, but just as a breach of the rules could not form the basis of a private law claim for damages, nor could such a breach defeat the statutory defence to a claim for false imprisonment that the detention was justified under s 12 of the 1952 Act (see p 703 g h, p 708 g and p 710 d f, post); dicta of Tudor Evans J in Williams v Home Office (No 2) [1981] 1 All ER 1211 at 1240–1242 applied.

(5) A claim for damages for false imprisonment could lie against the prison authorities

a at the suit of a prisoner who had been lawfully committed to prison and whose term of imprisonment had not expired but only if the prisoner was held under physical conditions so intolerable that the detention was rendered unlawful. However, bad faith on the part of the prison authorities was not a necessary ingredient of the tort. Since there was no evidence that the appellant had been detained under intolerable conditions, it followed that he had no claim in damages for false imprisonment (see p 707 d f to j, p 708 b c g, p 709 b to g and p 710 a b f g, post); *Weldon v Home Office* [1990] 3 All ER 672 b considered; *Middleweek v Chief Constable of the Merseyside Police* (1985) [1990] 3 All ER 662 doubted.

Notes

For treatment of prisoners and prison discipline, see 37 Halsbury's Laws (4th edn) paras 1139, 1141.

c For special control and restraint, see ibid para 1166, and for cases on the subject, see 37(3) Digest (Reissue) 402, 5320–5321.

For the Prison Act 1952, s 12, see 34 Halsbury's Statutes (4th edn) 651.

For the Prison Rules 1964, r 43, see 18 Halsbury's Statutory Instruments (4th reissue) 20.

d **Cases referred to in judgments**

Arbon v Anderson [1943] 1 All ER 154, [1943] KB 252.
Becker v Home Office [1972] 2 All ER 676, [1972] 2 QB 407, [1972] 2 WLR 1193, CA.
Bourgoin SA v Ministry of Agriculture Fisheries and Food [1985] 3 All ER 585, [1986] QB 716, [1985] 3 WLR 1027, QBD and CA.
Cardinal v Director of Kent Institution (1985) 24 DLR (4th) 44, Can SC.
e *Cobbett v Grey* (1850) 4 Exch 729, 154 ER 1409.
Hoffmann-La Roche (F) & Co AG v Secretary of State for Trade and Industry [1974] 2 All ER 1128, [1975] AC 295, [1974] 3 WLR 104, HL.
Kanda v Government of Malaya [1962] AC 322, [1962] 2 WLR 1153, PC.
Leech v Deputy Governor of Parkhurst Prison [1988] 1 All ER 485, [1988] AC 533, [1988] 2 WLR 290, HL.
f *Middleweek v Chief Constable of the Merseyside Police* (1985) [1990] 3 All ER 662, [1990] 3 WLR 481, CA.
Osborne v Milman (1886) 17 QBD 514; *rvsd* (1887) 18 QBD 471, CA.
Payne v Lord Harris of Greenwich [1981] 2 All ER 842, [1981] 1 WLR 754, CA.
Public Service Board of New South Wales v Osmond [1987] LRC (Const) 681, Aust HC.
R v Chief Constable of the Merseyside Police, ex p Calveley [1986] 1 All ER 257, [1986] QB g 424, [1986] 2 WLR 144, CA.
R v Comr of Police of the Metropolis, ex p Nahar (1983) Times, 28 May, DC.
R v Deputy Governor of Camphill Prison, ex p King [1984] 3 All ER 897, [1985] QB 735, [1985] 2 WLR 36, CA.
R v Gaming Board for GB, ex p Benaim [1970] 2 All ER 528, [1970] 2 QB 417, [1970] 2 WLR 1009, CA.
h *R v Gartree Prison Board of Visitors, ex p Sears* (1985) Times, 20 March.
R v Hull Prison Board of Visitors, ex p St Germain [1979] 1 All ER 701, [1979] QB 425, [1979] 2 WLR 42, CA.
R v Panel on Take-overs and Mergers, ex p Datafin plc (Norton Opax plc intervening) [1987] 1 All ER 564, [1987] QB 815, [1987] 2 WLR 699, CA.
j *R v Secretary of State for the Home Dept, ex p Swati* [1986] 1 All ER 717, [1986] 1 WLR 477, CA.
R v Secretary of State for Social Services, ex p Connolly [1986] 1 All ER 998, [1986] 1 WLR 421, CA.
Raymond v Honey [1982] 1 All ER 756, [1983] 1 AC 1, [1982] 2 WLR 465, HL.
Weldon v Home Office [1990] 3 All ER 672, [1990] 3 WLR 465, CA.
Williams v Home Office (No 2) [1981] 1 All ER 1211; *affd on other grounds* [1982] 2 All ER 564, CA.

Cases also cited

Anisminic Ltd v Foreign Compensation Commission [1969] 1 All ER 208, [1969] 2 AC 147, HL.

Chief Constable of the North Wales Police v Evans [1982] 3 All ER 141, [1982] 1 WLR 1155, HL.

Cooper v Wandsworth Board of Works (1863) 14 CBNS 180, 143 ER 414.

Dean v Wiesengrund [1955] 2 All ER 432, [1955] 2 QB 120, CA.

Dunlop v Woollahra Municipal Council [1981] 1 All ER 1202, [1982] AC 158, PC.

Grunwick Processing Laboratories Ltd v Advisory Conciliation and Arbitration Service [1978] 1 All ER 338, [1978] AC 655, CA and HL.

Isaacs v Robertson [1984] 3 All ER 140, [1985] AC 97, PC.

Jones v Swansea City Council [1989] 3 All ER 162, [1990] 1 WLR 54, CA.

Language Rights under the Manitoba Act 1870, Reference re (1985) 19 DLR (4th) 1, Can SC.

London and Clydeside Estates Ltd v Aberdeen DC [1979] 3 All ER 876, [1980] 1 WLR 182, HL.

Lovelock v Minister of Transport (1980) 40 P & CR 336, CA.

McInnes v Onslow Fane [1978] 3 All ER 211, [1978] 1 WLR 1520.

Mee v Cruikshank (1902) 86 LT 708, Assizes.

O'Connor v Isaacs [1956] 2 All ER 417, [1956] 2 QB 288, CA; *affg* [1956] 1 All ER 513, [1956] 2 QB 288.

Osborne v Angle (1835) 2 Scott 500.

Padfield v Minister of Agriculture Fisheries and Food [1968] 1 All ER 694, [1968] AC 997, HL.

R v Secretary of State for the Environment, ex p Hackney London BC [1984] 1 All ER 956, [1984] 1 WLR 592, CA.

R v Secretary of State for the Home Dept, ex p McAvoy [1984] 3 All ER 417, [1984] 1 WLR 1408.

R v Secretary of State for the Home Dept, ex p Singh [1987] Imm AR 489, DC; *affd* [1988] Imm AR 480, CA.

R v Thomas [1892] 1 QB 426, DC.

Ridge v Baldwin [1963] 2 All ER 66, [1964] AC 40, HL.

Russell v Duke of Norfolk [1949] 1 All ER 109, CA.

Smith v East Elloe RDC [1956] 1 All ER 855, [1956] AC 736, HL.

Town Investments Ltd v Dept of the Environment [1977] 1 All ER 813, [1978] AC 359, HL.

Wershof v Comr of Police for the Metropolis [1978] 3 All ER 540.

Whittaker v Roos, Morant v Roos [1912] App D 92, SA App Div.

Wiseman v Borneman [1969] 3 All ER 275, [1971] AC 297, HL.

Appeal

Christopher Hague appealed against the decision of the Divisional Court of the Queen's Bench Division (Ralph Gibson LJ and Nolan J) given on 28 July 1989 dismissing his application for judicial review of the decisions made on 8 July 1988 to transfer and segregate him pursuant to the provisions of prison department circular instruction 10/1974 and to continue the segregation for 28 days. The respondents to the appeal were the deputy governor of Parkhurst Prison, the Board of Visitors of Wormwood Scrubs Prison and the Secretary of State for the Home Department. The facts are set out in the judgment of Taylor LJ.

Stephen Sedley QC and *Timothy Owen* for the appellant.
John Laws and *David Pannick* for the respondents.

Cur adv vult

25 May. The following judgments were delivered.

a **TAYLOR LJ** (giving the first judgment at the invitation of Sir Nicolas Browne-Wilkinson V-C). This case raises important questions concerning prison management and in particular the rules and practice for segregating prisoners and transferring them between prisons.

It will be necessary to refer to a number of statutory provisions, rules and prison **b** department circulars, but it is convenient to start by setting out those which are at the heart of this case.

The Prison Rules 1964, SI 1964/388, as amended, are made pursuant to s 47 of the Prison Act 1952. Rule 43 provides as follows:

'(1) Where it appears desirable, for the maintenance of good order or discipline or in his own interests, that a prisoner should not associate with other prisoners, either generally or for particular purposes, the governor may arrange for the **c** prisoner's removal from association accordingly.

(2) A prisoner shall not be removed under this Rule for a period of more than 24 hours without the authority of a member of the board of visitors, or of the Secretary of State. An authority given under this paragraph shall be for a period not exceeding one month, but may be renewed from month to month.

d (3) The governor may arrange at his discretion for such a prisoner as aforesaid to resume association with other prisoners, and shall do so if in any case the medical officer so advises on medical grounds.'

Circular Instruction 10/1974, as amended, from the Prison Department of the Home Office to all prison establishments, provides as follows so far as is relevant:

e 'DISPERSAL POLICY—PROVISION OF CELLS IN LOCAL PRISONS

1. One of the decisions arising out of the review of dispersal policy is that a small number of secure cells in local prisons should be set aside for the use of governors of dispersal prisons to accommodate troublemakers temporarily and at short notice for a cooling off period.

f 2. The arrangement will be that each dispersal prison will have available two such cells, one in each of two different local prisons...

CRITERIA FOR USE OF LOCAL CELLS

3. The purpose of this facility offered to dispersal governors is to provide a brief "cooling off" period for a troublemaker who needs to be removed from normal location because of an imminently explosive situation caused by either his actual or **g** impending disruptive behaviour, and for whom placement in the segregation unit is inappropriate or impracticable, either because the prisoner would still be able to exercise a disruptive influence from the segregation unit (because of inadequate insulation between the segregation unit and the main prison), or because the extent to which the prisoner provides a focal point for prisoner unrest would mean that the mere act of placement in the segregation unit could have a provocative and **h** explosive effect on the rest of the establishment.

AUTHORITY FOR TRANSFER AND LENGTH OF STAY

4. Transfer will be at the discretion of the dispersal governor concerned; but will be for a period of not more than 28 days. The normal presumption will be that the prisoner will thereafter (or before if the situation permits) return to his parent prison...

j TRANSFER ARRANGEMENTS

5. Before transferring a prisoner under these arrangements, the dispersal governor should telephone the governor of the local prison to confirm that there are no exceptional problems that make it impossible for the prisoner to be accommodated and that his transfer would not bring him into contact with any prisoners from

whom he should be kept apart. If there are cases of difficulty which cannot be resolved locally the advice of the Regional Director should be sought.

6. Although dispersal governors will be regarded as having an automatic lien on these designated cells, the cells need not necessarily be kept empty when not being used by the dispersal prison in question . . .

7. The dispersal governor should ensure that the F1150 containing a full record of the behaviour which led to the transfer accompanies the prisoner to the local prison . . . In any event, the F1150, with a full report, should be sent within 24 hours: for obvious reasons it is essential that the governor of the local prison should have full background information about those difficult individuals that they will be having to accommodate, even though only for a very short time.

CONDITIONS

9. Prisoners transferred under these arrangements will always be made subject to the provisions of Prison Rule 43, and the necessary authority for their continued segregation for the remainder of the 28 day period, will be obtained by the dispersal prison governor from the Regional Director (who will act on behalf of the Secretary of State).

10. While in a local prison, men from dispersal prisons will be treated in the same way as any other prisoner on Rule 43 of the same security category in that prison. In particular they will do the same work, and receive pay on the same basis as their fellows, and enjoy no greater privileges than any other Rule 43 "subversive" prisoner. Prisoners transferred under these arrangements will bring with them none of the additional possessions normally allowed to long term prisoners.'

Facts

The appellant, Christopher Hague, was sentenced on 23 May 1985 to a term of 15 years' imprisonment for a number of offences including robbery, using a firearm with intent to resist arrest and escape from custody. He was assessed as a category A prisoner having regard to his offences and his record. After periods in several prisons he was transferred to Parkhurst on 3 October 1986.

In 1987 two prisoners escaped from Gartree Prison by helicopter. In consequence various precautionary measures were taken in prisons generally. At Parkhurst anti-helicopter wires were erected over the exercise yard. In addition, evening exercise for category A prisoners was made unpredictable. On occasion, it would be cancelled at short notice. This was resented and the appellant amongst others protested.

On 6 July 1988 the appellant was found to be in the exercise yard despite a notice on his wing indicating 'No CAT A exercise'. He had done the same on a previous occasion. On 7 July the appellant was seen by the assistant governor, Mr Rees. The appellant was aggressive, unco-operative and uncompromising; he made it clear that he would continue with his actions. Mr Rees said that, if he persisted, one option would be to remove him to another prison.

On 8 July, the deputy governor, Mr Wood was in charge of the prison. On the recommendation of Mr Rees, he decided to transfer the appellant to Wormwood Scrubs pursuant to the provisions of CI 10/1974. In accordance with para 9 of that circular the decision was to transfer the appellant subject to r 43 and to apply to the regional director to continue segregation beyond the 24-hour period which could be imposed by Mr Wood.

Prison Officer Cooper was sent by Mr Wood to tell the appellant what was to happen and the reasons. The appellant had barricaded himself in his cell. The door had to be opened by means of a jack. The appellant then walked out voluntarily, was handcuffed and taken to a prison van for transfer. Mr Cooper believes that he carried out his instructions to tell the appellant the reasons for this transfer, but because of the circumstances cannot be absolutely sure.

The Divisional Court resolved some disputed issues of fact and before us counsel for

the appellant has not sought to challenge those findings. Indeed, in the absence of any
a cross-examination of the deponents he accepts that he must proceed on the basis of the
respondents' affidavits where there is conflict.

The findings of the Divisional Court and the respondents' evidence are to the following
effect. Mr Wood telephoned the regional office and obtained oral authorisation from the
deputy regional director for the appellant's transfer and for the continuation of his
segregation for not more than 28 days pursuant to CI 10/1974. That authorisation was
b put in writing by an entry in the register.

On arrival at Wormwood Scrubs the appellant was placed in the segregation unit
under r 43. On 11 July he was seen by Mrs Burnaby, a member of the board of visitors.
The Divisional Court found that she told the appellant the reasons for his segregation.
She signed the form authorising his segregation for up to 28 days, although this was
unnecessary since it had already been authorised by the deputy regional director.

c On 14 July the appellant asked and was allowed to see another member of the board
of visitors, Mr Baines, who advised him to press on with the application for judicial
review that he said he intended to make.

Subsequently the appellant made applications to the full board of visitors to see him
and to give reasons for his segregation at Wormwood Scrubs. He also petitioned the
Secretary of State.

d On 4 August the appellant was transferred from Wormwood Scrubs to Gartree Prison,
where he was placed on normal location. He had spent 28 days in segregation at
Wormwood Scrubs and it is that regime which is the basis of all his complaints.

The appellant sought judicial review of the decisions made on 8 July 1988 to transfer
and segregate him pursuant to CI 10/1974 and to continue the segregation for 28 days.
The case came before the Divisional Court (Ralph Gibson LJ and Nolan J) and on 28 July
e 1989 the appellant's application was dismissed. He now appeals against that dismissal.

The challenge to the lawfulness of the appellant's segregation was argued before us
under four distinct heads. It is necessary to consider each separately.

(1) Transfer under r 43
f First, counsel for the appellant submits para 9 of CI 10/1974 is contrary to the Prison
Rules 1964 in requiring that transfers will always be made subject to r 43. He advances
two arguments. The first is that para 9 fetters the discretion of the dispersal prison
governor by obliging him to apply r 43 to a prisoner whom he proposes to transfer. This
constitutes an unlawful interference with his discretion to decide whether the transferee
should be withdrawn from association on transfer or not. However, the arrangements
made available to a governor by CI 10/1974 are intended to apply only when he has
g already exercised his unfettered discretion and has decided that a troublemaker needs to
be removed from association for a cooling-off period. The only question then for that
governor, at prison A, is where the prisoner should be segregated. If he can be
accommodated in the segregation block of prison A without prejudicing good order and
discipline, CI 10/1974 is unnecessary. If not, arrangements under the circular are available
h so as to provide a cell at prison B in which he can be segregated. So far as his jurisdiction
extends, therefore, no occasion arises for the governor of prison A to make a second
decision as to the need for segregation. He has already decided the question. Had the
circular provided for special cells to be available in an annex to prison A under the same
governor, albeit some distance away from the main prison, no problem would have
arisen as to the propriety of the initial segregation in that annex. However, the
j arrangement provides for transfer to a different prison with a different governor. This
prompts counsel's second and more fundamental argument under this head.

He submits that the governor at the dispersal prison has no power to order a prisoner
to be made subject to r 43 at another prison. The jursidiction and powers of a governor
derive from the Prison Act 1952. Section 7(1) provides that every prison shall have a
governor. Section 12 provides as follows, so far as relevant:

'(1) A prisoner, whether sentenced to imprisonment or committed to prison on remand or pending trial or otherwise, may be lawfully confined in any prison.
(2) Prisoners shall be committed to such prisons as to the Secretary of State may from time to time direct; and may by direction of the Secretary of State be removed during the term of their imprisonment from the prison in which they are confined to any other prison . . .'

Section 13 of the 1952 Act provides:

'(1) Every prisoner shall be deemed to be in the legal custody of the governor of the prison.
(2) A prisoner shall be deemed to be in legal custody while he is confined in, or is being taken to or from, any prison and while he is working, or is for any other reason, outside the prison in the custody or under the control of an officer of the prison.'

The scheme of those sections is that each prison has its own governor who is in charge only of that prison and its inmates. Consistently with that scheme, r 43(1) permits a governor to remove a prisoner within his prison from association with other inmates there; r 43(3) empowers, and may on medical advice require, the governor to return the prisoner to association. Counsel for the appellant submits that paras (1) and (3) were clearly intended to apply to the same governor at the same prison and to the management solely of the inmates there. It cannot, he says, be open to the governor of prison A to order that a transferee to prison B shall there be subject to r 43(1). Nor could he be authorised to do so by the Secretary of State, because, as Ralph Gibson LJ said in the Divisional Court: 'Rule 43(1) provides that the power to segregate is given to the governor and no one else.'

In *Williams v Home Office (No 2)* [1981] 1 All ER 1211 Tudor Evans J took the view that the Secretary of State could exercise a residual power vested in him to initiate segregation under r 43. He said (at 1228–1229):

'It is quite clear that r 43 provides an administrative power to remove a prisoner wholly or in part from association with other prisoners and that in the vast majority of cases it is the governor who uses the power in the ordinary day-to-day life of the prison. I do not think that the initial exercise of power can only be for 24 hours. Rule 43(2) provides that a prisoner shall not be removed without the authority of the board of visitors or the Secretary of State for more than 24 hours. It seems to follow that if an authority is given the prisoner may initially be removed for more than 24 hours, but not for more than one month. There may therefore be an authority by the Secretary of State in the first instance to remove for one month. It would therefore not be correct to hold that the role of the Secretary of State is simply confined to supervising the exercise of the governor's power only after a period of 24 hours. But if the Secretary of State can give an initial authority for a month, is he precluded from initiating the process? Is this process simply confined to the governor? I do not think so. The language of r 43(1) is not sufficiently precise to lead to a construction that the initial exercise of power is confined to the governor. It would be surprising if the Secretary of State, who by statute is responsible for prisons and prisoners, could not tell a governor of a prison that a prisoner or a class of prisoners ought to be segregated in a r 43 regime.'

Later the judge went on (at 1229):

'As I have already said, the Secretary of State has an over-all responsibility for prisons and prisoners. Section 1 of the 1952 Act confers on him all the powers and jurisdiction in relation to prisons and prisoners which, before the Prison Act 1877, were exercisable by other authorities. It is clear that he is ultimately responsible for prisoners, including their control. By s 47(1) of the 1952 Act the Secretary of State a has power to make rules for the regulation and management of prisons and other places of detention and, amongst other matters, for the classification, discipline and control of prisoners. It was in pursuance of this power that the 1964 rules were made. I do not think that it can be said that he is unable to exercise power under the rules made by him and approved by Parliament. I hold that the Secretary of State has power to act under r 43 . . .'

b I see the force of the practical considerations which led Tudor Evans J to his conclusions. It would clearly make for administrative sense and convenience if the movement and segregation of prisoners were not hampered by technical problems as to which governor has the power of decision. But, whether or not the Secretary of State retains an overall power to segregate a prisoner, he cannot, in my judgment, exercise it under r 43 because that rule gives powers specifically to the governor. Rule 43(2) provides for authority to
c be given to the governor to segregate for more than 24 hours by either a visitor or the Secretary of State. But that authority is merely clothing for the governor. The decision 'under this rule' is still his. I do not accept, therefore, that the Secretary of State can act under r 43 to initiate segregation any more than can a member of the board of visitors. Counsel for the respondents did not seek to rely on the reasoning in *Williams v Home Office (No 2)* on this point.
d The Secretary of State can delegate to a governor his power under s 12(2) of the 1952 Act to transfer a prisoner to another prison. Under s 13(2) a transferee from prison A is deemed to be in the custody of the governor of that prison all the way to the gates of prison B. But, once he enters prison B, he is in the custody of the governor there. Counsel for the appellant submits that at that stage the governor of prison A no longer has any gubernatorial power over the transferee. Whether he is segregated or put into association
e becomes a question for the governor of prison B to decide.

In my judgment this analysis is correct. Rule 43 was clearly drafted to apply to the powers of one governor in one prison. Seeking to apply it to a transfer between two prisons under CI 10/1974 overstrains its language. Moreover, it would, at least in theory, undermine the authority of the governor at prison B if the disposition of a transferee at his prison were to be decided by the transferring governor. I say 'at least in theory'
f because para 5 of the circular envisages that the agreement or acquiescence of the governor at prison B should be sought by telephone before the transfer is made and he would be unlikely, if a cooling-off period were necessary, to differ from the transferring governor as to the need, at least initially, to segregate the transferee.

g *(2) Authority of regional director*
The second head of challenge is that para 9 of CI 10/1974 is contrary to r 43(2) in providing:

'. . . the necessary authority for [the prisoners'] continued segregation for the remainder of the 28 day period, will be obtained by the dispersal prison governor from the Regional Director (who will act on behalf of the Secretary of State).'

h Counsel for the appellant submits that the phrases 'remainder of the 28 day period' and 'will be obtained' exclude separate consideration by the regional director of the merits of each individual case. Paragraph 9 contemplates that authority to segregate for the full 28-day period will routinely be granted whenever a prison governor opts to use CI 10/1974, without any reasoned decision whether a lesser period would suffice. It could be
j that the perceived need to segregate the prisoner from fellow inmates at prison A will quickly evaporate when he reaches prison B. It may therefore be unnecessary to segregate him there for the maximum period of 28 days permitted under r 43(2) and assumed to be routine under para 9. Counsel for the appellant says that it is incumbent on the regional officer to make a reasoned decision not only whether authority for continued segregation should be granted but for how long it should be granted. It is true that the

governor at the receiving prison has discretion to return the prisoner to association, but
that does not relieve the regional officer from making a reasoned decision in the first *a*
place. Moreover if the regional officer has authorised segregation for up to 28 days, there
may tend in practice to be a presumption by the receiving governor against exercising
his power to end it under r 43(3). In my judgment the submissions of counsel for the
appellant under this head are well founded. I bear in mind that the words of CI 10/1974
are not to be construed like a statute. But it is not possible fairly to read words into para
9 consistent with the regional director making a reasoned decision as to the grant and the *b*
period of the required authority. It is common ground that he cannot merely rubber-
stamp the governor's request for authority, yet the plain purport of the words used is
that when the dispersal governor applies, he will be routinely granted authority for
continued segregation 'for the remainder of the 28 day period'. That is inconsistent with
the making of a reasoned decision.

c

(3) *Right to be heard*
   Next, counsel for the appellant contends that the appellant had a right to be heard and
was not heard before the regional director granted authority to extend the period of
segregation. The question is: does a prisoner have a right to make representations before
he is made subject to r 43? The Divisional Court held that he does not. I agree.
   Counsel for the appellant does not contend for a right to be heard before the governor *d*
makes his initial decision to invoke r 43(1) for 24 hours. He concedes that such a decision
will usually be a matter of urgency and to seek the views of the prisoner who is, ex
hypothesi, considered troublesome and a threat to good order and discipline is unrealistic.
By that concession counsel recognises that the application of natural justice principles,·
and in particular the right to be heard, must depend in each situation on the subject
matter and the circumstances.   *e*
   This was made clear in *Payne v Lord Harris of Greenwich* [1981] 2 All ER 842, [1981] 1
WLR 754. A prisoner sought a declaration that he was entitled to be given the reasons
for refusing him parole so that he could make representations in rebuttal. This court
rejected his appeal. Lord Denning MR said ([1981] 2 All ER 842 at 845, [1981] 1 WLR
754 at 757):
                                                                                    f
   'No doubt it is the duty of all those concerned, from the member of the local
   review committee, to the Parole Board, to the Secretary of State, to act fairly. That is
   the simple precept which now governs the administrative procedure of all public
   bodies. But the duty to act fairly cannot be set down in a series of set propositions.
   Each case depends on its own circumstances.'

Shaw LJ said ([1981] 2 All ER 842 at 850, [1981] 1 WLR 754 at 764):   *g*

   'In the well-known case of *R v Gaming Board of Great Britain, ex parte Benaim* [1970]
   2 All ER 528 at 533, [1970] QB 417 at 430, Lord Denning MR said: "It is not
   possible to lay down rigid rules as to when the principles of natural justice are to
   apply; nor as to their scope and extent. Everything depends on the subject-matter."
   In a context in which the public interest may be put at risk by the inopportune *h*
   release of a prisoner on licence, no constraints or pressures should weigh on the
   Parole Board in coming to what must in the end be a decision in which expediency
   must be an important influence.'

Brightman LJ referred to the same passage from *Benaim*'s case and said ([1981] 2 All ER
842 at 852, [1981] 1 WLR 754):   *j*

   'The scope and extent of the principles of natural justice depend on the subject
   matter to which they are sought to be applied . . .'

Apart from the urgency of decisions under r 43, there may well be other public policy
grounds for not giving reasons in advance to the prisoner so as to enable him to make

representations. Giving reasons would often require unwise disclosure of information.
a Such disclosure could reveal to prisoners the extent of the governor's knowledge about
their activities. It would reveal the source of such information, thereby putting
informants at risk. It could cause an immediate escalation of trouble.

Counsel for the appellant claims, however, that after the governor has ordered a 24-
hour segregation under r 43(1) the urgency is abated and although some information
may need to be withheld from the prisoner on public policy grounds, he should still be
b heard as to why the period of segregation should not be extended. In fact there is still
urgency at that stage because the decision whether to authorise continued segregation
has to be made within 24 hours.

Counsel for the appellant relies on *Leech v Deputy Governor of Parkhurst Prison* [1988] 1
All ER 485, [1988] AC 533. There a prisoner complained of impropriety in proceedings
before a deputy governor under the Prison Rules 1964 (rr 47, 48 and 49). The House of
c Lords held that the court has jurisdiction to entertain an application for judicial review
of a prison governor's award where the principles of natural justice have been breached.
However, there was never any issue in that case as to the application of those principles.
They are written into r 49 in the following terms:

'Rights of prisoners charged
d   **49.**—(1) Where a prisoner is charged with an offence against discipline, he shall
be informed of the charge as soon as possible and, in any case, before the time when
it is inquired into by the governor.
(2) At any inquiry into a charge against a prisoner he shall be given a full
opportunity of hearing what is alleged against him and of presenting his own case.'

No such provisions are laid down in relation to r 43. Thus *Leech's* case, whilst relevant
e to the scope of the court's jurisdiction, does not assist counsel for the appellant as to a
right to be heard under r 43. On the contrary, the specific inclusion of natural justice
requirements in r 49 and their absence from r 43 afford powerful support to the
respondents' case. In disciplinary proceedings which may result in punitive action, the
full panoply of natural justice principles is appropriate and Parliament has provided that
f it should apply. Although the consequences of r 43 are in some respects akin to those
imposed as punishment, the object of the rule is not punitive. Indeed, where it is invoked
at the prisoner's request it is specifically aimed at protecting him from illegal punishment
at the hands of fellow prisoners. So, in the context of r 43, although the governor and the
regional director must act fairly and make reasoned decisions, the principles of natural
justice are not invoked in the rules.

g Instead, alternative safeguards are provided to protect the prisoner's rights. Segregation
can only exceed 24 hours by authority from the Secretary of State or the board of visitors
(r 43(2)). By r 43(3) the governor may in his discretion terminate the segregation at any
time. The prisoner has the right to see the governor and a member of the board of
visitors (r 8). The latter is required to hear any complaint or request the prisoner wishes
to make (r 95(1)). The prisoner may petition the Secretary of State (r 7(1)).

h Counsel for the appellant relied on the decision of the Supreme Court of Canada in
Cardinal v Director of Kent Institution (1985) 24 DLR (4th) 44, a case also concerned with
the segregation of prisoners. Regulations provided for a classification board to review the
segregation of any prisoner at least once a month and recommend whether it should end.
The director declined for some four months to accept the board's repeated recommendations to end the appellants' segregation. The court granted the appellants' application to
j be returned into association, partly because the director had not given his reasons for
rejecting the recommendations of the board or heard the appellants' representations.
Apart from the obvious difference in circumstances from those in the present case, there
is no indication in the Canadian report that the regulations provided, as do the Prison
Rules 1964, a right to be heard in other contexts and other opportunities for prisoners to
air their views and complaints.

Reliance was also placed on *Kanda v Government of Malaya* [1962] AC 322; but there, art 135(2) of the Malayan Constitution specifically ordained that before a police officer could be dismissed he had a right to be heard.

By contrast, in *Williams v Home Office (No 2)* [1981] 1 All ER 1211 Tudor Evans J had to consider problems similar to those arising in the present case. The appellant had brought an action for damages for false imprisonment and for a declaration that a Home Office circular setting up a control unit with segregation for troublemakers was ultra vires. One issue was whether the prisoner had a right to be heard before transfer to the unit. Tudor Evans J said (at 1247):

> 'It seems to me that Parliament, as reflected in the Prison Act and the Prison Rules, drew a clear distinction between r 43 cases and cases of offences against discipline. In the former case the prisoner has no voice in the decision which is to be taken. When a man is transferred to a segregation unit he is not able to make any representation. In para 166 of the Radzinowicz report [report of a subcommittee of the Advisory Council on the Penal System (chairman Professor Radzinowicz) (1968)] it is said that before transferring a prisoner to a segregation unit it is not necessary for them to have been guilty of an offence, and it therefore follows that there is no right to be heard or to make any representation against the decision ... In all the circumstances of this case, I do not consider that the principles of natural justice required that the plaintiff should have been given notice of what was intended and the opportunity to make representations that he should not be transferred to the unit. Such a step is not within the contemplation of the Prison Act or the Prison Rules and would be damaging to the exercise of the administrative power under r 43.'

In the Divisional Court in the present case, Ralph Gibson LJ said:

> 'In our view, having due regard to the interests of the prisoner and of society at large, including the due administration of the prisons, fairness does not require that a prisoner be given the right to be heard before a decision affecting him is made under r 43.'

With that view I agree for the reasons already set out.

(4) *Reasons*

The appellant's fourth and final complaint is that he should have been, but was not, given the reasons for his transfer and segregation after, if not before, they occurred. On this issue the Divisional Court held (a) that he was entitled to know the reasons for invoking CI 10/1974 but (b) that he did know and was specifically told.

As to (b) I fully agree. The appellant knew very well from his discussion with Mr Rees on 7 July what complaint the authorities made against him. When he made it clear on that occasion that he would continue his actions he was plainly told that one option would be to transfer him. Further, Mr Cooper believes that he told the appellant the reasons for transfer on 8 July although he cannot now be sure. The clinching matter, however, is that the Divisional Court accepted that Mrs Burnaby told the appellant the reasons for his transfer and segregation when she saw him at Wormwood Scrubs.

As to (a), entitlement in law to be given reasons, I would differ from the Divisional Court. No doubt in many cases the governor will be able, as here, to give reasons at the time of the decision or shortly after. But the same considerations of public policy as persuaded me, and indeed the Divisional Court, to hold that reasons are not in law required as a matter of course before a decision to segregate may apply with equal force after the decision. Again, the guiding factors must be the subject matter and the circumstances.

Counsel for the respondents argued that there is no general rule in public law that reasons must be given for administrative decisions. He supported that proposition by

reference to *Payne v Lord Harris of Greenwich* [1981] 2 All ER 842, [1981] 1 WLR 754, *R*
a *v Secretary of State for Social Services, ex p Connolly* [1986] 1 All ER 998 at 1006, [1986] 1
WLR 421 at 431 and *Public Service Board of New South Wales v Osmond* [1987] LRC (Const)
681. The appellant has the right under the rules to see a member of the board of visitors.
If he does not know the reason for his segregation he can ask. The member can then
inquire of the governor and relay to the prisoner any information which security permits
to be given.

b   I would not be prepared to hold that in all cases a prisoner has a legal right to be given
the reason for his segregation.

One further ground of complaint was raised in the Divisional Court. It was a
contention that the governor has used r 43 improperly to avoid bringing disciplinary
proceedings. He had achieved the punitive effect of such proceedings without bringing
them. This argument was abandoned; rightly so in my view, since there was no evidence
c to support it.

In summary, I would uphold only the first two of the appellant's four heads of
challenge.

Did the appellant suffer injustice?
d   Both these successful challenges are based on the chosen wording in para 9 of CI 10/
1974. However, the purpose of the circular could have been achieved perfectly lawfully.
The decision whether to segregate the transferee at the receiving prison could have been
required to be made by the receiving governor. Alternatively, arrangements might have
been made to transfer a troublesome prisoner from the main dispersal prison to an annex
under the control of the same governor. Regrettably, the draftsman seems to have fallen
between two stools. It is said that cells should be 'set aside for the use of governors of
e dispersal prisons', that transfer is to be at such a governor's discretion, that he is to be
'regarded as having an automatic lien on' cells but the transferee is to be in the custody of
the local prison governor. Conversely, despite having to accept the transferee into his
custody, the latter governor receives him already under r 43 and probably, by the time
of his arrival, with a 28-day authorisation for extended segregation from the regional
f director. Thus custody of the prisoner and the decision as to the conditions of that
custody have been inappropriately allotted to different governors.

As to the second limb of para 9, concerning extension of segregation, words could have
been used to accord with r 43(2). Had that limb read 'and authority for any continued
segregation should, in accordance with Rule 43(2), be sought from the Regional Director
who will act on behalf of the Secretary of State', it would not have been bad on its face
g which, as drafted, it is.

However, in my view no injustice seems to have resulted to the appellant in the
present case. The governor of Wormwood Scrubs was consulted about his transfer in
accordance with para 5 of CI 10/1974. He acquiesced and made out a fresh form 1299A
although one had already been completed at Parkhurst. Form 1299A is prescribed by
para 8 of CI 15/1974, a circular dealing with the procedure under r 43. Paragraph 8 reads
h as follows:

'Authority for segregation beyond 24 hours will normally be obtained from a
member of the board of visitors. This may be done by telephone initially; but
written confirmation should be sought as quickly as possible, and certainly not later
than 24 hours after the receipt of oral authority. For this purpose a new form
F1299A is being introduced. A copy of this is attached as Annex A ... The form
j should be completed in duplicate. One copy should be sent to regional office; the
second copy should be placed in the prisoner's F1150 ... It is important that an
adequate description of the reasons for segregation should be given. It is not
sufficient merely to record "own request" or "for good order and discipline". Some
account of the circumstances is required. Where authority for segregation is

obtained from the regional director or headquarters, acting on behalf of the Secretary
of State, eg under paragraph 9 of CI 10/74, the date of authorisation, the name of *a*
the authorising officer and his location should be recorded at the bottom of F1299A.'

The Wormwood Scrubs F1299A was given to Mrs Burnaby who, having been told the
reasons for the appellant's segregation and having seen and told the appellant himself,
proceeded to authorise an extension of segregation for a month. Had procedure under
para 9 of CI 10/1974 not been flawed, I do not think that the outcome would have been
any different. It is highly unlikely in my judgment that the governor of Wormwood *b*
Scrubs would have been willing to place in association with his own prisoners an
aggrieved troublemaker from another prison deemed by the governor there to be in
need of segregation and additionally aggrieved by being transferred.

Again, if the discretion as to the period of segregation to be authorised by the regional
director had been unfettered in accordance with r 43(2), I think it unlikely that a period
less than the permitted 28 days would have been chosen. Only at governor level could it *c*
be known whether or not it was appropriate for the transferee to be either released into
association or returned to Parkhurst.

Jurisdiction

In these circumstances, to what relief, if any, is the appellant entitled? First it is *d*
necessary to consider the court's jurisdiction. In *R v Hull Prison Board of Visitors, ex p St
Germain* [1979] 1 All ER 701, [1979] QB 425 this court held that challenge by way of
judicial review was open in respect of decisions of boards of visitors in disciplinary
proceedings. In *Leech v Deputy Governor of Parkhurst Prison* [1988] 1 All ER 485, [1988]
AC 533 the House of Lords held that judicial review was similarly available in respect of
a disciplinary award made by a prison governor, thereby overruling a decision of this *e*
court to the contrary in *R v Deputy Governor of Camphill Prison, ex p King* [1984] 3 All ER
897, [1985] QB 735. In this case the appellant claims still wider jurisdiction to grant
judicial review of managerial decisions relating to the transfer and segregation of
prisoners. Before the Divisional Court counsel for the respondents contended that the
court had no jurisdiction to entertain an application for judicial review of such decisions.
That argument was rejected in principle by the Divisional Court although no relief was *f*
granted to the appellant. The argument has not been renewed as a legal submission
before this court. Instead, counsel for the respondents, whilst conceding that the court
has such jurisdiction, sought to urge the utmost circumspection in exercising it. He
submitted that the court should distance itself from operational and managerial decisions
in prisons by declining to entertain direct challenges to them. The court's supervisory
jurisdiction should be invoked only after rejection of a complaint to the board of visitors *g*
or of a petition to the Secretary of State, and only by review of such rejection.

It is true that the court will not generally grant judicial review if an applicant has not
exhausted established appeal procedures, although it will do so in exceptional
circumstances: see *R v Chief Constable of the Merseyside Police, ex p Calveley* [1986] 1 All ER
257, [1986] QB 424 and *R v Secretary of State for the Home Dept, ex p Swati* [1986] 1 All ER
717, [1986] 1 WLR 477. A prisoner aggrieved at being 'put on r 43' has avenues by *h*
which to seek redress. He may complain to the visitors or petition the Home Secretary.
This appellant did both. But those avenues do not constitute established appeal procedures.
In *Leech's* case [1988] 1 All ER 485 at 496, [1988] AC 533 at 562 Lord Bridge made it clear
that the mere existence of other remedies did not oust the court's jurisdiction:

'To invoke the Secretary of State's general statutory duty to ensure compliance *j*
with prison legislation to oust the jurisdiction of the court on the ground that the
Secretary of State's duty obviates the need for any such jurisdiction in relation to the
governor's awards is to stand the doctrine by which the limits of jurisdiction in this
field are determined on its head. When the court comes to the question of how to
exercise discretion, it may well be proper to ask whether, in the particular case, the

a court's intervention is needed. But neither principle nor authority lend any support
to the view that the court must identify some element of necessity as the basis of its
jurisdiction. Just as the allegation of a wrong of a kind recognised as remediable by
private law is sufficient to found the court's ordinary jurisdiction, so the allegation
of a wrong of a kind recognised as remediable by public law is sufficient to found
jurisdiction in judicial review . . .'

b Lord Oliver too rejected the contention that the self-contained nature of prison
administration, providing for overview by the Secretary of State, obviates the need for
intervention by the court. He said ([1988] 1 All ER 485 at 511, [1988] AC 533 at 581):

'There is in my judgment, a basic fallacy in this approach, quite apart from the
fact that it is entirely unsupported by authority. It has never previously, so far as I
am aware, been suggested that the mere existence of an alternative remedy, of itself
c and by itself, ousts the jurisdiction of the court, though it may be a powerful factor
when it comes to the question of whether the discretion to review should be
exercised.'

Lord Bridge also pointed out that a review by the Secretary of State of a governor's
disciplinary award under r 50 might well provide an inadequate remedy since the
d Secretary of State could only remit or mitigate the award. He could not quash it, so it
would remain on the prisoner's record. In the present case Ralph Gibson LJ said:

'In our judgment the remedy by way of petition and by judicial review of the
decision of the Secretary of State in the case of the unlawful use of power under r 43,
possibly resulting in prolonged segregation of a prisoner without his consent, is no
more an adequate substitute for judicial review of the governor's decision, or of the
e decisions to grant authority for continued segregation, than in the case of review of
a governor's decision on a disciplinary charge under r 50.'

I agree with that conclusion, and accordingly cannot accept counsel's argument for
confining judicial review to supervision of 'second-stage' decisions by visitors or by the
Secretary of State. Of course, as both Lord Bridge and Lord Oliver recognised in the
f passages cited, the question whether any relief and what relief should be granted is a
matter of discretion in each case. Considerations of public policy may well arise in
relation to prison management which would not arise elsewhere. The need to maintain
good order and discipline and the need to make speedy decisions often in an emergency
are important considerations in the special context of prison management. I would agree
therefore with counsel's less bold proposition for the respondents, that the court should
g approach the exercise of discretion with great caution. The well-known proposition that
managers should be left to manage applies a fortiori in regard to prisons, save where a
clear case is made out for relief ex debito justitiae.

Remedies
h In the Divisional Court, and indeed at the start of this appeal, the only relief sought by
the appellant in public law consisted of certain declarations. Since CI 10/1974 is still in
force and being implemented, I consider that the appellant is entitled to declarations in
accordance with the two findings in his favour made above concerning that circular.
Originally, he did not seek to have quashed the orders which placed him under r 43
and extended its operational period. Presumably this was because, once he had been
j moved to Gartree, the segregation at Wormwood Scrubs was mere history. However,
counsel for the appellant applied for leave, which we granted, to amend his notice of
appeal to seek certiorari and for the orders to be quashed. This was solely to lay the
foundation for his private law claim for damages. During argument, counsel for the
appellant accepted that it was or may be necessary for the orders to be quashed before the
damages claim could succeed, whatever other obstacles it might encounter.

For my part, I would not exercise the court's discretion in the public law field to grant certiorari to quash these orders. As indicated earlier, I do not consider that the appellant   *a* has shown that he suffered any injustice. Had the procedure for deciding whether and for how long he should be segregated been impeccable, I do not, for reasons already given, consider that the outcome would have been different. If, therefore, it is necessary for the orders to be quashed before damages could be awarded, I would hold that the damages claim fails in limine.

b

Damages for false imprisonment

However, there are two other issues relevant to the appellant's private law claim for damages. (1) Can an action for false imprisonment succeed where it relies on a breach of the Prison Rules 1964 to rebut a defence of lawful detention? (2) In the present case, is there any basis for contending that the appellant was unlawfully imprisoned within   *c* imprisonment?

(1) At the end of the hearing the sole basis of the claim for damages was false imprisonment. The claim for misfeasance in a public office was rightly abandoned since there was no evidence to support it. The appellant claims that he was falsely imprisoned in that the procedure whereby he was segregated was flawed and he was thereby deprived of those residual liberties, especially freedom of association, which he would otherwise   *d* have enjoyed even in prison. Counsel for the appellant argues that s 12 of the Prison Act 1952 does not afford the respondents a defence because that Act and the 1964 rules should be read together and there were breaches of r 43. He does not suggest that a claim for damages could be based directly on breaches of the 1964 rules, but relies on the breaches to deprive the respondents of a defence to the tort of false imprisonment.

That a plaintiff cannot rely on a breach of the rules to establish or support a cause of   *e* action is supported by a number of authorities, including *Arbon v Anderson* [1943] 1 All ER 154, [1943] KB 252 and *Becker v Home Office* [1972] 2 All ER 676, [1972] 2 QB 407. In *Arbon v Anderson* Goddard LJ said ([1943] 1 All ER 154 at 156, [1943] KB 252 at 254):

'With regard to the prison rules, it would be enough to say that I find there were no breaches; but in case a higher court should take a different view, I should say   *f* that, in my opinion, neither do these rules confer rights upon prisoners which can be enforced by action. They are made under the Prison Act, 1898, s. 2, for the "government" of prisons ... The real question which falls to be determined is whether it is intended by the statute to confer an individual right. I am clearly of opinion, that neither the Prison Act nor the rules were intended to confer any such right.'

g

There is no reason to take any different view about rules made under the Prison Act 1952 which, by s 47(1) of that Act, may be made by the Secretary of State 'for the regulation and management of prisons ... and for the classification, treatment, employment, discipline and control of persons required to be detained therein.'

In *Becker v Home Office* [1972] 2 All ER 676, [1972] 2 QB 407 the plaintiff complained   *h* inter alia that, whilst she was a prisoner, a cheque had been delivered to the prison for her and had not been delivered to her or otherwise dealt with in accordance with r 42(3) of the Prison Rules 1964. Lord Denning MR said ([1972] 2 All ER 676 at 682, [1972] 2 QB 407 at 418):

'The Prison Rules are regulatory directions only. Even if they are not observed, they do not give rise to a cause of action. So I hold that in point of law Mrs Becker   *j* cannot claim.'

Edmund Davies LJ said ([1972] 2 All ER 676 at 683, [1972] 2 QB 407 at 420):

'... I hold (as Lord Denning MR has done) that a breach of these Prison Rules a does not per se, create any civil liability at the suit of a party who claims to have been damnified thereby.'

Stephenson LJ agreed with both.

In *Williams v Home Office (No 2)* [1981] 1 All ER 1211 at 1218 Tudor Evans J, having referred to these authorities, posed the very question which arises in the present case. He said:

b 'But, although the plaintiff cannot support his action by relying on a breach of the rules, it is submitted that the defendant cannot justify the detention of the plaintiff in a regime which constituted a breach of the rules. On this part of the case I shall have to consider the status of the Prison Rules and whether any breaches of them can have any effect of the lawfulness of the plaintiff's detention.'

c He said (at 1240–1241):

'What, if at all, is the relevance of the conditions of imprisonment to the lawfulness of the detention? (iii) What, if at all, is the relevance of a breach or non-compliance with the Prison Rules with respect to the issue of lawful detention? Section 12(1) of the Act empowers the Secretary of State lawfully to confine a prisoner in any prison. Counsel for the plaintiff submits, as I understand him, that
d the subsection is concerned only with the place of imprisonment and not with any tortious act done within it. This means that the subsection is not capable of justifying the detention of a prisoner when the nature of the imprisonment differs from that in the remainder of the system and where there is a breach of the Prison Rules. In my judgment, the sentence of the court and the provisions of s 12(1) always afford a defence to an action of false imprisonment. The sentence justifies the fact of
e imprisonment and the subsection justifies the confinement of a prisoner in any prison. How then can it be unjustifiable and unlawful to confine him there? I accept the submission of counsel for the defendant that the sentence of the court and the provisions of s 12(1) provide a defence to this action . . .'

Having referred again to *Arbon v Anderson* and *Becker v Home Office*, Tudor Evans J stated
f his conclusion on this issue as follows (at 1242):

'The observations in both of these cases were concerned with the question whether a prisoner could sue for a breach of the rules, but they indicate the nature of the rules. In my judgment, a breach of the rules is not relevant to the question, can the defendant justify in law the detention of the plaintiff. The defendant pleads the sentence of the court, the Prison Act and Rules in the amended defence. Reliance
g on the rules was unnecessary. It is the sentence of the court and the Act that are relevant to the issue of lawful detention and not the rules.'

I agree with those observations. In my judgment, decisions made under the Prison Rules which are regulatory and bear on administrative action in the public law domain, are open to judicial review and can give rise in an appropriate case to public law remedies.
h But, just as a breach of them cannot form the basis of a private law claim for damages, nor can such a breach defeat the statutory defence to a claim for false imprisonment that the detention was justified under s 12 of the Prison Act 1952.

(2) More broadly the question raised is whether an action for false imprisonment can lie at all when the plaintiff is confined in a prison pursuant to s 12. Can there, in short, be false imprisonment within lawful imprisonment?

j Counsel for the appellant bases his argument on the well-known principle that a convicted prisoner 'retains all civil rights which are not taken away expressly or by necessary implication': see *Raymond v Honey* [1982] 1 All ER 756 at 759, [1983] 1 AC 1 at 10 per Lord Wilberforce. He submits that to segregate a prisoner is to deprive him of such rights of movement and association as would normally be retained by a prisoner. If

it is done without lawful excuse it amounts to false imprisonment. He relies on certain
venerable cases.

    In *Cobbett v Grey* (1850) 4 Exch 729, 154 ER 1409 the plaintiff had been committed to
prison for failing to pay costs in a Chancery suit. Whilst he was in custody in that part of
the prison appropriate to his offence, an order was made compelling him to file a schedule
of his property. When he failed to do so he was removed to a part of the prison set aside
for class 1 debtors, being those who had failed to provide a schedule when ordered.
Conditions there were said to be 'more confined, dark, and insalubrious'. The plaintiff's
action for damages against the Secretary of State and the prison keeper for false
imprisonment and assault was tried by Pollock CB and a jury. He directed a verdict for
the defendant and the plaintiff moved for a new trial. The essence of the plaintiff's case
was that he had been committed to prison for not paying costs. It was therefore wrong
for him to be confined in that part of the prison reserved for those committed on the
ground that they had failed to file a schedule. In ordering a fresh trial Parke B said (4
Exch 729 at 736, 154 ER 1409 at 1412):

> 'The removal of a person from one part of a prison to another, in which by law he
> ought not to be confined, is primâ facie a trespass.'

Although some of the reasoning is difficult to follow from the report, it is clear that the
decision was based on the strict classification of prisoners and the parts of a prison in
which they could lawfully be confined. Even so, Pollock CB, who sat on the application
despite having been the trial judge, was unrepentant. He said (4 Exch 729 at 745, 154
ER 1409 at 1416):

> 'If [a gaoler] confines [prisoners] in wrong places, with reference to certain rules
> and regulations made by the Secretary of State, I think that is a question between
> the gaoler and the superior authority who gives out those rules and issues those
> commands; and that prisoners do not get a right of action for false imprisonment
> merely because they are put in a part of a gaol called A, instead of being put in
> another part called B—in ward A instead of ward B.'

Whatever was the correct view under the strict classifications in 1850, the arguments on
which that case turned are no longer relevant in view of the broad scope of s 12 of the
Prison Act 1952.

    In *Osborne v Milman* (1886) 17 QBD 514 the plaintiff had practised as a solicitor
although not qualified to do so. He was committed to Holloway prison, where he was
treated as a convicted criminal and placed on the criminal side. In an action for false
imprisonment, he claimed that as he had not been convicted of any criminal offence his
detention on that side of the prison was unlawful. The trial judge upheld that submission
and awarded damages, ruling that there was no statutory power to detain the plaintiff on
the criminal side. In general, the decision turned on the statutory requirement to place a
prisoner only in that part of the prison appropriate to his classification.

    That this is the proper reading of these two cases is clear from the decision of Goddard
LJ in *Arbon v Anderson* [1943] 1 All ER 154 at 156, [1943] KB 252 at 254–255, where he
said:

> 'It is significant that there is no trace of any action based on alleged breaches of
> prison rules ever having been brought in this country unless *Cobbett* v. *Grey* and
> *Osborne* v. *Milman* are to be so regarded, though, in my opinion, they are clearly
> distinguishable. The former case related to imprisonment in the wrong place.
> Under a rule having the force of statute different parts of prisons were set apart for
> the imprisonment of debtors of different categories. The plaintiff being in one of
> those parts was—it was assumed wrongly—removed by the warden of the prison to
> another and worse place of detention and this was held to be a trespass in spite of a
> somewhat vigorous dissent by Pollock, C.B. In *Osborne* v. *Milman*, the plaintiff was

imprisoned in Holloway Gaol and treated as a criminal prisoner. He contended that he was imprisoned on civil process and, therefore, ought to have been treated as a first class misdemeanant which is the only form of imprisonment that can be imposed on a prisoner on civil process. DENMAN, J., decided in his favour and awarded him damages. On appeal this decision was reversed on the ground that the prisoner was properly treated as a criminal prisoner, though obviously, if the court had thought that he should have been treated as a civil prisoner, the judgment would have been upheld. But both these cases relate to the nature of the imprisonment. Here the prisoners were lawfully imprisoned and the questions relate to the conditions of their imprisonment.'

In *Williams v Home Office (No 2)* [1981] 1 All ER 1211 at 1227 Tudor Evans J referred to that part of the judgment in *Arbon v Anderson* as follows:

'Counsel for the plaintiff submitted that the reference in this passage to the "nature of the imprisonment" means that Goddard LJ was of the opinion that the earlier cases were not only dealing on the issue in tort with the wrong place of confinement, but with the nature of the imprisonment in the sense of the conditions of the imprisonment. I do not read the judgment in this way. I think that Goddard LJ was merely saying that the nature of the imprisonment was tortious because it was in a place not authorised by law.'

After indicating that the modern textbook writers regard the older cases as authority for the limited proposition identified by Goddard LJ (and they still do), Tudor Evans J concluded:

'I hold that there is no authority in modern law to support the plaintiff's submission that although a detention may be lawful it can become unlawful if the nature (meaning the conditions) of the imprisonment changes.'

Further authority for the proposition that variation in the conditions of confinement adverse to the prisoner will not found an action for false imprisonment is provided by the judgment of Mann J in *R v Gartree Prison Board of Visitors, ex p Sears* (1985) Times, 20 March. The applicant for judicial review sought damages in respect of eight days' cellular confinement and eight days' loss of privileges awarded by the board of visitors. Mann J said:

'If a person is imprisoned in the place where he is lawfully so imprisoned, then it does not seem to me that a variation in conditions of confinement can constitute the tort of false imprisonment at common law.'

The judgments of Tudor Evans and Mann JJ were considered by this court in *Middleweek v Chief Constable of the Merseyside Police* (1985) [1990] 3 All ER 662, [1990] 3 WLR 481, in which Ackner LJ gave the judgment of the court on 24 July 1985. The plaintiff was a solicitor who had been arrested by the police on suspicion of theft. He sought damages for various torts including false imprisonment and his case was tried by judge and jury. One issue in this court was whether, assuming that he was lawfully arrested, the judge was justified in leaving to the jury the issue whether detaining him in a police cell was reasonable. Ackner LJ observed that had the judge's attention been drawn to the decided cases he would not have left that issue to the jury and he should not have done so. Ackner LJ referred to *Williams v Home Office (No 2)* and *Sears's* case with apparent approval, but did recognise one possible qualification to the general rule that conditions of imprisonment will not found an action for false imprisonment if detention of the plaintiff is lawful. He quoted from the judgments in the Divisional Court in an application for habeas corpus in *R v Comr of Police of the Metropolis, ex p Nahar* (1983) Times, 28 May. Both Stephen Brown and McCullough JJ indicated that there must be some minimum standard in the conditions of prison detention below which that detention would be unlawful. Ackner LJ went on ([1990] 3 All ER 662 at 668, [1990] 3 WLR 481 at 487):

'We agree with the views expressed by the Divisional Court that it must be possible to conceive of hypothetical cases in which the conditions of detention are so intolerable as to render the detention unlawful and thereby provide a remedy to the prisoner in damages for false imprisonment. A person lawfully detained in a prison cell would, in our judgment, cease to be so lawfully detained if the conditions in that cell were such as to be seriously prejudicial to his health if he continued to occupy it, eg because it became and remained seriously flooded, or contained a fractured gas pipe allowing gas to escape into the cell. We do not therefore accept as an absolute proposition that, if detention is initially lawful, it can never become unlawful by reason of changes in the conditions of imprisonment.'

Presumably, this proposition must depend on an implied requirement that conditions in prison must not be intolerable. Alternatively, it may be based on the provision in the Bill of Rights (1688) prohibiting the infliction of 'cruele and unusuale punishments', an argument addressed to Tudor Evans J in *Williams v Home Office (No 2)*. Whatever the legal basis for an action relying on intolerable conditions, it would not seem to be an action for false imprisonment simpliciter. The tort of false imprisonment is constituted by a complete deprivation of liberty for any time, however short, without lawful excuse (see *Clerk and Lindsell on Torts* (16th edn, 1989) p 972). It is the deprivation of liberty to move at will which is the essence of the tort, not intolerable conditions.

Since *Middleweek's* case there have been the judgment of the Divisional Court in the present case and the judgments of this court in *Weldon v Home Office* [1990] 3 All ER 762, [1990] 3 WLR 465. In the latter case Ralph Gibson LJ gave the first judgment and conveniently summarised what he had said in the present case and went on to consider Weldon's appeal. The latter raised a preliminary point, whether a claim for damages for false imprisonment against a prison officer should be struck out of the statement of claim on the grounds that in law it is not possible for a prison officer to commit the tort of false imprisonment against a convicted prisoner lawfully in custody in prison. Ralph Gibson LJ said ([1990] 3 All ER 672 at 681–682, [1990] 3 WLR 465 at 475):

'In *R v Deputy Governor of Parkhurst Prison, ex p Hague* (1989) Independent, 11 August, the Divisional Court, Nolan J and myself, in a passage of the judgment which was obiter and not necessary for the decision, expressed the opinion that an act, unauthorised but in good faith, which caused the prisoner to lose part of his remaining freedom as a prisoner and subjected him to the worsened conditions of segregation, was not an actionable wrong of false imprisonment. It is not necessary, in my judgment, on this appeal, for this court to reach a final conclusion of that question. It is sufficient to say that it is not clear to me, merely by reference to the nature of the tort of false imprisonment itself, having due regard to any appropriate policy considerations, that the court must hold on an application to strike out that a convicted prisoner cannot in any circumstances claim against a prison officer for false imprisonment. The allegations made by the plaintiff sufficiently allege want of good faith on the part of the prison officers concerned, if that is, as I am disposed to think that it is, a necessary ingredient in the claim.'

Ralph Gibson LJ went on to consider the 'intolerable conditions' factor referred to in *Middleweek's* case and said ([1990] 3 All ER 672 at 685–686, [1990] 3 WLR 465 at 479–480):

'Lastly, it was submitted that the decision in *Middleweek's* case was directed to, and should be restricted to, a prisoner under arrest and is not applicable to a convicted prisoner. I do not accept that submission. I see no reason why the principles stated in *Ex p Nahar* should not apply to the detention of a convicted

prisoner who is confined in intolerable circumstances on the ground that Parliament
a cannot have intended the 1952 Act, and the 1964 rules made thereunder, to
authorise confinement of a prisoner in physical circumstances which are intolerable.
The question whether a prisoner so confined is entitled thereby to damages for false
imprisonment, irrespective of the good faith of those who have been responsible for
his continued confinement, was not considered in *Ex p Nahar*, which was not a case
of false imprisonment. The prisoner's remedy in a particular case might not go
b beyond the making of an order that the prisoner be no longer confined in those
intolerable circumstances. For the reasons explained above I think that the better
view is that, to support a claim for false imprisonment on such a ground, it would
at least be necessary for the complainant to prove that the defendant had continued
the confinement of the prisoner in intolerable circumstances with knowledge that
the circumstances were intolerable. In this case, the allegation is that the intolerable
c conditions were imposed on the plaintiff deliberately with knowledge of them. It is
not necessary for the purpose of this case to deal more precisely with the necessary
elements of a claim based on this ground.'

Thus, the action contemplated by Ralph Gibson LJ involved adding to the ordinary
definition of false imprisonment not only detention under intolerable conditions but
d knowledge on the part of the defendant that the conditions were intolerable, ie bad faith.
Again I observe that bad faith has never been a necessary ingredient in the tort of false
imprisonment. Moreover, if the plaintiff can show bad faith his proper cause of action
would probably be for misfeasance in a public office, assuming that he could bring his
case within the criteria laid down in *Bourgoin SA v Ministry of Agriculture Fisheries and
Food* [1985] 3 All ER 585, [1986] QB 716.
e I am not persuaded by the argument which appealed to Parker LJ in *Weldon v Home
Office*, that if no action for false imprisonment can be brought by a prisoner serving a
sentence even though he be confined in unusual and disagreeable conditions, he would
be at the mercy of his fellow prisoners, who could lock him in some confined space with
impunity. In such a situation an action for false imprisonment would surely lie (for what
f it was worth), since the fellow prisoners would have no defence under s 12 of the Prison
Act 1952.
On the authorities, therefore, the position is as follows. On the view most favourable
to a potential prisoner plaintiff, he could only bring an action for false imprisonment if
he was detained under intolerable conditions and possibly also if those intolerable
conditions were being imposed on him knowingly and wilfully by the authorities. None
g of those conditions applies in the present case and it follows that the appellant can have
no claim in damages for false imprisonment. That is sufficient to decide this case.
However, I am not convinced that any added ingredient can be grafted on to the
established definition of false imprisonment so as to make a claim possible in a prison
context. To allow such a claim where conditions are intolerable can be reconciled with
the established definition. Such conditions would negative the statutory defence of
h lawful detention. For reasons already stated, a breach of the Prison Rules 1964 would not
defeat that defence, but a breach of the statute itself could. The rationale of both judges
in *R v Comr of Police of the Metropolis, ex p Nahar* (1983) Times, 28 May, and accepted in
Middleweek's case, was that there is to be implied in the Prison Act 1952 a term making
intolerable conditions unlawful.
But as to the suggestion of bad faith being a necessary ingredient in the tort, different
j considerations apply. To require proof of bad faith would be to alter the tort of false
imprisonment and in effect to create a new tort special to prisons and prisoners. Moreover,
acting in bad faith to keep a prisoner in intolerable conditions would in most cases
amount to misfeasance in a public office, so an action for false imprisonment would not
be necessary. In *Weldon's* case this court was required to consider only whether the
plaintiff's allegation of false imprisonment in his statement of claim should be struck
out. The court declined to hold that in no circumstances could a prisoner sue a prison

officer for false imprisonment. Ralph Gibson LJ made it clear that he was not reaching any final conclusion on the question. Parker LJ indicated that given extreme *a* circumstances, which he postulated and which would probably amount to intolerable conditions, he was not driven to conclude that no action for false imprisonment could lie.

In my view, save where a prisoner is held under intolerable conditions, the general power under s 12 of the Prison Act 1952 would afford defence to such an action by a prisoner against the prison authorities.   *b*

My conclusions on the present case are that I would not exercise the court's discretion to quash the challenged decision, that the claim for damages for false imprisonment cannot succeed since there is no evidence of intolerable conditions, nor, if it be relevant, was there any evidence of bad faith. The defence of lawful detention cannot be defeated by breaches of the Prison Rules.

A further point was argued before us which raises important and difficult issues. If an *c* action for false imprisonment is open to a prisoner, absent intolerable conditions, and if the court were to quash the challenged decisions what would be the retrospective effect of the decisions struck down? It has been held in a number of cases that an administrative decision or order is good unless and until set aside. Once set aside such a decision or order has been said to be and to have been of no effect. What is not clear is the validity or otherwise of acts done on the authority of or in obedience to the decision or order before *d* it is struck down. The subject is bedevilled by words and phrases such as 'void', 'voidable', 'nullity', 'interim validity' and 'de facto validity'. Would a prison governor obeying CI 10/1974 and prison officers carrying out his instructions thereunder be protected from civil action if the circular is ultimately decided ultra vires and their decisions are quashed? The contrasting approaches to the question can be found in, on the one hand, the speech of Lord Diplock in *F Hoffmann-La Roche & Co AG v Secretary of State for Trade and Industry* *e* [1974] 2 All ER 1128 at 1153–1154, [1975] AC 295 at 365 and, on the other, the judgment of Sir John Donaldson MR in *R v Panel on Take-overs and Mergers, ex p Datafin plc (Norton Opax plc intervening)* [1987] 1 All ER 564 at 578–579, [1987] QB 815 at 840, 842. In view of the conclusions that I have already reached ruling out the appellant's claim for damages in this case, it is unnecessary to decide this last and most difficult issue. *f* I refer to it partly because it was the subject of much interesting and cogent argument by counsel on both sides and partly because should this case go further and a different view be taken, the issue may need to be decided.

I would grant declarations in accordance with the findings made earlier in this judgment. Otherwise, I would dismiss this appeal.

NICHOLLS LJ. I agree that an order should be made in the terms proposed by Taylor *g* LJ for the reasons given by him. I add some comments only on the question of whether a claim for damages for false imprisonment can lie against the prison authorities at the suit of a prisoner who has been lawfully committed to prison and whose term of imprisonment has not expired.

The law seeks to protect individuals against various kinds of physical assault, principally *h* through causes of action falling under the generic head of trespass to the person. False imprisonment is one particular type of trespass to the person. Battery and assault are others. Although these causes of action all fall within the same overall heading of trespass to the person, the ingredients of each of these torts differ. False imprisonment is not necessarily accompanied by an assault or battery. Conversely, and obviously, there can be assault or battery without false imprisonment. The law also affords protection against *j* physical injury through claims in negligence.

When lawfully committed to prison, a prisoner thereby loses some, but not all, of the protection which otherwise he would enjoy against the various types of trespass to his person. Certain acts done by the prison authorities which would normally constitute trespass will not do so, so long as the prisoner is lawfully committed to prison. Thus,

a prison officers can use reasonable force to compel a prisoner to comply with instructions given to him in the normal, orderly conduct of the prison, for example if he refuses to go where he is told. The application of reasonable force for this purpose will not found a cause of action in battery or assault. But committal to prison does not carry with it any right for the prison authorities to apply excessive force, or to apply force for an improper purpose; for example a prisoner cannot be beaten up by prison officers. If prison officers do so conduct themselves, the prisoner's status as a prisoner provides no defence if he sues
b them for damages for battery or assault.

The same approach is to be applied to false imprisonment: to what extent does committal to prison leave scope for an individual to retain a residual liberty which the law can still protect by giving him a remedy for false imprisonment? For my part, subject only to one apparent exception, I can see no room in principle, in respect of the tort of false imprisonment, for the retention of any residual right against the prison
c authorities. False imprisonment is the wrongful deprivation of a person of his liberty: P is wrongfully detained by D in a particular place (or places). Thus if P is *lawfully* detained by D in a particular place, ex hypothesi the detention cannot constitute wrongful imprisonment by D. But that is precisely what occurs when a person is committed to prison. When a person is committed to prison, the prison authorities may lawfully detain him in any place authorised by statute, viz today, in any prison. Likewise, it is for the
d prison authorities to decide whereabouts within a prison an inmate shall be confined. A prisoner's loss of freedom to go where he will is total. In this way it is inherent in lawful committal to prison that, in law, the prisoner has no right of action arising from the fact of his being detained by the prison authorities in any prison or in any particular place within a prison.

On the authorities, and in particular *Middleweek v Chief Constable of the Merseyside Police*
e (1985) [1990] 3 All ER 662, [1990] 3 WLR 481, this is subject to one limitation: where the prisoner is kept in intolerable physical conditions (for example conditions which are seriously dangerous to health). It is, perhaps, possible to rationalise this apparent exception. It is implicit in the Prison Act 1952 that the place within a prison within which a prisoner will be detained will be physically suitable for that purpose. Thus he cannot lawfully be kept in a place which is not physically suitable, even though it is
f within a prison. If he is kept in such a place, his detention there is unlawful: his imprisonment there is wrongful.

What, then, of a prisoner who (a) is kept within a prison to which he has been lawfully committed in a cell which is physically suitable for the purpose, (b) is not subject to any assault or battery, (c) is not negligently injured, but (d) is deprived of association with his fellow-prisoners in breach of the Prison Rules 1964, SI 1964/388? He is not falsely
g imprisoned: see (a). He has not been assaulted or battered: see (b). He has no claim in negligence: see (c). What is his cause of action in respect of (d)? In my view, none.

This can be tested by considering what is the underlying complaint of a prisoner wrongfully 'put on r 43'. He is in solitary confinement. But the governor's decision not to put him into a cell with another prisoner is, quite simply, not a complaint about the
h fact of his imprisonment or the place where he is imprisoned; it is a complaint about the treatment being accorded to him in the course of his imprisonment. Such a decision is on all fours with, say, a decision restricting the number of letters or visits a prisoner may receive, or a refusal to let a prisoner have with him a radio or other personal belongings. None of those decisions is a decision depriving the prisoner of his liberty of movement which, in any event, he has already lost. The feature of the r 43 regime which comes
j closest to 'imprisonment' is the restriction imposed on the prisoner against leaving his cell, as do other prisoners, and associating with them for meals, work or recreation. But, even here, the complaint is about treatment.

In order to found a complaint of false imprisonment based on his treatment, such as a refusal to permit him to associate with others in the prison, a prisoner has to base his claim on the prison rules. He has to assert that they have not been applied properly in his

case. But I do not think that the rules were intended to be more than regulatory. They
regulate the manner in which prisons shall be run and prisoners shall be treated while in *a*
prison. Prisoners are entitled to have the rules duly observed. If they are not, prisoners
can have recourse to the remedies provided by the law where persons entrusted with
powers and duties under statutory authority err in the exercise of those powers or in the
fulfilment of those duties. But the rules cannot have been intended to have the effect that
any breach of them would render the imprisonment to that extent tortiously unlawful.
I cannot, for example, accept that a prisoner transferred without proper authority from *b*
one prison to another is, in consequence, falsely imprisoned, even though in accordance
with s 12(2) and the rules, he is being imprisoned in the 'wrong' place.

This approach is supported by the observations of Goddard LJ in *Arbon v Anderson*
[1943] 1 All ER 154 at 156–157, [1943] KB 252 at 254–255, although the availability of
judicial review today in respect of disciplinary decisions and, now, r 43 decisions
undermines part of his reasoning. However, it is one thing to accord to prisoners access *c*
to the discretionary remedies applicable to misuse of statutory powers. It is quite a
different matter to regard prison rules as derogating from the defences otherwise available
to a prison officer if sued in an action for assault, battery, or false imprisonment. If the
rules did so derogate, breaches of them would be actionable even though committed in
good faith. That cannot have been intended.

For completeness I add that, for the same reasons, it seems to me that a breach of the *d*
Prison Rules does not give rise to a cause of action in damages for breach of a statutory
obligation: see the *Arbon* decision.

In my view, therefore, a prisoner wrongly placed on r 43 has remedies, but they do
not include a claim for damages for false imprisonment. His remedies are threefold.
First, he has the remedy, provided by the rules, of complaint to the visitors. He may also
petition the Secretary of State, who is under a statutory obligation to ensure that the rules *e*
are duly complied with (s 4(2) of the 1952 Act). Second, he has the remedies provided by
way of judicial review of the decisions made under r 43, either by the governor, or by a
member of the board of visitors, or by the Secretary of State. Third, if the prison
authorities have not erred in good faith, but they have abused their power, the prisoner
has a cause of action in damages for misfeasance in public office.

It follows that the appellant has no cause of action in damages in the instant case *f*
despite the breach of r 43 which occurred.

SIR NICOLAS BROWNE-WILKINSON V-C. I agree with both judgments.

Appeal allowed in part; declarations granted. Leave to appeal and to cross-appeal to the
House of Lords granted.   *g*

Solicitors: *B M Birnberg & Co* (for the appellant); *Treasury Solicitor.*

Celia Fox   Barrister.

Merlin and another v British Nuclear Fuels plc

QUEEN'S BENCH DIVISION

GATEHOUSE J

2–6, 12, 13, 16, 18, 23, 24, 26, 27, 30, 31 OCTOBER, 6–10, 13–17, 20–24, 27–30 NOVEMBER, 1, 4 DECEMBER 1989, 2 APRIL 1990

Nuclear installation – Licensee – Liability to pay compensation – Ionising radiation emitted from waste matter discharged from nuclear site – Plaintiffs selling family home because of high level of radioactive contamination and perceived increase in health risks to children – Plaintiffs selling home for substantially less than expected – Plaintiffs claiming compensation for damage to property and increased risk of injury to health due to radioactive contamination from licensee's site – Whether plaintiffs entitled to compensation – Whether licensee in breach of statutory duty to secure that no ionising radiations emitted from discharge of nuclear waste caused personal injury or damage to property – Whether licensee's liability extending to risk or increased risk of personal injury or damage to property – Nuclear Installations Act 1965, ss 7(1)(b)(ii), 12(1) – Convention on Civil Liability for Nuclear Damage 1963, art I(k)(i).

In 1973 the plaintiffs, a married couple, purchased a house overlooking an estuary some six miles south of a nuclear reprocessing plant operated by the defendants. In 1977 a public inquiry was held to examine the defendants' plans to extend the plant. The inquiry attracted the interst of the media and a number of anti-nuclear pressure groups and, in the wake of that interest, the plaintiffs were alerted to the possibility of radioactive contamination in their home. At the suggestion of a member of one of the pressure groups, the plaintiffs collected a sample of house dust from their vacuum cleaner which was sent to the United States for analysis. In October 1981 the plaintiffs learnt that the tests carried out on their house dust sample indicated high levels of radioactive contamination which gave cause for concern. The plaintiffs decided to move from their home because they were concerned about the health risks to their children which they believed would result from long-term occupation of the house. The plaintiffs purchased a suitable property further away from the nuclear site in May 1982 and put their house on the market for £65,000. They experienced difficulty in selling the property, but it was eventually sold at auction in November 1984 for £35,500. The plaintiffs subsequently issued a writ against the defendants, claiming compensation under s 12(1)[a] of the Nuclear Installations Act 1965 for financial loss represented by the diminution in value of the house caused by the level of radioactive contamination in the house emanating from the discharge of nuclear waste from the defendants' site and their perception of the risk to the health of their children. The plaintiffs contended that the defendants were in breach of their duty under s 7(1)(b)(ii)[b] of the 1965 Act, which imposed a duty on the licensee of a nuclear site to secure that 'no ionising radiations emitted . . . from any waste discharged (in whatever form) on or from the site, cause injury to any person or damage to any property of any person other than the licensee', and alleged that there was a direct link between exposure to radiation and the risk of injury to health and that the ingress of radiation into their house constituted damage to property within the meaning of s 7. The defendants contended that s 7 of the 1965 Act was to be interpreted according to art I(k)(i)[c] of the Vienna Convention on Civil Liability for Nuclear Damage 1963, because

---

a   Section 12(1), so far as material, provides: 'Where any injury or damage has been caused in breach of a duty imposed by section 7 . . . compensation in respect of that injury or damage shall be payable . . .'

b   Section 7(1), so far as material, is set out at p 720 *f*, post

c   Article I, so far as material, is set out at p 720 *b c*, post

the Act was enacted to fulfil the United Kingdom's obligations under that convention, and, since art I(k)(i) defined nuclear damage as loss of life, personal injury or loss of or damage to property arising out of or resulting from the radioactive properties of nuclear fuel, radioactive products or waste from nuclear installations, the Act was restricted to providing compensation for actual personal injury and damage to property and did not extend to compensation for increased risk of either or to compensation for economic loss.

Held – On its true construction, s 7 of the 1965 Act did not extend liability for nuclear damage beyond that provided for in art I(k)(i) of the Vienna Convention and accordingly liability under the Act for nuclear damage did not extend to any loss or damage other than proved physical or mental personal injury and physical damage to property caused by either an occurrence involving nuclear matter or an emission of ionising radiations on or from the nuclear site. It followed that the ingress of radiation into a house, viewed in terms of the risk or increased risk of damage to property, and any consequent increase in the risk of injury to the health of its inhabitants did not amount to 'injury to any person or damage to any property' within s 7 on which a claim for compensation could be founded against the licensee of the nuclear site from which the radioactivity had emanated. Moreover, there was no reason why compensation under the 1965 Act should extend to pure economic loss when such loss would not be recoverable at common law. Since the mere presence of radioactive contamination in the plaintiffs' house was not enough to constitute damage amounting to a breach of the defendants' duty under s 7 which would found a right to compensation, the plaintiffs' action against the defendants would be dismissed (see p 719 a to c, p 720 e g to j, p 721 d g to j and p 722 e g, post).

Notes
For duties of nuclear site licensees, see 16 Halsbury's Laws (4th edn) paras 381–382.
    For the Nuclear Installations Act 1965, ss 7, 12, see 47 Halsbury's Statutes (4th edn) 793, 796.

Cases referred to in judgment
Hedley Byrne & Co Ltd v Heller & Partners Ltd [1963] 2 All ER 575, [1964] AC 465, [1963] 3 WLR 101, HL.
Rylands v Fletcher (1868) LR 3 HL 330, [1861–73] All ER Rep 1.
Simaan General Contracting Co v Pilkington Glass Ltd (No 2) [1988] 1 All ER 791, [1988] QB 758, [1988] 2 WLR 761, CA.

Cases also cited
Ashby v White (1703) 1 Bro Parl Cas 62, 1 ER 417.
Blyth v Birmingham Waterworks Co (1856) 11 Exch 781, [1843–60] All ER Rep 478, 56 ER 1047.
Bwllfa and Merthyr Dare Steam Collieries (1891) Ltd v Pontypridd Waterworks Co [1903] AC 426, [1900–3] All ER Rep 600, HL.
Crofter Hand Woven Harris Tweed Co Ltd v Veitch [1942] 1 All ER 142, [1942] AC 435, HL.
Dodd Properties (Kent) Ltd v Canterbury City Council [1979] 2 All ER 118; rvsd [1980] 1 All ER 928, [1980] 1 All ER 433, CA.
Drane v Evangelou [1978] 2 All ER 437, [1978] 1 WLR 455, CA.
Dreyfus (Louis) & Cie v Parnaso Cia Naviera SA, The Dominator [1959] 1 All ER 502, [1959] 1 QB 498; rvsd [1960] 1 All ER 759, [1960] 2 QB 49, CA.
Earnshaw-Wall, Re [1894] 3 Ch 156.
Fothergill v Monarch Airlines Ltd [1980] 2 All ER 696, [1981] AC 251, HL.
Home Office v Dorset Yacht Co [1970] 2 All ER 294, [1970] AC 1004, HL.
Jones v Skinner (1835) 5 LJ Ch 87.
Junior Books Ltd v Veitchi Co Ltd [1982] 3 All ER 201, [1983] 1 AC 520, HL.
Lawton v BOC Transhield Ltd [1987] 2 All ER 608.

Liesbosch (owners) v Edison (owners) [1933] AC 449, [1933] All ER Rep 144, HL.

a *Metropolitan Asylum District Managers v Hill* (1881) 6 App Cas 193, [1881–5] All ER Rep
   536, HL.

McGhee v National Coal Board [1972] 3 All ER 1008, [1973] 1 WLR 1, HL.

Millington v Duffy (1984) 17 HLR 232, CA.

Nokes v Doncaster Amalgamated Collieries Ltd [1940] 3 All ER 549, [1940] AC 1014, HL.

Rookes v Barnard [1964] 1 All ER 367, [1964] AC 1129, HL.

b *Secretary of State for Education and Science v Tameside Metropolitan Borough* [1976] 3 All ER
   665, [1977] AC 1014, CA and HL.

Smith v Brown (1871) LR 6 QB 729.

Smith v Eric S Bush (a firm), Harris v Wyre Forest DC [1989] 2 All ER 514, [1990] 1 AC 831,
   HL.

Swansea Corp v Harpur [1912] 3 KB 483, CA; *affd* [1913] AC 597, HL.

c *W (an infant), Re* [1971] 2 All ER 49, [1971] AC 682, HL.

Ward v Cannock Chase DC [1985] 3 All ER 537, [1986] Ch 546.

Wilsher v Essex Area Health Authority [1988] 1 All ER 871, [1988] AC 1074, HL.

Action

By writ issued on 14 August 1985 as reissued on 6 September 1988 as amended pursuant
d to the order of Master Creightmore, and by reamended particulars of special damage
served by leave of the trial judge, the plaintiffs, Christopher Peter Merlin and his wife
Christine Ann Merlin, brought an action against the defendants, British Nuclear Fuels
plc, claiming compensation under s 12(1) of the Nuclear Installations Act 1965 for
diminution in the value of their home, Mountain Ash, Ravenglass, Cumbria, allegedly
caused by radioactive contamination from the defendants' nuclear installation at Sellafield.
e The facts are set out in the judgment.

Stephen Sedley QC and *Matthias Kelly* for the plaintiffs.
Kenneth Rokison QC, Antony Edwards-Stuart and *Emma Griffiths* for the defendants.

Cur adv vult

f 2 April. The following judgment was delivered.

GATEHOUSE J. In this action the plaintiffs, Mr and Mrs Merlin, claim statutory
compensation from the defendants as owners and occupiers of the nuclear fuel
reprocessing plant at Sellafield in respect of damage to their property alleged to have been
caused by radioactive contamination emanating from the plant. The claim is brought
g under s 12 of the Nuclear Installations Act 1965, which gives a right to compensation
where any injury or damage has been caused in breach of a duty imposed by, inter alia,
s 7 of the Act. It will in due course be necessary to look more closely at the provisions of
the Act but in brief s 7 imposes on the licensee of a nuclear site, in this case the defendants,
a duty to secure that no ionising radiations emitted from any waste discharged from the
h site cause damage to any property of any person other than the licensee. Of course, the
Act also provides for the payment of compensation where the licensee's activities, in
breach of its duties under s 7 cause death or personal injury, but no such claim arises in
the present case.

   The plaintiffs claim that damage has been caused to their property, namely their
former home, a house called Mountain Ash in the village of Ravenglass some six miles
j south of Sellafield. They say that as a result of the discharge of waste material from the
defendants' operations into the Irish Sea via a pipeline radioactive matter has, by the
turbulence of the sea, found its way back to the coastline and become deposited in the
mud of the Ravenglass estuary and thence, by the action of the wind and the carriage of
the sediment on the feet of the plaintiffs, their family and their dogs, into their house.

   By paragraph 6(i) of the reamended statement of claim the plaintiffs allege that owing
to the contamination of their premises by artificial radionuclides the premises ceased to

be of any use or value to the first and second plaintiffs as a home and/or the first and
second plaintiffs were obliged and/or reasonably decided to sell the same on 14 December   *a*
1984 at an undervalue. They claim as special damage the loss in value of the house and
various other matters said to be consequential on the sale and they also claim general
damages in respect of annoyance and inconvenience.

The prayer of the statement of claim includes a claim for aggravated damages but
counsel for the plaintiffs abandoned this at an early stage. The above resume sets out the
basis of the claim. I add these further points. From the outset, counsel based his case   *b*
exclusively on the statute and emphasised this is not a claim founded in negligence. The
1965 Act, he argued, imposed an absolute liability on the defendants to pay statutory
compensation for any damage to property proved to have been caused in breach of the
duties imposed by s 7. There is, he argued, no other cause of action (see the wording of
s 12(1)) and, therefore, the claim in para 5 in the statement of claim, based on strict
liability at common law under the principle in *Rylands v Fletcher* (1868) LR 3 HL 330,   *c*
[1861–73] All ER Rep 1 does not arise.

I set out, as briefly as I can but necessarily at some length, the facts of the case as
admitted or established by the evidence. The first plaintiff, Mr Merlin, was at the date of
the hearing aged 48. After leaving school he obtained a diploma in automobile
engineering and worked for a company which made go-karts. Go-karting was his hobby.
He became the British champion and he established an international reputation both as   *d*
driver and as engine builder.

In 1968 he started his own business at Isleworth, which prospered well and quickly
and he and his wife were able to move to the Surrey countryside. But Mr Merlin's great
love was the sea. During his early childhood while his father, a naval surgeon, was away
on war service he lived on Saltcoats on the Ravenglass estuary and came to know and love
the area. After the war his family returned to Ravenglass on regular holidays. Mr Merlin   *e*
and his wife married in 1963 and they spent their honeymoon there and thereafter spent
a number of long weekends and longer breaks at Christmas in each year staying in the
local hotel. In 1972 the plaintiffs heard that the post office and general store in the main
street at Ravenglass was for sale.

By this time Mr Merlin, having worked very hard in his business, had, as he put it,   *f*
burnt himself out and he and his wife were attracted by the idea of getting out of the rat
race and moving to the wilds and a quieter life. They also wanted to start a family. The
post office had enough living space above and behind it to accommodate the two of them
until they could find something larger and they, therefore, sold their Surrey house and
bought the post office. In fact, they never did live on the premises because within a short
time they learnt that Mountain Ash was to be put on the market in the spring of 1973.   *g*

Mr Merlin knew the house well and had been a regular visitor since early childhood.
It had an incomparable position overlooking the estuary and he was determined to buy
it if he possibly could. As appears from the photographs and plans, Mountain Ash is
indeed a singular property. It is a substantial house built about 1910 situated at the very
end of the village and with views over the estuary and on the other side to Scafell and the
mountains. It has direct access from its garden to the beach. Mr Merlin was an   *h*
enthusiastic observer of the birdlife on the estuary and he and his family enjoyed walking
both on the estuary and in the mountains behind.

It was in every way a very desirable property for Mr Merlin and in the spring of 1973
he purchased it at auction, together with a small adjoining house called Rose Cottage and
a certain amount of garden and land, against a number of competitive bidders. Thereafter
the position was this: Mr Merlin had sold his Surrey home and a half interest in his   *j*
business. With the proceeds he bought the post office and general store and, with a
mortgage, Mountain Ash and Rose Cottage, which was then occupied by protected
tenants. Mrs Merlin ran the store and became the postmistress. Mr Merlin made exhaust
systems in the garage at Mountain Ash. The post office accommodation was let.

In 1974 the Merlins were offered a small property adjacent to the post office called

Ashley Cottage. This they purchased, Mr Merlin using the proceeds from the sale of the
a remaining half interest in the business. The Merlins' first surviving son was born on 29
December 1976 and their second on 23 March 1978.

In 1977 the public inquiry into the defendants' plans to extend the Sellafield plant was
held. The inspector was Parker J. The proceedings were widely reported, particularly in
the local press, but the general issues raised caused no great concern to the plaintiffs.

The planning inquiry, however, gave rise to three incidents that did affect them. One
b of the possible pathways by which radioactive material can find its way into humans was
by the consumption of locally caught fish and the Merlins were among a number of
volunteers who were tested for this with some positive but in no way startling results.

More significant, one of the groups at the inquiry opposed to the extension, Network
for Nuclear Concern (NNC), suggested that an analysis of radioactivity in house dust
should be carried out. An air monitoring device was placed in the Merlins' garden for 30
c days by the National Radiological Protection Board (NRPB) and attracted a certain
amount of media interest in the house and its occupants. As it was being removed at the
end of the test period, the Merlins were told they had nothing to worry about, a remark
which Mr Merlin said struck him as being too glib to be convincing but clearly it caused
little concern at the time.

The third incident arose out of the second and was to have much more far-reaching
d consequences. As a result of the temporary installation of the outdoor monitoring device,
a Mr Thompson called on the Merlins. He was a local biology teacher and a member of
NNC. He was concerned that only the outdoor air was being monitored and, as a result
of discussions with Professor Radford (of whom much more later), suggested that a
Hoover bag of house dust should be analysed for radioactive material.

A bagful was in due course collected by Mrs Merlin and handed over to Mr Thompson.
e This was in the latter months of 1977. That was, so far as Mr Merlin was concerned, the
last he heard of the matter until 1981. Meanwhile the next significant event was the
appearance in 1979 of a German scientist, Dr Sonhoff, at the Merlins' house with a small
camera team. He was apparently making a TV film on the environmental impact of the
Sellafield plant on the surrounding area.

There had, since the Parker inquiry, been regular monitoring of the air, local seafood
f and the sediments in the estuary and the Merlins were becoming uneasy, so Mr Merlin
put it, as they began to realise that 'to some extent we were living in the outskirts of a
sort of open laboratory'. The unease was considerably more on the part of Mrs Merlin
than her husband. Dr Sonhoff's visit caused her positive alarm, particularly when he
advised her against hoovering her house and expressed surprise that the Ravenglass area
had not been evacuated. The advice about hoovering was because dust on the floor which
g may contain adherent radionuclides can become resuspended in the cleaning operation
and thus capable of being inhaled by humans.

Dr Sonhoff tested their cat, a heavy consumer of local fish, with a Geiger counter,
producing positive results and amusement to the owners at the time, but some concern
when they thought about it afterwards.

Mrs Merlin was seriously upset by Dr Sonhoff's visit, but her husband regarded him as
h alarmist. He had no intention of moving at that time, and told his wife so. What changed
Mr Merlin's mind, he said, was a telephone call from Mr Thompson in 1981, following
his visit in late 1977, an incident which by the time of the telephone call Mr Merlin had
almost entirely forgotten.

The Hoover bag of dust had been sent by Mr Thompson to a distinguished
j epidemiologist in the United States, Professor Radford, for analysis. Mr Thompson knew
Professor Radford, who had given expert evidence on behalf of NNC at the Parker
inquiry. The professor encountered considerable difficulties in having the contents of
the bag analysed, and it took a very long time to obtain the results, but eventually, on 27
February 1981, he wrote to Mr Thompson enclosing a summary of the analyses. This
confirmed the latter's expectations. The material part of the letter read:

'It was good to talk to you, and I am enclosing a summary of the analyses as I have them at present. As you can see, the alpha activity totals about 11 pCu/gm, as I said, *a* with substantially more gamma activity. The alpha activity is of primary concern in terms of biological effects, but these effects cannot be accurately assessed unless we have a further evaluation of the size, distribution and chemical form of the activity . . . It is evident that much additional work is needed before the hazard can be adequately defined, although I think we can say that there is sufficient reason to be concerned. This additional work would be virtually impossible for me to get *b* done here. Too many questions would be asked and there would probably be considerable expense. We have to find some way to get the matter looked into in Britain.'

He then discussed various ways in which this might be done and continued:

'In any case, I think you should discuss the problem with your friend. Talk over *c* these possibilities. I await further word from you.'

Unfortunately, Mr Thompson has since died, but it was his account to Mr Merlin of Professor Radford's letter which was the turning point in the plaintiffs' lives. The only evidence of this is that of Mr Merlin, who said this:

'But in October 1981 dear Joe Thompson, who I had totally forgotten about, and *d* when he mentioned his name I could only just kind of place him, rang up. I was in my workshop, and I think he rang up about 7 o'clock one evening. He said, "I have heard back from my colleague in America", who at that time he had put a name to as Professor Radford. He said, "I am afraid the news isn't very good, Chris. You are not going to like this, but there are levels of radioactivity which give cause for *e* concern, particularly as I understand you now have two boys and your family is growing up. Mr Radford does express grave concern. I can't tell you more than that. What you do is up to you".'

Mr Merlin's evidence continued:

'We actually had something which I had heard about at the time of the inquiry, *f* and that was plutonium, in the house. I could not really hold this from my wife, but I did for two or three days, because I knew that now I had run out of reasons to stay in the village. I was absolutely heartbroken, but I knew that there was absolutely no excuse for staying any longer, no reason for staying any longer.'

There was a dispute whether this telephone call was in October 1981, as Mr Merlin said, or March. That was the date given in Mrs Merlin's affirmation made at the RSC *g* Ord 14 stage in these proceedings. She changed this to October in her evidence before me, one of the unsatisfactory parts of her evidence. Further urgent efforts were then made to support the October date. Mr Cattley, the plaintiffs' accountant, said that he had not been aware of the discovery of contamination at the time of the sale of Rose Cottage, which was in July 1981, but that does not assist. There was no particular reason why he *h* should have been told.

The late Mr Thompson's widow said he was in a dilemma whether to pass on the news to the Merlins and she said he waited for some months before doing so, putting it off, although she apparently kept trying to persuade him to do so. I cannot place much reliance on Mrs Thompson's memory for detail, stirred for the first time some eight years after the event, and I do not accept that her husband waited for what must have amounted *j* to a further eight months before relaying Professor Radford's views. On balance of probability, although Mr Thompson may have havered for while before bringing himself to pass on the bad news, I find that he did so in about March rather than in October. Probably it does not matter very much.

Having brooded alone for a few days on Mr Thompson's message, Mr Merlin decided

that he no longer had any good reason for opposing his wife's desire to move. He
a therefore told her the unwelcome news and they jointly decided to move from Mountain
Ash because, according to them, they were not prepared to expose their children to the
health risk which they believed would result from long-term occupation of the house.

They did not take any urgent steps to this end. They did not visit any estate agents but
they regularly scanned the local paper's property columns, and similar sources. They
visited one house in Kirkudbrightshire in late 1981 and another house near Hexham in
b early 1982 but otherwise took no active steps to find an alternative home. On this subject,
· again, I find Mrs Merlin's evidence to the contrary unsatisfactory.

Eventually they heard from the postman that a farm in the Duddon Valley, some 15
miles inland, was coming on the market. This was Grass Gars Farm, their present address.
It was remote, in attractive countryside, it was a working farm and it had a large detached
barn which Mr Merlin could convert to a workshop.

c With their accountant they attended the auction in May 1982 and with little
competitive bidding they purchased it for £43,000 plus £2,000 for some 35 acres of
grazing land for the 20 breeding ewes which they also bought. The price of the farm was
substantially less than they feared they might have to pay.

Thereafter, in the same month, the plaintiffs put Mountain Ash into the hands of at
first two, then three and finally four estate agents. The original asking price was £65,000.
d In July this was reduced to £62,000. In December it was again reduced to 'offers over
£59,950' and in March 1983 to £55,000. Quite a number of people came to look at the
house, some more than once, but no offers were made until October 1983.

In September 1982 completion on Grass Gars Farm took place and this was financed
by means of a bridging loan from the plaintiffs' bank.

In about April 1983 a team from Yorkshire Television embarked on the making of a
e documentary to be entitled, 'Sellafield—the Nuclear Dustbin' and they persuaded the
Merlins to take part. The Merlins and their children, and Mountain Ash, featured quite
prominently in the film, which was broadcast on 1 November 1983. It must have been
obvious to the plaintiffs that once broadcast the documentary would be unhelpful in
their efforts to sell the house, and so it proved.

I should mention here as an important part of the chronology that Dr Philip Day,
f senior lecturer in chemistry at Manchester University and an expert witness on behalf of
the plaintiffs, also played a part in the documentary. He was shown accepting for analysis
another Hoover bag of house dust from Mrs Merlin. That was shot in April and about a
month later, in May 1983, Mrs Merlin sent Dr Day a third bag. The results were analysed
for radioactivity and the average figures derived from both bags are those pleaded in
g para 4(b) of the statement of claim.

In June or July 1983 the plaintiffs consulted Messrs Cameron Markby on their legal
position vis-à-vis the defendants and they were advised, inter alia, that they were under a
legal obligation to disclose to prospective purchasers the facts so far as then known
relating to contamination of the house. They said that this reinforced the moral
obligation which they felt to make such disclosure. I think it is understandable that they
h did not, in fact, make such disclosure to any of the potential buyers who merely looked
at the house between May 1982 and September 1983 but in late September or early
October 1983, a Mr Hayward, a local solicitor, and his fiancée became seriously interested
and offered £53,100 for the property, including carpets and curtains, and together with
the adjacent building plot.

The Yorkshire Television documentary was to be shown on the 'First Tuesday' slot on
j 1 November and so the Mountain Ash contamination would then become public
knowledge. There is some doubt as to the exact moment when Mr Hayward and his
fiancée learnt of it, whether disclosed by the plaintiffs before the broadcast or whether
only as a result of the broadcast, but on balance I accept the plaintiffs' account of this,
namely that as Mr Hayward was almost at the point of agreeing unconditionally to
purchase they did disclose the facts to him prior to the broadcast. I do not think it is of

much importance because, accepting the plaintiffs' account, the discharge of their obligation of disclosure was, in any case, also recognising the inevitable that in a matter a of two or three weeks Mr Hayward and his fiancée were almost certain to learn the true facts.

To begin with, they were apparently unconcerned but after the broadcast they withdrew from the negotiations, not specifically because of the contamination, but because Mr Hayward was concerned at his ability to resell the house at a future date. Another potential purchaser, a Mr Nuttall, was also apparently prepared to buy at around b £53,000 but he too withdrew after the broadcast.

By this time, if not before, the plaintiffs' bank was becoming restive. The bridging loan for the purchase of Grass Gars Farm remained outstanding. The expected repayment from the sale of Mountain Ash had not materialised, and the plaintiffs had to realise their other Ravenglass asset, the post office and general store, in order to discharge or reduce the loan. The agreement for sale was concluded in November 1983, although completion c was delayed until May 1984 for reasons which are not relevant.

Mr Merlin transferred his workshop to one of the barns at Grass Gars Farm and, as I understand the position, he lived there and continued to attend to his increasingly successful operation of building exhaust systems. The children were now at day school at Gosforth and they and their mother continued to live at Mountain Ash, joining Mr Merlin at weekends. After completion of the sale of the post office the whole family d went to live at Grass Gars Farm in May 1984 and Mountain Ash was shut up.

By now the plaintiffs were falling further behind in their interest payments to the bank and the bank were putting increasing pressure on them to sell Mountain Ash. It was accordingly put up for auction in November 1984. The auction was poorly attended (apparently television camermen and the press outnumbered the public) and Mountain Ash (but without the building plot which the plantiffs retained) was sold for £35,500 to e a Sellafield employee who was unconcerned at the now much publicised contamination of the house and expressed the view that he had got a bargain.

That is a summary of the main facts and I now turn to consider the issues, but adding two factual concessions made by the defendants for the purposes of this action.

The defendants accept, first, that the levels of activity in Mountain Ash were as pleaded f in para 4 of the statement of the claim, and that those levels can be assumed to have been present at all times during the plaintiffs' occupancy. Second, the defendants accept that the radionuclides so found in Mountain Ash originated in waste emitted from the Sellafield pipeline.

So the essential nature of the plaintiffs' claim is this: it is for the financial loss resulting from their decision to sell Mountain Ash. That decision was based on the advice given to them by the late Mr Thompson as to the level of contamination in the house emanating g from the defendants' site and their perception of the consequent increased risk to health, particulary the health of their children were they to remain in Mountain Ash for any substantial period of time.

The plaintiffs' primary argument is that, as there is a linear relationship between exposure to radionuclides and risk to health, the ingress into the plaintiffs' house of h radionuclulides from the defendants' plant ipso facto constitutes damage to property within the meaning of the 1965 Act and entitles the plaintiffs to compensation. Although he seemed reluctant to qualify this by the de minimis principle, counsel for the plaintiffs accepted that there must be a limit below which the damage was so trivial as to attract no compensation. But, subject only to this, his primary case is the simple one set out above.

The defendants' primary case is that as there is no question of personal injury or j physical damage to the fabric of the plaintiffs' property, there is no breach of statutory duty and the plaintiffs have no claim to compensation under the 1965 Act. They say that apart from a minor claim for general damages for annoyance and inconvenience the plaintiffs' claim is in respect of economic loss consequent on their decision to leave

Mountain Ash, that on the plaintiffs' own case that decision was taken because of the
a plaintiffs' perception that to remain in the house would be to expose themselves, but
more particularly their young children, to an additional risk of future physical injury.
The defendents say that the 1965 Act provides for compensation in respect of proved
personal injury or damage to property: it does not provide compensation in respect of
the risk, or increased risk, of either; it does not compensate for mere economic loss,
which is the essence of the plaintiffs' claim and the presence of radionuclides in Mountain
b Ash does not of itself constitute damage.

My initial reaction to the defendants' primary case was unfavourable: it appeared to
limit drastically the ambit of the compensation provisions of the 1965 Act, and to give
no remedy for a case such as the present which might be the typical result of an accidental
emission of radioactive material from a nuclear site. Furthermore, although this is by no
means clear and the point was not argued, it may be that a plaintiff's only remedy is
c confined to a claim for statutory compensation under s 12 of the Act. But I am convinced
by counsel's arguments that the defendants' approach is right. There are several reasons.

First, I refer to the terms of the Vienna Convention on Civil Liability for Nuclear
Damage (Vienna, 21 May 1963; Misc 9 (1964); Cmnd 2333). It is not in dispute that the
1965 Act was passed in order to fulfil the United Kingdom's obligations under the Vienna
Convention.
d I was referred in some detail to the Vienna Convention on which reliance was placed
by both parties. The preamble recites that:

'THE CONTRACTING PARTIES HAVING RECOGNISED the desirability of establishing some
minimum standards to provide financial protection against damage resulting from
certain peaceful uses of nuclear energy, . . . have agreed as follows . . .'

e
Article II (and I will return to art I in a moment) provides:

'1. The operator of a nuclear installation shall be liable for nuclear damage upon
proof that such damage has been caused by a nuclear incident . . . (*b*) involving
nuclear material coming from or originating in his nuclear installation, and
f occurring . . .'

and then four qualifying matters are set out which I need not read. Article IV(1) provides:

'The liability of the operator for nuclear damage under this Convention shall be
absolute.'

g
Article IV(3)(*b*) provides:

'Except in so far as the law of the Installation State may provide to the contrary,
the operator shall not be liable for nuclear damage caused by a nuclear incident
directly due to a grave natural disaster of an exceptional character.'

Article V entitles the contracting parties to limit the operator's financial liability in
h respect of any one nuclear incident subject to a minimum figure. Article VI provides for
limitation periods for the bringing of claims but provides that the contracting parties
may extend these periods in certain defined circumstances. Article VIII provides:

'Subject to the provisions of this Convention, the nature, form and extent of the
compensation, as well as the equitable distribution thereof, shall be governed by the
j law of the competent Court.'

Article I contains definitions. I need only refer to the following:

'(*g*) "Radioactive products or waste" means any radioactive material produced in,
or any material made radioactive by exposure to the radiation incidental to, the

production or utilisation of nuclear fuel, but does not include radioisotopes which have reached the final stage of fabrication so as to be usable for any scientific, *a* medical, agricultural, commercial or industrial purposes.

(*h*) "Nuclear material" means—(i) nuclear fuel, other than natural uranium and depleted uranium, capable of producing energy by a self-sustaining chain process of nuclear fission outside a nuclear reactor, either alone or in combination with some other material; and (ii) radioactive products or waste . . .

(*k*) "Nuclear damage" means—(i) loss of life, any personal injury or any loss of, or *b* damage to, property which arises out of or results from the radioactive properties or a combination of radioactive properties with toxic, explosive or other hazardous properties of nuclear fuel or radioactive products or waste in, or of nuclear material coming from, originating in, or sent to, a nuclear installation . . . (ii) any other loss or damage so arising or resulting if and to the extent that the law of the competent court so provides . . . *c*

(*l*) "Nuclear incident" means any occurrence or series of occurrences having the same origin which causes nuclear damage.'

The pattern of the Vienna Convention is clear. In accordance with the preamble referring to the establishment of minimum standards, the Vienna Convention imposed obligations on the contracting parties in respect of certain matters, but left it to the *d* parties to take their individual decisions in respect of others. Accordingly, and as an example, the 1965 Act has extended the minimum limitation period required by the Vienna Convention, and has imposed liability in respect of unforeseeable natural disasters, as permitted by art IV, para 3(*b*).

But most significant for present purposes the 1965 Act has not extended liability for nuclear damage beyond the requirements of para (*k*)(i) of art I. *e*

Section 7(1) of the Act imposes a duty on the licensee to secure that—

'(*a*) no such occurrence involving nuclear matter as mentioned in subsection (2) of this section causes injury to any person or damage to any property of any person other than the licensee . . . (*b*) no ionising radiations emitted . . . (ii) from any waste discharged (in whatever form) on or from the site, cause injury to any person or *f* damage to any property of any person other than the licensee.'

Section 26 of the Act provides that 'injury' means personal injury and includes loss of life. 'Damage', more particularly 'damage to . . . property', is not defined.

Thus, read with the qualifications set out in sub-s (2), sub-s (1) of s 7 of the 1965 Act covers the various alternatives which are contained in para (*k*)(i) of art I of the Vienna *g* Convention.

The Act therefore provides as required by the Vienna Convention for compensation for loss of life, personal injury or damage to any property of any person other than the licensee, caused by breach of statutory duty. It does not provide for compensation for 'any other loss or damage' as it could have done in accordance with art I(*k*)(ii).

'Personal injury or damage to property' is a familiar enough phrase and in my *h* judgment it means, as it does in other contexts, physical (or mental) injury or physical damage to tangible property. The word 'property' alone may well have a wider meaning in some contexts (eg in testamentary dispositions, or in the field of company law, where the expression 'all the company's property', and so on, will extend to incorporeal property) but where it is used in the Vienna Convention and the 1965 Act it does not in my judgment extend to incorporeal property or property rights. The plaintiffs' argument *j* that 'property' included the air space within the walls, ceilings and floors of Mountain Ash, that this has been damaged by the presence of radionuclides and the house rendered less valuable as the family's home, seems to me to be too far-fetched.

The 1965 Act contains compromises. The principal compromises are these. It imposes

absolute liability on the licensee irrespective of negligence, and a greatly extended period
a for the bringing of claims; no doubt because, typically, the various types of cancer that
can arise may take many years to manifest themselves. To balance this extended exposure
of the licensee and his strict liability, there is introduced a maximum money liability in
respect of any one occurrence (s 16) and, in my judgment, a restriction on the nature of
the harm which qualifies for compensation, namely injury, including fatal injury, to the
person or physical damage to tangible property.

b   It is true, and the evidence of Dr Phillips made this plain, that the dose required to
produce any detectable damage to the molecular structure of inanimate objects such as
building materials, furniture etc is enormous, infinitely greater than the level of
radionuclides present in the plaintiffs' house. If 'damage to property' is restricted to
physical damage to tangible property, it might be argued that in reality this is so unlikely
to occur that there is really nothing to which the phrase would apply. But one obvious
c answer given by counsel for the defendants is that it would cover injury to livestock,
which is probably just as likely to occur in the vicinity of a nuclear installation as injury
to humans, and would clearly be an important head of compensation to local farmers.

I reject the argument that contamination of the plaintiffs' house per se amounts to
damage to their property. All that such contamination as was admitted in this case
amounts to is some increased risk to the health of its occupants. The 1965 Act compensates
d for proved personal injury, not the risk of future personal injury. If the Act were
concerned with risk, a number of very difficult questions would arise. For instance, risk
to whom? Is it the plaintiffs' health risk that has to be evaluated, or, (and this was their
concern) that of their children? Or is it that of potential purchasers of the house? The
degree of risk depends, among other factors, on the length of time over which the
individual is exposed to radioactivity. Is the court to attempt to forecast how many years
e each individual concerned is likely to live in the house?

Again, counsel for the plaintiffs conceded that there must be a cut-off line of
contamination below which no compensation would be payable. How is the court to
judge where this should be drawn? The Act provides no guidance. Is compensation to
depend on whether plaintiffs' reaction to the advice they happened to receive was at least
a reasonable response? Or is the test the reaction of a reasonable person in their position,
f which is not necessarily the same thing? Or is it a wholly objective test, based not on the
particular advice given to the particular plaintiffs, but on the actual level of risk as assessed
by the court as a result of expert evidence? In the present case, and because my
construction of the statute may be wrong, I read the reports of twelve experts,
supplemented by a vast mass of supporting documentation, and I heard oral evidence
from nine of them, extending over many days, in order to attempt to evaluate the actual
g increased level of risk in the plaintiffs' house.

Other questions would arise. The selection above is far from exhaustive. I therefore
conclude on the wording of the 1965 Act, and in the context of the Vienna Convention,
that damage to property has the limited meaning contended for by the defendants and
that the facts of this case do not entitle the plaintiffs to statutory compensation.

h   I have noted above what seems to me the deliberate choice of Parliament not to extend
the liability of the operator beyond the obligatory requirements of art I(k)(i) of the Vienna
Convention. Counsel for the plaintiffs argued that this was unnecessary because the
jurisprudence of the English court would fill the gap and extend to the facts of this case.
I do not agree. Although this is not a case founded on negligence, I can see no reason why
compensation under the 1965 Act should extend to pure economic loss when such loss
j would not be recoverable at common law.

No special relationship existed between the defendants and the plaintiffs, who were
merely part of the general public living in the Sellafield area, such as would give rise to a
duty of the *Hedley Byrne* type, so it seems to me that any such claim at common law must
have failed (see *Hedley Byrne & Co v Heller & Partners* [1963] 2 All ER 575, [1964] AC

465). See, for example, the judgments of the Court of Appeal and particularly Bingham LJ in *Simaan General Contracting Co v Pilkington Glass Ltd (No 2)* [1988] 1 All ER 791, *a* [1988] QB 758.

A further argument in favour of the defendants' construction is this: I bear in mind the dangers of acceding to a 'floodgates' argument, nevertheless I incline away from a construction of the Act which would result in the operator being in continual breach of the statutory duty to a possibly very large number of people. It is in the nature of nuclear installations that there will be some additional radionuclides present in the houses of the *b* local population, over and above the naturally occurring radionuclides to which every one of us is continually exposed. If the mere presence of this additional source is enough to constitute damage under s 7, the result would inevitably be that the defendants were indeed in breach of their statutory duty every day to possibly thousands of citizens, each of whom would have a claim for compensation.

Whether there would in fact be an award in every case would then involve a long and *c* complex inquiry into the particular facts, such as has been carried out in this case, to ascertain objectively whether the resulting additional risk did or did not reach a level justifying a monetary award, and with no guidance as to what that level should be.

Another reason why in my view the Act has no application here is the wording of s 7, which imports the element of causation. For there to be a breach of statutory duty, carrying with it a right to compensation, the plaintiff must establish that he has suffered *d* injury or damage to his property *caused*, and I emphasise the word 'caused', by either an occurrence involving nuclear matter (s 7(1)(*a*)) or an emission of ionising radiations on or from the site (s 7(1)(*b*)).

Although there was some dispute whether the present facts fell within para (*a*) as well as para (*b*), I am satisfied that this is a para (*b*)(ii) case, but it does not appear to matter: in either case there must be cause and effect. The mere presence of ionising radiations *e* within the plaintiffs' property emitted from waste discharged from the site is not enough to constitute a breach of statutory duty. There must be consequential damage. The radionuclides with which this case is concerned, plutonium isotopes and americium, are alpha emitters. These cannot do any significant damage to persons or property externally, but when inhaled, ingested or otherwise enabled to enter the body they may induce *f* cancers, but, of course, will not necessarily do so. The presence of alpha emitting radionuclides in the human airways or digestive tracts or even in the bloodstream merely increases the risk of cancer to which everyone is exposed from both natural and artificial radioactive sources. They do not per se amount to injury.

I therefore conclude that the facts of this case do not disclose any breach of duty by the defendants and the action must fail on that ground.

[His Lordship then made various findings of fact which do not call for report.] *g*

Action dismissed.

Solicitors: *Leigh Day & Co* (for the plaintiffs); *Freshfields* (for the defendants).

h

K Mydeen Esq   Barrister.

a # Shearson Lehman Hutton Inc and another v Maclaine Watson & Co Ltd and others (No 2)

QUEEN'S BENCH DIVISION (COMMERCIAL COURT)

b WEBSTER J

28, 29, 30 NOVEMBER, 1, 4, 21 DECEMBER 1989

Contract – Damages for breach – Sale of goods – Available market by which to ascertain difference between contract price and market price on date of breach – Contract for purchase of large quantity of tin – Purchaser refusing to accept goods – Assessment of damages for breach of
c *contract – Whether 'available market' for notional sale of goods if only one available buyer on date of breach – Whether there must be ready demand by sufficiently large pool of potential buyers either immediately or within reasonable time for 'available market' to be constituted – Sale of Goods Act 1979, s 50(3).*

Interest – Damages – Commercial cases – Appropriate rate of interest on damages – Commercial
d *court practice – Practice of Commercial Court to award interest at base rate plus 1% – Practice no more than mere presumption – Whether court can depart from usual rate where it would be substantially unfair to either party.*

Between 25 July and 30 September 1985 the defendants entered into forward contracts to purchase 7,755 tonnes of standard grade tin from the plaintiffs for a total price of some
e £70m for delivery on 12 March 1986. The defendants refused to perform the contracts and were subsequently found to be liable for breach of contract as at 12 March. On the issue of the measure of damages for the breach the questions arose whether, having regard to the amount of tin involved, the damages were to be assessed according to a hypothetical sale of all the tin on 12 March or whether it was permissible to take into account the price that could have been negotiated over a longer period and, if so, whether
f fluctuations in price during that period were to be taken into account. It was agreed that the correct measure of damages was prescribed by s 50(3)[a] of the Sale of Goods Act 1979, ie prima facie the difference between the contract price and the market price on the date of the breach if there was an 'available market'. The plaintiffs contended that there was an 'available market' on 12 March within s 50(3) even if there was only one available buyer for the goods on that day and that the appropriate price was the price which the
g goods would fetch in an outright sale for cash on that day. The defendants contended that there had to be a ready demand by a sufficiently large pool of potential buyers either immediately or within a reasonable time for an 'available market' to be constituted and that the appropriate price was that which would be paid by the potential buyers in those circumstances. The issue also arose as to the appropriate rate of interest on the damages
h from the date of breach to the date of judgment.

Held – (1) In assessing damages under s 50(3) of the 1979 Act for failure to perform a contract for the purchase of goods the measure of damages payable by the defaulting buyer was the difference between the contract price and the current or market price at the date of breach based on a hypothetical sale of the particular amount of the goods in
j question in the available market but disregarding any characteristics of the seller which might have led to a lower price being obtained. In determining whether there was an 'available market' for the goods in question, if the seller actually offered the goods for sale there was no available market unless there was one actual buyer on that day at a fair

a Section 50(3) is set out at p 726 *a b*, post

price. If, on the other hand, there was only a notional or hypothetical sale there was no available market unless on the relevant day there were in the market sufficient traders *a* potentially in touch with each other to evidence a market in which the seller could if he had wished have sold the goods. Furthermore, the market price on a hypothetical sale was the fair market price for the total quantity of the goods if they had to be sold on the relevant day but taking into account the price which might be negotiated within a few days with other potential buyers who were not part of the market on that day only because of difficulties in communication. It followed that the plaintiffs were entitled to *b* damages based on the fair market or current price on the date of the breach for 7,755 tonnes of standard grade tin but that price in turn would be based on both the price which would have been obtained by a sale of all the tin on 12 March 1986 and the price which would have been obtained by sales negotiated over a short period before or after that date (see p 726 *e f*, p 730 *j*, p 731 *a* to *h* and p 732 *b* to *d*, post); *Garnac Grain Co Inc v H M F Faure & Fairclough Ltd and Bunge Corp* [1967] 2 All ER 353 followed.   *c*

(2) The practice of the Commercial Court to award interest at the base rate plus 1% was no more than a presumption which could be displaced if its application would be unfair to either party. However, since the defendants had not produced any evidence that the award of interest at the base rate plus 1% would be unfair, interest would be awarded on that basis (see p 733 *g h* and p 734 *b c*, post).

d

Notes
For the prima facie rule as to damages for non-acceptance of goods sold, see 41 Halsbury's Laws (4th edn) para 870, and for cases on the subject, see 39(2) Digest (Reissue) 510–515, 4292–4323.

For the Sale of Goods Act 1979, s 50, see 39 Halsbury's Statutes (4th edn) 143.

e

Cases referred to in judgment
ABD (Metals and Waste) Ltd v Anglo Chemical and Ore Co Ltd [1955] 2 Lloyd's Rep 456.
BP Exploration Co (Libya) Ltd v Hunt (No 2) [1982] 1 All ER 925, [1979] 1 WLR 783; *affd* [1982] 1 All ER 925, [1981] 1 WLR 232, CA; *affd* [1982] 1 All ER 925, [1983] 2 AC 352, [1982] 2 WLR 253, HL.
Charter v Sullivan [1957] 1 All ER 809, [1957] 2 QB 117, [1957] 2 WLR 528, CA.   *f*
Dunkirk Colliery Co v Lever (1878) 9 Ch D 20, CA.
FMC (Meat) Ltd v Fairfield Cold Stores Ltd [1971] 2 Lloyd's Rep 221.
Garnac Grain Co Inc v H M F Faure & Fairclough Ltd and Bunge Corp [1967] 2 All ER 353, [1968] AC 1130, [1967] 3 WLR 143, HL.
General Tire and Rubber Co v Firestone Tyre and Rubber Co Ltd [1975] 2 All ER 173, [1975] 1 WLR 819, HL.   *g*
Jamal v Moolla Dawood Sons & Co [1916] 1 AC 175, PC.
Polish Steam Ship Co v Atlantic Maritime Co, The Garden City [1984] 3 All ER 59, [1985] QB 41, [1984] 3 WLR 300, CA.
Tate & Lyle Food and Distribution Ltd v Greater London Council [1981] 3 All ER 716, [1982] 1 WLR 149.   *h*
Thompson (W L) Ltd v R Robinson (Gunmakers) Ltd [1955] 1 All ER 154, [1955] Ch 177, [1955] 2 WLR 185.

Assessment of damages
In 1986 the plaintiffs, Shearson Lehman Hutton Inc (former Shearson Lehman Bros Inc) and Shearson Lehman Metal Ltd (formerly Shearson Lehman Commodities Ltd), brought *j* two actions (which were subsequently consolidated) against the defendants, Maclaine Watson & Co Ltd and nine others, claiming damages and interest for breach of contracts made before and on 24 October 1985 for the purchase of quantities of tin ore. On 16 March 1989 Webster J gave judgment for the plaintiffs on the issue of liability and

a adjourned the hearing for the assessment of damages. The facts are set out in the judgment.

Peter Scott QC, Ian Glick QC and *Mary Morgan* for Shearsons.
Richard Aikens QC and *Adrian Hughes* for Maclaines.

Cur adv vult

b 21 December. The following judgment was delivered.

WEBSTER J. On 16 March 1989 I gave judgment on the issue of liability in this action, and decided that the defendants, to whom I shall refer as 'Maclaines', were not entitled to refuse to perform, in accordance with their terms, the contracts made before and on c 24 October 1985 under which they had agreed to buy tin from the first plaintiffs, to whom I shall refer as 'Shearsons'; and my preliminary conclusion was that the date by reference to which damages should be assessed is 12 March 1986. This has been the trial on the issue of damages; and both parties have agreed that damages are to be assessed by reference to that date.

d There were two groups of contracts which Shearsons and Maclaines made with each other, the 'cash and carries' and the 'general trades'. Between 25 July 1985 and 30 September 1985 Shearsons sold to Maclaines, as cash and carries, 7,755 tonnes of tin for a total price of about £70,203,130; on 20 September and 24 October 1985 Shearsons sold to Maclaines, as general trades, 100 tonnes of tin for a total price of £868,250; and between 30 July and 23 September 1985 Shearsons bought from Maclaines, as general trades, 610 tonnes of tin for a total price of £5,570,100. All the cash and carries were e standard tin; the general trades were a mixture of standard and high grade. It is common ground that the damages to which Shearsons are entitled for Maclaines' failure to accept the cash and carries and the general trades are to be assessed on the same basis; and that Maclaines are entitled to set off, against the damages payable to Shearsons, damages for Shearsons' non-acceptance of the general trades sold to them by Maclaines, also assessed on the same basis.

f It has always been common ground on the pleadings that there was an available market for tin on 12 March 1986; and during the trial of this issue it has been common ground that there was an available market for the quantity of tin held by Shearsons, which was 19,750 tonnes, of which 8,150, including the 7,755 sold to Maclaines, was standard grade.

The common ground has extended still further; for it is Shearsons' primary case, and g Maclaines' only case, that the measure of damages is that prescribed by s 50(3) of the Sale of Goods Act 1979, ie prima facie the difference between the contract prices and the market or current price on 12 March. Shearsons' alternative case is that the measure is that prescribed by s 50(2), which, in this case, would be the difference between the contract prices and the prices at which they sold the tin, plus carrying costs (financing costs, warehousing and insurance), the cost of swapping certain quantities of standard tin h for high grade tin, or vice versa, and the cost of buying new tin, all as part of their selling strategy. But in my judgment Shearsons may not rely on this alternative case because it would only arise if there were no available market for tin on 12 March 1986 within the meaning of that expression in s 50(3), because it has been common ground on the pleadings that there was such an available market and because, even if it were not common ground, I would in any event find that there was an available market on that j date, for reasons hereinafter appearing. But if Shearsons had been able to rely on their alternative case Maclaines admit the prices at which Shearsons sold the tin and they admit both that Shearsons incurred the actual costs which they would seek to recover and that those costs were reasonably incurred.

Thus, since all relevant figures are agreed, the only issues are the current or market price on 12 March 1986 and the rate of interest to which Shearsons are entitled from that date until the date of judgment; and I turn now to the first of those issues.

Section 50(3), under the rubric 'Damages for non-acceptance', provides:

> 'Where there is an available market for the goods in question the measure of damages is prima facie to be ascertained by the difference between the contract price and the market or current price at the time or times when the goods ought to have been accepted or (if no time was fixed for acceptance) at the time of the refusal to accept.'

Although a number of particular issues have arisen about the meaning and effect of this subsection, the parties agree on its general effect. Thus they agree (or if they do not the contrary is beyond argument) that the object of the provision is to avoid uncertainty by the arbitrary insertion, into the assessment of damages, of a presumption that if there is an available market the plaintiff seller can obtain the market or current price of the goods on the date of the breach, that his damages are to be measured by reference to that price whether or not it would have been reasonable or sensible for him to have waited before going into the market and selling the goods, and that neither party is to be adversely affected by price fluctuations either before or after the date of the breach. For these reasons the requirements of reasonable mitigation, which would ordinarily apply to a claim for damages, do not apply when the measure of damages is governed by s 50(3).

The parties also agree that the test for determining the market or current price is an objective one, but they do not agree about the extent of its objectivity. Shearsons contend that, if, as one of the witnesses said, they were less skilled in negotiating sales of tin than some of their competitors, that fact should be taken into account in determining the market or current price of the tin on 12 March 1986. But I reject that contention. The section refers to 'the market or current price' of the goods, meaning 'the goods in question', not 'the goods in question in the hands of the seller'; and, although the quantity of goods is clearly a relevant factor, a characteristic of the seller is not: to conclude otherwise would be to dilute the element of certainty and objectivity which the subsection otherwise achieves, and would come very close to necessitating consideration of what would be reasonable conduct on the part of the plaintiff seller, which, as I have said, is irrelevant for this purpose. In short, in my view, where as in this case the seller did not in fact sell or offer the goods for sale on the date of the breach, the subsection contemplates a hypothetical sale by a hypothetical seller of the amount in question of the goods in question.

There is also limited agreement about the relevance of the expression 'prima facie' in the subsection. Neither party argues, nor could it successfully argue, that the application of that expression to the facts of this case has the effect that the measure of damages prescribed by s 50(3) does not apply at all. But Maclaines could argue, I think, that the expression could affect the literal application of the words which follow it, a point to which I return later in this judgment.

As will be seen when I consider it, the evidence establishes that it would have been impossible to sell the greater part of the standard tin on 12–13 March to consumers of tin (as distinct from merchants), and that, for that and other reasons, a better price would have been obtained if the sale were to have been negotiated over a few days than if it were to have taken place all within 24 hours, ie by the end of 13 March. The central issues, therefore, are first whether it could be said, given the proper meaning of 'available market', that there was an available market on 12–13 March, on which dates most consumers would not have been accessible to a seller of 7,755 tonnes of standard tin; and second (and I shall refer hereafter to this issue as the 'appropriate price' issue) whether it is necessary, for the purpose of determining the market or current price on 12–13 March, to consider only prices at which the tin could have been negotiated and sold on that day or whether it is permissible to consider the price which could have been negotiated over

a slightly longer period. I have referred in this paragraph to 12–13 March because the
a   time for delivery expired at midnight on 12 March, so that 13 March would have been
the first date on which Shearsons could have sold the tin in question.

As to the meaning of 'available market' counsel for Shearsons submits that it is an
essential characteristic of an available market that there is *an* immediate buyer for the
goods in question, ie that there is an available market even if there is only one buyer.
Counsel for Maclaines submits that there are three relevant characteristics of an available
b   market: first, that there should be a ready demand for the goods in question, second, that
this ready demand should be present either immediately or within a reasonable time of
the breach and, third, that the demand should be supplied by a sufficiently large pool of
potential buyers who can be said to constitute the market.

As to the appropriate price issue, counsel for Shearsons submits: that the market or
current price is to be taken as the price that the goods in question would fetch in an
c   outright sale for cash on the date of the breach; that it is not permissible to consider a sale
on any other day, because on subsequent days the prices might be different; that to allow
a consideration of the price other than that on the day of the breach would produce all
the problems which it is the objective of the subsection to avoid, in that it would be
inconsistent with the requirements of certainty and with the irrelevance of mitigating
conduct; that it overlooks the principle underlying the subsection, namely that the seller
d   should receive the proceeds of sale on the day on which he would have received them,
not a few days later; and (reflecting his submission on 'appropriate price') that a sale to
any purchaser is sufficient provided that there is *a* purchaser in the market on the day.

The submissions of counsel for Maclaines are: that, although it is not necessary for
every potential buyer to be in the market, the market or current price can only be
ascertained by reference to a sufficient number of them; that the court is concerned not
e   with one sale but with a market or current price; that it would be quite unreasonable, if
mitigation were relevant, even in the interests of certainty, for a seller to be obliged to
sell on one day when everyone concerned would know that he would get a better price if
he were to be given a few days to negotiate it; and that a price negotiated in this way
would more truly reflect the market or current price on the day in question.

Six decisions were cited or referred to which bear on these two issues. Except in one
f   case (*Garnac Grain Co Inc v H M F Faure & Fairclough Ltd and Bunge Corp* [1967] 2 All ER
353, [1968] AC 1130) none of the facts or issues in any of those cases were similar to the
facts or issues in this case, and none of them contained any general statement of principle
by reference to which I can decide the appropriate price issue.

In *Dunkirk Colliery Co v Lever* (1878) 9 Ch D 20 the defendant had failed to perform an
agreement to purchase 15,000 tons of coal at the rate of 300 tons per week, and a question
g   arose whether at the relevant time there was an available market. James LJ said (at 25):

> 'What I understand by a market in such a case as this is, that when the Defendant
> refused to take the 300 tons the first week or the first month, the Plaintiffs might
> have sent it in waggons somewhere else, where they could sell it, just as they sell
> corn on the *Exchange*, or cotton at *Liverpool*: that is to say, that there was a fair market
h   > where they could have found a purchaser either by themselves or through some
> agent at some particular place. That is my notion of the meaning of a market under
> those circumstances.'

I note the reference to 'a fair market where they could have found a purchaser'. I note
also that in that case, although the seller had actually sold the coal to a third party, many
j   of the relevant facts had not been established, so that the court was enunciating a
statement of principle largely in the abstract.

In *Jamal v Moolla Dawood Sons & Co* [1916] AC 175 a seller of shares, after default by
the buyer, sold the shares not on the day of default but on various subsequent days. Lord
Wrenbury, giving the opinion of the Judicial Committee of the Privy Council, said (at
179) that the loss to be ascertained was the loss at the date of the breach and said (at 180):

'The seller's loss at the date of the breach was and remained the difference between contract price and market price at that date.' Counsel for Shearson relies, of course, on a
those last three words, the effect of which is, in any event, expressed in s 50(3) in the words 'at the time or times when the goods ought to have been accepted', subject possibly to the effect of the qualifying expression 'prima facie'.

In *W L Thompson Ltd v R Robinson (Gunmakers) Ltd* [1955] 1 All ER 154, [1955] Ch 177 the defendant company had refused to accept delivery of a new Vanguard motor car, which they had contracted to buy from the plaintiffs, who were dealers in motor cars. b
The plaintiff sellers returned the car to their suppliers and claimed their loss of profits on the ground that, as they alleged, there was no available market within the meaning of s 50(3). Upjohn J, having cited the dictum of James LJ which I have myself just cited, continued ([1955] 1 All ER 154 at 159–160, [1955] Ch 177 at 187):

> 'I think that . . . the decision of the Court of Appeal in *Dunkirk Colliery Co.* v. *Lever* c
> is binding on me, and, therefore, unless one finds something in the nature of a market in the sense used by JAMES, L.J., s. 50(3) has no further application. However, the point seems to me of somewhat academic interest in this case, because, if one gives to the word "market" an extended meaning, in my view on the facts which I have to consider, a precisely similar result is reached. Had the matter been res integra, I think I should have found that an "available market" merely means that d
> the situation in the particular trade in the particular area was such that the particular goods could freely be sold, and that there was a demand sufficient to absorb readily all the goods that were thrust on it, so that if a purchaser defaulted the goods in question could readily be disposed of.'

Upjohn J, applying the dictum of James LJ and his own principle, concluded that there was no available market for the sale of new motor cars and that there was no demand, in e
the plaintiff sellers' area, which could readily absorb all the Vanguards available for sale.

In *ABD (Metals and Waste) Ltd v Anglo Chemical and Ore Co Ltd* [1955] 2 Lloyd's Rep 456 the question also arose, on facts which are immaterial, whether there was an available market. Sellers J cited both the dictum of James LJ and of Upjohn J (which seemed to him to be 'a very acceptable definition and in accordance with the authorities') and f
applied those standards, i e the standards established by each of the two dicta, to the facts of the case (at 465). Having decided that the evidence established, 'within the ambit of these authorities which I have quoted', that there was an available market, Sellers J went on to add (at 466):

> 'It is not necessary to establish a market that it should have a fixed place or building, but there must be sufficient traders who are in touch with each other to g
> evidence a market, and I think that is so here.'

I note the reference to 'sufficient traders who are in touch with each other'.

In *Charter v Sullivan* [1957] 1 All ER 809, [1957] 2 QB 117 the defendant refused to accept delivery of a Hillman Minx motor car which could only be sold at the retail price fixed by the manufacturers. The plaintiff seller sold the car some seven to ten days after h
the date on which the defendant had refused to accept delivery, and the issue turned on the question whether there was an 'available market' within the meaning of s 50(3). Jenkins LJ said ([1957] 1 All ER 809 at 813, [1957] 2 QB 117 at 128):

> 'I doubt if JAMES, L.J.'s observations in *Dunkirk Colliery Co.* v. *Lever* should be literally applied as an exhaustive definition of an available market in all cases. On j
> the other hand, I do not find UPJOHN, J.'s definition entirely satisfactory. I will not, however, attempt to improve on it, but will content myself with the negative proposition that I doubt if there can be an available market for particular goods in any sense relevant to s. 50(3) of the Sale of Goods Act, 1893, unless those goods are available for sale in the market at the market or current price in the sense of the

a
price, whatever it may be, fixed by reference to supply and demand as the price at which a purchaser for the goods in question can be found, be it greater or less than or equal to the contract price. The language of s. 50(3) seems to me to postulate that in the cases to which it applies there will, or may, be a difference between the contract price and the market or current price, which cannot be so where the goods can only be sold at a fixed retail price.'

b
In that case, therefore, Jenkins LJ defined the meaning of 'available market' negatively by reference to the meaning of 'market or current price', which in turn he defined as a price 'fixed by reference to supply and demand as the price at which a purchaser for the goods in question can be found . . .'

Counsel for Shearsons relies on the words 'a purchaser for the goods . . . can be found', emphasising the indefinite article. Hodson LJ expressed no opinion on this point, but Sellers LJ said ([1957] 1 All ER 809 at 817, [1957] 2 QB 117 at 133–134):

c

'. . . counsel for the defendant placed great reliance on s. 50(3) of the Sale of Goods Act, 1893, and submitted that there was an available market for the car at the one fixed or current price, which was also the contract price, and therefore there could be no loss of profit recoverable as that sub-section established the measure of damages. No evidence was given as to anything the plaintiff might have done to
d
bring about a resale of the rejected car except that which he did, viz., place it in his showroom and await a new buyer. Having regard to his success within ten days, the submissions on the meaning of "available market" seem to me to be somewhat theoretical and academic. The Act does not attempt to define a market and it may be conceded that one can exist in a variety of circumstances and apart, of necessity, from a defined place, but, since its trading has to serve as a factor in measuring the
e
damages, it must at least be a market in which the seller could, if he wished, sell the goods left on his hands. At the time of the defendant's refusal to accept . . . it has not been shown that there was any real market where the rejected car could have been offered for sale and sold. There was no available market. No doubt the current retail price was known and ascertained but there was no immediate buyer.'

f Counsel for Shearsons again relies on those last three words submitting that there is an available market if there is an immediate buyer. It seems from this passage that Sellers LJ decided that there was no available market because there was no immediate buyer until seven to ten days after the defendant's refusal to accept delivery; but I note the words 'a market in which the seller could, if he wished, sell the goods left on his hands'.

The last decision cited is *Garnac Grain Co Inc v H M F Faure & Fairclough Ltd and Bunge*
g *Corp* [1967] 2 All ER 353, [1968] AC 1130. In that case a seller failed to deliver 15,000 tons of lard at a price of $193 per ton. The trial judge had assessed the damages at £254,464 being the difference between the contract price and the market price on 4 February 1964, which he took at $242·50 per ton of the goods in question. Lord Pearson, in a speech with which the other members of their Lordships' House all agreed, said ([1967] 2 All ER 353 at 359, [1968] AC 1130 at 1138):

h

'. . . it was contended that no assessment could properly be made on the basis of the difference between the contract price and the market price on Feb. 4, 1964 (or any other date that might be material), because there was then no market in the United Kingdom for fifteen thousand tons of lard for immediate delivery, and the evidence did not reveal any other basis for assessing damages. There was evidence
j
that at all material times (towards the end of January and early in February, 1964), one could not buy that quantity for immediate delivery in the United Kingdom. There was, however, evidence that one could buy smaller quantities—up to two thousand tons at a time—in the U.S.A. for delivery to ports for shipment to the United Kingdom; and there was a market price, given by one witness as 242·50 dollars and by another witness as 243·60 dollars per ton, for such purchases on Feb.

4, 1964. If one wished to buy fifteen thousand tons at those prices one would have
to do so over a period. According to one witness, if one were able to buy fifteen   *a*
thousand tons of lard at one time, one would have to pay a higher price. There was
thus some evidence on which MEGAW, J., could find that there was a market price
and that it was 242·50 dollars per ton on Feb. 4. No argument to the effect that there
was no market price proved was presented at the trial of the action. No such point
was included in the "respondents' notice" given by Garnac to the Court of Appeal. It
may have been raised in the Court of Appeal, but it is not mentioned in the   *b*
judgments. In these circumstances I do not think that the finding of fact of MEGAW,
J., on this point can be successfully challenged.'

That case concerned, in substance if not in form, the application of s 51(3), which
prescribes the measure of damages for non-delivery where there is an available market
for the goods in question. Although the point in issue in this case appears not to have   *c*
been argued, the decision of the trial judge that the appropriate market price was $242·50
per ton appears to support, and is certainly consistent with, the following propositions.

First, where a seller defaults, and where the market price exceeds the contract price, in
assessing the buyer's recoverable damages a court may take into account, as evidence
relevant to the market or current price on the date of the default, the price at which a
buyer could obtain the goods over a period of days rather than the price that he would   *d*
have to pay if required to make an immediate purchase, and, second, the court may, or
possibly should, adopt the price which would produce the lower of two alternative
awards.

The text in *Benjamin's Sale of Goods* (3rd edn, 1987) para 1294 under the rubric 'The
temporal test of availability' reads:

'The "ready" or "immediate" accessibility to substitute buyers or sellers should not   *e*
be taken too literally. In *Charter v. Sullivan* the Court of Appeal found that the
demand for the goods exceeded the supply, but (apart from the question of a fixed
retail price) Sellers L.J. held that the fact that the resale of a car was made some seven
to ten days after the breach prevented there being an available market: "There was
no immediate buyer". It is submitted that the temporal test should be one of a   *f*
reasonable time after the breach, given the nature of the goods in question and the
business situation of the plaintiff; and that the opinion of Sellers L.J. is wrong on
this point.'

It will be seen, however, that there is no express reference in any of the cases which I
have cited to the test being 'one of a reasonable time after the breach', although those
words are consistent with the effect of the *Garnac Grain* case; and I would not, even if it   *g*
was open to me, conclude that the conclusion of Sellers LJ, that there was no available
market because there was no available buyer (at all) until some seven to ten days after the
breach, was wrong.

What, in the light of these decisions, is the meaning of 'available market'? In
attempting to answer this question, I shall go no further than is necessary for the purpose
of applying the answer to the particular issue in this case, except in so far as it is necessary   *h*
to demonstrate that I have not overlooked any of the authorities to which I have been
referred.

Approached in this way, the answer seems to me to be: that if the seller actually offers
the goods for sale there is no available market unless there is one actual buyer on that day
at a fair price; that if there is no actual offer for sale, but only a notional or hypothetical   *j*
sale for the purposes of s 50(3), there is no available market unless on that day there are
in the market sufficient traders potentially in touch with each other to evidence a market
in which the actual or notional seller could if he wished sell the goods: see *ABD (Metals
and Waste) Ltd v Anglo Chemical and Ore Co Ltd* [1955] 2 Lloyd's Rep 456 at 466 per
Sellers LJ and *Charter v Sullivan* [1957] 1 All ER 809, [1957] 2 QB 117.

What is the answer to the second question, ie the appropriate price issue? The answer
a seems to me to be: that, where there is no actual sale, the market price must be a fair
market price for the total quantity of goods assuming them to have been sold by a seller
on the relevant date; but that, since it might be unfair to the defendant purchaser to
confine the price so established to the price obtainable if an actual sale had to be concluded
on that day, it is permissible to take into account the price which would be negotiated
within a few days with persons who were members of the market on that day and who
b could not be taken into account as potential buyers on the day in question only because
of difficulties of communication. If account is taken of the price which would have been
negotiated after a few days, no account can be taken of any price fluctuations after the
date of the breach, ie for that purpose it has to be assumed that the price remained
constant during the period of the negotiations.

The same result can be achieved in practice by assuming, for the purpose of establishing
c a fair price, that all the potential buyers who were members of the market on that day
were actually accessible, as potential buyers, to a seller of the quantity of goods in question
on the day of the breach, or that the hypothetical seller of the goods in question, knowing
that he would have to make the sale on that day, had begun to negotiate it sufficiently
far ahead to enable him to make contact with all potential buyers so as to achieve a sale,
on that day, at a fair market price for that day. Neither of these assumptions, if they have
d to be made, seems to me to be inconsistent with the objects of the subsection or with the
application, to the facts in such a case, of the general measure of damages under s 50(2);
there seems to be nothing wrong in making limited fictitious assumptions when the sale
relied on for ascertaining the market price is itself a notional or fictitious sale; and the
assumption that the notional seller was negotiating the sale for a few days before the day
in question is not, as counsel for Shearsons submits, inconsistent with the principle that
e considerations of mitigation are irrelevant to the assessment of damages under s 50(3),
because one is not making the assumption that the plaintiff ought to have acted in such
a way so as to mitigate his damage, but that, if a court is to ascertain what would have
been a fair market price on the day in question, in certain circumstances it is necessary to
assume that the sale of the goods in question could have been negotiated over the period
of a few days immediately preceding that day.
f   All these conclusions seem to me to be consistent with the decision in the *Garnac Grain*
case and not inconsistent with any of the other authorities; and I would, if necessary,
justify them by resorting to the expression 'prima facie' in the subsection, implicit in
which, in my view, is a licence to avoid a literal application of the following words in
circumstances in which literal application of them would not lead to the establishment
of a fair market or current price on the day of the breach, given that there is an available
g market. In other words, the expression 'prima facie' enables the court, in an appropriate
case where it would be unfair to confine a notional sale to a sale which could only have
been made, in practice, on the day in question, to determine what would have been in
substance a fair price on that day in all the circumstances.
     But I also conclude that the price which would have been obtained if it were necessary
h to assume that the notional sale had actually been concluded in one day should also be
taken into account unless the effect of doing so would be to arrive at an unfair market or
current price, or unless, in the view of the court in the light of the evidence as a whole, it
would appear to be wholly irrelevant to the determination of that price.
     I now turn to the facts; and the first question, applying these conclusions, is whether
there was an available market on 12–13 March. The fact that it is common ground on
j the pleadings that there was such a market is not conclusive of the question, partly
because the question is one of mixed fact and law and partly because Maclaines have not
alleged or established that Shearsons are estopped by their pleading from denying that
there was an available market. But in my judgment there was one, because it has not
been suggested, still less established, that on 12–13 March there were not in the market,
as distinct from actually accessible to the plaintiffs for the purpose of negotiating a sale of

the quantity of goods in question, sufficient traders potentially in touch with each other to evidence a market in which the notional seller could, if he wished, have sold all of the *a* 7,755 tonnes of standard tin. The fact that all of the potential buyers would not have been immediately accessible to the notional seller on that very day does not, in my view, mean that there was on that day no available market for the goods.

What was the fair market or current price on 12–13 March 1986 for 7,755 tonnes of standard grade tin? For the reasons that I have already expressed, in answering this question I shall take into account both the price which, I conclude, would have been *b* obtained if a sale had taken place all on 12–13 March, and the price which would have been obtained if it had taken place after negotiations of a few days up to a week, either before 12–13 March at a price fixed on that date and without reference to previous fluctuations, or on a sale or sales concluded up to a week after that date but on the assumption that the price had remained constant since 12–13 March. It seems to me to be impossible, in the circumstances of this case, to determine a fair market or current *c* price without taking into account, inter alia, the evidence about both those prices; in this case the fair market price can only first be determined by reference to a range, and necessarily a fairly wide range, of possible prices; and I cannot conclude that the price which would have been obtained if the whole tonnage had to be sold on 13 March is irrelevant to the determination of that range.

[His Lordship then considered the expert evidence and continued:]   *d*

It is obviously easier to be more confident about a fair market price range than about a specific fair market price; but taking into consideration the evidence as a whole, and in particular the various factors to which I have expressly referred, in my judgment a fair market price range on 13 March 1986 for standard tin was from £3,000 to £4,000. Although a number of the figures, purely as figures, might point to a fair price slightly higher than the midpoint of that range, I am quite satisfied that the fair price is not above *e* that point when account is taken of the very large tonnage involved; and having at first tentatively concluded that the fair price was *at* the midpoint, after rereading the evidence more than once I have concluded that the midpoint would be somewhat too high and that the fair market or current price of 7,755 tonnes of standard tin on 12–13 March 1986 was £3,400 per tonne. That figure is consistent with, but by no means determined *f* by, the price of £3,400 obtained by Rudolf Woolf by 25 March, and Mr Goldsobel's $5,000 per tonne trading at the time.

Interest

It is common ground that I should award interest on Shearsons' damages as from 12–13 March 1986. There is an issue as to the appropriate rate.

Shearsons' case is that I should follow what they contend is the practice of the *g* Commercial Court and award interest at base rate (London and Scottish Clearing Banks' Lending Rate, commonly referred to as the UK Clearing Banks' Base Lending Rate) plus 1%. Maclaines contend that the rate should be LIBOR (London Inter-Bank Offer Rate) plus one-eighth.

'The fundamental principle is that interest is not awarded as a punishment, but simply *h* because the plaintiff has been deprived of the use of the money which was due to him': see Robert Goff J in *BP Exploration Co (Libya) Ltd v Hunt (No 2)* [1982] 1 All ER 925 at 974, [1979] 1 WLR 783 at 845, citing the speech of Lord Salmon in *General Tire and Rubber Co v Firestone Tyre and Rubber Co Ltd* [1975] 2 All ER 173 at 192, [1975] 1 WLR 819 at 841.

There is good authority for the proposition that the practice in the Commercial Court (and now the Admiralty Court) is to award interest at base rate plus 1%: see *FMC (Meat)* *j* *Ltd v Fairfield Cold Stores Ltd* [1971] 2 Lloyd's Rep 221 at 227 per Donaldson J, where he described an award of interest at 1% over the bank rate as his 'usual course' and added: 'If one can draw money at less than 1 per cent. below the bank rate, best of luck to [the defendant].' In *BP Exploration Co (Libya) Ltd v Hunt (No 2)* [1982] 1 All ER 925 at 979, [1979] 1 WLR 783 at 849 Robert Goff J said that an award of interest at base rate plus 1%

was 'in accordance with the usual practice in this court', ie the Commercial Court; and
a Kerr LJ in *Polish Steam Ship Co v Atlantic Maritime Co* [1984] 3 All ER 59 at 77, [1985] QB
41 at 66–67, in a judgment with which, on this point, Eveleigh and Griffiths LJJ agreed,
said that an award at base rate plus 1% was in accordance with the practice of the
Commercial Court and, by that date, of the Admiralty Court.

Maclaines support their contention for LIBOR plus one-eighth in reliance on a
judgment of Forbes J in *Tate & Lyle Food and Distribution Ltd v Greater London Council*
b [1981] 3 All ER 716 at 722–723, [1982] 1 WLR 149 at 154–155 and Shearsons' case on
damages. Forbes J said:

c   'I feel satisfied that in commercial cases the interest is intended to reflect the rate
    at which the plaintiff would have had to borrow money to supply the place of that
    which was withheld. I am also satisfied that one should not look at any special
    position in which the plaintiff may have been; one should disregard, for instance,
    the fact that a particular plaintiff, because of his personal situation, could only
    borrow money at a very high rate or, on the other hand, was able to borrow at
    specially favourable rates. The correct thing to do is to take the rate at which
    plaintiffs in general could borrow money. This does not, however, to my mind,
    mean that you exclude entirely all attributes of the plaintiff other than that he is a
d   plaintiff. There is evidence here that large public companies of the size and prestige
    of these plaintiffs could expect to borrow at 1% over MLR, while for smaller and less
    prestigious concerns the rate might be as high as 3% over MLR. I think it would
    always be right to look at the rate at which plaintiffs with the general attributes of
    the actual plaintiff in the case (though not, of course, with any special or peculiar
    attribute) could borrow money as a guide to the appropriate interest rate. If
e   commercial rates are appropriate I would take 1% over MLR as the proper figure for
    interest in this case . . . I should add, perhaps, that the proper question is: at which
    rate could the plaintiff borrow the required sum and not what return could the
    plaintiff have expected if he had invested it?'

And, in conclusion, he awarded interest at 1% over base rate.

f   Although the decision of Forbes J in the *Tate & Lyle* case was neither referred to in the
judgment nor cited in the *Polish Steam Ship Co* case I do not conclude that the cases which
refer to the practice in the Commercial and Admiralty Courts have the effect of
precluding evidence as to the rate at which persons with the general attributes of the
plaintiff could have borrowed the money. In the *FMC (Meat) Ltd* case and the *Polish Steam
Ship Co* case no evidence had been adduced on this question. In the *BP Exploration* case no
g   evidence had been adduced in relation to the sterling part of the award; but evidence was
adduced, and admitted by Robert Goff J, on the dollar element.

I conclude, therefore, that the practice of the Commercial Court amounts to no more
than a presumption which can be displaced if its application would be substantially
unfair to either one party or the other. I do not treat Donaldson J's short dictum 'If one
can draw money at less . . . best of luck to them' as inconsistent with this conclusion.

h   But if the presumption is to be displaced the burden must clearly lie on the party who
seeks to displace it. In this case no evidence has been called by either party; but Maclaines
rely on the following passage from Shearsons' case on damages at para 4.5:

j   'If . . . the appropriate rate in a Commercial case is that at which a plaintiff with
    the general attributes of Shearsons could have borrowed the money with any special
    position of Shearsons being disregarded . . . then Shearsons say that that rate is
    LIBOR plus one-eighth.'

The question, therefore, is whether Maclaines are entitled to treat that paragraph as
evidence which displaces the normal presumption.

I am sure that it is right to treat the document containing Shearsons' case on damages
as a pleading. It was signed by their solicitors, and served in accordance with an order

that I made at the conclusion of the trial on the issue of liability. It is therefore to be read as containing a formal allegation. But, in my view, unless evidence is given to support it **a** or unless it can be treated as a formal admission, Maclaines cannot rely on it as evidence in the case, unless they seek to set up an estoppel. Counsel for Maclaines did not, as I understood him, argue that it constituted a formal admission; but even had he done so I would not have accepted the argument. Counsel for Shearsons withdrew the passage in his opening of Shearsons' case on damages, and neither before that moment nor after it had Maclaines ever made any formal admission of it. Moreover, at no stage have **b** Maclaines sought to contend, still less to establish sufficient evidence to prove, that Shearsons are estopped from resiling from that paragraph.

I conclude, therefore, that there is no evidence which enables me to depart from the normal presumption and I have no knowledge, let alone judicial knowledge, relevant to the point. I therefore award interest on the damages at the base rate prevailing from time to time from 13 March 1986 until today, plus 1%.   **c**

It has been agreed that at this stage I should not attempt, myself, to convert my conclusions as to the market or current price and the rate of interest into specific figures.

Damages and interest accordingly.

Solicitors: *Simmons & Simmons* (for Shearsons); *Allen & Overy* (for Maclaines).   **d**

K Mydeen Esq   Barrister.

     e

Practice Direction

FAMILY DIVISION

Probate – Practice – Copies of wills and grants – Postal applications – Applications to be dealt with by York sub-registry – Applications direct to district registries or York sub-registry – **f** *Supreme Court Act 1981, ss 124, 125(c).*

As from 3 December 1990 requests for copies of wills and grants deposited in accordance with s 124 of the Supreme Court Act 1981 received through the post in the Principal Registry of the Family Division will be forwarded to the York probate sub-registry for the necessary search to be undertaken.   **g**

The probate registry identified by the search as that from which the grant issued will be requested to forward to the applicant the copies required.

There may be some advantage in terms of saving time for an applicant who knows that the will was proved in, or that the grant issued from, a district probate registry to apply direct to that registry or direct to York Probate Sub-Registry, Duncombe Place, York YO1 2EA, DX 61543 York, instead of the Principal Registry.   **h**

I continue to give my approval in accordance with s 125(c) of the 1981 Act to the practice of allowing applicants who attend in person at the Principal Registry to obtain copies of wills and grants from the Principal Registry regardless of the fact that the will may have been proved in, or the grant issued from, a district probate registry.

C F TURNER   **j**
31 October 1990   Senior Registrar.

Note

J v C

FAMILY DIVISION

THORPE J

8, 9 FEBRUARY 1990

Declaration – Procedure – Declaration as to lawfulness of proposed conduct – Proposed medical treatment – Medical treatment of person unable to consent thereto – Mentally handicapped person – Sterilisation – Originating summons – Directions – Evidence – Evidence by affidavit – Hearsay etc normally inadmissible – Directions for trial in complex and uncertain cases – Disposal without adjournment in straightforward and uncontentious cases – Ex parte applications to court in cases of emergency – Appearance by Official Solicitor – RSC Ord 28, rr 1A(1) (4), 4.

THORPE J, after giving specific directions in chambers on an application by the plaintiff, the sister and next friend of the defendant, a severely mentally handicapped woman, for a declaration that the proposed sterilisation of the defendant would not amount to an unlawful act by reason only of the absence of the defendant's consent, adjourned the application into open court to give general guidance on the appropriate procedure in such applications. This is the first application since the judgment of the House of Lords in *F v West Berkshire Health Authority (Mental Health Act Commission intervening)*[1989] 2 All ER 545, [1990] 2 AC 1 for a declaration that a proposed operation of sterilisation on a defendant of severe mental subnormality would be lawful.

The application was made by way of originating summons filed in the Principal Registry on 29 October 1989. On issuing the application, the court appointed a directions hearing before Mr Registrar Conn on 5 December 1989. The registrar was clearly mindful of the words of Lord Brandon in *F v West Berkshire Health Authority* [1989] 2 All ER 545 at 558, [1990] 2 AC 1 at 65 where he said:

'In my opinion there will, in cases of this kind, have to be a summons for directions heard by a judge, and it should be left to him to decide, on the hearing of such summons, whether any, and, if so what, further and more detailed directions should be given in the particular case before him.'

He therefore ordered that a further appointment be obtained before a judge of the Family Division for further directions and the application now comes before me, both the plaintiff sister and the defendant patient being represented. On behalf of the defendant patient, the Official Solicitor not only makes submissions as to the appropriate directions for the further preparation of this case, but also invites general guidance as to the appropriate procedure in amplification of the general rules formulated by Lord Brandon in his speech. The specific directions in this case having been dealt with in chambers, I have adjourned into open court in response to the Official Solicitor's invitation.

An originating summons seeking a declaration is issued pursuant to RSC Ord 28. The defendant has 14 days to file an acknowledgment of service, and the plaintiff 14 days thereafter to file his evidence: see Ord 28, r 1A(1). The defendant's evidence is to be filed 28 days thereafter: Ord 28, r 1A(4). The provisions as to directions are contained in Ord 28, r 4, but none seems particularly appropriate to these cases. In my judgment the registry, on issuing the originating summons, should fix a date for directions before a judge of the Family Division on the first open date after the passage of eight weeks. In that time the parties will be able to file their evidence in accordance with Ord 28, r 1A, and the judge at the directions appointment will be able to review the broad cases advanced by the parties.

If the case appears complex and uncertain in its outcome, he may give further directions including directions for trial; but, if the case appears straightforward and *a* without contention, he may dispose of it there and then without further adjournment. For although the gravity of the issues and consequences in sterilisation cases call for appropriate safeguards against hasty or ill-considered conclusions, many such cases involve a real degree of urgency. The longer the litigation, the longer the period in which the patient may be exposed to risk. Furthermore, in cases of emergency the originating summons can always be preceded by an initial application ex parte when the *b* court, on an undertaking to issue the originating summons forthwith, may consider abridging time limits or dispensing with procedures generally appropriate.

As to evidence, in my judgment all evidence, including expert evidence, should be on affidavit whether adduced by the plaintiff or the Official Solicitor. Hearsay or exhibited reports from other sources should not ordinarily be regarded as admissible. The Official Solicitor should be free to present his case in the same way as the plaintiff, relying on *c* affidavits and submissions. He should not feel himself under an obligation to submit a report.

In response to the judgment in *F v West Berkshire Health Authority* the Official Solicitor, with the aid of leading counsel, drafted a practice note. This has been reported in *Practice Note (Official Solicitor: sterilization)* [1989] 2 FLR 447[1]. He has also drafted a questionnaire *d* and, on receiving notice of any application for the sterilisation of a patient, it is his practice to dispatch a copy of both the practice note and the questionnaire to the solicitors for the plaintiff.

As to the practice note, it was issued for the guidance of practitioners and was not intended to be a mandatory code. As far as para 5 suggests that there will always be two hearings before a judge of the Family Division, I have already said that, in my judgment, *e* it will be appropriate in certain cases to elide the two hearings into one.

As to the last sentence of para 6, it is not to be interpreted as precluding or restricting the possibility that straightforward cases may be disposed of without oral evidence or dissent.

Finally the first sentence of para 7 needs to be expanded to make plain that, as well as acting as the patient's guardian ad litem in most cases, the Official Solicitor will also *f* appear as ex officio defendant in some. Whichever his role, all that follows in para 7 is of equal application.

As to the questionnaire, it is issued to indicate the matters which the Official Solicitor would hope to see brought out in the presentation of the plaintiffs' case. An answer to the questionnaire is certainly not obligatory, but if it is answered then the answer should be settled by the solicitors for the plaintiff, with or without the assistance of counsel, and *g* should reflect the evidence obtained both from the family and from the experts.

Bebe Chua   Barrister.

h

1   Editor's note: The Official Solicitor's practice note has since been amended to take account of the judgment reported herein: see [1990] NLJR 1273

Jones v Swansea City Council

HOUSE OF LORDS
LORD TEMPLEMAN, LORD GRIFFITHS, LORD ACKNER, LORD OLIVER OF AYLMERTON AND LORD LOWRY
24, 25, 26 APRIL, 15 NOVEMBER 1990

Public office – Abuse of – Misfeasance by public officer – Exercise of private contractual power – Council owning freehold premises – Plaintiff holding premises under agreement for lease made with council – Council refusing consent for change of use for premises – Plaintiff alleging council's action motivated by malice on part of majority councillors because of plaintiff's husband's political activities in opposition to majority – Whether plaintiff having good cause of action against council if malice on part of majority of councillors established.

In 1978 a council advertised for tenders for a 99-year lease of a vacant site which it owned with permission for the erection of a shop or an office and showroom. The plaintiff, who was in business with her husband who was then one of the councillors representing the majority Ratepayers Party on the council, submitted the only tender, which was accepted by the council. The plaintiff took possession in September 1978 and in January 1979 she applied for a change of use to that of a club. In April, after an acrimonious debate, the council approved the change of use. During the debate the leader of the Labour group stated that if he was returned at the forthcoming local government elections he would put down a motion to have the council's decision reversed. In May 1979 the local government elections resulted in a decisive Labour victory and the leader of the Labour group became the leader of the council. The plaintiff's husband did not stand for re-election. On 28 June the council voted to rescind the consent for a change in the use of the plaintiff's premises to that of a club, the resolution being proposed by the leader of the Labour group and carried by 28 to 15, the majority being made up of all 28 members of the Labour group present. The plaintiff brought an action against the council claiming, inter alia, that by maliciously refusing consent to the change of use with the object of injuring the plaintiff and her husband the council had been guilty of the tort of misfeasance in public office when passing the resolution of 28 June. The council contended that the plaintiff could not succeed against it on such a cause of action, even if it was otherwise justified on the evidence, because the council was acting as the plaintiff's landlord in circumstances in which, under private law, no cause of action based on malice would lie. The judge rejected that submission but dismissed the plaintiff's action on the ground that malice had not been proved against the leader of the Labour group or any other members of the Labour group. The plaintiff appealed to the Court of Appeal, which allowed the appeal, holding that the plaintiff had a good cause of action in tort for misfeasance in a public office on the part of the council and that the judge's finding that the leader and the other members of the Labour group had not been actuated by personal malice towards her and her husband when voting for the resolution could not be sustained. The court ordered a retrial because it was not in a position to substitute a positive finding of malice in place of the judge's finding that there had been no malice. The council appealed to the House of Lords.

Held – The plaintiff would have had a good cause of action against the council for misfeasance in a public office if she had alleged and proved that a majority of the councillors present, having voted for the resolution, had done so with the object of damaging her. However, since her case as pleaded was that all the Labour councillors who voted for the resolution were infected by their leader's malice and since that had not been proved, her case was bound to fail even if malice were proved against the leader of the Labour group. The appeal would accordingly be allowed and the judgment and order

of the judge restored (see p 739 *a* to *d*, p 741 *d* to *f*, p 744 *e f*, p 749 *f* to *j*, p 751 *b* to *d*,
p 753 *d* to *f* and p 756 *d* to *g*, post).   *a*
    Dunlop v Woollahra Municipal Council [1981] 1 All ER 1202 considered.
    Per curiam. To reach a conclusion founded on an alternative assumption is a common
and useful feature of civil trial by a judge without a jury and only exceptional
circumstances will justify an appellate court in refusing to accept supportable conclusions
pronounced by a judge on such a basis (see p 739 *a* to *d* and p 755 *g*, post).
    Decision of the Court of Appeal [1989] 3 All ER 162 reversed.   *b*

Notes
For abuse of public office, see 1(1) Halsbury's Laws (4th edn reissue) para 203.

Cases referred to in judgments
Dunlop v Woollahra Municipal Council [1981] 1 All ER 1202, [1982] AC 158, [1981] 2   *c*
    WLR 693, PC.
Gautret v Egerton (1867) LR 2 CP 371.
R v Waltham Forest London BC, ex p Baxter [1987] 3 All ER 671, [1988] QB 419, [1988] 2
    WLR 257, CA.
Watt (or Thomas) v Thomas [1947] 1 All ER 582, [1947] AC 484, HL.
                                                                                                    d

Appeal
The defendant, Swansea City Council, appealed with leave of the Appeal Committee of
the House of Lords given on 8 May 1989 against the decision of the Court of Appeal
(Nourse and Stuart-Smith LJJ, Slade LJ dissenting) ([1989] 3 All ER 162, [1990] 1 WLR
54) on 3 March 1989 allowing the appeal of the plaintiff, Margaret Elizabeth Jones,
against the judgment of Roch J given on 4 February 1988 whereby he dismissed the   *e*
plaintiff's claim against the council for damages for misfeasance in a public office. The
facts are set out in the opinion of Lord Lowry.

John Lindsay QC and *Kenneth Thomas* for the council.
John R Macdonald QC and *Philip Rees* for the plaintiff.   *f*

Their Lordships took time for consideration.

15 November. The following opinions were delivered.

LORD TEMPLEMAN. My Lords, the salient features of this unfortunate litigation
appear from the judgments in the Court of Appeal ([1989] 3 All ER 162, [1990] 1 WLR   *g*
54) and the comprehensive speech of my noble and learned friend Lord Lowry.
    This case presents some puzzling and disquieting features, namely the enmity
displayed against Cllr Jones because he was prominent in the Ratepayers group for 1979
when a Labour leader was prosecuted for corruption, the rejection of an offer by Mrs
Jones to pay a substantially increased rent for change of use, the public display of anger   *h*
and threats made by Cllr Tyssul Lewis at the council meeting on 26 April 1979, the
observation by the judge that 'this is not a case in which I can say that the evidence of
Cllr Tyssul Lewis satisfies me that he was not motivated by malice . . . for reasons of
personal antipathy . . .', the acceptance by the judge of the evidence that nothing relevant
was said at the meeting of the Labour group prior to the council meeting on 28 June
1979 and the inference that the members of the Labour group spontaneously and   *j*
independently came to the same conclusion as their leader. In these circumstances, I have
every sympathy with the penetrative observation of Nourse LJ that to deny that it was
open to the judge to infer group malice 'would in my view be to disregard the realities of
decision-taking by councillors in local government' (see [1989] 3 All ER 162 at 187,
[1990] 1 WLR 54 at 86). But the disputed events took place in 1979, the writ was not

issued until 1985, and the trial took place in 1988. A second trial in 1990, raking over
a the unsavoury history of the Swansea City Council, would be oppressive and unfair on
the witnesses and any result would be suspect. Accordingly, with some misgivings I
concur in allowing this appeal. The moral of this story is that a councillor and any close
relative of a councillor should avoid any business transactions with the council.

LORD GRIFFITHS. My Lords, I have had the advantage of reading in draft the speech
b prepared by my noble and learned friend Lord Lowry and for the reasons which he has
given I would allow the appeal.

LORD ACKNER. My Lords, for the reasons summarised by my noble and learned
friend Lord Lowry in the final two paragraphs of his speech, which I have had the
advantage of reading in draft, I too would allow this appeal, restore the judgment and
c order of the trial judge.

LORD OLIVER OF AYLMERTON. My Lords, I have had the advantage of reading
in draft the speech prepared by my noble and learned friend Lord Lowry. I agree with it
and would allow the appeal for the reasons which he has given.

d **LORD LOWRY.** My Lords, this appeal is concerned with an alleged tort of misfeasance
in public office by Swansea City Council against Mrs Margaret Elizabeth Jones (whom I
shall call 'the plaintiff'). The facts are set out admirably and in considerable detail by
Slade LJ in the Court of Appeal ([1989] 3 All ER 162 at 164ff, [1990] 1 WLR 54 at 57ff),
and I shall not weary your Lordships by restating them. It is enough to say that the
council owned a vacant site at 88–89 High Street, Swansea and in March 1978 advertised
e for tenders for a 99-year lease of the site under the heading 'Development Site at High
Street with permission for erection of a shop or an office and showroom'. The plaintiff
was in business with her husband Benjamin Jones, then one of the councillors representing
the majority Ratepayers group or party on the council, and on 4 May 1978 she submitted
the only tender, which was accepted by the council in June 1978. The effect of the
council's planning permission (granted to itself on 23 February 1978), when read with
f the terms of the tender, limited the use of the site to that of an office and showroom. In
September 1978 the plaintiff took possession of the site with the council's consent and
started building. She wished to change the use to that of a club, and this involved the
need for both planning permission and the council's permission *as her landlord* to alter
the use of the premises. The council's dual function helps to explain the large number of
meetings referred to in Slade LJ's summary. It was, of course, for the council ultimately
g to consider the respective recommendations of the planning committee and the estates
committee and to make a decision.

On 9 March 1979 the council and the plaintiff entered into a written agreement for a
lease in which the user clause conformed with the existing planning permission. On 13
March the planning committee by nine votes to three and on 14 March the estates
h committee by seven votes to five (subject to an increased rent being agreed) approved the
change of use to that of a club.

On 29 March the council confirmed by a single vote the resolution of the planning
committee but by a majority of 22 to 18 rejected the resolution of the estates committee.
The majority was of a cross-party character, since it included two independents, two
Conservatives and at least four of the Ratepayers group. On 3 April the plaintiff's
j solicitors wrote to the council's chief executive asking that her request for change of use
consent be reconsidered and on 11 April, despite the council's decision of 29 March, the
estates committee by eight votes to six again resolved in favour of a change of use to that
of a club.

On 26 April the council by 24 votes to 18 confirmed the estates committee resolution
of 11 April, thereby reversing its own decision of 29 March, and, as the factual summary

of Slade LJ shows, this was an important council meeting, to which I shall presently refer.
On 6 May 1979 the local government elections were held and resulted, so far as   *a*
Swansea City Council was concerned, in a decisive Labour victory. Mr Jones did not
stand for re-election, several of the Ratepayers group lost their seats and shortly after the
election Cllr Tyssul Lewis became the leader of the council.

In that capacity he attended the estates committee meeting on 13 June and, consistently
with his attitude at the council meeting on 26 April, was instrumental in having the city
estate agent's recommendation for a new rent (consequent on the proposed change of   *b*
use) disapproved by eleven votes to five.

At the council meeting on 28 June 1979 Cllr Tyssul Lewis proposed and carried a
resolution to rescind the council's resolution of 26 April. All 28 Labour members present,
but no others, voted in favour of that resolution, which was carried by 28 to 15 and
which became the basis for the cause of action against the council when the plaintiff
issued her writ on 27 June 1985, five years and 364 days later.   *c*

The summary of facts given in the Court of Appeal has described the events and the
litigation which followed the council's reversion to its position of 29 March (see [1989] 3
All ER 162 at 170–171, [1990] 1 WLR 54 at 65–67). I need not now refer to this, but the
summary also contains a sketch of the political background to which I call your Lordships'
attention ([1989] 3 All ER 162 at 165, [1990] 1 WLR 54 at 58–59):

   d

> 'Neither the plaintiff nor Mr Jones had been concerned in politics prior to the
> local government elections in May 1976. Before that date the council had been
> controlled by the Labour group of councillors for some forty years. Shortly before
> those elections, allegations of corruption in its affairs had been made which involved
> the leader of the Labour group at that time, Mr Gerald Murphy, and certain officers
> of the council. He was one of three councillors who represented the Landore ward.   *e*
> The local government election for the council held in May 1976 followed a bitter
> election campaign. It resulted in the Labour group being reduced to only 8
> councillors out of a total of 51. Following that election, a new group of councillors,
> calling themselves the Ratepayers Party, had an overall majority. Mr Jones was one
> of the three new Ratepayer councillors who replaced Mr Gerald Murphy and two
> others as representatives of the Landore ward. He had taken a leading part in the   *f*
> campaign, making available money, office accommodation and secretarial facilities
> to the Ratepayers Party. Between 1976 and 1979 the atmosphere on the council was
> an unhappy one. In 1976 or 1977 Mr Murphy was convicted of corruption in
> connection with his conduct as a councillor and sentenced to a term of imprisonment.
> Then, in 1978 or 1979, the leader of the Ratepayers group of councillors, the then
> leader of the council, was himself convicted of corruption in regard to his behaviour   *g*
> as a councillor and sentenced to a term of imprisonment.'

I should also mention that, when the plaintiff on 30 March learnt of the council's
decision of 29 March, she complained to the local commissioner of the Commission for
Local Administration in Wales the same day that 'it had become clearly apparent that
there was a personal vendetta being carried out against her husband, who was also a local   *h*
councillor in the Ratepayer group of councillors in Swansea' (see [1989] 3 All ER 162 at
167, [1990] 1 WLR 54 at 62). She referred by name to two Ratepayer councillors and to
the wife of an independent councillor (but not to any Labour councillors) as displaying
particularly vindictive attitudes towards Mr Jones and claimed that these councillors
would most vigorously oppose her project, aided by the entire Labour group of
councillors simply because her husband had an interest in the project. As requested, the   *j*
commissioner conducted an inquiry into the decision, in the course of which he also
considered what had happened at subsequent council and committee meetings. He
reported on 12 February 1981, rejecting the plaintiff's allegations. I mention this because,
by consent of the parties, the commissioner's findings were put in evidence at the trial
before Roch J, who concluded his judgment by saying:

'I make this comment: that the local commissioner at the end of his investigations
reached conclusions which are broadly consistent with those which I have reached,
after careful consideration of the evidence that I have received in this case.'

In the statement of claim and particulars the plaintiff alleged that all the Labour
councillors who voted for the resolution on 28 June 1979 were motivated by the desire
to damage the plaintiff and Mr Jones and that they all bore a grudge against him, and her
case was presented on that basis both at the trial and in the Court of Appeal. The proof of
that allegation naturally depended in the first place on proving that Cllr Tyssul Lewis
had been activated by malice and also on showing that, either directly or indirectly,
expressly or by implication from the circumstances, he as an individual and as leader of
the Labour group had caused the other Labour councillors to vote as they did. Indeed,
apart from him, Cllr McDonald-Murray, who had been deputy leader of the Labour
group before, but not after, the local government election of 6 May 1979, was the only
councillor against whom the plaintiff seriously attempted at the trial to prove express
malice.

Having regard to *Dunlop v Woollahra Municipal Council* [1981] 1 All ER 1202, [1982]
AC 158 and the cases mentioned in Wade *Administrative Law* (6th edn, 1988) p 777, I
apprehend that a local authority can be sued for misfeasance in a public office, but
counsel argued at the trial and in the Court of Appeal that the plaintiff could not succeed
against it on such a cause of action, even if it were otherwise justified by the evidence,
because in this case the council was acting as a landlord in circumstances in which,
according to private law, no cause of action based on malice would lie. The trial judge
and the Court of Appeal both rejected this argument for reasons with which I am
respectfully inclined to agree. This point, however, which constituted the council's first
submission on the appeal, was by agreement left on one side in this House until the other
points in the case had been argued and, in the event, your Lordships did not require to
hear argument on it. Accordingly, I do not propose on this occasion to discuss the bounds
of misfeasance committed by a body such as a local council or to compare the remedy for
that tort with an application for judicial review, but I consider that, generally speaking,
if a plaintiff *alleges and proves* that a majority of the councillors present, having voted for
a resolution, did so with the object of damaging the plaintiff, he thereby proves *against
the council* misfeasance in a public office.

The trial judge was not satisfied that malice had been proved against Cllr Tyssul Lewis
or against any Labour councillors and accordingly he dismissed the action. Before
considering, in the light of such high authorities as *Watt (or Thomas) v Thomas* [1947] 1
All ER 582, [1947] AC 484, whether it was open to the Court of Appeal to set aside his
judgment, it is important to see what he decided.

I would make two preliminary observations. The case was concerned almost entirely
with oral evidence given, by witnesses who were closely involved, almost nine years after
the event. Feelings in a charged political atmosphere might remain sharp but memories,
even of honest witnesses, must have dimmed. If the plaintiff, on whom lay the burden
of proof, delayed for six years to bring her action, the council and its witnesses can
scarcely be blamed if some of what they had to say was not entirely clear. Second, the
trial judge, when he was not sure of the answer, rightly based his conclusion on where
the burden of proof of an issue lay. I have, moreover, received a fairly clear impression
that, in delivering judgment in this very political case, he had well in mind the maxim
'Least said, soonest mended', which I suspect he applied, so far as he could consistently
with his duty to decide the case. This procedure, however, did not entirely satisfy the
Court of Appeal, which was for its part equally anxious to penetrate the mist and arrive
at the truth.

The plaintiff relied on negligence as well as misfeasance. This was rightly regarded as
a hopeless mission and she did not persevere with negligence in the Court of Appeal. Her
main point on misfeasance in the statement of claim as amended was:

'The controlling party voted en bloc . . . [and] Each member thereof was affected
by malice the principal instigators whereof were E. Tyssul Lewis; A. Lloyd; and L. *a*
Hopkins. Their intended victims were Benjamin Jones and through him his wife
the Plaintiff.'

The plaintiff's counsel at the trial and also in the Court of Appeal put the case of malice
against the councillors as a body in several different ways, but at all times they stuck
tenaciously to the allegation that all the councillors were infected by malice. This stand *b*
combined both logic and weakness; logic because, once the plaintiff was forced to concede
that there could have been councillors who voted for the resolution without being so
infected, the blanket effect of her case would disappear; weakness because three
councillors called as witnesses said that they voted for what they considered to be good
reasons, that they had not been instructed by Cllr Tyssul Lewis or anyone else how they
should vote and that there had been no group decision or party whip in operation. The *c*
judge accepted this evidence and it was, in my opinion, clearly open to him to do so.
   Giving judgment Roch J said:

   'In his closing submissions, [counsel for the plaintiff] put the plaintiff's case on
   this issue in this way: that Cllr Tyssul Lewis was malicious and as a consequence
   everybody who voted for the resolution on 28 June 1979 was affected by his malice, *d*
   he being the leader of the Labour Party, the majority party, on the Swansea City
   Council in June 1979. I do not accept the soundness of that submission. In my
   judgment, if one councillor is activated by malice, then that councillor's malice will
   only taint the actions of fellow councillors if either they know of that malice and
   acquiesce in it or the councillor who is malicious is in a position to, and does, apply
   a party whip so that the whole of his party group votes in the way he desires at his *e*
   direction.'

In my opinion that statement did at least full justice to the plaintiff's legal position and,
as your Lordships have seen, the facts as found by the judge did not match the plaintiff's
requirements for a decision in her favour.
   The judge in the course of narrating the history of the affair made certain findings of *f*
fact. Those findings have been accepted on behalf of the plaintiff. They include the
finding 'on the balance of probability' (which indicates a careful and scrupulous approach
to the evidence) that a meeting in the Bayview Hotel in July 1979, as deposed to by Mr
Jones, did not take place and that what was alleged to have been said on the occasion of
that alleged meeting was not said. In reality, when one reads the judgment, the evidence
against this meeting having happened appears very convincing. The judge then turned *g*
to deal with the issues, describing as the foremost issue in the case the question whether
Cllr Tyssul Lewis, either alone or with other leading members of the Labour group, was
activated by malice towards the plaintiff at the meeting of 28 June 1979.
   He disposed, rightly, as the Court of Appeal concedes, of the plaintiff's first point that
the decision at that meeting was so unreasonable that it could only be explained by the *h*
presence of malice. On this issue, as well as generally, your Lordships will recall (1) that
there were rational grounds (entertained by witnesses whose evidence was accepted by
the judge) for not allowing an alteration of use and (2) that the council's first resolution
passed at a time when Mr Jones's party was in control but reversed four weeks later, while
that party was still in control, had been against granting permission.
   The judge noted, as already mentioned, that, when complaining to the local *j*
commissioner, the plaintiff did not name any member of the Labour group as having
been actuated by malice and that on 29 March those who voted against giving permission
included members of every political group. He then in a manner indicative of great care
and anxious thought reviewed the different meetings which had been held and proceeded
to make his assessment of Cllr Tyssul Lewis. The judge's review involved in particular a

consideration of the council meetings held on 29 March, 26 April and 28 June 1979 and
a the estates committee meeting of 13 June.

He noted that there had been three broad grounds of objection to the use of the
premises as a club: (1) inadequate parking facilities, a ground in which he thought there
was no substance; (2) the likelihood of disturbance to residents, a ground which derived
some support from a petition and from approaches made by residents and traders to
councillors; (3) the fact that the site had originally been advertised on the basis of use as a
b shop and offices and the likelihood that the plaintiff's would not have been the sole
tender if the use contemplated in the advertisement had been wider. The first two
grounds were really planning considerations, but it is worth recalling that the planning
committee's recommendation was approved on 29 March by only one vote. The rejection
at the same council meeting of the estates committee's recommendation indicates that
the third ground listed above swayed the balance. The judge pointed out that witnesses
c for the plaintiff regarded this ground of objection as reasonable, if honestly held, and he
also noted another reason advanced by objecting councillors, namely that the applicant
for the lease on the original terms was the wife of a member of the majority group on
the council and therefore ought not to appear to have received preferential treatment.

He then considered the plaintiff's argument that, even if the decision against her could
be justified rationally, there was clear evidence pointing to malice on the part of the
d Labour councillors, in particular Cllr Tyssul Lewis. At the estates committee on 14
March, when the question of permitting a change of use was discussed, Cllr Hawkins
(Labour) was noted as saying:

> 'Speak on behalf of Ward member—objects strongly—car parking—enough
> pubs in area. Not personal vendetta. Club won't uplift area.'

e   There being no earlier context to evoke any denial of a vendetta, the plaintiff submitted
that Cllr Hawkins's denial itself indicated a vendetta. I note that the same point, for what
it is worth, could have been, but was not, made in regard to what Cllr McDonald-Murray
is recorded as having said about the proposal at the planning committee on 13 March: 'I
have no axe to grind—speaking from a planning viewpoint only.' A less sinister
f explanation could be that political opponents sometimes introduce their remarks in this
self-exculpatory way.

At the council meeting on 29 March, when the planning committee minutes were
passed by 12 to 11, part of the note reads:

> '*Cllr E T Lewis.* Should take cognisance of petition.
> *Cllr L A Evans.* You are opposed to Developer not the Development.
> *g*   *Cllr P F MacDonald-Murray.* Wrong—you should withdraw that remark.
> *Cllr L A Evans.* I will not—this matter has been discussed democratically and at
> length.
> *Cllr S Percival.* What is all this noise about?'

Councillors Greep and Coode (Ratepayers group) and Councillor Ball (Plaid Cymru) as
h well as Cllrs Hawkins, Tyssul Lewis and McDonald-Murray (Labour) spoke against
change of use. Councillor Greep said: 'Application smells of the Mafia', while Cllr
Edwards said, inter alia: 'Let it be quite clear that a councillor of this Council is involved
in this application and ever since it has been scheduled there have been rumours that
there is something going on.' Having regard to what I have said above, three other
remarks may be noted:

j   '*Cllr Ayres.* I have never brought personalities into it. I would have been against
it no matter who it was.
Cllr Coode. I am concerned with advert not the person.
Cllr Greep ... not concerned with personality...'

(This last remark was made on 26 April.)

The following extract from the note of the council meeting held on 26 April is of importance and the remarks of Cllr Tyssul Lewis were noted in the judgment: a

'*Cllr Lewis.* This decision stinks—man getting preference because he is member of Council—preferential treatment—Councillor P.H. Valerio always speaks of clubs—were the previous premises of this applicant used for group meetings of the Ratepayers Association?—have everything open.
Cllr Mrs Smith. Nothing about this in Minutes.
Cllr E T Lewis. Residents against having club in this area—this Authority as b ground landlord can say no to this—if I get back on Council I will put Notice of Motion on this to rescind it. This is preferential treatment to applicant and hope Council think about this and reject it.
Cllr C Hadley. Yes the applicant's premises was used for Ratepayers group some time ago—unfortunate that this is a personal battle amongst members—is there c anything legally or morally wrong about this?
Chief Executive and Town Clerk. Can't answer moral aspect and at last Council gave legal position.
Cllr L A Evans. Whole situation makes me feel sick—Councillor E.T. Lewis is sanctimonious hypocrite—talk about things being made in open—does not know meaning of word—if this man Joe Bloggs he would have got it. d
Cllr Phillips. Wish Councillor P.H. Valerio more? re. community centres—other application turned down by other applicant—so Joe Bloggs turned down . . .'

The meeting of 26 April was clearly an acrimonious one. The judge considered it carefully and reviewed the evidence of Cllrs Smith, Evans, Meager and Wesley, who were called as witnesses for the plaintiff. On studying such parts of the transcript of evidence as the parties have chosen to rely on, my view is that the judge was not at all bound to e find that Cllr Tyssul Lewis was motivated by malice against the plaintiff or her husband. The judge saw and heard all the witnesses, which conferred on him a most valuable advantage in a case which depended so much on the veracity and accuracy of recollection of the witnesses. Councillor Tyssul Lewis's attitude is readily attributable to indignation and to his determination to put right, if he could, a decision which he regarded as f completely wrong.

Passing to the estates committee meeting of 13 June, given the genuineness of the attitude expressed by Cllr Tyssul Lewis at the council meeting of 26 April, it may be regarded as perfectly natural for him to take the first official opportunity of pursuing his stated objective. Counsel for the plaintiff submitted that it was strange that 11 councillors should vote for a proposal for which no reasoned argument had been advanced and g inferred that the decision must have been taken before the meeting, but presumably the minutes of the previous meeting were available and even the brief note of the discussion indicates that the participants knew what they were debating about.

At the council meeting of 28 June Cllr Tyssul Lewis's proposal was consistent with the line he had already adopted. Again the judge noted the plaintiff's submission that the proposal to rescind the decision of 26 April had gone through strictly on party lines after h only a short debate without an elaborate justification. But again the note of the meeting tends to show that the point at issue was fully appreciated by those taking part. The judge records that Cllr Tyssul Lewis gave four reasons for his attitude, namely the nuisance to residents, the parking problem (admittedly these were planning points but would continue as relevant arguments in the mind of anyone who opposed the change of use), the principle of holding the (only) tenderer to the advertised use and the feeling j that the council, having rejected the change of use application in March 1979, ought not to have changed its mind in April.

The judge continued:

'He claimed that he held those views genuinely and acted as he did because of those views and not out of any personal antipathy for Mr Jones or Mrs Jones. The third and fourth reasons he gave would be consistent with my view of him as being something of a puritan.'

The judge's subsequent conclusions included the following passages:

'This is not a case in which I can say that the evidence of Cllr Tyssul Lewis satisfies me that he was not motivated by malice or that in acting as he did at the meetings of 26 April, 13 June and 28 June, he was not so acting for reasons of personal antipathy to Mr Benjamin Jones. I do not accept his evidence that at the meeting of 26 April, which was the last full council meeting prior to the local government elections, he was not out to get a good press for the local government elections. If he was not out to get a good press for his own party, I find that he was out to get a bad press for the Ratepayers group and part of that bad press was his assertion that the decision stank and that Mr Jones was getting preference because he was a member of the council. Those remarks implied that the plaintiff and Mr Jones were behaving in an improper manner. As I have already said, I have received no evidence which would indicate that, nor was any such suggestion put to the plaintiff or to Mr Jones when they were cross-examined, nor was it put forward by any witness who gave evidence, including Cllr Tyssul Lewis himself. Those remarks should not have been made at that meeting. In my judgment, they were made for party political reasons and were made for the effect that it was known that they would have, in the light of the recent history of councillors of the defendant council being convicted and imprisoned for corruption. Having said that, the conclusion that I have reached is that, although there are grounds for suspicion, it has not been proved on the balance of probability by the evidence that I have heard the Cllr Tyssul Lewis or any other member of the Labour group was motivated by malice towards the plaintiff or Mr Benjamin Jones in the strict legal sense of wishing and intending to cause them harm. I accept the evidence of the other Labour councillors whom I heard as witnesses, namely Cllrs Ayres, Lorna Josephine Aldron and Mary Ilene Chilcott, that they were not activated by personal malice towards Mr and Mrs Jones, that they were not instructed to or asked to vote in a particular manner, that there was no party whip in operation at the meeting of 28 June or at any of the earlier meetings and that they voted in accordance with their beliefs and consciences. Councillors Ayres and Aldron impressed me greatly as witnesses. It is significant that witnesses called on behalf of the plaintiff, such as Mr Leslie Arthur Evans and Cllr Murphy, spoke warmly of Cllr Ayres, saying that they respected his integrity and his judgment. Had Cllr Tyssul Lewis done anything behind the scenes to obtain the vote that he desired to obtain on 28 June 1979, then I do not believe that Cllrs Ayres, Aldron and Chilcott would have given the evidence that they did give. In reaching the conclusion that I have reached on this part of the case, I find that the motives which led Cllr Tyssul Lewis to act as he did, which included disregarding the standing orders of the Labour Party for Labour groups on local authorities, as well as ignoring the standing orders of the defendant council in his haste to have the decision of 26 April 1979 reversed, were his desire to have his own way on this issue, to fulfil the pledge which he had made at the meeting of 26 April to have the matter reversed and to be seen, as he somewhat pompously put it at the meeting of 28 June 1979, to be doing justice. I accept that he had an honest and sincere belief that a developer of property who had acquired a lease from the defendant council should be obliged to keep to the use for which that property had been originally advertised.'

Clearly the judge's conclusion about the motivation of Cllr Tyssul Lewis, although not very positively expressed, defeats the plaintiff's claim if it cannot be upset.

The judge's general verdict on the other Labour councillors must be noted here:

'Further, I do not find it proved that other Labour councillors were activated by
malice towards the plaintiff or Mr Benjamin Jones. In my judgment, it has not been　*a*
proved that Labour councillors on 28 June 1979 were voting on this matter in the
way they did under a party whip or because they knew that certain of their leaders
had a personal vendetta against the plaintiff or Mr Benjamin Jones and they wished
to support such leaders in carrying out such a personal vendetta. It follows that,
assuming that it had been established that Cllr Tyssul Lewis was motivated by
malice towards the plaintiff, the plaintiff has failed to prove either that the other　*b*
Labour councillors who voted at the meeting on 28 June 1979 knew of that malice
and acquiesced in it or that Cllr Tyssul Lewis applied a party whip to ensure that his
fellow Labour councillors voted in the way he desired.'

This was a negative finding, fully justified, in my opinion, by the evidence and not
capable of being attacked on logical grounds. Accordingly, it destroys the plaintiff's case　*c*
against the council, whether Cllr Tyssul Lewis was actuated by malice or not.

How then does the plaintiff cope with this twofold difficulty? In the Court of Appeal
Slade LJ, while conceding (as he must) that it was, on the evidence, open to the judge to
find for or against the plaintiff on the issue of Cllr Tyssul Lewis's malice, was dissatisifed
with the judge's finding against the plaintiff on that issue and accordingly held that, if
this were the only relevant issue, he would have been prepared to set aside the judge's　*d*
finding and order a new trial, although he would not enter judgment for the plaintiff
because, if he had adopted a correct approach, the trial judge could still have decided the
issue of malice either way. The other members of the court agreed with Slade LJ on this
point, to which I will return.

So far as the attitude of the other councillors was concerned, on the assumption that
malice had been, or might at a new trial be, found against Cllr Tyssul Lewis and, for　*e*
what it was worth, Cllr McDonald-Murray, Slade LJ pointed out that the plaintiff's case
was that *all* the councillors voting for the resolution on 28 June were infected by malice.
On this basis, having regarded to the evidence of Cllr Ayres, Aldron and Chilcott, which
was accepted by the judge, the plaintiff could not possibly succeed. He would hold the
plaintiff to her case as pleaded and presented but he further considered that, even if one
were to adopt a flexible approach and only look for proof that 22 councillors (a bare　*f*
majority) were malicious or infected by malice, the plaintiff still could not succeed in
proving her case, having regard to what the trial judge had quite legitimately found.
This is where the difference of opinion arose in the Court of Appeal, because the majority
regarded the insistence on '28 councillors infected' as a mere pleading point and were
also of the further opinion that, once the finding of no malice on the part of Cllr Tyssul
Lewis was set aside, there should be a new trial in view of the possibility that he might at　*g*
that new trial be found guilty of malice and that at least 21 other councillors might be
found to have been infected by malice.

My Lords, I come back to the question of malice on the part of Cllr Tyssul Lewis. Slade
LJ professed 'considerable unease' concerning the manner in which the judge dealt with
this issue 'for at least four reasons advanced in argument by counsel for the plaintiff'.　*h*
These are set out in detail (see [1989] 3 All ER 162 at 177–179, [1990] 1 WLR 54 at 73–
76), and can be summarised thus: (1) that it was difficult to reconcile the judge's
favourable findings as to Cllr Tyssul Lewis's motives with his inability to make a positive
finding that the councillor was not motivated by malice; (2) that there were some
grounds for supposing that the judge may have misunderstood the essential thrust of the
plaintiff's allegation of malice against Cllr Tyssul Lewis and correspondingly did not deal　*j*
adequately with the question of his motives; (3) (which Slade LJ found to be linked to
reason (2)) that the judge had failed to draw from the evidence and from the defendant's
omission to call Cllr McDonald-Murray (who had been in court at some stage) an
inference of malice against that councillor and had failed to say whether he accepted the
evidence of Cllr Leslie Evans; (4) that the judge, when finding that malice had not been

proved against Cllr Tyssul Lewis, failed to deal explicitly with the evidence of Cllrs
a Margaret Smith and Meager, since he merely recited it but did not say whether he
accepted it or appear to consider its significance.
   My comments on these points are as follows.
   (1) The burden of proof was on the plaintiff and the judge found that it had not been
discharged.
   (2) The entire trial was infused with political acrimony and the judgment read as a
b whole shows that the judge fully appeciated the significance of the political background.
That is why he recounted it. His recital of the evidence confirms that he could not have
failed to recognise the two-pronged nature of the plaintiff's attack, particularly when so
much of what was relied on by the plaintiff happened or was alleged to have happened at
meetings of the council. As Slade LJ himself said ([1989] 3 All ER 162 at 177–178, [1990]
c 1 WLR 54 at 74):

   'Counsel for the council submitted that the judge must have had both these
   reasons in mind, even though he only referred to one. I see the force of this
   submission. The point was argued. It was clearly pleaded. It was referred to in the
   evidence of a number, though not all, of the plaintiff's witnesses. The judge had set
   out the political background in an earlier part of his judgment.'

d   Slade LJ's misgivings are illustrated by what he said next ([1989] 3 All ER 162 at 178,
[1990] 1 WLR 54 at 74–75):

   'Nevertheless, I think it surprising that the judge did not explicitly refer to the
   point when dealing with the plaintiff's explanation of the alleged malice. It seems
   by no means impossible that, in the course of writing his judgment, he was directing
e   his attention primarily to the evidence of those of the plaintiff's witnesses who had
   referred to Mr Jones's abrasiveness and outspokenness (which gave offence even to a
   number of his own political colleagues) without also referring to the bitterness to
   which his activities of 1976 had given rise among his political opponents. The
   relevance of this point is that, if it was overlooked, it makes it significantly less likely
   that the judge would have found both malice on the part of Cllr Tyssul Lewis and
f   his associates, since he would have overlooked the significant suggested element of
   revenge. In particular, he might well have given greater weight to evidence of a
   long-standing grudge from witnesses such as Cllrs Valerio, Williams, Murphy,
   Meager and Margaret Smith and the plaintiff herself. As it is, we cannot tell whether
   or not the judge did in truth have this "revenge" point in mind.' (Slade LJ's
   emphasis).

g
   But, I feel bound to say, the whole atmosphere of the case was that the council had
been divided by political animosity and that Mr Jones was seen as not only an abrasive
and dislikeable man but an abrasive and dislikeable political opponent. I find it hard to
believe that the judge could have overlooked these obvious facts or failed to take account
of them and I consider that it is much more probable that he was resolved not to
h highlight or revive political differences any more than he was obliged to.
   (3) The principle is well established that an inference may, but must not, be drawn
when a witness who was available has not been called to contradict unfavourable
evidence, but its application varies with the circumstances. Councillor Evans, as the
judge put it, 'gave evidence of a conversation he said [sic] he had with a Labour councillor,
Cllr McDonald-Murray, at a planning committee meeting'. The judge proceeded:

j
   'He said that Cllr McDonald-Murray was bitterly opposed to this application, that
   he hated Mr Jones anyway, and that he had said: "We're going to stop him, make no
   mistake. We're going to stop him." He then asked Cllr McDonald-Murray what if
   it had been him, that is Cllr Evans, making the application and Cllr McDonald-
   Murray had replied: "If it was you or anyone else, there would be no hassle at all." '

The first observation which Cllr Evans attributed to Cllr McDonald-Murray was
consistent with a strong but sincere determination to prevent something wrong but the   *a*
last remark, if it was made, would tend to show malice in the shape of an intention to
thwart Mr Jones on grounds personal to him. With regard to this alleged incident, the
judge later said:

> 'I did not hear evidence from two Labour councillors who might have assisted me
> on this matter, namely Cllrs McDonald-Murray and Hawkins. It is right that the   *b*
> alleged conversation between Cllr McDonald-Murray and Mr Leslie Evans at a
> planning committee meeting was not particularised in the plaintiff's pleadings, nor
> was it mentioned during the opening of the plaintiff's case. Further, counsel for the
> plaintiff accepted that Mr Leslie Evans was not the most dispassionate of witnesses
> and invited me to discount his evidence, although not to reject facts about which he
> had told me. In a case of this kind, where serious allegations are being made against   *c*
> persons holding public elected offices, I do not consider it right to draw adverse
> inferences from the absence of certain potential witnesses from the witness box. In
> my judgment, I must decide this matter on the evidence that I have heard or have
> received in documentary form.'

Slade LJ commented ([1989] 3 All ER 162 at 178, [1990] 1 WLR 54 at 75–76):   *d*

> 'I assume that the judge made this reference to Cllr Hawkins because the notes of
> some of the meetings show that he had been a strong opponent of the plaintiff's
> proposed change of user of the premises, and in particular, at the estates committee
> meeting of 14 March 1979 had volunteered the observation that "this is not a
> personal vendetta". Presumably also, the "adverse inferences" which the judge was   *e*
> declining to draw were the inferences that Cllrs McDonald-Murray and Hawkins
> had voted for the resolution of 28 June 1979 with malicious intent towards the
> plaintiff and her husband. The judge was, I think, plainly right to refuse to draw
> such an inference against Cllr Hawkins. In the case of Cllr McDonald-Murray the
> question is much more difficult. Accepting that the judge should have decided the
> matter on the evidence which he had heard or had received in documentary form,   *f*
> why should he have declined to draw the inference of malice against Cllr McDonald-
> Murray? If Cllr Evans's evidence as to what Cllr McDonald-Murray said at the
> meeting of 26 April 1979 was to be believed, and he was not cross-examined on it,
> this was clear prima facie evidence of personal malice on the part of the latter
> towards Mr Jones: the words attributed to him, taken in their ordinary sense, would
> clearly indicate an intent to injure.'   *g*

After noting counsel's arguments he continued ([1989] 3 All ER 162 at 179, [1990] 1
WLR 54 at 76):

> 'The task of the court in dealing with this point would have been a much easier
> one if the judge had explicitly stated whether or not he accepted the relevant part of   *h*
> Cllr Evans's evidence. If he did accept it, his failure to draw an inference of malice
> against Cllr McDonald-Murray in the absence of evidence to rebut it, would not in
> my judgment have been justifiable. If, however, he intended to reject the material
> part of Cllr Evans's evidence, he should, in my judgment, have given reasons beyond
> a mere statement that he was "not the most dispassionate of witnesses".'

This was a fair comment, but the passage quoted above from the judgment of the trial   *j*
judge seems to me to contain a broad hint that he did not altogether accept Cllr Evans's
testimony, in which case the failure to call Cllr McDonald-Murray would be less
important. Moreover, the significance of point (3) was at best indirect. As Slade LJ said
([1989] 3 All ER 162 at 179, [1990] 1 WLR 54 at 76):

a
'The principal relevance of this evidence relating to Cllr McDonald-Murray in the present context is that, if the judge had found that the deputy leader of the Labour group had been actuated by malice in voting for the relevant resolution, he might have been the more willing to hold that Cllr Tysull Lewis's vote was similarly born of a grudge.'

b
(4) In his treatment of the evidence of Cllrs Margaret Smith and Meager the judge furnished another example of conclusions stated without the intermediate findings on which they were based. It would have been much more helpful if the judge had been more explicit, but again he seems to have chosen the path of reticence. I concede the aptness of Slade LJ's comment ([1989] 3 All ER 162 at 179, [1990] 1 WLR 54 at 77):

c
'This evidence, as summarised by the judge, was in my view of crucial importance because, if it was accepted, the words attributable by the witnesses to Cllr Tysull Lewis were clear prima facie evidence of an intention on his part to injure Mr Jones. I am inclined to think that the judge, in finding that malice on the part of the councillor had not been proved, must by necessary implication have rejected the evidence that these words were spoken. Nevertheless, with all respect to him, I think it is far from satisfactory that he should have found that malice on the part of
d
Cllr Tysell Lewis had not been proved without at the same time explicitly dealing with the critically important evidence of Cllrs Smith and Meager, beyond a bare recital of it, and indeed, so far as his judgment shows, without considering its significance.'

e
In fairness to this careful judge, I submit that your Lordships will readily concur in Slade LJ's assessment that the judge must have rejected the evidence that the words relied on were said, or will at least conclude that he must not have found the alleged words proved. The key words in Slade LJ's last sentence are 'so far as his judgment shows'. I would be confident that the judge considered the significance of these councillors' evidence but I agree that his judgment, elliptical here as elsewhere, does not *show* that he did so.

f
Reverting to point (1), the fact that the judge found the accusation of malice 'not proven' shows that he was careful and conscientious and also partly accounts for the greyness of his presentation. Points (2), (3) and (4) do not reveal any misdirections in point of law nor, except with the aid of what I would deem unwarranted speculation, can they in my opinion give rise to any misgivings about the judge's comprehension of the evidence that could justify a new trial of the issue of malice, which, as is conceded, the judge could properly have decided either way.

g
My Lords, that conclusion would, for my part, be enough to dispose of the appeal in the council's favour, but I shall now consider the case, as the judge and the Court of Appeal did, on the assumption that malice is proved on the part of Cllr Tyssul Lewis and, for good measure, Cllr McDonald-Murray as well. On this aspect of the case I respectfully and entirely agree with the judgment of Slade LJ.

h
According to her case as pleaded, the plaintiff had to show that all the Labour councillors were either motivated or infected by malice. The judge accepted the evidence of Cllrs Ayres, Aldron and Chilcott. Another judge might have taken a different view of the evidence of all or any of these witnesses, but the judge's findings, based on his acceptance of their evidence, cannot be challenged. That, in the opinion of Slade LJ and also in my opinion, is an end of the case, whatever view one takes about Cllr Tyssul
j
Lewis. As was said in *Gautret v Egerton* (1867) LR 2 CP 371, under our system the plaintiff must recover secundum allegata et probata. There is no other way: this was not a case where the course of the trial would have dictated or justified an amendment of the pleadings to conform with the reality, on the footing that the case as pleaded should be disregarded. The 'bare majority' solution was never propounded by the plaintiff; it only emanated at a late stage from the bench in the Court of Appeal. To require proof of

unanimity among the 28 Labour councillors is not making a mere pleading point, because at the trial the council refuted the plaintiff's case by calling Cllrs Ayres, Aldron *a* and Chilcott and might well have called another four councillors who, if they had given evidence to the same effect and been believed, would have established the maximum possible number of malicious or infected councillors at a figure below the bare majority of 22.

Slade LJ, moreover, although he considered that the plaintiff, in order to succeed, would have had to prove that all 28 Labour councillors were motivated or infected by *b* malice, went on to consider the claim on the further assumption that a bare majority (22) of malicious or infected councillors would have been enough. And even on this basis he held, rightly in my view, that the plaintiff could not succeed.

I respectfully indorse and adopt everything which Slade LJ has said on the attribution of malice (see [1989] 3 All ER 162 at 180–186, [1990] 1 WLR 54 at 77 and 84) and it would be pointless for me to repeat or rephrase that part of his judgment. I would just *c* refer to and comment on three passages.

He said ([1989] 3 All ER 162 at 183, [1990] 1 WLR 54 at 81):

> 'For the purposes of this appeal, in the light of the judge's findings of fact, counsel for the plaintiff explicitly accepted that (a) none of Cllrs Ayres, Aldron and Chilcott bore any personal malice towards the plaintiff or her husband, (b) there was no *d* discussion of the relevant resolution at the Labour group meeting on 26 June 1979, (c) there was no formal party whip applied with a view to ensuring there would be a uniform bloc vote by the members of the Labour group on the relevant resolution at the council meeting of 28 June 1979.'

This extract serves to emphasise not only the strength of the council's position in relation to Cllrs Ayres, Aldron and Chilcott, but also the adverse effect of their evidence, believed *e* by the judge and explicitly accepted by the plaintiff's counsel, on any attempt to prove that even a bare majority of Labour councillors were in the state of mind required by the plaintiff's case.

Then ([1989] 3 All ER 162 at 185, [1990] 1 WLR 54 at 83–84):

> 'On what basis could the judge have properly inferred that the other members of *f* the Labour group, or even a majority of them, were *not* motivated by their beliefs and consciences? I can see no sufficient basis. I accept that as a matter of common sense and political reality, he could readily have inferred that, all other things being equal, members of the Labour group would be likely to follow their leader and deputy leader in casting their votes as a matter of "group discipline" (see the introduction to the standing orders), whether or not they considered that r 7(c) *g* applied so as to place them under a party whip. Nevertheless, I do not see on what basis the judge, even if he had made this inference, and even if he had found personal malice on the part of Cllrs Tyssul Lewis and McDonald-Murray, would have been entitled to find (either as a matter of fact or of law or of mixed fact and law) that such malice affected all (or even a majority) of the other members of the Labour group concerned. It had not been shown that all (or any) such other *h* members were personally malicious or knew of the (assumed) malice of their leader and deputy leader. It had not been shown that, in the words of para 4 of the amended notice of appeal: "The proper inference from the evidence was that all Labour Councillors at the said meeting of the 28th June 1979 [or even a majority of them] knew that they had to vote in the way desired by Cllr. Tyssul Lewis in order *j* to redeem the said pledge and that they did so thus being tainted by the malice complained of." Thus, even if, contrary to my view, the pleadings did not make it incumbent on the plaintiff to show that *all* the members of the Labour group who voted in favour of the relevant resolution were in some way or other affected by the (assumed) malice of their two leaders, the evidence adduced at the trial would not,

a   in my view, have established that even the majority of such members were thus
      affected. The pleading point is therefore far from being the only reason for my
      ultimate conclusion.'

(Slade LJ's emphasis. I think that in this passage the word 'majority' must be taken to
mean, not 15 out of 28, but 20 which, if added to the names of Cllrs Tyssul Lewis and
McDonald-Murray, would bring the number to 22 out of 43.)

b   Finally ([1989] 3 All ER 162 at 185, [1990] 1 WLR 54 at 84):

      'For the reasons stated, even if the judge had found personal malice on the part of
      Cllrs Tyssul Lewis and/or McDonald-Murray proved, he would in my judgment
      still have been bound to dismiss the action, as was his own opinion. I have already
      expressed the view that there are grounds for criticising the manner in which he
      dealt with the allegations of malice against Cllrs Tyssul Lewis and McDonald-
c   Murray. However, even if such grounds are well founded, it would not in my
      judgment be right for this court to order a new trial, when the plaintiff could
      succeed at a new trial (if at all) only on the basis of a new case which was not pleaded
      or explored in evidence at the trial before Roch J.'

I entirely agree.
d   The majority in the Court of Appeal, as your Lordships will recall, held, agreeing with
Slade LJ, (1) that, if the necessary malice had been proved, the plaintiff would have had a
good cause of action and (2) that the judge's finding in favour of Cllr Tyssul Lewis could
not be sustained but, disagreeing with Slade LJ, they ordered a new trial because (1) they
did not consider that the failure to show that all the Labour councillors were infected,
proved by the evidence of Cllrs Ayres, Aldron and Chilcott, destroyed the plaintiff's case
e   and (2) they considered that it had been, and on a new trial would be, open to the judge
to find not only that Cllr Tyssul Lewis was guilty of malice but also that a majority of
the 43 councillors who voted were infected with Cllr Tyssul Lewis's malice, assuming
that malice to be proved. It will be convenient to consider first the judgment of
Stuart-Smith LJ.
      Stuart-Smith LJ introduced his consideration of the councillors' malice with the
f   following observations ([1989] 3 All ER 162 at 188, [1990] 1 WLR 54 at 87–88):

      'In effect the plaintiff's case was in the alternative. First, each of the councillors
      had a grudge against the plaintiff and Mr Jones and each was malicious. This case
      was rejected by the judge, who held that he was satisfied that three who so voted
      and gave evidence, namely Cllrs Ayres, Aldron and Chilcott were not malicious.
      There is no appeal from this finding. Alternatively, it was said that each of the
g   councillors was affected by the malice of the principal instigators, including Cllr
      Tyssul Lewis. At the trial this was said to arise in three alternative ways. First, that
      each member of the Labour Party knew of and acquiesced in the malice of Cllr
      Tyssul Lewis, and perhaps others of the Labour leadership. This case was rejected by
      the judge and that finding is not appealed. He found in terms that the three
h   councillors who gave evidence for the defence, other than Cllr Tyssul Lewis, did not
      know this and voted in accordance with their beliefs and conscience. Second, the
      members of the Labour Party voted under a party whip. Again, the judge rejected
      this: he found that there was no whip; there is no appeal from this finding. The
      third way is that which counsel for the plaintiff seeks to persuade us was established
      on the evidence; it can be summarised as follows: Cllr Tyssul Lewis made an election
j   pledge at the April council meeting that if Labour were returned to power he would
      see that the decision in favour of the plaintiff was rescinded. Under Labour's
      standing orders, or the Labour tradition, when Cllr Tyssul Lewis sought to redeem
      that pledge at the June meeting all Labour councillors would have been bound to
      vote for this resolution, if they had not raised the matter at the group meeting. The
      election pledge had the same status as a group decision. None of the newly elected

councillors had been involved in the detailed debate. There was no discussion and
they did not have enough information from the minutes to know why they should   a
reject the recommendation of the council officers. They followed their leaders as
they were expected to do. It is clear that this submission was not in the forefront of
the plaintiff's case at trial but was only an alternative or fall-back position if the
main contention that there had been a group decision and formal whip failed.
Indeed, it is a proposition that only emerged at a late stage in the case. It was not put
in cross-examination to Cllrs Ayres, Aldron or Chilcott. It is unfortunate that it was   b
not put to these witnesses; but in my judgment the reason why it was not is
understandable. At that stage of the case the plaintiff's counsel were concentrating
on trying to establish that a group decision had been taken and to this end they
sought to discover the minutes of the meeting. In the event it eventually transpired
that there were no minutes kept at the relevant time. Secondly, it was not till Cllr
Tyssul Lewis gave evidence that the Labour Party standing orders were produced in   c
evidence. The case was clearly put to Cllr Tyssul Lewis in cross-examination. There
was no application to recall the other witnesses so that the matter could be put to
them. I am satisfied that this case was open to the plaintiff on the amended pleading
and no objection was taken on this ground at the trial. It is also clear that counsel
for the plaintiff argued the point in his final submissions.'

Then, noting that the judge had held that one councillor's malice will only taint the   d
actions of fellow councillors if either they know of that malice and acquiesce in it or the
councillor who is malicious is in a position to, and does, apply a party whip so that the
whole of his party group votes in the way he desires at his direction, he continued ([1989]
3 All ER 162 at 189, [1990] 1 WLR 54 at 88–89):

'This recital does not fully record counsel's submissions for the plaintiff, since it   e
makes no reference to the pledge to have the previous decision rescinded or the
standing orders. But I think that this may well be because this was the plaintiff's
alternative and fall-back position. I do not therefore accept the submission of counsel
for the council that this case was not adequately pleaded or developed at the trial,
though I think it is unfortunate that what was an alternative case at trial has now
assumed critical importance when the plaintiff's primary case was rejected. In my   f
judgment the question that has to be posed is: why did all the Labour councillors
vote the way they did on 28 June 1979? There would appear to be three possible
explanations. First, there was a formal whip as a result of a group decision; although
this might seem the most obvious explanation, the council's witnesses said that
there was not and the judge so found. Second, each one of the Labour councillors
exercised his own independent judgment and voted on the merits. Third, they did   g
so for the reason submitted by counsel for the plaintiff, namely that they followed
their leaders who had given a pledge that the matter would be rescinded. I have not
understood counsel for the council to submit that, if this is the explanation, it would
not in law amount to a sufficient affection of the Labour councillors who voted as
they did on 28 June 1979 to constitute the tort in question. His submissions were,   h
first, that this case was not opened on the pleadings or properly presented at the
trial, second, that Cllr Tyssul Lewis was not malicious and, third, that this third case
was negatived by the judge's acceptance of the evidence of Cllrs Ayres, Aldron and
Chilcott. For the reasons I have given I do not accept the first of these submissions;
the second has been dealt with by Slade LJ in his judgment.'

Referring to the April council meeting Stuart-Smith LJ said: j

'Second, at the April meeting of the council Cllr Tyssul Lewis had stated that, if
Labour were returned, the decision then taken would be rescinded. Whether one
dignifies this statement with the term "election pledge" seems to me to matter little.
What does matter is that it was a plain declaration that Cllr Tyssul Lewis would use

a

his power and influence as leader of the party to see that, if and when Labour had a majority on the council, that majority would be used to rescind the decision. This statement was widely reported in the press.'

Your Lordships will see that Stuart-Smith LJ has with conspicuous clarity reduced the plaintiff's case to the 'third way' in which it was presented ([1989] 3 All ER 162 at 188, [1990] 1 WLR 54 at 87): Cllr Tyssul Lewis, the plaintiff said, made an 'election pledge'
b and, under Labour's standing orders or the Labour tradition, all Labour councillors would have been bound to support him at the June meeting, the 'pledge' having the status of a group decision. It is something like this case which the majority in the Court of Appeal seemed to be disposed to accept. This case was not put to Cllrs Ayres, Aldron and Chilcott. Having put it to Cllr Tyssul Lewis, the plaintiff did not ask leave to put it to those other witnesses. I do not accept the implication raised in the judgment that it
c was for the council to recall them to 'rebut' a case which Cllr Tyssul Lewis had rejected and as to which the burden lay on the plaintiff (see [1989] 3 All ER 162 at 192, [1990] 1 WLR 54 at 92). Furthermore, as Stuart-Smith LJ noted (see [1989] 3 All ER 162 at 189–190, [1990] 1 WLR 54 at 89–90), the standing orders were not in force and in any case no group decision had been made. The highly coloured description 'election pledge' was in my view calculated to confer on Cllr Tyssul Lewis's forceful statement a binding effect
d on his fellow councillors which it did not possess.

It has already been conceded on both sides that it was open to the judge to find either way on the question of Cllr Tyssul Lewis's alleged malice. It is therefore difficult to infer that the other Labour councillors *knew* that he was malicious, especially since there existed grounds for genuinely holding and supporting the view which he expressed and which the Ratepayer controlled council had adopted on 29 March. When one also takes
e into account the evidence of Cllrs Ayres, Aldron and Chilcott, there is in my opinion no room for anything more than speculation that a majority of councillors voted 'as directed' without using their own judgment. Moreover (depending on the view which your Lordships take of the pleading point) the plaintiff had to prove either that all the Labour councillors or that at least 22 of them failed to exercise their own judgment and vote in good faith on the merits.
f   After referring to R v Waltham Forest London BC, ex p Baxter [1987] 3 All ER 671, [1988] QB 419, Stuart-Smith LJ continued ([1989] 3 All ER 162 at 191, [1990] 1 WLR 54 at 91):

g

'I would accept by analogy with that case that the mere fact that all Labour councillors voted the same way in the present case, if it stood alone, does not raise any inference such as counsel for the plaintiff invites us to draw. But it does not stand alone; there are the other matters to which I have drawn attention. Moreover, this can hardly have been a matter of party policy, on which unity was an important consideration. It was only a party consideration inasmuch as Cllr Tyssul Lewis had sought to get a bad press for the Ratepayers Party or a good press for the Labour
h Party by making the wholly unfounded suggestion at the April council meeting that the plaintiff, Mr Jones, and other members of the Ratepayers Party had acted in an improper manner. It seems to me to stretch one's credulity to an unacceptable extent to suppose that all the Labour councillors voted as they did because they accepted the validity of the objections. In essence these were two: the first was a planning matter; it related to the objections of local residents to a club in the area.
j That had been resolved in favour of the plaintiff by the grant of planning permission for change of use to that of a club, which could not be rescinded. I am very doubtful if it was a valid reason to deny a change of use as landlord. The second was the fact that the premises had been offered and tendered for as shops and offices and it was wrong in principle to change. Although the judge found this was an honest and genuine reason, I confess it does not seem to me a very persuasive one, since it was

clear that the plaintiff was going to have to pay a substantially increased rent for the change of use.'

As to the 'wholly unfounded suggestion', the clerk's note of the 26 April council meeting, which was accepted by Cllr Tyssul Lewis, recorded him as follows:

> 'This decision stinks—man getting preference because he is member of Council—preferential treatment ... were the previous premises of this applicant used for group meetings of the Ratepayers Association—have everything open ... residents against having club in area—this Authority as ground landlord can say no to this—if I get back on Council I will put Notice of Motion on this to rescind it. This is preferential treatment to applicant and hope Council think about this and reject it.'

I have already drawn attention to the judge's refusal to accept Cllr Tyssul Lewis's denial that he was out to get a good press for his own party and a bad press for the Ratepayers group. But no one has suggested that what Cllr Tyssul Lewis said at the meeting was something from which malice against the plaintiff and Mr Jones *must* be inferred. If his feelings were genuine (always remembering that the same council had turned down the proposal in March), he could have wished to get the Ratepayers group a bad press and the fact that the judge did not accept his denial does not amount to a finding of malice or an inference that other Labour councillors knew that he was activated by malice.

In the passage I have cited Stuart-Smith LJ said: 'It seems to me to stretch one's credulity to an unacceptable extent to suppose that all the Labour councillors voted as they did because they accepted the validity of the objections.' No doubt, but, taking her case at its lowest, the plaintiff had to prove that at least 21 councillors in addition to Cllr Tyssul Lewis voted for unacceptable reasons. Stuart-Smith LJ then goes further and by implication casts doubt on the genuineness of the vote by criticising the two essential objections to the proposal. Witnesses called for the plaintiff had already agreed that it was possible to object on genuine grounds and it has also been conceded that the objections raised were not so innately unreasonable as to be evidence of malice. I respectfully disagree with Stuart-Smith LJ's comment on the second objection, the thrust of which was that a single tenderer (who was for good measure married to a councillor) was obtaining an unfair advantage over persons who might have tendered for the lease if the new proposed use had been advertised in the first place. A higher rent would not have remedied that apparent injustice.

Immediately after the passage in his judgment on which I have been commenting, Stuart-Smith LJ said:

> 'If the matter had rested there, I would be disposed to draw the inference that counsel for the plaintiff invites us to draw. But it does not rest there because the judge accepted the evidence of the three councillors that they voted in accordance with their beliefs and consciences. Does this destroy the plaintiff's case? I do not find it possible to accept the submission of counsel for the plaintiff that these three were nevertheless affected by malice. I do not see how in the light of this finding it can be said that these three voted as they did to fulfil Cllr Tyssul Lewis's pledge and simply out of party solidarity. But I do not think the fact that these three had proper and valid reasons for voting as they did necessarily rebuts the inference that the others did not. The decision was carried by a majority of 28 to 15; if the votes of the other 25 who formed the majority can be impugned, it seems to me that this is sufficient to undermine the decision.'

As to the opening sentence, for the reasons I have given, I respectfully consider the inference to be unwarranted. But this question becomes academic when one considers the adverse affect, not only on the plaintiff's case as presented but on the 'majority voting' case suggested by the Court of Appeal, of the judge's acceptance of the Ayres-Aldron-Chilcott evidence. Having referred to that evidence, Stuart-Smith LJ said: 'But I do not

think the fact that these three had proper and valid reasons for voting as they did
a necessarily rebuts the inference that the others did not.' I must observe that the 'proper
and valid reasons' motivating the three councillors were not peculiar to them but could
have influenced any of the councillors. There was on the evidence *no* inference to be
rebutted that all the other councillors, or even 22 of them, had voted for improper and
invalid reasons.

Stuart-Smith LJ proceeded to deal with the pleading point by which, he confessed, he
b had been troubled, but concluded that the plaintiff did not have to prove that all the
Labour councillors had been infected with malice. I have already given my reasons for
taking a different view.

I come to the last decisive passage in the judgment ([1989] 3 All ER 162 at 192, [1990]
1 WLR 54 at 92):

c   'In addition to these considerations, I am by no means certain that the judge
would have come to the same conclusion on this aspect of the case if he had found
malice established on the part of Cllr Tyssul Lewis and perhaps also Cllr McDonald-
Murray. Although I accept that intellectually it is possible that the leadership could
have been activated by malice while the other 26 councillors who voted for the
amendment were not, once it is accepted, if it is, that Cllr Tyssul Lewis said, "We'll
d   get him," it seems to me to imply not only an intent to injure the plaintiff through
Mr Jones but a determination to see that it is done. To my mind this determination
is a powerful ingredient to be taken into account when considering this question of
whether other councillors were affected by the malice. It adds great force to the
submission of counsel for the plaintiff that the result of the vote on 28 June 1979
was a foregone conclusion. There is an air of unreality in trying to consider the
e   question in the abstract, divorced from an actual finding of malice. In my judgment,
if the judge had found malice on the part of the Labour leadership, he might very
well have concluded this issue in favour of the plaintiff as well. I certainly do not
feel confident that we can dismiss the appeal on the basis that this issue must be
resolved in favour of the council.'

f   I agree that, if the judge had found malice against Cllr Tyssul Lewis and perhaps Cllr
McDonald-Murray, he might have found that some other Labour councillors were
infected, but the judge himself denied this proposition by considering the case on the
assumption that Cllrs Tyssul Lewis and McDonald-Murray were activated by malice. To
reach a conclusion founded on an alternative assumption is a common and useful feature
of civil trial by a judge without a jury and only exceptional circumstances will justify an
g appellate court in refusing to accept supportable conclusions pronounced by a judge on
such a basis. The proposition that one ought to accept the judge's conclusions as to the
alleged malice of the remaining councillors is in the present case strengthened by
reference to the conclusions which he reached with regard to the evidence of Cllrs Ayres,
Aldron and Chilcott; the latter conclusions appear very unlikely to have been different,
even if the judge had found malice proved against the two leaders. Finally, the reference
h by Stuart-Smith to the other 26 councillors who voted prompts me to say that the council
was under no duty to establish how many councillors were *not* infected by Cllr Tyssul
Lewis's (assumed) malice.

Nourse LJ agreed with Stuart-Smith LJ, observing that Cllrs Ayres, Aldron and Chilcott
were all found to have voted from motives which entirely acquitted them of malice
towards the plaintiff, whether direct or by affection. He then said ([1989] 3 All ER 162
j at 187, [1990] 1 WLR 54 at 86):

     'But that finding does not throw any light on the motives of the other members
of the majority. Nor could the three councillors who gave evidence of their own
motives have been expected to give anything but speculative evidence of the motives
of others.'

I agree, but this ought not to help the plaintiff. What those three witnesses proved, which did affect the position of the other councillors, was that the witnesses were not instructed *a* or asked to vote in a particular manner and that there was no party whip in operation at the council meeting on 28 June 1979 or at any of the earlier meetings. Moreover, there was no group decision at the meeting of the Labour Party group before the June council meeting.

Nourse LJ took the view that to deny that it was open to the judge 'to infer that the other 24 members of the council who voted for the resolution did so out of an informal *b* allegiance to Cllr Tyssul Lewis and his well publicised election pledge' would be 'to disregard the realities of decision-taking by councillors in local government' (see [1989] 3 All ER 162 at 187, [1990] 1 WLR 54 at 86). Again, with respect, this observation appears to replace the judge's conclusion on the evidence by a subjective assessment. The fact that the Labour councillors voted on party lines at the June council meeting did not justify the conclusion that they were infected by the (assumed) malice of Cllr Tyssul *c* Lewis; where a good case (as it seemed to Cllr Ayres, Aldron and Chilcott) had been made by a respected leader for reverting to a decision originally reached at the March meeting and later abandoned, it could be regarded as normal to vote the same way.

My Lords, I have felt bound to note and comment on a number of individual points which were made by the members of the Court of Appeal. It may therefore be useful to sum up my view. (1) It is agreed that it was open to the judge to find for or against the *d* charge of malice brought against Cllr Tyssul Lewis. To prove that charge was the essential basis of the plaintiff's case. For the reasons I have given, the plaintiff's criticisms of the judgment lack the strength and validity to justify setting it aside on this point. (2) If, contrary to my own view but consistently with that of Slade LJ, I assume that the judgment on Cllr Tyssul Lewis's malice is fit to be set aside, I would still refuse to order a new trial, because the plaintiff's case as pleaded, presented and argued in both courts *e* below was that *all* the Labour councillors who voted for the June resolution were (at the least) infected by their leader's malice. That case failed, and indeed was disproved. It would be wrong now to give the plaintiff a further opportunity, which was open to her at the trial, of making a new case based on the submission that a majority of the council, in voting for the June resolution, were infected by Cllr Tyssul Lewis's malice (if any). (3) No one suggests that judgment could *now* be given for the plaintiff and, even if both of *f* the points made above were wrong, I would still refuse a new trial, because the evidence of Cllrs Ayres, Aldron and Chilcott, accepted by the judge, disposed not only of the plaintiff's case as presented but also of the alternative case which was proffered to her by the Court of Appeal. It would have been entirely inconsistent for the judge to accede to that case while accepting the evidence of the three councillor witnesses.

Accordingly, for the reasons I have given, I would allow the council's appeal and *g* restore the judgment and order of the trial judge.

Appeal allowed.

Solicitors: *Sharpe Pritchard*, agents for *A K B Boatswain*, Swansea (for the council); *Allan* *h* *Jay & Co*, agents for *Robertsons*, Cardiff (for the plaintiff).

Mary Rose Plummer   Barrister.

a

Re Norman Holding Co Ltd

CHANCERY DIVISION (COMPANIES COURT)
MERVYN DAVIES J
1, 2, 8 OCTOBER 1990

b *Company – Winding up – Proof of debt – Set-off – Mutual dealings – Secure debt – Whether creditor of insolvent company required to set off money owed by him to company against secured debt – Insolvency Rules 1986, r 4.90.*

Although a creditor who proves in the liquidation of an insolvent company for an unsecured debt is required by r 4.90[a] of the Insolvency Rules 1986 to set off money owed c by him to the company against that debt, he is not required to set off the amount owed against any secured debt unless he elects to prove that debt in the liquidation, since r 4.90 requiring an account to be taken of mutual debts only applies to debts proved in the liquidation and a secured debt does not need to be proved in the liquidation (see p 761 c to f, post).

d **Notes**

For mutual credits and set-off in a liquidation, see 3(2) Halsbury's Laws (4th edn reissue) paras 535–540, and for cases on the subject of set-off, see 4 Digest (Reissue) 428–457, 3736–3943.

For the Insolvency Rules 1986, r 4.90, see 3 Halsbury's Statutory Instruments (Grey Volume) 311.

e

Cases referred to in judgment

Barnett, Ex p, re Deveze (1874) LR 9 Ch App 293 LC and LJJ.
Daintry, Re, ex p Mant [1900] 1 QB 546, [1895–9] All ER Rep 657, CA.
Hiley v Peoples Prudential Assurance Co Ltd (in liq) (1938) 60 CLR 468, Aust HC.
f *Keller (Samuel) (Holdings) Ltd v Martins Bank Ltd* [1970] 3 All ER 950, [1971] 1 WLR 43, CA.
Law, Ex p, re Kennedy (1846) 1 De G 378.
McColl's Wholesale Pty Ltd v State Bank of New South Wales [1984] 3 NSWLR 365, NSW SC.

Preliminary issue

On 24 April 1990 Harrowby Street Properties Ltd (Harrowby) applied to the court for an g order that within seven days of the order of the court the sum of £400,000 together with interest be paid to Harrowby from the balance of the proceeds of sale of Norman Holding Co Ltd's interest in the property known as Herbert House in Birmingham. The respondents to the application were (1) the liquidator of Norman Holding Co Ltd (Norman), (2) Bank in Liechtenstein (UK) Ltd, (3) Control Securities plc and (4) Damina Stiftung (Damina). On 9 July 1990 Vinelott J ordered that there be a trial of the following h preliminary issue: whether the sum claimed by Harrowby under its second charge fell to be reduced by way of set-off in respect of those sums, if any, due from Harrowby to Norman arising from alleged breaches of an agreement dated 30 March 1984 between Harrowby and Norman. The facts are set out in the judgment.

Robin St John Knowles for Harrowby.
j *Richard Hacker* for Damina.
Mark Arnold for the liquidator.
The second and third respondents were not represented.

Cur adv vult

a   Rule 4.90 is set out at p 759 d to f, post

8 October. The following judgment was delivered.

MERVYN DAVIES J. The matter before me arises in the winding up of a company
called Norman Holding Co Ltd. Hoffmann J made a winding-up order on 8 December
1988. There is an application in the winding up dated 24 April 1990. The applicant is
Harrowby Street Properties Ltd (Harrowby). The respondents to the application are (1)
the liquidator, (2) Bank in Liechtenstein (UK) Ltd, (3) Control Securities plc and (4)
Damina Stiftung (Damina). Before me respondent (2) did not appear and I am told that
that company is now no longer interested in the matter. On 9 July 1990 Vinelott J
ordered the trial of a preliminary issue. A statement of facts has been agreed by
Harrowby, the liquidator and Damina. I understand that respondent (3) will accept the
decision on the preliminary issue.

The statement of facts, agreed as above, is as follows. (1) Norman Holding Co Ltd (the
company) is in insolvent liquidation pursuant to a winding-up order made by Hoffmann J
on 8 December 1988.

(2) Prior to the commencement of its liquidation, the company became indebted to
Harrowby in the sum of £400,000 together with interest at an agreed rate. The
indebtedness represents part of the outstanding purchase price of a property known as
Herbert House (the property) which the company purchased from Harrowby pursuant
to a written agreement dated 30 March 1984 (the agreement).

(3) The indebtedness referred to in para (2) above remains outstanding. As security for
that indebtedness the company gave Harrowby a second legal charge over the property.
The first chargee has been paid off and plays no part in the present dispute.

(4) In addition to relying on its security, Harrowby has submitted a proof of debt in
the liquidation of the company.

(5) For the purposes of the preliminary issue it is to be assumed, as alleged by Damina,
that (a) at the commencement of the company's liquidation the company was entitled to
assert a cross-claim against Harrowby in respect of sums due under a rental warranty
given by Harrowby in the agreement and (b) the indebtedness remains outstanding and
is secured.

(6) For the purposes of the preliminary issue it is to be further assumed, as alleged by
Damina, that it is entitled (by subrogation) to a valid third charge over the property.

(7) Pursuant to an order of Warner J made on 11 July 1988 (on the company's
application under s 127 of the Insolvency Act 1986) the property was sold and its proceeds
are held subject to further order of the court, security rights over the property being
expressly treated as attaching to the proceeds of sale as they did to the property itself.

(8) The present preliminary issue arises for decision in the context of an application by
Harrowby for an order that it be paid out from the proceeds of sale the sums secured by
its second charge. That application is opposed by Damina, which contends that
Harrowby's secured claim has been discharged (either in whole or in part) by the
operation of set-off.

(9) The issue to be tried, pursuant to the order of Vinelott J made on 9 July is whether,
on those assumed facts:

'. . . the sum claimed by [Harrowby] under its second charge falls to be reduced
by way of set off in respect of those sums . . . due from [Harrowby] to the
Company . . .'

(10) This statement of facts is agreed for the purpose of the trial of the preliminary
issue only and its contents do not bind any party to the application save in relation to the
trial of that issue. The trial of the preliminary issue is to be without prejudice to
Harrowby's entitlement, in the future, to argue that the assumptions set out in paras (5)
and (6) above are incorrect.

That is the end of the statement of facts.

I was told that the debt mentioned in para (4) of the statement is a debt relating to an

unsecured claim, that is to say it is a debt separate and apart from the secured debt
a referred to in paras (2) and (3). The position therefore is (a) Harrowby is a secured creditor
of the company in the sum of £400,000, (b) Harrowby is an unsecured creditor of the
company for an unspecified sum and (c) the company is a creditor of Harrowby for an
unspecified sum. From that basis one reads the issue as set out in para (9) of the statement
and the issue becomes whether Harrowby's secured debt falls to be reduced by way of
set-off by the sum (unspecified) which Harrowby owes to the company.

b   Counsel for Harrowby contended that there should be no set-off. Counsel for Damina
contended for set-off. It was agreed that were there no liquidation there would be no set-
off. It was so agreed by reference to *Samuel Keller (Holdings) Ltd v Martins Bank Ltd* [1970]
3 All ER 950 esp at 952–953, [1971] 1 WLR 43 esp at 51 per Russell LJ, including the
words quoted from Megarry J in the court below. However, when liquidation supervenes
counsel for Damina said that the position was otherwise. One turns to r 4.90 of the
c Insolvency Rules 1986, SI 1986/1925. The rule is as follows:

> '(1) This Rule applies where, before the company goes into liquidation there have
> been mutual credits, mutual debts or other mutual dealings between the company
> and any creditor of the company proving or claiming to prove for a debt in the
> liquidation.
d
> (2) An account shall be taken of what is due from each party to the other in
> respect of the mutual dealings, and the sums due from one party shall be set off
> against the sums due from the other.
> (3) Sums due from the company to another party shall not be included in the
> account taken under paragraph (2) if that other party had notice at the time they
> became due that a meeting of creditors had been summoned under section 98 or (as
e
> the case may be) a petition for the winding up of the company was pending.
> (4) Only the balance (if any) of the account is provable in the liquidation.
> Alternatively (as the case may be) the amount shall be paid to the liquidator as part
> of the assets.'

Thus there is to be set-off as between Harrowby and the company if and to the extent
f that the rule applies. The rule applies (see para (1)) when there have been mutual credits
etc. That there were is agreed. But then the mutual credits etc must have been between
the company 'and any creditor of the company proving or claiming to prove for a debt
in the liquidation'. Harrowby is a creditor 'proving . . . for a debt in the liquidation' in
that it has proved for the sum owing to it that is unsecured, ie (b) above. Thus it is said
that r 4.90 applies as respects all the mutual debts as between Harrowby and the company
g so that there can be set-off not only as against the Harrowby unsecured debt but also as
against the Harrowby secured debt. The Insolvency Rules 1986 themselves give no clear
answer to the question whether or not set-off operates against a secured debt. I was
referred to r 13.12, which, defining 'debt', does not distinguish between debts secured
and debts unsecured. I was also referred to rr 4.73 (meaning of 'prove'), 4.88 (secured
creditors), 4.96 (surrender for non-disclosure) and 4.97 (redemption by liquidator); but
h none of those rules seem to me to be of much help in considering the question before
me, ie does set-off operate against a secured debt?

I refer to some of the authorities that were read. In *Ex p Law, re Kennedy* (1846) 1 De G
378 at 380 it appears to be assumed (when another question was under consideration), in
the briefest of sentences, that in bankruptcy a secured debt may be the subject of set-off.
I cannot regard *Ex p Law* as authority for answering the question before me. Another
j case in bankruptcy is *Ex p Barnett, re Deveze* (1874) LR 9 Ch App 293. Lord Selborne LC
says (at 295–296):

> 'We think that the judgment is not right in this case. The section in the *Bankruptcy
> Act*, 1869, is, no doubt, somewhat different from what would have been the law in
> the absence of bankruptcy, and it is a rule to be administered in bankruptcy. As I

understand it, it says, without noticing the subject of security at all, that when there have been mutual credits, debts, or mutual dealings—I say nothing at present upon any distinct meaning of "mutual dealings"—and a proof is to be made in bankruptcy, there is to be a rule of set-off, not, as I understand it, at the option of either party, but an absolute statutory rule—"The balance of such account, and no more, shall be claimed or paid on either side respectively." This is clearly a case of mutual credits at the time of the bankruptcy; on the one hand, there was a large debt maturing, though not matured, to *Barnett & Co.*, and there was a small debt actually due from them to the bankrupt. That being so, *Barnett & Co.* come in to prove, and the statute expressly says that the amount of their proof shall be ascertained by writing off the small debt from the larger, and as debt can co-exist with security, and often does, the fact that nothing is said about security or lien one way or the other in the section seems to me only to shew that the existence of security is not to affect its operation.'

To my mind the words quoted do not dispose of the question before me because, as counsel for Harrowby pointed out, (i) the secured debt in that case was the secured debt of the insolvent (compare here Harrowby) and (ii) the creditor, asserting set-off, was proving for a debt whereas Harrowby is not proving in respect of its secured debt. In the Australian case of *Hiley v Peoples Prudential Assurance Co Ltd (in liq)* (1938) 60 CLR 468 at 498 Dixon J said:

'In the fourth place, secured debts or liabilities are no less the subject of set-off than unsecured debts as mutual debts, credits or dealings. To the extent that the secured debt is answered by set-off the security is freed . . .'

The judge then referred to *Ex p Barnett* and *Ex p Law*. Those words are weighty but I observe that they were used in the context of the secured debt being in the hands of the insolvent company. Another Australian case, *McColl's Wholesale Pty Ltd v State Bank of New South Wales* [1984] 3 NSWLR 365, suggests that set-off is maintainable against a secured debt: see per Powell J (at 380) with reference to *Hiley's* case.

Ex p Barnett and *Hiley's* case are cases in which, as I have said, the security was held by the insolvent estate; whereas here the security is held not by the liquidator but by Harrowby. With that distinction in mind I do not see that *Ex p Barnett* is authority for saying that there must be set-off against a secured creditor such as Harrowby. If one takes a situation A with (i) company X having security for a debt of £A owed to it by Y and (ii) company X owing Y £B, then with X in liquidation the proceeds of the sale of X's security will necessarily be funds in the liquidator's hands plainly susceptible to set-off. But if one takes situation B with (i) company X owed £C by Y and (ii) company X owing £D to Y for which Y has security, then Y may elect not to prove in the liquidation; instead he may realise his security, take his money and account for any balance to the liquidator.

My conclusion so far, therefore, is that the express words of the Insolvency Rules 1986 do not say whether or not set-off arises in the circumstances of the case before me, and further that the authorities give no sure guidance. In this situation the following considerations seem to apply.

(1) Reading r 4.90, it seems that there is no set-off unless the creditor proves (or claims to prove) for his debt in the liquidation. Had Harrowby only its secured debt there would thus be no set-off because Harrowby has not proved and does not intend to prove for its secured debt.

I should say that in this connection counsel for Damina, referring to *Re Daintry, ex p Mant* [1900] 1 QB 546 at 568, [1895–9] All ER Rep 657 at 670–671, suggested that a creditor claiming to prove a debt is a creditor who has a right to prove a debt. He then said, as I understand, that a secured creditor has a right to prove and, therefore, Harrowby is 'claiming to prove' within r 4.90 as respect its secured debt. I do not accept that suggestion. No doubt Harrowby has a right to elect to prove for its secured debt but it is choosing not to do so.

(2) If it is right, as mentioned in (1) above, that there is no set-off against a secured creditor who does not prove, it would be a curious circumstance if, the secured creditor having as well an unsecured debt, the proving of the unsecured debt operated to involve the creditor in set-off not only as respects his unsecured debt but also as respects his secured debt.

(3) On the other hand, one reading of r 4.90 as a whole suggests that if there is an unsecured as well as a secured debt then the creditor has to submit to set-off as respects both his debts. For the set-off rule applies when there are mutual debts between the company and 'any creditor proving . . . for a debt.' Harrowby is proving for a debt, ie its unsecured debt.

(4) I do not think that r 4.90 should be read so literally as is set out in (3) above. A r 4.90 set-off operates in the course of a liquidation. But a secured creditor who does not prove is not involved in the liquidation as respects his secured debt, even if he is involved in the litigation as respects another debt which he has and which happens to be unsecured and for which he has to prove. The secured debt must be considered separate and apart from the unsecured debt because the secured debt is not a debt 'in the liquidation'. As a secured creditor he does not (unless he so elects) prove or claim to prove for his debt in the liquidation. He relies on and realises his security. But as an unsecured creditor he proves in the liquidation and so is caught by set-off as to the unsecured debt. Thus I read r 4.90 as affecting debts proved in the liquidation and not as affecting debts that are elected not to be proved therein. The position is that a creditor with two debts, one secured and the other unsecured, is obliged to submit to set-off in respect of his unsecured debt but is not obliged so to submit as to his second debt, because for that debt he is not proving in the liquidation.

Having regard to the considerations set out above I take the view, with some hesitation, that, while r 4.90 set-off applies to an unsecured creditor who proves in the liquidation, that creditor is not obliged to bring into account any secured debt owing to him by the insolvent company if the secured debt is not proved in the liquidation. As I have said, r 4.90 affects debts proved in the liquidation but does not affect debts that are elected not to be proved. It follows that I answer the question framed in para 9 of the statement in the negative.

Question answered in the negative.

Solicitors: *Simmons & Simmons* (for Harrowby); *Norton Rose* (for Damina); *Dibb Lupton Broomhead & Prior* (for the liquidator).

Jacqueline Metcalfe   Barrister.

Derby & Co Ltd and others v Weldon and others (No 8)

CHANCERY DIVISION
VINELOTT J
4, 6, 9 APRIL 1990

COURT OF APPEAL, CIVIL DIVISION
DILLON, BUTLER-SLOSS AND LEGGATT LJJ
25, 27 JULY 1990

Discovery – Legal professional privilege – Waiver – Documents created by plaintiffs for purpose of civil proceedings – Inadvertent disclosure of privileged documents to defendants during course of discovery – Defendants ignoring advice that they should clarify whether disclosure had occurred by mistake and obtaining copies of privileged documents – Whether plaintiffs' privilege waived by disclosure – Whether court should restore privileged status of documents.

Document – Admissibility in evidence – Privileged and confidential document – Copy coming into possession of party to litigation – Loss of privilege – Inadvertent disclosure of document – Claim for protection of confidentiality – Court's discretion – Whether court required to exercise discretion by balancing conflicting public policy considerations.

The plaintiffs were seven associated companies which were all part of a United States banking group. In 1981 the plaintiff group purchased a London commodity dealer, CML, from the first and second defendants, who were the directors and effective owners of CML. The sale of CML was made through the third and fourth defendants, a Panamanian company and a Luxembourg company, both of which were controlled by the first and second defendants. After the sale CML continued to be managed by the first and second defendants and while under their management CML offered very extensive credit to a Far Eastern commodity dealer which in 1984 became insolvent owing over £35m to CML. The plaintiff group recovered less than £1·5m in the insolvency and brought an action against the four defendants alleging deceit, conspiracy to defraud and fraudulent breach of fiduciary duty and seeking delivery up of secret profits, and against seven other defendants on the basis that they had been parties to the conspiracy or had assisted in the commission of unlawful acts by the first four defendants or had received assets for which they were accountable. In the course of discovery by the plaintiffs their solicitors compiled lists of documents in the usual form, but inadvertently included in the schedule to the list 14 documents which they later claimed fell within the scope of legal professional privilege. Solicitors representing the first and second defendants inspected a number of documents on the list, including some which were identified as privileged. Disregarding advice from leading counsel that they should inquire whether the plaintiffs' solicitors had intended to disclose privileged documents or whether there had been a mistake, the defendants' solicitors asked for and obtained copies of a range of documents including the 14 privileged documents. The inadvertent disclosure of the privileged documents came to the attention of the plaintiffs' solicitors when they were exhibited to an affidavit filed in support of an application by the first and second defendants for further and better discovery. The plaintiffs subsequently sought an order for delivery up of any copies of the privileged documents in the possession of the first and second defendants and an injunction restraining them from relying on any information contained in those documents and for leave to amend their list of documents by deleting reference to them. The defendants contended (i) that the plaintiffs' solicitors had waived any privilege attaching to the relevant documents when they allowed the defendants to inspect and take copies of them, (ii) that, if not, then before granting any injunctive relief the court should balance the legitimate interest of the plaintiffs in seeking to prevent disclosure and use of the confidential information against the public interest and the legitimate interest of the defendants in having all the salient facts put forward at the trial and (iii) that the defendants ought not to be put at a disadvantage in their conduct of the litigation by reason of the plaintiffs' carelessness. The judge held (i) that the plaintiffs had not lost the right to claim privilege in respect of 11 of the 14 documents since they were so plainly directed to obtaining legal advice for the purpose of legal proceedings that the defendants' solicitors should have realised that they had been inadvertently disclosed, and the plaintiffs were therefore entitled to the relief sought for those 11 documents, and (ii) that the court was not required to balance conflicting public policy considerations in determining whether to restore the privileged status of documents which had been inadvertently disclosed. The judge held that the three remaining documents did not appear on their face to be privileged and therefore did not have to be returned. The plaintiffs appealed in respect of the three documents, contending that the defendants should not be permitted to take advantage of an inadvertent disclosure which they knew to be a mistake. The defendants cross-appealed against the judge's failure to carry out a balancing exercise in respect of each document before granting injunctive relief.

Held – (1) Where privileged documents belonging to one party to an action were inadvertently disclosed to, and inspected by, the other side in circumstances such that the inspecting party must have realised that a mistake had occurred but sought to take advantage of the inadvertent disclosure, the court had power under its equitable jurisdiction to intervene and order the inspecting party to return all copies of the privileged documents and to grant an injunction restraining him from using information contained in or derived from the documents, even if it was not immediately obvious that the documents were privileged. Since the conduct of the defendants' solicitors made it plain that they were seeking to take advantage of an obvious mistake, the court would order them to return all copies of the privileged documents which they had obtained as a result of the mistake, including the three documents in issue. Accordingly, the order of the judge would be extended to include all 14 documents. The plaintiffs' appeal would therefore be allowed (see p 782 b j to p 783 b j and p 784 c, post); dicta of Slade LJ in *Guinness Peat Properties Ltd v Fitzroy Robinson Partnership (a firm)* [1987] 2 All ER 716 at 729–731 applied.

(2) Where an injunction was sought in aid of legal professional privilege the court was not required to exercise its discretion by balancing conflicting public policy considerations but would instead act to preserve an absolute privilege and would only refuse an injunction in aid of the privilege on general principles that qualify the grant of a discretionary remedy. Accordingly, where the court granted the restoration injunctive relief in aid of legal professional privilege it would not qualify the restoration of privileged status by reference to the importance of the documents to the inspecting party, since to do so would in effect enable important documents and return only those which were unimportant. There was no basis on which any of the privileged documents could be excluded from the order of the court, the defendants' cross-appeal would be dismissed (see p 784 c, post).

Notes

For legal professional privilege, see 13 Halsbury's Laws (4th edn) paras 71–75, and for cases on the subject (2nd reissue) 154–169, 1379–1482.

For confidential communications between solicitor and client, see 44 Halsbury's

Laws (4th edn) para 74, and for cases on the subject, see 44 Digest (Reissue) 38–40, 359–367.

For waiver of privilege, see 13 Halsbury's Laws (4th edn) para 84, and for cases on the subject, see 18 Digest (2nd reissue) 253–254, 2256–2267.

Cases referred to in judgments

Aegis Blaze, The [1986] 1 Lloyd's Rep 203, CA.
Ashburton (Lord) v Pape [1913] 2 Ch 469, [1911–13] All ER Rep 708, CA.
Briamore Manufacturing Ltd (in liq), Re [1986] 3 All ER 132, [1986] 1 WLR 1429.
British Coal Corp v Dennis Rye Ltd (No 2) [1988] 3 All ER 816, [1988] 1 WLR 1113, CA.
Calcraft v Guest [1898] 1 QB 759, [1895–9] All ER Rep 346, CA.
English and American Insurance Co Ltd v Herbert Smith [1988] FSR 232.
Goddard v Nationwide Building Society [1986] 3 All ER 264, [1987] QB 670, [1986] 3 WLR 734, CA.
Great Atlantic Insurance Co v Home Insurance Co [1981] 2 All ER 485, [1981] 1 WLR 529, CA.
Guinness Peat Properties Ltd v Fitzroy Robinson Partnership (a firm) [1987] 2 All ER 716, [1987] 1 WLR 1027, CA.
Nocton v Lord Ashburton [1914] AC 932, [1914–15] All ER Rep 45, HL.
Roberts (A) & Co Ltd v Leicestershire CC [1961] 2 All ER 545, [1961] Ch 555, [1961] 2 WLR 1000.
Webster v James Chapman & Co (a firm) [1989] 3 All ER 939.

Motion

The plaintiffs, Derby & Co Ltd, Cocoa Merchants Ltd (CML), Philbro-Salomon Finance AG, Philbro-Salomon Ltd, Philipp Bros Inc, Philipp Bros Ltd and Salomon Inc (the holding company of the other plaintiff companies), by a writ issued on 25 June 1987 brought an action against, inter alia, (1) Anthony Henry David Weldon, (2) Ian Jay, (3) Milco Corp, a Panamanian company, and (4) CML Holding SA of Luxembourg, claiming damages for breach of contract, misrepresentation, negligence, conspiracy to defraud and fraudulent breach of fiduciary duty arising out of the trading activities of CML between June 1981 and February 1984 while under the management of the first and second defendants as executive directors of CML after it had been purchased by Salomon Inc from the liquidator of a subsidiary of the third defendant, which was itself a subsidiary of the fourth defendant. Seven other companies and individuals were subsequently joined as defendants on the basis that they had been parties to the conspiracy or had assisted in the commission of unlawful acts by the first four defendants or had received assets for which they were accountable, namely (5) Wollstein Stiftung, a Liechtenstein stiftung which was the ultimate owner of a Liberian company, Cocoa Merchants (Far East) Ltd, and the holder of profits made from foreign exchange dealings with CML and Derby & (6) Tim Schneider, (7) Ernst Aeschbacher and (8) Peter Ritter, the trustees of two Liechtenstein trusts (the Lagor trust and the Ralgo trust), (9) Steelburg Management Inc, (10) Pilgrim Enterprises Inc, two companies owned by the two trusts, and (11) Rohner, the Swiss lawyer for the fourth and fifth defendants. In the course of the proceedings the plaintiffs applied for (i) an order for the delivery up of 14 documents in the evidence as documents A to N, which they alleged fell within the scope of the privilege and had been inadvertently included in the schedule to the list of documents compiled by the plaintiffs' solicitors, copies of which had been supplied to the defendants, (ii) an injunction restraining the first and second defendants from relying on any information contained in those documents or representing the first and second defendants took no part in this stage by deleting reference to them. The third defendants to amend their list of documents of the proceedings although they were interested. The facts are set out in the judgment.

Michael Lyndon-Stanford QC and *J Stephen Smith* for the plaintiffs.
Nicholas Chambers QC and *Mark Hapgood* for the defendants.

Cur adv vult

9 April. The following judgment was delivered.

VINELOTT J. In the course of discovery by the plaintiffs in this action, their solicitors, Messrs Lovell White Durrant (Lovells), compiled lists of documents in the usual form. They inadvertently included in part 1 of schedule 1 to the list documents which it is now said come within the scope of legal professional privilege. The solicitors acting for the first and second defendants, Messrs Hopkins & Wood, inspected some of the documents included in the list. The documents inspected included some which are now said to be within the scope of legal professional privilege. They were supplied at their request with copies of them. There are 14 documents which have so far been identified as privileged documents inadvertently disclosed. They have been referred to in the evidence as documents A to N. The inadvertent disclosure of these documents came to the attention of Lovells when they were exhibited to an affidavit filed in support of an application by the first and second defendants for further and better discovery.

In this application the plaintiffs seek an order for the delivery up of any copies of these documents in the possession of the first and second defendants and an injunction restraining them from relying on any information contained in those documents and for leave to amend their list of documents by deleting reference to them.

It is apparent from the evidence filed in this application that copies of the documents in question have been seen by the third to eleventh defendants and that they have made some use of them. However, they are not joined as parties to this application and, although invited to appear and to take part in it, they have not done so. I shall have to come back to consider the position of the third to eleventh defendants at the end of this judgment. For convenience, until I reach that point, I shall refer to the first and second defendants alone as 'the defendants'.

In the course of argument it became clear that the defendants are content to return all copies of all documents except documents E, K, L and M, and, in relation to documents other than E, K, L and M, to give undertakings in the terms of the injunction sought. However, discovery by the plaintiffs has been very extensive indeed and the plaintiffs fear that other privileged documents may have escaped detection and may have been inadvertently disclosed and inspected. Both the plaintiffs and defendants are therefore anxious that I should decide the questions of principle that have been raised so that the course that should be taken if any other documents have been inadvertently disclosed can be agreed without a further application to the court.

The defendants oppose this application on two grounds. They say, first, that the plaintiffs' solicitors when they allowed them to inspect and take copies of the relevant documents waived any privilege that may have attached to them. They say, second, that even if privilege has not been waived the only ground on which the plaintiffs can claim to recover the documents and to enjoin the defendants from relying on them is that they contain confidential information and that, in any case where a plaintiff seeks to protect confidential information, the court, before making an order, must balance on the one hand the legitimate interests of the plaintiff in seeking to prevent the disclosure and use of confidential information, and on the other the public interest and the legitimate interest of defendants in seeking to make use of it.

The defendants only invite the court to carry out this balancing exercise in relation to one document, document E. As regards documents K, L, M and N, the defendants accept that unless the privilege has been waived, the plaintiffs are entitled to the relief they seek.

Although the first of these two submissions is the more extensive in that it applies to all the documents in issue, it will be convenient to deal with the second submission first.

It brings into focus the principles on which the court has in the past compelled restoration of privileged documents which have come into the hands of the party to existing litigation or into the hands of a third party.

The balancing exercise

The first case in which a plaintiff successfully sought an order for the recovery of copies of privileged documents and an injunction restraining defendants from making use of them is *Lord Ashburton v Pape* [1913] 2 Ch 469, [1911–13] All ER Rep 708. The defendant Pape was a bankrupt. He applied for his discharge. Lord Ashburton, a substantial creditor, opposed the application. Pape served a clerk, Brooks, employed by Lord Ashburton's former solicitor, Nocton, with a subpoena duces tecum to produce letters written by Lord Ashburton to Nocton which were admittedly privileged. Nocton is referred to in the judgment of Cozens-Hardy MR as Lord Ashburton's 'late' solicitor, but it is clear from the decision of the House of Lords in *Nocton v Lord Ashburton* [1914] AC 932, [1914–15] All ER Rep 45 that he was in fact still living. Brooks attended the court. Before the subpoena was called, he complained of feeling ill and left the court. Before leaving the court, he handed the documents to Pape who gave them to his solicitor who copied them and returned them to Pape. Lord Ashburton started an action against Pape and his solicitor to recover the documents and the copies made of them and to restrain the defendant from disclosing or allowing any other person to disclose the documents or informing any other person of their contents.

The case is often referred to as one in which the possession of privileged documents had been obtained by a trick. The facts suggest that Cozens-Hardy MR's description of the case as one in which documents were 'by collusion between Pape and the clerk, obtained from their proper custody' may be more apt (see [1913] 2 Ch 469 at 471, [1911–13] All ER Rep 708 at 709). Lord Ashburton, having started his action, applied for an interim injunction in the same terms. The application came before Neville J. He made an order restraining the defendant from making use of the copies or of any information contained in them, but with the qualification, 'except for the purpose of the pending proceedings in the defendant Edward James Pape's bankruptcy and subject to the direction of the Bankruptcy Court'.

The reason for including that qualification is that it had been held in a number of cases, culminating in the decision of the Court of Appeal in *Calcraft v Guest* [1898] 1 QB 759, [1895–9] All ER Rep 346, that if a party to proceedings is entitled to object to the production of a document on the ground that it is privileged and if the other party has obtained a copy of it by any means, the copy can be produced as secondary evidence of the contents of the original.

Lord Ashburton appealed and sought a variation of the order by striking out the words I have cited. At the hearing before the Court of Appeal Pape did not appear. His solicitor appeared but took no part in the argument.

I have set out the facts and the history of the litigation fully because it is important to bear in mind that the appeal was an appeal by Lord Ashburton against the inclusion of the excepting words. There was no cross-appeal. There was no dispute and could be no dispute that the documents were both confidential and privileged and that Lord Ashburton was entitled to recover them and the copies made of them and to prevent the use of information derived from them, subject only to the exception. So in the Court of Appeal the only question was whether, in the light of *Calcraft v Guest*, the exception ought to be included. All the members of the Court of Appeal, Cozens-Hardy MR, Kennedy and Swinfen Eady LJJ, in answering this question in favour of Lord Ashburton, founded their decision on the confidential nature of the letters and on the jurisdiction of the court to restrain use of confidential information even in the hands of third parties, though Cozens-Hardy MR also referred to the fact that the documents were also privileged. He said ([1913] 2 Ch 469 at 473, [1911–13] All ER Rep 708 at 710):

'The rule of evidence as explained in *Calcraft* v. *Guest* merely amounts to this, that
a   if a litigant wants to prove a particular document which by reason of privilege or
some circumstance he cannot furnish by the production of the original, he may
produce a copy as secondary evidence although that copy has been obtained by
improper means, and even, it may be, by criminal means. The Court in such an
action is not really trying the circumstances under which the document was
produced. That is not an issue in the case and the Court simply says "Here is a copy
b   of a document which cannot be produced; it may have been stolen, it may have
been picked up in the street, it may have improperly got into the possession of the
person who proposes to produce it, but that is not a matter which the Court in the
trial of the action can go into." But that does not seem to me to have any bearing
upon a case where the whole subject-matter of the action is the right to retain the
originals or copies of certain documents *which are privileged*. It seems to me that,
c   although Pape has had the good luck to obtain to a copy of these documents which
he can produce without a breach of this injunction, there is no ground whatever in
principle why we should decline to give the plaintiff the protection which in my
view is his right as between him and Pape, and that there is no reason whatever why
we should not say to Pape in pending or future proceedings, "You shall not produce
these documents which you have acquired from the plaintiff surreptitiously, or
d   from his solicitor, who plainly stood to him in a confidential relation."'

I stress the words 'which are privileged'.
Counsel for the defendants submitted that the decision of the Court of Appeal is direct
authority for the proposition that the court acts in these circumstances solely on the
principles on which the court acts in preventing the use of confidential information.
e   Accordingly, the court must perform the same balancing exercise in deciding whether
or not to grant an injunction as it has to perform in other cases where it is sought to
prevent the disclosure and use of confidential information, an exercise with which the
courts have become familiar in recent years.
I do not think that the decision in *Lord Ashburton v Pape* can be taken to have been
founded solely on the ground that the letters in question were confidential. The exception
f   in Neville J's order would have been justified if the only ground for the order sought by
Lord Ashburton had been the confidential nature of the letters. Confidentiality is not a
separate head of privilege and, apart from the injunctions sought, oral evidence of their
contents could have been adduced at the hearing and use could have been made of the
information derived from them in cross-examination even if the copies had been
returned.
g   The unrestricted order which Lord Ashburton sought and which he obtained in the
Court of Appeal, although less fully spelled out than the order made by the Court of
Appeal in *British Coal Corp v Dennis Rye Ltd (No 2)* [1988] 3 All ER 816, [1988] 1 WLR
1113, was clearly designed and apt not only to secure the return of any copies of the
letters made by Pape's solicitors but to prevent Pape from giving oral evidence of their
h   contents or otherwise making use of any information derived from them in the
bankruptcy proceedings.
That that is the correct analysis of the decision of the Court of Appeal is strongly
supported by the decision of the Court of Appeal in *Goddard v Nationwide Building Society*
[1986] 3 All ER 264, [1987] QB 670, in particular by the judgment of Nourse LJ. The
plaintiffs in that case had bought a house with the assistance of a loan from the defendant
building society. The same solicitor had acted for the plaintiffs and the building society
j   on the purchase of the house. The plaintiffs later sued the building society for damages
for negligence on the part of its surveyor. The solicitor who acted for the plaintiffs and
the building society on the purchase of the house did not act for the plaintiffs or the
building society in the litigation. But he sent a copy to the building society's solicitors of
a memorandum recording a conversation with one of the plaintiffs at the time of the

purchase. The main question was whether the plaintiffs could claim that the memorandum was within the scope of legal professional privilege, that is whether, when *a* he made the memorandum, the solicitor was acting for the plaintiffs or one of them alone.

That question was answered by the Court of Appeal in favour of the plaintiffs. Then the question was whether in the light of *Lord Ashburton v Pape* [1913] 2 Ch 469, [1911–13] All ER Rep 708 the plaintiffs were entitled to strike out the part of the defence in which the memorandum was pleaded, and to an injunction calling for the delivery up of *b* copies of the memorandum in the hands of the building society and its solicitors and restraining them from using information derived from it. This question was also answered in favour of the plaintiffs.

May LJ referred to the ratio of *Lord Ashburton v Pape* as founded on the confidential nature of the contents of the letters written by Lord Ashburton to Nocton ([1986] 3 All ER 264 at 268, [1987] QB 670 at 680):   *c*

'The Court of Appeal was concerned to protect that confidence, in the same way, for instance, as the courts protect the trade secrets of an employer against the unauthorised use of them by an employee, both while he remains such, as well as after he has left the employment.'

However, he later stated his conclusion in rather different terms. He said ([1986] 3 All *d* ER 264 at 270, [1987] QB 670 at 683):

'I confess that I do not find the decision in *Lord Ashburton v Pape* logically satisfactory, depending as it does on the order in which applications are made in litigation. Nevertheless I think that it and *Calcraft v Guest* are good authority for the following proposition. If a litigant has in his possession copies of documents *to which* *e* *legal professional privilege* attaches, he may nevertheless use such copies as secondary evidence in his litigation: however, if he has not yet used the documents in that way, the mere fact that he intends to do so is no answer to a claim against him by the person in whom the privilege is vested for delivery up of the copies or to restrain him from disclosing or making any use of any information contained in them.' (My emphasis.)   *f*

Nourse LJ made a number of general observations which he prefaced by saying that they were in general confined to a case where the communication is both confidential and privileged. I should cite the first four of these observations in full ([1986] 3 All ER 264 at 271–272, [1987] QB 670 at 684–685):

'Firstly, it is desirable to emphasise that the proceedings in which the rule of *g* evidence denies protection to the confidential communication are not proceedings whose purpose is to seek that protection. The question is an incidental one which arises when the party who desires the protection asserts a right to it as if he was the plaintiff in an action seeking to invoke the equitable jurisdiction. When *Lord Ashburton v Pape* was decided, the practice and procedures of our courts were no *h* doubt such that it was first necessary to issue fresh proceedings. Nowadays I think that we would, at the most, require an undertaking to issue a pro forma writ, perhaps not even that, a consideration which no doubt explains the agreement not to require fresh proceedings in the present case. The crucial point is that the party who desires the protection must seek it before the other party has adduced the confidential communication in evidence or otherwise relied on it at trial.   *j*

Secondly, although the equitable jurisdiction is of much wider application, I have little doubt that it can prevail over the rule of evidence only in cases where privilege can be claimed. The equitable jurisdiction is well able to extend, for example, to the grant of an injunction to restrain an unauthorised disclosure of confidential communications between priest and penitent or doctor and patient. But those

communications are not privileged in legal proceedings and I do not believe that
equity would restrain a litigant who already had a record of such a communication
in his possession from using it for the purposes of his litigation. It cannot be the
function of equity to accord a de facto privilege to communications in respect of
which no privilege can be claimed. Equity follows the law.

Thirdly, the right of the party who desires the protection to invoke the equitable
jurisdiction does not in any way depend on the conduct of the third party into
whose possession the record of the confidential communication has come ... This
view seems to give effect to the general rule that equity gives relief against all the
world, including the innocent, save only a bona fide purchaser for value without
notice. It is directly in point in the present case and our decision necessarily affirms
it.

Fourthly, once it is established that a case is governed by *Lord Ashburton v Pape*,
there is no discretion in the court to refuse to exercise the equitable jurisdiction
according to its view of the materiality of the communication, the justice of
admitting or excluding it or the like. The injunction is granted in aid of the
privilege which, unless and until it is waived, is absolute. In saying this, I do not
intend to suggest that there may not be cases where an injunction can properly be
refused on general principles affecting the grant of a discretionary remedy, for
example on the ground of inordinate delay.'

As regards the first of these observations a separate application may have been necessary
because, as I understand it, the Bankruptcy Court was not part of the High Court when
Lord Ashburton v Pape was decided. The practical effect of *Ashburton v Pape* as interpreted
in *Goddard v Nationwide* is that the rule in *Calcraft v Guest* will have little if any application
if the person entitled to privilege is a party to the proceedings in which it is sought to
adduce secondary evidence of the contents of a privileged document.

There are three subsequent decisions which I must briefly mention. First, *Re Briamore
Manufacturing Ltd (in liq)* [1986] 3 All ER 132, [1986] 1 WLR 1429. In that case a
liquidator's solicitor inadvertently included letters for which privilege could have been
claimed in the liquidator's list of documents. They were inspected by the defendant's
solicitors who took notes of their contents and made a copy of one of them. The
liquidator's solicitors discovered their mistake the following day and telephoned the
defendant's solicitors to say that privilege was claimed for them. Later the liquidator
applied to the court for leave to amend his list. The defendant's solicitors applied for an
order for delivery of copies of the documents as documents included in the unamended
list. Both applications came before Hoffmann J. At the hearing *Calcraft v Guest* was cited,
Lord Ashburton v Pape was not. It was conceded by counsel for the liquidator that the
solicitors for the defendant could give secondary evidence of the contents of the
documents and could produce the photocopy of the one he had copied and could be cross-
examined on them. Hoffmann J concluded that if secondary evidence of the contents of
the documents could be given, it would be—

'illogical that having carried out the inspection, but not gone through the physical
process of making copies at the time, he should now be disentitled from obtaining
the best evidence of the documents which he has seen. Accordingly, on this very
narrow point, namely whether the process can be put into reverse between the
moment of inspection and the request for copies of the documents inspected, I
would respectfully disagree with the registrar and hold that once inspection has
taken place, it is too late to correct the mistake and that the respondent is entitled to
his copies.'

(See [1986] 3 All ER 132 at 134, [1986] 1 WLR 1429 at 1432.)

That conclusion, it seems to me, follows inevitably from the concession that was made.
What is in issue in the instant case is whether the concession was rightly made.

In *English and American Insurance Co Ltd v Herbert Smith* [1988] FSR 232 the clerk to counsel acting for the plaintiffs in pending litigation inadvertently allowed instructions to counsel, which included statements by witnesses and his opinion, to be collected by the defendants' solicitors. They read them and took notes of their contents before returning them. The plaintiffs sought an injunction restraining the defendants from making any use of any information derived from the documents. Sir Nicolas Browne-Wilkinson V-C summarised the decision in *Goddard v Nationwide Building Society* as showing that (at 236):

'The position therefore depends, following the decision in the *Nationwide* case, on whether proceedings are taken before the document is tendered in evidence or not. If such proceedings are taken before the document is tendered, then the person entitled to the legal professional privilege is entitled to delivery up of the documents and the copies and to an injunction restraining the other side from making any use of them, including use of them in the proceedings which are pending.'

He rejected an argument advanced on behalf of the defendants that *Lord Ashburton v Pape* and *Goddard v Nationwide* could be distinguished on the ground that in those cases the recipient of the confidential information had been in some way wrongfully implicated in obtaining it, as inconsistent with the third of the observations in the judgment of Nourse LJ which I have cited. He added (at 239):

'I therefore hold that I am bound by the decisions in *Ashburton v Pape* and *Goddard v Nationwide Building Society* to grant the relief sought against both defendants. I confess that that is a result which gives me some satisfaction. Legal professional privilege is an important safeguard of a man's legal rights. It is the basis on which he and his advisers are free to speak as to matters in issue in litigation and otherwise without fear that it will subsequently be used against him. In my judgment, it is most undesirable if the security which is the basis of that freedom is to be prejudiced by mischances which are of everyday occurrence leading to documents which have escaped being used by the other side.'

That observation is of particular importance in the instant case. Discovery by the plaintiffs has been unusually if not uniquely extensive. The plaintiffs have disclosed 4,200 files, some containing hundreds of documents. They have instituted a system under which a room has been made available to the defendants and staff have also been made available to inspect and copy any documents in the plaintiffs' list which the defendants wish to see. The task of searching through and isolating privileged documents in the files and ensuring that they are not made available for inspection has presented exceptional difficulty.

I must now turn to the decision on which counsel for the defendants primarily relies. Recently in *Webster v James Chapman & Co (a firm)* [1989] 3 All ER 939 Scott J took the view that the second and third of the observations I have cited from the judgment of Nourse LJ in *Goddard v Nationwide* [1986] 3 All ER 264 at 271–272, [1987] QB 670 at 684–685 were not part of the ratio decidendi of that case and that he was not bound by them. He held that the principle established in *Lord Ashburton v Pape* rests solely on the confidential nature of the communication which it is sought to protect and that ([1989] 3 All ER 939 at 945):

'The court must, in each case where protection of confidential information is sought, balance on the one hand the legitimate interests of the plaintiff in seeking to keep the confidential information suppressed and on the other hand the legitimate interests of the defendant in seeking to make use of the information. There is never any question of an absolute right to have confidential information protected. The protection is the consequence of the balance to which I have referred coming down in favour of the plaintiff.'

Having referred to *Goddard v Nationwide* and to *Guiness Peat Properties Ltd v Fitzroy*
a *Robinson Partnership (a firm)* [1987] 2 All ER 716, [1987] 1 WLR 1027, to which I shall
later refer, and to the decision of Hoffmann J in *Re Briamore Manufacturing Ltd (in liq)*
[1986] 3 All ER 132, [1986] 1 WLR 1429, he concluded that ([1989] 3 All ER 939 at
946–947):

'Nothing in these judgments, in my view, detracts from the analysis of the
principles underlying *Calcraft v Guest* and *Lord Ashburton v Pape* to which I have
b already referred. If a document has been disclosed, be it by trickery, accident or
otherwise, the benefit and protection of legal privilege will have been lost. Secondary
evidence of the document will have come into the possession of the other side to the
litigation. The question then will be what protection the court should provide given
that the document which will have come into the possession of the other side will
be confidential and that use of it will be unauthorised. If the document was
c obviously confidential and had been obtained by a trick or by fraud, it is not difficult
to see that the balance would be struck in favour of the party entitled to the
confidential document. If the document had come into the possession of the other
side not through trick or fraud but due to a mistake or carelessness on the part of
the party entitled to the document or by his advisers, the balance will be very
d different from the balance in a fraud case. Suppose a case where the privileged
document has come into possession of the other side because of carelessness on the
part of the party entitled to keep the document confidential and has been read by
the other party, or by one of his legal advisers, without realising that a mistake has
been made. In such a case the future conduct of the litigation by the other party
would often be inhibited or made difficult were he to be required to undertake to
e shut out from his mind the contents of the document. It seems to me that it would
be thoroughly unfair that the carelessness of one party should be allowed to put the
other party at a disadvantage. I do not think that this branch of the law is one where
any firm rules as to how the balance should come down should be stated.'

He went on to consider the other considerations that are relevant in deciding how the
balance should be struck and gave reasons for deciding that in that case the balance came
f down against making the order sought.
I need say very little about the facts of that case. The plaintiff's solicitors had
inadvertently disclosed a copy of an expert's report. The expert had been asked to
reconsider his report in the light of further instructions. The original report was enclosed
in a letter to the defendants' solicitors; in their letter they said that they were seeking
instructions and that if they proposed to rely on the report they would disclose a copy.
g The defendants' solicitor in affidavit evidence said that when he received the report he
did not know whether the disclosure had been intentional or accidental and thought that
the plaintiff's solicitors 'might well have chosen to rely on the report despite its
deficiencies and to disclose it. Nevertheless, I suspected the disclosure may have been
accidental'.
h However, although the decision in *Guinness Peat v Fitzroy Robinson Partnership* was
cited, it was not apparently suggested on behalf of the plaintiff that the defendant's
solicitor when he received the report must have known that it had been sent by mistake;
equally, as I understand it, it was not contended on the part of the defendants that the
privilege had been waived. In reaching his conclusion that the injunction sought ought
not to be granted, Scott J placed considerable weight on the fact that if expert evidence
j were relied on, experts' reports would have to be exchanged and that the plaintiff's
expert might be cross-examined as to matters on which he had expressed an opinion in
his original report, and that the conduct of the defendants' case would be seriously
embarrassed if the defendants and their legal advisers were not able to make use of their
knowledge of the contents of the original report, knowledge that had come into their
possession through no fault of theirs.

Although I differ from Scott J on a matter of this kind with the greatest diffidence and
reluctance, I am unable to share his view that the observations I have cited from the *a*
judgment of Nourse LJ in *Goddard v Nationwide* were obiter dicta. Both Nourse and May
LJJ took the view that the principle applied in *Lord Ashburton v Pape* concerned documents
to which legal professional privilege attaches, and the injunctions granted in *Lord
Ashburton v Pape* and in *Goddard's* case, in so far as they prevented, in *Lord Ashburton v
Pape* disclosure of the contents of the correspondence between Nocton and Lord
Ashburton in the bankruptcy proceedings, or, in *Goddard v Nationwide* using or relying *b*
on the solicitors' memorandum in the action, could not, as I see it, have been founded
solely on the ground that the information contained in them had been imparted in
confidence. If the injunction is sought, in the words of Nourse LJ, 'in aid of legal
professional privilege', no balancing act is called for. As Croom-Johnson LJ pointed out
in *The Aegis Blaze* [1986] 1 Lloyd's Rep 203 at 211, the balance between conflicting public
policy considerations, that of completeness of the evidence before the court and that of *c*
legal professional privilege—

> 'should not be done in any circumstances where legal professional privilege
> attaches. The balancing act has already been done by the making of the rule of legal
> professional privilege; and to do what counsel for the respondents submitted should
> be done in subsequent litigation, would be to deny, in effect, the existence of that *d*
> rule.'

Waiver

In *Guinness Peat Properties Ltd v Fitzroy Robinson Partnership* [1987] 2 All ER 716, [1987]
1 WLR 1027 one question was whether permitting the inspection of a privileged *e*
document inadvertently included in the defendants' list of documents could be relied on
by the plaintiffs as an implied waiver of privilege by the defendants' solicitors. The first
plaintiff was a building developer. The action was brought against a firm of architects for
negligence in the design of a building. After the plaintiffs had warned the defendants
that a claim might be made, the defendants' administrative partner, Mr McLeish, notified
their insurers. He included with the letter a number of memoranda setting out his views *f*
and the views of another partner as to, amongst other things, the merits of the plaintiffs'
claim. One of the issues in the Court of Appeal was whether the plaintiffs were entitled
to claim legal professional privilege for the letter (the McLeish letter). It was held in the
Court of Appeal that the plaintiffs were so entitled on the ground that the letter had
come into existence for the dominant purpose of being used by the insurers with whom
the defendants shared a common interest in obtaining legal advice in relation to the *g*
impending claim. The question then arose whether the legal professional privilege had
been lost.

It is important in understanding the reasoning of the Court of Appeal on this point to
have in mind the factual context in which this question arose. After the defendants had
served their first list of documents, which contained the usual general description in *h*
part 2 of schedule 1 of documents for which legal professional privilege was claimed, the
plaintiffs' solicitors sought further discovery. The defendants' solicitors gave notice of
their intention to serve a supplementary list of documents and offered inspection of the
documents prior to service of the list. On 9 December 1986 a Mr Hardy, a solicitor
employed by the firm acting for the plaintiffs, a Mr Crocker, the plaintiffs' expert
architect, and another expert attended at the defendants' solicitors' offices and were *j*
handed four correspondence files. The solicitors who gave them the files thought they
contained no more than correspondence between the first plaintiffs and the defendant.
Unfortunately one file, no 3, which had not then been paginated, included a copy of the
McLeish letter. Mr Crocker took a copy of it. He flagged some documents of which he
wanted to obtain copies but did not flag the McLeish letter. He sent a copy of that letter

to Mr Hardy. The defendants then served their supplementary list of documents. The
a list included the documents in file no 3 which by then had been paginated.

On 7 January 1987 Mr Hardy attended at the defendants' solicitors' offices to inspect
the documents disclosed in the supplemental list and on the same day he wrote requesting
a copy of the McLeish letter. Of course he had already had a copy. His evidence was that
his purpose in writing was to obtain a copy with the page number and to test the reaction
of the defendants' solicitor. He received no response. The mistake came to light when
b experts' reports were exchanged and the defendants saw a reference to the McLeish letter
in Mr Crocker's report.

Slade LJ having analysed the decisions of, amongst others, Hoffmann J in *Re Briamore
Manufacturing Ltd (in liq)* [1986] 3 All ER 132, [1986] 1 WLR 1429 and of the Court of
Appeal in *Goddard v Nationwide* [1986] 3 All ER 264, [1987] QB 670 and of Sir Nicolas
Browne-Wilkinson V-C in the *Herbert Smith* case [1988] FSR 232, found that ([1987] 2 All
c ER 716 at 729, [1987] 1 WLR 1027 at 1043):

> 'The evidence shows clearly that there was never any intention on the part of the
> defendant's solicitors to abandon the privilege which they regarded as attaching to
> the McLeish letter. As the judge found, the disclosure was due to inadvertence on
> the part of the defendants' solicitors. As soon as the error occurred, they applied for
d > delivery up of the letter.'

Then, having cited *Great Atlantic Insurance Co v Home Insurance Co Ltd* [1981] 2 All ER
485, [1981] 1 WLR 529 as illustrating the proposition that 'a mere plea of inadvertence
does not by itself necessarily enable a party to litigation to avoid a loss of privilege.
Privilege may be lost by inadvertence', he summarised the submission of counsel for the
plaintiff in these terms ([1987] 2 All ER 716 at 729–730, [1987] 1 WLR 1027 at 1044):
e

> '. . . in his submission, privilege is essentially privilege from compulsory
> disclosure. By analogy with the *Great Atlantic Insurance Co* case, he submitted, once
> a privileged document has not only been disclosed but also inspected in the course
> of discovery, it is too late to put the clock back: the privilege is lost. The essential
> distinction between the present case and the *Goddard* and *Herbert Smith* cases, counsel
f > for the plaintiffs contended, is that neither of those two cases dealt with a loss of
> privilege occurring as a result of a step taken in the litigation by the party entitled
> to the privilege. In all cases where inspection has been given in the course of
> discovery, he submitted, the court should follow the *Briamore* decision. This provides
> a simple practical rule. It places the onus on the party giving discovery, who should
> ensure that only documents in respect of which no claim of privilege is made should
g > be disclosed. It avoids the practical problems involved in attempting to restore the
> previous status quo by prohibiting a party and his experts from using information
> obtained in the normal course of discovery.'

Having summarised those submissions he continued:

> 'With one important reservation, I would entirely accept the submission
h > summarised in the immediately preceding paragraph. Care must be taken by parties
> to litigation in the preparation of their lists of documents and no less care must be
> taken in offering inspection of the documents disclosed. Ordinarily, in my
> judgment, a party to litigation who sees a particular document referred to in the
> other side's list, without privilege being claimed, and is subsequently permitted
> inspection of that document, is fully entitled to assume that any privilege which
j > might otherwise have been claimed for it has been waived. Let there be no doubt
> about that.'

However, he found that, on the balance of probabilities, the plaintiffs' experts, when
offered inspection of the relevant file on 9 December 1986 must have realised that the
McLeish letter had been included in it by mistake and that the plaintiffs' solicitor when

offered inspection of the letter must similarly have realised that it was done by reason of
the mistake and that the contents would have made him, as a trained lawyer, realise that   *a*
the defendants' solicitors, as soon as they became aware of the mistake, would wish to
claim privilege for the letter. He concluded that the plaintiffs' solicitors had sought to
take advantage of what they must have known was a mistake and that ([1987] 2 All ER
716 at 730–731, [1987] 1 WLR 1027 at 1045–1046):

> 'Though in the field of contract law, the intentions of the parties are usually   *b*
> judged from an objective standpoint, the courts are prepared to depart from this
> standpoint where one party seeks to take advantage of an obvious mistake on the
> part of the other party of which he was aware. I can see nothing to prevent this
> court from applying similar principles in exercising its equitable jurisdiction in the
> field of discovery, and, indeed, think that this is the manner in which justice will
> best be served.'
>   *c*

He than summarised his conclusions in a passage which I should cite in full:

> 'In my judgment, the relevant principles may be stated broadly as follows.
> (1) Where solicitors for one party to litigation have, on discovery, mistakenly
> included a document for which they could properly have claimed privilege . . .
> without claiming privilege, the court will ordinarily permit them to amend the list   *d*
> under RSC Ord 20, r 8, at any time before inspection of the document has taken
> place.
> (2) However, once in such circumstances the other party has inspected the
> document in pursuance of the rights conferred on him by RSC Ord 24, r 9, the
> general rule is that it is too late for the party who seeks to claim privilege to attempt
> to correct the mistake by applying for injunctive relief. Subject to what is said in (3)   *e*
> below, the *Briamore* decision is good law.
> (3) If, however, in such a last-mentioned case the party or his solicitor either (a)
> has procured inspection of the relevant document by fraud, or (b) on inspection,
> realises that he has been permitted to see the document only by reason of an obvious
> mistake, the court has the power to intervene for the protection of the mistaken
> party by the grant of an injunction in exercise of the equitable jurisdiction illustrated   *f*
> by the *Ashburton*, *Goddard* and *Herbert Smith* cases. Furthermore, in my view it
> should ordinarily intervene in such cases, unless the case is one where the injunction
> can properly be refused on the general principles affecting the grant of a discretionary
> remedy, for example, on the ground of inordinate delay . . .'

Woolf LJ agreed with the judgment of Slade LJ. Sir George Waller also agreed with
one minor exception.   *g*
There is one aspect of the judgment of Slade LJ that has troubled me. Although legal
professional privilege is the privilege of the client, his legal advisers have ostensible
authority to bind him to any matter which arises in or is incidental to the litigation and
that ostensible authority extends to the waiver of privilege: see *Great Atlantic Insurance Co
v Home Insurance Co Ltd* [1981] 2 All ER 485 at 494, [1981] 1 WLR 529 at 540 per   *h*
Templeman LJ. But a party to litigation cannot claim to have relied on the ostensible
authority to waive privilege in respect of a document disclosed on discovery if he knew
that the document was disclosed by mistake. And if the document was obviously
privileged and if he made no inquiry, the court may infer that he must have known that
the document was disclosed by mistake. So also I would think if the circumstances
otherwise found the inference that the solicitor to a party to whom disclosure was made   *j*
must have suspected that the document was disclosed by mistake and refrained from
making inquiry in case his suspicions were confirmed. A solicitor should not in these
circumstances be allowed to take advantage of the mistake. The courts expect a high
standard of probity and care on the part of its officers in the conduct of litigation, and a
solicitor must be taken to be aware of the importance of legal professional privilege and,

in the words of Sir Nicolas Browne-Wilkinson V-C, of the mischances that are likely to
occur in the course of discovery in a complex case: see the *Herbert Smith* case [1988] FSR
232 at 239. These principles must be borne in mind even in the heat of contested
litigation.

The point that has troubled me is that a principal is not in general bound by an act
done by his agent within the scope of his ostensible authority but without his actual
authority, save at the suit of someone who has acted to his detriment on the faith of the
implied representation that the agent had authority. The question is: at what stage can it
be said that a party to whom a privileged document has inadvertently been disclosed has
acted to his detriment? The answer given by Slade LJ is: at the time when he or his
representative is permitted to inspect it save when it should have been obvious that it
was disclosed by mistake. That seems to me to give rise to a paradoxical result. The
detriment can only be found in the fact that the person reading the document may have
learned something which he cannot thereafter put out of his mind. The possession of
that information, if he is not to be entitled to use it, may inhibit the conduct of the action
or otherwise embarrass him. The difficulty is that the detriment, if it is a relevant
consideration, is the same whether or not it should have been obvious to him reading the
document that privilege could have been claimed and that the document had probably
been disclosed by mistake. This difficulty would be particularly acute in a case where it
would only have become apparent that the document was obviously privileged and had
probably been disclosed by mistake when the solicitor had read it to the end, or if that
fact would only have become apparent once he had read the next document in the file
and had related it to the circulation list or to another document that he had also read.

Counsel for the plaintiffs submitted that it was unnecessary for the Court of Appeal to
decide at what point a party on whose behalf a privileged document is disclosed is bound
by the implied waiver of privilege, since the Court of Appeal held in that case that the
mistake must have been obvious to the plaintiffs' advisers. He submitted it is open to me
to hold that a waiver only becomes effective if the document is actually adduced in
evidence in court and so enters the public domain, as in the *Great Atlantic Insurance* case,
or if the party to whom the disclosure is made makes such use of it, for instance by
showing it to a prospective witness, that it would be inequitable for the other party to
assert the privilege.

I was at first attracted by this submission and if this point were free from authority I
would have accepted it. However, I have come to the conclusion after anxious
consideration that I must accept the clear and unambiguous opinion expressed by Slade
LJ with which the other members of the court concurred.

I must now turn to the documents in dispute. It is, of course, undesirable that I should
say more about them than is necessary to determine the issues that have been raised. I
should, however, observe that counsel for the defendants made it clear that he did not
rely on any use of the documents made by his client when they exhibited them to an
affidavit in support of their application for further and better discovery, or to any use
made in this application.

Documents A, B, C and D   These are all letters written by Mr Julian Lee, the finance
director of one of the plaintiff companies which is the principal subsidiary in the United
Kingdom of the Salomon Group, to a partner in the firm of solicitors then acting for the
plaintiffs. They were written at a time when a release of claims by the plaintiff companies
or some of them against the first and second defendants, later embodied in an agreement
dated 11 May 1984, which is referred to in the pleadings as the 'May agreement', was
being negotiated. Although the contents are banal, it is also clear on the most cursory
reading that they are within the scope of legal professional privilege, being confidential
communications in the course of obtaining legal advice. Counsel for the defendants
submitted that the defendants' solicitors might reasonably have taken the view that
because the contents were so banal, the plaintiffs' advisers had decided to waive privilege.

I cannot accept that submission. It would be both wrong and dangerous for the solicitor to a party to litigation to sort through a file of privileged correspondence and to disclose letters which were either innocuous or favourable to his client's case while claiming privilege for others. In my judgment, given the circumstances in which discovery took place, the defendants' solicitors should have appreciated that these letters had been inadvertently disclosed.

Document E This is a file note of Mr Julian Lee made shortly before the execution of the May agreement recording advice given by the plaintiffs' then solicitors as to the effect of the agreement, if executed, and as to a question which had arisen concerning the drafting of one clause. It is patently privileged. That was conceded by counsel for the defendants. He submitted that the defendants' solicitors might reasonably have taken the view that this document was disclosed deliberately so as to give a fair picture of the state of mind of those concerned with the May agreement on behalf of the plaintiffs. I do not think that any such belief could have been entertained for a moment.

Counsel then submitted that if the court is entitled to carry out a balancing exercise of the kind considered by Scott J, the balance comes down against the grant of the injunction sought by the plaintiffs. The ground of that submission was again that the memorandum is of importance as revealing the state of mind of Mr Lee at the time when the May agreement was executed. For the reasons I have given I do not think that it is open to the court to carry out any balancing exercise. The court acts in these circumstances to preserve an absolute privilege. If a balancing exercise did have to be carried out, I would nonetheless grant the injunction sought. I am not persuaded that the note would be admissible on the construction of the May agreement and, if it were admissible as part of surrounding matrix of facts, its probative value would be negligible.

This document has been seen by the solicitors acting for the third to eleventh defendants and it is said in an affidavit sworn by the solicitors acting for the first and second defendants that the solicitors acting for the third to eleventh defendants have shown it to a witness. The date when and circumstances in which it was shown to the witness are not explained. In my judgment, the solicitors acting for the third to eleventh defendants ought also to have seen that this document was privileged and had been disclosed inadvertently.

The third to eleventh defendants are not parties to this application. I think the right course in the circumstances, if the plaintiffs' privilege is to be protected, is to grant an injunction ex parte against the third to eleventh defendants as regards this document and to give them liberty to apply to discharge it.

Document F This is a memorandum written by Mr Lee to the plaintiffs' principle inhouse legal adviser, Mr Bernstein. It is common ground that the defendants and their advisers knew of Mr Bernstein's role. The memorandum contains Mr Lee's comments on the latest draft of the May agreement embodying revisions by the solicitors then acting for the first and second defendants. It is patently privileged. Counsel for the defendants did not submit to the contrary and he accepted that if a balancing exercise falls to be carried out, the balance would come down in favour of the grant of the injunction sought.

Document G This is a memorandum written by Mr Lee with his comments on a letter received by Mr Bernstein from New York attorneys acting for insurers against whom a claim had been made under a fidelity policy protecting the plaintiffs from loss and misconduct of, amongst others, the first and second defendants. Counsel for the defendants conceded that although it is less obviously privileged, the defendants' solicitors must be taken to have appreciated that it was privileged and that the plaintiffs are entitled to the injunction sought.

Document H This document is the most obviously privileged document of them all. It is again a note by Mr Lee and was sent to Mr Bernstein and to senior management in New York. It contains a lengthy account of advice which Mr Lee had been given by an

eminent solicitor with experience in the field of criminal law who had been consulted
a concerning the possibility that the May agreement could be set aside on the ground of
fraud, and Mr Lee's recommendations to, amongst others, Mr Bernstein, as to the course
the plaintiffs might take in the light of that advice. Counsel for the defendants conceded
that the document is obviously privileged and did not submit that if a balancing exercise
has to be carried out, there is any factor which would weigh against the grant of the
injunction sought.

b   There is another remarkable feature of this document. The defendants admit that
when inspected and copied it had on it a yellow sticker carrying the legend 'Privileged'.
The plaintiffs' solicitors explanation is that when they went through the files, they put
yellow stickers bearing this legend on privileged documents intending that if the
defendants asked to inspect a file, those with yellow stickers could be removed. During
the laborious and protracted task of inspection by the defendants, necessarily assisted by
c comparatively junior staff employed by the plaintiffs' solicitors, this document escaped
detection. The plaintiffs suspect that other documents with yellow stickers may have
escaped detection and cannot now be identified because the stickers were removed in the
course of photocopying. There is some support for that in other evidence filed on behalf
of the defendants where the witness says there was more than one document with a
yellow sticker on it.

d   Whether any of the documents now in dispute originally had yellow stickers on them
or not, the defendants' solicitors should have been put on notice by the yellow sticker on
document H even if it had not been obvious from the contents that it was privileged and
had been inadvertently disclosed. At the very least they should not have inspected or
taken any copy of that document without first inquiring whether it had been
inadvertently disclosed.

e   *Documents I and J*   These are questionnaires addressed to a member of the plaintiffs'
accounting staff by another of the plaintiffs' inhouse lawyers, Mr Levy, who was dealing
on behalf of the plaintiffs with an investigation by a body known as the Commodity
Futures Trading Commission, which is concerned with the regulation of commodity
trading in the United States of America and which has power to enforce its regulations. I
understand that the investigation of the plaintiffs has been completed but that an
f investigation into the conduct of the first and second defendants is still proceeding. The
questionnaire is again banal. Counsel for the defendants did not accept that it would
have been obvious to Mr Hopkins, who inspected all the documents, that it was
privileged, in particular that he would have known Mr Levy's role. However, he accepted
that in any balancing exercise there were no factors that would weigh against the grant
of the injunction sought and without conceding that privilege had not been waived
g made it clear that the defendants did not object to the return of copies of these documents.

Documents K, L and M   Document K is headed 'Programme for review of Allied
Cocoa'. Allied Cocoa was a group of companies which were customers of the plaintiff
Cocoa Merchants Ltd (CML) until February 1984 when the Allied Group defaulted. CML
was left with very large debts due from the Allied Group and little prospect of recovery.
h The defendants' responsibility for that state of affairs was the subject of the claim under
the fidelity insurance policy and of the May agreement. Document K sets out a
programme to be followed as a guide in conducting an audit of transactions with the
Allied Group. Documents L and M are responses to that programme by accountants
employed in the Salomon Group. They are addressed to Mr Bernstein.

The defendants' solicitors initially claimed that these documents are not within the
j scope of legal professional privilege. They referred in their evidence to a very large
number of accounting documents relating to audits carried out by external auditors, and
internally, in relation to the Allied Group and to inquiries as to the adequacy of the
plaintiffs' credit controls, all of which had been disclosed. However, counsel for the
defendants conceded, in the light of evidence filed in this application on behalf of the

plaintiffs, that these documents were part of an inquiry instituted by Mr Bernstein for the dominant purpose of getting together evidence on which a claim against the Allied *a* Group could be mounted, and that they are privileged documents.

The difficulty which confronts the plaintiffs is that it cannot be said that document K is, on its face, a privileged document, and although documents L and M are addressed to Mr Bernstein, they are not, in my judgment, so plainly directed to obtaining evidence for the purpose of legal proceedings as to alert the defendants' solicitor to the fact that they had been inadvertently disclosed. *b*

Put shortly, an explanation of the activities of the plaintiff companies is needed before it can be seen that they are within the scope of legal professional privilege. Not all documents submitted to an inhouse legal adviser fall within that category. If I am right in my analysis of the decision of the Court of Appeal in *Guinness Peat Properties Ltd v Fitzroy Robinson Partnership* [1987] 2 All ER 716, [1987] 1 WLR 1027, the conclusion must, I think, follow that privilege was waived when these documents were inspected by *c* the defendants even though no use has been made of them by the first and second defendants.

It is also said in affidavits filed on behalf of the first and second defendants that the solicitors acting for the third to eleventh defendants have made use of these documents by submitting them to their expert witnesses. When and in what circumstances that was done, whether before or after the plaintiffs' claim to recover them was made, is not clear. *d* However, if I am right in thinking that I am bound to hold that privilege must be taken to have been lost when these documents were inspected, this question is not relevant.

Document N This is a lengthy memorandum sent to Mr Bernstein from a senior director of one of the plaintiff companies in New York. It is part of the same series of inquiries and is headed 'Private and Confidential'. It relates to the loss resulting from the insolvency of the Allied Group. It is conceded by counsel for the defendants that it should *e* have been apparent on inspection that it was a privileged document and that if a balancing exercise had to be carried out, there could be no factor that could weigh against the grant of the injunction sought. The curious feature of this document is that it would not, to my mind, have been apparent to the reader that the document was part of a process of collecting information with a view to legal proceedings against the receiver of *f* the Allied Group and so entitled to privilege on that or any other ground, until he reached the middle of page 2 of a two and a half page memorandum. As I have said, it is not clear whether the application of the principle in the *Guinness Peat* case leads to the conclusion that privilege has been waived for the whole or slightly less than half of the whole. However, counsel did not oppose the grant of the relief sought as regards this document and I need say no more about it.

In my judgment, therefore, the plaintiffs are entitled as against the first and second *g* defendants to the relief sought as regards all the documents except K, L and M. If the plaintiffs wish to challenge my decision in the Court of Appeal I think they should be entitled to do so, and an injunction should be granted to restrain further use of these documents pending the appeal, if that can be arranged in the near future. If the plaintiffs so require, I will extend this injunction to the third to the eleventh defendants but will *h* give them liberty to apply to discharge it.

Application allowed in part.

Jacqueline Metcalfe   Barrister.

Appeal and cross appeal *j*
The plaintiffs appealed. The defendants cross-appealed.

Michael Lyndon-Stanford QC and *J Stephen Smith* for the plaintiffs.
Nicholas Chambers QC for the defendants.

DILLON LJ. This is an appeal by the plaintiffs, in this well-known action, against an
a order of Vinelott J made on 9 April 1990. The effective respondents to the appeal are the
first two defendants in the action. There have been a number of interlocutory applications
and interlocutory appeals. Happily we are told that the action is due to come on for trial
at the beginning of October 1990.

This appeal is concerned with the question of discovery of documents which were
within the scope of legal professional privilege. It is unnecesary to indicate the issues in
b the action; they are complex. The trial is expected to last for several months and discovery
has been voluminous.

We were given evidence as to the number of shelf yards of files of documents that fell
to be disclosed. During the course of discovery the files were listed in the list of
documents simply as files, without setting out the details of all their contents, and when
inspection was requested the defendants' solicitors were allowed to inspect all those files.
c Unfortunately, among the documents still included in the files when they came to be
inspected were a number which are privileged documents. When this particular
application was launched there were 14 documents which, as the judge put it, have so far
been identified as privileged documents inadvertently disclosed. They have been referred
to in the evidence as documents A to M. The inadvertent disclosure came to the attention
of the plaintiffs' solicitors when copies of some of the inadvertently disclosed documents
d were exhibited to an affidavit filed in support of an application by the defendants for
further and better discovery. It is now accepted that all the documents A to M were
privileged.

The judge granted injunctions requiring the return of all copies and requiring that
information contained in the documents should not be used in respect of all the
documents except K, L and M. He distinguished those three from others of the 14 on the
e ground that, though in truth they were privileged as documents prepared with a view to
instructing lawyers to advise, it did not appear from the face of the document that that
was the reason why they had been prepared and therefore it was not immediately obvious
that these were privileged documents. With all the others in A to M it was immediately
obvious that they were privileged documents.

The plaintiffs say that, although they made a mistake, they should be allowed to have
f K, L and M in addition to those that they got back under the judge's order. The
defendants say that the judge was right about K, L and M, but the judge should also have
refused to require the defendants to return document E, even though that is on its face a
privileged document, because the judge should have carried out a balancing exercise in
respect of each privileged document before ordering copies to be returned, and the
importance to the defendants at the trial of the action of document E, and the importance
g of having all the salient facts available at the trial in the interests of justice, override its
privileged, or previously privileged, nature.

We have been referred in the course of argument to all the principal authorities which
are concerned with what may happen where a copy of a privileged document gets into
the hands, by one route or another, of the other party to the litigation, such as *Calcraft v
h Guest* [1898] 1 QB 759, [1895–9] All ER Rep 346 and *Lord Ashburton v Pape* [1913] 2 Ch
469, [1911–13] All ER Rep 708, where the court in advance of the trial granted an
injunction, following the authorities on restraining disclosure of confidential information,
to restrain a party from making any use of privileged documents which he had got either
by fraud or by trick.

Counsel for the plaintiffs has submitted, in a very carefully reasoned exposition of the
j authorities, that in truth, save for certain views expressed by Slade LJ in *Guiness Peat
Properties Ltd v Fitzroy Robinson Partnership (a firm)* [1987] 2 All ER 716, [1987] 1 WLR
1027, the authorities in this court all lead to the view that the correct position in law is
that, if one party has disclosed privileged documents by mistake, then on application to
the court the mistake can and will be set aside and the other party will be ordered to

return all copies of the documents in question and not make use of any information contained in them.

I take the view that it is not open to us in this court to adopt such a broad approach as that, because we are bound by the *Guiness Peat* case, which is a considered judgment of another division of this court. The earlier authorities relied on by counsel, such as *Goddard v Nationwide Building Society* [1986] 3 All ER 264, [1987] QB 670 and *English and American Insurance Ltd v Herbert Smith* [1988] FSR 232, were cases where there was no question of the privilege having been waived by the party entitled to the privilege. The documents in question had got into the hands of the other party to the litigation, despite the wishes of the person entitled to privilege and in circumstances which could not amount to a waiver of privilege.

In the *Guinness Peat* case, as I read the judgment of Slade LJ (with which the other members of this court agreed), the court was impressed by certain observations of Templeman LJ in *Great Atlantic Insurance Co v Home Insurance Co* [1981] 2 All ER 485, [1981] 1 WLR 529. That was a case where solicitors in their list of documents and on inspection had disclosed two paragraphs of a copy of a memorandum in a way that had not suggested that there were other parts of the memorandum. The memorandum was initially a privileged document. Counsel for the plaintiff, whose document it was, read to the judge at the trial the two paragraphs which had been disclosed in ignorance that the memorandum contained any other paragraphs, let alone that there were other paragraphs which had not been disclosed. It was held that, as part of the document had been read at the trial, the other party was entitled to see and put in evidence the whole of the document and, as privilege existed in the document as a whole, rather than in parts, the waiver of privilege extended to the whole of the document. Templeman LJ said ([1981] 2 All ER 485 at 494, [1981] 1 WLR 529 at 540):

'... when counsel in the course of the trial introduces into the record a document or part of a document he thereby effectively waives any privilege attaching to that document which could otherwise be asserted by his client.'

But he also said ([1981] 2 All ER 485 at 494, [1981] 1 WLR 529 at 541):

'The court has no jurisdiction to relieve the plaintiffs from the consequences of their own mistakes particularly as those consequences cannot be wholly eradicted; part of the memorandum has in fact been read to the trial judge.'

Slade LJ went on ([1987] 2 All ER 716 at 729–730, [1987] 1 WLR 1027 at 1043–1044):

'Counsel for the plaintiffs in the present case did not seek to suggest that the defendants had waived or otherwise lost their privilege simply by including the McLeish letter [that was the document in question in the *Guinness Peat* case] in Pt 1 of Sch 1 to the first supplementary list of documents. He accepted that they would have been entitled to serve an amended list claiming privilege for it at any time before inspection took place. However, in his submission, privilege is essentially privilege from compulsory disclosure. By analogy with the *Great Atlantic Insurance Co* case, he submitted, once a privileged document has not only been disclosed but also inspected in the course of discovery, it is too late to put the clock back: the privilege is lost. The essential distinction between the present case and the *Goddard* and *Herbert Smith* cases, counsel for the plaintiffs contended, is that neither of those two cases dealt with a loss of privilege occurring as a result of a step taken in the litigation by the party entitled to the privilege. In all cases where inspection has been given in the course of discovery, he submitted, the court should follow the *Briamore* decision [*Re Briamore Manufacturing Ltd (in liq)* [1986] 3 All ER 132, [1986] 1 WLR 1429]. This provides a simple practical rule. It places the onus on the party giving discovery, who should ensure that only documents in respect of which no claim of privilege is made should be disclosed. It avoids the practical problems

involved in attempting to restore the previous status quo by prohibiting a party and
his experts from using information obtained in the normal course of discovery.

  With one important reservation, I would entirely accept the submissions
summarised in the immediately preceding paragraph. Care must be taken by parties
to litigation in the preparation of their lists of documents and no less great care must
be taken in offering inspection of the documents disclosed. Ordinarily, in my
judgment, a party to litigation who sees a particular document referred to in the
other side's list, without privilege being claimed, and is subsequently permitted
inspection of that document, is fully entitled to assume that any privilege which
might otherwise have been claimed for it has been waived. Let there be no doubt
about that.'

Then Slade LJ expressed his reservation ([1987] 2 All ER 716 at 730, [1987] 1 WLR 1027
at 1044):

  'My one reservation is this. I do not think that after inspection has taken place in
  the course of discovery, the court is inevitably and invariably powerless to intervene
  by way of injunction in exercise of the equitable jurisdiction exemplified by the
  Ashburton, Goddard and *Herbert Smith* cases if the particular circumstances warrant
  such intervention on equitable grounds. I do not doubt, for example, that the court
  would be prepared so to intervene where one party to litigation had obtained
  inspection of a privileged document by fraud, albeit in what purported to be the
  normal course of discovery.'

  On the facts of the case, he said that he had little hesitation in drawing the inference of
fact that—

  'The plaintiffs' experts, when offered inspection of the relevant correspondence
  file . . . must have realised that the McLeish letter had been included in that file by
  mistake.'

He gave the reasons for that and referred to the fact that the mistake was not pointed out
to the plaintiffs' solicitors; indeed they were careful not to draw it to the attention of the
plaintiffs' solicitors, but sought to take advantage of it. He summarised the rules broadly
at the end of his judgment ([1987] 2 All ER 716 at 730–731, [1987] 1 WLR 1027 at
1045–1046):

  '(1) Where solicitors for one party to litigation have, on discovery, mistakenly
  included a document for which they could properly have claimed privilege in Pt 1
  of Sch 1 to a list of documents without claiming privilege, the court will ordinarily
  permit them to amend the list under RSC Ord 20, r 8 at any time before inspection
  of the document has taken place.

  (2) However, once in such circumstances the other party has inspected the
  document in pursuance of the rights conferred on him by RSC Ord 24, r 9, the
  general rule is that it is too late for the party who seeks to claim privilege to attempt
  to correct the mistake by applying for injunctive relief. Subject to what is said in (3)
  below, the *Briamore* decision is good law.

  (3) If, however, in such a last-mentioned case the other party or his solicitor either
  (a) has procured inspection of the relevant document by fraud, or (b) on inspection,
  realises that he has been permitted to see the document only by reason of an obvious
  mistake, the court has the power to intervene for the protection of the mistaken
  party by the grant of an injunction in exercise of the equitable jurisdiction illustrated
  by the *Ashburton, Goddard* and *Herbert Smith* cases. Furthermore, in my view it
  should ordinarily intervene in such cases, unless the case is one where the injunction
  can properly be refused on the general principles affecting the grant of a discretionary
  remedy, for example, on the ground of inordinate delay (see *Goddard v Nationwide
  Building Society* [1986] 3 All ER 264 at 272, [1986] 3 WLR 734 at 745 per Nourse LJ).'

Possibly there may be other exceptions to the general rule set out in (2) above. However, in my judgment, the exception set out in (3) above suffices to cover the *a* present case. Save where it is too late to restore the previous status quo (eg on facts similar to those of the *Great Atlantic* case), I do not think the law should encourage parties to litigation or their solicitors to take advantage of obvious mistakes made in the course of the process of discovery.'

I would indorse that last sentence of a passage which is anyhow, in my judgment, *b* binding on this court.

The judge below ordered, and indeed the defendants did not strenuously resist, the return of copies of the documents, other than K, L and M, on the ground that all those documents were palpably privileged and directly within Slade LJ's rule (3). But he declined to make a similar order in respect of documents K, L and M because on their face it did not appear that they were privileged. *c*

It is necessary to look a little further into the facts. When these documents were disclosed, several of them, particularly, if not entirely, in file 3347, had squares of yellow paper stuck to them, the sort which are conveniently used nowadays as markers, and on the paper was the word 'privileged'. These included document H, which is a most obviously privileged document, setting out advice which had been received from lawyers. It is a memorandum from Mr Julian Lee, the finance director of the plaintiff companies, *d* as are many others of these privileged documents. It sets out advice received from the solicitors who formerly acted for the plaintiffs and also discussions of the matter with another solicitor querying the advice received from the first solicitors. But among the other memoranda of Mr Lee there were others equally obviously privileged which, so far as is known, did not have yellow stickers on them, such as document C, which was a letter to a partner in the firm of Messrs Herbert Smith at a time when they were acting *e* as solicitors for the plaintiffs in respect of matters which are in issue in this action. It is not entirely clear which of the documents in issue did, and which did not, have yellow stickers, because it seems that they have been photocopied quite a few times since the disputes arose and the yellow stickers have at some stage become detached. It is only known for certain that document H was one of those with yellow stickers. In the same *f* bundle as document C (bundle 3345) is document M, which is also in issue on this appeal. There are other privileged documents among the total of A to M in various other bundles.

What the defendants' solicitors prudently did, as they have candidly disclosed in evidence that has been filed, when they saw that there were apparently privileged documents (with yellow stickers or not) in the bundle was to seek advice from the defendants' leading counsel. The advice that leading counsel predictably gave the *g* solicitors was that they should get in touch with the plaintiffs' solicitors and ask them whether they had intended to disclose privileged documents or whether there was a mistake. The solicitors for the defendants, however, discarded leading counsel's advice. Instead, without disclosing even a suspicion that there had been a mistake, they asked the plaintiffs' solicitors to supply copies of a range of documents, which included some of these obviously privileged documents. The plaintiffs' solicitors left the copying to what *h* we are told are referred to as paralegals who are not expected to look closely at documents which they are asked to copy and test whether they are or are not in law privileged, and so the copies sought were sent. Because the plaintiffs' solicitors were not alerted to any possibility that they had made a mistake they did not appreciate it at that stage.

That conduct on the part of the defendants' solicitors, after the advice they had had from leading counsel, makes it plain to me that they must have realised that these *j* documents had been disclosed to them by mistake and therefore Slade LJ's rule (3) is satisfied.

Counsel for the defendants says that that might apply to documents which were in bundle 3347 which had yellow stickers, but there is no warrant for assuming that there was a mistake in respect to any other document. But it is quite clear that some of the other documents, which were not in bundle 3347, are blatantly privileged documents, again, such as documents C and E. It is plain that the system for excluding privileged a documents which had been applied by the plaintiffs' solicitors had broken down and the defendants' solicitors had appreciated this.

Counsel for the defendants says, 'Even so, they should only be required to return documents which are on their face privileged.' I do not see why the relief should be so limited. They are seeking to take advantage of an obvious mistake and they should give up all the documents which they have obtained as a result of that mistake. Accordingly, they must also give up documents K, L and M.

b Counsel submits that there should be a balancing exercise in respect of document E. Document E records certain advice given by the plaintiffs' solicitors at a time a compromise agreement was entered into which the plaintiffs are claiming to have set aside in the action on grounds of fraud. I see no reason why any such balancing exercise should be carried out. The court does not, so far as privileged documents are concerned, weigh the privilege and consider whether the privilege should outweigh the importance c that the document should be before the court at the trial, or the importance that possession of the document and the ability to use it might have for the advocate; and, again, where the privilege is being restored because the inspection was obtained by fraud or by taking advantage of a known mistake, there is to my mind no logic at all in qualifying the restoration of the status quo by reference to the importance of the document. 'You have taken advantage of an obvious mistake to obtain copies of d documents; we will order you to return all the ones that are unimportant but you can keep the ones that are important' would be a nonsensical attitude for the court to adopt.

The view expressed by Slade LJ in the *Guinness Peat* case in his reservation over mistake seems to me to be in accordance with the view expressed by Pennycuick J in *A Roberts & Co Ltd v Leicestershire CC* [1961] 2 All ER 545 at 551–552, [1961] Ch 555 at 570 in the e context of rectification, where he said:

> 'The second ground rests on the principle that a party is entitled to rectification of a contract on proof that he believed a particular term to be included in the contract, and that the other party concluded the contract with the omission or a variation of that term in the knowledge that the first party believed the term to be included.
> f Counsel appearing for the council formulated the principle in slightly different terms, as follows, viz., the plaintiff must show that his intention was that the term sought to be introduced by rectification should be included in the contract and (so far as now relevant) that the omission of the term was occasioned by the dishonest conduct of the defendant in acceptance of the formation of the contract without the term, in the knowledge that the plaintiff thought the term was included. Counsel thus introduces into his formulation of the principle the word "dishonest", but he g accepts that such conduct by the defendant in his formulation is of its nature dishonest, so that the word "dishonest" appears to carry the matter no further. I do not think that there is any substantial disagreement as to the scope of the principle.'

Then he refers to the principle as stated in Snell's *Principle of Equity* (25th edn, 1960) p 569:

h > 'By what appears to be a species of equitable estoppel, if one party to a transaction knows that the instrument contains a mistake in his favour but does nothing to correct it, he (and those claiming under him) will be precluded from resisting rectification on the ground that the mistake is unilateral and not common.'

That, in the context of rectification, has been approved by this court.

j I see no reason why the first and second defendants should not be deprived of all the benefit from their having in those circumstances knowingly taken advantage of an obvious mistake. I would therefore allow this appeal and make the same order in respect of documents K, L and M as was made in respect of document E and I would reject the cross-appeal in respect of document E.

BUTLER-SLOSS LJ. I agree entirely with the judgment of Dillon LJ, but would add one short comment on disclosure of documents by mistake.

The solicitors for the first and second defendants raised the question of privileged documents with their leading counsel, who advised that the matter be taken up with *a* plaintiffs' solicitors. This advice they chose not to follow, but preferred to ask for copies at the same time they asked for many other documents in the massive discovery exercise which has taken place in this case. In my view, whilst put on their guard, as these solicitors clearly were, that mistakes had been made and privileged documents had been inadvertently disclosed, they were at risk in continuing to retain these documents. I would respectfully indorse the words of Slade LJ in *Guinness Peat Properties Ltd v Fitzroy* *b* *Robinson Partnership (a firm)* [1987] 2 All ER 716 at 731, [1987] 1 WLR 1027 at 1045 in his rule (3), already referred to by Dillon LJ. Those words are equally applicable to this case. Nothing exceptional has arisen in this case to deny to the plaintiffs the remedy they seek. I can see no reason not to include documents K, L and M, nor to exclude document E. I would allow the appeal and dismiss the cross-appeal.

                                                          c

LEGGATT LJ. I agree with both judgments that have been delivered and, notwithstanding that we are differing from the judge, I desire to add nothing of my own.

Appeal allowed. Cross-appeal dismissed.

Solicitors: Lovell White Durrant (for the plaintiffs); *Hopkins & Wood* (for the defendants).   *d*

                                       Carolyn Toulmin   Barrister.

R v Porter

COURT OF APPEAL, CRIMINAL DIVISION   *e*
LORD LANE CJ, ROSE AND GARLAND JJ
17 JULY 1990

Drugs – Drug trafficking – Confiscation order – Joint drug trafficking venture – Whether court can make joint and several confiscation orders against each defendant – Whether court required *f* *to determine respective shares arising from joint benefit and make separate confiscation orders – Drug Trafficking Offences Act 1986, s 1.*

Where two or more persons have been convicted of drug trafficking offences arising out of a joint venture the sentencing court when deciding to make a confiscation order under s 1[a] of the the the Drug Trafficking Offences Act 1986 must as between the co-defendants *g* determine their respective shares arising from any joint benefit which they received from their drug trafficking and should then make separate confiscation orders according to their means rather than joint and several confiscation orders against each of the accused (see p 786 *e* to *g*, post).

Notes

For assessing the proceeds of drug trafficking, see 11(2) Halsbury's Laws (4th edn reissue) para 1306.

     For the Drug Trafficking Offences Act 1986, s 1, see 12 Halsbury's Statutes (4th edn) (1989 reissue) 989.

---

a   Section 1, so far as material, provides: *j*
      '(1) . . . where a person appears before the Crown Court to be sentenced in respect of one or more drug trafficking offences . . . the court shall act as follows.
      (2) The court shall first determine whether he has benefited from drug trafficking . . .
      (4) If the court determines that he has so benefited, the court shall, before sentencing or otherwise dealing with him in respect of the offence . . . determine . . . the amount to be recovered in his case . . .'

Case referred to in judgment

a   *R v Dickens* [1990] 2 All ER 626, [1990] 2 QB 102, [1990] 2 WLR 1384, CA.

Appeal against sentence

The appellant, Jeremy Porter, and another pleaded guilty on 15 May 1989 in the Crown Court at St Albans before his Honour Judge Hickman of supplying a controlled drug, namely cannabis resin, and of possessing a controlled drug with intent to supply. On

b   9 June 1989 they were each sentenced by his Honour Judge Colston QC to nine months' imprisonment of which four months were to be served, the balance to be held in suspense, and a confiscation order was made under the Drug Trafficking Offences Act 1986 requiring the appellant and his co-defendant to pay the sum of £9,600 jointly and severally within nine months with a period of six months' imprisonment in default of payment. The appellant sought an extension of time in which to appeal against sentence,

c   and that application was referred direct to the Full Court. The court granted the application and gave leave to appeal. The ground of appeal was that the trial judge erred in making the confiscation order joint and several. The facts are set out in the judgment of the court.

Louise Varty (who did not appear below) (assigned by the Registrar of Criminal Appeals)

d   for the appellant.
Philip Rueff for the Crown.

GARLAND J delivered the following judgment of the court. On 18 May 1989 in the Crown Court at St Albans the appellant and a co-defendant by the name of Rolph pleaded guilty to supplying cannabis resin and to possessing cannabis resin with intent to supply.

e   They were put back for sentence until 9 June, when they were both sentenced to nine months' imprisonment, four months to be served and five months to be held in suspense. In addition, and this is the subject of the present proceedings, a confiscation order pursuant to the provisions of the Drug Trafficking Offences Act 1986 was made in the sum of £9,600 against both of the defendants jointly and severally to be paid within nine months, and with six months' imprisonment consecutive in default of payment.

f   The appellant was originally advised that the confiscation order had been properly made. Both he and the co-defendant served that part of their sentence which involved immediate custody. The appellant then took the advice of other counsel, who pointed out that should his co-defendant fail to pay any money in part satisfaction of the order, the appellant would, as one severally liable, be responsible for discharging the whole sum, £9,600, and be in peril of imprisonment if he failed to do so.

g   On 8 and 9 June there was a hearing pursuant to the provisions of the Drug Trafficking Offences Act 1986 to determine to what extent, if at all, the two co-defendants had benefited from their drug trafficking. The judge found as a fact that the two co-defendants had jointly benefited in accordance with s 1(2), and then pursuant to ss 1(4) and 4(1) that the extent of that benefit was £9,600, and that the amount they should be ordered to pay jointly and severally was that same amount. The figure was based on a

h   calculation of benefit from the sale of 4 oz of cannabis resin per week at £120 per ounce for 20 weeks, the judge finding that it was at all times a joint venture. That determination of the sum was in accordance with s 2(1)(a).

The two defendants fortuitously had a joint asset, a house at 7 Shelley Close, Royston in Hertfordshire, which they bought in January 1988 for £49,000 subject to mortgage which, by the time of the hearing, was in arrear, but it was thought that the equity was

j   worth between £25,000 and £30,000. It was assumed throughout that the house was 'realisable property' within the terms of the 1986 Act, and the nine months which the co-defendants were given in which to pay the confiscation order was based on the contemplated sale of that property after the defendants had been released from their custodial sentences.

The position has in fact changed. The house, we are told, has been sold for £54,000, and, after redemption of the mortgage and the payment of estate agents' and solicitors' fees, there will be very little left indeed to discharge the confiscation order.   *a*

The appellant has in fact made an application to the High Court, Judge J, under s 14 of the 1986 Act for the order to be varied due to the change of financial circumstances. That is a matter with which this court cannot concern itself today.

However, what is before us today is the issue whether or not the order could properly be joint and several, or whether it should be several, each of the two co-defendants being   *b* required to pay £4,800, rather than jointly and severally twice that amount.

The trial judge at the conclusion of the hearing under the 1986 Act, having recited that he had arrived at the figure of £9,600, said:

> 'That is the figure which I shall use in due course when I make the confiscation order. I also make it plain now that it appears to me, having heard argument about it, that the order which I must make, this being a joint venture, is one which is   *c* against these two defendants jointly and severally. To make it a several order, using 50% of that figure against each, in my judgment, would fly in the face of the clear words of the section, which make it plain that it is the aggregate figure which I am concerned with, and to make the order against each of these defendants severally in the total sum seems to me would fly in the face of justice because that would involve   *d* confiscation of twice the figure which I have indicated already I find as a fact to be the proper aggregate figure.'

Then he repeated that he would make the order jointly and severally.

The Drug Trafficking Offences Act 1986 has not been without difficulties in its application. In April 1990 in *R v Dickens* [1990] 2 All ER 626, [1990] 2 QB 102 this court sought to give some guidance to those who have to grapple with those difficulties. Where   *e* property is jointly owned, particular problems may arise. In this case there was quite fortuitously both a joint enterprise and a joint asset.

However this court takes the view that the 1986 Act does not contemplate, as the judge thought, joint penalties even though there has been a joint venture. There must be certainty in sentencing. A convicted person is entitled to know the extent of his monetary liability; a fortiori when he is liable to lose his liberty if he fails to discharge a   *f* monetary penalty.

It appears to us that, in assessing benefit in accordance with the provisions of s 1 of the 1986 Act, the court must, as between co-defendants, determine their respective shares of any joint benefit that they may have received as a result of drug trafficking. In the absence of any evidence, whether from the co-defendants or elsewhere, a court is entitled to assume that they were sharing equally. Then, when it comes to arriving at the amount   *g* of the confiscation order pursuant to s 4 of the Act, s 4(3) makes it quite clear that, if the means of the co-defendants differ, then the amount of the confiscation order can be tailored to those means.

Having regard to those provisions of the 1986 Act, we take the view that the joint and several confiscation order was unsound. We will quash it and substitute several orders   *h* for £4,800 in respect of each of the two co-defendants, with three months' imprisonment in default. The time for payment of the order is extended for six months from today.

Appeal allowed in part. Confiscation order varied.

Solicitors: *Crown Prosecution Service, St Albans.*

N P Metcalfe Esq   Barrister.

R v Iqbal

COURT OF APPEAL, CRIMINAL DIVISION
WATKINS LJ, NOLAN AND WARD JJ
12 FEBRUARY, 7 MARCH 1990

Criminal evidence – Document – Document forming part of record compiled by person under duty – Witness statement – Admissibility – Statement taken in connection with proceedings other than those in which document sought to be admitted – Whether record must be made contemporaneously with occurrence of facts recorded – Police and Criminal Evidence Act 1984, s 68, Sch 3, para 7.

The appellant was a judge in Pakistan who came to the United Kingdom on holiday. On his arrival customs officers discovered that two suitcases which he was carrying had false bottoms, each containing about 1·4 kg of heroin. He was charged with being knowingly concerned in the fraudulent evasion of the prohibition on importation of a class A drug. At his trial he denied knowledge of the drugs and sought to have admitted in evidence, under s 68[a] of the Police and Criminal Evidence Act 1984, an affidavit and signed statement of a police inspector in Pakistan, with confession statements taken by the inspector from the appellant's servant and brother-in-law, all made some months after the appellant's arrest, in which they admitted having substituted the suitcases containing the heroin for the appellant's own suitcases without his knowledge. All three witnesses were outside the jurisdiction and it was not practicable to secure their attendance at the trial. The trial judge refused to admit the statements, on the ground that the inspector had not been compiling a 'record' within the meaning of s 68 since the inspector's affidavit and signed statement were not a contemporaneous record kept by a person acting in the performance of a duty to record facts and events as they occurred. The appellant was convicted. He appealed against his conviction on the ground that the trial judge's refusal to admit the evidence was wrong and rendered the conviction unsafe and unsatisfactory.

Held – The confession statements were admissible in evidence under s 68 of the 1984 Act since they were part of the record of a criminal investigation into drug dealing compiled by the inspector in the execution of his duty, and although that duty arose in connection with the preparation of a case which might lead to a criminal prosecution it was independent of the issues in the appellant's trial and had therefore not been created for the purpose of the trial in which the statements were sought to be admitted. It was not a necessary prerequisite for the admission of such a record that the recording officer was under a duty to record contemporaneous facts since under para 7[b] of Sch 3 to the 1984 Act the question whether the record was compiled contemporaneously was a question going to weight rather than admissibility. Since the information supplied to the inspector had been supplied by persons who had or might reasonably be supposed to have had personal knowledge of the matters set out in the confessions the trial judge had been wrong to exclude the statements, and, since the information they contained went to the heart of the defence, the jury's verdict had thereby been rendered unsafe and unsatisfactory. The appeal would therefore be allowed and the conviction quashed (see p 793 *j* to p 794 *j*, post).

R v Martin [1988] 3 All ER 440 distinguished.

Notes

For the written statement of a witness as evidence, see 11(2) Halsbury's Laws (4th edn reissue) para 1102.

---

a Section 68, so far as material, is set out at p 790 *d e*, post
b Paragraph 7 is set out at p 790 *j* to p 791 *a*, post

Mrs Iqbal had promptly and responsibly reported these matters to the police authority and a criminal investigation began. Sarwar and Azhar were arrested and made full *a* confessions to Inspector Hussain. Azhar confessed that he bought identical suitcases, gave them to the dealer in heroin in Lahore who concealed the drugs, whereupon Azhar effected the substitution in the expectation that one way or another the dealer's associates in England would successfully recover the suitcases. When seen by the servant making that switch, Azhar threatened Sarwar with violence if he revealed what had happened. Sarwar began to blackmail him, which led to the altercation witnessed by Mrs Iqbal. *b* Sarwar confirmed that he had observed the exchange of suitcases, that he was threatened with a pistol but was promised some financial reward, which was slow in being paid. Both men were averring that the appellant had no knowledge of what had been done to his suitcases. Although the statement of the inspector was silent as to the fate of the arrested men, it was the appellant's case that they had absconded in breach of their conditions of bail and that their whereabouts were unknown.   *c*

So far as is material s 68 of the 1984 Act provides as follows:

'(1) . . . a statement in a document shall be admissible in any proceedings as evidence of any fact stated therein of which direct oral evidence would be admissible if—(a) the document is or forms part of a record compiled by a person acting under a duty from information supplied by a person (whether acting under a duty or not) *d* who had, or may reasonably be supposed to have had, personal knowledge of the matters dealt with in that information; and (b) any condition relating to the person who supplied the information which is specified in subsection (2) below is satisfied.

(2) The conditions mentioned in subsection (1)(b) above are—(a) that the person who supplied the information . . . (ii) is outside the United Kingdom and it is not reasonably practicable to secure his attendance . . . (c) that, the identity of the person *e* who supplied the information being known, all reasonable steps have been taken to find him, but that he cannot be found . . .'

By s 70(1) Pt I of Sch 3 to the 1984 Act shall have effect for the purpose of supplementing s 68 above. The relevant paragraphs in Sch 3 are as follows:

'2. Where—(a) a document setting out the evidence which a person could be *f* expected to give as a witness has been prepared for the purpose of any pending or contemplated proceedings; and (b) it falls within subsection (1) of section 68 above, a statement contained in it shall not be given in evidence by virtue of that section without the leave of the court, and the court shall not give leave unless it is of the opinion that the statement ought to be admitted in the interests of justice, having regard—(i) to the circumstances in which leave is sought and in particular to the *g* contents of the statement; and (ii) to any likelihood that the accused will be prejudiced by its admission in the absence of the person who supplied the information on which it is based.'

We do not read para 3 in full. It permits the admissibility of evidence to test the credibility and consistency of the person supplying the information. Schedule 3 *h* continues:

'. . . 6. Any reference in section 68 above . . . to a person acting under a duty includes a reference to a person acting in the course of any trade, business, profession or other occupation in which he is engaged or employed or for the purposes of any paid or unpaid office held by him.

7. In estimating the weight, if any, to be attached to a statement admissible in *j* evidence by virtue of section 68 above regard shall be had to all the circumstances from which any inference can reasonably be drawn as to the accuracy or otherwise of the statement and, in particular—(a) to the question whether or not the person who supplied the information from which the record containing the statement was

compiled did so contemporaneously with the occurrence or existence of the facts
dealt with in that information; and (b) to the question whether or not that person,
or any other person concerned with compiling or keeping the record containing the
statement, had any incentive to conceal or misrepresent the facts.'

Section 68 above replaced s 1 of the Criminal Evidence Act 1965, which was enacted
to overcome the difficulties faced by the prosecution in *Myers v DPP* [1964] 2 All ER
881, [1965] AC 1001. That Act by s 1(1)(a) rendered admissible documents which were
or formed part of 'a record relating to any trade or business and compiled, in the course
of that trade or business, from information supplied . . . by persons who have . . . personal
knowledge'. The emphasis there is on business records. Much wider powers are conferred
by s 4(1) of the Civil Evidence Act 1968, the terms of which are virtually identical with
s 68 above. To complete our statutory review, we observe that s 68 is repealed by the
Criminal Justice Act 1988 and documentary evidence in criminal proceedings is now
governed by Pt II of that Act, which, stated broadly, will admit certain business or
professional documents unless the interests of justice require otherwise.

The judge at the trial had the advantage, as we have had, of the helpful submissions of
both counsel. He gave careful consideration to *R v Martin* [1988] 3 All ER 440, [1988] 1
WLR 655. He held that this was a document written by the inspector, who was writing
down the confessors' words, that he was under a duty to write down those words, that
the information contained in those words was supplied by the confessors, who claimed
to have knowledge of the matters described, and that the confessors were abroad and
could not be brought here to give evidence. In his judgment, however, the inspector was
not compiling a record within the meaning of s 68, as he understood it, that is to say a
contemporaneous record kept by a person acting in the performance of a duty to record
as things occur the facts and events at the time of their occurrence. He, therefore, refused
to admit that evidence. Counsel for the appellant now challenges that finding.

The courts have been careful not to give any exhaustive definition of 'record'. In what
may be the earliest decision of the criminal courts Lord Widgery CJ said in *R v Tirado*
(1974) 59 Cr App R 80 at 90 with reference to the 1965 Act:

> 'The language of section 1 seems on its face to contemplate the making or
> compilation of a record. That means the keeping of a book or a file, or a card index,
> into which information is deliberately put in order that it may be available to others
> another day. A cash book, a ledger, a stock book: all these may be records because
> they contain information deliberately entered in order that the information may be
> preserved. We think it at least widely open to question whether a file of the kind
> referred to in this case [being a file of correspondence maintained simply as a file of
> correspondence], either as a whole or when its individual documents are looked at,
> can come within the definition of a record within the meaning of the Act.'

In *R v Jones, R v Sullivan* [1978] 2 All ER 718 at 721, [1978] 1 WLR 195 at 199 per
Geoffrey Lane LJ it was held that 'record', again in the context of the 1965 Act, means 'a
history of events in some form which is not evanescent'. Accordingly, a bill of lading and
cargo manifest were admitted. That case also established that the Act did not require that
the document should be compiled in this country, and we agree that s 68 of the 1984 Act
likewise has no territorial limitation. In *H v Schering Chemicals Ltd* [1983] 1 All ER 849 at
852, [1983] 1 WLR 143 at 146 Bingham J held that the intention of the Civil Evidence
Act 1968, which, given the similarity of language, must be the intention which governed
s 68 of the 1984 Act, was:

> '. . . to admit in evidence records which a historian would regard as original or
> primary sources, that is documents which either give effect to a transaction itself or
> which contain a contemporaneous register of information supplied by those with
> direct knowledge of the facts.'

In *Savings and Investment Bank Ltd v Gasco Investments (Netherlands) BV* [1984] 1 All ER 296 at 307, [1984] 1 WLR 271 at 284–285 Peter Gibson J held:

'. . . a report by inspectors [appointed under the Companies Act], containing as it does a selection of the evidence put before the inspectors and their comments and conclusions thereon, is not a record in any ordinary sense of the word. It falls short of simply compiling the information supplied to them in the sense that some information will not be included in the report, and it goes beyond such a compilation in that it expresses opinions thereon.'

One can, therefore, readily see that the following were held not to be records: the file in the Land Registry containing a collection of inquiries and reports on the rights to the waters of a Cyprus river as in *Thrasyvoulos Ioannou v Papa Christoforos Demetriou* [1952] 1 All ER 179, [1952] AC 84, the file of correspondence in *R v Tirado* and the inspectors' report in the *Savings and Investment Bank* case.

Of more direct relevance to the matters before us the Court of Appeal held in *Taylor v Taylor (Taylor intervening, Holmes cited)* [1970] 2 All ER 609, [1970] 1 WLR 1148 that the transcript of criminal proceedings leading to a father's conviction of incest was 'a record' admissible under s 4(1) of the Civil Evidence Act 1968 to establish his adultery. As an even closer analogy, the Court of Appeal in *Edmonds v Edmonds* [1947] P 67 upheld the admissibility under the Evidence Act 1938 of a statement by a commissioner sitting in India which incorporated a note he took of the evidence of a witness in the proceedings he was there hearing which evidence was then sought to be admitted in English divorce proceedings. It is difficult to find any distinction between the commissioner or judge in the performance of his duty recording the information supplied to him by a witness giving evidence and this inspector of police in the execution of his duty in recording the confessions placed before us.

Counsel for the Crown, anxious not to open floodgates through which the unscrupulous will pour, relies on the authorities where this particular section has been considered. In *R v O'Loughlin* [1988] 3 All ER 431 Kenneth Jones J, having decided in the exercise of his discretion not to admit depositions to be read under s 13(3) of the Criminal Justice Act 1925, went on to hold that he would have to exercise his discretion in the same way with regard to the application to admit the depositions under s 68 of the 1984 Act. He found that the words of s 68 were not apt to include a deposition and he was strengthened in that view by the consideration that the reading of a deposition was clearly dealt within by s 13 of the 1925 Act and that there was no indication in the 1984 Act of any intention on the part of Parliament to add to the 1925 Act.

The matter was more fully argued in *R v Martin* [1988] 3 All ER 440, [1988] 1 WLR 655. This was a case where it was sought to admit under s 68 of the 1984 Act the statements taken by the investigating police officers from visiting seamen who complained that their money had been stolen in the course of the burglary of their ships moored at the docks. Giving the judgment of the court, Purchas LJ held ([1988] 3 All ER 440 at 446, [1988] 1 WLR 655 at 664):

'The fact that s 13(3) of the 1925 Act continues unrepealed and only amended in detail by the Criminal Procedure (Attendance of Witnesses) Act 1965, which was passed subsequently to the Criminal Evidence Act 1965, makes it impossible to construe s 68(1)(a) to extend to witness statements taken by police officers for the purpose of impending criminal proceedings. It cannot be reasonably argued that Sch 3, Pt I, para 2 of the Criminal Procedure Attendance of Witnesses Act 1965 avails to extend s 68(1). Paragraph 2(a) does refer to cases where "a document setting out the evidence which a person could be expected to give as a witness has been prepared for the purpose of any pending or contemplated proceedings", but para 2(b) provides that the document must *also* fall "within subsection (1) of section 68". The judge relied on these paragraphs as extending the meaning of "document" in

s 68(1); but the paragraphs are confined to documents falling within s 68(1) in any
event. The judge also overlooked the result of his construction of s 68(1), namely
that it would deprive an accused person of the protection of the stringent
requirements of s 13(3) of the 1925 Act (as amended); although this was emphasised
by Kenneth Jones J in *R v O'Loughlin* to which the judge was referred. In our
judgment the document must have come into existence as a record or part of a
record kept by a person acting in the performance of a duty to record
contemporaneous facts independent of the issues raised in the proceedings in which
it is sought to introduce the document as evidence. The section does not therefore
apply to statements incorporating the complaints of witnesses to an offence.'
(Purchas LJ's emphasis.)

Because of the importance Judge Slot placed on the duty to record *contemporaneous*
facts, we find it necessary to stress that the ratio of this decision is restated in these terms
(see [1990] 3 All ER 440 at 447, [1988] 1 WLR 655 at 664):

'The provisions of Sch 3, Pt I, paras 1 and 2 clearly relate back to the definition of
a document contained in s 68(1) and, in our judgment, are not a satisfactory vehicle
to construe the meaning of the section in any wider sense than it would otherwise
be construed, namely relating to some kind of record kept in the ordinary course of
business or the execution of a duty apart from the preparation of a case leading to
criminal prosecution.'

Finally I turn to *R v Cunningham* (1989) Times, 24 March, decided in the Court of
Appeal, Criminal Division on 3 March 1989, a transcript of which judgment is before
us. The appellant there, as here, had been convicted, inter alia, of being knowingly
concerned in the fraudulent evasion of the prohibition on importation of drugs. There,
as here, the only issue was whether he knew that his luggage contained the drugs which
were later found. There his solicitor had gone to Swaziland and taken statements in
accordance with the provisions of s 9 of the Criminal Justice Act 1967 from a servant
who had assisted in the packing of the appellant's belongings and who had included the
cannabis 'as a joke' without knowledge of the appellant. The issue was whether the
appellant's solicitor, in making those inquiries, making his attendance notes and taking
the statements, was compiling a record for the purposes of s 68. The court held:

'However, if the effect of para 2 of Sch 3 is that for which [counsel for the
appellant] contends [namely that it clearly envisages that a proof of evidence falls
within s 68(1)], it is difficult to see why Parliament did not make its meaning plain
in the body of the statute, as it has done now in s 23 of the Criminal Justice Act
1988. Having regard to the statutory history to which we have referred it seems
clear to us that it was not until 1988 that Parliament rendered potentially admissible
the sort of witness statements which [counsel] asked the judge to admit in the
present case.'

The court there gave the word 'record' a restricted meaning which also excluded the
solicitor's attendance notes, which had only come into existence because the defendant's
solicitor was preparing the defendant's case for trial. We have at all times had at the
forefront of our minds the dangers adverted to by the judge which would arise from too
liberal an admission of evidence of this kind in cases of this sort, but, as a matter of
construction of the act, we conclude as follows.

(1) The confession statements are documents which form part of a record, as we
interpret that word. It is a record because it is a compilation of facts supplied by those
with direct knowledge of the facts which is preserved in writing or other permanent
form, in order that it is not evanescent, and which will serve as an original source or
memorial or register of those facts and thus be evidence of them or of the transaction to
which the document gives effect. In saying that, we do not intend it to be an exhaustive

definition of the word 'record'. In plain language these documents were part of the record
of a criminal investigation into an allegation of dealing in drugs. They are as much a part *a*
of the police records as would be the occurrence book in which the desk sergeant notes
what is said to him across the counter of a police station.

(2) This record was compiled by the inspector in the execution of his duty in the
occupation in which he was engaged and so falls within para 2 of Sch 3 to the 1984 Act.

(3) His duty to record the facts supplied to him arose independently of the issues
which were raised far away from him in the Crown Court at Guildford. True it may be *b*
that the taking of the statements arose in the execution of his duty to prepare a case
which would or might lead to a criminal prosecution, but not this prosecution. The
records were not created for the purpose of the trial in which they are now sought to be
admitted, which is the governing limitation in R v Martin and R v Cunningham. It is not,
in our judgment, anomalous to hold that a confession taken by a police officer is
admissible, but one taken by the defendant's solicitor is not. Without seeking in any way *c*
to impugn the integrity of the solicitor, we see the very independence of the recording
officer who is performing his separate duty at one remove or further from the
transcription of the evidence into documentary form for the sole purpose of its
introduction into a specific criminal trial as a small but necessary safeguard for the
integrity of that evidence and thus the interests of justice.

(4) Judge Slot erred in holding that the duty is one to record contemporaneous facts, *d*
that is 'a duty to record as they occur facts and events at the time of their occurrence', as
he described it. In so holding, he no doubt relied on that passage in the judgment in R v
Martin to which we have already drawn attention. Their Lordships' judgment in that
case was, however, founded on the nature of the duty of the recording officer, not the
nature of the facts that he was recording, and we very much doubt whether the court
was attempting to define 'record' in the way the judge does. Section 68 contains no such *e*
limitation. On the contrary, para 7 of Sch 3, which is incorporated into s 68, makes it
plain that there is no such limitation to the admissibility of, as opposed to the weight to
be given to, the evidence. Weight will be affected by the question 'whether or not the
person who supplied the information from which the record containing the statement
was compiled did so contemporaneously with the occurrence or existence of the facts
dealt with in that information'. That paragraph clearly recognises that facts recorded at *f*
the time of their occurrence are more likely to be accurately recorded and so more
reliable than facts recorded long after their occurrence.

(5) The information supplied to the inspector was supplied by persons who had, or
might reasonably be supposed to have had, personal knowledge of the matters set out in
the confessions to which they subsequently put their hand.

(6) These confessors are outside the United Kingdom and it is not reasonably *g*
practicable to secure their attendance.

(7) Consequently the judge was wrong to conclude that the statement of the inspector
and the confessions it exhibited were inadmissible in evidence in law. Had he correctly
directed himself, he would undoubtedly have borne in mind that the defendant through
his solicitors had disclosed those matters to the prosecution in January, some six months *h*
or so before the trial, giving ample opportunity for the prosecution to investigate the
circumstances and gather such evidence as they could to cast doubt on the credibility and
consistency of the information. An officer of the Department of Customs and Excise did
visit Pakistan, though with what result we do not know. There would not seem to be
any good reason why the judge should have exercised his discretion to exclude the
statement. The information set out in the documents goes to the heart of the defence *j*
and, notwithstanding some features of the appellant's case which we find curious, we
hold that the verdict of the jury has been rendered unsafe and unsatisfactory and we
allow the appeal.

Lest the unscrupulous seize on this judgment to manufacture evidence to pervert the
course of justice, we remind them that s 68 of the 1984 Act has been repealed. The

interests of justice require that the court operate fairly, not just to the accused but also to the prosecution. The court will be vigilant, especially in cases of this kind, to ensure that any relaxation of the rules of hearsay evidence does not lead to any abuse of the due process of law.

Appeal allowed. Conviction quashed.

Solicitors: *Solicitor to the Customs and Excise.*

Kate O'Hanlon   Barrister.

Re K (a minor) (ward: care and control)

COURT OF APPEAL, CIVIL DIVISION
FOX LJ AND WAITE J
23 NOVEMBER 1989

Ward of court – Care and control – Contest between natural parent and foster parents – Test to be applied – Whether welfare of child positively demands displacement of natural parent's normal role in care and upbringing of child – Who would provide better home irrelevant.

In determining whether care and control of a ward of court who is the child of unmarried parents, one of whom has died, should vest in foster parents or the surviving natural parent the correct test is whether the welfare of the child positively demands that the natural parent's normal role in the care and upbringing of the child should be displaced by the foster parents rather than who would provide the better home for the child (see p 798 *b* to *d*, p 799 *a g* and p 800 *b c*, post).

Notes
For the court's jurisdiction to give directions as to the care and custody of wards of court, see 24 Halsbury's Laws (4th edn) para 595.

Cases referred to in judgments
J v C [1969] 1 All ER 788, [1970] AC 668, [1969] 2 WLR 540, HL.
K D (a minor) (ward: termination of access), Re [1988] 1 All ER 577, [1988] AC 806, [1988] 2 WLR 398, HL.
O'Hara, Re [1900] 2 IR 232, Ir CA.

Interlocutory appeal
The natural father of a child, R K, appealed against the decision of his Honour Judge Hyam sitting as a judge of the High Court by which the judge ordered that care and control vest in foster parents, Mr and Mrs E. The facts are set out in the judgment of Fox LJ.

Timothy Townshend for the father.
Timothy McLoughlin for Mr and Mrs E.

FOX LJ. This is an appeal by the father from a decision of his Honour Judge Hyam sitting as a judge of the High Court, giving care and control of a boy, R, born on 4 March 1985 to Mr and Mrs E, the plaintiffs in the proceedings.
    The father began to live with the mother at the beginning of 1985. They lived at various addresses and for various periods until the mother obtained a council house in Norwich in January 1987. Thereafter the father and the mother lived together at that

must act cautiously, not as if it were a private person acting with regard to his own child, and acting in opposition to the parent only when judicially satisfied that the welfare of the child requires that the parental right should be suspended or superseded.'

The judge properly directed himself as to the existence of that principle, but in my view he did not apply it. What he did was to apply a quite different test. In effect he asked himself the question: who would provide a better home for R? The father or Mr and Mrs E? Thus the judge sought to balance the consideration of normal family life in an exceptionally good home (which he concluded would be provided by Mr and Mrs E) against the fostering of the natural relationship which exists between a father and son. He said a risk attached to the fostering of the natural relationship with the father, and that it was possible R would not be likely to obtain the same high level of care which he said 'I am convinced he would get from Mr and Mrs E.' That, in my view, was the wrong approach. The question was not: where would R get the better home? The question was: was it demonstrated that the welfare of the child positively demanded the displacement of the parental right? The word 'right' is not really accurate in so far as it might connote something in the nature of a property right (which it is not) but it will serve for present purposes. The 'right', if there is one, is perhaps more that of the child.

In my view the circumstances did not demonstrate any such requirement. The father is a man aged 23; he is in work and in fact has always been. He occupies the council house, not at present as a tenant but if he has care and control of R it is not in doubt that he will be given tenancy of that house. At all times he has kept in close touch with R, having weekend access together with Wednesday evenings. His affection for R, and the affection that R has for him is not in doubt on the evidence or on the findings of the judge. R and the father have had an unhappy and difficult time consequent on the death of the mother, but the father has come through that, and in my view there is no reason to suppose that he is other than a stable and hard-working young man who, with the support of his parents (which is going to be available to him), will do his very best to provide a good home for R.

The welfare officer was of the opinion that he had an important part to play in R's life and there was nothing to indicate that he was not fit to have the care of R. He thought that the father would indeed rise to the occasion. It is right to say, however, for completeness, that the welfare officer had not seen R with his father.

In addition, the psychiatric social worker who attended R's mother said that she thought that the father was mature and had commitment, and she had no fears for the future of R if he went to live with his father.

There were three matters to which the judge referred as affecting his view of the case. First, the change might cause a great psychological harm to R, particularly having regard to the emotional disturbance he has gone through in his short life. As to that, I should observe that R has at all times kept in close contact with his father and has seen him regularly, so that there is a close affection between them. Further, he will not lose touch with the E family, and access arrangements to that end are accepted by the father as being necessary and will have to be made. Moreover, there was no expert evidence of a risk of great psychological harm to R if the changeover took place. As I have indicated, this is not a sudden change from one family well known to the child to another family, more or less unknown: it is a change from a family where R has indeed been well looked after to his father, with whom he has always been in touch and where a suitable home can be offered and where there will be no total break with the relationship which has been established with Mr and Mrs E.

Second, the judge was convinced that the father could not give the same high level of care as did Mr and Mrs E. He said that the level of care which could be offered by Mr and Mrs E would in his view be incomparably higher. In my view there is no evidence that the level of care which could be offered by the father and his parents would be inadequate a to this child's needs. Comparisons with the care of Mr and Mrs E are, in my view, not in point. What the court is concerned with is the case of a father who has always been in touch with his child and who can provide adequate housing and care for his son.

Third, the father, it was said, might form a new relationship and thus change the place of R in his father's home. Of course any parent who for the time being is unmarried may marry or establish a new relationship. But that is not necessarily to the disadvantage of R at all. It may expand and enrich the family life, but in any event it is something which is
b not, by itself, a reason for displacing the position of the natural parent who is able to offer a satisfactory home for his child.

As I have mentioned, the judge expressed some doubt as to the long-term commitment of the paternal grandmother in relation to the care of R. The judge did not indicate what had formed the basis for those doubts. I therefore do not feel able to place weight on them. He did not doubt the grandmother's ability to provide adequate care for R, as long
c as she was there. The judge referred to what I have mentioned as the 'strand of evidence' which he thought confirmed to some extent his doubts about the relationship of R with the grandmother, namely with regard to R following his father to the lavatory. As I have indicated, I regard that as altogether too slight and ambiguous a circumstance on which to base any conclusion adverse to the father's proposals for the care of R.

Looking at the whole matter, I can see no ground for ordering that the father should
d be displaced from his normal role in the care and upbringing of his child. In my opinion the judge did not direct himself properly as to the law to be applied to the case and, properly directed, he would not, in my view, have been entitled to reach the conclusion which he did. That is because, in my view, no circumstances had been demonstrated which made it necessary that, in the interests of the welfare of the child, the father's 'right' to bring him up should be displaced.
e I therefore come, with respect, to a conclusion differing from the judge but, having said that, I should add that the judge delivered a very full and sensitive judgment in which his concern for R was evident throughout. Though reaching a conclusion different from that of the judge, I have found his exposition of the facts very helpful in dealing with this appeal.

f As regards Mr and Mrs E, they have rendered great assistance to R and his father, for which both must be profoundly grateful. Mr and Mrs E will continue to have a part to play in R's life, and arrangements for access by them will be provided for.

For the reasons which I have indicated, I would allow this appeal and give care and control to the father. Arrangements for access by Mr and Mrs E are matters which we can consider with counsel.

g

WAITE J. I agree, and only wish to add a few words of my own because we are differing from a judge who approached an unusual and delicate case with evident care and sensitivity.

The tragic loss which this boy suffered through the death of his young mother when
h he was only three and a half years old has had one mercifully alleviating feature: he is surrounded by a concerned and loving natural family which, in its extended form, takes in two sets of grandparents, an aunt and uncle, and a father. They all live in the same locality; they are all anxious to play their part in seeing that R is brought up in an atmosphere of love and security; and they all, to their credit, acknowledge the important role to be played by each one of them in that process.

j The choice which the judge was called on to make in awarding care and control of R to Mr and Mrs E (his aunt and uncle), on the one hand, or to the father, on the other hand, therefore involved only a choice of primary carer. If that were to be Mr and Mrs E, R would continue to see a great deal of his father. If it were to be the father, he would continue to see a great deal of Mr and Mrs E. In either case his four grandparents would be at hand and closely involved in his life.

The judge correctly referred to *Re K D (a minor) (ward: termination of access)* [1988] 1 All ER 577, [1988] AC 806 for the guidance of principle which it afforded to him in making that choice. The principle is that the court in wardship will not act in opposition to a natural parent unless judicially satisfied that the child's welfare requires that the parental rights should be suspended or superceded. The speeches in the House of Lords make it plain that the term 'parental right' is not there used in a proprietary sense, but rather as describing the right of every child, as part of its general welfare, to have the ties of nature maintained wherever possible with the parents who gave it life.

Having at the outset correctly stated that guiding principle, the judge proceeded, however, in the remainder of his judgment, as though the question before him had been: which claimant will provide the better home? The question he ought of course to have been asking was: are there any compelling factors which required him to override the prima facie right of this child to an upbringing by its surviving natural parent?

That approach led him to embark on a careful and detailed assessment of the merits of the two competing households with a view to deciding in which of them R would have a better prospect of achieving a sense of security and stability, qualities, certainly, which he will badly need after his sufferings. That comparative exercise was conscientiously undertaken and involved the most careful weighing of minutiae such as the age differences between the parties, of imponderables such as the father's future marriage prospects, and even of wholly unknown quantities such as the emotional effect of a change of primary carer which the judge undertook in the absence of any medical or psychiatric evidence one way or the other. It was, despite its thoroughness, an exercise misconceived in law. The clear evidence of the court welfare officer and the mother's psychiatric social worker in support of the father's qualities of steadfastness and concern, as well as the father's record as a man who had made considerable efforts to match loyalty with realism throughout the ups and downs of a family relationship marred by the tragic impact of mental illness, made this a case in which a risk of physical or emotional damage to the child of a very high order would have been necessary to dislodge the primary claim on R's welfare of an upbringing by his father.

The judge had no such evidence before him, and if properly directed in law he could not have reached the decision which he did.

I agree with Fox LJ that the judge's error of principle in his approach to this case gives this court jurisdiction to intervene and to substitute its own discretion, which should be exercised by reversing the judge's order and committing care and control of the minor until further order to the father, with appropriate access to Mr and Mrs E. Their unselfish dedication to R during the past crucial 12 months of his life has been outstanding. It is heartening to be assured that he will remain close to them and to his young cousins, and that he will grow up in time to appreciate the debt he owes to them, and to join his father in acknowledging it. I too would allow the appeal.

Appeal allowed.

Solicitors: *Overbury Steward & Eaton*, Norwich (for the father); *Daynes Hill & Perks*, Norwich (for Mr and Mrs E).

Frances Rustin   Barrister.

Morris v Murray and another

COURT OF APPEAL, CIVIL DIVISION

FOX, STOCKER LJJ AND SIR GEORGE WALLER

10, 11, 12 JULY, 3 AUGUST 1990

Negligence – Volenti non fit injuria – Knowledge of risk – Passenger in light aircraft piloted by drunken pilot – Plaintiff aware that pilot very drunk – Plaintiff seriously injured when aircraft crashed – Whether plaintiff's claim against pilot's estate barred by defence of volenti non fit injuria.

The plaintiff, after having two or three drinks at a public house, met the deceased at another public house and, together with others, continued drinking with the deceased for some hours until the deceased suggested that they go on a joyride in the deceased's light aircraft. The plaintiff and the deceased drove to the aerodrome, where the plaintiff assisted in preparing the aircraft for take-off. The aircraft, piloted by the deceased, took off down wind and uphill, a highly dangerous manoeuvre, in conditions of poor visibility, low cloud and drizzle when other flying at the aerodrome had been suspended. The aircraft only just managed to get airborne and crashed soon afterwards. The deceased was killed and the plaintiff was seriously injured in the crash. An autopsy on the deceased showed that he had consumed the equivalent of 17 whiskies and his blood-alcohol level was more than three times the legal limit for driving a motor vehicle. The plaintiff brought an action against the deceased's estate claiming damages for personal injury. The judge awarded him £130,900 damages. The estate appealed against the award.

Held – A passenger who appreciated the risk he was taking in embarking on a joyride with a pilot whose drunkenness was so extreme and so glaring that to go on the flight was like engaging in an intrinsically and obviously dangerous operation was barred by the defence of volenti non fit injuria from claiming damages for personal injury sustained in a crash caused by the pilot's negligence because in such circumstances the passenger had thereby implicitly waived his right to damages. Since the plaintiff although drunk was aware of the risk he was taking flying with the deceased and had thereby knowingly and willingly embarked on a flight with a drunken pilot his claim against the deceased's estate was barred by the defence of volenti non fit injuria. The appeal would accordingly be allowed (see p 807 *b c h j*, p 808 *c* to *h*, p 809 *a c*, p 816 *b f* to *j*, p 817 *j* to p 818 *e*, p 819 *d g* and p 820 *f* to *h*, post).

Dictum of Asquith J in *Dann v Hamilton* [1939] 1 All ER 59 at 64 applied.

Notes

For the standard of care generally in negligence, see 34 Halsbury's Laws (4th edn) paras 10–12, and for cases on the subject, see 36(1) Digest (2nd reissue) 381–399, 3054–3211.

For negligence in relation to dangerous operations, see 34 Halsbury's Laws (4th edn) paras 35–36, and for cases on the subject, see 36(1) Digest (2nd reissue) 237–245, 1746–1782.

For the defence of volenti non fit injuria, see 34 Halsbury's Laws (4th edn) paras 62–65, and for cases on the subject, see 36(1) Digest (2nd reissue) 65–79, 333–442.

Cases referred to in judgment

Ashton v Turner [1980] 3 All ER 870, [1981] QB 137, [1980] 3 WLR 736.

Bennett v Tugwell (an infant) [1971] 2 All ER 248, [1971] 2 QB 267, [1971] 2 WLR 847.

Car and General Insurance Corp Ltd v Seymour (1956) 2 DLR (2d) 369, Can SC.

Dann v Hamilton [1939] 1 All ER 59, [1939] 1 KB 509.

Donoghue (or M'Alister) v Stevenson [1932] AC 562, [1932] All ER Rep 1, HL.

Hall v Brooklands Auto-Racing Club [1933] 1 KB 205, [1932] All ER Rep 208, CA.

Imperial Chemical Industries Ltd v Shatwell [1964] 2 All ER 999, [1965] AC 656, [1964] 3
    WLR 329, HL.
Insurance Comr v Joyce (1948) 77 CLR 39, Aust HC.
Kelly v Farrans Ltd [1954] NI 41, NI CA.
Lehnert v Stein (1962) 36 DLR (2d) 159, Can SC.
Morrison v Union Steam Ship Co of New Zealand Ltd [1964] NZLR 468, NZ CA.
Nettleship v Weston [1971] 3 All ER 581, [1971] 2 QB 691, [1971] 3 WLR 370, CA.
Owens v Brimmell [1976] 3 All ER 765, [1977] QB 859, [1977] 2 WLR 943.
Pitts v Hunt [1990] 3 All ER 344, [1990] 3 WLR 542, CA.
R v Warburton-Pitt (1990) Independent, 14 July, CA.
Slater v Clay Cross Co Ltd [1956] 2 All ER 625, [1956] 2 QB 264, [1956] 3 WLR 232, CA.
Smith v Baker & Sons [1891] AC 325, [1891–4] All ER Rep 69, HL.
Williams v Port of Liverpool Stevedoring Co Ltd [1956] 2 All ER 69, [1956] 1 WLR 551.
Wooldridge v Sumner [1962] 2 All ER 978, [1963] 2 QB 43, [1962] 3 WLR 616, CA.

Appeal
The defendants, Henry Murray and Janice Ellen Morey (now Mrs Gibbins), the
administrators of the estate of Harry Henry Murray deceased, appealed against the
decision of his Honour Judge Rice sitting as a judge of the High Court on 26 May 1989
whereby he awarded the plaintiff, Gary Morris, the sum of £130,900 damages for
personal injuries sustained in the crash of a light aircraft owned and piloted by Mr
Murray. The facts are set out in the judgment of Fox LJ.

Ivan Krolick for the defendants.
Walter Aylen QC and *Stephen Lennard* for the plaintiff.

Cur adv vult

3 August. The following judgments were delivered.

FOX LJ. This is an appeal by the defendants from an order of his Honour Judge Rice
(sitting as a judge of the High Court) whereby he awarded the plaintiff a sum of £130,900
damages for personal injuries sustained in the crash of a light aircraft owned and piloted
by the late Mr H H Murray (Mr Murray).
    On 3 March 1981 the plaintiff, Mr Morris, was drinking with a Mr Moran at a public
house in Harlow called the Red Lion. The plaintiff was then about 25 years old. How
much they drank there is uncertain. The plaintiff says that they were short of money.
He thinks they had two half pints. Mr Moran thinks it was two pints. The barman, Mr
Aldington, who was a friend of theirs, thinks it was three or four pints.
    At about midday, the barman received a telephone call from Mr Murray, who was a
regular customer at the Red Lion and a friend of the plaintiff and Mr Moran. Mr Murray
was in a public house called the Blue Boar about 25 minutes drive from the Red Lion.
He asked if somebody could collect him from the Blue Boar and take him to the Red
Lion. The plaintiff and Mr Moran accordingly drove to the Blue Boar. They drove in Mr
Moran's car but since Mr Moran had been disqualified from driving the plaintiff drove.
    When they arrived at the Blue Boar, they were given further drinks by Mr Murray.
Subsequently, as neither the plaintiff nor Mr Moran had any money, Mr Murray lent
each of them £10 so that they should not feel embarrassed by not being able to buy
rounds of drinks.
    The party was at some point enlarged by the landlord and his wife. Drinking continued
until about four o'clock in the afternoon. They drank spirits. Asked in evidence in chief
'Do you remember what you were doing at the Blue Boar?', the plaintiff replied 'Drinking
heavily'. By the end of the afternoon the plaintiff and Mr Moran had each spent their
£10 or most of it.

There seems to have been a suggestion by Mr Murray that the landlord and his wife
a should go on a flight with him. He had a pilot's licence and kept a light aircraft at a flying
club at Stapleford. The offer was declined. In the end the plaintiff and Mr Murray agreed
to go on a flight together and the plaintiff drove Mr Murray and Mr Moran to Stapleford.
The plaintiff remembered the car drawing up alongside the aircraft. He agreed in
cross-examination that he was anxious to start the engine and go on the flight. He tried
to start the engine by turning the propeller but was unable to do so. Either Mr Moran or
b the plaintiff and Mr Moran together did start the engine. The plane needed fuel and it
was filled up at a pump by the plaintiff, Mr Murray paying for it by cheque.

Flying conditions were poor. Mr R G Matthew, who conducted an inquiry into the
crash on behalf of the chief inspector of accidents says (in a written statement which,
with others, was read at the trial) that there was a wind of some 20 knots with poor
visibility, low cloud and occasional drizzle. The chief instructor at the Stapleford Flying
c Club had cancelled all club flying. Mr Murray, as I understand it, was not aware of this,
but, in any event, it did not prevent him flying his own aircraft if he chose to. The
plaintiff asked Mr Murray while they were in the aircraft whether he (Mr Murray)
needed to 'radio in' to flying control before taking off but Mr Murray said he did not.
That was apparently correct according to the statement of Mr P I Brand, a flying inspector.

The flight was short and chaotic. Mr Murray took off down wind. The runway was
d wet and was uphill. These factors would make take-off more difficult. In Mr Brand's
view, Mr Murray should have taken off on a different runway and into the wind.

Mr Reith, a consulting engineer who holds a pilot's licence, was driving on a nearby
road when he saw the plane. He said in his statement that when he saw the plane his
initial reaction was that he was looking at a model plane. He could not initially reconcile
the flying attitude of the plane, that is to say its almost vertical climb and its close
e proximity to the ground, with anything other than a model aircraft. The plane was
evidently recovering from a descent which brought it close to the ground. It climbed to
about 300 feet, then stalled and dived into the ground. Mr Reith's opinion from his
observation was that the pilot was not in control of the aircraft.

Mr Murray was killed and the plaintiff was severely injured. The plaintiff in the
f statement which he made to the police after the accident said that he had flown with Mr
Murray on two previous occasions and thought him a good pilot. He said in evidence at
the trial that, although he remembered making a statement and signing it he did not
remember saying that he had flown with Mr Murray twice before. The judge found that
since the accident, his memory was episodic.

The autopsy on Mr Murray showed that from the concentration of ethanol in his body
g and from his blood alcohol content he had consumed the equivalent of 17 whiskies. The
concentration of alcohol was more than three times the limit permitted for a car driver.

Mr Murray had for some five years prior to his death lived with a lady, now Mrs
Gibbins, who gave birth to his child on 30 March 1981, about three weeks after the
accident.

Letters of administration to the estate of Mr Murray were granted to Mrs Gibbins and
h to Mr Murray's father on 16 October 1981. The net value of the estate was sworn at about
£43,000 for the purposes of the grant.

The child, Ricky, is the person entitled to the estate on the intestacy.

The writ in this action was issued on 29 February 1984 and served in August 1984.
The defendants pleaded volenti non fit injuria and, in the alternative, contributory
negligence. The judge rejected the plea of volenti but held that there was contributory
j negligence to the extent of 20% only.

As to volenti the judge, after referring to *Dann v Hamilton* [1939] 1 All ER 59, [1939] 1
KB 509 and to the judgments of Lord Denning MR and Salmon LJ in *Nettleship v Weston*
[1971] 3 All ER 581, [1971] 2 QB 691, then continued as follows:

'In this case it is right to say that the plaintiff was aware that Mr Murray had been

drinking heavily, but Mr Murray was able, as it were, to start this aeroplane. He
even taxied the aeroplane to the place where petrol was sold, paid for the petrol and
then was able, albeit in a somewhat inexpert way because his faculties were clearly
affected by drink, but he was able to get the plane into the air, albeit it only flew for
some three or four minutes before crashing in the way I have described. But, in my
view, this is not a case where one can say that the plaintiff consented to run the risk
of the actual injuries that he subsequently suffered. This case falls far short of what
would be necessary in order to successfully defend the action on the grounds of
volenti non fit injuria. This is a case where, in my view, certainly there was
contributory negligence by the plaintiff in that he boarded a plane and allowed
himself to be flown when he knew that [Mr Murray] had consumed a considerable
amount of alcohol. In many ways it is analogous to the facts that prevailed in *Owens
v Brimmell* [1976] 3 All ER 765, [1977] QB 859 because in that case the plaintiff had
been in the defendant's company for most of the evening visiting one public house
after another. The defendant had there consumed eight to nine pints of bitter. In
that case the judge, having considered the question of negligence of the plaintiff in
that he agreed to be carried in a car driven by a person whose judgment he must
have known would be affected by alcohol, assessed the plaintiff's contributory
negligence at 20%. That is what I propose to do here.'

I should now refer to certain authorities. In *Dann v Hamilton* [1939] 1 All ER 59, [1939]
1 KB 509 the defendant, Mr Hamilton, drove the plaintiff and her mother from the area
of Staines into London to see the Coronation decorations. They all had tea in London at
about 6 pm. Between 9.30 pm and 10 pm they had some beer at a public house in
London. How much Hamilton drank was not known. They then drove quite safely to
another public house called the Milford Arms near Hounslow. It was about 10.30 pm
and the premises were just closing, but they met a Mr Taunton there whom they all
knew. Taunton and Hamilton had a drink at the Milford Arms. Hamilton's condition at
that time was described thus by Taunton: 'He wasn't drunk but I could see that he had
had one or two drinks.' It was then suggested that they should go to the Osterley Park
Club which they did. Hamilton drove. Taunton thought he drove rather fast and
swerved slightly but he did not appear to be driving dangerously. At the club Hamilton
ordered a round of drinks including a pint of beer for himself, which he drank quickly
and then ordered another round.

They returned to the car. Taunton was asked by the women to drive but Hamilton
would not let him. He agreed to drive Taunton to his house about a mile away. Taunton
said that he drove at excessive speed and there was talk in the car that they were going
too fast. Hamilton stopped the car after a while and he and Taunton went to the roadside.
Taunton said he thought that Hamilton was very drunk but agreed to return to the car
after obtaining a promise from him. Asquith J doubted whether, if Hamilton was as
drunk as Taunton suggested, he would have accepted Hamilton's promise. The remainder
of the drive on the way to Taunton's house seems to have been safe enough except for a
burst of high speed near the end. When Taunton got out he said to the two women 'You
two have more pluck than I have', to which the plaintiff replied 'You should be like me.
If anything is going to happen it will happen'. The car then drove on and was involved
in a very bad accident shortly afterwards in which Hamilton was killed and the plaintiff
was injured. Asquith J held that the volenti defence was not applicable and gave
judgment for the plaintiff. Contributory negligence which at that time would have been
a complete defence to the action was not pleaded and despite the judge's invitation to the
defendant's counsel to amend (see the note by Lord Asquith in (1953) 69 LQR 317) was
never relied on.

The decision has been criticised (see eg Dixon J in *Insurance Comr v Joyce* (1948) 77
CLR 39 at 59, Salmon LJ in *Nettleship v Weston* [1971] 3 All ER 581 at 590, [1971] 2 QB
691 at 704 and Fleming *Law of Torts* (7th edn, 1987) pp 272, 274). But I need not

examine the question of its correctness since it was approved by this court in *Slater v Clay*
a *Cross Co Ltd* [1956] 2 All ER 625, [1956] 2 QB 264 (though I do not read that approval as
going beyond the decision on its facts). The present case is, however, far removed on its
facts from *Dann v Hamilton*. In that case the plaintiff was engaged in a quite ordinary
social outing to London and back, with a driver who was not drunk when the drive
started and, indeed, who was not drunk until quite a late stage when it was not very easy
for the plaintiff to extricate herself without giving offence. The whole situation seems to
b me to bear little resemblance to the drunken escapade, heavily fraught with danger from
the first, on which the plaintiff and Mr Murray embarked in this case. It is said on behalf
of the plaintiff that *Dann v Hamilton* was a stronger case than the present for the
application of the volenti maxim having regard to the fatalistic reply given by the
plaintiff to Taunton when he finally left the car. That remark might be a good reason for
saying that the case should have been decided in favour of the defendant (see, for
c example, *Fleming* p 272, note 55) but Asquith J, in fact, gave no weight to it.
    The reasoning of Asquith J was that a person who voluntarily travels as a passenger
with a driver who is known to the passenger to have driven negligently in the past cannot
properly be regarded as volens to future acts of negligence by the driver. Should it then
make any difference that the driver is likely to drive negligently on the material occasion,
not because he is shown to have driven negligently in the past, but because he is known
d by the plaintiff to be under the influence of drink? Asquith J thought not and held that
the plaintiff by embarking in the car, or re-entering it with the knowledge that through
drink the driver had materially reduced his capacity for driving safely, did not implicitly
consent to or absolve the driver from liability from any subsequent negligence on his
part whereby she might suffer harm.
    Having reached that conclusion, however, Asquith J continued as follows ([1939] 1 All
e ER 59 at 64, [1939] 1 KB 509 at 518):

> 'There may be cases in which the drunkenness of the driver at the material time
> is so extreme and so glaring that to accept a lift from him is like engaging in an
> intrinsically and obviously dangerous occupation, inter-meddling with an unex-
> ploded bomb or walking on the edge of an unfenced cliff. It is not necessary to
f > decide whether in such a case the maxim *volenti non fit injuria* would apply, for in
> the present case I find as a fact that the driver's degree of intoxication fell short of
> this degree.'

    The question before us, I think, is whether, as a matter of law, there are such cases as
Asquith J refers to and, if so, whether this present case is one of them.
    As to the first of these questions there is a fundamental issue whether the volenti
g doctrine applies to the tort of negligence at all. In *Wooldridge v Sumner* [1962] 2 All ER
978 at 990, [1963] 2 QB 43 at 69 Diplock LJ said:

> 'In my view, the maxim, in the absence of express contract, has no application to
> negligence simpliciter where the duty of care is based solely on proximity or
> "neighbourship" in the Atkinian sense [see *Donoghue v Stevenson* [1932] AC 562 at
h > 580, [1932] All ER Rep 1 at 11 per Lord Atkin]. The maxim in English law pre-
> supposes a tortious act by the defendant. The consent that is relevant is not consent
> to the risk of injury but consent to the lack of reasonable care that may produce that
> risk . . . and requires on the part of the plaintiff at the time at which he gives his
> consent full knowledge of the nature and extent of the risk that he ran . . .'

j   Asquith J himself raised the same question in *Dann v Hamilton* [1939] 1 All ER 59 at
63, [1939] 1 KB 509 at 516–517. He drew a distinction between two kinds of case. First,
where a dangerous physical condition has been brought about by the negligence of the
defendant and, after it has arisen, the plaintiff fully appreciating its dangerous character
elects to assume the risk. In that sort of case Asquith J regarded the volenti maxim as
capable of applying. That, however, is not this case. Diplock LJ indeed would not have

regarded the maxim as truly applicable and was of the opinion that the correct test of liability of the person creating the risk was whether it was reasonably foreseeable by him that the plaintiff would so act in relation to it as to endanger himself, which is the principle of the 'rescue' cases.

The second class of case was where the act of the plaintiff relied on as a consent precedes and is claimed to licence in advance a possible subsequent act of negligence. *Dann v Hamilton* itself was an instance of that class in which Asquith J held on the facts the maxim not to be applicable. But as I have indicated he left open the question of extreme cases. Diplock LJ's observations in *Wooldridge v Sumner* [1962] 2 All ER 978 at 988, [1963] 2 QB 43 at 67 were in relation to a case which was concerned with injury to a spectator at a sporting event. He said:

> 'The matter has to be looked at from the point of view of the reasonable spectator as well as the reasonable participant; not because of the maxim volenti non fit injuria, but because what a reasonable spectator would expect a participant to do without regarding it as blameworthy is as relevant to what is reasonable care as what a reasonable participant would think was blameworthy conduct in himself. The same idea was expressed by SCRUTTON, L.J., in *Hall v. Brooklands Auto-Racing Club* ([1933] 1 KB 205 at 214, [1932] All ER Rep 208 at 213): "What is reasonable care would depend on the perils which might be reasonably expected to occur, *and the extent to which the ordinary spectator might be expected to appreciate and take the risk of such perils.*"' (Diplock LJ's emphasis.)

But a participant may, to the damage of a spectator, do something which a reasonable spectator in the context of the sport as it is normally understood would never anticipate. That may be negligence simpliciter and, since the spectator could not contemplate it, he could not be met by the defence of volenti. But in a case, such as the present, where a person voluntarily decided to participate in something which is itself necessarily dangerous, it seems to me that different considerations must arise.

Nettleship v Weston [1971] 3 All ER 581, [1971] 2 QB 691 was a case of a driving instructor injured by the negligent driving of the pupil. It is not, as a decision, of much relevance to the present case since, before giving the lesson, the instructor had asked for and obtained an assurance that there was in existence a policy of insurance. He was in fact shown a comprehensive policy which covered a passenger. That was unhopeful ground for a volens plea. There are, however, observations of Lord Denning MR and Salmon LJ to which I should refer. Lord Denning MR said ([1971] 3 All ER 581 at 587, [1971] 2 QB 691 at 701):

> 'Knowledge of the risk of injury is not enough. Nor is a willingness to take the risk of injury. Nothing will suffice short of an agreement to waive any claim for negligence. The plaintiff must agree, expressly or impliedly, to waive any claim for any injury that may befall him due to the lack of reasonable care by the defendant: or more accurately, due to the failure of the defendant to measure up to the standard of care that the law requires of him.'

Salmon LJ in the same case adopted, in a dissenting judgment, a different approach (see [1971] 3 All ER 581 at 589, [1971] 2 QB 691 at 704). He said that if, to the knowledge of the passenger, the driver is so drunk as to be incapable of driving safely, a passenger having accepted a lift cannot expect the driver to drive other than dangerously. The duty of care, he said, springs from relationship. The relationship which the passenger has created in accepting a lift in such circumstances cannot entitle him to expect the driver to discharge a duty of care which the passenger knows that he is incapable of discharging. The result is that no duty is owed by the driver to the passenger to drive safely. The difficulty about this analysis is that it may tend to equate 'sciens' with 'volens', which is not the law. However, there must be cases where the facts are so strong that 'volens' is the only sensible conclusion. Salmon LJ said that, alternatively, if there is a duty owed to the passenger to drive safely, the passenger by accepting the lift clearly assumed the risk

a of the driver failing to discharge that duty.

I doubt whether the gap between Lord Denning MR's approach and that of Salmon LJ is a very wide one. On the one hand you may have an implicit waiver of any claims by reason of an exhibited notice as to the assumption of risk (see *Bennett v Tugwell (an infant)* [1971] 2 All ER 248, [1971] 2 QB 267 which was decided before the Road Traffic Act 1972). On the other hand, if it is evident to the passenger from the first that the driver is

b so drunk that he is incapable of driving safely, the passenger must have accepted the obvious risk of injury. You may say that he is volens or that he has impliedly waived the right to claim or that the driver is impliedly discharged from the normal duty of care. In general, I think that the volenti doctrine can apply to the tort of negligence, though it must depend on the extent of the risk, the passenger's knowledge of it and what can be inferred as to his acceptance of it. The passenger cannot be volens (in the absence of some

c form of express disclaimer) in respect of acts of negligence which he had no reason to anticipate and he must be free from compulsion. Lord Pearce in *Imperial Chemical Industries Ltd v Shatwell* [1964] 2 All ER 999 at 1013, [1965] AC 656 at 687–688 said:

> 'So far as concerns common law negligence, the defence of volenti non fit injuria is clearly applicable if there was a genuine full agreement, free from any kind of
d pressure, to assume the risk of loss. In *Williams v. Port of Liverpool Stevedoring Co., Ltd.* ([1956] 2 All ER 69 at 72, [1956] 1 WLR 551 at 555), LYNSKEY, J., rejected the defence where one stevedore was injured by the deliberate negligence of the whole gang (to which the plaintiff gave "tacit consent") in adopting a dangerous system of unloading. There was an overall duty on the master to provide a safe system of work, and it is difficult for one man to stand out against his gang. In such
e circumstances one may not have that deliberate free assumption of risk which is essential to the plea and which makes it as a rule unsuitable in master and servant cases owing to the possible existence of indefinable social and economic pressures. If the plaintiff had been shown to be a moving spirit in the decision to unload in the wrong manner it would have been different; but these matters are questions of fact and degree.'

f We were referred to *Slater v Clay Cross Co Ltd* [1956] 2 All ER 625, [1956] 2 QB 264 but in that case the plaintiff, while she could be regarded as accepting the risks of walking down a narrow railway tunnel (which she and other villagers had long been in the habit of using as a short cut) she did not accept the risk that the driver would drive the train negligently.

Before coming to the facts it is perhaps worth noting how the volenti doctrine is stated.
g Lord Herschell said in *Smith v Baker & Sons* [1891] AC 325 at 360, [1891–4] All ER Rep 69 at 87):

> 'The maxim is founded on good sense and justice. One who has invited or assented to an act being done towards him cannot, when he suffers from it, complain of it as a wrong.'

h If the plaintiff had himself been sober on the afternoon of the flight it seems to me that, by agreeing to be flown by Mr Murray, he must be taken to have accepted fully the risk of serious injury. The danger was both obvious and great. He could not possibly have supposed that Mr Murray, who had been drinking all the afternoon, was capable of discharging a normal duty of care.

j But as he himself had been drinking, can it be assumed that he was capable of appreciating the risks? The matter was not very deeply examined at the trial, but he was certainly not 'blind drunk'. In cross-examination, he agreed with the description 'merry'. He was capable of driving a car from the Blue Boar to the airfield; and he did so for the purpose of going on a flight with Mr Murray. He helped to start the aircraft and fuel it. Immediately before take-off he asked Mr Murray whether he should not 'radio in' (a sensible inquiry). None of this suggests that his faculties were so muddled that he was incapable of appreciating obvious risks. Moreover, he gave no specific evidence to the effect 'I was really too drunk to know what I was doing'. Nor did anyone else give such evidence about him.

He was asked, and answered as follows:

'Q. Looking back on it now, Mr Morris, you must have been aware that Murray had been drinking too much, do you agree? A. As I had had too much to drink I probably had not noticed that he had.
Q. Well, I understand that, but I ask you to look back on it. A. Looking back, yes, definitely.'

In my opinion, on the evidence the plaintiff knew that he was going on a flight, he knew that he was going to be piloted by Mr Murray and he knew that Mr Murray had been drinking heavily that afternoon. The plaintiff's actions that afternoon, from leaving the Blue Boar to the take-off suggest that he was capable of understanding what he was doing. There is no clear evidence to the contrary. I think that he knew what he was doing and was capable of appreciating the risks. I do not overlook that the plaintiff's evidence was that, if he had been sober, he would not have gone on the flight. That is no doubt so but it does not establish that he was in fact incapable of understanding what he was doing that afternoon.

If he was capable of understanding what he was doing, then the fact is that he knowingly and willingly embarked on a flight with a drunken pilot. The flight served no useful purpose at all; there was no need or compulsion to join it. It was just entertainment. The plaintiff co-operated fully in the joint activity and did what he could to assist it. He agreed in evidence that he was anxious to start the engine and to fly. A clearer source of great danger could hardly be imagined. The sort of errors of judgment which an intoxicated pilot may make are likely to have a disastrous result. The high probability was that Mr Murray was simply not fit to fly an aircraft. Nothing that happened on the flight itself suggests otherwise, from the take-off down wind to the violence of the manoeuvres of the plane in flight.

The situation seems to me to come exactly within Asquith J's example of the case where—

'the drunkenness of the driver at the material time is so extreme and so glaring that to accept a lift from him is like engaging in an intrinsically and obviously dangerous occupation . . .'

(See *Dann v Hamilton* [1939] 1 All ER 59 at 64, [1939] 1 KB 509 at 518.)

I think that in embarking on the flight the plaintiff had implicitly waived his rights in the event of injury consequent on Mr Murray's failure to fly with reasonable care.

The facts go far beyond *Dann v Hamilton*, *Nettleship v Weston* and *Slater v Clay Cross Co Ltd*. It is much nearer to the dangerous experimenting with the detonators in *Imperial Chemical Industries Ltd v Shatwell* [1964] 2 All ER 999, [1965] AC 656. I would conclude, therefore, that the plaintiff accepted the risks and implicitly discharged Mr Murray from liability from injury in relation to the flying of the plane.

The result, in my view, is that the maxim volenti non fit injuria does apply in this case. The judge appears to have been influenced by the fact that Mr Murray managed to get the plane airborne. He did, but the take-off down wind was irregular and the bizarre movements of the plane in flight must raise the greatest doubts whether he was in proper control of it. The judge thought that the case was analogous to *Owens v Brimmell* [1976] 3 All ER 765, [1977] QB 859. But the volenti defence was not in issue in that case.

Considerations of policy do not lead me to any different conclusion. Volenti as a defence has, perhaps, been in retreat during this century, certainly in relation to master and servant cases. It might be said that the merits could be adequately dealt with by the application of the contributory negligence rules. The judge held that the plaintiff was

only 20% to blame (which seems to me to be too low) but if that were increased to
a so that the plaintiff's damages were reduced by half, both sides would be substanti
penalised for their conduct. It seems to me, however, that the wild irresponsibility of t.
venture is such that the law should not intervene to award damages and should leave the
loss where it falls. Flying is intrinsically dangerous and flying with a drunken pilot is
great folly. The situation is very different from what has arisen in motoring cases.

I should mention that the defence of volenti has been abrogated in relation to
b passengers in motor vehicles covered by comprehensive insurance (see s 148 of the Road
Traffic Act 1972). It is not suggested, however, that there is any similar enactment
relating to aircraft and applicable to this case.

In the circumstances I do not need to deal with the quantum of damages on which the
defendants appeal. As to the question of devastavit by the administrators on which there
has been argument before us, I do not think that this is a matter for this action. This is
c an action for damages for personal injuries. The question of devastavit, it seems to me, is
one to be raised in administration proceedings if damages were awarded but not paid or
not paid in full.

I would allow the appeal.

STOCKER LJ. I adopt with gratitude the exposition of the facts set out in the judgment
d of Fox LJ, which I have read in draft. I add observations of my own since we are differing
from the conclusion of the judge and in deference to the detailed arguments which have
been addressed to us by counsel on both sides and because, so far as I am aware, the facts
of the case are unique and raise matters of some importance.

This appeal is not concerned with precise formulation of the elements necessary to
support a plea of volenti non fit injuria. It is sufficient for the purpose of this case to
e accept, as counsel on both sides have done, that in order to defeat an otherwise valid
claim on the basis that the plaintiff *was* volens the defendant must establish that the
plaintiff at the material time knew the nature and extent of the risk and voluntarily
agreed to absolve the defendant from the consequences of it by consenting to the lack of
reasonable care that might produce the risk. It is common ground and long established
that knowledge of the risk is not sufficient but there must also be consent to bear the
f consequences of it. This appeal is concerned with the application of the doctrine to the
facts of the case. We have been referred to a number of cases illustrative of the application
of the maxim to the facts of the case in question. It is clear that there are two
categories of case in which this problem falls to be considered, viz (1) where the
breach of duty precedes the exposure of the victim to the risk of injury. Such
involve a 'rescue' situation, but in general present problems which are
g than the second category since the nature and the extent of the risk can
assessed where the dangerous situation has already been created. The
which the application of the maxim falls to be considered arises in
the question of volenti arises in advance of the negligent act which
such cases the question is whether or not there is some factor
h which he should conclude that a risk is likely to be created
In the instant case and in several of the cases in which
examined the relevant factor is the state of intoxicatise.
also includes cases in which the person injured is a
the public are admitted. Though of assistance to
a case usually involves considerations which
j intoxication of the defendant constitut
application of the doctrine is to be consi
the injured plaintiff is a passenger in a
a greater or lesser degree of intoxic
We have been referred to a n
and in Dominion jurisdiction

se formulation of the doctrine and its legal effect they are relevant to the issues that
e in this appeal in three respects. (1) To the question whether the maxim can ever be
plied in cases in which the negligence ie, the breach of duty of care, arises solely out of
he *Donoghue v Stevenson* concept of a duty owed by one person to another without that
duty being imposed by any special relationship such as master and servant or occupier
and licensee (see *Donoghue v Stevenson* [1932] AC 562, [1932] All ER Rep 1). (2) Whether
or not the appropriate method of reflecting the plaintiff's own responsibility in such
circumstances is through contributory negligence rather than through the principle of
volenti. (3) As examples of the application of the maxim in comparable situations. It is
in respect of these matters that the authorities cited to us fall to be considered.

The appropriate starting point is *Dann v Hamilton* [1939] 1 All ER 59, [1939] 1 KB 509.
The facts of that case were that the plaintiff knew that the driver of the car in which she
was a passenger was under the influence of drink and therefore the chances of an accident
were substantially increased. Nevertheless, she chose to remain in the car and was injured
owing to the negligent driving of the defendant. She had previously made a remark 'if
anything is going to happen, it will happen'.

Asquith J considered textbook and other authorities to the effect that the maxim had
no application to the law of negligence and to the fact that most authorities were
concerned with what I have described as the first category of case in which the maxim
has arisen, viz where the negligent act has already occurred before the plaintiff is exposed
to risk from it. The judge did not deal with contributory negligence since he was not
invited by counsel to do so. He expressed his decision in these terms ([1939] 1 All ER 59
at 64–65, [1939] 1 KB 509 at 518–519):

'Then, to take the last step, suppose that such a driver is likely to drive negligently
on the material occasion, not because he is known to the plaintiff to have driven
negligently in the past, but because he is known to the plaintiff to be under the
influence of drink. That is the present case. Ought the result to be any different?
After much debate, I have come to the conclusion that it should not, and that the
plaintiff, by embarking in the car, or re-entering it, with knowledge that through
drink the driver had materially reduced his capacity for driving safely, did not
impliedly consent to, or absolve the driver from liability for, any subsequent
negligence on his part whereby the plaintiff might suffer harm. There may be cases
in which the drunkenness of the driver at the material time is so extreme and so
glaring that to accept a lift from him is like engaging in an intrinsically and
obviously dangerous occupation, inter-meddling with an unexploded bomb or
lking on the edge of an unfenced cliff. It is not necessary to decide whether in
a case the maxim *volenti non fit injuria* would apply, for in the present case I find
ce that the driver's degree of intoxication fell short of this degree. I therefore
wi that the defence fails, and the claim succeeds. I arrive at this conclusion
sho the ff reluctance in that it would be unjust that the deceased man's estate
his es ected from suit by the mere fact that he got drunk before committing
egligence, whereas, if he had committed the same act when sober,
It seems t ve been liable.

clearly envisa
plaintiff's clain s judgment was one of fact rather than law since Asquith J
judges in subse in which the application of the maxim could defeat a
rejected.
In *Insurance Com* has met with criticism both by academic writers and by
a situation which d ome cases his decision has been applied and in others
was caused by the n
passenger, the plainti CLR 39 the High Court of Australia was faced with
evidence there was cons from the facts in *Dann v Hamilton*. An accident
iver of a car due to his intoxication and his
either the plaintiff nor the defendant gave
the proper finding on causation and it was

this fact which induced Dixon J to dissent from the views of his brethren. The majority
a of the court, Latham CJ and Rich J, held that the plaintiff's claim failed though they
differed as to their grounds for so holding. Dixon J considered *Dann v Hamilton* and cited
the passage already set out in this judgment and said (at 57):

> 'If he knowingly accepts the voluntary services of a driver affected by drink, he
> cannot complain of improper driving caused by his condition, because it involves
> no breach of duty.'
b

A little later he said:

> 'The second principle that has been applied is that referred in English law to the
> title *volenti non fit injuria*, under which is placed the voluntary assumption of risk
> which in the United States seems to exist as a separate rule. Here, too, some actual
> notice of the state of the driver must be necessary. But of course knowledge of what
c > is apparent may readily be inferred. The result of the application of this principle, it
> may be thought, should not differ from the result brought about by the first.'

And later he considers the decision of *Dann v Hamilton* and cites the passage which has
already been set out in this judgment (see 77 CLR 39 at 59). He concludes:

> 'No doubt the issue his Lordship propounded for decision was one of fact but,
d > with all respect, I cannot but think that the plaintiff should have been precluded.
> Every element was present to form a conscious and intentional assumption of the
> very risk for which she suffered.'

It is clear there that Dixon J would have found the maxim established in *Dann v Hamilton*
and have rejected the plaintiff's claim, though in fact he preferred the solution to the
e problem based on the duty which arose out of the relationship of driver to his passenger.
Although not a case involving a motor vehicle or a state of intoxication *Dann v Hamilton*
was considered by the Court of Appeal in *Slater v Clay Cross Co Ltd* [1956] 2 All ER 625,
[1956] 2 QB 264. Stated shortly the facts were that the plaintiff, a pedestrian, used a short
tunnel as a walkway in accordance with local usage known to the defendants, who had a
f small gauge railway line running through it. The plaintiff was injured by a train, the
driver of which had failed to comply with his instructions with regard to speed and
warning signals. Denning LJ cited *Dann v Hamilton* together with the explanation given
by Asquith J that he considered contributory negligence would have been applied if
raised and said ([1956] 2 All ER 625 at 628, [1956] 2 QB 264 at 270–271):

> 'In so far as he decided that the doctrine of volenti did not apply, I think the
g > decision was quite correct. In so far as he suggested that the plea of contributory
> negligence might have been available, I agree with him. Applying that decision to
> this case, it seems to me that, when the plaintiff walked in the tunnel, although it
> may be said that she voluntarily took the risk of danger from the running of the
> railway in the ordinary and accustomed way, nevertheless she did not take the risk
> of negligence by the driver. Her knowledge of the danger is a factor in contributory
h > negligence, but is not a bar to the action.'

In my view this case raised questions similar to those which arise in the 'spectator
sports' cases and involves the question whether or not the negligence giving rise to the
injury occurred outside the ambit of the risks inherent in the general use of the tunnel.
I do not read Denning LJ's words as meaning more than he approved the decision of
j Asquith J in *Dann v Hamilton* on its facts.
In 1956 the Supreme Court of Canada in *Car and General Insurance Corp Ltd v Seymour*
2 DLR (2d) 369 considered the position of a passenger injured by the negligent driving
of a person who was under the influence of drink. The journey was a long one and the
driver did not exhibit symptoms of intoxication at the outset of the journey but did so
later. The importance of the position for the purposes of the instant appeal is that the

court held that the time at which the application of the maxim volenti non fit injuria is to be considered is the knowledge and consent of the passenger at the time of the *a* inception of the journey. Rand J rejected the criticism of *Dann v Hamilton* by Dixon J in *Joyce's* case on this basis.

In *Wooldridge v Sumner* [1962] 2 All ER 978, [1963] 2 QB 43, again a spectator sports case, in which a photographer attending the National Horse Show was injured by a horse ridden by a very experienced rider, the object of the competition was to complete the appropriate circuit in the fastest time and the rider was attempting to achieve this and *b* the court found that that rider through an error of judgment had taken a corner too fast and that thereafter, for some other reason, the horse became temporarily out of control. This case is relied on by the plaintiff in the instant appeal in support of the proposition that the maxim has no application to the tort of negligence simpliciter. In his judgment Sellers LJ said ([1962] 2 All ER 978 at 983, [1963] 2 QB 43 at 57):

c

'If the conduct is deliberately intended to injure someone whose presence is known, or is reckless and in disregard of all safety of others so that it is a departure from the standards which might reasonably be expected in anyone pursuing the competition or game, then the performer might well be held liable for any injury his act caused. There would, I think, be a difference, for instance, in assessing blame which is actionable between an injury caused by a tennis ball hit or a racket *d* accidentally thrown in the course of play into the spectators at Wimbledon and a ball hit or a racket thrown into the stands in temper or annoyance when play was not in progress. The relationship of spectator and competitor or player is a special one, as I see it, as the standard of conduct of the participant, as accepted and expected by the spectator, is that which the sport permits or involves. The different relationship involves its own standard of care.'   *e*

Diplock LJ said ([1962] 2 All ER 978 at 990, [1963] 2 QB 43 at 69):

'In my view, the maxim, in the absence of express contract, has no application to negligence simpliciter where the duty of care is based solely on proximity or "neighbourship" in the Atkinian sense [see *Donoghue v Stevenson* [1932] AC 562 at *f* 580, [1932] All ER Rep 1 at 11, per Lord Atkin]. The maxim in English law presupposes a tortious act by the defendant. The consent that is relevant is not consent to the risk of injury but consent to the lack of reasonable care that may produce that risk (see *Kelly v. Farrans Ltd.* ([1954] NI 41 at 45), per LORD MACDERMOTT), and requires on the part of the plaintiff at the time at which he gives his consent full *g* knowledge of the nature and extent of the risk that he ran . . . In *Dann v. Hamilton*, ASQUITH, J., expressed doubts whether the maxim ever could apply to license in advance a subsequent act of negligence, for, if the consent precedes the act of negligence, the plaintiff cannot at that time have full knowledge of the extent as well as the nature of the risk which he will run. ASQUITH, J., however, suggested that the maxim might, nevertheless, be applicable to cases where a dangerous physical condition had been brought about by the negligence of the defendant, and *h* the plaintiff with full knowledge of the existing danger elected to run the risk thereof.'

It is clear that Diplock LJ was expressing this view in the context of the facts of the case then before him and it seems to me that the meaning that he was seeking to express is to be derived by earlier passages in his judgment. Diplock LJ said ([1962] 2 All ER 978 at *j* 988, [1963] 2 QB 43 at 66–67):

'. . . *Hall v. Brooklands Auto-Racing Club* ([1933] 1 KB 205, [1932] All ER Rep 208) [is one of the cases] in which the actual participants in the game or competition have been sued as well as the occupiers of the premises on which it took place, but juries

have acquitted the participants of negligence and the cases are reported only on the
a duty owed by an occupier of premises to invitees. Such duty is not based on
negligence simpliciter, but flows from a consensual relationship between the
occupier and the invitee; there is thus no conceptual difficulty in implying a term
in that consensual relationship (which, in the reported cases, has in fact been a
contractual relationship) that the occupier need take no precautions to protect the
invitee from all or from particular kinds of risks incidental to the game or
b competition which the spectator has come on the premises to watch. In the case of a
participant, however, any duty of care which he owes to the spectator is not based
on any consensual relationship between them but on mere "proximity", if I may use
that word as a compendious expression of what makes one person a "neighbour" of
another in the sense of LORD ATKIN's definition in Donoghue v. Stevenson ... The
matter has to be looked at from the point of view of the reasonable spectator as well
c as the reasonable participant; not because of the maxim volenti non fit injuria, but
because what a reasonable spectator would expect a participant to do without
regarding it as blameworthy is as relevant to what is reasonable care as what a
reasonable participant would think was blameworthy conduct in himself. The same
idea was expressed by SCRUTTON, L.J., in Hall v. Brooklands Auto-Racing Club ([1933] 1
KB 205 at 214, [1932] All ER Rep 208 at 213): "What is reasonable care would
d depend on the perils which might be reasonably expected to occur, *and the extent to
which the ordinary spectator might be expected to appreciate and take the risk of such
perils.*" (Diplock LJ's emphasis.)

It seems to me that the sense in which Diplock LJ, therefore, was making the remarks
cited in the first passage from his judgment is that he was drawing a distinction between
e dangers created in the actual course of the game or contest, even if through some casual
lack of care or skill, and the situation which arises where a spectator is injured by some
negligent or reckless act by a participant which occurs quite outside the ambit of the
game in question. In such a case the spectator's cause of action will necessarily have to be
based on the Atkinian neighbour principle since that is the nature of the duty which the
competitor would owe to the spectator in those particular circumstances. It seems to me,
f therefore, that the maxim would not apply in those circumstances since whereas the
spectator would anticipate danger from the performance of the game itself he could not
anticipate or condone in advance something which he could not possibly foresee as being
likely to occur.

For my part I do not derive great assistance from Nettleship v Weston [1971] 3 All ER
581, [1971] 2 QB 691 since although it concerned a claim by a passenger against a driver
g it was not a case of intoxication. The passenger had offered to give driving lessons to the
wife of a friend. Before doing so he had inquired whether or not there was in force a
policy of insurance and he was given the assurance that there was and was shown a fully
comprehensive policy which covered a passenger in the event of accident. It therefore
seems to me quite clear that the maxim would have no application: he did not consent
to accept the risk of injury or condone in advance the learner's negligence. I find it
h therefore surprising that reliance was placed on the maxim at all. Observations by the
members of the court have to be read in the light of those facts. Lord Denning MR said
([1971] 3 All ER 581 at 587–588, [1971] 2 QB 691 at 701–702):

'The plaintiff must agree, expressly or impliedly, to waive any claim for any
injury that may befall him due to the lack of reasonable care by the defendant: or
j more accurately, due to the failure of the defendant to measure up to the standard
of care that the law requires of him. That is shown in England by Dann v Hamilton
and Slater v Clay Cross Co Ltd; and in Canada by Lehnert v Stein ((1962) 36 DLR (2d)
159); and in New Zealand by Morrison v Union Steamship Co of New Zealand Ltd
([1964] NZLR 468). The doctrine has been so severely curtailed that in the view of
Diplock LJ ...'

and he cites the passage in *Wooldridge v Sumner* [1962] 2 All ER 978 at 990, [1963] 2 QB
43 at 69 which I have already set out in this judgment. Lord Denning MR continued: *a*

'Applying the doctrine in this case, it is clear that Mr Nettleship did not agree to
waive any claim for injury that might befall him. Quite the contrary. He enquired
about the insurance policy so as to make sure that he was covered.'

Salmon LJ said ([1971] 3 All ER 581 at 589–590, [1971] 2 QB 691 at 703–704):   *b*

'Any driver normally owes exactly the same duty to a passenger in his car as he
does to the general public, namely to drive with reasonable care and skill in all the
relevant circumstances. As a rule, the driver's personal idiosyncrasy is not a relevant
circumstance. In the absence of a special relationship what is reasonable care and
skill is measured by the standard of competence usually achieved by the ordinary
driver. In my judgment, however, there may be special facts creating a special   *c*
relationship which displaces this standard or even negatives any duty, although the
onus would certainly be on the driver to establish such facts. With minor
reservations I respectfully agree with and adopt the reasoning and conclusions of Sir
Owen Dixon in his judgment in *Insurance Comr v Joyce*. I do not however agree that
the mere fact that the driver has, to the knowledge of his passenger, lost a limb or
an eye or is deaf can affect the duty which he owes the passenger to drive safely. It is   *d*
well known that many drivers suffering from such disabilities drive with no less
skill and competence than the ordinary man. The position, however, is totally
different when, to the knowledge of the passenger, the driver is so drunk as to be
incapable of driving safely. Quite apart from being negligent, a passenger who
accepts a lift in such circumstances clearly cannot expect the driver to drive other
than dangerously. The duty of care springs from relationship. The special   *e*
relationship which the passenger has created by accepting a lift in the circumstances
postulated surely cannot entitle him to expect the driver to discharge a duty of care
or skill which ex hypothesi the passenger knows the driver is incapable of
discharging. Accordingly in such circumstances, no duty is owed by the driver to
the passenger to drive safely, and therefore no question of volenti non fit injuria can
arise. The alternative view is that if there is a duty owed to the passenger to drive   *f*
safely, the passenger by accepting a lift has clearly assumed the risk of the driver
failing to discharge that duty. What the passenger has done goes far beyond
establishing mere "scienter". If it does not establish "volens", it is perhaps difficult
to imagine what can. Such a case seems to me to be quite different from *Smith v
Baker & Sons* [1891] AC 325, [1891–4] All ER Rep 69 and *Slater v Clay Cross Co Ltd*.
Like Sir Owen Dixon, I prefer to rest on the special relationship between the parties   *g*
displacing the prima facie duty on the driver to drive safely rather than on the
ground of volenti non fit injuria. Whichever view is preferable, it follows that, in
spite of the very great respect I have for any judgment of Lord Asquith, I do not
accept that *Dann v Hamilton* was correctly decided . . . I should like to make it plain
that I am not suggesting that whenever a passenger accepts a lift knowing that the
driver has had a few drinks, this displaces the prima facie duty ordinarily resting on   *h*
a driver, let alone that it establishes volenti non fit injuria. Indeed, Sir Owen Dixon
dissented in *Joyce's* case, because he did not agree that the evidence was capable of
establishing that the plaintiff passenger knew that the driver was so drunk as to be
incapable of exercising ordinary care and skill. In practice it would be rare indeed
that such a defence could be established.'   *j*

In *Bennett v Tugwell (an infant)* [1971] 2 All ER 248, [1971] 2 QB 267 Ackner J
considered the effect of the maxim volenti non fit injuria in the light of an express notice
'Passengers travelling in this vehicle do so at their own risk' which had been exhibited by
the defendant on his father's motor car which he was driving. The relevance of the
decision to the instant appeal lies in the view which Ackner J took to the question

whether or not an injured passenger is volens is an objective and not subjective one. He
a said ([1971] 2 All ER 248 at 252, [1971] 2 QB 267 at 273):

> 'Can the defendant invoke the defence of volenti non fit injuria? The gist of this
> defence is not so much the assent to the infliction of injury as the assumption of the
> risk of such injury (see Fleming on Tort ((2nd edn, 1961) p 253), cited by Salmond
> on the Law of Torts ((15th edn, 1969) p 668)). Counsel for the plaintiff submits that
> a subjective test is the appropriate one and that I am concerned with what was in
b > the innermost recesses of the parties' minds. I do not accept that this is so. What is
> required is an objective approach. Legal enquiry into a person being "volens" is not
> into what he feels or inwardly consents to, but into what his conduct or words
> evidence that he is consenting to.'

This is a matter which arises on this appeal and I will have to consider it hereafter when I
c turn to the more detailed facts of this case.

Support for the proposition that the appropriate method by which to reflect a
passenger's voluntary assumption of risk is by apportionment on the basis of contributory
negligence rather than the application of the volenti maxim is to be derived from the
judgment of Watkins J in *Owens v Brimmell* [1976] 3 All ER 765, [1977] QB 859. In my
view the judge based his conclusion on the fact that the authorities entitled him to treat
d the matter as one of contributable negligence rather than a finding that the claim was
barred by the application of the principle of volenti. Other authorities base the decision
on the application of that maxim.

In *Ashton v Turner* [1980] 3 All ER 870, [1981] QB 137 Ewbank J having found against
the plaintiff on the basis of public policy also found that the volenti maxim would have
defeated his claim also since the plaintiff knew that the driver was in an intoxicated
e condition.

The last authority to which I feel it is necessary to refer is a recent case in this court,
Pitts v Hunt [1990] 3 All ER 344, [1990] 3 WLR 542. The facts were that the plaintiff,
who was 18 years of age, was a pillion passenger on a motor cycle driven by the defendant,
who was 16 years of age. To the plaintiff's knowledge the defendant rider of the motor
f cycle was neither insured nor had he a licence. The driving followed nearly four hours of
attendance at a disco in which a substantial amount of drink had been taken by both.
The judge described the driving as 'reckless, irresponsible and idiotic', and it was found
that the method of driving was deliberate in order to frighten the public. The judge and
the Court of Appeal dismissed the plaintiff's appeal against the rejection of his claim on
three grounds. Firstly that they were engaged in a joint illegal enterprise and that the
g claim was barred by the maxim ex turpi causa non oritur actio. The judge also found
that the claim would be defeated on the basis of the maxim volenti non fit injuria, but
for the fact that that defence was not possible in the context of a motor accident by virtue
of s 148(3) of the Road Traffic Act 1972. Beldam LJ clearly found that this statutory
provision did prevent the operation of the maxim but equally clearly was of the view
that, but for the provision, the maxim would have operated to defeat the plaintiff's claim.
h He said ([1990] 3 All ER 344 at 356, [1990] 3 WLR 542 at 556):

> 'As to the defence raised that the plaintiff voluntarily undertook to run the risk of
> injury by taking part in such a foolhardy, risky and illegal activity, I would have
> been prepared to say that it was obvious from the description of the plaintiff's
> behaviour whilst he was participating that he had done so. However the judge
> accepted that the effect of s 148(3) of the Road Traffic Act 1972 was that any
j > agreement or understanding that the risk of injury would be the plaintiff's was of
> no effect.'

He then continued by considering whether or not the judge was correct in so interpreting
that provision of the Road Traffic Act 1972. Balcombe and Dillon LJJ both considered
that the defence of volenti could not be relied on by virtue of that statutory provision,

but neither dissented from the view expressed by Beldam LJ as to the application of the maxim had it not been for that statutory provision.

I have referred to these authorities at some length in order to resolve the questions to which I have already referred.

As to the first and second questions, is the maxim volenti non fit injuria available as a defence in a case which is concerned with the tort of negligence? Or is the appropriate procedure to deal with the matter on the basis of contributory negligence?

I have no doubt that in appropriate cases the maxim can apply so as to defeat the plaintiff's claim. It has been held to be so in a number of cases which have been cited and was so held in the recent case of *Pitts v Hunt* to which I have just referred. For the reasons that I have already given I consider that Diplock LJ's dicta, approved as it was by Lord Denning MR in *Nettleship v Weston*, was not intended to apply to a driver/passenger situation. This is so because, as I believe, it was not intended so to apply or on the basis that a special relationship does exist between a driver and his passenger. Where a plaintiff is aware that his driver is to some extent intoxicated his responsibility can be reflected by an apportionment on the basis of contributory negligence. Whether such a course is appropriate or whether the maxim volenti applies depends on the facts of each case. In particular it is relevant to consider the degree of intoxication and the nature of the act to be performed by the driver. In motoring cases it may well be that an apportionment on the basis of contributory negligence will usually be the appropriate course but in my view to pilot an aircraft requires a far higher standard of skill and care than driving a motor car and the effect of intoxication becomes all the more important. It seems to me from the authorities cited that this is the approach which the courts ought to apply to this problem: how intoxicated was the driver? How obvious was this to the plaintiff, and the extent of the potential risk to the plaintiff if he voluntarily accepts the offer of carriage?

In the light of these observations I turn next to the crucial issue in this case. Did the plaintiff voluntarily accept the risk of injury, and of the defendant's likely breach of duty in negligence with full knowledge of the facts?

I therefore first consider the position on the basis that the plaintiff himself was sober, or at least not so intoxicated as the result of alcohol as to be incapable of assessing the risk. I would unhesitatingly answer this question 'Yes'. The facts were: (1) the deceased pilot had consumed at least the equivalent of 17 whiskies and when absorption rate is considered over the period of time involved must, in fact, have consumed rather more. (2) The plaintiff was drinking with him over several hours and knew how much the deceased pilot had had to drink. (3) The risk of accident was manifest to any sober person when the activity to be carried out involves flying an aeroplane. The risk is far greater than driving a car in a similar condition of insobriety. The plaintiff had flown with the deceased pilot before; he co-operated and, indeed, encouraged the deceased pilot throughout; he drove the pilot to the airfield and filled the aeroplane with aviation spirit. The purpose of going to the airfield can only have been to fly in the aircraft. That the pilot was in fact incapable of flying the aircraft is demonstrated by a number of factors. Firstly he took off down wind and uphill, a highly dangerous manoeuvre itself, and in fact only just managed to get airborne shortly before the end of the runway. Evidence suggests that the aircraft was out of control virtually at all times thereafter. (4) The plaintiff not only accepted the offer of being taken for a joyride in the aircraft, but actively sought it. Discussion as to this possibility had taken place at the first public house, the Red Lion in Harlow, and again took place at the Blue Boar when the deceased pilot was present. Without the plaintiff's co-operation the flight in the aircraft could never have taken place at all since the deceased pilot had no motor car and the other man was disqualified from driving.

Thus on the basis that the plaintiff himself was capable of appreciating the full nature and extent of the risk and voluntarily accepted it, I would have no doubt whatever that this maxim would have applied to defeat his claim. If this was not a case of volenti non fit injuria I find it very difficult to envisage circumstances in which that can ever be the case.

However, the position is that the plaintiff himself must have consumed an amount of drink not dissimilar to that consumed by the deceased pilot and, therefore, the question falls to be considered whether or not his own condition was such as to render him incapable of fully appreciating the nature and extent of the risk and of voluntarily accepting it.

This matter does not seem to have been canvassed to any great extent in evidence and was not argued in any great detail before this court. Passages possibly relevant to it appear from the transcript of the evidence:

'Q. Looking back on it now, Mr Morris, you must have been aware that Murray had been drinking too much, do you agree? A. As I had had too much to drink, I probably had not noticed that he had . . .

Q. Do you think now, I know you have had an accident, perhaps it is a bit unfair, do you accept that flying in a private aeroplane is an intrinsically dangerous pastime? Do you agree with that? A. Yes, I do.

Q. What do you think about flying in a private aeroplane with a drunken pilot? What is your view about that? A. It is a silly thing to do.

Q. Do you say that had you been sober you would not have done it, is that what you say? A. No doubt.

Q. But you say the reason why you went was because you yourself had been drinking, is that right? A. That is correct.

Q. You were not so drunk that you were unconscious, were you? You were merry, is that a way of putting it? A. I would say so.

Judge Rice. Who drove to the aerodrome? A. I do not recall, but I assume it was me . . .

Q . . . you were anxious to get on this flight, were you not? A. I was anxious to start the engine.

Q. And to fly? A. Well, I imagine so.

Q. Had you been sober you would have been aware that if you fly with a drunken pilot there is a danger that you could crash? A. I agree.

Q. Had you been sober you would not have gone, is that correct? A. Yes, I believe so.

These answers in my view have to be read in the context of the express finding of fact by the judge that the plaintiff's memory was episodic by reason of his injuries. Unhappily, the judge did not seem to consider at all the problem which arises in the context of the plaintiff's own state of intoxication. This may well be because it does not seem to have been canvassed except in the sense indicated by the passages cited above. It has been submitted to this court that the proper test of this, that is to say the plaintiff's appreciation of the risk, and his consent to it, is an objective one and the passage which I have cited from Ackner J in *Bennett v Tugwell (an infant)* [1971] 2 All ER 248, [1971] 2 QB 267 is relied on. I do not, for my part, go so far as to say that the test is an objective one (though if it is not a paradoxical situation arises that the plaintiff's claim could be defeated by the application of the maxim if he was sober, but he could recover damages if he was drunk), but unless there is specific evidence either from the plaintiff himself or from some other source that the plaintiff was in fact so intoxicated that he was incapable of appreciating the nature and extent of the risk and did not in fact appreciate it, and thus did not consent to it, it seems to me that the court is bound to judge the matter in the light of the evidence which is put before it for consideration. In this case the plaintiff did not say, 'I did not appreciate the risk as I was too drunk.' What he did say was that, looking back on it, he would not have gone on the flight had he not been drunk. This is a wholly different proposition. The evidence seems to me to establish that the plaintiff was not so drunk as to be incapable of appreciating the risk or of knowing the state of intoxication of the deceased pilot. Amongst the factors which tend to this conclusion seem to me to be that he himself drove the car to the aerodrome with no other object than of going on a flight *a* with the deceased pilot. He himself assisted to start the engine by swinging the propeller and filling it with petrol. He queried with the pilot whether he should 'radio in' to control. I do not feel that he could have done these things if he was seriously incapacitated by alcohol or unaware of knowing just what it was he was doing. He must have known a number of facts such as the amount of drink the deceased pilot had taken and the risks in general terms at least of flying in an aircraft. He was not himself so drunk as to be in a *b* state of incomprehension. He himself assented to the proposition that he was 'merry'. In my view, therefore, there was no evidence before the judge, even if the matter had been fully canvassed, which could have justified the proposition that the plaintiff's own condition was such as to render him incapable of appreciating the nature of the risk and its extent or indeed that he did in fact fail to appreciate the nature and extent of such risk. My conclusion, therefore, is that this case does fall within the exceptional *c* circumstances stated by Asquith J in *Dann v Hamilton* [1939] 1 All ER 59 at 64, [1939] 1 KB 509 at 518. I quote again:

> 'There may be cases in which the drunkenness of the driver at the material time is so extreme and so glaring that to accept a lift from him is like engaging in an intrinsically and obviously dangerous occupation . . .'   *d*

To accept a flight in an aeroplane piloted by a pilot who has had any significant amount of drink, let alone the amount which manifestly this pilot had had, is to engage in an intrinsically and obviously dangerous occupation. For these reasons, in my judgment, the judge ought to have found that the plaintiff's claim should be rejected on the basis of the application of the maxim volenti non fit injuria. It is, in my view, not necessary to *e* refer in any detail to the judgment of the judge. He gave his judgment, perhaps unwisely, impromptu. He was referred to *Dann v Hamilton* but drew the conclusion that the proper approach in the case was to apply contributory negligence principles rather than those of volenti. Part of his reasons are clearly wrongly expressed, either by reason of false transcription or perhaps because he omitted certain sentences from his own note. Although he purported to consider *Insurance Comr v Joyce* (1948) 77 CLR 39 and *Nettleship* *f* *v Weston* [1971] 3 All ER 581, [1971] 2 QB 691 it does not appear that, in fact, he drew any appropriate conclusions from either. Although he cited from the passage of Salmon LJ in *Nettleship v Weston* he did not point out that Salmon LJ considered that *Dann v Hamilton* was wrongly decided. The conclusion of the judge is expressed in these terms in the judgment:

> In this case it is right to say that the plaintiff was aware that Mr Murray had been *g* drinking heavily, but Mr Murray was able, as it were, to start this aeroplane. He even taxied the aeroplane to the place where petrol was sold, paid for the petrol and then was able, albeit in a somewhat inexpert way because his faculties were clearly affected by drink, but he was able to get the plane into the air, albeit it only flew for some three or four minutes before crashing in the way I have described. But, in my *h* view, this is not a case where one can say that the plaintiff consented to run the risk of the actual injuries that he subsequently suffered. This case falls far short of what would be necessary in order to successfully defend the action on the grounds of volenti non fit injuria. This is a case where, in my view, certainly there was contributory negligence by the plaintiff in that he boarded a plane and allowed himself to be flown when he knew that [Mr Murray] had consumed a considerable *j* amount of alcohol.'

In my view the judge clearly drew the wrong conclusion from the fact that the pilot did succeed in getting the aircraft airborne. The correct conclusion, it seems to me, was the fact that he took off down wind, a highly dangerous procedure, indicated he was not capable of flying the aircraft properly.

In my view the judge really did not consider the full implications of such authorities
a as were cited to him and for the reasons I have endeavoured to give I think the conclusion
that he reached was an incorrect one.

If I am wrong about this and the matter should be considered on the basis of
contributory negligence it seems to me that the judge was again in error in his
apportionment. On the facts that have been recited I could not find that the plaintiff's
own share of responsibility could be assessed at less than 50% and that is the apportionment
b that for my part I would have made.

In my view of the conclusion that I have reached it is not necessary to express any
views on any of the other issues. I would simply say that so far as the assessment of
damages is concerned it does seem to me that the judge's conclusion was over-favourable
to the plaintiff with regard to his assessment of past and future earnings and did not
sufficiently take into account the full cost of maintaining an infant child over a period of
c some years. For these reasons I doubt whether the assessment of damage was correct, but
express no further view on the matter.

None of the other issues arise in my view. There was no point in the judge assessing
the extent of the deceased pilot's estate, this was not an issue which arose in the case. His
task was simply to find liability and assess the damages. The other issues such as plene
administravit and the question of devastavit were matters for the Chancery Division and
d should not have been considered by the judge in this action however laudable the attempt
to do so in order to save court time may have been.

For these reasons I would allow this appeal and hold that the plaintiff's claim fails.

I should add that I agree with the comment made (a few weeks ago) by this court
sitting in its criminal jurisdiction that urgent steps should be taken to ensure that no
aircraft can be flown at all unless there is in force, in relation to all risks a policy of
e insurance in favour of any third party including a passenger (see *R v Warburton-Pitt*
(1990) Independent, 14 July). The aircraft concerned in this accident crashed on
agricultural land with minimal damage to crops. It was out of control and might have
crashed anywhere. It does not require any exercise of imagination to envisage that had it
crashed on a main road, or in the centre of a village, that the consequent damage might
have been of disaster proportion. Whether the appropriate steps can be taken through
f administrative channels, eg by the refusal of a licence without there being in force a
comprehensive policy of insurance of the type to which I have referred, or whether
legislation will be required to achieve this end I do not know, but I would hope that
urgent consideration will be given to this problem.

g **SIR GEORGE WALLER**. I agree with the judgments of Fox and Stocker LJJ. I will
briefly express my reasons. I do not repeat the account of what happened which has
already been set out by Fox and Stocker LJJ. I would just emphasise certain of the facts
before the aircraft took off. The deceased, Mr Murray, lent the plaintiff and Mr Moran
each £10 so that they could each pay for a round of drinks in turn and so between
lunchtime and 4 pm each one of the three would have the same number of drinks. Mr
h Murray had at least the equivalent of 17 whiskies and the plaintiff would have had a
similar amount. At 4 pm the plaintiff drove the other two to the airfield for the plaintiff
to fly with Mr Murray. The plaintiff agreed that it was a joyride. According to his inquest
statement the plaintiff had twice flown with Mr Murray before. When they arrived at
the aircraft the plaintiff helped to start it and also to refuel it.

j These facts show that the plaintiff was actively co-operating; it was a joyride for the
plaintiff piloted by Mr Murray, who the plaintiff must have known had had a great deal
to drink. To fly an aircraft having taken drink is adding to the risk of flying. It is difficult
to conceive anything more dangerous than to fly with a pilot who has consumed the
equivalent of 17 whiskies. The evidence was that Mr Murray took off down wind, a
major and very dangerous error on his part. With a 20-knot wind he was fortunate to

Application for judicial review

Andrew Caesar-Gordon, the chairman of the University of Liverpool Conservative *a*
Association, applied, with leave of Otton J given on 15 May 1989, for judicial review of
(i) decisions made on 8 November 1988 to withdraw permission for the association to
hold a meeting on 11 November 1988, (ii) decisions made on 7 December 1988 and 13
January 1989 to impose certain conditions in relation to a meeting to be held on 20
January 1989 and (iii) decisions made on 18 and 19 January 1989 to withdraw permission
for the meeting to be held on 20 January 1989 by way of declarations that the decisions *b*
were ultra vires being in breach of s 43 of the Education (No 2) Act 1986. In the course
of the hearing the applicant sought other relief in place of part of that sought in his
notice of motion under RSC Ord 53 (see p 824 *j* to p 825 *a*, post). The facts are set out in
the judgment of the court.

Richard Slowe for the applicant. *c*
Andrew Sander for the university.

Cur adv vult

25 May. The following judgment of the court was delivered.

WATKINS LJ. The applicant, the chairman of the University of Liverpool Conservative *d*
Association, applies by leave of Otton J for judicial review of decisions of the respondents,
the University of Liverpool, made in 1988 and 1989. The history giving rise to the
application can be shortly stated.

On 18 October 1988 the association applied to the University Guild of Undergraduates
for permission to hold a meeting on 11 November 1988 to be attended and addressed by
a member of the South African Embassy in London. On 19 October 1988 provisional *e*
permission to hold the meeting was granted subject to special conditions and 'co-
operation of the police outside the building'. Thereafter officers of the university were in
contact with the Merseyside Police Force. In particular on 4 November 1988 the
university security officer met and had a discussion with officers of that force. This was
followed by a meeting on 7 November 1988 between the senior assistant registrar, the
university security manager and police officers. In consequence on 8 November 1988 the *f*
registrar of the university wrote to the applicant informing him that he had decided to
withdraw permission for holding the meeting. The letter states, inter alia:

> 'Having made extensive enquiries and having considered such conditions which
> might be imposed, I am satisfied that in the circumstances of this case it is not
> reasonably practicable to make adequate arrangements to ensure that good order
> will be maintained. Pursuant to paragraph 2(i) of the University's Code of Practice *g*
> on Freedom of Speech you have the right to appeal against this decision to the Vice-
> Chancellor who will then determine the matter in consultation with the President
> of the Council.'

On 9 November Mr Baldwin, predecessor of the applicant as chairman of the association
lodged an appeal to the vice-chancellor against this decision. At the appeal the registrar *h*
and senior registrar confirmed that they had received representations from a wide range
of people concerning the proposed visits. They stated:

> 'The indications given by all of these were that, bearing in mind the strong
> emotive feelings that racial matters always aroused in the residential area adjacent
> to the University, a demonstration of major proportions against the visit would take *j*
> place.'

The vice-chancellor and the vice-president of the council of the university were
informed of the meetings which had taken place between university officers and the
police. The vice-chancellor, with whom the vice-president agreed, determined that, in
the light of all the circumstances, the decision of the registrar should stand.

a On 9 November 1988 the vice-chancellor by letter informed Mr Baldwin he had determined that the decision of the registrar should stand and that the invitation to the South African speaker must be withdrawn. Thus, the proposed meeting of 11 November 1988 did not take place.

On 30 November 1988 the association made an application to the Guild of Undergraduates for permission to hold a meeting on 20 January 1989 to be addressed by 'two first secretaries from the South African Embassy'. By letter dated 9 December 1988 b Mr Baldwin was informed that the application was—

'provisionally agreed, subject to special conditions and co-operation of the Police outside the Building . . .'

The special conditions were, as later revised and as relevant, as follows:

c '1. Attendance at the meeting is to be confined to students and staff of the University of Liverpool. Admission tickets may be personally issued to members of the University of Liverpool Conservative Association by an Officer of the Association no earlier than 13 January 1989. Publicity advertising the meeting to all members of the University should only be issued in accordance with paragraph 2 below.

d 2. Other than the issuing of invitations to members of the University of Liverpool Conservative Association as indicated above, there is to be no publicity of any kind for this meeting (including the production of leaflets and posters and the issuing of press releases), except that notices advertising the meeting may be posted within University premises, provided that such notices are not displayed before 9.00 a.m. on 20 January 1989 and that the wording of such notices has been cleared with the Permanent Secretary and Bursar in advance. The intention to hold such a meeting e should not be disclosed to any person other than a bona-fide Officer of the Association or an authorised Officer of the University. Any requests for information should be referred to the Registrar, without comment.

3. The number of people attending the meeting will be limited to the capacity of the venue (320 persons in the case of the Stanley Theatre). These persons will only be permitted to enter on production of a valid University of Liverpool Student or f Staff Card.'

On 12 January 1989 Mr Baldwin, on behalf of the association, appealed against the imposition of the original conditions. Having heard representations the vice-chancellor, in consultation with the president of the council, decided to vary the conditions attached to the proposed meeting of 20 January 1989. By letter dated 13 January 1989 the vice-chancellor informed Mr Baldwin of the conditions as revised. Between 13 January 1989 g and 18 January 1989 officers of the university received information from the police regarding the likely effect of the meeting of 20 January 1989 were it to take place. The police were very concerned about what in particular might happen in nearby Toxteth with its large coloured population. The university paid careful heed to that. By letter dated 18 January 1989 the registrar informed Mr Baldwin that he had decided to h withdraw permission for the meeting of 20 January 1989. He stated:

'Since the Vice-Chancellor's letter to you of 13 January, revising the special conditions, I consider that there has been a material change in the circumstances, which renders it likely that good order will not be maintained at the proposed meeting scheduled for 20 January.'

j Having set out matters of particular concern the registrar concluded:

'Having considered the situation most carefully, I have therefore decided that the material change in circumstances that has now occurred is such that it is no longer reasonably practicable to make adequate arrangements to ensure that good order will be maintained (reference special condition 10 and paragraph 2(h) of the Code of Practice on Freedom of Speech). Permission for the meeting is hereby withdrawn.'

Pursuant to paragraph 2(i) of the University's Code of Practice on Freedom of Speech, you have the right to appeal against the decision to the Vice-Chancellor who will *a* then determine the matter in consultation with the President of the Council.'

On 18 January 1989 Mr Baldwin appealed against this decision. The appeal was heard by the vice-chancellor and the president of the council in the presence of the senior assistant registrar on 19 January 1989. Later that day the vice-chancellor wrote to Mr Baldwin and stated:

b

'In consultation with the President I have reviewed the decision of the Registrar to withdraw permission for the meeting. Having carefully considered all the evidence and the representation you have made, I have decided to uphold the Registrar's decision. I confirm therefore that permission for the meeting is withdrawn. We shall notify the South African Embassy accordingly.'

As before, permission was in fact withdrawn because the university feared that in the *c* event of the meeting taking place public violence would erupt in Toxteth.

In this court the following concessions were made. (1) The university concedes that when deciding to impose conditions on the holding of the two LUCA speaker meetings and then subsequently deciding to ban each of them it took into account the risk of public disorder, that is to say: (i) disorder which might occur other than within the *d* university's private precincts or otherwise affect its private property; (ii) and, disorder there occasioned by members of the general public, being persons over whom the university had no control. (2) The applicant concedes that the university quite properly took into account when making its various decisions: (i) that there was also a risk of disorder in the university precincts or otherwise affecting its property, students and members; (ii) and, also the risk of disorder occasioned (wherever that might occur) by *e* persons over whom it did have control.

By his notice of application the applicant sought review of the following decisions: (1) The decisions made on 8 November 1988 to withdraw permission for the association to hold a meeting on 11 November 1988. (2) The decisions made on 7 December 1988 and 13 January 1989 to impose certain conditions in relation to a meeting to be held by the association on 20 January 1989. (3) The decisions made on 18 and 19 January 1989 to *f* withdraw permission for the meeting to be held on 20 January 1989.

The relief sought was as follows:

'1. A declaration that the decisions to withdraw permission for the meeting to be held on 11th November 1988 were ultra vires the University of Liverpool being in breach of the provisions of Section 43 of the Education (No 2) Act 1986.
2. A declaration that the following conditions imposed in relation to the meeting *g* to be held on 20th January 1989 were ultra vires the University of Liverpool being in breach of Section 43 of the said Act: 2.1 Requiring that information about the meeting be treated as confidential until 9.00 am on the day of the meeting. 2.2 In the circumstances of such restriction, requiring that attendance at the meeting only be permitted to those producing a valid student or staff card. 2.3 The decision to *h* reserve the right to charge the Association with the cost of security at such meetings.
3. A declaration that the decisions on 18th and 19th January 1989 to withdraw permission for the meeting to be held on 20th January 1989 were ultra vires being in breach of Section 43 of the said Act.'

In this court the applicant abandoned the relief sought under paras 1 and 3. Instead he seeks in addition to a declaration under para 2 by what we shall call para 4 a declaration *j* that:

'In the performance of its duty imposed under section 43(1) of the Education (No. 2) Act 1986, a University shall not take into account any risk of public disorder, being disorder which might occur other than within the University's private precincts or otherwise affecting its private property and disorder there occasioned by members of the general public, being persons over whom the University had no

control save and unless and to the extent that such public disorder gives rise to a risk
of disorder in the University precincts or otherwise affecting its property, students
or members, or the risk of disorder occasioned (wherever that might occur) by
persons over whom it did have control.'

The legislation to be considered is, so far as material, as follows:

'**43.** *Freedom of speech in universities, polytechnics and colleges.*—(1) Every individual
and body of persons concerned in the government of any establishment to which
this section applies shall take such steps as are reasonably practicable to ensure that
freedom of speech within the law is secured for members, students and employees
of the establishment and for visiting speakers.

(2) The duty imposed by subsection (1) above includes (in particular) the duty to
ensure, so far as is reasonably practicable, that the use of any premises of the
establishment is not denied to any individual or body of persons on any ground
connected with—(a) the beliefs or views of that individual or of any member of that
body; or (b) the policy or objectives of that body.

(3) The governing body of every such establishment shall, with a view to
facilitating the discharge of the duty imposed by subsection (1) above in relation to
that establishment, issue and keep up to date a code of practice setting out—(a) the
procedures to be followed by members, students and employees of the establishment
in connection with the organisation—(i) of meetings which are to be held on
premises of the establishment and which fall within any class of meeting specified
in the code; and (ii) of other activities which are to take place on those premises and
which fall within any class of activity so specified; and (b) the conduct required of
such persons in connection with any such meeting or activity; and dealing with
such other matters as the governing body consider appropriate.

(4) Every individual and body of persons concerned in the government of any
such establishment shall take such steps as are reasonably practicable (including
where appropriate the initiation of disciplinary measures) to secure that the
requirements of the code of practice for that establishment, issued under subsection
(3) above, are complied with.

(5) The establishments to which this section applies are—(a) any university; (b)
any establishment which is maintained by a local education authority and for which
section 1 of the 1968 (No. 2) Act (government and conduct of colleges of education
and other institutions providing further education) requires there to be an
instrument of government; and (c) any establishment of further education
designated by or under regulations made under section 27 of the 1980 Act as an
establishment substantially dependent for its maintenance on assistance from local
education authorities or on grants under section 100(1)(b) of the 1944 Act . . .'

The university code of practice made pursuant to sub-s (3), in our view local in its
scope, so far as material states:

'1. *Purpose of the Code of Practice*
. . . That any individual or body of persons shall be free, within the law, to hold
meetings or engage in such other activities of the type set out in Appendix II on the
premises of the University (including premises occupied by the Students' Union),
regardless of the beliefs, views, policies or objectives of that individual or body.

This Code sets out: (a) the procedures to be followed by members, students and
employees of the University in connection with the organisation of any public or
private meeting or activity which is to be held or take place on University premises.
(b) the conduct required in connection with any such meeting or activity; and (c)
steps which the University must take to secure compliance with the requirements
of this Code including, where appropriate, disciplinary measures.

All members, students and employees of the University shall be under a duty to
assist the University in securing freedom of speech within the law in the University
and promoting the principle set out above.

2. *Procedures for the Organisation of Meetings and Activities Involving the Use of University Premises*

...(f) The Registrar or his appointed officer will grant permission provided that he is satisfied that: (i) all reasonable steps can or will be taken to prevent any infringement of the law; and (ii) such conditions as he may reasonably require will be complied with; If the Registrar or his appointed officer withholds permission, he will explain in writing to the applicant the reasons for his decision.

(g) The conditions referred to in f(ii) above may include requirements that: (i) admissions tickets be issued...

(h) The Registrar or his appointed officer has discretion to lay down further conditions, if appropriate, after consultation with the police and the organising body. Thus he may, for example, require the designated meeting or activity to be declared public (which would permit a police presence); he may also arrange for employees of the University or (where appropriate) of the Guild of Undergraduates to be responsible for all security arrangements connected with the meeting or activity and appoint a member of staff as "controlling officer" for the occasion. If not satisfied that adequate arrangements can be made to maintain good order, he may refuse or withdraw permission for the meeting or activity. Such a step will normally only be taken after the police have been consulted...'

Against this background we have considered the applicant's principal submission, namely that in the performance of its duty under s 43(1) the university was not entitled to take into consideration a threat of public disorder outside the confines of the university by persons not in statu pupilari or otherwise within the control of the university.

Succinctly stated s 43(1) imposes on the university a positive duty to take steps to ensure that freedom of speech within the law is secured for members, students and employees and visiting speakers. This duty is of course qualified. The university need only take: 'Such steps as are reasonably practicable to ensure that freedom of speech within the law is secured...'

In our opinion the words 'reasonably practicable' qualify the steps which must be taken to ensure freedom of speech. The extent of that duty is made clear by sub-ss (3) and (4), which define the manner in which the duty imposed by sub-s (1) is to be discharged. The governing body of the university is required to issue a code of practice to be followed by *members of the university* in connection with the organisation of meetings and other activities *held on the premises of the university*. And the governing body of the university must take such steps as are reasonably practicable to secure that the requirements of the code of practice (*which apply to its members and its premises*) are complied with. Thus, we conclude, that on a true construction of s 43 the duty imposed on the university by sub-s (1) is local to the members of the university and its premises. Its duty is to ensure, so far as is reasonably practicable, that those whom it may control, that is to say its members, students and employees, do not prevent the exercise of freedom of speech within the law by other members, students and employees and by visiting speakers in places under its control. To require the university in the discharge of its duty under sub-s (1) to take into consideration persons and places outside its control would be, in our view, to impose on it an intolerable burden which Parliament cannot possibly have intended the university to bear.

It is stated in para 2(h) of the code as to the registrar:

'If not satisfied that adequate arrangements can be made to maintain good order, may refuse or withdraw permission for the meeting or activity.'

'Good order' can only, in our opinion, relate to good order within the precincts of the university. The code is concerned with procedures to be followed at meetings on university premises and does not envisage the university taking steps to ensure good order elsewhere. Such steps would be beyond the de facto powers of the university in any event.

Thus in discharging its duty under s 43(1) the university is not enjoined or entitled to a take into account threats of 'public disorder' outside the confines of the university by persons not within its control. Were it otherwise, the purpose of the section to ensure freedom of speech could be defeated since the university might feel obliged to cancel a meeting in Liverpool on the threat of public violence as far away as, for example, London, which it could not possibly have any power to prevent.

So we find as a matter of construction, that the applicant is entitled to a declaration in the terms sought by para 4. Counsel for the university submitted that it would have b been artificial and irresponsible for the university to ignore threatened disorder outside its precincts in Toxteth. The university, he submitted, was not entitled to divorce itself from the risk of disorder affecting property not its own and persons not its members. While this submission explains the reasons of the university authorities it does not, we think, deal with the meaning of s 43 on its true construction. In our view no possible criticism can attach to the well-meaning attitudes adopted finally by the university in c respect of the two meetings in question. The Act was recent and s 43 is not without its difficulties. We accept that the university authorities acted with the best possible motives to prevent breaches of the peace which they had good reason to believe would occur on and off their premises in the event of the meetings taking place.

Had they confined their reasons when refusing permission for the meetings to take place to the risk of disorder on university premises and among university members, it d may be that no objection could have been taken to either of their decisions. Where, however, the threat was of public disorder without the university, then, unless the threat was posed by members of the university, the matter was, in our opinion, entirely for the police.

It would be, in those circumstances, for the police to consider whether a meeting arranged at the university ought in the public interest on the grounds of an apprehended e breach of the peace to be forbidden or cancelled, and to consult with the university authorities and those organising the meetings to that end if needs be.

Doubtless they would, if necessary, in any event, use whatever powers they possess to ensure as well as they can that a breach of the peace did not occur. Of course, they might endeavour to insist that such a meeting did not take place. The scope of their powers, if any, in that context is not in point here and was not canvassed before us. Accordingly, f we do not attempt any definition of those they might be considered to possess under statute, or otherwise.

By para 2 of the original application to this court the applicant sought a declaration that the following conditions imposed in relation to the meeting to be held on 20 January 1989 were ultra vires the university by being in breach of s 43 of the 1986 Act:

g '2.1 Requiring that information about the meeting be treated as confidential until 9.00 am on the day of the meeting. 2.2 In the circumstances of such restriction, requiring that attendance at the meeting only be permitted to those producing a valid student or staff card. 2.3 The decision to reserve the right to charge the Association with the cost of security of such meetings.'

h It is submitted on behalf of the applicant that conditions 2.1 and 2.2 would hinder free speech and are therefore ultra vires the 1986 Act. It is further submitted that the relief sought under condition 2.3 is inconsistent with the duty imposed on the university to ensure free speech. We reject those submissions. On the information available to the officers of the university we are satisfied that the conditions in question could be considered to be necessary in the interests of free speech and good order in the event of j the meeting taking place. In our view in imposing these conditions the university was not acting ultra vires in breach of s 43 of the 1986 Act.

Declaration accordingly. No order as to costs.

Solicitors: *White & McDevitt* (for the applicant); *Alsop Wilkinson*, Liverpool (for the university).

Dilys Tausz   Barrister.

R v Parole Board, ex parte Bradley

QUEEN'S BENCH DIVISION
STUART-SMITH LJ AND SIMON BROWN J
12, 13, 14 MARCH, 4 APRIL 1990

Prison – Release on licence – Refusal to release on licence – Danger to public safety – Test of dangerousness to the public to be applied by Parole Board – Prisoner serving discretionary life sentence – Prisoner having served period necessary to satisfy requirements of deterrence and rehabilitation – Parole Board refusing to recommend applicant for release because of risk to public – Whether Parole Board applying correct test of dangerousness in refusing to recommend prisoner for release – Whether correct test likelihood that prisoner would probably commit further serious offences.

Prison – Release on licence – Refusal to release on licence – Reasons for refusal – Prisoner serving discretionary life sentence – Whether Parole Board required to inform discretionary life prisoner of reasons for refusal to recommend release – Whether contrary to rules of natural justice not to inform prisoner of reasons.

In 1976 the applicant was sentenced to life imprisonment, having pleaded guilty to offences of indecent assault and assault occasioning actual bodily harm on a 14-year-old girl and attempted murder of a 17-year-old girl. When the applicant was arrested on the attempted murder charge he told the police that he had wanted 'to see what it was like to kill somebody'. On his first review for parole in June 1986 the Parole Board decided not to recommend the applicant for release on licence. Later that year the applicant was assessed by a consultant forensic psychiatrist who reported to the board that in her opinion there was no evidence to suggest that the applicant would present a danger to the public if released. In 1987 the applicant's case was again considered by the board. The applicant believed, based on what he had been told by probation and prison officers, that he had received favourable reports from the prison and that none of the reports available to the board indicated that he any longer represented a danger to the public. However, the board again refused to recommend the applicant for release since they were not satisfied that, in view of the nature of his offences, the risk to the public in relation to the applicant's dangerousness in the community had been reduced to an acceptable level. The applicant's request to be given the reasons for the board's decision was refused. He applied for judicial review of the board's refusal to recommend him for release on licence or to disclose the reasons for that decision, contending (i) that the test of dangerousness to be applied by the board in determining whether to recommend for release discretionary life prisoners once they had served the period advised by the Lord Chief Justice and the trial judge as the minimum necessary to satisfy the requirements of deterrence and retribution (the tariff period) was the test of likelihood that the prisoner would probably commit further serious offences if released, ie the test controlling the imposition of discretionary life sentences, and not the test of risk to the public adopted by the board, which was less favourable to the prisoner, and (ii) that the board's refusal to give reasons was contrary to natural justice.

Held – The application would be dismissed for the following reasons—

(1) The imposition of a life sentence could only be justified by a very high degree of perceived public danger, but, once lawfully imposed, the life sentence then justified the prisoner's continued detention even though the risk to the public as ultimately perceived was substantially less than the actual probability of the prisoner committing further serious offences on release. Accordingly, the test to be applied by the Parole Board in deciding whether to recommend for release on licence a prisoner serving a discretionary life sentence was not the same as that which applied when the sentence was imposed but was instead a lower test, less favourable to the prisoner, involving an assessment of the

risk to the public in relation to the prisoner's dangerousness in the community and
a whether such risk was acceptable. It followed that the board had applied the correct test
in refusing to recommend the applicant for release on licence. Moreover, the board had
reached a reasonable decision since, in the absence of any clear explanation of motivation,
the applicant's offences clearly indicated a danger to the public, and although the applicant
had completed his tariff period it was not clear that he presented less danger to the public,
particularly in view of his remark to the police that he had wanted to see what it was like
b to kill someone (see p 838 a to f and p 839 j to p 840 a, post).

(2) The Parole Board were not under a duty to inform a prisoner of their reasons not to
recommend him for release on licence, regardless of whether he was serving a mandatory
life sentence or a discretionary life sentence, and consequently the board had not acted
contrary to natural justice in refusing to inform the applicant of their reasons for so
deciding (see p 841 a b and p 842 d e, post); Payne v Lord Harris of Greenwich [1981] 2 All
c ER 842 followed.

Per curiam. Although the level of risk required to justify the continued detention of a
discretionary life prisoner who has served the tariff period necessary to satisfy the
requirements of deterrence and rehabilitation must remain undefined, the risk must be
sufficient to be unacceptable in the subjective judgment of the Parole Board, to whom
Parliament has entrusted the decision to release on licence. In exercising their judgment
d as to the level of risk acceptable the board must clearly have in mind all material
considerations, including the intrinsic and increasing unfairness of continuing the
prisoner's detention beyond the tariff period unless there is sufficient public risk to justify
that detention (p 838 g h, post).

Notes

e For parole of prisoners serving life sentences, see 37 Halsbury's Laws (4th edn) paras
1187–1188, 1190–1191, and for a case on the subject, see 37(3) Digest (Reissue) 406,
5341.

For the Criminal Justice Act 1967, s 61, see 34 Halsbury's Statutes (4th edn) 699.

Cases referred to in judgment

f Associated Provincial Picture Houses Ltd v Wednesbury Corp [1947] 2 All ER 680, [1948] 1
KB 223, CA.
CEMI Ltd, Re (18 February 1989, unreported), QBD.
Council of Civil Service Unions v Minister for the Civil Service [1984] 3 All ER 935, [1985] AC
374, [1984] 3 WLR 1174, HL.
Gunnell and Wilson v UK (7 September 1989, unreported), E Comm HR.
g IRC v National Federation of Self-Employed and Small Businesses Ltd [1981] 2 All ER 93,
[1982] AC 617, [1981] 2 WLR 722, HL.
Payne v Lord Harris of Greenwich [1981] 2 All ER 842, [1981] 1 WLR 754, CA.
Puhlhofer v Hillingdon London BC [1986] 1 All ER 467, [1986] AC 484, [1986] 2 WLR 259,
HL.
R v Dempster (1987) 9 Cr App R (S) 176, CA.
h R v Gaming Board for GB, ex p Benaim [1970] 2 All ER 528, [1970] 2 QB 417, [1970] 2
WLR 1009, CA.
R v Hodgson (1968) 52 Cr App R 113, CA.
R v O'Dwyer (1986) 86 Cr App R 313, CA.
R v Pither (1979) 1 Cr App R (S) 209, CA.
R v Secretary of State for the Home Dept, ex p Benson (1988) Independent, 16 November,
j DC.
R v Secretary of State for the Home Dept, ex p Gunnell (1984) Times, 7 November, [1984] CA
Transcript 391.
R v Secretary of State for the Home Dept, ex p Handscomb (1987) 86 Cr App R 59, DC.
R v Secretary of State for the Home Dept, ex p Harrison [1987] CA Transcript 1246.
R v Stewart (1989) 11 Cr App R (S) 132, CA.
R v Wilkinson (1983) 5 Cr App R (S) 105, CA.

Cases also cited
British Airways Board v Laker Airways Ltd [1984] 3 All ER 39, [1985] AC 58. HL.   a
Davies v Taylor [1972] 3 All ER 836, [1974] AC 207, HL.
Findlay v Secretary of State for the Home Dept [1984] 3 All ER 801, [1985] AC 318, HL.
Lonrho plc v Secretary of State for Trade and Industry, [1989] 2 All ER 609, [1989] 1 WLR
    525, HL.
Parkin v Norman [1982] 2 All ER 583, [1983] QB 92, DC.
R v Birch (1989) 90 Cr App R 78, CA.   b
R v Blogg (1981) 3 Cr App R (S) 114, CA.
R v De Havilland (1983) 5 Cr App R (S) 109, CA.
R v Mental Health Review Tribunal, ex p Clatworthy [1985] 3 All ER 699.
R v Secretary of State for the Home Dept, ex p Brind [1990] 1 All ER 469, [1990] 2 WLR 787,
    CA.
R v Secretary of State for the Home Dept, ex p Swati [1986] 1 All ER 717, [1986] 1 WLR 477,   c
    CA.
R v Secretary of State for Social Services, ex p Connolly [1986] 1 All ER 998, [1986] 1 WLR
    421, CA.
Weeks v UK (1987) 10 EHRR 293, E Ct HR.
Williams v Home Office [1981] 1 All ER 1151.
    d

Application for judicial review
William Russell Bradley, a prisoner serving a discretionary life sentence, applied, with
the leave of Otton J given on 15 June 1989, for judicial review by way of orders of
certiorari to quash the decisions of the Parole Board given in or about January 1988 and
on 6 July 1988 refusing to recommend the applicant for parole and refusing to inform
him of the reasons for the board's decision or to disclose the reports made available to   e
them, and for declarations (i) that the applicant was entitled to know the reasons for the
board's decision to refuse to recommend him for parole, (ii) that the applicant was
entitled to know the specific nature of the danger which the board considered him to
represent to the public and (iii) that the applicant was entitled to see and comment on
any reports that suggested or concluded that he continued to represent a danger to the
public. The facts are set out in the judgment of the court.   f

Edward Fitzgerald for the applicant.
David Pannick and Robert Howe for the board.

Cur adv vult
    g
4 April. The following judgment of the court was delivered.

STUART-SMITH LJ. This is the judgment of the court, to which both members have
contributed. This is an application for judicial review of two decisions of the Parole
Board. By the first taken in about January 1988 the board refused to recommend the
applicant for parole. By the second, given by letter dated 6 July 1988, the board refused   h
to give the applicant the reasons for their decision.

The history
    The applicant was born on 25 February 1958. On 9 February 1975 he was convicted
of the rape of a 15-year-old girl and sentenced to three months' detention. On 18 April
1976 he committed offences of indecent assault and assault occasioning actual bodily   j
harm on a 14-year-old girl and on 8 May 1976 he attempted to murder a 17-year-old girl.
He pleaded guilty to these three offences in the Crown Court at Cardiff on 4 October
1976 and was sentenced to life imprisonment, with concurrent sentences of 9 and 15
months for the indecent and actual bodily harm assaults. It is necessary to relate the facts
of the attempted murder in a little more detail. The applicant met the girl at a party and
they subsequently went to a disco; after the disco the girl allowed a certain amount of
sexual petting; however, when the applicant tried to have sexual intercourse with her,

she made it plain that she did not want it and pushed him off. When she tried to go he
a put his hands round her throat and started to throttle her, saying that he would kill her.
After a while he let go, she struggled to her feet and tried to escape. However, the
applicant pursued her, dragged her back to the bus shelter where the first assault had
taken place and again started to throttle her. She tried to struggle and again escaped for a
few moments; but in her flight she fell into a bramble bush and again the applicant
pulled her to the ground and tried to throttle her. On each occasion that he had his hands
b round her neck she said she was unable to breathe and thought she was going to pass out.
Eventually, however, she got away and sought help.

   When he was arrested the applicant told the police that he had nearly strangled her.
He is recorded as saying:

   'I tried to kill her. I wanted to see what it was like to kill somebody. People are
c   saying that I am a rapist, they are playing on my nerves. If I don't kill someone I'll
      kill myself.'

A little later he said: 'I don't know how to describe it. Something like snapped in my
head and I sort of attacked her.' He was asked if the girl had done anything to offend him
and he said: 'Nothing. I think I am going mad.' And he said: 'I lost control, it was like as
if I was somebody else. I put my hands on her neck and squeezed. I wanted to see what
d it would be like.'

   There were available at the Crown Court three medical reports on the applicant. Two
are not material for present purposes; they were concerned with a possible defence of
automatism based on epilepsy; there was no evidence to support this conclusion. The
third doctor, Dr Reeves, a psychiatrist, said this of the applicant:

   'He denies any sadistic or aggressive fantasies when masturbating. He does not
e   think he is oversexed. He does say that when he has sex with a girl, he finds that he
      is more excited when he digs his nails into the girl's back, and has specifically grown
      his nails long for this purpose. He used to dig his nails into the back of his fiancée. I
      do not think any sinister interpretation should be put on this. I have interviewed
      him a number of times, and formed the impression that there is more to learn about
      him than he is prepared to say. At a recent interview, I told him I did not believe
f   him and I felt that he was someone who once having become sexually excited was
      unable to exert sufficient self control to stop himself. He was very angry at this, and
      stormed out of my office, swearing and slamming the door. The next day he
      returned to apologise. There is no evidence of any great disordered personality. He
      denies any sadistic interest. He tells me that at school he was in a fight with a boy
      and the lad hit him quite severely over the head; there was a fuss and the boy
g   subsequently claimed that [the applicant] had tried to touch him up and spread
      around the school that [the applicant] was queer. [The applicant] said he could not
      cope with this and missed a lot of school because of it. He says that he is not
      homosexual and has no homosexual interest. He says he did not knock his fiancee
      around during sex. I feel that there is more to learn about this young man and he
h   has more to tell us in due course. In my opinion, it would be in his own interests
      and the general public's interests, if he spent a period of his sentence at Grendon
      Underwood. I think he needs to talk at length about those offences and discuss how
      they came to be performed as this is essential to restore his self respect. The danger
      is of course that because of the offences he will not form a stable relationship with
      the opposite sex and in his frustration have further sexual intercourse by force. He
j   could go to Grendon as a [young person] or serving a borstal sentence. I must point
      out to the Court however, that whilst I can recommend this as the Medical Officer,
      there is absolutely no guarantee that he will go to Grendon. In view of the absence
      of grossly unstable personality or psychopathic disorder, I consider the prognosis to
      be good, but this is providing that he gets help during his prison sentence should
      the Court imprison him. If, of course, it transpired that he was sadistically inclined,
      then the prognosis is not so good, but there is even greater reason why he should tell
      the doctor the truth and receive help, if this is in fact his problem.'

Counsel for the applicant submits, correctly in our view, that Dr Reeves was expressing two areas of concern: sadism and suppressed sexual orientation leading to frustration and *a* further sexual intercourse by force. If these matters could be resolved and he received help in prison the prognosis was good.

At trial the applicant's counsel realistically accepted that a life sentence was inevitable. In passing sentence Watkins J said:

> 'That is what I shall do for the reasons that follow: two experienced psychiatrists have examined you and have seen you on a number of occasions, if not numerous *b* occasions and they are baffled about your mental state, neither saying anything as far as any specific mental illness recognised under the provisions of the Act, recognised under the relevant Act of Parliament, namely the Mental Health Act 1959, and both of them feel that they are not able to. It is best that you should be put in some secure place so that other psychiatrists could take a prolonged look at you in order to see what has been responsible for provoking in you such terrible *c* violence when your desires for sexual intercourse are thwarted. Accordingly, on the indictment, and in reference to those counts to which you have pleaded guilty, the sentence of the court on count 2, the indecent assault, on the 14-year-old girl, you will serve 9 months' imprisonment, count 4, causing actual bodily harm on a girl, 15 months' imprisonment, count 5, attempted murder of a 17-year-old girl, life imprisonment. The amount of time you will spend in prison as a result of these *d* offences, which will be concurrent, is a matter for the authorities, guided no doubt by medical opinion.'

Between 1977 and 1980 the applicant was at Grendon Underwood Prison. He says that, while there, he came to terms with a lot of his problems and amongst other things realised that he was homosexual. For part of 1981 he was at Bristol Prison, where he *e* accepts that he behaved emotionally and anti-socially at times and was subject to disciplinary charges. He spent the next six months at Dartmoor, where he believes that he did well. He then returned to Bristol, being transferred to Featherstone Prison in 1982. There is a letter dated March 1988 before the court from a Mr Hawkins, who is a psychologist and knew the applicant when he was at Bristol and has corresponded with him subsequently. He describes the applicant as an increasingly thoughtful and sensitive *f* person. He expresses the opinion that the offences were—

> 'committed . . . as a result of a conflict between his immature personality at the time and the kind of behaviour the hard drinking, 'womanising' society in which he lived expected of him.'

He thought the problems were very much past history.   *g*

In 1984 came the first parole review. In June 1986 the Parole Board decided not to recommend parole. The applicant was very upset at this; he spoke to Dr Washbrooke, the prison psychiatrist, who told him that he had suggested that the applicant was suitable for open conditions.

In August and November 1986 the applicant was seen by Dr Rosemarie Cope, a consultant forensic psychiatrist, who reported to the Parole Board in December of that *h* year. Her opinion was as follows:

> 'This 28 year old man has served 10 years of a life sentence for attempted murder and there was a previous history of assaults on young women. These occurred during a period of emotional instability and heavy drinking when he lost control of his aggressive feelings during sexual encounters with young women. Although he *j* did not consider it a problem at the time he has had considerable conflict about his sexual orientation being bisexual since his early adolescence. He appears to have resolved these conflicts now and there is evidence of maturation and a greater ability to express and understand his emotions. There is no evidence to suggest that he has sadistic propensities nor in my opinion is there any evidence to suggest that he would present a danger if he were released. I would support a move to more open conditions.'

In so far as the explanation of the offences is heavy drinking, it should be pointed o. that the applicant was not drunk at the time the offences were committed; although he had had a few drinks, he told the police at the time that he was very sober. Counsel for the applicant, however, points out that areas of concern expressed by Dr Reeves are to some extent resolved in this report on the resolution of his sexual orientation and the absence of evidence of sadism.

In May 1987 the applicant's case was again considered by the local review committee. It is the applicant's belief, based on what he was told by probation and prison officers, that he received favourable reports from the prison. Dr Cope reported again in June 1987; but she had nothing to add to her previous report. The Parole Board again considered his case in November 1987; they did not recommend parole. Thereafter, the applicant sought to obtain the reasons for the decision, but he was met with a refusal. He was told by the Home Secretary:

'As you are aware from the replies to your earlier petitions, the Parole Board do not give reasons for their recommendations. However, as outlined above, the question of risk is the predominant factor in the release of any life sentence prisoner, and it therefore seems likely that the Parole Board were not satisfied, taking account of the nature of your offences as well as your progress in prison, that any risk to the public which might result from release was at an acceptable level.'

In April 1988 the applicant was moved to Verne Prison. He is a category C prisoner. He says that he was told by the assistant governors of both Featherstone and Verne Prisons that the reason that the Parole Board still consider him dangerous is the remark he made to the police about wanting to know what it is like to kill somebody.

I have set out the facts as they emerge from the evidence before the court in some detail because it is essential to the submission of counsel for the applicant that, so far as is known, all those who have submitted reports to the Parole Board, whether they be psychiatrists, probation officers or prison governors, have submitted favourable reports on the applicant and have expressed the opinion that he is no longer dangerous. Counsel for the applicant has sought in these proceedings discovery of those reports which, apart from that of Dr Cope, have not been seen by the applicant or the court. We shall deal with this application later in this judgment. But there is no dispute that the gist of these reports is as I have indicated; there is no suggestion in them that the applicant is regarded by any of the authors of them as being a danger.

The challenge

In these proceedings the applicant challenges both the refusal to recommend him for parole and the refusal to give reasons on that decision. As to the first challenge, it is submitted, first, that the Parole Board applied the wrong test in assessing the risk of danger that he presented if he was released and, second, that the decision was unreasonable in the *Wednesbury* sense (see *Associated Provincial Picture Houses Ltd v Wednesbury Corp* [1947] 2 All ER 680, [1948] 1 KB 223) because it was contrary to all the advice and opinion of those who had reported on him and was taken by the board without any interview by any member of the board with the applicant. As to the second challenge, it is submitted that the refusal to give reasons is contrary to natural justice and that the decision of the Court of Appeal in *Payne v Lord Harris of Greenwich* [1981] 2 All ER 842, [1981] 1 WLR 754 is distinguishable.

The statutory framework

The Parole Board was set up under the Criminal Justice Act 1967, s 59. Its duties are to advise the Secretary of State with respect to release on licence under s 60(1) (those serving a determinate term of imprisonment) or s 61 (those serving life sentences) and the recall under s 62 (revocation of licences and conviction of prisoners on parole) of those whose cases are referred to the Parole Board by the Home Secretary. Section 61(1), as amended, provides:

'The Secretary of State may, if recommended to do so by the Parole Board, release on licence a person serving a sentence of imprisonment for life or custody for life or a person detained under section 53 of the Children and Young Persons Act 1933 (young offenders convicted of grave crimes), but shall not do so in the case of a person sentenced to imprisonment for life or custody for life or to detention during Her Majesty's pleasure or for life except after consultation with the Lord Chief Justice of England together with the trial judge if available.'

It is plain, therefore, that the Secretary of State cannot release a prisoner on licence unless he is recommended to do so by the Parole Board. The complaint in this case is that the Parole Board, by their refusal to recommend the applicant for parole, have denied him the opportunity of his case being considered for parole by the Secretary of State.

The members of the Parole Board include a person who holds or has held judicial office, and in the case of panels considering those sentenced to life imprisonment this is a High Court judge, a psychiatrist, a person who has knowledge and experience of the supervision and after-care of discharged prisoners, who is normally a probation officer, and a person who has made a study of the causes of delinquency and the treatment of offenders: see Sch 2, para 1.

The first stage of the procedure is consideration by the local review committee.

In a statement to Parliament on 30 November 1983 the Secretary of State has made it clear that he looks to the judiciary for advice as to the appropriate length of time that a prisoner should serve to satisfy the requirements of deterrence and retribution, sometimes called the tariff. He looks to the Parole Board for advice on the continued danger to the public presented by the prisoner. He said (see 49 HC Official Report (6th series) written answers col 507):

'These new procedures will separate consideration of the requirements of retribution and deterrence from consideration of risk to the public, which always has been, and will continue to be, the pre-eminent factor determining release. They will enable the prison and other staff responsible for considering and reporting on life sentence cases, the Local Review Committees and the Parole Board, to concentrate on risk. The judiciary will properly advise on retribution and deterrence. But the ultimate discretion whether to release will remain with me.'

In a further statement to Parliament on 23 July 1987, following the decision in *R v Secretary of State for the Home Dept, ex p Handscomb* (1987) 86 Cr App R 59, the Home Secretary explained when the review would take place (see 120 HC Official Report (6th series) written answers cols 347–349). So far as discretionary life sentences are concerned, the review will begin three years before the time when the prisoner will have served two-thirds of the tariff advised by the Lord Chief Justice and the trial judge. Thus, if the tariff so advised is twelve years, the review will begin after the prisoner has served five years.

It is common ground in this case that the applicant had served sufficient time to satisfy the tariff. His continued detention is only justified on the grounds of risk of danger to the public.

The test of dangerousness

What should be the test applied by the Parole Board in the case of discretionary life prisoners in the post-tariff period? In particular, what degree of risk must exist to justify their continued detention?

Before turning to the rival contentions, we pause to observe that, despite the growing body of jurisprudence in this field, this particular issue does not appear hitherto to have arisen.

Certainly we derive no real assistance on it from the various decisions which we have been shown, both in our courts and in Strasbourg, not even from *R v Secretary of State for the Home Dept, ex p Benson* (1988) Independent, 16 November, albeit the general question of risk was there at the very forefront of the court's deliberations. It is convenient to note

what was there said about risk. Having outlined the basic facts giving rise to a general
Wednesbury challenge, Lloyd LJ said (and we read from the transcript):

'One can see why, in those circumstances, Mr Benson may feel that something
must have gone wrong, that the Secretary of State must have misdirected himself in
some way, that he must have misunderstood the purpose of discretionary life
sentence or that he must have taken some factor into account which is irrelevant to
the question of dangerousness and therefore irrelevant to the only question which
remains for his consideration. Dangerousness is of course an elusive quality and
difficult to forecast. It is not made easier by substituting risk as a synonym. Risk
was the word used by the Secretary of State in his statement of 30 November 1983.
But there is a potential ambiguity: risk of what? Not, obviously risk, that the
prisoner will be a nuisance or engage in petty crime. The matter can be tested in
this way. Suppose when the trial judge passed sentence he had had before him a
medical report which said that Mr Benson was in no way dangerous. Suppose also
that he had throughout his adult life been a persistent petty thief. The judge would
have sentenced Mr Benson to a determinate sentence of, let us say, twelve years for
the attempted grievous bodily harm with intent; after eight years Mr Benson having
earned remission would have been released. There could have been no question of
keeping him in prison just because he was likely, even certain, to return to his life
of petty crime. If risk to the public is the test, risk must mean risk of dangerousness.
Nothing less will suffice. It must mean there is a risk of Mr Benson repeating the
sort of offence for which the life sentence was originally imposed; in other words
risk to life or limb. This is to say no more than was said by Lord Lane CJ when he
was giving guidance on the discretionary life sentence in R v Wilkinson (1983) 5 Cr
App R (S) 105 at 108–109: "It seems to us that the sentence of life imprisonment,
other than for an offence where the sentence is obligatory, is really appropriate and
must only be passed in the most exceptional circumstances. With a few exceptions,
of which this case is not one, it is reserved, broadly speaking, as Lawton L.J. pointed
out [in R v Pither (1979) 1 Cr App R (S) 209 at 213] for offenders who for one reason
or another cannot be dealt with under the provisions of the Mental Health Act
[1959], yet who are in a mental state which makes them dangerous to the life or
limb of members of the public. It is sometimes impossible to say when that danger
will subside, and therefore an indeterminate sentence is required, so that the
prisoner's progress may be monitored by those who have him under their supervision
in prison and so that he will be kept in custody only so long as public safety may be
jeopardised by his being let loose at large." I would only add that when Lord Lane
CJ refers to danger to life or limb he must also have been intending to include as a
proper use for the discretionary life sentence the non-violent but persistent rapist.'

Clearly, no part of that indicates the actual level as opposed to the nature of the risk
which justifies continued detention.

Equally is that so when one turns, perhaps illicitly, for guidance from the European
Commission on Human Rights. Their report in Gunnell and Wilson v UK (7 September
1989, unreported) goes no further than to say (para 74):

'... the commission considers that once the national "tariff" period has been
served by the applicants the justification for continued detention depends on
whether they remain a danger to the public.'

At one stage of his argument counsel for the applicant suggested that a useful parallel
might be found in the mental health legislation governing the continued detention of
patients. It is therefore convenient to see what, if any, guidance is available from that
source.

In making hospital orders under s 37 of the Mental Health Act 1983 there is no
requirement that the court has to be satisfied that the defendant is a risk to the public.
Where, however, the court in addition makes a restriction order under s 41, it has to
appear to the court—

'having regard to the nature of the offence, the antecedents of the offender and the risk of his committing further offences if set at large, that it is necessary for the *a* protection of the public from serious harm ...'

The Secretary of State has power under s 42 to direct that the patient shall cease to be subject to special restriction if he is 'satisfied that ... a restriction order is no longer required for the protection of the public from serious harm'. And where a restriction order is in force he can direct his absolute or conditional discharge from hospital in his discretion, if he thinks fit.   *b*

Section 72(1)(b) of the Mental Health Act 1983, so far as relevant, requires mental health review tribunals to—

'direct the discharge of a patient ... if they are satisfied ... (ii) that it is not necessary ... for the protection of other persons that he should receive ... treatment; or (iii) [in cases under ss 66(1)(g) and 25 where the responsible medical officer has *c* certified that the patient, if discharged, 'will be likely to act in a manner dangerous to other persons'] that the patient, if released, will not be likely to act in a manner dangerous to other persons ...'

Section 72(1)(b) applies both to patients who are not subject to restriction orders and (subject to ss 73 and 74) to those who are.

All that can be derived from these various provisions governing release is that the *d* Secretary of State or the tribunal (as the case may be) has to be satisfied of a negative, that is that detention is 'not necessary' (or 'is no longer required') for the protection of others. Again, the precise level of risk is not (surely cannot be) spelt out. All that is clear is that the authorities have to be satisfied that it does not exist, the burden being placed unfavourably on the detainee.

Accordingly, we are not persuaded that the procedures under the Mental Health Act *e* 1983 provide reliable guidance.

Against that general background, we now come to the argument. Counsel for the applicant contends for a test of 'likelihood': that the prisoner will probably commit further serious offences (injury to life or limb or serious sexual assault) if released.

This test has its origins in a well-established line of Court of Appeal, Criminal Division *f* authority controlling the imposition of discretionary life sentences. The current approach was formulated in *R v Hodgson* (1968) 52 Cr App R 113 at 114 as follows:

'When the following conditions are satisfied, a sentence of life imprisonment is in our opinion justified: (1) where the offence or offences are in themselves grave enough to require a very long sentence; (2) where it appears from the nature of the offences or from the defendant's history that he is a person of unstable character *g* likely to commit such offences in the future; and (3) where if the offences are committed the consequences to others may be specially injurious, as in the case of sexual offences or crimes of violence.'

In *R v Dempster* (1987) 9 Cr App R (S) 176 at 179 the court noted that those three criteria had been reiterated ipsissima verba by Lord Lane CJ in *R v O'Dwyer* (1986) 86 Cr App R 313 at 315 and added: *h*

'In order to be satisfied that the second of the three criteria is established, there must be clear evidence, usually but not essentially medical evidence, of mental instability which would indicate that the defendant is likely to be a danger to the public.'

A yet more recent statement of the principle is to be found in *R v Stewart* (1989) 11 Cr *j* App R (S) 132 at 136, in which Watkins LJ, giving the judgment of the court, said (in the case of a chronic alcoholic):

'So the main consideration must we think inevitably be: has it been displayed by the medical evidence that given a fairly protracted stay in prison he will be a person who when released is a serious risk to the general public? ... We do not believe it is right to say after a protracted stay in prison he will remain a danger to the public and a main likely to reoffend ...'

a The test stated by Mr Wilkie (the Secretary to the board) to be that in fact adopted by the Parole Board is of—

'the risk to the public in relation to [the prisoner's] dangerousness in the community, and whether any such risk was acceptable. In the present case dangerousness relates to the risk of him causing death or serious injury or serious sexual assaults if released.'

b The touchstone of acceptability remains unclear. Counsel for the board on instruction tells us only that the Parole Board would not regard a risk which is merely 'perceptible' as sufficient to justify the continued detention of a post-tariff discretionary lifer. That test of 'perceptible risk' found expression in the Parole Board's report for 1988. It appears, however, in a passage specifically commenting on the Carlisle Committee's report, itself confined to considerations of parole in the case of determinate prisoners (see the report of

c the review committee on The Parole System in England and Wales (Cm 532) (1988)). It is, we are told, the test applied by the Parole Board solely in relation to that category of prisoners, regarding whom quite different considerations apply; they, after all, are seeking release back into society during the tariff period of sentences and are thus truly at mercy.

d Underlying all the contentions of counsel for the applicant is the central consideration that, after completing the tariff period, discretionary lifers are, in the words of Professor Thomas (lecturer in criminology at the University of Cambridge) in his affidavit sworn in this case, 'effectively serving "extra time" that is only justified if there is a reasonable case that they continue to constitute a danger to the public'. Implicit in their sentence, submits counsel, is a promise that, once the tariff for punishment has been served, the sentence will be reviewed and they will be released unless public safety truly demands

e their continued incarceration. And, the argument runs, the test should be no lower than that which has to be satisfied in the first place when the discretionary life sentence is imposed. A great weight of authority establishes the test at that stage as one of the 'likelihood' of the accused committing serious offences in the future. By the same token, it is submitted, no less stringent a test ought to be applied at the later stage of the Parole Board's decision whether, the requirements of punishment satisfied, continued

f imprisonment is justified.

Although not essential to that basic argument, counsel submits further that discretionary life prisoners should be considered more sympathetically and treated more favourably not merely than determinate sentence prisoners but than mandatory lifers too. Whereas it is apt in their case to talk of parole in terms of merciful release, the grant of parole reducing the life term which Parliament itself has fixed, it is wholly

g inappropriate so to characterise release on licence in discretionary life cases.

The argument is a serious one, persuasively advanced. It requires careful analysis.

The rationale or justification for a discretionary life sentence must surely be this: that in exceptional cases the interests of public safety cannot sufficiently be protected by imposing a determinate sentence even to the maximum extent permissible, ie the tariff

h sentence merited in the way of punishment, uplifted to a limited extent allowed by established case law for the protection of the public. Rather it is necessary to cater for the presently perceived risk that, on completion of any lawful determinate sentence, the prisoner would, if freed, remain a grave danger to society. This is achieved by passing a life sentence so as to ensure that the public will be protected and the risk reassessed after the tariff period expires.

j But it is one thing to say, as the authorities clearly appear to do, that only the likelihood (in the sense of probability) of further serious offending justifies the imposition of a life sentence. It is quite another to say, as counsel for the applicant does, that justice demands that the identical test be applied at the later stage of Parole Board assessment.

We had thought at one stage of the argument that a possible answer to that submission lay in the very elasticity of a life sentence. It occurred to us that the risk of continued imprisonment beyond the expiry of the tariff period might be justified by the countervailing hope of release before it. But that will not do: release is simply not these days contemplated until the tariff has been served. Whatever may be said by a sentencing court, it can seldom if ever be the case that a life sentence is truly passed in mercy, i e as being more beneficial to the accused than any proper determinate sentence.

The real answer to counsel's submission we have concluded to be this: the sentencing court recognised that passing a life sentence may well cause the accused to serve longer, and sometimes substantially longer, than his just deserts. It must thus not expose him to that peril unless there is compelling justification for such a course. That compelling justification is the perception of grave future risk amounting to an actual likelihood of dangerousness. But, of course, the court's perception of that future risk is inevitably imprecise. It is having to project its assessment many years forward and without the benefit of a constant process of monitoring and reporting such as will be enjoyed by the Parole Board. When at the post-tariff stage the assessment comes to be made by that board they are thus much better placed to evaluate the true extent of the risk which will be posed by the prisoner's release. And they are a more expert body, custom-built by Parliament for the purpose. Given those considerations, and given too that their recommendation for release on licence, if accepted by the Secretary of State, will have immediate effect in terms of endangering public safety, quite unlike the decision of the trial judge whose sentence would in any event have protected society for an appreciable time, it seems to us perfectly appropriate for the Parole Board to apply some lower test of dangerousness, i e one less favourable to the prisoner.

In short, the true position is in our judgment this. The imposition of the life sentence itself can only be justified by a very high degree of perceived public danger: there would otherwise be the temptation to impose it altogether too often simply in the interests of long-term public safety. But, once lawfully imposed, the life sentence then justifies the prisoner's continued detention, even though the risk as ultimately perceived is substantially less than an actual probability of his seriously reoffending on release. And common sense surely supports such a conclusion. Were it otherwise, the Parole Board would be required to release back into society a relatively high risk group, some of whom (although logically, of course, less than 50%) would commit further serious offences of violence. Parliament cannot be thought to have intended such an approach. We certainly do not feel driven to circumscribe the Parole Board's discretion in such a fashion.

It follows that we reject counsel's contention for the applicant that the Parole Board is fixed with the same standard as the sentencing judge. But that leaves still wholly undefined the level of risk required to justify continued detention of post-tariff discretionary lifers. Yet undefined we fear it must remain. Unless the required test is expressed in percentage terms (in the same way that likelihood arguably implies more than 50%), which is surely impossible, it seems inevitable that one can say really no more than this. First, the risk must indeed be 'substantial' (counsel's fall-back position), but this can mean no more than that it is not merely perceptible or minimal. Second, it must be sufficient to be unacceptable in the subjective judgment of the Parole Board, to whom Parliament has of course entrusted the decision, the decision, that is, whether to recommend release on licence, which recommendation is itself a necessary precondition to the exercise of the Secretary of State's final discretion. Third, in exercising their judgment as to the level of risk acceptable, the Parole Board must clearly have in mind all material considerations. Certainly one such consideration should be the intrinsic and increasing unfairness of leaving the prisoner languishing in gaol, ex hypothesi for longer than punishment requires, unless there is sufficient public risk to justify this.

What it all comes to is this. The Parole Board have to carry out a balancing exercise between the legitimate conflicting interests of both prisoner and public. They must clearly recognise the price which the prisoner personally is paying in order to give proper effect to the interests of public safety. They should recognise too that it is a progressively higher price. Accordingly, the longer the prisoner serves beyond the tariff period, the clearer should be the Parole Board's perception of public risk to justify continued deprivation of liberty involved.

The one document, we would observe, which has given us the greatest cause for

concern in this case is a letter from the Prison Department dated 26 January 1988. It
a states as follows:

> 'No life sentence prisoner will be released, however long he may have served,
> unless the Home Secretary is personally as satisfied as it is reasonably possible to be
> that the degree of risk is acceptable.'

Both counsel agree that the Secretary of State and the Parole Board should and in
b practice do follow the same approach. Only thus can the board properly and effectively
discharge their advisory function. Undoubtedly, one *could* draw from the quoted sentence
the inferences (a) that the Home Secretary does not release life sentence prisoners unless
he is sure that they will pose no risk at all and (b) that that remains his approach however
long beyond the requirements of punishment the prisoner may have served. But it
cannot properly be said that those inferences must inevitably be drawn from the letter.
c Rather the propriety of the approach described depends on precisely what is encompassed
within the word 'acceptable'. Of itself, it provides no benchmark by which to gauge the
level of risk in mind and leaves unclear just what considerations are brought into account.
Thus the letter in the end cannot assist the applicant, and we are left with no reason to
doubt the propriety of the Parole Board's declared test either in its formulation or its
application.
d

Irrationality
Was the decision of the Parole Board to refuse to recommend parole unreasonable in
the *Wednesbury* sense? In *R v Secretary of State for the Home Dept, ex p Benson* (1988)
Independent, 16 November, where the applicant sought judicial review of the Home
Secretary's decision not to grant parole notwithstanding the Parole Board's recommen-
e dation, Lloyd LJ, after referring to the dicta of Lord Diplock in *Council of Civil Service
Unions v Minister for the Civil Service* [1984] 3 All ER 935 at 951, [1985] AC 374 at 410 ('a
decision so outrageous in its defiance of logic or common sense') and Lord Brightman in
Puhlhofer v Hillingdon London BC [1986] 1 All ER 467 at 474, [1986] AC 484 at 518 (one
that verges on the absurd), said (and we read from the transcript):

f   'I suspect that the degree of unreasonableness (so outrageous) which an appellant
must show in order to succeed on irrationality may have been pitched higher in
recent decisions; or it may be that in certain types of administrative decision the
courts will be even more reluctant to intervene than in others. If the latter is the
case, then the release of discretionary life sentence prisoners on parole would surely
come at the higher end of the scale. The responsibility given by Parliament to the
g   Secretary of State is indeed grave. It is easy enough for courts to condemn a decision
refusing parole as unreasonable. But it is the Secretary of State who, if the decision
to grant parole goes wrong, has to answer for it.'

In our judgment, similar considerations apply to the decision of the board itself. Theirs
too is a grave responsibility fraught with anxiety especially in the field of those serving
h life sentences for grave crimes. We must bear in mind that the panel considering their
cases will be presided over by a High Court judge, and includes others having relevant
knowledge and experience in judging risk.
Counsel for the applicant developed two lines of attack on the decision. First, he
submitted that it must prima facie be perverse since it included rejection of all the advice
from those who had seen and been in touch with the applicant. The board have not seen
j the applicant, although there is power for them to have him interviewed by one of their
number: see the Criminal Justice Act 1967, s 59(4)(b). We have no hesitation in rejecting
this submission. If, as we hold they did, the Parole Board applied the correct test, then it
is their decision and not that of their advisers; the latter give advice but do not make or
take responsibility for the decision. Moreover, it is perfectly possible to discern a rational
explanation of the board's decision. In the absence of any clear explanation of motivation
the series of offences against teenage girls, culminating in the attempted murder, speak

for themselves and quite clearly indicate a risk of danger to the public. It by no means follows that, simply because a defendant has served a period in prison to satisfy the tariff, he presents any less of a danger, still less that there is any presumption to that effect. It is perfectly possible to take the view that Dr Cope's opinion is open to question on the ground that she has accepted too readily that the offences were committed under the influence of heavy drinking; that may be something that the applicant now believes, but it is not supported by the contemporary evidence. It is clear that the board have attached significance to the applicant's remark to the police that he wanted to see what it was like to kill someone. Counsel for the applicant criticises them for doing so and this forms the second limb of his attack. But, subject to that, we can see no reason why the board should not attach significance to this statement.

Failure to disclose the importance attached to the remark, 'I wanted to see what it was like to kill someone'

Counsel for the applicant submits that the Parole Board acted perversely and in breach of the principles of natural fairness in failing either to seek the applicant's comments on this remark by interviewing him or to ask Dr Cope to inquire into it. He submits that, if this remark was the main or even one of the board's grounds of concern as to his continued danger, then it is incumbent on the board to hear what he had to say about it directly or indirectly. For our part, we certainly consider that it would be good practice for the board to discover either directly or indirectly what the applicant's reaction is to a matter that is troubling them, if they consider that the applicant may have some relevant contribution to make. And we were gratified to hear that, when the next review of the applicant's case begins in March this year, it is their intention to seek, through Dr Cope, to find the applicant's reaction to this remark and, perhaps more importantly, Dr Cope's opinion as to the significance of that reaction. But we are not persuaded that the circumstances here show any procedural unfairness in what has or has not happened, still less that the Parole Board have acted perversely in reaching their 1987 decision without having taken these steps. We say this for two reasons. Firstly, we in fact know what the applicant's reaction is: he denies having made the remark. Since it can hardly be suggested that the board would be acting perversely if they took the view that the remark probably was made, it does not seem to us that the applicant's reaction would greatly assist his case. Secondly, it is not clear at what stage this remark became a matter of critical concern to the board. If it did not arise until the 1987 review, which seems probable since the board have now directed specific inquiry to it, we cannot see that the board can be criticised for not asking Dr Cope to deal with it specifically in her earlier reports.

Counsel for the applicant pointed out that Dr Kellam, who was one of the doctors who examined the applicant in July 1976 with a view, in particular, to seeing if there was a defence of automatism, said that he did not consider this remark at all believable and that he thought that the applicant must have made this up on the spur of the moment to satisfy the police. That is a view he is perfectly entitled to hold. It does not follow that it is one that must be shared by the board.

In short, we reject the contention that the board's decisions thus far can be categorised as *Wednesbury* unreasonable. Whether, of course, their decision on the imminent 1990 review will remain the same will depend both on the further medical evidence they are obtaining and the weight they give to the considerations above referred to, that a prisoner as long past his tariff sentence as this applicant ought not to be further detained unless a clearly recognisable risk to the public exists to justify that course.

Failure to disclose reasons for the refusal to recommend parole

Counsel for the applicant recognises that, unless he can distinguish it, there is binding authority of the Court of Appeal in *Payne v Lord Harris of Greenwich* [1981] 2 All ER 842, [1981] 1 WLR 754 to the effect that the board do not have to give reasons. The only difference between that case and this is that Payne was serving a mandatory life sentence for murder. That, submits counsel for the applicant, makes all the difference because such a man is not entitled to release after serving the tariff sentence, provided he is no

a longer dangerous, whereas a discretionary lifer is. In our judgment, this is not a valid or logical distinction because it is quite clear that the board and the Home Secretary apply the same approach both to the mandatory and discretionary life prisoners, namely that, after they have served the tariff period, as decided by the Home Secretary after consultation and advice from the judiciary, the sole question that justifies detention in either case is risk to the public. It is plain that all members of the court in *Payne*'s case

b must have appreciated that discretionary life sentences were passed for grave crimes other than murder, and Shaw LJ expressly adverts to the point (see [1981] 2 All ER 842 at 848, [1981] 1 WLR 754 at 762). But there is no suggestion that what they were saying applied only to mandatory life sentences and the reasoning of the judgment applies equally to both.

Moreover, in *R v Secretary of State for the Home Dept, ex p Gunnell* (1984) Times,

c 7 November, the Court of Appeal was dealing with a man who had been sentenced to life imprisonment for rape and was, therefore, a discretionary life prisoner. The Court of Appeal rejected the submission that *Payne*'s case did not apply. Eveleigh LJ said (and we read from the transcript):

'. . . I agree with what was said by Watkins LJ in his judgment in the Divisional

d Court. He quoted the words of Brightman LJ in *Payne v Lord Harris of Greenwich* [1981] 2 All ER 842 at 852, [1981] 1 WLR 754 at 766 where he said: "The scope and extent of the principles of natural justice depend on the subject matter to which they are sought to be applied; see *R v Gaming Board for Great Britain, ex parte Benaim* [1970] 2 All ER 528 at 533, [1970] 2 QB 417 at 430. They apply to the present case, as conceded, to the extent that they impose on the board and the committee, and each member of it, a duty to act fairly. That duty does not, in my judgment, require

e that any disclosure is made to the prisoner of adverse material which the board and the committee have in their possession to assist them in their advisory and reporting functions." [Counsel for Gunnell] submitted that there is a difference in this case and that case, because that case was dealing with an initial release on parole and not with a consideration of the matter by the board after recall. It is true factually that

f there is that distinction, but in my judgment that distinction results in one difference and one difference only from the point of view of the consideration of the matter by the board, that is that the prisoner himself, in the case of recall, is entitled to have been told the reasons for his recall. So there is some information to which he is entitled, but to my mind this is the only distinction between the two cases. The principle of natural justice on which reliance has been placed in this case, ie an

g alleged principle of full disclosure, does not in my judgment apply.'

It is true that the argument presently advanced on behalf of the applicant by counsel was not advanced by him or his leader when they appeared for Gunnell in that case. But that reflects the tenuousness of the argument now advanced, rather than oversight by counsel in that case of an arguable distinction.

h Counsel for the applicant argues that we should not extend *Payne*'s case, particularly in the light of recent developments. These include the following.

(1) The passing of the Mental Health Act 1983 setting up the system of mental health review tribunals. As already indicated, the task of such tribunals under s 72 is in some ways analogous to that of the Parole Board in that they must direct the discharge of a patient if they are satisfied that his detention is not necessary for the protection of other

j persons. Where applications are made to the tribunal it is the practice, save in exceptional cases, that disclosure to the patient is made of medical reports so that he knows the reason for his continued detention. The evidence before the court from Dr Grounds, a forensic psychiatrist shows that this has worked well and had a beneficial effect.

(2) In 1988 the Carlisle report on the parole system recommended open reporting and the giving of reasons in fixed-term parole cases (see paras 331–336).

(3) In the government's White Paper *Crime, Justice and Protecting the Public* (Cm 965 (1990)) these passages are to be found:

'6.25 The Government agrees with the Carlisle Committee's view that the parole decision-making process should be made more open. This will be easier if there are *a* published criteria for the parole decision, since the reports prepared for the Board and the Board's own decisions should focus on the criteria . . .

6.26 The Government will give further consideration to the detailed arrangements for making the parole decisions in future, with the aim of moving towards disclosing reports made to the Board and the Board giving reasons for its decisions. The Government believes that greater openness could improve the quality of decision- *b* making. It would encourage a careful weighing of the evidence and arguments linked to the parole criteria. A detailed record of earlier decisions is likely to help future decisions and to encourage the development of clear policies and the consistent approach to parole decisions. This is particularly important because decisions are taken by panels of members of the Board. However, there is a risk that openness could lead to less full and telling reports and so to less well informed *c* decisions. Disclosing reports is likely to fuel demands for even more disclosure and the information could be used to contest adverse decisions through judicial review and any other available means. On balance, the Government believes that the likely benefits of greater openness outweigh its disadvantages.'

We acknowledge that there is much force in the argument that reasons and reports should be made available to those who are considered for parole; these can be set against *d* the policy reasons to the contrary to be found in the judgments of the Court of Appeal in *Payne's* case. But, unless we can distinguish *Payne's* case, which we cannot, it is not open to us to embark on the public policy considerations of whether natural justice requires disclosure of reports and reasons. This is a matter for Parliament.

Discovery of documents   *e*

The applicant sought an order for discovery of documents. These were the reports, including psychiatric reports, made on the applicant to the Parole Board and the record of the reasons for the refusal of a recommendation for parole. We refused to make an order; we now shortly give our reasons.

As to the reports, counsel for the applicant argued that they were plainly relevant and *f* would assist the applicant in advancing his case that the board's decision was perverse, because it ignored the views of those reporting that the applicant was no longer dangerous. But it is a cardinal principle of discovery that it will only be ordered if it is necessary for disposing fairly of the cause or matter or for saving costs: RSC Ord 24, r 8. The same principles apply to discovery under Ord 53, r 8. In this case there is no dispute of fact, which for these purposes includes opinion; it is accepted by the board that none *g* of the reports before the board indicate that in the opinion of the maker the applicant still represents a danger.

As to the reasons for the refusal to recommend parole, counsel for the applicant submits that it is unclear what test the Parole Board applied. He submits that the court should not accept what is said in para 15 of Mr Wilkie's first affidavit, namely that the criterion adopted by the Parole Board for release on licence in the applicant's case is the *h* risk of dangerousness to the public and that the board is not satisfied that there is an acceptable risk to the public in relation to the dangerousness of the applicant if he were released into the community.

But only if there is material before the court which suggests that what is said on affidavit is untrue will the court order discovery so that it can determine the facts. In this case, in our judgment, there is no such evidence. Moreover, it is quite unnecessary for *j* there to be discovery on this point. Either the test adopted by the Parole Board is correct in law, as we have held, or it is not. If it is not, the decision falls to be quashed; if it is, the application is dismissed. It will not assist the court to see the document from which it might deduce the test. Moreover, we would respectfully adopt what was said by Glidewell LJ in the Court of Appeal in *R v Secretary of State for the Home Dept, ex p Harrison* [1987] CA Transcript 1246. In that case the challenge to the decision was *Wednesbury* unreasonableness. Glidewell LJ said:

a

b

c

d

e

f

g

'What that ground is asserting, says [counsel for the Home Secretary], is that one only needs to look at the decision itself to see that it is so unreasonable that the process by which it was reached must be flawed in one or all of the ways set out. That, [counsel] submits, does not demand any examination of the route. In other words, he says that the claim is that the court should consider the terminus. If it finds that the terminus is irrational, then the route must be wrong, the decision maker must have set off on the wrong road somewhere. For myself I agree with that argument. What [counsel for the Home Secretary] is submitting is, to use Lord Roskill's phrase [in *IRC v National Federation of Self-Employed and Small Businesses Ltd* [1981] 2 All ER 93 at 121, [1982] AC 617 at 664], that either what is being sought is discovery in relation to something which is not within the grounds of the application for judicial review or this is a fishing expedition. It is asserted that the decision is so unreasonable that it must be flawed and then what is sought is discovery which it is hoped will turn up something on which another allegation can be based, for instance that the Secretary of State did take into account an irrelevant consideration or took into account some matter adverse to Mr Harrison without giving him the right to see it and counter it. As I say, I agree with that submission. If this is a fishing expedition, as I suspect it is, that is not a proper object of discovery. To put it another way, [counsel for the Home Secretary] says in a pungent phrase that there can be no discovery on judicial review on a contingent basis. The question of whether or not there should be judicial review at all and, if so, whether, for instance, the Home Secretary owed to Mr Harrison a duty of fairness which would oblige him to disclose to Mr Harrison any material of which he had possession which contained comment adverse to the applicant, are both questions which are in issue in these proceedings themselves. If the arguments for the Home Office succeed there will be no question of discovery, because there will be nothing to be disclosed. If there is no duty of fairness there is no need to disclose the documents which were not disclosed to Mr Harrison ... [Counsel for the Home Secretary] suggests that to a not immaterial extent what is being sought here is material which it is hoped by the applicant will, at least in part, contradict matter contained in Mr Caffarey's affidavit [Mr Caffarey was the head of the division in the criminal policy department at the Home Office who dealt with Mr Harrison's application for compensation]. In other words what is being sought is documents which can be used to check the accuracy of what Mr Caffarey asserts in his affidavit. [Counsel for the Home Secretary] submits that an applicant is not entitled to go behind an affidavit in order to seek to ascertain whether it is correct or not unless there is some material available outside that contained in the affidavit to suggest that in some material respect the affidavit is not accurate. If there is such material it may be right to order discovery to follow that up. But without some prima facie case for suggesting that the affidavit is in some respects incorrect it is improper to allow discovery of documents the only purpose of which, as I have said, would be to act as a challenge to the accuracy of the affidavit. With that submission also, which is of general application, I agree.'

h See also the judgment of Henry J in *Re CEMI Ltd* (18 February 1989, unreported).

The observations of Glidewell LJ are apposite to this case. Either the decision to refuse to recommend parole is perverse on its face for the reasons advanced by counsel for the applicant or it is not; either the test applied by the Parole Board is wrong in law or it is not. Moreover, the court will not order discovery, if that is in effect the very relief that is sought in the substantive application, and which we cannot grant because of the decision in *Payne's* case.

j For these reasons the application is refused.

Application dismissed. No order as to costs.

Solicitors: *B M Birnberg & Co* (for the applicant); *Treasury Solicitor.*

Dilys Tausz   Barrister.

Re Beatty's Will Trusts
Hinves and others v Brooke and others

CHANCERY DIVISION
HOFFMANN J
27, 28, 29 JUNE 1990

Will – Testamentary disposition – Delegation of will-making power – Whether will-making power may be delegated.

Power of appointment – Exercise by will – General power – Power to allocate among such persons as trustees think fit – Whether rule against delegation of making of will – Whether power valid.

By cll 3(a) and 4(a) of her will the testatrix bequeathed her personal estate and a legacy of £1·5m to her trustees to 'allocate . . . to or among such person or persons . . . as they think fit' and by cll 3(b) and 4(b) she requested the trustees 'to give effect to any memorandum . . . which may be deposited with . . . my will or left among my papers . . . or . . . to any wishes of mine of which they shall be aware . . .' The residuary beneficiaries challenged the validity of distributions made by the trustees under cll 3(b) and 4(b) on the ground that the gifts to the trustees infringed the rule that a testator could not delegate the making of his will to his trustees. The trustees issued a summons to determine the validity of the distributions.

Held – There was no rule of law that a testator could not delegate the making of his will to his trustees since that would prevent the use of wide powers of appointment in wills. On the other hand, there was a rule that a gift which was expressed in language too vague to be enforced could not be rescued by giving the executor a power of choice. Since cll 3(a) and 4(a) would have been valid powers of appointment if they had been inserted in a settlement and gave effect to the testatrix's will, rather than permitting the trustees to make a will when she had failed to do so, the distributions made by the trustees under cll 3(b) and 4(b) were valid (see p 848 c d, p 849 d j and p 850 b, post).

Re Park, Public Trustee v Armstrong [1931] All ER Rep 633, *Re Jones, Public Trustee v Jones* [1945] Ch 105 and *Re Abrahams's Will Trusts, Caplan v Abrahams* [1967] 2 All ER 1175 followed.

Blair v Duncan [1902] AC 37, *Grimond v Grimond* [1904–7] All ER Rep 445, *Houston v Burns* [1918–19] All ER Rep 817, *A-G v National Provincial and Union Bank of England* [1923] All ER Rep 123, *A-G of New Zealand v New Zealand Insurance Co Ltd* [1936] 3 All ER 888 and dicta of Lord Macmillan and Lord Simonds in *Chichester Diocesan Fund and Board of Finance Inc v Simpson* [1944] 2 All ER 60 at 62–63, 74 explained.

Tatham v Huxtable (1950) 81 CLR 639 not followed.

Notes

For delegation of will-making power, see 50 Halsbury's Laws (4th edn) para 209.

For general nature and construction of powers, see 36 ibid paras 801, 818, and for cases on the subject, see 37(2) Digest (Reissue) 6–20, 22–24, 1–121, 140–145.

Cases referred to in judgment

A-G v National Provincial and Union Bank of England [1924] AC 262, [1923] All ER Rep 123, HL.

A-G of New Zealand v New Zealand Insurance Co Ltd [1936] 3 All ER 888, PC.

Abrahams's Will Trusts, Re, Caplan v Abrahams [1967] 2 All ER 1175, [1969] 1 Ch 463, [1967] 3 WLR 1198.

Blair v Duncan [1902] AC 37, HL.

a *Carville, Re, Shone v Walthamstow BC* [1937] 4 All ER 464.

Chichester Diocesan Fund and Board of Finance Inc v Simpson [1944] 2 All ER 60, [1944] AC 341, HL.

Eyre, Re, Eyre v Eyre (1883) 49 LT 259.

Grimond v Grimond [1905] AC 124, [1904–7] All ER Rep 445, HL.

Gulbenkian's Settlement Trusts, Re, Whishaw v Stephens [1968] 3 All ER 785, [1970] AC 508,

b   [1968] 3 WLR 1127, HL.

Horan v James [1982] 2 NSWLR 376, NSW CA.

Houston v Burns [1918] AC 337, [1918–19] All ER Rep 817, HL.

Jones, Re, Public Trustee v Jones [1945] Ch 105.

Manisty's Settlement, Re, Manisty v Manisty [1973] 2 All ER 1203, [1974] Ch 17, [1973] 3 WLR 341.

c *Nicholls, Re* (1987) 34 DLR (4th) 321, Ont CA.

Park, Re, Public Trustee v Armstrong [1932] 1 Ch 580, [1931] All ER Rep 633.

Pugh's Will Trusts, Re, Marten v Pugh [1967] 3 All ER 337, [1967] 1 WLR 1262.

Tatham v Huxtable (1950) 81 CLR 639, Aust HC.

Yeap Cheah Neo v Ong Cheng Neo (1875) LR 6 PC 381.

d **Cases also cited**

Combe, Re, Combe v Combe [1925] Ch 210, [1925] All ER Rep 159.

Drake v A-G (1843) 10 Cl & Fin 257, 8 ER 739, HL.

Gerhardy v South Australian Auxiliary to the British and Foreign Bible Society Inc (1982) 30 SASR 12, S Aust SC.

Gestetner (decd), Re, Barnett v Blumka [1953] 1 All ER 1150, [1953] Ch 672.

e *Hastilow v Stobie* (1865) LR 1 P & D 64.

Hay's Settlement Trusts, Re [1981] 3 All ER 786, [1982] 1 WLR 202.

Hughes, Re, Hughes v Footner [1921] 2 Ch 208, [1921] All ER Rep 310.

Lutheran Church of Australia South Australia District Inc v Farmers' Co-op Exors and Trustees Ltd (1970) 121 CLR 628, Aust HC.

McEwen (decd), Re, McEwen v Day [1955] NZLR 575, NZ SC.

f *McPhail v Doulton* [1970] 2 All ER 228, [1971] AC 424, HL.

Morris (decd), Re, Lloyds Bank Ltd v Peake [1970] 1 All ER 1057, [1971] P 62.

Platt v Routh (1840) 6 M & W 756, 151 ER 618.

Smith's Goods, Re (1869) LR 1 P & D 717.

Summons

g By summons dated 27 February 1990 Herbert James Hinves, Anthony Robert Bishop and Cynthia Joyce Smith, the trustees of the will of Helen Gertrude Beatty deceased (the testatrix) sought the determination of the question whether the powers conferred on the trustees by cll 3(a) and 4(a) of the testatrix's will were valid. The defendants to the summons were the residuary beneficiaries, namely (1) Guy David Greville Brooke, (2) Charlotte Fraser, (3) Charles Fulke Chester Greville Brooke, (4) Daisy Rosamond Fraser,

h (5) Laura Alfreda Fraser (the third, fourth and fifth residuary beneficiaries appearing by Andrew Fraser, their guardian ad litem), (6) Anthony John Tennant, (7) Hamish Wallace and (8) Harrington Ltd, and (9) the person entitled on an intestacy, Rosamund Mary Hersilia Morris. The facts are set out in the judgment.

j *Jonathan Parker QC* and *M I Waters* for the trustees.

J Maurice Price QC and *Alastair Norris* for the residuary beneficiaries.

Sir William Goodhart QC and *Bernard Weatherill* for the ninth defendant.

HOFFMANN J. The testatrix died on 4 January 1986 leaving an estate valued at £32m, including a very valuable collection of paintings. By this summons, of which only the first paragraph is presently before me, her executors and trustees ask the court to pronounce on the validity of cll 3 and 4 of her will dated 1 December 1983. They read as follows: *a*

> '3. (*a*) I BEQUEATH all my personal chattels as defined by the Administration of Estates Act 1925 (including any car or cars that I may own at the time of my death) to my Trustees who shall at any time or times (but nevertheless within the period of two years following my death or such shorter period as they my Trustees in writing decide) allocate divide or make over all or any such personal chattels to or among such person or persons (whether individual or corporate) as they think fit And any of my said personal chattels not so allocated divided or made over shall fall into and become part of my residuary estate (b) I REQUEST my Trustees to give effect to any memorandum of mine as to my said personal chattels which may be deposited with this my Will or left among my papers at my death and failing or in addition to any such memorandum to any wishes of mine of which they shall be aware with regard to them but the foregoing expression of my wishes shall not create any trust or legal obligation even if the same may have been communicated in my lifetime to my Trustees or to any other person . . .
>   4. (*a*) I BEQUEATH a legacy of ONE MILLION FIVE HUNDRED THOUSAND POUNDS to my Trustees who shall at any time or times (but nevertheless within the period of two years following my death or such shorter period as they my Trustees in writing decide) allocate and pay over the same to or among such person or persons (whether individual or corporate) as they think fit And any part of the said legacy not so allocated or paid over shall fall into and become part of my residuary estate (b) I REQUEST my Trustees to give effect to any memorandum of mine as to the said legacy which may be deposited with this my Will or left among my papers at my death and failing or in addition to any such memorandum to any wishes of mine of which they shall be aware with regard to them but the foregoing expression of my wishes shall not create any trust or legal obligation even if the same may have been communicated in my lifetime to my Trustees or to any other person . . .'

Subject to these gifts, the testatrix left the residue of her estate in three equal shares, subject to certain trusts and gifts over, to the daughter and grandchildren of her late *f* husband by an earlier marriage.

During the two years following the death of the testatrix the trustees distributed personal chattels to the value of about £150,000 to about 87 people, and cash amounting to £1·2m to about 50 people in accordance with the wishes communicated in confidence by the testatrix pursuant to cll 3(b) and 4(b). Subsequently, however, solicitors acting for the residuary beneficiaries challenged the validity of these distributions and the ninth *g* defendant, who is a nephew of the testatrix, has been appointed to represent all the persons who have received chattels or money under cl 3 or cl 4.

Clauses 3 and 4 do not impose any trusts to distribute the chattels or money over which they operated. That is shown by the gift over to residue of the property which has not been distributed within the two-year period. They confer instead fiduciary powers which require the trustees to give consideration to whether they should be exercised and *h* to act in accordance with what they honestly consider to have been the purpose for which the testatrix created the powers.

The rule that a trustee cannot profit from his trust would ordinarily exclude the trustees themselves from the ambit of the powers, but cl 12(c) of this will allows the trustees to exercise any power conferred by the will, notwithstanding that they may have *j* a direct personal interest in the mode of its exercise. This arguably allows the trustees, subject to having proper regard to their overall fiduciary duties, to make gifts or payments to themselves. They have in fact paid themselves £10,000 each in accordance with the express wish of the testatrix that they should do so.

But the powers, being fiduciary, are not general powers in the sense of the traditional

classification which equates such a power with an outright beneficial disposition to the
a the trustee himself. Nor are they special powers in the traditional sense. The objects of
the powers can hardly be described as a class. They are intermediate or hybrid powers of
the kind considered in *Re Park, Public Trustee v Armstrong* [1932] 1 Ch 580, [1931] All ER
Rep 633.

Nevertheless, counsel for the residuary beneficiaries accepted that they satisfy the
modern requirement of certainty as laid down by the House of Lords in *Re Gulbenkian's
b Settlement Trusts, Whishaw v Stephens* [1968] 3 All ER 785, [1970] AC 508, namely that
the trustees must be able to say whether any given person is an object of the power or
not. In this case there is no difficulty because there is no one who is not.

Counsel therefore conceded that if they had appeared in a settlement, cll 3 and 4 would
have been valid powers, but he said that as part of a will, they were invalidated by the
rule that a testator cannot delegate the making of his will. This, he said, was a rule of
c common law distinct from the equitable rules concerning the certainty requirements for
trusts and powers. The common law rule reflected the view that the right to make a will
was a personal privilege, to be exercised with care and circumspection and not lightly
delegated to others. The formalities of the Wills Act 1837 would have little point if the
will was a mere enabling document leaving the real choice of the beneficiaries to be made
by the executors.

d In support of the existence of such a rule counsel cited a number of statements by
eminent judges in the House of Lords. Two passages from *Chichester Diocesan Fund and
Board of Finance Inc v Simpson* [1944] 2 All ER 60, [1944] AC 341 are sufficiently typical
to make further citation unnecessary. Lord Simonds said ([1944] 2 All ER 60 at 74,
[1944] AC 341 at 371):

e   'It is a cardinal rule, common to English and to Scots law, that a man may not
delegate his testamentary power: to him the law gives the right to dispose of his
estate in favour of ascertained or ascertainable persons. He does not exercise that
right if in effect he empowers his executors to say what persons or objects are to be
his beneficiaries. To this salutary rule there is a single exception: a testator may
validly leave it to his executors to determine what charitable objects shall benefit, so
f   long as charitable and no other objects may benefit.'

In the same case Lord Macmillan said ([1944] 2 All ER 60 at 62–63, [1944] AC 341 at
349):

          'The choice of beneficiaries must be the testator's own choice; he cannot leave the
g   disposal of his estate to others. The only latitude permitted is that, if he designates
with sufficient precision a class of persons or objects to be benefited, he may delegate
to his trustees the selection of individual persons or objects within the defined class.
The class must not be described in terms so vague and indeterminate that the
trustees are afforded no effective guidance as to the ambit of their power of
selection . . .'

h
If these remarks are divorced from their context, they can cause considerable difficulty.
Lord Simonds, as we have seen, emphasised that there was only a single exception to his
rule against delegation, namely that a testator could allow his trustee to choose the
specific recipients of a general gift to charity. But Lord Simonds must also have known,
as Lord Macmillan expressly acknowledged, that for centuries testators had been creating
j special powers of appointment. Furthermore, they had also been creating general powers
of appointment. It could be said of the latter that because they were equivalent to gifts to
the donee beneficially, no delegation was involved: the exercise of the power was a
disposal of the donee's property rather than that of the testator. This would be consistent
with the way such powers were treated for the purposes of the rule against perpetuities.
But Lord Simonds would almost certainly also have known that in *Re Park* Clauson J had

upheld the validity of a power to appoint to anyone but the donee, which is not susceptible of a similar explanation.

I find it hard to imagine that Lord Simonds regarded his remarks as casting doubt on the validity of testamentary powers of appointment, whether special, general or intermediate. The context in which he spoke was the consideration of a gift for purposes ('charitable or benevolent') which was expressed in language so conceptually vague that it would be impossible for the court to say whether any specific application was within the terms of the will or not. If an application of money in accordance with such a gift were to be upheld, it would not be giving effect to the will of the testator because that, ex hypothesi, was incapable of being enforced. It would be giving effect to the autonomous act of the executor. In this sense, it would be truly a delegation of the testamentary power. But the execution of an otherwise valid general, special or intermediate power is giving effect to the testator's will and not making a will for a testator who has failed to do so himself.

The reason why Lord Simonds said that charitable gifts were the only exception to his rule was because they are, indeed, the only case in which the court will uphold a gift in terms which would otherwise be regarded as too vague. Thus it seems to me that Lord Simonds, like other judges in earlier cases concerning gifts void for uncertainty, was intending to do no more than to state in forceful and dramatic terms the rule that a gift which is expressed in language too vague to be enforced cannot be rescued by giving the executor a power of choice. Lord Simonds would, I think, have been astonished to learn that he had just outlawed the use of widely expressed powers, or perhaps even any powers at all, in wills.

No such thoughts seem to have been entertained at the time in Lincoln's Inn. In *Re Jones, Public Trustee v Jones* [1945] Ch 105, which was decided some six months after Lord Simonds had delivered his speech, Vaisey J followed *Re Park* and upheld the validity of a broad intermediate power in a will. The legendary Mr Wilfrid Hunt, who appeared for the residuary beneficiaries to challenge the validity of the power, made no mention of a rule against testamentary delegation and did not cite the *Chichester Diocesan Fund* case.

I have taken the remarks of Lord Simonds by way of example, but I think that the same explanation can be given for the other similar statements cited by counsel: see *Blair v Duncan* [1902] AC 37, *Grimond v Grimond* [1905] AC 124, [1904–7] All ER Rep 445, *Houston v Burns* [1918] AC 337, [1918–19] All ER Rep 817, *A-G v National Provincial and Union Bank of England* [1924] AC 262, [1923] All ER Rep 123 and *A-G of New Zealand v New Zealand Insurance Co Ltd* [1936] 3 All ER 888. All those were cases in which the testator had purported to give his executors a power of choice among objects expressed in language held to be too uncertain to be capable of enforcement. The statements made in those cases were, in my view, likewise intended to go no further than to state the familiar rule which invalidates such gifts.

Re Carville, Shone v Walthamstow BC [1937] 4 All ER 464 and *Re Pugh's Will Trusts, Martan v Pugh* [1967] 3 All ER 337, [1967] 1 WLR 1262, on which counsel relied, as well as *Yeap Cheah Neo v Ong Cheng Neo* (1875) LR 6 PC 381, were each decided on the assumption, which does not appear in any of those cases to have been contested, that unless the language of the will could be construed as a beneficial gift to the executors, it was too uncertain to constitute an enforceable trust. I do not need to say whether in each case I would have regarded that assumption as justified. It is sufficient that the principle on which they were decided was in my view the rule of uncertainty and not any distinct rule against testamentary delegation.

What would the scope of such a rule be? Counsel for the residuary beneficiaries did not say that it prohibited all special powers, which a literal reading of Lord Simonds and some of the other House of Lords dicta (though not that of Lord Macmillan) would suggest. It was, he submitted, misleading to try to relate the test to the traditional classification of powers. It should rather be derived from the purpose of the rule, which was to require a testator to make his own will. This meant that the will should give

sufficient guidance, either from the nature of the class or from its other terms, to enable
a one to say that the testator had truly made a choice and had not left everything to the
executor. Thus it would prohibit powers expressed in such wide terms as that upheld in
the case of a settlement by Templeman J in *Re Manisty's Settlement, Manisty v Manisty*
[1973] 2 All ER 1203, [1974] Ch 17, where the trustees were given a power to add any
persons whom they thought fit to the class to which appointments could be made.

In my view such a rule, which no court has ever formulated, would itself be vague and
b uncertain. The question of what would constitute sufficient guidance to the executors is
so much a matter of degree that I think it would be quite impossible to say in advance
whether the power was valid or not. There is in fact no trace of a specific rule against
testamentary delegation in any case before the present century and at least one (see *Re
Eyre, Eyre v Eyre* (1883) 49 LT 259) in which one might have expected it to be mentioned.
Counsel submitted that the rule had only slept. Until recent times testators were modest
c in their use of special powers and the requirements of certainty were all that was
necessary to control their pretensions. But now that they commonly employ such wide
powers as those upheld in *Re Manisty's Settlement*, the time had come for the rule to
awaken and assert its strength.

It seems to me, however, that a common law rule against testamentary delegation, in
the sense of a restriction on the scope of testamentary powers, is a chimera, a shadow cast
d by the rule of certainty, having no independent existence. This was in effect the view
taken by Cross J in *Re Abrahams's Will Trusts, Caplan v Abrahams* [1967] 2 All ER 1175,
[1969] 1 Ch 463, where the judge was specifically invited to say that cases like *Re Park*
and *Re Jones* were inconsistent with the supposed rule against delegation as stated in the
cases in the House of Lords to which I have referred. The judge refused to do so and
upheld the validity of a testamentary power which, although dealing with fairly remote
e trusts, was expressed in the broadest possible terms. Counsel for the residuary beneficiaries
invited me not to follow *Re Abrahams's Will Trusts* and the two earlier cases, saying that
they were only extempore judgments by judges of first instance. I am afraid that I have
now added another to the list, though probably after the benefit of fuller argument than
my predecessors heard. Nevertheless, I respectfully think that Cross J was right.

The one jurisdiction in which the House of Lords dicta have apparently succeeded in
f generating an independent rule against testamentary delegation is in the High Court of
Australia, where it received the support of Fullagar J in his judgment in *Tatham v Huxtable*
(1950) 81 CLR 639. The judge there decided unequivocally that whether or not the
power in question might have been valid if conferred by deed, it was invalid because it
amounted to a testamentary delegation. Of the other two judges who constituted the
court, Kitto J decided that the power failed the certainty test and Latham CJ dissented,
g holding that it was valid as a general power.

Tatham v Huxtable has given rise to a good deal of discussion, most of it critical, in
Australian and Canadian legal literature and it was followed with some reluctance by the
Court of Appeal of New South Wales in *Horan v James* [1982] 2 NSWLR 376. I respectfully
think that Fullagar J found more in the House of Lords cases than was actually there.
h More recently, in *Re Nicholls* (1987) 34 DLR (4th) 321, the Ontario Court of Appeal has
rejected the existence of any rule against delegation which would preclude the use of
general powers in wills.

The result of this survey of the authorities, for which I am greatly indebted to counsel,
is that once it is conceded that cll 3 and 4 qualify as powers which would be valid if
created by deed, there is in my judgment no rule of law to invalidate them because they
j happen to be in a will. Nor can I think of any good reason why such a distinction should
exist. The solemn nature of a will, the interests of the next of kin in default and the
provisions of the 1837 Act, seem to me insufficient grounds for introducing one. Of
course, there are many distinctions between wills and settlements. But, like the Ontario
court in *Re Nicholls*, I can see no reason why these should dictate a special restriction on
the breadth of powers which can be created by will.

Furthermore, the invalidation of wide testamentary powers of appointment would involve considerable injustice to the beneficiaries of testators who, relying on cases like *Re Park* which have stood without adverse criticism for nearly 60 years, have conferred such powers on their trustees. For example, as counsel for the trustees in this case pointed out, the latest edition of *Williams on Wills* (6th edn, 1987) contains a precedent for a testamentary power in the widest possible terms to take advantage of the inheritance tax relief obtainable under the Inheritance Tax Act 1984, s 144, on a rearrangement of the beneficial interests within two years of the death. There is no warning in the book that such a power might be invalid and in my judgment no reason why there should have been.

So I shall accordingly declare that cll 3 and 4 of the will are valid.

Order accordingly.

Solicitors: *Birkbeck Montagu's* (for the trustees); *Theodore Goddard* (for the first to fifth defendants); *Thomson Snell & Passmore*, Tunbridge Wells (for the sixth to eighth defendants); *Wedlake Bell* (for the ninth defendant).

Evelyn M C Budd　Barrister.

Schott Kem Ltd v Bentley and others

COURT OF APPEAL, CIVIL DIVISION
NEILL AND GLIDEWELL LJJ
4, 5 DECEMBER 1989, 23 FEBRUARY 1990

Practice – Pre-trial or post-judgment relief – Interim payment – Jurisdiction to order interim payment – Evidence of need or prejudice – Applicant obtaining joint and several orders for interim payments against defendants without producing evidence of need or prejudice – Whether court having power to order interim payments in absence of evidence of need or prejudice – Whether court having power to make joint and several orders for interim payments against a number of defendants – RSC Ord 29, rr 11, 12.

The plaintiff company was a plumbing contractor with special expertise in the supply and installation of glass drainline, which was used primarily in hospitals and by public authorities for the disposal of corrosive waste material. In 1988 the plaintiffs' parent company decided to carry out investigations into the rapidly deteriorating financial position of its subsidiary. The investigations revealed that the joint managing directors of the plaintiff company, with the assistance of the contracts manager, had been dishonestly diverting contracts for the supply and installation of glass pipework and for large-scale plumbing works from the plaintiff company to two companies which they owned and controlled. The plaintiffs brought an action against the joint managing directors, the contracts manager and others claiming damages under various heads including conspiracy to defraud, breach of contract, misuse of confidential information, and seeking an account of profits obtained from the diverted contracts. The plaintiffs subsequently applied for interim payments under RSC Ord 29, rr 11[a] and 12[b] to be made by the six principal defendants to mitigate hardship and prejudice pending trial of the action. The judge treated the liability of the six defendants as a joint liability in respect

---

a　Rule 11, so far as material, is set out at p 855 *d e*, post
b　Rule 12, so far as material, is set out at p 855 *f g*, post

of each of the five heads of claim and made joint and several orders for interim payments
a against them, the aggregate of which exceeded his assessment of the total award
recoverable by the plaintiffs if the action proceeded to trial. In making interim payment
orders against four of the defendants the judge did not indicate how the payments were
to be apportioned under each head of claim. The defendants appealed against the interim
payment orders, contending (i) that Ord 29, rr 11 and 12 required a plaintiff to satisfy
the court of his need for an interim payment or that he would suffer prejudice if he did
b not obtain one and that since the plaintiffs had failed to produce any evidence of need or
prejudice the court should have refused to make the interim payment orders, and (ii)
that the court should not make joint and several orders for interim payments against a
number of defendants, since there was no procedure for apportionment pending trial
and such orders would enable a plaintiff to select the defendant from whom to recover
the interim payment, or alternatively, if joint and several orders were allowable, the total
c payments should equal an amount thought by the court to be 'just' in accordance with
rr 11 and 12.

Held – (1) On their true construction , RSC Ord 29, rr 11 and 12 conferred a discretion
on the court whether to order an interim payment at all, but where an interim payment
was ordered the amount of the payment should be such amount as the court thought
d 'just', with the additional limitation in the case of damages that the amount was not to
exceed a 'reasonable proportion' of the damages which in the opinion of the court were
likely to be recovered by the plaintiff, after taking into account any set-off, cross-claim or
counterclaim on which the defendant might be entitled to rely. Accordingly, the court
had jurisdiction to make an order for an interim payment under rr 11 and 12 without
requiring the plaintiff to satisfy the court either of his need for an interim payment or
e that he would suffer prejudice if he did not obtain it, since there was no restriction
implicit in the rules which would prevent an interim payment being made in the
absence of evidence of need or prejudice (see p 858 c to e and p 864 d, post); Shearson
Lehman Bros Inc v Maclaine Watson & Co Ltd [1987] 2 All ER 181 considered.

(2) The court also had jurisdiction to make orders for interim payments against two
f or more defendants in respect of the same liability and in respect of the same sum if it
was satisfied as to the liability of each of the defendants against whom the order was
made. Moreover, there was no objection in principle to the making of orders for interim
payments against two or more defendants for different proportions of the total amount
thought to be just, provided it was made clear that if the aggregate of the proportions
awarded against the defendants exceeded the 'just amount' the sum actually recoverable
g by the plaintiff could not exceed the just amount and that, in the case of a claim for
damages, the sum actually recoverable by the plaintiff could not exceed the reasonable
proportion of the damages likely to be awarded at trial. Additionally, where joint and
separate claims were made against a number of different defendants and some of the
claims were alternative to other claims, an order for interim payments had to make it
clear whether the payments ordered against different defendants in respect of the same
h liability were intended to be for the same sum or in respect of different proportions and,
where claims were made against two defendants in the alternative, the order also had to
make it clear whether the court was satisfied that the plaintiff would recover against one
of the defendants and, if so, which one. Accordingly, when making the order for interim
payments against the defendants, the judge should have indicated how the payments
were to be apportioned under each head of claim and whether the sum ordered against
j each individual defendant was intended to be in respect of a separate proportion of the
relevant liability. Since the aggregate of the payments ordered by the judge exceeded his
assessment of their total liability, the appeal would be allowed to the extent that the
interim payments to be made by the defendants would be reduced and that where the
total liability assessed by the judge under one head of claim was joint the sums ordered
to be paid would relate to separate proportions of that liability (see p 858 g j, p 859 b,
p 863 c and p 864 d, post).

whereby a company to be formed by Mr Bentley and Mr Buckley might take over the
Schott Kem plumbing business. On 30 June the proposal was finally rejected.   *a*

By this time, however, the German directors including Dr Schott had become very
suspicious of the activities of Mr Bentley and Mr Buckley and were also much concerned
by the rapidly deteriorating financial position of Schott Kem itself. The German directors
decided to carry out an investigation into the past activities of Mr Bentley and Mr
Buckley.

In July 1988 redundancies were declared in Schott Kem and Mr Bentley and Mr   *b*
Buckley were told that their futures were under review.

By August 1988 the investigations which were being carried out appeared to suggest
that Mr Bentley and Mr Buckley had been making fraudulent claims for expenses. In the
following month it came to the notice of Dr Van Den Broek, the general manager of
Schott Glass, that a company called Mileforge Ltd was competing for business with Schott
Kem and that Mr Buckley was the contact man for that company at Schott Kem's own   *c*
premises. It subsequently came to light that Mileforge had been incorporated by Mr
Bentley and Mr Buckley through nominee directors and shareholders on 11 July 1988.

Matters came to a head in October 1988. On 21 October both Mr Bentley and Mr
Buckley were dismissed. Before that Anton Piller orders had been granted against these
two defendants and also against Mileforge and the third and fifth defendants.

The writ in the present proceedings was issued on 10 October 1988 and has been   *d*
subsequently amended to include further defendants and further claims.

In broad terms the case for Schott Kem is that Mr Bentley and Mr Buckley, while still
directors of Schott Kem, dishonestly diverted contracts for the supply and installation of
pipework and for large-scale plumbing work from Schott Kem to Mileforge and to SGD,
being companies which were owned and controlled by Mr Bentley and Mr Buckley. It is
alleged that these two defendants were assisted by Mr Anderson, who was employed by   *e*
Schott Kem until 31 August 1988 as contracts manager.

I shall have to return later to consider in more detail the various heads of claim with
which this appeal is concerned. At this stage it is sufficient to note that there are five
relevant claims to which the following headings can be given: (1) the Chelsea contract;
(2) the Hastings contract; (3) the Drainline contracts; (4) the Mursa claim, and (5) stolen
material. It is also to be noted that Schott Kem relies on various causes of action including   *f*
conspiracy to defraud, breach of contract and misuse of confidential information. It also
claims an account of profits obtained from diverted contracts.

Before turning to consider the claims in more detail, however, I must first examine
the power of the court to order interim payments and the general submissions which
have been put forward on behalf of the defendants as to the limitations on the exercise of
that power.   *g*

The power to order interim payments

The power to make rules of court to enable a court in which any proceedings are
pending to make an order requiring a party to the proceedings to make an interim
payment was first conferred by s 20 of the Administration of Justice Act 1969. The court   *h*
has no inherent power to order an interim payment: *Moore v Assignment Courier Ltd*
[1977] 2 All ER 842, [1977] 1 WLR 638. This section gave effect, with modifications, to
recommendations which had been made in the report of the Winn Committee on
Personal Injuries Litigation (Cmnd 3691).

The power to make rules was first exercised in 1970 in relation to actions for damages
for death or for personal injury. In 1977 RSC Ord 29 was extended to provide for interim   *j*
payments in actions for possession of land. In 1980, however, Ord 29 was further
amended and the power to make interim payments in pending proceedings is now very
wide. The statutory basis for the jurisdiction is contained in s 32 of the Supreme Court
Act 1981. It is not necessary, however, to refer to s 32 of the 1981 Act and I can turn at
once to the relevant rules contained in Pt II of Ord 29.

By Ord 29, r 9 an interim payment is defined in relation to a defendant as—

'a payment on account of any damages, debt or other sum (excluding costs) which he may be held liable to pay to or for the benefit of the plaintiff.'

Order 29, r 10, as far as material, provides:

'(1) The plaintiff may, at any time after the writ has been served on a defendant and the time limited for him to acknowledge service has expired, apply to the Court for an order requiring that defendant to make an interim payment.
(2) An application under this rule shall be made by summons but may be included in a summons for summary judgment under Order 14 or Order 86.
(3) An application under this rule shall be supported by an affidavit which shall— (a) verify the amount of damages, debt or other sum to which the application relates and the grounds of the application; (b) exhibit any documentary evidence relied on by the plaintiff in support of the application . . .'

Order 29, r 11, so far as is material, provides:

'(1) If, on the hearing of an application under rule 10 in an action for damages, the Court is satisfied . . . (c) that, if the action proceeded to trial, the plaintiff would obtain judgment for substantial damages against the respondent or, where there are two or more defendants, against any of them, the Court may, if it thinks fit and subject to paragraph (2), order the respondent to make an interim payment of such amount as it thinks just, not exceeding a reasonable proportion of the damages which in the opinion of the Court are likely to be recovered by the plaintiff after taking into account any relevant contributory negligence and any set-off, cross-claim or counterclaim on which the respondent may be entitled to rely.
(2) No order shall be made under paragraph (1) in an action for personal injuries if it appears to the Court that the defendant is not a person falling within one of the following categories, namely—(a) a person who is insured in respect of the plaintiff's claim; (b) a public authority; or (c) a person whose means and resources are such as to enable him to make the interim payment.'

Order 29, r 12, so far as material, provides:

'If, on the hearing of an application under rule 10, the Court is satisfied . . . (c) that, if the action proceeded to trial, the plaintiff would obtain judgment against the defendant for a substantial sum of money apart from any damages or costs, the Court may, if it thinks fit, and without prejudice to any contentions of the parties as to the nature or character of the sum to be paid by the defendant, order the defendant to make an interim payment of such amount as it thinks just, after taking into account any set-off, cross-claim or counterclaim on which the defendant may be entitled to rely.'

Order 29, r 17, provides:

'Where a defendant has been ordered to make an interim payment or has in fact made an interim payment, whether voluntarily or pursuant to an order, the Court may, in giving or making a final judgment or order, or granting the plaintiff leave to discontinue his action or to withdraw the claim in respect of which the interim payment has been made, or at any other stage of the proceedings on the application of any party, make such order with respect to the interim payment as may be just, and in particular—(a) an order for the repayment by the plaintiff of all or part of the interim payment, or (b) an order for the payment to be varied or discharged, or (c) an order for the payment by any other defendant of any part of the interim payment which the defendant who made it is entitled to recover from him by way of contribution or indemnity or in respect of any remedy or relief relating to or connected with the plaintiff's claim.'

The power of the court to order interim payments under Pt II of Ord 29 has been considered in recent years in a number of cases in the Court of Appeal, including *Shearson Lehman Bros Inc v Maclaine Watson & Co Ltd* [1987] 2 All ER 181, [1987] 1 WLR 480, *Shanning International Ltd v George Wimpey International Ltd* [1988] 3 All ER 475, [1989] 1 WLR 981, *Ricci Burns Ltd v Toole* [1989] 3 All ER 478, [1989] 1 WLR 993 and *British and Commonwealth Holdings plc v Quadrex Holdings Inc* [1989] 3 All ER 492, [1989] QB 842.

From the wording of the relevant rules and from these authorities the following seems clear.

(1) Rules 11 and 12 of Ord 29 form part of a single code: see the *Shearson Lehman* case [1987] 2 All ER 181 at 190, [1987] 1 WLR 480 at 492 per Nicholls LJ.

(2) Under both rules the court approaches the matter in two stages.

(3) At the first stage the court has to consider whether it is 'satisfied' of one of the matters set out in sub-paras (a), (b) and (c) of the rules. Thus, for example, in a case where r 11(1)(c) is relied on the court has to be satisfied—

'that, if the action proceeded to trial, the plaintiff would obtain judgment for substantial damages against the respondent or, where there are two or more defendants, against any of them.'

In a case where Ord 29, r 12(1)(c) is relied on the court has to be satisfied—

'that if the action proceeded to trial, the plaintiff would obtain judgment against the defendant for a substantial sum of money apart from any damages or costs.'

(4) In order for the court to be satisfied that the plaintiff would obtain judgment—

'something more than a prima facie case is clearly required, but not proof beyond reasonable doubt. The burden is high. But it is a civil burden on the balance of probabilities, not a criminal burden.'

(See the *Shearson Lehman* case [1987] 2 All ER 181 at 187, [1987] 1 WLR 480 at 489 per Lloyd LJ.)

Furthermore, even where conditional leave to defend is given under Ord 14 the court may nevertheless order an interim payment in an appropriate case. Thus in *British and Commonwealth Holdings plc v Quadrex Holdings Inc* [1989] 3 All ER 492 at 511, [1989] QB 842 at 866 Sir Nicolas Browne-Wilkinson V-C put the matter as follows:

'. . . in cases where on the evidence then before it, the court entertains sufficient doubts as to the genuineness of the defence to give only conditional leave to defend, it is possible for a court to be satisfied that the plaintiff will succeed at trial. Although in such a case it does not automatically follow that it is appropriate to make an order for interim payment, if in all the circumstances such payment appears sensible and desirable, in my judgment it can be ordered.'

(5) At the second stage the court, if satisfied that the plaintiff would recover a substantial sum, may then proceed, if it thinks fit, to order an interim payment 'of such amount as it thinks just'. At this stage under r 11(1) the payment must not exceed—

'a reasonable proportion of the damages which in the opinion of the court are likely to be recovered by the plaintiff after taking into account any relevant contributory negligence and any set-off, cross-claim or counterclaim on which the respondent may be entitled to rely.'

Under r 12 the payment ordered must take account of 'any set-off, cross-claim or counterclaim on which the defendant may be entitled to rely'.

(6) Where a plaintiff makes alternative claims against a defendant, eg, for rent with an alternative claim for mesne profits, or for the price of goods with an alternative claim for damages, the court can order an interim payment without reaching a conclusion at that stage as to which of the alternative claims against the defendant will succeed at the trial, provided it is satisfied that the plaintiff will recover a substantial sum under one

head or the other: see the *Shearson Lehman* case [1987] 2 All ER 181, [1987] 1 WLR 480.

a Indeed, as Nicholls LJ pointed out in the *Shearson Lehman* case [1987] 2 All ER 181 at 191, [1987] 1 WLR 480 at 493:

> '... it is apparent from the express terms of r 12 that it is not intended that, as a prerequisite to making an interim payment order, the court must be satisfied in every case on the precise legal label to be attached to the sum in question.'

b It would seem, however, that if there is a doubt whether the sum claimed will prove to be recoverable as damages or under some other heading the court should apply a discount when ordering an interim payment to take account of the provision as to 'a reasonable proportion of the damages' in r 11(1).

(7) Where, however, claims are made in the alternative against two or more defendants it seems that an order for interim payment cannot be made if the court is satisfied merely *c* that the plaintiff will recover against one of these defendants but is not satisfied of recovery against any particular one. It will be remembered that it is provided in Ord 29, r 11(c) that in an action for damages the power to make an order for interim payment can arise if the court is satisfied that 'the plaintiff would obtain judgment for substantial damages ... where there are two or more defendants, against any of them'. But in *Ricci Burns Ltd v Toole* [1989] 3 All ER 478 at 485, [1989] 1 WLR 993 at 1002 Ralph Gibson LJ *d* (with whom Butler-Sloss LJ agreed) held that these words—

> 'do not on their true construction permit an order to be made against one or other of two defendants on the ground that the court is satisfied that the plaintiff will succeed against one or other of them. Proof of success to the necessary standard against any defendant is required before an order can be made against him.'

e And in *Breeze v R McKennon & Son Ltd* (1985) 32 Build LR 41 at 49 Croom-Johnson LJ said:

> 'What the court must be satisfied of under rule 11(1)(c) is that the plaintiff will recover substantial damages from the respondent against whom the order is made, and the damages "likely to be recovered" means recovered from that respondent and *f* not from somebody else.'

(8) In an action for personal injuries r 11(2) makes express provision concerning the means and resources of the defendant. Thus r 11(2)(c) places an absolute embargo on the making of an order for interim payment in personal injury cases where the means and resources of an uninsured defendant are inadequate. In other cases the means of the defendant are relevant though they are not decisive. Thus if a defendant's resources are *g* such that an order for interim payment would cause irremediable harm which cannot be made good by an eventual adjustment or repayment under r 17, that is a very relevant factor to be taken into account in fixing the amount of any interim payment: see the *Quadrex* case [1989] 3 All ER 492 at 511, [1989] QB 842 at 867 per Sir Nicolas Browne-Wilkinson V-C.

h (9) Interim payment procedures are not suitable where the factual issues are complicated or where difficult points of law arise which may take many hours and the citation of many authorities to resolve.

I turn now to the two general submissions made by counsel for the defendants concerning the operation of Pt II of Ord 29.

The first submission was that it is for a plaintiff to satisfy the court of his need for an *j* interim payment or that he will suffer prejudice if he does not obtain one, and that in the present case Schott Kem had produced no evidence of need or prejudice.

In support of this submission counsel relied on the dictum of Croom-Johnson LJ in *Breeze v R McKennon & Son Ltd* (1985) 32 Build LR 41 at 50 where he said that the plaintiff's evidence should explain why the order is required and cover 'the need for the plaintiff to have the money'. In addition reliance was placed on the following passage in the judgment of Nicholls LJ in the *Shearson Lehman* case [1987] 2 All ER 181 at 190, [1987] 1 WLR 480 at 492, where he said:

'... the underlying purpose of the two rules [rr 11 and 12] is the same: to mitigate hardship or prejudice to a defendant which may exist during the period from the commencement of an action to the trial.'

Moreover, reference might also have been made to a similar dictum as to the underlying purpose of the rules of Ralph Gibson LJ in *Ricci Burns Ltd v Toole* [1989] 3 All ER 478 at 485, [1989] 1 WLR 993 at 1002.

Counsel for Schott Kem, on the other hand, relied on the fact that in the *Shearson Lehman* case Lloyd LJ rejected an argument on behalf of the defendants that this Part of Ord 29 was only intended to apply in very special circumstances where the plaintiff can show real hardship.

As I understand the present practice, it is customary in personal injury actions for interim payments to be limited to sums for which the plaintiff can show a need. This is a sensible course because large interim payments in such cases may lead to difficulties if an order for repayment is subsequently made under Ord 29, r 17.

I am not satisfied, however, that there is any restriction implicit in the rules which prevents an interim payment order being made in the absence of evidence of need or prejudice. By the use of the words 'if it thinks fit', both rr 11 and 12 confer a discretion on the court whether to order an interim payment at all. Moreover the amount of the payment is expressed to be 'of such amount as [the court] thinks just', with the additional limitation in the case of damages that the amount is not to exceed 'a reasonable proportion of the damages which in the opinion of the Court are likely to be recovered by the plaintiff' after taking into account the matters specified. For my part I can see no basis for any further limitation on the jurisdiction of the court to order interim payments than those set out in Ord 29 itself.

I would therefore reject the argument that it is necessary for Schott Kem to produce evidence of need or prejudice.

The second general submission made on behalf of the defendants was to the effect that the court should not make joint and several orders for interim payments against a number of defendants. It was pointed out that there is no procedure for apportionment at this stage and that such orders would enable a plaintiff to select the defendant from whom to recover the interim payment.

In the alternative it was submitted that if joint and several orders are made the total of these orders should not exceed the amount thought to be 'just' in accordance with rr 11 and 12.

For my part I can see no objection to the making of orders for interim payments against two or more defendants in respect of the same liability and in respect of the same sum if the court is satisfied as to the liability of each of the defendants against whom an order is made. The payment of this sum or a proportion of it by any of the defendants will relieve the other defendants of their liability to the plaintiff either wholly or pro tanto, though there may of course be rights of recovery between the defendants.

Nor can I see any objection in principle to the making of orders for interim payments against two or more defendants for different fractions of the total amount thought to be 'just', provided (a) it is made clear that if the aggregate of the fractions awarded against the defendants exceeds the 'just amount' the sum actually recoverable by the plaintiff cannot exceed the 'just amount', (b) in the case of a claim for damages it is made clear that the sum actually recoverable by the plaintiff cannot exceed the 'reasonable proportion of the damages' and (c) the order otherwise complies with the rules. Thus the rules are to be applied flexibly and there may well be cases where one defendant will, for example, have a cross-claim which is not available to the other defendants.

I would only add that where fractions of the total amount thought to be 'just' are ordered by way of interim payments against different defendants it may often be simpler

in practice, in order to avoid any risk of confusion or duplication of recovery, to provide
a that the aggregate of the fractions does not exceed the 'just amount' or the 'reasonable
proportion' as the case may be.

More difficult questions arise, however, where, as in the present case, claims both joint
and separate are made against a number of different defendants and where some of the
claims are alternative to other claims. In such a case it is necessary for the order to make
clear (a) whether the payments ordered against different defendants in respect of the
b same liability are intended to be for the same sum or in respect of fractions and (b) where
claims are made against two defendants in the alternative, whether the court is satisfied
that the plaintiff will recover against one of the defendants and, if so, which. I shall
return to this matter again later when I come to the orders made in this case.

The heads of claim
c   With this general introduction I can turn to the heads of claim with which we are
presently concerned.

1. *The Chelsea contract*
In December 1987 Schott Kem was invited to tender for a sub-contract for the supply
of mechanical services at the New Brompton and National Heart Hospital in Chelsea. In
d due course a tender was put forward by Schott Kem in the sum of £561,000, which the
judge described as 'wholly unrealistic'. The main contractors invited Schott Kem to
submit a revised quotation, but the contract was diverted by Mr Bentley and Mr Buckley
to SGD. On 6 July 1988 the main contractor placed an order with SGD in the sum of
£291,840.

It is not in dispute that SGD received payments from the main contractor in respect of
e this work despite the fact that the labour costs were paid by Schott Kem. It is alleged in
the amended defence of Mr Bentley, Mr Buckley, Mileforge, SGD and Mursa (General
Engineering) Ltd (Mursa) that—

'SGD and Bentley and Buckley always intended to pay Schott Kem for the work
done on the job, as part of an overall agreement by them to take over Schott Kem's
f   plumbing business.'

The judge rejected this assertion (which was repeated in the affidavits) and also the
other defences put forward including a defence that the contract had been transferred to
SGD with the tacit approval of Schott Kem given through Mr Thiele, a director.

In the end the judge came to the conclusion that judgment should be entered against
Mr Bentley, Mr Buckley, SGD and Mr Anderson jointly and severally for a sum at least as
g great as the minimum figure of £94,000 for labour costs. In addition he concluded that
judgment should be entered against Mr Bentley, Mr Buckley and SGD for a further sum
of £6,386·85 for quantity surveyor's fees which had been paid by Schott Kem.

The judge did not reach any conclusion as to the basis of the claim against the four
defendants. He said:

h   'The claim in relation to the Chelsea contract is put in a number of ways. As
against Mr Bentley and Mr Buckley, damages under various heads are sought and,
in the alternative, an account of money paid under a mistake of fact. Adopting the
approach to which I have already referred in the *Shearson Lehman* case, I am not
required precisely to designate the label under which judgment would be obtained:
it suffices to say that I am satisfied that under this head of claim judgment will be
j   entered against them jointly and severally ... I am further satisfied that they have
admitted liability for these claims, although not the amount of damages or money
paid.'

For the purposes of this appeal it is not challenged on behalf of Mr Bentley, Mr Buckley
or SGD that they are likely to be found liable in respect of the Chelsea contract for

£100,386·85. Under this heading the appeal on their behalf is limited to the general
contentions that Schott Kem has not demonstrated a need for the payments to be made
and in any event that each of the three defendants has insufficient assets to meet the
interim payments ordered. I shall return to the question of assets later.

On behalf of Mr Anderson on the other hand the order for interim payment is
challenged on a wider ground. Thus it is asserted on his behalf that he was not involved
in the dishonest scheme, if such it was, to charge the labour costs to Schott Kem. The
claim, it is said, is for restitution for which Mr Anderson is not liable in law.

In his judgment the judge considered the position of Mr Anderson and said:

> 'The claim against Anderson does not include an account of money paid under a
> mistake of fact. But I am satisfied that in signing the time sheets in particular, and
> in other ways to which I have already referred, he was a party, despite his denials,
> with Mr Bentley and Mr Buckley in deceiving [Schott Kem] into paying the labour
> costs on the Chelsea contract. In my opinion, at least £94,000 will be awarded
> against him as damages.'

Earlier in the judgment the judge had already examined the nature of the case against
Mr Anderson. The judge expressed the conclusion that he was satisfied on consideration
of all the affidavits and the documents exhibited to them that Mr Anderson was 'a full
party, although in a subordinate position, to the activities of Mr Bentley, Mr Buckley,
SGD and Mileforge'. It is true that there are a number of matters of fact which are
challenged by Mr Anderson. It is also true that as a general proposition a court will be
very slow to reach conclusions about disputed facts in interlocutory proceedings. On the
other hand it is to be remembered that Mr Anderson was an employee of Schott Kem
and one of the claims against him is based on the fact that he owed duties to Schott Kem
in his position as an employee.

I have felt some anxiety about the position of Mr Anderson but in the end I have
concluded that there was sufficient material to entitle the judge to order an interim
payment against him under this head of claim. I shall have to return to the question of
amount later.

2. *The Hastings contract*

The Hastings contract was for work at the Hastings General District Hospital site. The
complaint by Schott Kem in the action is that the contract for this work was diverted by
Mr Buckley and Mr Bentley with the assistance of Mr Anderson first to SGD and then to
Mileforge.

The claims by Schott Kem in respect of the Hastings contract are pleaded in a number
of ways. For the purpose of the present applications, however, the relevant head of claim
relied on is that the defendants (other than Mursa) are liable as constructive trustees
either to account for the profits made by Mileforge or in respect of the losses made by
Schott Kem.

A number of factual defences are relied on. It is said that there is no proof that
Mileforge made any profit and that in any event the profits lie in the future. It is said
that consent to the diversion of this contract was given by Mr Zuber, the managing
director of Schott Kem. It is also alleged that there is no proof that Schott Kem would
have undertaken this contract itself or, if it had done so, that it would have made a profit.

In addition on behalf of the defendants reliance is placed on the decision of the House
of Lords in *Regal (Hastings) Ltd v Gulliver* [1942] 1 All ER 378, [1967] 2 AC 134. In that
case it was held that a director of the company who had acted in breach of his fiduciary
duty to his company but who had not been guilty of any wilful misconduct was not
liable to account for profits made by other persons as a result of his breach.

The judge came to the conclusion, having considered all the evidence, that there was
sufficient material in the documents, which included a transcript of taped telephone

calls, to satisfy him that Mr Bentley and Mr Buckley had acted dishonestly. He further
a concluded that the opportunity to participate in the Hastings contract was a form of trust
property and that Mr Bentley and Mr Buckley were liable to account for the profits as
constructive trustees even though they had not obtained the profit themselves. He took
the same view of the position of Mr Anderson.

In the result the judge concluded from the evidence that he was sure to a high degree
of probability that the profit to Mileforge on the Hastings contract would be considerable
b and that judgment would be obtained against Mr Bentley, Mr Buckley, Mr Anderson
and Mileforge for a sum of not less than £100,000. This liability, he decided, would be
joint and several.

I do not consider that it would be helpful at this stage to attempt to make a detailed
analysis of the cases to which we were referred and in particular of the decisions in *Barnes
v Addy* (1874) LR 9 Ch App 244 and *Belmont Finance Corp Ltd v Williams Furniture Ltd
c (No 2)* [1980] 1 All ER 393. Having considered the evidence before the judge, however, I
think there was material on which he could be satisfied for the purpose of RSC Ord 29,
r 12 as to the liability of Mileforge, Mr Bentley and Mr Buckley. It also seems to me that
he was entitled to assess liability at a round figure of £100,000. On the other hand I
regard the case against Mr Anderson as less clear. Though the point may be academic, I
would not uphold an interim payment in so far as it reflects any liability by him to
d account for profits made by Mileforge on the Hastings contract.

3. *The Drainline contracts*
The judge, in dealing with these contracts, said:

'A large number of contracts for the supply and installation of drainline pipework
e   were simply diverted by Mr Bentley and Mr Buckley to SGD. In some instances, the
tender documents sent to Schott Kem were made available to SGD, together with
Schott Kem's tender price. Letters under the signature of Mr Ruane [the eighth
defendant and a director of SGD] were then sent to the customers, making an
unsolicited tender at a price of 10% to 15% below the known Schott Kem price. As
they grew bolder, trade inquiries were simply switched to SGD directly, thereby
f   denying any knowledge of the inquiry to Schott Kem. SGD would then tender as a
company which was a subsidiary of or associated with Schott Kem.'

The claims by Schott Kem against Mr Bentley, Mr Buckley and SGD were for damages
and an account of profits on these contracts by SGD. The judge made his order, however,
only on the basis of the profits on the contracts which were not in dispute. On this basis
he concluded that the profit on the four relevant contracts was £31,124·81 and that the
g minimum sum recoverable against these three defendants would be £30,000.

Mr Bentley and Mr Buckley challenged the orders made against them on the basis that
they did not receive any of the profit themselves: cf *Regal (Hastings) Ltd v Gulliver* [1942]
1 All ER 378, [1967] 2 AC 134. But I consider that the judge was entitled to be satisfied
at this interlocutory stage that Schott Kem would recover against the two directors as
h persons who had knowingly and dishonestly diverted the contracts to SGD: cf Goff and
Jones *The Law of Restitution* (3rd edn, 1986) p 642 and *Snell's Principles of Equity* (28th edn,
1982) p 194.

4. *The Mursa claim*
Mursa is the ninth defendant. The claim against it is for money had and received and
j relates to sums paid by Schott Kem for materials which were invoiced but never delivered
to Schott Kem. It is conceded that some at least of these materials were used to perform
an SGD contract. The judge's conclusion on this claim was as follows:

'... Mursa has not performed its part of the contract at all and is liable to restore
the money paid to it. The case against Mr Bentley, Mr Buckley, Mr Anderson and

SGD can be put, again on the admissions which have been made, on the basis of damages for a conspiracy to defraud. It is not necessary for me to determine the precise ground on which Schott Kem would succeed under this head or to decide the factual issue as to how much has actually been paid.'

It seems to me, however, that the claim against Mursa for money had and received may properly be regarded as an alternative claim to the claim for damages for conspiracy against the other defendants. The primary liability would appear to be that of Mursa, which received the money. I would not uphold an interim payment under this heading against any defendants other than Mursa.

5. *The stolen material*

On 30 June 1988 48 rolls of cast iron belonging to Schott Kem were taken from the Schott Kem site at HMS Osprey on the instructions of Mr Anderson. There is a dispute about the value of this material. The four defendants against whom an order was made also dispute liability on the general grounds that Schott Kem has not proved either need or prejudice and that the defendants lack the means to make the payments ordered. The judge concluded that Schott Kem would recover damages of at least £5,000 against each of the four defendants as there was some room for dispute about the value of the claim which was put by Schott Kem at £9,183·77. Under this heading the judge made orders against Mr Bentley, Mr Buckley, Mr Anderson and SGD. I would uphold this order.

Summary of the judge's order

The judge concluded in respect of the five claims that Schott Kem would recover the following sums:

(1) *The Chelsea contract*
   (a) Against Mr Bentley, Mr Buckley and SGD   £100,386·85
   (b) Against Mr Anderson   £94,000·00
(2) *The Hastings contract*
   Against Mr Bentley, Mr Buckley,
   Mileforge and Mr Anderson   £100,000·00

In my judgment the case against Mr Anderson was not sufficiently clear to justify a finding at this stage on which to base an interim order.

(3) *The Drainline contracts*
   Against Mr Bentley, Mr Buckley and SGD   £30,000·00
(4) *The Mursa claim*
   Against Mr Bentley, Mr Buckley, SGD,
   Mr Anderson and Mursa   £12,471·03

In my judgment there is an argument that the claims against Mursa for money had and received and the claims against the other defendants for damages for conspiracy should be regarded as alternative claims. I consider therefore that any interim order under this heading should be limited to an order against Mursa.

(5) *The stolen material*
   Against Mr Bentley, Mr Buckley,
   Mr Anderson and SGD   £5,000·00

The total of the claims against the six relevant defendants can now be recalculated as follows:

Mr Bentley and Mr Buckley (1, 2, 3 and 5)   £235,386·85
Mr Anderson (1 and 5)   £99,000·00
SGD (1, 3 and 5)   £135,386·85
Mileforge (2)   £100,000·00
Mursa (4)   £12,471·03

On the basis of the somewhat larger assessments of liability made by the judge, he
a ordered the following interim payments:

Mr Bentley	£75,000·00
Mr Buckley	£75,000·00
Mileforge	£50,000·00
Mr Anderson	£10,000·00
SGD	£75,000·00
Mursa	£12,471·03

b

It is to be observed (a) that the judge treated the liability of the defendants as joint in
respect of each head of claim and (b) that in making the orders for interim payments
against the defendants other than Mileforge and Mursa the judge did not indicate how
the payments were to be apportioned under each head of claim. It seems to me that in
c the present case it was necessary for the judge to make clear in the order the sums ordered
under each head of claim and to indicate whether or not the sum ordered against each
individual defendant was intended to be in respect of a separate fraction of the relevant
liability. Thus there is force in the criticism on behalf of the defendants that the aggregate
of the payments ordered exceeds the total liability of which the judge was satisfied at this
stage.
d

The means of the defendants and cross-appeal
The judge made his assessments of the payments on the following basis:

> 'My final task is to assess an interim payment in respect of each defendant of such
> amount as I consider to be just, not exceeding, where the claim sounds in damages,
e > a reasonable proportion of those damages. I consider that the means of the respective
> defendants play a part in that determination. It is not my intention by this order to
> ensure the immediate bankruptcy of any one defendant or to drive either of the two
> companies out of business. If that is the unfortunate result, it can only be due to the
> lack of any satisfactory and up-to-date evidence of means provided to me by the
> defendants.'

f   In my view no valid criticism can be made of the judge's general approach. He had no
up-to-date evidence of means. This court, however, has some further information,
though even this information is far from complete or satisfactory. But it is enough to
enable and indeed require the court to look at the interim payments afresh.
      On the basis of the evidence of means before us, I see no sense in extending the ambit
of the orders to include other contracts or additional liabilities, and for this reason I would
g not give effect to any of the matters set out in Schott Kem's cross-notice. But I do not
criticise Schott Kem for putting these arguments forward because it is fully entitled to
scrutinise any evidence of means tendered by the defendants with great care.
      Looking at the matter afresh and having regard to such information as is now before
us, I would vary the judge's order as follows:

h   Mr Bentley   Interim payment of   £70,000
            This order to be apportioned as follows:
                  Chelsea contract   £30,000
                  Hastings contract   £30,000
                  Drainline contracts   £9,000
                  stolen material   £1,000

j   Mr Buckley   Interim payment of   £50,000
            This order to be apportioned as follows:
                  Chelsea contract   £20,000
                  Hastings contract   £20,000
                  Drainline contracts   £9,000
                  stolen material   £1,000

Mr Anderson	Interim payment of	£6,000

This order to be apportioned as follows:

Chelsea contract	£5,000
stolen material	£1,000

SGD	Interim payment of	£40,000

This order to be apportioned as follows:

Chelsea contract	£30,000
Drainline contracts	£9,000
stolen material	£1,000

Mileforge	Interim payment of	£30,000

in respect of the Hastings contract.

Mursa	Interim payment of	£12,471·03

in respect of the Mursa claim.
It is to be noted there is no up-to-date
evidence about this company.

These interim payments are intended to be cumulative.

Accordingly where the total liability assessed by the judge under one head of claim is joint the sums to be paid relate to separate fractions of that joint liability.

I would therefore vary the judge's order to this limited extent.

GLIDEWELL LJ. I agree and have nothing to add.

Appeal allowed.

Solicitors: *Knight & Sons*, Newcastle under Lyme (for the defendants); *Frere Cholmeley* (for Schott Kem).

Raina Levy   Barrister.

Telnikoff v Matusevitch

a

COURT OF APPEAL, CIVIL DIVISION
LLOYD, GLIDEWELL AND WOOLF LJJ
7, 8 MARCH, 24 APRIL, 16 MAY 1990

b *Libel and slander – Fair comment – Comment or fact – Communication to press – Letter in response to newspaper article complaining of author's racialist and anti-semitic views – Whether words complained of in letter capable of being understood as comment or fact – Whether words complained of to be read in isolation or in context of letter and/or article – Whether defence of fair comment capable of being based on extrinsic evidence.*

c *Libel and slander – Fair comment – Honest expression of opinion – Test of fair comment – Burden of proof – Criticism of newspaper article – Criticism contained in letter to newspaper – Whether test of fair comment subjective as well as objective – Whether defendant required to prove not only that comment was reasonable but also that it was honest expression of opinion.*

The plaintiff and the defendant were Russian emigrés who were both employed by the *d* BBC's Russian service, although they were unknown to each other. The plaintiff wrote an article on the importance of distinguishing between Russia and communism which was published in a national daily newspaper. In the course of the article he criticised the BBC's Russian service for recruiting too many employees from the ethnic minorities of the Soviet Union and not enough from among those people who 'associate themselves ethnically, spiritually or religiously with the Russian people'. The defendant was a *e* Russian Jew who, like the plaintiff, had suffered persecution before arriving in England as an emigré. He was incensed by the plaintiff's article and wrote a letter, which was published in the same newspaper, in which he indicated that the article was racialist and anti-semitic in content and complained that the plaintiff was advocating that in the interest of more effective broadcasts the management of the BBC's Russian service should 'switch from professional testing to a blood test' and that 'ethnically alien' employees *f* should be dismissed from the Russian service, however high their professional standards and integrity might be. The plaintiff considered the defendant's letter to be libellous and brought an action against him, claiming that the natural and ordinary meaning of the defendant's letter was that the plaintiff advocated the introduction of blood testing as part of the recruitment process of the Russian service in order to maintain racial purity, ie recruitment on the basis of ethnic origin and not professional merit, and the dismissal *g* of all ethnically alien employees. The defendant pleaded fair comment on a matter of public interest, but did not seek to justify. In reply the plaintiff alleged that the defendant had been actuated by express malice. At the trial the judge held that the matters complained of in the letter, construed as a whole, were to be understood as comment on a matter of public interest and not as statements of fact since it was clear that the defendant was doing no more than commenting that if effect were given to the plaintiff's *h* views the logical outcome would be that the BBC's Russian service would pursue a strictly racialist staffing policy and, applying the objective test of fair comment, the judge further held that an honest-minded man might honestly hold the views stated as comments on the facts on which those comments were made. The judge concluded that since any reasonable jury, properly directed, would be bound to uphold the defence of fair *j* comment and since there was no evidence of express malice, the plaintiff's action should be dismissed. The plaintiff appealed, contending (i) that in deciding the question whether the words complained of were statements of fact or comment the court was confined to a consideration of the words themselves without reference to the letter or article and (ii) that the test of fair comment required the defendant to satisfy not only the objective test that his letter expressed views which an honest man could hold but also the subjective test that his comment represented the honest expression of his view and that therefore the judge should not have withdrawn the case before the defendant had discharged the *a* subjective burden of proof.

Held – The appeal would be dismissed for the following reasons—

(1) On questions of construction where the court was required to determine whether an alleged libel was capable of being understood as containing statements of fact rather than comment, it was always permissible and indeed was essential for the court to have *b* regard to the context of the libel. In most cases it would be apparent from the publication itself whether the words complained of were comment or not, but in some cases it would be necessary for the court to have regard to the wider context, for example to documents which were incorporated in the publication by reference. Accordingly, where proceedings were brought in respect of an allegedly libellous letter published in response to a newspaper article, it was permissible for the court to look at the article in the context of *c* which the letter had been written as well as the letter itself in determining whether the words complained of were capable of being understood as statements of fact rather than comment. Moreover, it would be wrong in principle to answer the question of construction by reference to the letter alone since to do so would mean that, if the question whether the words complained of were fact or comment had fallen to be decided by the jury, the judge would have had to direct the jury that they had to refer to *d* the article in deciding whether any comment was fair or not, but could not refer to that wider context in deciding whether the words complained of amounted to comment in the first place. When the words complained of were considered in the context of the defendant's letter and the article which prompted that letter, it was clear that they were to be understood as comment and not as statements of fact (see p 870 *j* to p 871 *a e* to p 872 *a d e*, p 880 *d h*, p 881 *a e g j* and p 882 *a*, post). *e*

(2) Where a defendant raised the defence of fair comment in libel proceedings the burden lay on him to establish that the facts on which his comment was based were true and that it was objectively fair, but he was not required also to prove that the comment was an honest expression of his opinion, since the subjective issue of the defendant's state of mind or motive only arose where the plaintiff sought to counter the defence of fair comment by alleging that the comment was published maliciously, in which case it was *f* for the plaintiff to prove, in support of his allegation, that the defendant did not believe in the truth of his comment. Accordingly, where the defendant's comment was fair by the objective test, it was presumed to be the honest expression of his view unless the plaintiff pleaded and proved express malice, thereby obviating the need for any subjective test of fair comment. On the facts, it was not incumbent on the defendant to give evidence as to his state of mind since the burden of proof that the letter did not represent *g* the defendant's honest opinions lay on the plaintiff. It followed that since no reasonable jury could have held that the defendant's dominant motive had been to injure the plaintiff there was no evidence of malice to go to the jury. Accordingly, the judge had been right to withdraw the case from the jury when he did and to dismiss the plaintiff's action (see p 874 *a b*, p 875 *f g*, p 876 *j* to p 877 *a*, p 878 *h* to p 879 *b*, p 880 *c d*, p 881 *c e* *h* and p 882 *a*, post); dictum of Lord Porter in *Turner v Metro-Goldwyn-Mayer Pictures Ltd* [1950] 1 All ER 449 at 461 applied; *Cherneskey v Armadale Publishers Ltd* [1979] 1 SCR 1067 not followed.

Notes

For the defence of fair comment in libel proceedings, see 28 Halsbury's Laws (4th edn) *j* paras 131–144, and for cases on the subject, see 32 Digest (Reissue) 271–286, 2238–2332.

For malice generally and in relation to fair comment in particular, see 28 Halsbury's Laws (4th edn) paras 145–148, 152, and for cases on the subject, see 32 Digest (Reissue) 288–298, 2347–2432.

Cases referred to in judgments

a *Adams v Sunday Pictorial Newspapers (1920) Ltd* [1951] 1 All ER 865, [1951] 1 KB 354, CA.

   Cherneskey v Armadale Publishers Ltd [1979] 1 SCR 1067, Can SC; *rvsg* (1977) 79 DLR (3d) 180, Sask CA.

   Control Risks Ltd v New English Library Ltd [1989] 3 All ER 577, [1990] 1 WLR 183, CA.

   Egger v Viscount Chelmsford [1964] 3 All ER 406, [1965] 1 QB 248, [1964] 3 WLR 714, CA.

b *Horrocks v Lowe* [1974] 1 All ER 662, [1975] AC 135, [1974] 2 WLR 282, HL.

   Hunt v Star Newspaper Co Ltd [1908] 2 KB 309, [1908–10] All ER Rep 513, CA.

   Jones v Skelton [1963] 3 All ER 952, [1963] 1 WLR 1362, PC.

   Kemsley v Foot [1952] 1 All ER 501, [1952] AC 345, HL.

   Lyon v Daily Telegraph Ltd [1943] 2 All ER 316, [1943] 1 KB 746, CA.

c *McQuire v Western Morning News Co* [1903] 2 KB 100, [1900–3] All ER Rep 673, CA.

   Merivale v Carson (1887) 20 QBD 275, [1886–90] All ER Rep 261, CA.

   Slim v Daily Telegraph Ltd [1968] 1 All ER 497, [1968] 2 QB 157, [1968] 2 WLR 599, CA.

   Somerville v Hawkins (1851) 10 CB 583, 138 ER 231.

   Thomas v Bradbury Agnew & Co Ltd [1906] 2 KB 627, [1904–7] All ER Rep 220, CA.

   Turner v Metro-Goldwyn-Meyer Pictures Ltd [1950] 1 All ER 449, HL.

d

Cases also cited

Adam v Ward [1917] AC 309, [1916–17] All ER Rep 157, HL.

Aga Khan v Times Publishing Co [1924] 1 KB 675, CA.

Clark v Molyneux (1877) 3 QBD 237, CA.

Everett v Griffiths [1921] 1 AC 631.

e *London Artists Ltd v Littler* [1969] 2 All ER 193, [1969] 2 QB 375, CA.

Stuart v Bell [1891] 2 QB 341, CA.

Walker (Peter) & Son Ltd v Hodgson [1909] 1 KB 239, CA.

Appeal

f The plaintiff, Vladimir Telnikoff, appealed against the judgment of Drake J given on 14 May 1989 upholding a submission by the defendant, Vladimir Matusevitch, in an action for libel brought by the plaintiff, that there was no case to go to the jury in respect of a letter published in the Daily Telegraph on 18 February 1984 in which the defendant complained that an article written by the plaintiff and published in the Daily Telegraph on 13 February was racialist and anti-semitic. The judge dismissed the action on the grounds (i) that any reasonable jury, properly directed, would be bound to uphold the

g defence of fair comment and (ii) that there was no evidence of express malice. The facts are set out in the judgment of Lloyd LJ.

Desmond Browne QC for the plaintiff.
Edward Garnier for the defendant.

h
                                                                    Cur adv vult

16 May. The following judgments were delivered.

LLOYD LJ. In this case we are concerned with a dispute between two Russian emigrés.
j It raises an important question as to the scope of the defence of fair comment in an action for libel.

On 13 February 1984 the Daily Telegraph published an article written by the plaintiff, Mr Vladimir Telnikoff. He was then employed by the BBC Russian service as a probationer. The article was in many ways prophetic. The main thrust of the article was the importance of distinguishing between Russia on the one hand and communism on the other. The article traced the history of Russian broadcasting since the early 1970s, *a* and continued:

'But still, after three decades of gradually becoming aware of the significance of Russian language broadcasting, I believe its general concept has never been set right. It continues to reflect the fatal confusion of the West, which has yet to clarify to itself whether it is threatened by Russia or by Communism. We fail to understand *b* that Communism is as alien to the religious and national aspirations of the Russian people as those of any other nation.'

The article then makes a different point. I set out the next three paragraphs in full in order to put the matter in context. But it is the first of the following paragraphs which has given rise to all the trouble:

'This confusion further manifests itself in the policy of recruitment for the *c* Russian Service. While other services are staffed almost exclusively from those who share the ethnic origin of the people to whom they broadcast, the Russian Service is recruited almost entirely from Russian-speaking national minorities of the Soviet empire, and has something like 10 per cent of those who associate themselves ethnically, spiritually or religiously with Russian people. However high the *d* standards and integrity of that majority there is no more logic in this than having a Greek Service which is 90 per cent recruited from the Greek-speaking Turkish community of Cyprus.

When broadcasting to other East European countries, we recognise them to be enslaved from outside, and better able to withstand alien, Russian, Communism through our assertion of their own national spirit and traditions. However, this *e* approach leaves room for flirting with Euro-communism or "socialism with a human (non-Russian) face" as a desirable future alternative, and well suits the Left in the West.

Resisting the ideological advance of Communism by encouraging anti-Russian feelings is of less obvious value with a Russian audience. Making "Russian" synonymous with "Communist" alienates the sympathetic Russian listeners. It stirs *f* up social resentment in others against the Russians. Making those words synonymous also makes sympathy for Russia into support for the Communist system.'

So the plaintiff is making two separate, and at first sight unrelated, points. He draws a distinction, as I have said, between the Russian threat and the communist threat. But he also draws a distinction between Russia on the one hand and the national minorities of the Soviet empire on the other. He criticises the Russian service of the BBC for treating *g* Russia as synonymous with communism. But he also criticises the service for employing too many recruits from among the ethnic minorities of the Soviet empire, and not enough from among those who 'associate themselves ethnically, spiritually or religiously with Russian people'.

The defendant is Mr Vladimir Matusevitch. He is a Russian Jew, who, like the plaintiff, *h* suffered persecution in Russia before coming as an emigré to this country. Like the plaintiff, he too was employed at the relevant time by the Russian service of the BBC. But he had never met the plaintiff. He was much incensed by the plaintiff's article. He regarded it as racialist and anti-semitic. He wrote a letter to the Daily Telegraph which was published on 18 February 1984 as follows:

'sir—having read "Selecting the Right Wavelength to Tune into Russia" (Feb 13) *j* I was shocked, particularly by the part on alleged inadequacies of the BBC's Russian Service recruitment policies.

Mr Vladimir Telnikoff says: "While other services are staffed almost exclusively from those who share the ethnic origin of the people to whom they broadcast, the

Russian Service is recruited almost entirely from Russian-speaking national minorities of the Soviet empire".

Mr Telnikoff must certainly be aware that the majority of new emigrés from Russia are people who grew up, studied and worked in Russia, who have Russian as their mother-tongue and have only one culture—Russian.

People with Jewish blood in their veins were never allowed by the Soviet authorities to feel themselves equal with people of the same language, culture and way of life. Insulted and humiliated by this paranoic situation, desperate victims of these Soviet racialist (anti-Semitic) policies took the opportunity to emigrate.

Now the BBC's Russian Service, as well as other similar services of other Western stations broadcasting to Russia, who are interested in new staff members (natives), employ those people in accordance with common democratic procedures, interested in their professional qualifications and not in the blood of the applicants.

Mr Telnikoff demands that in the interest of more effective broadcasts the management of the BBC's Russian Service should switch from *professional testing* to a *blood* test.

Mr Telnikoff is stressing his racialist recipe by claiming that no matter how high the standards and integrity "of ethnically alien" people Russian staff might be, they should be dismissed.

I am certain the DAILY TELEGRAPH would reject any article with similar suggestions of lack of racial purity of the writer in any normal section of the British media.

One could expect that the spreading of racialist views would be unacceptable in a British newspaper.' (The defendant's emphasis.)

The plaintiff took great exception to the defendant's letter, and in particular to the statement that he, the plaintiff, was advocating the introduction of blood testing and the dismissal of ethnically alien members of the BBC Russian service. On 12 March the plaintiff's solicitors wrote demanding an apology. On 18 April they issued a writ, and served a statement of claim the following day. The natural and ordinary meaning pleaded in para 4 was that the plaintiff:

'(i) Advocated the introduction of blood-testing as part of the recruitment process of the BBC Russian Services, in order to maintain racial purity.

(ii) Advocated the dismissal of employees of the BBC Russian Services, on racial grounds.

(iii) Had made statements inciting racial hatred and/or racial discrimination.

(iv) Was a racialist and/or an anti-semite and/or a supporter and/or proponent of doctrines of racial superiority or racial purity.'

By his amended defence the defendant pleaded fair comment on a matter of public interest. He did not seek to justify. In reply, the plaintiff alleged that the defendant was actuated by express malice.

The case came on for trial before Drake J in May 1989. The plaintiff appeared in person. At the conclusion of the plaintiff's case, there was a submission of no case to go to the jury, on the ground (1) that any reasonable jury properly directed would be bound to uphold the defence of fair comment and (2) there was no evidence of express malice. The judge upheld the submission. There is now an appeal to this court.

Fact or comment?

The first question is whether the words complained of were capable of being understood as a statement of fact or facts, rather than comment: see *Turner v Metro-Goldwyn-Mayer Pictures Ltd* [1950] 1 All ER 449 at 461 per Lord Porter. If they were so capable, then it would have been the judge's duty to leave that question to the jury.

Counsel for the plaintiff submitted that there were three distinct allegations of fact contained in the words complained of, namely (i) that the plaintiff had demanded that

the management of the BBC's Russian service should switch from professional testing to
blood tests; (ii) that the plaintiff had claimed that no matter how high the standards and *a*
integrity of 'ethnically alien' Russian staff might be they should be dismissed; and
(iii) that the plaintiff had spread racialist views, and was a racist and an anti-semite.

Counsel for the defendant submitted that the words complained of were comment.
He particularised the comment, in accordance with the recent decision of this court in
Control Risks Ltd v New English Library Ltd [1989] 3 All ER 577, [1990] 1 WLR 183, as
follows: *b*

> 'The plaintiff's opinions regarding the personnel employed by the BBC Russian
> Service and the recruitment policy of that station are shocking for their racialism
> and, if taken to their logical conclusion, could lead to the selection or even dismissal
> of broadcasters on grounds of race or ethnic origin rather than on the basis of
> professional qualifications.' *c*

The judge was in no doubt that, reading the letter as a whole, the words complained
of should be regarded as comment. He said it would be artificial to regard the words as a
statement of fact:

> 'Read in the context of the rest of the letter, I think that the defendant was doing
> no more than to make the comments that, if [the plaintiff's] views as stated in his *d*
> article were given effect to, then the logical outcome would be that the BBC would,
> when interviewing applicants to join the Russian service, concentrate on the ethnic
> origins of the applicant rather than their expertise as broadcasters.'

Before coming to counsel's submissions for the plaintiff, there is a preliminary question
for our consideration. Certain questions in a defamation action are questions for the
judge alone. If, for example, the defence is qualified privilege, it is a question for the *e*
judge alone whether the occasion is privileged. So also, where the defence is fair
comment, whether the matter is one of public interest. There are some slight indications,
no more, that the judge may have regarded the question, 'statement of fact or comment?',
as also being a question for him alone. Thus at the start of the relevant passage in his
judgment he said: *f*

> 'I must consider whether the defendant's letter was purely comment on the article
> or whether it also contained statements of fact.'

At the conclusion he says:

> 'Having decided that the letter amounts to comment on a matter of public
> interest, I next turn to consider whether there is evidence to go to the jury that any *g*
> of the comments are unfair.'

I do not think it would be right to infer from these passages, or the judgment as a
whole, that this very experienced judge mistook his function. He was applying the law
as stated in 28 Halsbury's Laws (4th edn) para 228 as follows:

> 'The question whether all or some of the words complained of are statements of *h*
> fact or comments is a question of construction for the judge. If, in his opinion, there
> is no reasonable doubt, he must direct the jury accordingly; but if, in his view, there
> is reasonable doubt as to whether the words are statements of fact or expressions of
> opinion he must leave it to the jury to decide.'

When the judge said that he had no doubt that the letter was comment, he was saying *j*
that a reasonable jury would be bound so to conclude, no less and no more.

Next counsel for the plaintiff submitted that the judge was wrong to construe the
letter as a whole. This was a case where by concentrating on the wood, the judge
overlooked the trees. I do not agree. When any question of construction is involved the
courts always have regard to the context. In other words, the courts have regard to the

document as a whole. I cannot regard the question whether words are a statement of fact
a or comment as being an exception to this universal rule.

Then it was said that the defendant had failed to distinguish clearly between the
comment, if it was comment, and the facts on which it was based: see *Hunt v Star
Newspaper Co Ltd* [1908] 2 KB 309 at 319, [1908–10] All ER Rep 513 at 517 per Fletcher
Moulton LJ. Again I disagree. The defendant makes clear in the first paragraph of his
letter that the facts on which he is commenting are the plaintiff's article, from which he
b then goes on to quote in the second paragraph. The comment begins with the words 'Mr
Telnikoff must certainly be aware . . .' Facts and comment are thus clearly distinguished.

There remains the fundamental question whether the words in question were capable
of being understood as a statement of fact. If they were, they are defamatory, since there
is no attempt to justify. Although this is not the most important question in the appeal,
it is in some ways the most difficult. The dividing line between a statement of fact and
c comment is never easy.

Somewhat to my surprise, counsel for the defendant at first conceded that in deciding
that question we are confined to a consideration of the letter itself. We are not entitled to
look at the article. Counsel's reason for making that concession was that a man might
read the letter without having read the article, or without being able to remember what
the article said. The letter must therefore be judged on its own.
d
We were not happy to decide the case on the basis of this concession. So we invited
further argument on the point. On further consideration, counsel withdrew his
concession. He submitted that the question whether words are a statement of fact or
comment is a question of construction, albeit a question of construction of a special kind.
On questions of construction, it is always permissible, indeed essential, to have regard to
the context. In most cases it will be apparent from the publication itself whether the
e words complained of are comment or not. But in some cases it may be necessary to have
regard to the wider context, for example to documents which are, as it were, incorporated
in the publication by reference. This is permissible when a question arises as to the
meaning of the alleged libel: see *Gatley on Libel and Slander* (8th edn, 1981) para 102. It
should also be permissible where the question is whether words complained of are
f statement of fact or comment.

Counsel for the plaintiff submitted that we are confined to the four corners of the
letter. He conceded that the subject matter on which the defendant was commenting,
namely the article, was sufficiently indicated in the letter: see *Kemsley v Foot* [1952] 1 All
ER 501 at 504–505, [1952] AC 345 at 355–356 per Lord Porter. But the letter might, he
said, have been read by someone who had no ready access to the article. Accordingly, the
g question of construction, which he described as purely linguistic or grammatical, must
be answered by reference to the letter alone.

I cannot accept the argument of counsel for the plaintiff. It is not only wrong in
principle, it would also lead to all sorts of unfortunate consequences. It would mean that
if the question, statement of fact or comment, had fallen to be decided by the jury, the
judge would have had to direct the jury that they must refer to the article in deciding
h whether any comment was fair or not, but must *not* refer to the article in deciding
whether it was comment at all. I cannot regard that as a desirable result. Similarly, it
would mean that a correspondent, before commenting on an article, would be wise to
repeat the whole of the article on which he was commenting, in case any reader might
read the letter without having read the article. No newspaper editor would accept that
condition; and free discussion of matters of public interest would thus be restricted.
j The answer might be different if the reference were to some 'obscure publication', to
use Lord Porter's words in *Kemsley v Foot* [1952] 1 All ER 501 at 505, [1952] AC 345 at
356. But that was not the case here.

So I would allow counsel for the defendant to withdraw his original concession, and
hold that it is permissible for us to look at the article as well as the letter in deciding
whether the words complained of are a statement of fact or comment.

The judge was, however, able to decide the question without reference to the article. I find myself in the same position. The strongest argument of counsel for the plaintiff in favour of the view that the words complained of contain a statement of fact or facts is based on the judgment of Bowen LJ in *Merivale v Carson* (1887) 20 QBD 275 at 284, [1886–90] All ER Rep 261 at 265, quoted by Collins MR in *McQuire v Western Morning News Co* [1903] 2 KB 100 at 110, [1900–3] All ER Rep 673 at 675. If a man imputes that an author has written something which he has not written, he travels outside the realm of fair comment. As Bowen LJ said, positive misdescription is a question not of opinion but of fact.

On the other hand, it is well settled that a comment does not lose its quality as such merely because it is stated as a fact, providing it is apparent from the context that the fact so stated is an inference from the facts on which the comment is based: see *Kemsley v Foot* per Lord Porter [1952] 1 All ER 501 at 505, [1952] AC 345 at 356–357 and *Gatley* para 706.

The third of the three facts identified by counsel for the plaintiff is to my mind quite obviously an inference of fact in this sense. The same is also true, if not quite so obviously, in relation to the two other 'facts'. Take the statement 'Mr Telnikoff demands that [the BBC] should switch from professional testing to a blood test'. Contrary to what might appear from the particulars in the statement of claim, counsel for the plaintiff concedes that the reference to a blood test is not to be taken literally. The same is surely true of the plaintiff's 'demand'. It should not be taken literally. Any fair-minded man reading the letter as a whole would regard it as an inference drawn by the author from the quotations set out in the second paragraph of the letter. It is true that the defendant does not prefix the statement with the words 'I infer'. But this is not conclusive. The sense of the words is 'Mr Telnikoff *in effect* demands . . .' This is how the words must have been understood by a reasonable reader. It is for this reason that I agree with the judge on the first question. The words are comment, and are not reasonably capable of being understood as statements of fact.

The matter becomes all the clearer if, as I have held, one is entitled to look at the article as well as the letter in deciding the question of construction.

Fair comment: introduction

The second question is whether there was any evidence that the comment was unfair. If the case had been left to the jury, would the jury be bound to find that the comment was fair comment on a matter of public interest? It is common ground that the matter was one of public interest. So the question for the jury would be whether the comment was fair.

The judge adopted a conventional approach to this question. He referred to a number of well-known authorities, and concluded:

'It is clear from the authorities that the test for fair comment is an objective one, and that the vital question to be considered is whether an honest-minded man might honestly hold the views stated as comments on the facts on which those comments were made.'

I agree with that formulation. It is based on the language of Lord Esher MR in *Merivale v Carson* (1887) 20 QBD 275 at 281, [1886–90] All ER Rep 261 at 264, with the modification suggested by Lord Porter in *Turner v Metro-Goldwyn-Mayer Pictures Ltd* [1950] 1 All ER 449 at 461. In an earlier passage the judge had said:

'Where a comment is made on a matter of public interest, the defendant who relies on the plea of fair comment does not have to prove that the comment is an honest expression of his view.'

As authority for that proposition the judge quoted *Gatley* para 792, as follows:

'In the same way, the defendant who relies on a plea of fair comment does not have to show that the comment is an honest expression of his views.'

There is no challenge to this proposition in the notice of appeal. On the contrary, para 3 of the notice of appeal presupposes that the sole test for fair comment in the absence of express malice is an objective one. Nor is there any hint of anything other than an objective test in the original skeleton argument of counsel for the plaintiff.

But, as the argument was developed before us, another test began to take shape. By the end of his reply counsel for the plaintiff was contending that in every case where a defendant relies on fair comment, he has a twofold burden to discharge, as follows: (1) he must satisfy the objective test; and (2) he must prove that the comment represented his real opinion.

The reason for this change of direction in the plaintiff's case will appear hereafter. At present it is sufficient to note that it is this change of direction which has brought us face to face with a question of major importance in the law of defamation, namely whether the decision of the majority of the Supreme Court of Canada in *Cherneskey v Armadale Publishers Ltd* [1979] 1 SCR 1067 represents the law of England. Before coming to that, however, I should deal first with counsel's arguments on the judge's application of the objective test.

Fair comment: the objective test

It has been said from time to time that the expression 'fair comment' is unhelpful and potentially misleading. How can comment which is ex concessis prejudiced, wrong-headed and grossly exaggerated, be fair? It is anything but fair. It is for this reason that it is occasionally suggested that a better name for the defence would be honest comment, or more simply comment. But to introduce honesty into the name of the defence might be even more misleading. As will appear later, it risks confusion between the elements of the defence on which the burden rests on the defendant, and express malice, where the burden is on the plaintiff.

So in my view it is better to retain the traditional name of the defence. I have found it helpful to remind myself that the question is not whether the comment is fair in the ordinary sense of that word, but whether the words complained of can fairly be regarded as comment. The observations of an honest crank on a matter of public interest may fairly be regarded as comment, so as to attract the defence, even though the substance of his comment is grossly unfair.

There is a further virtue in retaining the name 'fair comment'. It serves to distinguish comment from what cannot fairly be regarded as comment at all, namely mere abuse or invective.

And so I come to counsel's submissions for the plaintiff on the objective test. Could any man, however prejudiced and obstinate, honestly hold the view expressed by the defendant in his letter? Counsel submits that it would have been open to the jury to answer the objective test in favour of the plaintiff. He relies on three main considerations. First, nowhere in the article does the plaintiff refer to Jews by name. He refers to Russian-speaking national minorities. Nor does the plaintiff advocate testing of any kind to exclude Jews. Second, nowhere does the plaintiff say that ethnically alien people should be dismissed. He does not even use the expression 'ethnically alien'. It follows that there was no justification for putting those words in inverted commas, thus suggesting that he had. Third, and most important, the plaintiff does not say in the article that only 10% of those employed by the Russian service are ethnically pure. He says that only 10% are among those who *associate themselves* 'ethnically, spiritually or religiously with the Russian people'. This is not a racial test, but a cultural test, or a test as to where a man's sympathies lie.

I hope I have stated the argument correctly. As to the third consideration, I can understand well enough that a man may associate himself culturally with the Russian

people. But how can he associate himself ethnically, without being a Russian? So it may
be that counsel reads too much into the word 'associate'.

Be that as it may, the question remains whether it would have been open to the jury
to find that the view expressed by the defendant was one which no honest man could
hold. I am quite unable to reach that conclusion. The plaintiff was complaining that 90%
of those employed by the Russian service came from national minorities of the Soviet
empire. If that was indeed his complaint, I do not see how it could be corrected except
by discrimination against national minorities in recruiting new staff in the future, or
dismissing existing staff. It was not disputed that Jews are a national or ethnic minority.
How, in those circumstances, could any reasonable jury regard the comment as other
than 'fair' in the objective sense? There is no other possible view. That was the opinion
of the judge. It is sufficient to say that I agree.

Fair comment: subjective test

I have already foreshadowed counsel's argument for the plaintiff under this head. He
contends that no comment can be fair unless it is the honest opinion of the person
making the comment. It is not enough, therefore, for the view expressed to be one which
an honest man could hold, ie the objective test: the defendant must hold the view
himself. Since the burden is on the defendant to prove fair comment, there must be
some evidence that the comment represents his own honest view. Otherwise he fails.
Counsel draws a distinction between the subjective test of honesty, on which the burden
is on the defendant, and malice, on which he accepts that the burden is on the plaintiff.

It may be thought that it matters little whether the honesty of the defendant comes in
at what I will call the fair comment stage or whether it comes in at the express malice
stage. The burden of proof may not be the same. But very few cases turn on the burden
of proof. But in the present case, as it happens, it does make a difference, because of the
unusual feature that the judge stopped the case before the defendant gave evidence. If
the burden was on the defendant to show that the letter was his honest opinion, he failed
to discharge that burden. The judge should not have stopped the case when he did. It
might have been open to the judge to stop the case *after* the defendant had given
evidence, but not before.

It is in this way that the great question in the present case is raised. Is the test of fair
comment subjective as well as objective? If so, is the burden on the defendant at both
stages?

A very similar question came before the Canadian Supreme Court in *Cherneskey v
Armadale Publishers Ltd* [1979] 1 SCR 1067. In that case the facts were curiously similar.
The defendants were a newspaper. They published a letter to the editor in which the
writer accused the plaintiff of holding racist views. The trial judge refused to leave the
defence of fair comment to the jury on the ground that there was no evidence that the
view expressed in the letter was the honest view of the writer; and the defendants had
given positive evidence that the letter did not represent the editor's views, or the views
of the newspaper. The defence of fair comment having been withdrawn, the jury found
in favour of the plaintiff, and awarded $Can25,000 damages. The defendants appealed.
The appeal was allowed. But, on further appeal to the Supreme Court, the decision of the
judge was restored by a majority over a strong dissenting judgment of Dickson J.

The majority view was that it is an essential ingredient of the defence of fair comment
that the view expressed should be the honest view of the author. Honesty of belief was
held to be the 'cardinal test' of fair comment (a phrase quoted from Lord Denning MR's
judgment in *Slim v Daily Telegraph Ltd* [1968] 1 All ER 497 at 503, [1968] 2 QB 157 at
170). The majority applied the cardinal test of honesty not only to the writer of the letter,
but also (if I follow the judgment correctly) to the newspaper which published the letter.
The decision is summarised in the following paragraph ([1979] 1 SCR 1067 at 1091 per
Ritchie J):

a   '. . . in the absence of any proof of the honest belief of the writers, and *having regard to the denial of honest belief by the defendants themselves,* the defence of fair comment cannot, in my view, prevail.' (My emphasis.)

This would at first sight seem to impose a very severe restriction on freedom of discussion. It would mean that no newspaper could safely publish a letter containing views with which it did not agree.

b   But in the very next paragraph the majority disclaim any such intention (at 1091):

    'This does not mean that freedom of the press to publish its views is in any way affected, nor does it mean that a newspaper cannot publish letters expressing views with which it may strongly disagree. Moreover, nothing that is here said should be construed as meaning that a newspaper is in any way restricted in publishing two diametrically opposite views of the opinion and conduct of a public figure. On the

c   contrary, I adopt as descriptive of the conclusion which I have reached, the language used by Brownridge, J.A., in the following excerpt from his reasons for judgment in the Court of Appeal, where he said ((1977) 79 DLR (3d) 180 at 192): "What it does mean is that a newspaper cannot publish a *libellous* letter and then disclaim any responsibility by saying that it was published as fair comment on a matter of public interest but it does not represent the honest opinion of the newspaper."' (Brownridge

d   JA's emphasis.)

This paragraph has the appearance of having been, as it were, tacked on to the majority judgment in order to meet the very real fears expressed by the minority that freedom of discussion of matters of public interest would be severely restricted.

I do not pause to consider the consequences of the majority view, or the complications

e   which arise when, as in *Cherneskey v Armadale Publishers Ltd*, a defendant, and in particular a newspaper, publishes the comments of another. These complications are discussed in *Gatley* para 730 and the very extensive footnotes to that paragraph. They do not arise in the present case.

The importance of *Cherneskey v Armadale Publishers Ltd* for present purposes is whether the majority were right in asserting that honesty of belief is an essential in the defence of

f   fair comment, *on which the burden rests on the defendant.* I can find no support for this view in the English authorities to which the majority refer. In my judgment the correct view of English law is that where the defendant's comment is fair by the objective test, it is presumed to be the honest expression of his view unless the plaintiff pleads and proves express malice. This would tie in with other branches of the law of defamation. Thus, where the defence is qualified privilege, the law presumes honest belief in the truth of

g   what is published, unless the contrary is proved: see *Horrocks v Lowe* [1974] 1 All ER 662 at 669, [1975] AC 135 at 150 per Lord Diplock. The same should be true of the defence of fair comment.

Before considering the English authorities, I would quote in full a passage from the minority judgment in *Cherneskey* [1979] 1 SCR 1067 at 1098–1099 which explains the position with admirable clarity and accuracy:

h

    'There is in some of the cases confusion between the requirement that a comment be "fair" and that it not be made with malice. In fact, these two requirements are quite distinct. Shortly stated, the test of whether a comment is "fair comment" in law is an "objective" test, *i.e.,* is the comment one that an honest, albeit prejudiced, person might make in the circumstances? The cases of *Merivale v. Carson* ((1887) 20

j   QBD 275, [1886–90] All ER Rep 261); *Lyon et al. v. Daily Telegraph, Ltd.,* ([1943] 2 All ER 316, [1943] 1 KB 746), and *Slim et al. v. Daily Telegraph, Ltd. et al.,* ([1968] 1 All ER 497, [1968] 2 QB 157) in my opinion, support this view. Even if the comment passes this test, the defence of fair comment will fail if it does not pass the subjective test of whether the publisher himself was actuated by malice: see *Thomas v. Bradbury, Agnew & Co., Ltd.* ([1906] 2 KB 627, [1904–7] All ER Rep 220). There would be no point in having the second test if the first one included the ingredient *a* of the subjective test. Many cases merge these two elements to ask whether the statement in question is the publisher's real opinion. This works passably well when the defendant is the writer, but it does not work at all if he is not, as in the case where, as here, a newspaper has printed a letter in its Letters to the Editor space. In my view, the legal position is this: If a defendant raises the defence of fair comment, he has the burden of establishing that the facts on which it is based are true and that *b* it is *objectively* fair; if he discharges this burden he will, nevertheless, lose the defence if the plaintiff proves that the comment was published maliciously. It is this second stage of the analysis which raises the *subjective* issue of the defendant's stage of mind or motive.' (Dickson J's emphasis.)

The only textbook authority relied on by the plaintiff is *Gatley* para 729:   *c*

'(e) *Honest opinion published without malice* Comment must be published honestly in that it is the expression of the defendant's real opinion. The law does not protect the expression of an opinion not honestly held, even if it is an opinion which someone else might honestly have expressed.'

It was this paragraph which was quoted in part by the majority in *Cherneskey v* *d* *Armadale Publishers Ltd* [1979] 1 SCR 1067 at 1072–1073. That case is now referred to in a footnote as authority for the proposition in the text.

I am not convinced that para 729 means what it appears to mean. In any event it is not dealing with the burden of proof. The editors are not saying, at any rate in terms, that honesty of belief is an essential element in the defence of fair comment on which the burden of proof lies on the defendant irrespective of malice. If they are (and I admit that *e* the cross-heading creates some uncertainty) then I find para 729 impossible to reconcile with paras 747 and 792. Paragraph 747 reads:

'The burden of proving that the words were published maliciously, *or were not the* *honest opinion of the critic*, is on the plaintiff.' (My emphasis.)

Paragraph 792 reads: *f*

'In the same way, the defendant who relies on a plea of fair comment does not have to show that the comment is an honest expression of his views.'

As they stand, paras 747 and 792 are simple and correct statements of English law. But the matter is complicated by a footnote to para 792, which reads: 'see § 729. See however, *Cherneskey v. Armadale Publishers* ([1979] 1 SCR 1067 at 1079–1084).'   *g*

In this somewhat confused state, I cannot regard para 729 in *Gatley* as authoritative. It was described by the minority in *Cherneskey v Armadale Publishers Ltd* [1979] 1 SCR 1067 at 1100 as 'unfortunate', and as being 'belied by the numerous passages in the same text which surround it'.

Turning to the cases, there are, of course, numerous references to honesty as being 'the cardinal test', and other similar expressions. But all these references, without exception, *h* fall into one or other of two classes. They are either cases where a contrast is being drawn between what is fair for the purposes of fair comment and what is reasonable. This appears most clearly from Lord Porter's modification in *Turner v Metro-Goldwyn-Mayer Pictures Ltd* [1950] 1 All ER 449 at 461 of Lord Esher MR's test in *Merivale v Carson* (1887) 20 QBD 275 at 281, [1886–90] All ER Rep 261 at 264. Despite the substitution of 'honest' for 'fair' ('would any honest man, however prejudiced he may be . . .'), Lord *j* Esher MR's test remains objective. The defendant's state of mind (in the absence of malice) is irrelevant.

Alternatively, they are cases where the court is using the term 'fair comment' in a comprehensive sense, to include the absence of malice. Once the plaintiff has pleaded

express malice in reply, then of course the defendant's state of mind becomes critical.
a The fact that a defendant does not himself believe in the truth of his comment is the
strongest possible evidence of malice. It is sometimes said to be conclusive. Once malice
is proved, what would otherwise be fair comment by the objective test becomes 'unfair'
overall.

It was these considerations which Lord Denning MR had in mind when he said in *Slim
v Daily Telegraph Ltd* [1968] 1 All ER 497 at 503, [1968] 2 QB 157 at 170 that honesty is
b the cardinal test. That this must be so is shown by what Denning LJ (as he then was)
himself said in *Adams v Sunday Pictorial Newspapers (1920) Ltd* [1951] 1 All ER 865 at
868, [1951] 1 KB 354 at 360:

'If [the defendant] proves that the facts were true and that the comment,
objectively considered, was fair—that is, if it was fair when considered without
c regard to the state of mind of the writer—I should not have thought that the
plaintiff had much about which to complain. Nevertheless, it has been held that the
plaintiff can still succeed if he can prove that the comments, subjectively considered,
were unfair because the writer was actuated by malice.'

To the same effect is Lord Denning MR's observation in *Egger v Viscount Chelmsford*
d [1964] 3 All ER 406 at 412, [1965] 1 QB 248 at 265:

'If the plaintiff seeks to rely on malice to aggravate damages, or to rebut a defence
of qualified privilege, or to cause a comment, otherwise fair, to become unfair, then
he must prove malice . . .'

Of the other English authorities, counsel for the plaintiff relied in particular on *Turner
e v Metro-Goldwyn-Mayer Pictures Ltd* [1950] 1 All ER 449, to which I have already referred
several times. But, rightly understood, the speech of Lord Porter is strongly against the
plaintiff. The defendants in that case were sued for libel. The principal question was
whether there was evidence of malice to go to the jury to rebut the defence of qualified
privilege. But the plaintiff had an alternative claim in slander, to which the defence was
fair comment. Counsel for the plaintiff relied on a sentence in Lord Porter's speech as
f follows ([1950] 1 All ER 449 at 461):

'Here again, as in the case of malice, the question is not whether the comment is
justified in the eyes of judge or jury, but whether it is the honest expression of the
commentator's real view and not mere abuse or invective under the guise of
criticism: see *McQuire v. Western Morning News Co* ([1903] 2 KB 100 at 111, [1900–
3] All ER Rep 673 at 676) . . .'

g But it is clear from the context that Lord Porter is treating the question comprehensively;
in other words he is including absence of malice within an overall test whether the
comment is 'fair'. In the very next paragraph Lord Porter says:

'The only foundation in the present case for the assertion that the comment is
h unfair, lies in the suggestion that it does not represent the real view of the speaker,
but was uttered with a dishonest object of injuring the appellant and driving her
from the occupation of film critic. I have already dealt with this question in
considering whether there is any evidence of malice which would defeat the
qualified privilege enjoyed in respect of the letter. Having regard to the opinion
there expressed, it is plain that I see no evidence from which unfairness could be
j derived. In alleging unfairness the plaintiff takes on him or herself the onus, also
taken by an allegation of malice, to prove that the criticism is unfair either from the
language used or from some extraneous circumstance.'

The last sentence of this passage is in direct opposition to counsel's main arguments on
burden of proof.

The majority in *Cherneskey v Armadale Publishers Ltd* [1979] 1 SCR 1067 quoted extensively from Lord Porter's criticism of the summing up in *Turner v Metro-Goldwyn-Mayer Pictures Ltd*. But the point which Lord Porter is making is whether the jury may have been misled into thinking that the reasonableness of the defendant's comments might in some way be relevant. This is clear from the following sentence ([1950] 1 All ER 449 at 462):

> 'My Lords, in the course of his summing-up in the present case the learned judge undoubtedly in places used language which accurately states the law as I conceive it to be, and, indeed, as it is accepted to be by both parties, *viz*., that it is the honesty of the witnesses' views, not their reasonableness, which decides whether they are malicious or not.'

I do not understand how this passage could be said to help counsel or to support the majority judgment in *Cherneskey v Armadale Publishers Ltd*.

Finally counsel for the plaintiff relied on a passage from Lord Morris's speech in *Jones v Skelton* [1963] 3 All ER 952 at 965, [1963] 1 WLR 1362 at 1379, as follows:

> 'Accordingly if a defendant publishes of a plaintiff words which a jury might on the one hand hold to be fact or might on the other hand hold to be comment and if a plaintiff does not accept that any of the words are true, or does not accept that any of them are comment, and if a defendant chooses to assert that some of the words are fair comment (made in good faith and without malice) on facts truly stated it must (assuming that the judge rules in regard to the public interest) be for the defendant to prove that which he asserts. If a plaintiff does not acknowledge that there are any words of comment, and if the words are reasonably capable of being held by a jury to be statements of fact, the plaintiff's overall burden of proving his case does not involve a duty of proving that comment (the existence of which he denies) is unfair.'

I do not read Lord Morris in this passage as saying that the burden of proving the absence of malice is on the defendant. He is saying (1) that the overall burden is on the plaintiff and (2) that the burden of proving fair comment is on the defendant, since that is the defence which he 'asserts'. Lord Morris does not deal specifically with the burden of proving express malice. But he would have had well in mind the long-established rule that the burden of proving express malice is on the plaintiff; see eg 24 Halsbury's Laws (3rd edn) para 131:

> 'In the case of a defence of fair comment on a matter of public interest the burden is on the defendant to show that the facts are true and, if there is any evidence of unfairness, that the comment is objectively fair, and it is then open to the plaintiff to prove that the defendant made the comment maliciously, for example from a motive of spite or ill-will.'

(See now 28 Halsbury's Laws (4th edn) para 145.)

Fair comment: conclusion

My conclusion is that the law is correctly stated in *Duncan and Neill on Defamation* (2nd edn, 1983) para 12.02 as follows:

> '(a) the comment must be on a matter of public interest; (b) the comment must be based on fact; (c) the comment, though it can consist of or include inferences of fact, must be recognisable as comment; (d) the comment must satisfy the following objective test: could any fair minded man honestly express that opinion on the proved facts? (e) even though the comment satisfies the objective test the defence can be defeated if the plaintiff proves that the defendant was actuated by express malice.'

In the light of the present case I would add a rider, already implicit in paras (a) to (e),
a   that the absence of honest belief in the truth of the comment is relevant to para (e), and
not otherwise. Thus the burden of proof in the present case that the letter did not
represent the defendant's genuine views lay on the plaintiff. It was not incumbent on the
defendant to give evidence as to his state of mind. It follows that the judge was entitled
to withdraw the case when he did, if he was not persuaded by the plaintiff that there was
evidence of malice to go to the jury.

b   Before leaving fair comment, I should add that it was not suggested by counsel for the
plaintiff that the defendant had imputed any dishonourable or corrupt motive to the
plaintiff so as to take the case out of the ordinary run of cases, or affect the defence of fair
comment in any way.

Malice: correct test

c   Again there is a preliminary question whether the judge was guilty of usurping the
role of the jury. The sentence which is criticised is as follows:

> 'In order for the plaintiff to have the question of malice submitted to the jury, it
> is necessary that the evidence should raise a probability of malice and be more
> consistent with its existence than its non-existence.'

d   This sentence shows, so it is said, that the judge was weighing up the evidence of malice,
which was a task for the jury, not for him. Even if the judge was open to criticism in this
respect, it is to be noticed that, in answering the question which he had set himself, he
held that there was *no* evidence to go to the jury that the defendant was actuated by
malice.

But in truth the judge did not misdirect himself. He was quoting from *Gatley* paras
e   794–795. The language of those paragraphs is taken from the decision of Maule J in
Somerville v Hawkins (1851) 10 CB 583, 138 ER 231. Counsel for the plaintiff seeks to
discredit that authority, or at any rate to cast doubt on the test which the judge derived
from *Somerville v Hawkins*. This overlooks the fact that the language which the judge
used was taken from a passage in Maule J's judgment which was quoted with express
f   approval by Lord Porter in *Turner v Metro-Goldwyn-Mayer Pictures Ltd* [1950] 1 All ER
449 at 455. So it cannot be said that the judge adopted the wrong test. The point is quite
simple. If a piece of evidence is equally consistent with malice and the absence of malice,
it cannot as a matter of law provide evidence on which the jury could find malice. The
judge would be bound so to direct the jury. If there are no pieces of evidence which are
more consistent with malice than the absence of malice, there is no evidence of malice to
g   go to the jury.

Malice: the facts

Counsel for the plaintiff relies on two letters dated 25 February and 8 May 1984, which
contain much exaggerated language, and some wildly extravagant allegations. As to the
exaggerated language, counsel submits that the judge erred in law when he held that
h   mere exaggeration is not evidence of express malice. Once again, he referred us to the
speech of Lord Porter in *Turner v Metro-Goldwyn-Mayer Pictures Ltd*. But it was *gross*
exaggeration which Lord Porter said in that case might constitute evidence of malice (see
[1950] 1 All ER 449 at 455). If *mere* exaggeration were sufficient, then the objective test
in *Merivale v Carson* (1887) 20 QBD 275, [1886–90] All ER Rep 261 would have to be
rephrased. Indeed, it was in *Merivale v Carson* 20 QBD 275 at 281, [1886–90] All ER Rep
j   261 at 264 that Lord Esher MR said: 'Mere exaggeration, or even gross exaggeration,
would not make the comment unfair.'

I do not find it necessary to consider the terms of the two letters in detail. They were
given careful consideration by the judge. The judge's conclusion as to the letter of
25 February was:

'These exaggerated or untrue statements as to the plaintiff's past do in my view provide a scintilla of evidence of malice on the part of the defendant towards the *a* plaintiff, but in my judgment it is no more than a scintilla.'

I find myself in complete agreement with the judge. I agree also with his view as to the letter of 8 May 1984.

Some reliance was also placed on a letter written three years later in March 1987, in which the defendant said: 'I knew and know nothing against him personally and *b* willingly accept that he is a decent human being.'

If the defendant always regarded the plaintiff as a decent human being, how, it was asked, could he truthfully have held the view that the plaintiff was a racist? I am unimpressed by this argument. The letter of March 1987 was written in a praiseworthy attempt to resolve the dispute between the parties. The defendant was holding out an olive branch, or twig at least. The sentence I have quoted is not evidence on which the *c* jury could hold that the defendant did not believe in the truth of his comment. Two things stand out. First, the defendant believed passionately in the evil of anti-semitism. Second, he and the plaintiff were total strangers. In those circumstances no reasonable jury could have held that the defendant's dominant motive was to injure the plaintiff, rather than express his own honest, if misguided views.

A number of other peripheral matters were mentioned. But they do not amount to *d* anything of substance. I agree with the judge that there was no evidence of malice to go to the jury. I would dismiss the appeal.

GLIDEWELL LJ. I have had the advantage of reading in draft the judgment of Lloyd LJ. I gratefully adopt and need not repeat his statement of the facts. In order for *e* Drake J at the trial of this action to uphold the submission that there was no case to go to the jury, it was necessary for him to decide that any reasonable jury properly directed would be bound to hold: (1) that the words of which the plaintiff complains in the defendant's letter were comment and not statements of fact; (2) that they were 'fair comment'; and (3) that there was no evidence to go to the jury of express malice which *f* would defeat the defence of fair comment.

As Lloyd LJ says, the question whether the jury would be bound to find that the words complained of were comment and not statements of fact raises the issue whether, in deciding the question, a jury if it were left to them would be, or the judge in the circumstances was, entitled to consider the whole of the plaintiff's article in the Daily Telegraph of 13 February 1984, or only the short extract from it contained in the *g* defendant's letter published on 18 February 1984.

The defendant's letter started by referring to the plaintiff's article, giving its title and the date on which it was published. While, of course, it may well be that many people who read the letter would not have read the earlier article, those who were sufficiently concerned about the content of the letter would have been able, if they wished, to refer back to the article. The Daily Telegraph is a newspaper with a wide circulation, and even *h* a few days after publication copies are readily available. In the circumstances of this case, I therefore agree with Lloyd LJ that in deciding the question, 'fact or comment?', the judge was entitled, and a jury would have been entitled, to consider the text of the whole article. I am strengthened in this view by realising that if this were not the case, the judge would have to direct the jury not to consider the article in deciding whether what was contained in the letter was comment or a statement of fact, but then if they decided *j* it was comment to look at the article in order to decide whether the comment was fair. This would be a most unsatisfactory basis for a direction and I cannot think it would correctly represent the law. Accordingly, in my view, it was permissible to consider the whole article in deciding both questions.

Considering the whole article in this way, I also agree with Lloyd LJ that the jury
a would have been bound to conclude that the matters of which complaint is made in the
letter were, though expressed as if they were statements of fact, in reality comment on
the content of the article, or of part of it.

If, however, it were not permissible when answering this question to look at the article
but only at the passage contained in the letter, then I would be of a different view. It
would in my view then be arguable whether the statements in the letter were statements
b of fact or comment, and I would not have thought it right for the judge to withdraw this
question from the jury. On this point, I find myself in disagreement with the view
expressed by Lloyd LJ. However, this disagreement is of no consequence.

In every other respect I agree with the judgment of Lloyd LJ, both with his reasoning
and with his conclusion. I wish particularly to emphasise my agreement with that part
of his judgment which considers whether, in English law, it is an essential ingredient of
c the defence of fair comment that the view expressed by the author should be his honest
view. Like Lloyd LJ, I am firmly of the opinion that this question only arises when the
next stage is reached, i e consideration of the question whether malice has been proved.

As I have said, I agree entirely with Lloyd LJ's reasoning on this matter, and it is
unnecessary for me to express the same reasons in words of my own. I emphasise,
however, that like him I regard the statement of the law in *Duncan and Neill on Defamation*
d (2nd edn, 1983) para 12.02 as accurate, subject to the rider to which Lloyd LJ refers. I
also regard the passage from the minority judgment of Dickson J in *Cherneskey v Armadale
Publishers Ltd* [1979] 1 SCR 1067 at 1098–1099 which Lloyd LJ has set out in his
judgment as accurately representing the law of England on this issue.

Agreeing as I do with Lloyd LJ's reasoning, I also agree with him that this appeal
should be dismissed.
e

WOOLF LJ. I have had the opportunity of reading the judgments of Lloyd and
Glidewell LJJ. Subject to what I say hereafter I agree with those judgments.

If the words contained in the letter about which complaint is made are *capable* of being
f regarded as statements of fact this appeal must succeed since it would then be for the jury
to decide whether the words amounted to comment or statements of fact. Considering
the letter alone, I have difficulty in deciding whether the words complained of are
comment or statements of fact. Therefore if I am required to determine this issue by
considering the letter alone I would have difficulty in accepting the approach adopted by
the judge.

However, having heard the further argument, I am quite satisfied that the question as
g to whether the words complained of are comment or statements of fact has to be decided
by looking at the whole of the contents of the letter and the article to which the letter
refers. This is the context in which the letter is to be construed and when the letter is
construed in this context, it is in my view clear that the words complained of are
comment and not statements of fact.

h In coming to my conclusion that you are entitled to look at the article in deciding
whether the words complained of are statements of fact or comment I have in mind that
it would unduly restrict the defence of fair comment if you were not entitled to look at
the material on which it is alleged that the words complained of were commenting. I am
not impressed by the argument that you are not entitled to look at the subject matter of
the comment because the reader of the allegedly defamatory statement may not be aware
j of its contents. The ability of the defendant to comment should not depend on whether
or not the reader is aware of the material which is the subject of the comment. The
defence of fair comment is based on the principle that you should be entitled to comment
on a matter of public interest and the fact that the publication is limited does not affect
the public interest.

As the statements complained of were comment I would dismiss the appeal for the reasons given by Lloyd LJ.

Appeal dismissed. Leave to appeal to the House of Lords granted.

Solicitors: *Peter Carter-Ruck & Partners* (for the plaintiff); *Bindman & Partners* (for the defendant).

L I Zysman Esq   Barrister.

R v Gullefer

COURT OF APPEAL, CRIMINAL DIVISION
LORD LANE CJ, KENNEDY AND OWEN JJ
4, 20 NOVEMBER 1986

Criminal law – Attempt – Acts preparatory to offence – When attempt begins – Defendant attempting to disrupt greyhound race in order to get back stake on losing dog – Whether defendant guilty of attempted theft of stake – Whether defendant's actions merely preparatory – Criminal Attempts Act 1981, ss 1(1), 4(3).

The appellant jumped onto the track at a greyhound racing stadium and waved his arms in an attempt to distract the greyhounds during the running of a race. He later admitted that he had acted in the hope that the stewards would declare 'no race' and that he would be able to recover the stake he had placed on a dog that was losing the race. He was charged with and convicted of attempted theft of his stake under s 1(1)[a] of the Criminal Attempts Act 1981, which provided that if with intent to commit an offence a person did an act which was 'more than merely preparatory to the commission of the offence' he was guilty of attempting to commit the offence. He appealed, contending that his actions were not sufficiently proximate to the complete offence of theft to be capable of comprising an attempt to commit theft.

Held – The appellant's action in jumping onto the track during the running of the race could not properly be said to be an action which had gone beyond mere preparation and to be part of the process of committing theft from the bookmaker. The appeal would therefore be allowed and the conviction quashed (see p 884 *f g* and p 885 *g*, post).
    Per curiam. (1) Section 1(1) gives clear guidance as to when an attempt begins, namely when merely preparatory acts come to an end and the defendant embarks on the crime proper (see p 885 *f g*, post); *R v Eagleton* [1843–60] All ER Rep 363 and dictum of Lord Diplock in *DPP v Stonehouse* [1977] 2 All ER 909 at 917 considered.
    (2) By virtue of s 4(3)[b] of the 1981 Act it is for the judge to decide whether there is sufficient evidence that the defendant went beyond the realm of mere preparation and embarked on the commission of the offence; if there is, it is then for the jury to decide whether the defendant in fact went beyond mere preparation (see p 884 *d e*, post).

Notes
For the actus reus of an attempt to commit a crime, see 11(1) Halsbury's Laws (4th edn reissue) para 72, and for cases on the subject, see 14(1) Digest (Reissue) 107–111, 723–749.

---

a Section 1(1) is set out at p 884 *b c*, post
b Section 4(3) is set out at p 884 *d*, post

a   For the Criminal Attempts Act 1981, ss 1, 4, see 12 Halsbury's Statutes (4th edn) (1989 reissue) 776, 779.

Cases referred to in judgment
Davey v Lee [1967] 2 All ER 423, [1968] 1 QB 366, [1967] 3 WLR 105, DC.
DPP v Stonehouse [1977] 2 All ER 909, [1978] AC 55, [1977] 3 WLR 143, HL.
Hope v Brown [1954] 1 All ER 330, [1954] 1 WLR 250, DC.
b   *R v Eagleton* (1855) Dears CC 515, [1843–60] All ER Rep 363, 169 ER 826, CCR.
    R v Ilyas (1983) 78 Cr App R 17, CA.

Appeal against conviction and sentence
Ian John Gullefer appealed against his conviction on 26 February 1986 in the Crown Court at Snaresbrook before his Honour Judge Stable QC and a jury of attempted theft for which he was sentenced to six months' imprisonment. He appealed against conviction
c   on a certificate from the trial judge. He appealed against sentence by leave of the single judge. The facts are set out in the judgment of the court.

Ian Copeman (assigned by the Registrar of Criminal Appeals) for the appellant.
Vivian Robinson QC for the Crown.

d   *Cur adv vult*

20 November. The following judgment of the court was delivered.

LORD LANE CJ. On 26 February 1986 before the Crown Court at Snaresbrook the appellant was convicted of attempted theft and sentenced to six months' imprisonment.
e   The judge certified that the case was fit for appeal on the ground that—

> 'a submission was made that the action alleged as constituting the attempt (as to which there was no dispute, because his action was filmed on video tape, which the jury and I saw) could not amount to an attempt to steal, even if the jury were satisfied that what the defendant did was done with the object of dishonestly
f   receiving a sum of money equivalent to his stake from a bookmaker.'

He also appeals against sentence by leave of the single judge.
    The facts were as follows. On 5 March 1985 the appellant attended the greyhound racing stadium at Romford. During the last race, as the dogs rounded the final bend, he climbed the fence onto the track in front of the dogs, waving his arms and attempting to distract them. His efforts were only marginally successful, and the stewards decided that
g   it was unnecessary to declare 'no race'. Had they made such a declaration, by the rules the bookmakers would have been obliged to repay the amount of his stake to any punter, but would not have been liable to pay any winnings to those punters who would have been successful if the race had been valid.
    When interviewed by the police the appellant said the reasons for his behaviour were
h   partly that a year earlier he had lost a large bet at the stadium by reason of one of the stadium's staff leaning over the rails and distracting the dog on which he had gambled. He also admitted that he had attempted to stop the race because the dog on which he had staked £18 was losing. He hoped that by his actions the dogs would be distracted, that the stewards would declare 'no race' and that he would therefore recover his stake from the bookmaker.
j   The perfected grounds of appeal contained four grounds: first, that the property which was the subject of the alleged attempted theft was not 'property belonging to another' within the meaning of the Theft Act 1968; second, that, even if the appellant had successfully completed his plan and had recovered the £18 from the bookmaker, that would not have amounted to an 'appropriation of property belonging to another'. Those two grounds of appeal were abandoned by counsel for the appellant at the outset of his

submissions to this court. In the light of our decision on the third ground of appeal, it is
unnecessary for us to inquire whether that abandonment was proper. The main burden *a*
of counsel's submission to us has been the third ground of appeal, namely that the acts
proved to have been carried out by the appellant were not 'sufficiently proximate to the
completed offence of theft to be capable of comprising an attempt to commit theft'.

We have been referred to a number of decisions, many of them of respectable
antiquity, which show, if nothing else, the difficulties which abound in this branch of
the criminal law. The present law is, however, now enshrined in the words of the *b*
Criminal Attempts Act 1981. Section 1(1) provides:

> 'If, with intent to commit an offence to which this section applies, a person does
> an act which is more than merely preparatory to the commission of the offence, he
> is guilty of attempting to commit the offence.'

Section 4(3) provides: *c*

> 'Where, in proceedings against a person for an offence under section 1 above,
> there is evidence sufficient in law to support a finding that he did an act falling
> within subsection (1) of that section, the question whether or not his act fell within
> that subsection is a question of fact.'

Thus the judge's task is to decide whether there is evidence on which a jury could *d*
reasonably come to the conclusion that the defendant had gone beyond the realm of
mere preparation and had embarked on the actual commission of the offence. If not, he
must withdraw the case from the jury. If there is such evidence, it is then for the jury to
decide whether the defendant did in fact go beyond mere preparation. That is the way
in which the judge approached this case. He ruled that there was sufficient evidence.
Counsel for the appellant submits that he was wrong in so ruling.   *e*

The first task of the court is to apply the words of the 1981 Act to the facts of the case.
Was the appellant still in the stage of preparation to commit the substantive offence, or
was there a basis of fact which would entitle the jury to say that he had embarked on the
theft itself? Might it properly be said that when he jumped on to the track he was trying
to steal £18 from the bookmaker?

Our view is that it could not properly be said that at that stage he was in the process of *f*
committing theft. What he was doing was jumping onto the track in an effort to distract
the dogs, which in its turn, he hoped, would have the effect of forcing the stewards to
declare 'no race', which would in its turn give him the opportunity to go back to the
bookmaker and demand the £18 he had staked. In our view there was insufficient
evidence for it to be said that he had, when he jumped onto the track, gone beyond mere
preparation.   *g*

So far at least as the present case is concerned, we do not think that it is necessary to
examine the authorities which preceded the 1981 Act, save to say that the sections we
have already quoted in this judgment seem to be a blend of various decisions, some of
which were not easy to reconcile with others.

However, in deference to the arguments of counsel, we venture to make the following *h*
observations. Since the passing of the 1981 Act, a division of this court in *R v Ilyas* (1983)
78 Cr App R 17 has helpfully collated the authorities. As appears from the judgment in
that case, there seem to have been two lines of authority. The first was exemplified by
the decision in *R v Eagleton* (1855) Dears CC 515, [1843–60] All ER Rep 363. That was a
case where the defendant was alleged to have attempted to obtain money from the
guardians of a parish by falsely pretending to the relieving officer that he had delivered *j*
loaves of bread of the proper weight to the outdoor poor, when in fact the loaves were
deficient in weight.

Parke B, delivering the judgment of the court of nine judges, said (Dears CC 515 at
538, [1843–60] All ER Rep 363 at 367):

'Acts remotely leading towards the commission of the offence are not to be considered as attempts to commit it, but acts immediately connected with it are; and if, in this case, after the credit with the relieving officer for the fraudulent overcharge, any *further step* on the part of the defendant had been necessary to obtain payment, as the making out a further account or producing the vouchers to the Board, we should have thought that the obtaining credit in account with the relieving officer would not have been sufficiently proximate to the obtaining the money. But, on the statement in this case, no other act on the part of the defendant would have been required. It was the last act, *depending on himself*, towards the payment of the money, and therefore it ought to be considered as an attempt.' (Parke B's emphasis.)

Lord Diplock in *DPP v Stonehouse* [1977] 2 All ER 909 at 917, [1978] AC 55 at 68, having cited part of that passage from *R v Eagleton* (1855) Dears CC 515, [1843–60] All ER Rep 363, added: 'In other words the offender must have crossed the Rubicon and burnt his boats.'

The other line of authority is based on a passage in *Stephen's Digest of the Criminal Law* (5th edn, 1894) art 50:

'An attempt to commit a crime is an act done with intent to commit that crime, and forming part of a series of acts which would constitute its actual commission if it were not interrupted.'

As Lord Edmund-Davies points out in *DPP v Stonehouse* [1977] 2 All ER 909 at 933, [1978] AC 55 at 85–86, that definition has been repeatedly cited with judicial approval: see Byrne J in *Hope v Brown* [1954] 1 All ER 330 at 332, [1954] 1 WLR 250 at 253 and Lord Parker CJ in *Davey v Lee* [1967] 2 All ER 423 at 425, [1968] 1 QB 366 at 370. However, as Lord Parker CJ in the latter case points out, *Stephen's* definition falls short of defining the exact point of time at which the series of acts can be said to begin.

It seems to us that the words of the 1981 Act seek to steer a midway course. They do not provide, as they might have done, that the *R v Eagleton* test is to be followed, or that, as Lord Diplock suggested, the defendant must have reached a point from which it was impossible for him to retreat before the actus reus of an attempt is proved. On the other hand the words give perhaps as clear a guidance as is possible in the circumstances on the point of time at which *Stephen's* 'series of acts' begins. It begins when the merely preparatory acts come to an end and the defendant embarks on the crime proper. When that is will depend of course on the facts in any particular case.

Counsel for the appellant advanced certain other arguments before us on the basis that the judge had been guilty of misdirections in his summing up to the jury. In the light of our decision on the main ground of appeal it is unnecessary for us to consider whether those complaints are justified or not.

The appeal against conviction is allowed and the conviction quashed.

Appeal allowed. Conviction quashed.

Solicitors: *Crown Prosecution Service*, Snaresbrook.

Kate O'Hanlon   Barrister.

R v Jones (Kenneth)

COURT OF APPEAL, CRIMINAL DIVISION
TAYLOR LJ, MARS-JONES AND WAITE JJ
13 MARCH, 3 APRIL 1990

Criminal law – Attempt – Acts preparatory to offence – When attempt begins – Defendant pointing loaded gun at victim with intention of killing him – Safety catch of gun not released and defendant's finger not on trigger – Whether defendant guilty of attempted murder – Whether defendant's actions merely preparatory – Criminal Attempts Act 1981, s 1(1).

The appellant got into a car driven by his ex-mistress's new lover and pointed a loaded sawn-off shotgun at him. The victim managed to wrest the gun from the appellant in the course of a struggle, threw it out of the car and then escaped. The appellant was charged with attempted murder under s 1(1)[a] of the Criminal Attempts Act 1981, which provided that if with intent to commit an offence a person did an act which was 'more than merely preparatory to the commission of the offence' he was guilty of attempting to commit the offence. At his trial there was evidence that the safety catch of the gun was on at the time of the attack, and the victim was unable to say that the appellant's finger had ever been on the trigger. The appellant submitted that the charge of attempted murder should be withdrawn from the jury since the full offence of murder could not have been committed until the appellant performed at least three more acts, namely released the safety catch, put his finger on the trigger and then pulled it. The trial judge rejected the submission and the appellant was convicted. He appealed, contending that the correct test to be applied was whether the defendant had committed the last act prior to the full offence being committed and that the appellant had not committed that last act.

Held – Although the appellant's actions in obtaining the shotgun, shortening it and going to the victim's car were merely preparatory, his actions in getting into the car, taking out the loaded gun and pointing it at the victim with the intention of killing him provided sufficient evidence for the jury to consider whether those acts were more than merely preparatory. The judge had accordingly rightly left the charge of attempted murder to the jury and the appeal would be dismissed (see p 890 j to p 891 a, post).

R v Gullefer [1990] 3 All ER 882 applied.

R v Eagleton [1843–60] All ER Rep 363 not followed.

Notes

For the actus reus of an attempt to commit a crime, see 11(1) Halsbury's Laws (4th edn reissue) para 72, and for cases on the subject, see 14(1) Digest (Reissue) 107–111, 723–749.

For the Criminal Attempts Act 1981, s 1, see 12 Halsbury's Statutes (4th edn) (1989 reissue) 776.

Cases referred to in judgment

Bank of England v Vagliano Bros [1891] AC 107, [1891–4] All ER Rep 93, HL.
Davey v Lee [1967] 2 All ER 423, [1968] 1 QB 366, [1967] 3 WLR 105, DC.
DPP v Stonehouse [1977] 2 All ER 909, [1978] AC 55, [1977] 3 WLR 143, HL.
Hope v Brown [1954] 1 All ER 330, [1954] 1 WLR 250, DC.
R v Boyle (1986) 84 Cr App R 270, CA.
R v Eagleton (1855) Dears CC 515, [1843–60] All ER Rep 363, 169 ER 826, CCR.
R v Gullefer (1986) [1990] 3 All ER 882, CA.

---

a Section 1(1) is set out at p 888 e, post

R v Ilyas (1983) 78 Cr App R 17, CA.

a   *R v Linneker* [1906] 2 KB 99, [1904–7] All ER Rep 797, CCR.
    R v Robinson [1915] 2 KB 342, CCA.
    R v Widdowson (1986) 82 Cr App R 314, CA.

    Cases also cited
    Comer v Bloomfield (1970) 55 Cr App R 305, DC.
b   *R v Fulling* [1987] 2 All ER 65, [1987] QB 426, CA.
    R v White [1910] 2 KB 124, [1908–10] All ER Rep 340, CCA.

Appeal against conviction and sentence
Kenneth Henry Jones appealed against his conviction on 28 July 1988 in the Crown
Court at Leicester before Leonard J and a jury of attempted murder for which he was
c   sentenced to 12 years' imprisonment. He also appealed against the sentence. The facts
are set out in the judgment of the court.

D J Farrer QC for the appellant.
John Mitting QC and *Richard Gaskell* for the Crown.

d
                                                                    Cur adv vult

3 April. The following judgment of the court was delivered.

TAYLOR LJ. This case raises a point of law as to the true construction of s 1 of the
e   Criminal Attempts Act 1981.
    On 28 July 1988 in the Crown Court at Leicester the appellant was convicted of
attempted murder on count 1 of an indictment and pleaded guilty to count 3, shortening
a shotgun. He was sentenced to 12 years' imprisonment on count 1 and two years'
imprisonment concurrently on count 3. Count 2 of the indictment, which charged the
appellant with possession of a loaded shotgun with intent to endanger life, was withdrawn
f   from the jury.
    The appellant, a married man, started an affair with a woman named Lynn Gresley in
1985. She lived with him in Australia during 1986. In September 1987, back in England,
she began a relationship with the victim, Michael Foreman. She continued, however, to
see the appellant, to whom she was still very attached. In November 1987 she decided to
break off the relationship with the appellant, but he continued to write to her, begging
g   her to come back to him.
    On 12 January 1988 the appellant applied for a shotgun certificate, and three days later
bought two guns in company with two companions. He bought two more guns a few
days later on his own. On 23 January he shortened the barrel of one of them and test
fired it twice the following day.
    The appellant told a colleague at work that he would be away on Tuesday, 26 January.
h   On 24 January he phoned Lynn Gresley in a distraught state. The next day he apologised,
but she again refused his invitation to resume their relationship. The appellant then told
his wife that he had packed a bag as he was going to Spain to do some work on their
chalet. On 26 January he left home dressed normally for work, saying that he would
telephone his wife whether he was leaving for Spain that evening.
    That same morning, the victim, Michael Foreman, took his daughter to school by car
j   as usual. After the child left the car, the appellant appeared, opened the door and jumped
into the rear seat. He was wearing overalls, a crash helmet with the visor down, and was
carrying a bag. He and the victim had never previously met. He introduced himself, said
he wanted to sort things out and asked the victim to drive on. When they stopped on a
grass verge, the appellant handed over a letter he had received from Lynn. Whilst the
victim read it, the appellant took the sawn-off shotgun from the bag. It was loaded. He
pointed it at the victim at a range of some ten to twelve inches. He said, 'You are not

going to like this' or similar words. The victim grabbed the end of the gun and pushed it
sideways and upwards. There was a struggle during which the victim managed to throw   *a*
the gun out of the window. As he tried to get out, he felt a cord over his head pulling
him back. He managed to break free and run away, taking the gun with him. From a
nearby garage he telephoned the police.

Meanwhile, the appellant drove off in the victim's car. He was arrested jogging away
from it carrying his holdall. He said that he had done nothing and only wanted to kill
himself. His bag contained a hatchet, some cartridges and a length of cord. He also had a   *b*
sharp kitchen knife which he threw away. In the appellant's car parked near the school
was £stg1,500 together with a quantity of French and Spanish money. The evidence
showed that the safety catch of the shotgun had been in the on position. The victim was
unclear whether the appellant's finger was ever on the trigger. When interviewed, the
appellant declined to make any comment.

At the end of the prosecution case, after the above facts had been given in evidence, a   *c*
submission was made to the judge that the charge of attempted murder should be
withdrawn from the jury. It was argued that since the appellant would have had to
perform at least three more acts before the full offence could have been completed, ie
remove the safety catch, put his finger on the trigger and pull it, the evidence was
insufficient to support the charge. The was a discussion as to the proper construction of
s 1(1) of the Criminal Attempts Act 1981. After hearing full argument, the judge ruled   *d*
against the submission and allowed the case to proceed on count 1. Thereafter, the
appellant gave evidence. In the result, the jury convicted him unanimously of attempted
murder. It follows that they found that he intended to kill the victim.

The sole ground of appeal is that the judge erred in law in his construction of s 1(1)
and ought to have withdrawn the case. Section 1(1) of the 1981 Act provides as follows:
                                                                                        e
'If, with intent to commit an offence to which this section applies, a person does
an act which is more than merely preparatory to the commission of the offence, he
is guilty of attempting to commit the offence.'

Section 4(3) of the 1981 Act provides:

'Where, in proceedings against a person for an offence under section 1 above,   *f*
there is evidence sufficient in law to support a finding that he did an act falling
within subsection (1) of that section, the question whether or not his act fell within
that subsection is a question of fact.'

Counsel for the appellant puts forward three broad propositions. First, he says that for
about a century, two different tests as to the actus reus of attempt have been inconsistently
applied by the courts. In *R v Eagleton* (1855) Dears CC 515, [1843–60] All ER Rep 363   *g*
the defendant was charged with attempting to obtain money from the guardians of a
parish by falsely pretending to the relieving officer that he had delivered loaves of bread
of proper weight to the poor when in fact the loaves were underweight. In the course of
giving the judgment of the court Parke B said (Dears CC 515 at 538, [1843–60] All ER
Rep 363 at 367):
                                                                                        h
'Acts remotely leading towards the commission of the offence are not to be
considered as attempts to commit it, but acts immediately connected with it are;
and if, in this case, after the credit with the relieving officer for the fraudulent
overcharge, any *further step* on the part of the defendant had been necessary to obtain
payment, as the making out a further account or producing the vouchers to the
board, we should have thought that the obtaining credit in account with the   *i*
relieving officer would not have been sufficiently proximate to obtaining the
money. But, on the statement in this case, no other act on the part of the defendant
would have been required. It was the last act, *depending on himself* towards the
payment of the money, and therefore it ought to be considered as an attempt.'
(Parke B's emphasis.)

Accordingly, the test deriving from *R v Eagleton* was said to be the 'last act' test. It was
a adopted in a number of cases, e g *R v Robinson* [1915] 2 KB 342. In *DPP v Stonehouse* [1977]
2 All ER 909 at 917, [1978] AC 55 at 68 Lord Diplock referred to *R v Eagleton* as the locus
classicus, adopted some of the words of Parke B and summarised them in the graphic
phrase: 'In other words the offender must have crossed the Rubicon and burnt his boats.'

The other test referred to by counsel for the appellant derives from *Stephen's Digest of
the Criminal Law* (5th edn, 1894) art 50, where it was stated thus:

b
'An attempt to commit a crime is an act done with intent to commit that crime,
and forming part of a series of acts which would constitute its actual commission if
it were not interrupted.'

Lord Edmund-Davies noted in *DPP v Stonehouse* [1977] 2 All ER 909 at 933, [1978] AC
55 at 85–86 that *Stephen's* definition has been repeatedly cited with approval. He referred
c to its adoption in *Hope v Brown* [1954] 1 All ER 330 at 332, [1954] 1 WLR 250 at 253 and
Davey v Lee [1967] 2 All ER 423, [1968] 1 QB 366. It was also applied in *R v Linneker*
[1906] 2 KB 99, [1904–7] All ER Rep 797, where *R v Eagleton* was not cited.

In some cases, including three since the 1981 Act, both tests have been considered, and
the court has found it unnecessary to decide between them, holding that the result in
those cases would have been the same, whichever applied (see *R v Ilyas* (1983) 78 Cr App
d R 17, *R v Widdowson* (1986) 82 Cr App R 314 and *R v Boyle* (1986) 84 Cr App R 270).

The second proposition of counsel for the appellant is that s 1(1) of the 1981 Act has
not resolved the question which is the appropriate test. Third, he submits that the test
deriving from *R v Eagleton* should be adopted.

This amounts to an invitation to construe the statutory words by reference to previous
conflicting case law. We believe this to be misconceived. The 1981 Act is a codifying
e statute. It amends and sets out completely the law relating to attempts and conspiracies.
In those circumstances the correct approach is to look first at the natural meaning of the
statutory words, not to turn back to earlier case law and seek to fit some previous test to
the words of the section. In *Bank of England v Vagliano Bros* [1891] AC 107 at 144–145,
[1891–4] All ER Rep 93 at 113 Lord Herschell, referring to a codifying Act, said:

f
'I think the proper course is in the first instance to examine the language of the
statute and to ask what is its natural meaning, uninfluenced by any considerations
derived from the previous state of the law, and not to start with inquiring how the
law previously stood, and then, assuming that it was probably intended to leave it
unaltered, to see if the words of the enactment will bear an interpretation in
conformity with this view. If a statute, intended to embody in a code a particular
g branch of the law, is to be treated in this fashion, it appears to me that its utility will
be almost entirely destroyed, and the very object with which it was enacted will be
frustrated. The purpose of such a statute surely was that on any point specifically
dealt with by it, the law should be ascertained by interpreting the language used
instead of, as before, by roaming over a vast number of authorities in order to
discover what the law was ... I am of course far from asserting that resort may
h never be had to the previous state of the law for the purpose of aiding in the
construction of the provisions of the code. If, for example, a provision be of doubtful
import, such resort would be perfectly legitimate.'

This approach was adopted by Lord Lane CJ presiding over this court in *R v Gullefer*
(1986) [1990] 3 All ER 882. Having set out ss 1(1) and 4(3) of the 1981 Act, Lord Lane CJ
j went on ([1990] 3 All ER 882 at 884):

'The first task of the court is to apply the words of the 1981 Act to the facts of the
case. Was the appellant still in the stage of preparation to commit the substantive
offence, or was there a basis of fact which would entitle the jury to say that he had
embarked on the theft itself? ... So far at least as the present case is concerned, we
do not think that it is necessary to examine the authorities which preceded the 1981

Act, save to say that the sections we have already quoted in this judgment seem to be a blend of various decisions, some of which were not easy to reconcile with others.'

Lord Lane CJ then, in deference (as he said) to the arguments of counsel, reviewed the two lines of authority already mentioned and concluded as follows ([1990] 3 All ER 882 at 885, [1990] 1 WLR 1063 at 1066):

'It seems to us that the words of the 1981 Act seek to steer a midway course. They do not provide, as they might have done, that the *R v Eagleton* test is to be followed, or that, as Lord Diplock suggested, the defendant must have reached a point from which it was impossible for him to retreat before the actus reus of an attempt is proved. On the other hand the words give perhaps as clear a guidance as is possible in the circumstances on the point of time at which *Stephen's* "series of acts" begins. It begins when the merely preparatory acts have come to an end and the defendant embarks on the crime proper. When that is will depend of course on the facts in any particular case.'

We respectfully adopt those words. We do not accept counsel's contention that s 1(1) of the 1981 Act in effect embodies the 'last act' test derived from *R v Eagleton*. Had Parliament intended to adopt that test, a quite different form of words could and would have been used.

It is of interest to note that the 1981 Act followed a report from the Law Commission on *Attempt, and Impossibility in Relation to Attempt, Conspiracy and Incitement* (Law Com no 102). At para 2.47 the report states:

'The definition of sufficient proximity must be wide enough to cover two varieties of cases; first, those in which a person has taken all the steps towards the commission of a crime which he believes to be necessary as far as he is concerned for that crime to result, such as firing a gun at another and missing. Normally such cases cause no difficulty. Secondly, however, the definition must cover those instances where a person has to take some further step to complete the crime, assuming that there is evidence of the necessary mental element on his part to commit it; for example, when the defendant has raised the gun to take aim at another but has not yet squeezed the trigger. We have reached the conclusion that, in regard to these cases, it is undesirable to recommend anything more complex than a rationalisation of the present law.'

In para 2.48 the report states:

'The literal meaning of "proximate" is "nearest, next before or after (in place, order, time, connection of thought, causation, etc.)". Thus, were this term part of a statutory description of the actus reus of attempt, it would clearly be capable of being interpreted to exclude all but the "final act"; this would not be in accordance with the policy outlined above.'

Clearly, the draftsman of s 1(1) must be taken to have been aware of the two lines of earlier authority and of the Law Commission's report. The words 'an act which is more than merely preparatory to the commission of the offence' would be inapt if they were intended to mean 'the last act which lay in his power towards the commission of the offence'.

Looking at the plain natural meaning of s 1(1) in the way indicated by Lord Lane CJ, the question for the judge in the present case was whether there was evidence from which a reasonable jury, properly directed, could conclude that the appellant had done acts which were more than merely preparatory. Clearly his actions in obtaining the gun, in shortening it, in loading it, in putting on his disguise and in going to the school could only be regarded as preparatory acts. But, in our judgment, once he had got into the car,

taken out the loaded gun and pointed it at the victim with the intention of killing him,
a there was sufficient evidence for the consideration of the jury on the charge of attempted
murder. It was a matter for them to decide whether they were sure that those acts were
more than merely preparatory. In our judgment, therefore, the judge was right to allow
the case to go to the jury, and the appeal against conviction must be dismissed.

I turn to the appeal against sentence. The appellant is now aged 49. He is a man of
previous good character. For the last 20 years he has held a responsible job as a personnel
b manager, and his employers describe him as excellent, trustworthy and competent. It is
clear that at the time of the offence he was emotionally disturbed by jealousy and
disappointment. A recent psychiatric report based on visits to the appellant in prison
indicates that he suffers from severe depression and is at times suicidal. It is urged on his
behalf that the incident in the car was of very brief duration and no physical harm
resulted to the victim. On the other hand, but for the courage, speed and success of the
c victim's action in deflecting and seizing the gun, he would probably have died. Clearly
the judge was bound to pass a substantial sentence of imprisonment. However, we are
persuaded that in the circumstances of the case a sentence of twelve years' imprisonment
was too long. We accordingly reduce it and substitute a sentence of eight years'
imprisonment on count 1. The concurrent sentence of two years' imprisonment on
count 3 will stand. The total sentence will thus be reduced from twelve years to eight
d years. To that extent this appeal against sentence is allowed.

Appeal against conviction dismissed. Sentence varied.

Solicitors: *Headleys,* Hinckley (for the appellant); *Crown Prosecution Service,* Leicester.

Kate O'Hanlon   Barrister.

R v Hyde and others

COURT OF APPEAL, CRIMINAL DIVISION
LORD LANE CJ, ROSE AND TUCKER JJ
27 JULY, 26 SEPTEMBER 1990

Criminal law − Murder − Concerted action − Joint unlawful enterprise − Mental element of secondary party − Joint attack on victim − Victim dying after attack by three defendants − Impossible to say which defendant struck fatal blow − Direction to jury − Judge directing jury that secondary party guilty of murder if he foresaw real possibility that joint enterprise might result in murder but continued to participate − Whether all three defendants guilty of murder − Whether direction to jury correct.

The three appellants kicked and punched a man outside a public house. The victim died from a kick to the head. The appellants were charged with murder. At their trial the prosecution alleged that the appellants had carried out a joint attack on the victim and were equally responsible for his death, even though it was impossible to say which of the three had inflicted the fatal blow or blows, and that either their intention had been to cause serious injury or each knew that such was the intention of the others when he took part. All three appellants gave evidence denying that there had been any joint enterprise or any intent to do serious harm to the victim. The appellants submitted that since the jury could not be sure whose act caused the death none of them should be convicted of murder. The judge directed the jury that if all three appellants intended to do grievous bodily harm to the victim then all three were guilty of murder; if they did not so intend but one of them decided to do it, then if either of the others could be shown to have had the same intention, inasmuch as he foresaw the real possibility that that might be the result of the fight which he was putting in train, then he too shared the responsibility. The jury convicted all three of murder. They appealed against their conviction on the ground that the jury had not been properly directed on joint enterprise.

Held − If a secondary party realised, without agreeing to such conduct being used, that a fellow assailant in a fight might kill or intentionally inflict serious injury, but nevertheless continued to participate with the assailant in the fight, then that amounted to a sufficient mental element for the secondary party to be guilty of murder if the assailant, with the requisite intent, killed the victim in the course of the fight, since in those circumstances the secondary party had lent himself to the enterprise and by so doing had given assistance and encouragement to the assailant in carrying out an enterprise which the secondary party realised might involve murder. It followed that the trial judge had been correct in directing the jury as he did. The appeals would therefore be dismissed (see p 896 *d e*, post).

Dictum of Sir Robin Cooke in *Chan Wing-siu v R* [1984] 3 All ER 877 at 880−881 applied.

R v Slack [1989] 3 All ER 90 explained.

Notes

For secondary parties and collateral acts in relation to criminal liability, see 11(1) Halsbury's Laws (4th edn reissue) paras 46−47, and for cases on the subject, see 14(1) Digest (Reissue) 73−77, 93−97, 421−457, 594−639.

For criminal liability in joint enterprise, see 11(1) Halsbury's Laws (4th edn reissue) para 435, and for cases on the subject, see 14(1) Digest (Reissue) 77−80, 458−488.

Cases referred to in judgment

Chan Wing-siu v R [1984] 3 All ER 877, [1985] AC 168, [1984] 3 WLR 677, PC.

R v Anderson and Morris [1966] 2 All ER 644, [1966] 2 QB 110, [1966] 2 WLR 1195, CCA.
R v Slack [1989] 3 All ER 90, [1989] QB 775, [1989] 3 WLR 513, CA.
R v Wakely [1990] Crim LR 119, CA.

Cases also cited

R v Barr (1986) 88 Cr App R 362, CA.
R v Moloney [1985] 1 All ER 1025, [1985] AC 905, HL.
R v Smith [1988] Crim LR 616, CA.
R v Ward (1986) 85 Cr App R 71, CA.

Appeal against conviction and sentence

David Charles Hyde, Philip James Sussex and Henry John Collins, appealed with leave of the court against their convictions on 28 February 1989 in the Crown Court at Winchester before Ian Kennedy J and a jury of murder for which they were sentenced to life imprisonment on the ground that the judge had misdirected the jury on the law of joint enterprise. The appellants also appealed against, inter alia, the sentence of four years' imprisonment imposed for assault occasioning actual bodily harm, to which they had pleaded guilty. The facts are set out in the judgment of the court.

Anthony Donne QC and *Christopher Critchlow* (assigned by the Registrar of Criminal Appeals) for the appellant Hyde.
John Perry QC and *Karen Hammond* (assigned by the Registrar of Criminal Appeals) for the appellant Sussex.
Nigel Pascoe QC and *Andrew Barnett* (assigned by the Registrar of Criminal Appeals) for the appellant Collins.
Jeremy S Gibbons for the Crown.

Cur adv vult

26 September. The following judgment of the court was delivered.

LORD LANE CJ. This is the judgment of the court. On 28 February 1989 these three applicants, David Charles Hyde, Phillip James Sussex and Henry John Collins, were convicted of murder and sentenced to life imprisonment. Each pleaded guilty to assault occasioning actual bodily harm on the victim of the killing, one Gallagher. Hyde also pleaded guilty to two further counts of assault occasioning actual bodily harm on other unconnected occasions. Each was sentenced to four years' imprisonment concurrent in respect of the assault on Gallagher. Hyde was sentenced to further terms of three and two years' imprisonment, each consecutive, in respect of the other assaults, making a total of nine years' imprisonment to run concurrently with the life sentence.

Their applications for leave to appeal against conviction and sentence have been referred to this court by the single judge. The grounds of appeal against conviction raise arguable points of law, and we give leave in respect both of conviction and sentence. We treat this accordingly as the appeal.

The incident resulting in the death of Gallagher took place outside the Merlin Public House, Andover, at about 10.25 pm on 3 June 1988. There was no dispute that Gallagher sustained a violent blow to the forehead, consistent with a heavy kick from a shod foot, which crushed the front of his skull. He died 73 days later, having never regained consciousness.

The prosecution case was that the three appellants carried out a joint attack on the victim and were all equally responsible for his death, even though it was not possible to say who had actually struck the fatal blow or blows; furthermore, that their intention had been to cause serious injury, or that each knew that such was the intention of the others when he took part.

By 10 o'clock that evening all three, who were regular customers at the Merlin Public House, had probably had too much to drink. Sussex and Collins were both overheard making unspecific threatening remarks. When Gallagher left he was closely followed by Hyde and Sussex, and then Collins. Other customers, in the belief that serious trouble was about to break out, gathered on the balcony to watch events unfold.

Gallagher was accompanied by a man called Burkwood, who related how Hyde had said to Gallagher, 'Hey, feller, you've got a problem.' When Gallagher asked 'Why?', he was felled by a blow. Collins told Burkwood, 'Get out if you know what's good for you.' Burkwood was then knocked against a car, and when he recovered his breath he saw all three appellants round Gallagher, who was already on the ground, kicking him. Other witnesses saw Hyde kicking Gallagher's legs from under him, Sussex punching Gallagher's head, Hyde kicking him between the legs, saying, 'This is for Norma [or Nora]', and Collins running back for five yards as they left and kicking Gallagher on the head.

Witnesses spoke of Hyde and Sussex going back into the public house with blood on their hands and clothes. It was said that they looked pleased with themselves, and later that evening Hyde told someone, 'It was a favour for a friend.' Collins told a friend of his the following day that he had kicked Gallagher twice.

Each of the three men was questioned by the police. Hyde agreed that he had hit Gallagher, asserting that no one else was involved. He said that he had had a bad day and Gallagher kept picking on him in the public house. He was asked if Gallagher had remained conscious, to which he replied, 'Don't think so, not the way I hit him.' He was then asked how he had hit him, and replied, 'With my fist on his face, square on his face with all my bloody weight behind it.'

Sussex said that he had been drunk and had punched Gallagher a few times. Collins said that there was a fight between Hyde and Gallagher with Sussex present. He, Collins, did not hit Gallagher and accompanied the other two after the incident back to the public house.

All three gave evidence before the jury denying that there was any joint enterprise or any intent to do serious harm to Gallagher. Hyde and Sussex said each had acted on his own with no intention beyond a simple assault. Collins, according to them, was responsible for the fatal blow. His actions and intention were nothing to do with them, nor did they foresee what he might intend or do. Collins for his part maintained that there was no joint attack or, if there was, it involved only Hyde and Sussex.

The jury, it was submitted, could not be sure whose act caused the death, and that therefore no one should be convicted as the killer.

The first ground of appeal in Hyde's notice was a complaint of excessive interventions by the judge during the course of the evidence. This ground was abandoned, and rightly abandoned, at the outset of the hearing before this court. It is a pity that it was ever advanced. It was without foundation. The case was not an easy one for the judge, but his handling of it was even-handed and skilful.

Before us the primary ground advanced by counsel was the contention that the judge misdirected the jury on the law of joint enterprise. The passages in the summing up of which complaint is made are these:

'As I say ordinarily speaking if he does something which is beyond the scope of the agreement, that is as you might say the end of the agreement. But, what if the others anticipated that he might do some such thing? and here we have to apply common sense. Fights do get out of hand and escalate. A man who starts by punching may get excited and decide to kick. If there was a tacit agreement to punch and kick, a man who is kicking may decide to give a kick like that which was allegedly given by Collins and which has been described as a place-kick or a penalty kick, a description which if the basic facts are right is not a bad description of the

a   kick. If either of the other two, and you have to consider the case of each of them
     separately, foresaw and contemplated a real possibility that one of his fellows might
     in the exictement of the moment go beyond the actual plan and intend to do and
     do grievous bodily harm, then you have to consider whether that man, the one who
     had the foresight, did not in truth intend that result himself.'

     The judge then went on to explain to the jury the distinction which may, in some
b   cases, exist between what a man desires should happen and what a man intends should
     happen. He explained to the jury that foresight that something will happen is not
     necessarily the same as an intention that it should happen, though it may be powerful
     evidence of such intention. The judge concluded this part of his summing up with the
     following words:

c   'We may summarise it shortly by saying that if all three intended to do grievous
          bodily harm, then that is that, they are all guilty of murder. If they did not but one
          of them decided to do it, then if either of the others can be shown to have had the
          same intention, inasmuch as he foresaw the real possibility that that might be the
          result of the fight which he was putting in train, then he too shares in the
          responsibility as in common sense he must.'

d   The specific complaints as set out in the notice of appeal are as follows. (1) The judge,
     in the circumstances of the case, erred in directing the jury on foreseeability, such a
     direction being unnecessary and confusing. (2) Alternatively, the judge erred in directing
     the jury that the defendant's foresight of the state of mind of another defendant was a
     relevant consideration in determining whether the defendant having that foresight had
     the intention to do grievous bodily harm. (3) Alternatively, the judge's direction on
e   foreseeability did not sufficiently distinguish between foreseeability and intention and/
     or did not sufficiently underline the necessity for the prosecution to prove the specific
     intent required for the offence of murder.
     The judgment of this court in R v Slack [1989] 3 All ER 90, [1989] QB 775 was not
     delivered until some four months after the conclusion of the hearing of the instant case.
     Consequently the judge here did not have before him the distinction which we
f   endeavoured to draw in R v Slack between the mental element required to be proved vis-
     à-vis the secondary party (hereinafter called 'B') and that required in the case of the
     principal party, the actual killer (hereinafter called 'A'). In the passages we have cited
     from the summing up of which complaint is made, the judge was endeavouring to apply
     the principles which were, prior to R v Slack, thought to apply to cases of joint enterprise.
     The question is whether the directions in the present case were sufficient to comply
g   with the law as it now stands.
     There are, broadly speaking, two main types of joint enterprise cases where death
     results to the victim. The first is where the primary object of the participants is to do
     some kind of physical injury to the victim. The second is where the primary object is not
     to cause physical injury to any victim but, for example, to commit burglary. The victim
     is assaulted and killed as a (possibly unwelcome) incident of the burglary. The latter type
h   of case may pose more complicated questions than the former, but the principle in each
     is the same. A must be proved to have intended to kill or to do serious bodily harm at
     the time he killed. As was pointed out in R v Slack [1989] 3 All ER 90 at 94, [1989] QB
     775 at 781, B, to be guilty, must be proved to have lent himself to a criminal enterprise
     involving the infliction of serious harm or death, or to have had an express or tacit
     understanding with A that such harm or death should, if necessary, be inflicted.
j   We were there endeavouring, respectfully, to follow the principles enunciated by Sir
     Robin Cooke in Chan Wing-siu v R [1984] 3 All ER 877 at 880–881 [1985] AC 168 at 175:

          'The case must depend rather on the wider principle whereby a secondary party
          is criminally liable for acts by the primary offender of a type which the former
          foresees but does not necessarily intend. That there is such a principle is not in

doubt. It turns on contemplation or, putting the same idea in other words, authorisation, which may be express but is more usually implied. It meets the case *a* of a crime foreseen as a possible incident of the common unlawful enterprise. The criminal culpability lies in participating in the venture with that foresight.'

It has been pointed out by Professor Smith, in his commentary on *R v Wakely* [1990] Crim LR 119 at 120–121, that in the judgments in *R v Slack* [1989] 3 All ER 90, [1989] QB 775 and also in *R v Wakely* itself, to both of which I was a party, insufficient attention *b* was paid by the court to the distinction between on the one hand tacit agreement by B that A should use violence, and on the other hand a realisation by B that A, the principal party, may use violence despite B's refusal to authorise or agree to its use. Indeed in *R v Wakely* we went so far as to say:

'The suggestion that a mere foresight of the real or definite possibility of violence being used is sufficient to constitute the mental element of murder is prima facie, *c* academically speaking at least, not sufficient.'

On reconsideration, that passage is not in accordance with the principles set out by Sir Robin Cooke which we were endeavouring to follow and was wrong, or at least misleading. If B realises (without agreeing to such conduct being used) that A may kill or intentionally inflict serious injury, but nevertheless continues to participate with A in *d* the venture, that will amount to a sufficient mental element for B to be guilty of murder if A, with the requisite intent, kills in the course of the venture. As Professor Smith points out, B has in those circumstances lent himself to the enterprise and by so doing he has given assistance and encouragement to A in carrying out an enterprise which B realises may involve murder.

That being the case it seems to us that the judge was correct when he directed the jury *e* in the terms of those passages of the summing up which we have already quoted. It may be that a simple direction on the basis of *R v Anderson and Morris* [1966] 2 All ER 644, [1966] 2 QB 110 would, in the circumstances of this case, have been enough, but the direction given was sufficiently clear and the outcome scarcely surprising. That ground of appeal, which was in the forefront of the arguments of each of the appellants, therefore fails.   *f*

[The court then considered certain subsidiary grounds of appeal against conviction and continued:] We do not consider that any of the grounds of appeal are substantiated so far as conviction is concerned, and the appeals against conviction are accordingly dismissed.

[The court then considered the appeals against sentence and held that in the light of the conviction for murder there was no necessity to impose any separate sentence in respect of the offence of assault occasioning actual bodily harm and that therefore the *g* sentence of four year's imprisonment would be quashed.]

Appeal against conviction for murder dismissed. Sentences varied.

Solicitors: *Crown Prosecution Service*, Winchester.

                                                                                                              h

N P Metcalfe Esq   Barrister.

Foster v British Gas plc

(Case C-188/89)

COURT OF JUSTICE OF THE EUROPEAN COMMUNITIES
JUDGES SIR GORDON SLYNN (PRESIDENT OF CHAMBER, ACTING AS PRESIDENT), KAKOURIS, SCHOCKWEILER AND ZULEEG (PRESIDENTS OF CHAMBERS), MANCINI, JOLIET, O'HIGGINS, MOITINHO DE ALMEIDA, RODRÍGUEZ IGLESIAS, GRÉVISSE AND DÍEZ DE VELASCO
ADVOCATE GENERAL VAN GERVEN
15 MARCH, 8 MAY, 12 JULY 1990

European Economic Community – Equality of treatment of men and women – Equal working conditions – Dismissal – Dismissal on attaining retirement age – Retirement age fixed by employer by reference to qualifying age for state pension – Qualifying age different for men and women – Retirement policy contrary to Equal Treatment Directive – Whether employer a public body – Whether employee entitled to rely on directive as against employer – Whether European Court having jurisdiction to determine question – Council Directive (EEC) 76/207, art 5(1).

The appellants were former female employees of the British Gas Corp who had been compulsorily retired on reaching the age of 60 in accordance with the corporation's general policy of retiring employees at the age at which the state retirement pension became payable, ie 60 for women and 65 for men. The appellants made complaints to an industrial tribunal of unlawful discrimination on the ground of sex and, in particular, that the corporation's policy, although not prohibited by national legislation, was contrary to art 5(1)[a] of Council Directive (EEC) 76/207, which guaranteed the same working conditions for men and women without discrimination on grounds of sex. The industrial tribunal dismissed their applications on the ground that the corporation was not a state authority and therefore that the directive could not be relied on as against it. On appeal the Employment Appeal Tribunal and the Court of Appeal upheld that decision. The appellants appealed to the House of Lords, which considered that the dispute raised questions on the interpretation of Community law and accordingly referred to the Court of Justice of the European Communities the question whether the corporation was a body of such a type that the appellants were entitled to rely directly on the directive so as to be entitled to claim damages on the ground that the corporation's retirement policy was contrary to the directive. The corporation had been a statutory corporation responsible for developing and maintaining a supply of gas in Great Britain, the members of which were appointed by the Secretary of State, who had power to give directions of a general character in relation to matters affecting the national interest and instructions concerning management. The corporation was required to submit reports to the Secretary of State which were laid before Parliament, and also had the right, with the consent of the Secretary of State, to submit proposed legislation to Parliament. It was also required to run a balanced budget and the Secretary of State could order it to pay certain funds over to him or to allocate funds to specified purposes. The question also arose whether the Court of Justice had jurisdiction to determine the question referred to it.

Held – (1) The Court of Justice had jurisdiction in proceedings for a preliminary ruling to determine the categories of persons against whom the provisions of a directive might be relied on since that question necessarily involved interpretation of the articles of the

---

a   Article 5(1) is set out at p 920 h, post

EEC Treaty concerning measures adopted by the institutions of the Community. However, it was for the national court to decide whether the party to the proceedings *a* before that court fell within one of those categories (see p 921 *e*, post).

(2) Article 5(1) of Directive 76/207 could be relied on by an individual in a claim for damages against a body, whatever its legal form, which had been made responsible, pursuant to a measure adopted by a member state, for providing a public service under the control of the state and which had for that purpose special powers beyond those resulting from the normal rules applicable in relations between individuals. Accordingly, *b* the appellants were entitled to rely on the directive in their claim against the corporation (see p 921 *g* to p 922 *a c* to *e g*, post); *Marshall v Southampton and South West Hampshire Area Health Authority (Teaching)* Case 152/84 [1986] 2 All ER 584 followed.

Notes

For the principle of equal treatment for men and women as regards working conditions, *c* including conditions governing dismissal, see 52 Halsbury's Laws (4th edn) para 21·13.

For the direct effect of Community law, see 51 ibid paras 3·41–3·48.

Cases cited

Auer v Ministére Public Case 271/82 [1983] ECR 2727.
Barber v Royal Exchange Assurance Case C-262/88 [1990] 2 All ER 660, CJEC. *d*
Becker v Finanzamt Münster-Innenstadt Case 8/81 [1982] ECR 53.
Beets-Proper v F Van Lanschot Bankiers NV Case 262/84 [1986] ECR 773.
Bodson v Pompes funébres des régions libérées Case 30/87 [1988] ECR 2479.
Burton v British Railways Board Case 19/81 [1982] 3 All ER 537, [1982] QB 1080, [1982] 3 WLR 387, [1982] ECR 555, CJEC.
Defrenne v Sabena Case 149/77 [1978] ECR 1365, CJEC. *e*
Defrenne v Sabena Case 43/75 (1976) [1981] 1 All ER 122, [1976] ECR 455, CJEC.
DPP v Holly, DPP v Manners [1977] 1 All ER 316, [1978] AC 43, [1977] 2 WLR 178, HL.
Duke v GEC Reliance Ltd [1988] 1 All ER 626, [1988] AC 618, [1988] 2 WLR 359, HL.
EC Commission v Belgium Case 149/79 [1980] ECR 3881.
EC Commission v Ireland Case 249/81 [1982] ECR 4005.
EC Commission v Italian Republic Case 118/85 [1987] ECR 2599. *f*
ECSC v Acciaierie e Ferriere Busseni SpA (in liq) Case C-221/88 (22 February 1990, unreported), CJEC.
Flli Constanzo SpA v Comune di Milano Case 103/88 [1990] 3 CMLR 239, CJEC.
Gebroeders Beentjes BV v Netherlands Case 31/87 [1988] ECR 4635.
Johnston v Chief Constable of the Royal Ulster Constabulary Case 222/84 [1986] 3 All ER 135, [1987] QB 129, [1986] 3 WLR 1038, [1986] ECR 1651, CJEC. *g*
Kolpinghuis Nijmegen BV, Criminal proceedings against Case 80/86 [1987] ECR 3969.
Kwekerij Gebroeders van der Kooy BV v EC Commission Joined cases 67, 68 and 70/85 [1988] ECR 219.
Marshall v Southampton and South West Hampshire Area Health Authority (Teaching) Case 152/84 [1986] 2 All ER 584, [1986] QB 401, [1986] 2 WLR 780, [1986] ECR 723, *h* CJEC.
Oberkreisdirektor des Kreises Borken v Handelsonderneming Moormann BV Case 190/87 [1988] ECR 4689.
Pubblico Ministero v Ratti Case 148/78 [1979] ECR 1629.
RC Commission v Italian Republic Case 118/85 [1987] ECR 2599.
Roberts v Tate & Lyle Industries Ltd Case 151/84 [1986] 2 All ER 602, [1986] ECR 703, *j* CJEC.
Rolls-Royce plc v Doughty [1987] ICR 932, EAT.
Société Nouvelle des Usines de Pontlieue Aciéries du Temple (SNUPAT) v High Authority of ECSC Joined cases 32 and 33/58 [1959] ECR 127.
Turpie v University of Glasgow (19 September 1986, unreported), Industrial Tribunal at Glasgow.

Ufficio Distrettuale delle Imposte Dirette di Fiorenzuola d'Arda v Comune di Carpaneto Piacentino
Joined cases 231/87 and 129/88 OJ 1989 C288, p 4, CJEC.
von Colson and Kamann v Land Nordrhein-Westfalen Case 14/83 [1984] ECR 1891.
Worms v High Authority of ECSC Case 18/60 [1962] ECR 195.

Reference

By order dated 4 May 1989 the House of Lords referred to the Court of Justice of the European Communities for a preliminary ruling under art 177 of the EEC Treaty a question (set out at p 921, post) on the interpretation of Council Directive (EEC) 76/207 of 9 February 1976 on the implementation of the principle of equal treatment for men and women as regards access to employment, vocational training and promotion and working conditions. The question was raised in the course of an appeal by Mrs A Foster, Mrs G A H M Fulford-Brown, Mrs J Morgan, Mrs M Roby, Mrs E M Salloway and Mrs P Sullivan, to the House of Lords against the decision of the Court of Appeal (Lord Donaldson MR, Nourse and Mann LJJ) ([1988] ICR 584) on 13 May 1988 dismissing their appeals against the decision of the Employment Appeal Tribunal (Popplewell J, Mr A C Blyghton and Mr A D Scott) ([1987] ICR 904) on 6 July 1987 whereby it dismissed their appeals against the decision of an industrial tribunal sitting at London (South) on 24 and 25 September 1986 dismissing their complaints of unlawful discrimination on the ground of sex against their employers, British Gas Corp (now British Gas plc). Mrs Foster and the other appellants, British Gas plc, the United Kingdom and the Commission of the European Communities submitted written observations to the court. The language of the case was English. The facts are set out in the report for the hearing presented by the Judge Rapporteur.

The Judge Rapporteur (G F Mancini) presented the following report for the hearing.

I—FACTS AND PROCEDURE
1. *Relevant legal provisions*
Article 5(1) of Council Directive (EEC) 76/207 on the implementation of the principle of equal treatment for men and women as regards access to employment, vocational training and promotion, and working conditions provides:

> 'Application of the principle of equal treatment with regard to working conditions, including the conditions governing dismissal, means that men and women shall be guaranteed the same conditions without discrimination on grounds of sex.'

Under English law, s 6(2)(b) of the Sex Discrimination Act 1975, which was in force at the material time, made it unlawful for any employer to discriminate against a woman employed in Great Britain 'by dismissing her or subjecting her to any other detriment'. Section 6(4) of the Act, however, provided that s 6(2) did not apply to any 'provision in relation to death or retirement'. Section 6(4) was repealed, with effect from 7 November 1986, by s 2 of the Sex Discrimination Act 1986.

The House of Lords has decided, in *Duke v GEC Reliance Ltd* [1988] 1 All ER 626, [1988] AC 618, that it is impossible in an action between workers and a private employer, to interpret the Sex Discrimination Act 1975 as it applied before the amendments introduced by the Sex Discrimination Act 1986 in such a way as to make it consistent with Directive 76/207, as interpreted by the court in its judgment in *Marshall v Southampton and South West Hampshire Area Health Authority (Teaching)* Case 152/84 [1986] 2 All ER 584, [1986] QB 401. In that judgment the court ruled ([1986] 2 All ER 584 at 601, [1986] QB 401 at 423):

> 'art 5(1) of EC Council Directive 76/207 must be interpreted as meaning that a general policy concerning dismissal involving the dismissal of a woman solely because she has attained or passed the qualifying age for a state pension, which age is different under national legislation for men and women, constitutes discrimination on grounds of sex, contrary to that directive.'

The court also ruled that the aforesaid provision—

> 'may be relied on as against a state authority acting in its capacity as employer, in *a*
> order to avoid the application of any national provision which does not conform to
> art 5(1).'

2. *The facts*

Mrs A Foster, Mrs G A H M Fulford-Brown, Mrs J Morgan, Mrs M Roby, Mrs E M *b*
Solloway and Mrs P Sullivan (hereinafter referred to as 'the appellants') are former
employees of the British Gas Corp (hereinafter referred to as 'the BGC'), the rights and
liabilities of which have been transferred to British Gas plc (hereinafter referred to as 'the
respondent').

At the material time, the BGC was governed by the Gas Act 1972, which vested in it
all the rights and obligations previously vested in the Gas Council and the area boards by *c*
virtue of the provisions of the Gas Act 1948, by which the gas industry had been
nationalised in the United Kingdom. Subsequently, the industry was privatised with
effect from 24 August 1986 by the Gas Act 1986 which established British Gas plc, the
respondent in the main proceedings.

Under the Gas Act 1972, the BGC was a statutory corporation granted a monopoly of
the supply of gas, whose duty was to develop and maintain an efficient, co-ordinated and *d*
economical system of gas supply for Great Britain and to satisfy all reasonable demands
for gas (ss 2(1) and 29 of the Gas Act 1972). It had power to carry on all such activities as
might appear to it to be requisite, advantageous or convenient for it to carry on for or in
connection with the discharge of its duty (s 2 (2)).

The members of the BGC were appointed by the Secretary of State (s 1(2)). He was
empowered to give to the BGC directions concerning its management and directions of *e*
a general character as to the exercise of the functions conferred on it in relation to matters
affecting the public interest (ss 4(2) and 7(1)).

The BGC was required to submit to the Secretary of State, at the latter's request or on
its own initiative, periodic reports concerning its management. It was also required to
make to the Secretary of State an annual report on the exercise of its functions and its
policy and programmes. These reports were laid before both Houses of Parliament (ss 4 *f*
and 8).

It was the duty of the BGC to balance its budget (s 14); the Secretary of State could also
direct the BGC to allocate amounts to reserves or to allocate for a specified purpose
amounts allocated to reserves (s 15). He also had power to direct the BGC to pay over to
him any surplus revenues obtained from certain of its activities (s 16).

Under s 6(6) the BGC was empowered to promote Bills in Parliament with the consent *g*
of the Secretary of State.

As a matter of English law, the BGC was a 'public body' and a 'public authority' for the
purposes of various domestic statutes and in English common law (as regards the
situation under the Gas Act 1948, see the judgment of the House of Lords in *DPP v Holly,
DPP v Manners* [1977] 1 All ER 316, [1978] AC 43). The BGC was not regarded as an *h*
agent of the Secretary of State and its employees were not in Crown employment for the
purposes of United Kingdom employment law.

The appellants were required to retire by the BGC on dates between 27 December
1985 and 22 July 1986, that is to say on attaining the age of 60, in accordance with the
BGC's general policy of requiring its employees to retire on their attainment of the age at
which they were entitled to a state pension. In the United Kingdom that age is 60 for *j*
women and 65 for men.

Since the appellants wished to continue working beyond the age of 60 and were not
allowed to do so, they presented complaints to the industrial tribunal in London (South),
claiming that they had been subject to unlawful discrimination on grounds of sex. They
claimed in particular that BGC's general policy of making male workers and female
workers retire at different ages, though not prohibited by national rules, was contrary to

art 5(1) of Directive 76/207, and that the latter provision could be relied on as against the

a BGC. By its decision of 25 September 1986 the industrial tribunal dismissed their applications on the ground that the BGC was not a 'state authority' within the meaning of the operative part of the judgment in *Marshall's* case and that Directive 76/207 therefore could not be relied on as against it (see [1987] ICR 52).

That decision was confirmed by the Employment Appeal Tribunal by a judgment of 6 July 1987 (see [1987] ICR 904) and by the Court of Appeal by a judgment of 13 May

b 1988 (see [1988] ICR 584), which dismissed the appeals brought by the appellants.

3. The question referred for a preliminary ruling

On 18 October 1988 the House of Lords gave the appellants leave to appeal against the decision of the Court of Appeal. Since it considered that the dispute raised a question on the interpretation of the Community rule at issue, the House of Lords, by order of 4 May

c 1989, decided pursuant to art 177 of the EEC Treaty to stay the proceedings and request the Court of Justice for a preliminary ruling on the following question:

'Was the British Gas Corporation (at the material time) a body of such a type that the appellants are entitled in English courts and tribunals to rely directly upon Council Directive 76/207 of 9 February 1976 on the implementation of the principle

d of equal treatment for men and women as regards access to employment, vocational training and promotion, and working conditions so as to be entitled to a claim for damages on the ground that the retirement policy of the British Gas Corporation was contrary to the directive?'

In the order for reference, the House of Lords states that it is not in dispute between the parties that, if Directive 76/207 was applicable, the BGC's practice of making men

e and women retire at different ages was illegal. It is further common ground that, if the directive did not have direct effect, there was nothing unlawful in BGC's retirement policy.

4. Procedure

f The order of the House of Lords was lodged at the court registry on 29 May 1989. In accordance with art 20 of the Protocol on the statute of the Court of Justice, written observations were submitted: on 27 July 1989, by Mrs A Foster and the other appellants, represented by James Goudie QC and John Cavanagh, barrister, instructed by Bruce Piper, solicitor; on 11 September 1989, by British Gas plc, the respondent, represented by Michael Beloff QC and Elizabeth Slade, barrister, instructed by C E H Twiss, Headquarters Director of Legal Services, British Gas plc; on 19 September 1989, by the

g United Kingdom, represented by Susan Hay, of the Treasury Solicitor's Department, acting as agent, assisted by John Laws and David Pannick, barristers; on 1 September 1989, by the Commission of the European Communities, represented by Karen Banks, a member of its legal department, acting as agent.

On hearing the report of the Judge Rapporteur and the views of the Advocate General,

h the court decided, by decision of 17 January 1990, to open the oral procedure without any preparatory inquiry.

II—WRITTEN OBSERVATIONS SUBMITTED TO THE COURT

Mrs Foster and others, appellants, consider that, in deciding whether a body is a 'state authority' for the purposes of relying on a directive, the term 'state' must be taken

j broadly as including all the organs of the state, including those engaged in commercial and similar activities. They refer in this regard to the opinion of Advocate General Sir Gordon Slynn in *Marshall's* case, and more recently, to the judgment of the court in *Flli Costanzo SpA v Comune di Milano* Case 103/88 [1990] 3 CMLR 239.

In the appellants' submission, it is clear from an analysis of the judgments in *Marshall's* case and *Johnston v Chief Constable of the Royal Ulster Constabulary* Case 222/84 [1986] 3 All ER 135, [1987] QB 129 that the court used the words 'state', 'organ of the state', 'emanation of the state', 'state authority' and 'public authority' interchangeably. The BGC, as a nationalised industry and public authority, is therefore among the bodies referred to in para 2 of the operative part of the ruling in *Marshall's* case.

In its judgments the court has ruled out completely the existence of an intermediate category between, on the one hand, the state and its organs and, on the other hand, private individuals. On the contrary, in *Johnston's* case, the court used 'public authority' in contradistinction to 'private individual'. Such a dichotomy appears equally clearly in *Marshall's* case and *Criminal proceedings against Kolpinghuis Nijmegen BV* Case 80/86 [1987] ECR 3969.

If an intermediate category exists, a number of tests may be suggested to identify those public authorities which are also state authorities. However, there are no grounds for applying such tests to determine the direct effect of directives, and their application in practice would cause great difficulty.

First of all, there is no justification for limiting the direct effect of directives to public authorities 'charged by the state with the performance of any of the classic duties of the state', as did the Court of Appeal in its judgment in this case. This limitation is incompatible with the judgments of the court and, in particular, with its judgment in *Marshall's* case [1986] 2 All ER 584 at 600, [1986] QB 401 at 422 (para 49), in which it stated that the direct effect of the directive was necessary to prevent the state from taking advantage of its own failure to comply with Community law. There is no reason why a directive should not have direct effect against bodies which have been constituted by the state but which perform duties other than the classic duties of the state. Moreover, such limitation would give rise to a number of practical difficulties: the classic duties of the state may vary from state to state and may change over time, so that the use of this test would lead to a situation that is incompatible with the uniform application of Community law and with legal certainty. If, however, such a test were to be applied in this case, it would lead to the conclusion that the BGC is a state authority for the purposes of the direct effect of directives. Since the BGC had a state monopoly from 1948, its functions must have become classic duties of the state, since only the state was able to perform them.

Second, the idea expressed by the industrial tribunal in its decision in this case that the direct effect of directives should be limited to bodies exercising the powers of the Crown must be rejected. This view is incompatible in particular with the judgment in *Johnston's* case, in which the court held that the Chief Constable of the Royal Ulster Constabulary was a state authority even though he was constitutionally independent of the state and whatever his relations might be with other organs of the state. In any event, the appellants consider that since the Crown is a peculiarly British concept, it cannot provide a test of general application for all the member states of the Community. Moreover, since such a test would be purely formal, it would enable the state to evade the consequences of direct effect by not giving certain bodies the status of Crown bodies.

Third, there are no grounds for limiting the application of the direct effect of directives to public authorities of a non-commercial character. Such a test would be contrary to the principle that a member state must not take advantage of its own failure to comply with Community law. Furthermore, it would be difficult to apply in certain cases such as, for example, the provision of medical services, which may be of a commercial character even though it is a nationalised service financed by the state.

Fourth, it is clear from the judgments of the court in *Becker v Finanzamt Münster-Innenstadt* Case 8/81 [1982] ECR 53 and in the *Marshall* and *Johnston* cases that directives may be relied on against bodies which do not themselves have power to legislate. This test is therefore also unacceptable.

The appellants therefore propose that the court should answer the question asked by the House of Lords as follows:

'The BGC (at the material time) was a body of such a type that its employees are entitled in English courts and tribunals to rely directly on Council Directive (EEC) 76/207 so as to found a claim for damages on the fact that the BGC's retirement policy was contrary to the directive.'

British Gas plc, respondent, considers that in order to decide on the definition and characteristics of the body against which directives can be relied on in proceedings it is necessary to examine the principle which enables individuals to rely on a directive in a municipal forum. It is clear from the judgments of the court in the *Becker, Marshall* and *Johnston* cases that the basis for this principle is that a state may not plead or take advantage of its own failure to perform the obligations imposed on it by directives.

In this regard, the judgments of the court are consistent with the classic idea of the state as comprising the legislature, the executive and the judiciary. The court has consistently held that the state is responsible for the failures of the executive and the legislature. Equally, in *von Colson and Kamann v Land Nordrhein-Westfalen* Case 14/83 [1984] ECR 1891 the court held that the member states' obligation arising from a directive to achieve the result envisaged by the directive is also binding on the courts, for matters within their jurisdiction.

So far as other organs or emanations of the state are concerned, the respondent contends that individuals may rely on a directive in claims against them only because they are agents of the state and the state has delegated to them certain functions. That would seem to be borne out by the judgments in the *Marshall* and *Johnston* cases. Furthermore, the respondent states that those judgments provide no support for the view that all employees who were not private employees were necessarily state employees and thus able to rely on Directive 76/207 in a municipal forum.

In that regard, reference should be made to the judgments in *Société Nouvelle des Usines de Pontlieue Aciéries du Temple (SNUPAT) v High Authority of ECSC* Joined cases 32 and 33/58 [1959] ECR 127 and *Worms v High Authority of ECSC* Case 18/60 [1962] ECR 195. There, the court defined the concept of an 'organ' of the High Authority by reference to the existence of a delegation of powers. If that approach is applied in this case, the BGC is not to be regarded as an organ or agent of the state.

The respondent states that on the basis of these principles, in order for directives to be directly effective against a body, that body must be part of the legislature, executive or judiciary or carry out its powers, duties or functions as agent for the state. However, the extent of control by the state is not important in determining whether a body may be considered to be the state for these purposes: a body may be an organ of the state even if it is constitutionally independent of the state. Conversely, the fact that a body is subject to a substantial degree of state control, for example through the appointment of administrators, does not lead to its being considered the state for these purposes.

So far as the BGC is concerned, in particular, it did not have the powers of the Secretary of State but merely acted as his agent. It had original powers and duties, subject only to a degree of control by the Secretary of State.

The express power to promote Bills in Parliament gave the BGC no greater power than that of a public limited company authorised to do so by its memorandum and articles. In any event, the BGC had no power to promote legislation other than a private Bill affecting its own interests, outside the area covered by Directive 76/207.

Unlike area health authorites, which perform the duties of the Minister of Health as his agents and which are part of the state in the sense of the Crown, the BGC was a nationalised industry which, according to the decisions of the English courts, was not part of the state in the sense of the Crown.

In conclusion, the respondent proposes that the question asked by the House of Lords should be answered in the negative. In the alternative, if the court were to hold that individuals may rely on a directive as against the BGC, the respondent states that it is only if the domestic courts refuse to interpret domestic legislation so as to comply with the directive that an individual can assert and rely on an independent right of action under Community law. Moreover, the court should limit the effects of the preliminary ruling ratione temporis, as it did in *Defrenne v Sabena* Case 43/75 (1976) [1981] 1 All ER **a** 122. That would be necessary in view of the serious financial consequences which the judgment of the court would have and on grounds of legal certainty.

The United Kingdom states, first, that it is not a matter for the Court of Justice, but a matter for the national courts, to determine whether the BGC is a part of the state in the context of the United Kingdom legal system: in support of that view, it refers to the judgment of the court in *Marshall's* case, in which the court stated that it was for the **b** national court to apply the considerations referred to by the court to the circumstances of each case.

To the extent that this is a matter of Community law, the United Kingdom states that the BGC is not part of the state since it does not perform the functions of the state directly or as an agent or delegate. That is the criterion which corresponds to the principle that a state may not take advantage of its own wrong in failing to implement the directive. By **c** contrast, whether or not the body in question is public or private is irrelevant.

This analysis is confirmed by distinctions made in other areas of Community law. Thus art 2 of Commission Directive (EEC) 80/723 on the transparency of financial relations between member states and public undertakings distinguishes between 'public authorities', defined as 'the State and regional or local authorites', and 'public undertakings', defined as: **d**

> 'any undertaking over which the public authorities may exercise directly or indirectly a dominant influence by virtue of their ownership of it, their financial partnership therein, or the rules which govern it'.

In Council Directive (EEC) 71/305 concerning the co-ordination of procedures for the award of public works contracts, as amended by Council Directive (EEC) 89/440, the **e** term 'a body governed by public law' is defined as any body 'established for the specific purpose of meeting needs in the general interest, not having an industrial or commercial character'. The BGC was not included in Annex 1 to the directive as a body governed by public law.

Last, the judgments of the court on the exception contained in art 48(4) of the EEC **f** Treaty for 'employment in the public service', and, in particular, its judgment in *EC Commission v Belgium* Case 149/79 [1980] ECR 3881, show that this term does not extend to authorities which are established by public law but which have an economic or commercial function. The same approach is reflected in the Commission communication entitled 'Freedom of movement of workers and access to employment in the public service of the Member States—Commission action in respect of the application of Article **g** 48(4) of the EEC Treaty' (OJ 1988 C 72, p 2). There the Commission stated:

> 'the functions involved in certain forms of public employment are for the most part sufficiently remote from the specific activities of the public service as defined by the Court of Justice that they would only in very rare cases be covered by the exception in Article 48(4) of the Treaty.'

h

On the basis of these considerations, the Commission stated that it intended to give priority in its proposed action to bodies responsible for administering commercial services, and gave as an example gas supply.

As regards the situation of the BGC, the United Kingdom states that the BGC was a statutory corporation which was performing its function of supplying gas on its own behalf, and not on behalf of the Crown. The BGC had a discretion in the running of its **j** daily operations. It was a body having a commercial character and was not performing any of the central functions of the state, such as legislative, judicial, or law and order functions.

As a matter of English law, the employees of the BGC were not Crown servants. It is well established in English law that a nationalised industry is not an organ of the Crown.

The Secretary of State had powers of control over the BGC but had no power to interfere
a in the ordinary business management of the corporation. In any event, the existence of a
power of control is not the determining factor of whether a body is part of the state. For
reasons of public policy, a wide variety of bodies, such as banks, insurance companies,
independent schools, are regulated, to various degrees and in various ways, by the state,
without those bodies thereby becoming part of the state.

Furthermore, there is a clear and significant contrast between the functions and status
b of the BGC and those of the bodies considered by the court in the Marshall and Johnston
cases. Unlike the BGC, the health authorites are agents of the minister; they are
dependent on public funding and their employees (like those of the Royal Ulster
Constabulary) are Crown servants whose conditions of service and pay are approved by
the minister.

If, however, the court were to consider that the BGC was part of the state and that the
c appellants were therefore entitled in English courts and tribunals to rely on Directive 76/
207 to claim relief against the respondent, the United Kingdom states that the appellants
would be entitled to compensation up to the level of the statutory maximum provided
for by s 65 of the Sex Discrimination Act 1975.

In conclusion, the United Kingdom proposes that the court should answer the question
raised by the House of Lords as follows:
d
'The BGC was not part of the state and therefore was not a body of such a type
that the appellants are entitled in English courts and tribunals to rely directly on
Council Directive (EEC) 76/207 so as to be entitled to claim any relief on the ground
that the retirement policy of the BGC was contrary to the directive.'

The Commission states by way of preliminary that this is not an isolated case. Similar
e questions have already been considered in at least two cases decided by tribunals in the
United Kingdom. In the first, Turpie v University of Glasgow (19 September 1986,
unreported), an industrial tribunal in Glasgow held that the university was not an organ
of the state, although some 80% of its funding came from the state. The industrial
tribunal based its decision on the considerable freedom enjoyed by universities in the
f organisation of their teaching and research and on their long tradition of independent
thought. In the second case, Doughty v Rolls-Royce plc, an industrial tribunal in
Birmingham held that Directive 76/207 could be relied on against Rolls-Royce on the
ground that the state owned 100% of the shares in Rolls-Royce and therefore had real
power over the company's decision-making. That decision was overturned, however, by
the Employment Appeal Tribunal (see Rolls-Royce plc v Doughty [1987] ICR 932), which
g emphasised that a company was to be regarded as entity separate and distinct from its
shareholders. It therefore took the view that the mere possibility of influencing Rolls-
Royce, without the control resulting from a legal obligation, was not enough to make
Rolls-Royce an organ of the state. Lastly, it emphasised that Rolls-Royce was not carrying
out a state function.

Second, the Commission states that, although in Marshall's case the court appears to
h confer on the national courts the task of determining what constitutes a state authority,
it appears from the present case and the cases referred to above that the national courts
would come to very divergent conclusions on the matter, conclusions which would not
necessarily be in conformity with the reasoning of the court in Marshall's case. This is
because each national legal system contains within it detailed technical rules and fine
distinctions which, when applied to so general an expression as 'organ of the state', may
j yield some surprising results. As the court has constantly emphasised in its case law (see
EC Commission v Belgium Case 149/79 [1980] ECR 3881), recourse to provisions of national
law to restrict the scope of the provisions of Community law would have the effect of
impairing the unity and efficacy of that law and consequently cannot be accepted.

It is therefore necessary for the court to give some further guidance in relation to the
types of body which may be considered to be 'state authorities' within the meaning of

that expression as used by the court in *Marshall's* case. It would then be for the national courts to determine whether the term so defined may be applied to a given body in an individual case.

The Commission considers that the expressions 'public authority', 'state authority', 'organ of the state' and 'emanation of the state' used by the court in its judgments are interchangeable. It is clear that the court intended to provide for only two categories of employer: on the one hand, the state (and its emanations), which could not be heard to plead as against individuals its own failure to legislate in order to implement a directive, and on the other hand, private employers who were not the addressees of the directive and who had no responsibility in relation to national legislation. There is therefore no third, intermediate category of entities which, while being 'public authorities', are not 'state authorities'.

As regards the BGC, it can be deduced from numerous aspects of its status that it was an organ of the state carrying out a state policy. It is clear that the BGC cannot be considered a private enterprise and, moreover, the national courts have acknowledged the 'public' character of the BGC. It would therefore be possible to dispose of this case on its particular facts and give to the House of Lords an answer which would cover only bodies akin to the BGC. However, since the same issue has arisen in other similar cases and may be raised in other contexts, it is perhaps worthwhile to formulate more general criteria for determining the bodies against which Directive 76/207 may be relied on.

Since the principle of equal treatment for men and women is one of the fundamental principles of Community law (see the *Defrenne* and *Marshall* cases), it would not be appropriate to give the concept of 'state authority' an over-restrictive meaning. To do so would be to limit the possibilities for enforcing the right laid down by art 5(1) of Directive 76/207.

As regards the specific content of this concept, the Commission states that the court has already included in it local authorities (see *Flli Constanzo SpA v Comune di Milano* Case 103/88 [1990] 3 CMLR 239) and public authorities carrying out a state function (see *Johnston's* Case). The court has not yet had occasion to pronounce on the situation of a body closely connected with, and even subject to directions from, the state, which is charged by the state with carrying out a function which could just as well be carried out by private enterprise. However, in *Marshall's* case the court showed no hesitation in accepting the view of the national court and treating as a 'public authority' a body carrying out functions in the field of public health, which is not necessarily a state function. This may lead one to conclude that wherever a body is carrying out a public function on behalf of the state, it is to be regarded as a 'state authority'. This view receives support from the judgment of the court in *Auer v Ministère Public* Case 271/82 [1983] ECR 2727 at 2745 (para 19), in which the court referred to professional societies as 'bodies entrusted with a public duty' which were therefore required to recognise a professional qualification to the extent that this was provided for in the directive.

However, the criterion in question does not cover commercial companies in which the state owns all or the majority of the shares, or even a blocking minority, although in reality it is likely that the state exercises a great degree of control over them. It is not easy to formulate a precise criterion which would allow these situations to be covered as well. An approach based on the existence of control on the part of the state in relation to the matter at issue, similar to that followed in the field of state aids (see *Kwekerij Gebroeders van der Kooy BV v EC Commission* Joined cases 67, 68 and 70/85 [1988] ECR 219), would pose substantial evidential difficulties. It might therefore be better to formulate the reply to the question in such a way that national courts would have a clear rule to apply, which was at the same time of sufficient breadth to avoid the danger of narrow legal constructions based on national law.

This rule could not refer to the funding by the state, since mere subvention alone could not affect the private character of an undertaking. A test based on the ability of the state to compel a particular body to act in the way it wished would also be too wide, since

the state can, generally speaking, achieve this result in relation to any private person by
a way of legislation. Conversely, a test based on the existence of a legal right to control the
policy of a particular entity might result in the exclusion of a number of the cases in
relation to which common sense tells us that real control exists. The 'economic reality'
approach, consisting in checking whether the state really could exercise control over the
policy of a body, though not a precise legal test, would have the advantage of being in
conformity with the court's approach in other areas.

b   It must be recognised, however, that any test based on the existence of control will fail
to cover a number of public authorities, such as bodies that are constitutionally
independent, professional societies and universities. It therefore appears that no one
criterion can be formulated which will cover all the situations which may arise. The
House of Lords should therefore be given a specific answer, dealing solely with the case
of the BGC and other bodies of the same type.

c   The Commission therefore proposes that the court reply to the question put by the
House of Lords as follows:

'1. Article 5(1) of Council Directive (EEC) 76/207 may be relied on as against any
body exercising a public function on behalf of the state, in order to avoid the
application of any national provision which does not conform to art 5(1). 2. It is for
d   the national courts to apply this rule to the circumstances of each case.'

James Goudie QC and *John Cavanagh* for the appellants.
Michael Beloff QC and *Elizabeth Slade* for the respondent.
John Laws and *David Pannick* for the United Kingdom.
Karen Banks for the EC Commission.

e 8 May. **The Advocate General (Walter Van Gerven)** delivered the following
opinion[1]. Mr President, Members of the Court,
    1.   The House of Lords has submitted the following question to the court for a
preliminary ruling under art 177 of the EEC Treaty:

'Was the British Gas Corporation (at the material time) a body of such a type that
f   the appellants are entitled in English courts and tribunals to rely directly upon
Council Directive 76/207 of 9 February 1976 on the implementation of the principle
of equal treatment for men and women as regards access to employment, vocational
training and promotion, and working conditions so as to be entitled to a claim for
damages on the ground that the retirement policy of the British Gas Corporation
was contrary to the directive?'

g   Mrs Foster and the other appellants in the main proceedings are women who were
employed by the British Gas Corp (the BGC); on reaching the age of 60 on various dates
between 27 December 1985 and 22 July 1986 they were required to retire, in accordance
with the general policy of the BGC. During the same period male employees of the BGC
were required to retire only at the age of 65.
    In its judgments in *Defrenne v Sabena* Case 149/77 [1978] ECR 1365, *Burton v British*
h *Railways Board* Case 19/81 [1982] 3 All ER 537, [1982] QB 1080, *Roberts v Tate & Lyle
Industries Ltd* Case 151/84 [1986] 2 All ER 602, *Marshall v Southampton and South West
Hampshire Area Health Authority (Teaching)* Case 152/84 [1986] 2 All ER 584, [1986] QB
401 and *Beets-Proper v F Van Lanschot Bankiers NV* Case 262/84 [1986] ECR 773 the court
ruled that an age limit applied for the purpose of terminating an employment
relationship constitutes a working condition and more particularly a condition governing
j dismissal whose validity must be examined in the light of Directive 76/207 on equal
treatment. (See also my opinion in *Barber v Guardian Royal Exchange Assurance Group*
Case C-262/88 [1990] 2 All ER 660 at 683, 686–687 (para 26 in fine and also paras 32 and
33).

---

[1]   Translated from the Dutch

Article 5(1) of that directive provides:

'Application of the principle of equal treatment with regard to working conditions, including the conditions governing dismissal, means that men and women shall be guaranteed the same conditions without discrimination on grounds of sex.'

The House of Lords points out that during the material period the United Kingdom had not yet brought its national law into conformity with the equal treatment directive. Section 6(4) of the Sex Discrimination Act 1975, which was then in force, provided that the prohibition, laid down in s 6(1)(b) and (2) of the Act, of discrimination against women in respect of conditions of recruitment or dismissal applied by employers or any other unfavourable treatment did not apply to provisions regarding death or retirement (amended by s 2(1) of the Sex Discrimination Act 1986 with effect from 7 November 1987). I shall not here discuss the duty of national courts to interpret provisions of national law in accordance with Community law (see *von Colson and Kamann v Land Nordrhein-Westfalen* Case 14/88 [1984] ECR 1891 and *Criminal proceedings against Kolpinghuis Nijmegen BV* Case 80/86 [1987] ECR 3969) since the House of Lords has not submitted any question in that respect (see also my opinion in *Barber's* case [1990] 2 All ER 660 at 693 (para 50)).

2.   The parties in the main proceedings are agreed that the distinction between men and women in the BGC's pension policy is unlawful notwithstanding s 6(4) of the Sex Discrimination Act 1975 if art 5(1) of Directive 76/207 is directly applicable to the conditions of dismissal of the appellants in the main proceedings, but that otherwise the BGC's policy is valid.

In *Marshall's* case [1986] 2 All ER 584 at 600, [1986] QB 401 at 422 (para 49) the court stated that persons may only rely on provisions such as art 5(1) of Directive 76/207 in their relations with 'the state', in its capacity as 'employer or public authority', since 'it is necessary to prevent the state from taking advantage of its own failure to comply with Community law'. In para 48, on the other hand, the possibility of relying on such a provision against an individual is excluded, inasmuch as a directive may not of itself impose obligations on an individual. In academic terminology, that means that where the period for their implementation has expired, provisions of directives which from the point of view of their content are unconditional and sufficiently precise (see [1986] 2 All ER 584 at 601, 600, [1986] QB 401 at 423, 422 (paras 55, 52)) have 'vertical direct effect' but no 'horizontal direct effect'.

The reference for a preliminary ruling thus concerns the issue whether at the material time the BGC was 'the state' or 'an individual'. In the first hypothesis the appellants in the main proceedings can rely on art 5(1) of Directive 76/207 but in the second they cannot.

3.   At the material time the BGC was a nationalised gas undertaking; since then it has been privatised by the Gas Act 1986, under which British Gas plc (the respondent in the main proceedings) was established and on 24 August 1986 it succeeded to the rights and liabilities of the BGC. (Following the abolition of the monopoly on the supply of gas through pipes, British Gas plc is one of the 'public gas suppliers': ss 3 and 7 of the Gas Act 1986.)

The status of the BGC, the employer of the appellants in the main proceedings at the relevant time, must be viewed in the context of the nationalisation of gas production and supply by the Gas Act 1948, which was later replaced by the Gas Act 1972. Under the Gas Act 1948 property, rights and liabilities were allocated to 'area boards' or to the 'Gas Council'. Under the Gas Act 1972 the Gas Council became the BGC and the property, rights and liabilities were vested in it. The BGC was a body with legal personality operating under the supervision of the authorities and having a monopoly on the supply of gas to homes and businesses in Great Britain. The members of the BGC were appointed by the Secretary of State, and he also determined their remuneration (s 1(2) and (3)). The task of the BGC was to develop and maintain an efficient, co-ordinated and economical

system of gas supply for Great Britain and to satisfy, so far as it was economical to do so,
a all reasonable demands for gas in Great Britain (s 2(1)). It was its duty to settle from time
to time, in consultation with the Secretary of State, a general programme of research into
matters affecting gas supply (s 3(3)).

The Secretary of State was empowered to required the BGC to report on its activities
and, after laying that report before both Houses of Parliament, to give the BGC such
directions as he considered appropriate, on the basis of that report, for the most efficient
b management of the undertaking (s 4). The BGC was obliged to give effect to any such
directions (s 4(3)). The Secretary of State could also, after consultation with the BGC, give
the BGC general directions for the exercise and performance of its functions, including
the exercise of its rights as a shareholder, where in his view the national interest so
required, and the BGC was obliged to give effect to any such directions (s 7). The BGC
was obliged, as soon as possible after the end of each financial year, to submit a report to
c the minister on the exercise and performance of its functions during that year and on its
policy and programmes (s 8).

The BGC was obliged so to perform its functions and so to exercise its control over its
subsidiaries as to ensure that, taking one year with another, the combined revenues of
the BGC and its subsidiaries were at least sufficient to meet total operating costs and
constitute the necessary reserves in order to be able to comply with any directions given
d by the Secretary of State (s 14). The Secretary of State could from time to time, after
consultation with the BGC and with the approval of the Treasury, require the BGC to
allocate certain amounts to reserves, whether or not for a specific purpose, and the BGC
was obliged to comply with any such directions (s 15). If in any financial year there was
a significant excess of income over total costs, the minister, with the approval of the
Treasury, could require the BGC to pay over to him the portion of that income which
e was surplus to the BGC's requirements, and the BGC was required to comply.

Under the Gas Act 1972 the BGC was not an agent of the Secretary of State. The
employees of the BGC were not in Crown employment for the purpose of United
Kingdom employment law. The BGC had no legislative functions.

f *The basis of the judgment in Marshall's case: nemo auditur*
4.   For the sake of convenience let me begin by quoting the central passage of the
Marshall judgment [1986] 2 All ER 584 at 600–601, [1986] QB 401 at 421–423 (paras
47–49 of the judgment and the second paragraph of its operative part):

'47.   That view is based on the consideration that it would be incompatible with
the binding nature which art 189 of the EEC Treaty confers on the directive to hold
g as a matter of principle that the obligation imposed thereby cannot be relied on by
those concerned. From that the court deduced that a member state which has not
adopted the implementing measures required by the directive within the prescribed
period may not plead, as against individuals, its own failure to perform the
obligations which the directive entails.

48.   With regard to the argument that a directive may not be relied on against
h an individual, it must be emphasised that according to art 189 of the EEC Treaty
the binding nature of a directive, which constitutes the basis for the possibility of
relying on the directive before a national court, exists only in relation to "each
Member State to which it is addressed". It follows that a directive may not of itself
impose obligations on an individual and that a provision of a directive may not be
relied on as such against such a person. It must therefore be examined whether, in
j this case, the authority must be regarded as having acted as an individual.

49.   In that respect it must be pointed out that where a person involved in legal
proceedings is able to rely on a directive as against the state he may do so regardless
of the capacity in which the latter is acting, whether employer or public authority.
In either case it is necessary to prevent the state from taking advantage of its own
failure to comply with Community law.

The court therefore held:

> 'art 5(1) of EC Council Directive 76/207 of 9 February 1976, which prohibits any *a*
> discrimination on ground of sex with regard to working conditions, including the
> conditions governing dismissal, may be relied on as against a state authority acting
> in its capacity as employer, in order to avoid the application of any national provision
> which does not conform to art 5(1).'

5. In *Marshall's* case the possibility of relying on an unconditional and sufficiently *b*
precise provision of a directive against a member state was thus clearly linked to the
failure of the member state to implement the directive in national law correctly and at
the proper time (see also the judgment in *Pubblico Ministero v Ratti* Case 148/78 [1979]
ECR 1629 at 1642 (para 22) and the opinion of Mr Advocate General Reischl in that case
(at 1653), and the judgment in *Becker v Finanzamt Münster-Innenstadt* Case 8/81 [1982]
ECR 53 at 71 (para 24). Accordingly, the principle that 'the state cannot plead its own *c*
wrong' (relied on by the health authority at the hearing in *Marshall's* case), or the
principle nemo auditur propriam turpitudinem allegans, was held to constitute the basis
for vertical direct effect. At the same time, however, the principle was interpreted
broadly: the failure to act can be relied on by individuals against the member state
regardless of the capacity in which the state acts as 'employer or public authority';
moreover, as also appears from later judgments which will be discussed below, the failure *d*
to act can be relied on by individuals against independent and/or local authorities which
are not themselves responsible for the failure to implement the directive in national law.

As I have already had the opportunity to explain in my opinion in *Barber's* case [1990]
2 All ER 660 at 694–695 (para 52), the relevant provision of the directive was thus given
some restricted effect with regard to third parties, that is to say against authorities other
than the defaulting authority. The rationale is (and remains) the desire to prevent the *e*
member state in question from deriving any advantage whatsoever from its failure to
comply with Community law. (In its judgment in *Oberkreisdirektor des Kreises Borken v
Handelsonderneming Moormann BV* Case 190/87 [1988] ECR 4689 at 4722 (paras 22, 24)
the court indicated the provisions of the Treaty which provide a basis for that conclusion,
namely art 189, third paragraph, and art 5 of the EEC Treaty.)

6. By giving the term 'state' so wide a meaning the court followed the opinion of *f*
Advocate General Sir Gordon Slynn, in which he stated ([1986] 2 All ER 584 at 594,
[1986] QB 401 at 413):

> '... (even if contrary to the trend of decisions in cases involving sovereign
> immunity where the exercise of imperium is distinguished from commercial and
> similar activities) as a matter of Community law ... the "state" must be taken *g*
> broadly as including all the organs of the state. In matters of employment ... this
> means all the employees of such organs and not just the central civil service.'

That the court did in fact wish to give the term 'state' a sense going beyond the
'personal default' of the authority concerned is clear from the actual circumstances. That
is to say, the issue was the possibility of relying on art 5(1) of Directive 76/207 against a *h*
local health authority which was certainly an 'agent for the Ministry of Health' (while its
employees, including hospital doctors and nurses and administrative staff, were 'Crown
servants') but was in no way concerned in or could be responsible for the failure of the
legislature in the relevant member state to implement the directive in national law.

Indeed, such a broad interpretation is also suggested by the choice of words in the
judgment: in the language of the case, and also in the other languages, expressions such *j*
as 'emanation of the state', 'organ of the state', 'public authority' and 'state authority' are
used as overlapping and synonymous terms. (In paras 12, 49, 50, 51 and 56 of the
judgment and in the second paragraph of the operative part four synonyms are used in
English, French, German, Danish and Italian, and five in Dutch. The manner in which
those four or five terms are distributed among the six passages cited, in which expressions

are repeated differently in different languages, confirms the broad meaning that must be
a given to the concept of 'the state' and also demonstrates that it is not correct to conclude
from the use of words in any one language that a basis for the definition of the 'state' can
be sought in the legal terminology of any one member state.)

Later cases

b   7.   A few months after the *Marshall* judgment the court gave judgment in *Johnston v
Chief Constable of the Royal Ulster Constabulary* Case 222/84 [1986] 3 All ER 135, [1987] QB
129, concerning the possibility for an employee of relying on arts 3(1) and 4 of Directive
76/207 against the Chief Constable of the Royal Ulster Constabulary. The British
government, arguing that those provisions could not be relied on, referred to the fact
that the chief constable is constitutionally independent of the state (see [1986] 3 All ER
c   135 at 160, [1987] QB 129 at 153 (para 49)). That did not prevent the court, referring to
the *Marshall* judgment, from stating ([1986] 3 All ER 135 at 161, [1987] QB 129 at 154
(para 56)):

> 'The court also held in *Marshall's* case that individuals may rely on the directive as
> against an organ of the state whether it acts qua employer or qua public authority.
d   > As regards an authority like the Chief Constable, it must be observed that, according
> to the industrial tribunal's decision, the Chief Constable is an official responsible for
> the direction of the police service. Whatever its relations may be with other organs
> of the state, such a public authority, charged by the state with the maintenance of
> public order and safety, does not act as a private individual. It may not take
> advantage of the failure of the state, of which it is an emanation, to comply with
e   > Community law.'

In that quotation it is striking to see the manner in which the relations between the head
of a local police force and 'other organs of state' are considered irrelevant, which again
shows that autonomous authorities which are independent of other organs of the state,
regardless of the level at which they operate, be it central or local, do indeed fall under
the broad expression 'the state'. It is also striking that the judgment states that the chief
f   constable is 'charged by the state with the maintenance of public order' and infers from
that that he 'does not act as a private individual'. I assume that in that judgment, unlike
in *Marshall's* case, the court referred to the specific public duties of the chief constable
because the maintenance of public order is regarded as a public function in all the
member states, which is not so clear in respect of health care. That may suggest that
although the nature of the duty is not conclusive in determining the public nature of an
g   authority, that is to say in distinguishing it from a private individual, it may nevertheless
be a useful pointer.
     Finally, the last sentence of the quoted paragraph is also worthy of attention, since it
takes up the theme of the 'advantage' that the state must not derive from its default and
expressly relates it to a constitutionally independent local authority, the Chief Constable
of Northern Ireland.
h   8.   The point of view expressed by the court in *Marshall's* case was applied again in its
judgment in *Flli Costanzo SpA v Comune di Milano* Case 103/88 [1990] 3 CMLR 239. That
case concerned a directive on public works contracts. The court was asked whether a
municipal authority was obliged, in examining individual tenders, to refrain from
applying national rules incompatible with the directive concerned, the period for whose
implementation had expired.
j   The court held (at 259 (para 31)):

> '... when the conditions under which the court has held that individuals may
> rely on the provisions of a directive before the national courts are met, all organs of
> the administration, including decentralised authorities, such as municipalities, are
> obliged to apply those provisions.'

Even outside the area of fundamental rights (equal treatment for men and women), then, the court has a very broad conception of the 'state' (a similar broad interpretation *a* may be seen in a judgment prior to the *Marshall* case, namely the judgment in *Auer v Ministère Public* Case 271/82 [1983] ECR 2727 esp at 2751 in the opinion of Mr Advocate General Mancini, in which he stated that a directive may be pleaded against institutions which, although they are not organs of the state in the true sense of the term, in one way or another implement the policy of the state. The case concerned professional organisations of veterinary surgeons which were responsible for the exercise of public *b* authority, namely the recognition of professional qualifications obtained in other member states): all administrative authorities, at every level of the territorial division of a member state, form part of 'the state' for the purposes of the *Marshall* judgment.

It is also clear that the 'state' does not cover only authorities whose powers are 'delegated' from the central authority. The criterion of delegation of powers is not always compatible with the legal situation of municipal authorities in different member states *c* and is in any event completely inappropriate to the situation in member states which have a federal structure.

A twofold or a threefold classification?

9.   In what I have said up to now I have tacitly assumed that what the court must do is draw a dividing line in Community law which will assist national courts in *d* distinguishing the concept of 'the state' from the concept of 'individual'. That point of departure is implicit in the cases discussed above, although in the *Marshall* and *Johnston* cases the court could rely to some extent on findings in that respect made by the national court itself. In the present case that is clearly not so: the House of Lords has made no assessment of the nature of the BGC, that is to say whether or not it formed part of 'the state'; on the contrary, in the questions which it has submitted to the court it assumes *e* that it is for *the court* to set out a Community framework *within* which the national courts may determine whether the direct effect of provisions of a directive may be relied upon against this or that body.

I would subscribe to that point of view, which indeed has not been disputed by any of the parties that have submitted observations. If the court itself did not lay down a basis in Community law, the result would be a complete lack of uniformity among the *f* member states with regard to the direct effect of provisions of directives.

10.   In outlining a Community framework for defining the 'state' a fundamental question arises. Are the concepts 'state' and 'individual' together exhaustive or is there, in between them, a third category of persons or bodies? Such an intermediate category might include bodies such as public undertakings (for instance, the BGC in this case), state universities or even private universities that are financed wholly or virtually wholly *g* by the state, and the like. If the existence of such a category is accepted, the question arises whether with regard to the possible direct effect of provisions of directives it must be put on the same footing as the category 'state' or the category 'individuals'.

As the appellants in the main proceedings have stated, no support can be found in the judgments of the court referred to above for the existence of an intermediate category. *h* Paragraph 48 of the judgment in *Marshall*'s case assumes a twofold and not a threefold classification when it states in its last sentence: 'It must therefore be examined whether, in this case, the authority must be regarded as having acted as an individual.' Similarly, in the passage of his opinion in that case quoted above Advocate General Sir Gordon Slynn appears to bring both 'the exercise of imperium' and 'commercial and similar activities' under the concept of 'the state' in Community law (see [1986] 2 All ER 584 at *j* 594, [1986] QB 401 at 413). That point of view is also supported in later judgments of the court in *Criminal proceedings against Kolpinghuis Nijmegen BV* [1987] ECR 3969 (the case concerned a member state which sought to rely in proceedings against an individual on a directive which had not yet been implemented in national law; the court naturally

refused to permit it to do so, in the light of the judgment in *Marshall*'s case; there is no
a indication in this judgment that the court proceeded on the basis of anything but a
twofold classification) and in *ECSC v Acciaierie e Ferriere Busseni SpA (in liq)* Case C-221/88
(22 February 1990, unreported) (paras 22–24). (This concerned recommendations under
the ECSC Treaty; in para 21 the court stated that these are measures of the same nature
as directives under the EEC Treaty.)

The advantage of a twofold classification is that the problem of definition can be
b approached from two sides. We may ask on the one hand who is the state and on the
other who must be regarded as an individual. It seems easier to decide who is an
individual and who is not, on the basis of the prevailing conceptions: thus public
undertakings are not private parties in the sense in which that is understood in everyday
language, which leads to the conclusion, in the hypothesis of a twofold classification, that
they are part of the 'state'.

c Although it is my view that there is no basis in the court's case law in this regard for a
threefold classification, I shall not use such complementary and mutually supporting
definitions of 'individuals' and 'state'. The point is not who is the state or an individual in
the abstract but against whom the failure of a member state to implement a directive
correctly and in good time in its own legal system can be pleaded, having regard to the
underlying reasons. According to the *Marshall* and *Johnston* cases the basic thinking is
d that a member state, and any public body charged with functions by the state, regardless
of the capacity in which it acts or its relations with other public bodies, may in no event
derive advantage from the failure of the member state to comply with Community law.

It must now be considered whether, having regard to that reasoning, a public
undertaking such as the BGC must not benefit from the default of its member state and
in that sense must be brought under the concept of 'the state'.
e

Analogies from other areas of Community law
   11.   Before discussing the positions of the parties and giving my own views, I should
like by way of comparison to discuss briefly a few areas of Community law in which
some notion of public authority plays a role. The most important general conclusion to
f be drawn from this comparison is that an interpretation is sought of each measure which
is most in keeping with its place in the Treaty and thus with the purpose of the concept
of public authority which is used. That conclusion suggests that in the present context
too an approach should be chosen which will give the concept of 'the state' the meaning
that corresponds most closely to the underlying reasoning, discussed above, of the
Marshall judgment. The comparison also elicits a number of criteria which may be useful
g in the present context.
   12.   Reference may be made first of all to the concept of an aid measure under art 92
of the EEC Treaty. As the court has consistently held, no distinction may be drawn
'between cases where aid is granted directly by the State and cases where it is granted by
public or private bodies established or appointed by the State to administer the aid' (see,
for example, the judgment in *Kwekerij Gebroeders Van der Kooy BV v EC Commission* Joined
h cases 67, 68 and 70/85 [1988] ECR 219 at 272 (para 35)). As concrete indications of the
public nature of the aid measure reference has been made for example to the fact that a
member state held directly or indirectly 50% of the shares in the undertaking granting
the aid and appointed half the members of the supervisory board, and that the tariffs
applied by the undertaking granting the aid had to be approved by a government
minister (see para 36). That was sufficient to show that in determining its tariffs the
j undertaking in no way enjoyed full autonomy, but acted under the control and on the
instructions of the public authorities (see para 37). It could therefore be concluded that
the fixing of the contested tariff was the result of action by the member state and thus
fell within the concept 'aid granted by a member state' for the purposes of art 92 (see para
38).

That definition of the state as the author of aid measures reflects a broad interpretation which corresponds to the purpose of art 92(1) of the Treaty, that of encompassing *all* aid *a* measures: 'any aid granted by a Member State or through State resources *in any form whatsoever*'.

A somewhat different intention lies behind Commission Directive (EEC) 80/723 on the transparency of financial relations between member states and public undertakings (extended by Commission Directive 85/413). It appears from the sixth recital in the *b* preamble to the directive that its purpose is to 'enable a clear distinction to be made between the role of the State as public authority and its role as proprietor'. Accordingly, art 2 defines, first, 'public authorities' ('the state and regional or local authorities') and then 'public undertakings' ('any undertaking over which the public authorities may exercise directly or indirectly a dominant influence by virtue of their ownership of it, their financial participation therein, or the rules which govern it'). (As Advocate General Mischo stated in his opinion in *EC Commission v Italian Republic* Case 118/85 [1987] ECR *c* 2599 at 2617, in applying that definition of 'public undertakings', 'greater importance must . . . be attached to function than to form'; see also paras 7–15 of the judgment (at 2621–2623).)

13.   A second area of Community law that may offer an analogy is that of public works contracts. In Council Directive (EEC) 71/305 concerning the co-ordination of procedures for the award of public works contracts (most recently amended by Directive *d* (EEC) 89/440) 'the State, regional or local authorities, bodies governed by public law, associations formed by one or several such authorities or bodies governed by public law' are described as 'contracting authorities'.

A 'body governed by public law' means any body (i) established for the specific purpose of meeting needs in the general interest, not having an industrial or commercial character and (ii) having legal personality and (iii) financed, for the most part, by the state, or *e* regional or local authorities, or other bodies governed by public law; or subject to management supervision by those bodies; or having an administrative, managerial or supervisory board more than half of whose members are appointed by the state, regional or local authorities or by other bodies governed by public law (see art 1 of the directive). Article 1a of the directive goes on to provide that contracting authorities which subsidise *f* directly by more than 50% a works contract awarded by an entity other than themselves must ensure compliance with the directive. This concept of the state, too, is interpreted by the court in a flexible manner in accordance with the aim of the measure (see the judgment in *Gebroeders Beentjes BV v Netherlands* [1988] ECR 4635 at 4655, 4662 (paras 11, 40); see also the opinion of Mr Advocate General Darmon (at 4644–4646 (paras 10–20)).)

14.   A third possible point of departure is the exceptional provision in the first sub- *g* paragraph of art 4(5) of the Sixth Council Directive on VAT (Council Directive (EEC) 77/388 on the harmonisation of the laws of the member states relating to turnover taxes: Common system of value added tax: uniform basis of assessment). As its wording indicates, that provision is restricted to the activities or transactions in which state, regional and local authorities and other bodies governed by public law engage 'as public *h* authorities'. That is also apparent from the case law of the court. (In its judgment in *Ufficio Distrettuale delle Imposte Dirette di Fiorenzuola d'Arda v Comune di Carpaneto Piacentino* Joined cases 231/87 and 129/88 OJ 1989 C288, p 4 the court emphasised that the provision in question seeks to draw a distinction between the activities of the bodies concerned which are governed by public law and those which are governed by private law.) The important distinction here is thus the capacity in which the public authority *j* acts: as an authority or as a normal taxable person.

15.   A final point of comparison can be found in the case law of the court on art 30 of the EEC Treaty, in which it is determined whether a particular restrictive practice can be ascribed to the authorities. (I shall not discuss the expression 'employment in the public service' in art 48(4) of the Treaty; as an exception from a fundamental principle of the Treaty it must be interpreted narrowly and thus has little relevance to the concept of 'the

state' at issue here.) In the *Buy Irish* judgment (*EC Commission v Ireland* Case 249/81 [1982]

a ECR 4005 at 4023 (paras 29–30)) it was demonstrated that the restrictive practice in question (a promotional campaign for the purchase and sale of Irish products) could be ascribed to the government and that Ireland had therefore failed to comply with its obligations under art 30. Proof that the campaign in question was a 'measure' for the purposes of art 30 was inferred from the carefully thought out and coherent set of initiatives emanating from the government, although the actual implementation of

b those initiatives was left to an association governed by private law.

Again in connection with the free movement of goods, reference may be made to the meaning given by the court to the concept of state monopolies of a commercial character within the meaning of art 37; that article applies to all—

c 'situations in which the national authorities are in a position to supervise, determine or even appreciably influence trade between Member States through a body established for that purpose or a monopoly delegated to others.'

That includes 'a situation in which the monopoly in question is operated by an undertaking or a group of undertakings, or by the territorial units of a State such as communes' (see *Bodson v Pompes funèbres des régions libérées* Case 30/87 [1988] ECR 2479

d at 2511 (para 13)). Every means at the disposal of national authorities for influencing trade in goods, regardless of whether the body 'used' is governed by private or public law, thus falls under art 37.

16.   As I have said, all these examples illustrate the desire to ensure that the concept of 'the state' is given full and proper effect, that is to say a meaning which achieves the goals of the measure in question. Depending on the aim of the measure the term 'state'

e may be interpreted broadly (for example, in connection with aid measures governed by art 92 (para 12 above) or in connection with public works contracts (para 15 above)), or a distinction may be drawn according to the role played by the state (for example, in connection with the transparency of relations between member states and public undertakings, by distinguishing between the state qua authority and qua owner (para 12 above), and in connection with the levying of VAT, by distinguishing between its

f activities as an authority and its activities as a taxable individual (para 14 above)).

A further point should be emphasised: whenever, in the light of the underlying purpose of the measure, the concept of 'the state' is given a broad interpretation, reference is made to the criterion of actual control, dominating influence and the possibility on the part of the authorities to give binding directions, regardless of the manner in which such control is exercised (by means of ownership, financial participation, dependence for

g purposes of management or finance, or through legislative provisions (paras 12, 13 and 15 above)). Somewhat different but nevertheless parallel reasoning lies behind the criterion used in the *Buy Irish* judgment (para 15 above) of whether a particular practice can be attributed to the government. In each case the assumption is thus that there is a 'core' of authority (broadly defined to include all central, regional and local authorities) which, for the purpose of the measure concerned, imparts a public character by its

h control and influence to other bodies or transactions, even where these are governed by private law.

The positions of the parties

17.   In the light of the foregoing I should now like briefly to discuss and comment

j on the observations submitted to the court.

The appellants in the main proceedings support a broad interpretation of the concept of 'the state'. They rely on the opinion of Advocate General Sir Gordon Slynn in *Marshall's* case [1986] 2 All ER 584 at 603, [1986] QB 401 at 403 and on the judgment in *Costanzo's* case [1990] 3 CMLR 239. They reject a criterion of public authority based strictly on 'the classics duties of the state' since an evaluation of what constitute 'duties of the state' would give rise to differences between member states and uncertainty in application. They also

82 [1983] ECR 2727 at 2745 (para 19), and the opinion of Advocate General Mancini (at 2751) which preceded them) there can be no doubt that they all fall under the concept of 'the state', and there is no need for any criterion of delegation or control by other public authorities. That much is certain.

The question in the case now before us is how much further the application of those judgments can extend, in particular with regard to undertakings, in this case public undertakings, which as such exercise no authority in the strict sense over individuals. I think the answer is this: it may extend as far 'the state' (in the broad sense described in the preceding paragraph) has given itself powers which place it in a position decisively to influence the conduct of persons, whatever their nature, public or private, or their sphere of activity, with regard to the subject matter of the directive which has not been correctly implemented. It is immaterial in that regard in what manner 'the state' can influence the conduct of those persons: de jure or de facto, for example because the organ of authority has a general or specific power (or is simply able as a matter of fact) to give that person binding directions, whether or not by the exercise of rights as a shareholder, to approve its decisions in advance or suspend or annul them after the fact, to appoint or dismiss (the majority of) its directors, or to interrupt its funding wholly or in part so as to threaten its continued existence, with, however, the provisos that (1) the possibility of exercising influence must stem from something other than a general legislative power (since otherwise all individuals subject to such general legislative power would be brought within the scope of *Marshall's* case and related judgments, which would go beyond their purpose), and (2) as I have already said, the possibility of exercising influence must exist, inter alia (or in particular), in connection with the matter to which the provision of a directive which has not yet been implemented relates or can relate.

Once the state (in the broad sense) has retained such a power to exercise influence over a person (in this case the BGC) with regard, inter alia, to the subject matter of the relevant provision of a directive, from the point of view of individuals it has brought that person within its sphere of authority. For that reason individuals may then rely against that person on the member state's failure to implement a directive. The reasoning lying behind *Marshall's* case and the related cases implies that the state may not benefit from its default in respect of anything that lies within the sphere of responsibility which by its own free choice it has taken on itself, irrespective of the person through whom that responsibility is exercised.

22. On the basis of the foregoing I propose that the following answer should be given to the House of Lords. Individuals may rely on an unconditional and sufficiently precise provision such as art 5(1) of Directive 76/207 against a person or body, in this case a public undertaking, in respect of which the state (understood as any body endowed with public authority, regardless of its relationship with other public bodies or the nature of the duties entrusted to it) has assumed responsibilities which put it in a position decisively to influence the conduct of that person or body in any manner whatsoever (other than by means of general legislation) with regard to the matter in respect of which the relevant provision of a directive imposes an obligation which the member state has failed to implement in national law.

It is for the national courts to apply that criterion in specific cases. I may, however, be permitted to point out that in the case of the BGC the competent Secretary of State had the power at the material time to give the BGC binding directions with regard both to the most efficient management of its activities and to the exercise and performance of its functions in general if the national interest so required (see para 3 above). It seems to me that compliance with the law, including Community law binding on the member state, is an objective of national interest, so that binding instructions *could* have been given to the BGC to comply with the provisions of Directive 76/207, which at the material time had not yet been formally implemented in national law. It was also the Secretary of State who appointed the members of the BGC and, I assume, could compel them to resign, a and he could also exercise pressure on the management of the corporation by appropriate financial arrangements.

In that connection I should also point out that the answer suggested above is in accordance, mutatis mutandis, that is to say having regard to the difference in the objectives of the various measures, with the legislation and case law in other areas of Community law where the concept of 'the state', as in the present situation, must be given a broad scope: in those areas too bodies other than those endowed with public
b authority are brought under the measure in question when their conduct can be influenced by the authorities (see para 16 above).

The question of damages

23.   In the second part of its question the House of Lords seeks to determine whether the appellants, if they can rely on the equal treatment directive against the BGC, have 'a
c claim for damages on the ground that the retirement policy of the BGC was contrary to the directive'. In the absence of any specific rule in Community law that is in principle a question which must be answered in accordance with the national law of the member state. Even so, there are restrictions in Community law on the liberty left to the member states to determine the substantive and procedural aspects of the sanctions associated with the obligations which result for a member state from a directive. More specifically, with
d regard to the sanctions on the obligation arising from art 5(1) of Directive 76/207, which is in issue in this case, the court held in *von Colson and Kamann v Land Nordrhein-Westfalen* Case 14/88 [1984] ECR 1891 at 1909 (para 28):

'. . . although Directive No 76/207/EEC, for the purpose of imposing a sanction for the breach of the prohibition of discrimination, leaves the Member States free to
e choose between the different solutions suitable for achieving its objective, it nevertheless requires that if a Member State chooses to penalize breaches of that prohibition by the award of compensation, then in order to ensure that it is effective and that it has a deterrent effect, that compensation must in any event be adequate in relation to the damage sustained and must therefore amount to more than purely nominal compensation . . .'
f
(See also at 1909, 1908 (paras 26, 23).)

It is for the national court to find a means, within its own legal system, of meeting that requirement under Community law.

Decision

g 24.   I propose that the question referred by the House of Lords should be answered as follows:

'Individuals may rely on an unconditional and sufficiently precise provision such as art 5(1) of Directive 76/207 against an undertaking in respect of which the state (understood as any body endowed with public authority, regardless of its relationship
h with other public bodies or the nature of the duties entrusted to it) has assumed responsibilities which put it in a position decisively to influence the conduct of that undertaking in any manner whatsoever (other than by means of general legislation) with regard to the matter in respect of which the relevant provision of a directive imposes an obligation which the member state has failed to implement in national law. Although Directive 76/207, for the purpose of imposing a sanction for breach
j of the prohibition of discrimination, leaves the member states free to choose between the different solutions suitable for achieving its objective, it nevertheless requires that if a member state chooses to penalise breaches of that prohibition by the award of compensation, then in order to ensure that it is effective and that it has a deterrent effect, that compensation must in any event be adequate in relation to the damage

sustained. It is for the national court to find a means within its own legal system of
meeting that requirement under Community law.'

a

12 July. **THE COURT OF JUSTICE** delivered the following judgment.

1.   By an order of 4 May 1989 which was received at the court on 29 May 1989, the
House of Lords referred to the court for a preliminary ruling under art 177 of the EEC
Treaty a question on the interpretation of Council Directive (EEC) 76/207 on the
implementation of the principle of equal treatment for men and women as regards access
to employment, vocational training and promotion, and working conditions.

b

2.   That question was raised in proceedings between A Foster, G A H M Fulford-
Brown, J Morgan, M Roby, E M Salloway and P Sullivan (hereinafter referred to as 'the
appellants in the main proceedings'), women who were formerly employed by the British
Gas Corp (hereinafter referred to as the 'BGC'), and British Gas plc (hereinafter referred
to as the 'respondent in the main proceedings'), the successor to the rights and liabilities
of the BGC, in respect of their compulsory retirement from the BGC.

c

3.   By virtue of the Gas Act 1972, which governed the BGC at the material time, the
BGC was a statutory corporation responsible for developing and maintaining a system of
gas supply in Great Britain, and had a monopoly of the supply of gas.

4.   The members of the BGC were appointed by the competent Secretary of State. He
also had the power to give the BGC directions of a general character in relation to matters
affecting the national interest and instructions concerning its management.

d

5.   The BGC was obliged to submit to the Secretary of State periodic reports on the
exercise of its functions, its management and its programmes. Those reports were then
laid before both Houses of Parliament. Under the Gas Act 1972 the BGC also had the
right, with the consent of the Secretary of State, to submit proposed legislation to
Parliament.

e

6.   The BGC was required to run a balanced budget over two successive financial
years. The Secretary of State could order it to pay certain funds over to him or to allocate
funds to specified purposes.

7.   The BGC was privatised under the Gas Act 1986. Privatisation resulted in the
establishment of British Gas plc, the respondent in the main proceedings, to which the
rights and liabilities of the BGC were transferred with effect from 24 August 1986.

f

8.   The appellants in the main proceedings were required to retire by the BGC on
various dates between 27 December 1985 and 22 July 1986, on attaining the age of 60.
These retirements reflected a general policy pursued by the BGC, that of requiring its
employees to retire on reaching the age at which they were entitled to a state pension
pursuant to British legislation, that is to say 60 years of age for women and 65 for men.

9.   The appellants in the main proceedings, who wished to continue to work, brought
proceedings for damages before the British courts asserting that their retirement by the
BGC was contrary to art 5(1) of Directive 76/207. According to that provision:

g

'Application of the principle of equal treatment with regard to working conditions,
including the conditions governing dismissal, means that men and women shall be
guaranteed the same conditions without discrimination on grounds of sex.'

h

10.   According to the order of the House of Lords, the parties to the main proceedings
are agreed that on the basis of the judgment of the court in *Marshall v Southampton and
South West Hampshire Area Health Authority (Teaching)* Case 152/84 [1986] 2 All ER 584,
[1986] QB 401 the dismissals were contrary to art 5(1) of Directive 76/207. They are also
agreed that those dismissals were not unlawful under the British legislation in force at
the material time and that according to previous judgments of the House of Lords that
legislation cannot be interpreted in a manner consistent with Directive 76/207. The
parties are in dispute over the issue whether art 5(1) of the directive may be relied on
against the BGC.

j

11.   It was in those circumstances that the House of Lords stayed the proceedings and
a   referred the following question to the court for a preliminary ruling:

'Was the British Gas Corporation (at the material time) a body of such a type that
the appellants are entitled in English courts and tribunals to rely directly upon
Council Directive 76/207 of 9 February 1976 on the implementation of the principle
of equal treatment for men and women as regards access to employment, vocational
training and promotion, and working conditions so as to be entitled to a claim for
b   damages on the ground that the retirement policy of the British Gas Corporation
was contrary to the directive?'

12.   Reference is made to the report for the hearing for a fuller account of the facts of
the case, the relevant Community legislation, the course of the procedure and the written
observations submitted to the court, which are mentioned or discussed hereinafter only
c   in so far as is necessary for the reasoning of the court.

The jurisdiction of the court
13.   Before considering the question referred by the House of Lords, it must first be
observed as a preliminary point that the United Kingdom has submitted that it is not a
matter for the Court of Justice but for the national courts to determine, in the context of
d   the national legal system, whether the provisions of a directive may be relied on against
a body such as the BGC.
14.   The question what effects measures adopted by Community institutions have
and, in particular, whether those measures may be relied on against certain categories of
persons necessarily involves interpretation of the articles of the Treaty concerning
measures adopted by the institutions and the Community measure in issue.
e   15.   It follows that the Court of Justice has jurisdiction in proceedings for a
preliminary ruling to determine the categories of persons against whom the provisions
of a directive may be relied on. It is for the national courts, on the other hand, to decide
whether a party to proceedings before them falls within one of the categories so defined.

f   *Reliance on the provisions of the directive against a body such as the BGC*
16.   As the court has consistently held (see *Becker v Münster-Innenstadt Finanzamt* Case
8/81 [1982] ECR 53 at 70–71 (paras 23–25)), where the Community authorities have, by
means of a directive, placed member states under a duty to adopt a certain course of
action, the effectiveness of such a measure would be diminished if persons were prevented
from relying on it in proceedings before a court and national courts were prevented from
taking it into consideration as an element of Community law. Consequently, a member
g   state which has not adopted the implementing measures required by the directive within
the prescribed period may not plead, as against individuals, its own failure to perform
the obligations which the directive entails. Thus, wherever the provisions of a directive
appear, as far as their subject matter is concerned, to be unconditional and sufficiently
precise, those provisions may, in the absence of implementing measures adopted within
the prescribed period, be relied on as against any national provision which is incompatible
h   with the directive or in so far as the provisions define rights which individuals are able to
assert against the state.
17.   The court further held in *Marshall's* case [1986] 2 All ER 584 at 600, [1986] QB
401 at 422 (para 49) that where a person is able to rely on a directive as against the state
he may do so regardless of the capacity in which the latter is acting, whether as employer
j   or as public authority. In either case it is necessary to prevent the state from taking
advantage of its own failure to comply with Community law.
18.   On the basis of those considerations, the court has held in a series of cases that
unconditional and sufficiently precise provisions of a directive could be relied on against
organisations or bodies which were subject to the authority or control of the state or had

special powers beyond those which result from the normal rules applicable to relations between individuals.

19. The court has accordingly held that provisions of a directive could be relied on against tax authorities (see the judgments in *Becker's* case and *ECSC v Acciaierie e Ferriere Busseni (in liq)* Case C-221/88 (22 February 1990, unreported)), local or regional authorities (see *Flli Costanzo SpA v Comune di Milano* Case 103/88 [1990] 3 CMLR 239), constitutionally independent authorities responsible for the maintenance of public order and safety (see *Johnston v Chief Constable of the Royal Ulster Constabulary* Case 222/84 [1986] 3 All ER 135, [1987] QB 129) and public authorities providing public health services (see *Marshall's* case).

20. It follows from the foregoing that a body, whatever its legal form, which has been made responsible, pursuant to a measure adopted by the state, for providing a public service under the control of the state and which has for that purpose special powers beyond those which result from the normal rules applicable in relations between individuals is included in any event among the bodies against which the provisions of a directive capable of having direct effect may be relied on.

21. With regard to art 5(1) of Directive 76/207 it should be observed that in *Marshall's* case [1986] 2 All ER 584 at 600, [1986] QB 401 at 422 at (para 52) the court held that that provision was unconditional and sufficiently precise to be relied on by an individual and to be applied by the national courts.

22. The answer to the question referred by the House of Lords must therefore be that art 5(1) of Directive 76/207 may be relied on in a claim for damages against a body, whatever its legal form, which has been made responsible, pursuant to a measure adopted by the state, for providing a public service under the control of the state and which has for that purpose special powers beyond those which result from the normal rules applicable in relations between individuals.

Costs
23. The costs incurred by the United Kingdom and by the Commission of the European Communities, which submitted observations to the court, are not recoverable. Since these proceedings are, in so far as the parties to the main proceedings are concerned, a step in the action pending before the national court, the decision as to costs is a matter for that court.

On those grounds, the court in answer to the question referred to it by the House of Lords by order of 4 May 1989, hereby rules that art 5(1) of Council Directive (EEC) 76/207 on the implementation of the principle of equal treatment for men and women as regards access to employment, vocational training and promotion, and working conditions may be relied on in a claim for damages against a body, whatever its legal form, which has been made responsible, pursuant to a measure adopted by the state, for providing a public service under the control of the state and has for that purpose special powers beyond those which result from the normal rules applicable in relations between individuals.

Agents: *Bruce Piper* (for the appellants); *C E H Twiss*, Headquarters Director of Legal Services, British Gas plc (for the respondent); *Susan Hay*, Treasury Solicitor's Department (for the United Kingdom); *Karen Banks*, Legal Adviser, EC Commission (for the Commission).

Mary Rose Plummer   Barrister.

a

Paragon Group Ltd v Burnell and others

CHANCERY DIVISION
HARMAN J
9 APRIL 1990

b *Practice – Service – Substituted service – Notice of writ – Court's discretion – Personal service 'impracticable' – Relief claimed in writ – Whether relief claimed in writ and terms of agreement sued on good reasons for permitting substituted service – RSC Ord 65, r 4.*

An order under RSC Ord 65, r 4[a] permitting substituted service of a writ or a document which is required to be served personally, on the grounds that 'it appears to the Court that it is impracticable for any reason to serve that document in the manner prescribed', *c* will only be made if there is evidence about the difficulties in effecting service in the prescribed manner. The relief claimed in the writ or the terms of any agreement being sued on, providing for example for waiver of any claim if not brought within a specified date, are not reasons which may make it impracticable to effect service in the prescribed manner and are therefore not grounds on which the court will permit substituted service *d* (see p 924 *j* to p 925 *b d g* and p 926 *d* to *f h j*, post).

Dictum of Goulding J in *Re Conan Doyle's Will Trusts, Harwood v Fides Union Fiduciaire* [1971] 2 All ER 1377 at 1379 doubted.

Notes

For substituted service, see 37 Halsbury's Laws (4th edn) para 153, and for cases on the *e* subject, see 37(2) Digest (Reissue) 258–263, 1684–1714.

Cases referred to in judgment

Conan Doyle's Will Trusts, Re, Harwood v Fides Union Fiduciaire [1971] 2 All ER 1377, [1971] Ch 982, [1971] 2 WLR 1408.
El Sombrero Ltd, Re [1958] 3 All ER 1, [1958] Ch 900, [1958] 3 WLR 349.

f

Motion

By motion dated 28 February 1990 Digby Michael McLaren Burnell, Nigel Anthony Plumptre Gaymer and Ralph Walter Simms, the defendants in an action brought by the plaintiff, Paragon Group Ltd, sought the trial as a preliminary issue of the question whether on the proper construction of RSC Ord 65, r 4 it was material for the court to *g* take into account, for the purpose of deciding whether to make an order for substituted service, cl 4.5 of an agreement dated 21 May 1987, which provided that any claim in respect of the matters therein referred to would be unconditionally waived on the last day of the sixth calendar month immediately following the applicable date if proceedings should not by then have been commenced and served on the defendants. The facts are set out in the judgment.

h

Robert Webb QC and *Richard M Sheldon* for the plaintiff.
Anthony D Colman QC and *Richard Jacobs* for the defendants.

HARMAN J. I have to decide whether, on the true construction of RSC Ord 65, r 4, the court should take into account, as material to the issue whether an order for substituted *j* service should be made, the terms of the agreement sought to be sued on in this case.

The action is brought by writ specially indorsed, as I would say, with the statement of claim issued on 30 January 1989. The statement of claim runs to nearly 50 pages with

---

a Rule 4, so far as material, is set out at p 924 *d*, post

schedules and the action concerns a claim under various different heads of liability by the
plaintiff company against the three individual defendants. The claims are put on at least
three, if not four, alternative bases: firstly, as misrepresentations, secondly, specific
breaches of contract and, thirdly, damages for the tort of negligent misrepresentation.
The writ was served on 31 January pursuant to an order for substituted service which
was made in somewhat peculiar circumstances by what is said to have been a Court of
Appeal, although as far as I understand it they never purported to meet together and
listen to counsel's submission. The Court of Appeal has directed that, that order having
been made by it ex parte, the application to discharge it should be made to a puisne
judge, who should approach it simply on the basis not that he is bound by any decision
of the Court of Appeal on any point of law or principle, but as if he were considering an
ordinary exercise of a discretion ex parte under Ord 65, r 4 on an inter partes application
to have the order set aside.

The matter is raised in motions by the plaintiff, which seeks in particular to have
discovery of documents and cross-examination of the defendants on the affidavits which
they have sworn in support of their application to set aside, on the ground that these
matters are material to the court's consideration whether it should set aside the order for
substituted service made ex parte. Order 65, r 4(1) provides:

> 'If, in the case of any document which . . . is required to be served personally or a
> document to which Order 10, rule 1, applies, it appears to the Court that it is
> impracticable for any reason to serve that document in the manner prescribed, the
> Court may make an order for substituted service of that document.'

In this case the document is one to which the provisions of Ord 10, r 1 apply. That
order provides, in the old fashioned classic way, that:

> '(1) A writ must be served personally on each defendant by the plaintiff or his
> agent.'

It then goes on in a fairly modern adaptation of 1962 to provide:

> '(2) A writ for service on a defendant within the jurisdiction may, instead of
> being served personally on him, be served—(a) by sending a copy of the writ by
> ordinary first-class post to the defendant at his usual or last known address, or (b) if
> there is a letter box for that address, by inserting through the letter box a copy of
> the writ enclosed in a sealed envelope addressed to the defendant . . .'

This is a case where the document is one to which that rule applies. I have to consider
whether 'it is impracticable for any reason to serve that document in the manner
prescribed,' and that must mean prescribed by the provisions of Ord 10, r 1. It is notable
that Ord 10, r 1(3) provides:

> '. . . (a) the date of service shall, unless the contrary is shown, be deemed to be the
> seventh day . . . after the day on which the copy was sent to or . . . inserted through
> the letter box . . . (b) any affidavit proving due service of the writ must contain a
> statement to the effect that—(i) in the opinion of the deponent . . . the copy of the
> writ . . . will have come to the knowledge of the defendant within 7 days thereafter.'

Those sub-paragraphs plainly show that service by post or by pushing the writ through
the letter box can only be effected when the deponent has reason to believe that the
document will come to the knowledge of the person whom it is sought to be served.

With that background knowledge I turn back to consider when the court may make
an order for substituted service. It may do so when 'it appears to the Court', so plainly
the court must have evidence before it showing what has to be made to appear. That
evidence must show to the court, I suppose on a balance of probabilities, that 'it is
impracticable for any reason' to serve that document in the manner prescribed. So the
reason which may be set out in the evidence may be any reason why that is so in a general
way, but in my judgment it is quite plain that what is required at the end is that the
evidence must show that it is impracticable to serve the document and serve it in the

manner prescribed. In my view that requires evidence that the server cannot properly
a serve it personally or serve it by post because perhaps he has no last known address, or
that he cannot serve it by placing it through the letter box at the premises because he has
no reason to believe that within seven days it will come to the intended defendant's
notice. Any evidence which goes to those matters plainly is proper evidence which a
judge must consider, but in my view what must be shown to be impracticable remains,
and remains only, that service 'in the manner prescribed' is impracticable. I cannot see
b that r 4 requires the court to consider any matters other than why and how it is said that
service in the manner prescribed is impracticable. Thus, any amount of evidence may be
admitted as to what the defendant is doing and how he is evading service, if that were
the case, and the court must then consider what that material amounts to and decide
whether it warrants the making of an order for service in some other manner than the
manner prescribed.

c   Plainly, simply to swear an affidavit that the post nowadays is very erratic and therefore
the deponent cannot rely on it to produce the document to the defendant within seven
days would be admissible and might convince a judge that service by post was
impracticable. If in addition there was no letter box at the premises and personal service
was not effected, then substituted service could be permitted. To my mind there is
nothing whatever in Ord 65 which is directed to matters other than evidence about the
d difficulties in service in the prescribed manner.

I have had shown to me two authorities. In the first, *Re El Sombrero Ltd* [1958] 3 All
ER 1, [1958] Ch 900, Wynn-Parry J had to consider the meaning of the word
'impracticable' in s 135(1) of the Companies Act 1948, and that, by then extremely
experienced, company judge held that the word 'impracticable' was not synonymous
with the word 'impossible'. Wynn-Parry J said ([1958] 3 All ER 1 at 4, [1958] Ch 900 at
e 904):

'... the question necessarily raised by the introduction of the word "impracticable"
is ... Examine the circumstances of the particular case and answer the question
whether, as a practical matter, the desired meeting of the company can be conducted,
there being no doubt, of course, that it can be convened and held. On the face of
f s. 135(1), there is no express limitation which would operate to give those words "is
impracticable" any less meaning than that which I have stated ...'

I entirely follow and, with respect, agree with, and in any event would adopt Wynn-
Parry J's reasons, but what he was considering there was: is it for any practical reason, not
as a practical matter, possible to conduct the meeting of the company? So, here what has
g to be considered is: is it for any practical reason not practicable to serve the document in
the manner prescribed? The width of the word 'practicable' does not alter the question
of what it is one must judge is practicable or not practicable, and in my view under Ord
65, r 4 it is service that one must examine and the methods of service to see what
practicality follows.

I was also shown *Re Conan Doyle's Will Trusts, Harwood v Fides Union Fiduciaire* [1971] 2
h All ER 1377, [1971] Ch 982, where Goulding J had a point much closer to this case. In
that case Goulding J held ([1971] 2 All ER 1377 at 1379, [1971] Ch 982 at 985):

'... the requirement ... that personal service must be shown to be impracticable
for one reason or another has to be tested according to the circumstances of any
particular case at the time when the request for an order for substituted service is
j made.'

That seems to me to be impeccable and sound and I wholly accept it. Goulding J
continued:

'If, as appears probable from the evidence, personal service cannot be effected
until early in May, it will not be possible for the plaintiff to bring the defendant
before the court in time for the court to consider whether or not to restrain the
projected sale by tender.'

I should say that the case concerned a proposed sale by a foreign trustee of the assets of Sir Arthur Conan Doyle's estate to the detriment of a beneficiary under that estate.

As it seems to me, Goulding J was misled in considering that that was the position because he was not referred to Ord 45, r 7(5), which provides that an order restraining an act can be made effective by giving notice of it by manners prescribed by the court. Traditionally such notice is usually by telegram. That rule appears not to have been called to Goulding J's attention. Indeed, an opposite submission was made to him by the extremely distinguished conveyancer who appeared before him in the matter and he accepted that submission, in my view, wrongly. The conclusion which Goulding J went on to draw from that submission was that he had thought at one time that in the circumstances that might mean that personal service was impracticable because the court could make some kind of ex parte order:

> 'On reflection and on hearing counsel's submissions . . . it appears to me that that does not really solve the problem . . . Accordingly, I have formed the view that, in the circumstances of this case as it stands today . . . and having regard to the relief claimed in the writ, personal service is, on the evidence, impracticable, and therefore I have power to make an order for substituted service.'

(See [1971] 2 All ER 1377 at 1379, [1971] Ch 982 at 985.)

With the greatest respect to Goulding J, I cannot follow that reasoning and it seems to me that the relief claimed in a writ does not affect the nature of the service and whether it is practicable or not to effect service by one of the ways prescribed at all. The relief in the writ sets out the remedies which the plaintiff seeks and they have nothing to do, that I can see, with matters of service and whether service can or cannot be effected in a proper way. It seems to me that Goulding J was under great pressure because he believed that he had no powers other than to allow substituted service which could bring the court's control over this foreign trustee of an English trust into effect, and he was misled, as I fear many on the Bench are from time to time, into misconstruing the rule because he thought that justice would otherwise be defeated. In my view that was, as I say, because he was misinformed by counsel as to the scope of the rules; but in any event it leads, in my view, to an unsound construction of Ord 65, r 4 and I would not follow it. As it seems to me, the only matters that are relevant to Ord 65, r 4 are matters about service. Any evidence and any reasons affecting service can be brought in but the relief claimed in the writ cannot in any way impinge on that service, nor the likelihood whether service is to be achieved or not.

As counsel for the defendants observed to me in argument that this writ contains claims based on three different causes of action at least. It plainly is a good writ and could be properly and regularly served by any ordinary process after 30 January to obtain those forms of relief. It seems likely that one particular cause of action which is sought to be enforced, that of breaches of express contract, may be unenforceable because the contract apparently provides a waiver if the process of enforcing it is not brought within a limited time. Thus, it appears, the writ is a perfectly good writ perfectly well served for some purposes between these very parties affecting this very contract, but is not adequately served for another purpose. It seems to me that that cannot be a distinction which turns on the practicability of service: that turns on matters which are nothing to do with service but are the consequences of the agreement discussed. In my judgment there is nothing that ought to be put before the court on evidence other than reasons why service is not practicable, and that is my conclusion on the preliminary issues.

Order accordingly.

Solicitors: *Linklaters & Paines* (for the plaintiff); *Travers Smith Braithwaite* (for the defendants).

Evelyn M C Budd   Barrister.

Re B (a minor) (wardship: medical treatment)

COURT OF APPEAL, CIVIL DIVISION

TEMPLEMAN AND DUNN LJJ

7 AUGUST 1981

Ward of court – Jurisdiction – Medical treatment – Child born with Down's syndrome and having intestinal blockage – Child requiring operation to remove blockage in order to live – Parents refusing consent to operation – Local authority making child ward of court and applying to court for authority to direct that operation be carried out – Whether court required to determine whether operation in child's best interest or whether parents' wishes should be respected.

A baby girl who was born suffering from Down's syndrome also had an intestinal blockage which could be cured without great difficulty. However, if she did not have the operation she would die within a few days. If she had the operation her life expectancy would be about 20 to 30 years. Her parents, believing that it was not in her best interests to have the operation because she would be very handicapped both mentally and physically if she survived, refused their consent to the operation. Although it could not be said to what extent her mental and physical defects would be apparent if she lived, the probability was that she would not be a person whose faculties were entirely destroyed. The local authority made her a ward of court and applied to the court to authorise it to direct that the operation be carried out. The judge held that the parents' wishes should be respected and that it was not in the child's best interests that the operation be performed. He accordingly refused to authorise the operation. The local authority appealed.

Held – The question which the court had to determine was whether it was in the child's best interests to have the operation and live as a mongoloid child or to die within a week, and not whether the parents' wishes should be respected. Since there was evidence that if the operation took place and was successful the child would live the normal life span of a mongoloid child with the handicaps and defects and life of such a child and since it had not been demonstrated that a life of that description ought to be extinguished, the court would authorise the local authority to direct the operation to be carried out. Accordingly, the local authority's appeal would be allowed (see p 929 b e to p 930 b, post).

Notes

For the court's jurisdiction over wards of court, see 24 Halsbury's Laws (4th edn) para 576, and for cases on the subject, see 28(3) Digest (2nd reissue) 305–328, 2881–2969.

For the duties of the Official Solicitor, see 10 Halsbury's Laws (4th edn) para 950, and for cases on the subject, see 16 Digest (Reissue) 238, 2347–2248.

Case cited

J v C [1969] 1 All ER 788, [1970] AC 668, [1969] 2 WLR 540, HL.

Appeal

The local authority appealed against the decision of Ewbank J on 7 August 1981 refusing to authorise an operation to be performed on a minor, B, a baby who was a ward of court, on the application of the local authority in whom B's care and control were vested. The parents of B and the Official Solicitor as the guardian ad litem of B were defendants to the application. The facts are set out in the judgment of Templeman LJ.

Anita Ryan for the local authority.
H W Turcan for the Official Solicitor.
Roger Gray QC and *Mark Cunningham* for the parents.

TEMPLEMAN LJ. This is a very poignantly sad case. Although we sit in public, for reasons which I think will be obvious to everybody in court, and if not will be obvious in the course of this judgment, it would be lamentable if the names of the parents of the child concerned were revealed in any way to the general public. The press and people who frequent these courts are usually very helpful in referring to names by initials, and this is a case where nothing ought to be leaked out to identify those concerned with the case.

It concerns a little girl who was born on 28 July 1981. She was born suffering from Down's syndrome, which means that she will be a mongol. She was also born with an intestinal blockage which will be fatal unless it is operated on. When the parents were informed of the condition of the child they took the view that it would be unkind to this child to operate on her, and that the best thing to do was for her not to have the operation, in which case she would die within a few days. During those few days she could be kept from pain and suffering by sedation. They took the view that that would be the kindest thing in the interests of the child. They so informed the doctors at the hospital, and refused to consent to the operation taking place. It is agreed on all hands that the parents came to that decision with great sorrow. It was a firm decision; they genuinely believed that it was in the best interests of this child. At the same time, it is of course impossible for parents in the unfortunate position of these parents to be certain that their present view should prevail. The shock to caring parents finding that they have given birth to a child who is a mongol is very great indeed, and therefore while great weight ought to be given to the views of the parents they are not views which necessarily must prevail.

What happened then was that the doctors, being informed that the parents would not consent to the operation, contacted the local authority, who very properly made the child a ward of court and asked the judge to give care and control to the local authority and to authorise them to direct that the operation be carried out, and the judge did so direct. But when the child was moved from the hospital where it was born to another hospital for the purposes of the operation a difference of medical opinion developed. The surgeon who was to perform the operation declined to do so when he was informed that the parents objected. In a statement he said that when the child was referred to him for the operation he decided he wished to speak to the parents of the child personally and he spoke to them on the telephone and they stated that in view of the fact that the child was mongoloid they did not wish to have the operation performed. He further stated:

'I decided therefore to respect the wishes of the parents and not to perform the operation, a decision which would, I believe (after about 20 years in the medical profession), be taken by the great majority of surgeons faced with a similar situation.'

Therefore the local authority came back to the judge. The parents were served in due course and appeared and made their submissions to the judge, and in addition inquiries were made and it was discovered that the surgeon in the hospital where the child was born and another surgeon in a neighbouring hospital were prepared and advised that the operation should be carried out. So there is a difference of medical opinion.

This morning the judge was asked to decide whether to continue his order that the operation should be performed or whether to revoke that order, and the position now is stark. The evidence, as I have said, is that if this little girl does not have this operation she will die within a matter of days. If she has the operation there is a possibility that she will suffer heart trouble as a result and that she may die within two or three months. But if she has the operation and it is successful, she has Down's syndrome, she is mongoloid, and the present evidence is that her life expectancy is short, about 20 to 30 years.

The parents say that no one can tell what will be the life of a mongoloid child who survives during that 20 or 30 years, but one thing is certain. She will be very handicapped mentally and physically and no one can expect that she will have anything like a normal

existence. They make that point not because of the difficulties which will be occasioned
to them but in the child's interest. This is not a case in which the court is concerned with
whether arrangements could or could not be made for the care of this child, if she lives,
during the next 20 or 30 years; the local authority is confident that the parents having
for good reason decided that it is in the child's best interests that the operation should not
be performed, nevertheless good adoption arrangements could be made and that in so far
as any mongol child can be provided with a happy life then such a happy life can be
provided.

The question which this court has to determine is whether it is in the interests of this
child to be allowed to die within the next week or to have the operation in which case if
she lives she will be a mongoloid child, but no one can say to what extent her mental or
physical defects will be apparent. No one can say whether she will suffer or whether she
will be happy in part. On the one hand, the probability is that she will not be a 'cabbage',
as it is called when people's faculties are entirely destroyed. On the other hand, it is
certain that she will be very severely mentally and physically handicapped.

Counsel for the parents has submitted very movingly, if I may say so, that this is a case
where nature has made its own arrangements to terminate a life which would not be
fruitful and nature should not be interfered with. He has also submitted that in this kind
of decision the views of responsible and caring parents, as these are, should be respected,
and that their decision that it is better for the child to be allowed to die should be
respected. Fortunately or unfortunately, in this particular case the decision no longer lies
with the parents or with the doctors, but lies with the court. It is a decision which of
course must be made in the light of the evidence and views expressed by the parents and
the doctors, but at the end of the day it devolves on this court in this particular instance
to decide whether the life of this child is demonstrably going to be so awful that in effect
the child must be condemned to die, or whether the life of this child is still so
imponderable that it would be wrong for her to be condemned to die. There may be
cases, I know not, of severe proved damage where the future is so certain and where the
life of the child is so bound to be full of pain and suffering that the court might be driven
to a different conclusion, but in the present case the choice which lies before the court is
this: whether to allow an operation to take place which may result in the child living for
20 or 30 years as a mongoloid or whether (and I think this must be brutally the result) to
terminate the life of a mongoloid child because she also has an intestinal complaint.
Faced with that choice I have no doubt that it is the duty of this court to decide that the
child must live. The judge was much affected by the reasons given by the parents and
came to the conclusion that their wishes ought to be respected. In my judgment he erred
in that the duty of the court is to decide whether it is in the interests of the child that an
operation should take place. The evidence in this case only goes to show that if the
operation takes place and is successful then the child may live the normal span of a
mongoloid child with the handicaps and defects and life of a mongol child, and it is not
for this court to say that life of that description ought to be extinguished.

Accordingly, the appeal must be allowed and the local authority must be authorised
themselves to authorise and direct the operation to be carried out on the little girl.

DUNN LJ. I agree, and as we are differing from the view expressed by the judge I
would say a few words of my own. I have great sympathy for the parents in the agonising
decision to which they came. As they put it themselves: 'God or nature has given the
child a way out.' But the child now being a ward of court, although due weight must be
given to the decision of the parents which everybody accepts was an entirely responsible
one, doing what they considered was the best, the fact of the matter is that this court now
has to make the decision. It cannot hide behind the decision of the parents or the decision
of the doctors; and in making the decision this court's first and paramount consideration
is the welfare of this unhappy little baby.

One of the difficulties in the case is that there is no prognosis as to the child's future,
except that as a mongol her expectation of life is confined to 20 or 30 years. We were told
that no reliable prognosis can be made until probably she is about two years old. That in

itself leads me to the route by which the court should make its decision, because there is no evidence that this child's short life is likely to be an intolerable one. There is no *a* evidence at all as to the quality of life which the child may expect. As counsel for the Official Solicitor said, the child should be put into the same position as any other mongol child and must be given the chance to live an existence. I accept that way of putting it.

I agree with Templeman LJ that the court must step in to preserve this mongol baby's life. I would allow the appeal and I agree with the order proposed by Templeman LJ.

b

Appeal allowed.

Solicitors: *C T Mahoney* (for the local authority); *Official Solicitor*; *Jolliffe & Co*, Chester (for the parents).

Mary Rose Plummer   Barrister. *c*

Re J (a minor) (wardship: medical   *d*
treatment)

COURT OF APPEAL, CIVIL DIVISION
LORD DONALDSON OF LYMINGTON MR, BALCOMBE AND TAYLOR LJJ
15, 19 OCTOBER 1990

e

Ward of court – Jurisdiction – Medical treatment – Grossly handicapped baby – Baby neither on point of death nor dying – Nature of medical treatment to be administered to ward – Reventilation likely to be fatal if baby collapsed – Whether deliberate steps should be taken artificially to prolong life whatever pain and suffering caused to child – Whether court should withhold consent to reventilation – Test to be applied in assessing course to be adopted in best interests of child – *f* *Whether relevant that child a ward of court – Whether court required to exercise a higher or different standard from that of reasonable and responsible parents.*

J was a ward of court who had been born very prematurely. He suffered very severe and permanent brain damage at the time of his birth, the brain tissue then lost being irreplaceable. He was epileptic and the medical evidence was that he was likely to develop serious spastic quadriplegia, would be blind and deaf and was unlikely ever to be able to *g* speak or to develop even limited intellectual abilities, but it was likely that he would feel pain to the same extent as a normal baby. His life expectancy was uncertain but he was expected to die before late adolescence, although he could survive for a few years. He had been ventilated twice for long periods when his breathing stopped, that treatment being both painful and hazardous. The medical prognosis was that any further collapse which *h* required ventilation would be fatal. However he was neither on the point of death nor dying. The question arose whether if he suffered a further collapse the medical staff at the hospital where he was being cared for should reventilate him in the event of his breathing stopping. The judge, exercising the court's parens patriae jurisdiction, made an order that J should be treated with antibiotics if he developed a chest infection but should not be reventilated if his breathing stopped unless the doctors caring for him *j* deemed it appropriate given the prevailing clinical situation. The Official Solicitor appealed against the order, contending that except where a child was terminally ill the court could never be justified in approving the withholding of life-saving treatment from a ward of court whatever the quality of the life being preserved or, alternatively, that it ought to do so only if it was certain that the child's life was going to be so intolerable that such a drastic conclusion was justified but that that had not been shown in the case of J.

Held – Where a ward of court suffered from physical disabilities so grave that his life
a would from his point of view be so intolerable if he were to continue living that he
would choose to die if he were in a position to make a sound judgment, the court could
direct that treatment without which death would ensue from natural causes need not be
given to the ward to prolong his life, even though he was neither on the point of death
nor dying. However, the court would never sanction positive steps to terminate the life
of a person. In deciding whether to authorise that treatment need not be given the court
b had to perform a balancing exercise in assessing the course to be adopted in the best
interests of the child, looked at from his point of view and giving the fullest possible
weight to his desire, if he were in a position to make a sound judgment, to survive, and
taking into account the pain and suffering and quality of life which he would experience
if life was prolonged and the pain and suffering involved in the proposed treatment.
Having regard to the invasive and hazardous nature of reventilation, the risk of further
c deterioration if J was subjected to it and the extremely unfavourable prognosis with or
without the treatment, it was in J's best interests that authority for reventilation be
withheld. The appeal would therefore be dismissed (see p 936 *f* to p 937 *a*, p 938 *c* to *j*,
p 939 *e* to *g*, p 940 *a*, p 942 *d f h j*, p 943 *c d* and p 944 *d e j* to p 945 *a c* to *e j*, post).

Dictum of McKenzie J in *Re Superintendent of Family and Child Service and Dawson*
(1983) 145 DLR (3d) 610 at 620–621 adopted.
d
Re B (a minor) (wardship: medical treatment) (1981) [1990] 3 All ER 927, *McKay v Essex
Area Health Authority* [1982] 2 All ER 771 and *Re C (a minor) (wardship: medical treatment)*
[1989] 2 All ER 782 considered.

Per Lord Donaldson MR. (1) A child who is a ward of court should be treated medically
in exactly the same way as one who is not, the only difference being that the doctors will
be looking to the court rather than the parents for any necessary consent (see p 934 *g*,
e post).

(2) In allocating limited resources to particular patients the fact that a child is or is not
a ward of court is irrelevant (see p 934 *j* to p 935 *a*, post).

Per Balcombe LJ. In deciding in any given case what is in the best interests of a ward,
the court adopts the same attitude as the responsible parent would do in the case of his or
her child; the court, exercising the duties of the sovereign as parens patriae is not expected
f to adopt any higher or different standard than that which, viewed objectively, a reasonable
and responsible parent would do (see p 941 *g*, post).

Per Taylor LJ. In deciding against treatment, the court must be satisfied to a high
degree of probability that its decision is in the child's best interests; certainty of proof is
not required (see p 945 *j*, post).

g
Notes
For the court's jurisdiction over wards of court, see 24 Halsbury's Laws (4th edn) para
576, and for cases on the subject, see 28(2) Digest (Reissue) 911–916, 2220–2248.

For the duties of the Official Solicitor, see 10 Halsbury's Laws (4th edn) para 950, and
for cases on the subject, see 16 Digest (Reissue) 238, 2347–2348.

h
Cases referred to in judgments
B (a minor) (wardship: medical treatment), Re (1981) [1990] 3 All ER 927, [1981] 1 WLR
1421, CA.
B (a minor) (wardship: sterilisation), Re [1987] 2 All ER 206, [1988] AC 199, [1987] 2 WLR
1213, HL.
j *Bolam v Friern Hospital Management Committee* [1957] 2 All ER 118, [1957] 1 WLR 582.
C (a minor) (wardship: medical treatment), Re [1989] 2 All ER 782, [1990] Fam 26, [1989] 3
WLR 240, CA.
McKay v Essex Area Health Authority [1982] 2 All ER 771, [1982] QB 1166, [1982] 2 WLR
890, CA.
Superintendent of Family and Child Service and Dawson, Re (1983) 145 DLR (3d) 610, sub
nom *Re S D* [1983] 3 WWR 618, BC SC.
Weberlist, Re (1974) 79 Misc 2d 753, 360 NYS 2d 783, NY SC.

Cases also cited or referred to in skeleton argument

D (a minor) (wardship: sterilisation) [1976] 1 All ER 326, [1976] Fam 326.

R v Adams (Bodkin) [1957] Crim LR 365.

S v S, W v Official Solicitor [1970] 3 All ER 107, [1972] AC 24, HL.

Wellesley v Duke of Beaufort (1827) 2 Russ 1, 38 ER 236, LC; affd sub nom Wellesley v Wellesley (1828) 2 Bli NS 124, HL.

X (a minor) (wardship: restriction on publication), Re [1975] 1 All ER 697, sub nom Re X (a minor) (wardship: jurisdiction) [1975] Fam 47, CA.

Appeal

The Official Solicitor, as guardian ad litem of the third defendant, a baby, J, who was a ward of court, appealed against para 6 of the order of Scott Baker J made in chambers on 11 October 1990 ordering that the plaintiffs, the local authority, should direct the relevant health authority to continue to treat J within the parameters of the opinion expressed by Dr W in his report dated 4 October 1990. The Official Solicitor sought an order that in place of para 6 there should be substituted an order that the hospital authority should continue to treat the ward with the object of sustaining and preserving his life, provided that if it should become necessary for him to be treated by means of intensive care procedures the matter should as soon as practicable be referred to the court as a matter of the utmost urgency. The judge also granted an injunction restraining publication of anything calculated to lead to identification of J, his parents (the first and second defendants), his carers or his whereabouts. The facts are set out in the judgment of Lord Donaldson MR.

James Munby QC and P A B Jackson for the Official Solicitor.
Shirley Ritchie QC and Colin Anderson for the local authority.
Timothy Clark for the parents.

At the conclusion of the argument their Lordships stated that they proposed to dismiss the appeal in substance and would give their reasons later.

19 October. The following judgments were delivered.

LORD DONALDSON OF LYMINGTON MR. Baby J has suffered almost every conceivable misfortune. He was a very premature baby, born after 27 weeks' gestation on 28 May 1990. He weighed only 1·1 kg (2·5 lb) at birth. He was not breathing. Almost immediately he was placed on a ventilator and given antibiotics to counteract an infection. He was put on a drip. His pulse rate frequently became very low and for ten days it was touch and go whether he survived.

One month later, on 28 June, the doctors were able to take him off the ventilator, but he was, and still is, a very sick and handicapped baby. There followed recurrent convulsions and episodes when he stopped breathing (apnoea). As a result he was oxygen-dependent until early August. At the end of August the doctors thought that he could be allowed to go home, although the prognosis was gloomy in the extreme. Four days later, on 1 September 1990, he had to be readmitted to hospital because he had choked and become cyanosed.

The subsequent history of J has been traumatic both for him, his parents and those professionally involved in caring for him. On 3 September it was noted that J had become cyanosed when he cried. On 5 September he collapsed suddenly and was again cyanosed. He was without a pulse, but was resuscitated. Two days later he again collapsed and had to be put on a ventilator. Between then and 23 September he was continuously on a ventilator. During that period four attempts were made to wean him from it. The first three failed because he suffered fits which interfered with the efficiency of the ventilator and on one occasion the doctors had to paralyse him in order to make his oxygen level safe. Since 23 September J has been breathing independently and in some

ways his condition has slightly improved. However this improvement is from a base line
a which can only be described as abysmally low.

Needless to say the doctors have been concerned to discover what are likely to be J's
long-term disabilities. As a result it is clear that he has suffered very severe brain damage
due to shortage of oxygen and impaired blood supply around the time of his birth. This
is no one's fault, but stems from his prematurity. Ultrasound scans of his brain were
conducted on 22 August and 10 September. They showed a large area of fluid-filled
b cavities where there ought to have been brain tissue. The body is incapable of making
this good. Of the three neo-natalogists who have been concerned with his care, the most
optimistic is Dr W. His view is that J is likely to develop serious spastic quadriplegia, that
is to say paralysis of both his arms and legs. It is debatable whether he will ever be able to
sit up or to hold his head upright. J appears to be blind, although there is a possibility
that some degree of sight may return. He is likely to be deaf. He may be able to make
c sounds which reflect his mood, but he is unlikely ever to be able to speak, even to the
extent of saying 'Mum' or 'Dad'. It is highly unlikely that he will develop even limited
intellectual abilities. Most unfortunately of all, there is a likelihood that he will be able
to feel pain to the same extent as a normal baby, because pain is a very basic response. It
is possible that he may achieve the ability to smile and to cry. Finally, as one might
expect, his life expectancy has been considerably reduced at most into his late teens, but
d even Dr W would expect him to die long before then.

This assessment of J's present state and likely future development is not based only on
the skills and experience of the doctors caring for him. It is supported by the ultrasound
scans to which I have already referred and by other objective scientific testing.

The problem which now has to be faced by all concerned is what is to be done if J
suffers another collapse. This may occur at any time, but is not inevitable. In most cases
e this would be a matter to be discussed and decided by the doctors in consultation with
the parents. By this I do not mean that the parents could tell the doctors what to do, but
they would have the right to withhold consent to treatment, subject to the right of the
doctors to apply to make the child a ward of court and to seek the guidance of the court.
In practice it might be expected that the parents would have confidence in the doctors
and that the doctors, recognising the agonising dilemma facing the parents, would take
f all the time that was necessary to explain the very limited options which were available
and, if at all possible, would agree with the parents on a course of action or inaction. In
the present case there has been no real difference of opinion between the doctors and the
parents, but for extraneous reasons into which it is unnecessary to go J has in fact been
made a ward of court and, accordingly, the right and duty to give or refuse consent to
treatment is vested in the court.
g On 11 October Scott Baker J made an order authorising the hospital to treat J within
the parameters of the opinion expressed by Dr W in his report of 4 October 1990, subject
to amendments to paras 24, 25 and 26 made in the course of his oral evidence. This
opinion, as amended and explained in the course of the hearing before this court, was as
follows:

h '24 I am of the opinion that it would not be in [J's] best interests to re-ventilate
him [using a ventilation machine] in the event of his stopping breathing, unless to
do so seems appropriate to the doctors caring for him given the prevailing clinical
situation. However, I think it would be reasonable to suck out his airway to remove
any plug of mucous or milk and to give oxygen by his face mask.
j 25 If he developed a chest infection I would recommend treatment with
antibiotics and maintenance of hydration, but not prolonged [manual] ventilation.
26 [Various recommendations to take effect on the assumption that baby J did
not in the event have to face a critical condition as a result of his stopping breathing
or otherwise.]'

The Official Solicitor has appealed against this decision. The parents do not formally
appeal, but naturally and very reasonably feel that they are in a dilemma. Their solicitor
took immense trouble to explain Scott Baker J's decision to them and at that time they

were minded to accept it as being a decision taken in the best interests of their son. However, the fact that the Official Solicitor has appealed has caused them to wonder *a* whether they were right.

The Official Solicitor submits that there are two justifications for an appeal. (i) *Re C (a minor) (wardship: medical treatment)* [1989] 2 All ER 782, [1990] Fam 26 gives guidance on the approach which it is appropriate to adopt in relation to the medical treatment of children who are dying and whose deaths can only be postponed for a short while. *Re B (a minor) (wardship: medical treatment)* (1981) [1990] 3 All ER 927, [1981] 1 WLR 1421 *b* gives similar guidance in relation to severely, but not grossly, handicapped children with a shortened, but nevertheless substantial, expectation of life. In the Official Solicitor's view, the present case illustrates a different category falling between these two on which guidance should be given. (ii) Whilst Scott Baker J rightly directed himself that he must act in what he considered to be the best interests of the child, in the Official Solicitor's submission he erred in that a court is never justified in withholding consent to treatment *c* which could enable a child to survive a life-threatening condition, whatever the quality of the life which it would experience thereafter. This is the absolutist approach. Alternatively, he submits that the judge erred in that a court is only justified in withholding consent to such treatment if it is certain that the quality of the child's subsequent life would be 'intolerable' to the child, 'bound to be full of pain and suffering' and 'demonstrably . . . so awful that in effect the child must be condemned to die' (see *Re* *d* *B* [1990] 3 All ER 927 at 929, 930, [1981] 1 WLR 1421 at 1424 per Dunn and Templeman LJJ). In this case, in the Official Solicitor's submission, this has not been shown.

Before considering these submissions, it is sensible to define the relationship between the court, the doctors, the child and its parents.

The doctors owe the child a duty to care for it in accordance with good medical practice recognised as appropriate by a competent body of professional opinion (see *Bolam v Friern* *e* *Hospital Management Committee* [1957] 2 All ER 118, [1957] 1 WLR 582). This duty is, however, subject to the qualification that, if time permits, they must obtain the consent of the parents before undertaking serious invasive treatment.

The parents owe the child a duty to give or to withhold consent in the best interests of the child and without regard to their own interests.

The court when exercising the parens patriae jurisdiction takes over the rights and *f* duties of the parents, although this is not to say that the parents will be excluded from the decision-making process. Nevertheless in the end the responsibility for the decision whether to give or to withhold consent is that of the court alone.

It follows from this that a child who is a ward of court should be treated medically in exactly the same way as one who is not, the only difference being that the doctors will be looking to the court rather than to the parents for any necessary consents. *g*

No one can *dictate* the treatment to be given to the child, neither court, parents nor doctors. There are checks and balances. The doctors can recommend treatment A in preference to treatment B. They can also refuse to adopt treatment C on the grounds that it is medically contra-indicated or for some other reason is a treatment which they could not conscientiously administer. The court or parents for their part can refuse to consent *h* to treatment A or B or both, but cannot insist on treatment C. The inevitable and desirable result is that choice of treatment is in some measure a joint decision of the doctors and the court or parents.

This co-operation is reinforced by another consideration. Doctors nowadays recognise that their function is not a limited technical one of repairing or servicing a body. They are treating people in a real life context. This at once enhances the contribution which *j* the court or parents can make towards reaching the best possible decision in all the circumstances.

Finally, mention should be made of one problem to the solution of which neither court nor parents can make any contribution. In an imperfect world resources will always be limited and on occasion agonising choices will have to be made in allocating those resources to particular patients. It is outwith the scope of this judgment to give any

guidance as to the considerations which should determine such an allocation, save to say
a that the fact that the child is or is not a ward of court is a total irrelevance.

Against this background I return to the submissions of counsel for the Official Solicitor.
His first, or absolutist, submission is that a court is never justified in withholding consent
to treatment which could enable a child to survive a life-threatening condition, whatever
the pain or other side effects inherent in the treatment and whatever the quality of the
life which it would experience thereafter. In making this submission, he distinguishes a
b case such as that of *Re C (a minor) (wardship: medical treatment)* [1989] 2 All ER 782, [1990]
Fam 26, where the child was dying and no amount of medical skill or care could do more
than achieve a brief postponement of the moment of death. He submits, rightly, that in
such a case neither the parents nor the court, in deciding whether to give or to withhold
consent, nor the doctors in deciding what treatment they recommend or would be
prepared to administer, are balancing life against death. In such a case death is inevitable,
c not in the sense that it is inevitable for all of us, but in the sense that the child is actually
dying. What is being balanced is not life against death, but a marginally longer life of
pain against a marginally shorter life free from pain and ending in death with dignity.
He also distinguished and excepted from his proposition the case of the child whose
faculties have been entirely destroyed, the so-called 'cabbage' case.

In support of this submission counsel for the Official Solicitor draws attention to the
d decision of this court in *McKay v Essex Area Health Authority* [1982] 2 All ER 771, [1982]
QB 1166. There a child suffered severe and irreversible damage before birth, as a result
of her mother contracting rubella (German measles). She sued the health authority
claiming damages under two heads. First, she claimed that if her mother had received
appropriate treatment her disabilities would have been less. She therefore claimed
damages based on the difference between the quality of her life as it was and the quality
e of life which she would have enjoyed if her mother had received that treatment. That
claim was allowed to proceed. However, the child also claimed damages on a different
basis. This was founded on the proposition that her mother should have been advised to
seek an abortion and that, if this advice had been given and accepted, she would never
have been born at all. The damages claimed under this head were necessarily based on a
f comparison between her actual condition and her condition if, as a result of an abortion,
she had never been born at all.

This court struck out the second claim as disclosing no cause of action and it is on the
reasoning which underlay this decision that counsel for the Official Solicitor relies.
Stephenson LJ said ([1982] 2 All ER 771 at 781, [1982] QB 1166 at 1180):

g
> 'To impose such a duty towards the child [to give the child's mother an
> opportunity to terminate the child's life] would, in my opinion, make a further
> inroad on the sanctity of human life which would be contrary to public policy. It
> would mean regarding the life of a handicapped child as not only less valuable than
> the life of a normal child, but so much less valuable that it was not worth
> preserving . . .'

h Later he said ([1982] 2 All ER 771 at 781–782, [1982] QB 1166 at 1181):

> 'But how can a court of law evaluate that second condition [where "the child's
> embryonic life has been ended before its life in the world had begun"] and so
> measure the loss to the child? Even if a court were competent to decide between the
> conflicting views of theologians and philosophers and to assume an "afterlife" or
j > non-existence as the basis for the comparison, how can a judge put a value on the
> one or the other, compare either alternative with the injured child's life in this
> world and determine that the child has lost anything, without the means of knowing
> what, if anything, it has gained?'

Ackner LJ said ([1982] 2 All ER 771 at 787, [1982] QB 1166 at 1189):

> 'But how can a court begin to evaluate non-existence, "The undiscovered country

from whose bourn No traveller returns?" No comparison is possible and therefore
no damage can be established which a court could recognise. This goes to the root
of the whole cause of action.'

Similarly, Griffiths LJ said ([1982] 2 All ER 771 at 790, [1982] QB 1166 at 1192):

'To my mind, the most compelling reason to reject this cause of action is the
intolerable and insoluble problem it would create in the assessment of damage.'

I do not regard this decision as providing us with either guidance or assistance in the
context of the present problem. The child was claiming damages and the decision was
that no monetary comparison could be made between the two states. True it is that it
contains an assertion of the importance of the sanctity of human life, but that is not in
issue.

Counsel for the Official Solicitor then turns to the decision of the Supreme Court of
British Columbia in *Re Superintendent of Family and Child Service and Dawson* (1983) 145
DLR (3d) 610, which is also reported and referred to in *Re C* sub nom *Re SD* [1983] 3
WWR 618. There the issue was whether a severely brain damaged child should be
subjected to a relatively simple kind of surgical treatment which would assure the
continuation of his life or whether, as the parents considered was in the child's best
interests, consent to the operation should be refused with a view to the child being
allowed to die in the near future with dignity rather than to continue a life of suffering.
Counsel for the Official Solicitor relies on the first paragraph of the judgment of
McKenzie J, but I think that that paragraph read in isolation is capable of being
misleading. The full quotation is (145 DLR (3d) 610 at 620–621):

'I do not think that it lies within the prerogative of any parent or of this court to
look down upon a disadvantaged person and judge the quality of that person's life
to be so low as not to be deserving of continuance. The matter was well put in an
American decision—*Re Weberlist* ((1974) 360 NYS 2d 783 at 787), where Justice
Asch said: "There is a strident cry in America to terminate the lives of *other* people—
deemed physically or mentally defective . . . Assuredly, one test of a civilization is
its concern with the survival of the 'unfittest', a reversal of Darwin's formulation . . .
In this case, the court must decide what its ward would choose, if he were in a
position to make a sound judgment." This last sentence puts it right. It is not
appropriate for an external decision maker to apply his standards of what constitutes
a liveable life and exercise the right to impose death if that standard is not met in
his estimation. The decision can only be made in the context of the disabled person
viewing the worthwhileness or otherwise of his life in its own context as a disabled
person—and in that context he would not compare his life with that of a person
enjoying normal advantages. He would know nothing of a normal person's life
having never experienced it.'

I am in complete agreement with McKenzie J that the starting point is not what might
have been, but what is. He was considering the best interests of a severely handicapped
child, not of a normal child, and the latter's feelings and interests were irrelevant. I am
also in complete agreement with his implied assertion of the vast importance of the
sanctity of human life. I cavil mildly, although it is a very important point, with his use
of the phrase 'the right to impose death'. No such right exists in the court or the parents.
What is in issue in these cases is not a right to impose death, but a right to choose a course
of action which will fail to avert death. The choice is that of the patient, if of full age and
capacity, the choice is that of the parents or court if, by reason of his age, the child cannot
make the choice and it is a choice which must be made solely *on behalf of* the child and in
what the court or parents conscientiously believe to be his best interests.

In my view the last sentence of the passage which I have quoted from the judge's
judgment shows that he was rejecting a particular comparison as a basis for decision
rather than denying that there was a balancing exercise to be performed. I do not
therefore think that this decision supports the absolutist approach which I would in any

event unhesitatingly reject. In real life there are presumptions, strong presumptions and
a almost overwhelming presumptions, but there are few, if any, absolutes.

I turn, therefore, to the alternative submission of counsel for the Official Solicitor that
a court is only justified in withholding consent to treatment which could enable a child
to survive a life-threatening condition if it is certain that the quality of the child's
subsequent life would be 'intolerable to the child', 'bound to be full of pain and suffering'
and 'demonstrably so awful that in effect the child must be condemned to die'. As I have
b already mentioned, this submission owes much to the decision of this court in Re B
(1981) [1990] 3 All ER 927, [1981] 1 WLR 1421.

It is, I think, important to remember the facts of that case and what was in issue. B
was born suffering from Down's syndrome and was a mongol. At birth she also had an
intestinal blockage. Nothing could be done to reverse the effect of Down's syndrome,
but the intestinal blockage could be cured without great difficulty and, if this was not
c done, the child would die. The parents with great sorrow came to the conclusion that it
was not in the best interests of the child that the intestinal blockage should be relieved,
as to do so would lead to their child experiencing 20 to 30 years of life with severe mental
and physical handicaps.

From the point of view of the parents, this was an immensely difficult decision and in
truth they were in no position to take it. They were suffering from the shock of finding
d that they had a mongoloid child and they may well have had little or no experience of
the quality of life of such a child, viewed from its own point of view. The decision
devolved on the court when the local authority made the child a ward.

There was no issue between the doctors that the operation could and, subject to the
views of the parents, should be performed. The difference of medical opinion arose out
of those views. One surgeon declined to operate saying that he would wish to respect the
e wishes of the parents and that in the light of 20 years' experience in the profession he
though that the great majority of surgeons would adopt the same attitude. Two other
surgeons said that they would operate, subject to obtaining the consent of the court and
notwithstanding the expressed wishes of the parents.

The judge originally decided to give the court's consent to the operation, but changed
his mind in the light of the arguments adduced by the parents and the fact that the
f parents did not wish the operation to be performed. This court held that whilst the
arguments adduced by the parents were of the utmost relevance in deciding where the
best interests of the child lay, their wishes (perhaps their evaluation of the child's best
interests is a better description) were irrelevant, since the duty of decision had passed
from them to the court.

This court then gave consent. Templeman LJ said ([1990] 3 All ER 927 at 929, [1981]
g 1 WLR 1421 at 1424):

> '... at the end of the day it devolves on this court in this particular instance to
> decide whether the life of this child is demonstrably going to be so awful that in
> effect the child must be condemned to die, or whether the life of this child is still so
> imponderable that it would be wrong for her to be condemned to die. There may
> h be cases, I know not, of severe proved damage where the future is so certain and
> where the life of the child is so bound to be full of pain and suffering that the court
> might be driven to a different conclusion, but in the present case the choice which
> lies before the court is this: whether to allow an operation to take place which may
> result in the child living for 20 or 30 years as a mongoloid or whether (and I think
> this must be brutally the result) to terminate the life of a mongoloid child because
> j she also has an intestinal complaint. Faced with that choice I have no doubt that it is
> the duty of this court to decide that the child must live.'

Dunn LJ said ([1990] 3 All ER 927 at 930, [1981] 1 WLR 1421 at 1424–1425):

> 'One of the difficulties in the case is that there is no prognosis as to the child's
> future, except that as a mongol her expectation of life is confined to 20 to 30 years.

We were told that no reliable prognosis can be made until probably she is about two years old. That in itself leads me to the route by which the court should make its decision, because there is no evidence that this child's short life is likely to be an intolerable one. There is no evidence at all as to the quality of life which the child may expect. As counsel for the Official Solicitor said, the child should be put into the same position as any other mongol child and must be given the chance to live an existence. I accept that way of putting it.'

Again I have to cavil at the use of such an expression as 'condemn to die' and 'the child must live' in Templeman LJ's judgment, which, be it noted, was not a reserved judgment. 'Thou shalt not kill' is an absolute commandment in this context. But, to quote the well-known phrase of Arthur Hugh Clough in *The Latest Decalogue*, in this context it is permissible to add 'but need'st not strive officiously to keep alive'. The decision on life and death must and does remain in other hands. What doctors and the court have to decide is whether, in the best interests of the child patient, a particular decision as to medical treatment should be taken which *as a side effect* will render death more or less likely. This is not a matter of semantics. It is fundamental. At the other end of the age spectrum, the use of drugs to reduce pain will often be fully justified, notwithstanding that this will hasten the moment of death. What can never be justified is the use of drugs or surgical procedures with the primary purpose of doing so.

Re B seems to me to come very near to being a binding authority for the proposition that there is a balancing exercise to be performed in assessing the course to be adopted in the best interests of the child. Even if it is not, I have no doubt that this should be and is the law.

This brings me face to face with the problem of formulating the critical equation. In truth it cannot be done with mathematical or any precision. There is without doubt a very strong presumption in favour of a course of action which will prolong life, but, even excepting the 'cabbage' case to which special considerations may well apply, it is not irrebuttable. As this court recognised in *Re B*, account has to be taken of the pain and suffering and quality of life which the child will experience if life is prolonged. Account has also to be taken of the pain and suffering involved in the proposed treatment itself. *Re B* was probably not a borderline case and I do not think that we are bound to, or should, treat Templeman LJ's use of the words 'demonstrably so awful' or Dunn LJ's use of the word 'intolerable' as providing a quasi-statutory yardstick.

For my part I prefer the formulation of Asch J in *Re Weberlist* (1974) 360 NYS 2d 783 at 787 as explained by McKenzie J in the passage from his judgment in *Dawson's* case (1983) 145 DLR (3d) 610 at 620–621 which I have quoted, although it is probably merely another way of expressing the same concept. We know that the instinct and desire for survival is very strong. We all believe in and assert the sanctity of human life. As explained, this formulation takes account of this and also underlines the need to avoid looking at the problem from the point of view of the decider, but instead requires him to look at it from the assumed point of view of the patient. This gives effect, as it should, to the fact that even very severely handicapped people find a quality of life rewarding which to the unhandicapped may seem manifestly intolerable. People have an amazing adaptability. But in the end there will be cases in which the answer must be that it is not in the interests of the child to subject it to treatment which will cause increased suffering and produce no commensurate benefit, giving the fullest possible weight to the child's, and mankind's, desire to survive.

I make no apology for having spent time on the generality of the problem which faces doctors and the court in cases of this nature. The Official Solicitor invited us to do so and if we can succeed in achieving any degree of clarification, it will be worthwhile in terms of assisting those who have to make these very difficult decisions at short notice and in distressing circumstances. However, I now turn to the instant appeal.

The issue here is whether it would be in the best interests of the child to put him on a mechanical ventilator and subject him to all the associated processes of intensive care, if

at some future time he could not continue breathing unaided. Let me say at once that I
a   can understand the doctors wishing to ascertain the court's wishes at this stage, because it
is an eventuality which could occur at any time and, if it did, an immediate decision
might well have to be made. However, the situation is significantly different from being
asked whether or not to consent on behalf of the child to particular treatment which is
more or less immediately in prospect. The judge has found that the odds are about even
whether the need for artificial ventilation, whether mechanical or manual, will ever
b   arise. If it does arise, the very fact that it has arisen will mean that the more optimistic
end of the range of prognoses, pessimistic though the whole range is, will have been
falsified. On the other hand, the child's state of health might change at any time for the
better as well as for the worse, even though there are distinct limits to what could be
hoped for, let alone anticipated.

The doctors were unanimous in recommending that there should be no mechanical
c   reventilation in the event of his stopping breathing, subject only to the qualifications
injected by Dr W and accepted by the judge that in the event of a chest infection short
term manual ventilation would be justified and that in the event of the child stopping
breathing the provisional decision to abstain from mechanical ventilation could and
should be revised, if this seemed appropriate to the doctors caring for him in the then
prevailing clinical situation.
d   There can be no criticism of the judge for indorsing this approach on the footing that
he was thereby abdicating his responsibility and leaving it to the doctors to decide. He
had reviewed and considered the basis of the doctors' views and recommendations in the
greatest detail and with the greatest care. Nothing could be more inimical to the interests
of the child than the judge should make an order which restricted the doctors' freedom
to revise their present view in favour of more active means to preserve the life of the
e   child, if the situation changed and this then seemed to them to be appropriate.

The basis of the doctors' recommendations, approved by the judge, was that mechanical
ventilation is itself an invasive procedure which, together with its essential accompani-
ments, such as the introduction of a naso-gastric tube, drips which have to be resited and
constant blood sampling, would cause the child distress. Furthermore, the procedures
f   involve taking active measures which carry their own hazards, not only to life but in
terms of causing even greater brain damage. This had to be balanced against what could
possibly be achieved by the adoption of such active treatment. The chances of preserving
the child's life might be improved, although even this was not certain and account had
to be taken of the extremely poor quality of life at present enjoyed by the child, the fact
that he had already been ventilated for exceptionally long periods, the unfavourable
g   prognosis with or without ventilation and a recognition that if the question of
reventilation ever arose, his situation would have deteriorated still further.

I can detect no error in the judge's approach and in principle would affirm his decision.
This is subject to two qualifications. (i) Although all concerned have, as they know,
liberty to apply to the judge at any time and he had arranged to review his decision in
December, I think that he should have asked for periodic reports meanwhile on J's
h   condition, so that he could, if he thought it appropriate, review the matter before then
of his own motion. (ii) I do not think that his order should have been in the form of 'The
[local authority] shall direct the relevant health authority to continue to treat . . .' because
neither the court in wardship proceedings nor, I think, a local authority having care and
control of the baby is able to require the authority to follow a particular course of
treatment. What the court can do is to withhold consent to treatment of which it
j   disapproves and it can express its approval of other treatment proposed by the authority
and its doctors. There is ample precedent for the judge's formula, but I think that it is
wrong and obscures the co-operative nature of the relationship between court and
medical authorities. I would prefer 'Approval is given to the continuance of the treatment
of . . .'

I would continue the order restraining identification of the ward, his parents, his carers
or his whereabouts made by Scott Baker J.

Subject to the minor variations in his order which I propose, I would dismiss the appeal.

a

BALCOMBE LJ. This appeal from an order dated 11 October 1990 made by Scott Baker J sitting in chambers raises again the question of the nature of medical treatment to be given to, or withheld from, a seriously handicapped child who is a ward of court. Questions of this nature have previously been considered by this court in *Re B (a minor) (wardship: medical treatment)* (1981) [1990] 3 All ER 927, [1981] 1 WLR 1421 and *Re C (a minor) (wardship: medical treatment)* [1989] 2 All ER 782, [1990] Fam 26 and by the Supreme Court of British Columbia in *Re Superintendent of Family and Child Service and Dawson* (1983) 145 DLR (3d) 610. We were told that there have been similar cases before courts in the United States of America but we were not referred to any of those cases. The cases are invariably tragic and difficult.

b

Baby J, the ward in the present case, was born on 28 May 1990, some 12 weeks premature. Lord Donaldson MR, whose judgment I have had the advantage of reading in draft, summarises J's medical history to date, and I need not repeat it here in any detail. However, it is relevant to note that J has already been ventilated on two occasions for a total period of about six weeks and the judge found, on the evidence he heard, that this is itself exceptional. The present position of J is that he suffered very severe brain damage around the time of his birth which is permanent, and the brain tissue then lost is irreplaceable. The consensus of the medical evidence is that J is likely to develop serious spastic quadriplegia (paralysis of both arms and both legs), and it is likely that he will be both blind and deaf. While he may be able to make sounds, he is unlikely to be able to speak. It is unlikely that he will develop even limited intellectual abilities. He is epileptic. He can probably feel pain, which is a very basic response. His life expectancy is uncertain: none of the doctors expects him to live beyond his late 'teens and all expect him to die before then, though he may survive for a few years. In so far as there is any doubt as to the prognosis any further collapse which might lead to ventilation points to the pessimistic end of the scale. However, and this is where the present case differs from that of *Re C*, J is neither on the point of death or dying.

c

d

e

As J is a ward of court no major step in his life may be taken without the leave of the court. J has already stopped breathing on a number of occasions during his short life and while at the moment he appears to be stable a crisis could occur again at any time. The doctors who are responsible for his care are concerned to know what treatment they should then give him if he again collapses since a decision might have to be made within minutes: an hour could be too long. All three doctors who gave evidence before the judge were unanimous that they would not wish to give J further prolonged ventilation and intensive care, although one thought it conceivable that a situation might arise where very short term ventilation might be appropriate.

f

g

Ventilation is a procedure that is invasive to the child and which carries its own hazards. No doctor would subject a child to it if it were not for the good of that child. In J's case, if further ventilation were necessary, he would have to be fed by a nasogastric tube or intravenously; the latter method would probably be the safer. Drips have to be resited from time to time. Constant blood sampling is necessary to ensure that the oxygen levels are neither too high nor too low. External cardiac massage may be necessary with the injection of drugs directly into the heart. There are no half measures to intensive support and the evidence was that there is a risk that these procedures may cause significant distress to J who is thought to feel pin pricks and other forms of pain. There is also the risk that the ventilation procedure itself could affect J's condition and hence the prognosis as to his future.

h

j

On this evidence the judge held that the doctors should not be required to keep J, 'this gravely damaged child', alive by yet further prolonged ventilation. He also held that, in view of the urgency with which any decision would have to be taken, it was not necessary to come back to the court for a ruling in the event of a further collapse on the part of J. From this order the Official Solicitor, as J's guardian ad litem, has appealed to this court. The appeal has been presented as raising important questions of principle; it is possible

that the precise wording of the order made by the judge may require consideration, but
a I propose first to consider the issues of principle.

Before I do so, however, I should mention the position of J's parents. J's mother has
many problems and cannot cope on her own. J's father has a better comprehension of
what is here at stake. The parents have at times been prepared to accept the doctors'
recommendations, as indorsed by the judge, but at other times have followed the line
taken by the Official Solicitor. Before us the parents' counsel said (on the instructions of
b the father who was present in court) that the father wants J to have any chance there may
be. This is a wholly understandable attitude, but not one which is of direct assistance to
this court in the decision we now have to make.

Counsel for the Official Solicitor presented his argument on two alternative bases. The
first, or 'absolute', submission was that, save in a case where the ward is already terminally
ill (as in Re C), the court can never be justified in approving the withholding of life-
c saving treatment on the basis of the quality of the ward's life. The second, or 'qualified',
submission was that the court can only approve the withholding of life-saving treatment
if it is certain that the life of the child is going to be so intolerable that, on the facts of the
case, the court was justified in reaching so drastic a conclusion; that there was here no
sufficient finding of fact by the judge, or evidence before him, which entitled him to
make the order which he did.

d Before I consider these two submissions I should state certain general principles. The
origin of wardship as it is at present understood lies in the concept that the sovereign as
parens patriae has a duty to protect his subjects, particularly those such as children who
are unable to protect themselves. This duty was entrusted to the Lord Chancellor and
through him to the Court of Chancery; it is now entrusted primarily to the Family
Division of the High Court: see, generally, Lowe and White *Wards of Court* (2nd edn,
e 1986) pp 3–5. Further:

> 'There is no doubt that, in the exercise of its wardship jurisdiction, the first and
> paramount consideration is the well-being, welfare, or interests (each expression
> occasionally used, but each, for this purpose, synonymous) of the human being
> concerned, that is the ward herself or himself . . . In particular there is no issue of
f > public policy other than the application of the above principle which can conceivably
> be taken into account . . .'

(See *Re B (a minor) (wardship: sterilisation)* [1987] 2 All ER 206 at 212, [1988] AC 199 at
202 per Lord Hailsham LC.)

In deciding in any given case what is in the best interests of the ward, the court adopts
the same attitude as a responsible parent would do in the case of his or her own child; the
g court, exercising the duties of the sovereign as parens patriae, is not expected to adopt
any higher or different standards than that which, viewed objectively, a reasonable and
responsible parent would do.

I turn now to consider the two submissions of counsel for the Official Solicitor.

(1) *The 'absolute' submission*   This submission was based on the following propositions.
h (a) The court is unable to evaluate the consequence of death, ie non-existence: see *McKay
v Essex Area Health Authority* [1982] 2 All ER 771 at 781–782, 787, 790, [1982] QB 1166,
1181, 1189, 1192–1193 per Stephenson, Ackner and Griffiths LJJ. But this was said in
the context of a claim for damages by a child born disabled as the result of an infection
of German measles suffered by the mother while the child was in the womb. The basis
of the claim was that the defendants were negligent in allowing the child to be born
j alive, ie that in the circumstances of the case the doctors should have performed an
abortion and terminated the life of the foetus. This court decided that the child's claim
was contrary to public policy as being a violation of the sanctity of human life and a
claim which could not be recognised and enforced because the court could not evaluate
non-existence *for the purpose of awarding damages for the denial of it*. In my judgment, the
facts of that case, and the issues to which those facts gave rise, are wholly different from
the facts and issues in the present case, and the views expressed by the members of that
court do not assist us in dealing with a wholly different problem. In particular, it cannot

be too firmly stressed that, notwithstanding the somewhat emotive language used by Templeman LJ in *Re B (a minor) (wardship: medical treatment)* (1981) [1990] 3 All ER 927 *a* at 929, [1981] 1 WLR 1421 at 1424, for example 'condemned to die', in none of the wardship cases has there ever been, as there was in *McKay*'s case, a proposal that a positive step should be taken to terminate a life: the issue in every case is whether or not treatment which might save or prolong a life should be withheld. (b) Respect for the sanctity of human life and the requirements of public policy preclude attempts by the court to evaluate the quality of a disabled person's life. This submission also was supported by *b* citations from *McKay*'s case and from the judgment of McKenzie J in the Canadian case of *Re Superintendent of Family and Child Service and Dawson* (1983) 145 DLR (3d) 610. (c) The 'slippery slope' argument: that it is unsafe to permit any erosion in the principle of the absolute sanctity of human life.

Both the submissions summarised under paras (b) and (c) above depend on the assertion that public policy precludes any inroad on the sanctity of human life. I have already cited *c* the passage from the speech of Lord Hailsham LC in *Re B (a minor) (wardship: sterilisation)* [1987] 2 All ER 206 at 212, [1988] AC 199 at 202 which established that issues of public policy, as such, cannot prevail over the interests of the ward. In my judgment there is no warrant, either on principle or authority, for the absolute submission. There is only the one test: that the interests of the ward are paramount. Of course the court will approach those interests with a strong predilection in favour of the preservation of life, because of *d* the sanctity of human life. But there neither is, nor should there be, any absolute rule that, save where the ward is already terminally ill, ie dying, neither the court nor any responsible parent can approve the withholding of life-saving treatment on the basis of the quality of the ward's life. (For my part I would not accept that the so-called 'cabbage' cases could be treated as an exception to this suggested rule, since in deciding that a child whose faculties have been destroyed is a 'cabbage' of itself involves making a judgment *e* about the quality of that child's life.) I say that there is no such rule because there is no authority to that effect: indeed the judgments in *Re B (a minor) (wardship: medical treatment)* (1981) [1990] 3 All ER 927, [1981] 1 WLR 1421 are consistent only with there being no 'absolute' rule. I say that there should be no such rule because it could in certain circumstances be inimical to the interests of the ward that there should be such a requirement: to preserve life at all costs, whatever the quality of the life to be preserved, *f* and however distressing to the ward may be the nature of the treatment necessary to preserve life, may not be in the interests of the ward.

(2) *The 'qualified' submission*   Here again I cannot accept the submission in the terms in which it was framed, which treats the language used by Templeman and Dunn LJJ in *Re B (a minor) (wardship: medical treatment)* [1990] 3 All ER 927 at 929–930, [1981] 1 WLR 1421 at 1424 as if they had intended to lay down a test applicable to all *g* circumstances, which clearly they did not. Further, I would deprecate any attempt by this court to lay down such an all-embracing test since the circumstances of these tragic cases are so infinitely various. I do not know of any demand by the judges who have to deal with these cases at first instance for this court to assist them by laying down any test beyond that which is already the law: that the interests of the ward are the first and *h* paramount consideration, subject to the gloss on that test which I suggest, that in determining where those interests lie the court adopts the standpoint of the reasonable and responsible parent who has his or her child's best interests at heart.

I turn finally to the question which arises in the instant appeal: should we overturn the substance of the order made by Scott Baker J? We would only be justified in so doing if we were satisfied that he had exercised his undoubted discretion on wrong principles *j* or that there was no sufficient finding of fact, or evidence, which entitled him to make the order. In my judgment, the judge exercised his discretion on proper principles. There was no error in his approach and he found facts, which I have referred to briefly above and which are set out in greater detail by Lord Donaldson MR, which fully entitled him to make the decision which he did. Subject to the two qualifications which Lord

Donaldson MR proposes, and with which I agree, I agree that this appeal should be
dismissed.

TAYLOR LJ. The plight of baby J is appalling and the problem facing the court in the
exercise of its wardship jurisdiction is of the greatest difficulty. When should the court
rule against the giving of treatment aimed at prolonging life?

b   Three preliminary principles are not in dispute. First, it is settled law that the court's
prime and paramount consideration must be the best interests of the child. That is easily
said but not easily applied. What it does involve is that the views of the parents, although
they should be heeded and weighed, cannot prevail over the court's view of the ward's
best interests. In the present case the parents, finding themselves in a hideous dilemma,
have not taken a strong view so that no conflict arises.

c   Second, the court's high respect for the sanctity of human life imposes a strong
presumption in favour of taking all steps capable of preserving it, save in exceptional
circumstances. The problem is to define those circumstances.

Third, and as a corollary to the second principle, it cannot be too strongly emphasised
that the court never sanctions steps to terminate life. That would be unlawful. There is
no question of approving, even in a case of the most horrendous disability, a course
d aimed at terminating life or accelerating death. The court is concerned only with the
circumstances in which steps should not be taken to prolong life.

Two decisions of this court have dealt with cases at the extremes of the spectrum of
affliction. *Re C (a minor) (wardship: medical treatment)* [1989] 2 All ER 782, [1990] Fam 26
was a case in which a child had severe irreversible brain damage such that she was
hopelessly and terminally ill. This court held that the best interests of the child required
e approval of recommendations designed to ease her suffering and permit her life to come
to an end peacefully with dignity rather than seek to prolong her life.

By contrast, in the earlier case of *Re B (a minor) (wardship: medical treatment)* (1981)
[1990] 3 All ER 927, [1981] 1 WLR 1421, the court was concerned with a child suffering
from Down's syndrome, who quite separately was born with an intestinal obstruction.
Without an operation this intestinal condition would quickly have been fatal. On the
f other hand, the operation had a good chance of successfully removing the obstruction,
once and for all, thereby affording the child a life expectation of some 20 to 30 years as a
mongol. The parents genuinely believed it was in the child's interests to refrain from
operating and allow her to die. The court took a different view. Templeman LJ said that
the court had to decide—

g   'whether the life of this child is demonstrably going to be so awful that in effect
the child must be condemned to die, or whether the life of this child is still so
imponderable that it would be wrong for her to be condemned to die. There may
be cases, I know not, of severe proved damage where the future is so certain and
where the life of the child is so bound to be full of pain and suffering that the court
might be driven to a different conclusion, but in the present case the choice which
h lies before the court is this: whether to allow an operation to take place which may
result in the child living for 20 or 30 years as a mongoloid or whether (and I think
this must be brutally the result) to terminate the life of a mongoloid child because
she also has an intestinal complaint. Faced with that choice I have no doubt that it is
the duty of this court to decide that the child must live ... The evidence in this case
only goes to show that if the operation takes place and is successful then the child
j may live the normal span of a mongoloid child with the handicaps and defects and
life of a mongol child, and it is not for this court to say that life of that description
ought to be extinguished.'

(See [1990] 3 All ER 927 at 929, [1981] 1 WLR 1421 at 1424.)
Dunn LJ said ([1990] 3 All ER 927 at 930, [1981] 1 WLR 1421 at 1424–1425):

'. . . there is no evidence that this child's short life is likely to be an intolerable one. There is no evidence at all as to the quality of life which the child may expect. As counsel for the Official Solicitor said, the child should be put into the same position as any other mongol child and must be given the chance to live an existence. I accept that way of putting it.'

Those two cases thus decide that where the child is terminally ill the court will not require treatment to prolong life; but where, at the other extreme, the child is severely handicapped although not intolerably so and treatment for a discrete condition can enable life to continue for an appreciable period, albeit subject to that severe handicap, the treatment should be given.

I should say that, in my view, the phrase 'condemned to die' which occurs twice in the passage cited from the judgment of Templeman LJ is more emotive than accurate. As already indicated, the court in these cases has to decide, not whether to end life, but whether to prolong it by treatment without which death would ensue from natural causes.

It is to be noted that Templeman LJ did not say, even obiter, that where the child's life would be bound to be full of pain and suffering there would come a point at which the court should rule against prolonging life by treatment. He went no further than to say there may be cases where the court might take that view.

This leads to the arguments presented by counsel for the Official Solicitor. His first submission propounded an absolute test, that, except where the ward is terminally ill, the court's approach should always be to prolong life by treatment if this is possible, regardless of the quality of life being preserved and regardless of any added suffering caused by the treatment itself. I cannot accept this test which in my view is so hard as to be inconsistent at its extreme with the best interests of the child. Counsel for the Official Solicitor submits that the court cannot play God and decide whether the quality of life which the treatment would give the child is better or worse than death. He referred to dicta in *McKay v Essex Area Health Authority* [1982] 2 All ER 771, [1982] QB 1166. That case involved a quite different situation since a claim was being made for damages for negligence against doctors for allowing a gravely damaged infant plaintiff to be born at all after his mother had contracted German measles. The exercise of weighing the disability against the alternative of not being born at all was, therefore, in a damages context. But Stephenson LJ said ([1982] 2 All ER 771 at 781, [1982] QB 1166 at 1180):

'Like this court when it had to consider the interests of a child born with Down's syndrome in *Re B (a minor) (wardship: medical treatment)* ([1990] 3 All ER 927, [1981] 1 WLR 1421), I would not answer until it is necessary to do so the question whether the life of a child could be so certainly "awful" and "intolerable" that it would be in its best interests to end it and it might be considered that it had a right to be put to death.'

Again there is reference in that passage to the possibility of a child being 'put to death'. I repeat, because of its importance, the debate here is not about terminating life but solely whether to withhold treatment designed to prevent death from natural causes.

Ackner LJ said ([1982] 2 All ER 771 at 787, [1982] QB 1166 at 1189):

'But how can a court begin to evaluate non-existence, "The undiscovered country from whose bourn no traveller returns?" No comparison is possible and therefore no damage can be established which a court could recognise.'

Despite the court's inability to compare a life afflicted by the most severe disability with death, the unknown, I am of the view that there must be extreme cases in which the court is entitled to say: 'The life which this treatment would prolong would be so cruel as to be intolerable.' If, for example, a child was so damaged as to have negligible use of its faculties and the only way of preserving its life was by the continuous

administration of extremely painful treatment such that the child either would be in
a continuous agony or would have to be so sedated continuously as to have no conscious
life at all, I cannot think counsel's absolute test should apply to require the treatment to
be given. In those circumstances, without there being any question of deliberately
ending the life or shortening it, I consider the court is entitled in the best interests of the
child to say that deliberate steps should not be taken artificially to prolong its miserable
life span.

b Once the absolute test is rejected, the proper criteria must be a matter of degree. At
what point in the scale of disability and suffering ought the court to hold that the best
interests of the child do not require further endurance to be imposed by positive
treatment to prolong its life? Clearly, to justify withholding treatment, the circumstances
would have to be extreme. Counsel for the Official Solicitor submitted that if the court
rejected his absolute test, then at least it would have 'to be certain that the life of the
c child, were the treatment to be given, would be intolerably awful'.

I consider that the correct approach is for the court to judge the quality of life the child
would have to endure if given the treatment and decide whether in all the circumstances
such a life would be so afflicted as to be intolerable to that child. I say 'to that child'
because the test should not be whether the life would be tolerable to the decider. The test
must be whether the child in question, if capable of exercising sound judgment, would
d consider the life tolerable. This is the approach adopted by McKenzie J in *Re Superintendent
of Family and Child Service and Dawson* (1983) 145 DLR (3d) 610 at 620–621 in the passage
cited with approval by Lord Donaldson MR. It takes account of the strong instinct to
preserve one's life even in circumstances which an outsider, not himself at risk of death,
might consider unacceptable. The circumstances to be considered would, in appropriate
cases, include the degree of existing disability and any additional suffering or aggravation
e of the disability which the treatment itself would superimpose. In an accident case, as
opposed to one involving disablement from birth, the child's pre-accident quality of life
and its perception of what has been lost may also be factors relevant to whether the
residual life would be intolerable to that child.

Counsel for the Official Solicitor argued that, before deciding against treatment, the
court would have to be *certain* that the circumstances of the child's future would comply
f with the extreme requirements to justify that decision. Certainty as to the future is
beyond human judgment. The courts have not, even in the trial of capital offences,
required certainty of proof. But, clearly, the court must be satisfied to a high degree of
probability.

In the present case, the doctors were unanimous that in his present condition, J should
not be put back on to a mechanical ventilator. That condition is very grave indeed. I do
g not repeat the description of it given by Lord Donaldson MR. In reaching his conclusion,
the judge no doubt had three factors in mind. First, the severe lack of capacity of the
child in all his faculties which even without any further complication would make his
existence barely sentient. Second, that, if further mechanical ventilation were to be
required, that very fact would involve the risk of a deterioration in B's condition, because
h of further brain damage flowing from the interruption of breathing. Third, all the
doctors drew attention to the invasive nature of mechanical ventilation and the intensive
care required to accompany it. They stressed the unpleasant and distressing nature of
that treatment. To add such distress and the risk of further deterioration to an already
appalling catalogue of disabilities was clearly capable in my judgment of producing a
quality of life which justified the stance of the doctors and the judge's conclusion. I
j therefore agree that, subject to the minor variations to the judge's order proposed by
Lord Donaldson MR, this appeal should be dismissed.

Appeal dismissed. No order for costs.

Mary Rose Plummer   Barrister.

Richard Saunders & Partners (a firm) v Eastglen Ltd

QUEEN'S BENCH DIVISION

HIS HONOUR JUDGE DOBRY QC SITTING AS A JUDGE OF THE HIGH COURT

27 JUNE, 4 JULY 1989

Evidence – Exchange of witnesses' statements – Statement of oral evidence – Direction by court – Application for order for exchange before trial of written statements of oral evidence – Factors to be considered by court in deciding whether to order exchange of witness statements – Whether exchange limited to cases involving source or technical evidence – Whether order for exchange limited to specialised courts – RSC Ord 38, r 2A.

Where a party seeks an order under RSC Ord 38, r 2A[a] for the exchange of witness statements of all oral evidence which the parties intend to lead at trial, the normal practice in all divisions of the High Court is for the court to order simultaneous exchange of proofs of oral evidence irrespective of whether the evidence is technical or is source material, unless it is inappropriate for such an order to be made. However, the court will not make an order under Ord 38, r 2A in cases in which the full disclosure principle does not apply, eg where fraud is alleged and it may be necessary to preserve the element of surprise regarding witnesses and their evidence, where the exchange of proofs of oral evidence would be oppressive because there would be great difficulty and expense in obtaining a statement from a particular witness, or where the application is made too late and the preparation of witness statements immediately prior to the trial would add to rather than save costs thereby defeating one of the main purposes of r 2A (see p 949 *g h* and p 950 *j* to 951 *a g* to *j*, post).

Comfort Hotels Ltd v Wembley Stadium Ltd (Silkin and ors, third parties) [1988] 3 All ER 53 considered.

Notes

For exchange of witnesses' statements, see Supplement to 37 Halsbury's Laws (4th edn) para 457A.

Cases referred to in judgment

Ballantine (George) & Son Ltd v FER Dixon & Son Ltd [1974] 2 All ER 503, [1974] 1 WLR 1125.

Comfort Hotels Ltd v Wembley Stadium Ltd (Silkin and ors, third parties) [1988] 3 All ER 53, [1988] 1 WLR 872.

Naylor v Preston Area Health Authority [1987] 2 All ER 353, [1987] 1 WLR 958, CA.

White & Co v Credit Reform Association and Credit Index Ltd [1905] 1 KB 653, CA.

Appeal

The plaintiffs, Richard Saunders & Partners (a firm), appealed against the refusal by Master Lubbock on 13 March 1989 to make an order under RSC Ord 38, r 2A that within 14 days of setting down the action in which the plaintiffs claimed damages for breach of contract against the defendant, Eastglen Ltd, the parties should exchange written statements of the oral evidence which they intended to lead on any issues of fact to be decided at the trial. The appeal was heard in chambers but judgment was given by his Honour Judge Dobry QC in open court. The facts are set out in the judgment.

Charles Graham for the plaintiffs.
Rory McAlpine for the defendant.

Cur adv vult

---

a   Rule 2A, so far as material, is set out at p 947 *e f*, post

4 July. The following judgment was delivered

HIS HONOUR JUDGE DOBRY QC. This is an appeal by the plaintiffs, Richard Saunders & Partners (a firm), from an order of Master Lubbock, who refused an application by the plaintiffs under RSC Ord 38, r 2A, as amended, for an order that within 14 days of setting down, the parties exchange written statements of the oral evidence which they intended to lead on any issues of fact to be decided at the trial. This is one of the first appeals arising from RSC (Amendment No 2) 1988, SI 1988/1340, which came into force on 1 October 1988 and, as far as I know, there was only one other decision given in open court. The master said that he had never dealt with this precise point before and recommended that his decision should go to appeal. He felt that in the present case the order sought *would* expedite the disposal of the matter and *save* costs but he decided that he ought not to make the order, possibly because of the far-reaching effect on all litigation in the High Court.

Paragraph (1) of r 2A prior to the amendment read as follows:

'This rule applies to any cause or matter which is proceeding in the Chancery Division, the Commercial Court, the Admiralty Court or as official referees' business, and in this rule "the court" includes an official referee.'

I shall read the amended paragraph presently but must refer at this stage, somewhat out of context, to the amending rules, which read as follows. I will only cite rr 2 and 3 of the rules under the heading of 'Exchange of witnesses' statements'. Rule 2: 'Order 38, rule 2A shall be amended by omitting paragraph (1).' Rule 3: 'Order 38, rule 2A shall be further amended by deleting the words "to which this rule applies" in paragraph (2).' The first paragraph of r 2A now reads:

'At any stage in any cause or matter, the Court may, if it thinks fit for the purpose of disposing fairly and expeditiously of the cause or matter and saving costs, direct any party to serve on the other parties, on such terms as the Court shall think just, written statements of the oral evidence which the party intends to lead on any issues of fact to be decided at the trial.'

As an aid to construction the following should be noted: (a) this rule applies to all High Court litigation and not to any special business; and (b) the purpose of an exchange order is to dispose fairly *and* expeditiously of the cause or matter *and* saving costs. The meaning of para (2) itself is plain: the aim is expedition and saving costs if the exchange is not unfair in the particular circumstances of the case.

Paragraph (3) adds flexibility to this streamlining procedure: different directions may be given for some issues of fact or for different witnesses. It means that some issues may be too delicate for pre-trial disclosure; and in other cases exchange may be restricted by exclusion of highly controversial witnesses. Further, the court may require that a written statement be signed by the intended witness, and also that statements be filed with the court.

There are safeguards and procedural aids: where a witness whose statement had been exchanged is not called, the statement may not be put in evidence (para (4)); and normally no evidence-in-chief not contained in the statement can be added. The statement itself or part of it can stand as evidence-in-chief; whether or not this is ordered, the statement may be used in cross-examination.

By way of explanation of the objects of the order, part of *The Supreme Court Practice 1988* vol 1, para 38/2A/2 should be cited in full:

'The rule is designed to ahieve several beneficial objectives, including: (1) the fair and expeditious disposal of proceedings and the saving of costs (para. (2)). It is aimed at accelerating the process and reducing costs in the fair disposal of actions in the High court; (2) the elimination of any element of "surprise" before or at the trial as to the witnesses each party intends to call at the trial or as to the substance of their evidence. The parties will no longer be able to spring or to be exposed to surprises as to the trial witnesses or their evidence, but will be required to "place their cards on the table"; (3) the promotion of a fair settlement between the parties. With all or substantially all the factual evidence before them, subject to cross-examination, the parties will be able to make a more realistic appraisal of the strengths and weaknesses of their own and each other's cases, which should contribute towards the fair and expeditious disposal of the proceedings by settlement or otherwise; (4) the avoidance of a trial, thereby saving a great deal of wasteful time, effort and cost on the part of the practitioners, the judiciary and the court staff, as well as the parties and their witnesses; (5) the identification of the real issues and the elimination of unnecessary issues; (6) the encouragement of the parties to make admission of facts, which they are often reluctant to do; (7) the reduction in the number of pre-trial applications, such as for further and better particulars of pleadings or for further discovery of documents or for interrogatories; (8) the provision of the framework whereby routine and evidence-in-chief can be given in summary form, see para. 5(*b*). (9) the improvement of the process of cross-examination; (10) the concentration of both the parties and the trial Judge on the real matters in controversy between the parties.'

The pleadings

I now turn to the pleadings. The claim and defence are fully and clearly pleaded. The claim is for damages for breach of contract, together with interest, based on an oral agreement made in May 1982 between a Mr Bell and a Mr Smith. A joint venture is relied on: the plaintiffs, who are a well-known firm of City surveyors, were to introduce to the defendant the opportunity of purchasing a particular property in the City in consideration of payment of professional fees in connection with the purchase, development and sale of the property and, further, 50% of the profits. The venture having been carried out, the property was sold on 20 April 1987; the defendant paid the plaintiffs professional fees but not the share of profits. The claim alleging a joint venture is denied.

An alternative claim for contractual payment of interest is based on a telephone conversation between Mr Bell and Mr Smith in April 1987, in which a payment of £125,000 plus interest on account was agreed and admitted to be due; and, further, it is alleged that payment of interest on the balance of sums due was implied from this agreement. The relief sought is for an account, damages and interest.

The facts pleaded in the defence are (1) that the property was sold by tender by the City corporation and the defendant secured it as the result of a competitive bid, (2) that the plaintiffs' retainer was solely in respect of professional fees and the joint venture with the plaintiffs is, as I have said, denied; the partner in the venture was Sunley Holdings Ltd. As to the April 1987 agreement, this is also denied; and it is alleged that in any event the consideration was past.

Submissions

I now turn to counsel's submissions. (a) The main submission of counsel for the defendant is that the exchange of written statements should be ordered sparingly. The repealed para (1) of r 2A applied to (a) the Commercial Court, (b) official referees', (c) the Admiralty Court and (d) the Chancery Division. There were special reasons why the exchange of proofs was suitable in those cases. 'Commercial action' is defined, inter alia, as any cause relating to construction of a mercantile document (Ord 72, r 1(2)) and pleadings should be 'as brief as possible' (Ord 72, r 7(1)). His further analysis shows why exchange of proofs is particularly suitable in the commercial list; to give one example, the judge (not a master) hears interlocutory applications and, therefore, with his knowledge of the issues, is well equipped to decide an application for exchange. As to the official referees' list, counsel makes the point that much of the evidence is expert opinion, and there is no conceivable reason against exchange of statements. Further, technical evidence falls into a special category; and the official referee who tries the case also deals

a cases in which fraud is alleged
ER 799) or other cases, such a
close to the chest might be just
in showing that the defendar
Authority [1987] 2 All ER 353 a
a case dealing with exchange
might be appropriate. This is e

b for simultaneous pre-trial disc
professional negligence. Sir Jo
360, [1987] 1 WLR 958 at 967

'... whilst a party is e
once he has put his hand
c face up on the table ... th

Orders 37 and 38 have since
and not evidence in general, b
exercise its discretion under t
WLR 958 at 967):

d 'The exercise of discre
that the basic objective
account of time, money a
as well as of a just outco
the courts must be, and i
of methods, of which a
e desirable. Accordingly,
strength or weakness of
same time enables them
to achieve a consensual

f *Conclusions*
In my view, the argume
making of the rule, rather
submissions of counsel for t
(1) First, the court's discr
matter of practice, the party
g should be made.
(2) A *normal* order is for
may be appropriate under t
(3) This is because as a m
of the cause or matter and s
(4) It follows that there i
h *is source or technical evidence*
all Divisions, not limited to s
Directions already made sh
(5) An order for exchang
principle would not apply
alleged or the exchange o
j application is made too late
the order should not be ma
There is no need to exa
the defendant accepted th
normal rule applies. As hi
cases has been rejected by

---

a with interlocutory applications. Counsel also submits that the Admiralty Court is 'a law unto itself'; perhaps 'a world apart' would have been an equally apt expression. The Chancery Division has most specialist jurisdiction (Pt II of the Landlord and Tenant Act 1954 is an obvious example) and much of it is commenced by originating process in which affidavits filed pursuant to RSC Ord 28, r 1A take the place of pleadings. Counsel also referred to wardship proceedings; but these by their very nature are so particular that they provide no guidance for practice in this division.

b (b) The analysis of the facts and issues by counsel for the defendant is important. The issues as pleaded need not be restated; they are, as he said, a 'classic conflict of facts' as to whether a contract was made. I agree with counsel that the facts are not complex or 'of some sophistication'. Thus the summary of his submissions is that exchange of proofs would not normally achieve the stated objectives because: (i) the number of witnesses will be a constant; (ii) settlement is not likely to be promoted; (iii) as to expeditious c disposal and saving of costs, the effect of r 2A(5)(a) preventing the parties from leading evidence-in-chief in addition to the recorded statement or proof will in a *straightforward* case like this result in a time-consuming preparation of proofs, an intricate process which would increase costs. He relies on what Hoffmann J said in *Comfort Hotels Ltd v Wembley Stadium Ltd (Silkin and ors, third parties)* [1988] 3 All ER 53 at 55, [1988] 1 WLR 872 at 875.

d (c) Counsel for the defendant concludes that the 1988 amendment must be construed in the light of previous practice and case law: these indicate that exchange should be ordered where there is source material which by its nature should be disclosed. And the applicant must justify the order by identifying that material. He also submitted that, if no further material, ie other than the facts as pleaded, is adduced, it will result in the exercise being vacuous; and the advantage of spontaneity is lost. As to the construction e of the rule, he accepted that, if the exchange achieves expedition and saves costs and the factor of 'disposing fairly' is 'neutral', an order can be made, but it should only be made in cases where there is technical evidence and thus a difficulty in giving coherent oral evidence.

The basic submissions of counsel for the plaintiffs are as follows. (i) Order 38, r 2A has been amended so that it now applies to any cause or matter, including any action begun f in the Queen's Bench Division. (ii) There exists considerable guidance for the court as to exercising its discretion, ie (a) the Practice Direction in the Commercial Court dated 23 October 1987 (*Practice Note* [1987] 3 All ER 799 set out, as far as material, in *Comfort Hotels Ltd v Wembley Stadium Ltd (Silkin and ors, third parties)* [1988] 3 All ER 53 at 56, [1988] 1 WLR 872 at 875–876) and the direction for the Chancery Division (*Practice Direction* [1988] 1 All ER 764, [1989] 1 WLR 133); (b) the judgment of Hoffmann J in g the *Comfort Hotels* case; (c) comparison with the construction of the relevant rules and practice in respect of discovery and interrogatories; (d) the notes to r 2A in *The Supreme Court Practice 1988* vol 1, para 38/2A/2, some of which I have already referred to. (iii) The effect of the construction of the rule and the guidance is that the court should *normally* make the order unless it is established that it would be inappropriate for an order to be made. This last submission is central to the issue. Is the *normal* approach to be 'cards on h the table' or, as counsel for the defendant argues, is it restricted to special jurisdictions and other appropriate cases such as where technical evidence is involved?

The Practice Directions
Counsel for the plaintiffs examined the Practice Directions which have already been issued. These are to the effect that an exchange order should *normally* be made (see the j Commercial Court *Practice Note* [1987] 3 All ER 799, set out, so far as material, in the *Comfort Hotels* case [1988] 3 All ER 53 at 56, [1988] 1 WLR 872 at 875–876 and the Chancery Division *Practice Direction* [1989] 1 All ER 764, [1989] 1 WLR 133). The last-mentioned direction states:

'Henceforward on the hearing of the summons for directions the master will *normally* make an order under RSC Ord 38, r 2A ... Any party who objects to the

making of such or
summons for directi

The submission is that th
be applied in the Quee
generally.

The Comfort Hotels case
   I now turn to the *Comt*
follows. The plaintiff clai
the plaintiff was appoint
for a term of ten years. T
because the party who |
second, because the boarc
was invalidated by the
transaction and, third, be
in connection with the p
   The court declined t
application was so close
other point taken by the
against the rule that a pa
made to his legal advise
contention. But the judg
the Commercial Court I
as to the exercise of juris
   Most importantly, th
made in good time, the
All ER 53 at 58, [1988]
suggested that (but for t
rejected) the case was n
rule.

The relevant rule
   Lastly, counsel for th
'may ... direct' give th
These words are split by
expeditiously of the cau
a named purpose. This
ordered 'either for the
costs'. The same words
under Ord 38, r 2A 'th
alternative ground for t
All ER 53 at 59, [1988]
   Nevertheless, notwit
some of the decisions ar
Ltd [1974] 2 All ER 50
passing-off action; the
that it should not be o
matter of discretion sin
for saving costs but w
established that in respe
v Credit Reform Associat
order might be oppress
statement from a parti

---

exercise my discretion in the defendant's favour. The appeal is allowed and the order prayed for before the master must be made.

Appeal allowed.

Solicitors: *Nabarro Nathanson* (for the plaintiffs); *Turner Kenneth Brown* (for the defendant).

K Mydeen Esq   Barrister.

Re Citro (a bankrupt) and another appeal

COURT OF APPEAL, CIVIL DIVISION
NOURSE, BINGHAM LJJ AND SIR GEORGE WALLER
5 APRIL, 23 MAY 1990

Bankruptcy – Property available for distribution – Matrimonial home – Sale under trust for sale – Exceptional circumstances justifying postponement of sale – Husband and wife joint tenants – Husband bankrupt – Wife in occupation of home with young children – Rights of creditors and spouse in occupation – Whether hardship to wife resulting from eviction an exceptional circumstance – Law of Property Act 1925, s 30.

In 1985 two brothers who carried on business together were adjudicated bankrupt in respect of partnership debts of £99,150 and individual debts of £11,353 and £12,638. Receiving orders were made jointly and individually against them. Their only assets were their half shares in their respective matrimonial homes, which shares were valued at £27,490 and £38,859. One brother was separated from his wife, who occupied the matrimonial home with their three children, the youngest of whom was aged 12 years. The other brother occupied his matrimonial home with his wife and three children, the youngest of whom was aged 10 years. The trustee of the bankrupts' estates applied to the court for orders under s 30[a] of the Law of Property Act 1925 that the matrimonial homes be sold and the bankrupts' share of the proceeds be used to reduce the deficiency on their estates. The judge made a declaration that the beneficial interest in each house was owned by the bankrupt and his wife in equal shares and made orders for the possession and sale of the houses subject to a proviso in each case that the order for sale was not to be enforced until the youngest child reached the age of 16 years. The trustee appealed against the provisos attached to the orders.

Held – Where a spouse who had a beneficial interest in a matrimonial home became bankrupt owing debts which could not be paid without the realisation of that interest the rights of the creditors would usually prevail over the rights of the other spouse and, regardless of whether the property was still being used as the matrimonial home or whether the spouses had separated or were divorced, an order would be made under s 30 of the 1925 Act for the sale of the home within a short period unless there were exceptional circumstances. In determining what were exceptional circumstances the fact (Sir George Waller dissenting) that the other spouse was a wife with young children who faced eviction in circumstances which would cause hardship was not an exceptional circumstance, but, on the other hand, the fact that it was highly unlikely that the postponement of payment of their debts would cause any great hardship to any of the creditors could amount to an exceptional circumstance. It followed that the fact that an

---

a   Section 30, so far as material, is set out at p 957 *a b*, post

order under s 30 of the 1925 Act for the sale of the matrimonial homes would cause
_a_ hardship to the wives of the bankrupts was not a valid reason for postponing the
enforcement of the order until the youngest child reached the age of 16 years.
Accordingly (Sir George Waller dissenting), the appeal would be allowed and the judge's
order varied to provide that the sale of the houses was to be postponed for no longer than
six months (see p 961 g to p 962 b, p 963 c to e j, p 964 a to d and p 965 b to d f, post).

Jones v Challenger [1960] 1 All ER 785 applied.
_b_ Re Holliday (a bankrupt), ex p the trustee of the bankrupt v The bankrupt [1980] 3 All ER
385 distinguished.

Notes

For orders for possession of a matrimonial home occupied by the spouse of a bankrupt,
see 3(2) Halsbury's Laws (4th edn reissue) paras 635–637, and for cases on the subject, see
_c_ 5 Digest (Reissue) 681, 5964–5965.

For the Law of Property Act 1925, s 30, see 37 Halsbury's Statutes (4th edn) 108.

Cases referred to in judgments

Bailey (a bankrupt), Re, ex p the trustee of the bankrupt v Bailey [1977] 2 All ER 26, [1977] 1
WLR 278.
_d_ Boydell v Gillespie (1970) 216 EG 1505.
Buchanan-Wollaston's Conveyance, Re, Curtis v Buchanan-Wollaston [1939] 2 All ER 302,
[1939] Ch 738, CA.
Burke v Burke [1974] 2 All ER 944, [1974] 1 WLR 1063, CA.
Debtor, Re a, ex p the trustee v Solomon [1966] 3 All ER 255, [1967] Ch 573, [1967] 2 WLR
172.
_e_ Densham (a bankrupt), Re, ex p the trustee of the bankrupt v Densham [1975] 3 All ER 726,
[1975] 1 WLR 1519.
Hardy's Trust, Re, Sutherst v Sutherst (1970) 114 SJ 864.
Harman v Glencross [1986] 1 All ER 545, [1986] Fam 81, [1986] 2 WLR 637, CA.
Holliday (a bankrupt), Re, ex p the trustee of the bankrupt v The bankrupt [1980] 3 All ER 385,
_f_ [1981] Ch 405, [1981] 2 WLR 996, CA.
Jones v Challenger [1960] 1 All ER 785, [1961] 1 QB 176, [1960] 2 WLR 695, CA.
Kleinwort Benson Ltd v Barbrak Ltd [1987] 2 All ER 289, [1987] AC 597, [1987] 2 WLR
1053, HL.
Lowrie (a bankrupt), Re, ex p the trustee of the bankrupt v Lowrie [1981] 3 All ER 353, DC.
Mayo, Re, Mayo v Mayo [1943] 2 All ER 440, [1943] Ch 302.
_g_ Rawlings v Rawlings [1964] 2 All ER 804, [1964] P 398, [1964] 3 WLR 294, CA.
Turner (a bankrupt), Re, ex p the trustee of the bankrupt v Turner [1975] 1 All ER 5, [1974] 1
WLR 1556.

Cases also cited

Austin-Fell v Austin-Fell [1990] 2 All ER 455, [1990] 3 WLR 33.
_h_ Bernard v Josephs [1982] 3 All ER 162, [1982] Ch 391.
Lowery v R [1973] 3 All ER 662, [1974] AC 85, PC.

Appeals

Re Domenico Citro (a bankrupt)

The trustee in bankruptcy of Domenico Citro appealed against the order of Hoffmann J
_j_ made on 15 June 1989 by which the judge (i) declared that the beneficial estate and
interest in freehold property at 24 Dryfield Road, Burnt Oak, Edgware, Middlesex,
registered in the joint names of Domenico Citro, the first respondent, and his wife, Mary
Catherine Citro, the second respondent, was owned by them in equal shares, and (ii)
made an order for the sale and possession of the property in favour of the trustee in
bankruptcy subject to a proviso that the order was not to be enforced until their youngest
child had attained the age of 16. The facts are set out in the judgment of Nourse LJ.

Re Carmine Citro (a bankrupt)

The trustee in bankruptcy of Carmine Citro appealed against the order of Hoffmann J made on 15 June 1989 by which the judge (i) declared that the beneficial estate and interest in freehold property at 109 Bell Lane, Hendon, London NW4, registered in the joint names of Carmine Citro, the first respondent, and his wife, Josephine Violet Citro, the second respondent, was owned by them in equal shares, and (ii) made an order for the sale and possession of the property in favour of the trustee in bankruptcy subject to a proviso that the order was not to be enforced until their youngest child had attained the age of 16. The facts are set out in the judgment of Nourse LJ.

Bernard Devlin for the trustee.

James Cameron for the bankrupts and their wives.

Cur adv vult

23 May. The following judgments were delivered.

NOURSE LJ. In the leading case of *Jones v Challenger* [1960] 1 All ER 785, [1961] 1 QB 176 it was held by this court that on an application under s 30 of the Law of Property Act 1925 in relation to property acquired jointly as a matrimonial home neither spouse has a right to demand a sale while that purpose still exists. That is now a settled rule of law, applicable to property owned jointly by joint occupants, whether married or unmarried. But its application depends on the whole of the beneficial interest being vested in the occupants. If one of them has become bankrupt, so that part of the beneficial interest is vested in his or her trustee, there arises a conflict between the interests of the occupants and the statutory obligation of the trustee to realise the bankrupt's assets for the benefit of the creditors.

In a series of bankruptcy decisions relating to matrimonial homes subject to *Jones v Challenger* it has been held that the interests of the husband's creditors ought usually to prevail over the interests of the wife and any children and, with one exception, *Re Holliday (a bankrupt), ex p the trustee of the bankrupt v The bankrupt* [1980] 3 All ER 385, [1981] Ch 405, a sale within a short period has invariably been ordered. It has also been assumed that no distinction ought to be made between a case where the property is still being enjoyed as the matrimonial home and one where it is not. That distinction, if it ought to be made, would be of no significance on these appeals, which relate to the matrimonial homes of two bankrupt brothers, one of whom is still living there with his wife and the other of whom has been judicially separated and living elsewhere since 1984. It should be stated at the outset that s 336 of the Insolvency Act 1986 has no application to either case.

The two brothers are Domenico and Carmine Citro. Prior to 22 October 1984 they carried on business together in partnership as panel beaters and car sprayers under the name or style of Broadley Continental Garage. On that date receiving orders, and on 15 April 1985 adjudication orders, were made against the brothers, both individually and in respect of their joint estate. On 29 May 1987 Mr R A Powdrill, an insolvency practitioner and a partner in the firm of Spicer & Oppenheim practising from their Croydon office, was appointed as trustee of the brothers' separate and joint estates.

Domenico Citro's only asset is his half share of the beneficial interest in the former matrimonial home, 24 Dryfield Road, Burnt Oak, Edgware, Middlesex, which he owns jointly with his wife, Mary Catherine Citro, from whom he was judicially separated by an order made on 4 December 1984. She still lives there, together with their three children, who are now aged 20, 17 and 12 years. In November 1988 the house was valued at between £75,000 and £85,000, subject to a building society mortgage on which about £20,020 was then owing. In a statement of affairs prepared by the trustee as at 14 November 1988 Domenico Citro's half share of the beneficial interest in the house (taking the lower value of £75,000) was accordingly valued at £27,490. Against that he

a was shown as having unsecured debts of £4,824, of which £1,069 is owed to the Inland
Revenue and £3,755 to other creditors. In addition, estimated amounts were shown for
costs and expenses, fees and remuneration and statutory interest at 4% to date, making a
total of £11,353 as the estimated amount required to obtain a full discharge in respect of
Domenico Citro's separate estate.

b Carmine Citro's only asset is his half share of the beneficial interest in the matrimonial
home, 109 Bell Lane, Hendon, London NW4, which he owns jointly with his wife,
Josephine Violet Citro, with whom he lives there, together with their three children,
who are now aged 15, 13 and 10 years. Although Josephine Citro has thought of taking
proceedings for divorce and has sought advice from a solicitor about it, no proceedings
have been commenced and a decision has been postponed until the outcome of these
proceedings is known. In November 1988 a valuer instructed by the trustee hoped that
the house would realise about £110,000, subject to mortgages in favour of a building
c society and an insurance company on which an aggregate sum of about £32,083 was
then owing. (Josephine Citro has said in evidence that she has been advised that the
house is worth £130,000.) In a second statement of affairs prepared by the trustee as at
14 November 1988 Carmine Citro's half share of the beneficial interest in the house
(taking the valuation of £110,000) was accordingly valued at £38,859. Against that he
was shown as having unsecured debts of £5,342, of which £567 is owed to the Inland
d Revenue and £4,475 to other creditors. When the estimated amount for costs and
expenses, fees and remuneration and interest were added in a total of £12,638 was shown
as the estimated amount required to obtain a full discharge in respect of Carmine Citro's
separate estate.

In a third statement of affairs prepared by the trustee as at 14 November 1988 the joint
estate was shown as having no assets to satisfy unsecured debts of £72,970, of which
e £65,272 is owed to the Inland Revenue and the Customs and Excise in respect of Pay As
You Earn income tax and value added tax respectively. When the estimated amounts for
costs and expenses, fees and remuneration and interest were added in, a total of £99,150
was shown as the estimated amount required to obtain a full discharge in respect of the
joint estate.

f Accordingly, as at 14 November 1988, the following estimated amounts were required
to obtain full discharges in respect of the separate and joint estates:

	Domenico Citro	Carmine Citro
Separate estate	£11,353	£12,638
Joint estate (half share)	£49,575	£49,575
	£60,928	£62,213

g

Against these liabilities must be set the estimated net assets of £27,490 and £38,859
respectively, leaving a deficiency of £33,438 in the case of Domenico and £23,354 in the
h case of Carmine. Even if it had been right to take the higher house values of £85,000
and £130,000, the deficiencies would still have been £28,438 and £13,354 respectively.
That is the position as between the two bankrupts. Vis-à-vis the creditors they are jointly
and severally liable for the deficiency on the joint estate, which, after crediting the
surpluses on the separate estates, would be £56,792 on the lower values of the houses and
£41,792 on the higher.

j By notices of motion dated 14 and 16 December 1988, to each of which one of the
bankrupts and his wife were made respondents, the trustee sought declarations as to the
beneficial interests in the houses and orders for sale and possession, together with ancillary
and consequential relief. Those applications came on for hearing before Hoffmann J,
who, on 15 June 1989, declared that the beneficial interest in each house was owned by
the bankrupt and his wife in equal shares and made orders for sale and possession, subject
to a proviso in each case that the order was not to be enforced until the youngest child of
the bankrupt and his wife had attained the age of 16 years. The youngest child of

Domenico and Mary Citro was born on 20 May 1978 and the youngest child of Carmine and Josephine Citro on 4 November 1979. In other words, if the judge's orders stand, *a* their enforcement will, in all normal circumstances, be postponed until 20 May 1994 in the one case and 4 November 1995 in the other. The trustee has now appealed in both cases. He contends that, in attaching the provisos to his orders, the judge erred in principle or exercised his discretion in a manner which was plainly wrong. He seeks their detachment accordingly. Although Mary Citro contended below that her share of the beneficial interest in 24 Dryfield Road was larger than a half, she has not cross- *b* appealed against the judge's declaration on that question.

The evidence before Hoffmann J consisted of affidavits sworn by the trustee, his solicitor and the two wives, each of the latter giving additional oral evidence in chief and then being cross-examined. The judge was referred to two authorities, *Re Holliday (a bankrupt)* [1980] 3 All ER 385, [1981] Ch 405 and *Re Lowrie (a bankrupt), ex p the trustee of the bankrupt v Lowrie* [1981] 3 All ER 353. From the first of these he drew the guiding *c* principle which Goff LJ stated in these words ([1980] 3 All ER 385 at 394, [1981] Ch 405 at 420):

> 'So we have to decide having regard to all the circumstances, including the fact that there are young children . . . whose voice, that of the trustee seeking to realise the debtor's share for the benefit of his creditors or that of the wife seeking to *d* preserve a home for herself and the children, ought in equity to prevail.'

In applying that principle to the facts which were before him, Hoffmann J carefully considered the personal circumstances of each wife and her children. He observed that they had very little money coming in and that Mary Citro was not well. In evidence they had both said that their children's education would be upset if they had to move. The *e* judge was clearly concerned, more so perhaps in the case of Mary Citro, that, if the houses had to be sold, the half shares of the proceeds received by the wives would not enable them to find proper accommodation for themselves and their families. He expressed his decision thus:

> 'The balancing which one is required to do between the interests of the creditors *f* and the interests of the wives and families, who are of course entirely innocent parties, is by no means an easy thing to do. The two interests are not in any sense commensurable. On the one hand, one has the financial interests of the Crown, some banking institutions and a few traders. On the other, one has personal and human interests of these two families. It is very hard to see how they can be weighed against each other except in a way which involves some value judgment on the part *g* of the tribunal. If one was considering the rights of these two wives to their matrimonial homes in the event of a breakdown of their marriages, I think that it would be accepted that, in so far as the Family Division did not order the interest of the husband to be transferred to the wife, it would be unlikely to make an order for the sale of the house to allow the husband to realise his share until at any rate such time as the youngest child of the marriage had attained the age of 16. It is of course *h* true that the vesting of the husband's share in the trustee brings a new factor into the equation. It requires the interests of the creditors too to be taken into account. Nevertheless the normal practice in the Family Division seems to me a fair indication of the way in which the court might deal with the husband's property rights as property rights, and it is after all to his property rights that the trustee has succeeded. It therefore appears to me that it would be wrong to refuse altogether to make an *j* order for sale. That would be treating the wives as having a permanent right to reside in the houses and to prevent the husband or his trustee from realising their interests. That, in my view, would be inequitable. On the other hand, I think it would be equally wrong to make an immediate order for sale, having regard to the hardship which this would cause to the two families.'

In order to see whether the judge's decision can be supported, it is necessary to give
a   close consideration to the earlier authorities. So far as material, s 30 of the Law of
Property Act 1925 provides.

'If the trustees for sale refuse to sell . . . any person interested may apply to the
court . . . for an order directing the trustees for sale to give effect thereto, and the
court may make such order as it thinks fit.'

b   One of the consequences of the 1925 property legislation is that the legal estate in any
property which is beneficially owned jointly or in common is necessarily held on trust
for sale and is thus subject to the jurisdiction of the court under s 30. From its inception
the section was one of wide application. But it seems that before Jones v Challenger it had
not been the means of making an order for the sale of a former matrimonial home (see
[1960] 1 All ER 785 at 787, [1961] 1 QB 176 at 180).
c   In that case Devlin LJ considered the earlier authorities on the section and distinguished
between those where the purpose behind the joint acquisition had been investment and
no more and those where there had been a secondary or collateral purpose, either
expressed or to be inferred from the circumstances. In the first category was Re Mayo,
Mayo v Mayo [1943] 2 All ER 440 at 441, [1943] Ch 302 at 304, where Simonds J
said: 'The trust for sale will prevail, unless all three trustees agree in exercising the
d   power to postpone.' Chief amongst the authorities in the second category was Re
Buchanan-Wollaston's Conveyance, Curtis v Buchanan-Wollaston [1939] 2 All ER 302 at 308,
[1939] Ch 738 at 747, where Lord Greene MR said that the court must ask itself 'whether
or not the person applying for execution of the trust for sale is a person whose voice
should be allowed to prevail'.
Devlin LJ said ([1960] 1 All ER 785 at 789, [1961] 1 QB 176 at 183–184):
e
'In the case we have to consider, the house was acquired as the matrimonial home.
That was the purpose of the joint tenancy and, for so long as that purpose was still
alive, I think that the right test to be applied would be that in Re Buchanan-Wollaston.
But with the end of the marriage, that purpose was dissolved and the primacy of the
duty to sell was restored. No doubt there is still a discretion. If the husband wanted
f   time to obtain alternative accommodation, the sale could be postponed for that
purpose . . . If he was prepared to buy out the applicant's interest, it might be proper
to allow it . . . Let it be granted that the court must look into all the circumstances;
if when the examination is complete, it finds that there is no inequity in selling the
property, then it must be sold. The test is not what is reasonable. It is reasonable for
the husband to want to go on living in the house, and reasonable for the wife to
g   want her share of the trust property in cash. The true question is whether it is
inequitable for the wife, once the matrimonial home has gone, to want to realise
her investment? Nothing said in the cases which I have cited can be used to suggest
that it is, and in my judgment it clearly is not. The conversion of the property into
a form in which both parties can enjoy their rights equally is the prime object of the
trust; the preservation of the house as a home for one of them singly is not an object
h   at all. If the true object of the trust is made paramount, as it should be, there is only
one order that can be made.'

Before turning to the subsequent bankruptcy decisions, I should state that, with regard
to the distinction made in Jones v Challenger, I look on the secondary purpose behind the
joint acquisition of Domenico and Mary Citro's home as having come to an end, whereas
j   the secondary purpose behind the joint acquisition of Carmine and Josephine Citro's
home still exists.
In Re a debtor, ex p the trustee v Solomon [1966] 3 All ER 255, [1967] Ch 573 the
husband's trustee in bankruptcy applied for an order for the sale of the matrimonial
home under s 30. Although the marriage was still subsisting, the husband had deserted
the wife more than ten years earlier. Goff J gave four reasons for his conclusion that a sale

of the property ought to be ordered (see [1966] 3 All ER 255 at 264, [1967] Ch 573 at 588–589). His first reason, in line with *Jones v Challenger* and *Rawlings v Rawlings* [1964] 2 All ER 804, [1964] P 398, was that the marriage, thought not legally at an end, was in fact virtually so. His fourth reason was ([1966] 3 All ER 255 at 264, [1967] Ch 573 at 589):

> '. . . because this is not a question between the husband and the wife, but between the wife and the trustee in bankruptcy on behalf of the husband's creditors.'

In *Boydell v Gillespie* (1970) 216 EG 1505 the husband had executed a deed of arrangement whereby he assigned to a trustee for his creditors a number of interests, including his half share of the beneficial interest in the matrimonial home where he and his wife were living. On the application of the trustee, Plowman J ordered a sale of all the properties, including the matrimonial home. He distinguished an earlier decision, *Re Hardy's Trust, Sutherst v Sutherst* (1970) 114 SJ 864, where it had been the simple case of a dispute between husband and wife, and continued (at 1507):

> 'Here it was not the husband who was trying to get the wife out of the matrimonial home; it was a husband and wife who were united in trying to prevent the trustee under the deed of arrangement from selling the house with vacant possession for the benefit of [the husband's] creditors. There was no dispute in the matter as between the defendants themselves. He [his Lordship] did not think that [the wife] was entitled to pray this doctrine in aid for the purpose of depriving [the husband's] creditors of their rights under the deed of arrangement.'

Re Turner (a bankrupt), ex p the trustee of the bankrupt v Turner [1975] 1 All ER 5, [1974] 1 WLR 1556, another decision of Goff J, was also a case where a bankrupt husband was living with his wife in the matrimonial home. The husband's trustee in bankruptcy sought an order for sale. The trustee was represented by counsel, but the husband and wife appeared in person. In applying the guiding principle, Goff J thought that the trustee's claim based on his statutory duty gave him the stronger claim and required his voice to be treated as the one which ought to prevail in equity. The judge found support in *Boydell v Gillespie* (1970) 216 EG 1505, although he observed that it did not appear whether *Jones v Challenger* [1960] 1 All ER 785, [1961] 1 QB 176 and *Solomon* case's had been brought to Plowman J's attention. Having quoted from the report of Plowman J's judgment, Goff J continued ([1975] 1 All ER 5 at 8, [1974] 1 WLR 1556 at 1559):

> 'Plowman J there rejected the claim of the wife to pray in aid the doctrine of *Re Hardy's Trust* and I think that I ought to follow the conclusion of Plowman J and say that, in the circumstances of this case, the wife is not entitled to pray in aid the *Jones v Challenger* line of cases, and is not entitled to deprive the husband's creditors in the bankruptcy of their share in the matrimonial home.'

Re Densham (a bankrupt), ex p the trustee of the bankrupt v Densham [1975] 3 All ER 726, [1975] 1 WLR 1519, a third decision of Goff J, was yet another case where a bankrupt husband was living with his wife in the matrimonial home, although there the wife's beneficial interest in it was less than a half. Goff J made an order for sale, but his reasoning did not add anything of general value to the earlier authorities. However, for the first time in the bankruptcy cases, consideration was given to the effect of there being young children of the marriage. Counsel for the husband and the wife stressed the possible harmful effects on the children, but Goff J, following *Burke v Burke* [1974] 2 All ER 944, [1974] 1 WLR 1063, thought that that had only an indirect bearing on the matter (see [1975] 3 All ER 726 at 738, [1975] 1 WLR 1519 at 1531).

In *Re Bailey (a bankrupt), ex p the trustee of the bankrupt v Bailey* [1977] 2 All ER 26, [1977] 1 WLR 278 the parties had been divorced in 1974 and the husband became bankrupt in 1975. On an application by the husband's trustee in bankruptcy, the wife contended that the order for sale should be postponed until the son of the marriage had completed his full-time education in the summer of 1978. The Divisional Court in bankruptcy, on appeal from the county court, rejected that contention and ordered a sale

within a short period. Much of the judgments were taken up with a discussion as to how
a   far the interests of children could be taken into account and both Megarry V-C and
Walton J, also following *Burke v Burke* [1974] 2 All ER 944, [1974] 1 WLR 1063, thought
that their interests were only incidentally to be taken into consideration. Megarry V-C
said that the matrimonial property cases were not cases in which matters of commercial
obligation arose, as in the case of bankruptcy, where the claims of the creditors as asserted
through the trustee in bankruptcy must be considered (see [1977] 2 All ER 26 at 30,
b   [1977] 1 WLR 278 at 282). Walton J, having accepted that the children's welfare was a
very big factor to be taken into account in the matrimonial cases, said ([1977] 2 All ER
26 at 31, [1977] 1 WLR 278 at 283):

> 'But when one has cases which are between the trustee in bankruptcy and a
> former spouse, or indeed, an existing spouse (because it sometimes works out that
c   > way) of the bankrupt then the situation is vastly different . . .'

I now come to *Re Holliday* [1980] 3 All ER 385, [1981] Ch 405, which, as I have said, is
the only reported bankruptcy decision in which a sale within a short period has not been
ordered. It is also the only previous case in which the bankruptcy decisions have been
considered by this court. It must therefore be examined with some care.

So far as material, the facts in *Re Holliday* were these. The parties were married in 1962
d   and had three children, born in 1965, 1968 and 1973. The matrimonial home was jointly
acquired in 1970. In 1974 the husband left the wife and ceased to live in the matrimonial
home. The wife petitioned for divorce and a decree nisi was pronounced in 1975. On or
shortly before 3 March 1976 the wife gave notice of her intention to bring on her
application for ancillary relief, whereupon, on that same day, the husband filed his own
bankruptcy petition, asking for immediate adjudication. A receiving order was then and
e   there made against him and he was at once adjudicated bankrupt. In due course his
trustee in bankruptcy applied to the court for an order for the sale of the matrimonial
home. The wife responded by launching a motion to annul the adjudication. Foster J
dismissed the wife's application and later made an order for the sale of the matrimonial
home within a short period.

The wife's appeal to this court came first before Buckley, Goff LJJ and Sir David Cairns.
f   It was held that Foster J had been correct in deciding that the husband could not pay his
debts and that the bankruptcy petition had not been an abuse of the process of the court.
That appeal was dismissed accordingly. The leading judgment was given by Goff LJ,
who, in turning to the wife's appeal against the order for sale, dealt with the position
where there has been no bankruptcy ([1980] 3 All ER 385 at 391, [1981] Ch 405 at 415):

g   > 'Where the property in question is a matrimonial home, then the provision of a
> home for both parties is a secondary or collateral object of the trust for sale (see per
> Devlin LJ in *Jones v Challenger* [1960] 1 All ER 785 at 787, [1961] 1 QB 177 at 181)
> and the court will not ordinarily order a sale if the marriage be still subsisting and
> no question of bankruptcy has supervened. Where, however, the marriage has come
> to an end by divorce or death of one of the parties, or is dead in fact, though still
h   > subsisting at law, then apart from any question how far the secondary or collateral
> object can be said to be still subsisting if there are young or dependent children,
> though there remains a discretion it is one in which, as I see it, some very special
> circumstances need to be shown to induce the court not to order a sale (see *Jones v
> Challenger* and *Rawlings v Rawlings* [1964] 2 All ER 804, [1964] P 398).'

j   Goff LJ then considered how far the interests of children were to be taken into
consideration where no bankruptcy had supervened. Again he preferred the view
expressed by Buckley LJ in *Burke v Burke* [1974] 2 All ER 944, [1974] 1 WLR 1063, that
is to say that the existence of young or dependent children did not prolong the secondary
purpose, but was a factor incidentally to be taken into account so far as it affected the
equities in the matter (see [1980] 3 All ER 385 at 392, [1981] Ch 405 at 417). Next, he
held that, where the beneficial interest of one of the parties to a marriage was vested in a
trustee in bankruptcy, the matter could be dealt with in the Chancery Division under

s 30, even though proceedings for ancillary relief were pending in the Family Division. Having then referred to the previous bankruptcy decisions, he concluded that the court had to exercise its discretion in accordance with the guiding principle (see above), for which purpose there ought to be an adjournment so that the parties could consider the position and file further evidence, if advised.

Sir David Cairns agreed with the judgment of Goff LJ. Buckley LJ also agreed and added some short observations of his own. He said ([1980] 3 All ER 385 at 395, [1981] Ch 405 at 421):

'When considering whether in the existing circumstances a sale should be ordered or not, the conflicting legal and moral claims to be taken into account and weighed against each other are, as I am at present inclined to think, those of the creditors asserted through the trustee in bankruptcy on the one hand (rather than any claim of the trustee in bankruptcy) and those of the wife on the other, taking all relevant facts, including the existence of the children, into account.'

The matter came back for further consideration on fresh evidence in May 1980. Goff LJ having died in the meantime, the parties agreed that the matter should be disposed of by the other two members of the court. In the course of stating the facts, Buckley LJ said that the value of the equity of redemption in the matrimonial home might be taken to be of the order of £26,500. The only creditors who called for consideration in the husband's bankruptcy were his former solicitors, to whom he owed about £1,260 for costs, his bank, to whom he owed about £5,000, and the wife's mother, to whom he owed about £250 in respect of a loan. Those debts added up to about £6,500 and about £7,500 was needed in order fully to discharge the obligations and expenses under the bankruptcy. On the other side, the wife would have needed something between £20,000 and £25,000 to buy another house of comparable capacity in the neighbourhood, she was without capital and her present income was of the order of £87 per week.

Buckley LJ, having said that the wife's situation was attributable to the husband's former conduct, which seemed to afford the wife strong and justifiable grounds for saying that it would be unfair to her to enforce the trust for sale at that juncture, continued ([1980] 3 All ER 385 at 397, [1981] Ch 405 at 424):

'Of course, the creditors are entitled to payment as soon as the debtor is in a position to pay them. They are entitled to payment forthwith; they have an unassailable right to be paid out of the assets of the bankrupt. But in my view, when one of those assets is an undivided share in land in respect of which the debtor's right to an immediate sale is not an absolute right, that is an asset in the bankruptcy which is liable to be affected by the interest of any other party interested in that land, and if there are reasons which seem to the court to be good reasons for saying that the trust for sale of the land should not be immediately enforced, then that is an asset of the bankruptcy which is not immediately available because it cannot be immediately realised for the benefit of the creditors.'

He concluded that the house should not be sold, without the consent of the wife or pursuant to an order of the court, before 1 July 1985, some five years in the future.

Sir David Cairns agreed that in all the circumstances of the case the voice of the wife, on behalf of herself and the children, should prevail to the extent that the sale of the house should be deferred for a substantial period. He continued ([1980] 3 All ER 385 at 398, [1981] Ch 405 at 425):

'I reach that view because I am satisfied that it would at present be very difficult, if not impossible, for the wife to secure another suitable home for the family in or near Thorpe Bay; because it would be upsetting for the children's education if they had to move far away from their present schools, even if it were practicable, having regard to the wife's means, to find an alternative home at some more distant place; because it is highly unlikely that postponement of the payment of the debts would a cause any great hardship to any of the creditors; and because none of the creditors thought fit themselves to present a bankruptcy petition and it is quite impossible to know whether any one of them would have done so if the debtor had not himself presented such a petition.'

In referring to the earlier cases, he said that the trustee had succeeded there because no sufficiently substantial case of hardship of dependants had been established.

b Finally, there is Re Lowrie (a bankrupt) [1981] 3 All ER 353, another case where the husband and wife were living in the matrimonial home. The husband having been adjudicated bankrupt in 1979, his trustee applied to the county court for an order for sale, which order was made but suspended for 30 months. The trustee appealed successfully to the Divisional Court in bankruptcy, which ordered a sale within a short period. In giving the first judgment, Walton J said (at 355–356):

c '... one must always look at the whole of the circumstances of the case, and in exceptional circumstances there is no doubt that the trustee's voice will not be allowed to prevail in equity and the sale will not be ordered. A brilliant example of just such a situation is to be found in Re Holliday (a bankrupt) [1980] 3 All ER 385, [1981] Ch 405, where the petition in bankruptcy had been presented by the husband himself as a tactical move, and quite clearly as a tactical move, to avoid a transfer of property order in favour of his wife, or ex-wife, at a time when no creditors
d whatsoever were pressing and he was in a position in the course of a year or so out of a very good income to discharge whatever debts he had. He had gone off leaving the wife in the matrimonial home, which was the subject matter of the application, with responsibility for all the children on her own. One can scarcely, I think, imagine a more exceptional set of facts, and the court gave effect to those exceptional
e facts.'

He then reviewed the facts in detail and concluded that there were no exceptional circumstances which justified a postponement of the order for sale. Although Goulding J had more difficulty in coming to that conclusion, he agreed with Walton J that the appeal must be allowed. He continued (at 358–359):

f 'In all cases where a home is the subject of co-ownership between a trustee in bankruptcy for the benefit of the bankrupt's creditors on the one hand and the wife of the bankrupt on the other, the court, in exercising its discretionary jurisdiction to order or not to order a sale pursuant to s 30 of the Law of Property Act 1925, has to effect a comparison of merits and hardship which in its nature is very difficult, because the position of creditors on the one hand and a family on the other are in
g themselves hard to compare.'

In my view Walton J, in describing the circumstances in which the trustee's voice will not prevail as 'exceptional', stated a correct test. Alternatively, he might have described them as 'special', which to my mind means exactly the same thing.

The broad effect of these authorities can be summarised as follows. Where a spouse
h who has a beneficial interest in the matrimonial home has become bankrupt under debts which cannot be paid without the realisation of that interest, the voice of the creditors will usually prevail over the voice of the other spouse and a sale of the property ordered within a short period. The voice of the other spouse will only prevail in exceptional circumstances. No distinction is to be made between a case where the property is still being enjoyed as the matrimonial home and one where it is not.
j What then are exceptional circumstances? As the cases show, it is not uncommon for a wife with young children to be faced with eviction in circumstances where the realisation of her beneficial interest will not produce enough to buy a comparable home in the same neighbourhood, or indeed elsewhere; and, if she has to move elsewhere, there may be problems over schooling and so forth. Such circumstances, while engendering a natural sympathy in all who hear of them, cannot be described as

exceptional. They are the melancholy consequences of debt and improvidence with which every civilised society has been familiar. It was only in *Re Holliday* that they helped the wife's voice to prevail; and then only, as I believe, because of one special feature of that case.

One of the reasons for the decision given by Sir David Cairns was that it was highly unlikely that postponement of payment of the debts would cause any great hardship to any of the creditors, a matter of which Buckley LJ no doubt took account as well. Although the arithmetic was not fully spelt out in the judgments, the net value of the husband's half share of the beneficial interest in the matrimonial home was about £13,250, against which had to be set debts of about £6,500 or £7,500 as the sum required to obtain a full discharge. Statutory interest at 4% on £6,500 for five years would have amounted to no more than £1,300, which, when added to the £7,500, would make a total of less than £9,000, well covered by the £13,250. Admittedly, it was detrimental to the creditors to be kept out of a commercial rate of interest and the use of the money during a further period of five years. But, if the principal was safe, one can understand that that detriment was not treated as being decisive, even in inflationary times. It must indeed be exceptional for creditors in a bankruptcy to receive 100p in the pound plus statutory interest in full and the passage of years before they do so does not make it less exceptional. On the other hand, without that special feature, I cannot myself see how the circumstances in *Re Holliday* could fairly have been treated as exceptional. I am confirmed in that view by the belief that it would be shared by Balcombe LJ, who in *Harman v Glencross* [1986] 1 All ER 545 at 556, [1986] Fam 81 at 95 said that the decision in *Re Holliday* was very much against the run of the recent authorities. I would not myself have regarded it as an exceptional circumstance that the husband had presented his own petition, even 'as a tactical move'. That was not something of the creditors' choosing and could not fairly have been held against them. I do not say that in other cases there might not be other exceptional circumstances. They must be identified if and when they arise.

If *Re Holliday* is put on one side, are the bankruptcy cases, all of which were decided at first instance or in the Divisional Court in bankruptcy, consistent with the principles stated in *Jones v Challenger*? I will take first the case where the property is no longer being enjoyed as the matrimonial home, either because the marriage has been dissolved or because the bankrupt spouse has gone to live elsewhere and the marriage is dead in fact if not in law. The decisions in this category are *Solomon's* case [1966] 3 All ER 255, [1967] Ch 573 and *Re Bailey* [1977] 2 All ER 26, [1977] 1 WLR 278. Here it is clear that there is no inconsistency, because, even if he was not bankrupt, the husband would usually be entitled to demand a sale. His trustee in bankruptcy cannot be in any worse position than he himself.

The more interesting question is whether there is an inconsistency in the case where the property is still being enjoyed as the matrimonial home, as it was in *Boydell v Gillespie* (1970) 216 EG 1505, *Re Turner* [1975] 1 All ER 5, [1974] 1 WLR 1556, *Re Densham* [1975] 3 All ER 726, [1975] 1 WLR 1519 and *Re Lowrie* [1981] 3 All ER 353. It would have been open to the wife in each of those cases to argue that the secondary purpose was still existing, that the husband's beneficial interest to which the trustee had succeeded was, in the words of Buckley LJ in *Re Holliday* [1980] 3 All ER 385 at 397, [1981] Ch 405 at 424, 'an asset in the bankruptcy which is liable to be affected by the interest of any other party interested in that land' and that the trustee had no greater right to demand a sale than the husband himself. That argument may have been advanced in *Boydell v Gillespie* and I think it likely that Goff J had it in mind in *Re Turner*. Perhaps it was unfortunate that there the husband and wife represented themselves, because after that the point appears to have got lost. In none of the decisions is there to be found any overt consideration of the argument or any reasoned explanation of its rejection. They simply assume that there is no distinction between the two cases.

Here I should state that counsel who appears for the bankrupts and their wives has not argued for any distinction between these two cases, notwithstanding that the secondary purpose behind the joint acquisition of Carmine and Josephine Citro's home still exists.

a Having been puzzled by the point myself and having thought it right to consider it, I have come to a clear conclusion that the assumption made in the earlier decisions is correct. Shortly stated, my reasoning is this. In the husband and wife cases exemplified by *Jones v Challenger* it is held that neither spouse has a right to demand a sale of the property while the purpose of its enjoyment as a matrimonial home still exists. In order to be so enjoyed it must be occupied by the spouses jointly. As a matter of property law,

b the basis of their joint occupation is their joint ownership of the beneficial interest in the home. Although the vesting of one of their interests in a trustee for creditors does not in itself destroy the secondary purpose of the trust, the basis for their joint occupation has gone. It must, I think, be implicit in the principle of *Jones v Challenger* that the secondary purpose can only exist while the spouses are not only joint occupiers of the home but joint owners of it as well.

c   I am therefore of the opinion that the earlier authorities, as I have summarised them, correctly state the law applicable to the present case. Did Hoffmann J correctly apply it to the facts which were before him? I respectfully think that he did not. First, for the reasons already stated, the personal circumstances of the two wives and their children, although distressing, are not by themselves exceptional. Second, I think that the judge erred in fashioning his orders by reference to those which might have been made in the

d Family Division in a case where bankruptcy had not supervened. That approach, which tends towards treating the home as a source of provision for the children, was effectively disapproved by the earlier and uncontroversial part of the decision of this court in *Re Holliday* [1980] 3 All ER 385, [1981] Ch 405. Third, and perhaps most significantly, he did not ask himself the critical question whether a further postponement of payment of their debts would cause hardship to the creditors. It is only necessary to look at the

e substantial deficiencies referred to earlier in this judgment in order to see that it would. Since then a further 18 months' interest has accrued and the trustee has incurred the costs of these proceedings as well.

    In all the circumstances, I think that these cases are clearly distinguishable from *Re Holliday* and ought to have been decided accordingly. Part at least of the reason why they were not was that the points with which we have been concerned were not as fully

f argued below as they have been here. In particular, a close examination of the figures in order to see whether a postponement would cause increasing hardship to the creditors was not undertaken. That is not to imply any criticism of counsel. It is a characteristic of our system that the higher court often seems partial toward thinking that the important point is the one which was not taken in the lower court.

    Finally, I refer to s 336 of the Insolvency Act 1986, which, although it does not apply

g to either of these cases, will apply to such cases in the future. In sub-s (5) of that section the court is required, in the circumstances there mentioned, to 'assume, unless the circumstances of the case are exceptional, that the interests of the bankrupt's creditors outweigh all other considerations'. I have no doubt that that section was intended to apply the same test as that which has been evolved in the previous bankruptcy decisions, and it is satisfactory to find that it has. I say that not least because s 336 only applies to

h the rights of occupation of those who are or have been married. The case law will continue to apply to unmarried couples, who nowadays set up house together in steadily increasing numbers. A difference in the basic tests applicable to the two classes of case would have been most undesirable.

    I would allow both appeals by deleting the provisos for postponement from the orders

j of Hoffmann J and substituting short periods of suspension, the length of which can be discussed with counsel.

BINGHAM LJ. I have had the opportunity of reading in draft the judgment of Nourse LJ and I agree with it.

    Section 30 of the Law of Property Act 1925 confers two discretions. First, it confers a discretion on 'any person interested' to 'apply to the court . . . for an order directing the trustees for sale to give effect thereto'. Second, it confers a discretion on the court to 'make such order as it thinks fit'.

The section contains no express limitation on the exercise of these discretions but neither is altogether unfettered. Where a trustee in bankruptcy is a person interested, his statutory duty to realise the bankrupt's assets for the benefit of the creditors may well require him in the ordinary way to seek an order for sale of the trust property where such sale is likely to raise money available for distribution. Where the court is asked by a trustee in bankruptcy to make an order of sale, the authorities show that it usually does so (see *Re Holliday (a bankrupt), ex p the trustee of the bankrupt v The bankrupt* [1980] 3 All ER 385 at 394, [1981] Ch 405 at 419–420). In deciding whether (on the breakdown of a marriage) the voice of the trustee or the voice of a wife ought in equity to prevail, the court must consider all relevant circumstances, including the conflicting legal and moral claims of the creditors asserted through the trustee in bankruptcy on the one hand and those of the wife and her children on the other (see [1980] 3 All ER 385 at 394–395, [1981] Ch 405 at 420–421). But if the court is not to order a sale it seems that the wife must show 'very special circumstances' (see [1980] 3 All ER 385 at 391, [1981] Ch 405 at 415) or 'good reasons' (see [1980] 3 All ER 385 at 397, [1981] Ch 405 at 424) or 'a substantial case of hardship' (see [1980] 3 All ER 385 at 394, [1981] Ch 405 at 425) or 'exceptional circumstances' (see *Re Lowrie) (a bankrupt), ex p the trustee of the bankrupt* [1981] 3 All ER 353 at 355). I should for my part have inclined to think that a test of exceptional circumstances was, in the absence of statutory guidance, more stringent than was warranted (as, in a quite different context, the House of Lords held in *Kleinwort Benson Ltd v Barbrak Ltd* [1987] 2 All ER 289 at 300, [1987] AC 597 at 622), but I have to acknowledge that in enacting s 336(5) of the Insolvency Act 1986 Parliament appears to have expressly approved it.

The only case drawn to our attention in which the voice of the wife has been held to prevail over that of the trustee was *Re Holliday*. If the judge was entitled to treat the present cases as fairly comparable with that case, then his exercise of discretion may not be disturbed. But Walton J in *Re Lowrie* [1981] 3 All ER 353 at 356 observed of *Re Holliday*: 'One can scarcely, I think, imagine a more exceptional set of facts . . .'; and one must examine the circumstances of that case to decide whether those of the present case are indeed fairly comparable.

Sir David Cairns listed the factors in *Re Holliday* [1980] 3 All ER 385 at 398, [1981] Ch 405 at 425 which led him to conclude that the wife's voice should prevail). They were: (1) that it would be difficult if not impossible for the wife to secure another suitable home for the family in or near her then home; (2) that it would be upsetting for the children's education if they had to move far away from their present schools, even if it were practicable, having regard to the wife's means, to find an alternative home at some more distant place; (3) that it was highly unlikely that postponement of the payment of the debts would cause any great hardship to any of the creditors; (4) that none of the creditors thought fit themselves to present a bankruptcy petition and it was quite impossible to know whether any one of them would have done so if the debtor had not himself done so. Although less explicitly stated, the same factors were no doubt in the mind of Buckley LJ.

Whether these factors quite merit the description applied to them by Walton J may be debatable, but it is to be observed: (i) that in *Re Holliday* (unlike the present case) there might well have been no bankruptcy at all but for the debtor's action; (ii) that after the moratorium imposed by the court all the creditors could be paid in full with interest (albeit at the anachronistic statutory rate), which will not be the case here; (iii) that the sum available to the wife on sale was expected to be much smaller, even allowing for inflation, than would be available to either of these wives; (iv) that the children in that case were younger than those in these cases.

Even so, the moratorium ordered by the Court of Appeal in *Re Holliday* was shorter than that ordered by Hoffmann J in the present case.

None of these matters was mentioned by Hoffmann J. As I read his judgment, he

treated *Re Holliday* as entitling or obliging him simply to balance the interests of the
a creditors against those of his wife, the creditors' prima facie entitlement to their money
being simply one element in the scales (and not a particularly weighty one at that). I
would willingly adopt this approach if I felt free to do so. It is in my view conducive to
justice in the broadest sense and it reflects the preference which the law increasingly
gives to personal over property interests. I do not, however, think it reflects the principle
which, as I conclude, clearly emerges from the cases, that the order sought by the trustee
b must be made unless there are (at least) compelling reasons, not found in the ordinary
run of cases, for refusing it. I find it impossible to reach that conclusion on the present
facts, which I would expect to be substantially repeated in many other cases of this kind.

As I have, I think, made clear, I regret this conclusion. But we must apply the law as
we understand it, and where authority has indicated how a discretion should be exercised
in the unexceptional case it is desirable that it should be followed, unless overruled, if
c arbitrariness is to be avoided. I do not think we are free to overrule the authority relevant
to these appeals, and indeed it would be improper given the terms of s 336(5) of the
Insolvency Act 1986.

I would allow the appeal and invite submissions on the length of the moratorium we
should grant.

d

SIR GEORGE WALLER. I regret to say that I do not agree with the conclusions of
Nourse and Bingham LJJ and I will shortly and respectfully state my reasons.

In these two cases the trustee in bankruptcy is appealing against the judgment of
Hoffmann J that under s 30 of the Law of Property Act 1925 there should be an order for
the sale of the two houses but that it should not be enforced in each case until the
e youngest child of the marriage reaches the age of 16, ie in one case five years and in the
other case six years. It was submitted that there was no sufficient evidence of exceptional
circumstances in either case to justify such an order.

Although s 30 says the court 'may' make an order the authorities show that the court
will make an order for sale unless the circumstances are exceptional. There are cases of
joint ownership by husband and wife where parties have sought to persuade the court
f that the wife (or husband) will suffer hardship if a sale is ordered but in the absence of
children the court has not been persuaded.

The principal Court of Appeal case to which we were referred was *Re Holliday (a
bankrupt), ex p the trustee of the bankrupt v The bankrupt* [1980] 3 All ER 385, [1981] Ch
405, but before considering it I should just refer to three of the cases mentioned by Goff
LJ and previously decided by him, *Re a Debtor, ex p the trustee v Solomon* [1966] 3 All ER
g 255, [1967] Ch 573 and *Re Turner (a bankrupt), ex p the trustee of the bankrupt v Turner*
[1975] 1 All ER 5, [1974] 1 WLR 1556, where there was no mention of children, and *Re
Densham (a bankrupt), ex p the trustee of the bankrupt v Densham* [1975] 3 All ER 726, [1975]
1 WLR 1519, where there were children but Goff J considered that in that case that had
only an indirect bearing. Nourse LJ also mentioned *Re Bailey (a bankrupt), ex p the trustee
of the bankrupt v Bailey* [1977] 2 All ER 26, [1977] 1 WLR 278, where there was a son, but
h Megarry V-C said in that case that the evidence of interference with education was very
slight. In *Re Holliday* Goff LJ referred to the cases I have set out above, in all of which he
had made an order for sale, and said that there would have to be 'some very special
circumstances' to induce the court not to order a sale. He then said ([1980] 3 All 385 at
394, [1981] Ch 405 at 420):

j   'Nevertheless there is a discretion, and I would hear argument according to these
principles on the question whose voice in the circumstances of this case ought to
prevail, and in this connection it will be necessary to consider the schooling
arrangements at present obtaining, and what could be done if the house were sold,
but the evidence at present does not cover this very adequately.'

Goff LJ then set out the various inquiries about schooling which should be made. Both
Buckley LJ and Sir David Cairns agreed with this judgment. Although he was fully

aware of the position of the creditors and the fact that the debtor had presented his own petition, it is, I think, clear from the judgment of Goff J that had it not been for the education of the children the court would not have given further consideration to the case.

After the death of Goff LJ, when the facts were finally considered by Buckley LJ and Sir David Cairns, Buckley LJ set out fully the facts relating to the children's education. Then, after summarising the relative considerations of the creditors and the wife, he said ([1980] 3 All ER 385 at 397, [1981] Ch 405 at 424):

> 'Balancing the interest of the creditors and interest of the wife, burdened, as I say, with the obligation to provide a home for the three children of the marriage, in my view the right attitude for the court to adopt is that the house should not be sold at the present juncture.'

A decision was made in favour of the wife, Sir David Cairns emphasising that to do otherwise would be 'upsetting for the children's education' and Buckley LJ, also mentioning the children's education while not finally deciding the case, clearly thought that the education of the children was a matter to be taken into consideration, and Buckley LJ and Sir David Cairns postponed the sale for five years because 'the hardship for the wife and children would be much less or would have disappeared altogether [by then]'.

In *Re Lowrie (a bankrupt), ex p the trustee of the bankrupt v Lowrie* [1981] 3 All ER 353 the appeal against an order of postponement for 30 months was allowed but the two children were aged 3½ years and 18 months and Walton J did say in the course of his judgment that, if their schooling had been involved, it might have been different.

In this case the judge set out the interests which had to be balanced, the creditors and the two wives and their children who were very much at the critical age for their education, in Mary Citro's case one son wanting to stay at school and to do A levels and another son wanting to start at the same school. In Josephine Citro's case the eldest at school was 14. This can only have been mentioned because the sale of the house in each case would create educational difficulties. He set out fully in his judgment the situation of the families which fell clearly within the situation described in the judgments which I have quoted above. The circumstances relating to the two wives set out by the judge, the housing difficulty, education, difficulties of which were before him, and his description of their position as being 'extremely unenviable' in different words describe exactly that which in *Re Holliday* was described as 'hardship' or 'very special circumstances'. That education was a fundamental element of the judge's order is clear from the order itself, namely the sixteenth birthday of the youngest child in each family.

The judge had to exercise his discretion and he followed the decision in *Re Holliday*. *Re Holliday* was a decision of the Court of Appeal which may possibly go further than earlier authorities, but it is a decision of this court and, although Goff LJ was not party to the final decision, he clearly had in mind in his judgment the possibility of such a decision. I have no difficulty in regarding the circumstances as very special; there has been no similar case with such problems.

Although the judge's words may not have precisely followed the words of the judgments in *Re Holliday*, in my opinion he covered exactly the same points and I would dismiss the appeal in both cases.

Appeal allowed. Orders for sales of properties within six months. Leave to appeal to the House of Lords refused. Stay of orders pending hearing of petitions for leave to appeal.

Solicitors: *Stoneham Langton & Passmore* (for the trustee); *Phelps & Lawrence*, Swindon (for the bankrupts and their wives).

Raina Levy　Barrister.

a
Cia Portorafti Commerciale SA v Ultramar Panama Inc and others
The Captain Gregos

COURT OF APPEAL, CIVIL DIVISION
b SLADE, STOCKER AND BINGHAM LJJ
30 NOVEMBER, 1, 14 DECEMBER 1989

Shipping – Carriage by sea – Damages for breach of contract – Time limit for bringing action – Wrong or misdelivery of cargo – Cargo interests bringing action against carrier claiming damages for short delivery of cargo – Cargo interests alleging theft by carrier – Action brought outside one-
c *year limitation period prescribed by Hague Visby Rules for claims in respect of carriage of goods – Whether claim subject to one-year limitation period – Carriage of Goods by Sea Act 1971, Sch, art II, art III, para 6.*

The owners of a cargo of crude oil which was to be shipped from Egypt to Rotterdam sold it to P, which then resold it under a processing deal to B. The cargo was subsequently
d loaded at an Egyptian port onto a vessel chartered from the shipowners. The contract of carriage contained in the two bills of lading incorporated the Hague Visby Rules, as set out in the schedule to the Carriage of Goods by Sea Act 1971. More than one year after the cargo had been discharged at Rotterdam, the cargo interests, P and B, brought an action for damages against the shipowners, claiming that the shipowners had stolen a quantity of the oil by diverting it into a gathering space on board the vessel and not
e delivering it to B, the party entitled to it. The shipowners issued an originating summons against the cargo interests, seeking the determination by the court of the question whether the one-year limitation period prescribed by art III, para 6[a] of the Hague Visby Rules discharged the shipowners from all liability in respect of the short delivery of the cargo arising out of the alleged theft because the action had been brought more than one year after the cargo should have been delivered and was therefore extinguished. The
f judge dismissed the shipowners' summons, holding that since delivery and the concepts of possessory or proprietary rights associated with it were outside the scope of art II[b], which made the carrier subject to the responsibilities and liabilities set out in art III in relation to 'the loading, handling, stowage, carriage, custody, care and discharge' stages in the transportation of a cargo, it followed that wrong or misdelivery of any kind was outside the scope of art III, para 6 and that therefore the cargo interests' claim was not
g subject to the one-year limitation period. The shipowners appealed.

Held – A cargo owner who was party to a bill of lading contract incorporating the Hague Visby Rules was barred from claiming for misdelivery due to deliberate or negligent misappropriation of cargo by the carrier if he failed to bring suit against the carrier
h within the one-year time limit laid down in art III, para 6, since although art II defined the scope of the operations to which the responsibilities, liabilities, rights and immunities in the rules applied, the carrier's central obligation, in accordance with art III, para 2, was 'properly and carefully [to] load, handle, stow, carry, keep, care for and discharge the goods carried' and therefore any failure by the carrier properly to keep and care for goods during transportation fell within art III, para 2 and claims in respect of such failure were
j subject to the time limit imposed by art III, para 6. Moreover, the inference that the one-year time bar was intended to apply to all claims arising out of the carriage or miscarriage of goods by sea under bills of lading subject to the Hague Visby Rules was strengthened

---

a   Article III, so far as material, is set out at p 970 e to h, post
b   Article II is set out at p 970 d, post

e consideration that art III, para 6, like any time bar, was intended to achieve
ity. Accordingly, the cargo owners were barred from claiming for short delivery due   *a*
he alleged theft of part of the cargo by the shipowners, since they had failed to bring
oceedings within the one-year limit laid down in art III, para 6 even though they would
ave known of the short delivery at or about the time of delivery and could have been
ready to sue well within the one-year time limit (see p 973 *f* to p 974 *a g* to *j*, p 977 *f h* to
p 978 *a c d*, post).

Per curiam. On the proper construction of the 1971 Act and the Hague Visby Rules   *b*
the mandatory contractual regime set out therein is clearly intended to regulate the
rights and duties of parties to a bill of lading contract and not to regulate relations
between non-parties and, accordingly, the issue of a bill of lading to which the rules apply
is a necessary, but not in itself a sufficient, condition of the right of the cargo owner or
carrier to rely on the rules (see p 976 *h* to p 977 *c f* and p 978 *a d f*, post); dictum of Lord
Brandon in *Leigh & Sillavan Ltd v Aliakmon Shipping Co Ltd, The Aliakmon* [1986] 2 All ER   *c*
145 at 155–156 applied.

Decision of Hirst J [1989] 2 All ER 54 reversed.

Notes

For time limits for bringing actions for loss or damage under the Hague Visby Rules, see   *d*
43 Halsbury's Laws (4th edn) para 773, and for cases on the subject, see 43 Digest (Reissue)
597, 11084–11086.

For the Carriage of Goods by Sea Act 1971, Sch, arts II, III, see 39 Halsbury's Statutes
(4th edn) 836.

Cases referred to in judgments

Aries Tanker Corp v Total Transport Ltd, The Aries [1977] 1 All ER 398, [1977] 1 WLR 185,   *e*
    HL.
Gillespie Bros & Co Ltd v Roy Bowles Transport Ltd [1973] 1 All ER 193, [1973] QB 400,
    [1972] 3 WLR 1003, CA.
Hollandia, The [1982] 3 All ER 1141, [1983] 1 AC 565, [1982] 3 WLR 1111, HL.
Kenya Railways v Antares Pte (Nos 1 and 2), The Antares [1987] 1 Lloyd's Rep 424, CA.   *f*
Leigh & Sillavan Ltd v Aliakmon Shipping Co Ltd, The Aliakmon [1986] 2 All ER 145, [1986]
    AC 785, [1986] 2 WLR 902, HL; *affg* [1985] 2 All ER 44, [1985] QB 350, [1985] 2
    WLR 289.
Photo Production Ltd v Securicor Transport Ltd [1980] 1 All ER 556, [1980] AC 827, [1980]
    2 WLR 283, HL.
Port Jackson Stevedoring Pty Ltd v Salmond & Spraggon (Australia) Pty Ltd, The New York Star   *g*
    [1980] 3 All ER 257, [1981] 1 WLR 138, PC.
Suisse Atlantique Société d'Armement Maritime SA v NV Rotterdamsche Kolen Centrale [1966]
    2 All ER 61, [1967] 1 AC 361, [1966] 2 WLR 944, HL.
Thomas National Transport (Melbourne) Pty Ltd v May & Baker (Australia) Pty Ltd (1966)
    115 CLR 353, Aust HC.
    h

Appeal

The plaintiffs, Cia Portorafti Commerciale SA of Panama (the shipowners), appealed
against the decision of Hirst J ([1989] 2 All ER 54) given on 21 December 1988 whereby
he held that a claim in tort brought against them by the defendants, Ultramar Panama
Inc of Panama, Phibro Energy AG of Switzerland and BP Oil International Ltd (the cargo   *j*
owners), in respect of a cargo of crude oil carried by the shipowners on board the vessel
Captain Gregos pursuant to a contract of carriage contained in or evidenced by two bills
of lading dated 31 May and 1 June 1984 which incorporated the Hague Visby Rules for
damages arising out of an alleged theft of part of the cargo had not been extinguished by
art III, para 6 of the Hague Visby Rules on the ground that suit was not brought within
one year of the date when the cargo should have been delivered since misdelivery was

David Johnson QC and Nigel Teare for the shipowners.
Iain Milligan for the cargo owners.

outside the scope of that article. The first defendant took no part in the proceedings since it had sold its interest in the cargo to the second defendant on 25 May 1984, several days prior to the date of the contract of carriage. The facts are set out in the judgment of Bingham LJ.

Cur adv vult

14 December. The following judgments were delivered.

BINGHAM LJ (giving the first judgment at the invitation of Slade LJ). In June 1984 the vessel Captain Gregos carried a cargo of crude oil from Egypt to Rotterdam under bills of lading which incorporated the Hague Visby Rules. Discharge at Rotterdam was completed on 17 June 1984.

In December 1985 Messrs Clyde & Co, who had recently been instructed by owners of the cargo, complained that the ship had made short delivery. The shipowners' P & I club replied that the claim was barred by the one-year time limit in art III, para 6 of the Hague Visby Rules.

On 28 January 1987 the shipowners issued an originating summons in the Commerical Court seeking determination of the question:

'whether a claim in tort by the owners of a cargo of crude oil carried on board the vessel CAPTAIN GREGOS pursuant to the contract of carriage contained in or evidenced by 2 bills of lading ref. no. LN-A-84-42 dated 31 May 1984 and 1 June 1984 which incorporate the Hague-Visby Rules for damages arising out of an alleged theft of part of the said cargo has been extinguished by Article III rule 6 of the said Rules on the ground that suit was not brought within one year of the date when the cargo should have been delivered.'

As later amended this summons was issued against Ultramar Panama Inc, Phibro Energy AG and BP Oil International Ltd. Ultramar has never been served and has played no part in the proceedings. Phibro and BP contested the summons, which was heard by Hirst J in December 1988. He determined the question in favour of the cargo owners (see [1989] 2 All ER 54) and made a declaration—

'that the claim for wrong or misdelivery by the [ship] Owners . . . for damages arising out of an alleged theft of part of the said cargo has not been extinguished by Article III rule 6 of the said Rules.'

Counsel for Phibro and BP, whom I shall together call 'the cargo owners', accepts that the expression 'theft' used in the summons and the declaration does not properly describe his civil causes of action, which must lie in conversion (or wrongful interference with goods) and negligence. To reflect this admission, leave was sought and given to reamend the originating summons by deleting 'theft' and substituting 'conversion, or negligence resulting in the loss . . .' It is, however, the essence of the cargo owners' case that the short delivery of which they complain was caused not by normal evaporation or wastage or inadvertent or accidental loss, but by deliberate misappropriation. In their counterclaim served on 30 January 1989 and the particulars given under it the cargo owners allege that the shipowners used part of the cargo to bunker the vessel, transhipped part of the cargo during the voyage and deliberately omitted to discharge the full cargo at Rotterdam, concealing part of it in hidden recesses aboard the vessel and sailing away with that part of the cargo still on board for their own use. If it is necessary to do so, the cargo owners stigmatise the shipowners' conduct as dishonest.

By virtue of s 35(1)(b) of the Limitation Act 1980 the cargo owners' counterclaim is deemed to have been commenced on the same date as the shipowners' original action, 28

January 1987. But that was over 18 months after the expiry of the one-year time limit in art III, para 6. The shipowners now appeal against the judge's ruling that that time limit *a* does not apply. Our first task is to decide whether it does or not. For purposes of this inquiry I assume that the shipowners and the cargo owners were respectively parties to a bill of lading contract incorporating the Hague Visby Rules.

The starting point of this inquiry must lie in the rules themselves, scheduled to the Carriage of Goods by Sea Act 1971 and having effect in this country as if part of 'directly enacted statute law' (see *The Hollandia* [1982] 3 All ER 1141 at 1145, [1983] 1 AC 565 at *b* 572). The whole scheme and effect of the rules is in some sense relevant to our task of construction, since the rules represent a negotiated bargain between shipowners whose interest lies in maximum immunity and cargo owners whose interest lies in maximum redress. But I must confine my citations to those provisions which appear to be most strictly germane to the present problem:

c

'ARTICLE I
... (*e*) "Carriage of goods" covers the period from the time when the goods are loaded on to the time they are discharged from the ship.

ARTICLE II
Subject to the provisions of Article VI, under every contract of carriage of goods *d* by sea the carrier, in relation to the loading, handling, stowage, carriage, custody, care and discharge of such goods, shall be subject to the responsibilities and liabilities, and entitled to the rights and immunities hereinafter set forth.

ARTICLE III
... 2. Subject to the provisions of Article IV, the carrier shall properly and *e* carefully load, handle, stow, carry, keep, care for, and discharge the goods carried
...
6. Unless notice of loss or damage and the general nature of such loss or damage be given in writing to the carrier or his agent at the port of discharge before or at the time of removal of the goods into the custody of the person entitled to delivery thereof under the contract of carriage, or, if the loss or damage be not apparent, *f* within three days, such removal shall be prima facie evidence of the delivery by the carrier of the goods as described in the bill of lading.

The notice in writing need not be given if the state of the goods has, at the time of their receipt, been the subject of joint survey or inspection.

Subject to paragraph 6*bis* the carrier and the ship shall in any event be discharged from all liability whatsoever in respect of the goods, unless suit is brought within *g* one year of their delivery or of the date when they should have been delivered. This period may, however, be extended if the parties so agree after the cause of action has arisen.

In the case of any actual or apprehended loss or damage the carrier and the receiver shall give all reasonable facilities to each other for inspecting and tallying the goods. *h*

ARTICLE IV
... 5. (*a*) Unless the nature and value of such goods have been declared by the shipper before shipment and inserted in the bill of lading, neither the carrier nor the ship shall in any event be or become liable for any loss or damage to or in connection with the goods in an amount exceeding [a specified limit]... (*e*) Neither *j* the carrier nor the ship shall be entitled to the benefit of the limitation of liability provided for in this paragraph if it is proved that the damage resulted from an act or omission of the carrier done with intent to cause damage, or recklessly and with knowledge that damage would probably result.

ARTICLE IV BIS

a   1. The defences and limits of liability provided for in these Rules shall apply in any action against the carrier in respect of loss or damage to goods covered by a contract of carriage whether the action be founded in contract or in tort . . .

4. Nevertheless, a servant or agent shall not be entitled to avail himself of the provisions of this article, if it is proved that the damage resulted from an act or omission of the servant or agent done with intent to cause damage or recklessly and
b   with knowledge that damage would probably result . . .'

As compared with the Hague Rules scheduled to the Carriage of Goods by Sea Act 1924, these rules contain two changes relevant for present purposes. (1) Whereas art III, para 6 of the Hague Rules had provided: 'In any event the carrier and the ship shall be discharged from all liability in respect of loss or damage unless suit is brought . . .', the Hague Visby Rules provide: '. . . the carrier and the ship shall in any event be discharged
c   from all liability whatsoever in respect of the goods, unless suit is brought . . .' (2) Article IV bis is entirely new.

The judge summarised the respective arguments of the parties very fully in his judgment (see [1989] 2 All ER 54 at 57–62) and arguments to very much the same effect were addressed to us. The main thrust of the shipowners' argument was to this effect.
d   The conduct alleged against the shipowners (if established) amounted to incontestable breaches of their duty under art II and art III, para 2. Article IV bis, para 1 showed clearly that a cargo owner could not improve his position by framing his claim in tort. Article III, para 6 discharges the shipowner from all liability whatsoever in respect of the goods unless suit is brought within one year. Reference to the travaux préparatoires which led to the amendment of art III, para 6 showed that the object of the amendment (as defined
e   by the chairman of the relevant sub-committee at the Stockholm Conference) was—

'to give the text a bearing as wide as possible, so as to embody within the scope of application of the one year period, even the claims grounded on the delivery of the goods to a person not entitled to them, ie even in the case of what we call a wrong delivery.'

f   Since the plain intention of art III, para 6 was to achieve finality, the time limit would apply even if the conduct alleged against the shipowners did not amount to breaches of Hague Visby obligations.

Counsel for the cargo owners accepted that there had on his case been some breaches by the shipowners of their obligations under art III, para 2 but contended that art III, para 6 did not apply because (1) he was relying on causes of action in tort which were outside
g   the rules and therefore not governed by them and (2) the causes of action in part arose after discharge (when the ship sailed away with his clients' cargo on board) and so outside the period of time defined by art I, para (e) which ended with discharge. If a claim which could be framed as a breach of the rules were framed in a manner not falling within the rules, the time bar in art III, para 6 did not apply. The rules did not protect a shipowner guilty of intentional wrongdoing. This was a case of intentional misdelivery, and the
h   rules did not apply to that. The travaux préparatoires showed no clear legislative intention, and in any event were not concerned with deliberate misappropriation.

The crux of the judge's decision in favour of the cargo owners is to be found in his judgment ([1989] 2 All ER 54 at 62):

'Conclusions   The first question which I have to decide is whether delivery is in
j   any way within the scope of the art II "package". Article II described the various stages at which the carrier bears responsibilities and liabilities, and is entitled to rights and immunities; this begins with loading and ends with discharge of goods, with the intermediate stages of handling, stowage, carriage, custody and care in between. All these are functions of transportation, beginning at the moment when

the goods start to be put on board and ending with the moment when they are
finally unloaded. The "package" so described thus seems to me inherently inapt to   *a*
embrace delivery, which imports concepts of possessory or proprietary rights, alien
in my judgment to these carefully listed transportational stages. This view seems to
me to be reinforced by the definition of "Carriage of goods" in art I, para (*e*). Once
the conclusion is reached that delivery is outside the scope of art II, which is of
course the key article, it must inexorably follow that misdelivery of whatever kind
is outside the scope of art III, para 6, since the carrier is under no "liability" in that   *b*
respect. There is, moreover, in consequence no need for any saving clause comparable
to art IV, para 5(*e*).'

The judge found support for his conclusion in an article written by Mr Michael Mustill
QC, 'Carriage of Goods by Sea Act 1971' (1972) 11 Arkiv Sjorett 684 at 706, and in a
footnote (to uncannily similar effect) in *Scrutton on Charterparties* (19th edn, 1984) p 441,   *c*
footnote 32, and was unpersuaded by an article by Mr Anthony Diamond QC, 'The
Hague-Visby Rules' [1978] Lloyd's MCLQ 225 at 256 tentatively to the contrary effect.
Having reached that conclusion, he held that the travaux préparatoires could not possibly
be invoked to support a contrary view. Misdelivery, whether dishonest, honestly
intentional or merely mistaken, was (he held) entirely outside the scope of the rule
(meaning, I think, art III, para 6). If, however, it was appropriate to have regard to the   *d*
travaux préparatoires, he recognised that they tended to demonstrate a legislative
intention to apply the time limit to cases of wrong delivery, but held there was no
legislative intention that the time limit should apply in cases of theft by the carrier. If,
contrary to his main conclusion, wrong delivery was within the scope of the rules, he
would have declined to hold that the theft by the carrier himself was within their scope.
Very clear words would be required to cover even deliberate misdelivery by the carrier,   *e*
let alone theft by the carrier, and such words were not to be found.

We were referred to one authority not cited to the judge, namely *Port Jackson
Stevedoring Pty Ltd v Salmond & Spraggon (Australia) Pty Ltd, The New York Star* [1980] 3
All ER 257, [1981] 1 WLR 138. In that case goods were carried under bills of lading
which were not governed by the Hague or the Hague Visby Rules but which contained
a clause which provided: *f*

'17. In any event the Carrier and the ship shall be discharged from all liability in
respect of loss or damage unless suit is brought within one year after the delivery of
the goods or the date when the goods should have been delivered . . .'

This reproduces (with one wholly immaterial difference) the Hague Rule version of art
III, para 6. The goods were stolen while in the custody of the second defendant stevedores   *g*
through their negligence. There was argument on the effect of cl 17. Giving the advice
of the Judicial Committee of the Privy Council Lord Wilberforce said ([1980] 3 All ER
257 at 261–262, [1981] 1 WLR 138 at 144–145):

'Third, as to "fundamental breach". The proposition that exemption clauses may
be held inapplicable to certain breaches of contract as a matter of construction of the   *h*
contract, as held by the House of Lords in *Suisse Atlantique Société d'Armement
Maritime SA v NV Rotterdamsche Kolen Centrale* [1966] 2 All ER 61, [1967] 1 AC 361
and *Photo Production Ltd v Securicor Transport Ltd* [1980] 1 All ER 556, [1980] AC
827, and indorsed in Australia by Windeyer J in *Thomas National Transport
(Melbourne) Pty Ltd v May & Baker (Australia) Pty Ltd* (1966) 115 CLR 353 at 376, was
not disputed. But counsel for the consignee put forward a special, and ingenious,   *j*
argument that, because of the fundamental nature of the breach, the stevedore had
deprived itself of the benefit of cl 17 of the bill of lading, the time bar clause. A
breach of a repudiatory character, which he contended that the breach in question
was, entitles the innocent party, unless he waives the breach, to claim to be released
from further performance of his obligations under the contract. So far their

Lordships of course agree. One of these obligations, counsel proceeded to argue, ʋ
to bring any action on the breach within a period of one year, and the innoceʌ
party was released from this obligation. An alternative way of putting it was tha
the bringing of suit within one year was a condition with which the innocent party
was obliged to comply; the repudiatory breach discharged this condition. A further
point made was that cl 17 applied at most to actions for breach of contract; the
stevedore's negligence as bailee, however, gave rise to an action in tort which was
not governed by the time bar. Their Lordships' opinion on these arguments is clear.
However adroitly presented, they are unsound, and indeed unreal. Clause 17 is
drafted in general and all-embracing terms: "In any event the Carrier and the ship
shall be discharged from all liability in respect of loss or damage unless suit is
brought within one year after the delivery of the goods or the date when the goods
should have been delivered. Suit shall not be deemed brought until jurisdiction
shall have been obtained over the Carrier and/or the ship by service of process or by
an agreement to appear." The reference to delivery of the goods shows clearly that
the clause is directed towards the carrier's obligations as bailee of the goods. It cannot
be supposed that it admits of a distinction between obligations in contract and
liability in tort; "all liability" means what it says.'

It seems strange that the important point raised in this appeal has not been the subject
of foreign decision or learned discussion abroad, which would be of obvious importance
to us in seeking to put the correct construction on an English statute embodying an
international convention. We were however told that the researches of counsel had
unearthed nothing further to help us.

Despite the cogent submissions of counsel for the cargo owners, and with considerable
diffidence, I have for my part reached a conclusion which differs from that of the judge.

The contract of carriage here was of an entirely normal kind. The cargo owners
counterclaim as parties to the bill of lading (which I shall at this stage assume them to
have been) against the shipowners as carriers. It is a paradigm situation.

The definition in art I, para (e) does, I accept, assign a temporal term to the 'carriage of
goods' under the rules, supporting an argument that the rules do not apply to events
occurring before loading or after discharge. (See also art VII.) I read art II as defining the
scope of the operations to which the responsibilities, liabilities, rights and immunities in
the rules apply. Apart from the obligation of seaworthiness imposed by art III, para 1
(not in issue here), the carrier's central obligation is (per art III, para 2) properly and
carefully to load, handle, stow, carry, keep, care for and discharge the goods carried.

It seems to me that the acts of which the cargo owners complain are the most obvious
imaginable breaches of art III, para 2. A bailee does not properly and carefully carry, keep
and care for goods if he consumes them in his ship's boilers or delivers them to an
unauthorised recipient during the voyage. A bailee does not properly and carefully
discharge goods if, whether negligently or intentionally, he fails to discharge them and
so converts them to his own use. If the cargo owners were to establish the facts they
allege, and had brought suit within the year, I cannot see how a claim based on breach of
the rules could fail. Both the cargo owners and the judge tended to treat their claim as
one of misdelivery, but that does not strike me as an apt or helpful way of characterising
it.

Article III, para 6 provides that the carrier and the ship shall 'in any event be discharged
from all liability whatsoever in respect of the goods' unless suit is brought within the year. I
do not see how any draftsman could use more emphatic language. It is even more
emphatic than the language Lord Wilberforce considered 'all-embracing' in The New York
Star. Like him, I would hold that 'all liability whatsoever in respect of the goods' means
exactly what it says. The inference that the one-year time bar was intended to apply to all
claims arising out of the carriage (or miscarriage) of goods by sea under bills subject to
the Hague Visby Rules is in my judgment strengthened by the consideration that art III,

a 6 is, like any time bar, intended to achieve finality and, in this case, enable the
powner to clear his books (see *Aries Tanker Corp v Total Transport Ltd, The Aries* [1977] **a**
All ER 398 at 402, [1977] 1 WLR 185 at 188).

I think the cargo owners' construction poses some (albeit minor) practical problems,
for if the time bar in art III, para 6 does not apply to claims such as this it would seem the
first and last paragraphs would not apply either. But these paragraphs would ordinarily
come into play at a stage when the cargo owner knew no more than that he had not
received the cargo he should have done, with no knowledge how or why the shortage **b**
had come about. It would seem to me that in cases such as this those paragraphs might
be more than ordinarily relevant.

If one were to accept that the cargo owners could escape the time bar by declining to
sue for breach of the rules and instead framing the claim in tort, one would have also to
accept that this was permitted by art IV bis, para 1. This is a provision which the judge
cited, but did not in this context allude to or discuss. It seems to be specifically directed **c**
to answering an argument such as the cargo owners' and I think it effective to do so. The
editors of *Scrutton* p 458 describe its principal object as being to ensure that a cargo owner
is no better off suing in tort than he would be if he sued in contract. I respectfully agree.
But that seems to me to be exactly what the cargo owners are seeking to achieve.

There is an obvious attraction in the argument that a party should not be able to rely
on a one-year time bar to defeat a claim based on his own dishonesty. It is, however, to **d**
be remembered that claims such as these are made not infrequently (although how often
they are established I do not know). I would moreover be slow to suppose that the
experienced shipping interests represented at the conferences which led to these rules
were not alert to the possibility of almost any form of skulduggery. But I think the rules
themselves provide the solution. If damage to the goods is caused by wilful or reckless
misconduct the shipowner loses the benefit of the financial limitation (art IV, para 5(e)). **e**
If a servant or agent of the carrier damages the goods by wilful or reckless misconduct he
cannot rely on the provisions of art IV (art IV bis, para 4), although still perhaps able to
rely on the time bar (see the commentary in *Scrutton* p 459). There is, however, no
provision which deprives the shipowner of his right to rely on the time bar, even where
he has been guilty of wilful or reckless misconduct. I cannot regard the omission as other
than deliberate. This approach gains some small support from the Court of Appeal **f**
decision in *Kenya Railways v Antares Pte (Nos 1 and 2), The Antares* [1987] 1 Lloyd's Rep
424.

I would be more reluctant to accept the shipowners' argument if I thought it would
lead to injustice. A limitation provision can lead to injustice if a party's cause of action
may be barred before he knows he has it. But that should not, as it seems to me, happen
here. A cargo owner should know whether he has received short delivery at or about the **g**
time of delivery. With a cargo of crude oil such as this he will quickly be able to consider,
and if necessary investigate, whether the shortage is reasonably explicable by evaporation,
wastage, clingage, unpumpable residue etc. He can investigate what quantity was loaded.
If he finds an unjustifiable shortage during carriage he is in a position to sue, and it is not
crucial how or why the shortage occurred. He should be ready to sue well within the **h**
year, as the rules intend. The only reason why the cargo owners seek to found on the
ship owners' alleged misconduct rather than on the breaches of the rules is, as I infer, that
for whatever reason they let the year pass without bringing suit. That is in my view
precisely the result the rules were intended to preclude.

For these reasons I differ from the judge and conclude that he was wrong to make the
declaration he did on the ground he did. In reaching my conclusion I am not greatly **j**
influenced by the travaux préparatoires, which seem to me to have been concentrating
on a different problem, namely delivery to a party who does not present the bills, but I
hold the view, if it be relevant, that the travaux préparatoires certainly do disclose the
legislative intention which the judge found. I am pleased to find that my conclusions

broadly reflect those of Mr Brian Davenport QC in 'Limits on the Hague Rules' (1989,
105 LQR 521, of which it would have been helpful to be reminded.

There were other points raised before the judge with which, because of his finding on
this first point, he found it unnecessary to deal. These now fall, a little unhappily, to be
considered by this court sitting in effect as a court of first instance.

The cargo owners contend that on the facts they were not, and are not to be treated as,
parties to the bills of lading, with the result that they are not bound by the Hague Visby
Rules statutorily incorporated in the bills. To this the shipowners reply (a) that the cargo
owners were, or are to be treated as, parties to the bills and so bound thereby and (b) that
on a proper construction of the 1971 Act and the rules the cargo owners are bound even
if the shipowners could not establish (a).

Lack of time and the impending reconstitution of the court have deprived us of the
opportunity to hear argument on (a) at this stage. But we have heard full argument on
the issue raised by (b) and it is convenient to give judgment on that issue at once. For
purposes of that issue the only essential fact is that the shipowners did issue bills of lading
to which the 1971 Act and the Hague Visby Rules applied, whether or not the cargo
owners became actual or deemed parties to them.

Again, the solution of this problem must be found in a just construction of the 1971
Act and the rules, for which purpose further citations are called for.

Section 1(2) of the 1971 Act provides:

> 'The provisions of the Rules, as set out in the schedule to this Act, shall have the
> force of law.'

Section 1(4) provides:

> '. . . nothing in this section shall be taken as applying anything in the Rules to any
> contract for the carriage of goods by sea, unless the contract expressly or by
> implication provides for the issue of a bill of lading or any similar document of
> title.'

Our attention was in this context drawn to the following rules set out in the schedule:

> 'ARTICLE I
> . . . (a) "Carrier" includes the owner or the charterer who enters into a contract of
> carriage with a shipper. (b) "Contract of carriage" applies only to contracts of carriage
> covered by a bill of lading or any similar document of title, in so far as such
> document relates to the carriage of goods by sea, including any bill of lading or any
> similar document as aforesaid issued under or pursuant to a charter party from the
> moment at which such bill of lading or similar document of title regulates the
> relations between a carrier and a holder of the same . . .

> ARTICLE II
>
> [As quoted above.]

> ARTICLE III
> . . . 8. Any clause, covenant, or agreement in a contract of carriage relieving the
> carrier or the ship from liability for loss or damage to, or in connection with, goods
> arising from negligence, fault, or failure in the duties and obligations provided in
> this article or lessening such liability otherwise than as provided in these Rules, shall
> be null and void and of no effect . . .

> ARTICLE IV BIS
>
> [As quoted above.]

> ARTICLE V
> A carrier shall be at liberty to surrender in whole or in part all or any of his rights
> and immunities or to increase any of his responsibilites and obligations under these

Rules, provided such surrender or increase shall be embodied in the bill of lading issued to the shipper...

ARTICLE VI

Notwithstanding the provisions of the preceding articles, a carrier, master or agent of the carrier and a shipper shall in regard to any particular goods be at liberty to enter into any agreement in any terms as to the responsibility and liability of the carrier for such goods, and as to the rights and immunities of the carrier in respect of such goods, or his obligation as to seaworthiness, so far as this stipulation is not contrary to public policy, or the care or diligence of his servants or agents in regard to the loading, handling, stowage, carriage, custody, care, and discharge of the goods carried by sea, provided that in this case no bill of lading has been or shall be issued and that the terms agreed shall be embodied in a receipt which shall be a non-negotiable document and shall be marked as such.

Any agreement so entered into shall have full legal effect.

Provided that this article shall not apply to ordinary commercial shipments made in the ordinary course of trade, but only to other shipments where the character or condition of the property to be carried or the circumstances, terms and conditions under which the carriage is to be performed are such as reasonably to justify a special agreement.

ARTICLE X

The provisions of these Rules shall apply to every bill of lading relating to the carriage of goods between ports in two different States if: (a) the bill of lading is issued in a contracting State, or (b) the carriage is from a port in a contracting State ...'

The shipowners' argument was in essence very brief. They could rely on the time bar in art III, para 6 because the rules have the force of law and apply to any bill covered by art X, as these bills admittedly were. Article IV bis, para 1 expressly provides that the rules shall apply in any action against the carrier in respect of loss or damage to goods covered by a contract of carriage whether the action be founded in contract or in tort. It would frustrate the purpose of an international convention if its application were to depend on questions of privity to which (as we know) different legal systems may yield different answers. The issue of a bill of lading to which the rules apply is a necessary but also a sufficient condition of the right of shipowner or cargo owner to rely on the rules, even though neither is a party to the bill. Reliance was placed in particular on views expressed by Mr Diamond QC in 'The Hague-Visby Rules' [1978] Lloyd's MCLQ 225 at 248–249 and on *Gillespie Bros & Co Ltd v Roy Bowles Transport Ltd* [1973] 1 All ER 193 at 198, [1973] QB 400 at 412, where Lord Denning MR cited art IV bis, para 1 to show how a non-party could become bound.

The cargo owners' response was even briefer. The effect of the 1971 Act is to give statutory force to a mandatory contractual regime. The language of the Act and the rules shows that they were intended to regulate the rights and duties of the parties to the bill of lading contract, not non-parties. That was what Mr Mustill QC thought in 'Carriage of Goods by Sea Act 1971' (1972) 11 Arkiv Sjorett 684 at 710. The issue of a bill of lading was a necessary, but not in itself a sufficient, condition of the application of the rules.

We are again (no doubt unavoidably) obliged to resolve this issue without the help which the decisions or opinions of foreign judges or jurists might have given us. I have not for my part found it an easy question. I am particularly concerned at the risk that idiosyncratic legal rules on privity might yield different results in different countries. But on balance I prefer the cargo owners' arguments for three main reasons.

(1) As s 1(4) of the 1971 Act and art I, para (b) and art X of the rules in particular make clear, the bill of lading is the bedrock on which this mandatory code is founded. A bill of lading is a contractual document with certain commercially well-known consequences

when indorsed and transferred. It is not clear to me why the code shou~

a existence of a bill of lading as a matter of such central and overriding importa~
code is to apply with equal force as between those who are not parties to the
which the bill contains or evidences.

(2) Much of the language in the Act and the rules suggests that the code is inten~
govern the relations between the parties to the bill of lading contract. Section 1(4) sp~
of applying the rules to a contract. Article I, para (*a*) defines the carrier as including ~

b party who enters into a contract of carriage with a shipper. Article I, para (*b*) speaks ~
regulating relations between a carrier and a holder of a bill or similar document of title.
Most significantly of all, art II defines the application of the rules 'under every contract of
carriage'. Articles V and VI are concerned with agreements between contracting parties.
Article X applies the rules to the bill of lading, not the carriage. If it had been intended
to regulate relations between non-parties to the bill of lading contract, it is hard to think

c the language would not have been both different and simpler.

(3) Whatever the law in other jurisdictions, the general principle that only a party to a
contract may sue on it is well established here. If the draftsmen of the 1924 and 1971
Acts had intended the respective rules to infringe that principle or appreciated that that
was their effect, I think they would have sought to make that clear in the Acts. It would
be strange if so fundamental a principle were to be so inconspicuously abrogated.

d In reaching this conclusion I recognise the unattractiveness to carriers of exposure to
claims by non-parties to bills not subject to limits in time or amount. But the notion that
bill of lading terms may be held to regulate relations between those who were not parties
to the bills was, as I understand, specifically disavowed by Lord Donaldson MR and the
House of Lords in *Leigh & Sullavan Ltd v Aliakmon Shipping Co Ltd, The Aliakmon* [1985] 2
All ER 44 at 54, [1985] QB 350 at 368; *affd* [1986] 2 All ER 145 at 155–156, [1986] AC

e 785 at 818.

I would accordingly determine this second issue in the cargo owners' favour. The fate
of the appeal as a whole cannot be determined until the remaining questions are ruled
on.

f **STOCKER LJ.** I agree.

I was, for most of the duration of the argument before this court, of the opinion that
despite the terms of art IV bis, para 1, the terms of art II and art III, para 2 were, in the
light of the temporal limitation in art I, para (*e*), confined to the functions of transportation
undertaken by the shipowners. In other words art II and art III, para 2 expressed in
contractual terms the duties and obligations which would arise in tort in respect of the
shipowners' duties in relation to the cargo in the course of transportation of that cargo

g from the time of loading until discharge and that these duties did not relate to a deliberate
denial of the cargo owners' proprietary rights by conversion of the goods to their own
benefit, or theft, and accordingly the judge was correct in his conclusion and in his
reasons for it.

I no longer find myself able to sustain this view. Article III, para 6, which imposes the

h limitation period, is prefaced by the words:

'Unless notice of loss or damage and the general nature of such loss or damage be
given . . . at the port of discharge before or at the time of the removal of the goods
into the custody of the person entitled to delivery . . .'

These words are apt to cover failure to deliver for any reason and the shortage should be

j apparent at the time of discharge. It is not disputed but that the cargo owners could have
framed their claim under the articles cited and no injustice can result from their failure
to give notice in the terms of art III, para 6 within the time limit.

I have had the advantage of reading in draft the judgment of Bingham LJ and although
we are differing from the judge I do not feel it would be of any assistance to add any
further comments of my own on a topic on which I have no great experience to the

.d reasoning contained in his judgment, and I would agree and respectfully
conclusion and his reason therefor on the issues argued before this court.

E LJ. I am in full agreement with the judgment of Bingham LJ and, though we
ffering from Hirst J on the issue considered by him, there is little which I can
.ully add.

As to the first issue, I have from the start found some difficulty in seeing how
onversion resulting in the loss of part of the cargo could be said not to be an obvious
breach of the obligations to 'keep, care for, and discharge' imposed on the carrier by art
III, para 2. Counsel's able submissions on behalf of the cargo owners have not persuaded
me otherwise. The fact that the cargo owners may choose to assert their claim by way of
a proprietary claim in tort seems to me irrelevant: see art IV bis, para 1. With all respect
to Hirst J, and due diffidence in a field of law which is not very familiar to me, I believe
that he may have been misled by treating the alleged acts complained of as involving no
more and no less than 'misdelivery'. While counsel further submitted that art III, para 6
does not on any footing apply to causes of action arising after termination of discharge,
the complaint here is in substance of a failure to discharge at the end of the voyage and
of a failure properly to keep and care for the goods during the voyage. Such failures, in
my judgment, fall within art III, para 2, and claims in respect thereof are correspondingly
subject to the time limit imposed by art III, para 6.

As to the second issue falling for our decision, I think that the wording of arts II and
VI, already quoted by Bingham LJ, lend very strong support to his conclusion and to the
cargo owners' argument. Article II, read by itself, gives rise to no rights or obligations. It
does no more than state the scope and purpose of all the succeeding articles. However, it
clearly shows that the purpose of those succeeding articles is, subject to the provisions of
art VI, to define (a) the responsibilities and liabilities to which the carrier shall be subject
'*under every contract of carriage of goods by sea*' and (b) the rights and immunities to which
the carrier shall be entitled *under every such contract*. Article VI, however, gives the
shipper and the carrier the liberty, within the limits stated in that article, to enter into an
agreement by way of variation of the responsibilities, liabilities, rights and immunities
which would otherwise attach to the carrier by virtue of the preceding articles. These
provisions, in my judgment, by themselves show fairly clearly that the purpose of all the
articles is to govern the relationship of *the parties to the contract* under a contract of carriage
of goods by sea. For these and other reasons given by Bingham LJ, I too would determine
the second issue in the cargo owners' favour.

As he has said, the outcome of the appeal as a whole will depend on the determination
of the outstanding questions. Meantime, I would welcome submissions as to the form of
the declarations (if any) which should now be made in accordance with the judgments of
this court on the two issues so far decided.

Order accordingly.

Solicitors: *Lewis Moore* (for the shipowners); *Clyde & Co* (for the cargo owners).

Celia Fox   Barrister.

a

Practice Note

QUEEN'S BENCH DIVISION
LORD LANE CJ, ALLIOTT AND AULD JJ
26 OCTOBER 1990

b

Magistrates – Summary trial – Offence triable summarily or on indictment – Matters to be taken into account in determining mode of trial – Guidelines – Duty of magistrates to consider each case individually and on its own merits – General considerations – Defendants to whom guidelines apply – Either way offences generally to be tried summarily unless certain features present or court's sentencing powers insufficient – Burglary – Theft and fraud – Handling – Social security frauds – Violence against the person – Public order offences – Violent disorder – Affray – Violence to and neglect of children – Indecent assault – Unlawful sexual intercourse – Drugs – Reckless driving – Criminal damage – Offences against the Person Act 1861, ss 20, 47 – Criminal Damage Act 1971, s 1 – Magistrates' Courts Act 1980, s 19, Sch 1, para 28(c), Sch 2 – Public Order Act 1986.

c

LORD LANE CJ gave the following guidelines at the sitting of the court. The purpose of these guidelines is to help magistrates decide whether or not to commit 'either way' offences for trial in the Crown Court. Their object is to provide guidance not direction. They are not intended to impinge on a magistrate's duty to consider each case individually and on its own particular facts.

d

These guidelines apply to all defendants *aged 17 and above.*

e   *General mode of trial considerations*

Section 19 of the Magistrates' Courts Act 1980 requires magistrates to have regard to the following matters in deciding whether an offence is more suitable for summary trial or trial on indictment: (1) the nature of the case; (2) whether the circumstances make the offence one of a serious character; (3) whether the punishment which a magistrates' court would have power to inflict for it would be adequate; (4) any other circumstances which appear to the court to make it more suitable for the offence to be tried in one way rather than the other; (5) any representations made by the prosecution or the defence.

f

Certain general observations can be made: (a) the court should never make its decision on the grounds of convenience or expedition; (b) the court should assume for the purpose of deciding mode of trial that the prosecution version of the facts is correct; (c) the defendant's antecedents and personal mitigating circumstances are irrelevant for the purpose of deciding mode of trial; (d) the fact that the offences are alleged to be specimens is a relevant consideration; the fact that the defendant will be asking for other offences to be taken into consideration, if convicted, is not; (e) where cases involve complex questions of fact or difficult questions of law, the court should consider committal for trial; (f) where two or more defendants are jointly charged with an offence and the court decides that the offence is more suitable for summary trial, if one defendant elects trial on indictment, the court must proceed to deal with all the defendants as examining justices in respect of that offence. A juvenile jointly charged with someone aged 17 or over should only be committed for trial if it is necessary in the interests of justice; (g) **in general, except where otherwise stated, either way offences should be tried summarily unless the court considers that the particular case has one or more of the features set out in the following pages *and* that its sentencing powers are insufficient.**

g

h

j

Features relevant to individual offences

Note: Where reference is made in these guidelines to property or damage of 'high value' it means a figure equal to at least twice the amount of the limit imposed by statute on a magistrates' court when making a compensation order (currently £2,000).

welling house. (1) Entry in the daytime when the occupier (or another) is present; (2) entry at night of a house which is normally occupied, whether or not the occupier (or owner) is present; (3) the offence is alleged to be one of a series of similar offences; (4) when soiling, ransacking, damage or vandalism occurs; (5) the offence has professional hallmarks; (6) the unrecovered property is of high value.

Note: Attention is drawn to para 28(c) of Sch 1 to the Magistrates' Courts Act 1980, by which offences of burglary in a dwelling *cannot* be tried summarily if any person in the dwelling was subjected to violence or the threat of violence.

2. Non-dwellings. (1) Entry of a pharmacy or doctor's surgery; (2) fear is caused or violence is done to anyone lawfully on the premises (e g nightwatchman, security guard); (3) the offence has professional hallmarks; (4) vandalism on a substantial scale; (5) the unrecovered property is of high value.

Theft and fraud

(1) Breach of trust by a person in a position of substantial authority, or in whom a high degree of trust is placed; (2) theft or fraud which has been committed or disguised in a sophisticated manner; (3) theft or fraud committed by an organised gang; (4) the victim is particularly vulnerable to theft or fraud, e g the elderly or infirm; (5) the unrecovered property is of high value.

Handling

(1) Dishonest handling of stolen property by a receiver who has commissioned the theft; (2) the offence has professional hallmarks; (3) the property is of high value.

Social security frauds

(1) Organised fraud on a large scale; (2) the frauds are substantial and carried out over a long period of time.

Violence (ss 20 and 47 of the Offences against the Person Act 1861)

(1) The use of a weapon of a kind likely to cause serious injury; (2) a weapon is used and serious injury is caused; (3) more than minor injury is caused by kicking, head-butting or similar forms of assault; (4) serious violence is caused to those whose work has to be done in contact with the public, e g police officers, bus drivers, taxi drivers, publicans and shopkeepers; (5) violence to vulnerable people, e g the elderly and infirm.

The same considerations apply to cases of domestic violence.

Public Order Act 1986 offences

1. Cases of *violent disorder* should generally be committed for trial.

2. *Affray.* (1) Organised violence or use of weapons; (2) significant injury or substantial damage; (3) the offence has clear racial motivation; (4) an attack on police officers, ambulancemen, firemen and the like.

Violence to and neglect of children

(1) Substantial injury; (2) repeated violence or serious neglect, even if the harm is slight; (3) sadistic violence, e g deliberate burning or scalding.

Indecent assault

(1) Substantial disparity in age between victim and defendant, and the assault is more than trivial; (2) violence or threats of violence; (3) relationship of trust or responsibility between defendant and victim; (4) several similar offences, and the assaults are more than trivial; (5) the victim is particularly vulnerable; (6) serious nature of the assault.

Unlawful sexual intercourse

a (1) Wide disparity of age; (2) breach of position of trust; (3) the victim is particularly vulnerable.

Note: Unlawful sexual intercourse with a girl *under 13* is triable only on indictment.

Drugs

1. Class A. (a) *Supply; possession with intent to supply:* these cases should be committed
b for trial. (b) *Possession:* should be committed for trial unless the amount is small and consistent only with personal use.

2. Class B. (a) *Supply; possession with intent to supply:* should be committed for trial unless there is only small scale supply for no payment. (b) *Possession:* should be committed for trial when the quantity is substantial.

c *Reckless driving*

(1) Alcohol or drugs contributing to recklessness; (2) grossly excessive speed; (3) racing; (4) prolonged course of reckless driving; (5) other related offences.

Criminal damage

(1) Deliberate fire-raising; (2) committed by a group; (3) damage of a high value;
d (4) the offence has clear racial motivation.

Note: Offences set out in Sch 2 to the Magistrates' Courts Act 1980 (which includes offences of criminal damage contrary to s 1 of the Criminal Damage Act 1971 which do not amount to arson) *must* be tried summarily if the value of the property damaged or destroyed is £2,000 or less.

e N P Metcalfe Esq   Barrister.

Practice Direction

f COURT OF APPEAL, CIVIL DIVISION

Court of Appeal – Practice – Civil Division – Receiving and processing appeals and applications – Reference of jurisdictional issues for legal scrutiny – Lodging of notices of appeal and applications – Functions of counter staff – Reference of papers to office lawyer or registrar – Appeals and applications lodged by post – Setting down – Setting down of appeal or application not precluding
g *other party or court from raising jurisdictional issues – Obligation to comply with rules and directions – Notification of defects in appeals or applications – Requirement to comply with time limits – Unrepresented litigants attending in person– Departure from arrangements in urgent cases – RSC Ord 59, r 14.*

Following the recent addition to the staff of the Civil Appeals Office of a team of office
h lawyers to assist the court in connection with the management of its case load, a number of changes have been made to the system for receiving and processing appeals and applications to the Civil Division of the Court of Appeal. These changes will come into effect on 29 October 1990. The details of the new arrangements are set out below.

The purpose of the new system is to ensure that jurisdictional issues, such as whether leave to appeal is required, are referred for legal scrutiny at an early stage and to have the
j progress of each appeal and application monitored by an office lawyer from the date of setting down to the point where it is ready for listing. Appeals and applications will be assigned to groups by reference to the subject matter of the case (eg public law, family law etc). The lawyer concerned, with the assistance of a member of the administrative staff, will be responsible for monitoring the progress of all appeals and applications assigned to that group.

The principal features of the new system are as follows.

(1) In the case of notices of appeal and applications which are lodged by personal attendance at the Civil Appeals Office, the staff on the counter will not, in future, carry out any check on whether leave to appeal is required or whether there is any other jurisdictional bar to the appeal or application being accepted.

The counter staff will continue to carry out a *preliminary* check on the following: (i) whether the relevant time limits have been complied with; (ii) whether a copy of the order being appealed has been lodged; (iii) in the case of applications (other than in-time applications for leave to appeal) whether an affidavit in support of the application is included with the papers; and (iv) whether the correct court fee has been paid.

If the person dealing with the matter at the counter considers that the appeal is out of time, or that any of the other requirements listed above have not been complied with, he/she will inform the solicitor, or solicitor's clerk, of this and will not take the papers in. If the solicitor who has the conduct of the case considers that all relevant time limits and other formalities have been complied with, that solicitor (not the clerk) should telephone the Civil Appeals Office or send a letter or fax, and the matter will be referred to the registrar.

If the member of the staff at the counter considers that the time limits and other formalities have been complied with, he/she will accept the papers; but they will then be referred to an office lawyer (and, if necessary, the registrar) to consider whether leave to appeal is required and whether the Civil Division of the Court of Appeal has jurisdiction to entertain the appeal or application concerned. If the relevant office lawyer considers that, for any reason, the appeal or application has not been validly instituted or is one which the court has no jurisdiction to entertain, the appellant's/applicant's solicitor (or the appellant/applicant if in person) will be informed of this, normally by letter. Any query concerning the office lawyer's decision will be referred to the registrar.

(2) It follows from the arrangements set out in para (1) above that the fact that the staff in the Civil Appeals Office have accepted the notice of appeal or application concerned must not be taken to be an indication, still less a guarantee, that the appeal or application is validly instituted or is one which the court has jurisdiction to entertain.

(3) Appeals and applications lodged by post will be similarly dealt with. The staff in the general office will carry out the preliminary check on time limits and formalities, and then the papers will be referred for legal scrutiny.

(4) If, after the preliminary check and legal scrutiny, the appeal or application is considered to be in order, it will be set down (ie entered in the records of the Court of Appeal) and given a reference number. The appellant's/applicant's solicitors (or the appellant/applicant if in person) will then be informed by a letter from the Civil Appeals Office that the appeal/application has been set down; that letter will give the appeal/application reference number (which should be quoted when writing or telephoning) and will specify what further steps must be complied with by the appellant's/applicant's side and within what timetable.

(5) It is important to emphasise that these procedures for vetting appeals and applications are intended to assist the court in the management of its case load and to ensure, so far as possible, that invalid appeals or applications are not accepted. They do not, however, relieve any party (whether represented or acting in person) of the obligation to comply with the requirements of all relevant rules and directions and that party's solicitor, or the party himself/herself, as the case may be, will remain solely responsible for all consequences, including the costs, of any failure to comply with any relevant requirement. It follows that the acceptance of an appeal or application by setting it down does not provide any guarantee that it is valid and it remains open to any other party, and the court of its own motion, if it thinks fit, to raise any jurisdictional issue or any failure to comply with any relevant rule of direction.

In *The Supreme Court Practice 1991* vol 1, para 59/1/6 there is a brief account of the steps to be taken to institute and proceed with an appeal, including cross-references to

the relevant rules and paragraphs in the commentary dealing with service of notices of
a appeal and setting down of appeals. For details of the cases where leave to appeal is
required, see paras 59/1/25 to 59/1/28; and for details of the requirements necessary in
respect of applications to the Court of Appeal, see RSC Ord 59, r 14, and paras 59/14/1 to
59/14/20.

(6) The staff in the Civil Appeals Office, both administrative and legal, have a heavy
workload, and there can be no guarantee that they will be able to notify the solicitors or
b litigants in person of defects in appeals or applications in time for those defects to be
rectified before the relevant time limit runs out, particularly if the papers are not lodged
with the Civil Appeals Office until shortly before the expiry of that time limit. It is
therefore unwise for solicitors, or litigants in person, to leave it until the last day, or even
close to the last day, of the period concerned before posting or bringing the requisite
documents to the Civil Appeals Office.

c (7) It has also been necessary to make changes in the arrangements for dealing with
unrepresented litigants who attend the Civil Appeals Office in person with a view to
bringing an appeal, or making an application, to the Court of Appeal. As in the past, it
will be necessary, before any steps can be taken, or any forms issued, for the litigant to
produce or send to the office a copy of the order against which he/she seeks to appeal; but
the past practice of handing out forms and notes for guidance at the counter to litigants
d in person will in future no longer be adopted. Instead, the litigant will be asked to leave
with (or post to) the Civil Appeals Office a copy of the order, together with a short
standard form giving his/her name, address and telephone number. The order will then
be passed to an office lawyer (or, if necessary, the registrar) to consider whether the
appeal/application is one which the Court of Appeal has jurisdiction to entertain, whether
leave to appeal is required and whether there are any other special procedural
e requirements applicable to that case.

When that scrutiny has been carried out the Civil Appeals Office will post the requisite
form and notes for guidance to the intending appellant/applicant or, if the appeal/
application is one which the Court of Appeal has no jurisdiction to entertain, a letter will
be sent to the litigant informing him/her of this and of the reasons for it.

f The purpose of this new system is to try to avoid incorrect forms or notes being sent,
or any jurisdictional issues being overlooked.

Again, it needs to be emphasised that the administrative and legal staff in the Civil
Appeals Office will need time to deal with these matters and litigants in person are
therefore advised to make sure that they communicate with the Civil Appeals Office as
soon as possible after the decision against which they wish to appeal has been given, and
well before the expiry of the four-week time limit for serving notice of appeal.

g (8) These arrangements will only be departed from in cases where the matter is so
urgent that it is necessary to make special arrangements. A case does not count as urgent
for this purpose merely because a party has left it too close to the expiry of the time limit
before taking the necessary steps to institute the appeal or application concerned. A case
will only be treated as urgent for this purpose if a direction to that effect is made by the
h registrar or the senior lawyer.

Issued with the concurrence of the Master of the Rolls.

J D R ADAMS
24 October 1990   Registrar of Civil Appeals.

Re a debtor (No 2389 of 1989), ex parte Travel and General Insurance Co plc v The debtor

a

CHANCERY DIVISION
VINELOTT J
23, 26 MARCH 1990

b

Insolvency – Proceedings on creditor's petition – Dismissal of petition – Voluntary arrangement proposed by debtor – Unreasonable refusal of offer – Whether proposed voluntary arrangement 'an offer to secure or compound for a debt in respect of which the petition is presented' – Whether proposed voluntary arrangement to be treated as offer to each creditor capable of being accepted or refused by petitioning creditor – Whether court having jurisdiction to dismiss petition on ground that petitioning creditor has unreasonably refused proposal if he votes against it or fails to vote – Insolvency Act 1986, s 271(3).

c

Although s 271(3)[a] of the Insolvency Act 1986 provides that the court may dismiss a bankruptcy petition if it is satisfied that an offer made by the debtor 'to secure or compound for a debt in respect of which the petition is presented ... has been unreasonably refused' and that acceptance of the offer 'would have required the dismissal of the petition', a voluntary arrangement proposed by the debtor pursuant to the provisions of Pt VIII of the 1986 Act to settle his affairs is not to be regarded as an offer to each creditor which is capable of being accepted or refused by the petitioning creditor within the meaning of s 271(3). Instead, the offer is made to the class of creditors affected by it and, as such, the consequences of acceptance or refusal are to be found in Pt VIII of the Act alone. Accordingly, a petitioning creditor the amount of whose debt is such that he could secure approval of a voluntary arrangement if he voted in favour of it is not to be taken as refusing his consent to the offer if he votes against the voluntary arrangement or fails to exercise his vote, and accordingly the court does not have jurisdiction under s 271(3) to dismiss the petition on the ground that he has thereby unreasonably refused the proposal (see p 988 *a b*, post).

d

e

f

Notes

For proceedings on creditor's petition, see 3(2) Halsbury's Laws (4th edn reissue) para 186.

For the Insolvency Act 1986, Pt VIII (ss 252–263), s 271, see 4 Halsbury's Statutes (4th edn) (1987 reissue) 897, 913.

g

Case referred to in judgment

Gilmartin (a bankrupt), ex p the bankrupt v International Agency and Supply Ltd [1989] 2 All ER 835, [1989] 1 WLR 513.

h

Appeal

Travel and General Insurance Co plc (the petitioning creditor) appealed against the order of Mr Registrar Scott dated 29 September 1989 dismissing its petition on the ground that the debtor's offer to secure or compound for the debt had been unreasonably refused within s 271(3) of the Insolvency Act 1986. The facts are set out in the judgment.

j

Raymond Davern for the petitioning creditor.
Kenneth Hamer for the debtor.

---

a Section 271(3) is set out at p 986 j, post

VINELOTT J. This is an appeal by a petitioning creditor against the decision of Mr
a   Registrar Scott dismissing the petition. It gives rise to a question of some importance in
the administration of the new insolvency legislation. The question is whether a voluntary
arrangement proposed by a debtor pursuant to the provisions in Pt VIII of the Insolvency
Act 1986 is an offer to the creditors to whom it is addressed within s 271(3) of that Act,
with the consequence that the court has jurisdiction under that subsection to consider
whether the proposal was unreasonably refused by the petitioning creditor and, if the
b   court concludes that it was unreasonably refused and if the conditions in s 271(3) are
otherwise satisfied, to dismiss the petition.

This question was not argued before the registrar. The only question argued before
him was whether the petitioning creditor, who held well over 25% in value of the
aggregate of the debtor's unsecured debt, had acted unreasonably in voting against a
voluntary arrangement that had been put forward at a meeting of the creditors. However,
c   the jurisdiction of the registrar to entertain that question has been challenged in this
appeal. It is not suggested that either of the parties would have wished to adduce further
evidence if this issue had been raised before the registrar, and as the question goes to the
jurisdiction of the court I must, I think, answer it before entering into the question
whether the petitioning creditor did, in fact, unreasonably refuse an offer by the debtor.

The facts which are relevant to this preliminary issue can be shortly stated. The debtor
d   carried on business as a travel agent. He carried on business through at least two
companies, Mandarin International Travel Ltd (which I will abbreviate to MIT) and ICSS
(London) Ltd (which I will abbreviate to ICSS). Both are now in liquidation. The
companies were registered with the International Air Transport Association (IATA) and,
through IATA, were able to purchase tickets on credit and to account for them (less
commission) monthly. But the companies had to obtain bonds from an insurance
e   company willing to accept liability. The petitioning creditor, Travel and General
Insurance Co plc, provided the necessary bonds. The debtor gave the petitioning creditor
a cross-guarantee. When the two companies went into liquidation two airlines, Singapore
Airways and Malaysian Airways, and IATA called on the petitioning creditor to meet the
liabilities of the companies. The petitioning creditor, having paid the sums due or
claimed under the bonds, claimed reimbursement from the debtor. Three separate
f   actions were commenced and in each action the petitioning creditor obtained summary
judgment under RSC Ord 14. The first judgment was on 5 December 1987 and was for
just over £20,000 (including interest and costs). The second and third were on
17 December 1987 and were for £10,000 plus interest and costs and £15,000 plus
interests and costs respectively.

On 18 December 1987 the petitioning creditor obtained a charging order over the
g   debtor's property, 101 Pennine Drive, London NW2, in respect of the sum for which
judgment had been given in the first action, and on 31 March 1988 it obtained charging
orders in respect of the sums for which judgment had been given in the second and third
actions.

On 26 April 1989 the petitioning creditor served a statutory demand for the sum (then
h   £19,272·24) due under the third judgment. The debt was not paid, and on 26 May the
petitioning creditor presented a petition. In the petition the security created by the
charging order was valued at nil. The petition was listed for hearing on 5 July 1989.

On 30 June the debtor gave notice of an application for an interim order under s 253
of the 1986 Act. That was supported by an affidavit exhibiting a proposal for a voluntary
arrangement. The nominee named for this purpose was a Mrs H T Phillips, a chartered
j   accountant and a licensed insolvency practitioner. I shall have to say more about the
substance of the proposals later. The petitioning creditor was given notice of the
application. It came before the registrar on 5 July. An interim order was made for 14
days, and the application was stood over until 19 July. The nominee's report was duly
submitted to the court, and on 19 July the interim order was extended to 17 August.
The registrar directed that a meeting of creditors should be convened for 11 August, as

proposed by the nominee. The petition and the application for an interim order were
stood over to 17 August in the expectation that the report of the meeting would be   *a*
lodged before the date.

The meeting of creditors on 11 August was attended by a legal executive of the firm
of solicitors acting for the petitioning creditor, who held a proxy for the petitioning
creditor, and by a representative of Barclays Bank plc, which had a first charge on the
debtor's property 101 Pennine Drive. Barclays Bank was treated as a secured creditor and
was not listed as voting or abstaining from voting on the resolution to approve the   *b*
voluntary arrangement. I shall have to say more about the position of Barclays Bank
later. One other creditor was represented, Abbey National Finance. The voting is
recorded as follows:

> 'The petitioning creditor—19,272—against.
> Surely Trust—4,236—for.
> United Dominions Trust—3,866—for.   *c*
> City Bank Trust Ltd.—7,200—for.
> Abbey National Finance—3,448—abstained.'

The figure of 19,272 was, of course, the amount of the debt on which the petition was
founded. The creditors who voted in favour of the voluntary arrangement were not
present or represented at the meeting and they must, I think, have given a proxy to the   *d*
proposed nominee as chairman. The proportion in value of the petitioning creditor's
debt, in respect of which its vote was cast, is 50·7% of the whole. The majority required
to secure the approval of a voluntary arrangement under s 258 of the 1986 Act is not
specified in Pt VIII of the Act, but under r 5.18 of the Insolvency Rules 1986, SI 1986/
1925, which are made under the powers conferred by s 412 of the Act, the passing of a
resolution approving a voluntary arrangement requires 'a majority in excess of three-   *e*
quarters in value of the creditors present in person or by proxy and voting on the
resolution'. So a creditor with a debt equal to only 25% of the aggregate of the debts, that
is of the debts owed to creditors affected by a voluntary arrangement, can ensure that it
is not approved.

On 17 August the application for an interim order and the petition came before Mr
Registrar Dewhurst, Mr Registrar Scott being absent on holiday. The debtor and the   *f*
nominee appeared and asserted that the petitioning creditor had unreasonably refused to
accept the voluntary arrangement. The registrar accordingly stood over the application
and the petition to 28 September and gave directions for the filing of evidence on this
issue. Nothing was heard from the debtor until 28 September, when the petitioning
creditor was served with a notice, dated 27 September, that at the hearing the debtor
would oppose the making of a bankruptcy order on the ground that he had made an   *g*
offer to secure or compound for the debt in respect of which the petition was presented,
that acceptance of that offer would have required the dismissal of the petition, and that
the offer had been unreasonably refused. That was supported by an affidavit sworn by
the debtor on 27 September and produced at the hearing on 28 September. The hearing
occupied two days, and overnight the petitioning creditor prepared a draft affidavit by
the legal executive who had attended the meeting on 11 August, which was admitted on   *h*
the usual undertakings as to being sworn and filed. That is all I need say at this stage
about the evidence.

Section 271(3) provides as follows:

> 'The court may dismiss the petition if it is satisfied that the debtor is able to pay
> all his debts or is satisfied—(*a*) that the debtor has made an offer to secure or   *j*
> compound for a debt in respect of which the petition is presented, (*b*) that the
> acceptance of that offer would have required the dismissal of the petition, and (*c*)
> that the offer has been unreasonably refused; and, in determining for the purposes
> of this subsection whether the debtor is able to pay all his debts, the court shall take
> into account his contingent and prospective liabilities.'

It was assumed at the hearing before the registrar by counsel who appeared for the

petitioning creditor and by counsel who appeared for the debtor (not counsel wh
a appeared for the debtor before me) that a voluntary arrangement proposed by a debtor is
an offer to the creditors to whom it is addressed within para (*a*) of s 271(3), that if a
petitioning creditor votes against acceptance of the voluntary arrangement he refuses his
consent to it and that if the amount of the petitioning creditor's debt is such that if he
had voted in favour of acceptance of the voluntary arrangement it would have been
approved then para (*b*) of s 271(3) is also satisfied. That last step is founded in s 260(5),
b which provides that if a voluntary arrangement is approved after the presentation of a
bankruptcy petition which has been stayed by an interim order then the 'petition is
deemed, unless the court otherwise orders, to have been dismissed'.

The initial submission of counsel for the petitioning creditor was that the proposition
that a proposed arrangement is an offer and that a creditor who votes against it must be
taken to have refused the offer leads to an absurd consequence; for a creditor with 25%
c of the debt affected by the arrangement who has made it clear to the debtor and the
nominee that he objects to the proposed arrangement may nevertheless abstain from
voting in the knowledge that another creditor, with more than 25% of the remainder of
the aggregate debt, will vote against it. The answer of counsel for the debtor to that
submission was that a creditor who abstains from voting on a proposal must be taken to
have refused to accept it; just as a person to whom an offer is made is taken as having
d refused it unless he accepts it within the time limited for acceptance or, if no time is
specified, within a reasonable time.

That does not wholly meet the difficulty pointed to by counsel for the petitioning
creditor. A petitioning creditor may abstain not from voting but from attending a
meeting knowing that another creditor will attend and vote against or has lodged a proxy
casting his vote against the proposed arrangement and that his vote will suffice to defeat
e it. If, for instance, the petitioning creditor held 25·5% in value of the debt affected by the
arrangement and B held 20% of the debt, the proposed arrangement would be defeated
by the exercise of B's vote against the proposed arrangement, provided that A does not
attend in person or by proxy. Is it to be said that A unreasonably withheld his consent
because he did not attend and outvote B? That is not a merely fanciful example. A and B
might be associated companies; moreover, companies which supply goods and services
f on a large scale may well consult each other as to the course each of them proposes to
take.

Faced with this difficulty, counsel for the debtor submitted that a petitioning creditor
must be taken to have refused to accept the offer made by a proposed voluntary
arrangement unless he takes steps to attend and vote in person or by proxy in favour of
its acceptance. That seems to be a situation unlikely to have been contemplated by the
g legislation. Moreover, a petitioning creditor with 25% of the debt affected by the
arrangement by some oversight might not have been given notice of the meeting to
consider a proposed voluntary arrangement. If the voluntary arrangement were not
approved, is the petitioning creditor then to be taken to have unreasonably refused to
accept it unless he takes steps under s 262(1)(*b*) to have the resolution set aside and a
further meeting convened?
h
This is not the only difficulty. Under s 271(3) the court can dismiss a petition if an
offer is unreasonably refused and if acceptance of the offer 'would have required the
dismissal of the petition'. But if a voluntary arrangement is accepted at the meeting of
creditors then, on the expiration of 28 days from the date when the report of the meeting
was made to the court, the bankruptcy petition 'is deemed, unless the court otherwise
j orders, to have been dismissed'.

Counsel for the debtor submitted that the words in para (*b*) of s 271(3) 'would have
required the dismissal of the petition' can be read as 'would have required or would have
resulted in the dismissal of the petition'. I accept, of course, that it would be wrong to
attach too great importance to the literal meaning of the words used in para (*b*). The
court must look at the scheme of the legislation as a whole and the purpose to be inferred
from it. However, in the instant case, the literal construction of para (*b*) avoids the
anomalies to which I have referred. The acceptance of a proposed voluntary arrangement

t the creditors' meeting does not itself require or have the consequence that the petition
falls to be dismissed. That consequence only follows if no application to the court is made *a*
under s 262(1).

In my judgment, therefore, a proposed voluntary arrangement is not to be treated as
an offer to each creditor capable of being accepted or refused by the petitioning creditor
within the meaning of s 271(3). The offer is made to the creditors affected by it as a class,
and the consequences of acceptance or refusal are to be found in Pt VIII of the Act alone.

It is suggested in *Muir Hunter on Personal Insolvency* (1986) pp 3050–3050/1 that so *b*
construed s 271(3) has very limited scope. The tender of payment in full with costs is
covered by s 271(1)(*a*), which must be read with r 6.25 of the 1986 rules; further, if a
composition for less than the full amount of the debt is accepted a petition cannot be
withdrawn without the leave of the court. It is difficult, therefore, to see how it can be
said that in such a situation acceptance would have required the dismissal of the petition.
That leaves only the possibility, in practice rare, where a creditor might offer to pay off *c*
one or more of the debts, leaving the balance of debt less than the statutory minimum;
for in such a situation the petition would have to be dismissed on that ground.

However, as I see it, construed in the sense I have indicated, there is a plain and
important area for the operation of s 271(3). If, after a petition has been presented, a
debtor were to offer a composition to all his creditors conditionally on acceptance by
them all, which was accepted by all the creditors except the petitioning creditor, it could, *d*
it seems to me, be said that the offer was an offer to each of the creditors individually and
that acceptance by the petitioning creditor (as well as the other creditors) 'would have
required the dismissal of the petition', since, if all the creditors had agreed to accept the
composition, there would be simply no ground on which the court could properly refuse
to dismiss the petition.

What the debtor cannot do, as I see it, is to invoke the coercive machinery in Pt VIII of *e*
the 1986 Act in order to bind dissentient or inactive creditors (creditors, that is, who do
not attend the meeting of creditors in person or by proxy) and then claim that a creditor
who votes against the resolution to approve the voluntary arrangement has unreasonably
withheld his consent to it. What the debtor can do in these circumstances (that is if all
except the petitioning creditor accept a proposed voluntary arrangement which provides
for payment by way of composition) is to offer the composition to each creditor *f*
conditionally on acceptance by all and then, if the petitioning creditor refuses, apply for
the dismissal of the petition. The court would have jurisdiction to stand over the petition,
if necessary, while these steps are being taken or completed.

[His Lordship then considered the facts on the basis of which the debtor had put
forward the voluntary arrangement and held that the registrar's conclusion could not be
supported because the debtor had not put all the relevant facts before the creditors and *g*
there was no evidence how the debtor proposed to finance his ability to pay £1,500 per
month towards his debts. In those circumstances the petitioning creditor had been
justified in taking the view that the interest of the creditors as a whole would be better
served if the affairs of the debtor were fully investigated by a trustee in bankruptcy. His
Lordship agreed with Harman J in *Re Gilmartin (a bankrupt), ex p the bankrupt v* *h*
International Agency and Supply Ltd [1989] 2 All ER 835 at 838, [1989] 1 WLR 513 at 516
that an appeal from a registrar was a 'true' appeal and that, since he was satisfied that the
registrar had erred in law, the court was therefore able to override the registrar's decision
that the petitioning creditor had unreasonably refused its consent. His Lordship
continued:]

In my judgment, therefore, this appeal succeeds. *j*

Appeal allowed.

Solicitors: *Harkavys* (for the petitioning creditor); *Fladgate Fielder* (for the debtor).

Jacqueline Metcalfe   Barrister.

a
R v Mearns

COURT OF APPEAL, CRIMINAL DIVISION
GLIDEWELL LJ, IAN KENNEDY AND FENNELL JJ
1 MAY 1990

b *Criminal law – Verdict – Alternative offence – Summary and indictable offences – Alternative verdict of guilty of summary offence where summary offence not included in indictment – Common assault and assault occasioning actual bodily harm –Whether defendant can be found guilty of common assault as alternative to assault occasioning actual bodily harm if charge of common assault not included in indictment – Criminal Justice Act 1988, ss 39, 40.*

Since by virtue of s 39^a of the Criminal Justice Act 1988 common assault is a summary
c offence and may no longer be tried either on indictment or summarily, an alternative verdict of guilty of common assault may not be brought in on an indictment charging assault occasioning actual bodily harm unless, as provided by s 40^b of the 1988 Act, a count charging the defendant with the summary offence of common assault founded on the same facts or evidence as a count charging an indictable offence such as assault occasioning actual bodily harm is included in the indictment (see p 990 j to p 991 b and
d p 992 e f, post).

Notes
For prosecutions for assault, see 11(1) Halsbury's Laws (4th edn reissue) para 489, and for counts in an indictment charging a summary offence, see 11(2) ibid para 922.
     For the Criminal Justice Act 1988, ss 39, 40, see 12 Halsbury's Statutes (4th edn) (1989
e reissue) 1161.

Case referred to in judgment
R v Wilson (Clarence), R v Jenkins (Edward John) [1983] 3 All ER 448, [1984] AC 242, [1983] 3 WLR 686, HL.

f
Appeal against conviction
John Mearns appealed against his conviction on 19 June 1989 in the Crown Court at Ipswich before his Honour Judge Sheerin and a jury of common assault following his trial on an indictment alleging assault occasioning actual bodily harm, contrary to s 47 of the Offences against the Person Act 1861, on the ground that, by virtue of ss 39 and 40
g of the Criminal Justice Act 1988, a verdict of common assault on an indictment not containing a count specifically charging common assault was not open to the jury. The charge arose out of a struggle with a police officer while the appellant was being arrested on suspicion of burglary. The facts are set out in the judgment of the court.

Carolyn Ludlow (assigned by the Registrar of Criminal Appeals) for the appellant.
h *Frederick Ferguson* for the Crown.

GLIDEWELL LJ delivered the following judgment of the court. On 19 June 1989 in the Crown Court at Ipswich the appellant pleaded not guilty to an indictment containing one count of assault occasioning actual bodily harm, contrary to s 47 of the Offences against the Person Act 1861. His trial commenced and on the following day he was
j found not guilty on that count but guilty of common assault.
     Before that happened, indeed as we understand it, at the outset of the trial, there was a discussion between counsel and the judge in which counsel, who appeared for the appellant then as she has before us, submitted to the judge that under the present

---

a   Section 39 is set out at p 990 *f*, post
b   Section 40, so far as material, is set out at p 990 *g h*, post

legislative provisions, to which I shall come in a moment, a verdict of common assault on an indictment not containing a count specifically charging common assault was not open to the jury. The judge rejected that submission, left it to the jury as an alternative and, as I have said, they convicted. The appellant was ordered to perform 200 hours' community service and has, we believe, successfully completed that sentence.

He now appeals against conviction as of right because what is urged on his behalf is a point of law.

The point of law arises out of some of the provisions of the Criminal Justice Act 1988, which came into force in October 1988. Those provisions apply to the offence alleged in this case.

There is no doubt that until the 1988 Act came into force common assault, which is a common law offence, was an offence of which a person charged, as the appellant was with the indictable offence of assault occasioning actual bodily harm in the Crown Court could be convicted as an alternative if he were acquitted of the charge laid in the count against him. That was so whether or not there was a specific count in the indictment alleging common assault as an alternative. That was the result of s 6(3) of the Criminal Law Act 1967, which provides:

'Where, on a person's trial on indictment for any offence except treason or murder, the jury find him not guilty of the offence specifically charged in the indictment, but the allegations in the indictment amount to or include (expressly or by implication) an allegation of another offence falling within the jurisdiction of the court of trial, the jury may find him guilty of that other offence or of an offence of which he could be found guilty on an indictment, specifically charging that other offence.'

Until October 1988 common assault was an offence which could be tried on indictment or could be tried summarily and thus fell within the jurisdiction of the Crown Court in every sense. However, the provisions of the 1988 Act which are relevant and which, as I say, came into force in time to catch this offence, are ss 39 and 40. Section 39 reads:

'Common assault and battery shall be summary offences and a person guilty of either of them shall be liable to a fine not exceeding level 5 on the standard scale, to imprisonment for a term not exceeding six months, or to both.'

Section 40 provides:

'(1) A count charging a person with a summary offence to which this section applies may be included in an indictment if the charge—(a) is founded on the same facts or evidence as a count charging an indictable offence; or (b) is part of a series of offences of the same or similar character as an indictable offence which is also charged, but only if (in either case) the facts or evidence relating to the offence were disclosed in an examination or deposition taken before a justice in the presence of the person charged.

(2) Where a count charging an offence to which this section applies is included in an indictment, the offence shall be tried in the same manner as if it were an indictable offence; but the Crown Court may only deal with the offender in respect of it in a manner in which a magistrates' court could have dealt with him.

(3) The offences to which this section applies are—(a) common assault . . .'

Then there are four other types of offences named.

Section 41 of the 1988 Act deals with the related powers of the Crown Court to deal with summary offences where a person is committed for an either way offence. It also deals with alternatives to either way offences.

The submission of counsel for the appellant which she advanced before the judge, and which she advances in her notice of appeal, is this. Since October 1988 common assault, a instead of being a common law offence which could be tried either on indictment or summarily, is now, by statute, a summary offence only. However, there is still the specific provision in s 40 which provides that in an indictment alleging assault occasioning actual bodily harm an alternative verdict of guilty to common assault may be given in appropriate circumstances, but only if a count to that effect is included in the indictment. That, submits counsel, is the effect of these two sections of the 1988 Act. In our view that submission is correct: these two provisions have effected a change in the law relating to

b the powers of the Crown Court to return alternative verdicts of lesser charges in relation to the offences specified in s 40(3) of the 1988 Act, of which common assault is one.

Counsel for the Crown, in his able argument to the contrary, submits that the submission for the appellant was based on a misreading of s 6(3) of the Criminal Law Act 1967. I have already read that subsection. It gives power to return a verdict of guilty of an alternative offence if the allegations in the indictment amount to or include an

c allegation of that other offence, but subject to the words, 'falling within the jurisdiction of the court of trial'. The point of counsel for the appellant is that those offences which are triable summarily only and may only be tried in the Crown Court if a specific count is added are not within the jurisdiction of the Crown Court unless a specific count is added, and so s 6(3) of the 1967 Act does not apply in such a situation, which was the case here, because no alternative count was ever added to this indictment. As I have said,

d counsel for the Crown submits that that is a misreading of the phrase in s 6(3), 'falling within the jurisdiction of the court of trial'. For that proposition he reminds us, first, of a very brief passage in the speech of Lord Roskill in *R v Wilson (Clarence), R v Jenkins (Edward John)* [1983] 3 All ER 448 at 451, [1984] AC 242 at 256. In that speech, with which all the other members of the House of Lords agreed, Lord Roskill, having quoted s 6(3) of the 1967 Act, said: 'The words "falling within the jurisdiction of the court of

e trial" can now be ignored since the creation of the Crown Court.'

We make two observations about that. The matter at issue in those appeals was not the question at issue in this case at all, or a point anywhere near it. His Lordship's observation, which was strictly obiter, was no doubt directed to the abolition of the distinction between misdemeanour and felony, and with the abolition of the distinction when the Crown Court was formed between the former powers of assizes and quarter sessions. In

f relation to those matters his Lordship's observation was entirely right. What he was not considering was any question of different jurisdiction between the Crown Court and the magistrates' court. With the greatest respect to him, the words in s 6(3), 'falling within the jurisdiction of the court of trial' are still relevant if what is in issue is the trial of a matter which is triable summarily only.

Counsel for the Crown also directed our attention to certain other statutory provisions.

g The Public Order Act 1986, by ss 2, 3 and 4, creates offences in s 2 of violent disorder, in s 3, affray, and by s 4(1) provides: 'A person is guilty of an offence if he—(a) uses towards another person threatening, abusive or insulting words or behaviour . . .' Then there is a provision in s 7(3), which reads:

h 'If on the trial on indictment of a person charged with violent disorder or affray the jury find him not guilty of the offence charged, they may (without prejudice to section 6(3) of the Criminal Law Act 1967) find him guilty of an offence under section 4.'

Similarly, in the Road Traffic Offenders Act 1988, s 24(1) provides:

j 'Where on a person's trial on indictment in England and Wales for an offence under section 1 (causing death by reckless driving), 2 (reckless driving) or 28 (reckless cycling) of the Road Traffic Act 1988 the jury find him not guilty of the offence specifically charged in the indictment, they may (without prejudice to section 6(3) of the Criminal Law Act 1967) find him guilty—(a) where the offence so charged is an offence under section 1 or 2 of the Road Traffic Act 1988, of an offence under section 3 (careless and inconsiderate driving) of that Act . . .'

a

Careless and inconsiderate driving under s 3 of that Act and using threatening, abusive or insulting words or behaviour under s 4 of the Public Order Act 1986 are offences which are triable summarily only. So those two statutory provisions in the two Acts to which I have just referred are specific provisions which have the effect that if the greater indictable offence is charged, the facts cover the lesser summary offence, and there is an acquittal on the greater offence, then nevertheless there may be a conviction in the Crown Court of the lesser offence. It will be seen that both the provisions to which counsel for the Crown drew our attention use the phrase, 'without prejudice to s 6(3) of the Criminal Law Act 1967'. Counsel submits that what that means is, 'without regard to the power to convict under s 6(3)'; in other words he submits that really what these sections are saying is despite the fact that there could be a conviction under s 6(3) of the 1967 Act, this is a specific statutory provision providing for conviction as an alternative of these summary offences. In our view, that is turning the meaning of the words on its head. The words in those two provisions to which he referred us, 'without prejudice to s 6(3) of the Criminal Law Act 1967' clearly import that but for these specific statutory provisions in s 7(3) of the 1986 Act and s 24(1) of the 1988 Act, it would not be possible to bring in an alternative verdict of the lesser summary charge because of the provisions of s 6(3). That is because, to come back to the words of that subsection, the words, 'another offence falling within the jurisdiction of the court of trial' would not apply to the specific statutory offences. In other words, the provisions to which counsel has drawn our attention are actually adverse to his submission and make it clear to our minds that the submission that counsel for the appellant has put forward is correct.

b

c

d

Whether the situation that results from all this is satisfactory is not for us to say. It does mean that for the future the Crown Court is going to have to be careful, if minded to allow a jury to consider bringing in an alternative verdict of some offence which clearly is comprehended within a greater offence which is included in an indictment, to see whether it falls within some such specific statutory provision as the Public Order Act 1986 provision to which I have referred, or the Road Traffic Offenders Act 1988 provision, in which case it can bring in an alternative verdict without having a count in the indictment; or whether it is an offence which comes within s 40 of the Criminal Justice Act 1988, in which case it can only bring in the alternative verdict if a count of the lesser offence is already contained within, or is added by amendment to, the indictment. Whether that is a satisfactory state of affairs is at least doubtful. But that it is the law is in our view quite clear.

e

f

For the reasons we have given this appeal must succeed and the conviction of common assault must be quashed.

g

Appeal allowed.   Conviction quashed.

Solicitors: *Crown Prosecution Service*, Ipswich.

Kate O'Hanlon   Barrister.

CANADA
IN COLOUR

Waterfalls on the Credit River, Caledon, Ontario

Printed and bound in Hong Kong by Serasia Limited

Canada in Colour

Text by Val Clery
Photographs by Bill Brooks/Chic Harris/Tom Hall

The Arctic

The Atlantic Coast

French Canada

Central Canada

The Great Western Plains

The Mountains

The Pacific Coast

Hounslow Press, Toronto, Canada

Old Quebec City Waterfront, Quebec

2

INTRODUCTION

Canada, because of its immensity, has always been difficult to grasp as a country. And always will be. Not just for people who come to visit, but for the people who consider it to be their country, Canadians themselves. Just as its political system of confederation seems inadequate at times to the task of bringing a unity to the conflicting interests of its provinces and territories, so the idea that its physical diversity has a geographical entity seems arbitrary and artificial. One of Canada's greatest prime ministers, Mackenzie King, summed up the dilemma when he said, "If other countries have too much history, we have too much geography."

Canada does have too much geography; far too much to allow anyone to claim that he has seen all of Canada and has come to know it as a country should be known by those who want to understand it. And so we must all accept, whether we're visitor or Canadian, that Canada is always going to evade our grasp, is going to remain forever the mysterious, "the unknown country".

As the second largest country in the world, of course Canada has gained in practical terms from the arrival of the jet era, but that gain may have lost many of us the opportunity of ever getting to know this country. Spanning the continent in a few convenient hours, as removed from actuality as our baggage in the freight compartment, gets us (in terms of understanding) nowhere. Experience takes time, and if we wish to know the rich and meaningful variations of reality that make up Canada, we must expose ourselves to them.

The young, who often do have an instinctive sense of what is true, seem to have rediscovered a basic human need. Their current urge to travel simply and slowly, hitchhiking across continents and even round the world, sleeping out, eating cheaply, in easy open community, may be restoring to them an essential in growing that their parents had allowed to lapse.

Canada needs to be travelled in such a way. It demands an unhurried journey from ocean to ocean, watchful and thoughtful through many dawns and noons and sunsets and throughout each of the seasons, with time to watch the sun grow on the Atlantic horizon, to stand by the St. Lawrence at spring runout, to feel the weight of midsummer in the bushland of Ontario, to sense the golden immensity of the Prairies, to end a day facing a Pacific sunset. Ideally, it is a journey that should be made to last a lifetime.

This book is not intended as a convenient substitute for such a journey, but perhaps as a rehearsal for a journey, or even as the encouragement to make one. The pictures and words that follow can offer only glimpses of the reality of Canada. But they are the produce of personal experience and much travel, and are brought together with care and reflection and feeling which we hope you can share in. Take time over the pages, look long and deeply, open yourself to what they say and you may find that your own journey through Canada has already begun.

The Arctic

The Canada that we intend to show lies along the 49th parallel from Atlantic to Pacific and extends only a few hundred miles to its north. Beyond this Canada, little known though it may be, is another Canada, ten times vaster and a thousand times more enigmatic, that extends in the form of a vast wedge to end in a point at the North Pole.

3

Polar Bear crossing between ice floes

Until recently most of us were content to people the Yukon and the Northwest Territories with stereotypes — a handful of Eskimos and white trappers urging their dog teams across limitless wastes of snow and ice, which they shared with only the loping menace of polar bears. There are still polar bears up there, and even a few dog teams that have not been superseded by snowmobiles, tractors and helicopters, but that Canada can no longer be held in actual or imaginative deep-freeze.

Eskimo with his dogs, Pond Inlet, Northwest Territories

Whether from sheer waste or real necessity, the developed world suddenly finds that it needs the metal and energy resources that nature has hoarded beneath the north. What we so long thought vaguely to be the Canada of the future has become the Canada of tomorrow. And so tomorrow the need to know that other immense Canada, to visit, and even to live in it will become as pressing as the need now to know the Canada of today.

4

The Atlantic Coast

Here is the first Canada—a landfall, wreathed in fogs, that conjured up for adventuring Vikings, imperious French, dispossessed Highlanders and hunger-thin Irish mirages of distant homelands. Atlantic and Arctic contend for it. Icebergs, like lost spirits from the shrunken empire of the Pole, still scout along the scarred battlements of the Labrador and Newfoundland coasts. Atlantic tides surge on daily forays deep into the arteries of the continent.

Puffins on an Atlantic cliff top

6

*The violent powers of weather and water tyrannize Newfoundland
—ceaselessly pummelling its broken coasts, forcing the waterfront
houses of St. John's to cling to the rocky security of its headland.*

An Atlantic storm glowers at the mouth of Ingonish Harbour on Cape Breton, Nova Scotia.

Early morning sunlight outshines the beacon on Machias Island.

8

9

Peggy's Cove, a much visited and very typical Nova Scotian fishing village. Beside its spindle-legged dock, an inshore boat takes its ease in the haven between rounds of the lobster traps. On the slope above, the morning wash is stretched and bleached by salty Atlantic airs that are as often threatening as playful.

Boats of the Nova Scotian fishing fleet balance on their own reflections in Halifax harbour.

12

The Town Clock, which has been measuring the hours of Halifax life since 1803.

13

Monuments to tomorrow—the bright new hoists that advertise Halifax's development as one of the continent's earliest and largest cargo-container ports.

14

Across the wide even flow of the St. John River, Fredericton, capital of New Brunswick, rests urbanely amongst its shade trees.

True to their title, the Maritime provinces constantly present fresh reminders of the ocean. The tidal flats of Fundy, scored by heavy tides that surge twice daily up the Bay between the shores of Nova Scotia and New Brunswick. And in Prince Edward Island, slow-motion herons glide over a salt water inlet.

16

The rich brick red soil of Prince Edward Island that nourishes potatoes below and thick pasture above

Farming and fishing remain the hard and simple bases of life along the Gaspé shore of the St. Lawrence. A boat throbbing homewards after trawling in the Gulf passes Percé Rock, famous as the first landfall of French explorers of the region.

19

French Canada

Quebec, a land originally marked out to aggrandize the Crown and the Church of France. Settlers managed to impose at first only a trim of ordered life to the vast hinterland of overgrown forest and rock-ribbed plain—isolated fortresses, an introvert capital, lonely villages . . . But from here the hopeful sweep of great rivers wooed voyageurs deeper to west and north, leaving wives and children to the chill comfort of prayers and patience.

22

The snow goose, as apt a symbol of Canada's realities as the beaver. An annual migratory reminder in the busy populated valley of the St. Lawrence that not far north wilderness takes over Quebec.

A wayside crucifix in Quebec

Sunset over the imposing parish church at St. Charles, Quebec

24

Spring warmth and the early passage of ships make embroidery of the ice on the broad St. Lawrence. At any season the breadth of the river is impressive; as far upstream as Trois Rivieres, it can still make freighters seem like toys.

The unchanging rhythm of life in Quebec's Eastern Townships

Sky blue and snow-white, the natural and national colours of French Canada highlight the distinctive architecture of a Quebec barn.

27

Quebec City

Quebec City, provincial capital, was sited originally on the top of a high bluff that could command the river. But trade, not war, makes a city grow. The huddled descent of old houses down the steep slope marks the early eagerness of merchants to profit from the St. Lawrence. The most uniquely French city on the continent (even its choice of such concessions to modernity as the car tend to be Gallic) it attracts more tourists now than traders. And tourists sustain artists and craftworkers, who have made many of the narrow streets of the Lower Town their own.

28 *Lower town*

29 *Artist's corner near the famous Chateau Frontenac Hotel*

30 *Old Quebec City street scene*

Montreal

Montreal is the living index of a changing Quebec. A volatile mixture of the distinctive spirits of Quebec, of Canada and of North America, spiked with the many matured flavours of Europe. Bilingual, multilingual, unilingual —it all depends who you are, who you're speaking to, and where you are in this city that straddles the St. Lawrence and its islands and drapes the lower slopes of the regal Mountain. Montreal style is a subtle blending of styles – one moment you can be passing through a district that is pure Quebecois in its architecture, the next along an avenue or across a square as stolidly respectable as in any city of English Canada; the new glittering ambitious heart of Montreal could be translated without alteration to the downtown core of any affluent city in the continent. What gives this vibrant city its uniqueness are things that cannot be measured – contrast, and rhythm and panache.

31 *Downtown snow scene*   **32** *Boutique window in Place Ville Marie*   **33** *The city at night from Mount Royal*

35 *The Trillium—Ontario's floral emblem*

Central Canada

The sturdy torso of Canada, rock-hard under a flesh of rich brown topsoil, powerfully-musculed by rivers and wide lakes. Ontario, showily overdressed in resources and energy, in wealth and influence and people, yet less than half a century from pioneer simplicity, and vast enough to contain both modern wasteland and untouched wilderness. The province that, for all its affluent pride, cherishes as its emblem the shy delicate trillium.

36 *Ivy Lea Bridge, stretching south across the border to New York State, straddles a fall tinted corner of Ontario's Thousand Islands.*

From the Federal Parliament Buildings in Ottawa, the national capital, the Peace Tower soars into the afternoon sky.

The Royal Military College stands sentinel before the City of Kingston on the north shore of Lake Ontario.

38

Toronto

In less than a decade Toronto has shed a reputation for the dour pursuit of work and wealth. New Canadian immigrants have refreshed Toronto, have stirred in its downtown heart a vigour that contrasts with the decay that has stricken the core of other cities. Italians, Greeks, Hungarians, West Indians, for whom streets are stages to strut and stare and live on, have lined them with taverns and restaurants and boutiques and exotic delicatessens. The symbols of their industry and ambition tower above the business district, their open attitude to living is caught perfectly by the soaring lines of their new City Hall.

39 *An interpretation of King Street*

40 *The new City Hall*

41 *Montage of lights on Yonge Street*

Glimpses of the other less obvious Ontario. The modest prettiness of an Edwardian family residence at Niagara-on-the-Lake and an autumn woodland near Kingston.

42

*The spray-plumed Horseshoe
Falls at Niagara, the wonder of
the world and of North
America's newlyweds.*

44

A white-tailed deer in the Ontario bush

The final fiery curtain of the day over Marie Louise Lake, Sibley Provincial Park, in Ontario's vacation country

Highway 17 stretches like a lifeline through a Lake Superior storm in northwestern Ontario

47   48

The Great Western Plains

The wide and wondering face of Canada—the wheatlands and pastures of Manitoba, Saskatchewan and Alberta. Miming each year long life cycle the same fleeting expressions—callow and green, fulfilled and golden, mellow and wearying, and finally deathly pale as the openhanded blows of winter strike. A sky always vast with promises, a soil unfaltering in response.

50 Plains Bison

*Lower Fort Garry, sedate and well preserved, once the centre of a
violent fur trade from which the City of Winnipeg grew to become
Manitoba's provincial capital.*

Manitoba Grain Elevators—the gold vaults of the Prairie wheat farmers

Near Brandon, Manitoba

Horses overlooking the Trans-Canada Highway west of Moose Jaw, Saskatchewan

Abandoned farmhouse, Pense, Saskatchewan

55

The wide open wheatbelt is a journal of its own development. Tractors, the workhorses of today, may claim a monopoly on the dirt sideroads as they putter tirelessly from one chore to the next. But horses are still cherished and still claim a pride of place on the Prairie skylines. People are less sure of their place here. Although the same weather moves across the same fertile soil and the same growth follows the seasons, abandoned farms mark the new necessity for what is bigger and more efficient.

54

Fences appear a petty and superfluous interruption of the apparently limitless cattle pastures outside of Medicine Hat, Alberta.

Gophers seem altogether out-of-scale as inhabitants of a land so enormous.

56

57

Rape seed, a lesser recently developed vein of prairie gold

The Alberta badlands, at Red Deer River, appropriate terrain for the Dinosaur Provincial Park

59

Calgary

Calgary still trades in the beef
cattle that produced its early for-
tunes, but the trade that most interests its millionaire barons
nowadays is in oil futures and real
estate, much of it situated thousands of miles to the north. They
affect stetsons still and cowboy
boots, and once a year, at Stam-
pede Week, they insist that this
city of office towers is still a cow
town.

*Calgary, Alberta, from the
Husky Tower*

The Mountains

The Rockies—arched like patient Atlas, the strong sinewed back of the continent. Invincible and poised, and insensible to aeons of snow and sunlight, unmoved by the recent nervous scurry of men and their machines across its vertebrae, indifferent to the animal loners and nomads that infest its rough clothing of forest.

61   62

Kokanee salmon "hold" at a stream mouth before the obsessive yearly struggle upcurrent to their spawning grounds

Grizzly Bears—the sweet-toothed-sour tempered hobos of the foothills

63

64

The thundering power of Helmcken Falls, British Columbia.

Mount Eisenhower, Alberta bronzed monumentally by the rising sun.

Mountain goats live beyond the law of gravity.

The Rockies command attention. The Prairie's impression of vaulting space can evade the eye and the camera. The rococo of the Ontario bush can become boring in its complexity. Only the mobile immensity of an ocean compares in fascination with the immense eternal stillness of these mountains. Both have the same power to woo you forward and yet stop you in your tracks. And to leave impressions that are ineffacable.

Near Mount Edith Cavell, Alberta

Sea Lions roaring off Long Beach, British Columbia

The Pacific Coast

The outside chance of Canada. An extremity full of extremes—deserts and rain forests, high cattle country above orchard valleys, ski slopes overlooking beach resorts, loggers' beerhalls beside English tearooms, power drunk torrents feeding placid lakes . . . British Columbia is the province where the unusual is the norm. Not many travellers who have come over the mountains have regretted the journey.

Vancouver Harbour Traffic

Goldstream River Rain Forest near Victoria, British Columbia

Vancouver

Vancouver makes no secret of the fact that it is proud of itself. Its sea-girdled downtown district has sprouted the office towers worthy of a province still booming in the enjoyment of natural resources. Homes are stacked up the slopes that surround its many shores like spectators around a stadium, and Vancouver people value their real estate on the view it will lend them of the spectacle of Vancouver.

Vancouver, British Columbia from the harbour

71

Joggers in Vancouver's Stanley Park

The enticing mysteries of tide and sea mist along the British Columbia coastline.

Bastion Square, Victoria, British Columbia

An antique store window, says it all in Victoria, the Provincial Capital.

To follow the daily path the sun takes across Canada seems the most natural order of travel. What more appropriate prelude to the journey than to watch the day grow from the eastern horizon of the Atlantic? What more fitting postscript than to see it slide below the Pacific to the west? At most only a few hours separate the departure of the sun from one end of Canada and its return at the other; as each journey ends the moment for another new journey to begin is close. Let this post-script be the prelude to your many journeys.

The futile bravado of Pacific surf against Long Beach, British Columbia

77 *Pacific Ocean freighters*

BILL BROOKS

Bill Brooks became serious about photography while working toward a degree in economics at the University of Toronto. After graduating in 1962, he managed a large Toronto portrait studio, sold books for an American publisher, and worked as a technical representative for a major producer of cameras and film.

He spent five years in charge of all photography and picture research for a major Canadian-owned publishing company. It was while working on a nine volume illustrated natural history series that he developed a love for his country and a passion to record its beauty and grandeur.

In the last few years he has travelled across Canada in a camper van taking many of the pictures that appear in this book.

Bill lives with his wife, Betty, in the Toronto, Ontario suburb of Scarborough, and works as a freelance photographer and consultant on illustrated books. His photographs have appeared regularly in numerous books and magazines and he has researched historical illustrations for many large gift books.

Bill Brooks photograph credits by plate number

1, 6, 8, 16, 17, 18, 22, 24, 25, 32, 35, 36, 37, 38, 39, 40, 41, 42, 43, 44, 45, 46, 47, 48, 49, 51, 53, 54, 55, 56, 57, 58, 59, 60, 67.

TOM HALL

Tom Hall has always had a keen interest in the outdoors. His work as Superintendent of Ground Communication Engineering for Air Canada took him across Canada many times. The hundreds of hours he spent looking down on the spectacular vastness and wilderness beauty of the country gave birth to an insatiable curiosity about the natural phenomena passing below.

In 1949 he moved to Edmonton to participate in the formation of Canadian Electronics Limited. He disposed of his business interests in 1962 and settled with his family in Penticton, British Columbia, which serves as headquarters for many miles of photographic safari through rugged back country from sea level to alpine tundra.

He has a large file of transparencies and negatives relating to natural history subjects. Over 1,000 of his photographs have been published.

Tom Hall photograph credits by plate number

50, 61, 62, 63, 64, 65, 66, 68, 69, 70, 72, 73, 74, 75, 76, 77.

CHIC HARRIS

Chic Harris, was born in England and graduated from London University in chemistry. He came to Canada in 1929 and worked for Canadian Industries Limited in their research department until his retirement in 1966.

The camera to him, is a tool to be used as a means of artistic expression and as an inducement to walk about with one's eyes open looking for those simple things which so often express real beauty. Much of his photography has been done in the Province of Quebec and in the Maritimes. He is a member of The National Association of Photographic Art, The Montreal Camera Club and The Toronto Guild of Colour Photography.

Chic makes his home in Beloeil, Quebec.

Chic Harris photograph credits by plate number

2, 5, 9, 10, 11, 12, 13, 14, 15, 19, 20, 21, 23, 26, 27, 28, 29, 30, 31, 33, 52.

VAL CLERY

Val Clery is Editor and co-founder of *Books in Canada*. A Dubliner by birth, he travelled widely through North Africa, Italy and the Balkans while serving as a commando in World War II.

Subsequently he settled in London and, after an initial spell as a short story writer, became interested in radio as a medium and joined the BBC. In 1959 he moved to the London bureau of the CBC and eventually came to Toronto as a public affairs producer. He has crossed Canada several times while assembling material for numerous radio documentaries.

Since leaving the CBC in 1970, he has continued broadcasting as a freelancer, has contributed to the Globe Magazine, and has been actively involved in the efforts to support Canadian writing and publishing.

ADDITIONAL PHOTOGRAPH CREDITS

Plate # 3– Information Canada Photothèque, photograph by Ted Grant.
Plate # 4– Information Canada Photothèque, photograph by Doug Wilkinson.
Plate # 7– Information Canada Photothèque, photograph by John de Visser.
Plate # 71–Information Canada Photothèque, photograph by Freeman Patterson.

This book was set in American Garamond
and Garamond Bold Italic monotype by Mono Lino
Typesetting Company Limited, Toronto, Canada

Paper: 150 gsm M/C Art.